THE ROLLING STONES COMPLETE RECORDING SESSIONS 1962-2012
50th ANNIVERSARY EDITION

A Sessionography and History of Studio and Select
Live Recordings, from the Famous Chart-Toppers to the
Infamous Rarities
More than 1,500 Tracks Listed
March 1962 – July 2012

MARTIN ELLIOTT

Foreword by Chris Kimsey

Edited by Chris Bartlett

THE ROLLING STONES COMPLETE RECORDING SESSIONS 1962-2012
50th ANNIVERSARY EDITION

Photo Courtesy of Graham Wiltshire, FRPS.

Ronnie Wood, Keith Richards, Mick Jagger and Charlie Watts.
27 August 2006, Don Valley Stadium, Sheffield, England.

Thank you also to Brian Jones, Ian Stewart, Bill Wyman, Mick Taylor
and the backing players without whom…

MARTIN ELLIOTT

First published in Great Britain in 2012 by Cherry Red Books, (a division of Cherry Red Records Ltd.), Power Road Studios, 114 Power Road, London W4 5PY.

ISBN: 978-1-901447-77-4

Design: Becky Stewart

Photos courtesy of Chris Kimsey, Barry Sage and Graham Wiltshire

CONTENTS

		PAGE
	Foreword - by Chris Kimsey	7
	Introduction, Special Thanks, Assistance and Contacts.	9
1	**DIDDLEY DADDY – THE FATHER OF THEM ALL** March 1962 – February 1964	13
2	**CHESS – FIRST MOVE TO THE TOP** March 1964 – April 1965	33
3	**SATISFACTION GUARANTEED** May 1965 – October 1966	57
4	**DANDELION AND THE FLOWER POWER GAME** November 1966 – October 1967	84
5	**HONKY TONK COWBELL SUMMONS HYDE PARK HERD** February 1968 – July 1969	97
6	**GIMME SHELTER FROM ALTAMONT** October 1969 – March 1971	122
7	**EXILES ENJOY STAR STAR TREATMENT** June 1971 – June 1974	142
8	**HAND OF FATE ENDS GUITARIST HUNT** December 1974 – August 1976	172
9	**PUNK AND THE EMOTIONAL YEARS** March 1977 – June 1982	188
10	**GIANTS ENTER A DEEP SLEEP** November 1982 – December 1985	235
11	**STEEL WHEELS ROLLIN' ON** January 1989 – July 1995	253
12	**NO BRIDGE TOO FAR FOR THE BABYLON BOYS** March 1997 – June 1999	307
13	**GET YOUR LICKS** May 2002 – September 2003	326
14	**A BIGGER BANG . . . FOR A SHINING LIGHT** June 2004 – August 2007	346
15	**ROLLED GOLD** April 2009 – July 2012	376
	Appendices:	
A	Session Tracks in date order	380
B	Live Tracks in date order	398
C	Alphabetic Song Title, Also Known As Index	406
	Interviews and Information Provision, Magazines and Books, Web Sources	419

CONTENTS

Foreword by Chris Kimsey

I was very pleased to be contacted by Martin Elliott, the author of this book, to discuss my history of working with the Rolling Stones. This led to a vast amount of information that I had first-hand knowledge of and which would help him in putting the record straight. It is so important to have a true historical documentation of the performances and recordings of the Rolling Stones, as they are and will always be, the most prolific rock 'n' roll band ever. Their like will never be seen again.

I found it quite wonderful to be able to discover some facts that I had forgotten on earlier recordings that I wanted to research, so it was a unique opportunity to meet the author, whose ethic is very clear and sound – to just provide the simple facts.

In the 1950s, the medium of recording would develop into the phonograph, which documented speech, theatre and then music. It started to illustrate a different part of history and document social change through the medium of song.

When songs were written and recorded they became popular, as people could relate and share the stories within them. The recordings were political, sexual and religious and the medium of song would facilitate the passing of folklore.

Folk and rock music began to defy and rebel against the social and political status quo regarding war and civil rights. The new medium had arrived with vinyl records. People's feelings that they could never share were captured by those who could. The Stones were on the cusp of this musical revolution.

History was one of my favourite subjects at school.

I liked the fact that people documented events in their lifetime, hoping that they would be preserved and passed on to future generations. I loved this and began to realise that this recording of events would feature in my life and career. The thrill of having a tape recorder and capturing a sound like the spoken voice, which could be played to many, anywhere, again and again, could be a picture of what was happening to society and the mood of the time.

This book has the most detailed and reliable source of information which validates the evolution of the band.

A lot of these events are not documented so become hearsay and flamboyant mythologising, purely to claim a bit of fame. This book is not based on gossip or tales but documentation of where the Stones went and where and how they recorded. During the 14 years (1977 – 1991) I worked and recorded with them, I tried to keep as much documentation as possible. We would record in different countries and studios and I was always trying to keep documenting as much as possible. The recording medium at that time was analogue tape - 8 track, 16 track and 24 track. A reel of 2" 16 / 24 track tape weighs 11lbs and would record 30 minutes of music; for example, the Some Girls sessions in Paris amassed some 150 reels of tape. Those 150 tapes would weigh 1,650lbs and take up the space of three huge steamer trunks. They would be flown from Paris to New York to Los Angeles to London, a logistical and customs nightmare. It cost a fortune to keep them mobile. That is some excess baggage charge!

I had a series of log books which detailed every reel, every take, every song and every jam.

Sadly, these were lost in a flood at the Stones' storage warehouse in Bermondsey. Then there was another occasion when the band had changed labels from Atlantic to Columbia. Columbia wanted to re-master some of the back catalogue but the stereo master mix tapes of one of the albums could not be found – so the re-master was made from a CD! Two months later the original tapes suddenly arrived on the doorstep of the Rolling Stones office in London, with no return address or documentation.

In moving from record company to record company there was always the danger of losing tapes.

Of course, Keith's attitude to recording was that, once they had been recorded, mixed and released, then you may as well destroy them so no one can play around with them again or lose them!

The other vital component to the 2" tape was the track sheet, which told you what was recorded on each of the 16 tracks and what speed it was recorded at, 15ips or 30ips, whether Dolby noise reduction was used, and the tape alignment recording curves of NAB or CCIR.

Unless there was a coherent tape operator whose handwriting could be deciphered, it could be a journey of discovery, trying to figure who was playing what!

Even within the band, sometimes Keith or Ronnie would play bass; people would switch from electric guitar to acoustic guitar and back again. Mick may play guitar or piano. Deciphering how a track came together, who played what, when and where, what was added and kept, what was added and not used.

It is fun to follow the trail of how a song would have been recorded in one studio then overdubbed in another studio and country then mixed in London or New York. Different musicians would add their parts, months later in another city.

Keeping the trail of all this was difficult so, with this book, it is as much fun for me as the reader to discover the complex series of events that made it all happen.

Martin has done a great job of tracking down who played what on what; sometimes it could be a bit of a guessing game as so many musicians passed through the studio.

You have to get to the source to put the story straight and Martin has done this better than anyone. His facts are highly accurate, I even find myself reading the book to remind me of dates and events!

My involvement with the Rolling Stones was over a 25 year period and for nine albums: Sticky Fingers (1971), Some Girls (1978), Emotional Rescue (1980), Sucking In The Seventies (1981), Tattoo You (1981), Undercover (1983), Steel Wheels (1989), Flashpoint (1991) and Stripped (1995) and the Live At The Max IMAX film soundtrack (1991). Ranging from tape operator, recording engineer, mixer, associate producer and co-producer, I learnt an awful lot from the world's best rock n roll band.

For Martin to find and document all of this information is a Holy Grail of the Rolling Stones from their conception until this day.

I know first-hand how difficult it is to keep track of all this information. It was memory that was used when the band wanted to see what tracks had not been released that I had recorded - and that's just my small part in the history of the Rolling Stones recordings. Before that, the early years of Rolling Stones recording must be really difficult to figure out what went down.

Martin has discovered and correlated so much information across the vast history of their recordings and put it all in this book. I am really happy that this has come together; people can trace and follow the map of how the world's greatest rock 'n' roll band first pressed RECORD and made history.

Chris Kimsey.
London, April 2012.

Chris Kimsey,
Barnes, London. 2012.

Introduction

"Ladies and Gentleman, the greatest rock and roll band in the World . . . The Rolling Stones."

The Stones' tour manager, Sam Cutler, uttered these words on stage to a Colorado audience on the first date of their USA tour in November 1969, before the band's opening number, *Jumpin' Jack Flash*. They were immortalised by dint of their inclusion on the 1970 live album Get Yer Ya Ya's Out. The words struck even more of a chord when reading Sam's 2008 volume of great rock and roll tales *You Can't Always Get What You Want*. Apparently Mick Jagger picked Sam up on the choice of words at the end of that 1969 show. Sam's bold reply was sharp and to the point: "Well, either you fuckin' are or you ain't. What the fuck is it gonna be?"

So the quote introduced the band for the rest of the tour. After having this potentially heavy mantle thrown at them by Sam Cutler, this "thrust upon" reputation is one they have aspired to for the next 40-plus years.

This is my third book on the recording works of the Rolling Stones. It reflects 50 years of their existence and almost 1,000 tracks from the studio, television appearances and rehearsals. In addition, some 500 live performances are accounted for. These include official releases, bootlegs and those considered unavailable.

Recently, in only the last few years, the archives have been opened in all their glory, in an unprecedented way, and we have been treated to re-releases, including bonus out-takes and live recordings re-mastered from their previous, inferior "bootleg" quality. We can only guess and look forward to what may be forthcoming.

In addition, the available research information (written and audio), releases and recordings have expanded greatly over the past 20-odd years and my data has also been improved by additional contacts and interviews. I am very grateful to the information providers who have helped me with direct research. As a result, this is another release to cover the Stones' career to date, coinciding with the golden anniversary of their first live performance and, in January 2013, with the coming together of the original six band members.

The book places the recordings in chronological order and in historical context. After all, as you would expect, six decades have manifested dramatic changes in freedom, politics, fashion and technology, not to mention the music that complemented each facet.

Each track is provided with background information and I summarise an example and description of each item:

435. **LIVE WITH ME** (Jagger, Richard) 3.33
12-31 May; 18 October - 3 November 1969: Place: Olympic Sound Studios, London, England; Sunset Sound Studios, Elektra Studios, Los Angeles, USA.
Played Live: 1969, 1970, 1971, 1973, 1994, 1995, 1998, 1999, 2002, 2003, 2005, 2006, 2007
Rolling Stones with Mick Taylor, Nicky Hopkins, Leon Russell, Bobby Keys.
Producer: Jimmy Miller.
Engineer: Glyn Johns.
Horn arrangement: Leon Russell, Bruce Botnick. Assistant Engineers: Bruce Botnick, Jerry Hansen, George Chkiantz, Vic Smith, Alan O'Duffy.
USA LP LET IT BLEED: 29 November 1969: No. 3 - 19 weeks UK LP LET IT BLEED: 5 December 1969: No. 1 - 29 weeks
UK LP SOLID ROCK: 13 October 1980

The session number (435 above) is simply a numerical sequence to refer to the track and is in date order of when the number was first recorded. The appendices refer to this number to help locate a track and do not reflect a page number. The songwriters are credited in parentheses. Keith Richards is known as Richard until the release of the 1978 SOME GIRLS album. The (s) was dropped at Andrew Oldham's suggestion at the start of their career in an attempt to modernise it and align it with the performer Cliff Richard.

The track time, where known, is shown in minutes and seconds but beware - different releases of the exact same track can vary by a second or two and silent lead-ins, introductions and fade-outs can also affect the length. The digital age has provided an automated listed length and the majority of the book's timings are taken from these. Live recordings will vary, too, depending on spoken introductions and concluding crowd noise. Should the track have been recorded in front of a live audience, then it is annotated with " ✗ " to differentiate it from true "sessions". For many recordings, the song may start out under a different working name and these are listed when known with "AKA" (Also known as). The date and place of the recordings are mentioned. Studio tracks recorded over multiple sessions at different venues are separated by a ';' (semi-colon) otherwise a ',' (comma) will signify a continuation or separation unknown. In the above example, there is a split in recording dates and studios ';' but a continuation from one studio to another - from Sunset Sound to Elektra - with no specific dates known other than it was during October and November 1969. Then the year when the track has been played live are documented.

Guest musicians are also credited. The use of the term Rolling Stones is a broad one. It always includes the band members, Mick Jagger, Keith Richards, Charlie Watts and the integral Ian Stewart, plus either Brian Jones, Mick Taylor, Ron Wood or Bill Wyman, depending on the period. As a guide, from 1962 to April 1969, Brian Jones was a credited member. Mick Taylor took over in June 1969 and resigned in December 1974. Ron Wood officially took over the mantle of second guitarist in December 1975. Bill Wyman left the band in January 1993 and Darryl Jones has mainly taken his place on subsequent tours but has not been afforded official Stones status. Ian Stewart is much missed by those who knew and heard him. All contacts who I have met only have glowing words to describe him. It cannot go unnoticed that the band's last documented entry within this sessionography was made in his name, albeit in the form of a tribute album by Ben Waters but with participation by all current band members.

The production team is named next, split between producers, engineers and other accreditations. Where a track has been released, the detail for British and USA albums are listed with the date of release and the chart position. Sometimes another country is mentioned, should it be significant in terms of rarity. The type of media is also identified as: Vinyl LP (Long Player), EP (Extended Play) or Single. Other media listed are Cassette, CD (Compact Disc), Film, Video, DVD (Digital Video or Versatile Disc). Recently, it has been necessary to prefix an album or single with an 'e' to show it is an electronic download source. Multiple re-releases of original material on vinyl, compact disc and download are not documented. For example, CBS/Colombia, Virgin and Universal have released multiple formats.

The highest position and length of weeks in the Top 100 is taken from the American Billboard and the "official" British charts, which have changed over the years. If the track is an out-take from a session and has only been available by an unauthorised (bootleg) release then this is labelled as "Bootleg only". Should the recording not be heard in any of these formats, then it is labelled as "Unavailable".

Within the text description, significant other versions are documented and also listed with times e.g. (* a – 3.22, b – 4.36). In the Session Appendix, they are given the label Version if released or listed as a Track or a Cut if not released. It is not intended to be a full list of out-take cuts because it is evident that bootleggers liberally cut and re-processed tracks. However, important out-takes and mixes are included, timed and described. All albums are labelled in CAPITALS; book names and track titles are identified by *Italics*.

The Stones first live performance took place on 12 July, 1962 so 2012 sees the 50th anniversary, although the band did not fully manifest itself until January 1963. This long tenure at the top of their game is unprecedented for a rock 'n' roll band. Since this inception they have marched on inexorably, delivering peaks and troughs of recorded and live works and performing gargantuan world tours and concerts. Does the Stones' amazing story await a final script writer to conjure up a suitable conclusion as we enter the sixth decade . . . or could their concluding years remain as an unfinished masterpiece, a legacy of the greatest rock 'n' roll band in the world?

Special Thanks

Wendy Elliott has given me her continued support and input, while friends Chris Bartlett (journalist and editor) and Mike Carvalho (www.sistersingrease.com) have provided their literary and musical help respectively. Ronald Elliott for your editorial help in the past (miss you). Greg and Russ Elliott gave me their perspectives too.

I would like to extend a special thanks to Chris Kimsey (chriskimsey.com), who has written the foreword to this book and given me full co-operation on his work with the Stones. He is full of enthusiasm for the band and it has been a pleasure to meet him and receive his on-going input to the project since. Thanks also to Barry Sage (barrysage.com) for being very patient with subsequent questions and provision of photographs.

I must also thank the publisher (Cherry Red), especially their Chairman Iain McNay, Richard Anderson and designer Becky Stewart. Kudos to Steve Carter for his help and advice. Thanks to Gary Galbraith of the Internet Rocks Off message board who gave me permission to use their Setlist information to determine which year a song was played live. I am very grateful to Graham Wiltshire FRPS for providing photographs ranging from 1973 to the present. He can be contacted at f4atpark.gaw@gmail.com for enquiries regarding prints.

Lastly, thank you to all those great people and friends in the land of glimmers.

Assistance and Contacts

Felix 'Prof' Aeppli, Andre, Arve, Nick Bartlett, Nandita Batra, Alan Brackett, Doug Corkhill, Ben Cragg, Dave Cross, Gaby Del Bianco, Dr Johannes Delmere, Dr Andrew 'Dem' Demery, Diane 'Altamont' Dibble, Bob Drummond, Werner Dwenger, Chris Eborn, Blake Eikenberry, Roland 'Eagle Eye' Erbs, Fabrice Fayolle, Richard Fox, Gary 'Gazza' Galbraith, Bill German, Dean Gray, Derik Hering, Margaret Hoehn, Jim Henning, Laura Hull, Steve Jezzard, Jo (BOgLiN), Philip Johnston, Dr Thierry Joubard, Mike Keane (friend of Dave Hassinger), Chris Koenig, Ken Kola, The Lamb Inn, Matt Lee, Mike Majewski, Ian McPherson, Lew 'Keno' Menechino, John Nicholls, Steve Portigal, Doug 'Stonesdoug' Potash, Philippe Puicouyoul, Vernon Purnell, Chris Ritchey, Axel Schumacher, Michael 'miXile' Shanahan, Sherill, Marcelo Sonaglioni, Dave Stevenson, Joyce Stoffelsma, Nicole Sumon, Doug Teramura, Gary Wheelock, Aidan Wylde, Paul Young, Clarence Yu and, last but not least, Nico "I write the facts, you tell the stories," Zentgraf.

1 DIDDLEY DADDY – THE FATHER OF THEM ALL
March 1962 – February 1964

1. AROUND AND AROUND (LITTLE BOY BLUE & THE BLUE BOYS) (Berry) 1.21
January - March 1962: Place: Bexleyheath, Kent, England.
Mike Jagger, Keith Richards, Bob Beckwith, Allen Etherington, Dick Taylor.
Bootleg only.

Like stars forming a constellation, the various members embarked on their unification coming together in 1961. Michael (Mike) Jagger and Keith Richards bumped into each other at Dartford train station in the early autumn on Wednesday 17 October, the two having not seen each other since primary school days.
They reminisced and then, due to some records held under Mike's arm (THE BEST OF MUDDY WATERS, Chuck Berry's ROCKIN' AT THE HOPS and a compilation of the NATIONAL JAZZ FESTIVAL), discovered music was their current common denominator - Jimmy Reed, Howlin' Wolf, John Lee Hooker, etc. To carry records around under your arm was like wearing a badge on your sleeve and to have USA Chess imports showed music dedication.
Both young men knew Dick Taylor (who later founded a successful mid-60s R 'n' B band, The Pretty Things) and consequently they started some rehearsals at Jagger's home. Bob Beckwith (guitar) and Allen Etherington (Mike's closest school friend who lived in the same street as Mike and was given a percussion role) joined them as their co-noise makers under the guise of Little Boy Blue and The Blue Boys ("Blue Boy" was an inscription on Keith Richards' first guitar).
The seeds were sown, the friendship renewed. Bill Perks was born in 1936 and raised in South London where, as a kid, he dodged World War Two bombs and bullets. In the late 50s he did his national service in the RAF and fell in love with rock and roll, and with some friends in late 1960 he formed a dance band who became known as The Cliftons with Tony Chapman as their drummer. By comparison, Brian Jones landed in London from the Cotswolds, propelled by meeting Alexis Korner after a Chris Barber gig which featured Sonny Boy Williamson in Brian's home-town of Cheltenham in late 1961.
Brian had gained valuable experience by occasionally playing guitar and saxophone on Duane Eddy-style numbers in Cheltenham band The Ramrods. On Monday 19 February 1962, The Ramrods supported The Delta Jazzmen (a band formed by Bill Nile who Brian had recorded with), Danny Rivers, Mike Berry, and The Outlaws at Cheltenham Town Hall. Brian had met Paul Pond (later Paul Jones, the front man for Manfred Mann) at parties in London where musical ideas were swapped, but Brian proudly refused to join Paul's band, wanting one of his own. Brian wanted to know what Alexis Korner felt about a tape (labelled "Elmo and Paul") which he and Paul Pond had sent him, but he could not remember receiving it.
As a result, Alexis listened to Brian's guitar playing and, duly impressed, invited him to London - where he regularly stayed as Korner's guest. Brian had a girlfriend and a son, which complicated his life somewhat, but he eventually moved to London in early 1962 and played occasionally with Blues Incorporated, guesting on slide guitar on his favourite Dust My Broom. In January 1962, Charlie Watts joined Alexis Korner's Blues Incorporated, which featured Cyril Davies. In the late 1950s, the Cyril Davies Jazz Band had launched skiffle and the career of Lonnie Donnegan. Charlie was from Wembley in North London and he learned his drum trade at night in coffee shops while working in an advertising agency having left Harrow Art School.
Alexis Korner's band played a mixture of jazz, rhythm and blues, even country blues and attracted press attention in musical journals like Disc, Jazz News and the Melody Maker. In early April, Mike Jagger, Keith Richards and the band investigated the West London, Ealing Jazz Club which was run by Alexis Korner and witnessed the slide blues player who was guesting with Blues Incorporated. After the gig they chatted with Brian Jones, who had adopted the alias Elmo Lewis - Elmo after his blues idol, Elmore James and Lewis his christened first name.

2. LITTLE QUEENIE (LITTLE BOY BLUE & THE BLUE BOYS) (Berry) 4.32
January - March 1962: Place: Bexleyheath, Kent, England.
Played Live: 1969, 1970, 1971, 1973, 1986, 1997, 1998
Mike Jagger, Keith Richards, Bob Beckwith, Allen Etherington, Dick Taylor.
Bootleg only.

In late 1961 (from November) or early 1962, Little Boy Blue and the Blue Boys recorded a number of tracks in two different sittings. A reel-to-reel Agfa tape of these tracks was sold at Christie's in 1995 by a school friend of the band, who regularly attended their informal sessions to provide feedback on their performance. His parents owned a reel-to-reel recorder so he taped some of their rehearsals. These tapes were edited to produce the auctioned version. The full track listing as specified at the auction was *Around And Around, Little Queenie, Beautiful Delilah, La Bamba, On Your Way To School, 'I'm Left, You're Right, She's Gone', Don't Want No Woman, I Ain't Got You, Johnny B. Goode, Little Queenie* (take 2) (* a - 4.11) and *Beautiful Delilah* (take 2).
They mainly consisted of Chuck Berry covers, but also Elvis Presley's version of *You're Right, I'm Left, She's Gone* and Bobby "Blue" Bland's 1957 song *Don't Want No Woman.* Jagger himself coughed up £52,000 for these 10 songs and 12 tracks which ensured his rightful ownership. The tracks were recorded at either Bob Beckwith or Alan Etherington's house in Bexleyheath, near Dartford, where, as well as Jagger's home they used to rehearse. *Around And Around* is not complete and was probably included in a medley. *Little Queenie* is obviously a favourite since there are two versions both lasting more than four minutes. A young Jagger can already be heard singing in different styles.

3. BEAUTIFUL DELILAH (LITTLE BOY BLUE & THE BLUE BOYS) (Berry) 2.58
January - March 1962: Place: Bexleyheath, Kent, England.
Mike Jagger, Keith Richards, Bob Beckwith, Allen Etherington, Dick Taylor.
Bootleg only.

Again there are two versions. One at 2.58 and another at 2.18 (* a).

4. LA BAMBA (LITTLE BOY BLUE & THE BLUE BOYS) (Valens) 0.18
January - March 1962: Place: Bexleyheath, Kent, England.
Played Live: 1962
Mike Jagger, Keith Richards, Bob Beckwith, Allen Etherington, Dick Taylor.
Bootleg only.

A short extract probably from a medley.

5. GO ON TO SCHOOL (LITTLE BOY BLUE & THE BLUE BOYS) (Reed) 2.02
AKA: On Your Way To School, Wee Baby Blues
January - March 1962: Place: Bexleyheath, Kent, England.
Mike Jagger, Keith Richards, Bob Beckwith, Allen Etherington, Dick Taylor.
Bootleg only.

Two minutes of this very rare track.

6. I'M LEFT, YOU'RE RIGHT, SHE'S GONE (LITTLE BOY BLUE & THE BLUE BOYS) (Kesler, Taylor) 2.31
January - March 1962: Place: Bexleyheath, Kent, England.
Mike Jagger, Keith Richards, Bob Beckwith, Allen Etherington, Dick Taylor.
Bootleg only.

The reel-to-reel tape was heard by Record Collector's Peter Doggett in 1995 and he stated: "Only when they move from black blues to white, with Elvis' Sun Record favourite *I'm Left, You're Right, She's Gone* does some of his certainty vanish. When they're tackling Chuck Berry though, Mick and Keith sound as if they're walking on solid ground." In 2011, a bootleg of this song came to light.

7. DOWN THE ROAD APIECE (LITTLE BOY BLUE & THE BLUE BOYS) (Raye) 2.12
January - March 1962: Place: Bexleyheath, Kent, England.
Mike Jagger, Keith Richards, Bob Beckwith, Allen Etherington, Dick Taylor.
Bootleg only.

8. DON'T WANT NO WOMAN (LITTLE BOY BLUE & THE BLUE BOYS) (Robey) 2.30
January - March 1962: Place: Bexleyheath, Kent, England.
Mike Jagger, Keith Richards, Bob Beckwith, Allen Etherington, Dick Taylor.
Bootleg only.

A version of this Bobby Bland hit written by Don Robey who owned Duke Records.

9. I AIN'T GOT YOU (LITTLE BOY BLUE & THE BLUE BOYS) (Carter, Carter) 2.00
January - March 1962: Place: Bexleyheath, Kent, England.
Played Live: 1962
Mike Jagger, Keith Richards, Bob Beckwith, Allen Etherington, Dick Taylor.
Bootleg only.

A version of *I Ain't Got You*, written by Calvin and Clarence Carter and recorded by Jimmy Reed in 1955. It was also performed by Bo Diddley's harmonica player Billy Boy Arnold.

10. JOHNNY B. GOODE (LITTLE BOY BLUE & THE BLUE BOYS) (Berry) 2.24
January - March 1962: Place: Bexleyheath, Kent, England.
Played Live: 1962, 1963
Mike Jagger, Keith Richards, Bob Beckwith, Allen Etherington, Dick Taylor.
Bootleg only.

Certainly, this shows some talent as an authentic version of a Chuck Berry classic.

11. REELIN' AND A ROCKIN' (LITTLE BOY BLUE & THE BLUE BOYS) (Berry)
January - March 1962: Place: Bexleyheath, Kent, England.
Mike Jagger, Keith Richards, Bob Beckwith, Allen Etherington, Dick Taylor.
Unavailable.

12. BRIGHT LIGHTS, BIG CITY (LITTLE BOY BLUE & THE BLUE BOYS) (Reed)
January - March 1962: Place: Bexleyheath, Kent, England.
Mike Jagger, Keith Richards, Bob Beckwith, Allen Etherington, Dick Taylor.
Unavailable.

At some point, *Reelin' And A Rockin'* and *Bright Lights, Big City* were recorded and along with *La Bamba* and *Around And Around*, sent to Alexis Korner to assist in the group's quest for a residency at his Ealing Club. Dick Taylor fondly remembers the version of *La Bamba* with Mike (who soon became known by the more credible street name Mick) having obtained the words off the record in pseudo-Spanish.
Alexis was not impressed by the recordings but still invited Mick Jagger to Ealing to sing and play harmonica as a guest on various blues songs with Blues

Incorporated at weekends and also at the Marquee Jazz Club on week-days. That is when Charlie Watts first got his view of Mick Jagger's bum! Their paths were getting closer and they each saw a March edition of Jazz News, which mentioned the Ealing Club and on 7 April, 1962 the pair attended for the first time and saw Brian Jones performing. Duly impressed by this talented and - in their eyes - a worldly-wise character, they got chatting.

It was Brian who put an advertisement in the May, 1962 edition of Jazz News asking for players to join him at a session with a view to the formation of a band. Ian Stewart was the first to reply followed by guitarist Geoff Bradford, who soon bowed out in June. Ian was working in a full-time job as a clerk with Imperial Chemical Industries (ICI) in the heart of London. Originally from Fife, in Scotland, he had been brought up to play the piano, his passion being the blues and the piano-orientated boogie-woogie style.

They practised in bars such as the White Bear, near Leicester Square, and the Bricklayer's Arms in Soho. Ian was not keen on pure rock 'n' roll initially but soon appreciated Johnnie Johnson's piano work with Chuck Berry and thus became a band co-founder.

Finally, Mick Jagger went with Keith Richards and Dick Taylor (now on bass) to jam at these sessions. Ian and Brian favoured Paul Jones who in their eye was a better vocalist and a more pure blues musician but eventually plumped for the more precocious talent. Rehearsals continued and Mick Avory (later of The Kinks) played drums with them but they settled for Tony Chapman, of The Cliftons. For the time being, Brian's band was formed and Little Boy Blue & The Blue Boys ceased to exist. Mick Jagger stopped playing with Blues Incorporated to concentrate on what was happening with Jones and the others. Meanwhile, as a well-known outfit, Blues Incorporated had convinced the BBC of their worth and were booked for a studio session to be recorded for The Jazz Club programme. Marquee owner, Harold Pendleton, warned that they would lose their residency if they did not show up. Relations with the band, in particular Keith, were fraught due to his favour of jazz. The BBC could only budget for six musicians and Jagger was the one too many but Alexis Korner compromised by suggesting that he could convince the young singer to play at the Marquee with his new band. Alexis spoke to Brian Jones who agreed to the gig, made aware - even if he had not seen it before - of Mick's potential impact.

Brian chose the name Rollin' Stones, after the Muddy Waters song *Rollin' Stone*, although *Mannish Boy* (another Waters song) also mentions, "I'm a rolling stone". The 1950 *Rollin' Stone* song was featured on THE BEST OF MUDDY WATERS album.

When booking the band for a gig, Brian was asked for their name and, after apparently seeing the album on the floor by the telephone, selected *Rollin' Stone*. The song was a re-interpretation of a Mississippi blues standard called *Catfish Blues*, so we can thank Muddy for the revised title.

The Marquee event which took place on 12 July, 1962 was promoted as "Mick Jagger and the Rolling Stones", the singer being joined by Keith Richards, Brian Jones (Elmo Lewis), Dick Taylor, Ian Stewart and Tony Chapman. They played mainly Jimmy Reed and Elmore James numbers with Keith featuring on three Chuck Berry songs. The main act on the bill were Long John Baldry's Kansas City Blue Boys. Harold Pendleton was not amused when fights started between Marquee jazz regulars locals and the young rhythm and blues fans attracted to the venue for their first time.

After a few more gigs at the Ealing Jazz Club and others at the Marquee, Charlie Watts was approached but was not prepared to commit to the band on a regular basis as he still worked full-time and played with Blues Incorporated - so Tony Chapman continued to help out.

13. YOU CAN'T JUDGE A BOOK BY THE COVER (Dixon) 0.36
27 October 1962: Place: Curly Clayton Sound Studios, Highbury, London, England.
Played Live: 1962, 1963
Brian Jones, Mike Jagger, Keith Richards, Tony Chapman, Ian Stewart.
Engineer: Curly Clayton.
Bootleg only.

In late August 1962, Mick Jagger, Keith Richards and Brian Jones moved into a house in Edith Grove, Kensington, where the autumn and winter turned out to be one of the coldest on record. Mick and Keith had put their days in Dartford behind them. For Keith, there was no more working as a 'weekend boy' at the Pricerite supermarket or as a temporary postman at Christmas.

In October, they went to session guitarist Curly Clayton's studio with Tony Chapman playing drums but with no bass guitar. By this time Dick Taylor, had returned to college, prompted by another band bust-up with Harold Pendleton and his desire to play lead guitar rather than bass. At the time, Keith's favoured guitar was a Hofner semi-acoustic which John Lennon and Paul McCartney were both using back in 1961 and 1962.

14. SOON FORGOTTEN (Oden)
27 October 1962: Place: Curly Clayton Sound Studios, Highbury, London, England.
Played Live: 1962, 1963
Brian Jones, Mike Jagger, Keith Richards, Tony Chapman, Ian Stewart.
Engineer: Curly Clayton.
Unavailable.

15. CLOSE TOGETHER (Reed)
27 October 1962: Place: Curly Clayton Sound Studios, Highbury, London, England.
Played Live: 1962, 1963
Brian Jones, Mike Jagger, Keith Richards, Tony Chapman, Ian Stewart.
Engineer: Curly Clayton.
Unavailable.

Three tracks - *Soon Forgotten, Close Together* and *You Can't Judge A Book By Its Cover* - were recorded at the studio which was a rival to Joe Meek's recording operations. Two of the songs have not been made available but *You Can't Judge A Book By The Cover* was broadcast on BBC Radio One's Simon Bates' programme in 1988.

The presenter interviewed a collector who had purchased an EMIDISC acetate of these three historic recordings in April 1988 for £6,000 by the Phillips auctioneers, the vendor having been given the acetate by Brian Jones in exchange for a shirt! The recordings were re-sold for £10,800 in 2003.

Mick Jagger's enunciation on the songs was distinctly non-British and leered in true Willie Dixon style, his vocals being the most distinctive instrument on the tape. The recordings were sent to jazz guitarist and talent spotter Neville Skrimshire at EMI, who rejected them and commented: "It would be fine if you could sing".

Brian Jones then wrote to Jazz News in October 1962 and attempted to explain that … "It must be apparent that Rock 'n' Roll has a far greater affinity for R & B, than the latter has for jazz, insofar as Rock is a direct corruption of Rhythm & Blues, whereas jazz is Negro music on a different plane, intellectually higher, though emotionally less intense." Brian Jones, London SW10. (Brian Jones plays guitar with The Rollin' Stones).

At this time, Charlie Watts was finding that playing so regularly with Blues Incorporated was affecting his day job so he left and started to play occasionally with Brian Knight's Blues By Six.

16. DIDDLEY DADDY (McDaniel) 2.38
11 March 1963: Place: IBC Studios, London, England.
Played Live: 1963
Engineer: Glyn Johns.
Bootleg only.

Tony Chapman had told Bill Perks of the Stones existence and that they did not have a full-time bass player. After meeting Ian Stewart in early December 1962, at a concert by Glyn John's Presidents, Bill, who became known as Wyman that was the surname of a friend which he thought was more stage-cool, was persuaded to attend a practice session at the Wetherby Arms on 7 December.

Brian Jones was more impressed by the size of Bill's VOX 30 amplifier than his playing on his fretless home-made bass guitar but, after a couple of rehearsals, the newcomer was invited to play at the next gig. Wyman's instrument which he made in 1959 from a standard Dallas Tuxedo bass was soon made fretless. This pre-empted manufacturers who caught up with the fretless style in 1966. The speaker cabinet, with cement at the bottom, was another contributory factor to the sound, even if it did take four people to carry it.

Tony Chapman was sacked by the band, early in January 1963, knowing that Charlie Watts was on the side-lines so on 12 January, 1963, the line-up of The Rolling Stones was established for the first time at a gig in Ealing. Bill Wyman recounts this date in his book *Rolling With The Stones*.

At this time, there was one more significant addition to the Stones scene as, at another gig in January, Mick advertised to the crowd that there was a spare bed going at Edith Grove for anyone willing to rent. After the band were packing up, James Phelge, who would later write a book of his memoirs with the Stones, agreed to move in. And so the stage was set for the greatest motion adventure for which anyone could care to wish or dream. The constellation would take many shapes and images over the years.

It was time to book themselves into the IBC (Independent Broadcasting Corporation) studios which were more commonly used for recording jingles since it was so small - the walls' sound buffers were egg boxes. The outcome of the sessions is a set of distinctly blues-flavoured tracks. *Diddley Daddy* is a Bo Diddley number and is performed in true rhythm and blues (R 'n' B) style. The Diddley bow is an African one-stringed guitar used by young American bluesmen to learn the guitar. The song, although rough in texture, is guided by Mick Jagger's roots vocals and features two instrumental breaks - the first by Brian Jones on the harmonica and the second by Ian Stewart, tinkering on the ivories to the fade out.

17. ROAD RUNNER (McDaniel) 3.02
11 March 1963: Place: IBC Studios, London, England.
Played Live: 1962, 1963, 1964
Engineer: Glyn Johns.
Bootleg only.

Road Runner, another well-known Ellis McDaniel (AKA Bo Diddley) number, was next on the list for the Stones' treatment and is played in a hard-rocking, non-compromising style. The guitar played by Brian Jones is the main lead instrument, supported by Keith Richards on rhythm, a harmonica from Mick Jagger and Ian Stewart on piano.

It was a popular stage favourite at their Crawdaddy Club residency in Richmond and was a small concession in attempting to put across some of the more commercial material onto tape in order to secure a recording contract. Their musical upbringing was in jazz clubs where they were used to playing sedate blues. Later, young entrepreneur Andrew Loog Oldham (referred to hereafter as Andrew Oldham), who was to become their manager, had his finger on the pulse of youth culture and knew that they had to stop sitting on bar stools, jazz style, and literally move with the music. They also had to make the music more accessible to the punter by playing more popular tunes.

Ironically, on their first British tour as a support act, they were to drop all Bo Diddley numbers in deference to the master himself - he was also on the tour, second on the bill to the Everly Brothers. An IBC Sound Recording acetate exists of *Road Runner*, coupled with *Diddley Daddy*. It sold for £1,500 in 1988.

18. I WANT TO BE LOVED (Dixon) 1.53
AKA: I Wanna Be Loved
11 March 1963: Place: IBC Studios, London, England.
Engineer: Glyn Johns.
Bootleg only.

This was later re-recorded as the B-side of the first single *Come On*. It is a leisurely mix indeed and again, instrumentally, Ian Stewart and Brian Jones on harmonica are prominently featured. The song is an authentic Willie Dixon R 'n' B standard. Mick Jagger's vocals are meaningful and interpret the senior blues man's desires in a way that only the young are able.

19. BABY, WHAT'S WRONG? (Reed, Reed) 3.24
AKA: Honey What's Wrong?
11 March 1963: Place: IBC Studios, London, England.
Played Live: 1962, 1963
Engineer: Glyn Johns.
Bootleg only.

This track was intended to wrap up the Stones' first recording session. The IBC sessions, although now famous and much sought after, were considered as a whole far too rough for a commercial release, much to the band's disappointment. *(Honey) Baby, What's Wrong* is a meandering song and double-tracked harmonies leave a lot to be desired. The mix of pop vocals with Keith Richards' R 'n' B lead guitar and Mick Jagger's harmonica did not quite gel.

Glyn Johns, who engineered the sessions, was a musician himself and detected the group's potential. He had sung with them at one of their concerts and offered to record them. It was only a two-track mono studio, with a Grundig tape recorder, but the band signed a six-month deal with IBC to record there free of charge in studio down-time. The studio was owned by band leader Eric Robinson and George Clouston, an orchestra player.

An acetate was made of the sessions - it was not liked by the management but it was touted by IBC amongst the record companies. EMI were one of the companies to reject the tracks - sincerity was detected in the music but the thin production quality and the lack of chart potential caused the end product to be suspect. The band were particularly critical of the lack of bass in the mix and wanted the tracks re-cut but this did not happen. A ten-inch acetate of the five tracks was sold by a friend of Brian Jones at an auction in April 1993.

20. BRIGHT LIGHTS, BIG CITY (Reed) 2.25
11 March 1963: Place: IBC Studios, London, England.
Played Live: 1962, 1963
Engineer: Glyn Johns.
Bootleg only.

An impressive version of Jimmy Reed's *Bright Lights, Big City*, despite the fact that it was recorded in the final five minutes of the session time. Keith Richards again played lead guitar with Mick Jagger on harmonica. The song epitomised a young Stones sound, Jagger performing in a relaxed manner while Ian Stewart provided an excellent piano background. Their enthusiasm could not be missed by anyone listening. Bill Wyman's *Rolling With The Stones* book states that Brian Jones was particularly proud of the five recordings and would often play them back to friends.

21. PRETTY THING (McDaniel)
20 April 1963: Place: R G Jones Studio, Morden, Surrey, England.
Played Live: 1962, 1963, 1964
Producer: Giorgio Gomelsky.
Engineer: R G Jones Junior.
Unavailable.

22. IT'S ALL RIGHT BABE (McDaniel)
20 April 1963: Place: R G Jones Studio, Morden, Surrey, England.
Played Live: 1963
Producer: Giorgio Gomelsky.
Engineer: R G Jones Junior.
Unavailable.

Giorgio Gomelsky was the promoter at the Station Hotel in Richmond which provided an alternative to the Ealing Jazz Club and the Marquee. The Stones were also playing regularly at the Ricky Tick Club at the Star and Garter in Windsor and the Red Lion in Sutton.

Giorgio was so enthusiastic about the Stones that he gained them a Station Hotel residency on Sunday evenings from the 3 March until the end of May, fresh after their afternoon session at Ken Colyer's Studio 51. Another residency followed at Eel Pie Island in Twickenham.

The Crawdaddy Club (named after the Bo Diddley song *Craw-Dad*) soon became a local phenomenon. The London hip squad and the press began to take notice, and membership of the club escalated - dance improvisation was rife on the hot, sweaty dance floor.

Ian McLagan who at the time was in a school band, recalls attending the Crawdaddy every week where he hung out under Brian Jones' slide guitar. The atmosphere was charged and seeing an incredible slide musician was an inspiring moment for him. Even the Beatles visited the club having been persuaded by Giorgio. Their third single *From Me To You* had just been released and was to become their first No. 1 in the UK.

Certainly Giorgio's interest in promoting the Rolling Stones was making him their manager by default, but it was not an official arrangement. His ambitions were big and he attempted to self-record a promotional film of the blues scene. The soundtrack was to include *Pretty Thing* and *It's All Right Babe*, both were recorded at the R G Jones Studio. The filming was done the next day on Sunday 21 April.

Peter Jones, the editor of Record Mirror, attended the concert where *Pretty Thing* and *Hey Crawdaddy* were stomping crowd pleasers used at the end of the show as a hypnotic climax. *It's All Right Babe* was a background track in the documentary but the film was never completed. All was not lost, though, as Peter Jones had tipped off Andrew Oldham as to what was happening in Richmond - he saw the concert, too, with Tony Calder, who was his co-PR worker and the yin to his yang.

They were suitably impressed and told Eric Easton, who they worked with and who, more importantly, had a promoter's license and an office. He wanted to see the Stones with his own eyes and the next week they all witnessed the Sunday 28 April performance. While Giorgio Gomelsky was out of the country due to a family funeral, a 19-year-old Andrew Oldham and Eric Easton offered the group a contract on 1 May 1963. A letter from Eric Easton to Brian Jones was sold at Christie's - it stated that Andrew wanted a three-year deal rather than the normal single year.

23. I'M MOVING ON (Snow)
23 April 1963: Place: BBC Radio, London, England.
Rolling Stones with Ricky Fenson, Carlo Little.
Unavailable.

24. I'M A HOG FOR YOU BABY (Leiber, Stoller)
23 April 1963: Place: BBC Radio, London, England.
Played Live: 1962, 1963
Rolling Stones with Ricky Fenson, Carlo Little.
Unavailable.

Brian Jones had written to the BBC in January 1963 to request a radio audition for the Jazz Club show, claiming that "in view of the vast increase of interest in rhythm and blues in Britain an exceptionally good future has been predicted for us by many people". The audition happened on a Tuesday which was not a good day since Charlie Watts, Bill Wyman and Ian Stewart were working. Ian got the day off and the rhythm section was quickly gained from Cyril Davies' band, namely Carlo Little and Ricky 'Fenson' Brown. They had played a number of gigs with the Stones over the winter period but this session was their final time.
The tracks are not available and were considered too "black" and not commercial enough in content for the BBC production panel. The performance was not considered suitable for BBC purposes. James Phelge, in *Phelge's Stones*, remembers the band returning from the session generally subdued due to the low-key interest shown in the band by the BBC staff. They were not to gain another BBC session until September 1963.

25. COME ON (Berry) 1.50
10 May 1963: Place: Olympic Studios, Carton St, London, England.
Played Live: 1963, 1964, 1965
Producer: Andrew Oldham, Eric Easton.
Engineer: Roger Savage.
UK Single: 7 June 1963: No. 21 - 14 weeks
UK Compilation LP THANK YOUR LUCKY STARS VOL 2: 27 September 1963
UK Compilation LP READY STEADY GO!: 24 January 1964: No. 20 - 1 week
UK Compilation LP BIG HITS (HIGH TIDE AND GREEN GRASS): 4 November 1966: No. 4 - 43 weeks
UK Compilation LP ROCK 'N' ROLLING STONES: 13 October 1972: No. 41 - 1 week
USA Compilation LP MORE HOT ROCKS (BIG HITS & FAZED COOKIES): 1 December 1972: No. 9 - 12 weeks
UK Compilation LP ROLLED GOLD: 14 November 1975: No. 7 - 50 weeks
German Compilation LP THE REST OF THE BEST: December 1983
UK & USA LP THE ROLLING STONES SINGLES COLLECTION - THE LONDON YEARS: 15 August 1989
USA Compilation CD MORE HOT ROCKS (BIG HITS & FAZED COOKIES): 3 September 2002
UK & USA CD box set THE ROLLING STONES SINGLES - 1963 - 1965: 4 May 2004
UK Compilation CD ROLLED GOLD +: 12 November 2007: No. 26 - 12 weeks

On 9 May 1963, a three-year management contract was confirmed between Brian Jones, Eric Easton and Andrew Oldham. Brian signed himself as L B Jones while Mick Jagger was described as a student. Oldham and Easton formed a company called Impact Sound to be the management and recording team behind the Rolling Stones. The deal was signed on 21 May by Brian Jones (as L B Jones) and Eric Easton for Impact Sound.
Brian's part in the negotiations was reflected in an extra £5 a week, a fact hidden in the detail. Overall, it was weighted on Impact's side - they received 14 per cent from Decca and paid the band six per cent. Oldham talked Jones into returning to IBC, paying them for the time spent in the studio and the return of their tapes, thereby nulling the contract with them.
This displeased Glyn Johns, who had thought he would be producing the Stones' early work. He did not in fact produce them until later in their career when Oldham was off the scene, relenting later to engineer live tapes in 1965 and work on the BETWEEN THE BUTTONS album.
Oldham booked the Olympic studios (a former Dutch reform church and a Synagogue in Carton Street, in London's West End) for the first recording session on 9 May 1963. It was agreed that Roger Savage would be the recording engineer in a £40-for- three-hours deal.
The studio manager, Keith Grant, remembered it differently. He described that the "rabbit" was a free session which they gave occasionally. He knew Roger was keen to record the Stones having seen them at the Crawdaddy club. Keith was not so sure, having also watched them with BBC's Jimmy Grant, from Saturday Club, and concluding: "They were dreadful." He was somewhat surprised and pleased, therefore, when he heard the session's result.
Come On is played at a frenetic pace, faster than the Chuck Berry version. Berry had a number of hits in the USA and UK in the 1950s but had not enjoyed chart success in the early 60s. *Come On* was virtually unknown and, to the public, it could have been construed as an original.
A harmonica guides the track throughout in a rail-road style. The outcome was a very clean recording with clearly defined instrumentation, unlike some of the Regent Sound. Ian Stewart, although present at the sessions, did not contribute to the recording since his microphone had been switched off at Oldham's instructions, according to the latter's *Stoned* book.
The recording was made on an Ampex with tambourine and vocals over-dubbed. Roger Savage asked Oldham to mix the track thinking that was his production role but he left Roger to perform the task. Andrew had no clue how to go about taking four tracks and creating an end result, hence most of the early tracks being mono. Besides he had more to think about and needed a record company to sell the product.
At the time there were only two major UK recording companies - EMI and Decca. Having been rejected by EMI there was only one more door to knock on. The Decca artiste and repertoire (A & R) man, Dick Rowe, who had previously turned down The Beatles in favour of Brian Poole and The Tremeloes, desperately wanted to rectify this mistake and recover some standing in the music industry. Ironically, Rowe had already been tipped off by George Harrison to sign the Stones. He saw the band live in early May and within a week had offered a recording contract. Oldham and Easton negotiated a shrewd recording contract with Rowe enabling the Stones to record independently and then sell the tapes to Decca.
The recording session for *Come On* was then arranged. Naturally, Decca were not convinced of the Impact Sound achieved on 10 May and requested that *Come On* be re-recorded at Decca's own studios on 18 May. Decca then listened to both versions and agreed to release the original Impact Sound/Roger Savage version.
The band themselves were not too convinced of the result created by "no mix" producer Oldham and sound engineer Savage. To back this up, the song was not played at concerts, the speed of the record being significant - it was too fast to dance to. However, it entered the lower echelons of the UK charts on 25 July 1963 and became their first "hit". The track was included on a THANK YOUR LUCKY STARS compilation of various artists released by Decca in September 1963.

26. I WANT TO BE LOVED (Dixon) 1.51
10 May 1963: Place: Olympic Studios, Carton St, London, England.
Played Live: 1963
Producer: Andrew Oldham, Eric Easton.
Engineer: Roger Savage.
UK B-side Come On: 7 June 1963
German Compilation LP THE REST OF THE BEST: December 1983
UK & USA LP THE ROLLING STONES SINGLES COLLECTION - THE LONDON YEARS: 15 August 1989
UK & USA CD box set THE ROLLING STONES SINGLES - 1963 - 1965: 4 May 2004

The equipment at Olympic was state of the art, as Keith Grant reflected in 2012: "We had the first four-track studio with an EMT reverb plate and equalisation on every channel. It was developed by our engineer Dick Swettenham."
The Olympic version of *I Want To Be Loved* is a faster guitar boogie than the original demo take and is also polished by a crisp quality studio finish. Again, the harmonica is used extensively and is featured in the instrumental break. Andrew Oldham was happy with the single sound and product and gave Keith £3 to pass on to Roger Savage for his effort in lieu of overtime.
The release, of which this was the flipside, was coupled by an appearance on the acclaimed Thank Your Lucky Stars TV show, where both sides were featured. As a result, a modest chart entry ensued. The TV recording is famous for the band wearing a set of appealing chequered suits, an image they attempted hastily to reject. In order to better project the Stones on camera, Andrew Oldham also decided that Ian Stewart should step down from on-stage work and not appear in publicity photos, becoming instead a studio player and their road manager. This was due to his somewhat staid, square-jawed appearance and, graciously, he agreed. Stewart had seen the signs when his piano had been moved further and further towards the dressing room while on stage. The Stones were starting to feel their way up the pop ladder by such compromises, whilst managing to retain their musical integrity.

27. FORTUNE TELLER (Neville) 2.18
9 July 1963: Place: Decca, West Hampstead, London, England.
Played Live: 1962, 1963
Producer: Andrew Oldham, Michael Barclay.
UK Compilation LP SATURDAY CLUB: 24 January 1964
USA Compilation LP MORE HOT ROCKS (BIG HITS & FAZED COOKIES): 1 December 1972: No. 9 - 12 weeks
UK LP SOLID ROCK: 13 October 1980
German Compilation LP THE REST OF THE BEST: December 1983
USA Compilation CD MORE HOT ROCKS (BIG HITS & FAZED COOKIES): November 1990
USA Compilation CD MORE HOT ROCKS (BIG HITS & FAZED COOKIES): 3 September 2002

Credited to Naomi Neville but some say written by Allen Toussaint, *Fortune Teller* was intended to be the B-side of *Poison Ivy* but, due to the non-release of this single, it was only made available to the public via a compilation album of the BBC radio programme Saturday Club.
The song was extensively produced to give it a commercial ring. Charlie Watts' drums are powerful and vibrant and crash during the track's bridges. There were background vocal "ah-ah's" and an accompanying harmonica on the more common SATURDAY CLUB release. There is another version which was released on early CD releases for MORE HOT ROCKS (844 478-2) which lacks the repeat of the last verse and the harmonica overdubs (* a - 2.06). It is also this version that appears overdubbed with crowd screams for the *Got Live If You Want It!* EP.
Such an early recording proves that, while naivety in musicians can be turned into spontaneity, when producers and engineers are also inexperienced in pop technique, as in this case, the end result can lose its potential. It was not as sweet as the American funk the Stones were attempting to imitate. However, it was not to be long before such problems were overcome.

28. POISON IVY (Leiber, Stoller) 2.36
15 July 1963: Place: Decca, West Hampstead, London, England.
Played Live: 1963
Producer: Andrew Oldham, Michael Barclay.
UK Compilation LP SATURDAY CLUB: 24 January 1964
UK LP SOLID ROCK: 13 October 1980
German Compilation LP THE REST OF THE BEST: December 1983
USA Compilation CD MORE HOT ROCKS (BIG HITS & FAZED COOKIES): 3 September 2002

Throughout June, July and August, while *Come On* was having modest chart success, the Rolling Stones were playing virtually every night on the local residency circuit of the Ricky Tick Club (Windsor), Eel Pie Island (Twickenham) and Ken Colyer's Studio 51.
Their last gig for the Crawdaddy Club, which had now been located at the ballroom of the Richmond Athletic Club, was in the late summer of 1963. A reel-to-reel tape recording of the performance was on sale at Christie's Auctions in 2004. The track list was *Route 66, Come On, Talkin' 'Bout You, Love Potion No.9, Roll Over Beethoven, Money, Pretty Thing, Jaguar & Thunderbird, Don't Lie To Me, Our Little Rendezvous* (Chuck Berry's rewrite of *Good Morning Little Schoolgirl*), *You Got Me Running, Brown Eyed Handsome Man, Diddley Daddy* and *Money*.
It was a unique glance at their performing repertoire and was purchased by an unknown buyer for £23,900. At this time, eager to soak up the group, Chrissie Shrimpton was on the scene dating Mick Jagger. On 11 August 1963 the Stones were paid £30 for playing the 3rd National Jazz Festival in Richmond, an event founded and organised by Harold Pendleton.
A young 16-year-old Ronnie Wood witnessed their performance at the bottom of the bill in a sweaty tent on a warm summer's day when, with jazz favourite Acker Bilk on the main stage, everyone disappeared to hear the Stones.
The band used the Ken Colyer Club and the Wetherby Arms to rehearse material for their next recording, such as a cover of the Shirelles' *Putty In Your Hands*. They were eager to capitalise on their recent chart position with *Come On*. After a lot of internal conflict, they considered The Coasters' *I'm A Hog For You Baby* before

compromising and settling for *Poison Ivy*. It was recorded at Decca's recording studios in North London where the Beatles had famously failed their audition for a contract on the basis that guitar bands were on their way out.

The song is a little rushed and also suffers from muffled studio problems. It was commercially viable but lacked the quality necessary to be a follow-up to *Come On*. Dick Rowe from Decca had attempted to use Michael Barclay at the session, an idea which failed miserably because Michael did not hit it off with the band. The Stones and Andrew Oldham were exasperated and Decca were left positively fuming - but it was worth being patient.

Decca went as far as issuing a catalogue number of F11742 and a release date of 26 August 1963 before the proposed single was scrapped. Two mixes are available, one on the SATURDAY CLUB album and a second alternative version recorded four months later on the USA MORE HOT ROCKS release. Andrew Oldham started to search frantically for a follow-up. He was aware that other popular groups, notably The Beatles, were recording their own songs and he pressurised Mick Jagger and Keith Richards to do the same.

29. YOU BETTER MOVE ON (Alexander) 2.40
8 August 1963: Place: Decca, West Hampstead, London, England.
Played Live: 1962, 1963, 1964
Producer: Eric Easton, Andrew Oldham.
UK EP The Rolling Stones: 10 January 1964
USA LP DECEMBER'S CHILDREN (AND EVERYBODY'S): 4 December 1965: No. 4 - 22 weeks
UK Compilation LP THROUGH THE PAST DARKLY (BIG HITS VOL 2): 12 September 1969: No. 2 - 37 weeks
UK LP SLOW ROLLERS: 9 November 1981
UK & USA CD box set THE ROLLING STONES SINGLES - 1963 - 1965: 4 May 2004

Inspired by such luminaries as The Drifters, a song in a similar vein, written by Arthur Alexander, was recorded at the Decca Studios. The lead vocals were double-tracked by Mick Jagger and Bill Wyman and Brian Jones performed backing vocals. Brian also played an acoustic guitar ballad-style and the song became an instant Stones classic being lapped up by the fans.

It soon became popular at their concerts and was released early in 1964. Plaintive and charged with emotion, this track received the most airplay on track one of side two of the EP. The EP produced by Impact Sound (Eric Easton and Andrew Oldham) soon outsold their previous two chart entries.

30. BYE BYE JOHNNY (Berry) 2.12
8 August 1963: Place: Decca, West Hampstead, London, England.
Played Live: 1963, 1964, 1972, 1986
Producer: Eric Easton, Andrew Oldham.
UK EP The Rolling Stones: 10 January 1964
UK Compilation LP ROCK 'N' ROLLING STONES: 13 October 1972: No. 41 - 1 week
USA Compilation LP MORE HOT ROCKS (BIG HITS & FAZED COOKIES): 1 December 1972: No. 9 - 12 weeks
USA Compilation CD MORE HOT ROCKS (BIG HITS & FAZED COOKIES): 3 September 2002
UK & USA CD box set THE ROLLING STONES SINGLES - 1963 - 1965: 4 May 2004

Keith Richards picks his fingers almost as nimbly through this song as did his hero Chuck Berry. He certainly copies the master's licks and the rest of the Stones rock along in fine style. Keith was asked to comment on Chuck Berry and stated: "To me, Chuck Berry always was the epitome of rhythm and blues playing, rock and roll playing. It was beautiful, effortless and his timing was perfection. He is rhythm man supreme. He plays that lovely double-string stuff, which I got down a long time ago but I'm still getting the hang of. Later I realised why he played that way - because of the sheer physical size of the guy. I mean, he makes one of those big Gibsons look like a ukulele!"

Bye Bye Johnny is a worthy contribution to their first EP and begins to show the potential of Mick Jagger's vocals. The release of this EP followed the *I Wanna Be Your Man* single and ensured a continued spotlight in the charts, so much so that it would remain in the EP listings for the rest of the year. The sleeve notes revealed: "Their approach to their music is far closer to the brash, hard-driving Chicago style rhythm and blues than the majority of the groups currently riding the beat wagon..." It proved the Stones' popularity and they were soon to enter a studio to record their first album.

31. MONEY (Gordy Junior, Bradford) 2.34
8 August; 14-15 November 1963: Place: Decca, West Hampstead; De Lane Lea Studios, Kingsway, London, England.
Played Live: 1963, 1964
Producer: Eric Easton, Andrew Oldham.
UK EP The Rolling Stones: 10 January 1964
USA Compilation LP MORE HOT ROCKS (BIG HITS & FAZED COOKIES): 1 December 1972: No. 9 - 12 weeks
UK Compilation LP NO STONE UNTURNED: 5 October 1973
German Compilation LP THE REST OF THE BEST: December 1983
USA Compilation CD MORE HOT ROCKS (BIG HITS & FAZED COOKIES): 3 September 2002
UK & USA CD box set THE ROLLING STONES SINGLES - 1963 - 1965: 4 May 2004

Mick Jagger recalled buying the 1960 American hit version by Barrett Strong and decided it could be worked upon for the English market. He was not the only one inspired by the song because The Beatles had recorded it in July for inclusion on their second LP, WITH THE BEATLES, which was subsequently released in November 1963. During the same month Bern Elliott and the Fenmen were at No. 14 in the UK charts with this Berry Gordy/Janice Bradford song and remained in the charts for 13 weeks. It emphasised the point that songwriters were few and far between at that juncture in pop culture.

The Stones created a loose feel to the track, but Brian Jones managed to hold it together with his excellent harmonica playing. Mick's vocals are a little undisciplined as though he needs some kind of restraint for his up-front voice. Considering it was only their second or third venture into a recording studio, The Rolling Stones were beginning to fuse into a tight unit.

32. MONEY (Gordy Junior, Bradford)
23 September 1963: Place: BBC Maida Vale Studios, London, England.
Unavailable.

33. I'M TALKIN' ABOUT YOU (Berry)
23 September 1963: Place: BBC Maida Vale Studios, London, England.
Unavailable.

34. COME ON (Berry) 2.02
23 September 1963: Place: BBC Maida Vale Studios, London, England.
Bootleg only.

The Chuck Berry lyrics were compromised with some "stupid jerk" changed to "stupid guy" as was the single.

35. MEMPHIS TENNESSEE (Berry) 2.20
23 September 1963: Place: BBC Maida Vale Studios, London, England.
Played Live: 1963, 1964
Bootleg only.

36. ROLL OVER BEETHOVEN (Berry) 2.17
23 September 1963: Place: BBC Maida Vale Studios, London, England.
Played Live: 1962, 1963, 1964, 1970
Bootleg only.

Television and especially radio played an important part in broadcasting and promoting the early 1960s rock-and-roll message. As much as anything, playing live on radio was proof that any recording was genuine.

The Stones were booked to appear in the third show of Ready Steady Go! to promote a playback of their first single *Come On* in August. An interview was conducted by 20-year-old presenter Cathy McGowan after producer Vicki Wickham booked them principally because Brian Jones looked gorgeous! Her other working colleagues were co-presenter Keith Fordyce and filmographer Michael Lindsay-Hogg.

The show contrasted directly with the more staid BBC Top Of The Pops. It was produced from a young, risk-taking viewpoint as Vicki Wickham proudly recalled in 2012: "Michael shot the show as a fan would want to see it . . . faces of the performers, short skirts and fashion on the dancers, lots of close-ups, fast cutting, it was way pre-MTV but had a cool, very hip and very exciting look."

As initial television coverage grew, the BBC production team at Saturday Club, Jimmy Grant and Bernie Andrews, were anxious to get the Stones on the show. This time the production team approved the audition tape and, following the recording, Bill Wyman and Charlie Watts backed Bo Diddley for his radio session transmitted on 5 October. They had come a long way since both being influenced by 50s icon Johnny Ray and played on *Bo Diddley*, *Road Runner*, *Pretty Thing* and *Hey Bo Diddley*.

The above tracks are testimony to the Stones' affiliation with Chuck Berry and were recorded for a Saturday Club radio broadcast on 26 October 1963. *Memphis Tennessee* and *Roll Over Beethoven* are notable as they have not been released on record. The Stones rock on all the Berry numbers despite Ian Stewart's piano again missing from the session. British beat music, in the form of R 'n' B, was ready to blossom and take over the "boring" pop market! *Come On* is played at more of a relaxed pace and compares very favourably with the single version.

At the end of September, following the BBC recording, the Stones embarked on their first UK tour supporting the Everly Brothers and their hero Bo Diddley. The set list was short, amounting to just six songs. This tour extended for the whole of October and offered two shows a day with only three or four days of rest. It was a great chance to fine tune their act and also witness the theatrical antics of Little Richard, who was brought in to increase ticket sales. Such was the success that, on 21 November 1963, Robert Stigwood signed the band for a four-week February 1964 tour at a fee of £1,000 per week.

37. I WANNA BE YOUR MAN (Lennon, McCartney) 1.43
7 October 1963: Place: De Lane Lea Studios, Kingsway, London, England.
Played Live: 1963, 1964
Producer: Eric Easton, Andrew Oldham.
UK Single: 1 November 1963: No. 12 - 16 weeks
UK Compilation LP READY STEADY GO!: 24 January 1964: No. 20 - 1 week
USA Single: 17 February 1964
USA B-side Not Fade Away: 6 March 1964
UK Compilation LP MILESTONES: 18 February 1972: No. 14 - 8 weeks
UK Compilation LP ROLLED GOLD: 14 November 1975: No. 7 - 50 weeks
UK Compilation LP GET STONED - 30 GREATEST HITS, 30 ORIGINAL TRACKS: 21 October 1977: No. 13 - 15 weeks
UK LP SOLID ROCK: 13 October 1980
UK & USA LP THE ROLLING STONES SINGLES COLLECTION - THE LONDON YEARS: 15 August 1989
UK & USA CD box set THE ROLLING STONES SINGLES - 1963 - 1965: 4 May 2004
UK Compilation CD ROLLED GOLD +: 12 November 2007: No. 26 - 12 weeks

The Stones, Andrew Oldham and Decca, having considered and refused the *Poison Ivy* single, sought a follow-up to *Come On*. On 10 September 1963, Andrew Oldham bumped into John Lennon and Paul McCartney following a Variety Club awards ceremony at the Savoy Hotel at which The Beatles had won "top vocal band". Andrew complained at the lack of suitable material for the Stones' second single release and John and Paul thought that they might be able to help. They were in the middle of recording their second album and had an unfinished R 'n' B song that was an instant hit!

Andrew took them into Ken Colyer's Studio 51 club, where he knew the Stones were practising and performing later. The bass and electric guitars were handed over to the Liverpool duo and Charlie provided a back beat to the first verse and chorus. Bill Wyman remembers in *Stone Alone* how amazed he was to witness Paul playing his bass backwards since Paul is left-handed.

The Stones liked the feel of the song so John and Paul disappeared into another room to finish it off. Much to everyone's surprise, they returned a few minutes later, with the finished product. Probably more than anything this song writing adeptness inspired the Stones to compose their own work and the royalties would be helpful too! Two weeks later, after personalising the song with slide guitar, the Stones entered De Lane Lea Studios.

From the opening chords the song is pure, high energy. Bill Wyman hits a hard-driving bass and Brian Jones delivers an electrifying lead guitar including a tight, relaxed bottleneck slide solo. The foundations had been laid for the Stones to establish their potential on the unassuming public by this gift from The Beatles and, indeed, the single reached No. 12 in the UK charts. It appeared as a promo only single in the United States and was not fully released, either because of a potential lack of sales or the fact that the contentious *Stoned* was on the B-side.

On Wednesday 1 January 1964, in a disused Manchester Church converted into a TV studio, the Stones (introduced by Jimmy Savile) promoted the single on the very first screening of a new BBC music programme, simply titled Top of The Pops - and so two musical legends were born. *I Wanna Be Your Man* was released in the United States with *Stoned* but soon withdrawn due to the B-side song title. It was then released as the flip side of their first US single in March 1964, but sales were poor and it only reached No. 48. It was coupled with *Not Fade Away*.

38. STONED (Nanker, Phelge) 2.09
AKA: Stones
7 October 1963: Place: De Lane Lea Studios, Kingsway, London, England.
Producer: Eric Easton, Andrew Oldham.
UK B-side I Wanna Be Your Man: 1 November 1963
USA B-side I Wanna Be Your Man: 17 February 1964
UK Compilation LP NO STONE UNTURNED: 5 October 1973
German Compilation LP THE REST OF THE BEST: December 1983
UK & USA LP THE ROLLING STONES SINGLES COLLECTION - THE LONDON YEARS: 15 August 1989
UK & USA CD box set THE ROLLING STONES SINGLES - 1963 - 1965: 4 May 2004

Twelve-bar improvisation yielded the so-called retake of Booker T and the MGs' *Green Onions*. It is basically an instrumental, with Mick Jagger occasionally uttering "stoned" followed by "outta my mind". Well, it was the end of a hard session! It is the very first song, albeit plagiarised, written by the group to end up on a single, which meant royalties were split amongst the band.

Ian Stewart was the piano player and Keith Richards was quick to promote him when talking about the single release. The writers of the track were stated as Nanker, Phelge and this pseudonym was to be used for future group-written songs. The title originates from publicity shots where they put their fingers up their noses and pulled their eyelids down (this was a nanker, although some say it involved Brian Jones and a chicken) and Phelge, their friend from Edith Grove, who had a dubious habit of wearing his stained underpants on his head.

The first few hundred copies of this single were entitled *Stones* and copies of these are now collectors' items. In the USA it was briefly released as a single flip-side to *I Wanna Be Your Man* (London L 9641) but withdrawn due to the song title connotations. James Phelge recalls in *Phelge's Stones* the time that he was shown the single and was asked to look at the flip side. All he could see was the song title *Stoned*; it was not until he was prompted that he saw the songwriter - Nanker, Phelge. James looked at their broad smiles and was proud that they had recognised his indirect contribution.

In order to gain songwriting rights for *Stoned*, Eric Easton used Southern Music, not offering to admit that this was a company that he was already involved with, increasing his pay back. The contract dated 11 October 1963 was between Southern Music Publishing Company Ltd and Mick Jagger and the rest of the band known as Nanker Phelge. Bill Wyman signed himself as W Perks. In *Stoned*, Andrew Oldham acknowledged that a few more songs were published that way before the band realised.

39. GO HOME GIRL (Alexander) 2.26
14-15 November 1963: Place: De Lane Lea Studios, Kingsway, London, England.
Producer: Eric Easton, Andrew Oldham.
Bootleg only.

Arthur Alexander's 1962 debut album of soulful music was not only an inspiration for the Beatles, who covered *Anna*, but also the Rolling Stones. The album led with his hit single *You Better Move On* but also included this number which was released as a single in 1963.

40. I'M TALKIN' ABOUT YOU (Berry)
AKA: Talkin' About You
14-15 November 1963: Place: De Lane Lea Studios, Kingsway, London, England.
Producer: Eric Easton, Andrew Oldham.
Unavailable.

A cover of the 1961 track by Chuck Berry but this version is not available. The song was a staple part of their full set list.

41. POISON IVY (Leiber, Stoller) 2.09
14-15 November 1963: Place: De Lane Lea Studios, Kingsway, London, England.
Producer: Eric Easton, Andrew Oldham.
UK EP The Rolling Stones: 10 January 1964
USA Compilation LP MORE HOT ROCKS (BIG HITS & FAZED COOKIES): 1 December 1972: No. 9 - 12 weeks
UK & USA CD box set THE ROLLING STONES SINGLES - 1963 - 1965: 4 May 2004
UK Compilation LP NO STONE UNTURNED: 5 October 1973
USA Compilation CD MORE HOT ROCKS (BIG HITS & FAZED COOKIES): 3 September 2002

The previous recorded version of this song was the track destined to be the second UK single but later cancelled because of poor sound quality. The Stones were still insistent that they wanted to record a version of *Poison Ivy* and this track therefore ended up on the UK EP released in January 1964. It is taken at a more leisurely pace than the first recording and overall is far superior in texture - even the annoying washboard-type ticking had been extracted and basic harmony vocals deployed at strategic places (Keith Richards' idea). It contains an extra repeated verse and a Charlie Watts drum flourish at the very end.

42. WILL YOU BE MY LOVER TONIGHT? (Jagger, Richard)
20-21 November, 7 December 1963: Place: Regent Sound Studios, London, England.
Producer: Andrew Oldham.
Unavailable.

One of the earliest Jagger/Richard compositions. Andrew Oldham was always after new talent provided the look was right - George Bean was someone who hung around Andrew's scene and sang on the backing track created by the Stones. The first track that Andrew recorded with him was *Secret Love* and Keith Richards played claves percussion on the song and recommended to everyone to buy the record in October 1963. Andrew used Richard without the "s" for the songwriter credits to be in line with the surname of British pop artist Cliff Richard.

43. SHANG A DOO LANG (Jagger, Richard) 0.10
20-21 November 1963; March 1964: Place: Regent Sound Studios; Olympic Studios, Carton St, London, England.
Producer: Andrew Oldham.
Engineer: Keith Grant
Bootleg only.

Understandably not Stones material, but a potential bubble gum pop hit. It was a demo for a young 15-year-old teenage actress Adrienne Poster (née Posta) and was recorded as her second single in March 1964. It was produced by Andrew Oldham with musical direction by Charles Blackwell. The song's style was of a re-hashed Phil Spector ilk. Adrienne related that this ploy was entirely deliberate. It was modelled on The Crystals' *He's Sure The Boy I Love*.
She was introduced to Andrew by Dick Rowe after a Stones gig, as a potential manager, and she remembered him to be entirely professional and business-like - a very nice guy. At the same time she met Keith Richards, Mick Jagger and Charlie Watts. Mick presented her with the lyrics for the song which were written on the back of a dry-cleaners tag from a shirt.
They all reconvened at the Olympia Sound Studios in front of about 60 people for a three-hour recording session. It was recorded completely live, Charlie playing drums and Andrew marching around the studio with an oily rag to dampen his drum sound. It was evident that Andrew was in awe of the man he called Uncle Phil and wanted to emulate the sound so much that there were even ringing bells at the start and close of the song.
The session was completed in the allotted time by Keith Grant after just two takes and the B-side *When A Girl Really Loves You* was also cut. Adrienne walked out of the studio with an acetate of the recording then appeared on the Ready Steady Go! television show to promote the single release.

44. MY ONLY GIRL (Richards, Jagger) 2.01
AKA: That Girl Belongs To Yesterday
20-21 November 1963: Place: Regent Sound Studios, London, England.
Producer: Andrew Oldham.
Bootleg only.

45. THAT GIRL BELONGS TO YESTERDAY (Richards, Jagger)
AKA: My Only Girl
20-21 November 1963: Place: Regent Sound Studios, London, England.
Producer: Andrew Oldham.
Unavailable.

On 17 November and 22 November, respectively, the band lip-synched a performance of *I Wanna Be Your Man* for the Thank Your Lucky Stars TV programme in Birmingham and also Ready, Steady, Go! in London. Gene Pitney was there to promote his Burt Bacharach hit *Twenty Four Hours From Tulsa* and remembers being in the same dressing room as the Stones when a man appeared at the door way. Gene thought he recognised him and asked if he was Mr Mancini. It was the great composer Henry Mancini, who had gone to the studios to see what all these youngsters were up to - he was not going to miss a trick.
Andrew Oldham was impressed that Gene had worked with Phil Spector on his second USA hit *Every Breath I Take* and also the Oscar-nominated movie soundtrack, *Town Without Pity*. Gene, an up and coming songwriter and performer, had first met Phil Spector in 1962. He heard the Crystals, was determined to write a song for them and did so with *He's A Rebel*. He took it to his publisher's office in New York when Phil walked in, heard the first eight bars and his eyes lit up - a classic pop song was born. They both proceeded to seal the deal at a 7th Avenue Chinese restaurant.
At the TV studios Andrew, in his typical style, hustled Gene into agreeing that Andrew could be his UK publicist and so another link in the chain was created. As a result, Gene recorded the Richards (with an "s" and appearing before Mick in the credits) /Jagger composition *My Only Girl*. It was intended for George Bean but Gene Pitney changed the melody and the chorus, left the lyrics as they were and recorded it for himself as *That Girl Belongs To Yesterday* in March 1964. It reached No. 7 in the charts, the first time a Jagger/Richards song had gone top ten in the UK.

46. LEAVE ME ALONE (Jagger, Richard) 1.57
20-21 November, 7 December 1963: Place: Regent Sound Studios, London, England.
Producer: Andrew Oldham.
Bootleg only.

An up-tempo piano-based track. The Regent Sound Studios were in the heart of London at No 4 Denmark Street, off Charing Cross Road, fondly known as "Tin Pan Alley". They were run by Bill Farley, who also worked as an engineer. In essence it was a low budget operation with a Vortexian valve mixing board and a four channel, two track Revox recorder pinned to a wall surrounded by egg cartons to dampen echo.

47. SURE I DO (Jones)
20-21 November, 7 December 1963: Place: Regent Sound Studios, London, England.
Producer: Andrew Oldham.
Unavailable.

A Brian Jones-penned number recorded by the Stones, but not available. It features Brian on vocals and is sung in a soft manner. Brian went as far as publishing the song with Posner Music Company. A US artiste was going to use the composition as their next "A" side. That could have been Gene Pitney and some say he co-wrote *Sure I Do* with Brian. Gene was asked by Andrew Oldham to give Brian help and advice but ultimately the Stones guitarist was too scared to put forward his songs for recording in case he was ridiculed by the rest of the band. Gene confirmed in 2002 that no actual song writing took place with him and Brian, he was simply offering advice. In an interview with EIL.COM in 2006, Oldham agreed that you cannot just write pop music: ". . . it smells out the fake. And in that department Brian was a fake. . ."

48. SO MUCH IN LOVE (Jagger, Richard) 0.11
20-21 November, 7 December 1963: Place: Regent Sound Studios, London, England.
Producer: Andrew Oldham.
Bootleg only.

A Jagger/Richard tune that was eventually released by the Mighty Avengers, produced by Andrew Oldham with musical direction from John Paul Jones. It became their only hit charting at No. 46 in the UK charts in November 1964. The Herd, with Mick Fleetwood, recorded the same song for release in February 1966. Another artist with the stage name of Charles Dickens (David Anthony), who toured with the Stones on their Spring 1965 tour, released the song on Oldham's Immediate label, also in 1966. An out-take is available of the Stones demo.

49. GIVE ME YOUR HAND (Jagger) 0.06
AKA: I'll Hold Your Hand
20-21 November, 7 December 1963: Place: Regent Sound Studios, London, England.
Producer: Andrew Oldham.
Bootleg only.

The Stones wanted to return the favour to the Beatles for their second single hit, *I Wanna Be Your Man*. *Give Me Your Hand* was given to the Beatles but was not recorded, although there is a strong resemblance to the next Beatles No. 1 (December 1963) hit *I Wanna Hold Your Hand*. However, they had already recorded *I Wanna Hold Your Hand* on 17 October and it was released on 29 November 1963.
The song originated by Mick Jagger (as can be seen on the Piccadilly Records label) was written for Teddy Green, who released it as the flip-side to his March 1964 single, *Always*. On 30 November 2006 an acetate of an out-take version of *Tell Me* (labelled as *You're Coming Back To Me*), coupled with *Give Me Your Hand*, sold at a Cooper, Owen auction for £4,000. The label has Regent Sound Ltd, 4 Denmark Street, London printed on it.

50. I WANT YOU TO KNOW (Jagger, Richard, Jones) 0.11
20-21 November, 7 December 1963: Place: Regent Sound Studios, London, England.
Played Live: 1963
Producer: Andrew Oldham.
Bootleg only.

Another early attempt by Brian Jones, who plays harmonica, was destroyed by false female background vocals. This is part of bootleg compendium of out-takes, most of the cuts lasting a few bars or even a few seconds, so the true song content cannot be fully commented upon. It was cut on to an acetate by itself but copies of these are extremely rare.

51. WHEN A GIRL LOVES A BOY (Jagger, Richard) 0.21
AKA: When A Boy Meets A Girl
20-21 November, 7 December 1963: Place: Regent Sound Studios, London, England.
Producer: Andrew Oldham.
Bootleg only.

The chorus has a passing resemblance to Susan Maughan's *Bobby's Girl,* recorded in 1962.

52. YOU MUST BE THE ONE (Jagger, Richard) 0.16
20-21 November, 7 December 1963: Place: Regent Sound Studios, London, England.
Producer: Andrew Oldham.
Bootleg only.

Recorded by the Greenbeats but failed to chart when released in November 1964. It had potential.

53. IT SHOULD BE YOU (Jagger, Richard) 1.45
20-21 November, 7 December 1963: Place: Regent Sound Studios, London, England.
Producer: Andrew Oldham.
Bootleg only.

Another track recorded for the late George Bean, but he was unable to bring any credibility to it, the lyrics being repetitive and the tune very basic. It was obvious that the Stones' creativity lay in R 'n' B not contemporary pop songs. The ultimate aim, of course, was to mould the two. George was a friend of James Phelge and was a big enthusiast of the music club scene, as well as a Stones fan.

54. TELL ME (YOU'RE COMING BACK) **(EARLY VERSION)** (Jagger, Richard) 2.47
AKA: You're Coming Back To Me
20-21 November, 7 December 1963: Place: Regent Sound Studios, London, England.
Producer: Andrew Oldham.
Engineer: Bill Farley.
UK LP THE ROLLING STONES (1st Pressing): 17 April 1964: No. 1 - 51 weeks
USA Single: 19 June 1964: No. 24 - 5 weeks
USA Compilation LP BIG HITS (HIGH TIDE AND GREEN GRASS): 1 April 1966: No. 3 - 35 weeks
USA Compilation LP MORE HOT ROCKS (BIG HITS & FAZED COOKIES): 1 December 1972: No. 9 - 12 weeks
UK & USA LP THE ROLLING STONES SINGLES COLLECTION - THE LONDON YEARS: 15 August 1989

This was the first Jagger/, Richard composition to be released and is essentially an experimental song, although fans of Doris Troy may have heard a similarity to *Whatcha Gonna Do About It*, released on her 1963 album, JUST ONE LOOK. The make-up of the song was club-based (Keith Richards referred to it as "dub"') and it gradually built itself up to a cut that was passable for release when it was re-recorded in January and February 1964.
It was released on an acetate with *Give Me Your Hand* as *You're Coming Back To Me*. It was also accidentally released on first pressings of the first album. The second line says, "I need your love" rather than "I want your love". It is shorter, at 2 minutes 47 seconds, and does not have a guitar solo, although the first pressing is slightly longer (* a - 3.02).

55. TO KNOW HIM IS TO LOVE HIM (Spector) 3.09
2 January 1964: Place: Regent Sound Studios, London, England.
Rolling Stones with Cleo Sylvestre.
Producer: Andrew Oldham.
Engineer: Bill Farley.
Musical Director: Mike Leander.
UK Single: January 1964

Andrew Oldham used the Stones as the backing band for his next protégé, Cleo Sylvestre. She had auditioned for the Stones back in the Bricklayer Arms days and was a good friend of the band. *To Know Him Is To Love Him* was a hit for the Teddy Bears in 1958 and was Phil Spector's first hit as group member/producer. It became a million seller and was a fitting track to be recorded by Andrew as he tried to emulate the Spector magic. The song was released simply under the name Cleo but failed to chart, the artist going on to become an actress and performing in English soap television - as Coronation Street's first ethnic character and also in Crossroads.

56. THERE ARE BUT FIVE ROLLING STONES (Leander, Oldham) 2.23
2 January 1964: Place: Regent Sound Studios, London, England.
Producer: Andrew Oldham. Musical Director: Mike Leander.
Engineer: Bill Farley.
UK B-side To Know Him Is To Love Him: January 1964

Phil Spector, in order to focus the radio stations on the A side, usually included an instrumental on the B side. Andrew Oldham copied this technique but went one step further and used it to promote his main band. The track title more than hints at the backing artists and the instrumental was credited to the session producer Mike Leander and Andrew himself. It was a B Bumble & The Stingers-type instrumental featuring the piano work of Ian Stewart, some nifty clap-back and a guitar break at the end.
The production style was more inspired by Kim Fowley, who had written the No. 1 instrumental *Nut Rocker* by B Bumble & The Stingers. On release, early copies of the single credited the B side to the Andrew Oldham Group. The rest of January 1964 was spent by The Rolling Stones touring the UK with the famous Ronettes. It was their second major UK tour and ensured that they were becoming a household name throughout the UK, not just in London and the home counties.

57. ROUTE 66 (Troup) 2.23
3 January 1964: Place: Regent Sound Studios, London, England.
Played Live: 1963, 1964, 1965, 1973, 1976, 1977, 1986, 1999
Producer: Andrew Oldham.
Engineer: Bill Farley.
UK LP THE ROLLING STONES: 17 April 1964: No. 1 - 51 weeks
USA LP ENGLAND'S NEWEST HIT MAKERS: 30 May 1964: No. 11 - 12 weeks
USA Compilation LP THE ROLLING STONES - PROMOTIONAL ALBUM: October 1969
UK Compilation LP ROCK 'N' ROLLING STONES: 13 October 1972: No. 41 - 1 week
UK LP SOLID ROCK: 13 October 1980

In January 1964, in between the Ronettes' tour, the Stones started work on their first album simply titled THE ROLLING STONES, which featured on the cover a simple but effective Nicholas Wright photograph of the five staring from a darkened background, plus the Decca logo. The studios were Bill Farley's Regent Sound, though they had rehearsed many of the songs on the album at Tin Pan Alley studios, also in Denmark Street.
Route 66, written by the late Bobby Troup, gets the album off to a rousing start, Keith Richards playing an excellent guitar with a tight clap-back track rhythm by Bill Wyman and Charlie Watts. It soon became a popular stage number. Later in June, on the same bill as Bobby Vee, The Chiffons, Bobby Goldsboro and Bobby Comstock, the Stones kicked off on the opening date of their first American tour.
The town was San Bernardino, which was mentioned in the lyrics of *Route 66*, providing an unintentional way to win over the fans, who were jiving and bopping in the aisles. Security police, a feature of that tour at some venues, went onto the stage and pushed over-exuberant fans back to their seats. At other gigs the shows

were not sold out, particularly in the middle of the country, but the word was spreading. Keith was glad he met Bobby Goldsboro since they both had a passion for the guitar, Bobby having played with Roy Orbison. Guitar talk included how Chuck Berry weaved his magic and Jimmy Reed who, Keith learned for the first time, played five-chord guitar.

58. MONA (I NEED YOU BABY) (McDaniel) 3.35
3 January 1964: Place: Regent Sound Studios, London, England.
Played Live: 1963, 1964, 1981
Producer: Andrew Oldham.
Engineer: Bill Farley.
UK LP THE ROLLING STONES: 17 April 1964: No. 1 - 51 weeks
USA LP THE ROLLING STONES, NOW!: 12 February 1965: No. 5 - 29 weeks

Known as either *Mona* or *I Need You Baby*, this is yet another inspired copy of a Bo Diddley number where the shuffle beat runs rife throughout the song. The Stones were beginning to prove that they were not only marketing figure-heads but also adequate musicians. Keith Richards was learning to improvise on every guitar lick in the R 'n' B catalogue and his understanding with Brian Jones created a tight rhythm.
They often said that the reason for their success was the unique rhythm they could produce. They were both able to play lead if required but could fall back into ensemble then trade licks with each other. *Mona* is such a number where Brian particularly excels in emulating the Diddley off beat. Surprisingly, the track was extracted from the American release of the album and replaced by *Not Fade Away*.

59. CAROL (Berry) 2.35
3 January 1964: Place: Regent Sound Studios, London, England.
Played Live: 1964, 1965, 1969
Producer: Andrew Oldham.
Engineer: Bill Farley.
UK LP THE ROLLING STONES: 17 April 1964: No. 1 - 51 weeks
USA LP ENGLAND'S NEWEST HIT MAKERS: 30 May 1964: No. 11 - 12 weeks
UK Compilation LP ROLLED GOLD: 14 November 1975: No. 7 - 50 weeks
UK LP SOLID ROCK: 13 October 1980
UK Compilation CD ROLLED GOLD +: 12 November 2007: No. 26 - 12 weeks

The riff recasts Chuck Berry's original song and produces one of the album's barnstormers. Keith Richards had an unnerving ability to continuously improve his guitar virtuosity. It worried someone like Brian Jones who, although extremely competent, tended to reach a peak on an instrument and then use his musical versatility quickly to master another. This is perhaps why the Stones fused together so well - their characters were diversified but, as a unit, their musical interpretation was superb. Ian Stewart referred to them as the "three-chord wonders". The Stones were all soloists in their own right, but first and foremost played for each other as a band. Such was the popularity of *Carol* as a live song, that it resurfaced in 1970 on the Stones' first official live LP, GET YOUR YA YA'S OUT.

60. NOT FADE AWAY (Petty, Hardin) 1.49
10, 28 January, 4 February 1964: Place: Regent Sound Studios, London, England.
Played Live: 1964, 1966, 1994, 1995
Rolling Stones with Gene Pitney, Phil Spector, Graham Nash, Tony Hicks, Allen Clarke.
Producer: Andrew Oldham.
Engineer: Bill Farley.
UK Single: 21 February 1964: No. 3 - 15 weeks
USA Single: 6 March 1964: No. 48 - 13 weeks
USA LP ENGLAND'S NEWEST HIT MAKERS: 30 May 1964: No. 11 - 12 weeks
USA Compilation LP BIG HITS (HIGH TIDE AND GREEN GRASS): 1 April 1966: No. 3 - 35 weeks
UK Compilation LP BIG HITS (HIGH TIDE AND GREEN GRASS): 4 November 1966: No. 4 - 43 weeks
UK Compilation LP MILESTONES: 18 February 1972: No. 14 - 8 weeks
USA Compilation LP MORE HOT ROCKS (BIG HITS & FAZED COOKIES): 1 December 1972: No. 9 - 12 weeks
UK Compilation LP ROLLED GOLD: 14 November 1975: No. 7 - 50 weeks
UK Compilation LP GET STONED - 30 GREATEST HITS, 30 ORIGINAL TRACKS: 21 October 1977: No. 13 - 15 weeks
UK LP SOLID ROCK: 13 October 1980
UK & USA LP THE ROLLING STONES SINGLES COLLECTION - THE LONDON YEARS: 15 August 1989
USA Compilation CD MORE HOT ROCKS (BIG HITS & FAZED COOKIES): 3 September 2002
UK CD LP FORTY LICKS: 30 September 2002: No. 2 - 45 weeks
USA CD LP FORTY LICKS: 1 October 2002: No. 2 - 50 weeks
UK & USA CD box set THE ROLLING STONES SINGLES - 1963 - 1965: 4 May 2004
UK Compilation CD ROLLED GOLD +: 12 November 2007: No. 26 - 12 weeks

From the opening bars, Keith Richards' acoustic guitar gave the song its feel and instant appeal. Keith had been improvising on this 1957 Buddy Holly and Norman Petty song - which had been performed by The Crickets - at the Willesden flat he shared with Mick Jagger and Andrew Oldham. Andrew recognised its potential and declared that he considered the song's style was perfect for the Stones. Keith had conceived the sound and revamped the riff back to the rawness of the Bo Diddley rhythm rather than Buddy Holly's version, which had originally copied the shuffle drum beat of Buddy Knox's *Party Doll*, amalgamated with Bo Diddley. The Stones turned the arrangement upside-down with the upfront guitar and incorporation of harmonica playing by Brian Jones.
In January, following a London show with the Ronettes, they returned to the studios to start work on a Stones classic. An early version from January has a different

guitar sound and more harmonica playing (* a - 1.49). *Not Fade Away* was the logical extension to what they had previously attempted on *Mona (I Need You Baby)*. From the all-important opening bars the atmosphere was right and, within a breath-taking two minutes, the basis of the track was complete. Andrew felt the first takes were too fast and asked them to slow things down, having learned a lesson from *Come On*. The harp playing of Brian Jones is full of energy and Phil Spector's "manic maracas" create an exciting rhythm track.

In *Stoned*, Andrew Oldham revealed that the maracas were in fact an empty cognac bottle with an American dime in it. The recording included Phil Spector's and possibly Gene Pitney's (he could not precisely recall if he contributed to *Not Fade Away*) presence on the final overdubs at a session on 4 February. Ian Stewart, who played piano, said it was Andrew's idea to credit Gene Pitney with publicity. Three of the Hollies - Allan Clarke, Tony Hicks and Graham Nash - were in an adjacent studio and were asked to lend a hand.

Allan Clarke gave his version to The Huffingham Post in 2011: "We were just walking past a studio where The Stones were recording and they asked us to come in because they needed some help. It was myself, Graham, and Gene Pitney. I think Gene was clinking a two-penny piece against a brandy bottle, and I was playing maracas." All of this excess obviously influenced Andrew Oldham's production and the sound quality was the best he had achieved so far. One wonders if Mick Jagger recalled, a few years previously, viewing with Dick Taylor an impressive performance of *Not Fade Away* by Buddy Holly at the Woolwich Granada in March 1958 during what was to be his only English tour.

61. (WALKIN' THRU THE) SLEEPY CITY (Jagger, Richard) 2.52
10 January; 1-10 July 1964, 31 August 1964 - 4 September 1964: Place: Regent Sound Studios; Greenford Studios, Greenford; Decca, West Hampstead, Regent Sound Studios, London, England.
Rolling Stones with Jim Sullivan, John McLaughlin, Jimmy Page, Joe Moretti, Andy White.
Producer: Andrew Oldham.
Engineer: John Paul Jones.
Other Production: Mike Leander.
UK Compilation LP METAMORPHOSIS: 6 June 1975: No. 45 - 1 week
USA Compilation LP METAMORPHOSIS: 6 June 1975: No. 8 - 8 weeks

Another experimental Jagger/Richard composition and basically a copy of The Crystals' *He's A Rebel* was given to British group, The Mighty Avengers; predictably it flopped. Andrew Oldham's idea of capitalising on the Stones' success by issuing these tracks to unsuspecting artists was not exactly a commercial success. The Stones version is ruined by being over-produced - simplicity, as they would soon learn, was the key to success. Oldham enlisted John Baldwin to assist with some arrangements and gave him a new name - John Paul Jones. These mid-summer recordings, sometimes referred to as the Sleepy City sessions, were primarily to provide Oldham with material for other artists.

Big Jim Sullivan was a well-known guitarist who had already played with Marty Wilde's Wildcats and backed Eddie Cochran with the Wildcats on the ill-fated tour of Britain. Jim's guitar session work reads like a who's who of British popular music. He was a talented guy who, in 1965, played with the Birds, featuring Ron Wood. John McLaughlin was guitarist for Georgie Fame and the Blue Flames and went on to explore eastern jazz fusion with the Mahavishnu Orchestra. James Page, aged 19, started working for Mike Leander at Decca Records and contributed guitar work to many sessions. His first guitar piece on Jet Harris & Tony Meehan's *Diamond* went to No. 1. He was known as Little Jim to avoid confusion with the other session guitarist Big Jim Sullivan. He went on to play with Van Morrison, The Kinks, The Who, The Yardbirds and later founded Led Zeppelin. Joe Moretti's musical pedigree was earned as a guitarist for Johnny Kidd and The Pirates. Andy White was a session drummer who was hired by George Martin to play on The Beatles' *Love Me Do*, much to Ringo Starr's disgust.

62. EACH AND EVERYDAY OF THE YEAR (Jagger, Richard) 2.49
10 January; 1-10 July 1964, 31 August 1964 - 4 September 1964: Place: Regent Sound Studios; Greenford Studios, Greenford; Decca, West Hampstead, Regent Sound Studios, London, England.
Rolling Stones with Jim Sullivan, John McLaughlin, Jimmy Page, Joe Moretti, Andy White.
Producer: Andrew Oldham.
Engineer: John Paul Jones.
Other Production: Mike Leander.
UK Compilation LP METAMORPHOSIS: 6 June 1975: No. 45 - 1 week
USA Compilation LP METAMORPHOSIS: 6 June 1975: No. 8 - 8 weeks

As the Jagger/Richard songwriting continued, Andrew Oldham looked out for other aspiring artists to record. Their version, with similar backing instruments, was released on METAMORPHOSIS. *Each And Everyday Of The Year* was recorded by young fresh-faced American rocker Bobby Jameson, who was introduced to Oldham by Kim Fowley. The track was released in January 1965 as the B-side to an Oldham/Richards song, named *All I Want Is My Baby*.
Jimmy Page played fuzz guitar on the track with Mick Jagger on backing vocals. Bobby had flown especially from Los Angeles to record the track. Later, another British combo The Thee, featuring Reg King, an employee of Oldham, recorded it as a single in May 1965. *Each And Everyday Of The Year* is an orchestrated track featuring horns and is reminiscent of a Spanish fiesta song - or rather, a siesta song, zzzzz.....

63. I JUST WANT TO MAKE LOVE TO YOU (Dixon) 2.19
28 January, 24-25 February 1964: Place: Regent Sound Studios, London, England.
Played Live: 1963, 1964, 1981, 1990, 1998, 2002, 2003
Producer: Andrew Oldham.
Engineer: Bill Farley.
UK LP THE ROLLING STONES: 17 April 1964: No. 1 - 51 weeks
USA LP ENGLAND'S NEWEST HIT MAKERS: 30 May 1964: No. 11 - 12 weeks
USA B-side Tell Me: 19 June 1964
UK Compilation LP MILESTONES: 18 February 1972: No. 14 - 8 weeks
UK Compilation LP ROCK 'N' ROLLING STONES: 13 October 1972: No. 41 - 1 week

UK & USA LP THE ROLLING STONES SINGLES COLLECTION - THE LONDON YEARS: 15 August 1989
UK & USA CD box set THE ROLLING STONES SINGLES - 1963 - 1965: 4 May 2004

The album is generally a mixture of American soul, Chuck Berry rock 'n' roll, Stones R 'n' B and inspirational blues but *I Just Want To Make Love To You* does not seem to fall into any category. Willie Dixon's delta blues song seems to have been misinterpreted and is driven home in a fast blues, Bo Diddley-type, rhythm. Mick Jagger is unable to bring feeling to the vocals at such a pace. Instrumentally, the song is fine, it just seems to be driven too close to the safety barriers. Brian Jones was the harmonica player, a role he is not often credited for.

Producer Andrew Oldham was an expert at pushing sensitivity to the limit. His sleeve notes on the reverse of the album cover show a certain controlled arrogance: "The Rolling Stones are more than just a group - they are a way of life". He was not so pleased at the way London released the album in the USA with the anonymous title ENGLAND'S NEWEST HIT MAKERS.

64. HONEST I DO (Reed) 2.12
28 January, 24-25 February 1964: Place: Regent Sound Studios, London, England.
Played Live: 1963
Producer: Andrew Oldham.
Engineer: Bill Farley.
UK LP THE ROLLING STONES: 17 April 1964: No. 1 - 51 weeks
USA LP ENGLAND'S NEWEST HIT MAKERS: 30 May 1964: No. 11 - 12 weeks

Jimmy Reed was an artist who inspired the Stones to promote the blues gospel. This was their first public release of a Reed song, although they had previously recorded the unreleased *Bright Lights Big City*. They managed to do justice to the work and produced a song deep in feeling, laid back in approach and charged with atmosphere. The song plods forward positively and Brian Jones plays beautiful harp to accompany Mick Jagger's gutsy vocals.

65. I'M A KING BEE (Harpo, Moore) 2.37
28 January, 24-25 February 1964: Place: Regent Sound Studios, London, England.
Played Live: 1963, 1964
Producer: Andrew Oldham.
Engineer: Bill Farley.
UK LP THE ROLLING STONES: 17 April 1964: No. 1 - 51 weeks
USA LP ENGLAND'S NEWEST HIT MAKERS: 30 May 1964: No. 11 - 12 weeks

I'm A King Bee was another straight copy. It surprised Mick Jagger that the public could listen to a pale imitation when the genuine Slim Harpo 1961 version was available. His wife Lovell Moore (the song's co-writer) said he was known as Slim because he was skinny as a rail while the Harpo moniker was because of his mouth-harp playing.

The Stones interpretation also incorporated the trademark harp near the song's end but predominantly revolves around Mick's powerfully-accentuated blues dialect. He spits out the sexual innuendoes and, when the vocals turn to stinging around the honey hive, Keith Richards drags out a riff at the bottom of the fret board to deliver the shadowed message.

66. YOU CAN MAKE IT IF YOU TRY (Jarrett) 2.03
28 January, 24-25 February 1964: Place: Regent Sound Studios, London, England.
Played Live: 1963, 1964
Producer: Andrew Oldham.
Engineer: Bill Farley.
UK LP THE ROLLING STONES: 17 April 1964: No. 1 - 51 weeks
USA LP ENGLAND'S NEWEST HIT MAKERS: 30 May 1964: No. 11 - 12 weeks

The late Theodore (Ted) Jarrett wrote the song about a girlfriend who had dumped him and Gene Allison had a Top 40 hit with it in 1958. Jarrett was a musician, label-owner and producer who brought R 'n' B and soul to Nashville. The Stones version is a slow, hollering blues song led by Mick Jagger's pleading vocals. Ian Stewart plays a gospel-type organ and Keith Richards and Brian Jones strum on acoustic guitars. Ian's style would not be suitable for all piano or organ works but, if it swung or did not have minor chords, then he would be the man - when it came to playing A minor, he would just leave it out.

The album as a whole was an immediate success and even knocked The Beatles off the top of the UK charts on 2 May 1964. It remained at the top for 12 weeks, only to be replaced by the release of the next Beatles album, A HARD DAY'S NIGHT. Based on the 51 weeks in the charts, it was their most successful album ever. The two-track Regent Sound Studios had produced a fresh and vibrant album and the blitz by the Stones had begun. While 1963 was the year of The Beatles, The Rolling Stones replaced them in the popularity polls in 1964. The British rock revolution had started.

67. WALKING THE DOG (Thomas) 3.11
28 January, 24-25 February 1964: Place: Regent Sound Studios, London, England.
Played Live: 1963, 1964, 1965
Producer: Andrew Oldham.
Engineer: Bill Farley.
UK LP THE ROLLING STONES: 17 April 1964: No. 1 - 51 weeks
USA LP ENGLAND'S NEWEST HIT MAKERS: 30 May 1964: No. 11 - 12 weeks
USA Compilation LP THE ROLLING STONES - PROMOTIONAL ALBUM: October 1969

The first Rolling Stones album in Britain did not produce any single releases, but individual tracks proved very popular in other countries. *Walking The Dog*, coupled with *Under The Boardwalk*, was belatedly released in Australia in 1965 and jumped to their first No. 1 position in that country. During the same week, the Stones also held top-five positions with *Little Red Rooster* and *Heart Of Stone*, a feat rarely achieved even now by the most popular of the pop and rock and roll fraternity.

Walking The Dog is a humorous Rufus Thomas song, complete with dog call whistles. It is given the Stones' fast R 'n' B treatment and is a high point on the album. There is a controlled rowdiness under the surface, which is only once released when Keith Richards delivers a fine guitar solo while Brian Jones adds some rowdy backing vocals. "England's Greatest Hit Makers" were expressing their identities and, at the same time, the aforementioned title was used for the Stateside album release.

68. TELL ME (YOU'RE COMING BACK) (Jagger, Richard) 3.49
AKA: You're Coming Back To Me
28 January, 24-25 February 1964: Place: Regent Sound Studios, London, England.
Played Live: 1964
Producer: Andrew Oldham.
Engineer: Bill Farley.
UK LP THE ROLLING STONES: 17 April 1964: No. 1 - 51 weeks
USA LP ENGLAND'S NEWEST HIT MAKERS: 30 May 1964: No. 11 - 12 weeks
UK Compilation LP GET STONED - 30 GREATEST HITS, 30 ORIGINAL TRACKS: 21 October 1977: No. 13 - 15 weeks
USA Compilation CD MORE HOT ROCKS (BIG HITS & FAZED COOKIES): 3 September 2002
UK & USA CD box set THE ROLLING STONES SINGLES - 1963 - 1965: 4 May 2004
UK Compilation CD ROLLED GOLD +: 12 November 2007: No. 26 - 12 weeks

The influences of *Tell Me* stemmed from commercial-type Beatles songs and those of their Merseyside counterparts. Surprisingly, in view of its Mersey beat influences, *Tell Me* was later to become the Stones' second American single and sprang up to a commendable No. 24 in the Billboard charts, coinciding with the first USA tour. This was the earlier and shorter November 1963 version - the later recording sounds much more polished and is extended by a Keith Richards guitar solo. On the corrected UK vinyl edition, it is longer by 15 seconds (* a - 4.05) than most other versions which are slightly edited or even speeded up. *Tell Me* plays on the same heart-strings as *You Better Move On* and manages to cross over into the pop mainstream. Keith plays a 12-string acoustic (he owned two) which, at the time, Big Jim Sullivan was unusually utilising in session work. The vocal technique was to sing harmony vocals into the same microphone while Brian Jones only contributed tambourine to the recording.

69. OH I DO LIKE TO SEE ME ON THE B-SIDE (Oldham, Watts, Wyman) 2.24
January 1964: Place: Regent Sound Studios, London, England.
Rolling Stones with Eric Ford, Andy White, Reg Guest.
Producer: Andrew Oldham. Musical Director: Mike Leander.
Engineer: Bill Farley.
UK B-side 365 Rolling Stones (One For Each Day Of The Year): 10 April 1964

70. 365 ROLLING STONES (ONE FOR EACH DAY OF THE YEAR) (Oldham, Leander) 2.01
January 1964: Place: Regent Sound Studios, London, England.
Rolling Stones with Eric Ford, Andy White, Reg Guest.
Producer: Andrew Oldham. Musical Director: Mike Leander.
Engineer: Bill Farley.
UK Single: 10 April 1964.

Recorded in January 1964, some of the Stones helped Andrew Oldham out on tracks that would end up on mostly B sides. Also featuring on the tracks were Eric Ford (guitar), Andy White (drums) and Reg Guest (piano), along with Jim Sullivan and Alan Weighle, they made up the Nashville 5. An instrumental song was released as a single by The Andrew Loog Oldham Orchestra on 10 April 1964. In order to create some mystique that the Stones were involved it was given the title, *365 Rolling Stones (One For Each Day Of The Year)*.
For a short time it became the soundtrack for Ready Steady Go! the ITV television programme launched to combat BBC's Top Of The Pops. Charlie Watts and Bill Wyman certainly appeared on the B side, *Oh, I Do Like To See Me On The B Side*, a pastiche on *I Do Like To Be Beside The Seaside*. A Bill Wyman-penned song, *Funky And Fleopatra*, ended up on the B-side of Jeannie and The Redheads classic (!) *Animal Duds*.

71. DON'T LIE TO ME (Whittaker) 1.43
3 February 1964: Place: BBC Maida Vale Studios, London, England.
Played Live: 1964, 1972
Bootleg only.

72. MONA (McDaniel) 2.11
3 February 1964: Place: BBC Maida Vale Studios, London, England.
Bootleg only.

73. WALKING THE DOG (Thomas) 2.35
3 February 1964: Place: BBC Maida Vale Studios, London, England.
Bootleg only.

74. BYE BYE JOHNNY (Berry) 2.11
3 February 1964: Place: BBC Maida Vale Studios, London, England.
Bootleg only.

75. I WANNA BE YOUR MAN (Lennon, McCartney) 1.49
3 February 1964: Place: BBC Maida Vale Studios, London, England.
Bootleg only.

76. YOU BETTER MOVE ON (Alexander) 2.35
3 February 1964: Place: BBC Maida Vale Studios, London, England.
Bootleg only.

Their second BBC session was for the Saturday Club, hosted by Brian Matthew. It consisted of a couple of tracks from their EP that had just been released, their last single *I Wanna Be Your Man*, two tracks from their yet to be unveiled album, *Mona, Walking The Dog* and a stage Chuck Berry tune, *Don't Lie To Me*. The latter was a quick run through of a stage favourite and enabled the crowd to get up and dance.
You Better Move On features an early attempt at background vocals, while *Walking The Dog* has a variation on the usual guitar solo. *Bye Bye Johnny* is a fun version of an old Chuck Berry favourite . . . its pace is faster than the original British EP track, though as ever the lead guitar wheels the song down the highway in the fast lane. Chuck Berry must have been quaking in his winkle-pickers! The session was broadcast on 8 February 1964.

77. ANDREW'S BLUES (Phelge, Spector) 3.03
AKA: And The Rolling Stones Met Phil And Gene, Fuckin' Andrew, Song For Andrew
4 February 1964: Place: Regent Sound Studios, London, England.
Rolling Stones with Phil Spector, Gene Pitney, Allan Clarke, Graham Nash.
Producer: Andrew Oldham.
Engineer: Bill Farley.
Bootleg only.

The session continued with this whimsical ditty, its lyrical content being a little too shocking for public release. This is the reason for it only being available on bootleg. It comprises of verses which generally describe Andrew Oldham's imagined sexual exploits with nursery-rhyme heroes Jack and Jill, and mimicry of the then Chairman of Decca Records. He describes Phil Spector, who cried, "The Rolling Stones are a load of shit, but now that I've heard them, I know they're a load of shit!" A load of fun and generally a good "Mick-take".
In 2002, Gene Pitney recalled with fondness the good fun and "pornographic" overtones of this track. On the METAMORPHOSIS album sleeve notes, Gene (along with Phil Spector, Allan Clarke and Graham Nash) is thanked for his contribution. This relates to Andrew's Blues which was planned to be released on the NECROPHILIA compilation project. Oldham had written the sleeve notes which ended up on METAMORPHOSIS. A 1964 acetate of *Not Fade Away*, backed by the politely named *Song For Andrew*, exists.

78. MR SPECTOR AND MR PITNEY CAME TOO (Phelge, Spector) 2.47
AKA: Aftermath
4 February 1964: Place: Regent Sound Studios, London, England.
Rolling Stones with Phil Spector, Gene Pitney, Allan Clarke, Graham Nash.
Producer: Andrew Oldham.
Engineer: Bill Farley.
Bootleg only.

This track perfectly encapsulates the uniqueness of the session. Laughter at the beginning and a female voice (possibly Veronica Bennett - later Ronnie Spector) shouts:, "I've never recorded before." A false piano intro is laughed at before Phil Spector takes control and starts it off with a "1-2, a 1-2-3-4". The band charge in with an infectious assault of R 'n' B. Harmonica, boogie piano and lead guitars with a bottle chiming in the background, provide an alternate take to *Now I've Got A Witness*. It was nearly released officially on the aborted 1972 NECROPHILIA ABKCO compilation project named as *Aftermath* which ABKCO own tapes of today.

79. LITTLE BY LITTLE (Phelge, Spector) 2.41
4 February 1964: Place: Regent Sound Studios, London, England.
Played Live: 1964
Rolling Stones with Phil Spector, Gene Pitney.
Producer: Andrew Oldham.
Engineer: Bill Farley
UK B-side Not Fade Away: 21 February 1964.
UK LP THE ROLLING STONES: 17 April 1964: No. 1 - 51 weeks
USA LP ENGLAND'S NEWEST HIT MAKERS: 30 May 1964: No. 11 - 12 weeks
UK & USA LP THE ROLLING STONES SINGLES COLLECTION - THE LONDON YEARS: 15 August 1989
UK & USA CD box set THE ROLLING STONES SINGLES - 1963 - 1965: 4 May 2004

The 4 February session was intended to complete the *Not Fade Away* single and to provide a B-side, since Decca were anxious to release a follow-up single. The session apparently did not start well - the Stones were a bit jaded and not talking to each other. Andrew Oldham rang Gene Pitney and told him he needed help because the band "hated" each other. Gene and Phil Spector had both been travelling in Europe and returned from Paris for an overnight stop before returning to the United States. Gene arrived at the studio and was followed later by Phil who discreetly arrived in a big black Rolls-Royce. There were the obligatory bottles of spirit brought from France, it was nearly Gene's birthday and he said it was a family custom to drink cognac.
The refreshments did the trick and, with Gene helping out on piano, revived a flagging session.
Two of the Hollies, Allan Clarke and Graham Nash, accompanied the Stones on backing vocals and Phil, eager to help, grabbed Mick's maracas. *Little By Little* was similar to *Now I've Got A Witness* for Phil Spector was there to add his prowess as a co-writer with the group (Phelge). While the American legend was obviously a

strong influence in the studio, production was firmly in the hands of Andrew Oldham (at least in name). Phil Spector created an ambience in the studio and a spirit, perhaps due to the empty bottles of cognac, which was hard to emulate.

As a result, the Stones, along with the maestro, manufactured a "wall of noise" as opposed to the famed "wall of sound" which Spector had created with the Crystals and Ronettes. Listen to the high screams in the background. *Little By Little* is a composition made up of selections from various parts of Jimmy Reed's *Shame, Shame, Shame*. It is essentially a 12-bar blues jam session made after the successful recording of *Not Fade Away* the same night, but it is one which does not allow the looseness of the gathering to infiltrate the song, written by Phil Spector and Mick Jagger in the darkened corridors of the IBC Studios. Gene recalls how small the studio actually was, hence the need to step outside its confines. Phil plays maracas with Ian Stewart and Gene is on the piano - and the session was back on course.

80. CAN I GET A WITNESS (Holland, Dozier, Holland) 2.58
4 February 1964: Place: Regent Sound Studios, London, England.
Played Live: 1963, 1964
Producer: Andrew Oldham.
Engineer: Bill Farley.
UK LP THE ROLLING STONES: 17 April 1964: No. 1 - 51 weeks
USA LP ENGLAND'S NEWEST HIT MAKERS: 30 May 1964: No. 11 - 12 weeks

Marvin Gaye had previously recorded this Motown classic and Andrew Oldham, keen to establish the band in a more pop-orientated mould, decided *Can I Get A Witness* was a suitable song for inclusion on the album. Consequently, Mick Jagger rushed down to Carlin Music and bought the song sheet to the Holland, Dozier, Holland hit. Ian Stewart pounds out the basic chords and Mick contributes particularly up-front vocals.

81. NOW I'VE GOT A WITNESS (LIKE UNCLE PHIL AND UNCLE GENE) (Phelge) 2.32
4 February 1964: Place: Regent Sound Studios, London, England.
Rolling Stones with Phil Spector, Gene Pitney.
Producer: Andrew Oldham.
Engineer: Bill Farley.
UK LP THE ROLLING STONES: 17 April 1964: No. 1 - 51 weeks
USA LP ENGLAND'S NEWEST HIT MAKERS: 30 May 1964: No. 11 - 12 weeks

Following the recording of *Can I Get A Witness*, Phil Spector again offered his production expertise and Gene Pitney played on Ian Stewart's prized piano on a basic re-working of the song. It is said the inclusion of the track was to fill up the album, due to lack of authentic material. Ian Stewart, having given away the piano to Uncle Gene, plays very prominent organ with Brian Jones on outstanding harp complementing Ian's prime drive. Keith Richards then sways into the song trading Chuck Berry chords whilst Mick Jagger hits the tambourine rhythmically on his gyrating hip. Bill Wyman and Charlie Watts create the basis for the jam.

82. WAKE UP IN THE MORNING (Jones, Thompson) 0.27
AKA: Rice Krispies Jingle
6 February 1964: Place: Star Sound Studios, London, England.
Producer: Jonathan Rollands.
Engineer: Glyn Johns.
Bootleg only.

Kellogg's, the manufacturers of breakfast cereal, wanted a soundtrack for their new Rice Krispies promotion. The JW Thompson agency supplied the lyrics (hence the credit) but the track was written and performed mainly by Brian Jones, with vocals undertaken by Mick Jagger. In his book *Rolling With The Stones*, Bill Wyman described it as a Jimmy Reed-style track.

It was used on television throughout Europe during 1964. The Stones were paid a sum of £400 for the 30-second recording, the contract being signed by Brian Jones on behalf of the group and witnessed by Eric Easton on 6 February 1964. Pye Studios are often quoted as the recording source, as well as the Star Sound, Hampstead studio.

83. ROLL OVER BEETHOVEN (Berry) ✏ 2.17
8 February - 7 March 1964: Place: UK Tour - Unknown venue, BBC Radio, London, England.
Bootleg only.

84. BEAUTIFUL DELILAH (Berry) ✏ 2.14
8 February - 7 March 1964: Place: UK Tour - Unknown venue, BBC Radio, London, England.
Bootleg only.

Two tracks recorded during the tour and broadcast on Brian Matthews' Saturday Club on 8 March.

85. GOOD TIMES, BAD TIMES (Jagger, Richard) 2.30
24-25 February 1964: Place: Regent Sound Studios, London, England.
Producer: Andrew Oldham.
Engineer: Bill Farley.
UK B-side It's All Over Now: 26 June 1964
USA B-side It's All Over Now: 25 July 1964
USA LP 12 X 5: 23 October 1964: No. 3 - 20 weeks
USA Compilation LP BIG HITS (HIGH TIDE AND GREEN GRASS): 1 April 1966: No. 3 - 35 weeks

USA Compilation LP MORE HOT ROCKS (BIG HITS & FAZED COOKIES): 1 December 1972: No. 9 - 12 weeks
UK Compilation LP GET STONED - 30 GREATEST HITS, 30 ORIGINAL TRACKS: 21 October 1977: No. 13 - 15 weeks
UK & USA LP THE ROLLING STONES SINGLES COLLECTION - THE LONDON YEARS: 15 August 1989
USA Compilation CD MORE HOT ROCKS (BIG HITS & FAZED COOKIES): 3 September 2002
UK & USA CD box set THE ROLLING STONES SINGLES - 1963 - 1965: 4 May 2004

A blues song fit for any Andrew Oldham "anthology" compilation, it strides along purposefully. Mick Jagger spreads his lips and illustrates the need for placing more trust in the world - the writing duo were beginning to broaden their horizons. The group were being forcefully led by Andrew Oldham's well-oiled publicity machine, which was laying the rock foundations and creating a group being developed as an exact antithesis of The Beatles.

The Stones were the group the parents loved to hate. Andrew even had a press name for Charlie Watts, calling him the "Beau Brummel" for his good dress sense. The Press acceded to the Oldham's strategy with stories of a headmaster who had suspended pupils for imitating the Stones' unruly mops and requested that they had them styled neatly like The Beatles. The Daily Mirror headline read: "Beatle Your Rolling Stone Hair". The pressure was mounting but still they played the blues and there were indeed "good times, bad times".

86. OVER YOU (Toussaint, Orange)
24-25 February 1964: Place: Regent Sound Studios, London, England.
Producer: Andrew Oldham.
Engineer: Bill Farley.
Unavailable.

Again, another track from this session and possibly a contender for the next single. It is not available as a bootleg but turned up in a 1995 auction on a 1964 Regent Sound acetate. It was an A side with *Good Times, Bad Times* on the flip. *Over You* was a cover of an Allen Toussaint/Allen Orange song recorded by Aaron Neville in 1960 and, as his debut single, reached No. 21 in the R 'n' B charts.

2 CHESS – FIRST MOVE TO THE TOP
March 1964 – April 1965

87. AS TIME GOES BY (Jagger, Richard, Oldham) 2.13
AKA: As Tears Go By
8-14 March 1964: Place: De Lane Lea Studios, Kingsway, Olympic, London, England.
Rolling Stones with Jim Sullivan, Eric Ford.
Producer: Andrew Oldham.
Bootleg only.

In various partnerships, the Stones continued to come up with songs which were mostly ballads in nature. This one shared a name with Dooley Wilson's 1931 song that appeared in the 1942 film *Casablanca* starring Humphrey Bogart and Ingrid Bergman - "play it again Sam!" In late March 1964, for the launch of Adrienne Poster's music career, Sid Posta (her father) organised a party at her house. Many guests attended and Adrienne recalled that this is where Andrew Oldham and Mick Jagger met Marianne Faithfull, who was accompanied by her husband John Dunbar. There was an instant attraction between Andrew and Marianne - so she was asked if she could sing (not that that appeared to matter) and so another young artist was signed to Andrew's stewardship. This party is also said to be where Keith Richards met Linda Keith who worked for Vogue magazine.
At a practice session, a Lionel Bart song was considered for Marianne's first release but Andrew asked if *As Time Goes By*, recorded earlier that month, could be worked upon. The original track features Jim Sullivan on 12-string guitar, Mick on vocals and Eric Ford on bass. Big Jim met Andrew Oldham and the Stones at the publishing company's offices in Denmark Street, where he was asked to work on the song for Marianne Faithfull and helped to contribute to its writing.
It started off as a simplistic demo with sufficient promise that Andrew considered that, along with Lionel Bart, he could work on the song's orchestral arrangement and instruments and lyrics. It also needed to be renamed to avoid any connection with the *Casablanca* film so the more poignant "tears" was substituted for "time". Released on 26 June, Marianne Faithfull obtained her first hit in August 1964, when the song reached No. 9 in Britain. In the States, in early 1965, it flirted with a top 30 position at No. 22. *As Tears Go By* was a highlight of Oldham's musical production career.

88. NO ONE KNOWS (Jagger, Richard) 0.09
8-14 March 1964: Place: De Lane Lea Studios, Kingsway, London, England.
Rolling Stones with Jim Sullivan, Eric Ford, Clem Cattini.
Producer: Andrew Oldham.
Bootleg only.

A short extract on a medley of songs from a similar era with female vocals in the background.

89. COME AND DANCE WITH ME (Jagger, Richard)
8-14 March 1964: Place: De Lane Lea Studios, Kingsway, London, England.
Rolling Stones with Jim Sullivan, Eric Ford, Clem Cattini.
Producer: Andrew Oldham.
Unavailable.

No One Knows is a very short demo track while *Come And Dance With Me* is generally unavailable. It was recorded on to an acetate and reputedly a copy emerged for sale in the 1990s. Jim Sullivan, who plays guitar on the recording, cannot recall their origin. He was aware that Keith Richards, Mick Jagger and Brian Jones were trying to write songs at the time. Andrew Oldham reckoned that Brian found it difficult to write because he always wanted to be original.
He put down some of Mick and Keith's efforts as being popular soft music. It was easier to write soft ballads to start with rather than up-tempo numbers. Oldham looked down the nose at that and, although he tried writing, Brian thought the public would see through non-genuine attempts. Brian, Charlie Watts or Bill Wyman were mostly not involved in these sessions since Oldham did not feel he could ask them to work for little money on their off-days.

90. LOOK WHAT YOU'VE DONE (McKinley, Morganfield)
18 March 1964: Place: Regent Sound Studios or IBC Studios, London, England.
Producer: Andrew Oldham.
Engineer: Bill Farley.
Unavailable.

These studio tracks were broadcast in four separate parts in April and May 1964 by Radio Luxembourg for their programme Top Swinging Groups. They were recorded to promote the release of the Stones' first album and were probably cut at IBC due to the potentially lower cost of hire. They were *Bye Bye Johnny, I Wanna Be Your Man, Diddley Daddy, Little By Little, Look What You've Done, Mona, Not Fade Away, Now I've Got A Witness, Pretty Thing, Walking The Dog, You Better Move On, Reelin' And A Rockin', Roll Over Beethoven* and *Route 66*. The above song would be recorded in 1964 many miles away.

91. ROUTE 66 (Troup) ✏ 2.45
19 March 1964: Place: Camden Theatre, London, England.
Bootleg only.

92. COPS AND ROBBERS (Harris) ✏ 3.55
19 March 1964: Place: Camden Theatre, London, England.
Bootleg only.

93. YOU BETTER MOVE ON (Alexander) 〰 3.01
19 March 1964: Place: Camden Theatre, London, England.
Bootleg only.

94. MONA (McDaniel) 〰 2.51
AKA: I Need You Baby
19 March 1964: Place: Camden Theatre, London, England.
Bootleg only.

The Stones had been touring persistently since early January 1964 with such artistes as The Ronettes (hence Phil Spector, the Ronettes' handy-man being available for the Regent Studio sessions), The Swinging Blue Jeans, Marty Wilde and The Wildcats, Dave Berry and The Cruisers, Johnny Kidd and The Pirates, Jet Harris, Mike Berry, Bern Elliott and The Fenmen and The Hollies. Inevitably sets were short, rarely exceeding a dozen songs for the Stones and many venues were treated to an early and a late show.

The Ronettes made a big impression, especially with Keith Richards and Mick Jagger, who had relationships with Ronnie and Estelle Bennett respectively. Keith told Jon Wilde, of Loaded magazine in 1995: "That's when I found rock n' roll. That's also when I learned about jealousy, 'cos I had Phil Spector chasing me around with a shotgun. That's when I started ducking and diving. It was a question of survival!" In all during the period, they had played 40 gigs from 6 January to 7 March 1964 and recorded at least 14 tracks, including a No. 1 album and a top three single. They were cruising from town to town, sleeping sometimes in Ian Stewart's van and occasionally grabbing a greasy egg and chips at a roadside cafe, as publicity photos testify.

A letter from Charlie Watts to a fan illustrates the touring fun: "The Rolling Stones van somewhere on the road England . . .It is very exciting, having a hit record, but it's rather a strain on the nerves and I am now a nervous wreck. I have bitten my nails so low that I now wear false hands, and I have to cut Stu's hair and make it into a wig as all my hair has fallen out. I am secretly married to the fan club secretary, Annabelle and the Queen Mother . . . It isn't a dance that Mick does you know, it is a nervous twitch . . . I daren't say anything about Brian as he has a knife in between my shoulder blades . . ." Ouch!

The four tracks detailed above were recorded during their hectic touring schedule and were destined for a future BBC broadcast transmission on 9 May 1964 at 9.30 am. The transmission on Network Radio 3 was innovative because it featured mock stereo, the television being used as one channel and the radio broadcast another - a unique method of creating a stereo mix. Ian Grant was the producer of the television-sound experiment. The show, titled Rhythm And Blues and featuring the Stones with Georgie Fame and his Bluenotes, was presented by Long John Baldry, who introduced the Rolling Stones as "charming deviationists".

Cops And Robbers, another strident Bo Diddley number with Brian Jones on harmonica, is of particular interest since it has not officially been made available, although it was broadcast on BBC World Services. In the 70s, it was the lead track on a famous 7-inch bootleg extended play single. In 1998, David Lister from the UK's Independent newspaper, gained access to the BBC's archive of sessions between October 1963 and September 1965. BBC archivists and retired producers had found more than 20 lost recordings that could be considered for potential release.

Two of these were announced as *Dust My Pyramids* (written by B Jones and Richards) and *I Wanna Love You* from the Rhythm and Blues session. The former was a short instrumental and the latter Jimmy Reed's *I'm A Love You*. All in all, the bootlegs amount to 50 recordings broadcast by the BBC in the two-year period.

95. NOT FADE AWAY (Petty, Hardin) 〰 2.04
10 April 1964: Place: Playhouse Theatre, London, England.
Bootleg only.

96. HIGH HEELED SNEAKERS (Higgenbotham) 〰 1.39
10 April 1964: Place: Playhouse Theatre, London, England.
Bootleg only.

97. LITTLE BY LITTLE (Phelge, Spector) 〰 2.30
10 April 1964: Place: Playhouse Theatre, London, England.
Bootleg only.

98. I JUST WANT TO MAKE LOVE TO YOU (Dixon) 〰 2.16
10 April 1964: Place: Playhouse Theatre, London, England.
Bootleg only.

99. I'M MOVING ON (Snow) 〰 2.08
10 April 1964: Place: Playhouse Theatre, London, England.
Bootleg only.

These tracks were played live for the Joe Loss Radio Show. He was famous for his big band Glenn Miller songs and his radio show also played that kind of style - at odds with the Stones. The show was broadcast at lunchtime on 10 April, which was a good time for increased listeners and exposure. Joe Loss made the band welcome and both the current single and the flip side were included as the tracks were still in the charts.

100. NOT FADE AWAY (Petty, Hardin) 2.07
13 April 1964: Place: BBC Maida Vale Studios, London, England.
Bootleg only.

101. WALKING THE DOG (Thomas) 3.00
13 April 1964: Place: BBC Maida Vale Studios, London, England.
Bootleg only.

102.   I JUST WANT TO MAKE LOVE TO YOU (Dixon) 2.11
13 April 1964: Place: BBC Maida Vale Studios, London, England.
Bootleg only.

103.   BEAUTIFUL DELILAH (Berry) 2.18
13 April 1964: Place: BBC Maida Vale Studios, London, England.
Bootleg only.

104.   HIGH HEELED SNEAKERS (Higgenbotham) 2.34
13 April 1964: Place: BBC Maida Vale Studios, London, England.
Played Live: 1964
Bootleg only.

105.   CAROL (Berry) 2.30
13 April 1964: Place: BBC Maida Vale Studios, London, England.
Bootleg only.

Recorded for The Saturday Club and broadcast on 18 April, 1964 just after the release of their first album. Three tracks taken from the album plus *Not Fade Away*, the current single, were featured along with the unreleased *Beautiful Delilah* and *High Heeled Sneekers*. The Stones were still touring extensively and, since The Ronettes shows in January, had been on the road with John Leyton during February and March. In April, they played more than 20 dates at various ballrooms throughout the UK.

106.   MONA (McDaniel)
20 April 1964: Place: ITV TV Ready Steady Go!, Montreux, Switzerland.
Unavailable.

107.   ROUTE 66 (Troup)
20 April 1964: Place: ITV TV Ready Steady Go!, Montreux, Switzerland.
Unavailable.

108.   NOT FADE AWAY (Petty, Hardin)
20 April 1964: Place: ITV TV Ready Steady Go!, Montreux, Switzerland.
Unavailable.

Recorded in Montreux for the Golden Rose International TV Awards, this was the first time the Stones had gone abroad to play. Ready Steady Go! Producer Vicki Wickham remembered the visit well: "Yes, their first trip and ours! I sat with Brian Jones and we were both terrified of flying and held hands the entire way. When we landed, the others were going to the venue across the lake in a boat - we opted to drive round."
Ronald Elliott, editor of the first Ready, Steady, Go! magazine, recollected this dramatic visit to Switzerland and business director Francis Hitching recalled: "The 40 dancers who had flown over with us on a special charter flight were almost as big stars as the Rolling Stones and Kenny Lynch. After the show they all got themselves free hospitality in a local night club just by demonstrating the Block, the Ticket, the Face-Twist and so on. The Stones and Kenny joined in the fun too. At one point Bill Wyman tried to get in a taxi that already had five kids - the legal maximum. 'Non, Madame, non', shouted the Swiss taxi driver. Men cut their hair short in Switzerland."

109.   NOT FADE AWAY (Petty, Hardin) ⚡ 2.01
26 April 1964: Place: NME Poll Winners Concert, Empire Pool Wembley, London, England.
Bootleg only.

110.   I JUST WANT TO MAKE LOVE TO YOU (Dixon) ⚡ 2.19
26 April 1964: Place: NME Poll Winners Concert, Empire Pool Wembley, London, England.
Bootleg only.

111.   I'M ALRIGHT (McDaniel) ⚡ 2.07
26 April 1964: Place: NME Poll Winners Concert, Empire Pool Wembley, London, England.
Bootleg only.

The British weekly musical magazine, New Musical Express, hosted an awards show at the Empire Pool, Wembley. The Beatles were there and congratulated the Stones on the success of their album which had incredibly gone straight to No. 1, replacing their second album WITH THE BEATLES. The show was broadcast in May 1964 on ABC television as "Big Beat 64". Jimmy Savile introduced a rowdy performance with the band interacting well. Brian Jones produces climactic, juxtaposed shouts to Mick Jagger's vocals.

112.   NOT FADE AWAY (Petty, Hardin) ⚡
27 April 1964: Place: The Royal Albert Hall, London, England.
Unavailable.

113. HIGH HEELED SNEAKERS (Higgenbotham) ∕
27 April 1964: Place: The Royal Albert Hall, London, England.
Unavailable.

114. I'M ALRIGHT (McDaniel) ∕
27 April 1964: Place: The Royal Albert Hall, London, England.
Unavailable.

Fame and adulation continued in earnest as, following the NME Poll Winners concert, they played at that great British institution, The Royal Albert Hall. The show was broadcast on radio and TV in a one-off BBC2 programme "Top Beat Pop Prom" on 25 May.

115. DON'T LIE TO ME (Whittaker) 2.02
AKA: Let's Talk It Over, Don't You Lie To Me
12 May 1964: Place: Regent Sound Studios, London, England.
Producer: Andrew Oldham.
Engineer: Bill Farley.
UK Compilation LP METAMORPHOSIS: 6 June 1975: No. 45 - 1 week
USA Compilation LP METAMORPHOSIS: 6 June 1975: No. 8 - 8 weeks

Don't Lie To Me is usually credited as being a Chuck Berry song since he made it popular. However, it was written in 1940 by Hudson Woodbridge, who assumed his grandfather's name of Whittaker. He was also known in the blues world as Tampa Red. It was incorrectly credited to Jagger, Richards on initial copies of the METAMORPHOSIS album sleeve.
Ian Stewart opens the song purposefully but it then lacks conviction and disintegrates into a studio work-out, despite Keith Richards occasionally plunging in with some impetuous lead guitar. Mick Jagger tries to convince the band to charge on this medium-packed rock and roll tune but it did not fulfil the band's expectations. *Don't Lie To Me* faltered only to resurface on an out-take compilation album in 1975.

116. CONGRATULATIONS (Jagger, Richard) 2.29
12 May, 24-26 June 1964: Place: Regent Sound Studios, London, England.
Played Live: 1964
Producer: Andrew Oldham.
Engineer: Bill Farley.
USA B-side Time Is On My Side: 25 September 1964
USA LP 12 X 5: 23 October 1964: No. 3 - 20 weeks
UK Compilation LP NO STONE UNTURNED: 5 October 1973
German Compilation LP THE REST OF THE BEST: December 1983
UK & USA LP THE ROLLING STONES SINGLES COLLECTION - THE LONDON YEARS: 15 August 1989
UK & USA CD box set THE ROLLING STONES SINGLES - 1963 - 1965: 4 May 2004

This track is not available in the United Kingdom but can be obtained on the reverse side of *Time Is On My Side*, the third American single, and second American album 12 X 5 (twelve tracks by five musicians). It obtained its first release in the UK on a compilation of recordings NO STONE UNTURNED in 1973.
Congratulations is a Mick Jagger and Keith Richards composition, a bit too predictable and lacking in direction. The initial releases in the United States were all of a slow tempo and *Congratulations* was added onto the *Time Is On My Side* single which continued the trend.

117. DOWN IN THE BOTTOM (Dixon) 2.46
25 May 1964: Place: BBC Broadcasting House, London, England.
Bootleg only.

118. YOU CAN MAKE IT IF YOU TRY (Jarrett) 2.13
25 May 1964: Place: BBC Broadcasting House, London, England.
Bootleg only.

119. ROUTE 66 (Troup) 2.27
25 May 1964: Place: BBC Broadcasting House, London, England.
Bootleg only.

120. CONFESSIN' THE BLUES (Brown, McShann) 3.00
25 May 1964: Place: BBC Broadcasting House, London, England.
Bootleg only.

121. DOWN THE ROAD APIECE (Raye) 2.05
25 May 1964: Place: BBC Broadcasting House, London, England.
Bootleg only.

Another Saturday Club radio show recording, featuring two tracks from the first album, namely *You Can Make It If You Try* and *Route 66*. The session, which was broadcast on 6 June 1964, also included *Down In The Bottom*, *Down The Road Apiece* and *Confessin' The Blues*, which were to be recorded the next month in the United States.

122. NOT FADE AWAY (Petty, Hardin) 1.55
3 June 1964: Place: Hollywood Palace TV Show, Los Angeles, California, USA.
Bootleg only.

123. I JUST WANT TO MAKE LOVE TO YOU (Dixon) 1.12
3 June 1964: Place: Hollywood Palace TV Show, Los Angeles, California, USA.
Bootleg only.

The Stones' first Stateside adventure was to last just over three weeks, playing 12 concerts at nine venues. Keith Richards later commented on the visit, saying: "It was a gift going to America." Bob Bonis, who became very well respected by the band, was their road manager for the tour, a promotional venture which was timed to coincide with the release of their first US album.

They arrived at JF Kennedy Airport on 1 June 1964 (it had been re-dedicated from its previous name New York International on 24 December 1963), to a modest reception compared to the hysterical greeting The Beatles had received four months earlier.

On arrival in the States, The Stones sadly lacked hit material, though one of their publicists did bring some hairy English sheepdogs to meet the band! Their first two American singles, *I Wanna Be Your Man* and *Not Fade Away*, released in January and March 1964 respectively, failed to make a great impression on the Billboard charts. They were trying to re-import the blues to America and that would be a severe test of their musical integrity.

They handled their first TV interviews with Les Crane comfortably on 2 June then, the next day, flew to Los Angeles to record two tracks for television, *Not Fade Away* and *I Just Want To Make Love To You* - the latter being the B-side of the forthcoming American single *Tell Me*.

The show, hosted by Dean Martin, was a compendium of clowns, cowboys and other doubtful entertainers. Mr Martin, pretending to be worse for drink (I've been rolled while I was stoned myself), delighted the older American viewers with snide comments about Stones/Beatles hair pulling contests and, prior to a commercial break, announced: "Now don't go away, you wouldn't want to leave me with these Rolling Stones would you?"

The Stones were antagonised but performed their second number *I Just Want To Make Love To You* with professional gusto in front of a limited group of teen screamers. Dean Martin had given the Stones their first taste of American publicity and their manager, Andrew Oldham, perversely loved every minute.

124. STEWED AND KEEFED (Nanker, Phelge) 4.12
AKA: Brian's Blues
10 June 1964: Place: Chess Studios, Chicago, USA.
Producer: Andrew Oldham.
Engineer: Ron Malo.
Bootleg only.

For the previous six months, the Stones had been trying to emulate their American blues and soul heroes. They had played hundreds of gigs and the BBC sessions had also tightened and fused their sound. The culmination of that period came when Phil Spector helped them to realise an ambition and actually record at the renowned Leonard and Phil Chess Studios, previously used by Muddy Waters, Howlin' Wolf, Little Walter, John Lee Hooker, Bo Diddley, Willie Dixon, Buddy Guy, Etta James and Chuck Berry (say no more).

Marshall Chess later likened it to having Beethoven, Bach and Mozart on the same label. In fact, the Stones were one of the first white acts to be recorded at Chess. Keith Richards recalls an incongruous situation when they met Muddy Waters, who was assisting with the upkeep of the studios and was up a ladder in white overalls, decorating the ceiling!

Keith still insists this was the case but Bill Wyman, Charlie Watts and Marshall Chess say they can remember no such thing. Bill, however, said Waters did help to carry their instruments when he saw them unloading outside.

The band were in their element with "magic fingers" Ron Malo at the controls on a classic Bill Putnam console and were not over-awed by the occasion. Malo worked as an engineer at Chess from 1959 to 1970 and was clearly very fond of his surroundings, remarking: "The studio at 2120 was an exceptional piece of engineering. It was a room within a room, adjustable walls and state of the art microphones."

The Chicago session was to produce a number of unreleased tracks, of which this was one. This was not necessarily because the product was below standard but perhaps due to the prolific output of a group who were on their first blues pilgrimage. It is an instrumental which features two duelling musicians - the bar room shuffling Ian Stewart and the lazy blues guitar of Keith Richards.

Like the Mississippi, the track meanders inexorably to the blues delta. *Stewed And Keefed* is undoubtedly a worthy jam track, typical of the laid-back ambience achieved at Chess. Brian Jones was unwell, hence his "blues" in the alternative title. Keef was a name that Keith referred to himself as amongst family friends.

125. I CAN'T BE SATISFIED (McKinley, Morganfield) 3.26
10 June 1964: Place: Chess Studios, Chicago, USA.
Producer: Andrew Oldham.
Engineer: Ron Malo.
UK LP THE ROLLING STONES NO 2: 15 January 1965: No. 1 - 37 weeks
USA Compilation LP MORE HOT ROCKS (BIG HITS & FAZED COOKIES): 1 December 1972: No. 9 - 12 weeks
USA Compilation CD MORE HOT ROCKS (BIG HITS & FAZED COOKIES): 3 September 2002

This Muddy Waters song was described as "nigger music" by the songwriter himself (tongue firmly in cheek) and discredited by radio personality Murray the K, who reckoned the Stones were on to a loser because white kids didn't listen to tunes by Waters and the rest of the blues fraternity. How wrong this was - as he soon realised.

As Muddy said: "The blues had a baby and called it rock 'n' roll". How true - the Stones created a song sentimental in approach, with the controlled methodical rhythm unit of Bill Wyman and Charlie Watts hardly breaking into sweat. Brian Jones is the instrumentalist on this particular track and he plays some inspirational bottleneck blues. Keith Richards stands in the background, supporting the rhythm with upfront acoustic, and lends a hand at the end, trading blues licks with Brian. The guitar roles were temporarily reversed but you cannot deny the sheer mastery of a skilful bottleneck player - and still only aged 22. *I Can't Be Satisfied* was not released in the States until the December 1972 MORE HOT ROCKS (BIG HITS AND FAZED COOKIES), a muddled collection of B-sides, single hits and album tracks.

126. TIME IS ON MY SIDE (Ragovoy, Norman) 2.56
10 June, 8 November 1964: Place: Chess Studios, Chicago, USA.
Played Live: 1964, 1965, 1966, 1981, 1982, 1998
Producer: Andrew Oldham.
Engineer: Ron Malo.
UK LP THE ROLLING STONES NO 2: 15 January 1965: No. 1 - 37 weeks
USA Compilation LP BIG HITS (HIGH TIDE AND GREEN GRASS): 1 April 1966: No. 3 - 35 weeks
UK Compilation LP BIG HITS (HIGH TIDE AND GREEN GRASS): 4 November 1966: No. 4 - 43 weeks
USA LP THE ROLLING STONES HOT ROCKS 1964-1971: 11 January 1972: No. 4 - 30 weeks
UK Compilation LP MILESTONES: 18 February 1972: No. 14 - 8 weeks
UK Compilation LP ROLLED GOLD: 14 November 1975: No. 7 - 50 weeks
UK Compilation LP GET STONED - 30 GREATEST HITS, 30 ORIGINAL TRACKS: 21 October 1977: No. 13 - 15 weeks
UK LP SLOW ROLLERS: 9 November 1981
UK Compilation CD ROLLED GOLD +: 12 November 2007: No. 26 - 12 weeks

Recorded in America and released only in Britain, this is the second version, featuring lead guitar with a gentle Hammond organ. An early take was recorded at their June session but the UK-released version was finally recorded on their second American visit. The guitar-led version was simply much better than the earlier one at Regent. It became a popular live song, even if the screams tended to drown this rousing ballad. The rhythm chord finale is by Keith Richards. While the vinyl version of HOT ROCKS contained the guitar version when ABKCO transferred the results to compact disc, the UK organ rendering was featured in 1986.

127. IT'S ALL OVER NOW (B and S Womack) 3.28
10 June 1964: Place: Chess Studios, Chicago, USA.
Played Live: 1964, 1965, 1967, 1973, 1994, 1995, 2007
Producer: Andrew Oldham.
Engineer: Ron Malo.
UK Single: 26 June 1964: No. 1 - 15 weeks
USA Single: 25 July 1964: No. 26 - 10 weeks
USA LP 12 X 5: 23 October 1964: No. 3 - 20 weeks
USA Compilation LP BIG HITS (HIGH TIDE AND GREEN GRASS): 1 April 1966: No. 3 - 35 weeks
UK Compilation LP BIG HITS (HIGH TIDE AND GREEN GRASS): 4 November 1966: No. 4 - 43 weeks
UK Compilation LP STONE AGE: 6 March 1971: No. 4 - 7 weeks
USA Compilation LP MORE HOT ROCKS (BIG HITS & FAZED COOKIES): 1 December 1972: No. 9 - 12 weeks
UK Compilation LP ROLLED GOLD: 14 November 1975: No. 7 - 50 weeks
UK Compilation LP GET STONED - 30 GREATEST HITS, 30 ORIGINAL TRACKS: 21 October 1977: No. 13 - 15 weeks
UK & USA LP THE ROLLING STONES SINGLES COLLECTION - THE LONDON YEARS: 15 August 1989
USA Compilation Promo CD THE ROLLING STONES REMASTERED: 30 May 2002
USA Compilation Promo CD ABKCO'S THE ROLLINGS STONES REMASTERED SERIES: 30 May 2002
USA Compilation CD MORE HOT ROCKS (BIG HITS & FAZED COOKIES): 3 September 2002
UK CD LP FORTY LICKS: 30 September 2002: No. 2 - 45 weeks
USA CD LP FORTY LICKS: 1 October 2002: No. 2 - 50 weeks
UK & USA CD box set THE ROLLING STONES SINGLES - 1963 - 1965: 4 May 2004
UK Compilation CD ROLLED GOLD +: 12 November 2007: No. 26 - 12 weeks

Murray the K, a popular American disc jockey and promoter, turned the Stones onto this Valentinos song. He had interviewed them on his New York radio show and had given Andrew Oldham the single by Bobby Womack, guaranteeing him it would be a hit if covered. The Stones decided to record it and, with Ron Malo's engineering technique, another Chess soul classic was created. Melody Maker (a British weekly music paper) reports that 14 takes of the song were made before the band were happy with the recording. There was also an argument between Andrew, Mick Jagger and Charlie Watts about how the song should start.
However, it went straight to No. 1 in Britain, Jagger nonchalantly admitting it was great that it had reached that position but he was looking for a worldwide hit with far more copies sold. His thoughts were probably on the United States, where the track was edited and only achieved a No. 26 position (* a - 2.48), despite eight weeks of promotional work and a brief tour of the Northern states.
On *It's All Over Now* Malo blends Keith's reverberating, earthy guitar with a country rhythm plucked by Brian Jones. Bobby Womack, the Valentinos' lead singer and songwriter had ignored the abrasive edge of the lyrics, which Jagger intuitively saw. Keith added a unique lead guitar solo, which provides the icing on the cake. At the time, Bobby Womack was an established soul artiste and was rather annoyed that the Stones should improvise on his song (little were they to know that 20 years later Womack would guest on the 1986 DIRTY WORK album). Despite this, *It's All Over Now* is a landmark in the Stones' recording history and is typical of the creative influence of the Chess Studios.
This was despite Andrew later feeling he had added too much echo to the underlying track but he sensed they had recorded a uniquely American sound with the song. Marshall Chess, the son of Leonard Chess, was present at the recording of *It's All Over Now* and was later to become the Stones' manager in the 1970s. In May 1974, Decca planned to release the track again with *Paint It Black* - it was given the matrix number DECCA F 13517.

128. REELIN' AND A ROCKIN' (Berry) 3.32
10-11 June 1964: Place: Chess Studios, Chicago, USA.
Producer: Andrew Oldham.
Engineer: Ron Malo.
Bootleg only.

Another Chuck Berry song performed at a sedate, relaxed pace, with two distinctive lead guitars. Charlie Watts' drum sound provides a metronome for the song as he perfectly controls the rest of the band. Mick Jagger's vocals are an intrinsic part of the three-and-a-half minute track as he guides the musicians through to the break of dawn.

On the first day of recording, Chuck himself came by the studio, as did Buddy Guy and Willie Dixon, who was proffering some of his songs. *Reelin' And A Rockin'* was not released and, apparently, some Chess tracks were recorded but Andrew Oldham managed to lose them - or perhaps they were saved for his pension trust fund! The session was completed around midnight before they headed off for a gig in Minneapolis. There were four tracks recorded on the first day and a further 11 on the second day, this information being recorded in Bill Wyman's diaries and his book *Rolling With The Stones*.

129. **IF YOU NEED ME** (Pickett, Bateman, Sanders) 2.05
11 June 1964: Place: Chess Studios, Chicago, USA.
Played Live: 1962, 1964
Producer: Andrew Oldham.
Engineer: Ron Malo.
UK EP Five By Five: 14 August 1964
USA LP 12 X 5: 23 October 1964: No. 3 - 20 weeks
UK Compilation LP STONE AGE: 6 March 1971: No. 4 - 7 weeks
UK & USA CD box set THE ROLLING STONES SINGLES - 1963 - 1965: 4 May 2004

If You Need Me is a medium tempo ballad which creates a soul-searching feel to the opening tracks of the British EP. Ian Stewart contributes a prominent organ which flows throughout the song in the background. The track, recorded by Wilson Pickett, had been given away by Jerry Wexler to Solomon Burke, who had a hit with it.

130. **EMPTY HEART** (Nanker, Phelge) 2.38
11 June 1964: Place: Chess Studios, Chicago, USA.
Played Live: 1964
Producer: Andrew Oldham.
Engineer: Ron Malo.
UK EP Five By Five: 14 August 1964
USA LP 12 X 5: 23 October 1964: No. 3 - 20 weeks
UK & USA CD box set THE ROLLING STONES SINGLES - 1963 - 1965: 4 May 2004

The band soaked up the Chicago city atmosphere, particularly Ian Stewart and Charlie Watts, who would visit venues such as the London House Jazz club, spending many a memorable night there. Feeling their way into the Chicago studio ambience, the boys' confidence bristled as they recorded a worthy band composition. Mick's vocals are powerful, backed by Keith Richards' distinctive voice. Brian Jones wails on the harmonica in the background and the track, which might have sounded pale captured in an English studio, seems to bloom with the undoubted enthusiasm of half-a-dozen blues devotees playing at the Chess "blues Mecca". It marked a new era in the Stones' recordings.

131. **2120 SOUTH MICHIGAN AVENUE** (Nanker, Phelge) 2.38
11 June 1964: Place: Chess Studios, Chicago, USA.
Producer: Andrew Oldham.
Engineer: Ron Malo.
UK EP Five By Five: 14 August 1964
USA LP 12 X 5: 23 October 1964: No. 3 - 20 weeks
UK Compilation LP NO STONE UNTURNED: 5 October 1973
USA Compilation Promo CD THE ROLLING STONES REMASTERED: 30 May 2002
UK & USA CD box set THE ROLLING STONES SINGLES - 1963 - 1965: 4 May 2004

This was essentially an instrumental studio jam session, with Bill Wyman opening the track and Ian Stewart pumping his organ into overdrive. Each member of the band takes his turn on an instrumental break as *South Michigan Avenue* escalates into a steam-rolling number, with Mick Jagger and Brian Jones sparring with each other on harmonicas.

The final cut, as released on the British EP, is shortened and the reason for that is endlessly debated. Those who own the long version, extended by an additional one-and-a-half minutes (* a - 3.39), believe that this was due to blues aficionado Muddy Waters joining in the jam, thereby causing contractual problems - not so. The more technically orientated simply adhere to the fact that only so much time can be filled on an early 1960s extended-play single. Bill Wyman, in fact, denies that any guest played on the track. In November 1982, a 12-inch version of the EP was released in the UK which contained the long version and, when 12 X 5 was remastered in 2002, it finally appeared in its full length.

Andrew Oldham stated on the sleeve notes: "This new EP was recorded in Chicago during the Stones' recent American tour and is yet another showcase for their exciting vocalising and unique instrumental sound. And by way of saying 'thank you' to their friends and fans, we have included an extra track on this, their latest disc outing." By the way, *2120 South Michigan Avenue* is the address of the Chess Studios!

132. **CONFESSIN' THE BLUES** (Brown, McShann) 2.48
11 June 1964: Place: Chess Studios, Chicago, USA.
Played Live: 1962, 1964, 1986
Producer: Andrew Oldham.
Engineer: Ron Malo.
UK EP Five By Five: 14 August 1964
USA LP 12 X 5: 23 October 1964: No. 3 - 20 weeks

UK Compilation LP STONE AGE: 6 March 1971: No. 4 - 7 weeks
UK & USA CD box set THE ROLLING STONES SINGLES - 1963 - 1965: 4 May 2004

Inspired by the Chess Studios, Brian Jones and Keith Richards started to record all the old blues standards that they knew so well from their record collections. *Confessin'* may have been the original big-band Jay McShann and Walter Brown version written in the 1940s or, more likely, the Chuck Berry song found on his aforementioned album ROCKIN' AT THE HOPS.

They both agreed later that Andrew Oldham did not seem to be into the blues scene and that the Chess sessions were held together by Ron Malo. *Confessin'* was slowed down and performed in true blue-bottle style, the song plodding along with ease. The band knew they had accomplished a transformation from the type of tracks already laid down in England, which were set for inclusion on the second album. There is a stereo version available on STONE AGE.

133. AROUND AND AROUND (Berry) 3.04
11 June 1964: Place: Chess Studios, Chicago, USA.
Played Live: 1963, 1964, 1965, 1966, 1976, 1977
Producer: Andrew Oldham.
Engineer: Ron Malo.
UK EP Five By Five: 14 August 1964
USA LP 12 X 5: October 1964: No 3 - 20 weeks
USA Compilation LP THE ROLLING STONES - PROMOTIONAL ALBUM: October 1969
UK Compilation LP STONE AGE: 6 March 1971: No. 4 - 7 weeks
UK & USA CD box set THE ROLLING STONES SINGLES - 1963 - 1965: 4 May 2004

Around And Around, an old Chuck Berry favourite, was said to be recorded in his presence. It was the first number Mick Jagger had sung live when he and Keith Richards had made an impromptu appearance with Blues Incorporated at the Ealing Club, London, in 1962. It had also been included in the first demo tape sent by Mick to Alexis Korner. By now a degree of maturity had replaced the initial inexperience and this version is nothing short of immaculate.
Keith Richards, whose guitar playing is excellent, leads the song, rocking and rolling in a manner that would inspire any "greased duck's quiff" and helps create an EP whose achievements have long since been copied but not emulated. In 1995, Keith commented on a Nicky Campbell BBC radio show that it is not called rock and roll for nothing: "the rock is only good if you have the roll for contrast." This song explains why.

134. HIGH HEELED SNEAKERS (Higgenbotham) 2.59
11 June 1964: Place: Chess Studios, Chicago, USA.
Producer: Andrew Oldham.
Engineer: Ron Malo.
Bootleg only.

It was not unusual during the two-day sessions at the Chess Studios for the band's idols to drop by, carry in their gear, and chat to them in between takes. Muddy Waters, Willie Dixon and Buddy Guy were among those who genially gave them advice. Generally, all this gave the Stones' Chess sessions a distinct blues flavour, but this particular Tommy Tucker track falls into no-man's land. It lacks the band's usual positive drive, needing a faster pace. Despite Mick Jagger's insistent vocals and Brian Jones's harmonica playing, which temporarily lifts the track, the take was not a success - the probable reason for it not being released.

135. TELL ME BABY (Broonzy) 1.57
AKA: *Tell Me Baby, How Many Times?*
11 June 1964: Place: Chess Studios, Chicago, USA.
Producer: Andrew Oldham.
Engineer: Ron Malo.
German Compilation LP THE REST OF THE BEST: December 1983

This time the Stones latch on to a Big Bill Broonzy song, playing a typical plodding blues with the obligatory wailing harmonica. It is certainly not a classic and has not officially been made available, either in the United States or the United Kingdom. In Germany, a 1983 boxed set of Stones material included *Tell Me Baby* - a fact which may have disconcerted some Decca personnel!
The basic attitude adopted at the Chess sessions was to have a good time and lay down as many tracks as possible, usually in just one take. *Tell Me Baby* catches the enthusiasm but not the skilful direction of other tracks.

136. DOWN IN THE BOTTOM (Dixon) 2.43
AKA: *Fat Old Man*
11 June 1964: Place: Chess Studios, Chicago, USA.
Played Live: 1964, 1986, 1995
Producer: Andrew Oldham.
Engineer: Ron Malo.
Bootleg only.

Possibly inspired by the presence of Willie Dixon himself - or at least his ribs and soul food, which were cooked for the Stones at his house during the visit. On *Down In The Bottom*, the band turn out an up-tempo number which streaks along. Keith Richards puts on his running shoes and gets to grips by laying down an atmospheric rhythm guitar while Ron Malo adds his studio expertise and helps to create a solid Stones performance.
Malo was a famed Chess engineer who had previously recorded classics by Chuck Berry, Muddy Waters, Bo Diddley and Howlin' Wolf at the very same studios. Word got around and, on a postcard that Bill Wyman sent back to the UK, it remarked that: "Bo Diddley is coming to see us and Muddy Waters too." He also confirmed that, on 11 June, they cut four tracks, one of which was their new single *(It's All Over Now)*.

137. DOWN THE ROAD APIECE (Raye) 2.51
11 June 1964: Place: Chess Studios, Chicago, USA.
Producer: Andrew Oldham.
Engineer: Ron Malo.
UK LP THE ROLLING STONES NO 2: 15 January 1965: No. 1 - 37 weeks
USA LP THE ROLLING STONES, NOW!: 12 February 1965: No. 5 - 29 weeks
UK Compilation LP ROCK 'N' ROLLING STONES: 13 October 1972: No. 41 - 1 week

It's clear that Keith Richards was particularly impressed by Chuck Berry. This Don Raye song had been performed and mastered by Berry, so the Stones were more than excited when Chuck himself called into the studio and caught them in the middle of one of his classics. He commended the Stones on the performance, remarking that they were really getting it on - "Swing on gentlemen, you are sounding so well if I may say so". Well, they had been performing it since 1962. He was also impressed by the immaculate playing of the guitarist (Keith Richards) and no wonder - this track is a notable example of his skill as he swings and boogies in unique style. Ian Stewart plays some great boogie piano.

138. LOOK WHAT YOU'VE DONE (McKinley, Morganfield) 2.16
11 June 1964: Place: Chess Studios, Chicago, USA.
Producer: Andrew Oldham.
Engineer: Ron Malo.
USA LP DECEMBER'S CHILDREN (AND EVERYBODY'S): 4 December 1965: No. 4 - 22 weeks
UK Compilation LP STONE AGE: 6 March 1971: No. 4 - 7 weeks
German Compilation LP THE REST OF THE BEST: December 1983

Yet another track recorded in the two-day Chicago visit. There was such a wealth of recording material that it was suggested a Chicago LP should be made but unfortunately this was not done. It would certainly have made an interesting album and Ian Stewart, in particular, felt the sessions were great. Indeed, a compilation album of Chess songs was put together in Japan in 1988 (ROLLING STONES CHICAGO CHESS SESSIONS).
Instead, an EP and a single were released which still left a lot of tracks on the shelf. Some, such as *Look What You've Done*, resurfaced on compilations (a 1971 album released by Decca, titled STONE AGE) and others on bootleg.
Look What You've Done is a slow blues featuring Ian Stewart on the ivories and Brian Jones's wailing harmonica, for which Ron Malo uses a subtle echo. The song plods along but the five instrumental breaks by Stewart and Jones are restricted by the song's indirection. *Look What You've Done* was written by Muddy Waters and released in July 1960 as the 'B' side to *Love Affair* so he might have been the one to suggest recording it while in the studio with the Stones. Rumour has it that a few days later a very young Don Fagenson (Was) was taken to see the band at the Detroit Olympic stadium, so beginning his lifelong affinity with them.

139. CAROL (Berry) 2.49
18 June 1964: Place: Mike Douglas Show, Cleveland, Ohio, USA.
Bootleg only.

140. TELL ME (YOU'RE COMING BACK) (Jagger, Richard) 2.35
18 June 1964: Place: Mike Douglas Show, Cleveland, Ohio, USA.
Bootleg only.

141. NOT FADE AWAY (Holly) 2.00
18 June 1964: Place: Mike Douglas Show, Cleveland, Ohio, USA.
USA Compilation DVD British Invasion - 1960's & 1970's: 8 November 2005
USA Compilation DVD Mike Douglas - Moments & Memories: 25 March 2008

The second USA television recording took the Stones to Cleveland on Lake Erie and was aired on 25 June 1964. Four songs were performed and two - *Carol* and *I Just Want To Make Love To You* - were played live. Unfortunately the latter is not available and has not been bootlegged while the playbacks were *Tell Me* (released as their second USA single on 13 June 1964) and *Not Fade Away*, which is available on a compilation DVD. By now Keith Richards had taken the *Not Fade Away* beat and was driving it forward hard with his lead rhythm style.
The chat show host, the late Mike Douglas, interviewed the whole band, asking them to introduce themselves and having a joke at the expense of Charlie's surname - "Charlie what? Oh Watts!" Three girls were asked to meet the band by Mike and they swooned over Keith Richards and Brian Jones. Bill Wyman was left holding his bass in his upright stage manner while Mick Jagger shook hands, laughing at the girls' reactions. A brief interview segment has Brian saying in response to the question: "Is there one of you five who seems to be more popular with the young ladies than the others?" . . . "Mick is more popular with the men". Just a little risky for the times, but taken by all in good humour. The show promoted the new American album ENGLAND'S NEWEST HIT MAKERS with *Carol* showcasing some great musical interaction as Brian's rhythm guitar complements the Berry riffs from Keith.
The Stones' next stop was Harrisburg, Pennsylvania, before a bout of partying in New York. That first night they were out into the early hours at various nightclubs before attending the Clay Cole TV studio, a bit worse for wear, for playbacks of *Tell Me, Carol* and *Not Fade Away*. The Saturday Show attained huge audience figures for Channel 11 (their biggest yet) since Clay Cole managed a scoop by having a live feed from a Beatles concert on the same broadcast, which he quickly dubbed "The Beatles vs. The Rolling Stones".
The show preceded the Stones' final live concerts of the tour, booked by promoter Sid Bernstein, at Carnegie Hall in New York on the same Saturday, 20 June, before they flew back to London. The illustrious, 19th-century Carnegie Hall was a venue made famous by, amongst others, George Gershwin, Yehudi Menuhin, Benny Goodman, Count Basie and Billie Holliday. The Beatles, again booked by Bernstein, played there in February 1964, but, after the Stones' appearance and the crowd's over exuberance, all rock acts were cancelled.

142. TIME IS ON MY SIDE (Ragovoy, Norman) 2.52
24-26 June 1964: Place: Regent Sound Studios, London, England.
Producer: Andrew Oldham.
Engineer: Bill Farley.
USA Single: 25 September 1964: No. 6 - 9 weeks
USA LP 12 X 5: 23 October 1964: No. 3 - 20 weeks
German Compilation LP THE REST OF THE BEST: December 1983
UK & USA LP THE ROLLING STONES SINGLES COLLECTION - THE LONDON YEARS: 15 August 1989
UK & USA CD box set THE ROLLING STONES SINGLES - 1963 - 1965: 4 May 2004

The Stones flew back to Britain and immediately that evening honoured a college ball booking in Oxford. Then they returned to the Denmark Street Regent Studios which provided a complete contrast to Chess - they were back to two-track after experiencing the new technology of the Ampex four-track.
Time Is On My Side was written in October 1963 by Jerry Ragovoy (alias Norman Meade) for original bebop, jazz artist and trombonist Kai Winding. The co-lyricist was named as Jerry Norman but this was a fact disputed by Jerry Ragavoy until his death. The Winding version (without any credit to Jerry Norman) was in a jazz soul style, the excellent vocals being supplied by The Gospelaires (Dionne and Dee Dee Warwick and also Cissy Houston - mother of Whitney). It was also covered expertly by Irma Thomas on the flip side of her 1964 single *Anyone Who Knows What Love Is (Will Understand)*.
Andrew Oldham had been given this slice of pop history vinyl at Liberty Records by record promoter Tony LiPuma and promotion man Bob Krasnow. The Stones had bought the song sheet (hence the Meade, Norman credit) and music for both songs on their recent trip to Los Angeles. The Stones version (almost a note for note copy) was recorded in Britain, and was destined to be an American single, appearing on the second USA album 12 X 5. Ironically the same song, recorded later in the year at the Chess Studios, was set for inclusion on a British album - definitely a transatlantic mix-up. The difference is that the UK recorded version has a full organ introduction and a more pronounced tambourine, while the Chess take has a guitar introduction and stinging guitar throughout.
It is a worthy ballad, poignant in context, and given the full Stones treatment. Ian Stewart supplies the gospel-type organ, helping the USA single, released in September 1964, to peak at an incredible No. 6 position in November/December 1964, providing a major breakthrough into the American market. They had accomplished the feat of transposing the song into a Stones original, just as they had cleverly done with *Not Fade Away*.

143. YOU'VE JUST MADE MY DAY (Trad) 0.38
24-26 June 1964: Place: Regent Sound Studios, London, England.
Producer: Andrew Oldham.
Engineer: Bill Farley.
Bootleg only.

A small segment of an organ-based song which was compiled into a medley.

144. OFF THE HOOK (Nanker, Phelge) 2.34
24-26 June, 2 September 1964: Place: Regent Sound Studios, London, England.
Played Live: 1964, 1965
Producer: Andrew Oldham.
Engineer: Bill Farley.
UK B-side Little Red Rooster: 13 November 1964
UK LP ROLLING STONES NO 2: 15 January 1965: No. 1 - 37 weeks
USA LP THE ROLLING STONES, NOW!: 12 February 1965: No. 5 - 29 weeks
USA Compilation LP THE ROLLING STONES - PROMOTIONAL ALBUM: October 1969
UK & USA LP THE ROLLING STONES SINGLES COLLECTION - THE LONDON YEARS: 15 August 1989
UK & USA CD box set THE ROLLING STONES SINGLES - 1963 - 1965: 4 May 2004

The Stones were at last formulating a style which set them apart from other so-called English beat acts, notably The Downliners Sect and Ron Wood, who at that time performed and wrote minor single successes with The Birds. *Off The Hook*, with its nifty, repetitive edge is a good example of this new sound, a mid-tempo rocker controlled by a clean lead guitar sound. Keith Richards and Brian Jones had the happy knack of being able to play black American blues music with a popular feel, illustrated well on this particular track.
Chess Studios thought it was too similar to one of their own recordings, Little Walter's *Off The Wall*, and sued the band for copyright, a compromise being reached for 50 per cent of the royalties. Chess Records might have contemplated that the success of The Rolling Stones was in turn having a good effect on their blues idols, who were increasing in popularity due to the resurgence of the genre in Britain. *Off The Wall* is an instrumental so there was no comparison of lyrics, the term was merely used to describe someone who was stupid. An early version was recorded in June and completed in September 1964 for the flip side of *Little Red Rooster*.

145. YOU CAN'T CATCH ME (Berry) 3.30
24-26 June, 28-29 September 1964: Place: Regent Sound Studios, London, England.
Producer: Andrew Oldham.
Engineer: Bill Farley.
UK LP THE ROLLING STONES NO 2: 15 January 1965: No. 1 - 37 weeks
USA LP THE ROLLING STONES, NOW!: 12 February 1965: No. 5 - 29 weeks

A wealth of material was being recorded in this period but a lot of the chosen tracks were still predominantly cover versions. *You Can't Catch Me* was originally played by Chuck Berry and provided Bill Wyman's first recollection of rock and roll, back in his RAF National Service days. This interpretation, destined for release on their second British and third American albums, is a real rocker. The rhythm section of Bill and Charlie Watts play 1950s style, while Keith Richards quite effortlessly picks the song's rhythm out on his guitar.

146. GODZI (Nanker, Phelge)
1-10 July 1964; 3-11 August 1966. Place: Greenford Studios, Greenford, Decca, West Hampstead, Regent Sound, London, England; RCA Studios, Hollywood, USA
Producer: Andrew Oldham.
Unavailable.

The only confirmation of this track's existence comes thanks to a reference from Bill Wyman, who wanted to include it on the BLACK BOX 1975 compilation album. It is also said to be registered with Broadcast Music, Inc. (BMI) as a band composition - Nanker, Phelge. The track's origin may also be from a 1966 RCA session.

147. MEMPHIS TENNESSEE (Berry) 2.28
1-10 July 1964: Place: Greenford Studios, Greenford, Decca, West Hampstead, Regent Sound, London, England.
Producer: Andrew Oldham, John Paul Jones.
UK LP 16 HIP HITS: Andrew Loog Oldham Orchestra and Chorus: 2 October 1964
German Compilation LP THE REST OF THE BEST: December 1983

Andrew Oldham would neither deny nor confirm that the Stones contributed to the 16 HIP HITS album. He knew that the very possibility of their inclusion would prosper his sales on an odd compilation of cover material and Andrew Oldham originals. *Memphis*, a Chuck Berry cover performed without vocals, has a hint of the Keith Richards/Brian Jones guitar work.
John Paul Jones (nicknamed Bambi), then only a young 18 year old session player whose music pedigree was as a cathedral choir master where he played organ, assisted Andrew Oldham in the production work. The basic tracks were laid down at Regent before the production was enhanced with additional instruments at Decca's studios by John Paul Jones or Mike Leander.

148. SOME THINGS JUST STICK IN YOUR MIND (Jagger, Richard) 2.27
1-10 July 1964: Place: Greenford Studios, Greenford, Decca, West Hampstead, Regent Sound, London, England.
Rolling Stones with Jim Sullivan, Jimmy Page, John McLaughlin.
Producer: Andrew Oldham.
UK Compilation LP METAMORPHOSIS: 6 June 1975: No. 45 - 1 week

Probably recorded at the same time as the Jimmy Page's version of *Heart of Stone*, due to its country flavours. Session musicians including John McLaughlin were possibly incorporated in this Andrew Oldham production. Pedestrian in approach, it allows Mick Jagger to twist his tongue around a western movie soundtrack. *Some Things Just Stick In Your Mind* emphasises the two-way struggle between attempting to write commercial pop songs and R 'n' B rockers. It was a demo for Vashti Bunyan, who released her version in May 1965 with Nicky Hopkins on piano as a debut single.
Ian Stewart was a particular fan of Nicky's piano playing from his days with Long John Baldry in the Cyril Davis and the All-stars band but all the Stones were familiar with him from the Marquee days. *Some Things Just Stick In Your Mind* was also recorded by Dick and Dee Dee, who simply sang over the Stones backing track, with Andrew Oldham producing for Warner Bros in America. The original was not released on the American version of METAMORPHOSIS.

149. WE'RE WASTIN' TIME (Jagger, Richard) 2.44
1-10 July 1964, 31 August 1964 - 4 September 1964: Place: Greenford Studios, Greenford, Decca, West Hampstead, Regent Sound, London, England.
Rolling Stones with Jim Sullivan, John McLaughlin, Jimmy Page, Joe Moretti, Andy White.
Producer: Andrew Oldham.
Engineer: John Paul Jones.
Other Production: Mike Leander.
UK Compilation LP METAMORPHOSIS: 6 June 1975: No. 45 - 1 week

This particular track, another demo, was not released on the American METAMORPHOSIS album. A version with studio background voices can be heard at the intro and the outro has a longer fade-out (* a - 2.53). Session musicians were probably used but their exact identity is unknown. At the end of June and the first week of July, most of the Stones were resting and taking a much-needed break from touring.
The song has a distinct country feel, which was Jim Sullivan's particular strength. In 2002, he remembered that, in the studio, Jimmy Page would tend to take the rock numbers while he would work on the country rock. One of Big Jim's credentials was to have the only 12-string guitar in Britain at the time and he did not feel ill at ease in the studio with the Stones. Quite to the contrary as he recalled: "I was more famous than Mick Jagger then!"
The going rate for sessions at that time was four pounds and ten shillings for three hours. While the Stones had some music pedigree, a lot of artists were lost in a studio and needed someone professional to help them out and many producers of that era knew that. Jack Good was the resident arranger at Decca's studios. The other two record label studios were EMI and Phillips/Fontana, then there were the privates such as Regent, Olympic, De Lane Lea and Advision.
Big Jim only got involved in demos for the Jagger/Richards songwriting partnership and was unaware that some tracks ended up on the released METAMORPHOSIS. Jimmy Tarbuck, by profession a comedian, had the dubious honour of recording this track and releasing it as a single.

150. BLUE TURNS TO GREY (Jagger, Richard) 2.29
1-10 July 1964, 31 August 1964 - 4 September 1964: Place: Greenford Studios, Greenford, Decca, West Hampstead, Regent Sound, London, England.
Producer: Andrew Oldham.
Bootleg only.

This track was floated amongst a number of artists and was recorded as a demo for the Mighty Avengers, being released by them in February 1965. It was re-recorded first for Dick and Dee Dee for release in 1965 the same year Dave Hassinger also recorded it at RCA Studios, Hollywood in 1965. Cliff Richard put out a version in 1966 and the Stones' track, with horns, was at one stage lined up for the unreleased compilation album NECROPHILIA.

151. TRY A LITTLE HARDER (Jagger, Richard) 2.19
1-10 July 1964, 31 August 1964 - 4 September 1964: Place: Greenford Studios, Greenford, Decca, West Hampstead, Regent Sound, London, England.
Rolling Stones with Jimmy Page, John McLaughlin, Reg Guest, Joe Moretti, Andy White.
Producer: Andrew Oldham.
Engineer: John Paul Jones.
Other Production: Mike Leander.
USA B-side I Don't Know Why: 23 May 1975
UK B-side I Don't Know Why: 23 May 1975
UK Compilation LP METAMORPHOSIS: 6 June 1975: No. 45 - 1 week
USA Compilation LP METAMORPHOSIS: 6 June 1975: No. 8 - 8 weeks
UK & USA LP THE ROLLING STONES SINGLES COLLECTION - THE LONDON YEARS: 15 August 1989
UK CD box set THE ROLLING STONES SINGLES - 1968 - 1971: 28 February 2005
USA CD box set THE ROLLING STONES SINGLES - 1968 - 1971: 1 March 2005

Another track, presumably an out-take, which is difficult to date. The track has a ring of the American Dave Hassinger soul production sound while the opening bass sounds by Jimmy Page are powerful and set a strident pace. The Motown feel is accentuated by back-up vocals and the inclusion of horns.

152. IT'S ALL OVER NOW (Womack, Womack) 3.29
17 July 1964: Place: Playhouse Theatre, London, England.
Bootleg only.

153. IF YOU NEED ME (Pickett, Bateman, Sanders) 2.01
17 July 1964: Place: Playhouse Theatre, London, England.
Bootleg only.

154. CONFESSIN' THE BLUES (Brown, McShann) 3.00
17 July 1964: Place: Playhouse Theatre, London, England.
Bootleg only.

155. CAROL (Berry) 2.38
17 July 1964: Place: Playhouse Theatre, London, England.
Bootleg only.

156. MONA (McDaniel) 2.58
17 July 1964: Place: Playhouse Theatre, London, England.
Bootleg only.

The preceding numbers were recorded and broadcast for the Joe Loss show on the same day. There were a couple of album tracks and songs from their imminent new EP from the Chicago sessions and also the then current No. 1 single *It's All Over Now*.

157. AROUND AND AROUND (Berry) 2.45
17 July 1964: Place: BBC Broadcasting House, London, England.
Bootleg only.

158. IF YOU NEED ME (Pickett, Bateman, Sanders) 2.02
17 July 1964: Place: BBC Broadcasting House, London, England.
Bootleg only.

159. I CAN'T BE SATISFIED (McKinley, Morganfield) 2.30
17 July 1964: Place: BBC Broadcasting House, London, England.
Played Live: 1964, 1965
Bootleg only.

160. CRACKIN' UP (McDaniel) 2.14
17 July 1964: Place: BBC Broadcasting House, London, England.
Played Live: 1963, 1977
Bootleg only.

Another radio session followed and was recorded the same day for Brian Matthew's Top Gear show, broadcast on 23 July 1964. This was used as an opportunity to record the rest of the songs from the next EP. *Around And Around* was strong material and would gain interest abroad as a single and was also a lead track for a German album. Mick Jagger's vocals on *Crackin' Up* have a tinge of American influence (he even gives a Mexican-type "brrrah" whoop) while Keith Richards sings a distinctive backing vocal. The track was officially recorded live in 1977 in Toronto and released on the LOVE YOU LIVE album.

161. HEART OF STONE (Jagger, Richard) 3.48
21 July-August 1964: Place: Regent Sound Studios, Decca, West Hampstead, London, England.
Rolling Stones with Jimmy Page.
Producer: Andrew Oldham.
UK Compilation LP METAMORPHOSIS: 6 June 1975: No. 45 - 1 week
USA Compilation LP METAMORPHOSIS: 6 June 1975: No. 8 - 8 weeks

This version was tried and tested in the UK before the RCA Hollywood sessions in autumn, 1964. It features a choral voice back-drop along with guest session musician Jimmy Page. The feel is country and western with "electric" steel guitar, making for an unusual version, generally influenced by the other Andrew Oldham-produced session tracks of the time.
It was released on the 1975 compilation out-take album METAMORPHOSIS. Keith Richards credits Jimmy Page, acknowledging that he copies Jimmy's guitar solo lick-for-lick for the RCA Hollywood version. Another UK rendition of the track exists without the country feel but with an extended guitar solo at the fade where Mick Jagger sings "I got to go" (* a - 4.11).

162. HEAR IT (Jones, Richard) 3.04
31 August 1964 - 4 September 1964: Place: Regent Sound Studios, Decca, West Hampstead, London, England.
Rolling Stones with Jim Sullivan.
Producer: Andrew Oldham.
Engineer: Mike Leander; Gus Dudgeon
Bootleg only.

Hear It - this may have been a Jones composition. It is typical Oldham territory, with violin accompaniment and Jim Sullivan guesting on guitar. At the time, Brian Jones was writing material for a possible solo single release and had formed a friendship with Jet Harris, who toured with the Stones in February and March 1964. Brian and Jet were rumoured to have written together but no recordings are available if indeed any were made. The track was lined up for the aborted NECROPHILIA album.

163. DA DOO RON RON (Spector, Greenwich, Barry) 2.21
1 September 1964: Place: Regent Sound Studios, London, England.
Producer: Andrew Oldham, John Paul Jones.
UK LP 16 HIP HITS: Andrew Loog Oldham Orchestra and Chorus: 2 October 1964
German Compilation LP THE REST OF THE BEST: December 1983

Again, it is unlikely that all the Stones were in attendance for this run through of a Phil Spector classic, although it is evident that Mick Jagger is the vocalist on this Crystals' cover. As well as Jagger, Andrew Oldham was working with the likes of Kim Fowley, John Paul Jones, John McLaughlin, Joe Moretti, Jimmy Page, Jim Sullivan and Andy White and seemed determined to construct a British mirror-image of the Phil Spector success story. Recording cover versions of Spector songs was not a subtle way of achieving this!

164. UNDER THE BOARDWALK (Resnick, Young) 2.46
2 September 1964: Place: Regent Sound Studios, London, England.
Played Live: 1965
Producer: Andrew Oldham.
Engineer: Bill Farley.
USA LP 12 X 5: 23 October 1964: No. 3 - 20 weeks
UK LP ROLLING STONES NO 2: 15 January 1965: No. 1 - 37 weeks
UK LP SLOW ROLLERS: 9 November 1981

The Stones' re-working of the Drifters' *Under The Boardwalk* featured Keith Richards on acoustic and electric guitar. It is an example of their effort to produce some authentic soul-based work but unfortunately this seems to be a hurried interpretation - as the baritone background vocals testify. Mick Jagger's vocals do have an effected quality, though. The Drifters' version charted in July 1964, reaching No. 4, but the Stones' arrangement is not solid and gradually falls by the wayside. The soul, perhaps due to the acoustic guitar, is lacking but, despite this, it was later to stomp to the top of the Australian singles charts for three weeks, coupled with *Walking The Dog*. It appeared on both the UK and USA album releases.

165. UNDER THE BOARDWALK (RHYTHMS DEL MUNDO REMIX) (Resnick, Young) 2.44
2 September 1964; 2008 - 2009: Place: Regent Sound Studios, London, England; Abdala Studios, Havana, Cuba.
Rolling Stones with Augusto Enriquez.
Producer: Andrew Oldham.
Engineer: Bill Farley.
UK CD CLASSICS - RHYTHMS DEL MUNDO: 20 July 2009
USA CD CLASSICS - RHYTHMS DEL MUNDO: 4 August 2009

The Rhythms Del Mundo were brought together following the 2004 Asian Tsunami to benefit climate change projects and charities - Artists Project Earth (APE). It features members of the Buena Vista Social Club, from Cuba, along with other local and world musicians. The successful combo has covered artists in their own unique style, this mambo version of *Under The Boardwalk* using the original Stones track mixed with the Latin sounds of Augusto Enriquez.

166. **LITTLE RED ROOSTER** (Dixon) 3.06
2-3 September 1964: Place: Regent Sound Studios, London, England.
Played Live: 1964, 1965, 1976, 1977, 1986, 1989, 1990, 1997, 1998, 2002, 2003
Producer: Andrew Oldham.
Engineer: Bill Farley.
UK Single: 13 November 1964: No. 1 - 12 weeks
USA LP THE ROLLING STONES, NOW!: 12 February 1965: No. 5 - 29 weeks
UK Compilation LP BIG HITS (HIGH TIDE AND GREEN GRASS): 4 November 1966: No. 4 - 43 weeks
UK Compilation LP ROLLED GOLD: 14 November 1975: No. 7 - 50 weeks
UK Compilation LP GET STONED - 30 GREATEST HITS, 30 ORIGINAL TRACKS: 21 October 1977: No. 13 - 15 weeks
German Compilation LP THE REST OF THE BEST: December 1983
UK & USA LP THE ROLLING STONES SINGLES COLLECTION - THE LONDON YEARS: 15 August 1989
UK & USA CD box set THE ROLLING STONES SINGLES - 1963 - 1965: 4 May 2004
UK Compilation CD ROLLED GOLD +: 12 November 2007: No. 26 - 12 weeks

This single displayed a return to mainstream blues and had advance orders of more than 200,000 copies in the UK, subsequently securing the group's second British No. 1 single. It was not released in America as a single due to its "farmyard sexual nature" but did appear on their next USA album. The softer *Heart Of Stone* was the USA single.

The Stones needed to consolidate the foundations they had already laid and many critics believed that this unadulterated blues song was risky in a commercial sense. Andrew Oldham agreed but the Stones insisted on its release, with Brian Jones later describing it as his favourite Stones track. No wonder, since he plays incredible bottleneck slide guitar and harmonica in one of his Stones finest moments, while Keith Richards adds supports on acoustic.

Brian's contribution, however, was not a totally happy experience. After running into The Pretty Things lead singer Phil May at the studio one evening just before the start of another British tour, he found a note from the rest of the Stones asking him to finish off this track that the other members had recorded the night before. Brian was requested to overdub slide guitar on specific bars of the song and, as this was probably not the most diplomatic way of communicating, he was upset by the move. However, his slide guitar, expertly emulating Hubert Sumlin, who played on the original Howlin' Wolf version, was the making of the song.

The Stones had succeeded in taking a pure blues song to the top of the charts, a feat that has never been repeated. Willie Dixon, the song's writer, was an acoustic bass guitarist who worked with Muddy Waters. His song writing was prestigious - *Hoochie Coochie Man, I Ain't Superstitious, My Babe, Spoonful, I Can't Quit You Baby, I Just Want To Make Love To You* - but he struggled to get his own recognition, let alone money royalties.

He wrote *Bring It On Home* which was released on LED ZEPPELIN II and the subsequent live album HOW THE WEST WAS WON. In his later years, Dixon's record company unsuccessfully sued Led Zeppelin for recompense, an action which was repeated for his song *You Need Love*, which Led Zeppelin had translated into *Whole Lotta Love*. He received out-of-court settlements relating to both songs.

Even Howlin' Wolf seemed to get more credit from *Little Red Rooster* when he recorded it as *The Red Rooster* in June 1961, with Dixon on bass, though he may have had good reason since some sources say he co-wrote "Rooster" with Dixon. In a 1970 interview, Mick Jagger referred to the song as a Son House recording, so it is likely to be one of those Mississippi Delta "traditional" songs made popular and laid claim to by many.

Interviewed in 2008 for a BBC documentary, *Blues Britannia: Can Blues Men Sing the Whites?*, Keith Richards summarised the band's thoughts on releasing the song: "We must have been wearing brass balls that day, when we decided to put that out as a single. I think we just thought it was our job to pay back, to give them what they've given us. They've given us the music and the friendship, and let's stand up, be men, and give them a blues - and it went to No. 1. Mr Howlin' Wolf, he didn't mind at all. It was maybe a moment of bravado, in retrospect, but it worked. We have been blessed by the music that we listened to, and let's see if we can actually spin it back around and make American white kids listen to *Little Red Rooster*. You had it all the time, pal, you know. You just didn't listen."

167. **I'M RELYING ON YOU** (Jagger, Richard) 0.24
AKA: **I'm Just A Funny Guy**
28-29 September 1964: Place: Regent Sound Studios, London, England.
Producer: Andrew Oldham.
Engineer: Bill Farley.
Bootleg only.

A short extract, available on bootleg, of a slow song with resonating guitar. It was intended for release and an acetate was prepared with another unreleased song, *We Were Falling In Love*.

168. **WE WERE FALLING IN LOVE** (Jagger, Richard) 1.20
AKA: **Waving Hair**
28-29 September 1964: Place: Regent Sound Studios, London, England.
Producer: Andrew Oldham.
Engineer: Bill Farley.
Bootleg only.

This song was made available on a 1964 acetate, coupled with *I'm Relying On You*, the label stating the composers were Jagger, Richard. It was given by Andrew Oldham to Mark Wynter's manager but never recorded. There is also a full female vocal version (possibly by Cleo Sylvestre), backed by the Andrew Oldham Orchestra, with distinct Phil Spector leanings, which was not released.

169. **GROWN UP WRONG** (Jagger, Richard) 1.59
28-29 September 1964: Place: Regent Sound Studios, London, England.
Producer: Andrew Oldham.
Engineer: Bill Farley.

USA LP 12 X 5: 23 October 1964: No. 3 - 20 weeks
UK LP ROLLING STONES NO 2: 15 January 1965: No. 1 - 37 weeks

Another abbreviated song which does not manage to fulfil itself, despite a promising start. The vocals do not blend with the instrumentation, the production is lacking and, despite Brian Jones trying to enliven the proceedings with his harmonica, it goes nowhere fast. Mick Jagger and Keith Richards were finding that the task of writing songs was not an easy one but it is clear that there was a dormant genius waiting to be unleashed.

There had been a brief taster on *Off The Hook* but the other self-penned songs seemed to lack inspiration. As Andrew Oldham said on the cover of the 12 X 5 album (with photos taken by David Bailey): "This is the new ROLLING STONES album and it's the best they've ever done (except for the one they're about to make)". The cover photo was also used on THE ROLLING STONES NO 2 album.

170. SUSIE Q (Hawkins, Lewis, Broadwater) 1.48
28-29 September 1964: Place: Regent Sound Studios, London, England.
Played Live: 1963, 1964
Producer: Andrew Oldham.
Engineer: Bill Farley.
USA LP 12 X 5: 23 October 1964: No. 3 - 20 weeks
UK LP ROLLING STONES NO 2: 15 January 1965: No. 1 - 37 weeks
USA Compilation LP THE ROLLING STONES - PROMOTIONAL ALBUM: October 1969

From Charlie Watts' opening beat, this track is full of R 'n' B spirit. It seems to be a mod "work out" featuring some particularly deranged guitar playing, unlike the Dale Hawkins original. Having made its point on the tail-end of the album, it quickly fades out, leaving the listener to wonder what would happen if the Stones were left to improvise on a more inspiring rocker. It appeared on the second US Stones album in October 1964, ahead of its eventual release in the UK in January 1965.

171. SURPRISE, SURPRISE (Jagger, Richard) 2.31
28-29 September 1964: Place: Regent Sound Studios, London, England.
Producer: Andrew Oldham.
Engineer: Bill Farley.
USA LP THE ROLLING STONES, NOW!: 12 February 1965: No. 5 - 29 weeks
UK Compilation LP 14: 21 May 1965
USA Compilation LP ENGLAND'S GREATEST HITMAKERS: May 1965
UK Track Maxi-single Street Fighting Man: 25 June 1971
UK B-side Street Fighting Man: 20 July 1971
German Compilation LP THE REST OF THE BEST: December 1983
UK & USA LP THE ROLLING STONES SINGLES COLLECTION - THE LONDON YEARS: 15 August 1989
UK CD box set THE ROLLING STONES SINGLES - 1968 - 1971: 28 February 2005
USA CD box set THE ROLLING STONES SINGLES - 1968 - 1971: 1 March 2005

Early attempts by Jagger, Richard to write popular, upbeat songs were unsuccessful as they seemed to have the Mersey sound too close to their hearts, instead of sticking to what they knew best. They were aware of this problem and the fact that *Surprise, Surprise* was little more than a demo, made it conveniently slot onto a Decca compilation album 14, the royalties of which were donated to the Lord Taverner's National Playing Fields Association.

However, it was released for the first time on the American album THE ROLLING STONES, NOW! concluding side two. Lulu and the Luvvers believed the track had some standing, though, and recorded it for single release in April 1965 - this was the historic final occasion that the tiny Regent Sound studios were used for recording. Around this time, in the same studio, Keith Richards recorded a guitar part on *House Of The Rising Sun* for the B-side of Marianne Faithfull's new single. At an after-show party for Ready Steady, Win! (a game show for aspiring musical talent produced by Rediffusion TV), a tipsy Mick Jagger, taken with Marianne's ample bosom, mischievously decided to tip some champagne down it - Marianne was not impressed, preferring Keith's attention. It could have been at the same show that Ron Wood and the Birds played their debut single.

172. DUST MY PYRAMIDS (Jones, Richard)
8 October 1964: Place: Playhouse Theatre, London, England.
Unavailable.

173. IF YOU NEED ME (Pickett, Bateman, Sanders)
8 October 1964: Place: Playhouse Theatre, London, England.
Unavailable.

174. AROUND AND AROUND (Berry)
8 October 1964: Place: Playhouse Theatre, London, England.
Unavailable.

175. AIN'T THAT LOVIN' YOU BABY (Reed) 1.54
8 October 1964: Place: Playhouse Theatre, London, England.
Bootleg only.

176. **I'M A LOVE YOU** (Reed)
8 October 1964: Place: Playhouse Theatre, London, England.
Unavailable.

177. **MONA** (McDaniel)
8 October 1964: Place: Playhouse Theatre, London, England.
Unavailable.

178. **2120 SOUTH MICHIGAN AVENUE** (Nanker, Phelge) 3.46
8 October 1964: Place: Playhouse Theatre, London, England.
Bootleg only.

Near the end of their September and October autumn tour with Mike Berry, The Mojos, Billie Davis and Inez and Charlie Foxx (a sister and brother soul act from the United States), the Stones recorded a radio session for Alexis Korner's Rhythm and Blues show, to be broadcast on 31 October 1964. It featured tracks from their EP - *Mona* and, famously, a short instrumental (*Dust My Pyramids*) in the style of Elmore James, where Brian Jones and Keith Richards jammed together at the start of the show.

Another unusual track was also played, the Jimmy Reed song *I'm A Love You*, which may have been confused with *Ain't That Loving You Baby*. *2120 South Michigan Avenue* is an exemplary piece of recording history and translated well in the UK studio.

On 10 September 1964, the band played Cheltenham Town Hall and Brian Jones - back on home territory - was reunited with the Ramrods, with whom he had occasionally played in 1962. His proud parents attended one of the two concerts performed on that day. Pathé News filmed a widely-distributed segment of the Hull concert on 21 September, which was shown at cinemas but also used within *25 X 5: The Continuing Adventures Of The Rolling Stones* video released in 1990. The British tour concluded on 11 October before a ground-breaking one-off gig at the Olympia in Paris on 20 October. At the end of that month, the United States beckoned for a second time.

179. **AROUND AND AROUND** (Berry) 2.23
25 October 1964: Place: Ed Sullivan TV Show, CBS Studio 50, New York, USA.
USA DVD 6 Ed Sullivan Shows Starring The Rolling Stones: 1 November 2011

Four months had passed since the Chess recording sessions in June. The Stones had toured consistently and gruellingly, performing in the Channel Islands and throughout England. This included August gigs at the home of Longleat's Lions near Warminster and the National Jazz and Blues Festival at Richmond, where this year they took a cool 50 per cent of the takings from Harold Pendleton. A young fan, 17-year-old Ron Wood, attended their festival performance. There was also a trip to the Netherlands for a one-off concert - where the crowd body-surfed in their excitement - and also shows in Northern Ireland, Scotland and Paris.

The Stones were even guest panellists on the infamous Juke Box Jury BBC "hit or miss" TV show where they created public controversy with some non-committal off-hand comments. In September, they had also appeared on an American television show during the Red Skeleton Hour, which featured a mock concert at London Palladium on 5 August 1964. There were accompanying comedy sections of entertainer Red Skeleton being passed by on the inside steps as fans flocked through to see the Stones, who mimed to playbacks of T*ell Me, Carol* and *It's All Over Now*. Drummer Charlie Watts, meanwhile, took time out of the busy schedule to marry Shirley Shepherd, whom he had met at a Alexis Korner gig, in a quiet ceremony in October.

The Stones were now all self-proclaimed celebrities and, in late October 1964, they returned to the States for their second tour. The ultimate TV media attraction in the USA was the Ed Sullivan Show and, on Friday 23 October, they started rehearsals for their appearance. Mass hysteria from armies of fans enveloped the studios for three days. *Around and Around,* a genuine rock and roller and the opening track on their just released 12 X 5 album, further inflamed the atmosphere and the Stones responded accordingly, with Keith Richards in especially fine form.

After the show, Ed Sullivan said he had received hundreds of letters from parents complaining about the long-haired Stones' performance. One telegram read: "Stop presenting crude, ignorant, demoralising, disgusting groups like the Rolling Stones." But he also received thousands of letters from excited teenagers who were more than into this British rock phenomenon. The presence of all these talented bands from across the Atlantic became known as the British Invasion.

180. **TIME IS ON MY SIDE** (Ragovoy, Norman) 2.44
25 October 1964: Place: Ed Sullivan TV Show, CBS Studio 50, New York, USA.
USA Compilation DVD Ed Sullivan's Rock 'n' Roll Revolution: 23 September 2003
UK DVD CD box set THE ROLLING STONES SINGLES - 1968 - 1971: 28 February 2005
USA DVD CD box set THE ROLLING STONES SINGLES - 1968 - 1971: 1 March 2005
USA DVD 6 Ed Sullivan Shows Starring The Rolling Stones: 1 November 2011

Time Is On My Side was the second song performed on the show. It is a slow number but, due to the excitement of the crowd, was speeded up as they screamed at every available lull in the proceedings. In part it can be seen on *25 X 5: The Continuing Adventures Of The Rolling Stone*s. Adult American TV viewers were alarmed at this apparent riot unfolding in their own homes and gradually the pressure mounted. Ed Sullivan, anxious to reaffirm his prestige, denied responsibility that he had anything to do with the booking of the Stones. He said was shocked by the performance and vowed to cancel all future rock and roll acts, claiming that his show had been built up over 17 years and he did not want it broken up by such unruly behaviour. The Stones were not like that other British act, The Dave Clark Five - such nice gentlemen!

The video gained an official release status when it appeared on the 2005 box set of singles along with three other DVD videos. This was followed in 2011 when the Andrew Solt company SOFA Entertainment finally released the entire Ed Sullivan performances with the Rolling Stones on DVD format. He had acquired the rights to the programme in 1990 and the programme was re-introduced to the American public in 1991.

The show was originally called Toast Of The Town but changed to carry the name of its famous presenter and was broadcast from 1948 to 1971. To this day, the currently named Ed Sullivan Theatre in Los Angeles is used for The David Letterman Show. Letterman came to the fore via The Tonight Show Starring Johnny Carson in 1978.

181. AROUND AND AROUND (Berry) ✏ 2.17
28-29 October 1964: Place: Santa Monica Civic Auditorium, California, USA.
USA DVD The T.A.M.I. Show Collector's Edition: 21 March 2010

182. OFF THE HOOK (Nanker, Phelge) ✏ 2.31
28-29 October 1964: Place: Santa Monica Civic Auditorium, California, USA.
USA DVD The T.A.M.I. Show Collector's Edition: 21 March 2010

183. TIME IS ON MY SIDE (Ragovoy, Norman) ✏ 2.34
28-29 October 1964: Place: Santa Monica Civic Auditorium, California, USA.
USA DVD The T.A.M.I. Show Collector's Edition: 21 March 2010

184. IT'S ALL OVER NOW (B and S Womack) ✏ 3.08
28-29 October 1964: Place: Santa Monica Civic Auditorium, California, USA.
USA DVD The T.A.M.I. Show Collector's Edition: 21 March 2010

185. I'M ALRIGHT (McDaniel) ✏ 3.02
28-29 October 1964: Place: Santa Monica Civic Auditorium, California, USA.
USA DVD The T.A.M.I. Show Collector's Edition: 21 March 2010

186. GET TOGETHER (Nanker, Phelge) ✏ 2.07
29 October 1964: Place: Santa Monica Civic Auditorium, California, USA.
USA DVD The T.A.M.I. Show Collector's Edition: 21 March 2010

The Santa Monica Civic Auditorium played host to the 1964 Teen Awards Music International (T.A.M.I.). Recordings for television broadcast under the title "Gather No Moss" were made of the principal teen stars and the Stones. Except for the finale, the soundtrack was recorded the day before. Other British performers were Gerry and the Pacemakers and Billy J Kramer and the Dakotas while the American acts featured were Marvin Gaye, Lesley Gore, Jan and Dean, Smokey Robinson and the Miracles and the Supremes. There were also formidable performances by James Brown, Chuck Berry and The Beach Boys.

It was unusual to see so many black and white acts together on the same bill but discrimination had been banned in public places in July 1964 by the introduction of the American Civil Rights Act. The Stones, who closed the concert, lived up to expectations and produced a set full of wild excitement, almost upstaging the magnificent preceding performance by James Brown. Andrew Oldham deliberately delayed their stage entry until the fervour had diminished.

During the *Around And Around* guitar solos Mick Jagger, having studied James Brown's moves earlier that year at the Harlem Apollo Theatre, shimmied and bopped, raising the crowd's reaction. *Off The Hook* sat well in the set and *I'm Alright*, introduced as *It's Alright*, provided the band's finale. It led onto *Get Together* and featured representatives from the other performers dancing hysterically to a Stones jam. What an honour to have James Brown and Chuck Berry bop to your music.

The performance was a landmark in the Stones' history and put Mick Jagger into a category alongside the likes of James Brown, who even congratulated the band on their performance having earlier warned that they would not want to return to the USA. They also impressed Bobby Vee's saxophone player Bobby Keys who later recalled, in Keith Richards' autobiography *Life*, that he was none too pleased that the Stones had covered his idol, fellow Texan Buddy Holly's song *Not Fade Away* - but was surprised at how well they performed it.

At last, in 2010, the video of the show footage was released officially on a USA DVD *The T.A.M.I. Show Collector's Edition*. The concert also proved to be historic since they met Jack Nitzsche, who was involved with the show production and joined them a few days later at RCA.

187. DOWN HOME GIRL (Leiber, Butler) 4.08
2 November 1964: Place: RCA Studios, Hollywood, USA.
Played Live: 1969
Rolling Stones with Jack Nitzsche.
Producer: Andrew Oldham.
Engineer: Dave Hassinger.
UK LP THE ROLLING STONES NO 2: 15 January 1965: No. 1 - 37 weeks
USA LP THE ROLLING STONES, NOW!: 12 February 1965: No. 5 - 29 weeks

Following the publicity coup on the Ed Sullivan Show the Stones tried to settle into the RCA studios in Hollywood (a venue used by Elvis after Memphis). The studios were huge compared to anything they had experienced before but they soon began to enjoy the experience.

Down Home Girl is a country blues song which typifies the "at home" approach to recording. Mick Jagger's vocal style accentuates the lyrics: "I can tell by your giant step you been walkin' through the cotton fields." The Stones were now competent musicians and recording artistes. Their astounding success was assured by two other factors - Andrew Oldham's hype and their own self-confidence. The song had been given to them by Seymour Stein, who worked at Red Bird Records, run by the great song writers Leiber, Stoller.

Keith Richards was a big fan but Jerry Leiber seemed reluctant to meet him so Seymour gave them a copy of the recently released single by Alvin Robinson - that was the best Keith could do at the time. *Down Home Girl* does not explore new land but it does reiterate the band's eclectic blues and soul status, with country leanings. The original has a more soulful approach in the style of Otis Redding.

The late Jack Nitzsche (then aged 27) is featured on piano after suggesting at the T.A.M.I. show that they record at RCA in his hometown between their San Diego and Cleveland dates. He helped to create Phil Spector's "wall of sound" and went on to contribute to the production of some of the Stones' greatest mid-1960s successes. Later, he did the music arrangement for the Mick Jagger featured *Performance* film before going on to Oscar-nominated movie scores such as *One Flew Over The Cuckoo's Nest*, *An Officer And A Gentleman* and *9 And A Half Weeks*.

188. EVERYBODY NEEDS SOMEBODY TO LOVE (Russell, Burke, Wexler) 5.00
2 November 1964: Place: RCA Studios, Hollywood, USA.
Played Live: 1965, 1981, 2002, 2003
Producer: Andrew Oldham.
Engineer: Dave Hassinger.
UK LP THE ROLLING STONES NO 2: 15 January 1965: No. 1 - 37 weeks
USA LP THE ROLLING STONES, NOW!: 12 February 1965: No. 5 - 29 weeks
USA Compilation LP THE ROLLING STONES - PROMOTIONAL ALBUM: October 1969
UK Track Maxi-single Street Fighting Man: 25 June 1971
UK Compilation LP ROCK 'N' ROLLING STONES: 13 October 1972: No. 41 - 1 week
USA Compilation CD MORE HOT ROCKS (BIG HITS & FAZED COOKIES): 3 September 2002
UK CD box set THE ROLLING STONES SINGLES - 1968 - 1971: 28 February 2005
USA CD box set THE ROLLING STONES SINGLES - 1968 - 1971: 1 March 2005

The Stones turned this Solomon Burke composition into an R 'n' B mini epic. Solomon Burke released "Everybody" as a single in 1964 but, despite previous hits in the States, it did not chart on that occasion. The Stones' take on the song provided an impressive opening to both their UK and USA second albums, albeit featuring different versions. In the USA, a three-minute track was released (* a - 2.57) which, it was claimed, had been put on THE ROLLING STONES, NOW! album in error. It is completely different to the longer, five-minute UK version, with a less disciplined arrangement and more ragged backing vocals.
The longer song is progressive in nature and does not rely on the typical three-minute pop formula. It almost reaches a standstill at one stage, until Jagger lurches the "jam" forward again. "Everybody" became a tour classic, even featuring at shows 40 years later and receiving a universal new lease of life when the Blues Brothers featured it within their 1980 musical comedy film and released it on the soundtrack album.

189. PAIN IN MY HEART (Redding, Walden) 2.05
2 November 1964: Place: RCA Studios, Hollywood, USA.
Played Live: 1965
Rolling Stones with Jack Nitzsche.
Producer: Andrew Oldham.
Engineer: Dave Hassinger.
UK LP THE ROLLING STONES NO 2: 15 January 1965: No. 1 - 37 weeks
USA LP THE ROLLING STONES, NOW!: 12 February 1965: No. 5 - 29 weeks
UK LP SLOW ROLLERS: 9 November 1981

Sonny Bono, who worked for Phil Spector, had met the Stones at the airport and took them to the Sunset Boulevard studio, where Jack Nitzsche was producing. They were amazed at the glamour of the RCA studios and the size of the limos, discovering that even Dave Hassinger, the studio engineer, had one. When they bopped into RCA, the place ground to a halt as studio hands stared open-mouthed at the unique appearance of this brash English band. The Stones researched local record shops to see what material was available and Hassinger was impressed by their uncanny method of recording as they transformed tempos of songs in order to get the perfect cut. Keith Richards recalled in 1995 that the mark of a good song was when you played it at a different tempo and it still worked.
Mick Jagger and Keith Richards gave Hassinger the Stones' approval and yet another track was in the can - if Keith smiled at the end of the playback, he knew he would get the nod to start a mix. This process was not something he was used to when working with other artists. He noted that Andrew Oldham did not get involved in the decision-making, leaving that to Mick and Keith.
Dave was a quiet, unassuming, very likeable guy, who confidently and competently got on with his work. *Pain in My Heart* tugs at the heart-strings in typical Jaggeresque fashion, with Jack Nitzsche playing a mini-piano on the track. It was written by Naomi Neville (one of the four Neville clan) but erroneously credited to Otis Redding and Phil Walden (his manager). Otis had recorded the number earlier in 1964 - it was a basic re-work of an Irma Thomas number called *Ruler Of My Heart*.

190. HEART OF STONE (Jagger, Richard) 2.51
2 November 1964: Place: RCA Studios, Hollywood, USA.
Played Live: 1964, 1965, 2002
Rolling Stones with Jack Nitzsche.
Producer: Andrew Oldham.
Engineer: Dave Hassinger.
USA Single: 19 December 1964: No. 19 - 5 weeks
USA LP THE ROLLING STONES, NOW!: 12 February 1965: No. 5 - 29 weeks
UK LP OUT OF OUR HEADS: 24 September 1965: No. 2 - 24 weeks
USA Compilation LP BIG HITS (HIGH TIDE AND GREEN GRASS): 1 April 1966: No. 3 - 35 weeks
Italian B-side Con Le Mie Lacrime: April 1966
UK Compilation LP BIG HITS (HIGH TIDE AND GREEN GRASS): 4 November 1966: No. 4 - 43 weeks
USA LP THE ROLLING STONES HOT ROCKS 1964-1971: 11 January 1972: No. 4 - 30 weeks
UK LP SLOW ROLLERS: 9 November 1981
UK & USA LP THE ROLLING STONES SINGLES COLLECTION - THE LONDON YEARS: 15 August 1989
UK & USA CD box set THE ROLLING STONES SINGLES - 1963 - 1965: 4 May 2004
UK Compilation CD ROLLED GOLD +: 12 November 2007: No. 26 - 12 weeks

This track was not released in Britain for a further 10 months but was a natural for the American market. As a single containing the slow Stateside mould, it is a well-managed Jagger, Richard composition in the blues tradition and was submerged in the USA charts by the Christmas holidays. The song lived up to the macho bad-boy image of grabbing girls as a typical young man's pursuit ... although attracted she would never break the heart of stone!

The guitar work is neat (Keith Richards remembered Jimmy Page's licks) and captured well by Dave Hassinger, who claims he was merely helping out the lads, knowing when to keep his mouth shut and allowing the positive nature of the group to dictate the session. Ian Stewart was on piano and Jack Nitzsche supported the percussion on tambourine, contributing to a successful take. A rare stereo mix is available on THE ROLLING STONES HOT ROCKS 1964-1971 (* a - 2.59).

191. HITCH HIKE (Gaye, Stevenson, Paul) 2.26
2 November 1964: Place: RCA Studios, Hollywood, USA.
Producer: Andrew Oldham.
Engineer: Dave Hassinger.
USA LP OUT OF OUR HEADS: 30 July 1965: No. 1 - 35 weeks
UK LP OUT OF OUR HEADS: 24 September 1965: No. 2 - 24 weeks

Hitch Hike was Marvin Gaye's first single and became a small success for him early in 1963. The Stones had heard Gaye perform the song at the T.A.M.I. concert only a week earlier, hence the cover at RCA. It is led by a full guitar entrance but the song plods in an indifferent manner, an intermittent slow guitar solo standing out.

192. OH, BABY (WE GOT A GOOD THING GOING) (Ozen) 2.09
2 November 1964: Place: RCA Studios, Hollywood, USA.
Played Live: 1964, 1965
Producer: Andrew Oldham.
Engineer: Dave Hassinger.
USA LP THE ROLLING STONES, NOW!: 12 February 1965: No. 5 - 29 weeks
UK LP OUT OF OUR HEADS: 24 September 1965: No. 2 - 24 weeks
UK Compilation LP ROCK 'N' ROLLING STONES: 13 October 1972: No. 41 - 1 week

This is supposed to be a song learned by playing the original Barbara Lynn Ozen single over and over. The slow blues is converted to a roaring R 'n' B track led by Mick Jagger's exasperated vocals, with Brian Jones and Keith Richards distinctive on guitar and Ian Stewart's piano faintly heard in the background. The first RCA session had ended but it started a pivotal moment for the Stones since Dave Hassinger was to be their engineer for the next few years as they consolidated their American studio recording period and learned so much that they would take back to the UK and beyond. Dave became a long-term friend and was pleased to meet them all backstage years later at a BRIDGES TO BABYLON concert.

193. LITTLE RED ROOSTER (Dixon)
8 November 1964: Place: Chess Studios, Chicago, USA.
Producer: Andrew Oldham.
Engineer: Ron Malo.
Unavailable.

In an interview recorded in Alan Lysaght's book *An Oral History*, Willie Dixon stated that *Little Red Rooster* was re-recorded at Chess while he was present and claims it is a better recording than the original. There is no evidence of its existence and, since the Regent version was just about to be released in a few days in the UK, it may have been discarded.

194. KEY TO THE HIGHWAY (Segar, Broonzy) 3.25
8 November 1964: Place: Chess Studios, Chicago, USA.
Played Live: 1976, 1986
Producer: Andrew Oldham.
Engineer: Ron Malo.
Bootleg only.

The band played a short second United States eleven tour with the Shangri-Las. As part of the 11-date trip, on the 1 November they appeared at Long Beach, south of Los Angeles, where Ike & Tina Turner were on the bill. After previously studying James Brown at the T.A.M.I. show, Mick Jagger paid careful attention to the dance moves of Tina Turner and a combination of these two American acts would mould the future of Mick's own stage persona.
The tour travelled to Chicago, which prompted another Chess session with Ron Malo on the 8 November. The visit was not quite as fulfilling as the previous time and, following the session, Brian Jones became ill and missed four tour dates due to severe respiratory and exhaustion problems, returning for the last concert in Chicago. It is rumoured that, on *Key To The Highway*, Howlin' Wolf played along but Bill Wyman has dismissed this as a myth.

195. GOODBYE GIRL (Wyman) 2.14
AKA: Get Back To The One You Love
8 November 1964: Place: Chess Studios, Chicago, USA.
Producer: Andrew Oldham.
Engineer: Ron Malo.
Bootleg only.

This was the first Bill Wyman song to be recorded by the Stones but was not released. It is an upbeat song and has Ian Stewart on piano and Keith Richards playing a hard blues guitar. It was registered for publishing rights by ABKCO with the songwriters named as Jagger, Richard.

196. WHAT A SHAME (Jagger, Richard) 2.59
8 November 1964: Place: Chess Studios, Chicago, USA.
Producer: Andrew Oldham.
Engineer: Ron Malo.
USA B-side Heart Of Stone: 19 December 1964
UK LP THE ROLLING STONES NO 2: 15 January 1965: No. 1 - 37 weeks
USA LP THE ROLLING STONES, NOW!: 12 February 1965: No. 5 - 29 weeks
UK & USA LP THE ROLLING STONES SINGLES COLLECTION - THE LONDON YEARS: 15 August 1989
UK & USA CD box set THE ROLLING STONES SINGLES - 1963 - 1965: 4 May 2004

What A Shame, featuring Ian Stewart on piano and Brian Jones on harmonica, was released as a flip side to the forthcoming American single *Heart of Stone*. It is a true attempt to conjure up some R 'n B magic and all the band are prominent in the mix, Bill Wyman playing almost jazz-style licks. At the time the Stones' songwriting team was up and down - and this was certainly a "down". In the UK music paper Melody Maker, Mick Jagger excused the recording saying it lacked atmosphere due to it being a Sunday in Chicago. The paper's main headline during that week of the article was "Beatles Feeling Just Fine" following pre-orders of 750,000 for their new single *I Feel Fine*. The Stones had some chasing to do to overtake them the following year.

197. MERCY MERCY (Covay, Miller) 2.44
AKA: Have Mercy
8 November 1964: Place: Chess Studios, Chicago, USA.
Producer: Andrew Oldham.
Engineer: Ron Malo.
Bootleg only.

Another attempt at a soul standard made popular during 1964 by Don Covay and His Goodtimers (with Jimi Hendrix on guitar). Unfortunately, Keith Richards' guitar interpretation did not emulate Jimi's sound and, six months later, the Stones were to return to Chicago to re-record it. The last date of the USA tour was on the 15 November and the band returned to the UK to honour a booking at the Glad Rag Ball, Wembley Empire Pool, plus TV recordings for Ready Steady Go! and Thank Your Lucky Stars. There was also a mix-up with some BBC radio sessions, for which the band failed to show up, the Stones claiming that they were unaware of them while the management team of Andrew Oldham and Eric Easton insisting they had been properly cancelled - the dispute with the BBC festered for some months. On a happier note, the obvious highlight at the end of 1964 was *Little Red Rooster*, which became their second No. 1 UK single.

198. OFF THE HOOK (Nanker, Phelge) 2.30
20 November 1964: Place: Ready, Steady, Go! TV Studio, London, England.
Video Ready, Steady, Go!, Volume Three: November 1984

199. LITTLE RED ROOSTER (Dixon) 2.58
20 November 1964: Place: Ready, Steady, Go! TV Studio, London, England.
Video Ready, Steady, Go!, Volume Three: November 1984

Off The Hook and *Little Red Rooster* have been entered into this Sessionography due to their inclusion on a compilation video released in 1984. They are, however, merely mimed playbacks of the officially released versions. The interview with Keith Fordyce before the start of *Rooster* explained that Brian Jones had contracted a virus whilst away in the States and was still recuperating. He had missed a few gigs in the States and the signs were ominous. It had been some year for the band - were bigger and better things beckoning?

200. THE LAST TIME (Jagger, Richard) 3.42
11-12; 17-18 January, 18 February 1965: Place: De Lane Lea Studios, Kingsway, London, England; RCA, Hollywood, USA.
Played Live: 1965, 1966, 1967, 1997, 1998
Rolling Stones with Jack Nitzsche.
Producer: Andrew Oldham.
Engineer: Dave Hassinger.
UK Single: 26 February 1965: No. 1 - 13 weeks
USA Single: 13 March 1965: No. 9 - 8 weeks
USA LP OUT OF OUR HEADS: 30 July 1965: No. 1 - 35 weeks
USA Compilation LP BIG HITS (HIGH TIDE AND GREEN GRASS): 1 April 1966: No. 3 - 35 weeks
UK Compilation LP BIG HITS (HIGH TIDE AND GREEN GRASS): 4 November 1966: No. 4 - 43 weeks
UK Compilation LP STONE AGE: 6 March 1971: No. 4 - 7 weeks
USA Compilation LP MORE HOT ROCKS (BIG HITS & FAZED COOKIES): 1 December 1972: No. 9 - 12 weeks
UK Compilation LP ROLLED GOLD: 14 November 1975: No. 7 - 50 weeks
UK Compilation LP GET STONED - 30 GREATEST HITS, 30 ORIGINAL TRACKS: 21 October 1977: No. 13 - 15 weeks
German Compilation LP THE REST OF THE BEST: December 1983
UK & USA LP THE ROLLING STONES SINGLES COLLECTION - THE LONDON YEARS: 15 August 1989
USA Compilation CD MORE HOT ROCKS (BIG HITS & FAZED COOKIES): 3 September 2002
UK CD LP FORTY LICKS: 30 September 2002: No. 2 - 45 weeks
USA CD LP FORTY LICKS: 1 October 2002: No. 2 - 50 weeks
UK & USA CD box set THE ROLLING STONES SINGLES - 1963 - 1965: 4 May 2004
UK Compilation CD ROLLED GOLD +: 12 November 2007: No. 26 - 12 weeks

In early January 1965, the Stones played a brief Irish tour (three dates, six shows) as well as a couple of concerts at the Hammersmith ABC Commodore with Zoot Money and Marianne Faithfull supporting. Following this, they went into the Kingsway studios to rehearse tracks for their new single, *The Last Time*, which was written at the end of 1964 in Mick and Keith's Hampstead flat. As the first self-penned single, they were nervous at presenting it to the band in case it was rejected - this was the first time they had the confidence to do so.

The Last Time was nonchalantly recorded at the RCA Studios prior to dropping in on the Australasian continent for an incredibly successful 16-date (33 concerts) tour, including stop-overs in such jet-set venues as Hawaii, Fiji, Singapore, Hong Kong and Japan. At the Singapore Badminton Hall, the crowd was so enthusiastic that a wall collapsed.

Mick Jagger was not sufficiently happy with the vocals on *The Last Time* so they returned in February to re-do them. The song signified a slight change in style - the sound was harder hitting, thriving on what was to become one of Keith Richards' trademark guitar riffs that repeated strongly and some surging backing vocals: "I don't know". This type of sound was later to evolve into the genre of rock music and represented a small step in the mid-1960s acceleration of different musical forms. The recording instantly satisfied Keith as he knew he had written and performed on an addictive, three-and-a-half minute, driving song and that this feel could be further developed. His contribution was the acoustic rhythmic chords, which helped to create the notable "wall of noise" electric charge, but he also took the lead solo. Brian Jones played the incessant lead guitar riff on his tear-shaped VOX Mark VI with two pick-ups, while Jack Nitzsche was on the tambourine. At that time, Mick Jagger was not fully part of the chord-writing process, although he clearly contributed an important part with some direct lyrics and ideas such as: "Well I told you once and I told you twice, that someone will have to pay the price."

Andrew Oldham was so pleased with the end result that he called Phil Spector to come and listen to it. In Oldham's book *2Stoned* he recalled that Spector listened and chuckled: "Number ten, guys, number ten." Lo and behold, in the USA charts, he was out by just one. The chorus and some of the song structure was taken from a traditional song made popular by the Five Blind Boys of Alabama in 1953 and the 1962 "gospel" Staple Singers' number *This May Be The Last Time*. An acetate from a UK recording has the lead guitars mixed down and the vocals heavily echoed in parts. A true corner had been turned with *The Last Time* and it gave Mick and Keith confidence to write further songs. The BBC's flagship music programme featured the song as a performance playback in March with a young 18-year-old footballer, George Best, dancing among the crowd.

201. PLAY WITH FIRE (Nanker, Phelge) 2.15
AKA: A Mess With Fire
11-12; 17-18 January, 18 February 1965: Place: De Lane Lea Studios, Kingsway, London, England; RCA, Hollywood, USA.
Played Live: 1965, 1966, 1989, 1990
Rolling Stones with Phil Spector, Jack Nitzsche.
Producer: Andrew Oldham.
Engineer: Dave Hassinger.
UK B-side The Last Time: 26 February 1965
USA B-side The Last Time: 13 March 1965
USA LP OUT OF OUR HEADS: 30 July 1965: No. 1 - 35 weeks
USA Compilation LP BIG HITS (HIGH TIDE AND GREEN GRASS): 1 April 1966: No. 3 - 35 weeks
USA LP THE ROLLING STONES HOT ROCKS 1964-1971: 11 January 1972: No. 4 - 30 weeks
UK Compilation LP GET STONED - 30 GREATEST HITS, 30 ORIGINAL TRACKS: 21 October 1977: No. 13 - 15 weeks
UK LP SLOW ROLLERS: 9 November 1981
German Compilation LP THE REST OF THE BEST: December 1983
UK & USA LP THE ROLLING STONES SINGLES COLLECTION - THE LONDON YEARS: 15 August 1989
UK & USA CD box set THE ROLLING STONES SINGLES - 1963 - 1965: 4 May 2004
UK Compilation CD ROLLED GOLD +: 12 November 2007: No. 26 - 12 weeks

At the time of recording their next single, the band released a second UK album, THE ROLLING STONES NO. 2, the front cover picture for which was taken by Mick Jagger's socialite friend David Bailey and had showed the band simply staring down the lens. Andrew Oldham wrote the sleeve notes which caused controversy as they advocated fans to knock a blind man on the head and steal his wallet to get the loot to buy the album - not the most sensitive of remarks.

Press interviews had Keith Richards saying his favourite track was *You Can't Catch Me* whilst Brian Jones preferred the blues of *I Can't Be Satisfied*. It's likely that more versions of *Play With Fire* were recorded and there is evidence of a more up-tempo number *A Mess With Fire*, which is not available. Chrissie Shrimpton, Andrew Oldham's assistant and Mick Jagger's girlfriend at the time, is rumoured to have delivered the wrong master to the studio and as a result this slower version, featuring Phil Spector on Zoom acoustic guitar resembling bass and Jack Nitzsche playing harpsichord and percussion, was released and *A Mess With Fire* was destroyed.

The rest of the Stones, apart from Mick and Keith, were apparently a little worse for wear because of the length of the session and their recent transatlantic flight and caught up with some sleep on the studio couches; apparently it was seven o'clock in the morning. Although a flip-side, *Play With Fire* still generated plenty of interest, being an atmospheric song, lyrically adventurous, reminiscent of Bob Dylan and seedy in approach. Mick's angry lyrics referred to a girlfriend's mother who lived in luxury in Knightsbridge but got her kicks in Stepney, a less well-heeled part of east London town. Keith Richards, who wrote most of the music, later referred to it as an Elizabethan blues. Roddy Krieger remarked that he wrote the classic Doors song *Light My Fire* with a little inspiration: "I'll write about the four elements: earth, air, fire or water. I picked fire because I like the Stones song *Play With Fire*.'"

202. I'D MUCH RATHER BE WITH THE BOYS (Oldham, Richard) 2.12
24 - 28 February 1965: Place: Decca Studios, West Hampstead, London, England.
Rolling Stones with Andy White, John McLaughlin, Joe Moretti.
Producer: Andrew Oldham.
Other Production: Mike Leander, Gus Dudgeon.
UK Compilation LP METAMORPHOSIS: 6 June 1975: No. 45 - 1 week
USA Compilation LP METAMORPHOSIS: 6 June 1975: No. 8 - 8 weeks

Another demo, but unusual since the songwriters are Andrew Oldham and Keith Richards, who composed it on the beach in Australia during a gap in the touring schedule. The Australia (marking a return to Mick Jagger's mother's birth place) and New Zealand tour was extremely successful, the band usually playing two shows a night and even some afternoon gigs. Their support acts included Roy Orbison, Rolf Harris and The Newbeats. *I'd Much Rather Be With The Boys* was also recorded by the Toggery Five at the Abbey Road Studios, the band featuring the late Paul Young (once of Sad Cafe and Mike & The Mechanics). He was new to the band and vocals were taken by lead guitarist Frank Renshaw with Alan Doyle (rhythm guitar), Ken Mills (bass) and drummer Graham Smith. It became their third single and was released in February 1965 but failed to chart.

Meanwhile, in Canada during the same month, Donna Lynn followed up her novelty hit *My Boyfriend Got A Beatle Haircut* with the Richard/Oldham song but re-named it *I'd Much Rather Be With The Girls* and performed it in a Shangri-La girl-group fashion. The track was featured on a compilation, GIRL GROUP SOUNDS LOST AND FOUND in January 2006.

The Stones version tends to be stilted and the country guitars generally lack inspiration. It ends in a rather embarrassing crescendo which leaves Mick Jagger entirely baffled. Bill Wyman humorously chose this track for inclusion on a proposed mid-1970s compilation album THE BLACK BOX. Decca and Allen Klein (their late 1960s manager) ignored the idea because there were too many covers, thereby reducing the songwriting royalties, but this track eventually ended up on the compilation album METAMORPHOSIS.

203. DOWN THE ROAD APIECE (Raye) 2.05
1 March 1965: Place: Playhouse Theatre, London, England.
Bootleg only.

Fresh from their American and Australian visits and the disputes with the BBC resolved, there was another appearance for the Top Gear show which was broadcast on 6 March 1965. The Stones also mimed lip-synched performances of *The Last Time* on the Ready, Steady, Go! show on 26 February 1965 and the Eamonn Andrews Show two days later. Their second UK album and the third in the USA, THE ROLLING STONES, NOW! had been released while they were away and the British album had gone to No. 1. The UK single *The Last Time* had just been released and was about to become No. 1.

The Last Time was a fresh song and, though its arrangement needed to be perfected, sounded fine on the Saturday Club broadcast while *Down The Road Apiece* was standard live fodder and was a good performance. In a Brian Matthews interview on Saturday Club, Mick Jagger was asked why they had waited so long before releasing a Jagger, Richard single. Mick just acknowledged that, as far as beat numbers were concerned, they simply had not recorded a good enough track.

204. EVERYBODY NEEDS SOMEBODY TO LOVE (Russell, Burke, Wexler) 3.31
1 March 1965: Place: Playhouse Theatre, London, England.
Bootleg only.

205. THE LAST TIME (Jagger, Richard) 3.07
1 March 1965: Place: Playhouse Theatre, London, England.
Bootleg only.

206. IF YOU NEED ME (Pickett, Bateman, Sanders)
1 March 1965: Place: Playhouse Theatre, London, England.
Unavailable.

207. EVERYBODY NEEDS SOMEBODY TO LOVE (Russell, Burke, Wexler) ✎ 0.33
5-16 March 1965: Place: IBC Mobile Unit, London Edmonton Regal, Liverpool Empire, Manchester Palace, England.
Producer: Andrew Oldham.
Engineer: Glyn Johns.
UK EP Got Live If You Want It!: 11 June 1965
German Compilation LP THE REST OF THE BEST: December 1983
UK & USA CD box set THE ROLLING STONES SINGLES - 1963 - 1965: 4 May 2004

This live track kicks off a completely spontaneous recording of the band on their sixth British tour. An IBC Mobile Unit with a two-track recorder, arranged by Andrew Oldham, was used, the aim being to record the band as though you were sat in the cinema watching them. He wanted to create a ball of sound which enveloped the listener, where no particular sound is more important than the other.

Glyn Johns masterminded the recording by dangling a few microphones over the balcony at selected gigs. It was the first time Glyn had agreed to record with them since the IBC studio sessions - it had taken three years for him to cool off. The decision to release these sparse recordings was a brave one but the record did not claim to be anything other than just a fair representation of the band at work. The rest of the tracks on the EP, which was released digitally for the first time on a CD box set of singles nearly 40 years later, follow.

208. PAIN IN MY HEART (Redding, Walden) ✎ 2.03
5-16 March 1965: Place: IBC Mobile Unit, London Edmonton Regal, Liverpool Empire, Manchester Palace, England.
Producer: Andrew Oldham.
Engineer: Glyn Johns.
UK EP Got Live If You Want It!: 11 June 1965
German Compilation LP THE REST OF THE BEST: December 1983
UK & USA CD box set THE ROLLING STONES SINGLES - 1963 - 1965: 4 May 2004

A slow interpretation of the song which permitted the screams to be properly heard! The EP contained all non-Jagger, Richards tracks so, to create some royalty credit, Andrew cited a 20-second track of the crowd chanting *We Want The Stones* as written by Nanker, Phelge, which secured at least some money from the release. It was not released digitally available until 2004.

209. ROUTE 66 (Troup) ✎ 2.36
5-16 March 1965: Place: IBC Mobile Unit, London Edmonton Regal, Liverpool Empire, Manchester Palace, England.
Producer: Andrew Oldham.
Engineer: Glyn Johns.
UK EP Got Live If You Want It!: 11 June 1965
USA LP DECEMBER'S CHILDREN (AND EVERYBODY'S): 4 December 1965: No. 4 - 22 weeks
German Compilation LP THE REST OF THE BEST: December 1983
UK & USA CD box set THE ROLLING STONES SINGLES - 1963 - 1965: 4 May 2004

A rabble rouser, in true "peppermint twist" (Joey Dee & The Starlighters) style.

210. I'M MOVING ON (Snow) ✎ 2.12
5-16 March 1965: Place: IBC Mobile Unit, London Edmonton Regal, Liverpool Empire, Manchester Palace, England.
Played Live: 1962, 1964, 1965, 1966
Producer: Andrew Oldham.
Engineer: Glyn Johns.
UK EP Got Live If You Want It!: 11 June 1965
USA LP DECEMBER'S CHILDREN (AND EVERYBODY'S): 4 December 1965: No. 4 - 22 weeks
UK Compilation LP NO STONE UNTURNED: 5 October 1973
German Compilation LP THE REST OF THE BEST: December 1983
UK & USA CD box set THE ROLLING STONES SINGLES - 1963 - 1965: 4 May 2004

This track was never attempted in the studio so this is the only available recording. It was a song by Hank (Clarence) Snow, a Canadian artist who had a country No. 1 with it when he moved to Nashville. *I'm Moving On* was also popular in the jazz clubs and Ray Charles secured a No. 40 chart position with it in 1959. The Stones' fast R 'n' B approach with slide guitar (closer to Ray Charles and quite at odds with the original), warmly lifted the EP. The EP's title was taken from an old Warren Smith rockabilly standard *I've Got Love If You Want It*, written by Slim Harpo and James Moore.
The Yardbirds (with band member Eric Clapton) included the track on their 1964 album FIVE LIVE YARDBIRDS and the Kinks recorded it on their 1965 album YOU REALLY GOT ME. The live Yardbirds album released in good sound may have prompted the Stones also to record live; it was an anomaly that they had not done so as yet.

211. TIME IS ON MY SIDE (Meade, Norman) ✎ 2.48
5-16 March 1965: Place: IBC Mobile Unit, London Edmonton Regal, Liverpool Empire, Manchester Palace, England.
Producer: Andrew Oldham.
Engineer: Glyn Johns.
USA LP GOT LIVE IF YOU WANT IT!: 9 December 1966: No. 6 - 11 weeks
UK Compilation LP GIMME SHELTER: 29 August 1971: No. 19 - 5 weeks

Two other songs from the same recordings are available on bootleg, *Down The Road Apiece* and *Time Is On My Side*. The latter was selected with overdubbed vocals for the 1966 album GOT LIVE IF YOU WANT IT! It has a wild lead guitar break and was credited to Ragovoy.

212. I'M ALRIGHT (Nanker, Phelge) ✎ 2.22
AKA: I Know (I'm Alright)
5-16 March 1965: Place: IBC Mobile Unit, London Edmonton Regal, Liverpool Empire, Manchester Palace, England.
Producer: Andrew Oldham.
Engineer: Glyn Johns.
UK EP Got Live If You Want It!: 11 June 1965
USA LP OUT OF OUR HEADS: 30 July 1965: No. 1 - 35 weeks
USA LP GOT LIVE IF YOU WANT IT!: 9 December 1966: No. 6 - 11 weeks
UK & USA CD box set THE ROLLING STONES SINGLES - 1963 - 1965: 4 May 2004
German Compilation LP THE REST OF THE BEST: December 1983

An adequate Stones (Nanker, Phelge) interpretation of a Bo Diddley song which ends the live EP in rapturous screams. Their replication of such a well-known 1962, Diddley song was close to the knuckle even for them. It is widely believed that a studio version of this song exists but it is certainly not the filler track on the American OUT OF OUR HEADS album - that is also this live take. Two other songs from the same recordings are available on bootleg, *Down The Road Apiece* and *Time Is On My Side*. The EP reached No. 13 in the UK single charts, the cover displaying band members in white-on-black mod pose - the Stones were credited for its arrangement. Strangely, *I'm Alright* was released on OUT OF OUR HEADS, the USA album version in 1965 and with re-recorded vocals was released on the GOT LIVE IF YOU WANT IT! album in 1966 (* a - 2.26).
The tour also included the notorious incident when, while travelling back from a show, a garage forecourt attendant refused permission for the Stones to use the staff toilet, prompting a few of them to relieve themselves against a wall. Remarks were exchanged, some comments were considered abusive and the story hit the papers two days later, followed by a court summons for Mick Jagger, Bill Wyman and Brian Jones. This resulted in a reprimand and a small fine - the first bust!

213. EVERYBODY NEEDS SOMEBODY TO LOVE (Russell, Burke, Wexler) 2.33
9 April 1965: Place: Ready, Steady, Goes Live, ITV Studio One, Wembley, London, England.
Bootleg only.

214. PAIN IN MY HEART (Redding, Walden) 2.01
9 April 1965: Place: Ready, Steady, Goes Live, ITV Studio One, Wembley, London, England.
Bootleg only.

215. I'M ALRIGHT (Nanker, Phelge) 3.28
9 April 1965: Place: Ready, Steady, Goes Live, ITV Studio One, Wembley, London, England.
Played Live: 1963, 1964, 1965, 1966
Bootleg only.

216. THE LAST TIME (Jagger, Richard) 2.59
9 April 1965: Place: Ready, Steady, Goes Live, ITV Studio One, Wembley, London, England.
Bootleg only.

Following the British live dates, with the Hollies, Dave Berry, Checkmates and Goldie and the Gingerbreads, The Stones went on a late March Scandinavian tour of Denmark, Sweden and Finland and, on their return, played live for a re-formatted version of the Ready, Steady, Go! show. A bigger studio was used, it was claimed the bands played live and Cathy McGowan became the main presenter. A Ready, Steady, Go! magazine contained an article by Cathy McGowan recalling how newspapers paired her off with many of the stars because she was seen dancing with them on the programme.
She wrote: "The best example of this concerns Mick Jagger, who asked me to dance with him between Rolling Stones numbers on the show. We were apparently having a laugh about something Mick had said earlier and it lit a fuse that brought about 100 postcards and letters into our office protesting. Some of them were so funny that I phoned Mick and asked him to come round and see them. He fell about laughing when he read them. One girl said I could dance with everyone, but to leave her gorgeous Mick alone!"

217. EVERYBODY NEEDS SOMEBODY TO LOVE (Russell, Burke, Wexler) ✕ 0.23
11 April 1965: Place: Empire Pool Wembley, London, England.
Bootleg only.

218. PAIN IN MY HEART (Redding, Walden) ✕ 1.58
11 April 1965: Place: Empire Pool Wembley, London, England.
Bootleg only.

219. AROUND AND AROUND (Berry) ✕ 2.20
11 April 1965: Place: Empire Pool Wembley, London, England.
Bootleg only.

220. THE LAST TIME (Jagger, Richard) ✕ 3.04
11 April 1965: Place: Empire Pool Wembley, London, England.
Bootleg only.

221. EVERYBODY NEEDS SOMEBODY TO LOVE (Russell, Burke, Wexler) ✕ 2.55
11 April 1965: Place: Empire Pool Wembley, London, England.
Bootleg only.

The annual NME Poll Winners concert was recorded and broadcast on an ABC TV show at Easter. *Everybody Needs Somebody To Love* was segued into *Pain In My Heart* then *Around And Around* followed by the single, *The Last Time*. The full version of *Everybody Needs Somebody To Love* was used as a finale to the performance. The Stones picked up awards for Best New Group, Best British R 'n' B Group and Mick Jagger won Best New Disc or TV Singer. The Beatles closed the show.

222. HEY CRAWDADDY (McDaniel) ✕ 5.52
AKA: Craw-Dad
17-18 April 1965: Place: Olympia Theatre, Paris, France.
Bootleg only.

A selection of tracks featuring, amongst others, their three latest singles which were recorded at a Paris concert on a quick promotional visit in April 1965 - the band's busiest year for worldwide concert promotions. Paris certainly erupted with Stones fever on this Easter holiday weekend, the performance culminating in an epic five-minute Bo Diddley number renamed *Hey Crawdaddy*, originally recorded in 1959 as a flipside single labelled *Craw-Dad*.
The track builds up intensely to a ritual climax, with Jagger enticing the crowd in a deep voice, encouraging the "Crawdaddy" chant. The atmosphere is electric and you can almost feel the sweat falling from the ceiling as the song stomps along to the end of a noteworthy set. *Hey Crawdaddy* is an essential collector's item. The concert was broadcast on French radio and has been extensively bootlegged.

223. THE LAST TIME (Jagger, Richard) 3.12
2 May 1965: Place: Ed Sullivan TV Show, CBS Studio 50, New York, USA.
Video The History Of Rock 'n' Roll Vol 7: 1995
USA DVD 4 Ed Sullivan Shows Starring The Rolling Stones: 4 October 2011
USA DVD 6 Ed Sullivan Shows Starring The Rolling Stones: 1 November 2011

224. LITTLE RED ROOSTER (Dixon) 2.34
2 May 1965: Place: Ed Sullivan TV Show, CBS Studio 50, New York, USA.
USA DVD 6 Ed Sullivan Shows Starring The Rolling Stones: 1 November 2011

225. EVERYBODY NEEDS SOMEBODY TO LOVE (Russell, Burke, Wexler) 2.18
2 May 1965: Place: Ed Sullivan TV Show, CBS Studio 50, New York, USA.
USA DVD 6 Ed Sullivan Shows Starring The Rolling Stones: 1 November 2011

226. 2120 SOUTH MICHIGAN AVENUE (Nanker, Phelge) 1.34
2 May 1965: Place: Ed Sullivan TV Show, CBS Studio 50, New York, USA.
USA DVD 6 Ed Sullivan Shows Starring The Rolling Stones: 1 November 2011

On 22 April 1965, the band flew out to Canada for performances in Quebec and Ontario. It is reputed that this is when Keith Richards first started working on *Satisfaction* on his cassette recorder. The band actually rehearsed for their second Ed Sullivan performance and were told to smarten up their appearance up, although the presenter's threat from the previous October was apparently forgotten: "Before even discussing the possibility of a contract, I would like to learn from you, whether your young men have reformed in the matter of dress and shampoo," was the statement.
The Ed Sullivan Show was the longest-running TV variety programme, being broadcast on Sunday evenings from 1948 to 1971, aimed at family audiences. He was a ham-fisted sometimes tongue-tied, monotone introducer but he had a knack of knowing what the audience wanted and showcased the most unusual entertainers, coupled with the most famous in the industry. The guests sat in the audience and were called up to the stage. It was a show that could not be ignored so some smart clothes were bought.
The Stones were not the only UK guests that night, the show also included Tom Jones and Morecambe and Wise (the famous UK comic duo). The Stones performed *The Last Time* - their current American single - *Little Red Rooster* and *Everybody Needs Somebody To Love*. Unusually at the end of the show, the normal signature tune was replaced by *2120 South Michigan Avenue*. The black and white footage is fascinating, showing Keith's solo on *The Last Time*, Brian Jones on slide guitar during *Rooster* and Mick doing fancy footwork and pointing during the "you, you, you" part of *Everybody Needs Somebody To Love*.

227. LITTLE RED ROOSTER (Dixon)
3 May 1965: Place: Clay Cole TV Show, New York, USA.
Unavailable.

The Stones had performed on the Clay Cole TV Show in October 1964 and found him to be supportive and likeable but slightly irritating. He was a DJ who won fame in 1962 by appearing in the Ronettes' film, *Twist Around The Clock*. On the last show in 1964, they had lip-synched their performance but this was an hour-long special TV programme to be broadcast on 22 May 1965. It was a Battle Of The Bands-style programme with The Beatles, as their compatriots, also in the ring. It is thought six tracks were cut at the session, with *The Last Time* and *Little Red Rooster* certain inclusions. In a cost-cutting measure, all tapes from the shows were destroyed in 1968.

228. MERCY MERCY (Covay, Miller) 2.46
10-11 May 1965: Place: Chess Studios, Chicago, USA.
Played Live: 1965, 1966, 1969
Producer: Andrew Oldham.
Engineer: Ron Malo.
USA LP OUT OF OUR HEADS: 30 July 1965: No. 1 - 35 weeks
UK LP OUT OF OUR HEADS: 24 September 1965: No. 2 - 24 weeks

The Stones performed in Chicago on 9 May as part of their tour of the States and another session was arranged at the Chess Studios. At that time, Brian Jones apparently felt some paranoia that his contribution was being minimised and threatened not to attend the Chess Sessions but, according to Bill Wyman's *Rolling With The Stones*, he convinced Brian to attend, warning that a boycott could have serious consequences.
The next few days were to represent a significant stepping stone in the band's recording career. *Mercy Mercy* is a satisfactory cover version of a song suitable for Mick Jagger's voice, although the harmony vocals appear a little stretched. Ron Malo places the guitar sound to the forefront of the track, allowing Keith Richards and Brian to diversify from the usual clear notes by using a more fulfilling valve sound, thereby making full use of the amplifiers.
The sound is unique and punchy, an indication perhaps that something rubbed off from listening to Don Covay's guitarist, Jimi Hendrix, on the March 1964, No. 35 hit. Covay had a gospel background and had played alongside Marvin Gaye and Little Richard, forming the Goodtimers as his backing band and writing songs for the 1964 MERCY album with Steve Cropper. He was to play later on the 1985 album DIRTY WORK. *Mercy Mercy* is co-written with jazz musician Don Miller. Mick studied this song and particularly liked the high-pitched style which he was later to imitate when falsetto vocals were added to tracks.

229. TRY ME (Brown) 2.25
10-11 May 1965: Place: Chess Studios, Chicago, USA.
Producer: Andrew Oldham.
Engineer: Ron Malo.
Unavailable.

Try Me, the title track from James Brown's first 1959 album, was re-released in 1964 under the brash title THE UNBEATABLE JAMES BROWN - 16 HITS. The Stones version can only be found on a nine-track mono red seal sound-tape which was researched for the 2002 ABKCO DSD/SACD recording project but disappointingly not released. Other tracks on the tape were *Have Mercy, That's How Strong My Love Is, Cry To Me, Satisfaction, My Girl, I've Been Loving You Too Long, Good Times* and *The Under Assistant West Coast Promotion Man*. A ten-inch RCA Victor acetate of the Stones playing an Everly Brothers song (title unknown) was also recorded, with no vocals, at these sessions. It was auctioned in 1990.

230. THE UNDER ASSISTANT WEST COAST PROMOTION MAN (Nanker, Phelge) 3.07
10-11 May 1965: Place: Chess Studios, Chicago, USA.
Producer: Andrew Oldham.
Engineer: Ron Malo.
USA B-side Satisfaction: 5 June 1965
USA LP OUT OF OUR HEADS: 30 July 1965: No. 1 - 35 weeks
UK LP OUT OF OUR HEADS: 24 September 1965: No. 2 - 24 weeks
UK Compilation LP ROCK 'N' ROLLING STONES: 13 October 1972: No. 41 - 1 week
UK & USA LP THE ROLLING STONES SINGLES COLLECTION - THE LONDON YEARS: 15 August 1989
UK CD box set THE ROLLING STONES SINGLES - 1965 - 1967: 12 July 2004
USA CD box set THE ROLLING STONES SINGLES - 1965 - 1967: 27 July 2004

Under Assistant, reminiscent of *Fanny Mae* and akin to *Off The Hook*, was recorded predominantly for the American market - and both Nanker, Phelge compositions deserve more credit than just being placed on a single flipside. London Records, Decca's wing in America were not exactly a large label and did not have a huge reputation among the industry. *The Under Assistant West Coast Promotion Man* is an adventurous composition which gently pokes fun at George Sherlock, who accompanied the band on the American tour as a representative of London. Did Andrew Oldham really have to resort to tongue-in-cheek jibes at the opposition?! This track has subsequently become an anthem for all aspiring promo men.
A longer version of the track was released on THE ROLLING STONES SINGLES COLLECTION - THE LONDON YEARS album. It is extended by a further 15 seconds with Mick Jagger jiving: "I have two clerks . . . I break my ass every day . . . Here comes the bus . . . I know I've got a dime here somewhere, I'm so sharp, you won't believe how sharp I really am, don't laugh at me." Evidently, Mick was dressed in a seersucker suit! This version appeared on very early pressings of the UK and USA OUT OF OUR HEADS album (* a - 3.20).

231. THAT'S HOW STRONG MY LOVE IS (Jamison) 2.25
10-11 May 1965: Place: Chess Studios, Chicago, USA.
Played Live: 1965, 1966, 2002, 2003
Producer: Andrew Oldham.
Engineer: Ron Malo.
USA LP OUT OF OUR HEADS: 30 July 1965: No. 1 - 35 weeks
UK LP OUT OF OUR HEADS: 24 September 1965: No. 2 - 24 weeks

Written by Roosevelt Jamison and made popular by Otis Redding, his version being released as a B-side on the classic *Mr Pitiful* in January 1965. *That's How Strong My Love Is* developed a new genre of power ballad. The Stones rendition is introduced by an acoustic guitar and almost certainly features Jack Nitzsche on organ and piano. Mick Jagger utters his normal explicit vocals from the bottom of his heart. Possibly sincere, but not a classic.
Andrew Oldham's heady sleeve notes on the album cover were also possibly sincere, certainly playing to the American market in a sycophantic manner: "In this world where minds have overtaken reason and every thought is potential treason the only message about this new ellpee is let's all live to enjoy it". Bob Dylan would surely be proud! In March 1965, the USA had contentiously entered the arena of war in Vietnam, sending in an army of troops which, over the next few years, would grow to 2.5 million. They supported the South Vietnamese against the communist-led North.

232. (I CAN'T GET NO) SATISFACTION (Jagger, Richard) 3.53
10-11 May 1965: Place: Chess Studios, Chicago, USA.
Producer: Andrew Oldham.
Engineer: Ron Malo
Bootleg only.

This monster of rock was conceived by Keith Richards one night in a hotel room, possibly on the Canadian and United States tour. Keith awoke the next morning, guitar in hand, to find the tape cassette at the end of the reel. He rewound it and found a snatch of the riff, followed by 40 minutes of snoring - he regrets not keeping that masterpiece. He also saw a pencilled note which said "I Can't Get No Satisfaction", recalled from the lyrics to a Chuck Berry song *Thirty Days* and an indication of the state of play with his current girlfriends. Keith claims he pinched the opening riff from Martha and The Vandellas' *Dancing In The Street*. More work on the lyrics followed as Keith and Mick got together at the Fort Harrison Hotel in Clearwater, Tampa Bay, Florida on 5 May 1965, by the swimming pool before a gig at a local stadium.
The many implications of this recorded rock anthem were obviously not realised at its inception. Keith wrote the music in a folk mould and, therefore, never believed that it could be anything other than a soft rock song. Mick, though, was aware of the possibilities of the anti-establishment lyrics that showed adolescent alienation and, after much persuasion, Keith permitted the switch to a rock 'n' roll beat. The lyrics were anarchic for the time and were atypical of the mid-1960s, speaking for a new generation - trying to "make" some girl was the safe way of expressing what was actually intended.

The mammoth recording programme began in Chicago at midday on 10 May, finished at 5am the next day and was completed in another take at RCA Studios, Hollywood, due to their concert commitments on the east coast. The Chess Studio version has an accompanying Brian Jones harmonica track and lacks the piano. When the song was completed, Keith felt that it was no more than a B-side or an album cut. The Chess recording, with a rapid fade-out, can be heard on the 26 May broadcast of the Shindig TV show and this was chosen as the backing track, with vocals, recorded on the 20 May.

233. (I CAN'T GET NO) SATISFACTION (Jagger, Richard) 3.44
12-13 May 1965: Place: RCA Studios, Hollywood, USA.
Played Live: 1965, 1966, 1967, 1968, 1969, 1971, 1972, 1976, 1978, 1981, 1982, 1989, 1990, 1994, 1995, 1997, 1998, 1999, 2002, 2003, 2005, 2006, 2007
Rolling Stones with Jack Nitzsche.
Producer: Andrew Oldham.
Engineer: Dave Hassinger.
USA Single: 5 June 1965: No. 1 - 14 weeks
USA LP OUT OF OUR HEADS: 30 July 1965: No. 1 - 35 weeks
UK Single: 20 August 1965: No. 1 - 12 weeks
USA Compilation LP BIG HITS (HIGH TIDE AND GREEN GRASS): 1 April 1966: No. 3 - 35 weeks
UK Compilation LP BIG HITS (HIGH TIDE AND GREEN GRASS): 4 November 1966: No. 4 - 43 weeks
USA LP THE ROLLING STONES HOT ROCKS 1964-1971: 11 January 1972: No. 4 - 30 weeks
UK Compilation LP MILESTONES: 18 February 1972: No. 14 - 8 weeks
UK Compilation LP ROLLED GOLD: 14 November 1975: No. 7 - 50 weeks
UK Compilation LP GET STONED - 30 GREATEST HITS, 30 ORIGINAL TRACKS: 21 October 1977: No. 13 - 15 weeks
UK LP SOLID ROCK: 13 October 1980
German Compilation LP THE REST OF THE BEST: December 1983
UK & USA LP THE ROLLING STONES SINGLES COLLECTION - THE LONDON YEARS: 15 August 1989
USA Compilation Promo CD THE ROLLING STONES REMASTERED: 30 May 2002
UK CD LP FORTY LICKS: 30 September 2002: No. 2 - 45 weeks
USA CD LP FORTY LICKS: 1 October 2002: No. 2 - 50 weeks
UK CD box set THE ROLLING STONES SINGLES - 1965 - 1967: 12 July 2004
USA CD box set THE ROLLING STONES SINGLES - 1965 - 1967: 27 July 2004
UK Compilation CD ROLLED GOLD +: 12 November 2007: No. 26 - 12 weeks

After a quick detour to Hollywood, recording resumed on May 12 and finished late evening May 13. Keith Richards was still reluctant to release the end product, feeling the riff was over-simplified as he intended that it would have been played by brass instruments rather like the February 1966 Otis Redding version. Indeed, the fuzz tone guitar was meant to merely sketch the part he saw the horns playing on the track.

Bill Wyman recalls that *Satisfaction* was eventually released following a democratic band vote, which included Dave Hassinger, Andrew Oldham and Ian Stewart (who was amazed at what they had achieved). Ironically, the two who voted against the release were Keith Richards and Mick Jagger. The decision was a monumental stepping stone in their career.

Generally the RCA studios offered four-track recording while the Chess studio had a three-track option, depending on which console was used. Both engineers recorded in stereo but mixed and ultimately released the final cut in mono. The outcome therefore features acoustic sounds on one track and a heavier electric sound, using Gibson fuzz-box techniques, on the other. Keith wanted the heavier sound and asked Ian Stewart to see what he could do. He bought a tone distortion box from a local store to enhance the dirty sound and this provided the fuzzy, sustained notes. The fuzz tone became the trademark sound of the song.

Perhaps Jack Nitzsche was familiar with the guitarist Chester (Chet) Atkins, who produced and played with a young female actress and singing artiste, Ann-Margret, who had a No. 17 USA single in 1961 titled *I Just Don't Understand*. This featured Chet's guitar effects with the pioneering fuzz guitar sound, a technique he had learnt in the 1950s. The Beatles covered Ann-Margret's song live at the London Paris Theatre for the Pop Goes The Beatles programme on 16 July 1963, a track later released on the 2001 album LIVE AT THE BBC. George Harrison was a huge fan of Chet Atkins.

Out-takes of *Satisfaction* exist and demonstrate some of the different cuts, one being an instrumental with pronounced piano playing by Ian Stewart (* a - 3.44). The one most readily available is the backing track for the Chess, Chicago version, while the released song features an outstanding Charlie Watts backing track, helped out by Jack Nitzsche on tambourine and a piano buried so far in the mix that it might not be there in the final cut.

Andrew Oldham felt the song was great but decided that the vocals should be submerged in the overall sound but was amazed that Mick had laid them down in one take. This would have been a deliberate ploy to avoid the double entendre critics who were eager to ban any subversive aggression, should it be released as a single. The vocals referring to "girl reaction" were often misheard as "girlie action" and older girls could relate to the need to ask, "Baby, better come back maybe next week 'cause you see I'm on a losing streak". Dave Hassinger recalled: "They kept telling me to bring the voice down more and more into the track. I thought they were crazy."

The combination of all these factors produced a synthesis of acoustic/electric sounds unique in style (although perhaps reminiscent of Bob Dylan) and helped to create a worldwide No.1 hit, even though British fans were upset by the late release of the single in the UK. It had already been No. 1 in the States (their first one) for two months, the tardiness of the release being due to a delay in negotiating a renewal of their contract with Decca. The effect ended up as a positive, however, as it produced advance orders of 250,000 and a guaranteed No. 1 hit.

Over the years the mono sound is so embedded in our senses that it is interesting to hear the unfamiliarity of the stereo version. This was not released until the 1980s on Japanese editions of HOT ROCKS. The wide separation enables the sound of Brian Jones' acoustic guitar to come more to the fore. A house DJ remix of *Satisfaction*, named *Rockerfaction*, was created by Norman Cook (alias Fatboy Slim), using the prominent guitar riff, Mick's vocal and Charlie's drum sound. For copyright reasons, it was not released.

234. THE SPIDER AND THE FLY (Nanker, Phelge) 3.39
12-13 May 1965: Place: RCA Studios, Hollywood, USA.
Played Live: 1965, 1966, 1995
Rolling Stones with Jack Nitzsche.
Producer: Andrew Oldham.
Engineer: Dave Hassinger.
USA LP OUT OF OUR HEADS: 30 July 1965: No. 1 - 35 weeks
UK B-side (I Can't Get No) Satisfaction: 20 August 1965
UK Compilation LP STONE AGE: 6 March 1971: No. 4 - 7 weeks
German Compilation LP THE REST OF THE BEST: December 1983
UK & USA LP THE ROLLING STONES SINGLES COLLECTION - THE LONDON YEARS: 15 August 1989

The Spider And The Fly is a eulogy of life on the road, encapsulating the tough decision facing a young rock 'n' roller on tour - do I sleep with the groupie? It is a slow country blues (Mick Jagger said it was in a Jimmy Reed style mixed with typically British pop lyrics) which was thought just right for the British market by Tony King, who worked as Andrew Oldham's UK promotion man, hence its UK release on the prestigious flip-side of *Satisfaction*. Mick Jagger relates the pitfalls awaiting a touring rock 'n' roll band which had a particular image to live up to. It obviously has to be tongue in cheek and was recorded at the end of a session having finalised their other recordings. Jack Nitzsche plays keyboards and percussion on this, the last Nanker, Phelge track. It was considered to be strong enough to be selected for re-recording on the STRIPPED acoustic collection. A handwritten transcription of the lyrics by Mick Jagger displays the phrase "some little girl will pass me by" with the "me" crossed out to leave the released "pass on by". Also, another set of words were toughened up on the final release, "about the blonde peroxide sitting on my left" changing to "about the rinsed out blond sitting on my left".

235. ONE MORE TRY (Jagger, Richard) 1.58
12-13 May 1965: Place: RCA Studios, Hollywood, USA.
Played Live: 1965
Producer: Andrew Oldham.
Engineer: Dave Hassinger.
USA LP OUT OF OUR HEADS: 30 July 1965: No. 1 - 35 weeks
UK Compilation LP STONE AGE: 6 March 1971: No. 4 - 7 weeks
German Compilation LP THE REST OF THE BEST: December 1983

A jaunty, discordant song led by guitar and the harmonica of Brian Jones. Mick Jagger ushers the track forward at an awkward pace, not seeming to match the song's rhythm, though it does conclude in record time and finished as the closing number on the USA OUT OF OUR HEADS! *One More Try* was not released in the UK until the unofficial collection STONE AGE.

236. GOOD TIMES (Cooke) 1.59
12-13 May 1965: Place: RCA Studios, Hollywood, USA.
Played Live: 1965
Producer: Andrew Oldham.
Engineer: Dave Hassinger.
USA LP OUT OF OUR HEADS: 30 July 1965: No. 1 - 35 weeks
UK LP OUT OF OUR HEADS: 24 September 1965: No. 2 - 24 weeks

The experiment with soul continued, this particular track being a cover of a song written by Sam Cooke. It was a Top 20 hit for him in June 1966, six months after he was tragically killed in a shooting incident. This tribute is a short, sharp reminder of 1950s soul employing Shirley and Lee's good time phrase "Let The Good Times Roll". The melody hooks the listener to this pleasant up-tempo song, which makes a positive contribution to the OUT OF OUR HEADS album, but also emphasises the album's disjointed song styles. A different version, with additional backing vocals, was considered for the NECROPHILIA album.
The great music photographer, Gered Mankowitz, took the album cover shot of the band in an alley way. Despite their previous album reaching No. 1 in the UK, it failed to do so this time due to the phenomenal popularity of the musical THE SOUND OF MUSIC. This Rodgers and Hammerstein film and soundtrack was an international sensation, entering the UK charts in March 1965 and staying for more than seven years (351 weeks). Even the Stones couldn't "climb every mountain".

237. CRY TO ME (Russell) 3.10
12-13 May 1965: Place: RCA Studios, Hollywood, USA.
Played Live: 1965
Producer: Andrew Oldham.
Engineer: Dave Hassinger.
USA LP OUT OF OUR HEADS: 30 July 1965: No. 1 - 35 weeks
UK LP OUT OF OUR HEADS: 24 September 1965: No. 2 - 24 weeks

Having had success with Solomon Burke's *Everybody Needs Somebody To Love*, the Stones turned their attentions to *Cry To Me*, an old stage number for the same artist. It reverts to the pleading soul songs so reverently included on the first and second albums. The guitar stings in painful tones and Mick Jagger's vocals try to comfort those harbouring any thoughts of loneliness. Coincidentally, another British R 'n' B band, the Pretty Things, (which included Keith Richards' old mate Dick Taylor), had recorded the song and charted with it in July prior to the release of the Stones' British version in September.

238. I'VE BEEN LOVING YOU TOO LONG (Redding, Butler) 2.57
AKA: I've Been Lonely Too Long
12-13 May 1965: Place: RCA Studios, Hollywood, USA.
Producer: Andrew Oldham.
Engineer: Dave Hassinger.
German LP COLLECTOR'S ONLY: 4 June 1980
German Compilation LP THE REST OF THE BEST: December 1983
USA Compilation CD MORE HOT ROCKS (BIG HITS & FAZED COOKIES): 3 September 2002

This Otis Redding ballad was recorded just a month before Otis himself obtained a No. 21 hit with it in the American Billboard charts. Due to this coincidence, it is unlikely the Stones actually wanted the track to be released and, although performed live, it never gained official status - except on a German 1980 collection of Stones material. This original recording, however, did serve a useful purpose and, with an organ and screams overdubbed, it was used to fill out the 1967 live album GOT LIVE IF YOU WANT IT. An unpopular ending to an otherwise excellent cover of an Otis Redding number. (Otis died, aged 26, in a plane crash in December 1967 and posthumously charted at No. 1 in February 1968 with the memorable *The Dock Of The Bay*).
An acetate contains some of the RCA 12 May sessions, labelled "Decca Group Advance Test Processing", with *Cry To Me* and *Satisfaction* on Side A and *My Girl, I've Been Loving You Too Long* and *Good Times* on Side B. It was finally released digitally on the 2002 MORE HOT ROCKS from a tape misnamed as *I've Been Lonely Too Long*.

239. MY GIRL (Robinson, White) 2.39
12-13 May 1965; 31 August-2 September 1966: Place: RCA Studios, Hollywood, USA; IBC Studios, London, England.
Producer: Andrew Oldham.
Engineer: Dave Hassinger.
Strings: Mike Leander.
USA Compilation LP FLOWERS: 15 July 1967: No. 3 - 18 weeks
UK Compilation LP STONE AGE: 6 March 1971: No. 4 - 7 weeks
German Compilation LP THE REST OF THE BEST: December 1983

A track made available by Decca in 1967 on a compilation album FLOWERS. It is a soft ballad previously performed by the Temptations, who reached No. 1 in the States with it in January 1965. Bill Wyman told Beat Magazine that he found the timing difficult to get to grips with but he liked the final take. At the mixing desk, unobtrusive orchestral strings were added to the recording track by Andrew Oldham at a following session in August 1966. He tried this on many other tracks in the hope that they would then become more marketable. This time, the result was not totally absurd.

240. LITTLE RED ROOSTER (Dixon) 3.04
18 May 1965: Place: RCA Studios, Hollywood, USA.
Producer: Andrew Oldham
Engineer: Dave Hassinger
Bootleg only.

241. THE LAST TIME (Jagger, Richard) 3.04
18 May 1965: Place: RCA Studios, Hollywood, USA.
Producer: Andrew Oldham
Engineer: Dave Hassinger
Bootleg only.

242. PLAY WITH FIRE (Jagger, Richard) 2.09
18 May 1965: Place: RCA Studios, Hollywood, USA.
Producer: Andrew Oldham
Engineer: Dave Hassinger
Bootleg only.

These three tracks were laid down especially for the TV show Shindig, which was recorded a couple of days later. An excerpt of *The Last Time* performance appears on the *25 X 5: The Continuing Adventures Of The Rolling Stones* video.

243. DOWN THE ROAD APIECE (Raye) 1.04
20 May 1965: Place: Shindig ABC TV Studios, Hollywood, Los Angeles, USA.
Rolling Stones with Billy Preston.
Bootleg only.

244. (I CAN'T GET NO) SATISFACTION (Jagger, Richard) 2.43
20 May 1965: Place: Shindig ABC TV Studios, Hollywood, Los Angeles, USA.
Bootleg only.

This Shindig performance (Show 37 of the ABC series aired on 26 May 1965) is both notorious and audacious. It was the Stones only live appearance on the show, although they were booked before and after, most of the playbacks being recorded a few days earlier at the RCA studios especially for broadcast by Shindig (an American noun for a good time). These good times started off at the show's introduction with a live version of *Down The Road Apiece*, accompanied by Billy Preston on piano and a group of go-go dancers - The Shin-Diggers - choreographed by dancer Toni Basil. Billy Preston was part of the Shin-Diggers house band for the show. Other members included Glen Campbell, James Burton, Delaney Bramlett and Leon Russell. The Stones then mimed to the pre-recorded versions of *Little Red Rooster* (filmed in a mock crypt), *The Last Time* and *Play With Fire*.

The Last Time, the band's current single, was sliding down the charts and *Satisfaction* was planned to be released in the States in early June. So they decided to perform the recently recorded song from Chess Studios on the 26 May broadcast at the show's fade-out finale. To do this, they used the Chess version of *Satisfaction*, which had no vocals. Mick Jagger then recorded some vocals and the band mimed to the backing track, with Brian Jones performing the harmonica role. Jack Good (the producer) and Jimmy O'Neill, the host of Shindig, could later proclaim in an August broadcast of *Satisfaction*: "Here's the No. 1 national hit song that was heard for the first time in the world right here on Shindig". Jack Good was a UK TV producer who was well-respected by the UK artists, hence bands like the Beatles agreeing to do the show.

Jack secretly booked Howlin' Wolf on to the same show because he knew the Stones were huge fans - he performed *How Many More Years* after being presented by Mick and Brian. Much to Keith Richards' amusement, Jack Good referred to Howlin' Wolf as Mr Wolf. Off camera, Howlin' Wolf introduced Mick to Son House, who was unassumingly sat in the audience. Son House had recorded *Little Red Rooster* and was Robert Johnson's mentor - a lovely gentleman, Mick recalls. The interview with Mick and Keith and an extract of *The Last Time* can be seen on the *25 X 5* video.

The Stones found that the publicity seed had been sewn and their remaining live performances for the rest of the month, along with the Shindig appearance, ensured that it entered the Billboard Top 40 the following month. It had been a busy time for the group as, a few days earlier, they had performed (playbacks only) on the late Gene Weed's Shivaree TV programme and shared the bill with Chuck Berry on the Hollywood A Go-Go TV show. They had narrowly escaped being crushed by fan hysteria when their limousine was literally swamped by over enthusiastic followers many of whom became casualties in the turmoil. The roof of the car had been dangerously close to cracking. It was time to return to Britain.

245. MERCY MERCY (Covay, Miller)
28 July 1965: Place: Twickenham Studios, London, England.
Unavailable.

246. HITCH HIKE (Gaye, Stevenson, Paul)
28 July 1965: Place: Twickenham Studios, London, England.
Played Live: 1965
Unavailable.

247. THAT'S HOW STRONG MY LOVE IS (Jamison)
28 July 1965: Place: Twickenham Studios, London, England.
Unavailable.

248. (I CAN'T GET NO) SATISFACTION (Jagger, Richard)
28 July 1965: Place: Twickenham Studios, London, England.
Unavailable.

A return to the UK enabled the Stones to make a short Scottish tour and another Scandinavian foray. Their live EP was also released. Mick Jagger, Ian Stewart and Bill Wyman participated in a session with Eric Clapton, Jimmy Page and Chris Winters. They recorded two tracks, *Snake Drive* and *West Coast Idea*, in June 1965. In addition to these tracks, recorded live for ABC TV's Shindig, *Good Times, Cry To Me, Spider And The Fly* and *I've Been Loving You Too Long* were also mimed. The backing track for *Satisfaction* had the "trying to make some girl" lyrics scrubbed from the vocal (unlike the May broadcast), so as not to offend the American public. *Satisfaction* was broadcast on 16 September 1965 (Show 52) and *Good Times* and *Mercy Mercy* on Show 67, 6 November 1965.

249. MERCY MERCY (Covay, Miller) 2.51
20 August 1965: Place: BBC Maida Vale Studios, London, England.
Bootleg only.

In what was to become their last BBC session, these tracks were broadcast on two different shows. *Oh Baby, Mercy Mercy, Satisfaction* and *The Spider And The Fly* were aired on the BBC Yeh! Yeh! Show on the 30 August 1965 while *Fanny Mae, Oh Baby, Cry To Me, Satisfaction* and *Spider And The Fly* appeared on the Brian Matthew Saturday Club show on 18 September 1965. *Mercy Mercy* has the start of the falsetto arrangements, as the backing vocals testify! Interviewed by Tony Hall, Mick Jagger commented that the American studios were a lot better in which to record and the producers and engineers contributed significantly to the output, a reference to the studio staff at Chess and RCA.

250. OH, BABY (WE GOT A GOOD THING GOING) (Ozen) 1.54
20 August 1965: Place: BBC Maida Vale Studios, London, England.
Bootleg only.

251. (I CAN'T GET NO) SATISFACTION (Jagger, Richard) 3.52
20 August 1965: Place: BBC Maida Vale Studios, London, England.
Bootleg only.

In an interview, Mick Jagger dismisses the fact that this had taken 38 hours to record - and that was without a hamburger break - claiming that it only took two hours and another hour to mix. The radio broadcast was on the day of release of the UK single. The stun guitar effects obviously sound different from the original recording. The latent potential of the track was being realised in its delivery. Mick's vocals position the harshness of the lyrics with a soft delivery until the crescendo - an ending had not been perfected.

252. THE SPIDER AND THE FLY (Jagger, Richard) 3.26
20 August 1965: Place: BBC Maida Vale Studios, London, England.
Bootleg only.

The radio session track is slightly heavier in approach and has a stronger boogie rhythm. In the introduction, Mick Jagger is interviewed by Brian Matthew and comments on Andrew Oldham's production input: "Sometimes he contributes a lot and sometimes nuthin'."

253. CRY TO ME (Russell, Burke, Wexler) 3.06
20 August 1965: Place: BBC Maida Vale Studios, London, England.
Bootleg only.

The radio session version available on bootleg is played at the same pace and, instead of fading out, drifts along for a few seconds more before the band ends the sad ordeal.

254. FANNY MAE (Brown) 2.11
20 August 1965: Place: BBC Maida Vale Studios, London, England.
Played Live: 1965
Bootleg only.

Bill Wyman attempted to get this recording released in 1975 under the Black Box title. *Fanny Mae* touched on old ground, a straight Buster Brown R 'n' B rocker featuring harmonica in a Sonny Terry mould. Buster Brown was famous for his electronic harmonica and, at the age of 50 in 1959, he charted with this classic. This Stones interpretation was a notable copy but had not been used greatly in the set list. It was Mick Jagger and Bill's choice to include it in the radio set and was viewed as a chance to try out something different, even if Mick had to repeat a verse or two since he could not remember the lyrics.
This was the last of the BBC sessions. There were 58 recordings made but it is arguable how many currently exist, as the BBC had a disastrous policy of re-using reel-to-reel tape - reports in 1999 suggested that 42 were officially still in existence. Mick Jagger has heard these recordings and believed that the quality was good enough for release. Stones fans still eagerly await the appearance of what would be an excellent product, along the lines achieved via the BBC by other contemporary artists!

255. OH, BABY (WE GOT A GOOD THING GOING) (Ozen) 1.21
2 September 1965: Place: Ready, Steady, Go! TV Show, Wembley, London, England.
Producer: Michael Lindsay-Hogg.
Bootleg only.

The 20 August 1965 radio session and this rendition, which was broadcast on TV on 10 September 1965, was the first time this Barbara Lynn Ozen composition had been aired since its recording in November 1964.

256. THAT'S HOW STRONG MY LOVE IS (Jamison) 1.56
2 September 1965: Place: Ready, Steady, Go! TV Show, Wembley, London, England.
Producer: Michael Lindsay-Hogg.
Bootleg only.

257. (I CAN'T GET NO) SATISFACTION (Jagger, Richard) 4.17
2 September 1965: Place: Ready, Steady, Go! TV Show, Wembley, London, England.
Producer: Michael Lindsay-Hogg.
Video Ready, Steady, Go! Volume Two: May 1984

This show predominately featured The Rolling Stones and was made famous by a mimed performance of *I Got You Babe*. It was introduced by Mick Jagger, who described the Stones' cameo performance as being by miming artists from Leighton Buzzard. Cathy McGowan played the Cher role, with Brian Jones opposite her as Sonny Bono, with Andrew Oldham and the rest of the Stones mimicking in the background. Keith Richards is featured in dark glasses on the trombone.
Among the letters to the Ready Steady Go! magazine is this one:
"Dear Cathy, Everyone says you are competing with us with your hairstyle - change it at once!"
It was signed by Mick Jagger. The three Stones numbers on this show emphasised their great contribution to R 'n' B with *Oh Baby* and *That's How Strong How My Love Is*, while *Satisfaction* is delivered with pep.
The camera employs staccato in and out fades and, at the climax, the stage is swamped by enthusiastic fans. Other techniques by the cameraman included highlighting faces and freeze frame shots. As Ready Steady Go! Producer Vicky Wickham revealed: "When the Walker Brothers were on . . . he had all three of them in one shot with their great hairs and faces. We were black and white and the lighting was theatrical in that just their faces were lit. It was mind-blowing. He captured Mick playing to the camera and used a technique which had only been used for sports before, which meant the camera could freeze on a shot. When we were rehearsing there was a wonderful and funny moment where the picture indeed froze and was stunning - but the sound also froze!"

258. CHARLIE IS MY DARLING (Trad) 3.16
AKA: Intermezzo
3-4 September 1965: Place: Adelphi Theatre, Dublin, Eire or ABC Theatre, Belfast, N Ireland.
Producer: Peter Whitehead.
USA DVD Charlie Is My Darling: 6 December 2005
UK DVD Charlie Is My Darling: 3 August 2009

Andrew Oldham had already met Allen Klein in London in 1964, having been introduced by James Alexander (the late Sam Cooke's manager). Allen had tried but failed to sign the Beatles and, desperate to grab a piece of the UK pie, turned his attention to the Stones. Andrew was suitably impressed with Allen's big money approach at a time when the Decca Record Company and Impact Sound (Andrew Oldham and Eric Easton Production Company) contract was due for renewal. Negotiations could so easily have been a formality when Eric Easton presented a concluding renewal contract worth £600,000 but Andrew smelt a rat and was enticed by Allen's "cheese".

Having met Allen Klein again at a record company convention on the third American tour, Andrew wanted to appoint him as the Stones' business manager. He offered him 20 per cent as opposed to the normal manager's 10 per cent but wanted Allen to negotiate a new recording deal for the USA and Canada, where royalties were currently half of the UK market. Finally the band met Allen Klein in London in late July and a ten-year deal with Decca (trading again as London in America) was struck by Klein without the band contacting any independent solicitor. In August 1965, Andrew Oldham, Mick Jagger and Keith Richards, on behalf of the other band members, formalised Allen Klein's US management position alongside Andrew Oldham, negating Eric Easton's role in the process.

Through Allen and Betty Klein's company (ABKCO), a $3 million US deal had been negotiated for the next five years, along with a £5 million contract with Decca to fulfil and record an unrealistic five films.

Without delay, Peter Whitehead was asked to record the first, a documentary of life on the road with The Rolling Stones, the opportunity presenting itself on a two-day tour of Ireland. The filming captured backstage rehearsals of *Get Off My Cloud* and a run through of *Salty Dog* but, most significantly, the jam on a traditional folk song, *Charlie Is My Darling*. The film *Charlie Is My Darling* was premiered in January 1966 and was offered to distributors but, apart from newsreel extracts, failed to get an official release until 2005. Immediately following the filming, the Stones returned to London then flew to Los Angeles specifically for their next recording session and, with the help of time-zone differences, that was the very next day!

259. GET OFF MY CLOUD (Jagger, Richard) 2.56
5 September 1965: Place: RCA Studios, Hollywood, USA.
Played Live: 1965, 1966, 1967, 1975, 1999, 2005, 2006, 2007
Producer: Andrew Oldham.
Engineer: Dave Hassinger.
USA Single: 25 September 1965: No. 1 - 11 weeks
UK Single: 22 October 1965: No. 1 - 12 weeks
USA LP DECEMBER'S CHILDREN (AND EVERYBODY'S): 4 December 1965: No. 4 - 22 weeks
USA Compilation LP BIG HITS (HIGH TIDE AND GREEN GRASS): 1 April 1966: No. 3 - 35 weeks
UK Compilation LP BIG HITS (HIGH TIDE AND GREEN GRASS): 4 November 1966: No. 4 - 43 weeks
USA LP THE ROLLING STONES HOT ROCKS 1964-1971: 11 January 1972: No. 4 - 30 weeks
UK Compilation LP MILESTONES: 18 February 1972: No. 14 - 8 weeks
UK Compilation LP ROLLED GOLD: 14 November 1975: No. 7 - 50 weeks
UK Compilation LP GET STONED - 30 GREATEST HITS, 30 ORIGINAL TRACKS: 21 October 1977: No. 13 - 15 weeks
UK LP SOLID ROCK: 13 October 1980
German Compilation LP THE REST OF THE BEST: December 1983
UK & USA LP THE ROLLING STONES SINGLES COLLECTION - THE LONDON YEARS: 15 August 1989
USA Compilation Promo CD THE ROLLING STONES REMASTERED: 30 May 2002
UK CD LP FORTY LICKS: 30 September 2002: No. 2 - 45 weeks
USA CD LP FORTY LICKS: 1 October 2002: No. 2 - 50 weeks
UK Compilation CD ROLLED GOLD +: 12 November 2007: No. 26 - 12 weeks

The trilogy of 1965 UK and USA hit singles continued with this track, which was again criticised by Keith Richards even though he wrote the melody, who felt the production let it down. The general mode was to produce the single with a lot of compression so that it sounded bright on radio. However, it became the first simultaneous No. 1 hit in the States and the UK and the band's fifth consecutive No. 1 hit in Britain, an achievement which had only been previously matched a year before by The Beatles. The purpose of the Hollywood session was to record a follow-up to *Satisfaction* and it is remarkable that this was achieved in such convincing style.

The track adopts a rock and roll approach (sometimes referred to as the "Twist and Shout" chord method) and was a contrast to the rock/soul sound of *Satisfaction*. The song title was a "fingers-up" response to record executives insisting on a quick follow-up to *Satisfaction* and also provided a defiant slogan for the era.

The lyrics perfectly illustrated the pill-popping age of the 1960s with the "heys" and "yous" resonating in distinctive tones. More people were letting their inhibitions go and the "stoned" age, whether by drugs or alcohol, was beginning to run away from the establishment. Appearances on the by now institutionalised BBC Top of The Pops TV show proved that the Stones had made their mark - *Get Off My Cloud* created a safe pedestal for a degree of experimentation on future single releases. Brian Jones contributes lead guitar. A stereo mix was released on THE ROLLING STONES HOT ROCKS 1964-1971.

260. BLUE TURNS TO GREY (Jagger, Richard) 2.29
6 September 1965: Place: RCA Studios, Hollywood, USA.
Producer: Andrew Oldham.
Engineer: Dave Hassinger.
USA LP DECEMBER'S CHILDREN (AND EVERYBODY'S): 4 December 1965: No. 4 - 22 weeks
UK Compilation LP STONE AGE: 6 March 1971: No. 4 - 7 weeks
German Compilation LP THE REST OF THE BEST: December 1983

Recorded earlier in 1964 in the UK as a demo, *Blue Turns To Grey* was again recorded for release on the USA DECEMBER'S CHILDREN album. Cliff Richard popularised this track (a Top 20 hit) by releasing his version as a British single in early 1966. The Stones were obviously not impressed with the song since it was not featured on an authorised UK release. It did, however, re-surface on a dubious UK Decca compilation of Stones so-called rarities in 1971.

The Stones were angry at the release just after the cessation of their contract with Decca. Indeed, they placed an advertisement in the British musical newspapers advising against purchase of an inferior product! The track has weak foundations, relying on vocal harmonies which sounded very experimental. This was one area that needed a certain amount of work - the arranger could be excused on this occasion.

261. **SHE SAID YEAH** (Roderick, Jackson, Christy) 1.35
6 September 1965: Place: RCA Studios, Hollywood, USA.
Played Live: 1965, 1966
Producer: Andrew Oldham.
Engineer: Dave Hassinger.
UK LP OUT OF OUR HEADS: 24 September 1965: No. 2 - 24 weeks
USA LP DECEMBER'S CHILDREN (AND EVERYBODY'S): 4 December 1965: No. 4 - 22 weeks
USA Compilation LP THE ROLLING STONES - PROMOTIONAL ALBUM: October 1969
UK Compilation LP MILESTONES: 18 February 1972: No. 14 - 8 weeks
e-Single: 9 August 2010

She Said Yeah is a rousing number which noisily opens the British OUT OF OUR HEADS and the American DECEMBER'S CHILDREN (AND EVERYBODY'S) albums. It portrayed the heavier beat/mod sound with which The Pretty Things, The Who and The Yardbirds were having so much success. The vocals are aggressive and slightly indistinct while the guitar sound is superb, with primitively sustained overdrive - imagine Keith Richards and Brian Jones fraternising with feedback! The track was brought to fame by the piano-pounding, Larry Williams in the late 1950s.
The band may have seen a cover of the song performed by UK boogie-woogie artist Roy Young (the English Little Richard) on a BBC TV show Drumbeat in 1959. The Roderick mentioned in the credit is Roddy Jackson, who wrote the song with Don Christy (Sonny Bono) in 1959. It was a flip-side to Williams' *Bad Boy* single. Martin Scorsese directed a one-minute advertisement for Bleu De Chanel in August 2010 which incorporated *She Said Yeah* within the soundtrack. As a result, the track was released as an electronic download single coupled with a video of the Stones' Hullabaloo television appearance in November 1965.

262. **GOTTA GET AWAY** (Jagger, Richard) 2.07
AKA: I've Gotta Get Away
6 September 1965: Place: RCA Studios, Hollywood, USA.
Rolling Stones with James Alexander
Producer: Andrew Oldham.
Engineer: Dave Hassinger.
UK LP OUT OF OUR HEADS: 24 September 1965: No. 2 - 24 weeks
USA LP DECEMBER'S CHILDREN (AND EVERYBODY'S): 4 December 1965: No. 4 - 22 weeks
USA B-side As Tears Go By: 18 December 1965
UK & USA LP THE ROLLING STONES SINGLES COLLECTION - THE LONDON YEARS: 15 August 1989
UK CD box set THE ROLLING STONES SINGLES - 1965 - 1967: 12 July 2004
USA CD box set THE ROLLING STONES SINGLES - 1965 - 1967: 27 July 2004

A Jagger, Richard composition which is just an album filler. The lyrics lack imagination and the folk/rock tune never gets off the ground. James W Alexander, who was the late Sam Cooke's producer and arranger, performed on tambourine on this number. *Gotta Get Away* does an injustice to the hidden talent of the group. They were going through an industrious period and inevitably some tracks would not satisfy the fans' expectations or the band's potential.

263. **TALKIN' 'BOUT YOU** (Berry) 2.32
6 September 1965: Place: RCA Studios, Hollywood, USA.
Played Live: 1962, 1963, 1964
Producer: Andrew Oldham.
Engineer: Dave Hassinger.
UK LP OUT OF OUR HEADS: 24 September 1965: No. 2 - 24 weeks
USA LP DECEMBER'S CHILDREN (AND EVERYBODY'S): 4 December 1965: No. 4 - 22 weeks
UK Compilation LP ROCK 'N' ROLLING STONES: 13 October 1972: No. 41 - 1 week

Covering Chuck Berry tunes was a happy pastime both in the studio and live but the decision to actually record them for release was brave, since they would always be compared to the master's original. The Stones, however, were progressing to their own inimitable style and, when covering Chuck Berry songs, the rhythm was usually the key to the success of the copy. The Stones describe it as "shuffle and eighths" as opposed to the more usual eight to the bar. *Talkin' 'Bout You* is played mid-tempo in a slow competent manner. It is not a classic Berry cover but is worthwhile due to its extempore nature.

264. **I'M FREE** (Jagger, Richard) 2.24
6 September 1965: Place: RCA Studios, Hollywood, USA.
Played Live: 1969, 2006
Rolling Stones with James Alexander.
Producer: Andrew Oldham.
Engineer: Dave Hassinger.
UK LP OUT OF OUR HEADS: 24 September 1965: No. 2 - 24 weeks
USA B-side Get Off My Cloud: 24 September 1965
USA LP DECEMBER'S CHILDREN (AND EVERYBODY'S): 4 December 1965: No. 4 - 22 weeks
USA Compilation LP THE ROLLING STONES - PROMOTIONAL ALBUM: October 1969
USA Compilation LP MORE HOT ROCKS (BIG HITS & FAZED COOKIES): 1 December 1972: No. 9 - 12 weeks
UK & USA LP THE ROLLING STONES SINGLES COLLECTION - THE LONDON YEARS: 15 August 1989
USA Compilation Promo CD THE ROLLING STONES REMASTERED: 30 May 2002
USA Compilation CD MORE HOT ROCKS (BIG HITS & FAZED COOKIES): 3 September 2002

UK & USA e-Single; 21 November 2006
UK Compilation CD ROLLED GOLD +: 12 November 2007: No. 26 - 12 weeks

It was noticeable that the musical style was beginning to shift from the r 'n' b of the early 'sixties to a rock foundation; *I'm Free* typifies this approach. It is predictive of the recordings to follow and also has distinct Beatle touches. A shimmering vibrato guitar riff glides through the song and percussion is supported by James W Alexander on tambourine later of Sam Cooke, Rufus Thomas and Bar-Kays fame. He was not on board the private plane that crashed and killed in 1967 his band colleagues in the Bar-Kays as well as Otis Redding. *I'm Free* is an optimistic number full of Jaggeresque teachings with a sexual undertone. It typified the impending freedom of the 'sixties. It was a stage favourite and was later performed at the 1969 Hyde Park concert. Chris Farlowe covered the song in 1966 and a British band The Soup Dragons had a No.5 hit with it in 1990. In 2006 a number of remixes appeared and were released for digital download. The Fatboy Slim version was featured in a television advertisement for a Chase credit card, although the company originally wanted DJ Shadow to do the re-mix but preferred Fatboy Slim's version. The original was used in a Renault advert the following year.

265. I'M FREE (HOT CHIP REMIX) (Jagger, Richard) 3.03
6 September 1965; 2006: Place: RCA Studios, Hollywood, USA; Various Studios.
Rolling Stones with James Alexander.
Producer: Andrew Oldham.
Engineer: Dave Hassinger.
Re-Mixed 2006: Hot Chip
UK & USA e-Single Track I'm Free: 21 November 2006

266. I'M FREE (MOBY REMIX) (Jagger, Richard) 3.43
6 September 1965; 2006: Place: RCA Studios, Hollywood, USA; Various Studios.
Rolling Stones with James Alexander.
Producer: Andrew Oldham.
Engineer: Dave Hassinger.
Re-Mixed 2006: Moby
UK & USA e-Single Track I'm Free: 21 November 2006

267. I'M FREE (THE POSTAL SERVICE REMIX) (Jagger, Richard) 2.27
6 September 1965; 2006: Place: RCA Studios, Hollywood, USA; Various Studios.
Rolling Stones with James Alexander.
Producer: Andrew Oldham.
Engineer: Dave Hassinger.
Re-Mixed 2006: The Postal Service
UK & USA e-Single Track I'm Free: 21 November 2006

268. I'M FREE (DJ SHADOW REMIX) (Jagger, Richard) 4.11
6 September 1965; 2006: Place: RCA Studios, Hollywood, USA; Various Studios.
Rolling Stones with James Alexander.
Producer: Andrew Oldham.
Engineer: Dave Hassinger.
Re-Mixed 2006: DJ Shadow
UK & USA e-Single Track I'm Free: 21 November 2006

269. I'M FREE (FATBOY SLIM REMIX) (Jagger, Richard) 3.58
6 September 1965; 2006: Place: RCA Studios, Hollywood, USA; Norman Cook Studio, Hove, Brighton, England.
Rolling Stones with James Alexander.
Producer: Andrew Oldham.
Engineer: Dave Hassinger.
Re-Mixed 2006: Fatboy Slim
UK & USA e-Single Track I'm Free: 21 November 2006

270. LOOKING TIRED (Jagger, Richard) 2.15
6 September, 8-10 December 1965: Place: RCA Studios, Hollywood, USA.
Producer: Andrew Oldham assisted by Jack Nitzsche.
Engineer: Dave Hassinger.
Bootleg only.

Looking Tired (probably a description of their current state of minds) was originally set for inclusion on an album titled COULD YOU WALK ON THE WATER? It is a mid-tempo rock song, featuring nimble acoustic guitar and a casually played piano. It avoided official release and is much sought after, more for its rarity appeal, rather than the musical quality. The sessions were used to finalise the *Get Off My Cloud* mix and recording and also tracks for the upcoming US DECEMBER'S CHILDREN album.

271. THE SINGER NOT THE SONG (Jagger, Richard) 2.23
6 September 1965: Place: RCA Studios, Hollywood, USA.
Producer: Andrew Oldham.
Engineer: Dave Hassinger.
UK B-side Get Off My Cloud: 22 October 1965
USA LP DECEMBER'S CHILDREN (AND EVERYBODY'S): 4 December 1965: No 4 - 22 weeks
UK Compilation LP NO STONE UNTURNED: 5 October 1973
German Compilation LP THE REST OF THE BEST: December 1983
UK & USA LP THE ROLLING STONES SINGLES COLLECTION - THE LONDON YEARS: 15 August 1989
UK CD box set THE ROLLING STONES SINGLES - 1965 - 1967: 12 July 2004
USA CD box set THE ROLLING STONES SINGLES - 1965 - 1967: 27 July 2004

An unremarkable track featuring acoustic guitars which duet in an amateurish fashion. The vocals lack the plush harmonies of their chart-topping counterparts, The Beatles, and the track sounds particularly off-key. This type of sound produced embarrassing smiles and was a temporary let-down for Andrew Oldham's creativity. It should have remained a studio out-take and it is unfortunate such lightweight material should be used as a single flip-side, though this was the prerogative tendency of the record company.

The British were lucky they did not have to contend with the American DECEMBER'S CHILDREN album, which was a compiler's nightmare. To fill it out, it even included two live tracks from the UK EP. Once the recordings were finished the exhausting schedule took them back to the UK for a pre-arranged date in Douglas, Isle Of Man. Then the tour went abroad to West Germany (this was when Anita Pallenberg joined the entourage after befriending Brian Jones in Munich) for just short of a week before ending in Vienna, Austria. This helped the Stones get their act together for a two-and-a-bit weeks of solid UK touring in late September and October, with The Spencer Davis Group and the Moody Blues supporting.

Mainly because touring was not really Andrew Oldham's "bag", Tito Burns (musician, agent and manager) was appointed their booking agent in Europe and he was impressed that the band were always on time and professional. Marianne Faithfull was asked to join the Stones for their Bristol Colston Hall gig on 26 September and, after a night chilling with the group, she found herself talking about poetry and books with Mick - the start of their relationship.

On the same tour, Tom Keylock took up his driving, minding and general fixer duties. Known as "Mr Get-It-Together", he had previously done similar work for film stars such as Shirley MacLaine. Keylock's training and World War II action with the Royal Army Service Corps would be useful dealing with the fans and ultimately he was a genuine, loyal guy. He found the Stones world different from his previous career.

272. CRY TO ME (Russell) 2.46
22 October 1965: Place: Ready, Steady, Go! TV Studio, Wembley, London, England.
Producer: Michael Lindsay-Hogg.
Bootleg only.

273. SHE SAID YEAH (Christy, Jackson) 2.13
22 October 1965: Place: Ready, Steady, Go! TV Studio, Wembley, London, England.
Producer: Michael Lindsay-Hogg.
Bootleg only.

274. GET OFF MY CLOUD (Jagger, Richard) 2.29
22 October 1965: Place: Ready, Steady, Go! TV Studio, Wembley, London, England.
Producer: Michael Lindsay-Hogg.
Bootleg only.

With *Satisfaction* fading in the UK charts and *Get Off My Cloud* already released in the States and at No. 1, another UK chart-topper No. 1 looked guaranteed. It certainly did no harm to promote the single on Ready, Steady, Go! on its day of release.

275. AS TEARS GO BY (Jagger, Richard, Oldham) 2.46
26 October 1965: Place: IBC Studios, London, England.
Played Live: 2005, 2006
Producer: Andrew Oldham.
Engineer: Glyn Johns.
Orchestra: Mike Leander. Arrangement: Keith Richard.
USA LP DECEMBER'S CHILDREN (AND EVERYBODY'S): 4 December 1965: No. 4 - 22 weeks
USA Single: 18 December 1965: No. 6 - 6 weeks
UK B-side 19th Nervous Breakdown: 4 February 1966
USA Compilation LP BIG HITS (HIGH TIDE AND GREEN GRASS): 1 April 1966: No. 3 - 35 weeks
UK Compilation LP BIG HITS (HIGH TIDE AND GREEN GRASS): 4 November 1966: No. 4 - 43 weeks
UK Compilation LP STONE AGE: 6 March 1971: No. 4 - 7 weeks
USA LP THE ROLLING STONES HOT ROCKS 1964-1971: 11 January 1972: No. 4 - 30 weeks
UK Compilation LP ROLLED GOLD: 14 November 1975: No. 7 - 50 weeks
UK Compilation LP GET STONED - 30 GREATEST HITS, 30 ORIGINAL TRACKS: 21 October 1977: No. 13 - 15 weeks
German Compilation LP THE REST OF THE BEST: December 1983
UK & USA LP THE ROLLING STONES SINGLES COLLECTION - THE LONDON YEARS: 15 August 1989
UK CD box set THE ROLLING STONES SINGLES - 1965 - 1967: 12 July 2004

USA CD box set THE ROLLING STONES SINGLES - 1965 - 1967: 27 July 2004
UK Compilation CD ROLLED GOLD +: 12 November 2007: No. 26 - 12 weeks

This is the first Jagger, Richard composition which also credited Andrew Oldham as a songwriter. It tends to confirm that the track, written in 1964, was intended as little more than a money-maker for Marianne Faithfull, who reached No. 9 in the UK with it in August 1964. Possibly it surprised not only Andrew Oldham but also Jagger, Richard by its success (not to mention Lionel Bart, Miss Faithfull's previous musical mentor). Originally recorded in July 1964 as a demo, it was re-recorded for a future single release in America, where the soft ballad was in mode. The lyrics were sentimental and soporific but were a brave attempt by Mick Jagger to convey a female viewpoint. A morose tale of watching children play doing things we all used to do.

In a 1995 interview with Jann Wenner, Mick Jagger refers to the fact that he was reading poems by Russian romantic writer Alexander Pushkin at the time. The song was a unique reminder of the softer Stones approach and, musically, was a milestone in their then short songwriting career. It was needed for inclusion on the DECEMBER'S CHILDREN album and would be released as a US single a week before Christmas. In Britain, The Stones were concerned that the release of such a commercial ballad would have British critics saying it was yet another Beatle imitation (particularly of the song *Yesterday*). Mick played almost a solo role in the song, backed only by Keith on guitar (he was also credited with the arrangements) and the Mike Leander Orchestra.

Although *As Tears Go By* had been written a year earlier, the arrangement of *Yesterday*, released on the HELP! Album, was very similar, Paul McCartney being the only artist featured on the song, accompanied by a string quartet. *Yesterday* had a low-key release in Britain, not even featuring on the HELP! Movie soundtrack, but in the United States it was released as a single in October 1965 and went to No. 1. In the UK, *As Tears Go By* was released as a low-key single B-side and did not reach the dizzy heights of *Yesterday* in the States, nevertheless notching an impressive No. 6. Just to extend the integral connection between the two songs, Marianne Faithfull released a version of *Yesterday* in November 1965.

276. SHE SAID YEAH (Jackson, Christy) 1.41
11 November 1965: Place: Hullabaloo TV, NBC Studios, New York, USA.
Producer: Steve Binder
USA Video Hullabaloo 5-8: 26 March 1996
e-Single Track She Said Yeah: 9 August 2010

The Rolling Stones set off with much increased ambivalence and confidence to again darken the doors of the United States for their fourth and most extensive so far North American tour. For most of the trip they were supported by Patti Labelle and the Blue Belles and The Rockin' Ramrods, the latter being one of Boston's premier garage rock bands. Brian Jones must have felt a twinge of memory for his own Cheltenham Ramrods. The Rockin' Ramrods, meanwhile, must not be confused with The Ramrods, from Connecticut, who had a 1961 UK and USA hit with *Riders In The Sky*.

Patti Labelle was a feisty soul singer who had minor chart success through the 1960s before achieving her biggest hit with *Lady Marmalade* in 1975. The Blue Belles consisted of Nona Hendryx and Sarah Dash, who later performed on STEEL WHEELS, Ronnie Wood's LIVE AT THE RITZ and Keith Richards' TALK IS CHEAP, LIVE AT THE HOLLYWOOD PALLADIUM and MAIN OFFENDER solo albums. Part way through the tour, the Stones performed on the new NBC Hullabaloo television variety programme, the tracks were (as yet) an unreleased playback of *She Said Yeah* and the recent single *Get Off My Cloud* with live vocals. A compendium volume of songs was released on video, featuring both tracks, in 1996.

The tour was a financial success, its only downer being an incident near the end of the tour, in Sacramento, California, when Keith Richards experienced a massive on-stage electric shock. "I woke up in the hospital an hour later," Richards recalled. "The doctor said [electrocution victims] come around or they don't." His trademark, rubber-souled, Hush Puppy shoes probably saved him. The whole dramatic episode was recorded on Super 8 film and sold in 2006 for $20,000.

It is rumoured that the after-tour celebrations included Keith Richards' and Brian Jones' first acid trips after they were led on by LA socialites' swinging parties. They took their girlfriends Linda Keith and Anita Pallenberg (to be) respectfully (no pun intended). After Sacramento and their last concerts in San Diego the Stones stayed in Los Angeles, where another recording revolution was about to commence in sessions for what would become the AFTERMATH album - their first to take full advantage of the stereo recording facility.

277. 19TH NERVOUS BREAKDOWN (Jagger, Richard) 3.57
8 December 1965: Place: RCA Studios, Hollywood, USA.
Played Live: 1966, 1967, 1997, 1998, 2005
Producer: Andrew Oldham assisted by Jack Nitzsche.
Engineer: Dave Hassinger.
UK Single: 4 February 1966: No. 2 - 8 weeks
USA Single: 11 February 1966: No. 2 - 9 weeks
USA Compilation LP BIG HITS (HIGH TIDE AND GREEN GRASS): 1 April 1966: No. 3 - 35 weeks
UK Compilation LP BIG HITS (HIGH TIDE AND GREEN GRASS): 4 November 1966: No. 4 - 43 weeks
USA LP THE ROLLING STONES HOT ROCKS 1964-1971: 11 January 1972: No. 4 - 30 weeks
UK Compilation LP ROCK 'N' ROLLING STONES: 13 October 1972: No. 41 - 1 week
UK Compilation LP ROLLED GOLD: 14 November 1975: No. 7 - 50 weeks
UK Compilation LP GET STONED - 30 GREATEST HITS, 30 ORIGINAL TRACKS: 21 October 1977: No. 13 - 15 weeks
German Compilation LP THE REST OF THE BEST: December 1983
UK & USA LP THE ROLLING STONES SINGLES COLLECTION - THE LONDON YEARS: 15 August 1989
UK CD LP FORTY LICKS: 30 September 2002: No. 2 - 45 weeks
USA CD LP FORTY LICKS: 1 October 2002: No. 2 - 50 weeks
UK CD box set THE ROLLING STONES SINGLES - 1965 - 1967: 12 July 2004
USA CD box set THE ROLLING STONES SINGLES - 1965 - 1967: 27 July 2004
UK Compilation CD ROLLED GOLD +: 12 November 2007: No. 26 - 12 weeks

The lengthy American tour in the autumn of 1965 was often described by Mick Jagger in jest as his "19th nervous breakdown", a phrase immediately appropriated by the band and put forward as a possible song title, the music being almost incidental. It did, however, display the anarchy of previous singles, continuing the heavy rock sound with a and slightly erratic pace. Keith Richards thought some of it was inspired by The Everly Brothers. *19th Nervous Breakdown* was certainly not as instantaneous or appealing as *Satisfaction* or *Get Off My Cloud*, though the alliteration in the title and chorus helped it to roll off the tongue. It focused so much on the band's thematic pills/mental breakdown saga, that Chrissie Shrimpton neurotically believed it was written about her.

Andrew Oldham told NME's Keith Altham in February 1966 that the song would be a good one to request for the BBC radio's light programme Housewife's Choice! References to drugs are surreptitiously included, continuing the theme of the album cut *Mother's Little Helper*. The vocals were, as usual, placed very much in the background by Andrew Oldham's arrangement. The public and the record company might, therefore, have missed the sole reference to "a teenager's first trip". Glyn Johns was given the chance to re-mix the track and to bring forward the vocals, but the band decided not to release it. Another earlier version has a more pronounced rhythm guitar track and the fuzz tone lead played by Keith is buried (* a - 4.03). A small amount of the vocal arrangement is different with added "heys". The song is famous for Bill Wyman's "dive bomb" bass lines at the end which he put together rather haphazardly but to great effect on his semi-acoustic Framus instrument. He describes it dismissively as a "Bo Diddley thing". Certainly you can hear strains of *Diddley Daddy* in Brian Jones' rhythm guitar.

In Britain, the single only managed a No. 2 position, breaking the run of five successive No 1s. The Beatles were at that time on their ninth consecutive British No 1 and so the battle for chart record supremacy was lost for ever. An out-take with a different vocal arrangement and backing track is available but is less disciplined than the released cut. There is also an unreleased stereo mix version. Pete Townshend was so impressed with the song that it inspired him to write *Substitute*.

278. MOTHER'S LITTLE HELPER (Jagger, Richard) 2.45
8-10 December 1965: Place: RCA Studios, Hollywood, USA.
Played Live: 1966
Producer: Andrew Oldham assisted by Jack Nitzsche.
Engineer: Dave Hassinger.
UK LP AFTERMATH: 15 April 1966: No. 1 - 28 weeks
USA Single: 2 July 1966: No. 8 - 8 weeks
USA Compilation LP FLOWERS: 15 July 1967: No. 3 - 18 weeks
UK Compilation LP THROUGH THE PAST DARKLY (BIG HITS VOL 2): 12 September 1969: No. 2 - 37 weeks
USA Compilation LP THROUGH THE PAST DARKLY (BIG HITS VOL 2): 13 September 1969: No. 2 - 16 weeks
USA LP THE ROLLING STONES HOT ROCKS 1964-1971: 11 January 1972: No. 4 - 30 weeks
UK Compilation LP GET STONED - 30 GREATEST HITS, 30 ORIGINAL TRACKS: 21 October 1977: No. 13 - 15 weeks
UK & USA LP THE ROLLING STONES SINGLES COLLECTION - THE LONDON YEARS: 15 August 1989
UK CD LP FORTY LICKS: 30 September 2002: No. 2 - 45 weeks
USA CD LP FORTY LICKS: 1 October 2002: No. 2 - 50 weeks
UK CD box set THE ROLLING STONES SINGLES - 1965 - 1967: 12 July 2004
USA CD box set THE ROLLING STONES SINGLES - 1965 - 1967: 27 July 2004
UK Compilation CD ROLLED GOLD +: 12 November 2007: No. 26 - 12 weeks

"What a drag it is getting old", as the song goes. Brian Jones was determined to refute this by exploring different musical sounds and this track featured the Indian sitar. It was not merely coincidental that The Beatles had just released RUBBER SOUL (recorded mid-October and early November) on 3 December 1965. *Norwegian Wood* was the first time the Indian instrument had been used on a popular record. *Mother's Little Helper* is an experimental song and prepares the way for future leanings of this kind - it has a dark, menacing quality, with Bill Wyman's bass warning of more sullen things to come. Brian's sitar adds a warmer, more optimistic feel. Mick Jagger's lyrical enunciation of housewives' boredom and depression which leads to popping yellow pills (valium or diazepam), was perhaps condescending. Feminists took a stronger line, calling it male chauvinism so the human tones of sympathy and understanding were missed! While included on the UK AFTERMATH album, *Mother's Little Helper* was not released as a single in the States until six months later, reaching No. 8 and proving a worthy follow-up to *Paint It Black*. The musical similarity must have also been a contributory factor. An out-take of the backing track is available and has a 1-2-3 countdown at the start. In 2002, when researching the source tapes for the re-released and re-mastered ABKCO catalogue, it transpired that the final cut was recorded on a tape machine at a slightly faster speed, resulting in a slow master when played back on equipment running at the correct speed. This mistake was corrected for the 2002 re-release.

279. DONCHA BOTHER ME (Jagger, Richard) 2.41
AKA: Don't Ya Follow Me
8-10 December 1965: Place: RCA Studios, Hollywood, USA.
Played Live: 1966
Producer: Andrew Oldham assisted by Jack Nitzsche.
Engineer: Dave Hassinger.
UK LP AFTERMATH: 15 April 1966: No. 1 - 28 weeks
USA LP AFTERMATH: 2 July 1966: No. 2 - 26 weeks

Back to the British recording roots of R 'n' B, *Doncha Bother Me* is played at a jaunty pace and includes Brian Jones' bottleneck guitar and Ian Stewart on piano with harmonica incorporated after a few verses. Mick Jagger's lyrics are dismissive: "I'm still waiting here for a single idea in your clothes and your hair . . . I wore it last year . . . don't you follow me no more." The result is a strange dichotomy of blues tinged with country leanings. There was no such unnecessary complication on the next track.

280. GOIN' HOME (Jagger, Richard) 11.14
8-10 December 1965: Place: RCA Studios, Hollywood, USA.
Played Live: 1967
Producer: Andrew Oldham assisted by Jack Nitzsche.
Engineer: Dave Hassinger.
UK LP AFTERMATH: 15 April 1966: No. 1 - 28 weeks
USA LP AFTERMATH: 2 July 1966: No. 2 - 26 weeks

The first track to reach rock marathon status, it lasted a whopping 11 minutes and 45 seconds - almost by accident. *Goin' Home* should have been a standard three-and-a-half minute song about returning from LA to London to see your girlfriend but Mick Jagger started grooving and so it expanded. Dave Hassinger was all for stopping the tape but Andrew Oldham sensed what might be happening and encouraged the Stones to improvise further. *Going Home* becomes a glorious feel-driven "open plan" blues jam which builds up incessantly in the style of John Lee Hooker. It was a precursor to what would be achieved with *Midnight Rambler* and reminiscent of early live epics like *Hey Crawdaddy*.

Mick leads the song's structure, thrusting the band forward and simmering them down as he feels appropriate against the background of Bill Wyman's hard bass. The whole band responds to Mick's rock jargon, reflecting their anticipation at going home following almost two months of American touring. Being on the road provided a vehicle for writing songs and, to immediately go into the studio, ensured the band were buzzing. Just before the climax of *Goin' Home*, Mick sits back for a few seconds and hums evocatively along to the melody before striking hard until the song has to relinquish. Mick also added a distant harmonica, the vibrato guitar being played entirely by Keith Richards, with Ian Stewart on piano and Charlie Watts feathering the bass drum jazz style with brushes.

The result swept aside the standard album cut format and was quite innovative. The fact that the band had managed to maintain interest throughout was significant and also characteristic of their live performance. Andrew Oldham had just witnessed a standout event where the Stones had broken the sound barrier with ease and though many fans would appreciate to hear it live, it was only featured on the March/April European tour in 1967.

On hearing *Goin' Home* for the first time, Love guitarist Johnny Echols, reckoned the number was similar in style to their own *Revelation* (aka John Lee Hooker). Echols recalled: "They would come into the Whisky and see us. They came back three times in a row when we were doing *Revelation*. Mick and Keith came in together and they sat in the back in the balcony just by themselves. When we heard (*Going Home*) we knew it was just a rip off because they just rushed in and did it." Dave Hassinger was engineer for both recordings. Love's version was recorded a few months earlier at the same studios.

281. TAKE IT OR LEAVE IT (Jagger, Richard) 2.47
8-10 December 1965: Place: RCA Studios, Hollywood, USA.
Rolling Stones with Jack Nitzsche.
Producer: Andrew Oldham assisted by Jack Nitzsche.
Engineer: Dave Hassinger.
UK LP AFTERMATH: 15 April 1966: No. 1 - 28 weeks
USA Compilation LP FLOWERS: 15 July 1967: No. 3 - 18 weeks
UK LP SLOW ROLLERS: 9 November 1981

A schmaltzy, embarrassing song, written with little imagination, it epitomized the current direction Andrew Oldham was keen to follow. He seemed determined to emphasise the production and also condone the terrible vocal harmony arrangements. The track was later released in America on the compilation album FLOWERS in June 1967 and, with a slower orchestral brass band colliery-type arrangement, it wound up on the horrible THE ARANBEE POP SYMPHONY ORCHESTRA album, under the direction of Keith Richard, released on Andrew Oldham's Immediate label in 1966. The Searchers had a No. 31 hit with the song in March 1966. At the time of recording, the British New Musical Express announced the filming of *Back, Behind And In Front*, another film project destined to commence in spring 1966 and said to feature songs cut at these sessions.

282. THINK (Jagger, Richard) 3.09
8-10 December 1965: Place: RCA Studios, Hollywood, USA.
Producer: Andrew Oldham assisted by Jack Nitzsche.
Engineer: Dave Hassinger.
UK LP AFTERMATH: 15 April 1966: No. 1 - 28 weeks
USA LP AFTERMATH: 2 July 1966: No. 2 - 26 weeks

Keith Richards leads the attack on this mediocre rocker. There are a number of different guitar parts, fuzz tone effects used to emulate background brass "stabs" over a clean rhythm sound. The song lacks the punch of other tracks with this technique, notably some of the single releases. This is despite some extensive lyrics, over four verses, such as: "I'm giving you a piece of my mind" and "You're getting much too old before your time". Chris Farlowe, a British R 'n' B performer, thought the song was sufficiently good to allow Jagger, Richards and Oldham to produce a version for him. It was released as a single and became a moderate UK hit for a newcomer when it charted at No. 37 in February 1966.

283. RIDE ON BABY (Jagger, Richard) 2.53
8-10 December 1965: Place: RCA Studios, Hollywood, USA.
Producer: Andrew Oldham assisted by Jack Nitzsche.
Engineer: Dave Hassinger.
USA Compilation LP FLOWERS: 15 July 1967: No. 3 - 18 weeks
German Compilation LP THE REST OF THE BEST: December 1983

Another out-take type of track, not available anywhere else, which managed to find its way onto the FLOWERS compilation album. Brian Jones experimented with a new instrument, the marimba, which gave the song a soft texture disguising the somewhat brash lyrics - "by the time you're 30 you'll look 65." Ian Stewart is on piano and bongo-style drums are tapped in the background, emphasising the newly-acquired 1960s nuance. A studio run-through of *Ride On Baby* is available on bootleg. The song was also released as a single by Chris Farlowe, so completing three successive Jagger, Richard covers. Mick was credited with the production.

284. SITTIN' ON A FENCE (Jagger, Richard) 3.02
8-10 December 1965: Place: RCA Studios, Hollywood, USA.
Producer: Andrew Oldham assisted by Jack Nitzsche.
Engineer: Dave Hassinger.
USA Compilation LP FLOWERS: 15 July 1967: No. 3 - 18 weeks
UK Compilation LP THROUGH THE PAST DARKLY (BIG HITS VOL 2): 12 September 1969: No. 2 - 37 weeks

USA Compilation LP MORE HOT ROCKS (BIG HITS & FAZED COOKIES): 1 December 1972: No. 9 - 12 weeks
UK LP SLOW ROLLERS: 9 November 1981
German Compilation LP THE REST OF THE BEST: December 1983
USA Compilation CD MORE HOT ROCKS (BIG HITS & FAZED COOKIES): 3 September 2002

In early December their next USA album DECEMBER'S CHILDREN was released to capitalise on the tour. It was a strange blend of tracks, including *You Better Move On* (recorded in 1963), two tracks from the UK live EP and a mixture of singles and B sides. This track is also available on the American compilation album FLOWERS. The prominent instruments are a classical sounding English "country garden" guitar and the background sound of Brian Jones' harpsichord. The song was written by Mick Jagger and Keith Richards while on the Scandinavian section of their spring 1965 tour. A British duo, Twice As Much, copied the same classical style and popularised the song in the British charts by reaching No. 25. Andrew Oldham was the producer and 'Little Jim' (Jimmy Page) played guitar.

285. SAD DAY (Jagger, Richard) 3.02
AKA: Sad Ol' Day
8-10 December 1965: Place: RCA Studios, Hollywood, USA.
Rolling Stones with Jack Nitzsche.
Producer: Andrew Oldham assisted by Jack Nitzsche.
Engineer: Dave Hassinger.
USA B-side 19th Nervous Breakdown: 11 February 1966
UK Single: 29 April 1973
UK Compilation LP NO STONE UNTURNED: 5 October 1973
German Compilation LP THE REST OF THE BEST: December 1983
UK & USA LP THE ROLLING STONES SINGLES COLLECTION - THE LONDON YEARS: 15 August 1989
UK CD box set THE ROLLING STONES SINGLES - 1965 - 1967: 12 July 2004
USA CD box set THE ROLLING STONES SINGLES - 1965 - 1967: 27 July 2004

Sad Day, a rocked-up ballad, was recorded and released as the flip-side for the next American single. It was overlooked by Decca, despite being lined up for inclusion on the COULD YOU WALK ON THE WATER? album. Seven years later it was eventually released on an inexplicable quick Decca, cash-in-hand, UK single in 1973. Mick Jagger seemed more at home with *Sad Day* than some of the more arranged sounds of *Ride On Baby* and *Sittin' On A Fence*. He was able to shout and cajole the lyrics and the band seemed happy to return to the more simple and familiar rock approach, Jack Nitzsche playing a sinister piano line or two. Finally the band split and went their separate ways for the Christmas break.

286. (I CAN'T GET NO) SATISFACTION (Jagger, Richard) 2.36
13 February 1966: Place: Ed Sullivan TV Show, CBS Studio 50, New York, USA.
USA Video The Very Best Of The Ed Sullivan Show: Volume One: April 1992
USA Video The History Of Rock 'n' Roll: Volume Three: June 1995
USA Compilation DVD Ed Sullivan's Rock 'n' Roll Revolution: 23 September 2003
USA DVD 4 Ed Sullivan Shows Starring The Rolling Stones: 4 October 2011
USA DVD 6 Ed Sullivan Shows Starring The Rolling Stones: 1 November 2011

287. AS TEARS GO BY (Jagger, Richard, Oldham) 2.18
13 February 1966: Place: Ed Sullivan TV Show, CBS Studio 50, New York, USA.
USA DVD 4 Ed Sullivan Shows Starring The Rolling Stones: 4 October 2011
USA DVD 6 Ed Sullivan Shows Starring The Rolling Stones: 1 November 2011

288. 19TH NERVOUS BREAKDOWN (Jagger, Richard) 4.11
13 February 1966: Place: Ed Sullivan TV Show, CBS Studio 50, New York, USA.
USA DVD 4 Ed Sullivan Shows Starring The Rolling Stones: 4 October 2011
USA DVD 6 Ed Sullivan Shows Starring The Rolling Stones: 1 November 2011

The Stones began 1966 with The New Year Starts Here, a Ready, Steady, Go! TV special also featuring a number of other bands playing out 1965 and playing in 1966. January was a month of comparative rest, purchasing of expensive homes and general shopping sprees. On 14 January, British musical newspaper New Musical Express hailed the announcement of an EP featuring *As Tears Go By* and also the release of the next album COULD YOU WALK ON THE WATER? (both were subsequently aborted).

The proposed album was said to include *19th Nervous Breakdown, Sad Day, Take It Or Leave It, Think, Looking Tired, Mother's Little Helper, Goin' Home, Sittin' On A Fence, Doncha Bother Me* and *Ride On Baby*, which were the tracks recorded in December 1965. A ten-page booklet of photos was prepared, the artwork for the album sleeve cover was also ready and was said to feature the group about to walk on water. The shots were taken at Lakeside, Beverly Hills, California, by Guy Webster. Release was planned for March 1966 but, when the product was presented to Decca, they predictably panicked at the risqué album title and the cover sleeve. The Stones became bored and left "the aftermath" to the record company. The album was, therefore, never released. The booklet of photos, however, did appear in April 1966 on the first official compilation album HIGH TIDE AND GREEN GRASS (BIG HITS) which featured their singles to date. The band then quickly flew to the States to promote the new single *19th Nervous Breakdown* plus their current Top Ten American single, *As Tears Go By* - for good measure *Satisfaction* was also included. The source of promotion was once again the Ed Sullivan TV show for which they received $5,000. Just Mick Jagger and Keith Richards don smart jackets to sit down and perform *As Tears Go By*, while *19th Nervous Breakdown* has Bill Wyman on stage left next to Brian Jones. Meanwhile, the Stones' TV performances were generating furore throughout America. The ecstatic scenes outside the television studios were unique and the actual recordings are, as usual, drowned by screams. The film marks the first time the Stones had been recorded in colour and some footage can be seen in the video compilation *25 X 5: The Continuing Adventures Of The Rolling Stones*, as in the first song performed *Satisfaction*. It was not released fully but appeared in snatches until the Ed Sullivan DVD was compiled in 2003 by David Solt. Mick Jagger and Keith Richards then simmer things down with *As Tears Go By*, which uses the single's orchestral back track, then the pace quickens as they launch into *19th Nervous Breakdown*, the American public's first taste of the band's just released new single. After this sojourn in New York, they flew Down Under via Los Angeles to undertake a nine-date tour of Australia and New Zealand.

289. OUT OF TIME (Jagger, Richard) 5.37
6-9 March 1966: Place: RCA Studios, Hollywood, USA.
Rolling Stones with Jack Nitzsche.
Producer: Andrew Oldham.
Engineer: Dave Hassinger.
UK LP AFTERMATH: 15 April 1966: No. 1 - 28 weeks
USA Compilation LP FLOWERS: 15 July 1967: No. 3 - 18 weeks
UK Compilation LP MILESTONES: 18 February 1972: No. 14 - 8 weeks
USA Compilation LP MORE HOT ROCKS (BIG HITS & FAZED COOKIES): 1 December 1972: No. 9 - 12 weeks
UK Compilation LP ROLLED GOLD: 14 November 1975: No. 7 - 50 weeks
UK & USA LP THE ROLLING STONES SINGLES COLLECTION - THE LONDON YEARS: 15 August 1989
USA Compilation CD MORE HOT ROCKS (BIG HITS & FAZED COOKIES): 3 September 2002
UK Compilation CD ROLLED GOLD +: 12 November 2007: No. 26 - 12 weeks

The return trip from Australia and New Zealand went via Fiji then back to Los Angeles. This gave the Stones the opportunity to enter the studio in March 1966 to complete the AFTERMATH sessions. Dave Hassinger and Jack Nitzsche again assisted with production, the latter contributing piano on *Out Of Time*, supporting Ian Stewart on organ. Mick Jagger later agreed that he thought that this was one of the better tracks available on the UK edition of the AFTERMATH album.
Brian Jones was again featured on the marimba, an African instrument whose name is translated as the "voice of wood" and played like a xylophone. Its sound is unique due to the wooden keys mounted above resonators. Brian's experimentation and virtuosity on such instruments continued the rock allegiance with RUBBER SOUL-period Beatles, the Liverpool band about to continue their innovative approach on their forthcoming REVOLVER album.
The Beatles were fully aware of the similarity and, in one publicity photo, John Lennon and George Harrison held high the covers of the AFTERMATH album and *19th Nervous Breakdown* single, proclaiming that they were attempting to come up with a couple of really original ideas!
Subtle rhythm changes and some pleasant, acoustic-sounding guitars are the keys to the song. Timed at more than five minutes, the track is over the standard length and as such is quite creditable, although the American releases on FLOWERS and MORE HOT ROCKS (* a - 3.42) were edited by more than a minute. The backing track exists as an out-take without the lead vocal (* b -4.58).

290. LADY JANE (Jagger, Richard) 3.08
6-9 March 1966: Place: RCA Studios, Hollywood, USA.
Played Live: 1966, 1967
Rolling Stones with Jack Nitzsche.
Producer: Andrew Oldham.
Engineer: Dave Hassinger.
UK LP AFTERMATH: 15 April 1966: No. 1 - 28 weeks
USA LP AFTERMATH: 2 July 1966: No. 2 - 26 weeks
USA B-side: Mother's Little Helper: 2 July 1966
UK Compilation LP BIG HITS (HIGH TIDE AND GREEN GRASS): 4 November 1966: No. 4 - 43 weeks
USA Compilation LP FLOWERS: 15 July 1967: No. 3 - 18 weeks
USA Compilation LP MORE HOT ROCKS (BIG HITS & FAZED COOKIES): 1 December 1972: No. 9 - 12 weeks
UK Compilation LP ROLLED GOLD: 14 November 1975: No. 7 - 50 weeks
UK Compilation LP GET STONED - 30 GREATEST HITS, 30 ORIGINAL TRACKS: 21 October 1977: No. 13 - 15 weeks
UK LP SLOW ROLLERS: 9 November 1981
UK & USA LP THE ROLLING STONES SINGLES COLLECTION - THE LONDON YEARS: 15 August 1989
USA Compilation CD MORE HOT ROCKS (BIG HITS & FAZED COOKIES): 3 September 2002
UK CD box set THE ROLLING STONES SINGLES - 1965 - 1967: 12 July 2004
USA CD box set THE ROLLING STONES SINGLES - 1965 - 1967: 27 July 2004
UK Compilation CD ROLLED GOLD +: 12 November 2007: No. 26 - 12 weeks

A tender, typically English ballad, which compromised Mick Jagger's stance on women. The publicity statements played on the Elizabethan feel to the record and claimed it was based on a letter written by Henry VIII to Jane Seymour, proclaiming his love for her and forecasting the end of his present wife by decapitation. Other much more plausible reasons for the song are Mick Jagger's flirtatious dealings with such British socialites as Jane Ormsby-Gore.
The contribution by Brian Jones was again significant, particularly after American folk singer Richard Farina had introduced him to the dulcimer. Farina had worked with Carolyn Hester (his first wife), Bob Dylan and Mimi Baez (his second wife and Joan Baez's sister) - Richard and Mimi's performance with dulcimer and Arabic drum at the 1965 Newport Folk Festival was a musical highlight. Tragically, Richard died in April 1966 in a motorcycle accident.
Brian's work was innovative once again and confirmed Andrew Oldham's belief that the band's mid-60s musical success was due to his instrumental elaboration. The Elizabethan feel is extended with Jack Nitzsche on harpsichord. The song was covered by Merseyside artist David Garrick in June 1966 and achieved a No. 28 position. In the rest of Europe, it was even more successful reaching No. 5 in the Netherlands. Glyn Johns also recorded a version during 1966 and, in Spain, it was released as a single coupled with *You Shall Be Gone Tomorrow Huge,* his name being mis-spelt on the cover and appearing as Glynt Johns.
Peter Whitehead used the *Lady Jane* soundtrack, while the film incorporated wild crowd scenes at a recording of *Have You Seen Your Mother Baby* with slow motion techniques. The outcome was included in his 1967 film *Tonight Let's All Make Love In London*, a documentary of the times, which included Stones interviews and footage.

291.   IT'S NOT EASY (Jagger, Richard) 2.56
6-9 March 1966: Place: RCA Studios, Hollywood, USA.
Producer: Andrew Oldham.
Engineer: Dave Hassinger.
UK LP AFTERMATH: 15 April 1966: No. 1 - 28 weeks
USA LP AFTERMATH: 2 July 1966: No. 2 - 26 weeks

One of the less inspired inclusions on the AFTERMATH album. A chug-along R 'n' B rhythm ploughs the song forward on lacklustre lyrics, though Bill Wyman is prominent on a dry fuzz bass. AFTERMATH was let down by these mediocre tracks and emphasised the necessity for songwriting consistency before album inclusion. However, it was a mighty achievement to release an album of all Jagger, Richard compositions as previous releases had, of course, included many covers. This was the way to turn their talents into gold and they must surely have been thankful to Andrew Oldham for insisting that they should write more of their own songs.

292.   STUPID GIRL (Jagger, Richard) 2.56
6-9 March 1966: Place: RCA Studios, Hollywood, USA.
Played Live: 1966
Producer: Andrew Oldham.
Engineer: Dave Hassinger.
UK LP AFTERMATH: 15 April 1966: No. 1 - 28 weeks
USA B-side: Paint It Black: 7 May 1966
USA LP AFTERMATH: 2 July 1966: No. 2 - 26 weeks
USA Compilation LP THE ROLLING STONES - PROMTIONAL ALBUM: October 1969
UK & USA LP THE ROLLING STONES SINGLES COLLECTION - THE LONDON YEARS: 15 August 1989
UK CD box set THE ROLLING STONES SINGLES - 1965 - 1967: 12 July 2004
USA CD box set THE ROLLING STONES SINGLES - 1965 - 1967: 27 July 2004

A better musical performance but the tongue-lashing lyrics again fall back on the female "put-down" notion. The band's association with this theme is much debated. It may have been derived from insecurity or simply the boredom of impersonal hotel groupies or another Chrissie Shrimpton unmaking . It created critical conflict and was politically derisory but nonetheless fuelled the publicity machine. Mick Jagger told Rolling Stone's Jan Wenner in 1994, "Obviously, I was having a bit of trouble. I wasn't in a good relationship. Or I was in too many bad relationships. I had so many girlfriends at that point. None of them seemed to care they weren't pleasing me very much. I was obviously in with the wrong group." Ian Stewart accompanies *Stupid Girl* on organ. In 1979, Ellen Foley covered the song for her album NIGHT OUT - she had been the backup vocalist on Meatloaf's BAT OUT OF HELL.

293.   PAINT IT, BLACK (Jagger, Richard) 3.20
AKA: Paint It Black
6-9 March 1966: Place: RCA Studios, Hollywood, USA.
Played Live: 1966, 1967, 1989, 1990, 1998, 1999, 2003, 2005, 2006, 2007
Rolling Stones with Jack Nitzsche.
Producer: Andrew Oldham.
Engineer: Dave Hassinger.
USA Single: 7 May 1966: No. 1 - 10 weeks
UK Single: 13 May 1966: No. 1 - 10 weeks
USA LP AFTERMATH: 2 July 1966: No. 2 - 26 weeks
UK Compilation LP BIG HITS (HIGH TIDE AND GREEN GRASS): 4 November 1966: No. 4 - 43 weeks
USA Compilation LP THROUGH THE PAST DARKLY (BIG HITS VOL 2): 13 September 1969: No. 2 - 16 weeks
UK Compilation LP STONE AGE: 6 March 1971: No. 4 - 7 weeks
USA Compilation LP HOT ROCKS 1964-1971: 11 January 1972: No. 4 - 30 weeks
UK Compilation LP ROLLED GOLD: 14 November 1975: No. 7 - 50 weeks
UK Compilation LP GET STONED - 30 GREATEST HITS, 30 ORIGINAL TRACKS: 21 October 1977: No. 13 - 15 weeks
German Compilation LP THE REST OF THE BEST: December 1983
UK & USA LP THE ROLLING STONES SINGLES COLLECTION - THE LONDON YEARS: 15 August 1989
USA 12-inch Single: 11 June 1990
UK Single: 11 June 1990: No. 61 - 3 weeks
USA Compilation Promo CD THE ROLLING STONES REMASTERED: 30 May 2002
UK CD LP FORTY LICKS: 30 September 2002: No. 2 - 45 weeks
USA CD LP FORTY LICKS: 1 October 2002: No. 2 - 50 weeks
UK CD box set THE ROLLING STONES SINGLES - 1965 - 1967: 12 July 2004
USA CD box set THE ROLLING STONES SINGLES - 1965 - 1967: 27 July 2004
UK Single: May 2007: No. 70 - 1 week
UK Compilation CD ROLLED GOLD +: 12 November 2007: No. 26 - 12 weeks

Keith Richards supplied the music to this, their next single, and Mick Jagger wrote the lyrics. Keith was not satisfied with the final take and amusingly reckoned it would sound good as a funky 18th-century sonata (!). Mick and Keith tried to sort out the problem in a corner while Bill Wyman, becoming bored with the delay, reproduced the melody by pedalling bass notes on a Hammond organ as an "impression" of their previous manager, Eric Easton. In his youth, Easton had played the organ in English cinemas during the intermission.

Andrew Oldham asked Bill to play it again and Keith picked up on the riff before Charlie Watts took up the beat and Brian Jones joined in on the sitar. Jack Nitzsche filled in the sound by playing what he claimed was a "gypsy-style piano". The song's transition was random and instantaneous. An instrumental version can be heard (* a - 2.22) and the album version is longer (* b - 3.45). Brian Jones' virtuoso performance on the sitar was inspirational, having accidentally been introduced to the instrument after it was played to them in the studio by a guy in a jazz group. His attack on the sitar was unique and provided a distinct contrast to George Harrison who reverently stroked the instrument. Brian irremissibly rocked it up - so much so that he deeply cut the tops of his fingers.

In a performance playback on the Ed Sullivan Show, Brian sits cross-legged in white trousers and shirt playing the Indian instrument while Mick, in an army jacket, conducts the live vocals. The vocals are sung in a sombre manner for the first few verses before being followed by a coarser rock approach. The delivery is reminiscent of the Supremes 1965 hit, *My World Is Empty Without You*. It is said the track is about a funeral, depression, or simply a broken relationship. Others, inspired by Andrew Oldham's comma in the title - not on the Decca single - reckoned it was a racial attack.

The humming incantation after the main verses has a hypnotic appeal and some of the musical arrangements of this track played live in 1990 would return to this hypnotic feel. The over-all musical transition was notable, particularly for the single only purchasers; the current public interest was intense and 300,000 advance orders produced a No. 1 single - both in Britain and the United States.

The single was released with a stereo mix on THE ROLLING STONES HOT ROCKS 1964-1971 (* c - 3.24) while the longer version appeared on FORTY LICKS. An out-take of the backing track has a couple of extra guitar licks before the normal kick-in (* d - 2.22). The 2007 digital releases by ABKCO prompted a few old single releases, one of which was *Paint It Black*, which charted six times for just one week from 2007 to 2009 with the highest entry at No. 70.

294. **LONG LONG WHILE** (Jagger, Richard) 3.01
6-9 March 1966: Place: RCA Studios, Hollywood, USA.
Rolling Stones with Jack Nitzsche.
Producer: Andrew Oldham.
Engineer: Dave Hassinger.
UK B-side Paint It Black: 13 May 1966
USA Compilation LP MORE HOT ROCKS (BIG HITS & FAZED COOKIES): 1 December 1972: No. 9 - 12 weeks
UK Compilation LP NO STONE UNTURNED: 5 October 1973
German Compilation LP THE REST OF THE BEST: December 1983
UK & USA LP THE ROLLING STONES SINGLES COLLECTION - THE LONDON YEARS: 15 August 1989
USA Compilation CD MORE HOT ROCKS (BIG HITS & FAZED COOKIES): 3 September 2002
UK CD box set THE ROLLING STONES SINGLES - 1965 - 1967: 12 July 2004
USA CD box set THE ROLLING STONES SINGLES - 1965 - 1967: 27 July 2004
UK B-side Paint It Black: May 2007

Keith Richards was again critical of the final sound created on *Paint It Black*. Somehow, it typified the band's current success, which was due to four factors: the musical integrity led by Keith Richards, a unique musician in Brian Jones, the publicity connivance of Mick Jagger and Andrew Oldham and lastly the rhythm backbone of the band, Charlie Watts and Bill Wyman. The latter duo provided the enthusiasm for this soul take. A boogie-woogie piano starts *Long Long While* off in Presleyesque style, augmented by Ian Stewart's gospel organ playing. The track develops a Righteous Brothers feel, which builds up unreservedly. It deserved to be more than just a banal flip-side but it can certainly not be classed as innovative. Another soul style sound, *Tracks Of My Tears* by Smokey Robinson and The Miracles, also was possibly recorded but there is no out-take.

295. **UNDER MY THUMB** (Jagger, Richard) 3.41
6-9 March 1966: Place: RCA Studios, Hollywood, USA.
Played Live: 1966, 1967, 1969, 1981, 1982, 1997, 1998, 2006
Producer: Andrew Oldham.
Engineer: Dave Hassinger.
UK LP AFTERMATH: 15 April 1966: No. 1 - 28 weeks
USA LP AFTERMATH: 2 July 1966: No. 2 - 26 weeks
USA Compilation LP THE ROLLING STONES - PROMOTIONAL ALBUM: October 1969
USA LP THE ROLLING STONES HOT ROCKS 1964-1971: 11 January 1972: No. 4 - 30 weeks
UK Compilation LP MILESTONES: 18 February 1972: No. 14 - 8 weeks
UK Compilation LP ROLLED GOLD: 14 November 1975: No. 7 - 50 weeks
USA Compilation Promo CD THE ROLLING STONES REMASTERED: 30 May 2002
UK CD LP FORTY LICKS: 30 September 2002: No. 2 - 45 weeks
USA CD LP FORTY LICKS: 1 October 2002: No. 2 - 50 weeks
UK Compilation CD ROLLED GOLD +: 12 November 2007: No. 26 - 12 weeks

A lyrically revelistic and chauvinistic song, inspired by late-night groupie encounters and the ability to exert control over "girls". The song has a strong rhythmic base, with almost African connotations, its primeval feel enhanced by Brian Jones' marimba, which provides a unique riff against Bill Wyman's tight bass sound and for Mick Jagger really made the song. Keith Richards plucks the guitar on the rhythm breaks and there is a de-tuned groaned chorus riff, in the style of the previous year's Spencer Davis Group's *Keep On Runnin'*. The song's groove speeds up at the end as Mick Jagger jives, "take it easy babe". *Under My Thumb* is musically one of the more inspiring tracks released on the AFTERMATH album.

296. **HIGH AND DRY** (Jagger, Richard) 3.08
6-9 March 1966: Place: RCA Studios, Hollywood, USA.
Producer: Andrew Oldham.
Engineer: Dave Hassinger.

UK LP AFTERMATH: 15 April 1966: No. 1 - 28 weeks
USA LP AFTERMATH: 2 July 1966: No. 2 - 26 weeks

Ever since the band's first visit to the States, Keith Richards' fondness and interest for country and western and Appalachian music had been developing. *High And Dry* is one of the first songs recorded that he had written in this style and they were to be featured more strongly in the future. There is a busker cymbal type sound that runs throughout the recording while a hillbilly harmonica accompanies the country hick drawl of Mick Jagger's vocals. Mick was quick to mimic any dialect dictated by a song's style and this was no exception. (He was to perfect and accentuate it on *Sweet Virginia* and *Far Away Eyes* in the 70s). The lyrical content of *High And Dry* was insignificant and the song as a whole paled embarrassingly in comparison to the likes of Bob Dylan's conscience songs.

297. FLIGHT 505 (Jagger, Richard) 3.27
6-9 March 1966: Place: RCA Studios, Hollywood, USA.
Producer: Andrew Oldham.
Engineer: Dave Hassinger.
UK LP AFTERMATH: 15 April 1966: No. 1 - 28 weeks
USA LP AFTERMATH: 2 July 1966: No. 2 - 26 weeks

Ian Stewart plays the opening chords filling one channel on the stereo with a distant bar-room piano. The band then join in using both channels on this medium-paced Chuck Berry sound-a-like rocker. The song depicts the story of Flight Number 505 which crashes into oblivion. The lyrics were written at the Beverly Wilshire Hotel, Beverly Hills, California, as a handwritten manuscript testified. It was auctioned in 1997 for £6,000.
This was the flight number of the first plane that took them from the UK to the United States. Their hectic touring schedule obviously produced its own nightmares. The track, despite fine piano playing, lacks the vivacious character of their more refined rockers. The album release in the UK and USA was separated by 10 weeks, although acetates were available from American Bell Sound in late May 1966.

298. I AM WAITING (Jagger, Richard) 3.11
6-9 March 1966: Place: RCA Studios, Hollywood, USA.
Rolling Stones with Jack Nitzsche.
Producer: Andrew Oldham.
Engineer: Dave Hassinger.
UK LP AFTERMATH: 15 April 1966: No. 1 - 28 weeks
USA LP AFTERMATH: 2 July 1966: No. 2 - 26 weeks
USA Compilation Promo CD THE ROLLING STONES REMASTERED: 30 May 2002

The soft tones of the dulcimer, played by Brian Jones, provide a unique pitch for Mick Jagger to articulate somewhat malevolent lyrics - don't fear the reaper. The song is a quiet one which lurches forth ("slow or fast") on chorus lines - again not a particularly strong track, but one which encapsulated the newly found direction of "art for art's sake". Jack Nitzsche contributes a piano line. It was played back with live Jagger vocals on Ready Steady Go! on 27 May 1966, Charlie Watts looking austere in glasses, Brian on dulcimer and Mick in a decorative army-style top.

299. WHAT TO DO (Jagger, Richard) 2.32
6-9 March 1966: Place: RCA Studios, Hollywood, USA.
Producer: Andrew Oldham.
Engineer: Dave Hassinger.
UK LP AFTERMATH: 15 April 1966: No. 1 - 28 weeks
USA Compilation LP MORE HOT ROCKS (BIG HITS & FAZED COOKIES): 1 December 1972: No. 9 - 12 weeks
USA Compilation CD MORE HOT ROCKS (BIG HITS & FAZED COOKIES): 3 September 2002

The final track on the British album, but not included on the American version due to the addition there of the hit single *Paint It Black*. This was the last track of a four-day long session which included the talents and merits of Jack Nitzsche, who was then the arranger/entrepreneur at Phil Spector's RCA Studios. The long stint produced the AFTERMATH album but was weighted in its attempts to progress musically.
The successful songs, however, produced a monumental transgression and can be credited to one man, Brian Jones - listen again to *Paint It Black, Mother's Little Helper* and *Lady Jane*. It is ironic that *What To Do* has become remarkable for the way in which a very ill-looking Brian crashed on the floor and it was left to Andrew Oldham to walk over and unplug his guitar and pull out the lead. Andrew tells this tale in his book *2Stoned* and quotes Keith Richards as saying in conclusion: "That's what happens when you fly without radar." *What To Do* tried to eulogise the ordinary man who struggles for recognition. *Paint It Black* was an excellent substitute. In the United States it was not released until the 1972 MORE HOT ROCKS compilation.

300. CON LE MIE LACRIME (Jagger, Richard, Oldham, Danpa) 2.44
AKA: Con Le Mie Lagrime Cosi, As Tears Go By
15 March 1966: Place: IBC Studios, London, England.
Played Live: 2006
Producer: Andrew Oldham.
Engineer: Glyn Johns.
Orchestra: Mike Leander. Arranger: Keith Richards, Mike Leander.
Italian Single: April 1966
UK LP SLOW ROLLERS: 9 November 1981
German Compilation LP THE REST OF THE BEST: December 1983

An unusual production of *As Tears Go By*, with Italian lyrics and a different backing track. Following the *Lady Jane* use of harpsichord at RCA, it was again employed for this arrangement. Mike Leander, who also played the harpsichord, and Keith Richards were credited as the arrangers, although the basic backing track is the same as the October 1965 version. It was released as an Italian single in April 1966, reaching the No.12 position. Another cut of the Italian version found on a bootleg has an acoustic guitar in place of the harpsichord (* a - 2-59). Dante Panzuti (pseudonym Danpa), a composer/lyricist who translated the song is credited on the single. At the end of March and early April, a brief seven-date European (Netherlands, Belgium, France, Sweden and Denmark) tour was conducted.

301. OUT OF TIME (Jagger, Richard) 3.22
27-30 April, 6 May 1966: Place: Pye Studios, London, England.
Rolling Stones with Jimmy Page, Joe Moretti, Eric Ford, Reg Guest, Andy White, Sydney Sax, Chris Farlowe.
Producer: Mick Jagger.
Engineer: Alan Florence.
Arranger: Art Greenslade.
UK Compilation LP METAMORPHOSIS: 6 June 1975: No. 45 - 1 week
USA Compilation LP METAMORPHOSIS: 6 June 1975: No. 8 - 8 weeks
USA Single: 12 August 1975
UK Single: 5 September 1975: No. 45 - 2 weeks
UK CD box set THE ROLLING STONES SINGLES - 1968 - 1971: 28 February 2005
USA CD box set THE ROLLING STONES SINGLES - 1968 - 1971: 1 March 2005

Take your pick on the huge backing cast. Andrew Oldham and Mick Jagger recorded the song principally for Chris Farlowe. The track is orchestrated (led by violinist Sydney Sax) and features unknown female backing vocals. Art Greenslade (pianist) arranged the backing track, which was also used for the Chris Farlowe single. The "band" included Jimmy Page and Joe Moretti on guitar, Eric Ford (drums), Earl (Reg) Guest (piano) and Andy White (early Beatles drummer).
Mick Jagger produced the single and thereby prompted a British No. 1 for Chris Farlowe in June 1966. The contemptuous lyrics fired yet another swipe at the demeanour of women. Decca released the track with Mick Jagger on vocals as a single in 1975 from the dubious METAMORPHOSIS compilation. At the same time Chris Farlowe's version was released and Dan McCafferty, the Nazareth Scottish rock singer, completed a bit of history with the unusual appearance of three versions of *Out Of Time* in the lower reaches of the British charts in September 1975.
The Stones take nearly received an earlier album release as an opening track. In 1972 Allen Klein, as part of his settlement with the Stones, was permitted to release one more album. Al Steckler proposed a release called NECROPHILIA and an acetate was made - the album contents were *Out Of Time, Don't Lie To Me, Have You Seen Your Mother Baby, Standing In The Shadow?, Think, Hear It, Some Things Just Stick In Your Mind, Aftermath, I'd Much Rather Be With The Boys, Andrew's Blues, Pay Your Dues, Let The Good Times Roll, Heart Of Stone, Each And Every Day Of The Year, Sleepy City, Try A Little Harder, Blue Turns To Grey, We're Wasting Time*. It received a catalogue number of ABKCO AB-4224 and the aforementioned tracks reached acetate stage in October 1972. Nine of the songs ended up on the METAMORPHOSIS project.

302. PAINT IT BLACK (Jagger, Richard) 2.13
12 May 1966: Place: BBC TV, London, England.
Bootleg only.

Following the AFTERMATH sessions, the hectic touring schedule continued in Europe. From the Netherlands the Stones travelled to Belgium, France (two more concerts at the Paris Olympia), Sweden and then Denmark where a chair flew from the audience, giving Mick Jagger a black eye. After the brief tour, May was a month of comparative rest in England. It was also time for the band's mounting frustrations to come to the surface. Although Brian Jones' instrumental virtuosity on AFTERMATH was faultless, his remoteness at recording sessions was causing them concern, as was his seeming lack of interest in the electric guitar.
Brian's problems revolved around Jagger and Richards' domination of the band, particularly the songwriting aspect. In the early days, Brian had formed the band and now felt he had been pushed to one side. This insecurity was to grow further and would lead to more problems for the Stones' stability. On 1 June, Brian attended the Beatles *Yellow Submarine* sessions and added instrumentation with Marianne Faithfull to the recording, albeit just clinking glasses for the submarine sound effects. The preview of the newly written *Paint It Black* was recorded live for Top Of The Pops. It was also featured at the annual New Musical Express May Day concert for poll winners which was not filmed due to a dispute with ABC TV regarding the sound quality. The Beatles also had the cameras turned off for what turned out to be their last live British performance, due to the same argument. On 27 May 1966 the Stones lip-synched performances of *Under My Thumb, I Am Waiting* and *Paint It Black* for Ready, Steady, Go! The recording is notable for Brian Jones, who mimes the playing of marimbas, dulcimer and sitar for the respective three songs. Mick Jagger was beginning to display a more eclectic fashion sense with an embroidered jacket top, demonstrating how much the band had moved on fashion wise from their previous appearance.
Michael Lindsay-Hogg related how, during *Paint It Black*, he asked Mick at the end of each verse to raise his hand and, as a result, a section of the lights would go out, exuding his control and power until all were in black. Touring recommenced in America in June and July. There were dramatic scenes of riot - including the use of tear gas - and general press antagonism, as the band threaded their way through the States. A double A-side single, featuring *Mother's Little Helper* and *Lady Jane*, was released in the States to complement the tour, along with the album AFTERMATH.

303. MOTHER'S LITTLE HELPER (Jagger, Richard) ✏ 2.32
28 July 1966: Place: Honolulu Stadium, Honolulu, Hawaii.
Bootleg only.

The fifth North American and Canadian tour, which started late in June 1966, culminated in the exotic location of Honolulu, Hawaii on 28 July. The preceding concert took place at the Hollywood Bowl on July 25 and, as fate would have it, Brian Jones would not play another live performance in the United States. Support acts for the tour had included "original punksters" Standells (who had just charted with their classic *Dirty Water*), The McCoys (featuring "Sloopy" Rick Derringer on vocals) and The Trade Winds, The Ronettes plus the newly-formed Buffalo Springfield and The Byrds at the final two shows.
The Honolulu concert was broadcast on local radio and is widely bootlegged. The show consisted of *Not Fade Away, The Last Time, Paint It Black, Lady Jane* (Charlie was asked to introduce this song and mistakenly announced *The Last Time* - Mick Jagger corrected him, to much laughter), *Mother's Little Helper, Get Off My Cloud,*

19th Nervous Breakdown and *Satisfaction* - the last two featured some wonderfully deranged and distorted guitar. Ronnie Schneider, who managed the USA tour, was asked to provide some lighting effects and different colour spotlights were used. The new found rock concert style was definitely emerging.

Mick Jagger confirmed his unique style during *Satisfaction*, where his vocals orchestrate the song's tempo. Mick announced before *Satisfaction* that this was their last concert - pausing for dramatic effect - ever! The era was unique as it combined their earlier single hit material and the new sounds created on AFTERMATH, requiring Brian Jones to play live instruments such as the sitar and dulcimer. *Mother's Little Helper* was their latest chart single in the States and, coupled with *Lady Jane*, reached No. 5 in July.

Keith Richards spent much of the tour alone as his girlfriend, Linda Keith, left him in May to move to New York. Their relationship was hanging in the balance and it was in the Big Apple that she saw, met and fell in love with Jimi Hendrix, introducing him to Chas Chandler in July. Hendrix moved to London in September, with one of Keith's guitars, and his solo career commenced.

304. PANAMA POWDER ROOM (Jagger, Richard)
3-11 August 1966: Place: RCA Studios, Hollywood, USA.
Producer: Andrew Oldham.
Engineer: Dave Hassinger.
Unavailable.

Panama Powder Room is an unavailable instrumental track, its session status confirmed by Bill Wyman wanting to release it on the aborted 1975 BLACK BOX compilation. It was recorded in celebration mood as England's footballers had just beaten West Germany in their only World Cup Final victory on the 30 July 1966. Hopefully some television station broadcast the match in Los Angeles.

305. WHO'S DRIVING YOUR PLANE? (Jagger, Richard) 3.13
AKA: Who's Driving My Plane?
3-11 August; 31 August - 2 September 1966: Place: RCA Studios, Hollywood, USA; IBC Studios, London England.
Rolling Stones with Jack Nitzsche.
Producer: Andrew Oldham.
Engineer: Dave Hassinger.
UK B-side: Have You Seen Your Mother, Baby, Standing In The Shadow?: 23 September 1966
USA B-side: Have You Seen Your Mother, Baby, Standing In The Shadow?: 23 September 1966
UK Compilation LP NO STONE UNTURNED: 5 October 1973
German Compilation LP THE REST OF THE BEST: December 1983
UK & USA LP THE ROLLING STONES SINGLES COLLECTION - THE LONDON YEARS: 15 August 1989
UK CD box set THE ROLLING STONES SINGLES - 1965 - 1967: 12 July 2004
USA CD box set THE ROLLING STONES SINGLES - 1965 - 1967: 27 July 2004

Just under half of the next album BETWEEN THE BUTTONS was recorded during the LA summer of 1966 following the tour. Some tracks would have orchestral overdubs created in London at the IBC studios by the Mike Leander Orchestra. It is rumoured that this happened to *Who's Driving Your Plane?* But, if this did occur, it is not available. *My Girl*, recorded in May 1965, had string arrangements added in September 1966 to prepare for its release on the FLOWERS album. The rest of the BETWEEN THE BUTTONS album would be created at the Olympic studios towards the tail-end of the year.

Who's Driving Your Plane? displays a heavier boogie approach to the blues. At the start you are almost waiting in anticipation for Dylan to come in and provide the vocals - it has that feel. The lyrics concern themselves with the problems of a girl who, because of dominant parents, has no mind of her own.

The vocals are sung with delayed echo, which gives a sophisticated edge to the song. This style was to pave the way for similar-sounding recordings made in the late 60s. The lead guitar is also a pre-cursor to some of the heavier influenced blues which would emerge from 1968. The *Have You Seen Your Mother, Baby, Standing In The Shadow?* (a bold attempt at a catchy title) single was released at the same time on both sides of the Atlantic. In the USA, the B-side was labelled as *Who's Driving My Plane?*

306. GET YOURSELF TOGETHER (Jagger, Richard) 3.10
AKA: I Can See It, I'll Feel A Whole Lot Better, Can't Believe It
3-11 August; 8 November - 6 December 1966: Place: RCA Studios, Hollywood, USA; Olympic Sound Studios, Barnes, London, England.
Producer: Andrew Oldham.
Engineer: Glyn Johns.
Bootleg only.

Get Yourself Together is a lively rock and roll jaunt that missed its vocation and has since become a sought-after recording. It portrays some harder guitar licks and an organ wavering in the background. Two versions exist - the original backing track (* a - 3.38) and an edited cut with vocals. The Chesterfield Kings released a version of it in 1994 on their LET'S GO GET STONED album under the title *Can't Believe It*.

307. MY OBSESSION (Jagger, Richard) 3.18
3-11 August; 8 November - 6 December 1966: Place: RCA Studios, Hollywood, USA; Olympic Sound Studios, Barnes, London, England.
Producer: Andrew Oldham.
Engineer: Dave Hassinger; Glyn Johns.
Assistant Engineer: Eddie Kramer.
UK LP BETWEEN THE BUTTONS: 20 January 1967: No. 3 - 22 weeks
USA LP BETWEEN THE BUTTONS: 11 February 1967: No. 2 - 19 weeks

The unique drum sound production on *My Obsession* provides a background for Keith Richards, who deploys a ricochet of stun guitar effects and also for Ian Stewart, who subtly taps R 'n' B rhythms on the keyboard. As a solo performance for Charlie Watts the song is impressive and he unwittingly inspired the album title, the cover photo displaying a fashion-conscious drummer. A longer instrumental out-take exists (* a - 4.08) where the clap back sounds and Ian Stewart's piano are even more prominent.

The "ooh baby" vocals were led by Brian Jones. Beach Boy Brian Wilson witnessed the Stones in the studio recording *My Obsession* and thought it so scarily good that he had to leave and stay in bed for two whole days, contemplating how he could compete. Perhaps his mind had been affected by the powerful smoke Mick Jagger had given him as he responded with the classic October 1966 release of *Good Vibrations* and the SMILE album, which was started in September but not released until 2004.

308. ALL SOLD OUT (Jagger, Richard) 2.18
AKA: All Part Of The Act
3-11 August; 8 November - 6 December 1966: Place: RCA Studios, Hollywood, USA; Olympic Sound Studios, Barnes, London, England.
Producer: Andrew Oldham.
Engineer: Dave Hassinger; Glyn Johns.
Assistant Engineer: Eddie Kramer.
UK LP BETWEEN THE BUTTONS: 20 January 1967: No. 3 - 22 weeks
USA LP BETWEEN THE BUTTONS: 11 February 1967: No. 2 - 19 weeks
UK LP SOLID ROCK: 13 October 1980

Essentially the music on BETWEEN THE BUTTONS reflects the Carnaby Street revolution and, musically, contemporary British bands such as Cream, The Kinks and The Yardbirds. In short, it is certainly derivative as opposed to innovative. *All Sold Out,* originally known as *All Part Of The Act,* has a progressive, heavy feel, with an undercurrent of electric guitar solos which somehow lead you to expect more, but only exasperate by fading out before improvisation starts.

The brevity of the track, at 2 minutes 15 seconds, heightens this effect, though the cymbal work and production of Charlie Watts' percussion sound is the high spot again. Brian Jones presumably plays the wistful recorder. The alternative title may have been the earlier RCA version. A backing track without vocals and a different guitar sound exists as an out-take (* a - 2.48).

Glyn Johns had worked for Andrew Oldham on his solo projects and was a good friend of Ian Stewart. He got on well with the band and became a natural choice for their work in a London studio of which the Olympic Studios was a perfect choice and became their first choice for the next four years.

309. SHE SMILED SWEETLY (Jagger, Richard) 2.45
3-11 August; 8 November - 6 December 1966: Place: RCA Studios, Hollywood, USA; Olympic Sound Studios, Barnes, London, England.
Played Live: 1967, 2002
Rolling Stones with Jack Nitzsche.
Producer: Andrew Oldham.
Engineer: Dave Hassinger; Glyn Johns.
Assistant Engineer: Eddie Kramer.
UK LP BETWEEN THE BUTTONS: 20 January 1967: No. 3 - 22 weeks
USA LP BETWEEN THE BUTTONS: 11 February 1967: No. 2 - 19 weeks

She Smiled Sweetly is a ballad which features Keith Richards in his first venture on the church organ and sounds as though he was determined not to miss a note, hence the methodical playing. Keith also contributes guitar and the bass lines while Jack Nitzsche is on piano. Mick Jagger utters the sweet lyrics which was intended to be a quasi-religious song with the subject a "he" instead of a "she". *She Smiled Sweetly* should have been saved for an out-take compilation such as FLOWERS but the Stones were being given complete artistic freedom by Andrew Oldham and out of this would come some failures, but also some works of genius. Keith remembered the song with affection and it was played at the Roseland Ballroom, New York, in September 2002, during the LICKS tour.

310. YESTERDAY'S PAPERS (Jagger, Richard) 2.05
3-11 August; 8 November - 6 December 1966: Place: RCA Studios, Hollywood, USA; Olympic Sound Studios, Barnes, London, England.
Played Live: 1967
Rolling Stones with Jack Nitzsche
Producer: Andrew Oldham.
Engineer: Dave Hassinger; Glyn Johns.
Assistant Engineer: Eddie Kramer.
UK LP BETWEEN THE BUTTONS: 20 January 1967: No. 3 - 22 weeks
USA LP BETWEEN THE BUTTONS: 11 February 1967: No. 2 - 19 weeks
UK Compilation LP MILESTONES: 18 February 1972: No. 14 - 8 weeks
UK Compilation LP ROLLED GOLD: 14 November 1975: No. 7 - 50 weeks
UK Compilation CD ROLLED GOLD +: 12 November 2007: No. 26 - 12 weeks

Although the lyrics return to the chauvinistic theme of discarding women as waste paper, instrumentally *Yesterday's Papers* is a cut above the rest on the album. It did become the death knell for Chrissie Shrimpton's relationship with Mick Jagger which ended in December 1966 - Marianne Faithfull was waiting in the wings. The harmonies sound as though they have been worked upon and Mick Jagger wrote most of the music - his first solo piece of composition. Keith Richards takes a prominent spot when playing a great guitar break which slashes with plenty of reverb and echo and the marimba is again used to astonishing effect by Brian Jones.

This suggests the initial track may have been put to tape earlier in the year by Dave Hassinger in Hollywood - supported by Jack Nitzsche playing harpsichord. It was evident that Brian Jones' contribution later in the year was limited due to ill health. Early versions exist, one seems to be a demo (* a - 2.06) and another has more monotone guideline vocals by Mick Jagger (* b - 2.12). The backing track without vocals is also available as an out-take (* c - 3.08). Chris Farlowe released a version, his fifth Jagger, Richards cover, on the Immediate label in May 1967. It failed to chart but the outcome was more like what Mick intended when writing it. The song was played live on the 1967 European tour in a medley with *Get Off My Cloud.*

311. PLEASE GO HOME (Jagger, Richard) 3.18
3-11 August; 8 November - 6 December 1966: Place: RCA Studios, Hollywood, USA; Olympic Sound Studios, Barnes, London, England.
Rolling Stones with Shirley Watts.
Producer: Andrew Oldham.
Engineer: Dave Hassinger; Glyn Johns.
Assistant Engineer: Eddie Kramer.
UK LP BETWEEN THE BUTTONS: 20 January 1967: No. 3 - 22 weeks
USA Compilation LP FLOWERS: 15 July 1967: No. 3 - 18 weeks

A roughneck, deranged *Not Fade Away* beat, inspired by the Diddley Daddy himself, accompanies this interpretation of late era mod music. Echoes on the vocals and Pete Townshend-type reverb feedback intermittently break into the song. It is a poor imitation of the aforementioned heroes but was an example of how their music was becoming progressive with textured sounds. Mick Jagger said in 1967 that the whining vocal in the background was Charlie Watts' wife Shirley. Brian Jones is prominent on the track with another unusual electronic instrument, the Theremin. *Please Go Home* was not released on the American version of BETWEEN THE BUTTONS but was included on FLOWERS, a compilation American LP released by London Records in June 1967. Again, an instrumental out-take exists (* a - 3.20).

312. MISS AMANDA JONES (Jagger, Richard) 2.48
3-11 August; 8 November - 6 December 1966: Place: RCA Studios, Hollywood, USA; Olympic Sound Studios, Barnes, London, England.
Producer: Andrew Oldham.
Engineer: Dave Hassinger; Glyn Johns.
Assistant Engineer: Eddie Kramer.
UK LP BETWEEN THE BUTTONS: 20 January 1967: No. 3 - 22 weeks
USA LP BETWEEN THE BUTTONS: 11 February 1967: No. 2 - 19 weeks
USA Compilation Promo CD THE ROLLING STONES REMASTERED: 30 May 2002

Miss Amanda Jones is refreshing, humorous, mischievous fun, if a little sexist - keep showing the suspenders . . . Miss Jones is a good-time girl who is the "darling of the discotheque crowd". She keeps going down and down . . . at least that is the straight version. There were rumours that the song may have been about Frenchman Alain Tapp, who in the early 60s had a sex change operation and married a Lear in London and thus became Amanda Lear.
She hung around the model crowd, naturally met people like Brian Jones and was wooed by Salvador Dali and fashion guru Ossie Clark. Later she was the model on the Roxy Music FOR YOUR PLEASURE album, before turning to music herself. The sound production enhances the humour, with lead guitar and piano parts cleverly thrown into the scenario. Indeed, Keith Richards' guitar sounds strong and abrasive as he plays a raunchy 12-bar beat.

313. BACK STREET GIRL (Jagger, Richard) 3.28
3-11 August; 8 November - 6 December 1966: Place: RCA Studios, Hollywood, USA; Olympic Sound Studios, Barnes, London, England.
Rolling Stones with Nick De Caro.
Producer: Andrew Oldham.
Engineer: Dave Hassinger; Glyn Johns.
Assistant Engineer: Eddie Kramer.
UK LP BETWEEN THE BUTTONS: 20 January 1967: No. 3 - 22 weeks
USA Compilation LP FLOWERS: 15 July 1967: No. 3 - 18 weeks
UK LP SLOW ROLLERS: 9 November 1981

Mick Jagger rated *Back Street Girl* his favourite track of the BETWEEN THE BUTTONS sessions. It has a chirping cricket type sound running throughout, appearing as though Morris dancers were in the studio providing the background bells. It is a melodic sound, described by critics as a valse musette, or, more understandably, a waltz time song à la française.
The French accordion, played by Nick De Caro, aids the Gallic atmosphere but does nothing to hide the contemptuous, vitriolic lyrics of prostitution and forbidden sex which are concealed from the participant's nice conventional home life. Jack Nitzsche suggested to Andrew Oldham, Nick De Caro who was an arranger and also an accomplished accordion player. *Back Street Girl* was not to feature on the American release of the album but again appeared on the FLOWERS album. It is a much hidden classic.

314. COOL, CALM AND COLLECTED (Jagger, Richard) 4.19
3-11 August; 8 November - 6 December 1966: Place: RCA Studios, Hollywood, USA; Olympic Sound Studios, Barnes, London, England.
Rolling Stones with Jack Nitzsche, Nicky Hopkins.
Producer: Andrew Oldham.
Engineer: Dave Hassinger; Glyn Johns.
Assistant Engineer: Eddie Kramer.
UK LP BETWEEN THE BUTTONS: 20 January 1967: No. 3 - 22 weeks
USA LP BETWEEN THE BUTTONS: 11 February 1967: No. 2 - 19 weeks

This composition is an audacious attempt at music-hall variety. The unlikely combination of instruments such as the kazoo by Keith Richards and the sitar, with a tinkering mad piano, featured on a rock album are too much to comprehend. Jack Nitzsche is often credited with this keyboard work but Nick Hopkins was adept at creating madcap piano lines. The speeded up finale includes this burst of piano with Brian Jones on harmonica. It loses any humour it was attempting to achieve and, as a new rock form, can be dismissed. Ray Davies and the Kinks had successfully carried it off to much better effect on *Dedicated Follower Of Fashion* and *Sunny Afternoon*.
Nicky Hopkins had played sessions with the Kinks and now turned his piano trade towards the Stones, contributing some overdubs during the final BETWEEN THE BUTTON sessions. Nicky's career commenced in 1962 with Screaming Lord Sutch's Savages and Cyril Davies' All Stars before playing on The Who's first album and their mammoth hit *My Generation* (Mick Jagger thought that his playing on *Anyway, Anyhow, Anywhere* was especially good), The Pretty Things, Rod Stewart and

on The Beatles' SGT PEPPER album. His session and solo work continued until his untimely death in 1994. Most notably he played on many Stones sessions and concert tours, becoming an integral contributor, much more of which will be documented later.

315. SOMETHING HAPPENED TO ME YESTERDAY (Jagger, Richard) 4.55
3-11 August; 8 November - 6 December 1966: Place: RCA Studios, Hollywood, USA; Olympic Sound Studios, Barnes, London, England.
Rolling Stones with Nicky Hopkins.
Producer: Andrew Oldham.
Engineer: Dave Hassinger; Glyn Johns.
Strings: Sydney Sax; Assistant Engineer: Eddie Kramer.
UK LP BETWEEN THE BUTTONS: 20 January 1967: No. 3 - 22 weeks
USA LP BETWEEN THE BUTTONS: 11 February 1967: No. 2 - 19 weeks

The "Vaudevillism" experiment continues on *Something Happened To Me Yesterday*. Brian Jones leads the hysterics on trombone and other brass and string instruments, possibly arranged by Sydney Sax. He also whistles a happy tune. This five-minute concept of mockery on BETWEEN THE BUTTONS illustrated the need to take stock of the situation, as the pressure of touring and incessant studio work began to take its toll artistically.

The Stones were recording products that they thought the "Carnaby Street" public would like and not concentrating on extending their artistic repertoire and swaggering performances. Keith Richards helps Mick Jagger out on the vocals as they take turns at discussing yesterday's trip, unsure of what it was or if it was against the law. Ironically, they soon would. The song ends as Mick Jagger thanks the band and producer "Reg Thorpe" (Andrew Oldham) and offers some road safety advice - "wear white, evening all!" - in the style of Dixon of Dock Green (a cosy, very popular British TV police series 1955 - 1976). Ian Stewart contributes a line or two of piano as did Nicky Hopkins, when he overdubbed his piece.

316. WHO'S BEEN SLEEPING HERE? (Jagger, Richard) 3.57
3-11 August; 8 November - 6 December 1966: Place: RCA Studios, Hollywood, USA; Olympic Sound Studios, Barnes, London, England.
Rolling Stones with Jack Nitzsche.
Producer: Andrew Oldham.
Engineer: Dave Hassinger; Glyn Johns.
Assistant Engineer: Eddie Kramer.
UK LP BETWEEN THE BUTTONS: 20 January 1967: No. 3 - 22 weeks
USA LP BETWEEN THE BUTTONS: 11 February 1967: No. 2 - 19 weeks

The influences of Bob Dylan were displayed on this track. The summer of 1966 had brought the release of Dylan's classic album, BLONDE ON BLONDE, and comparisons were detectable. The Stones were by no means the only group affected by his folk charms but the influences may have been stronger due to Brian Jones' friendship with Dylan. The excellent Dylan single *Like A Rolling Stone* was misconstrued to be written for Brian, who felt *Ballad Of A Thin Man* was also about him. Brian Jones' usual harmonica techniques were discarded on *Who's Been Sleeping Here?* as he plays in true Dylanesque style. The music is not strictly acoustic as Keith Richards delivers a lead guitar solo but the die of a Dylan pastiche had been well cast.

317. COMPLICATED (Jagger, Richard) 3.16
3-11 August; 8 November - 6 December 1966: Place: RCA Studios, Hollywood, USA; Olympic Sound Studios, Barnes, London, England.
Rolling Stones with Jack Nitzsche
Producer: Andrew Oldham.
Engineer: Dave Hassinger; Glyn Johns.
Assistant Engineer: Eddie Kramer.
UK LP BETWEEN THE BUTTONS: 20 January 1967: No. 3 - 22 weeks
USA LP BETWEEN THE BUTTONS: 11 February 1967: No. 2 - 19 weeks

The guitar and drum sound produced by Andrew Oldham on *My Obsession* was recreated again for the song *Complicated*. Keith Richards was obviously fond of this bumble-bee effect and a pleasing uplifting melody is played on the organ by Brian Jones. Was Mick Jagger's new found relationship with Marianne Faithfull providing some songwriting material or was it referring to a groupie having "many men in so short a time"? The lyric continues: "She treats me oh so kind . . . but she's very educated." An out-take without vocals exists and the high-toned organ is used to good effect (* a - 3.25).

318. CONNECTION (Jagger, Richard) 2.10
3-11 August; 8 November - 6 December 1966: Place: RCA Studios, Hollywood, USA; Olympic Sound Studios, Barnes, London, England.
Played Live: 1967, 1995, 2006
Producer: Andrew Oldham.
Engineer: Dave Hassinger; Glyn Johns.
Assistant Engineer: Eddie Kramer.
UK LP BETWEEN THE BUTTONS: 20 January 1967: No. 3 - 22 weeks
USA LP BETWEEN THE BUTTONS: 11 February 1967: No. 2 - 19 weeks
UK LP SOLID ROCK: 13 October 1980

The vocals are taken by Keith Richards on his first solo effort, although Mick Jagger helps out in the background while beating his hands on a bass drum. Ian Stewart plays piano and a bass line using organ pedals. The pace of the song seems to be a little fast. It was covered by American hard rock band Montrose to much better effect in 1974. Ramblin' Jack Elliott, one of Keith's favourite blues pickers, made a commercial attempt to boost his ratings, recording *Connection* in a medley with Bob Dylan's *Don't Think Twice, It's Alright* for his 1968 album YOUNG BRIGHAM. The lyrical content written by Keith evidently refers to drug taking, the morality of which would be severely tested within the next few months. It also reflects the busy life on the road and the desire to return home. The album was released in 1967 after acetates were produced in December 1966. Reflecting on the album, Mick thought it was sub-par but one of the good cuts was *Connection*, along with *Back Street Girl*.

319. HAVE YOU SEEN YOUR MOTHER, BABY, STANDING IN THE SHADOW? (Jagger, Richard) 2.36
3-11 August; 31 August; 8 September 1966: Place: RCA Studios, Hollywood, USA; IBC Studios, London, England; RCA Hollywood, USA.
Played Live: 1966
Rolling Stones with Jack Nitzsche.
Producer: Andrew Oldham.
Engineer: Dave Hassinger, Glyn Johns.
Brass: Mike Leander.
UK Single: 23 September 1966: No. 5 - 8 weeks
USA Single: 23 September 1966: No. 9 - 6 weeks
UK Compilation LP BIG HITS (HIGH TIDE AND GREEN GRASS): 4 November 1966: No. 4 - 43 weeks
USA Compilation LP FLOWERS: 15 July 1967: No. 3 - 18 weeks
USA Compilation LP THROUGH THE PAST DARKLY (BIG HITS VOL 2): 13 September 1969: No. 2 - 16 weeks
USA Compilation LP MORE HOT ROCKS (BIG HITS & FAZED COOKIES): 1 December 1972: No. 9 - 12 weeks
UK Compilation LP ROLLED GOLD: 14 November 1975: No. 7 - 50 weeks
UK Compilation LP GET STONED - 30 GREATEST HITS, 30 ORIGINAL TRACKS: 21 October 1977: No. 13 - 15 weeks
German Compilation LP THE REST OF THE BEST: December 1983
UK & USA LP THE ROLLING STONES SINGLES COLLECTION - THE LONDON YEARS: 15 August 1989
USA Compilation CD MORE HOT ROCKS (BIG HITS & FAZED COOKIES): 3 September 2002
UK CD LP FORTY LICKS: 30 September 2002: No. 2 - 45 weeks
USA CD LP FORTY LICKS: 1 October 2002: No. 2 - 50 weeks
UK CD box set THE ROLLING STONES SINGLES - 1965 - 1967: 12 July 2004
USA CD box set THE ROLLING STONES SINGLES - 1965 - 1967: 27 July 2004
UK Compilation CD ROLLED GOLD +: 12 November 2007: No. 26 - 12 weeks

The pattern of mid-60s singles releases culminated in *Have You Seen Your Mother?* a song described by Mick Jagger as the "ultimate freak-out". He added that he was not interested in the band's chart positions, which was just as well since the single was not a success in Rolling Stones terms - it just scraped a Top 10 position on both sides of the Atlantic. The recording was a move away from single commercialism, featuring guitar feedback at the beginning and end and also unaccredited trumpets which generate the song's attack.

Bill Wyman's bass line and a raving piano glide the song as it dips and climbs around Mick Jagger's surging vocals. Keith Richards was critical of the final product which he had written on the piano at his London pad and was never quite happy with its outcome, feeling it had been rushed to such an extent that the wrong mix was released. As a result the rhythm section was buried, thereby lacking punch and excitement. Producer Andrew Oldham explained that Mick, Keith and himself were finalising the song by taking the four-tracks and bouncing the recording to another reel. This opened up two further tracks for more overdubs which had the effect of damping the sound, particularly the guitar.

Keith asked for the guitar to be doubled but the base recording was just at too low a frequency so bringing up the level would provide background room noise. Vocals were overdubbed and that is when the nasal "na-na-na" sections were added, with Andrew trying to beef up the guitar. Charlie Watts thought they were mad but conceded it had worked. An out-take has a more upfront lead guitar, reverberating with the "Mother" hook (* a - 2.29). There is also a version with just backing vocals and finger clicks without the lead vocal (* b - 2.33). Additional arrangements were worked upon back at IBC by Mike Leander, including the trumpet and orchestral additions, in an attempt to give depth to the song. Other brass instrumentation was tried but trumpet was the one that worked.

Mick, Keith, Andrew and Ian Stewart attended a final mix session at RCA which concluded the track. It was also the final time the Stones recorded at RCA and with Dave Hassinger. A stereo version exists on MORE HOT ROCKS and THE ROLLING STONES SINGLES COLLECTION - THE LONDON YEARS (* c - 2.36). Andrew could not be faulted for his publicity coups to accompany the single and the band decided to produce promotional films to support the release, a revolutionary idea at the time. They used a young London Soho film maker, Peter Whitehead, who produced some unique footage of the band. He had been chosen for the *Charlie Is My Darling* film because he had a new camera which ran almost silently and did not require additional lights.

One of the promotional films starts with an apocalyptic stage entrance on the Ed Sullivan show and continues showing a clip of Mick Jagger inspecting some Paris street art and the band being made up for a drag photo session in New York. The resultant photos by Jerry Schatzberg became the sleeve for the American release but picturing the group in World War II drag garb caused concern and outrage in the USA, particularly for Bill Wyman, who was distastefully sat in a wheelchair. It was all good mother-mocking fun, even if Keith Richards did appear slightly embarrassed by it all.

The video finishes with the group adopting the same poses - this time out of drag - with Brian Jones yawning then smirking cheekily. Another black and white, partly slow motion film, shows the band being made up before the shoot. The footage, suffice to say, did not appear on the British television music programme Top Of The Pops. The USA compilation album BIG HITS released in Britain in February was delayed until November with the addition of this single. The album stayed in the charts for an extensive 43 weeks. The released track also suffered from the same mistake as *Mother's Little Helper*, in that it has a slightly slower speed than intended. The ABKCO re-mastered catalogue in 2002 corrects this error.

320. PAINT IT BLACK (Jagger, Richard) 2.17
9 September 1966: Place: Ed Sullivan TV Show, CBS Studio 50, New York, USA.
USA DVD Ed Sullivan's Rock 'N' Roll Classics - Chart Toppers Vol. 1 - Hits Of 1965-1967: 24 September 2002
USA DVD 6 Ed Sullivan Shows Starring The Rolling Stones: 1 November 2011

321. LADY JANE (Jagger, Richard) 3.07
9 September 1966: Place: Ed Sullivan TV Show, CBS Studio 50, New York, USA.
USA DVD 6 Ed Sullivan Shows Starring The Rolling Stones: 1 November 2011

322. HAVE YOU SEEN YOUR MOTHER, BABY, STANDING IN THE SHADOW? (Jagger, Richard) 2.28
9 September 1966: Place: Ed Sullivan TV Show, CBS Studio 50, New York, USA.
USA DVD 6 Ed Sullivan Shows Starring The Rolling Stones: 1 November 2011

The Stones made a whistle-stop visit to the States in September for four or five days, purely to visit the studio in Los Angeles. The band then returned to New York to record an Ed Sullivan TV appearance on 9 September 1966 which featured *Paint It Black*, *Lady Jane* and the forthcoming single, *Have You Seen Your Mother, Baby, Standing In The Shadow?* Mick Jagger, Charlie Watts and Keith Richards can be seen wearing mock military jackets. Brian Jones is more dapper with a smart black and white suit on the last two numbers.

The performance was made with Brian Jones suffering from a badly injured hand. Reportedly, this had happened as a result of a climbing accident whilst holidaying in Morocco but was in fact due to him trying to strike Anita Pallenberg - but missing and hitting an iron frame. As a result, the normal insistence of a live rendition had to be withdrawn to allow a "vocal only" performance to the released backing track. However, the audience's reaction to the performance was ecstatic, as usual drowning the melodic strains of *Lady Jane* and making it hard for the Stones to out-sing the backing track of *Have You Seen Your Mother, Baby?* They also mimed to *Paint It Black*.

323. UNDER MY THUMB (Jagger, Richard) ✏ 2.53
1 October 1966: Place: City Hall, Newcastle, England.
Producer: Andrew Oldham.
Engineer: Glyn Johns.
USA LP GOT LIVE IF YOU WANT IT!: 9 December 1966: No. 6 - 11 weeks
UK Compilation LP GIMME SHELTER: 29 August 1971: No. 19 - 5 weeks

324. GET OFF MY CLOUD (Jagger, Richard) ✏ 2.54
1 October 1966: Place: City Hall, Newcastle, England.
Producer: Andrew Oldham.
Engineer: Glyn Johns.
USA LP GOT LIVE IF YOU WANT IT!: 9 December 1966: No. 6 - 11 weeks

325. THE LAST TIME (Jagger, Richard) ✏ 3.07
1 October 1966: Place: City Hall, Newcastle, England.
Producer: Andrew Oldham.
Engineer: Glyn Johns.
USA LP GOT LIVE IF YOU WANT IT!: 9 December 1966: No. 6 - 11 weeks

326. 19TH NERVOUS BREAKDOWN (Jagger, Richard) ✏ 3.30
1 October 1966: Place: City Hall, Newcastle, England.
Producer: Andrew Oldham.
Engineer: Glyn Johns.
USA LP GOT LIVE IF YOU WANT IT!: 9 December 1966: No. 6 - 11 weeks

The Stones had not played live for two months and not for a year in Britain. Any fears of how the audience would react faded away as the opening number at The Royal Albert Hall on 23 September 1966 had to be stopped as the stage was swamped. The tour support acts included Ike and Tina Turner with the Ike-Ettes and their Kings of Rhythm Orchestra featuring Jimmy Thomas, Bobby Johns and Ray Cameron, Peter Jay & The New Jay Walkers (with Terry Reid on vocals) and The Yardbirds (Jeff Beck and Jimmy Page).

The Yardbirds had enjoyed many incarnations including a 1964 line-up with Eric Clapton. The troupe that played on the Stones tour was not a happy bunch and Jeff Beck left mid-tour shortly after an American gig. They were, however, a formidable live attraction with two lead guitarists playing loud, "heavy" R 'n' B music, even if the line-up did only last five months.

Next year this rock format was to explode further with the Jimi Hendrix Experience and the famous Cream. While the album cover insisted that the GOT LIVE IF YOU WANT IT! album originated at The Royal Albert Hall it was, in fact, recorded over two shows at Newcastle City Hall and Bristol Colston Hall. It was interesting to see how many of the newer songs were interpreted live - *19th Nervous Breakdown* was, of course, faster but with driving guitars and gutsy vocals. In the studio, overdubs were added to *Lady Jane, I'm Alright, Have You Seen Your Mother Baby?* and *Satisfaction*.

327. HAVE YOU SEEN YOUR MOTHER, BABY, STANDING IN THE SHADOW? (Jagger, Richard) 2.27
4 October 1966: Place: Ready, Steady, Go!, Wembley TV Studio, London, England.
Producer: Michael Lindsay Hogg.
Bootleg only.

This was a live recording transmitted on 7 October 1966.

328. UNDER MY THUMB (Jagger, Richard) ✏ 3.08
7 October 1966: Place: Colston Hall, Bristol, England.
Producer: Andrew Oldham.
Engineer: Glyn Johns.
USA CD GOT LIVE IF YOU WANT IT!: December 1986

329. LADY JANE (Jagger, Richard) ✏ 3.08
7 October 1966: Place: Colston Hall, Bristol, England.
Producer: Andrew Oldham.
Engineer: Glyn Johns.
USA LP GOT LIVE IF YOU WANT IT!: 9 December 1966: No. 6 - 11 weeks
UK Compilation LP GIMME SHELTER: 29 August 1971: No. 19 - 5 weeks

330. NOT FADE AWAY (Petty, Hardin) ✎ 2.03
7 October 1966: Place: Colston Hall, Bristol, England.
Producer: Andrew Oldham.
Engineer: Glyn Johns.
USA LP GOT LIVE IF YOU WANT IT!: 9 December 1966: No. 6 - 11 weeks

331. HAVE YOU SEEN YOUR MOTHER, BABY, STANDING IN THE SHADOW? (Jagger, Richard) ✎ 2.19
7 October 1966: Place: Colston Hall, Bristol, England.
Producer: Andrew Oldham.
Engineer: Glyn Johns.
USA LP GOT LIVE IF YOU WANT IT!: 9 December 1966: No. 6 - 11 weeks

332. (I CAN'T GET NO) SATISFACTION (Jagger, Richard) ✎ 3.04
7 October 1966: Place: Colston Hall, Bristol, England.
Producer: Andrew Oldham.
Engineer: Glyn Johns.
USA LP GOT LIVE IF YOU WANT IT!: 9 December 1966: No. 6 - 11 weeks
UK Compilation LP GIMME SHELTER: 29 August 1971: No. 19 - 5 weeks

Glyn Johns' reel to reels recorded the concerts and the end result was produced (!) by Andrew Oldham. The recordings are horribly contrived; at the time, recording techniques for live concerts were a little primitive with microphones literally dropped over the balconies to record the concert. In bootleg terms, this became known as an audience recording. More than one microphone was used, producing a three-track recording of vocals, crowd screams and the band in the background.
The sound is layered and mixed in that order and the end product is terrible, paling into insignificance compared with the raunchy British EP of the same name. Incredulously, *I've Been Loving You Too Long* and *Fortune Teller* are studio tracks with screams over-dubbed and the resulting album is a commercial "cop out", although *I'm Alright* was from the same source. The cover sleeve, however, is more imaginative, with evocative live photos taken by Gered Mankowitz. Charlie Watts can be seen at the microphone, not singing but introducing *Lady Jane*. Around that time, Mankowitz took the memorable BETWEEN THE BUTTONS album cover photograph on Primrose Hill in London, an image which centres on Charlie's coat buttons on a cold winter's day. In 1994, the venue and image was replicated pastiche-style for a photo of the then up-and-coming Oasis.
Despite the screams, the GOT LIVE IF YOU WANT IT! soundtrack lacks depth and atmosphere and certainly does not convey the near-riot conditions that aborted some shows. The Stones had the sense not to release the end product in Britain but it has, however, appeared via import shops and a few select tracks are available on an August 1971 compilation album, GIMME SHELTER, distributed by Decca in the UK.
This was designed to promote the release of the Albert and David Maysles' film *Gimme Shelter*. When the album was re-released in digital format in 1986, re-mastered by Steve Rosenthal and Andrew Oldham, there is a long intro with all the band members mentioned. Also, a different recording of *Under My Thumb* was selected from the Bristol Colston Hall concert, with the vocal levels adjusted and the audience merged with the band rather than at odds. In 2005, a promotional film of *Have You Seen Your Mother Baby?* was released on a box set of singles.

333. FORTUNE TELLER (Neville) 1.56
11-20 October 1966: Place: IBC Studios, London, England.
Producer: Andrew Oldham.
Engineer: Glyn Johns.
USA LP GOT LIVE IF YOU WANT IT!: 9 December 1966: No. 6 - 11 weeks
UK Compilation LP GIMME SHELTER: 29 August 1971: No. 19 - 5 weeks

334. I'VE BEEN LOVING YOU TOO LONG (Redding, Butler) 2.54
11-20 October 1966: Place: IBC Studios, London, England.
Producer: Andrew Oldham.
Engineer: Glyn Johns.
USA LP GOT LIVE IF YOU WANT IT!: 9 December 1966: No. 6 - 11 weeks
UK Compilation LP GIMME SHELTER: 29 August 1971: No. 19 - 5 weeks

The final mixing for the GOT LIVE IF YOU WANT IT! album project was done at the IBC studios by Glyn Johns and Andrew Oldham. There must have been a shortage of material for these two older tracks to be over-dubbed with audience noise as it was not as if they needed promoting. Other tour live material such as *Play With Fire*, *The Spider And The Fly*, *She Said Yeah* and *Mother's Little Helper* sounded more mouth-watering. When it was released digitally in 1986 and 2002, different masters located for transfer and consequently both studio tracks were used for over-dub purposes.

4 DANDELION AND THE FLOWER POWER GAME
November 1966 – October 1967

335. ENGLISH SUMMER (Jagger, Richard)
8 November - 6 December 1966: Place: Olympic Sound Studios, Barnes, London, England.
Producer: Andrew Oldham.
Engineer: Glyn Johns.
Unavailable.

No bootleg recordings are available to verify this track. At one point it was proposed as a single release.

336. TROUBLE IN MIND (Jones) 3.43
8 November - 6 December 1966: Place: Olympic Sound Studios, Barnes, London, England.
Producer: Andrew Oldham.
Engineer: Glyn Johns.
Bootleg only.

A Richard M Jones (traditional) standard recorded by Sonny Terry and Walter Brown "Brownie" McGhee on their 1963 album BROWNIE'S BLUES. The song is led by Brian Jones on kazoo, Ian Stewart is invited to do the first chorus, then they all join in on the riff and see what happens. It rambled and rolled in a Brian-inspired studio jam. Jack Nitzsche joined the Stones for these London sessions which would complete the BETWEEN THE BUTTONS album - and a few more recordings were made besides.

337. SOMETIMES HAPPY, SOMETIMES BLUE (Jagger, Richard) 2.05
AKA: Dandelion, Fairground
8 November - 6 December 1966: Place: Olympic Sound Studios, Barnes, London, England.
Producer: Andrew Oldham.
Engineer: Glyn Johns.
Bootleg only.

An early version of *Dandelion*, with just the accompanying words of *Sometimes Happy, Sometimes Blue* and la-la guideline vocals by Keith Richards. There are no other lyrics and the arrangement is restricted to acoustic guitars. Glyn Johns was known by Keith Grant and, from these sessions, worked extensively at Olympic. Keith was a strict disciplinarian, focussing on time-keeping and professionalism. He did not tolerate the use of alcohol or drugs by the engineers (at least when he was in the building) and there was a golden rule of no photographs or autographs, remarking: "It was very important for the engineer to be an equal of the artist". The studios had moved from Carton Street to Church Road, Barnes, where Olympic opened again in the middle of 1966.

338. DANDELION (Jagger, Richard) 3.33
AKA: Sometimes Happy, Sometimes Blue, Fairground
8 November - 6 December 1966, 12-13 June, 2 July, 19 July 1967: Place: Olympic Sound Studios, Barnes, London, England.
Producer: Andrew Oldham.
Engineer: Glyn Johns.
Assistant Engineer: Eddie Kramer.
UK B-side We Love You: 18 August 1967
USA Single: 18 August 1967: No. 14 - 6 weeks
UK Compilation LP THROUGH THE PAST DARKLY (BIG HITS VOL 2): 12 September 1969: No. 2 - 37 weeks
USA Compilation LP THROUGH THE PAST DARKLY (BIG HITS VOL 2): 13 September 1969: No. 2 - 16 weeks
USA Compilation LP MORE HOT ROCKS (BIG HITS & FAZED COOKIES): 1 December 1972: No. 9 - 12 weeks
UK Compilation LP GET STONED - 30 GREATEST HITS, 30 ORIGINAL TRACKS: 21 October 1977: No. 13 - 15 weeks
German Compilation LP THE REST OF THE BEST: December 1983
UK & USA LP THE ROLLING STONES SINGLES COLLECTION - THE LONDON YEARS: 15 August 1989
USA Compilation Promo CD THE ROLLING STONES REMASTERED: 30 May 2002
USA Compilation CD MORE HOT ROCKS (BIG HITS & FAZED COOKIES): 3 September 2002
UK CD box set THE ROLLING STONES SINGLES - 1965 - 1967: 12 July 2004
USA CD box set THE ROLLING STONES SINGLES - 1965 - 1967: 27 July 2004
UK Compilation CD ROLLED GOLD +: 12 November 2007: No. 26 - 12 weeks

The lyrics to *Dandelion* are loosely based on several nursery-rhyme theories. This enhanced the music, giving it a tender and progressive trippy feel, compatible with the "summer of love" period. Perhaps this was the reason why it was not released until the following year when it was to feature as the flip side of *We Love You*. The harmony vocals do seem a little stretched but the overall achievement was significant, Brian Jones being featured on the orchestral sounds - a saxophone and was it an oboe? Either he or Jack Nitzsche played harpsichord.
Once the song fades out, the track winds into a segment of *We Love You*, which finishes as quickly as it starts. The song was concluded in June and July 1967 when *We Love You* was recorded at sessions attended by Paul McCartney and John Lennon, their harmony vocals said to be used on *Dandelion*. A demo of the song recorded at least six months before the released version was known as *Sometimes Happy, Sometimes Blue* and only has those words on it, sung by Keith Richards in guide style.

339. **IF YOU LET ME** (Jagger, Richard) 3.18
8 November - 6 December 1966: Place: Olympic Sound Studios, Barnes, London, England.
Producer: Andrew Oldham.
Engineer: Glyn Johns.
UK Compilation LP METAMORPHOSIS: 6 June 1975: No. 45 - 1 week
USA Compilation LP METAMORPHOSIS: 6 June 1975: No. 8 - 8 weeks

Bill Wyman vetted this song in 1974/75 for inclusion on the Stones' version of a compilation album of out-takes provisionally titled BLACK BOX. The album was never released but *If You Let Me* was included on Allen Klein's METAMORPHOSIS compilation. The BLACK BOX product featured too many non-Jagger, Richard compositions and therefore the royalties to ABKCO Music (an Allen Klein subsidiary) would have been insignificant - this is the carousel of music politics. The song's appeal is its laid back approach to a summer's stroll in the country with Brian Jones' dulcimer epitomising the mood of the sessions at the time. That country folk feel, with some more blues leanings, was to come more to the fore during the next year.

340. **RUBY TUESDAY** (Jagger, Richard) 3.11
AKA: Title 8
16 November - 6 December 1966: Place: Olympic Sound Studios, Barnes, London, England.
Played Live: 1967, 1989, 1990, 1997, 1998, 1999, 2003, 2005, 2006, 2007
Rolling Stones with Jack Nitzsche
Producer: Andrew Oldham.
Engineer: Glyn Johns.
Assistant Engineer: Eddie Kramer.
USA Single: 13 January 1967: No. 1 - 9 weeks
UK B-side Let's Spend The Night Together: 13 January 1967
USA LP BETWEEN THE BUTTONS: 11 February 1967: No. 2 - 19 weeks
USA Compilation LP FLOWERS: 15 July 1967: No. 3 - 18 weeks
UK Compilation LP THROUGH THE PAST DARKLY (BIG HITS VOL 2): 12 September 1969: No. 2 - 37 weeks
USA Compilation LP THROUGH THE PAST DARKLY (BIG HITS VOL 2): 13 September 1969: No. 2 - 16 weeks
USA LP THE ROLLING STONES HOT ROCKS 1964-1971: 11 January 1972: No. 4 - 30 weeks
UK Compilation LP ROLLED GOLD: 14 November 1975: No. 7 - 50 weeks
UK Compilation LP GET STONED - 30 GREATEST HITS, 30 ORIGINAL TRACKS: 21 October 1977: No. 13 - 15 weeks
UK LP SLOW ROLLERS: 9 November 1981
German Compilation LP THE REST OF THE BEST: December 1983
UK & USA LP THE ROLLING STONES SINGLES COLLECTION - THE LONDON YEARS: 15 August 1989
USA Compilation Promo CD THE ROLLING STONES REMASTERED: 30 May 2002
UK CD LP FORTY LICKS: 30 September 2002: No. 2 - 45 weeks
USA CD LP FORTY LICKS: 1 October 2002: No. 2 - 50 weeks
UK CD box set THE ROLLING STONES SINGLES - 1965 - 1967: 12 July 2004
USA CD box set THE ROLLING STONES SINGLES - 1965 - 1967: 27 July 2004
UK Compilation CD ROLLED GOLD +: 12 November 2007: No. 26 - 12 weeks

The Rolling Stones followed their stint in America by returning for what was to become a three-year period in the tranquillity of their native recording studios. *Ruby Tuesday* launched a significant change in direction and fortified the band's recent innovative moves made on AFTERMATH. Keith Richards had written the melody on a piano at his flat in St. Johns Wood. Brian Jones had been working on a German film score with arranger Mike Leander for *Mord Und Totschlag (A Degree Of Murder)* starring Anita Pallenberg, his then girlfriend. The film, a German entry at the Cannes Film Festival, featured all manner of instrumentation that typically inspired Brian at the time.
It was recorded in late 1966 and early 1967 by Glyn Johns and also featured Jimmy Page, Nicky Hopkins and Peter Gosling. The soundtrack has guitar, piano and recorder, the latter played by Brian and later used on *Ruby Tuesday* to create a romantic atmosphere. The double bass or cello is played beautifully by Bill Wyman and Keith Richards (Bill could not get his hands on the top to hold the notes and to strike the string so Keith plucked the strings, having marked the notes on the neck with a white pencil) while the piano accompaniment by Jack Nitzsche is superb. When Andrew Oldham re-mastered the track for CD release he discovered additional bass guitar sounds and whispered count-ins for the cello.
It was a well-deserved American No. 1, becoming their third biggest single ever. The Stones had tended to serve the American public with the more tepid (in beat) sounds while rock which could be danced to had been reserved for the British public - hence the swap in A-sides in Britain. The song was written almost exclusively by Keith and Brian Jones and is said to be about their mutual love for Linda Keith. Keith and Linda's relationship was souring as a result of her over-indulgence with drugs and the fact that she was sleeping with Jimi Hendrix.
In 1967, Brian finally nurtured what was to be a tempestuous relationship with Linda. The Richards/Jones combination was a promising move to rekindle the band. An out-take of *Ruby Tuesday* exists without the vocals and has a 1-2-3-4 introduction (* a - 3.25). In it, the structure of the song can be witnessed at first hand while, before the final take, the cello was removed into the background. Mick Jagger always enjoyed singing the track, even though he had not written it. Female singer Melanie (Safka) charted at No. 9 in the UK and No. 52 in the USA with the song in 1970. When ABKCO remastered *Ruby Tuesday* in 2002, the wrong mix was used without extra overdubbed backing vocals (* b - 3.17).

341. **LET'S SPEND THE NIGHT TOGETHER** (Jagger, Richard) 3.39
16 November - 6 December 1966: Place: Olympic Sound Studios, Barnes, London, England.
Played Live: 1967, 1976, 1977, 1981, 1982, 1997, 1998, 2006, 2007
Rolling Stones with Jack Nitzsche

Producer: Andrew Oldham.
Engineer: Glyn Johns.
Assistant Engineer: Eddie Kramer.
UK Single: 13 January 1967: No. 3 - 10 weeks
USA B-side Ruby Tuesday: 13 January 1967
USA LP BETWEEN THE BUTTONS: 11 February 1967: No. 2 - 19 weeks
USA Compilation LP FLOWERS: 15 July 1967: No. 3 - 18 weeks
UK Compilation LP THROUGH THE PAST DARKLY (BIG HITS VOL 2): 12 September 1969: No. 2 - 37 weeks
USA Compilation LP THROUGH THE PAST DARKLY (BIG HITS VOL 2): 13 September 1969: No. 2 - 16 weeks
USA LP THE ROLLING STONES HOT ROCKS 1964-1971: 11 January 1972: No. 4 - 30 weeks
UK Compilation LP ROLLED GOLD: 14 November 1975: No. 7 - 50 weeks
UK Compilation LP GET STONED - 30 GREATEST HITS, 30 ORIGINAL TRACKS: 21 October 1977: No. 13 - 15 weeks
German Compilation LP THE REST OF THE BEST: December 1983
UK & USA LP THE ROLLING STONES SINGLES COLLECTION - THE LONDON YEARS: 15 August 1989
UK CD LP FORTY LICKS: 30 September 2002: No. 2 - 45 weeks
USA CD LP FORTY LICKS: 1 October 2002: No. 2 - 50 weeks
UK CD box set THE ROLLING STONES SINGLES - 1965 - 1967: 12 July 2004
USA CD box set THE ROLLING STONES SINGLES - 1965 - 1967: 27 July 2004
UK Compilation CD ROLLED GOLD +: 12 November 2007: No. 26 - 12 weeks

The mood of the session changes and returns to a pop-rock theme. The production, however, moved away from the familiar guitar thrash to a song led by the piano playing of Jack Nitzsche, supported by an incessant throbbing drum beat. It was one of the first songs that Keith Richards had written on the piano, which was a new instrument for him, and he also played bass guitar. The critics picked up the unashamed lyrics and developed them into a moralistic story, particularly in America, with radio stations either bleeping out the "night" on the single, or settling for *Ruby Tuesday* on the other side.

The fans were quick to point out that *Let's Spend The Night Together* was an honest love song depicting modern times. Perhaps it refers to Mick Jagger's affair with Marianne Faithfull that had gathered pace as he finished his relationship with Chrissie Shrimpton at the end of the year. Andrew Oldham recalls the actual recording in London when two traffic policemen decided to investigate the unusual noises emanating from the studio.

Eddie Kramer was at the four-track by the window when Mick Jagger was finishing off some vocals and he warned Glyn Johns that two "fuzz" had just climbed the stairs and were stood behind him. On the headphones Glyn warned Mick, who turned around and asked them to help him with his headphones which were not secure. Meanwhile, the control room was being fumigated! Mick was well aware of this and, anxious to avoid any possible drugs scandal, grabbed the police officers' truncheons and banged them together as though they were a long-lost tribal instrument. They can be heard on the vocal bridge. With autographs signed, the cops disappeared - "Evening all!"

A version exists with just backing vocals and not the lead vocal track (* a - 3.56) and there is also an early instrumental (* b - 3.46). The single take is shorter than that on the album. (* c - 3.26). To this day, Andrew Oldham views *Let's Spend The Night Together* as one of their best songs. The Stones felt honoured when Muddy Waters recorded it for his 1968 electric blues album ELECTRIC MUD. It was also covered by David Bowie and Jerry Garcia in 1973 and 1974 respectively. In 2007, ROLLED GOLD + was released and included a stereo version of the song (* d - 3.37).

342. RUBY TUESDAY (Jagger, Richard) 3.19
15 January 1967: Place: Ed Sullivan TV Show, CBS Studio 50, New York, USA.
USA DVD 4 Ed Sullivan Shows Starring The Rolling Stones: 4 October 2011
USA DVD 6 Ed Sullivan Shows Starring The Rolling Stones: 1 November 2011

343. LET'S SPEND SOME TIME TOGETHER (Jagger, Richard) 3.03
AKA: Let's Spend The Night Together
15 January 1967: Place: Ed Sullivan TV Show, CBS Studio 50, New York, USA.
USA DVD 4 Ed Sullivan Shows Starring The Rolling Stones: 4 October 2011
USA DVD 6 Ed Sullivan Shows Starring The Rolling Stones: 1 November 2011

The Stones flew to America on the weekend of 14 January to promote the release of the double A-sided single *Ruby Tuesday/Let's Spend The Night Together*. Ed Sullivan, eager not to corrupt his young audience, demanded, "either the song goes or you go" but a compromise of sorts was reached after some alterations to the lyrics to "Let's Spend Some Time Together". To this day, the alternative title was still being used for a DVD release (perhaps due to emphasis being placed on the original censored times). Mick Jagger later claimed he did not use this alternative version but the recording contradicts this, as revealed on *25 X 5: The Continuing Adventures Of The Rolling Stones*. Every time it came to the chorus Mick lifted his forehead to the ceiling in despair, something of which he was not proud and would not compromise again, except on album covers.

In rehearsals for the show, Mick did sing the normal version, otherwise the Stones mimed to the backing tracks. The show, broadcast on 15 January, traditionally closed with all the artists appearing with Ed Sullivan during the credits. Controversially, the Stones wore Nazi regalia but security did not allow them to get to the stage where, among others, The Muppets were waiting.

The Stones were finally banned from the show by Ed Sullivan but, at that point, had received all the publicity and promotion they needed. The band also mimed to a playback of *Ruby Tuesday*, Keith Richards sat playing the piano, with Brian Jones next to him on the recorder. Bill Wyman sweeps his bow along a cello while Charlie Watts does his best to miss his drum queue.

344. CONNECTION (Jagger, Richard) 2.25
20 January 1967: Place: Olympic Sound Studios, London, England.
Bootleg only.

345. RUBY TUESDAY (Jagger, Richard) 3.17
20 January 1967: Place: Olympic Sound Studios, London, England.
Bootleg only.

346. IT'S ALL OVER NOW (Womack, Womack) 3.18
20 January 1967: Place: Olympic Sound Studios, London, England.
Bootleg only.

347. LET'S SPEND THE NIGHT TOGETHER (Jagger, Richard) 2.44
20 January 1967: Place: Olympic Sound Studios, London, England.
Bootleg only.

The Ed Sullivan Show was not the Stones' only brush with television officialdom that January. After immediately flying back to England, they managed to upset British viewers when they appeared on Sunday Night At The London Palladium on, 22 January 1967. They played the single with unaltered lyrics but refused, at Mick Jagger's instigation, to stand with the rest of the artists at the finale and wave to the audience. The British public, whipped up by the press, were insulted by this brash gesture which prompted repercussions they might later regret.

It was a two-fingered salute that backfired on them - even the diehard fans were unhappy. Mick Jagger told NME writer Keith Altham that the band intended to hit the road soon with a young person's show, which would include a compendium of entertainment . . . "except at the end we'll go round on a revolving stage, leaping about for an hour to make up for the Palladium. Oh, and the ice creams will all have acid in them, that's my brother's idea!"

A unique performance of *It's All Over Now*, with a different arrangement and a slower, more James Brown-style approach and stinging lead guitar, was recorded for the London Palladium show. The backing tracks were laid down at the Olympic studios on 20 January (the date BETWEEN THE BUTTONS was released) for broadcast on 22 January. The new Olympic studios were in Church Road, Barnes, at the site of a former theatre and cinema, having moved there following the closure of the studio in Carton Street. The desk was initially a transistorised four-track until it was upgraded to eight tracks, with 32 channels, in 1969.

348. SHE SMILED SWEETLY (Jagger, Richard)
5 February 1967: Place: Eamonn Andrews Show, ATV Studios, London, England.
Unavailable.

The Stones turned up to promote the *Let's Spend The Night Together* single on the Eamonn Andrews TV Show and were told by the musicians' union that they could not lip-synch to a backing track. As a result, the band played a live version of *She Smiled Sweetly* from the BETWEEN THE BUTTONS album. The UK Sunday newspaper News Of The World was in the middle of a series of stories on the lives of flamboyant, decadent, drug-taking pop stars (Pop Stars and Drugs: Facts That Will Shock You). In an interview on the show Mick Jagger used the opportunity to announce he was issuing a writ to defend himself against the News Of The World, which had reported him as being in a London club in possession of drugs. It was a case of mistaken identity, as the Rolling Stone in question was in fact Brian Jones. This writ would have revengeful consequences.

349. BLUES 1 (Jagger, Richard)
11 February 1967: Place: Olympic Sound Studios, London, England.
Producer: Rolling Stones.
Unavailable.

The atmosphere around the Stones throughout 1967 was heavily charged and the weekend of the 11/12 February was to prove horrendous by anyone's standards. In Bill Wyman's *Stone Alone* book, he refers to the recording of a *Blues 1* track on the Saturday and there were others labelled as Blues Tracks laid down - none are available. After the session, Mick Jagger and Keith Richards travelled to Redlands, Keith's country home, for a get-together with, among others, Marianne Faithfull, Robert Fraser, Christopher Gibbs, Michael Cooper, George and Pattie Harrison (the latter two only turned up on Sunday afternoon).

The weekend inevitably involved drugs and great food prepared by a Moroccan cook. It was also said to involve Mick's first and probably last acid trip. On Sunday morning, the atmosphere mellowed with strolls on a local beach (as Michael Cooper's photos show). During the evening, just after George and Pattie's exit from the Redlands lane (conspiracy theories abound), police officers from Bognor Regis, apparently responding to a tip-off, arrived at Redlands at 8.15 pm. Mick, Keith and Robert Fraser were busted - Mick for possession of amphetamines (alias Italian pep pills), Keith for allowing the use of drugs in his home and Robert for possession of heroin. It was a "frame-up", instigated by the News Of The World Sunday newspaper. David Schneiderman was the main suspect, having also been at the party and allegedly being found to have drugs - but was not charged. He fled the country and later changed his identity. It would seem that despite an arrest warrant the police allowed him to depart. The band would be in a state of flux until the court case was heard. More than 30 years later, Schneiderman's involvement in that eventful weekend was hinted at by David Jove (his real name being Schneiderman) in a part confession. The full truth of the "Acid King" may never come to light since he died in 2004. Mick and Keith may have had a wry smile when the complete demise and closure of the News Of The World occurred in 2011 due to a huge phone hacking scandal.

350. 2000 LIGHT YEARS FROM HOME (Jagger, Richard) 4.45
AKA: Title 12, Toffee Apple, Aftermath, Loose Woman
11 February, 7-22 July, 10 August - 7 September 1967: Place: Olympic Sound Studios, London, England.
Played Live: 1989, 1990
Rolling Stones with Nicky Hopkins, Eddie Kramer, John Paul Jones.
Producer: Rolling Stones.
Engineer: Glyn Johns.
Other Production: Eddie Kramer.
UK LP THEIR SATANIC MAJESTIES REQUEST: 8 December 1967: No. 3 - 13 weeks
USA LP THEIR SATANIC MAJESTIES REQUEST: 9 December 1967: No. 2 - 13 weeks
USA B-side She's A Rainbow: 23 December 1967

UK Compilation LP THROUGH THE PAST DARKLY (BIG HITS VOL 2): 12 September 1969: No. 2 - 37 weeks
USA Compilation LP THROUGH THE PAST DARKLY (BIG HITS VOL 2): 13 September 1969: No. 2 - 16 weeks
USA Compilation LP MORE HOT ROCKS (BIG HITS & FAZED COOKIES): 1 December 1972: No. 9 - 12 weeks
UK Compilation LP GET STONED - 30 GREATEST HITS, 30 ORIGINAL TRACKS: 21 October 1977: No. 13 - 15 weeks
UK & USA LP THE ROLLING STONES SINGLES COLLECTION - THE LONDON YEARS: 15 August 1989
USA Compilation CD MORE HOT ROCKS (BIG HITS & FAZED COOKIES): 3 September 2002
UK CD box set THE ROLLING STONES SINGLES - 1965 - 1967: 12 July 2004
USA CD box set THE ROLLING STONES SINGLES - 1965 - 1967: 27 July 2004
UK Compilation CD ROLLED GOLD +: 12 November 2007: No. 26 - 12 weeks

Despite the problems encircling the band they returned to work. As well as many other working titles, such as *Loose Woman* and *Aftermath*, an early instrumental of *2000 Light Years* was made in February before the main recordings in the summer (* a - 2.05). The inspiration of psychedelia was genuinely captured on this track with echoes of those true hippy pilgrims, The Pink Floyd, whose first album PIPER AT THE GATES OF DAWN was released in August 1967. The *2000 Light Years From Home* lyrics were supposedly written by Mick Jagger during his stay in jail: "It's so very lonely, you're 2000 light years from home."

The track is opened by Brian Jones gently feeling his way on the mellotron, Glyn Johns stating later that Brian's spooky playing, along with the strings, generally saved the track from anonymity. Eddie Kramer was beginning to forge a reputation for himself after starting out with the Kinks in the Pye studios in 1964 then progressing to Olympic, where he recorded The Small Faces with Glyn Johns. That summer he worked on the July 1967 Beatles' *All You Need Is Love* single and with Jimmy Miller on Traffic's first album MR. FANTASY.

Eddie Kramer was the key to the introduction of Jimmy Miller to the Stones though his most notable musical contribution was as engineer during Jimi Hendrix's career. With Chas Chandler as producer, he had just recorded Jimi's debut May 1967 ARE YOU EXPERIENCED? Eddie later worked on BEGGARS'S BANQUET and LOVE YOU LIVE. On *2000 Light Years From Home* he plays the wooden percussion instrument, the claves and John Paul Jones helps with the arrangement. Keith Richards' abrasive contribution on electric guitar added to the eerie atmosphere and the song became a firm favourite, although Mick Jagger felt it lost a lot on its stereo mix. Many out-takes of *2000 Light Years* are available on an alternative SATANIC MAJESTIES bootleg (* b - 30.32).

The single version is shorter by a minute (* c - 3.27). As the B-side of a USA promo single it was further edited (* d - 2.51). An acetate of possible masters was cut on 15 September and an alternative title of *Aftermath* was used for *2000 Light Years*. A colour promotional film, directed by Peter Clifton, shows the band performing the track, Mick Jagger resplendent in druid head gear. It was seen in Clifton's 1969 film of 60s beat music *Popcorn - An Audio Visual Thing*. The song was dramatically featured on the 1989 STEEL WHEELS and 1990 URBAN JUNGLE tours.

351. IN ANOTHER LAND (Wyman) 3.15
AKA: Acid In The Grass, Bill's Tune
11 February, 13-22 July 1967: Place: Olympic Sound Studios, London, England.
Rolling Stones with Nicky Hopkins, Steve Marriott, Ronnie Lane, Pete Townshend.
Producer: Rolling Stones.
Engineer: Glyn Johns.
USA Single: 4 December 1967
UK LP THEIR SATANIC MAJESTIES REQUEST: 8 December 1967: No. 3 - 13 weeks
USA LP THEIR SATANIC MAJESTIES REQUEST: 9 December 1967: No. 2 - 13 weeks
UK & USA LP THE ROLLING STONES SINGLES COLLECTION - THE LONDON YEARS: 15 August 1989
UK CD box set THE ROLLING STONES SINGLES - 1965 - 1967: 12 July 2004
USA CD box set THE ROLLING STONES SINGLES - 1965 - 1967: 27 July 2004

Bill Wyman managed to break the band's dominant songwriting partnership during the "Satanic" sessions by recording on the Monday after the Redlands arrests. Glyn Johns had cancelled an evening's recording when Mick and Keith were indisposed and was unable to contact Bill Wyman or Charlie Watts, so they dutifully turned up on time with Brian Jones. The piano foundations of the track were originally put down by Bill while Small Faces pair Steve Marriott and Ronnie Lane, who were recording in the next studio, came in and placed down some lead guitar and vocals. It is also possible that Pete Townshend provided backing vocals to the track as, within an "extra" for the *Rock And Roll Circus* DVD, he has indicated that he sung with Ronnie Lane on a Stones number. Nicky Hopkins filled the tracks out by contributing some fine piano work.

The Small Faces had just signed to Andrew Oldham's Immediate label and were recording for their next single, *Itchycoo Park*, with Glyn Johns, George Chkiantz and Eddie Kramer at the controls. The end of that track has some *We Love You* similarities, as The Small Faces were experimenting with psychedelia. Ian McLagan recalled that Andrew Oldham and Immediate Records were like a breath of fresh air. The band were treated very well, unlike their previous management stint with Don Arden, which undeniably had brought them success. Also, with Andrew, they were encouraged to record freely and not be restrained and this they did gleefully, although the tapes would stop running when Glyn Johns went home at midnight.

George Chkiantz had been experimenting with tape phasing or flanging, a process where two master tapes are played side-by-side and one is flanged slightly to alter the sound and speed. This was evidently heard in mono on *Green Circles* by the Small Faces. George introduced this technique to George Martin and shared it with his colleagues at Olympic while Eddie Kramer transformed Jimi Hendrix's sound on the swirling stereo of *Bold As Love*.

As Keith Grant reiterated: "All the engineers were quite happy to share their techniques and there was no thought of keeping anything to oneself. We were a true family." Bill's vocals on *In Another Land* also involved studio wizardry as they were suitably disguised, with some Glyn Johns trickery, as the feathers floated by in the wind. It was a song about a dream within a dream with Bill having to record his vocal when everyone had left the studio due to his embarrassment.

The final mix was decided upon after a number of takes, twenty-three of which are on a bootleg (* a - 8.34, b - 12.54), among them are some heavily-featured piano versions. On the following day, the recordings were played back to the group and they had to admit that it was OK and in keeping with the "Satanic" mood. Backing vocals were overdubbed by Mick Jagger and Keith Richards, therefore maintaining the band's collectiveness.

This whole exercise proved that the songwriting duo would consider other material but the circumstances of the recording were coincidental to say the least. The Stones recognised the recording by releasing it as a single in America, but it flopped without even entering the Top 40. There was no promotional work to support its release. Was the overdubbed snoring at the end of the album cut an indication of Brian Jones' mounting boredom or actually Bill snoozing waiting for the band to show (in reality the latter!)?

352. SHE'S A RAINBOW (Jagger, Richard) 4.35
AKA: She Comes In Colours, Lady Fair, Pieces, Flowers, Flowers In Your Hair, Flowers In Your Barnet
16-20 May, 12-13 June 1967: Place: Olympic Sound Studios, London, England.
Played Live: 1997, 1998
Rolling Stones with John Paul Jones, Nicky Hopkins.
Producer: Rolling Stones.
Engineer: Glyn Johns.
UK LP THEIR SATANIC MAJESTIES REQUEST: 8 December 1967: No. 3 - 13 weeks
USA LP THEIR SATANIC MAJESTIES REQUEST: 9 December 1967: No. 2 - 13 weeks
USA Single: 23 December 1967: No. 25 - 4 weeks
UK Compilation LP THROUGH THE PAST DARKLY (BIG HITS VOL 2): 12 September 1969: No. 2 - 37 weeks
USA Compilation LP THROUGH THE PAST DARKLY (BIG HITS VOL 2): 13 September 1969: No. 2 - 16 weeks
UK Compilation LP MILESTONES: 18 February 1972: No. 14 - 8 weeks
USA Compilation LP MORE HOT ROCKS (BIG HITS & FAZED COOKIES): 1 December 1972: No. 9 - 12 weeks
UK Compilation LP ROLLED GOLD: 14 November 1975: No. 7 - 50 weeks
UK Compilation LP GET STONED - 30 GREATEST HITS, 30 ORIGINAL TRACKS: 21 October 1977: No. 13 - 15 weeks
UK & USA LP THE ROLLING STONES SINGLES COLLECTION - THE LONDON YEARS: 15 August 1989
USA Compilation Promo CD THE ROLLING STONES REMASTERED: 30 May 2002
USA Compilation Promo CD ABKCO'S THE ROLLINGS STONES REMASTERED SERIES: 30 May 2002
USA Compilation CD MORE HOT ROCKS (BIG HITS & FAZED COOKIES): 3 September 2002
UK CD LP FORTY LICKS: 30 September 2002: No. 2 - 45 weeks
USA CD LP FORTY LICKS: 1 October 2002: No. 2 - 50 weeks
UK CD box set THE ROLLING STONES SINGLES - 1965 - 1967: 12 July 2004
USA CD box set THE ROLLING STONES SINGLES - 1965 - 1967: 27 July 2004
UK Compilation CD ROLLED GOLD +: 12 November 2007: No. 26 - 12 weeks

Desperate to gain some peace from the press attention following the busts and at the advice of Allen Klein, Brian Jones, Keith Richards, Mick Jagger, Tom Keylock, Anita Pallenberg, Christopher Gibbs and Robert Fraser met up in Tangier, Morocco. Tom (who had been Bob Dylan's protector and driver on his "electric" 1966 world tour at Keith's suggestion) drove Brian, Keith and Anita and the girlfriend of Donald Cammell (director of the film Performance) from Paris to Tangier in his Blue Lena. However, Brian became ill en-route in France and was hospitalised. As a result Keith and Anita journeyed on and were able to "get it on". Brian recuperated and a guilty-feeling Anita went back to him, the pair returning to London, from where they took a flight with Marianne Faithfull. On a stopover in Gibraltar, Brian played extracts of his music from *A Soundtrack To Murder* to the Barbary apes on the top of the rock but they ran away, increasing his paranoia. In Tangier, details of the love tryst inevitably came out and Brian beat up Anita, injuring his hand in the process, before Tom fled with Keith and Anita in the car. This did not bode well for the atmosphere on the European tour in March and April 1967. Brian's father, Lewis Jones, said in 1971 that this was a pivotal moment in Brian's ultimate downfall - he had lost the girl he loved the most and never recovered emotionally.

The tour circle was widened with Italy, Poland and Greece being included while, in Zurich, Switzerland, on 14 April, Mick was hurled to the floor by a fan and nearly fell off the stage. Tom Keylock was involved in the skirmish and broke his hand. The Greek Panathinaikos date on 17 April was Brian's last concert date with the Stones, apart from an NME Poll Winners show. Customs inspections, riots, arrests, police lining stages and smoke bombs were part of the tour make up. Indeed the New Musical Express attended the unique concert in Poland where they reported on "battlefield" scenes outside the concert hall - with photographs backing this up. The communist-led Poles had distributed tickets to party members and workers.

Elsewhere, the Stones were almost embroiled in the Greek uprising that led to the deposing of King Constantine, the coup d'état occurring on 21 April. Bill Wyman recalls in *Rolling With The Stones* that he had decided to stay for a short holiday and heard gunfire. Because of the strife, the airport was shut and he could not get a flight out for a few days. News footage of the tour shows the mayhem but brief sound-bites also illustrate the intensity and rawness of the band's playing. The Australian band, The Easybeats, supported the Stones on the tour and featured songwriter George Young, who was the elder brother of Michael and Angus Young from the yet to be formed AC/DC.

On 10 May, Mick Jagger, Keith Richards and Robert Fraser went to the first court hearing when trial by jury was agreed for late June. As if to compound the conspiracy theories, Brian Jones was arrested for possession of cannabis at his flat the same day. He appeared in court in June and elected to be tried by jury later in the year. The SATANIC MAJESTIES sessions were spread through the summer of 1967 and were undoubtedly marred by these drug busts and various court appearances. The band were burnt out after the incessant touring and the police attention did nothing to help. Ironically, while other bands were reaching a creative peak, the Stones were hitting a lull and lack of enthusiasm in their output.

Sometimes Mick and Keith would not come to the studio until late in the evening. Quite often Glyn Johns would tell the punctual ones, such as Bill Wyman, Charlie Watts and Nicky Hopkins, to go and waste a few hours in the pub. Andrew Oldham became thoroughly disillusioned by the situation, resulting in a series of blazing disagreements with Mick. In his book *2Stoned* he said: "I would be unable to distinguish whether I was driving the plane or a passenger who has lost control of the ride." The Stones deliberately antagonised him by logging all-night sessions, playing bum sounds and generally freaking out. Andrew Oldham, frustrated at the growing arguments and his inability to contribute, gave up and walked out, leaving the Stones to Allen Klein and, on this occasion, to produce themselves. Besides, his attention was being taken more and more by the company he had formed with Tony Calder, Immediate Records.

She's A Rainbow was one of the first songs recorded at the sessions - demos originated from May 1967 as the alternative titles suggest - and continued the pretty Elizabethan sound started in *Ruby Tuesday* and *Dandelion*. The group Love released their second album DA CAPO in April 1967 - one of the final tracks being Arthur Lee's *She Comes In Colours*, which possibly inspired the Stones' *She's A Rainbow*. The song's prominent instruments are Nicky's beautiful piano melody and the discordant orchestral strings which were supplied by the aforementioned John Paul Jones, who later found considerable fame with British super group Led Zeppelin. There is a 25-second introduction with fairground background noises on what was a suitable flower-power type song, though it was not released as a single in Britain. The single came out in the USA, though, and it was also edited for a DJ-only promotional copy (* a - 2.51). Brian described it as "Indian with a touch of the Arabian nights." A rough mix out-take exists (* b - 4.10) along with seven early takes (* c - 12.15). An acetate was prepared of the possible final cut in September and the track was titled *Flowers*. Other tracks were *Aftermath (2000 Light Years From Home)*, *God Bless You (Sing This All Together)*, *After Five (Citadel)* and *Pieces*. There is a rare promotional film by Michael Lindsay-Hogg, a young producer who had worked on similar exercises the previous year with the Beatles (*Paperback Writer* and *Rain*) and the Who (*Happy Jack*).

353. TELSTAR II (Jagger, Richard)
16-20 May 1967: Place: Olympic Sound Studios, London, England.
Producer: Rolling Stones.
Engineer: Glyn Johns.
Unavailable.

354. MANHOLE COVER (Jagger, Richard)
16-20 May 1967: Place: Olympic Sound Studios, London, England.
Producer: Rolling Stones.
Engineer: Glyn Johns.
Unavailable.

These tracks, recorded at the same sessions as *She's A Rainbow*, were mentioned in Bill Wyman's book *Rolling With The Stones* but are unavailable. Another possibility for the studio location is RG Jones, Morden which was used for rehearsals. At Olympic, Keith Grant had a good relationship with George Martin and had assisted him in recording Matt Monro. In May they worked together again with the Beatles on *Baby You're A Rich Man* with Brian Jones rumoured to be playing the oboe. This was recorded at Olympic on 11 May by Keith Grant and Eddie Kramer. Keith's business-like style pushed the Beatles along and it was one of the few tracks they recorded in a six-hour non-stop session. Keith could not reliably say if the Stones contributed since he said the session was so busy. Geoff Emerick, who was assistant to George Martin at Abbey Road, commented that the sound captured by Keith was very good, particularly the low, bass frequencies which the Olympic console did so well. Brian also may have played saxophone on *You Know My Name (Look Up The Number)* in June.

355. CITADEL (Jagger, Richard) 2.50
AKA: After Five
9 June, 7-22 July, 10 August - 7 September 1967: Place: Olympic Sound Studios, London, England.
Rolling Stones with Nicky Hopkins, Rocky Dijon
Producer: Rolling Stones.
Engineer: Glyn Johns.
UK LP THEIR SATANIC MAJESTIES REQUEST: 8 December 1967: No. 3 - 13 weeks
USA LP THEIR SATANIC MAJESTIES REQUEST: 9 December 1967: No. 2 - 13 weeks
UK LP SOLID ROCK: 13 October 1980

The Stones' mid-summer recording stint became known as the *Citadel* sessions. There is a proliferation of bootleg recordings from this time and *Citadel* is one that has a number of instrumental takes available (* a - 25.21). Nicky Hopkins is in danger of overshadowing the song's structure on some cuts while Charlie Watts' cascading drum sounds introduce others. The lyrics mention, "Candy and Taffy, hope you are both well. Please come and see me in the citadel". This referred to two drag queens who hung out on the New York scene. *Citadel* centres around a Keith Richards heavy guitar riff which was copied by Bryan Ferry on his 1973 hit single *Street Life*. The song is said to be inspired by the early 1920s film *Metropolis*. Weird glockenspiel is played by Mick Jagger and mellotron - or even a child's ukulele - was later added by Brian Jones to what was originally quite a simple rock song. Other keyboards have Nicky Hopkins on an underlying harpsichord and piano. The track also features the first contribution by percussionist Rocky Dijon (Rocki Dzidzornu).

356. WE LOVE YOU (Jagger, Richard) 4.21
AKA: We Love You, Goodbye
13, 21 June, 2, 19 July 1967: Place: Olympic Sound Studios, London, England.
Rolling Stones with John Lennon, Paul McCartney, Nicky Hopkins.
Producer: Andrew Oldham.
Engineer: Glyn Johns.
UK Single: 18 August 1967: No. 8 - 8 weeks
USA B-side Dandelion: 18 August 1967
UK Compilation LP THROUGH THE PAST DARKLY (BIG HITS VOL 2): 12 September 1969: No. 2 - 37 weeks
USA Compilation LP MORE HOT ROCKS (BIG HITS & FAZED COOKIES): 1 December 1972: No. 9 - 12 weeks
UK Compilation LP ROLLED GOLD: 14 November 1975: No. 7 - 50 weeks
UK Compilation LP GET STONED - 30 GREATEST HITS, 30 ORIGINAL TRACKS: 21 October 1977: No. 13 - 15 weeks
German Compilation LP THE REST OF THE BEST: December 1983
UK & USA LP THE ROLLING STONES SINGLES COLLECTION - THE LONDON YEARS: 15 August 1989
USA Compilation CD MORE HOT ROCKS (BIG HITS & FAZED COOKIES): 3 September 2002
UK CD box set THE ROLLING STONES SINGLES - 1965 - 1967: 12 July 2004
USA CD box set THE ROLLING STONES SINGLES - 1965 - 1967: 27 July 2004
UK Compilation CD ROLLED GOLD +: 12 November 2007: No. 26 - 12 weeks

The drugs trial commenced on 27 June and full sentences were passed on 29 June. Mick Jagger was the first to take to the stand and was found guilty of drug possession, despite his doctor testifying that, while he did not prescribe the tablets, Mick had his moral blessing to use the Italian pills. Robert Fraser was also found guilty but sentence could not be passed until Keith Richards' trial was heard. Mick and Robert were remanded in custody, handcuffed and taken to Lewes prison. The more complicated trial for Keith commenced the next day but he too was found guilty.
The result was a preposterous three-month jail sentence for Mick and a year for Keith. Robert Fraser, an art gallery friend, was sentenced to six months. They were banged away separately in HMP Brixton and HMP Wormwood Scrubs (the latter with Robert Fraser). Eventually British justice awakened and, on 30 June, having

spent their respective time in jail, Mick and Keith were released on bail, awaiting appeal and with their passports held. An incensed Keith was advised not to sue Her Majesty for allowing drugs to be available in one of her establishments, since he had been offered them. On 1 July, The Times ran a famous leader article entitled "Who Breaks A Butterfly On A Wheel?", attacking the rough justice and questioning the reasoning of Judge Block, who had presided over the case.

In a move to keep the Stones' music in the public eye, The Who and Kit Lambert recorded *The Last Time* and *Under My Thumb*, with Jimmy Page on guitar, at De Lane Lea Studios, on the day before the sentences were announced. The single was rushed out on the day of Mick and Keith's release and reached No. 44 in the UK charts. That other British group, The Beatles, had spent a period at Olympic Studios in June recording their next single *All You Need Is Love*, with Mick and Keith contributing backing vocals. The friendship and that deed was reciprocated as John Lennon and Paul McCartney accompanied the Stones singing high harmonies on *We Love You* apparently transforming the song and session at one o'clock one morning. The result was a trippy, psychedelic song opened by heavy footsteps and clanging cell doors. Bill Wyman wanted to use a Goon Show (the comedy team of Michael Bentine, Spike Milligan, Harry Secombe and Peter Sellers) sketch soundtrack for the shutting gates. The February 1956 episode, repeated in April 1964, was entitled *Tales Of Old Dartmoor (HM Princetown Prison)* and a similar sound effect of someone walking along the corridor and a door opening and shutting featured in this story.

Bill's trickling bass sound is heard well on the mix while Nicky Hopkins' piano riff provides the song's structure and glue. The mellotron played by Brian launches in and the band turn the other cheek, declaring in typical hippy style "We Love You". They were trying to get as much done before the drugs trial so that there would be some legacy of their work if had spent any length of time in jail. The alternative title *We Love You, Goodbye* was even considered for a while.

As the song progresses, the sounds become weirder, with Brian obviously enjoying the off-beat Arabic brass arrangements and using the Olympic studio mellotron to excellent affect. In his book *Let It Bleed*, Sean Egan says quite simply that engineer George Chkiantz felt Brian's contribution was "a fucking miracle . . . he exceeded himself." Nicky Hopkins had the opening piano riff in his mind for weeks ahead of the recording and was looking for a song that it could work on. The single release has remnants of *Dandelion* during the fade out. An instrumental out-take has a more pronounced lead guitar arrangement, minus brass (* a - 3.02). An accumulation of five instrumental takes can also be heard (* b - 9.52). Keith had to ensure that the song was speeded up so it was not too dirge like. It was the last production by Andrew Oldham as the band officially split from his management in September.

Peter Whitehead, following his film work on *Have You Seen Your Mother?*, was contacted again and asked to produce a promotional film for *We Love You*. It was a pastiche based on The Trials of Oscar Wilde and, due to its anti-establishment, provocative nature, was banned by the BBC. Keith features as the Marquis of Queensbury and Marianne Faithfull also has a role, revealing Mick seemingly naked under a certain fur rug. Segments of the band in the studio at one point show Brian looking totally stoned. The film concluded that Mick and Keith had been lucky to avoid Wilde's fate of incarceration. Meanwhile, Robert Fraser continued his sentence devoid of a pardon or his freedom. The Manic Street Preachers were inspired by the arrogance of the song title and, on their 1992 debut album, they recorded a song called *You Love Us*.

357. SHE'S DOING HER THING (Jagger, Richard)
7-22 July, 10 August - 7 September 1967: Place: Olympic Sound Studios, London, England.
Producer: Rolling Stones.
Engineer: Glyn Johns.
Unavailable.

358. BLOW ME MAMA (Jagger, Richard)
7 - 22 July, 10 August - 7 September 1967: Place: Olympic Sound Studios, London, England.
Producer: Rolling Stones.
Engineer: Glyn Johns.
Unavailable.

It was registered by ABKCO for publishing credits which indicates recordings must have been made of the song.

359. BATHROOM (Jagger, Richard)
AKA: Toilet
7-22 July, 10 August - 7 September 1967: Place: Olympic Sound Studios, London, England.
Producer: Rolling Stones.
Engineer: Glyn Johns.
Unavailable.

Three other songs, said to be recorded during the SATANIC MAJESTIES sessions, were possibly given working titles but all are unavailable. Brian Jones referred to one out-take being labelled *Plum Blossom*. The Stones were evidently glad to see the end of 1967 as the year had been dominated by the drug busts, culminating with Brian Jones being given three years' probation and a fine on 12 December. Rest and recuperation was what was needed and, for a number of months, it became the longest period of inactivity since the Stones story began. They deserved it after the incessant pace, concert after concert, tour after tour, with recording studios in between.

360. SING THIS ALL TOGETHER (Jagger, Richard) 3.46
AKA: All Together, God Bless You
7-22 July, 10 August - 7 September 1967: Place: Olympic Sound Studios, London, England.
Rolling Stones with Nicky Hopkins, John Lennon, Paul McCartney.
Producer: Rolling Stones.
Engineer: Glyn Johns.
UK LP THEIR SATANIC MAJESTIES REQUEST: 8 December 1967: No. 3 - 13 weeks
USA LP THEIR SATANIC MAJESTIES REQUEST: 9 December 1967: No. 2 - 13 weeks

361. SING THIS ALL TOGETHER (SEE WHAT HAPPENS) (Jagger, Richard) 7.52
AKA: All Together, God Bless You
7-22 July, 10 August - 7 September 1967: Place: Olympic Sound Studios, London, England.
Rolling Stones with Nicky Hopkins, John Lennon, Paul McCartney.
Producer: Rolling Stones.
Engineer: Glyn Johns.
UK LP THEIR SATANIC MAJESTIES REQUEST: 8 December 1967: No. 3 - 13 weeks
USA LP THEIR SATANIC MAJESTIES REQUEST: 9 December 1967: No. 2 - 13 weeks

THEIR SATANIC MAJESTIES REQUEST was originally intended by Mick Jagger to be a concept album, inspired by the statement on British Passports: "Her Britannic Majesty's Principal Secretary of State for Foreign and Commonwealth Affairs Requests and Requires in the Name of Her Majesty . . ." but, for the sake of satirical brevity, this was altered to Her Satanic Majesty Requests and Requires. Decca were none too happy at this suggestion, hence the eventual title. At one stage, in readiness for a seasonal release, the album was entitled COSMIC CHRISTMAS, an idea also spurned.

Sing This All Together, separated by other album tracks, opens and closes Side One. Keith Altham confirmed in September 1967 that Brian Jones had played him, in the studio, a 15-minute instrumental track which made up the two halves of the song. At the time it was hip and psychedelic to introduce recurring themes, as in a dream - possibly the reason for the split in the track. The June 1967 Beatles' album SGT PEPPER had included a reprise of the opening track *Sgt Pepper's Lonely Hearts Club Band*. Musically, *Sing This All Together* spins around a lacklustre sing-along of "Why don't we sing this song all together". The non-resonant rhythms and instruments that accompany this give the song a psychedelic, intoxicating appeal.

In contrast to *Sing This All Together*, the seven-minute *See What Happens* is essentially a dream-like trippy sequence, featuring a jam on electric guitar and experimentation of various exotic instruments and substances. John Lennon and Paul McCartney feature on karma-like backing vocals and maybe some percussion. "Where's that joint?" can be heard at the beginning of *See What Happens* in studio chat, perhaps a remark aimed at antagonising the establishment! The flute and brass are played by Brian Jones while Nicky Hopkins is featured heavily on piano. Take seven of the song can be heard on bootleg sounding like an unedited version of the released mix (* a - 14.54).

362. GOMPER (Jagger, Richard) 5.08
AKA: Flowers In Your Hair, The Ladies The Lillies And The Lake
7-22 July, 5 August 1967: Place: Olympic Sound Studios, London, England.
Producer: Rolling Stones.
Engineer: Glyn Johns.
UK LP THEIR SATANIC MAJESTIES REQUEST: 8 December 1967: No. 3 - 13 weeks
USA LP THEIR SATANIC MAJESTIES REQUEST: 9 December 1967: No. 2 - 13 weeks

As the sessions progressed, they become increasingly weird and freakish as highlighted on *Gomper*. The flavour is demonstrably eastern, with Brian Jones playing the dulcimer and mellotron while tabla drums are gently tapped in the background by Mick Jagger. It was inspired by Tibetan monks who became induced into a "gomper" hypnotic state. An organ is played which resembles the sound of a synthesiser though these were only just being introduced into the music world. Once the vocals finish after less than two minutes, the track develops into a musical freak-out, lasting three or four more. This was proved by the rich number of out-takes from the *Gomper* session, two of which are more than eight minutes long (* a - 8.50, b - 8.56, c - 6.49).

Brian Jones had reached a difficult phase. Having helped to escalate the Stones to their current pitch with his contribution on various instruments and also unintentionally furthering the far-out public image by his acid trips with Jimi Hendrix and company, he now felt enough was enough. At one point he seriously considered leaving the band to work on solo projects but was convinced otherwise. He did not like the Stones' move away from the blues and thought it was time to divert his wiped-out talents elsewhere. This was unfortunately not helped by his current mental and physical state, which prompted various hospital visits from July to December following his drug bust in May 1967. His prison sentence was fortunately repealed in December 1967 following reports from his physician, Dr Green, which stated that imprisonment would throw Brian into the chasm of total despair.

363. MAJESTIES HONKY TONK (Jagger, Richard) 2.28
7-22 July, 10 August - 7 September 1967: Place: Olympic Sound Studios, London, England.
Producer: Rolling Stones.
Engineer: Glyn Johns.
Bootleg only.

One of the many instrumental out-takes available on bootleg. Various takes exist (*a - 20.41), the track name inspired by bootleggers.

364. 5 PART JAM (Jagger, Richard) 3.33
7-22 July, 10 August - 7 September 1967: Place: Olympic Sound Studios, London, England.
Producer: Rolling Stones.
Engineer: Glyn Johns.
Bootleg only.

Again an instrumental of which multiple takes exist on bootleg (* a - 25.51). If spliced together it may have extended past three minutes. Strictly for fans and maybe an embryo for *On With The Show*.

365. 2000 MAN (Jagger, Richard) 3.07
AKA: I Want All The People To Know
7-22 July, 5 August, 16, 21, 23 October 1967: Place: Olympic Sound Studios, London, England.
Rolling Stones with Nicky Hopkins.
Producer: Rolling Stones.
Engineer: Glyn Johns.

UK LP THEIR SATANIC MAJESTIES REQUEST: 8 December 1967: No. 3 - 13 weeks
USA LP THEIR SATANIC MAJESTIES REQUEST: 9 December 1967: No. 2 - 13 weeks
USA Compilation LP THE ROLLING STONES PROMOTIONAL ALBUM: October 1969

2000 Man, a relatively short three-minute song, begins with an acoustic guitar work-out and finishes as an electric thrash on organ and guitar. It is a heavy track which, at the end, is driven by Bill Wyman's bass while Charlie Watts plays an echoed beat and Nicky Hopkins is the man on organ. Were Mick Jagger's lyrics prophetic of the Internet with *2000 Man,* as he asks the question: "Am I having an affair with a random computer?" Meanwhile Mick Taylor, who had recently joined John Mayall's Bluesbreakers, was about to record his first album with him CRUSADE. He witnessed some of the SATANIC sessions and, at that time, bought Keith Richards' sunburst Gibson Les Paul original, acquired by the Stones man in 1961 from him. Mick Taylor could not recall meeting Keith since the transaction was done with Ian Stewart. Little did Keith realise that the instrument would later see Rolling Stones duty again.
In the studio Mick became aware of the friendly rivalry between the Stones and The Beatles which contributed to his determination to produce an album of at least equal quality to the newly-released SGT PEPPER'S LONELY HEARTS CLUB BAND. Musically the Stones failed as SGT PEPPER is melodic, whereas SATANIC MAJESTIES lacks true depth and continuity. However, some fans will still refer to individual songs as not being as bad as critical history has determined. The alternative title is from a studio engineer introduction on an out-take. There are more than ten tracks and some 15 takes of *2000 Man* (* a - 38.53) plus various introductions, middle parts and ends. An acetate was prepared of a possible final cut for SATANIC in September but excludes *2000 Man.*

366. TITLE 15 (Jagger, Richard) 4.05
7-22 July, 10 August - 7 September 1967: Place: Olympic Sound Studios, London, England.
Producer: Rolling Stones.
Engineer: Glyn Johns.
Bootleg only.

Two instrumental out-takes exist of this track. The first is purely electric rhythm guitar with light drums in the background (* a - 4.08) while the other one includes a second lead guitar. It has a couple of memorable riffs, possibly stashed away by Keith Richards and re-cycled in parts for *Honky Tonk Women* and *Luxury.*

367. TITLE 5 (Jagger, Richard) 1.47
7-22 July, 10 August - 7 September 1967; September - November; December 2009: Place: Olympic Sound Studios, London, England; One East Studio, New York, Henson Studios, Village Recording; Mix This!, Los Angeles, USA.
Producer: Don Was, The Glimmer Twins.
Engineer: Glyn Johns; Additional Engineering and Editing: Krish Sharma; Mixed by Bob Clearmountain.
UK CD EXILE ON MAIN ST (EXTRA TRACKS): 17 May 2010: No. 1 - 10 weeks
USA CD EXILE ON MAIN ST (EXTRA TRACKS): 18 May 2010: No. 1 - 3 weeks

A drum roll then Glyn Johns announces "Title 5 take one". It kicks off with a distinct guitar sound, almost like a Jews Harp vibrato effect through a Vox amplifier. The song's style is similar to *Title 15,* which was a Satanic era out-take. It is another instrumental with just drums, bass and guitars and is not to be confused with the same alternative title to *Jumpin' Jack Flash.* It rolls along to an unsophisticated riff and concludes with some guitar feedback.
The era of this two-minute track is not obvious and it sounds at odds to the rest of the numbers included for the extras on the re-release of EXILE ON MAIN ST in 2010. Perhaps it was as early as late 1966 but more likely from the SATANIC period. It finds itself at the end of the bonus tracks amongst other out-takes from 1970 which had no alterations or additions from 2009. It was well received since the track and its overall sound had not been heard before.

368. SATANIC ORGAN JAM (Jagger, Richard) 1.44
7-22 July, 10 August - 7 September 1967: Place: Olympic Sound Studios, London, England.
Rolling Stones with Nicky Hopkins.
Producer: Rolling Stones.
Engineer: Glyn Johns.
Bootleg only.

A track reminiscent of *She Smiled Sweetly.*

369. SOUL BLUES (Jagger, Richard) 3.53
7-22 July, 10 August - 7 September 1967: Place: Olympic Sound Studios, London, England.
Rolling Stones with Nicky Hopkins.
Producer: Rolling Stones.
Engineer: Glyn Johns.
Bootleg only.

The rhythm unit of bass and percussion, Bill Wyman and Charlie Watts, participate in this studio jam with some organ by Nicky Hopkins. Three out-takes exist from the SATANIC sessions (* a - 1.46, b - 2.05).

370. THE LANTERN (Jagger, Richard) 4.23
AKA: Fly High As A Kite, Fly My Kite, Dream Pipe
7-22 July, 5 August 1967: Place: Olympic Sound Studios, London, England.
Rolling Stones with Nicky Hopkins.
Producer: Rolling Stones.
Engineer: Glyn Johns.
USA B-side In Another Land: 4 December 1967
UK LP THEIR SATANIC MAJESTIES REQUEST: 8 December 1967: No. 3 - 13 weeks

USA LP THEIR SATANIC MAJESTIES REQUEST: 9 December 1967: No. 2 - 13 weeks
UK & USA LP THE ROLLING STONES SINGLES COLLECTION - THE LONDON YEARS: 15 August 1989
UK CD box set THE ROLLING STONES SINGLES - 1965 - 1967: 12 July 2004
USA CD box set THE ROLLING STONES SINGLES - 1965 - 1967: 27 July 2004

The recordings at the Olympic Studio continued with or without the presence of Brian Jones (due to his unstable health). *The Lantern* commences with a gothic funeral introduction and continues at a slow pace. Acoustic and lead guitar, supplied by Keith Richards, do not help the depressive weary "sea of light" philosophy. It was music designed to appeal to the intellect and mind, as Jagger related to Keith Altham, for the New Musical Express. The arrangement has some acoustic and piano parts that would be experimented with further on BEGGARS BANQUET. Again many versions are available on eight out-takes (* a - 26.45).

371. BLUES NO. 3 (Jagger, Richard) 3.02
7-22 July, 10 August - 7 September 1967: Place: Olympic Sound Studios, London, England.
Rolling Stones with Nicky Hopkins.
Producer: Rolling Stones.
Engineer: Glyn Johns.
Bootleg only.

This track was extensively worked upon but did not fit in with the others. Six cuts exist as the tapes keep running on over 25 multiple "try again" takes (* a - 19.21). It was a blues rock R 'n' B song with Nicky Hopkins on organ. It had a strong lead riff which, on some takes, went into a jam-like heavy blues boogie à la *Rock Me Baby*.

372. JAM ONE (Jagger, Richard) 4.05
7-22 July, 10 August - 7 September 1967: Place: Olympic Sound Studios, London, England.
Producer: Rolling Stones.
Engineer: Glyn Johns.
Bootleg only.

Three instrumental out-takes exist - for self-punishing fans only (* a - 6.20). More distorted heavy guitar riffs and a strong bass.

373. GOLD PAINTED FINGERNAILS (Jagger, Richard) 5.00
AKA: Gold Painted Nails
7-22 July, 5, 10 August - 7 September 1967: Place: Olympic Sound Studios, London, England.
Rolling Stones with Nicky Hopkins.
Producer: Rolling Stones.
Engineer: Glyn Johns.
Bootleg only.

Evidently a favourite of Bill Wyman's since he wanted it to be included on THE BLACK BOX project. Again this track was worked upon extensively, since there are ten out-takes and 23 takes available on bootleg (* a - 31.56). It is an instrumental only and features heavy organ playing from Nicky Hopkins, as well as mouth organ. Keith Richards plays on acoustic and Brian Jones contributes something (possibly mouth organ) since he is mentioned in the studio back-track. There does not seem to be any take that is passable for release, so one wonders which one Bill was partial to.

374. ON WITH THE SHOW (Jagger, Richard) 3.39
AKA: Surprise Me
7-22 July, 5 August, 2-5 October 1967: Place: Olympic Sound Studios, London, England.
Rolling Stones with Nicky Hopkins.
Producer: Rolling Stones.
Engineer: Glyn Johns.
UK LP THEIR SATANIC MAJESTIES REQUEST: 8 December 1967: No. 3 - 13 weeks
USA LP THEIR SATANIC MAJESTIES REQUEST: 9 December 1967: No. 2 - 13 weeks

On With The Show is possibly a forerunner of The Rock 'n' Roll Circus idea and was predominantly written by Keith Richards. Twenty-five minutes of out-takes are available (* a - 25.21). It concludes the album with images of *Yellow Submarine* and is a cacophony of unrehearsed mayhem, even Nicky Hopkins outdoing his own manic playing. It starts with a night-club greeter enticing people into a girlie show before proceeding with the upper class British tones of Mick Jagger, reminiscent of *Something Happened To Me Yesterday*. He says that: "Your hostess here is Wendy, you'll find her very friendly too", before making a fond adieu. Supposed over dubs of sounds from a night club - there was one just around the corner from the studio - run through the song.
The SATANIC project failed in terms of sales and was also a disaster critically. The album cover attempted to out-dress SGT PEPPER, the late Michael Cooper having designed and photographed the gatefold sleeve. Andrew Oldham knew his time was over when Mick told him the cover would be done by Michael Cooper instead of Andrew's preferred option, Gered Mankowitz. The photo session was in New York in late September. A 3D camera was used and the first album covers were sold with the animated band staring from their personalized Taj Mahal. Decca thankfully forbade a nude picture of Mick Jagger at the centre of the maze on the inner cover.
Pictures of The Beatles were timidly hidden on the cover, as The Beatles themselves had done to the Stones on the SGT PEPPER sleeve (respect reciprocated). The 3D design proved too expensive to mass produce and so it reverted to the normal one-dimensional image. The album was released with stereo and mono mixes, the latter being rarer. To this day, the Stones rate the album as one of their worst moments. Allen Klein negotiated a deal with Andrew Oldham to conclude his Stones participation. At Mick's instigation Klein also bought the masters to their recordings which Andrew owned. The proceeds were split evenly between the band and Andrew whose interest in the songwriting credits were retained at Allen Klein's insistence. Apparently at this time the Stones were offered the rights to the

master recordings but, according to Allen, they declined on the advice of their accountants as they could not afford them. An announcement was made of the split to the press by Les Perrin in late September.

Bill Wyman indicates that the band certainly came close to splitting up during the long recording marathon that led to the album. Bill was keen to progress with other initiatives and, in September 1967, recorded with The End, a band who had performed on the September/October 1965 tour with The Stones. Bill Wyman produced, recorded and co-wrote on two tracks which included *Shades Of Orange* and *Loving, Sacred Loving*. Nicky Hopkins played piano/harpsichord and Charlie Watts percussion and tabla. *Shades Of Orange* was released as the band's second single and both were included on the 1969 album INTROSPECTION.

It has since become a period piece integral to the psychedelic movement. Unfortunately the delay in its release to December 1969 was due to problems with Allen Klein. The guitarist who joined The End in 1967 was Terry Taylor, who formed a long-lasting relationship with Bill and plays with the latter's Rhythm Kings to this date. After The End collapsed in 1969, Terry Taylor formed Tucky Buzzard and Bill Wyman contributed and produced on their material until 1974. Their only self-titled album, released in June 1971, was made at Olympic Studios and engineered by Keith Harwood, assisted by Chris Kimsey and Jeremy Gee.

375. CHILD OF THE MOON (Jagger, Richard) 3.12
AKA: Child Of The Moon (rmk)
7-22 July, 16, 21, 23 October 1967, 23-29 March 1968: Place: Olympic Sound Studios, London, England.
Rolling Stones with Nicky Hopkins.
Producer: Jimmy Miller.
Engineer: Glyn Johns, Eddie Kramer.
UK B-side Jumpin' Jack Flash: 24 May 1968
USA B-side Jumpin' Jack Flash: 24 May 1968
USA Compilation LP MORE HOT ROCKS (BIG HITS & FAZED COOKIES): 1 December 1972: No. 9 - 12 weeks
UK Compilation LP NO STONE UNTURNED: 5 October 1973
German Compilation LP THE REST OF THE BEST: December 1983
UK B-side Jumpin' Jack Flash: 25 May 1987
UK 12-inch Track Jumpin' Jack Flash: 25 May 1987
UK & USA LP THE ROLLING STONES SINGLES COLLECTION - THE LONDON YEARS: 15 August 1989
USA Compilation CD MORE HOT ROCKS (BIG HITS & FAZED COOKIES): 3 September 2002
UK CD box set THE ROLLING STONES SINGLES - 1968 - 1971: 28 February 2005
USA CD box set THE ROLLING STONES SINGLES - 1968 - 1971: 1 March 2005

The most significant extract from the SATANIC MAJESTIES sessions was the emergent return to their roots, albeit with a nod to a rock resurgence as inspired by The Who, Cream, Traffic, and Jimi Hendrix. *Child Of The Moon* was recorded at these sessions as a couple of out-takes testify (* a - 9.57). Later in October, a four-minute acoustic version, with guitar and a classical piano by Nicky Hopkins, was cut (* b - 4.16). The song was reworked as the flip side to *Jumpin' Jack Flash* in March 1968. The original B-side has a different mix to the MORE HOT ROCKS and THE ROLLING STONES SINGLES COLLECTION - THE LONDON YEARS version but is not a separate take (* c - 3.11). This different mix was also released on a *Jumpin' Jack Flash* single in 1987. There is an out-take with no lead vocals from March 1968 (* d - 3.11).

On *Child Of The Moon*, Nicky Hopkins is on piano while Brian Jones again plays the "other" instrument, this time a soprano saxophone which sounds like a trumpet. Charlie Watts is very effective on percussion, exaggerating the effect that simplicity is the key. Bill Wyman plucks a dampened over-driven bass and Rocky Dijon is said to play percussion on the single version. The mood was of wizardry and sorcery, an interest ironically that would have been better suited to the SATANIC MAJESTIES album but the track did not fit in. Mick Jagger felt it was one of the most original songs they had done to date and that it would be very popular in the USA but it wasn't released there until December 1972. Brian Jones felt the song was commercial and good enough to be a single.

The sound texture created on *Child Of The Moon* was akin to their mod heroes, The Who, particularly the unintelligible Daltrey-type shouts (by Jimmy Miller) and the Townshend guitar reverb at the start. An incredibly lazy but effective electric guitar continues throughout, a style with which Keith Richards had recently been improvising. He was experimenting with open tuning, a technique that he felt blues musicians used effectively. The final chord sequence, incidentally, has to be the ultimate guitar chord finale to a rock song!

There is a rare promotional film, put together by USA producer Sanford 'Sandy' Lieberson and directed by Michael Lindsay-Hogg. It is filmed in the countryside and has the band stood in a lane with Mick perched in a tree and a white horse in the background. Brian spookily hides behind a tree - they are all intent and staring. The tone is eerie and has a vague storyline with a young child and two ladies seeming to search for the child. These images are cut into the video from an old 50s English movie film.

Sandy Lieberson went on to produce the *Rock 'n' Roll Circus* and *Performance* films. At one point, before Stanley Kubrick took on *A Clockwork Orange*, Lieberson was going to film the movie in Soho, casting Mick Jagger in the lead as Alex and the rest of the band playing supporting roles in the gang. The screenplay would have been written by Michael Cooper and Terry Southern and the soundtrack scored by the Rolling Stones but eventually the idea failed as they did not commit to the time needed for the project. Meanwhile, at their appeal sessions in court, Mick was given a conditional one-year discharge whilst Keith's sentence was quashed due to insufficient evidence.

376. COSMIC CHRISTMAS (Trad) 0.40
AKA: We Wish You A Cosmic Joke
16, 21, 23 October 1967: Place: Olympic Sound Studios, London, England.
Producer: Rolling Stones.
Engineer: Glyn Johns.
Arranged: Bill Wyman.
UK LP THEIR SATANIC MAJESTIES REQUEST: 8 December 1967: No. 3 - 13 weeks
USA LP THEIR SATANIC MAJESTIES REQUEST: 9 December 1967: No. 2 - 13 weeks

Towards the finale of *Sing This All Together (See What Happens)* there is a brief, slowed down electronic version of *We Wish You All A Merry Christmas* arranged by Bill Wyman. At the end of October, Brian Jones finally attended court regarding possession of cannabis and allowing his premises to be used for taking the drug.

Despite medical advice that he was ill, he received a sentence totalling 12 months. Similar to Mick Jagger and Keith Richards, though, he went to prison for one night. Immediately, friends and drug campaigners mounted a demonstration leading to the arrest of Chris Jagger which the front page of The Daily Mirror covered, along with Brian's sentence. The next day bail was granted pending an appeal for Brian.

It wasn't the summer of love all round for the band. Brian had befriended Jimi Hendrix and had introduced him to the crowd at the Monterey Pop Festival in June when Andrew Oldham was one of the pop artists promoting the concert. Apparently it was his choice to have Jimi Hendrix and the Who play the festival thereby changing the destiny of their careers. Also, Brian met musician Al Kooper in Monterey and he would play his own brief part in Stones history a year later.

In October, Brian and Jimi composed and recorded two takes of *My Little One* with producer Chas Chandler and Eddie Kramer engineering. The line-up featured Jimi on guitar, Dave Mason on sitar, Mitch Mitchell on drums and Brian playing sitar and various percussions. It is a shame that nothing more permanent was made of the recording - a lost opportunity from two huge talents.

On 12 December at the court appeal sitting, medical evidence was used yet again and it stated that Brian was potentially suicidal. The judge decided against handing out the normally prescribed prison sentence and opted for three years' probation with a fine. This would make his position with the band ultimately untenable for foreign travel. Brian was at a very low ebb and was again hospitalised shortly after his court appearance.

377. MY HOME IS A PRISON (Moore) 2.43
AKA: I'll Coming Home, Shot My Baby
21 February - 14 March 1968: Place: RG Jones Studios, Morden, Surrey, England.
Producer: Jimmy Miller.
Engineer: Eddie Kramer.
Bootleg only.

Brian Jones attended another session by Jimi Hendrix at Olympic Studios on 21 January 1968, the engineers being Eddie Kramer and George Chkiantz. The band included Mitch Mitchell (drums), Dave Mason (acoustic guitar) and Jimi on guitar and bass. It was during these sessions that *All Along The Watchtower* was recorded. Eddie found Brian very frustrating: "Brian Jones was the unsung hero of the band, by far the most prolific and imaginative musician among the Stones, pushing the musical boundaries with passion. His ability to master difficult instruments, such as the sitar and the Indian shenhai, made for very interesting sounds on the Stones records. He was a good friend of Jimi Hendrix's and would hang out on his sessions then fall into a heap on the control room floor."
After recording *Watchtower*, Jimi returned to the USA and, on 1 February 1968, played at the opening night of the Fillmore Auditorium in San Francisco, along with Albert King and John Mayall (including Mick Taylor).
Rehearsals for the next album had started in late January, at Keith Richards' Redlands home and RG Jones Studios, which were also used prior to the Stones' return to Olympic. Evidence of the sessions can be found on bootleg. The recordings have few passable tracks; instead they contain various untitled instrumentals. However, they do convey the idea that the Stones intended to shift their style back to the blues, with a harder rock edge and feel. The guitars are at times quite wild and distorted and one has the *Jumpin' Jack Flash* licks. *My Home Is A Prison* is a traditional Slim Harpo blues track, with harmonica and piano by Ian Stewart. There may also be extracts of Jimmy Reed's *Shoot My Baby* too.
With the tapes still rolling, guitar licks and drum rolls follow and include extracts of what would become *No Expectations* and *Stray Cat Blues*. Bill Wyman and Brian Jones were absent from some of the Surrey sessions. Indeed, an interview by NME writer Keith Altham from the sessions reveals that Brian Jones was away celebrating his birthday in Paris. Bill Wyman was apparently suffering with an anxiety attack. Keith Altham later handled press and publicity for the Stones following Les Perrin's death in 1978. He wrote a witty book, *The PR Strikes Back*, which included a chapter on his employee, Mick Jagger.

378. HOLD ON I'M COMING (Hayes, Porter) 4.08
21 February - 14 March 1968: Place: RG Jones Studios, Morden, Surrey, England.
Producer: Jimmy Miller.
Engineer: Eddie Kramer.
Bootleg only.

Sam and Dave had had a 1966 hit with *Hold On I'm Coming*. The song was run through more than once and some ad-lib *Satisfaction* lyrics were added by Mick Jagger. Mick is also featured on a heavy sounding guitar.

379. ROCK ME BABY (King, Josea, James, Taub) 0.41
21 February - 14 March 1968: Place: RG Jones Studios, Morden, Surrey, England.
Producer: Jimmy Miller.
Engineer: Eddie Kramer.
Bootleg only.

During the Surrey sessions this familiar BB "Blues Boy" King song was tried a number of times but a full version did not materialise. In an studio interview with Keith Altham, Keith Richards asks what is the purpose of rehearsing? Mick Jagger says you can't go into a studio under rehearsed. Keith Altham wonders if the reason Mick was performing on guitar was because he needed to replace Brian Jones. Mick commented that Brian was just on vacation in Paris. Another comment about them going out on the road again, brought an early reference by Mick to them using their wheel-chairs - only seven years into their career. Jimmy Miller was also interviewed and confirmed that he would be producing the next single and album. He was eager to participate and bring new ideas.

380. PAY YOUR DUES (Jagger, Richard) 3.05
AKA: Primo Grande, Did Everybody Pay Their Dues?
February - 14 March; 17-31 March 1968: Place: Rolling Stones Mobile, Redlands, Sussex, England; Olympic Sound Studios, London, England.
Rolling Stones with Nicky Hopkins, Dave Mason, Rick Grech, Jim King, Roger Chapman.
Producer: Jimmy Miller.
Engineer: Eddie Kramer.
Bootleg only.

Redlands, Keith Richards' new house in the country, was used as a base for rehearsing songs and laying ideas onto cassette in February 1968. The tapes were then played to Jimmy Miller for suggestions and eventually they would set about transferring the track from cassette to four-track in the studio. *Primo Grande* was the first working title for *Did Everybody Pay Their Dues*, until it eventually turned into *Street Fighting Man*. *Pay Your Dues* has a different set of lyrics which sound quite stilted and cumbersome compared with the well-known official release. Some of the backing track was carried through to *Street Fighting Man*, such as Nicky Hopkins' piano, Keith Richards' acoustic and Charlie Watts' percussion, achieved with a suitcase drum kit.
Keith's tuning was in open-G, a technique usually used for slide guitar, which had been shown to him by Ry Cooder. Other instruments include Brian Jones on sitar, Dave Mason (from Traffic) on shehnai and Rick Grech (Richard Roman Grechko) on a blistering electric viola. Backing vocals were performed by Jim King

and Roger Chapman. Grech, King and Chapman were all members of the group Family, who were in the same studios recording their debut album MUSIC IN A DOLL'S HOUSE. This was co-produced by Dave Mason and Jimmy Miller and engineered by Eddie Kramer and George Chkiantz. The Stones needed help and direction in the studio, that was clear from SATANIC, and Jimmy was selected, having been put forward by Glyn Johns, since he was an American with limited ego.

381. **NO EXPECTATIONS** (Jagger, Richard) 3.56
AKA: Untitled Slide Doodles
1-14, 17-31 March; 13-18 May, 4-10 June 1968: Place: RG Jones Studios, Morden, Surrey, England; Olympic Sound Studios, London, England.
Played Live: 1968, 1969, 1973, 1994, 1995, 1997, 2002, 2003, 2007
Rolling Stones with Nicky Hopkins.
Producer: Jimmy Miller.
Engineer: Eddie Kramer, Glyn Johns.
Assistant Engineer: Phill Brown.
USA B-side Street Fighting Man: August 1968
UK LP BEGGARS BANQUET: 6 December 1968: No. 3 - 12 weeks
USA LP BEGGARS BANQUET: 7 December 1968: No. 5 - 13 weeks
USA Compilation LP MORE HOT ROCKS (BIG HITS & FAZED COOKIES): 1 December 1972: No. 9 - 12 weeks
UK & USA LP THE ROLLING STONES SINGLES COLLECTION - THE LONDON YEARS: 15 August 1989
USA Compilation CD MORE HOT ROCKS (BIG HITS & FAZED COOKIES): 3 September 2002
UK CD box set THE ROLLING STONES SINGLES - 1968 - 1971: 28 February 2005
USA CD box set THE ROLLING STONES SINGLES - 1968 - 1971: 1 March 2005
UK Compilation CD ROLLED GOLD +: 12 November 2007: No. 26 - 12 weeks

No Expectations is a tranquil, pensive song and claimed by Keith Richards to have been written very quickly by him. It is a complete contrast to the electric riffs tried out during the Surrey sessions. At that time it was known as an *Untitled Slide Doodles*. From the end of the third verse, Nicky Hopkins lays down a soft, delicate melody on the piano, which rises an octave for the song's conclusion and there's a wonderfully skilful, effortless bottleneck steel guitar by Brian Jones. You can almost detect the atmospheric ripples of water, splashing on stone - it has that outdoors lazy Sunday morning feel and one of Brian's career highlights. He was thrilled at the return to Robert Johnson country blues. It was recorded one night when he was unusually on an emotional high.

An original out-take has studio conversation introducing *No Expectations* with no percussion (* a - 4.20). The take does not have the bottleneck guitar and has more use of the single key soft organ which is used in great juxtaposition with the piano. From this version, you can appreciate the acoustic guitar playing by Keith Richards and the subtle bass arrangement. Apparently Mick Jagger remembers the band sat cross legged on the floor in a circle recording with open microphones. *No Expectations* was released in the States as the flipside to *Street Fighting Man* and was certainly an excellent foretaste of the album release.

THE ROLLING STONES SINGLES COLLECTION - THE LONDON YEARS has a mono mix of the track. Many guest artists were to feature on the BEGGARS BANQUET sessions. Various guitar players, including possibly Dave Mason, lent a hand due to Brian Jones' general unreliability. Another participant was ace guitarist Ry Cooder, a friend of Jack Nitzsche's. Jimmy Miller and Glyn Johns were later to hint that Brian Jones contributed certain guitar passages on BEGGARS BANQUET and it is certain that this is one. In 1995, Mick Jagger told Rolling Stone magazine that this was Brian's last significant input to the Stones music.

382. **STRAY CAT BLUES** (Jagger, Richard) 4.37
1-14, 17-31 March; 13-18 May 1968: Place: RG Jones Studios, Morden, Surrey, England; Olympic Sound Studios, London, England.
Played Live: 1969, 1970, 1971, 1973, 1976, 2002, 2003
Rolling Stones with Nicky Hopkins.
Producer: Jimmy Miller.
Engineer: Eddie Kramer. Glyn Johns.
Assistant Engineer: Phill Brown.
UK LP BEGGARS BANQUET: 6 December 1968: No. 3 - 12 weeks
USA LP BEGGARS BANQUET: 7 December 1968: No. 5 - 13 weeks
UK Compilation LP MILESTONES: 18 February 1972: No. 14 - 8 weeks

The semi-pornographic overtones captured in the lyrics of *Stray Cat Blues* overshadow the excellent musical quality of the rock-styled rhythm and blues. The song concerns itself with sleazy under-age groupie sex with an older man even inviting the girl's friend along - "if she's so wild then she can join in too". The musical accompaniment is atmospherically excellent, enhancing the sordid message. Brian Jones plays an electronic keyboard, an excellent slide guitar while Keith Richards scratches out more than a few lead solos. He felt the song was reminiscent of Albert King, who had adopted a cutting electric blues style. Brian Jones can be heard on mellotron but well down in the mix.

The Stones failed to play live during 1968 but, on the 1969 tours, the song became a firm stage favourite. Mick Jagger claimed later that the "Velvet Underground sound" in tracks like *Heroin* was the inspiration and basis for some of the BEGGARS BANQUET vibe, but in particular *Stray Cat*. It is not an obvious comparison except for the intensity and aggression that was beginning to surface in the music. Eddie Kramer felt that Jimmy Miller was intrinsic to this rawness and renewed aggression. Early raucous versions of the guitar riff can be heard from the Surrey sessions. An out-take from Olympic has a false, faltering introduction and added vocals at the end of the track, where Mick shouts some "scratch my back" enticements (* a - 4.17).

383. **JUMPIN' JACK FLASH** (Jagger, Richard) 3.41
AKA: Title 5
12-13; 23-29 March 1968: Place: RG Jones Studios, Morden, Surrey, England; Olympic Sound Studios, London, England.
Played Live: 1968, 1969, 1970, 1971, 1972, 1973, 1975, 1976, 1977, 1978, 1979, 1981, 1982, 1989, 1990, 1994, 1995, 1997, 1998, 1999, 2002, 2003, 2005, 2006, 2007

Rolling Stones with Nicky Hopkins, Jimmy Miller.
Producer: Jimmy Miller. Engineer: Eddie Kramer, Glyn Johns.
UK Single: 23 May 1968: No. 1 - 11 weeks
USA Single: 24 May 1968: No. 3 - 11 weeks
UK Compilation LP THROUGH THE PAST DARKLY (BIG HITS VOL 2): 12 September 1969: No. 2 - 37 weeks
USA Compilation LP THROUGH THE PAST DARKLY (BIG HITS VOL 2): 13 September 1969: No. 2 - 16 weeks
UK Compilation LP GIMME SHELTER: 29 August 1971: No. 19 - 5 weeks
USA LP THE ROLLING STONES HOT ROCKS 1964-1971: 11 January 1972: No. 4 - 30 weeks
UK Compilation LP ROLLED GOLD: 14 November 1975: No. 7 - 50 weeks
UK Compilation LP GET STONED - 30 GREATEST HITS, 30 ORIGINAL TRACKS: 21 October 1977: No. 13 - 15 weeks
German Compilation LP THE REST OF THE BEST: December 1983
UK Single: 25 May 1987
UK 12-inch Single: 25 May 1987
UK & USA LP THE ROLLING STONES SINGLES COLLECTION - THE LONDON YEARS: 15 August 1989
USA Compilation Promo CD THE ROLLING STONES REMASTERED: 30 May 2002
UK CD LP FORTY LICKS: 30 September 2002: No. 2 - 45 weeks
USA CD LP FORTY LICKS: 1 October 2002: No. 2 - 50 weeks
UK CD box set THE ROLLING STONES SINGLES - 1968 - 1971: 28 February 2005
USA CD box set THE ROLLING STONES SINGLES - 1968 - 1971: 1 March 2005
UK Compilation CD ROLLED GOLD +: 12 November 2007: No. 26 - 12 weeks

As a complete contrast to the heady recording period of 1967, the sound created on *Jumpin' Jack Flash* just six months later was a monumental transformation from that realised during the SATANIC MAJESTIES sessions. The band's decision was to return to R 'n' B in English studios and this they did with the precision of Jimmy Miller at the controls at Olympic's four-track studios. He got on well with the Stones, so much so that he was to produce for them for the next six years. It was a relationship which would severely test him and put him in danger of being consigned to the control-room scrap heap.

The *Jumpin' Jack Flash* foundations were laid by Bill Wyman during the Surrey sessions as he "mucked around" with a chord sequence on the piano. Brian Jones and Charlie Watts improvised on it until Keith Richards and Mick Jagger entered the studio. The duo knew instantaneously that the sound had great possibilities. Mick had some nearly completed lyrics and Keith had some guitar riffs using open tuning - amazingly, they were both inspired by Jack Dyer, the gardener at Redlands. So they set about recording and bringing all the ideas together. The sparse lyrics contain magical imagery of a war baby in the crossfire of a hurricane. Mick later related, "It's about having a hard time and getting out. Just a metaphor for getting out of all the acid things." The heavy guitar chords which run throughout the track immediately assault the senses, being heavy but acoustically based.

Keith used to record his work on to cassette and then use that to play back to the rest of the band. On *Jumpin' Jack Flash* they decided that was the "sound" they wanted to re-create and so recorded two acoustic guitars onto the cassette with so much overload that it sounded electric. One was tuned to Open-D with a capo and another used Nashville tuning. Keith reckoned he was born with the main riff, either backwards or forwards (forgetting Bill's initial input). Jagger shouts "watch it" and the band join in, supplying an incessant riff around the uplifting vocal. Brian Jones shuffles his demonic maracas as Keith's wonderfully distorted lead guitar provides the Stones with their most powerful rock sound to date.

An instrumental out-take of *Jumpin' Jack Flash* from the Surrey sessions is much less sophisticated with heavy guitar riffing (* a - 2.17). Another out-take of *Jumpin' Jack Flash* illustrates the undeniable enthusiasm for the track as the band shout "yeah, yeah" and "woah" between the choruses (* b - 3.25), a style to be copied in future live performances. There is also a version with the released track but only accompanying backing vocals, which Jimmy Miller helps with (* c - 3.52). At the end of the released cut there are the brass-like sounds of a mellotron by Bill Wyman and distorted organ playing by Nicky Hopkins. Keith also played the bass lines and a floor tom-tom.

Brian Jones was so happy with the end result that, as soon as the session finished he contacted a friend, Ronny Money - wife of musician Zoot Money - and told her the Stones had returned to rock and roll with this thing called *Jumpin' Jack Flash*, it's a gas! They had extricated themselves from the tangled mire of SATANIC and the new song gave the Stones a British No. 1 single and a world-wide hit. Originally, it was intended for release on BEGGARS BANQUET, the next album, but the overwhelming enthusiasm created by the track brought an early single release. In the USA the single was edited by a minute (* d - 2.42).

Mick Jagger believes that the promotional film which accompanied the single's release ensured its success, but this was underestimating the Stones' now renewed rock popularity. The promo was shot by Michael Lindsay-Hogg on 28 April 1968 using audio from an Olympic session. George Chkiantz was the sound engineer assisted by Phill Brown. The musical backing track seems to be the same but with a different vocal by Mick and less of a fade-out (* e - 3.58). The partnership with Michael Lindsay-Hogg was the start of an affiliation which was to last many years. The video simply portrays the band performing the song live in front of a camera at Olympic's Studio One. It was an awesome sight.

The band, with the exception of Keith Richards, were heavily made up, including symbolic forehead tattoos. Jagger, decked in war paint, leered menacingly at the camera. Brian Jones played a Telecaster and atmospherically wore dark green-rimmed sunglasses and his orange lipstick complemented his dyed auburn hair. The band's overall appearance was unnerving but vividly exciting.

The video versions (and there are three) sometimes feature the original backing track but all use either of two different vocal tracks. One has no "watch it" intro and an extended vocal outro, uttering "oohs" and "bahs". Another has a "yeah, yeah" intro and claps at the end which is from a Peter Clifton 1969 film *Popcorn - An Audio Visual Thing*, celebrating 60s psychedelia. This version was also used for BBC's Top Of The Pops in June. In 2005, the promo film with the original single soundtrack was released on a box set DVD. In 1970, Ravi Shankar's cousin Ananka Shankar covered the tune for his album ANANKA SHANKAR. The album was mostly self-written Bangladeshi sitar-laced numbers but included a world-fusion version of *Jumpin' Jack Flash* and The Doors' *Light My Fire*. During the last few tours, Ron Wood has played the song with an electric sitar, as he does with *Street Fighting Man*.

384. JIGSAW PUZZLE (Jagger, Richard) 6.06
17-31 March; 6-25 July 1968: Place: Olympic Sound Studios, London, England; Sunset Sound Studios, Los Angeles, California, USA.
Rolling Stones with Nicky Hopkins.
Producer: Jimmy Miller.

Engineer: Eddie Kramer, Glyn Johns.
Assistant Engineer: Phill Brown.
UK LP BEGGARS BANQUET: 6 December 1968: No. 3 - 12 weeks
USA LP BEGGARS BANQUET: 7 December 1968: No. 5 - 13 weeks

Nicky Hopkins, since his introduction during the 'SATANIC' session, was beginning to contribute a more prominent role in the band's overall sound and they used him to good effect on this track. Ian Stewart did not contribute to BEGGARS BANQUET. The blues feel is still retained with some fine slide guitar by Keith Richards but the song's rhythm is controlled by Nicky Hopkins incessantly pounding on the ivory keys. The song, written by Mick Jagger, caused anxiety among critics who hinted at Dylan comparisons - the imagery is bizarre and unrelated, the jigsaw puzzle was left uncompleted.

It is more than six minutes long and has some amusing lyrics depicting a rock band - the singer looks so angry, the bass player looks nervous about the girls outside (oh yeah!), the drummer is shattered trying to keep on time and the guitar players look damaged (no way!). Keith thought the song was too long but he backed and went along with Mick's arrangement. There is a faint eastern style instrument low down in the mix which could be attributed to Brian Jones or even Bill Wyman on a synthesiser or mellotron. An out-take of *Jigsaw Puzzle* has a different bass arrangement from Keith and less echoed vocals (* a - 6.07). More than 50 minutes of *Jigsaw Puzzle* is available on 11 session tracks and 14 takes (* b - 53.35), illustrating how the song was built from the distinctive slide guitar and the piano playing of Nicky Hopkins.

385. PARACHUTE WOMAN (Jagger, Richard) 2.20
17-31 March 1968: Place: Olympic Sound Studios, London, England.
Played Live: 1968, 2002
Producer: Jimmy Miller.
Engineer: Eddie Kramer, Glyn Johns.
Assistant Engineer: Phill Brown.
UK LP BEGGARS BANQUET: 6 December 1968: No. 3 - 12 weeks
USA LP BEGGARS BANQUET: 7 December 1968: No. 5 - 13 weeks
UK LP SOLID ROCK: 13 October 1980

The foundations are very simple on this prototypical R 'n' B showcase. It was fun to make but the mood is purposeful and the formula of harmonica with steel guitar is successful. Electric guitar dubbed on at the end satisfactorily complete this up-tempo number, which Keith Richards recalls was initially put down in a rough form on a cassette and transferred to eight-track. Such was the vibrancy, it did not take long to record. The lyrics are lewdly plain, particularly the last verse. Mick Jagger jokingly referred to it as a song about relationships. There is a different mix with double tracked vocals (* a - 2.15).

386. HIGHWAY CHILD (Jagger, Richard) 5.02
AKA: The Vulture
17-31 March 1968: Place: Mobile at Redlands, Sussex, England.
Producer: Jimmy Miller.
Engineer: Glyn Johns.
Bootleg only.

Highway Child is a five-minute fast number which appears to only feature Mick Jagger on vocals and a runaway lead guitar and Charlie Watts on drums. It was during these sessions that Charlie's daughter Serafina was born.

387. NATURAL MAGIC (Nitzsche) 1.39
March-September 1968; July - August 1969: Place: Olympic Sound Studios, London, England; Elektra Studios, Los Angeles, USA.
Rolling Stones with Jack Nitzsche, Ry Cooder, Randy Newman, Bernard Krause, Lowell George, Amiya Dasgupta, Milt Holland, Gene Parsons, Russel Titelman
Producer: Jack Nitzsche.
Engineer: Glyn Johns.
UK LP PERFORMANCE (A motion picture sound-track): 19 September 1970
USA LP PERFORMANCE (A motion picture sound-track): 19 September 1970
UK B-Side Memo From Turner: 31 October 1970 (Credited as Mick Jagger only)
German Compilation LP THE REST OF THE BEST: December 1983
UK & USA LP THE ROLLING STONES SINGLES COLLECTION - THE LONDON YEARS: 15 August 1989
UK CD box set THE ROLLING STONES SINGLES - 1968 - 1971: 28 February 2005
USA CD box set THE ROLLING STONES SINGLES - 1968 - 1971: 1 March 2005

This short blues instrumental, with distinctive Ry Cooder slide bottleneck guitar, was released by Mick Jagger on the flip-side of *Memo From Turner* and is also included on the Stones' ABKCO production SINGLES COLLECTION. Originally recorded in 1968 with Ry Cooder, it was worked upon for the PERFORMANCE soundtrack album in Los Angeles mid-1969. This was at the time that Randy Newman was recording his album 12 SONGS with Ry Cooder, Gene Parsons (of Byrds fame) and Milt Holland, some of the artists credited on the soundtrack. The track has wispy wind sounds created by a synthesiser, probably featuring electronic expert, Bernard Krause. The soundtrack would be the last release by Decca of a Stones-related project.

388. SALT OF THE EARTH (Jagger, Richard) 4.47
AKA: Silver Blanket
9-10, 13-18 May; 6-25 July 1968: Place: Olympic Sound Studios, London, England; Sunset Sound Studios, Los Angeles, California, USA.
Played Live: 1968, 1989, 2003
Rolling Stones with Nicky Hopkins, Watts Street Gospel Choir, Dave Mason.
Producer: Jimmy Miller.

Engineer: Glyn Johns.
Assistant Engineer: Phill Brown.
UK LP BEGGARS BANQUET: 6 December 1968: No. 3 - 12 weeks
USA LP BEGGARS BANQUET: 7 December 1968: No. 5 - 13 weeks
USA Compilation Promo CD ABKCO'S THE ROLLINGS STONES REMASTERED SERIES: 30 May 2002

Acoustic guitar kicks off a rousing anthem to the working class. Keith Richards is in charge of the vocals on the opening verse. Nicky Hopkins is at the track's forefront when Mick Jagger sings the second verse along with a striking piano line. Hopkins was a man in demand - not only did he spend those few weeks in the studio with the Stones but he also recorded tracks like *Revolution* for the Beatles WHITE ALBUM. Another "first" is the inclusion of female singers who provide the vocal sustenance to the track's finale.

These vocals were added in July by the Watts Street Gospel Choir, when final mixing of the album was undertaken at Sunset Sound Studios in Los Angeles. Watts Town, in Los Angeles, was a trouble spot for racial tension and had seen a remarkable riot following the death of Martin Luther King, much of the town being set aflame. One has to acknowledge that *Salt Of The Earth* is the Stones' sing-along equal to the Beatles' *All You Need Is Love*. The song's melody and pace is driven by the choir, Charlie Watts' percussion and the ivory keys of Nicky at the climax. The poignant message contained is open to being misconstrued, since when did the Stones have any pretensions of being working class?

An alternate mix is available from the LA sessions which is very similar to the final release (* a - 4.48). The song was sensitively used to drink to the "salt of the earth", the tireless, hardworking New York fire department. This was for the memorial and fund-raising concert following terrorist attack on the World Trade Centre's twin towers in New York on 11 September 2001. The lyrics for Keith's first verse were altered that night. "Let's drink to the hard working people, let's drink to the lowly of birth, let's drink to the good not the evil, let's drink to the salt of the earth."

389. JUMPIN' JACK FLASH (Jagger, Richard) ✎
12 May 1968: Place: NME Poll Winners Concert, Empire Pool, Wembley, England.
Unavailable.

The Olympic sessions were literally cut in two when on, 12 May 1968, they had an opportunity to preview *Jumpin' Jack Flash* to an audience at the NME Annual Poll Winners' Concert. They were not included in the original bill and so their surprise performance of two numbers, including *Jumpin' Jack Flash* and *Satisfaction*, naturally created an amazing crowd reaction and renewed the band's vigour for going on the road. It was also the last performance with Brian Jones on any stage. Hosted by Jimmy Savile, Tony Blackburn and Roger Moore (who presented the Stones with the best R 'n' B act), it featured other popular artists such as Status Quo, The Move, Dusty Springfield, The Herd, The Association, The Bee Gees, The Showstoppers, Lulu, Don Partridge, The Love Affair, The Paper Dolls, Amen Corner, Cliff Richard and The Shadows, Dave Dee, Dozy, Beaky, Mick & Tich and The Tremeloes.

None was as popular as the Stones, though, and the single was to be released in just under two weeks' time. The show was caught on camera by Mike Mansfield and broadcast on ITV's *Time For Blackburn* a week before the single release on 18 May. This footage has since disappeared and is therefore much sought after. The audience were very excited and enthusiastic at seeing the Stones' first performance since 1966. At first they planned to play only one song, but also did *Satisfaction* due to the immense reaction.

390. (I CAN'T GET NO) SATISFACTION (Jagger, Richard) ✎
12 May 1968: Place: NME Poll Winners Concert, Empire Pool, Wembley, England.
Unavailable.

391. STREET FIGHTING MAN (Jagger, Richard) 3.16
13-18 May 1968: Place: Olympic Sound Studios, London, England.
Played Live: 1969, 1970, 1971, 1972, 1973, 1975, 1976, 1977, 1978, 1981, 1990, 1994, 1995, 1998, 2002, 2003
Rolling Stones with Dave Mason, Nicky Hopkins.
Producer: Jimmy Miller.
Engineer: Eddie Kramer, Glyn Johns.
Assistant Engineer: Phill Brown.
USA Single: 31 August 1968
UK LP BEGGARS BANQUET: 6 December 1968: No. 3 - 12 weeks
USA LP BEGGARS BANQUET: 7 December 1968: No. 5 - 13 weeks
UK Compilation LP THROUGH THE PAST DARKLY (BIG HITS VOL 2): 12 September 1969: No. 2 - 37 weeks
USA Compilation LP THROUGH THE PAST DARKLY (BIG HITS VOL 2): 13 September 1969: No. 2 - 16 weeks
UK Maxi-single Track Everybody Needs Somebody To Love: 25 June 1971
UK Single: 20 July 1971: No. 21 - 8 weeks
UK Compilation LP GIMME SHELTER: 29 August 1971: No. 19 - 5 weeks
USA LP THE ROLLING STONES HOT ROCKS 1964-1971: 11 January 1972: No. 4 - 30 weeks
UK Compilation LP ROLLED GOLD: 14 November 1975: No. 7 - 50 weeks
UK Compilation LP GET STONED - 30 GREATEST HITS, 30 ORIGINAL TRACKS: 21 October 1977: No. 13 - 15 weeks
UK & USA LP THE ROLLING STONES SINGLES COLLECTION - THE LONDON YEARS: 15 August 1989
UK CD LP FORTY LICKS: 30 September 2002: No. 2 - 45 weeks
USA CD LP FORTY LICKS: 1 October 2002: No. 2 - 50 weeks
UK CD box set THE ROLLING STONES SINGLES - 1968 - 1971: 28 February 2005
USA CD box set THE ROLLING STONES SINGLES - 1968 - 1971: 1 March 2005
UK Compilation CD ROLLED GOLD +: 12 November 2007: No. 26 - 12 weeks

Street Fighting Man is certainly "subversive", as Decca described it. It was inspired by the anti-government April/early May 1968 student riots in Paris, which almost toppled French President Charles de Gaulle and, more closely, the anti-Vietnam War demonstration at London's Grosvenor Square. The latter event, outside the American Embassy on 17 March, was attended by Mick Jagger for a short period, with minder Tom Keylock in close proximity. Mick wanted to contribute something to the desperate situation and, therefore, produced an urban guerrilla rock anthem. He was politically disappointed at governments' "compromise solution" but, as he sings in the lyrics, he was aware realistically that his vocation was to sing in a rock and roll band. He understood that revolution could not be started by a record alone. His contribution was limited to sympathetic voyeurism instead of practical participation, although he did voice meek discontent at the aforementioned protest march.

Street Fighting Man was recorded before the Beatles' *Revolution*, in 1968, the "year of revolution". The Soviet Union had just invaded Czechoslovakia and the war in Vietnam was reaching a low ebb as popularity for the offensive against communist Vietnam kept declining. Closer to home, France was undergoing sit-ins from students followed by civil unrest at class discrimination and the government's political powers over University funds. It led to general strikes and President Charles de Gaulle's government falling from power in April 1969. Sleepy London town was quiet in comparison. The song, based on *Did Everyone Pay Their Dues*, owes a lot to Keith Richards' acoustic guitar and acoustic overdubs by Jimmy Miller but the agitated atmosphere is created by the delivery of the lyrics by Mick. He lingers on notes for emphasis, which serves to build the song's aggression.

The menacing quality of *Street Fighting Man* was made even more pointed by the fact that the electric guitar was laid aside for Keith's subtle attack on the acoustic Gibson Hummingbird. Keith was employing the technique of using a mono cassette player overloaded by its own tiny microphone. He was already complaining that modern studio facilities were making rock and roll music too clean and he was keen to rough the edges. The cassette was played back through an amplifier where it was used to gain a startling effect and then transferred to the studio's four-track.

Keith also plays bass guitar, the only electric instrument on the song. Charlie Watts' drums consisted of a tiny fold-away 1930s London jazz kit, again recorded through the cassette. He also added African tom-tom recorded from the stairwell. Brian Jones' contribution was minimal as he performed almost unnoticed on sitar and percussively on the tamboura. Dave Mason is on the wailing shehnai, which is a wind-like reed instrument akin to the flute but with more of a likeness to that used by an African snake charmer.

Street Fighting Man was released in the States as a single in August due to the album's delay and was promptly banned in Chicago for fear of encouraging riot. It contains a slightly different vocal mix from the album version (* a - 3.10). Many other cities followed suit. The States were particularly unstable at that time after the Martin Luther King (4 April) and Robert Kennedy (5 June) assassinations. The authorities did not want to risk further fighting in the street, which the song's message conveyed. The original picture sleeve on the single showed demonstrators being beaten by police on the Sunset Strip in Hollywood, Los Angeles, during the summer of 1966, scenes which inspired the Buffalo Springfield hit *For What It's Worth*.

The *Street Fighting Man* single was quickly banned by worried distributors. Decca Records in Britain did not risk conflict and the song was not released as a single until 1970. It was re-released on a maxi single in 1972 when it eventually charted at No. 21. A low-cost promotional film of Mick Jagger lip-synching exists but is rarely seen. Rod Stewart and Ron Wood released their slide-guitar version in late 1969 in the USA and February 1970 in the UK on the ROD STEWART ALBUM and AN OLD RAINCOAT WON'T EVER LET YOU DOWN albums respectively.

392. DEAR DOCTOR (Jagger, Richard) 3.22
13-18 May 1968: Place: Olympic Sound Studios, London, England.
Rolling Stones with Nicky Hopkins, Dave Mason.
Producer: Jimmy Miller.
Engineer: Glyn Johns.
Assistant Engineer: Phill Brown.
UK LP BEGGARS BANQUET: 6 December 1968: No. 3 - 12 weeks
USA LP BEGGARS BANQUET: 7 December 1968: No. 5 - 13 weeks
UK LP SLOW ROLLERS: 9 November 1981

A certain maturity is displayed in this musical interpretation of a 'down in Virginia' country music song, played unusually in waltz-time and mainly written by Mick Jagger. *Dear Doctor* was very much a comical song which all the band contributed to, suggesting suitable lyrics. Again, it was an easy song to record in a booze-up type atmosphere. Mick practises his newly acquired affected drawl and illustrates an amusing scene of despair and happiness. A wedding is set for a poor unfortunate to a bow-legged, sow of a woman. Bourbon cannot drown the feeling of the wedding day and as he searches in his wedding suit pocket for the ring he finds a note which says the sow has run off with his cousin. There follow tears of relief - the doctor can put away his stethoscope; the blood pressure is now under control. The story was typically fashioned around the irony of the blues, a depressing but most up-lifting music form, a strange dichotomy derived from ethnic roots. The musical quality on the original album version is superb. Listen to the harmonica by Brian Jones, the tack piano and the stunning twelve-string acoustic guitar - one of the contributors was Dave Mason on guitar. There are a couple of out-takes, one with a slightly different faster tempo, different lead vocals without the high pitched delivery to the "Darling I'm so sorry to hurt you" verse the and without backing vocals (a - 3.28) and one take with both (* b - 3.24).

393. PRODIGAL SON (Wilkins) 2.52
AKA: That's No Way To Get Along
13-18 May, 24 June 1968: Place: Olympic Sound Studios, London, England.
Played Live: 1969, 1970, 1979
Producer: Jimmy Miller.
Engineer: Glyn Johns.
Assistant Engineer: Phill Brown.
UK LP BEGGARS BANQUET: 6 December 1968: No. 3 - 12 weeks
USA LP BEGGARS BANQUET: 7 December 1968: No. 5 - 13 weeks
USA Compilation LP THE ROLLING STONES PROMOTIONAL ALBUM: October 1969

The late 1967 and early 1968 break had allowed Keith Richards to listen to old records. He concentrated on some of the tunings and moved away from the normal six-string guitar. As he famously recalls, the five-string open G tuning allowed three notes, two fingers and one arse-hole to play it. Keith felt rejuvenated. The

Reverend Robert Wilkins' gospel song of biblical parallels, originally titled *That's No Way To Get Along*, was convincingly attempted by the band. Robert Wilkins (a herbal medicine practitioner and a World War One veteran) had written the original *Rollin' Stone* song about a girl back in 1928 - it was based on a parable, "the lost son", described in Luke 15. *Prodigal Son* was covered by Hank Williams in 1952 and in 1965 it appeared on a live album including other artists, BLUES AT NEWPORT VOL 2. Duelling acoustic guitars and wailing harmonica by Brian Jones provide the background for Jagger to sing on this Chicago blues track. The result is impressively impromptu, with Mick's vocals having a country blues lilt. The two guitarists were Keith Richards and, potentially, Brian. The recording sessions allowed the band to forget outside influences but for some there were rude awakenings. On 21 May 1968 Brian Jones was arrested and charged with possession of cannabis. The drugs were wrapped in a ball of wool but Brian genuinely claimed he knew nothing about it since he was staying at a friend's flat while his was being re-decorated. He was bailed but the pressure brought by the establishment (the plain-clothes detectives who constantly followed and harassed Mick, Keith and Brian) was taking its toll. In short, the prodigal son was cracking badly under the unfair imposed strain. His musical talents floundered, interest waned and he failed to turn up for many session dates. The band could do little to halt this decline. At court on 26 September 1968 he was fined but not jailed, even though he had a previous suspended sentence.

394. GIVE ME A HAMBURGER TO GO (Jagger, Richard) 3.25
AKA: Stuck Out All Alone
13-18 May 1968: Place: Olympic Sound Studios, London, England.
Producer: Jimmy Miller.
Engineer: Glyn Johns.
Bootleg only.

High pitched "ooh-ooh" vocals introduce this slow ballad. The song does not sound finished hence the ad-libbing - "yeah" and "my my". Bongo drums percussion can be plainly heard.

395. FAMILY (Jagger, Richard) 4.06
13-18 May, 28 June 1968: Place: Olympic Sound Studios, London, England.
Rolling Stones with Nicky Hopkins, Jimmy Miller.
Producer: Jimmy Miller.
Engineer: Glyn Johns.
Assistant Engineer: Phill Brown.
UK Compilation LP METAMORPHOSIS: 6 June 1975: No. 45 - 1 week
USA Compilation LP METAMORPHOSIS: 6 June 1975: No. 8 - 8 weeks

The creation of *Family* may be traced through collecting two out-takes on bootleg. They are obviously incomplete versions prior to the recording of the final take; the lyrics were certainly not completed. The final bizarre lyrics depict a family where the daughter wants to be a prostitute and her first intended customer is her father. There is an acoustic version (* a - 4.13) and an organ swirl entrance one (* b - 4.01). The electric end result, with Jimmy Miller on percussion, lacks the necessary Stones finish and it is easy to see why it was excluded from BEGGARS BANQUET. It does not have the recurrent R 'n' B theme which was so prevalent on BEGGARS BANQUET. It is rumoured that further songs were recorded on the 28 June, named *Power Cut*, *Thief For The Blues* and *Too Far To Walk*.

396. FACTORY GIRL (Jagger, Richard) 2.09
13-18 May 1968: Place: Olympic Sound Studios, London, England.
Played Live: 1990, 1997
Rolling Stones with Rick Grech, Rocky Dijon, Dave Mason.
Producer: Jimmy Miller.
Engineer: Glyn Johns.
Assistant Engineer: Phill Brown.
UK LP BEGGARS BANQUET: 6 December 1968: No. 3 - 12 weeks
USA LP BEGGARS BANQUET: 7 December 1968: No. 5 - 13 weeks
USA Compilation Promo CD THE ROLLING STONES REMASTERED: 30 May 2002

The working class sentiments tackled on *Salt Of The Earth* are repeated on *Factory Girl*, although in a much more dismissive manner. The track is a short acoustic finger-picking song with slight country/Appalachian hillbilly leanings using open tuning. Rick Grech's fiddle was Nicky Hopkins' idea and was encouraged by Jimmy Miller. Rocky Dijon plays the congas and Dave Mason the mandolin. Although adequate, *Factory Girl* would certainly not win the track of the album award. Mick Jagger admitted that it had been written quickly in the studio and was about waiting for your girl to come out of the factory, "curlers in her hair . . . wears scarves instead of hats".

With the album now complete, the task of sleeve design came next. Using the medieval banquets theme, photographs were taken by Michael Joseph in early June 1968, first at Sarum Chase, Hampstead - these can be seen within the inside cover, depicting a scene of the Stones revelling around a dinner feast. The following day they moved to Swarkestone Manor, in Derbyshire, for outside photos with a derelict pavilion as a backdrop and scenes of the band playing cricket in long grass. These were not selected for the cover but were later used for the compilation album HOT ROCKS in 1972. A cartoon design was also considered but dismissed in favour of a photograph taken by Barry Feinstein, showing a toilet decked in graffiti. The toilet location was in a car mechanic's repair shop on Hollywood Boulevard. The Stones liked the idea and did a quick redecorating job by producing their own graffiti, with track listings and acknowledgements on the back cover. When Decca Records were shown the design, they immediately rejected it on grounds of bad taste. Mick countered that it only showed half the toilet - a whole lavatory would have been rude. The ensuing argument held up the release of the album for a number of months. Mick suggested a compromise of packaging the sleeve in a plain paper bag and labelling it "Unfit for Children". Decca, however, insisted, as they did with the March 1966 cover for COULD YOU WALK ON THE WATER?, that the sleeve had to be changed if the recorded product was ever to be made available - so the Stones had to agree.

On reflection, perhaps they should have returned to Michael Joseph's earlier photo shoot. A simple plain white gatefold sleeve was chosen, which led to immediate parallels with the just released Beatles' WHITE ALBUM - could they never win? These hassles added to the pressure to search for another record company.

397. SISTER MORPHINE (Jagger, Richard, Faithfull) 5.34
13 May - June 1968; 22-31 March 1969: Place: Olympic Sound Studios, London, England.
Played Live: 1997, 1998
Rolling Stones with Ry Cooder, Jack Nitzsche.
Producer: Jimmy Miller.
Engineer: Glyn Johns.
Assistant Engineer: Phill Brown.
UK LP STICKY FINGERS: 23 April 1971: No. 1 - 25 weeks
USA LP STICKY FINGERS: 30 April 1971: No. 1 - 26 weeks

This song weaved a troubled life from 1968 to its eventual release in 1971. The riff for *Sister Morphine* was written by Mick Jagger in Rome, in 1968, and recorded by the band at the BEGGARS BANQUET sessions. This early version has different lyrics and Nicky Hopkins on piano (* a - 5.35). When Keith Richards, Anita Pallenberg, Mick Jagger and Marianne Faithfull went on a cruise from Lisbon, Portugal to Rio De Janeiro, Brazil in December 1968, Marianne re-wrote some of the lyrics inspired by the potential miscarriage of Anita, but her efforts were minimal. Mick recalls "cousin cocaine - meanwhile the sheets stain red" were on the original. The song must have brought back memories of her own miscarriage in November 1968.
Early versions, with Marianne on vocals, were cut on tape in the States in July 1968. Marianne considered recording it for the *Rock And Roll Circus* event but its lyrical content may have been a bit too close to the knuckle for TV release. Her version was released as a single in February 1969 but was withdrawn two days later by Decca bosses. This one (* a - 5.29) has a different arrangement to the Stones album cut but is said to include Jack Nitzsche, who tinkered on the organ and Ry Cooder, who excelled himself on the bottleneck slide guitar at the latter session. Another earlier "sparser sounding" version has a "ready" spoken part then two minutes of acoustic guitar before the slide enters.(* b - 5.35). Acoustic guitar tracks are made by Mick and Keith but at different times.
Once the song was released on STICKY FINGERS Marianne Faithfull saw that she was not credited as a songwriter. She put in a claim that she was the co-writer of the song and Jagger and Richards later signed an acknowledgement of this. *Sister Morphine* is a harrowing tale of a man, injured in an accident, who needs to score to ease the pain while recuperating. Due to its title, the song was, of course, linked with drug addiction and the ultimate overdose.
The version which appears on STICKY FINGERS, two or three years after its original recording, depicts the nightmare - so much so that the Spanish edition of the album substituted another track to avoid any youth subversion. In fact, it is musically quite beautiful, Charlie Watts' drums are lean and purposeful, the lead slide guitar is mean and it has an unusual keyboard sound, while the acoustic back-drop is resplendent.

398. BLOOD RED WINE (Jagger, Richard) 5.20
13-18 May 1968: Place: Olympic Sound Studios, London, England.
Rolling Stones with Nicky Hopkins.
Producer: Jimmy Miller.
Engineer: Glyn Johns.
Bootleg only.

Blood Red Wine is a slow track with a strumming acoustic guitar and a smooth piano providing the back-drop for Mick Jagger's mournful vocals. The lyrics offer contrasting imagery: "I got red blood, and I got blood red wine which I bring you, when the snow lies heavy on the ground. If you get cold I wrap my coat around . . . don't you stay on that snowy ground." Maybe some of the lyrics were carried over to 1973's track *Winter*.

399. STILL A FOOL (Morganfield) 6.43
AKA: Two Trains Running
13-18 May; 26-30 June 1968: Place: Mobile at Redlands, Sussex, Olympic Sound Studios, London, England.
Played Live: 1962, 1995
Rolling Stones with Nicky Hopkins.
Producer: Jimmy Miller.
Engineer: Glyn Johns.
Bootleg only.

Still A Fool, also known as *Two Trains Running*, is a return to the *Little Red Rooster* style blues. The song was a 1951 Muddy Waters (McKinley Morganfield) tune. Another British group, The Groundhogs, (named after a John Lee Hooker song), with Tony McPhee as their guitarist, recorded *Still A Fool* in 1968 for their debut album SCRATCHING THE SURFACE, released in November. The Groundhogs had blues connections - they were John Lee Hooker's backing group for a UK tour and, in 1965, recorded an album with him in London titled HOOKER & THE HOGS.
Slide guitar, wailing harmonica, piano and Jagger moaning in true southern delta fashion all adds up to create a track which should be sought by blues critics and Stones' official collectors alike. It returns to the past but also is predictive of the future. It must have given them confidence to tackle tracks like the impending *Midnight Rambler*. There is an extended slower version lasting almost ten minutes (* a 9.48) as well as the standard seven-minute track.

400. LADY (Jagger, Richard) 1.32
AKA: London Jam
4-10 June 1968: Place: Olympic Sound Studios, London, England.
Rolling Stones with Nicky Hopkins.
Producer: Jimmy Miller.
Engineer: Glyn Johns.
Bootleg only.

The BEGGARS BANQUET sessions in the Spring and Summer of '68 produced a number of unreleased tracks. *Lady*, is a blues number recorded during the *Sympathy For The Devil* session.

401. THE DEVIL IS MY NAME (Jagger, Richard)
AKA: Sympathy For The Devil
4-10 June 1968: Place: Olympic Sound Studios, London, England.
Rolling Stones with Nicky Hopkins.
Producer: Jimmy Miller.
Engineer: Glyn Johns. Assistant Engineer: Phill Brown.
Bootleg only.

The Devil Is My Name was the working title for *Sympathy For The Devil*, the sessions for which were captured during the filming of the Stones' cinematic debut. Jean-Luc Godard was a politically aware film producer whose anti-establishment reputation fitted in well with the band's image. The film cameras took over the Olympic Studios for two days and documented the rehearsals for *Sympathy For The Devil*. The film was provisionally titled *One Plus One* but was changed to attract more box office appeal. Uniquely, it captures the Stones' recording method, which is purposeful and spontaneous, but there also are also some long, tedious scenes. The track builds up from what was once a Dylanesque country song, to an insane samba rhythm, Rocky Dijon's played percussion driving it on to a faster pace. Mick Jagger is shown playing acoustic guitar and indicates how he feels the song should build up while, during difficult percussive pieces, he encourages Charlie Watts: "Try to make it a bit more lively - it sounds a bit dead".

The film emphasised the rift between the Stones and Brian Jones, who was very much the outsider. At times he sat in the corner and was offered only a small acoustic guitar part. Keith Richards was industriously playing bass lines and lead guitar while Nicky Hopkins, who was now into the Stones' recording groove, plays competently on his Hammond organ, again contributing significantly to the song-writing process. On later run-throughs he moves to alter the mood to a grand piano. One very interesting cut of *Sympathy For The Devil* includes echo on Jagger's vocals.

As a documentary of life in the studio, the film is an essential Stones recording artefact. Mysteriously, Jean-Luc Godard captured the ultimate climax when the roof of the studio caught fire from an exploding light bulb and the band hurriedly evacuated at 2am one morning. Jimmy Miller and Bill Wyman ensured the safety of the tapes as the fire brigade controlled the fire, drenching the studio. Phill Brown was asked to clear all Stones tapes from the store while Keith Grant ensured the studio opened on time as, by four in the morning, he had arranged a scaffolding company to secure the timbers and place tarpaulin over the structure. Further sessions were problematic as aircraft noises could be heard on the recordings.

During July, the band flew to Los Angeles to do overdubs and mixing for the BEGGARS BANQUET album, scheduled then for release late July/early August - but this was held up by the dispute over the album cover. The actual recording was mastered a little slower than intended, which was rectified when ABKCO re-mastered the catalogue in 2002. In August, Brian Jones went to Morocco with studio engineer George Chkiantz to record the album THE PIPES OF PAN OF JOUJOUKA played by the Master Musicians of Joujouka. It was Brian's intention that the recordings could be used on a Stones album but the others were not keen. Allen Klein was also not interested in the project and it dismayed Brian that he could not gain a release, the album eventually appearing after Brian's death, in October 1971, on The Rolling Stones' own label.

Mick Jagger spent September and October filming *Performance* in London, many of the scenes being filmed in Chester Square, where he lived and had written *Sympathy For The Devil*. Performance was produced by Sanford Leiberson, directed by Donald Cammell and Nicholas Roeg, starred James Fox and also featured Anita Pallenberg. It is a visually compelling look at the hippie, mystical lifestyle and the gangster underworld. The screenplay, written by Donald Cammell, sees James Fox, as Chas, taking refuge in a home where the bisexual Turner, played by Mick Jagger is living with Anita Pallenberg (Pherber) and her amourette Lucy (Michele Breton). The main characters delve into each other's worlds and create a film that is rich and symbolic, until the end when Chas murders Turner - the ultimate betrayal. The New York Times summarised the film: "You don't have to be a drug addict, pederast, sado-masochist or nitwit to enjoy *Performance*, but being one or more of those things would help." Donald Cammell took his own life by shooting himself in 1996.

402. SYMPATHY FOR THE DEVIL (Jagger, Richard) 6.18
AKA: The Devil Is My Name
4-10 June 1968: Place: Olympic Sound Studios, London, England.
Played Live: 1968, 1969, 1970, 1971, 1975, 1976, 1981, 1989, 1990, 1994, 1995, 1997, 1998, 1999, 2002, 2003, 2005, 2006, 2007
Rolling Stones with Nicky Hopkins, Anita Pallenberg, Suki Poitier, Marianne Faithfull, Rocky Dijon.
Producer: Jimmy Miller.
Engineer: Glyn Johns.
Assistant Engineer: Phill Brown.
UK LP BEGGARS BANQUET: 6 December 1968: No. 3 - 12 weeks
USA LP BEGGARS BANQUET: 7 December 1968: No. 5 - 13 weeks
USA Compilation LP THE ROLLING STONES PROMOTIONAL ALBUM: October 1969
UK Compilation LP GIMME SHELTER: 29 August 1971: No. 19 - 5 weeks
USA LP THE ROLLING STONES HOT ROCKS 1964-1971: 11 January 1972: No. 4 - 30 weeks
UK Compilation LP ROLLED GOLD: 14 November 1975: No. 7 - 50 weeks
UK Compilation LP GET STONED - 30 GREATEST HITS, 30 ORIGINAL TRACKS: 21 October 1977: No. 13 - 15 weeks
UK Track 12-inch Single Jumpin' Jack Flash: 25 May 1987
UK & USA LP THE ROLLING STONES SINGLES COLLECTION - THE LONDON YEARS: 15 August 1989
USA Track 12-inch Single Paint It Black: 11 June 1990
UK CD LP FORTY LICKS: 30 September 2002: No. 2 - 45 weeks
USA CD LP FORTY LICKS: 1 October 2002: No. 2 - 50 weeks
UK CD Track Sympathy For The Devil Neptunes Radio Edit: 1 September 2003
USA CD Single: Sympathy For The Devil Neptunes Radio Edit: 16 September 2003
UK CD box set THE ROLLING STONES SINGLES - 1968 - 1971: 28 February 2005
USA CD box set THE ROLLING STONES SINGLES - 1968 - 1971: 1 March 2005
UK Compilation CD ROLLED GOLD +: 12 November 2007: No. 26 - 12 weeks

The subject matter for *Sympathy For The Devil* is Satan and his madcap escapades into human life. Mick Jagger was influenced by Mikhail Bulgakov's novel *The Master And The Margarita*, in which Satan looks at the effects of the Russian Revolution. Marianne Faithfull was reading it at the time and, in her autobiography, labelled the song as "pure papier-mâché Satanism". Mick Jagger twists the tale further, evoking and inciting nightmare images. The tragic incident involving Robert F. Kennedy, who was shot and mortally wounded on 5 June 1968, prompted the line: "Who killed the Kennedys?", which was changed from the original, singular: "Who killed John Kennedy?" - a reference to Robert's brother, who had been assassinated in 1963.

Lyrically, *Sympathy For The Devil* is a rock and roll masterpiece which tells a dark tale, carrying on with type of images which were started in *Jumpin' Jack Flash*. It was, however, imagery that Mick Jagger did not want the band to dwell on, he did not want them to be labelled as "Satanists", though the tag did haunt them for years to come. The track starts gently enough as Mick Jagger and Charlie Watts play percussion to a samba beat before Nicky Hopkins enters on the piano and Mick invokes his irreligious taunts. Once the pace is right, Keith Richards bursts in with an electrifying solo guitar performance and also provides the bass, with Bill Wyman on maracas. The infamous background "whoo-whoo's", inspired by Jimmy Miller, are supplied by the band (including Brian Jones and Charlie Watts), Anita Pallenberg, Suki Poitier, Marianne Faithfull, Glyn Johns and Nicky Hopkins. Even "Mr Get It Together" was asked to join in.

The guitar wanes for a few verses before entering again to an understated climactic crescendo. In a BBC radio interview, Keith Richards said he felt that the essence of the Stones was captured on that song. He reckoned you had to hang on to its tail as it evolved and that it mirrored the society at the time. There is an out-take very similar to the final release but Mick Jagger misses out four lines from the second verse (* a - 6.23). An edited cut, with the backing vocals lower in the mix, can be heard (* b - 5.57). When the original track was released on the *Sympathy* remixes in 2003, it became the first Rolling Stones track to be given an airing in 5.1 DSD surround sound. The song was covered magnificently by the German group Laibach in 1988.

403. SYMPATHY FOR THE DEVIL (NEPTUNES REMIX) (Jagger, Richard) 5.55
4-10 June 1968; April - July 2003: Place: Olympic Sound Studios, London, England; The Hit Factory, New York, Hovercraft Studios, Mixstar Studios, Virginia, USA.
Rolling Stones with Nicky Hopkins, Anita Pallenberg, Suki Poitier, Marianne Faithfull, Rocky Dijon.
Producer: Jimmy Miller.
Engineer: Original: Glyn Johns. Remix: Brian Garten, Andrew Coleman
Remixed and Re-edited by The Neptunes, Additional Mixing by Serban Ghenea
UK CD Track Sympathy For The Devil Neptunes Radio Edit: 1 September 2003
USA CD Track Sympathy For The Devil Neptunes Radio Edit: 16 September 2003

404. SYMPATHY FOR THE DEVIL (NEPTUNES RADIO REMIX) (Jagger, Richard) 4.16
4-10 June 1968; April - July 2003: Place: Olympic Sound Studios, London, England; The Hit Factory, New York, Hovercraft Studios, Mixstar Studios, Virginia, USA.
Rolling Stones with Nicky Hopkins, Anita Pallenberg, Suki Poitier, Marianne Faithfull, Rocky Dijon.
Producer: Jimmy Miller.
Engineer: Original: Glyn Johns. Remix: Brian Garten, Andrew Coleman
Remixed and Re-edited by The Neptunes, Additional Mixing by Serban Ghenea
UK CD Single: 1 September 2003: No. 14 - 6 weeks
USA CD Single: 16 September 2003: No. 97 - 1 week
UK CD/DVD box set THE ROLLING STONES SINGLES - 1968 - 1971: 28 February 2005
USA CD/DVD box set THE ROLLING STONES SINGLES - 1968 - 1971: 1 March 2005

405. SYMPATHY FOR THE DEVIL (FATBOY SLIM REMIX) (Jagger, Richard) 8.25
4-10 June 1968; April - July 2003: Place: Olympic Sound Studios, London, England; HMS House, Brighton, England.
Rolling Stones with Nicky Hopkins, Anita Pallenberg, Suki Poitier, Marianne Faithfull, Rocky Dijon.
Producer: Jimmy Miller.
Engineer: Original: Glyn Johns. Re-mixed and Re-Edited by Fatboy Slim
Mixed and Engineered: Simon Thornton
UK CD Track Sympathy For The Devil Neptunes Radio Edit: 1 September 2003
USA CD Track Sympathy For The Devil Neptunes Radio Edit: 16 September 2003
UK CD box set THE ROLLING STONES SINGLES - 1968 - 1971: 28 February 2005
USA CD box set THE ROLLING STONES SINGLES - 1968 - 1971: 1 March 2005

406. SYMPATHY FOR THE DEVIL (FATBOY SLIM RADIO REMIX) (Jagger, Richard) 4.06
4-10 June 1968; April - July 2003: Place: Olympic Sound Studios, London, England; HMS House, Brighton, England.
Rolling Stones with Nicky Hopkins, Anita Pallenberg, Suki Poitier, Marianne Faithfull, Rocky Dijon.
Producer: Jimmy Miller.
Engineer: Original: Glyn Johns. Re-mixed and Re-Edited by Fatboy Slim
Mixed and Engineered: Simon Thornton
USA CD Track Sympathy For The Devil Neptunes Radio Edit: 16 September 2003
USA Compilation DVD Rock And Roll Circus: 12 October 2004
UK Compilation DVD Rock And Roll Circus: 25 October 2004

407. SYMPATHY FOR THE DEVIL (FULL PHATT REMIX) (Jagger, Richard) 5.26
4-10 June 1968; April - July 2003: Place: Olympic Sound Studios, London, England; Magic Shop, New York, Flava Lab, London, England.
Rolling Stones with Nicky Hopkins, Anita Pallenberg, Suki Poitier, Marianne Faithfull, Rocky Dijon.

Producer: Jimmy Miller.
Engineer: Original: Glyn Johns. Mix: Full Phatt
Re-mix and additional production by Matt Ward, Dean Gillard. Stereo Mix by Sgt Fury assisted by 'Dum Dum' Dugan. Additional mixing by Double D & Disco.
UK CD Track Sympathy For The Devil Neptunes Radio Edit: 1 September 2003
USA CD Track Sympathy For The Devil Neptunes Radio Edit: 16 September 2003

408. SYMPATHY FOR THE DEVIL (FULL PHATT RADIO REMIX) (Jagger, Richard) 3.42
4-10 June 1968; April - July 2003: Place: Olympic Sound Studios, London, England; Magic Shop, New York, Flava Lab, London, England.
Rolling Stones with Nicky Hopkins, Anita Pallenberg, Suki Poitier, Marianne Faithfull, Rocky Dijon.
Producer: Jimmy Miller.
Engineer: Original: Glyn Johns. Mix: Full Phatt
Re-mix and additional production by Matt Ward, Dean Gillard. Stereo Mix by Sgt Fury assisted by 'Dum Dum' Dugan. Additional mixing by Double D & Disco.
USA CD Track Sympathy For The Devil Neptunes Radio Edit: 16 September 2003
UK CD box set THE ROLLING STONES SINGLES - 1968 - 1971: 28 February 2005
USA CD box set THE ROLLING STONES SINGLES - 1968 - 1971: 1 March 2005

409. MEMO FROM TURNER (Jagger, Richard) 4.03
September-October 1968: Place: Olympic Sound Studios, London, England.
Mick Jagger with Jack Nitzsche, Ry Cooder, Steve Winwood, Jim Capaldi.
Producer: Jack Nitzsche.
Engineer: Glyn Johns.
UK LP PERFORMANCE: 19 September 1970
USA LP PERFORMANCE: 19 September 1970
UK Single: 31 October 1970 (Credited as Mick Jagger only): No. 32 - 5 weeks
German Compilation LP THE REST OF THE BEST: December 1983
UK & USA LP THE ROLLING STONES SINGLES COLLECTION - THE LONDON YEARS: 15 August 1989
UK CD box set THE ROLLING STONES SINGLES - 1968 - 1971: 28 February 2005
USA CD box set THE ROLLING STONES SINGLES - 1968 - 1971: 1 March 2005

While Mick Jagger was playing his first film role as Turner in *Performance*, Keith Richards felt creatively remote. His girlfriend Anita Pallenberg was playing opposite Mick Jagger, in a role involving some bedroom scenes, some of which were cut from the final film. The insecurity mounted and the Jagger, Richard composition, intended by writer and co-producer Donald Cammell to be the major score of the film, was still missing. Keith attempted to retaliate by delaying the sessions as long as possible then Mick countered by inviting a host of other players, including Traffic's Steve Winwood and Jim Capaldi. Ry Cooder overdubbed bottleneck slide guitar, possibly at a later date in Los Angeles. Steve Winwood had worked with Jimmy Miller before in The Spencer Davis Group.
The released version is without a prominent organ that can be heard on an out-take with a slow percussive start (* a - 3.54). The single became Mick Jagger's first solo single from the PERFORMANCE film but he did not want it to be released and refused to promote it, arguing that the song was not meant to be commercial and was done strictly as part of the soundtrack. While it was later released on Stones' album collections, this version does not feature the other band members. Amazingly, Mick told NME writer Roy Carr, in November 1970, that when the master was flown to the States, the original backing track was erased and had to be re-recorded by session people. Things became even more confused when Donald Cammell said that he should have had a co-writing credit with Jagger. Lyrically it does tell a convincing desperado's story and, if Keith had persevered, it may have ended up on the LET IT BLEED album.

410. YOU CAN'T ALWAYS GET WHAT YOU WANT (Jagger, Richard) 7.28
16-17 November 1968, 15 March; April - May 1969: Place: Morgan Studios, London, Olympic Sound Studios, London, England; CBS Studios, New York, USA.
Played Live: 1968, 1972, 1973, 1975, 1976, 1981, 1982, 1989, 1990, 1995, 1997, 1998, 2002, 2003, 2005, 2006, 2007
Rolling Stones with Al Kooper, London Bach Choir, Madeline Bell, Doris Troy, Nanette Workman, Rocky Dijon, Jimmy Miller.
Producer: Jimmy Miller.
Engineer: Glyn Johns.
Arranger: Jack Nitzsche. Assistant Engineers: Bruce Botnick, Jerry Hansen, George Chkiantz, Alan O'Duffy, Vic Smith, Andy Johns.
USA LP LET IT BLEED: 29 November 1969: No. 3 - 19 weeks
UK LP LET IT BLEED: 5 December 1969: No. 1 - 29 weeks
UK B-side Honky Tonk Women: 11 July 1969
USA B-side Honky Tonk Women: 11 July 1969
USA LP THE ROLLING STONES HOT ROCKS 1964-1971: 11 January 1972: No. 4 - 30 weeks
UK B-side Sad Day: 29 April 1973
UK LP SLOW ROLLERS: 9 November 1981
German Compilation LP THE REST OF THE BEST: December 1983
UK & USA LP THE ROLLING STONES SINGLES COLLECTION - THE LONDON YEARS: 15 August 1989
UK CD LP FORTY LICKS: 30 September 2002: No. 2 - 45 weeks
USA CD LP FORTY LICKS: 1 October 2002: No. 2 - 50 weeks
UK CD box set THE ROLLING STONES SINGLES - 1968 - 1971: 28 February 2005
USA CD box set THE ROLLING STONES SINGLES - 1968 - 1971: 1 March 2005
UK Compilation CD ROLLED GOLD +: 12 November 2007: No. 26 - 12 weeks

"Slightly over the top" is an understatement. The song includes Al Kooper on keyboards and French horn, producer Jimmy Miller plays on drums (Jimmy suggested a certain drum accent that Charlie Watts was not comfortable with) and Rocky Dijon adds some percussion, not to mention three female vocalists and a choir who help out Mick Jagger. Alan "Al" Kooper was holidaying in England with Denny Cordell (producer of *A Whiter Shade Of Pale* and Joe Cocker's *With A Little Help From My Friends*). The Stones office called him and asked whether Al would play on a couple of sessions. They needed a keyboard player as Nicky Hopkins was touring in the USA. Al had a groove in mind and Keith Richards played an acoustic part which complemented it. Once a passable cut was made, they added an organ and electric guitar. The French horn was overdubbed on to a master copy the next year in New York with some brass but Jagger only used the French horn introduction - Al admitted that was a good decision since he had not played the other horns well that evening. Jack Nitzsche had been brought back by Mick Jagger to score the *Performance* film (it was he who had introduced Ry Cooder to Mick) so it seemed natural that he would get involved with the Stones as well. He was a bit unnerved by the behaviour of Keith, who had turned inwardly to drugs such as heroin and all the hangers-on which that habit encouraged.

The end result of all the contributors is a production by the Stones unparalleled to this day, an adventurous attempt at a mini rock opera conceived by Mick, running in at over seven minutes. The choir was added in March and Mick had to work with them on the pronunciation of "want" - they were reluctant to move away from their English accents to the required drawl. The track was shortened for it to be featured as the flip side of *Honky Tonk Women* - it did not have the choir intro (* a - 4.52). The London Bach Choir (all 60 of them), although content with their contribution, were not over-impressed with the rest of the album (e.g. *Midnight Rambler*) and wished to renounce their role in it - but it was too late.

The original version was recorded by Andy Johns at Morgan Studios in London and is without the orchestral theatrics. Brian Jones does not contribute, probably unaware that Mick wanted his amp switched off while Al Kooper added the organ sounds. *You Can't Always Get What You Want* has been a tour favourite ever since, simply because it is a song that people can relate to. It is also a possible taunt at Keith by Mick, due to the latter and Anita Pallenberg's liaison on the *Performance* film set. Marianne Faithfull felt it was Mick chastising her for taking heroin. Who was Mr Jimmy who hung out at the Chelsea drug store? Mr Jimmy Miller (the obvious suspect) or a Mr Jimi Hendrix? According to the lyrics he looked pretty ill and said one word: "dead". A single-sided EMIDISC acetate was prepared on 11 July 1969, the date of its release on single as the flip side to *Honky Tonk Women*.

411. YOU CAN'T ALWAYS GET WHAT YOU WANT (SOULWAX FULL LENGTH REMIX) (Jagger, Richard) 6.07
16-17 November 1968, 15 March; April - May 1969; 2007: Place: Olympic Sound Studios, London, England; CBS Studios, New York, USA; Soulwax Studios, Ghent, Belgium.
Rolling Stones with Al Kooper, London Bach Choir, Madeline Bell, Doris Troy, Nanette Workman, Rocky Dijon, Jimmy Miller.
Producer: Jimmy Miller.
Engineer: Glyn Johns.
Vocal Arranger: Jack Nitzsche.
Assistant Engineers: Bruce Botnick, Jerry Hansen, George Chkiantz, Alan O'Duffy, Vic Smith, Andy Johns.
USA e-Single: 19 February 2008
USA Compilation CD MUSIC FROM THE MOTION PICTURE 21: 18 March 2008
UK Compilation CD MUSIC FROM THE MOTION PICTURE 21: 7 April 2008

David Sardy, the score composer for the Kevin Spacey drama film *21*, used the original initially, but felt it was out of sync with the rest of the 2008 soundtrack, which features Rihanna, U.N.K.L.E. and LCD Soundsystem, so remix specialists Soulwax (two Belgian mixers) were commissioned. Sardy told the Hollywood Reporter: "If you're offended, you're of a certain age and if you're not, you're definitely of a certain age." The download single was available for a limited one-week period and mainly played around the vocal delivery of the song title with sound bites of guitar, piano and choir from the original. A synthesised electronic backbeat of keyboards and percussion modernised the song. As Jody Klein commented in the ABKCO press release: "We are very excited to present our music in innovative ways to new generations of fans."

412. MEMO FROM TURNER (Jagger, Richard) 2.46
17 November 1968: Place: Olympic Sound Studios, London, England.
Rolling Stones with Al Kooper.
Producer: Jimmy Miller.
Engineer: Glyn Johns, George Chkiantz, Andy Johns.
UK Compilation LP METAMORPHOSIS: 6 June 1975: No. 45 - 1 week
USA Compilation LP METAMORPHOSIS: 6 June 1975: No. 8 - 8 weeks

Determined that Jagger improve upon the version already recorded for the PERFORMANCE soundtrack and since Al Kooper was in the studio, Mick invited him to play a guitar part with Keith Richards. However, interestingly, he jammed with Keith and showed him the open-G guitar technique, something that Ry Cooder claimed to have taught the Stones guitarist. It was based on the tuning used for five-string banjos sold by Sears, Roebuck & Co in their mail order catalogue in the early 1900s. They later sold guitars and the musicians who bought them, who were used to banjo playing, took off the sixth string and tuned it like a banjo. The Stones version of *Memo From Turner* was eventually released on METAMORPHOSIS and we assume Al was on the final cut, maybe with Keith with perhaps some Ry Cooder and Steve Winwood thrown in for good measure from the previous session. A demo version can be found (* a - 2.49). Confusing to say the least. During the recording of PERFORMANCE Mick Jagger bought a modular Moog synthesiser Series III in September 1968 but sold it in 1969 when he failed to get any coherent musical sounds from it. It was later sold to German keyboard specialist Christoph Franke from Tangerine Dream. It featured within the *Performance* film as a prop, when it was owned by Jack Nitzsche.

413. SYMPATHY FOR THE DEVIL (Jagger, Richard) 5.30
30 November 1968: Place: David Frost LWT TV Show, London, England.
Rolling Stones with Nicky Hopkins, Rocky Dijon.
UK Compilation DVD Frost On Saturday 1968: 4 October 2010

A playback of the Stones miming to their recent creation. Brian Jones sits at the piano and a rather self-conscious Mick Jagger begins to perfect his stage performance; he takes off his t-shirt and kneels before the song fades. This style was re-enacted in a couple of weeks' time.

414. ROUTE 66 (Troup)
10-11 December 1968: Place: Intertel Studios, Stonebridge, London, England.
Producer: Jimmy Miller.
Engineer: Glyn Johns.
Unavailable.

Pete Townshend explained that the original concept for *Rock And Roll Circus* was seeded at Olympic Studios by Ronnie Lane, Mick Jagger and who would form a travelling troupe that would go from town to town. The Small Faces were about to split, due to artistic wavering by Steve Marriott and his desire to work with Peter Frampton, so Ronnie Lane, Kenney Jones and Ian McLagan were considering their next move. Edward "Chip" Monck, who did the stage design for the Monterey festival, was asked to work on what might be necessary for three touring bands (The Stones, The Who and what was to become The Faces) to tour America on a train with a circus tent and recording facilities but it proved too unwieldy a project.

So the Circus turned into a smaller extravaganza recorded in December 1968 and was intended for a BBC TV Christmas special to promote the BEGGARS BANQUET album. The press were invited to a medieval party launch on 5 December at the Gore Hotel Bar 190 in Kensington, London with busty Elizabethan wenches serving drink, food and clay pipes before each person was given a box which consisted of meringue. This was duly flung liberally at people's faces, Mick Jagger slapping Brian Jones to commence the fight. The images reflected the inside cover of the album, taken earlier in June by Michael Joseph, Ron Wood replicating the scene fabulously for his Beggars Banquet painting in 2005.

The album was unusual in that there was no obvious single released to promote it. Tickets for the innovative show were free and distributed through an advertisement in the New Musical Express. Filming was directed by Ready, Steady, Go!'s Michael Lindsay-Hogg and the cinematographer was Tony Richmond. Nicky Hopkins had literally just hopped off a plane fresh from his tour with the Jeff Beck Group, which included Ron Wood. The star-studded array of performers was disguised in clown outfits, although the idea of dressing Mick Jagger typically dressed as a ring-master was incongruous and unreal. Originally they hoped Brigitte Bardot would perform this role but she was unavailable.

The Stones, in particular, were dissatisfied with the overall outcome - it was even considered that they were upstaged by The Who and wanted their part to be re-filmed, which never happened. "The Circus" was not released for 27 years when it finally appeared on video and a soundtrack album, the release being made in conjunction with ABKCO, whose and production included work by Jody Klein, son of Allen Klein. Re-arrange the letters in the credits of Lenne Allik to determine who he really was. The tape found was not perfect and the later DVD version taken from another recently found copy was in better quality.

The 1979 rockumentary film *The Kids Are All Right* had extracts from their performance from the original copy. The soundtrack included Jethro Tull, recommended by Charlie Watts and Bill Wyman and including new member Tony Iommi, The Who on startling form, Taj Mahal at Keith's request, Marianne Faithfull (who could resist?), Yoko Ono (Oh no!) and the super group The Dirty Mac. Michael, Lindsay-Hogg and Mick said no to another fledgling band Led Zeppelin because they wanted more musical variety. The Dirty Mac was formed very quickly when Steve Winwood could not get a group together. They performed John Lennon and Paul McCartney's *Yer Blues* and included Lennon on lead vocal (at one point Steve Winwood was considered, then Paul McCartney) and guitar, Eric Clapton on lead guitar and Mitch Mitchell on drums. For a number that included a wailing Yoko, a less than enthusiastic Frenchman Ivry Gitlis played the violin. The potential vacant guitar spot was for bass, Bill Wyman being disappointed that his place was taken by Keith Richards. At 2am on December 11, with energy levels low, the Stones hit the stage and warmed up with *Route 66* and *Confessin' The Blues*.

415. CONFESSIN' THE BLUES (Troup)
10-11 December 1968: Place: Intertel Studios, Stonebridge, London, England.
Producer: Jimmy Miller.
Engineer: Glyn Johns.
Unavailable.

416. LOOK ON YONDER WALL (Clark)
AKA: Yonders Wall
10-11 December 1968: Place: Intertel Studios, Stonebridge, London, England.
Producer: Jimmy Miller.
Engineer: Glyn Johns.
Unavailable.

417. WALKIN' BLUES (Johnson)
10-11 December 1968: Place: Intertel Studios, Stonebridge, London, England.
Producer: Jimmy Miller.
Engineer: Glyn Johns.
Unavailable.

In between breaks for the camera, Mick Jagger performs solo on a couple of old blues tunes.

418. JUMPING JACK FLASH (Jagger, Richard) 3.35
10-11 December 1968: Place: Intertel Studios, Stonebridge, London, England.
Rolling Stones with Rocky Dijon.
Producer: Jimmy Miller, Jody Klein, Lenne Allik.
Engineer: Glyn Johns.
Mixing Engineer: Steve Rosenthal. Assistant Engineer: Teri Landi, Joe Warda.
UK Compilation LP ROCK AND ROLL CIRCUS: 15 October 1996: No. 12 - 1 week
USA Compilation LP ROCK AND ROLL CIRCUS: 15 October 1996
USA Compilation DVD Rock And Roll Circus: 12 October 2004
UK Compilation DVD Rock And Roll Circus: 25 October 2004

The show was filmed at the Intertel Studios, Stonebridge, North West London and recorded by Olympic's Mobile truck. Intertel had done many television shows and were considered cutting edge for that time. The cameras were turned on and the Stones performed three versions of *Jumping Jack Flash* and *Parachute Woman*, each time getting louder and louder and more enthusiastic.

419. PARACHUTE WOMAN (Jagger, Richard) 2.58
10-11 December 1968: Place: Intertel Studios, Stonebridge, London, England.
Rolling Stones with Nicky Hopkins, Rocky Dijon.
Producer: Jimmy Miller, Jody Klein, Lenne Allik.
Engineer: Glyn Johns.
Mixing Engineer: Steve Rosenthal. Assistant Engineer: Teri Landi, Joe Warda.
UK Compilation LP ROCK AND ROLL CIRCUS: 15 October 1996: No. 12 - 1 week
USA Compilation LP ROCK AND ROLL CIRCUS: 15 October 1996
USA Compilation DVD Rock And Roll Circus: 12 October 2004
UK Compilation DVD Rock And Roll Circus: 25 October 2004

Keith Richards takes the lead solo, Brian Jones plays rhythm and Mick Jagger transforms the recently released track with his harmonica at the end.

420. NO EXPECTATIONS (Jagger, Richard) 4.13
10-11 December 1968: Place: Intertel Studios, Stonebridge, London, England.
Rolling Stones with Nicky Hopkins, Rocky Dijon.
Producer: Jimmy Miller, Jody Klein, Lenne Allik.
Engineer: Glyn Johns.
Mixing Engineer: Steve Rosenthal. Assistant Engineer: Teri Landi, Joe Warda.
UK Compilation LP ROCK AND ROLL CIRCUS: 15 October 1996: No. 12 - 1 week
USA Compilation LP ROCK AND ROLL CIRCUS: 15 October 1996
USA Compilation DVD Rock And Roll Circus: 12 October 2004
UK Compilation DVD Rock And Roll Circus: 25 October 2004

Nicky Hopkins can be heard but not seen on piano. Keith Richards plays acoustic guitar and, as on the record, Brian Jones plays an excellent bottleneck blues guitar. A good moment for him in an otherwise dejected, rather deflated performance.

421. YOU CAN'T ALWAYS GET WHAT YOU WANT (Jagger, Richard) 4.24
10-11 December 1968: Place: Intertel Studios, Stonebridge, London, England.
Rolling Stones with Nicky Hopkins, Rocky Dijon.
Producer: Jimmy Miller, Jody Klein, Lenne Allik.
Engineer: Glyn Johns.
Mixing Engineer: Steve Rosenthal. Assistant Engineer: Teri Landi, Joe Warda.
UK Compilation LP ROCK AND ROLL CIRCUS: 15 October 1996: No. 12 - 1 week
USA Compilation LP ROCK AND ROLL CIRCUS: 15 October 1996
USA Compilation DVD Rock And Roll Circus: 12 October 2004
UK Compilation DVD Rock And Roll Circus: 25 October 2004

The newly recorded *You Can't Always Get What You Want* was performed with a sparse arrangement. Brian Jones plays rhythm, with Keith Richards adds an excellent lead guitar.

422. SYMPATHY FOR THE DEVIL (Jagger, Richard) 8.38
10-11 December 1968: Place: Intertel Studios, Stonebridge, London, England.
Rolling Stones with Nicky Hopkins, Rocky Dijon.
Producer: Jimmy Miller, Jody Klein, Lenne Allik.
Engineer: Glyn Johns.
Mixing Engineer: Steve Rosenthal. Assistant Engineer: Teri Landi, Joe Warda.
UK Compilation LP ROCK AND ROLL CIRCUS: 15 October 1996: No. 12 - 1 week
USA Compilation LP ROCK AND ROLL CIRCUS: 15 October 1996
USA Compilation DVD Rock And Roll Circus: 12 October 2004
UK Compilation DVD Rock And Roll Circus: 25 October 2004

The climax to the performance was a rousing nine-minute version of *Sympathy For The Devil* with Mick Jagger really working out for the camera. Apparently the take before was not convincing enough and the band received a "bit of a bollocking" from the production crew. They react well and deliver a great cut, Mick taking off his red t-shirt to reveal a "painted on" demonic Satan tattoo. Pete Townshend and Keith Moon can be seen grooving to the tune, and at the end, John Lennon mischievously waves a ball of wool in front of the camera - surely not a reference to Brian's earlier drugs-related mishap? Brian plays maracas and Rocky Dijon supports the rhythm on bongo drums.
It is a shame that Nicky Hopkins' piano is not given more visual prominence since it has such a vital contribution to the overall sound. It was as though he was positioned in the orchestra pit at the bottom of Brian's feet. Keith Richards slides between playing rhythm and taking lead solos as the only guitar player for the track. The growing responsibility that Keith was taking for guitar playing was great but it was sad to see Brian's reduced role (maracas on *Sympathy*) and for much of the day he could be found with tears in his eyes. Marianne Faithfull felt Brian looked ill and very uncomfortable, perhaps realising subconsciously that this would be his last performance with the band. He told Michael Lindsay-Hogg a day before that he did not want to do the show because the rest of the band were not talking to him. Michael told Brian that the Stones would not be the Stones without him and he had to be there - which convinced him.

423. SALT OF THE EARTH (Jagger, Richard) 5.07
10-11 December 1968: Place: Intertel Studios, Stonebridge, London, England.
Rolling Stones with Nicky Hopkins, Rocky Dijon, The Who, John Lennon, Yoko Ono, Eric Clapton.
Producer: Jimmy Miller, Jody Klein, Lenne Allik.
Engineer: Glyn Johns.
Mixing Engineer: Steve Rosenthal. Assistant Engineer: Teri Landi, Joe Warda.
UK Compilation LP ROCK AND ROLL CIRCUS: 15 October 1996: No. 12 - 1 week
USA Compilation LP ROCK AND ROLL CIRCUS: 15 October 1996
USA Compilation DVD Rock And Roll Circus: 12 October 2004
UK Compilation DVD Rock And Roll Circus: 25 October 2004

Not strictly a session take since the musical accompaniment is in fact the released backing track recorded at Olympic, with the vocal inclusion of the *Rock And Roll Circus* cast. There was a live acoustic live version but it was not thought as good as this exhausted, sat down, party version. At 6am the *Rock And Roll Circus* was completed, Keith Richards singing the first verse and Jagger then taking over. Everyone is wearing ponchos and felt hats and swinging from side to side. Then Mick ushers them to stand up and smiles, albeit wearily, before they all headed home from the Wembley studios.
When the DVD was released in 2004, there were bonus features that incorporated extra cameos and songs by classical pianist Julius Katchen, three songs by Taj Mahal and also incorporated voice overs of the main film. They were by Michael Lindsay-Hogg, Tony Richmond, Ian Anderson, Pete Townshend, Taj Mahal, Marianne Faithfull, Yoko Ono, Bill Wyman, Keith Richards and Mick Jagger. This emphasised the fondness and historic nature placed on a film which captured the naivety and spirit of the era. "One of the classics of modern cinema", laughed Keith. Mick concluded by saying: "There was certainly this fantastic camaraderie which existed at that time that made this programme really special. It was a fantastic day though and I'm really pleased it still seems to stand the test of time and peculiarity." The story continued in 1968 when Marianne Faithfull, Keith Richards and Anita Pallenberg travelled to Lisbon before catching a cruise ship to spend Christmas in Brazil. Apparently on this trip, in a hotel bar, a lady was trying to pursue their identity with "Who are you? Won't you give us a glimmer?", thereby coining the Glimmer Twins production pseudonym. Brian Jones and Suki Poitier, meanwhile, headed for an extended six-week break in Ceylon.

424. MIDNIGHT RAMBLER (Jagger, Richard) 6.52
9-10 February, 10-11 March, 16 May; 18 October - 3 November 1969: Place: Olympic Sound Studios, London, England; Sunset Sound Studios, Elektra Studios, Los Angeles, USA.
Played Live: 1969, 1970, 1971, 1972, 1973, 1975, 1976, 1989, 1990, 1995, 1999, 2002, 2003, 2005, 2006, 2007
Producer: Jimmy Miller.
Engineer: Glyn Johns.
Assistant Engineers: Bruce Botnick, Jerry Hansen, George Chkiantz, Vic Smith, Alan O'Duffy.
USA LP LET IT BLEED: 29 November 1969: No. 3 - 19 weeks
UK LP LET IT BLEED: 5 December 1969: No. 1 - 29 weeks
USA LP THE ROLLING STONES HOT ROCKS 1964-1971: 11 January 1972: No. 4 - 30 weeks
UK Compilation LP ROLLED GOLD: 14 November 1975: No. 7 - 50 weeks
UK Compilation CD ROLLED GOLD +: 12 November 2007: No. 26 - 12 weeks

Inspired by *You Can't Always Get What You Want* and recovered from their extended holidays to South America and Ceylon, sessions for the new album commenced in February. The ceiling and roof had been repaired at Olympic and the opportunity taken to ensure the studio was sound-tight. *Midnight Rambler* is a gutsy reminder of the Boston Strangler, the lyrics even including part of Albert de Salvo's confessions. Keith Richards is the prime instrumentalist, over-dubbing guitar parts (it took a week to get the solo right) and creating subtle tempo changes that intensify Jagger's homicidal dialogue. He likened the sound to early Chicago blues. *Midnight Rambler* builds up menacingly until it reaches the "Don't do that" passage, Keith Richards controlling the direction as Mick Jagger blows away on the harmonica. The song's theatrical leanings allow anger to be vented in drama rather than insane violence. Live performances of the track allowed the song to be extended with plenty of rhythm changes. Keith Richards and Mick Jagger both enjoyed the malevolent atmosphere it created and it was a challenge to perform on stage. Brian Jones did not contribute any guitar work to *Midnight Rambler*, although he played some percussion.
The song was worked on during a brief writing trip that Mick and Keith took to Positano, Italy, in early March 1969. There was a session in May with Nicky Hopkins, Ry Cooder, Bill Wyman, Charlie Watts and Mick Jagger in attendance. Keith was not there because he had fallen out with Ry. Meanwhile, Keith attended sessions for a Billy Preston album and contributed bass guitar on two tracks for the George Harrison produced THAT'S THE WAY GOD PLANNED IT album.
One of the tracks recorded at the Ry Cooder session was *The Boudoir Stomp*, written by Nicky, Ry and Charlie. The content of this jam has more than a passing similarity to the riff and harp playing from *Rambler*. The resultant album from the sessions was released on Rolling Stones Records in January 1972 and was called JAMMING WITH EDWARD. Eric Clapton took the *Rambler* feel one step further when guesting with Delaney and Bonnie in late 1969 on his virtuoso song *I Don't Want To Discuss It*. It was released by them on the 1970 album ON TOUR WITH ERIC CLAPTON.

425. YOU GOT THE SILVER (Jagger, Richard) 2.50
AKA: You Got Some Silver Now
9-18 February 1969: Place: Olympic Sound Studios, London, England.
Played Live: 1999, 2006, 2007
Rolling Stones with Nicky Hopkins.
Producer: Jimmy Miller.
Engineer: Glyn Johns.
Assistant Engineers: Bruce Botnick, Jerry Hansen, George Chkiantz, Vic Smith, Alan O'Duffy.
USA LP LET IT BLEED: 29 November 1969: No. 3 - 19 weeks
UK LP LET IT BLEED: 5 December 1969: No. 1 - 29 weeks
USA Compilation Promo CD THE ROLLING STONES REMASTERED: 30 May 2002

This country love song was written by Keith Richards for Anita Pallenberg. One of Keith's influences was the preceding year's album Byrds album SWEETHEARTS OF THE RODEO and he performed the vocals not for one verse, as on *Salt Of The Earth*, but for the complete song. The reason for this is apparently that, at the point of delivering the master tapes, an engineer accidentally wiped Mick Jagger's vocals off the multi-track. Mick was in Australia during July, August and some of September recording his film Ned Kelly so Keith's vocals were used on top of the master track.

A version does exist with Mick singing but this is an earlier recording and slightly faster in vocal approach (* a - 2.51). Keith plays acoustic and electric slide-guitar. George Chkiantz remembers that at one point his hands were bleeding, such was his dedication as they made one take after another trying to get the drum sound right. Glyn Johns was the lead engineer and gained a well-respected role. Keith Grant reflected in 2012 that Glyn was a determined individual who got things done and seemed totally unaffected by anything around him other than the job in hand. Nicky Hopkins helps build the song's tempo with alternating piano and organ passages. It was an all-time favourite performance of his.

Brian Jones plays one of his last studio contributions on autoharp, a flat string instrument often played in bluegrass music. In Sean Egan's book *Let It Bleed*, George thinks that Brian was using car keys to strum the strings in order to create a high-up harmonic. The finished track was chosen by Michelangelo Antonioni for inclusion on the soundtrack of his film *Zabriskie Point*. While appearing in the film, it was not included in the album soundtrack, which included Pink Floyd and Jerry Garcia, of Grateful Dead fame.

426. LOVE IN VAIN (Payne) 4.19
9 February-31 March 1969: Place: Olympic Sound Studios, London, England.
Played Live: 1969, 1970, 1971, 1972, 1978, 1995, 1997, 1998, 2002, 2003, 2007
Rolling Stones with Ry Cooder, Nicky Hopkins.
Producer: Jimmy Miller.
Engineer: Glyn Johns.
Assistant Engineers: Bruce Botnick, Jerry Hansen, George Chkiantz, Vic Smith, Alan O'Duffy.
USA Compilation LP THE ROLLING STONES - PROMOTIONAL ALBUM: 31 October 1969
USA LP LET IT BLEED: 29 November 1969: No. 3 - 19 weeks
UK LP LET IT BLEED: 5 December 1969: No. 1 - 29 weeks
UK Compilation LP GIMME SHELTER: 29 August 1971: No. 19 - 5 weeks

Marianne Faithfull convinced Mick Jagger to record a song formerly played by one of his blue's idols, Robert Johnson. At that time there was only the one album of Johnson material, KING OF THE DELTA BLUES SINGERS, released in 1961. In the sleeve notes to Robert Johnson's THE COMPLETE RECORDINGS album, Keith Richards said that he first came across Robert Johnson when Brian Jones played that album to him. He could not believe that there were not two people on guitar but realised that "this guy must have three brains" to play like that.

A bootleg recording of other tunes surfaced in '67 or '68. Mick and Keith thought *Love In Vain* was perfect with the latter remarking: "It is such a beautiful song. Mick and I both loved it and at the time I was working and playing around with Gram Parsons, and I started searching around for a different way to present it, because if we were going to record it there was no point in trying to copy the Robert Johnson style or version. So I sat around playing it in all kinds of different ways and styles. We took it a little bit more country, a little more formalised and Mick felt comfortable with that. But in a way it was just like - we've got to do this song, one way or another. Because it was just so beautiful; the title, the lyrics, the ideas, the rhyme, just everything about it."

Keith had met Gram Parsons the summer before when the Byrds played a gig in London. Gram was just about to embark on a South African tour but immediately pulled out and quit the band when Keith explained the ills of apartheid. He ended up staying at Redlands for the next couple of months and taught Keith how to play the piano and the nuances of country music. In 1970, Robert Johnson's Volume 2 of KING OF THE DELTA BLUES SINGERS was released with *Love In Vain* recorded. For the Stones recording, to add another dimension, Ry Cooder was brought in to play an excellent mandolin passage (normally Brian would have filled this role) and the song evolved around the distinctive country blues format.

A purely acoustic version was recorded, which ended up on a much-sought-after promotional album, simply titled THE ROLLING STONES (* a). It features tracks from the early days such as *Walking The Dog* and leads up to the late 60s, culminating in the rare and yet to be released version of *Love In Vain*. Intended for promotional purposes only, copies were released to radio stations in the States and only 200 for the press in the UK. Decca have since released a version of the album in Australia which has a different track listing.

427. DOWNTOWN SUZIE (Wyman) 3.53
AKA: Downtown Lucy, Lisle Street Lucie
23-25 February, 15 March - 23 April 1969: Place: Olympic Sound Studios, London, England.
Rolling Stones with Ry Cooder, Jimmy Miller.
Producer: Jimmy Miller.
Engineer: Glyn Johns.
UK Compilation LP METAMORPHOSIS: 6 June 1975: No. 45 - 1 week
USA Compilation LP METAMORPHOSIS: 6 June 1975: No. 8 - 8 weeks

The good fortune of having his composition included on the SATANIC MAJESTIES album made Bill Wyman determined to write further songs. He knew the musical quality had to be maintained and he admitted that *Downtown Suzie* did not warrant inclusion on LET IT BLEED or earlier on BEGGARS BANQUET. How did the street working girl Lucy mentioned in the lyrics become Suzie in the song title?

Brian Jones did not respond quite so objectively to the Jagger/Richard dominance. Keith Richards indicates that Brian never actually came up with a finished product and, therefore, this part of his insecurity was mostly self-inflicted. The music on Suzie is good-time boogie with a portion of acoustic blues and open tuned slide guitar by Ry Cooder. The humorous lyrics pertain to the original working title - "Have you ever been had? Got a dose from Lisle Street Lucy." Also, "I heard the ringing of the bell. It's Lucy with the clientele" and "Oh Lucy kicked me in the hall - yeah yeah yeah. A tennis worth of aching balls." Lisle Street is in Chinatown, Soho, in London and was well-known for "walk-ups".

An out-take is available on bootleg which has the same vocal style but less instrumentation (* a - 3.45), the original being overdubbed in April 1969 and eventually appearing on the mid-70s Decca compilation, METAMORPHOSIS, making it only the second Wyman composition to feature on a Rolling Stones' album.

428. GIMMIE SHELTER (Jagger, Richard) 4.30
AKA: Give Me Some Shelter, Gimme Shelter
23-25 February, 15 March; 18 October - 3 November 1969: Place: Olympic Sound Studios, London, England; Sunset Sound Studios, Elektra Studios, Los Angeles, USA.
Played Live: 1969, 1970, 1972, 1973, 1975, 1989, 1990, 1995, 1997, 1998, 1999, 2002, 2003, 2006
Rolling Stones with Nicky Hopkins, Jimmy Miller, Merry Clayton.
Producer: Jimmy Miller.
Engineer: Glyn Johns.
Assistant Engineers: Bruce Botnick, Jerry Hansen, George Chkiantz, Vic Smith, Alan O'Duffy.
USA LP LET IT BLEED: 29 November 1969: No. 3 - 19 weeks
UK LP LET IT BLEED: 5 December 1969: No. 1 - 29 weeks
UK Compilation LP GIMME SHELTER: 29 August 1971: No. 19 - 5 weeks
USA LP THE ROLLING STONES HOT ROCKS 1964-1971: 11 January 1972: No. 4 - 30 weeks
UK Compilation LP ROLLED GOLD: 14 November 1975: No. 7 - 50 weeks
UK Compilation LP GET STONED - 30 GREATEST HITS, 30 ORIGINAL TRACKS: 21 October 1977: No. 13 - 15 weeks
UK CD LP FORTY LICKS: 30 September 2002: No. 2 - 45 weeks
USA CD LP FORTY LICKS: 1 October 2002: No. 2 - 50 weeks
UK Compilation CD ROLLED GOLD +: 12 November 2007: No. 26 - 12 weeks

Rock and roll excess does not get better than this. The song was written in 1968 while Mick Jagger was filming *Performance*. Sometimes Keith Richards would wait outside the recording venue for Anita to come out, apparently mulling over insecurity, destiny and the subject of war and storms. The USA was still in a brutal war in the Far East, supporting the South Vietnamese. Keith put together the song on a cassette recorder at Robert Fraser's flat one stormy day. Eventually, it was recorded in February/March 1969, under the title *Give Me Some Shelter*.

Gimme Shelter is a hard rock track with some strange scales which ride up and down just like a real storm. Some of the credit of the unique sound was credited to some new Triumph amps that had been acquired by Ian Stewart. Just as they got to overheat stage they started to produce an uncanny sound. The strong vocals of Merry (because she was born at Christmas) Clayton were added at Elektra by Bruce Botnick for the final mixing, at the suggestion of Jack Nitzsche.

Merry was a New Orleans session singer who had come more to the fore with Ray Charles and had worked with Jack before. She had literally been called very late at night to join the session as, apparently, Bonnie Bramlett was not well enough to perform, although a jealous Delaney Bramlett may have prevented her fraternising with the band. On meeting Mick for the first time Merry is said to have uttered those immortal words: "Man, I thought you was a man, but you nothing but a skinny little boy!" Her vocal accompaniment has reached legendary status, possibly beaten to the post by Lisa Fischer's strong and lascivious stage performances with the group since 1989. Apparently, following Merry's performance of just three takes and on her return home, legend says she suffered a miscarriage, so her memories of the session would be a bit painful. However, she did record *Gimme Shelter* herself for a 1970 single release.

The song centres around the heavy lead semi-acoustic Maton guitar of Keith's as it resonated through his Triumph amplifier; apparently, the guitar literally fell to bits after the recording was made. Keith related the playing style to a Jimmy Reed open-tuning move. Mick also plays harmonica and Nicky Hopkins is almost buried in the mix. Jimmy Miller enhances the percussion techniques with shakers and a type of washboard scratch, a knack which he was keen to develop on future Stones mixes.

Gimme Shelter is a very strong contemporary sound which stands the test of time and was ideal for the opening cut on the album. Andy Johns, who helped his brother Glyn on the sessions, said in 2002: "It was one of the most perfect mixes of all time. The groove is outstanding. Wonderful. You could listen to that forever." It was as though the Stones had kicked things around and had re-invented the blues, slightly charred but still well tasty.

An earlier out-take has some very different sounding vocals by Mick emphasising the "war, children", "rape, murder" and there are no vocals by Merry Clayton (* a - 4.22). A unique cut, with Keith Richards on vocals, provides an excellent alternative to the released version (* b - 4.31). It has the same backing track but is without Merry Clayton's vocals. The song name is open to debate, Americans would have it called *Gimme Shelter*, while Brits may say *Gimmie Shelter* - original copies have the latter. The song has been used for promotion purposes for the car emergency pick-up company RAC in 2000 and to promote the hugely popular computer war game Call Of Duty for its Black Operation release in 2010.

429. THE JIMMY MILLER SHOW (Jagger, Richard)
22-23 March 1969: Place: Olympic Sound Studios, London, England.
Producer: Jimmy Miller.
Engineer: Glyn Johns.
Unavailable.

This was a true out-take from the sessions but has not been made available. *Old Glory, French Gig, Mucking About* may be in the same category. *Pennies From Heaven* was another though this is considered to be a working title for another track.

430. I'M A COUNTRY BOY (Jagger, Richard) 4.30
AKA: And I Was A Country Boy, I Was Just A Country Boy
23 March 1969: Place: Olympic Sound Studios, London, England.
Rolling Stones with Nicky Hopkins.
Producer: Jimmy Miller.
Engineer: Glyn Johns.
Bootleg only.

An instrumental track but not, as you would expect, played in the country vein. It has a repetitive piano riff and acoustic guitar and may have been recorded as early as the BEGGARS BANQUET sessions. Keith Richards recalls it as an EXILE out-take.

431. GET A LINE ON YOU (Jagger, Richard)
AKA: Shine A Light
31 March 1969: Place: Olympic Sound Studios, London, England.
Rolling Stones with Nicky Hopkins.
Producer: Jimmy Miller.
Engineer: Glyn Johns.
Unavailable.

The early forerunner for *Shine A Light* was recorded during the LET IT BLEED sessions with different lyrics and the hook of "Get a line on you". In September and October 1969, Bill Wyman and Charlie Watts joined Leon Russell to help record his second album, at Olympic studios with Glyn. Leon was a renowned session musician who had played with Jerry Lee Lewis, Ronnie Hawkins and Phil Spector's band. With Ringo Starr on drums, Mick Jagger on vocals, he recorded *(Can't Seem To) Get A Line On You* for his album LEON RUSSELL. On an out-take Mick Jagger can be heard at the end saying, "that was quite nice". Certainly, after listening to the EXILE ON MAIN STREET version, the lines of "May the good Lord flash a light on you" seem very different. The slowed down sections sound very quiet compared to the gospel version. The slide guitar player was probably Mick Taylor but is not identified.

432. SO DIVINE (ALADDIN STORY) (Jagger, Richard) 4.32
AKA: Aladdin Stomp, Aladdin Story
March 1969, 21 - 31 October 1970; September - November; December 2009: Place: Olympic Sound Studios, London, England; One East Studio, New York, Henson Studios, Village Recording; Mix This!, Los Angeles, USA.
Rolling Stones with Bobby Keys, Jim Price, Nicky Hopkins.
Producer: Jimmy Miller, Don Was, The Glimmer Twins.
Engineer: Glyn Johns; Additional Engineering and Editing: Krish Sharma; Mixed by Bob Clearmountain.
Other Production: Andy Johns, Chris Kimsey, Keith Harwood.
UK CD EXILE ON MAIN ST (EXTRA TRACKS): 17 May 2010: No. 1 - 10 weeks
USA CD EXILE ON MAIN ST (EXTRA TRACKS): 18 May 2010: No. 1 - 3 weeks

The instrumental track, first known as *Aladdin Stomp* and reportedly referred to as such in ABKCO's archives, became bootlegged as *Aladdin Story*. It was reworked again in 1970 but picked up for the EXILE re-release in 2010, when it appeared without any mention of Aladdin but with "Aladdin Story" included in parentheses in the song title credit. The instrumental backing track was not changed for release but lyrics were written, overdubbed and multi-tracked by Mick Jagger. The main riff was by Bobby Keys on saxophone and the style is very much soft rock. There was also a lead guitar signature recorded and added by Keith Richards at One East Studio in 2009. In 1999, a British electronic group, Death In Vegas, recorded a faithful version with a two-line lyric on their album THE CONTINO SESSIONS.

433. MONKEY MAN (Jagger, Richard) 4.11
AKA: Positano Grande
17-22 April, 5 June - 3 July; 18 October - 3 November 1969: Place: Olympic Sound Studios, London, England; Sunset Sound Studios, Elektra Studios, Los Angeles, USA.
Played Live: 1994, 1995, 2002, 2003, 2006, 2007
Rolling Stones with Nicky Hopkins, Jimmy Miller.
Producer: Jimmy Miller.
Engineer: Glyn Johns.
Assistant Engineers: Bruce Botnick, Jerry Hansen, George Chkiantz, Alan O'Duffy, Vic Smith.
USA LP LET IT BLEED: 29 November 1969: No. 3 - 19 weeks
UK LP LET IT BLEED: 5 December 1969: No. 1 - 29 weeks
USA Compilation Promo CD THE ROLLING STONES REMASTERED: 30 May 2002

Monkey Man originated from some songwriting trips to Positano in Naples, Italy during March 1969 as the early instrumental "also known as" indicates. Powered by a heavy guitar and Nicky Hopkins' piano, the song pushes out a tongue-in-cheek stance of satanic messianism to entrap the fans: "Well I hope we're not too messianic or a trifle too satanic. We love to play the blues," as the song goes. Nicky Hopkins plays a delicate piano introduction, with Bill Wyman accompanying on a vibraphone (vibes) which resonated tremolo effects from its metal tubes. Jimmy Miller joins on tambourine until Charlie Watts hits home and the strong guitar riff plays. The lyrical message is over halfway through and the song develops into a piano and guitar workout as Nicky replies to Keith's slide and lead guitar charges. It has some delightful melody shifts until Mick re-joins the activity shouting: "I'm a Monkey."
Despite the outcome, all was not easy in the recording process. The decision to choose studio two over the larger "one" at Olympic proved problematic because the band needed more space and disliked the early playbacks. George Chkiantz became the scapegoat and finally had to give way to the more experienced but staid, Vic Smith. George was not happy, as he recalls to Sean Egan in his book *Let It Bleed*, but time has healed and he now appreciates the quality of the recording. He also believes that they never used studio two again. *Monkey Man* was not played live until the 1994 Voodoo Lounge tour.

434. HONKY TONK WOMEN (Jagger, Richard) 3.01
12 May - 8 June 1969: Place: Olympic Sound Studios, London, England.
Played Live: 1969, 1970, 1971, 1972, 1973, 1975, 1976, 1977, 1978, 1981, 1982, 1989, 1990, 1994, 1995, 1997, 1998, 1999, 2002, 2003, 2005, 2006, 2007
Rolling Stones with Mick Taylor, Nicky Hopkins, Steve Gregory, Bud Beadle, Nanette Workman, Madeline Bell, Reparata & The Delrons.
Producer: Jimmy Miller.
Engineer: Glyn Johns, Vic Smith.
UK Single: 4 July 1969: No. 1 - 17 weeks
USA Single: 11 July 1969: No. 1 - 14 weeks
UK Compilation LP THROUGH THE PAST DARKLY (BIG HITS VOL 2): 12 September 1969: No. 2 -37 weeks

USA Compilation LP THROUGH THE PAST DARKLY (BIG HITS VOL 2): 13 September 1969: No. 2 - 16 weeks
UK Compilation LP GIMME SHELTER: 29 August 1971: No. 19 - 5 weeks
USA LP THE ROLLING STONES HOT ROCKS 1964-1971: 11 January 1972: No. 4 - 30 weeks
UK Compilation LP ROLLED GOLD: 14 November 1975: No. 7 - 50 weeks
UK Compilation LP GET STONED - 30 GREATEST HITS, 30 ORIGINAL TRACKS: 21 October 1977: No. 13 - 15 weeks
UK LP SOLID ROCK: 13 October 1980
German Compilation LP THE REST OF THE BEST: December 1983
UK & USA LP THE ROLLING STONES SINGLES COLLECTION - THE LONDON YEARS: 15 August 1989
UK & USA B-side Paint It Black: 11 June 1990
USA Compilation Promo CD THE ROLLING STONES REMASTERED: 30 May 2002
USA Compilation Promo CD ABKCO'S THE ROLLINGS STONES REMASTERED SERIES: 30 May 2002
UK CD LP FORTY LICKS: 30 September 2002: No. 2 - 45 weeks
USA CD LP FORTY LICKS: 1 October 2002: No. 2 - 50 weeks
UK CD box set THE ROLLING STONES SINGLES - 1968 - 1971: 28 February 2005
USA CD box set THE ROLLING STONES SINGLES - 1968 - 1971: 1 March 2005
UK Compilation CD ROLLED GOLD +: 12 November 2007: No. 26 - 12 weeks

With Brian Jones contributing less and less and with plans to go back on the road, the band had to seriously think about his future inclusion. Brian was not keen on touring and had made this known to Mick Jagger. The Stones even considered playing the Memphis Blues festival in June 1969 with Eric Clapton as a replacement. Brian had hinted before that he wanted out, being generally dissatisfied with the band's heavier rock moves. On the lookout for a suitable replacement, Mick Jagger considered Ron Wood but Ian Stewart suggested Mick Taylor, from John Mayall's Bluesbreakers band. He had followed the pedigree of Eric Clapton and Peter Green in what had become renowned as a great stable for young British talent. Previously, Mick had played with school band The Juniors (with Ken Hensley) and very briefly The Gods - both line-ups spawning members of Jethro Tull and Uriah Heep. At some gigs the Gods would often support Ron Wood's Birds.

A short session in May 1969 enabled Mick to establish himself as suitable for an honorary guitar position with the Stones and one of the first songs he played on was *Honky Tonk Women*. Jimmy Miller taps out the first few beats on the cowbell picked up by Charlie Watts' drum microphones. Charlie then hits the snare and kicks into the bass drum with Keith Richards following shortly with that hugely recognisable guitar riff. *Honky Tonk* is a unique piece of rhythm artistry and, as a single, has not been equalled by the Stones to this day. Charlie later said that when he kicked in his drums it was not in time with the cowbell, "but Keith comes in right, which makes the whole thing right".

In Sean Egan's book *Let It Bleed*, Vic Smith stated that he oversaw the latter sessions that created the final cut. He believed there were many reasons for the success of the track but felt the percussion, which had a cavernous feel to it, was a significant one, the cowbell which played throughout the song and the rising twin rock guitars before each verse being other factors. The released take features Ian Stewart's piano and brass instruments, played by session musicians Steve Gregory and Bud Beadle, in the background with Keith rather than Bill Wyman on bass guitar. It is claimed that the backing singers were from the all-girl trio Reparata & The Delrons (Mary Aiese, Nanette Licari and Lorraine Mazzola) who were touring Europe off the back of their hit UK single, *Captain Of Your Ship*.

Madeline Bell has also been credited with backing vocals - she was a renowned solo singer, later that year a member of Blue Mink and a backing vocalist for the likes of Tom Jones and Dusty Springfield. The sleeve note from FORTY LICKS only confirmed Nanette Newman on backing vocals. She sang the harmony vocal which was originally intended for Keith. Nanette's actual name was Workman but it was changed for working permit reasons. *Honky Tonk Women* was written by Jagger, Richards during a visit to Brazil in late 1968. It was inspired by the native ranch workers skilled at herding their cattle. Earlier recordings of the track were written in the *Country Honk* style and may have featured Brian Jones on guitar, but it was later re-recorded on 1 July with the aspiring young blues musician Mick Taylor. Mick experimented and Keith changed the tuning and funked up the country song by bouncing the riff around.

An early version has some alternative lyrics, featuring a completely different second verse (* a - 3.06) with words centred on Paris ("I am strolling on the boulevards of Paris, as naked as the day that I will die"), rather than the officially-released much more sleazy New York version, where the male subject "laid a divorcee", continuing the theme of the first verse. The all-American lyrics reflected the nature of the song which had strong southern country blues tones and Mick's slightly slurred delivery accentuate this, as does Mick Taylor's overdubbed country guitar frills.

Another alternate vocal rendition has the woman putting up a fight in New York City - rather than with Mick - when he laid her (* b - 2.52). A slightly different mix with less guitars was used for the mono single release (* c - 3.02). Ry Cooder was also present at the early 1969 sessions and, once *Honky Tonk Women* was released, he argued that he had written the opening chords, a dispute which inevitably caused a rift between himself and Keith Richards, the credited writer. Keith used the open-G guitar tuning which had been inspired and copied either from Cooder's book of guitar riffs or by jamming with Al Kooper during the recording for *Memo From Turner*. On the other hand, the drum sound created by Charlie and the production team of Jimmy Miller and Glyn Johns, is recognised as one of the most original and best released on disc. It was a perfect foundation for the rest of the band to rock along to, creating an immensely successful dance record. The public echoed those sentiments ensuring a worldwide No. 1 hit. It was released on both UK and USA versions of a highly successful compilation album that September, titled THROUGH THE PAST DARKLY.

The cover was an unusual octagonal shape, with the band pictured, full face with long hair. The shape was inspired by an M.C. Escher artwork called Verbum. Indeed Mick Jagger wrote to Escher requesting him to do the artwork for an album but he declined. Andy Warhol was also approached but they settled for the octagonal design on this occasion, Andy later agreeing to do the STICKY FINGERS artwork. Mott The Hoople also used an Escher design, Reptiles, for their 1969 debut album. It was after the final mixing of *Honky Tonk Women* and the heady knowledge that they had just delivered a classic single that Mick, Keith and Charlie drove to Brian's house to discuss his departure.

435. LIVE WITH ME (Jagger, Richard) 3.33
12-31 May; 18 October - 3 November 1969: Place: Olympic Sound Studios, London, England; Sunset Sound Studios, Elektra Studios, Los Angeles, USA.
Played Live: 1969, 1970, 1971, 1973, 1994, 1995, 1998, 1999, 2002, 2003, 2005, 2006, 2007
Rolling Stones with Mick Taylor, Nicky Hopkins, Leon Russell, Bobby Keys.
Producer: Jimmy Miller.
Engineer: Glyn Johns.

Horn arrangement: Leon Russell, Bruce Botnick.

Assistant Engineers: Bruce Botnick, Jerry Hansen, George Chkiantz, Vic Smith, Alan O'Duffy.

USA LP LET IT BLEED: 29 November 1969: No. 3 - 19 weeks

UK LP LET IT BLEED: 5 December 1969: No. 1 - 29 weeks

UK LP SOLID ROCK: 13 October 1980

Live With Me is the forerunner of the sound so successfully captured later in the year on *Brown Sugar*. It was one of the first tracks Mick Taylor performed, along with *Honky Tonk Woman*. He did not appreciate that, when the session was finished, the Stones wanted him to join the band permanently. He felt he was just helping them out on the album and maybe a tour, since Mick Jagger and Keith Richards believed Brian Jones would not get an American visa. Ironically on 28 May, Mick and Marianne Faithfull were arrested for possession of cannabis, in what Mick believed was again a conspiracy setup.

Live With Me was conceived at the Olympic sessions in May and completed in Los Angeles in November. As well as electric guitar, Keith feeds the rhythm section with a strong attacking bass guitar and Charlie Watts provides a powerful back beat on what is a simple rock song. The lyrics are also bawdily simplistic of life in a country mansion ("the cook she is a whore, yes, the butler has a place for her behind the pantry door"), which caused some concern with the London Bach Choir when it was included on the LET IT BLEED album.

Leon Russell provides the inspiration for the saxophone arrangements and assists on piano. *Live With Me* features for the first time the talents of saxophonist Bobby Keys whose rock pedigree was undisputed, having played with Buddy Holly when he was still in his mid-teens. He was in the Elektra studios recording with Delaney & Bonnie on their single *Comin' Home*, with Eric Clapton and Leon Russell. Walking down the corridor he came face-to-face with Mick Jagger who asked him to pop into their studio to record on *Live With Me*. Bobby stated that Delaney Bramlett was none too pleased that he played on the track, predicting that he would join up more permanently with them. Coincidentally, Bobby shares the same birthday as Keith and was playing with Bobby Vee as support to the Stones on their USA '64 visit to San Antonio. He has consistently appeared with the Stones off and on ever since, contributing significantly to their sound and development.

436. COUNTRY HONK (Jagger, Richard) 3.07

12 May, 5 June - 3 July; 18 October - 3 November 1969: Place: Olympic Sound Studios, London, England; Sunset Sound Studios, Elektra Studios, Los Angeles, USA.

Played Live: 1976

Rolling Stones with Mick Taylor, Byron Berline, Nanette Workman.

Producer: Jimmy Miller.

Engineer: Glyn Johns.

Assistant Engineers: Bruce Botnick, Jerry Hansen, George Chkiantz, Vic Smith, Alan O'Duffy.

USA LP LET IT BLEED: 29 November 1969: No. 3 - 19 weeks

UK LP LET IT BLEED: 5 December 1969: No. 1 - 29 weeks

This was a version of *Honky Tonk Women* expressed as a typical 30s country song in the mould of Jimmy Rogers or Hank Williams (Hank had a hit in 1948 with *Honky Tonkin'* and *Honky Tonk Blues* in 1952 shortly before he died at the age of 29 on his way to a gig in 1953). Honky Tonks were drinking and dancing establishments where the workers wound down after a long day in the Texan oil fields. They were synonymous with country music and featured many women artists. The country sound had been inspired when Mick Jagger, Marianne Faithfull joined Keith Richards and Anita Pallenberg in Brazil for Christmas 1968 staying at a cattle ranch. The cowboy influence had also been pushed along by Keith's friendship with country rock artist Gram Parsons.

In Sean Egan's book *Let It Bleed*, Bruce Botnick says that, at the mixing stage in November, they re-recorded the whole song and did not use any of the Olympic masters. Gram Parsons suggested that they hire Byron Berline to play the fiddle and Bruce agreed. Byron was a bluegrass specialist who had played on the February 1969 Flying Burrito Brothers' debut album THE GILDED PALACE OF SIN. Gram, along with another ex-Byrd, Chris Hillman, was a founding member of the Flying Burritos. Recording began in the studio then, in order to gain a more authentic sound, Mick moved the bemused Mr Berline onto the boulevard's sidewalk (pavement) and recorded the traffic and car honk, which was mixed in at the beginning and end of the track. Bruce says that the honk was directed by Mick and played by Sam Cutler - well it was summer in the city on the La Cienega Boulevard!

An Olympic out-take naturally lacks the fiddle and subtle addition of the "honk" (* a - 3.04). *Country Honk*, with the lyrics changed in the first verse from a bar in Memphis to Jackson, is a country version of *Honky Tonk Women* and as such is a refreshing change. Mick Taylor is on a Selmer Hawaiian lap slide guitar played in standard tuning. On backing vocals is Nanette Workman, who performed with Doris Troy and Madeline Bell on *You Can't Always Get What You Want*.

437. GIVE ME A DRINK (Jagger, Richard) 6.39

AKA: Loving Cup

5 June - 3 July 1969: Place: Olympic Sound Studios, London, England.

Rolling Stones with Nicky Hopkins, Mick Taylor.

Producer: Jimmy Miller.

Engineer: Glyn Johns.

Bootleg only.

The beginnings of *Loving Cup*, released on EXILE ON MAIN STREET were first recorded on *Give Me A Drink*. It has a different emphasis with an additional verse and fade-out lyrics emphasising *Give Me A Little Drink*, Mick Jagger even slurring the lyrics affectedly. There are two lead guitars - one with Mick Taylor - and the piano work of Nicky Hopkins.

438. LOVING CUP - ALTERNATE TAKE (Jagger, Richard) 5.26

AKA: Give Me A Little Drink

5 June - 3 July 1969; September - November; December 2009: Place: Olympic Sound Studios, London, England; One East Studio, New York, Henson Studios, Village Recording; Mix This!, Los Angeles, USA.

Rolling Stones with Nicky Hopkins, Mick Taylor.

Producer: Jimmy Miller, Don Was, The Glimmer Twins.

Engineer: Glyn Johns; Additional Engineering and Editing: Krish Sharma; Mixed by Bob Clearmountain.
Other Production: Andy Johns.

UK CD EXILE ON MAIN ST (EXTRA TRACKS): 17 May 2010: No. 1 - 10 weeks
USA CD EXILE ON MAIN ST (EXTRA TRACKS): 18 May 2010: No. 1 - 3 weeks

The preceding track was taken and re-mixed in 2009, when the slurred lyrics at the end were also edited out. The track is cut around the two-minute mark and spliced with the entry of the "what a beautiful buzz" lyric and the outcome is a slower, more guitar-orientated song than the official version. Mick Taylor's rhythm is much more pronounced; Keith Richards' guitar stands out at the front of the mix and Bob Clearmountain was tempted to alter the timing to the piano but left it as it was.

Essentially, five tracks out of the eventual 18 on the album, were recorded at Olympic rather than in France. Mick Jagger had researched potential tracks for inclusion in the EXILE re-release project, which was to be unveiled with additional songs, and said in 2010: "I bought one of these books with all the Rolling Stones recording dates in . . ."

He researched that *Loving Cup* was the earliest such song and decided that songs from then until when EXILE was mastered three years later could be included in the project. Don Was relates that he received numerous tracks to listen to and that this out-take was his favourite. He felt that Mick Jagger's vocal conveyed such an attitude. On 16 May 2010, Don Was, in a series of interviews on USA radio station NPR, commented about *Loving Cup* that: "This song to me represents the furthest frontier of how far the beat can be stretched before it falls apart . . . it is everything rock 'n' roll should be."

439. LET IT BLEED (Jagger, Richard) 5.27
AKA: If You Need Someone
5 June - 3 July 1969: Place: Olympic Sound Studios, London, England.
Played Live: 1981, 1982, 1995, 1997, 1998, 2002, 2003, 2006, 2007
Producer: Jimmy Miller.
Engineer: Glyn Johns.
Assistant Engineers: Bruce Botnick, Jerry Hansen, George Chkiantz, Vic Smith, Alan O'Duffy.

USA LP LET IT BLEED: 29 November 1969: No. 3 - 19 weeks
UK LP LET IT BLEED: 5 December 1969: No. 1 - 29 weeks
USA Compilation LP MORE HOT ROCKS (BIG HITS & FAZED COOKIES): 1 December 1972: No. 9 - 12 weeks
USA Compilation CD MORE HOT ROCKS (BIG HITS & FAZED COOKIES): 3 September 2002
UK Compilation CD ROLLED GOLD +: 12 November 2007: No. 26 - 12 weeks

On 9 June 1969, the original line-up of the Rolling Stones was finally broken after it was publicly announced that Brian Jones was quitting the band due to the age-old "musical differences". Brian was listening to the likes of *Proud Mary*, by Creedence Clearwater Revival, and had started sessions with Alexis Korner, Mickey Waller (drummer for Cyril Davies, Little Richard's tour band and Jeff Beck - he even sat in for an absent Charlie Watts in 1964) and John Mayall at his house. Other visitors were Peter Sourup (New Church lead singer), Sappho (Alexis Korner's daughter) and also long-time friend Cleo Sylvestre. It was a jazz/blues fusion with Brian on saxophone, the instrument he played in his early music days. There was even a time when John Lennon stopped by to play a few songs with him. It was said that John Lennon and two other unknown (but well known - maybe even Jimi Hendrix) musicians recorded with him. He was also thought to have considered joining Trevor Burton (Move) and Noel Redding before Trevor created the short-lived supergroup Balls.

After the *Honky Tonk* session Mick Jagger, Keith Richards and Charlie Watts had visited Brian at his 10-acre East Grinstead home, formerly Winnie The Pooh's (i.e. A A Milne's) idyllic Cotchford Farm. Charlie felt as though they were taking the last thing away from him - "his band" but the Stones had not toured for two years and were eager to finalise details for an American visit to promote the forthcoming album LET IT BLEED. Brian agreed that a tough schedule was not what he needed so he thoughtfully declined and it was then that they hinted that Mick Taylor was ready and willing to join the band for just over £100 per week and that he had performed on *Honky Tonk Women*.

It was agreed that the split would be formally announced and Brian did not play any further part in recording sessions. However, it was left that Brian could come back in the future should he want to. It should be noted that, for sessionography purposes, Mick Taylor is now Rolling Stones "personnel". In Hyde Park, London, on 13 June 1969, the Stones held a press conference to confirm this and also that arrangements were underway for a free concert to be held at on 5 July 1969. Mick had attended a Blind Faith concert on 7 June in Hyde Park which inspired the announcement the following week.

On the album track of *Let It Bleed*, Ian Stewart replaces Nicky Hopkins momentarily on the "Joanna" playing a honky tonk style for an R 'n' B fashioned song that became the title track of the new album - it was his only contribution. Bill Wyman can be heard in the background, particularly at the start, on a spooky autoharp. Jimmy Miller recalls that Keith Richards was always at pains to arrive at a precise sound, over-dubbing various guitar parts to create the perfect sound, being in danger at times of overdoing it. He contributes acoustic and a slide lead guitar. As Dave Hassinger found in Los Angeles, Keith's sheer musical professionalism was one of the mainstays of the band.

The lyrics have some obvious sex and drugs connotations which Marianne Faithfull believed referred to her hazy existence. The song was said to have been written during the South American visit. The "parking lot" was a reference to Marianne's private parts while "when you need a little coke and sympathy" with "we all need someone we can lean on" are classic lines, even if "you can cream on me" isn't! The album was now complete, a wealth of material being included, literally spanning a decade. The cover was a circular surrealistic cake seated in turn on a tyre, pizza, clock, reel of tape box, plate and a record disc with a stylus. It was designed to resemble a turntable since the provisional album title was Auto Changer - a facility that allowed discs to drop when the previous one had finished. The sleeve was designed by American graphic designer Robert Brownjohn and the edible part cooked by Delia Smith, a now famous British chef who, at that time, was studying her trade at college. Another working title which found some space within the artwork was HARD KNOX AND DURTY SOX. Once released, the album leapt to No. 1 in Britain and remained in the UK charts well into the Summer of 1970. First pressings included a sticker on the front cover advertising a poster of the band within. On reflection, many will conclude that LET IT BLEED contains several elements of a classic rock album. A new re-master of the ABKCO catalogue for the CD format of SACD segues from track to track, closing the gaps as originally intended.

440. **I'M GOING DOWN** (Jagger, Richard, Taylor) 2.52
5 June - 3 July; 18 October - 3 November 1969; 14 - 15 July 1970: Place: Olympic Sound Studios, London, England; Sunset Sound Studios, Elektra Studios, Los Angeles, USA.; Olympic Sound Studios, London, England.
Rolling Stones with Mick Taylor, Bobby Keys, Stephen Stills, Rocky Dijon, Bill Plummer.
Producer: Jimmy Miller.
Engineer: Glyn Johns.
UK Compilation LP METAMORPHOSIS: 6 June 1975: No. 45 - 1 week
USA Compilation LP METAMORPHOSIS: 6 June 1975: No. 8 - 8 weeks

The current level of productiveness and the purposeful quality of the material had encouraged the Stones to think of a two-album release in 1969. They said in June that an album titled STICKY FINGERS would be released in September and another was set for Christmas release. What actually happened was that a compilation album was released in September named THROUGH THE PAST, DARKLY. It was subtitled Big Hits Vol 2 and was a compendium of 60s tracks, along with their most recent single, *Honky Tonk Women*.

The track listings did differ depending on which side of the Atlantic you were on but, to give some indication of the new album, a double-sided acetate was prepared of LET IT BLEED. Its tracks were *Midnight Rambler, Love In Vain, Let It Bleed, Monkey Man* (A side) and *Give Me Some Shelter, You Got Some Silver Now, Sister Morphine* and *Loving Cup* (Side B). The promise was broken, though, and certain material never made an official release at that time, including *I'm Going Down* which had to wait for the METAMORPHOSIS Decca compilation in 1975. *I'm Going Down* is a mid-tempo rock song featuring brass sounds and can be heard with a guitar miss-start (* a - 3.04) and features bassist Bill Plummer, who played in 1971 on *Rip This Joint*, Rocky Dijon on bongos and Stephen Stills on guitar. Keith Richards and Mick Jagger stayed with him as they mixed LET IT BLEED in Hollywood. The connection may have been inspired by engineer Andy Johns. *I'm Going Down* missed the boat and a certain amount of confusion remains over the credited songwriters. The disc's inner circle names Mick Taylor in addition to Jagger and Richards, whilst the sleeve prints only Jagger, Richard. The track has certain Taylor trademarks, a searing guitar for one. An out-take on bootleg is the same track, without fade-outs, that emerges on METAMORPHOSIS.

441. **JIVING SISTER FANNY** (Jagger, Richard) 3.25
5 June - 3 July 1969: Place: Olympic Sound Studios, London, England.
Rolling Stones with Mick Taylor, Nicky Hopkins.
Producer: Jimmy Miller.
Engineer: Glyn Johns.
UK Compilation LP METAMORPHOSIS: 6 June 1975: No. 45 - 1 week
USA Compilation LP METAMORPHOSIS: 6 June 1975: No. 8 - 8 weeks
USA B-side Out Of Time: 12 August 1975
UK B-side Out Of Time: 5 September 1975
UK & USA LP THE ROLLING STONES SINGLES COLLECTION - THE LONDON YEARS: 15 August 1989
USA Compilation Promo CD THE ROLLING STONES REMASTERED: 30 May 2002
UK CD box set THE ROLLING STONES SINGLES - 1968 - 1971: 28 February 2005
USA CD box set THE ROLLING STONES SINGLES - 1968 - 1971: 1 March 2005

A 12-bar blues tune, which was strangely placed as the flip side of a 1975 single *Out Of Time*. It is played in true chug along rock 'n' roll style and was so noticeably an anachronism that it was not included on an album of its own period. The vocals sound as though they are pure guide vocals since they do not make much sense. Mick Taylor features heavily on lead guitar - its non-release surely could not have anything to do with his prominent "jiving" role! Another version, with Mick Taylor guitar more in the mix, is available as an out-take (* a - 3.24). He had learned a masterful vibrato technique courtesy of his heroes, B.B. King and Jimi Hendrix.

442. **ALL DOWN THE LINE (ACOUSTIC)** (Jagger, Richard) 4.22
5 June - 3 July 1969: Place: Olympic Sound Studios, London, England.
Producer: Jimmy Miller.
Engineer: Glyn Johns.
Bootleg only.

All Down The Line was re-recorded in 1971 for the EXILE ON MAIN STREET album. This acoustic guitar version from June/July 1969 was principally instrumental. Mick Jagger only sang a brief vocal line for guide purposes, indicating the lyrics were unfinished, although the chorus was definitely *All Down The Line*. Testimony to this, the earlier recording date can be confirmed by reference to the copyright credits which were the same as other 60s material (Essex Music International Ltd, 19/20 Poland Street, London W1). Some of the Stones' best rockers were acoustic and this is no exception - a great out-take!

On 13 June, the press conference was held to announce the free concert at Hyde Park and also introduce Mick Taylor as the new official band member. It did not mention plans for a concert at Rome's Colosseum on 26 June to be filmed and intended to replace the Stones footage for the *Rock 'n' Roll Circus* project which Mick was not happy with - the Italian gig subsequently did not take place. A few days later the band performed to pre-recorded tracks of *You Can't Always Get What You Want* and *Honky Tonk Women* for the first time (Mick with live vocals) on the David Frost TV show, later broadcast in July and August. Mick Taylor looked confident and quite indifferent to the proceedings.

443. **I DON'T KNOW WHY** (Wonder, Riser, Hunter, Hardaway) 3.02
AKA: **Don't Know Why I Love You**
29-30 June - 3 July 1969: Place: Olympic Sound Studios, London, England.
Producer: Jimmy Miller.
Engineer: Glyn Johns.
UK Single: 23 May 1975
USA Single: 23 May 1975

UK Compilation LP METAMORPHOSIS: 6 June 1975: No. 45 - 1 week
USA Compilation LP METAMORPHOSIS: 6 June 1975: No. 8 - 8 weeks
UK & USA LP THE ROLLING STONES SINGLES COLLECTION - THE LONDON YEARS: 15 August 1989
UK CD box set THE ROLLING STONES SINGLES - 1968 - 1971: 28 February 2005
USA CD box set THE ROLLING STONES SINGLES - 1968 - 1971: 1 March 2005

It was early morning on 3 July and Mick Jagger, Keith Richards and Charlie Watts were busy mixing a version of Stevie Wonder's *I Don't Know Why*, when a 'phone call from Janet Lawson (Tom Keylock's friend) interrupted the session. She told Mick about the tragic events of Brian having drowned in his own swimming pool, just before midnight. Charlie called Bill Wyman at 3am to advise him. The band's sentiments and the reasons for Brian's death have been publicly aired and trawled for years. The national press still run stories about the circumstances of his death and in particular the apparent incomplete police investigation.

Janet was staying at the house to look after Brian and she felt that certainly not all the truth has been uncovered. Frank Thorogood was supervising building work on Brian's cottage and it has been since revealed that Janet was not comfortable with Frank's wayward attitude towards Brian. A death-bed confession by Frank to Tom in 1993 suggests that events got out of hands that evening but this was not corroborated. Anna Wohlin, Brian's girlfriend, was unceremoniously whisked out of the country by Tom. He was asked to arrange the funeral and many items at the cottage were inexplicably disposed of by him from the cottage, allegedly on behalf of the family - but these seem to have been "lost". Let's simply remember Brian's epitaph: "Please Don't Judge Me Too Harshly" and continue with the music he loved.

Bill Wyman touchingly summarises Brian in his book *Rolling With The Stones*: "When people think of the Stones now, Mick and Keith come to mind. Back then, it was as likely to have been Brian. He had style and, despite the way he was towards the end, he did more than anyone to glamorise hippy chic. He was probably a better natural musician than the rest of us put together - he played bloody great bottleneck guitar long before anyone else in Britain knew what it was . . . we were Brian's band and without him our little blues outfit wouldn't have become the greatest rock 'n' roll band in the world." Poignantly in late spring, Brian had invited his parents to stay at Cotchford for a weekend. His father later said that it was such a pleasure to have spent time with him and how he was so enthusiastic about the future.

Earlier, in March 1969, Stevie Wonder had had a small hit with *I Don't Know Why* (No. 14 UK, No. 39 USA). The Stones cover is played very much in Stevie fashion (with Ian Stewart on piano) and incorporates the now familiar brass sounds which were unaccredited. Also, it contains a searing guitar solo by Mick Taylor, an early reminder of what he would provide in the studio. Release on the intended '69 Christmas album did not materialise so it was picked up again by Decca in 1975, re-edited and released as a UK single. The first 1,000 copies were erroneously credited to Jagger, Richard. The American marketeers went one better declaring Jagger, Richard and Taylor as the songwriters!

444. I'M YOURS AND I'M HERS (Winter) ⟋ 3.17
AKA: I'm Yours, She's Mine
5 July 1969: Place: Hyde Park, London, England.
Producer: Jo Durden-Smith, Leslie Woodhead.
Engineer: Ray Prickett.
Pye Mobile Recording Unit.
UK Video The Stones In The Park: 1983
UK DVD The Stones In The Park: March 2001
UK DVD The Stones In The Park: 25 September 2006
USA DVD The Stones In The Park: 8 May 2007

At 6pm on the evening of 5 July 1969, the Stones prepared to take the stage in front of quarter of a million sun-drenched music revellers. They came to London's Hyde Park for a day of pop music, previously unparalleled in England. The crowd (more than twice the size of the annual Wembley FA Cup Final, as pointed out to the audience by future tour manager Sam Cutler), had been entertained by Screw, Battered Ornaments, Third Ear Band, Roy Harper, Alexis Korner's New Church, King Crimson and Family. Third Ear Band featured a youthful Paul Buckmaster, who later made string arrangements for the Stones.

A documentary, filmed by Granada TV with just six cameras, was broadcast on 2 September 1969 and captures the historic day. The footage was naturally edited and cut some of the music soundtrack. Sam Cutler, who worked for the promoters Blackhill Enterprises, informed Mick Jagger that there needed to be some budget to build a robust stage and make sure the event ran smoothly. Mick achieved this, with Granada providing money to fund the event. The film contrasts the celebration of the new Rolling Stones line-up and the mourning of a lost friend, Brian Jones.

Thanks to the Beatles, rehearsals for the gig had taken place at Apple Studios, in the basement of 3 Savile Row, London. Mid-afternoon on the day, the band was ensconced in a Park Lane hotel, looking over the massed crowd made up of mods, rockers, bikers (the security helpers who incongruously ushered the crowd, along with uniformed police constables), spaced-out hippies and ordinary people like you and me. The Stones were unusually nervous as they journeyed to the arena in an old army World War II ambulance, which belonged to recently-sacked Pete Brown from support act Battered Ornaments.

They entered just 15 minutes before show time, the bikers (there were no formal English Hells Angels until late 1969) clearing a path to the back-stage caravan where Mick Taylor and Keith Richards tuned up practising blues riffs. Charlie Watts handed apples and other provisions out of the window to some waiting fans. Among others, Ian Stewart and Tom Keylock prepared the stage and kept watchful eyes on the busy area from where Sam Cutler was managing and emceeing the event.

445. JUMPING JACK FLASH (Jagger, Richard) ⟋ 3.19
5 July 1969: Place: Hyde Park, London, England.
Producer: Jo Durden-Smith, Leslie Woodhead.
Engineer: Ray Prickett.
Pye Mobile Recording Unit.
UK Video The Stones In The Park: 1983
UK DVD The Stones In The Park: March 2001
UK DVD The Stones In The Park: 25 September 2006
USA DVD The Stones In The Park: 8 May 2007

446. **MERCY MERCY** (Covay, Miller) ✏ 2.55
5 July 1969: Place: Hyde Park, London, England.
Producer: Jo Durden-Smith, Leslie Woodhead.
Engineer: Ray Prickett.
Pye Mobile Recording Unit.
UK DVD The Stones In The Park: 25 September 2006
USA DVD The Stones In The Park: 8 May 2007

447. **DOWN HOME GIRL** (Leiber, Butler) ✏ 4.51
5 July 1969: Place: Hyde Park, London, England.
Bootleg only.

448. **STRAY CAT BLUES** (Jagger, Richard) ✏ 3.36
5 July 1969: Place: Hyde Park, London, England.
Producer: Jo Durden-Smith, Leslie Woodhead.
Engineer: Ray Prickett.
Pye Mobile Recording Unit.
UK DVD The Stones In The Park: 25 September 2006
USA DVD The Stones In The Park: 8 May 2007

Part recording only.

449. **NO EXPECTATIONS** (Jagger, Richard) ✏ 3.19
5 July 1969: Place: Hyde Park, London, England.
Producer: Jo Durden-Smith, Leslie Woodhead.
Engineer: Ray Prickett.
Pye Mobile Recording Unit.
UK DVD The Stones In The Park: 25 September 2006
USA DVD The Stones In The Park: 8 May 2007

Part recording only.

450. **I'M FREE** (Jagger, Richard) ✏ 2.49
5 July 1969: Place: Hyde Park, London, England.
Producer: Jo Durden-Smith, Leslie Woodhead.
Engineer: Ray Prickett.
Pye Mobile Recording Unit.
UK Video The Stones In The Park: 1983
UK DVD The Stones In The Park: March 2001
UK DVD The Stones In The Park: 25 September 2006
USA DVD The Stones In The Park: 8 May 2007

451. **GIVE ME A DRINK** (Jagger, Richard) ✏ 5.07
AKA: **Loving Cup**
5 July 1969: Place: Hyde Park, London, England.
Bootleg only.

452. **LOVE IN VAIN** (Payne) ✏ 4.33
5 July 1969: Place: Hyde Park, London, England.
Producer: Jo Durden-Smith, Leslie Woodhead.
Engineer: Ray Prickett.
Pye Mobile Recording Unit.
UK Video The Stones In The Park: 1983
UK DVD The Stones In The Park: March 2001
UK DVD The Stones In The Park: 25 September 2006
USA DVD The Stones In The Park: 8 May 2007

453. **(I CAN'T GET NO) SATISFACTION** (Jagger, Richard) ✏ 6.20
5 July 1969: Place: Hyde Park, London, England.
Producer: Jo Durden-Smith, Leslie Woodhead.
Engineer: Ray Prickett.
Pye Mobile Recording Unit.
UK Video The Stones In The Park: 1983
UK DVD The Stones In The Park: March 2001
UK DVD The Stones In The Park: 25 September 2006
USA DVD The Stones In The Park: 8 May 2007

454. HONKY TONK WOMEN (Jagger, Richard) ✏ 3.10
5 July 1969: Place: Hyde Park, London, England.
Producer: Jo Durden-Smith, Leslie Woodhead.
Engineer: Ray Prickett.
Pye Mobile Recording Unit.
UK Video The Stones In The Park: 1983
UK DVD The Stones In The Park: March 2001
UK DVD The Stones In The Park: 25 September 2006
USA DVD The Stones In The Park: 8 May 2007

455. MIDNIGHT RAMBLER (Jagger, Richard) ✏ 4.29
5 July 1969: Place: Hyde Park, London, England.
Producer: Jo Durden-Smith, Leslie Woodhead.
Engineer: Ray Prickett.
Pye Mobile Recording Unit.
UK Video The Stones In The Park: 1983
UK DVD The Stones In The Park: March 2001
UK DVD The Stones In The Park: 25 September 2006
USA DVD The Stones In The Park: 8 May 2007

456. STREET FIGHTING MAN (Jagger, Richard) ✏ 3.34
5 July 1969: Place: Hyde Park, London, England.
Producer: Jo Durden-Smith, Leslie Woodhead.
Engineer: Ray Prickett.
Pye Mobile Recording Unit.
Japan Blu-Ray DVD The Stones In The Park: 21 September 2011

457. SYMPATHY FOR THE DEVIL (Jagger, Richard) ✏ 10.18
5 July 1969: Place: Hyde Park, London, England.
Rolling Stones with Ginger Johnson's African Drummers
Producer: Jo Durden-Smith, Leslie Woodhead.
Engineer: Ray Prickett.
Pye Mobile Recording Unit.
UK Video The Stones In The Park: 1983
UK DVD The Stones In The Park: March 2001
UK DVD The Stones In The Park: 25 September 2006
USA DVD The Stones In The Park: 8 May 2007

At last the Stones were introduced to the crowd and Mick Jagger, resplendent in a Greek tunic, was given the unenviable task of quietening them down in order to say a few words about Brian. He spoke a few stanzas of a Shelley poem, then waiting helpers released thousands of white butterflies. The band promptly started the first sound *I'm Yours And I'm Hers*, a number not previously performed by them and written by Johnny Winter. It was played because it was one of Brian's recent favourite songs. It was available as the opening track on Johnny Winter's just-released second album JOHNNY WINTER.

Jumpin' Jack Flash followed as they moulded themselves into a format of loose rock. Nicky Hopkins was invited to attend but declined since he was in the USA, something which he later regretted since he felt he may have been offered a permanent role in the band at that time. He had earlier avoided Mick and Keith's requests to join. The sound showed the Stones were not performance fit and at times out of tune, but gradually their confidence grew. Some of the crowd actually sat down and listened to them while others hypnotically weaved.

The tracks played were mostly new and taken from the recent blues-tinged BEGGARS BANQUET and LET IT BLEED sessions. Only *I'm Free, Mercy Mercy*, a rare live *Down Home Girl*, with a blistering Mick Taylor performance, and an extended *Satisfaction* pre-dated 1968. *Midnight Rambler, Stray Cat Blues* and *Love In Vain* were improvised, extended and previewed from the new album whilst *Give Me A Little Drink* would need re-working. Keith played a Gibson Flying V, a five-string open G tuned guitar once owned by Albert King, on tracks like *Love In Vain. Give Me A Drink* was introduced as from the new album to be released in, oh . . . 10 years' time. Finally, the band launched into what Mick Jagger described as "a samba", Ginger Johnson's African bongo drummers tapping out the rhythm while the escalating guitars of Mick Taylor and Keith Richards came beautifully to a hypnotic climax. The show was a renowned success and has become a legend amongst concert goers. The transposition of the Granada documentary was first released on video in 1983 with eight out of the 14 songs played featuring.

In 2006, an extended version was released but only *Mercy, Mercy* was shown in full. A Japanese release in 2011 also showed for the first time a fully charged *Street Fighting Man*. For the Stones, the concert was a distinct turning point in their career. Mick Taylor had held his part down well. There was a nice touch by Sam Cutler, too . . . those who helped to clear up the park on the Sunday after the performance were given freebies of the newly released single *Honky Tonk Women*. This was promoted on the BBC Top Of The Pops programme and included unique different lead vocals with the single playback.

458. I DON'T KNOW THE REASON WHY (Jagger, Richard, Taylor) 11.29
AKA: Hillside Blues
18 October - 3 November 1969: Place: Sunset Sound Studios, Elektra Studios, Los Angeles, USA.
Rolling Stones with Bobby Keys.
Producer: Jimmy Miller.
Engineer: Glyn Johns.
Bruce Botnick.
Bootleg only.

Brian was buried in Cheltenham on Thursday 10 July, with Bill Wyman and Charlie Watts attending the funeral, Mick Jagger and Keith Richards sending wreaths. They had their own reasons not to attend. Mick and Marianne Faithfull had flown to Australia to take their parts in the film Ned Kelly. Mick loved the movie business, an interest which has continued to this day, and believed that one of the best ways to learn about the industry was to become an actor. He was not, however, joined by Marianne who, still distraught about Brian's death, had taken an overdose of sleeping tablets and had to be replaced.
Mick played the leading role of Ned Kelly, a famous figure from Australian folklore. The screen story told how his family had settled in Australia only to find hardship then, when a policeman made an accusation against his mother, Ned became a fugitive, stealing horses with his brothers to make ends meet. He was killed in a western-style (classic) shoot-out, dressed in a suit of armour, which protected him from initial impact until he fell for the last time. The film was judged mediocre when released in 1970.
As announced in July, the Stones' organisation had put together a tour of the United States of America for November. They asked Sam Cutler to handle band logistics for the tour since they were so impressed with his handling of the Hyde Park occasion. It was "one small step for a man, one giant leap for the band", since they had not toured there since July 1966 - the Apollo moon landing took place on 20 July.
I Don't Know The Reason Why is an 11-minute excursion into the blues recorded in Los Angeles, either at Sunset Sound or Elektra studios, as the band rehearsed for their USA tour. The Sunset and, principally Elektra, studios were used for overdubbing and mixing LET IT BLEED tracks. An abbreviated version is also available (* a - 5.57). Mick Taylor is evident on electric guitar playing in the traditional English "blues breakers" mould of Eric Clapton and John Mayall. The saxophone work of Bobby Keys can also be heard. The stereo recording elevates *I Don't Know The Reason Why* into a worthy collector's piece.

459. GIMME SHELTER (Jagger, Richard) 3.51
18 November 1969: Place: Ed Sullivan TV Show, CBS Studios, Los Angeles, USA.
USA DVD 6 Ed Sullivan Shows Starring The Rolling Stones: 1 November 2011

460. LOVE IN VAIN (Payne) 3.30
18 November 1969: Place: Ed Sullivan TV Show, CBS Studios, Los Angeles, USA.
USA DVD 6 Ed Sullivan Shows Starring The Rolling Stones: 1 November 2011

461. HONKY TONK WOMEN (Jagger, Richard) 2.57
18 November 1969: Place: Ed Sullivan TV Show, CBS Studios, Los Angeles, USA.
USA DVD 6 Ed Sullivan Shows Starring The Rolling Stones: 1 November 2011

In their last appearance on the Ed Sullivan Show, which was broadcast on 23 November 1969, the Stones performed *Gimme Shelter, Love In Vain* and *Honky Tonk Women* with live vocals to the original backing tracks. Keith Richards can be seen miming convincingly with his Dan Armstrong Ampeg Plexi guitar. Ed Sullivan was much more reverential toward the Stones by now and insisted that he was shown at the end of each recording shaking hands with Mick Jagger. Their fee had increased exponentially over a five-year period to $15,000.

462. STRAY CAT BLUES (Jagger, Richard) ✔ 3.40
26 November 1969: Place: Baltimore Civic Centre, Madison, USA.
Producer: Rolling Stones, Glyn Johns.
Engineer: Glyn Johns.
UK LP GET YER YA-YA'S OUT: 4 September 1970: No. 1 - 15 weeks
USA LP GET YER YA-YA'S OUT: 26 September 1970: No. 6 - 10 weeks
USA CD GET YER YA-YA'S OUT (40th Anniversary): 3 November 2009
UK CD GET YER YA-YA'S OUT (40th Anniversary): 30 November 2009

The 17-date tour of North America provided the Stones and their new member, Mick Taylor, a chance to fine-tune their act. Financially, due to their dispute with Allen Klein, they needed someone to look after the money, so Ronnie Schneider (Allen Klein's nephew) was asked to become the Tour Manager, having been involved in Stones' tours since 1966. Klein was not pleased at this family disloyalty. He had asked the long-established William Morris Agency to arrange dates for the tour and, being threatened by a different approach, they quickly negotiated to a lower rate with Ronnie to provide the bookings. Rolling Stones Limited were Ronnie's umbrella company for the first packaging tour, where everything remained in control of Ronnie and the Stones, particularly the gate money! At one point, Bill Graham, a well-known promoter pitched for the tour but was rejected and in order to appease him, he was given one show to promote in Oakland, California. Sam Cutler introduced the band to the crowd as he had done at Hyde Park. He uttered the immortal, introductory words: "Ladies and gentlemen, the greatest rock and roll band in the world - the Rolling Stones!" When Mick Jagger first heard this introduction in Fort Collins, Colorado, he approached Sam after the show, asking him not to utter those boastful words. Sam simply retorted: "Well, either you fuckin' are or you ain't. What the fuck is it gonna be?" His motives were to ensure they were at the top of their game. In his book *Let It Bleed*, Ethan Russell, the tour photographer summarised: "In a way the slogan just made them work harder right from the start. They knew they weren't going to play for three minutes and be mobbed by eight thousand screaming girls and rushed offstage. They had to play. And they did. That's one thing about the Rolling Stones: they've always worked hard at it." By the time the show reached New York, more than three years after they last played there, the Stones were ready and capable of delivering the proverbial goods. Touts increased the normal ticket prices, which ranged from $7.50 to $15, and celebrities such as Andy Warhol, Jimi Hendrix and Janis Joplin crowded back-stage areas.

463. LOVE IN VAIN (Payne) ✎ 4.56
26 November 1969: Place: Baltimore Civic Centre, Madison, USA.
Producer: Rolling Stones, Glyn Johns.
Engineer: Glyn Johns.
UK LP GET YER YA-YA'S OUT: 4 September 1970: No. 1 - 15 weeks
USA LP GET YER YA-YA'S OUT: 26 September 1970: No. 6 - 10 weeks
UK B-Side Single Little Queenie: December 1970
UK & USA Video Gimme Shelter: 15 September 1993
USA CD GET YER YA-YA'S OUT (40th Anniversary): 3 November 2009
UK CD GET YER YA-YA'S OUT (40th Anniversary): 30 November 2009

464. JUMPIN' JACK FLASH (Jagger, Richard) ✎ 4.02
27 November 1969: Place: Madison Square Garden, New York, USA.
Producer: Rolling Stones, Glyn Johns.
Engineer: Glyn Johns.
UK LP GET YER YA-YA'S OUT: 4 September 1970: No. 1 - 15 weeks
USA LP GET YER YA-YA'S OUT: 26 September 1970: No. 6 - 10 weeks
USA Compilation Promo CD ABKCO'S THE ROLLINGS STONES REMASTERED SERIES: 30 May 2002
USA CD GET YER YA-YA'S OUT (40th Anniversary): 3 November 2009
UK CD GET YER YA-YA'S OUT (40th Anniversary): 30 November 2009

465. PRODIGAL SON (Wilkins) ✎ 2.38
27 November 1969: Place: Madison Square Garden, New York, USA.
Producer: Rolling Stones, Glyn Johns.
Engineer: Glyn Johns.
UK & USA Video Gimme Shelter: 15 September 1993

466. UNDER MY THUMB (Jagger, Richard) ✎ 3.38
27 November 1969: Place: Madison Square Garden, New York, USA.
Producer: Rolling Stones, Glyn Johns.
Engineer: Glyn Johns.
USA CD & DVD GET YER YA-YA'S OUT (40th Anniversary): 3 November 2009
UK CD & DVD GET YER YA-YA'S OUT (40th Anniversary): 30 November 2009

467. I'M FREE (Jagger, Richard) ✎ 2.47
27 November 1969: Place: Madison Square Garden, New York, USA.
Producer: Rolling Stones, Glyn Johns.
Engineer: Glyn Johns.
USA CD & DVD GET YER YA-YA'S OUT (40th Anniversary): 3 November 2009
UK CD & DVD GET YER YA-YA'S OUT (40th Anniversary): 30 November 2009

468. HONKY TONK WOMEN (Jagger, Richard) ✎ 3.34
27 November 1969: Place: Madison Square Garden, New York, USA.
Producer: Rolling Stones, Glyn Johns.
Engineer: Glyn Johns.
UK LP GET YER YA-YA'S OUT: 4 September 1970: No. 1 - 15 weeks
USA LP GET YER YA-YA'S OUT: 26 September 1970: No. 6 - 10 weeks
USA CD GET YER YA-YA'S OUT (40th Anniversary): 3 November 2009
UK CD GET YER YA-YA'S OUT (40th Anniversary): 30 November 2009

469. JUMPIN' JACK FLASH (Jagger, Richard) ✎ 3.17
28 November 1969 (Show One): Place: Madison Square Garden, New York, USA.
Producer: Rolling Stones, Glyn Johns.
Engineer: Glyn Johns.
UK & USA Video Gimme Shelter: 15 September 1993

470. CAROL (Berry) ⟋ 3.46
28 November 1969 (Show One): Place: Madison Square Garden, New York, USA.
Producer: Rolling Stones, Glyn Johns.
Engineer: Glyn Johns.
UK LP GET YER YA-YA'S OUT: 4 September 1970: No. 1 - 15 weeks
USA LP GET YER YA-YA'S OUT: 26 September 1970: No. 6 - 10 weeks
UK Compilation LP ROCK 'N' ROLLING STONES: 13 October 1972: No. 41 - 1 week
UK & USA Video Gimme Shelter: 15 September 1993
USA CD GET YER YA-YA'S OUT (40th Anniversary): 3 November 2009
UK CD GET YER YA-YA'S OUT (40th Anniversary): 30 November 2009

471. SYMPATHY FOR THE DEVIL (Jagger, Richard) ⟋ 6.51
28 November 1969 (Show One): Place: Madison Square Garden, New York, USA.
Producer: Rolling Stones, Glyn Johns.
Engineer: Glyn Johns.
UK LP GET YER YA-YA'S OUT: 4 September 1970: No. 1 - 15 weeks
USA LP GET YER YA-YA'S OUT: 26 September 1970: No. 6 - 10 weeks
USA CD GET YER YA-YA'S OUT (40th Anniversary): 3 November 2009
UK CD GET YER YA-YA'S OUT (40th Anniversary): 30 November 2009

472. LITTLE QUEENIE (Berry) ⟋ 4.33
28 November 1969 (Show One): Place: Madison Square Garden, New York, USA.
Producer: Rolling Stones, Glyn Johns.
Engineer: Glyn Johns, Andy Johns.
UK LP GET YER YA-YA'S OUT: 4 September 1970: No. 1 - 15 weeks
USA LP GET YER YA-YA'S OUT: 26 September 1970: No. 6 - 10 weeks
UK Single: December 1970
UK Compilation LP ROCK 'N' ROLLING STONES: 13 October 1972: No. 41 - 1 week
USA DVD Gimme Shelter: 14 November 2000
USA CD GET YER YA-YA'S OUT (40th Anniversary): 3 November 2009
UK CD GET YER YA-YA'S OUT (40th Anniversary): 30 November 2009

473. (I CAN'T GET NO) SATISFACTION (Jagger, Richard) ⟋ 5.38
28 November 1969 (Show One): Place: Madison Square Garden, New York, USA.
Producer: Rolling Stones, Glyn Johns.
Engineer: Glyn Johns.
UK & USA Video Gimme Shelter: 15 September 1993
USA CD & DVD GET YER YA-YA'S OUT (40th Anniversary): 3 November 2009
UK CD & DVD GET YER YA-YA'S OUT (40th Anniversary): 30 November 2009

474. STREET FIGHTING MAN (Jagger, Richard) ⟋ 4.03
28 November 1969 (Show One): Place: Madison Square Garden, New York, USA.
Producer: Rolling Stones, Glyn Johns.
Engineer: Glyn Johns.
UK LP GET YER YA-YA'S OUT: 4 September 1970: No. 1 - 15 weeks
USA LP GET YER YA-YA'S OUT: 26 September 1970: No. 6 - 10 weeks
USA CD GET YER YA-YA'S OUT (40th Anniversary): 3 November 2009
UK CD GET YER YA-YA'S OUT (40th Anniversary): 30 November 2009

475. CAROL (Berry) ⟋ 3.29
28 November 1969 (Show Two): Place: Madison Square Garden, New York, USA.
Producer: Rolling Stones, Glyn Johns.
Engineer: Glyn Johns.
USA DVD Gimme Shelter: 14 November 2000

476. PRODIGAL SON (Wilkins) ⟋ 4.04
28 November 1969 (Show Two): Place: Madison Square Garden, New York, USA.
Producer: Rolling Stones, Glyn Johns.
Engineer: Glyn Johns.
USA DVD Gimme Shelter: 14 November 2000
USA CD & DVD GET YER YA-YA'S OUT (40th Anniversary): 3 November 2009
UK CD & DVD GET YER YA-YA'S OUT (40th Anniversary): 30 November 2009

477. **YOU GOTTA MOVE** (McDowell, Davis) 🎵 2.18
28 November 1969 (Show Two): Place: Madison Square Garden, New York, USA.
Producer: Rolling Stones, Glyn Johns.
Engineer: Glyn Johns.
USA CD & DVD GET YER YA-YA'S OUT (40th Anniversary): 3 November 2009
UK CD & DVD GET YER YA-YA'S OUT (40th Anniversary): 30 November 2009

478. **MIDNIGHT RAMBLER** (Jagger, Richard) 🎵 9.04
28 November 1969 (Show Two): Place: Madison Square Garden, New York, USA.
Producer: Rolling Stones, Glyn Johns.
Engineer: Glyn Johns.
UK LP GET YER YA-YA'S OUT: 4 September 1970: No. 1 - 15 weeks
USA LP GET YER YA-YA'S OUT: 26 September 1970: No. 6 - 10 weeks
USA Compilation Promo CD THE ROLLING STONES REMASTERED: 30 May 2002
USA CD GET YER YA-YA'S OUT (40th Anniversary): 3 November 2009
UK CD GET YER YA-YA'S OUT (40th Anniversary): 30 November 2009

479. **LIVE WITH ME** (Jagger, Richard) 🎵 3.02
28 November 1969 (Show Two): Place: Madison Square Garden, New York, USA.
Producer: Rolling Stones, Glyn Johns.
Engineer: Glyn Johns.
UK LP GET YER YA-YA'S OUT: 4 September 1970: No. 1 - 15 weeks
USA LP GET YER YA-YA'S OUT: 26 September 1970: No. 6 - 10 weeks
USA CD GET YER YA-YA'S OUT (40th Anniversary): 3 November 2009
UK CD GET YER YA-YA'S OUT (40th Anniversary): 30 November 2009

480. **HONKY TONK WOMEN** (Jagger, Richard) 🎵 3.02
28 November 1969 (Show Two): Place: Madison Square Garden, New York, USA.
Producer: Rolling Stones, Glyn Johns.
Engineer: Glyn Johns.
UK & USA Video Gimme Shelter: 15 September 1993

481. **STREET FIGHTING MAN** (Jagger, Richard) 🎵 3.41
28 November 1969 (Show Two): Place: Madison Square Garden, New York, USA.
Producer: Rolling Stones, Glyn Johns.
Engineer: Glyn Johns.
UK & USA Video Gimme Shelter: 15 September 1993

Mick entered the Madison Square Garden arena wearing a stars-and-stripes top hat, determined to test the mettle of the American public as well as Sam Cutler's claim. The stray 15-year-old girls in *Stray Cat Blues* became 13-year-olds and the rendition that day in New York of *Midnight Rambler* (still not released) confirmed its theatrical soft-porn status. The Stones had started to dress more resplendently and theatrically, with Keith in sequins and Mick wearing silk scarves - the times they were a-changing, markedly since Hyde Park. Closed circuit television footage of the performance, complete with close-ups, was shown on a large projection screen above the stage.

This additional presentation tool was something Pink Floyd had been experimenting with for a few years. Chip Monck, who looked after the stage and lights, had been involved with the Monterey Pop Festival and Woodstock, so had good references. One technique used, just before *Street Fighting Man*, was to physically lower the stage lights and change them from colour to bright white before hoisting them again above the stage - it was not yet possible to automatically change colours. The concerts in New York were recorded by Glyn Johns using techniques considerably more advanced than those on the 1966 GOT LIVE IF YOU WANT IT. The recording console was brought in from Wally Heider's Californian studio, the band being captured in electrifying form, Keith Richards and Mick Taylor pairing up well. *Sympathy For The Devil* enabled them to toss guitar solos back and forth while *Midnight Rambler* was extended to a work-out lasting eight-and-a-half minutes. It was full of subtle rhythm changes which built the crowd up to fever pitch.

For collectors, the album contains a version of *Little Queenie*, a Chuck Berry rock and roll standard not previously recorded. Ian Stewart played piano on this and the other Berry song in the set-list, *Carol*. Songs played on the tour that did not end up on the live album are *Under My Thumb, Prodigal Son, I'm Free, Gimme Shelter* and *Satisfaction*. *You Gotta Move*, as yet un-recorded, was also played at most venues during the acoustic blues set, along with *Love In Vain*. The concert recording was made available by Decca to cash in on a live market currently furnished by a new era of professional bootleggers - Bob Dylan, The Beatles and the Stones were their chief targets.

At Oakland, on 9 November, the second show was recorded by local promoter Bill Graham. This was the start of a long-standing, sometimes fraught, relationship with the band. Either this recording or a bootlegger's version surfaced on the legendary LIVER THAN YOU'LL EVER BE album and sold astonishingly well, helped by a review and support from Rolling Stone magazine. Bill Graham's soundboard recording was broadcast on local San Francisco KSAN radio in 1972.

In 1970, to counter the bootleg threat, Decca released GET YER YA-YA'S OUT, the title originating from a voodoo chant, although Charlie Watts' t-shirt on the cover may provide another meaning - "get yer tits out". The original Ethan Russell cover, featuring a suitcase with tour mementos, including Jagger's passport and Uncle Sam Wilson's top hat (with offending joint), was scrapped. The album title may also have been a passing reference to Blind Boy Fuller's song, *Get Your Yas Yas Out*. Mick Jagger wanted it to be a double album also featuring the tour's principal support acts, BB King and Ike and Tina Turner. At certain events, other support acts included Terry Reid and The Pack and even Chuck Berry himself.

Although a master was produced, Decca were not impressed. Financial logistics prevented the release so only the single album was made available. Needless to say, test pressings of the double album are extremely rare and valuable. The tracks were in a different order to the released version and lacked the obligatory guitar overdubs. Finally, Mick achieved the release of tracks by the support artists when the 40th Anniversary package was released in 2009. Steve Rosenthal, who was very keen to retain the 60s feel, re-mastered the new tracks *Prodigal Son, You Gotta Move, Under My Thumb, I'm Free* and *Satisfaction*.

He commented: "Anytime you deal with trying to recreate mixes from the '60s and '70s, it's funny because you're dealing with people's sense memories. If you think about it, some people have heard these songs so many times, and they have a particular sense of what they're supposed to sound like. So whenever you do something like this, you really need to respect that. You're marrying the technology you have today, but you don't want that to get in the way of the feel of what the records were like when they were first released."

The Madison Square Garden date was filmed for a documentary by David and Albert Maysles. They also filmed the Muscle Shoals sessions and the last concert at Altamont after being selected by Ronnie Schneider. There was a cinema release made in December 1970 under the title *Gimme Shelter*.

482. YOU GOTTA MOVE (McDowell) 2.34
2-4 December; 15 December 1969; March - May 1970: Place: Muscle Shoals, Alabama, USA; Rolling Stones Mobile, Stargroves, Newbury; Olympic Sound Studios, Trident Studios, London, England.
Played Live: 1969, 1970, 1975
Producer: Jimmy Miller.
Engineer: Jimmy Johnson, Andy Johns, Larry Hamby, Glyn Johns.
Other Production: Chris Kimsey, Keith Harwood.
UK LP STICKY FINGERS: 23 April 1971: No. 1 - 25 weeks
USA LP STICKY FINGERS: 30 April 1971: No. 1 - 26 weeks

On 30 November 1969, the Stones played at the three-day West Palm Beach Pop Festival at the Raceway Track in Florida for $100,000. They headlined the Palm Beach festival, which was meant to emulate Woodstock, which had been held in the summer. The Florida event featured, among others, Janis Joplin, Johnny Winter, Spirit and Grand Funk Railroad but the Stones were held up at the airport and did not play until well after midnight - it was cold, wet and muddy and the 50,000 crowd had dispersed to a mere 5,000. Mick Jagger had to be persuaded to forget the cold and play the event by Dave Rupp, the promoter.

The set list was the same as the rest of the tour, apart from the inclusion of *Gimme Shelter*.

The next day the band travelled north west to Alabama while Sam Cutler was told to fly to San Francisco to ensure the proposed free concert there was on track, as there had been rumours to the contrary. They had decided to record two recently-written compositions and one cover at the infamous home of southern soul music, the eight-track Muscle Shoals Studio in "sweet home" Alabama on the banks of the Tennessee River. They wanted to record while they were still hot and together from the tour.

Jimmy Miller was not present at the sessions and an engineer was asked to check things out in advance to ensure a good standard was reached. There was plenty of positive feedback, not surprising since artists such as Etta James, Arthur Conley, Aretha Franklin, Percy Sledge, Clarence Carter and Wilson Pickett had all placed their faith in Jimmy Johnson (the producer) in the 60s. At that time a license was granted to either play live or record in the studio - but not both. Muscle Shoals, though, was far enough away from the larger studios for anybody to care. Jimmy Johnson's assistant was Larry Hamby while Jimmy Miller and Glyn Johns were both used for post-production.

You Gotta Move is the cover, a short, simplistic tune written by a blues gospel artist, "Mississippi" Fred McDowell. It had been part of the set list for the tour and as such was familiar. The song contains Keith Richards on a National Steel and the languid slide guitar of Mick Taylor, using a 1954 Fender Telecaster, together with an acoustic 12-string, and the singular pounding of a bass drum. Bill Wyman plays electric piano. The gospel image is intensified as the whole band sing along camp-fire style.

An out-take does not have the over-dubbed bass drum but features vocal reverb and extra backing vocals (*a - 2.35). Despite the apparent simplicity of the tune, it took the Stones numerous attempts before the final master was made. Andy Johns (Glyn John's brother) was a teenage tape operator at Olympic during the late 60s and worked with Blind Faith, Free, Mott The Hoople, Ten Years After, Jethro Tull and Stevie Winwood before his career took off in 1970 when he engineered and mixed LED ZEPPELIN III. He was at Olympic Studios for a year (Keith Grant let him go as he was continually being late) and then at Morgan Studios where he was Chief Engineer. He went on to take a fuller role with the Stones but in particular engineered the EXILE sessions in France.

Talking of engineers, another future Stones producer was credited on this track. Chris Kimsey had been destined to be a shop-fitter until he attended a couple of interviews at Olympic with Keith Grant. Suitably impressed when he passed a practical test of how to wire a 13-amp plug, he joined the studio. Keith explained that the interview process ensured that all employees were enthusiastic, personable and affable. Their technical expertise was almost secondary since invariably young apprentices would not get on the desk for up to two years.

Under the auspices of Keith and his assistant Anna Menzies (later a Stones office manager in the 70s) and the great Glyn Johns, Chris started to learn the ropes. The mornings would be spent on commercial jingles, the afternoon on orchestras and the evening was turned over for rock and roll. Working with Alan O'Duffy and Glyn was a great way to learn fast. Kimsey's first major project was working on STICKY FINGERS as an assistant engineer before, later in the year, collaborating with Andy Johns on a project for Ten Years After. He was to make a more fundamental Stones contribution in the late 70s and early 80s.

483. BROWN SUGAR (Jagger, Richard) 3.49
AKA: Black Pussy
3-4 December; 14 December 1969, 24 April, December 1970: Place: Muscle Shoals, Alabama, USA; Olympic Sound Studios, London, England.
Played Live: 1969, 1970, 1971, 1972, 1973, 1975, 1976, 1977, 1978, 1981, 1982, 1989, 1990, 1994, 1995, 1997, 1998, 1999, 2002, 2003, 2005, 2006, 2007
Rolling Stones with Bobby Keys.
Producer: Jimmy Miller.
Engineer: Jimmy Johnson, Andy Johns, Larry Hamby, Glyn Johns.
Other Production: Chris Kimsey, Keith Harwood.
UK Single: 16 April 1971: No. 2 - 13 weeks
UK LP STICKY FINGERS: 23 April 1971: No. 1 - 25 weeks

USA LP STICKY FINGERS: 30 April 1971: No. 1 - 26 weeks
USA Single: 7 May 1971: No. 1 - 12 weeks
USA LP THE ROLLING STONES HOT ROCKS 1964-1971: 11 January 1972: No. 4 - 30 weeks
UK Compilation LP MADE IN THE SHADE: 6 June 1975: No. 14 - 12 weeks
USA Compilation LP MADE IN THE SHADE: 6 June 1975: No. 6 - 9 weeks
UK Compilation LP GET STONED - 30 GREATEST HITS, 30 ORIGINAL TRACKS: 21 October 1977: No. 13 - 15 weeks
UK Re-released Single: 29 June 1984: No. 58 - 2 weeks
UK Compilation LP REWIND 1971-1984 (THE BEST OF THE ROLLING STONES): 29 June 1984: No. 45 - 5 weeks
USA Compilation LP REWIND 1971-1984 (THE BEST OF THE ROLLING STONES): 2 July 1984: No. 86 - 11 weeks
UK & USA LP THE ROLLING STONES SINGLES COLLECTION - THE LONDON YEARS: 15 August 1989
UK Compilation LP JUMP BACK THE BEST OF THE ROLLING STONES '71 - '93: 22 November 1993: No. 16 - 26 weeks
USA Compilation Promo CD THE ROLLING STONES REMASTERED: 30 May 2002
USA Compilation Promo CD ABKCO'S THE ROLLINGS STONES REMASTERED SERIES: 30 May 2002
UK CD LP FORTY LICKS: 30 September 2002: No. 2 - 45 weeks
USA CD LP FORTY LICKS: 1 October 2002: No. 2 - 50 weeks
USA Compilation CD JUMP BACK THE BEST OF THE ROLLING STONES '71 - '93: 24 August 2004: No. 30 - 58 weeks
UK CD box set THE ROLLING STONES SINGLES - 1968 - 1971: 28 February 2005
USA CD box set THE ROLLING STONES SINGLES - 1968 - 1971: 1 March 2005
UK Compilation CD ROLLED GOLD +: 12 November 2007: No. 26 - 12 weeks
UK CD box set THE SINGLES COLLECTION 1971-2006: 45 X 45s: 11 April 2011
UK Vinyl Single: 16 April 2011
USA CD box set THE SINGLES COLLECTION 1971-2006: 45 X 45s: 26 April 2011

Brown Sugar is literally a rock and roll overdose. The lyrical message written in the studio is mixed and sordid. The brown, chemically-mixed opium powder of heroin known as "brown sugar" became the song title. It concerns the slave trade and the unsavoury bosses who buy girls for illicit purposes and, after their work is done in the cotton fields, "hear the boss whip the women and taste them just around midnight", while the boss's wife screws the black house boy: "House boy knows that he's doing all right. You shoulda heard him just around midnight". It was Jimmy Dickinson who told Jagger to keep the midnight reference since he was leaving it out when doing some vocal overdubs.

The song's working title derived from one of Mick Jagger's early lyrics but was soon dropped, although he denied later there was ever a reference to "pussy", apart from the lyrical "taste them". Claudia Lennear, an American singer from the Ikettes, has long been associated with the song, having met Mick on the 1969 tour as one of Ike and Tina Turner's backing vocalists and apparently made him weak at the knees - but then, so did his extended dalliance with Marsha Hunt. Mick remembers writing the classic song in the middle of the Australian outback while recuperating from a hand injury sustained during filming for Ned Kelly in 1969.

In January 1969, Sam & Dave had a minor hit with *Soul Sister, Brown Sugar* - "Keep on sockin' it to me all night long, soul sister, you're brown sugar" - which may have provided more inspiration. Reverend Jesse Jackson interpreted the song as being racist and demanded that it should be banned from the radio. Later, Mick contritely wondered what he had been on at the time to write such antagonistic and nasty lyrics. Jimmy Dickinson recalled the verses being written effortlessly by Mick.

Mick learned that it was well known that Duane Allman was known as "skydog" in Muscle Shoals (Wilson Pickett named him "skyman" when he played on his version of *Hey Jude*) where the Allman Brothers played sessions so the lyrics supposedly became "skydog slaver" and not "scarred old slaver", though most people's ears hear the latter on all versions.

Bobby Keys contributed enormously to the success of *Brown Sugar*, his driving sax so inspirational, but the rock riff merchant, Keith Richards, created the foundation for the huge hit single with his classic open-G riff supported by Mick Taylor on a Strat. Keith combined both the force of the riff with the rhythm driving, his hands gliding up and down the fret boards. Unusually, the chords and riff were claimed to be written by Mick. Bill Wyman played a Dan Armstrong Plexiglas body bass and the slightly echoed, dirty Gibson SG guitar sound was created by engineer Jimmy Johnson, who placed Keith's Fender twin amp in a backroom booth because it was too loud out front.

Keith, also on the acoustic guitar, emphasises the *Street Fighting* anthem similarity, while Mick's "Yeah, Yeah, Yeah, Woah" at the end prompts the ritual raised fist. Various out-takes exist, a few without the brass, which was added when it was re-mixed in April at Olympic. There is a Jagger vocal "free for all" with "yo" and other gutteral utterings continuing the whole track length, ending with an "oh baby" (* a - 3.43).

There is a very percussive, messy version with the guitars entering and jostling at will (* b - 3.49). Mick Taylor and Ian Stewart are much more prominent on the Muscle Shoals originals, the former's guitar sounding way back in the mix on the released version. There are nine tape rewinds of the introduction and cuts up to the first and second verses can also be heard (* c). These are taken from Glyn Johns' working tape reels that were sold at Sotheby's.

An early cut without brass, more pronounced castanets and an additional lead guitar by Mick Taylor, was accidentally released on early copies of THE ROLLING STONES HOT ROCKS 1964-1971 album and in part in the soundtrack of the *Gimme Shelter* movie (* d - 3.48). A similar version to this, but with an alternative Mick Taylor solo in the last 30 seconds, is also available on the Glyn Johns tape (* e - 3.52).

Finally there is an advanced mix, with sax, from the Sotheby's tape, which was studio polished and mixed for the final version (* f - 3.54). Ian Stewart plays a mean bar room rock and roll style piano. On release he thought it was a better single even than *Honky Tonk Women*. Mick Taylor echoed that sentiment in *The True Adventures Of The Rolling Stones* by Stanley Booth, who was present at the studios: "That's what makes a good rock and roll record, simplicity".

Mick wanted it to sound dirty and it did because witnesses said the whole building was shaking to the overall sound, recalled Jimmy Johnson. Keith, too, wanted to capture the rough and raw textures and get away from the new Crosby, Stills and Nash sound which he described as "clean music which is scrubbed and input through the shower and bath".

Stanley Booth mentioned the frustration felt by Ian Stewart during the recording of *Brown Sugar*. Even the drums were out of tune with each other as the tom-tom rubbed against the bass drum, with Charlie Watts protesting that there was no point tuning them if he was going to hit them a few times before going out of kilter again. But that is what made the so-called "shitty" sound that Mick and Keith wanted. Ultimately, Charlie was so impressed with the drum sound that he wanted to buy the high U47 microphone used for the session. Mick felt that the drum beat should sound like Freddy Cannon's *Way Down Yonder In New Orleans* and encouraged Charlie to perform in that manner. As well as vocals, Mick plays the shakers and what sounds like a scratch board/castanet in the left speaker.

Chris Kimsey, who had been a tape operator for Glyn Johns, worked on the final session and the saxophone overdub made by Bobby Keys. This came about after Jimmy Miller heard Bobby jamming with the Stones at Keith's birthday party at Olympic in December 1970, when the alternative version of *Brown Sugar* was recorded with Eric Clapton, and felt he should do the same on the STICKY FINGERS version. The brass part helped the song lift off enormously and became Bobby's trademark lick. The single was the first to be released on their own label, courtesy of Atlantic Records President Ahmet Ertegun, who was wooing the Stones to join his company upon expiry of their contract with Decca. It was no coincidence that he was in attendance at the Muscle Shoals sessions. Inevitably, there was a delay before agreement was reached and any new material could be issued, so 17 months passed before *Brown Sugar* hit the streets. Ahmet became a lifelong friend to the band until his untimely death following a backstage fall at their New York Beacon Theatre concert in 2006. A vinyl single was re-released in 2011 on the 40th anniversary of the original to coincide with Record Store Day.

484. WILD HORSES (Jagger, Richard) 5.42

3-4 December; 15 December 1969, 17 February, August 1970: Place: Muscle Shoals, Alabama, USA; Olympic Sound Studios, Trident Studios, London, England.
Played Live: 1971, 1975, 1976, 1994, 1995, 1997, 2002, 2003, 2005, 2006
Rolling Stones with Jimmy Dickinson.
Producer: Jimmy Miller.
Engineer: Jimmy Johnson, Andy Johns, Larry Hamby, Glyn Johns.
Other Production: Chris Kimsey, Keith Harwood.
UK LP STICKY FINGERS: 23 April 1971: No. 1 - 25 weeks
USA LP STICKY FINGERS: 30 April 1971: No. 1 - 26 weeks
USA Single: 12 June 1971: No. 28 - 5 weeks
USA LP THE ROLLING STONES HOT ROCKS 1964-1971: 11 January 1972: No. 4 - 30 weeks
UK Compilation LP MADE IN THE SHADE: 6 June 1975: No. 14 - 12 weeks
USA Compilation LP MADE IN THE SHADE: 6 June 1975: No. 6 - 9 weeks
UK Compilation LP GET STONED - 30 GREATEST HITS, 30 ORIGINAL TRACKS: 21 October 1977: No. 13 - 15 weeks
UK & USA LP THE ROLLING STONES SINGLES COLLECTION - THE LONDON YEARS: 15 August 1989
UK Compilation LP JUMP BACK THE BEST OF THE ROLLING STONES '71 - '93: 22 November 1993: No. 16 - 26 weeks
USA Compilation Promo CD THE ROLLING STONES REMASTERED: 30 May 2002
UK CD LP FORTY LICKS: 30 September 2002: No. 2 - 45 weeks
USA CD LP FORTY LICKS: 1 October 2002: No. 2 - 50 weeks
USA Compilation CD JUMP BACK THE BEST OF THE ROLLING STONES '71 - '93: 24 August 2004: No. 30 - 58 weeks
UK CD box set THE ROLLING STONES SINGLES - 1968 - 1971: 28 February 2005
USA CD box set THE ROLLING STONES SINGLES - 1968 - 1971: 1 March 2005
UK Compilation CD ROLLED GOLD +: 12 November 2007: No. 26 - 12 weeks
e-EP Single: 20 November 2009
UK CD box set THE SINGLES COLLECTION 1971-2006: 45 X 45s: 11 April 2011
USA CD box set THE SINGLES COLLECTION 1971-2006: 45 X 45s: 26 April 2011

Wild Horses is a soft country love ballad lasting a lengthy six minutes. It is played without the wry country irony which can be heard on other outings, such as *Dead Flowers*. Mick Taylor plays a Nashville strung guitar, a technique used by established country and western artistes, while Keith Richards plays the lead solo, the hook dedicated to Gram Parsons. The songwriting typified the band's approach - Keith had written the riff and chorus while Mick Jagger provided the verses. Jimmy Dickinson, a Memphis and Nashville session man who helped to arrange the booking of the eight-track studio, is featured on tack piano. He struggled to find a piano that was close in tuning to the Stones arrangement after Ian Stewart declined to play because the song was in a minor chord. Keith had given him a note of the chord structure but Jimmy struggled with them until Bill Wyman helped him out explaining that Keith did not know how to construct a chord chart: "Pay no attention to him . . . he has no idea what he is doing . . . he only knows where to put his fingers yesterday!" Jimmy had witnessed the sessions and was intrigued at the Stones' spontaneous methods with Mick writing lyrics on the fly, Charlie Watts and Keith both not tuning any instrument and the band recording take after take until the first cut without any mistakes, whereupon Charlie would signify a final take by standing up and walking away from his drum-set.
The lyrics apparently concern Keith's reluctance to go on the '69 tour because it left Anita alone to cope with their newly-born son, Marlon. The sentiments can, however relate to any strained relationship and they were also said to be similar to the demands placed on Mick Jagger by Marianne Faithfull following her suicide attempt in Australia in July 1969, an incident which led to the ending of the romance in early 1970.
In fact, the exact subject matter is not important. The moving quality of Mick's vocals, which twist and turn, serve their purpose, even if the call card line "wild, wild horses couldn't drag me away" was Marianne's opening remark when she came out of her coma. The backing vocals of Pete Townshend and Ronnie Lane were said to be on the final mix, but that is unlikely as Keith takes on that task magnificently.
One out-take of *Wild Horses* from Muscle Shoals of features the Flying Burritos' steel guitar player "Sneeky" Pete Kleinow (* a - 5.22), although there are rumours that it was Gram Parsons, or even both of them made a contribution. Gram would have been a more likely piano player should he have been present. He recorded *Wild Horses* himself with The Flying Burrito Brothers - Keith said that they had a magnetic attraction to each other. It was released on the Burritos' 1970 album BURRITO DELUXE before the Stones version which was released as a single in the States but only attained a No. 28 position, the Stones' most unsuccessful chart ranking to date. An edited version was released in June 1971 on a promotional single titled *Short Version* but copies are very rare (* b - 3.26). At one time, it was planned to release it as a single for the Christmas market on the Stones own label in 1970 but this could not be achieved. On first pressings of THE ROLLING STONES HOT ROCKS 1964-1971 album, an alternate take was released without backing vocals and Mick Taylor's distinctive lead guitar (* c - 5.45). Two guitar-only jams from the session, are known loosely as *Muscle Shoals Jam 1* and *2* and feature Mick Taylor on lead guitar.
While they were recording in Alabama Jo Bergman, who was in San Francisco, told Ian Stewart that all was not well and that Ronnie Schneider and Sam Cutler were trying to overcome some potentially insurmountable problems for the free concert. Mick Jagger wanted to provide an event on the scale of Woodstock but, at such short notice, the Stones and Sam were trying to achieve the impossible.

As they left the studios, Mick ensured that he had the master tapes and that there were no other tapes left, even destroying some. Chris Kimsey later recalled a harrowing moment while preparing the master tape of *Wild Horses,* transferring the eight-track recording from one machine to another in a separate room when the playback started to slur. He ran back to the master where he saw mountains of tape on the floor. He pressed stop and looked at how he could unravel the snagged part of the tape.

Keith Grant, one of the studio owners, helped him save the day by producing a heavy iron (doubtless used before for such a purpose) to press out the creases. An additional version from this session, with Billy Preston on organ, was recorded but not released (* d - 5.43). In 2009, the track was given another single re-release by the Stones following the success of a cover by quirky classical singer Susan Boyle and, more importantly, a payment for £1 million in royalties. She had been a contestant on the Britain's Got Talent TV show and her debut solo album, featuring her first single, *Wild Horses*, became the biggest selling album in the world in 2009.

485. THE SUN IS SHINING (Reed) ⤳ 3.44
6 December 1969: Place: Altamont Speedway, Livermore, California, USA.
Bootleg only.

Determined to put on a free show following press criticism about high ticket prices and in an attempt to out-do Woodstock, the Stones had agreed to play San Francisco at the end of the tour - it would still be warm there in December and a search started to find a suitable festival venue site. Rock Scully, the manager for Grateful Dead, agreed to help and secured Golden Gate Park, subject to there being no publicity until 24 hours before the show. Making matters worse, he found that the Stones were impossible to talk to as they were entrenched in layers of crooks, who were so-say "looking after the Stones' interests".

When the band announced the free gig, against the Golden Gate Park authorities' wishes, while in New York, another venue was required. Sear's Point Racetrack was put forward but, just 48 hours before the scheduled event, agreement could not be reached with the owners, who demanded a share of the film rights or a $100,000. Land was strangely put forward on behalf of the Catholic Knights of Columbus but, on inspection, Sam Cutler felt it was inaccessible. Strangely John Jaymes, who had helped out with tour cars but was now playing a more prominent role with security, had negotiated on behalf of the Stones as the Young American Enterprise Association, hence this weird suggestion which probably involved kick-backs. His role was likened to a Mafia-like figure who had infiltrated the band. Eventually, in return only for some free publicity, Altamont Speedway, located 60 miles east of San Francisco between Livermore and Tracy, was offered and Michael Lang, who had promoted Woodstock, agreed the venue but the late switch allowed little time to tear down the stage from Sear's Point and transfer it 80 miles to Altamont for such an extravagant event. The stage was not high since it was designed to be mounted on top of a hill at Sears Point with a drop to the audience. The Grateful Dead put out calls for helpers to help transfer the gear and Chip Monck, who was in charge of the Stones' stage, contacted Bill Graham a day or so before, pleading for his help. Graham's advice was to cancel as it was clear that there was no overall festival co-ordinator and organiser but still the message from the Stones camp was that the show must go on.

486. SYMPATHY FOR THE DEVIL (Jagger, Richard) ⤳ 6.02
6 December 1969: Place: Altamont Speedway, Livermore, California, USA.
Producer: Ronald Schneider. Associate Producer: Porter Bibb.
Engineer: Bob Matthews.
Alembic Recording Mobile. Director: Albert Maysles, David Maysles, Charlotte Zwerin.
UK & USA Video Gimme Shelter: 1993

487. UNDER MY THUMB (Jagger, Richard) ⤳ 3.31
6 December 1969: Place: Altamont Speedway, Livermore, California, USA.
Producer: Ronald Schneider. Associate Producer: Porter Bibb.
Engineer: Bob Matthews.
Alembic Recording Mobile. Director: Albert Maysles, David Maysles, Charlotte Zwerin.
UK & USA Video Gimme Shelter: 1993

488. GIMME SHELTER (Jagger, Richard) ⤳ 2.03
6 December 1969: Place: Altamont Speedway, Livermore, California, USA.
Producer: Ronald Schneider. Associate Producer: Porter Bibb.
Engineer: Bob Matthews.
Alembic Recording Mobile. Director: Albert Maysles, David Maysles, Charlotte Zwerin.
UK & USA Video Gimme Shelter: 1993

Support artists for an audience of more than 250,000 included Gram Parson's Flying Burrito Brothers, Crosby, Stills, Nash and Young, Santana and Jefferson Airplane. Grateful Dead were due to play but decided not to because of all the hold-ups. Nobody appeared to know who was distributing them but it was clear that spiked acid pills had been given free to the crowd, causing bad trips and vibes. The stage was set at the bottom of a hill and, because of its low height, was easily over-run and a front-of-stage mesh security fence was also pulled down. The Hell's Angels provided the band and equipment "security" for the event, paid for by a few kegs of potent liquid supplemented by murine bottles of acid, but they were nothing like the English bikers used at Hyde Park. Unfortunately, the hired security crew (John Jaymes' associates) diminished as the day progressed, claiming they had families waiting for them at home.

There had been some trouble from rednecks, bikers and greasers during the sets by Santana and Jefferson Airplane, with their singer Marty Balin knocked to the ground twice, so the cauldron was simmering at dusk as the Stones were awaited on stage. The situation was exacerbated because an important Hell's Angels chapter meeting had been taking place that day which caused the leaders to arrive late at the event.

There were chaotic scenes both backstage and on stage, Mick Jagger being punched as he arrived and the whole tone was not good. Angels mixed freely on stage with the Stones - even a dog wanders across the stage at one point in the film. Sam Cutler made a very brave attempt at holding it together but it was a hopeless task. The band scrambled their way to the incredibly low and inappropriate stage and, for a couple of numbers, all was OK, despite the poor sound quality.

It was during *Sympathy For The Devil* that outbursts of trouble started. Bikers, armed with pool cues, fought with the crowd and there was mayhem on and off stage as Angels freely knocked people off the stage. The music was halted while some kind of peace was restored before the Stones resumed with a Jimmy Reed number, *The Sun Is Shining*, which was intended to try and calm things down. Keith Richards bravely uttered some strong words against the trouble-makers but Mick had lost his usual "under my thumb" pull over the crowd.

The Stones eventually restarted and jammed, playing the blues for a few minutes. While a subdued, low-key rendition of *Under My Thumb* was sending out its strong bass rhythm, the infamous killing occurred at the end of the song. Meredith Hunter, an 18-year-old with gun in hand for self-defence, was seen trying to get away from a scuffle, but pointing a gun towards the stage. Instantly an Angel pounced on him to protect others and, in the ensuing struggle, the teenager was left dying from knife wounds.

After being charged with murder, an Angel (the late Alan Passaro) was acquitted when it was agreed by a jury that he had acted in self defence. The case was finally closed more than 35 years later when it could not be proven that a second angel was involved in the stabbing. Despite the chaos in the crowd, The Stones continued with the previously unreleased *Brown Sugar* as they did not want to incite further trouble by jumping ship. The crowd, fed by the acid, lazily accepted the Stones but the damage had been done and another nail had been placed in the coffin of the hippies' peace, love and understanding. After the event, Chip Monck, who was left to salvage the lights and equipment, saw one of the Angels try to walk off with the Stones' stage carpet, he defended it and lost two front teeth as a result.

The 1969 American tour had been filmed by the Maysles Brothers, who caught the killing of Meredith Hunter on camera, the footage being used as evidence in court. The Angels later insisted they wanted a copy of the film to check its contents and Sam Cutler was instrumental in ensuring that this request was granted. It was Mick's idea to record the concert and release it as soon as possible, thus pre-empting the *Woodstock* film. It was released under the title *Gimme Shelter* - one of the working titles was *Love In Vain* - and it still does the cinematic rounds to this day.

The visual impact of Charlie Watts' and Mick Jagger's comments on the tragedy of the concert is powerful cinematic viewing. One of the Maysles' favourite tools was to utilise facial close-ups because they believed they revealed the inner soul - and that was certainly the case in a few poignant moments. Another member of the crew, George Lucas, filmed the exodus from the festival in near apocalyptic scenes. The musical soundtrack was laid down by Bob Matthews, the Grateful Dead's recording engineer on the Alembic Recording mobile and he still owns the tapes to this day. Alembic was run by Deadhead friends, Ron and Susan Wickersham. A week after the concert Susan, badly tainted by the experience, was quoted as saying: "The Stones screwed us all over royally. The Dead paid us all of their own expenses to fly to Altamont and back by helicopter, and then they weren't allowed to play. They put out money that hasn't been reimbursed, and now they're flat broke. The Stones are just not nice people, you know . . ."

489. DEAD FLOWERS (Jagger, Richard) 4.05
15 December 1969, 24 April 1970: Place: Olympic Sound Studios, London, England.
Played Live: 1970, 1971, 1973, 1976, 1989, 1990, 1994, 1995, 1997, 1998, 1999, 2002, 2003, 2005, 2006, 2007
Producer: Jimmy Miller.
Engineer: Glyn Johns, Andy Johns.
Other Production: Chris Kimsey, Keith Harwood.
UK LP STICKY FINGERS: 23 April 1971: No. 1 - 25 weeks
USA LP STICKY FINGERS: 30 April 1971: No. 1 - 26 weeks

The Stones fled to the UK and left Sam Cutler to pick up the aftermath of Altamont. He was promised expenses and legal support by Mick Jagger but neither arrived, so, ever loyal to the cause, he negotiated with the Angels alone. Regrettably he did not hear from or work for the band again, instead being employed as the Grateful Dead's tour manager. Meanwhile Stones' representatives from London spoke with Meredith Hunter's relatives. An account of the Altamont free concert can be read in Sam Cutler's excellent, thought-provoking book *You Can't Always Get What You Want*.

Obliviously, the band went to Olympic to finish off the three tracks recorded at Muscle Shoals. In addition, treading now on ever more familiar ground, the first takes of *Dead Flowers* were recorded. The earlier recordings had a throwback to *Downtown Suzie*, Lucy taking the place of the chief character. *Dead Flowers* is another Nashville ringer but up-tempo with Mick Taylor on his electric Gibson. The song was written by Mick Jagger, who had rehearsed it 100 times at Stargroves before bringing it to the studio.

Was the inspiration Blind Willie McTell's *Lay Some Flowers On My Grave*? *Dead Flowers* features Ian Stewart on piano and the country-sloven vocals of Mick on some humorously ironic lyrics. The love for country and western was not simply a popular fashion or cheap imitation - the Stones seemed to have an in-built love for the music and country songs were included on most future albums, even if they were not treated as seriously as *Wild Horses*. *Dead Flowers* was completed in April 1970.

On 12 December 1969, the band attended a BBC TV recording for Top Of The Pops where they mimed to *Honky Tonk Women* and recorded *Let It Bleed* and *Gimme Shelter* for two 60s retrospectives. Mick did live vocal takes on all three numbers to the studio released track. Finally, 1969 ended with two concerts, on 14 and 21 December, at the Saville Theatre and the Lyceum Theatre respectively. They played two sell-out shows at each, the set lists being drawn from the USA tour. An attempt had been made to hire the Royal Albert Hall but the management had turned down the booking.

490. ROCK IT (Jagger, Richard)
March - May 1970: Place: Rolling Stones Mobile, Stargroves, Newbury, Olympic Sound Studios, London, England.
Producer: Jimmy Miller.
Engineer: Glyn Johns, Andy Johns.
Unavailable.

491. TRAVELLING TIGER (Jagger, Richard)
March - May 1970: Place: Rolling Stones Mobile, Stargroves, Newbury, Olympic Sound Studios, London, England.
Producer: Jimmy Miller.
Engineer: Glyn Johns, Andy Johns.
Unavailable.

This may have been an early version of *Travellin' Man*.

492. **AS NOW** (Jagger, Richard)
March - May 1970: Place: Rolling Stones Mobile, Stargroves, Newbury, Olympic Sound Studios, London, England.
Producer: Jimmy Miller.
Engineer: Glyn Johns, Andy Johns.
Unavailable.

The early part of the year was spent in the studio mixing and overdubbing the USA recordings aimed for release as a live album. From March to May and also in the autumn, time was spent between Mick Jagger's manor, Stargroves, and the Olympic studios. At the house, they used the Rolling Stones Mobile to record, not just rough demos, but passable takes for re-mix at Olympic. The sessions could sometimes be disrupted when Bianca Jagger peered around the door and Mick Jagger departed upstairs. Stargroves also became the location for recordings by the Who and Led Zeppelin. These three tracks have not been made available and could be working titles.

493. **MOONLIGHT MILE** (Jagger, Richard) 5.56
AKA: **The Japanese Thing**
March - May, 21 October - 2 November 1970: Place: Rolling Stones Mobile, Stargroves, Newbury, Olympic Sound Studios, Trident Studios, London, England.
Played Live: 1999
Rolling Stones with Paul Buckmaster, Jim Price.
Producer: Jimmy Miller.
Engineer: Glyn Johns, Andy Johns, Chris Kimsey.
Assistant Engineer: Keith Harwood.
UK LP STICKY FINGERS: 23 April 1971: No. 1 - 25 weeks
USA LP STICKY FINGERS: 30 April 1971: No. 1 - 26 weeks

Recording methods were changing considerably - the Stones had purchased their own mobile unit, within an air-conditioned Leyland truck, which was managed by Ian Stewart. It was used by the band early in 1970 to put some ideas (hence *The Japanese Thing*) on to tape for the next album. Andy Johns, when talking about the mobile, stated: "Stargroves was ideally suited because it was a big mansion and a kind of grand hall with a gallery around, with bedroom doors and a staircase. Big fireplace, big bay window - you could put Charlie in the bay window. And, off the main hall there were other rooms you could put people in. We did stuff like *Bitch* there, and you can hear *Moonlight Mile* when Mick is singing with the acoustic, it sounds very live, because it was! Four or five in the morning, with the sun about to come up, getting takes".

Mick Taylor first heard the song when Mick sang it to him in a first-class train compartment. In the studio he took the beginning and wrote the rest of the track and felt that deserved a co-writer credit - but the Glimmer Twins denied him, for which he was annoyed. Paul Buckmaster, who had helped to arrange David Bowie's *Space Oddity* and *Your Song* for Elton John, was called in to assist with *Sway*. He arranged the 24-piece string orchestra to create a beautiful track that was a significant change of direction for the band. Mick Taylor plays a haunting, acoustic 12-string guitar and the song gradually builds up under Paul Buckmaster's direction, Jim Price being used to great effect on piano.

Marshall Chess insisted that Mick Jagger kept on re-recording his vocals until he got the perfect cut. Keith Richards, who was present at the mixing stages, reckons that part of his original guitar workings were included near the end of the track - some way to get a songwriting credit! It was a fitting album closure with imagery of tiredness following a mad, mad day. Altamont could have been the subject matter or even the death of Brian Jones. *Moonlight Mile* was covered by American band 5th Dimension in 1975 for their album EARTHBOUND. They were well known for their 1969 hippy hit *Aquarius*. Later in 2004, DJ Mix and folk duo Turin Brakes mixed a compilation album of covers, LATE NIGHT TALES with their version of this song.

494. **I GOT THE BLUES** (Jagger, Richard) 3.54
March - May 1970: Place: Rolling Stones Mobile, Stargroves, Newbury, Olympic Sound Studios, Trident Studios, London, England.
Played Live: 1971, 1999
Rolling Stones with Bobby Keys, Billy Preston, Jim Price.
Producer: Jimmy Miller.
Engineer: Glyn Johns, Andy Johns, Chris Kimsey.
Assistant Engineer: Keith Harwood.
UK LP STICKY FINGERS: 23 April 1971: No. 1 - 25 weeks
USA LP STICKY FINGERS: 30 April 1971: No. 1 - 26 weeks

Billy Preston, who had found brief pop fame with the Beatles in 1969 when he had played keyboards on *Get Back* and *Don't Let Me Down*, joined the Stones to play organ on this tease of the Stax sound. *I Got The Blues* is played in a slow blues mould and includes the brass sounds of Bobby Keys and Jim Price. In his biography, *Every Night's A Saturday Night*, Bobby Keys revealed that Mick Jagger was very much into the sound of Otis Redding, Wilson Pickett and the Memphis Horns. He told Mick that he had his own Texan Horns - the Longhorns! Ian Stewart, who was a big fan of Leon Russell, also promoted their inclusion within the band set-up. The outcome, on this occasion, is not a classic but it did have a sincere delivery.

495. **CAN'T YOU HEAR ME KNOCKING** (Jagger, Richard) 7.15
March - May 1970: Place: Rolling Stones Mobile, Stargroves, Newbury, Olympic Sound Studios, Trident Studios, London, England.
Played Live: 2002, 2003, 2007
Rolling Stones with Bobby Keys, Billy Preston, Jimmy Miller, Rocky Dijon, Pete Townshend, Ronnie Lane.
Producer: Jimmy Miller.
Engineer: Glyn Johns, Andy Johns, Chris Kimsey.
Assistant Engineer: Keith Harwood.
UK LP STICKY FINGERS: 23 April 1971: No. 1 - 25 weeks
USA LP STICKY FINGERS: 30 April 1971: No. 1 - 26 weeks

Another awesome fuzzed-out, echoed guitar riff by Keith Richards provides the basis for *Can't You Hear Me Knocking*. Keith used it to test his new brother in arms, Mick Taylor, and also sparred with Bobby Keys' sax, Billy Preston's organ and the percussion sounds of Jimmy Miller and Rocky Dijon. Charlie Watts is perfectly at home in this free-flowing environment. It was a jazz-like jam in the vein of *Goin' Home*. It was not intended to be like this but the second part just developed as Mick Taylor continued to jam with Rocky Dijon and Bobby Keys, who joined in completely unrehearsed.

Mick Taylor's improvised, fluid and magnificent distant solos were made on his Gibson ES-345. Again, it is rumoured that Pete Townshend and Ronnie Lane joined the Stones on the brief backing vocals. The song's final guitar chords provide a unique exit and Jimmy Miller liked the song's extension, managing to persuade Mick Jagger that it would be a fitting release. The album, now almost complete, was left in the can until the outcome of the Klein publishing rights trials. STICKY FINGERS featured a host of musicians and took seven months to record but, due to protracted record company deals and various law suits, was not released for a further 10 to 12 months.

The Stones' relationship with Allen Klein had been strained for some time and the air following the cessation of the contract on 31 July 1970 was thick with law suits and counter law suits. The Stones claimed Klein had duped them, some of their payments having been deposited into his company, Nanker Phelge Music Inc, instead of Nanker Phelge Music Ltd. Klein invested the money until it was correctly apportioned years later, stating years that the rights were in his American company to protect the Stones for tax reasons.

A $29 million law suit was at issue and, in July 1970, the Stones officially divorced themselves from Klein though the settlement itself was not completed until May 1972, when the band agreed to a modest $2 million. There were conditions relating to further releases made, which included the inability for the band to release any ABKCO-owned songs re-recorded or live for five years. Keith had no regrets with Allen Klein; he had made them a global enterprise and the experience had all been part of their business education.

There are a few songs that are jointly owned by ABKCO and the Stones, such as *Brown Sugar* and *Wild Horses*. So Rolling Stones Records was created, within the Atlantic empire, and Mick Jagger was determined that what he saw at Apple Records with the Beatles would not be repeated by his band. As he said: "We're not going to build a skyscraper in Saville Row". In April 1969, Andy Warhol was asked by Jagger to help design the next album cover and he produced the controversial zip sleeve for STICKY FINGERS, which included the male "Levis" photograph. Warhol is often mistaken for having designed the Stones tongue logo too.

Marshall Chess suggested to Mick that the Stones needed a logo that was instantly recognisable like Shell Petrochemicals' yellow shell design. In an Indian calendar, Mick saw an image of Hindu Goddess Kali, who was the Goddess of destruction - she had a lascivious red tongue. This was given to London Royal College of Art student John Pasche, who came up with the first idea of the Stones tongue and was authorised by the band's London office to design the work in April 1970. Stones office manager Georgia "Jo" Bergman wrote: "We have also asked you [as well as the 1970 and 1972 tour posters] to create a logo or symbol which may be used on note paper, as a programme cover and as a cover for the press book."

On first meeting Mick to discuss the idea the first thing that struck Pasche was: "Face to face with him, the first thing you were aware of was the size of his lips and his mouth". The student was paid a one-off initial amount of £50 then, in 1972, a further £200 due to the success of the logo. He also received merchandising rights until selling the logo to the Stones in 1984.

Before the release of STICKY FINGERS, Marshall Chess commissioned a concept packaging company who asked design consultant Ernie Cefalu (famous for the Jesus Christ Superstar design), who produced a new incarnation for the tongue. Pasche's simple design was featured discretely on the inner sleeve of the album and the disc itself while Cefalu's was portrayed on all STICKY FINGERS merchandise and in various guises on every tour since. The sexual innuendo of Warhol's zip was not subtle but the only country to object was Spain which, at that time, was under a long-term dictatorship. The Spanish Group of Atlantic Records changed the cover and also substituted *Let It Rock* for the needle-inspired *Sister Morphine*. The Russian sleeve copy featured a female with jeans safely zipped up.

On the inside cover, there is an iconic Peter Webb photo of the band in their everyday gear, looking bored and entitled "the big yawn". This image was the intended cover for the record until the more elaborate design came along. The album became their biggest-selling release to date and topped the charts internationally. It heralded the arrival of a new business acumen and launched the Stones firmly into the 70s while their counterparts, The Beatles, remained lost in the 60s'. Still, "nothing is Beatle proof". Carlos Santana honoured Mick Taylor by covering the song, with Scott Weiland on vocals, in 2010, for his aptly-named album GUITAR HEAVEN: THE GREATEST GUITAR CLASSICS OF ALL TIME.

496. GOOD TIME WOMEN (Jagger, Richard) 3.21
AKA: Tumbling Dice

March - May; 21 -31 October 1970; September - November; December 2009: Place: Rolling Stones Mobile, Stargroves, Newbury, Olympic Sound Studios, London, England; One East Studio, New York, Henson Studios, Village Recording; Mix This!, Los Angeles, USA

Rolling Stones with Bobby Keys, Jim Price.
Producer: Jimmy Miller, Don Was, The Glimmer Twins.
Engineer: Glyn Johns; Additional Engineering and Editing: Krish Sharma; Mixed by Bob Clearmountain.
Other Production: Andy Johns, Chris Kimsey, Keith Harwood.

UK CD EXILE ON MAIN ST (EXTRA TRACKS): 17 May 2010: No. 1 - 10 weeks
USA CD EXILE ON MAIN ST (EXTRA TRACKS): 18 May 2010: No. 1 - 3 weeks

A strident bass guitar and a brief harmonica open this track. With a different set of lyrics, *Good Time Women* was the embryo of *Tumbling Dice*. References to red light women and honeys who like to party were reminiscent of *Honky Tonk Women*. It is played at a faster pace than *Tumbling Dice* and even accelerates towards the end, driven by the lead-guitar of Mick Taylor and the integral boogie piano power of Ian Stewart.

The marked difference between *Good Time Women* and the eventual outcome, *Tumbling Dice*, which is skilfully slovenly, is the rhythm artistry of Keith Richards. He performed the lead and rhythm guitar while Mick Taylor played the bass. In so doing (with changed lyrics more in keeping with the casino atmosphere), he transformed the track from anonymity to chart success. In 2009, while wading through the Rolling Stones' London archive sent to him on hard disc following transfer from tape, Don Was spotted this earlier version of *Tumbling Dice* (* a - 3.17). It was re-mixed and engineered to enhance the sound quality from an already-heard bootleg tape. As such it appeared on the EXILE extras disc which was mixed at Bob Clearmountain's Mix This! Studios in December 2009.

497. DANCING IN THE LIGHT (Jagger, Richard) 4.22
March - May 1970; September - November; December 2009: Place: Rolling Stones Mobile, Stargroves, Newbury Olympic Sound Studios, London, England; One East Studio, New York, Henson Studios, Village Recording; Mix This!, Los Angeles, USA.
Rolling Stones with Jimmy Miller.
Producer: Jimmy Miller, Don Was, The Glimmer Twins.
Engineer: Glyn Johns; Additional Engineering and Editing: Krish Sharma; Mixed by Bob Clearmountain.
Other Production: Andy Johns, Keith Harwood.
UK CD EXILE ON MAIN ST (EXTRA TRACKS): 17 May 2010: No. 1 - 10 weeks
USA CD EXILE ON MAIN ST (EXTRA TRACKS): 18 May 2010: No. 1 - 3 weeks

Dancing In The Light received a make-over in 2009 for the EXILE re-release. The original instrumental bootleg was put forward by Don Was as a potential track to be worked on for the project (* a - 2.44). Mick Jagger was in essence the executive producer and decision-maker for the bonus project. He added lyrics to the track and belatedly recorded his vocals and the outcome was a significant attempt at producing something of that genre. It was unlike Mick to take on a retrospective but he put significant time aside in 2009 to help Don Was to come up with a creditable re-release.
Mick's thoughts were revealed in the documentary *Stones In Exile* released to accompany the EXILE re-release, ". . . that old fucking recording sessions, boring, who gives a shit?" The original track had Ian Stewart on keyboards and the guitar work of Mick Taylor and Keith Richards - there was a juxtaposition of styles between the two Mick Taylor. The song had a riff struggling to get out, while a slide lead played with a country feel was riding on top. Jimmy Miller plays some percussion.
After the opening guitars, the new vocals immediately jump out at you but the delivery is distinctly Mick of recent times, rather than old. Once this inevitability is accepted and allowed for, the track becomes enjoyable but one of the weaker bonus efforts, just like the original out-take. The new lyrics fitted in with the out-take label and were about a lost love: "Sat here in the darkness, you're dancing in the light. You really hit the big time, I really took a dive". While re-mixing the master for the re-release, Don Was felt the bass guitar needed some filling on this recording. He hooked up a bass guitar but there was no way he could follow Bill's note pattern and style, which was unique.

498. WHO AM I? (Jagger, Richard) 3.49
AKA: See I Love You
March - May 1970; 14-15 July 1970: Place: Rolling Stones Mobile, Stargroves, Newbury, England; Olympic Sound Studios, London, England.
Producer: Jimmy Miller.
Engineer: Glyn Johns.
Other Production: Andy Johns, Chris Kimsey.
Bootleg only.

Rightly discarded as substandard, *Who Am I?* is played with a repetitive calypso beat. There are guide vocals from Mick Jagger and Keith Richards.

499. COCKSUCKER BLUES (Jagger, Richard) 3.28
AKA: Schoolboy's Blues, Lonesome Schoolboy
May 1970: Place: Rolling Stones Mobile, Stargroves, Newbury, Olympic Sound Studios, London, England.
Producer: Jimmy Miller.
Engineer: Glyn Johns.
Other Production: Andy Johns.
German Compilation LP THE REST OF THE BEST: December 1983

As the Stones terminated their contract with Decca, an executive reminded them that they still had to deliver one further single. The Stones duly obliged, presenting them with the master tape of *Cocksucker Blues*. They also included a bunch of much unfinished demos and titles named *Midnight In Hoboken, Seaside Blues, Brown Sugar, You Gotta Move* and *Wild Horses*. The music publishing for these numbers, except *You Gotta Move*, is owned by ABKCO records. It was the Stones' last two-finger salute to the record company who, through the years, continually censored album covers and product alike.
Decca were morally obliged not to release the X-rated *Cocksucker Blues*, a slow number featuring just acoustic guitar and Mick Jagger's wailful tones. Mick is the likely acoustic guitar player while the lyrics freely describe homosexual practices. The track was later retitled *Schoolboy Blues* when it was included in the stage production of The Trials of Oz by Geoff Robertson. Original demos were recorded in the mobile unit at Stargroves. Chris Kimsey thinks it unlikely that Olympic was used. There is also an electric version sometimes called *Schoolboy's Blues* (* a - 5.05).
In 1984, the German second edition box set of Decca material contained a bonus single featuring *Cocksucker Blues*. It was available for a short period and then, in 1985, was discontinued and Decca in Hamburg declined to comment. There was a session at Olympic early in May 1969 for Howlin' Wolf, who wanted to record a London-based album of covers of his older material. Those involved with the sessions were the rhythm unit of Charlie Watts and Bill Wyman, Ian Stewart on piano and Hubert Sumlin on guitar.
Other contributors were Eric Clapton, Steve Winwood, Lafayette Leake, John Simon, Phil Upchurch, Joe Miller, Jordan Sandke and Dennis Lansing. Keith Richards did not play but was very welcoming to Hubert Sumlin who did not have a passport. Eric Clapton told him he would not play if he did not attend, so he acquired the necessary document. The album, released in 1971, was THE LONDON HOWLIN' WOLF SESSIONS.

500. CANDLEWICK BEDSPREAD (Jagger, Richard)
16 June - 27 July 1970: Place: Olympic Sound Studios, London, England.
Producer: Jimmy Miller.
Engineer: Glyn Johns.
Unavailable.

Not available on bootleg.

501. **HEY MAMA** (Jagger, Richard)
16 June - 27 July 1970: Place: Olympic Sound Studios, London, England.
Producer: Jimmy Miller.
Engineer: Glyn Johns.
Unavailable.

These two tracks are not available on bootleg.

502. **STOP BREAKING DOWN** (Johnson - credited to 'trad arranged by Jagger, Richard' on album sleeve) 4.34
16 June, 21-31 October 1970; 7 June - October; 30 November - 19 December 1971; 10 January - 28 March 1972: Place: Olympic Sound Studios, London, England; RSM Nellcôte, France; Sunset Sound Studios, LA, USA.
Played Live: 1994
Rolling Stones with Nicky Hopkins.
Producer: Jimmy Miller.
Engineer: Andy Johns, Glyn Johns, Joe Zagarino, Jeremy Gee.
Assistant Engineer: Chris Kimsey, Keith Harwood.
UK LP EXILE ON MAIN ST: 12 May 1972: No. 1 - 16 weeks
USA LP EXILE ON MAIN ST: 22 May 1972: No. 1 - 17 weeks
UK CD EXILE ON MAIN ST (EXTRA TRACKS): 17 May 2010: No. 1 - 10 weeks
USA CD EXILE ON MAIN ST (EXTRA TRACKS): 18 May 2010: No. 1 - 3 weeks

A Robert Johnson classic arranged by Jagger, Richard, Wyman, Taylor and Watts into a semi rhythm 'n' blues mould. The recording for this song started in 1970 with Glyn Johns at the helm - the early version has altered lyrics in the second verse and the fourth verse swapped for the third. Robert Johnson recorded this standard on Sunday 20 June 1937 in Dallas, Texas and his song, released as *Stop Breakin' Down Blues*, also had two versions with different lyrics, both appearing on his THE COMPLETE RECORDINGS anthology. For the Stones cut, the instrumental lead is shared by Mick Taylor, who plays a rasping slide solo, and Ian Stewart's piano. Mick Jagger plays a rhythm guitar piece and blows the life out of his harmonica.
It was Andy Johns' idea to add the harp during the mixing. He felt that the track was one of the best on the album in true traditional white blues style. At the overdub stage, echoed compressed "oohs" were used to good effect. Robert Johnson did not copyright any of his compositions hence the songwriter being credited as a traditional. Mick later bought the rights to make a film about the life of Robert Johnson but it has never materialised. Originally recorded by Glyn Johns, his younger brother took on production for what is a favourite of his, though he remembered that the studio vibe was not always great. Mick really wondered whether recording at the French villa was such a good idea.

503. **LEATHER JACKET** (Taylor) 3.31
16 June - 27 July 1970: Place: Olympic Sound Studios, London, England.
Rolling Stones with Nicky Hopkins.
Producer: Jimmy Miller.
Engineer: Glyn Johns.
Bootleg only.

Leather Jacket is an instrumental, though vocals may have been intended at a later date. The track consists solely of a repetitive melody supplied by Mick Taylor and is obviously unfinished. It was re-worked and released on his debut album MICK TAYLOR in 1979. The lyrics of this later song give a clue as to Mick's mind-set: "You never keep your fortune, that you made in the south of France, all your leather jackets and your faded jeans, all you have left of your rock and roll dreams."

504. **ALL DOWN THE LINE (ELECTRIC)** (Jagger, Richard) 4.09
16 June - 27 July, 21 - 31 October 1970; September - November; December 2009: Place: Olympic Sound Studios, London, England; One East Studio, New York, Henson Studios, Village Recording; Mix This!, Los Angeles, USA.
Rolling Stones with Nicky Hopkins.
Producer: Jimmy Miller, Don Was, The Glimmer Twins.
Engineer: Glyn Johns; Additional Engineering and Editing: Krish Sharma; Mixed by Bob Clearmountain.
Other Production: Andy Johns, Chris Kimsey.
UK e-Single: 3 May 2010
Japan CD EXILE ON MAIN ST (EXTRA TRACKS): 19 May 2010

Collectors had to be quick to pick up this free internet download available through amazon.co.uk - it was there for just one week. Alternatively they could purchase the Japanese album version of the EXILE ON MAIN ST re-release containing this track. It had not been heard before and had very different unfinished lyrics with shouted vocals. The style of the song was almost country, with guitars picking their way rather than sliding and the piano very prominent.

505. **SWEET VIRGINIA** (Jagger, Richard) 4.26
30 June, 20 July, 21 - 31 October 1970; 7 June - October; 30 November - 19 December 1971; 10 January - 28 March 1972: Place: Olympic Sound Studios, London, England; RSM Nellcôte, France; Sunset Sound Studios, LA, USA.
Played Live: 1972, 1973, 1994, 1995, 1999, 2002, 2003, 2005, 2007
Rolling Stones with Bobby Keys, Jim Price.
Producer: Jimmy Miller.
Engineer: Andy Johns, Glyn Johns, Zagarino, Jeremy Gee.
Other Production: Andy Johns, Chris Kimsey.

UK LP EXILE ON MAIN ST: 12 May 1972: No. 1 - 16 weeks
USA LP EXILE ON MAIN ST: 22 May 1972: No. 1 - 17 weeks
UK CD EXILE ON MAIN ST (EXTRA TRACKS): 17 May 2010: No. 1 - 10 weeks
USA CD EXILE ON MAIN ST (EXTRA TRACKS): 18 May 2010: No. 1 - 3 weeks

A growing library of songs was being stored for additional work and *Sweet Virginia* may even have originated from 1969 sessions. The earlier out-take, probably from the 1970 session, has a different vocal style and a magnificent sax solo by Bobby Keys (* a - 4.23). Keith Richards' fraternisation with country and western music was evident at the "Jungle Disease" sessions - while band members were arriving or eating, he was usually seen playing "cowboy" songs. Engineer Andy Johns heard the outcome and was insistent that Keith should put out an album of his own songs. Keith claimed, though, that he would request the services of the band, thereby defeating the original purpose with a quasi-Stones product, a distorted logic which meant only the occasional release of a potential country classic. Ian Stewart managed to regain the piano seat momentarily from Nicky Hopkins on this pure country song, which stood apart from the other tracks on EXILE. He thought it was one of the outstanding EXILE tracks, along with *Loving Cup*. When recording *Sweet Virginia* in the south of France, one of the backing singers may have been Gram Parsons. An alternate mix lacking backing vocals is also available (* b - 4.32). It received full media attention via Wolfman Jack, the famous American disc-jockey. He played *Sweet Virginia* on his AM prime-network radio station KDAY. The song's reference to drugs with "speed", "shit" and popping pills ensured an air-wave hit with the youth, but it remained as an album cut only. Nashville survived to live another day!

506. SHINE A LIGHT (Jagger, Richard) 4.17
AKA: Get A Line On You
23 July 1970; 7 June - October; 30 November - 19 December 1971; 10 January - 28 March 1972: Place: Olympic Sound Studios, London, England; RSM Nellcôte, France; Sunset Sound Studios, LA, USA.
Played Live: 1995, 1997, 1998, 1999, 2006, 2007
Rolling Stones with Nicky Hopkins, Bobby Keys, Jim Price, Billy Preston, Clydie King, Joe Green, Venetta Fields, Jesse Kirkland, Jimmy Miller.
Producer: Jimmy Miller.
Engineer: Andy Johns, Glyn Johns, Joe Zagarino, Jeremy Gee.
Other Production: Andy Johns, Chris Kimsey.
UK LP EXILE ON MAIN ST: 12 May 1972: No. 1 - 16 weeks
USA LP EXILE ON MAIN ST: 22 May 1972: No. 1 - 17 weeks
UK CD EXILE ON MAIN ST (EXTRA TRACKS): 17 May 2010: No. 1 - 10 weeks
USA CD EXILE ON MAIN ST (EXTRA TRACKS): 18 May 2010: No. 1 - 3 weeks

The song had begun to transform from *Get A Line On You* to more of a gospel version when it was re-worked for the EXILE album. Featuring the expertise of Billy Preston on organ and piano, *Shine A Light* is essentially the anthem of the album. It incorporates gospel tones, torn images and sexual failings, all so prevalent on the album. It is played with a reggae beat and combines the talents of guitarist Mick Taylor, who contributes bass guitar as well as lead solo after solo and the undoubted rising star of the company, Billy Preston. At the mixing stage in Los Angeles, Venetta Fields recalls Mick Jagger was very tired when she recorded her vocals. He just wanted the session done and trusted the singers to do their thing.

507. ROLL OVER BEETHOVEN (Berry) ✎ 2.12
7 October 1970: Place: Grugahalle, Essen, Germany.
Rolling Stones with Bobby Keys, Jim Price.
Bootleg only.

Mick Jagger's relationship with Marianne Faithfull finally faltered during 1970. In late 1969, Mick had been courting a singer and dancer, Marsha Hunt, and she was expecting Mick's baby, Karis, in November 1970, although at the time that news was kept out of the press. The film *Ned Kelly* was released to lacklustre reviews in London and even Mick found a reason not to attend the opening night. STICKY FINGERS was well on its way so the next step was to tour Europe for the first time for more than three years. The twin Texan horns of Bobby Keys and Jim Price complemented the on-stage sound.
On the back of the release of the live album GET YER YA YA'S OUT in early September, the Stones started the tour in Malmo, Sweden, on 30 August, going on to Finland, Denmark, Germany, France, Austria and Italy before returning to France and Germany and finishing in the Netherlands on 9 October. The support artists were Buddy Guy and Junior Wells, except for the Amsterdam gig when they were joined by Stephen Stills on piano. Buddy Guy was a well-respected musician, having previously played with blues legends Willie Dixon, Otis Rush, Otis Span, Sonny Boy Williamson and Sonny Turner. He was also admired by likes of Jimi Hendrix and Eric Clapton.
During 1970, Buddy Guy and Junior Wells were recording with Ahmet Ertegun and Eric for the album BUDDY GUY & JUNIOR WELLS PLAY THE BLUES and Clapton joined Buddy on stage during one of the concerts. Buddy was one of those inspiring artists who was able to metamorphose the blues into electric rock and roll in a style that people like Eric, Jimi, Jimmy Page and Stevie Ray Vaughan had used as their musical platform.
This was the first Stones tour to include other stage personnel in order to enhance the sound - brass instrumentation was a standard part of the set on numbers like *Live With Me, Honky Tonk Women* and *Brown Sugar*. Mick Taylor's first European tour allowed him to stretch his identity, adding some improvisation to his reliable and precise guitar playing. The Stones included three Chuck Berry numbers on the tour - *Little Queenie* was well rehearsed and *Let It Rock* was played for the first time, as was the rock and rolling *Roll Over Beethoven* which, replaced *Carol* in the set list. The number sounded a little stilted as though the band were not quite comfortable with it - this also happened with their cover of *Chantilly Lace* in 1982.
Unique film footage exists from the Essen show and the tour was a relatively quiet affair, marred only by rioting and arrests in Milan, Italy on 1 October. Due to huge transportation costs, it would only break even and lessons would be learned. When the Stones rolled into Paris on 22 September 1970, Mick was introduced to Bianca Perez Morena de Macias for the first time and, such was the strong mutual attraction, that Bianca joined the tour for some of the last dates. Separate hotel rooms were booked, which emphasised the seriousness of the situation, and they started to live together at Stargroves after the tour finished.

508. **RED HOUSE** (Hendrix)
21 October - November 1970: Place: Rolling Stones Mobile, Stargroves, Newbury, Olympic Sound Studios, London, England.
Producer: Jimmy Miller.
Engineer: Glyn Johns.
Other Production: Andy Johns.
Unavailable.

Jimi Hendrix died of a sleeping pill overdose in London on 18 September 1970. This track was recorded only a few months later after his death but has not been made available.

509. **BITCH** (Jagger, Richard) 3.37
21 October - November 1970: Place: Rolling Stones Mobile, Stargroves, Newbury, Olympic Sound Studios, London, England
Played Live: 1971, 1972, 1973, 1989, 1990, 1997, 1998, 1999, 2002, 2003, 2005, 2006, 2007
Rolling Stones with Bobby Keys, Jimmy Miller, Jim Price.
Producer: Jimmy Miller.
Engineer: Glyn Johns, Andy Johns, Chris Kimsey.
Assistant Engineer: Keith Harwood.
UK B-side Brown Sugar: 16 April 1971, June 1984
UK LP STICKY FINGERS: 23 April 1971: No. 1 - 25 weeks
USA LP STICKY FINGERS: 30 April 1971: No. 1 - 26 weeks
USA B-side Brown Sugar: 7 May 1971
UK Compilation LP MADE IN THE SHADE: 6 June 1975: No. 14 - 12 weeks
USA Compilation LP MADE IN THE SHADE: 6 June 1975: No. 6 - 9 weeks
UK Compilation LP TIME WAITS FOR NO ONE - ANTHOLOGY 1971 - 1977: 1 June 1979
UK Compilation LP JUMP BACK THE BEST OF THE ROLLING STONES '71 - '93: 22 November 1993: No. 16 - 26 weeks
USA Compilation CD JUMP BACK THE BEST OF THE ROLLING STONES '71 - '93: 24 August 2004: No. 30 - 58 weeks
UK CD box set THE ROLLING STONES SINGLES - 1968 - 1971: 28 February 2005
USA CD box set THE ROLLING STONES SINGLES - 1968 - 1971: 1 March 2005
UK CD box set THE SINGLES COLLECTION 1971-2006: 45 X 45s: 11 April 2011
USA CD box set THE SINGLES COLLECTION 1971-2006: 45 X 45s: 26 April 2011
UK Vinyl B-side Brown Sugar: 16 April 2011

The Keith Richards/Bobby Keys partnership, that had started the year before on *Live With Me* and more recently on *Brown Sugar*, proved fruitful on *Bitch*. The track again centres on one of Keith's famous riffs but, on this occasion Jim Price was used to enhance the brass sound on trumpet. He was a friend of Bobby Keys, who had recently accompanied him on a Delaney and Bonnie tour. The brass meshed with the guitars compulsively, following them rather than playing independently. It would not have been the same without the thrust of brass, similar to another rhythm guitar on the cut.
The backing track was done at Olympic and the overdubs with brass were added at Stargroves. Originally the song lacked any involvement by Keith until he listened to and, according to Andy Johns, transformed the track into what we hear today. *Bitch* was good enough to merit its own single status but, due to some "sex" comments, was banned from the airwaves. The song was misunderstood since Mick Jagger was bemoaning the fact that love was a "bitch" rather than that he fancied a "bitch" - "when you lay me out, my heart is beating louder than a big bass drum". Mick Taylor's lead solo tears from the blocks following the last verse as the "hey hey's" come in.
An early out-take exists with guide vocals (* a - 3.39) and another near-complete version ends abruptly when the tape snags (* b - 2.24), the latter being from the Glyn Johns' Working Tapes and includes re-starts of *Bitch* up to the second verses. The released single version has a slightly different mix (* c - 3.42). *Bitch* has been played as an occasional tour favourite since.

510. **SWEET BLACK ANGEL** (Jagger, Richard) 2.58
AKA: **Black Angel, Bent Green Needles**
21 October - November 1970; 7 June - October; 30 November - 19 December 1971; 10 January - 28 March 1972: Place: Rolling Stones Mobile, Stargroves, Newbury, Olympic Sound Studios, London, England; RSM Nellcôte, France; Sunset Sound Studios, LA, USA.
Played Live: 1972
Rolling Stones with 'Amyl Nitrate' (Richard 'Didymus' Washington), Jimmy Miller.
Producer: Jimmy Miller.
Engineer: Andy Johns, Glyn Johns, Joe Zagarino, Jeremy Gee.
Other Production: Chris Kimsey, Keith Harwood.
UK B-side Tumbling Dice: 14 April 1972
USA B-side Tumbling Dice: 15 April 1972
UK LP EXILE ON MAIN ST: 12 May 1972: No. 1 - 16 weeks
USA LP EXILE ON MAIN ST: 22 May 1972: No. 1 - 17 weeks
UK CD EXILE ON MAIN ST (EXTRA TRACKS): 17 May 2010: No. 1 - 10 weeks
USA CD EXILE ON MAIN ST (EXTRA TRACKS): 18 May 2010: No. 1 - 3 weeks
UK CD box set THE SINGLES COLLECTION 1971-2006: 45 X 45s: 11 April 2011
USA CD box set THE SINGLES COLLECTION 1971-2006: 45 X 45s: 26 April 2011

Jimmy Miller provides a hypnotic percussive beat full of Caribbean flavour on this simple acoustic song. Mick Jagger saunters on the harmonica and a touch of "the Brian Jones sound" is created by "Amyl Nitrate" on the marimba. "Amyl", alias Richard "Didymus" Washington (a member of the Dr John Band), was not enamoured at all by the end product, concerned more by the lack of a personal credit on the album cover rather than the reference to a drug. The latter may have stemmed from the working title for the song, which started its life during the STICKY FINGERS sessions but is unavailable as an out-take.

At a concert on the North American Tour, on 24 June 1972, *Sweet Black Angel* was sympathetically dedicated to the exploits of black militant Angela Davis, who championed the causes of blacks in jail - it was on the day that she was released following a framed "conspiracy to murder" charge. One verse of the lyrics refer to "Ten Little Niggers" which was a literary reference to the title of Agatha Christie's 1939 book which was quickly re-titled to "Ten Little Indians" and related the mystery tale of ten strangers who on an island disappeared one by one. The authorities wanted Angela Davis to be one of the ten little niggers that would fall off the wall, just like the ten green bottles or the original ten little injuns. Mick Jagger argued, "Ten little niggers sitting on the wall, her brothers been falling, falling one by one. For a judge's murder in a judge's court, now the judge he going to judge her for all that he's worth." *Sweet Black Angel* became a foretaste of the album as it was placed on the flip-side of *Tumbling Dice*.

The song was captured on the slowest side of the double LP, Mick Jagger arguing that EXILE was an album of four single sides and should not be played collectively but in 20-minute bursts. An instrumental version of *Sweet Black Angel*, supposedly recorded on the lawn at Stargroves, is available, featuring Jimmy Miller's percussion skills, harmonica and a hard-working Bill Wyman on bass. (* a - 3.00)

511. SHAKE YOUR HIPS (Moore) 2.59
AKA: Hip Shake
21-31 October 1970; 7 June - October; 30 November - 19 December 1971; 10 January - 28 March 1972: Place: Olympic Sound Studios, London, England; RSM Nellcôte, France; Sunset Sound Studios, LA, USA.
Rolling Stones with Bobby Keys, Jim Price.
Producer: Jimmy Miller
Engineer: Andy Johns, Glyn Johns, Joe Zagarino, Jeremy Gee.
Other Production: Chris Kimsey, Keith Harwood.
UK LP EXILE ON MAIN ST: 12 May 1972: No. 1 - 16 weeks
USA LP EXILE ON MAIN ST: 22 May 1972: No. 1 - 17 weeks
UK CD EXILE ON MAIN ST (EXTRA TRACKS): 17 May 2010: No. 1 - 10 weeks
USA CD EXILE ON MAIN ST (EXTRA TRACKS): 18 May 2010: No. 1 - 3 weeks

This Slim Harpo (the late James Moore) composition is played in rockabilly fashion. Charlie Watts conservatively tick-tacks the rhythm throughout on the drum rim, while the lead guitars interweave authentic 50s sounds. Mick Jagger warbles on the harmonica as the song fades out. It was recorded first at Olympic Studios, or possibly Stargroves, in 1970, but really received the treatment at the EXILE sessions in France the following year. The phrasing on the vocals has all of Jagger's hallmark qualities - well accentuated but not over performed.

The Stones' vocal style was very much to use Mick as part of the songs instrumentation. Some lyrics were hardly understood at all as they would be lower in the mix or gutturally obscured deliberately. *Hip Shake* was a perfect accompaniment, sandwiched between *Rip This Joint* and *Casino Boogie*. An early, slightly extended version, has a lead electric guitar filling another minute until the band peter out (* 4 - 11).

512. TRAVELLIN' MAN (Jagger, Richard, Taylor) 5.58
21-31 October 1970: Place: Olympic Sound Studios, London, England.
Rolling Stones with Nicky Hopkins.
Producer: Jimmy Miller.
Engineer: Glyn Johns.
Other Production: Chris Kimsey, Keith Harwood.
Bootleg only.

An up-tempo number used by Mick Taylor to whip his guitar into action. He plays a lengthy solo which ducks and dives for the duration of the track. Nicky Hopkins plays organ and Mick Jagger indicates that the track was unfinished by doing his guideline vocals.

513. POTTED SHRIMPS (Jagger, Richard) 4.12
21-31 October 1970: Place: Olympic Sound Studios, London, England.
Rolling Stones with Nicky Hopkins.
Producer: Jimmy Miller.
Engineer: Glyn Johns.
Other Production: Chris Kimsey, Keith Harwood.
Bootleg only.

Another instrumental, this time featuring a Keith Richards' riff, with an air of familiarity, extracted from his extensive repertoire. It worried Keith that a riff he thought to be new may in fact have been a sound taken from his subconscious. The sessions that produced these tracks were strongly influenced by Mick Taylor. It is his wah-wah lead guitar that rocks most of the take against the piano playing of Nicky Hopkins. Charlie Watts was beginning to sound like a heavy rock drummer, pounding to keep up with the electric melodies.

514. TRIDENT JAM (Jagger, Richard, Taylor) 3.43
AKA: Untitled Instrumental, Untitled Jam
21-31 October 1970: Place: Olympic Sound Studios, London, England.
Producer: Jimmy Miller.
Engineer: Glyn Johns.
Other Production: Chris Kimsey, Keith Harwood.
Bootleg only.

A guitarist work-out, which looks to be another Mick Taylor jam. It was possibly recorded at the Trident Studios, in West London, where the first eight-track facility had even tempted The Beatles out of Abbey Road to record *Hey Jude*. During the early 70s, Trident was used extensively by Queen, Elton John, David Bowie and T. Rex. In 1970 Mick Jagger recorded there with Dr John. There was a bootleg release named the TRIDENT MIXES which encompasses a range of tracks from 1968 to 1970 - a very confused era for bootleg recordings.

515. SILVER TRAIN (Jagger, Richard) 4.26
21-31 October 1970; 25 November - 21 December 1972; 7 May - June 1973: Place: Olympic Sound Studios, London, England; Dynamic Sounds, Kingston, Jamaica; Olympic Sound Studios, Island Studios, London, England.
Played Live: 1973
Producer: Jimmy Miller.
Engineer: Andy Johns, Glyn Johns.
Assistant Engineer: Carlton Lee, Howard Kilgour, Doug Bennett, Chris Kimsey, Keith Harwood.
UK B-side Angie: 20 August 1973
USA B-side Angie: 28 August 1973
UK LP GOATS HEAD SOUP: 31 August 1973: No. 1 - 14 weeks
USA LP GOATS HEAD SOUP: 12 September 1973: No. 1 - 19 weeks
UK CD box set THE SINGLES COLLECTION 1971-2006: 45 X 45s: 11 April 2011
USA CD box set THE SINGLES COLLECTION 1971-2006: 45 X 45s: 26 April 2011

Mick Jagger and Keith Richards wrote *Silver Train* in 1970 so it is probably the same vintage as its "sister", *All Down The Line*. An out-take is available which illustrates how the earlier version had a different vocal delivery without harmonica and, because of more acoustic instrumentation, lacked the guitar punch of the final take (* a - 3.36). It also had unfinished lyrics and played on the "and I did not know her name" as if that was all right then.

A second out-take from 1973, offering a slightly different mix of the final cut (* b - 4.36), is closer to the final release with backing vocals. Johnny Winter, a talented white bluesman, got wind of the song and recorded it for single release in the Spring of 1973 for his album ALIVE AND WELL, which also includes *Let It Bleed*. It pre-empted the Stones' version which appeared as a flip-side antidote to the *Angie* single. Ian Stewart is hard rocking on piano while Mick honks an aggressive harp and plays more than a good lick or two of electric guitar and Charlie Watts thumps out a glorious back beat.

The bass role was probably taken by Keith Richards or Mick Taylor, the latter showing he liked the song as he recorded it for one of his later solo projects. The guitars of Mick Taylor on slide and Mick and Keith's rhythms all move furiously on what is a well-heeled southbound blues rocker. The final mix is with harmonica and an added guitar but without saxophone. The backing track was used with live vocals for the Don Kirshner's Rock Concert programme, filmed by Michael Lindsay Hogg in July 1973 and broadcast 29 September that year.

516. SWAY (Jagger, Richard) 3.52
21 October - November 1970; January 1971: Place: Rolling Stones Mobile, Stargroves, Newbury, Olympic Sound Studios; Island Studios, Trident Studios, London, England.
Played Live: 2005, 2006, 2007
Rolling Stones with Nicky Hopkins, Paul Buckmaster.
Producer: Jimmy Miller.
Engineer: Glyn Johns, Andy Johns, Chris Kimsey, Keith Harwood.
Strings: Paul Buckmaster.
UK LP STICKY FINGERS: 23 April 1971: No. 1 - 25 weeks
USA LP STICKY FINGERS: 30 April 1971: No. 1 - 26 weeks
USA B-side Wild Horses: 12 June 1971
UK CD box set THE ROLLING STONES SINGLES - 1968 - 1971: 28 February 2005
USA CD box set THE ROLLING STONES SINGLES - 1968 - 1971: 1 March 2005
UK CD box set THE SINGLES COLLECTION 1971-2006: 45 X 45s: 11 April 2011
USA CD box set THE SINGLES COLLECTION 1971-2006: 45 X 45s: 26 April 2011

Nicky Hopkins was rested on STICKY FINGERS, following his hefty contribution to the BEGGARS BANQUET and LET IT BLEED albums. *Sway* is the only track he appeared on, playing piano with Buckmaster's orchestra and leaving Ian Stewart to cope with Jim Price, Billy Preston and Jimmy Dickinson on the other cuts. Mick Jagger would often ask Nicky to provide what he called "diamond tiaras" to add magic dust to a session and this a fine example, from either Island or Trident Studios, in early 1971.

Mick Taylor uses his Gibson Les Paul to display some searing solo guitar work, a job with which Keith Richards felt uncomfortable. Keith was used to laying down riffs and providing the band with its unique rhythm while Mick Taylor was to add a heavier virtuoso dimension, as demonstrated on *Sway*. With Mick Taylor playing slide and lead together and Mick Jagger on rhythm, *Sway* was predominantly a Jagger, Taylor song. Taylor was told by Jagger that he would get a songwriting credit and was disappointed when he saw the cover . . . Keith helped out on vocals.

The origins of the track came from the mobile at Stargroves while the light orchestra arrangements and vocals were over-dubbed at Olympic. It is a roguish, swaggering song, full of loathing and not shedding a tear for those in the "burial ground", taken by the ways of "demon life". There is an alternate take and mix of *Sway*, without the final 15-second guitar solo and more of Keith's backing vocals, which was released as the B-side to *Wild Horses* (* a - 3.33).

Internet fan websites helped convince the band that the song should be played live and eventually it was, on the 2005 A BIGGER BANG tour. There is a great version of *Sway* performed by Mick Taylor on Carla Olson's 1991 live album TOO HOT FOR SNAKES, recorded at The Roxy in Los Angeles in March 1990. Other Stones songs recorded with Carla were *Winter*, *Silver Train* and *You Gotta Move*.

517. BROWN SUGAR (Jagger, Richard) 4.05
18 December 1970: Place: Olympic Sound Studios, London, England.
Rolling Stones with Eric Clapton, Bobby Keys, Al Kooper.
Producer: Jimmy Miller.
Engineer: Glyn Johns, Chris Kimsey, Alan O'Duffy.
Bootleg only.

Jimmy Miller announced a joint birthday party at the Olympic Studio for Keith Richards and Bobby Keys. Axe hero Eric Clapton was invited and soon the party developed into a jam session. This was fuelled by some hash cookies, with even the normally sober engineer Alan O'Duffy suffering from the consequences. Chris Kimsey ran the tapes for the session, during which the camaraderie would have been good because Eric had been on tour with Derek & The Dominos in 1970, with Bobby as the saxophone player. Although he was at the party, George Harrison declined to play. The tapes managed to cover this unique version of *Brown Sugar* and other blues jams and the result has always been classed as a unique piece of live studio work. The atmosphere is great, Al Kooper participating with a rhythm guitar piece, but the significant contribution was the sound of the slide guitar, purportedly added by Eric Clapton.
It is a distinctive, rasping performance, which may have been given by Eric, but he was not known for slide playing (Duane Allman starred on *Layla*) so could it have been Mick Taylor or, according to Chris Kimsey, even George Harrison, despite his denial? Keith is heard predominantly on the vocals for nobody had the heart to turn down his level! Although obviously a bit rough, the spontaneity caused the Stones to wonder if it should be released officially. Keith told Al that this would be the case but, technically, it was not as good as the original recorded in Muscle Shoals so this version remained on Olympic's dusty shelves. In January 1971, the STICKY FINGERS album was completed and mastered, with some minor overdubs, between the Trident Studios or Island Studios in London.

518. LET IT ROCK (Anderson) 2.47
13 March 1971: Place: RS Mobile, Leeds University, Leeds, England.
Rolling Stones with Nicky Hopkins, Bobby Keys, Jim Price.
Producer: Glyn Johns.
Assisted by: Rod Thear; Technical Assistant: Mick McKenna.
UK B-side Brown Sugar: 16 April 1971
German Single: January 1972
USA CD LP ROLLING STONES RARITIES 1971-2003: 22 November 2005: No. 76 - 6 weeks
UK CD LP ROLLING STONES RARITIES 1971-2003: 28 November 2005
UK CD box set THE SINGLES COLLECTION 1971-2006: 45 X 45s: 11 April 2011
UK Vinyl B-side Brown Sugar: 16 April 2011
USA CD box set THE SINGLES COLLECTION 1971-2006: 45 X 45s: 26 April 2011

In the meltdown from the end of Decca and Allen Klein, Mick Jagger had met Prince Rupert Loewenstein, who was managing director of the merchant bank Leopold Joseph. He agreed to handle the Stones' financial affairs which were in a mess, although each band member had done rather well in property . It was no coincidence that, to make ends meet, the proceeds from the 1969 USA and 1970 European tours had been deposited into a Swiss bank account, far away from Allen Klein's hands. With unpaid tax going back almost to the time when the band started, they were, for all intents and purposes, bankrupt. Prince Rupert recommended that, to pay back the arrears and avoid the punitive 83% tax and 15% non-earned surcharge, they would have to leave the country before the end of the tax year on 5 April 1971. He suggested that they move to France so the short, nine-date tour in March 1971, which was run by Marshall Chess, was billed as a "Good Bye Britain" farewell and thank you to the English fans who had not seen them play since 1969. The Groundhogs were the support act and, as well as Bobby Keys and Jim Price, the Stones and Ian Stewart were joined by Nicky Hopkins on piano - his first time on tour with the band.
Some reaction to the concerts was not favourable - the fans felt deserted and demanded to know the real state of affairs. As a compromise, the British were rewarded not only with this tour but also by way of a souvenir, *Let It Rock* being coupled (only in Britain) with *Bitch* on the flip-side of the new single *Brown Sugar*. It charted at No. 2 in the UK, kept off the top by Dawn's *Knock Three Times,* but gained another No. 1 in the USA. On the Spanish release of STICKY FINGERS, *Let It Rock* was put on the album instead of *Sister Morphine. Let It Rock* was also released as an A-sided Rolling Stones label single, with *Blow With Ry* as the B side, in January 1972, for a German charity in aid of Release and drug rehabilitation.
On the other side of the tax year the Stones eventually released *Brown Sugar* and STICKY FINGERS. The tour contained a foretaste of the new album (*Bitch, Can't You Hear Me Knocking, Dead Flowers, Wild Horses* and *Brown Sugar*) but was predominantly based on the maxim of good-time rock 'n' roll. *Let It Rock*, written by Chuck Berry under the pseudonym of Anderson, is a good example. Keith Richards is in hot form on electric guitar, playing Chuck Berry riffs, while lead solos by Mick Taylor bombard the "crawdaddy" senses - the piano and saxophone are also key elements. Nicky Hopkins was invited to make his first live appearances with the band on this tour.
As well as the stereo version released on single for the first time, there is also a mono mix available - an individual shouting for *Paint It Black (*but no "you devil") can be heard at the beginning. Keith reckoned it to be one of Berry's finest works and Chuck agreed, including it in a top ten list of his own compositions. *Satisfaction* has a distinctively different arrangement, the introduction being led by Charlie Watts until a more subtle guitar riff commences, then the brass kicks in with the same style of Otis Redding's arrangement, which Keith had so liked. *Little Queenie* captures the band in a hard-driving boogie frame of mind while Mick Taylor's lead solo during *Dead Flowers* is a significant moment.
The band did not get to grips with *Can't You Hear Me Knocking* during the free-format section and Bobby Keys recalled that the song disintegrated and was one of the few moments when he "died" on stage. The new single *Brown Sugar* is played and Mick reminded Bobby Keys not to improvise but to play it as he did on the record. Recordings from two concerts were bootlegged on the 1971 British tour, the aforementioned Leeds concert on 13 March, courtesy of a live BBC radio broadcast, and the "official" end of tour gig at the Roundhouse, London, the day after. The Leeds concert, named GET YOUR LEEDS LUNGS OUT - a Jagger demand at the start of *Honky Tonk Women* - is a classic bootleg stereo recording of the era.
Allen Klein and Decca released a compilation album titled STONE AGE on 5 March 1971, perhaps to retaliate against the *Cocksucker Blues* single. Mick Jagger, on behalf of the group, took an advertisement in the music papers stating: "Beware! Message from the Rolling Stones re: STONE AGE. We didn't know this record was going to be released. It is, in our opinion below the standard we try to keep up, both in choice of content and cover design". All the group's signatures featured in the advert and the ignominy was compounded by the cover having graffiti doodles on a wall in the style of the rejected (at Decca's request) BEGGARS BANQUET cover.

519. LIVE WITH ME (Jagger, Richard) ✎ 3.50
26 March 1971: Place: Marquee Club, London, England.
Rolling Stones with Nicky Hopkins, Bobby Keys, Jim Price.
Producer: Glyn Johns.
Bootleg only.

The final concert, a two-show finale, one for fans and another for family and friends, was at the Marquee on 26 March 1971. It was a much-needed return to a situation where the band could concentrate on the music, while larger concert halls required a performance event. The shows were filmed for a potential film release titled Ladies & Gentlemen, The Rolling Stones, Live At The Marquee. The shows were not as hot as the provincial gigs, although the atmosphere did bubble over when Keith Richards had a swipe at Marquee owner Harold Pendleton, with his guitar continuing their charged relationship. Mick Jagger had a go at Harold, too, since he had put up a banner behind the stage which was obscuring the cameraman's view. Before playing *Bitch* he said that this was one was "starring Harold Pendleton Junior".
Some individual clips, rather than the entire film, were bought for broadcast in the UK or USA, so it is not widely available. The 40-minute, produced by Derek Randal and directed by Bruce Gowers, did get played in its entirety in Europe, though. Mick was inspired to think about editing a compilation video cassette of all the films recorded of their live performances, including the Crawdaddy Club, concerts in Ireland, the aborted *Gimme Shelter* project and the Marquee club itself. There were tentative plans to promote STICKY FINGERS (which would be scuppered due to visa problems) and expand the tour to Japan in the summer, followed by a visit to USA and Canada in the autumn.

520. DEAD FLOWERS (Jagger, Richard) ✎ 3.58
26 March 1971: Place: Marquee Club, London, England.
Rolling Stones with Nicky Hopkins, Bobby Keys, Jim Price.
Producer: Glyn Johns.
Bootleg only.

521. I GOT THE BLUES (Jagger, Richard) ✎ 3.39
26 March 1971: Place: Marquee Club, London, England.
Rolling Stones with Nicky Hopkins, Bobby Keys, Jim Price.
Producer: Glyn Johns.
Bootleg only.

522. LET IT ROCK (Anderson) ✎ 2.25
26 March 1971: Place: Marquee Club, London, England.
Rolling Stones with Nicky Hopkins, Bobby Keys, Jim Price.
Producer: Glyn Johns.
Bootleg only.

523. MIDNIGHT RAMBLER (Jagger, Richard) ✎ 9.20
26 March 1971: Place: Marquee Club, London, England.
Rolling Stones with Nicky Hopkins, Bobby Keys, Jim Price.
Producer: Glyn Johns.
Bootleg only.

524. (I CAN'T GET NO) SATISFACTION (Jagger, Richard) ✎ 4.45
26 March 1971: Place: Marquee Club, London, England.
Rolling Stones with Nicky Hopkins, Bobby Keys, Jim Price.
Producer: Glyn Johns.
Bootleg only.

525. BITCH (Jagger, Richard) ✎ 4.05
26 March 1971: Place: Marquee Club, London, England.
Rolling Stones with Nicky Hopkins, Bobby Keys, Jim Price.
Producer: Glyn Johns.
Bootleg only.

526. BROWN SUGAR (Jagger, Richard) ✎ 4.16
26 March 1971: Place: Marquee Club, London, England.
Rolling Stones with Nicky Hopkins, Bobby Keys, Jim Price.
Producer: Glyn Johns.
Bootleg only.

In early April 1971, having done their duty in Britain, France beckoned (and called), in particular the French Riviera. Their exile period was brought about by a Special Tax (Surtax) that was introduced in 1967-68 to penalise those who had back-tax issues. Normal tax was 45% for high earners and 50% Surtax was levied - despite any agreement on arrangements for back-tax payments - so it was not worth earning a UK crust. Even the Tory election of Ted Heath, replacing the Harold Wilson Labour administration in June 1970, did nothing to persuade the band to stay, because it would take many years for the tax to become less punitive for high earners.

A press conference was held by the Stones in Cannes on 6 April (the commencement of the new UK tax year) to announce their arrival and also, more importantly, to promote the new "tongue" label with Ahmet Ertegun. In remembering Ahmet, who died in 2006, Mick said that the label negotiations were like a long negotiation over a carpet - a lot of wooing over dinner and drinks: "When Ahmet and I finally agreed on the deal, he was so drunk that he fell over backward in his chair. That was the deal clincher!"

STICKY FINGERS went to number one both sides of the Atlantic, while *Brown Sugar* topped the US charts but was kept off the No. 1 slot in the UK by Marc Bolan and T Rex's *Hot Love*. To continue the publicity and press spree, Mick Jagger formally hitched himself to Bianca Perez Morena de Macias in a Roman Catholic fisherman's chapel in St. Tropez on 12 May, 1971. Bianca, Nicaraguan by birth and an aspiring model/socialite, agreed to marry Mick just eight months after their first meeting in Paris. In July, Mick announced that Bianca was expecting their child in October but denied it had been a shotgun wedding.

The guests who descended on the French Riviera included John Lennon, Paul McCartney, Ringo Starr, Eric Clapton, Terry Reid, Stephen Stills, Keith Moon, Nicky Hopkins, Kenney Jones, Ron Wood and his wife Krissie. It was there that Ronnie met Bobby Keys for the first time, in a bathroom along with Keith Richards - say no more.

Keith, desperate to get back to work, had the mobile unit installed at his villa in Villefranche-sur-Mer. The mobile had been commissioned by the Stones in 1968 under Ian Stewart's control and was designed by Glyn Johns and Helios Electronics. It recorded in 16-track as opposed to Olympic's 8-track studio, a process which became useful later to identify recording eras. Helios was a company run by Dick Swettenham who designed Olympic's studio which paved the way for his creation of the Apple Studios. Helios are still alive today and Paul Weller's 2000 HELIOCENTRIC album was dedicated to their studio. The mobile was first used as an 8-track to record at Stargroves but was also used at Hyde Park before a 16-track upgrade, then used by Led Zeppelin, before it went to Villefranche. The band congregated again, a wholly different unit from their last sessions in October, but judging from their farewell tour they were ready artistically and to burst forth feverishly.

527. LOVING CUP (Jagger, Richard) 4.25
AKA: Give Me A Drink
7 June - October; 30 November - 19 December 1971; 10 January - 28 March 1972: Place: Rolling Stones Mobile, Nellcôte, France; Sunset Sound Studios, LA.
Played Live: 1969, 1972, 2002, 2003, 2006
Rolling Stones with Bobby Keys, Jim Price, Nicky Hopkins, Jimmy Miller, Clydie King, Venetta Fields.
Producer: Jimmy Miller.
Engineer: Andy Johns, Glyn Johns, Joe Zagarino, Jeremy Gee.
UK LP EXILE ON MAIN ST: 12 May 1972: No. 1 - 16 weeks
USA LP EXILE ON MAIN ST: 22 May 1972: No. 1 - 17 weeks
UK CD EXILE ON MAIN ST (EXTRA TRACKS): 17 May 2010: No. 1 - 10 weeks
USA CD EXILE ON MAIN ST (EXTRA TRACKS): 18 May 2010: No. 1 - 3 weeks

Villa Nellcôte, a mansion used by the Nazis in the 1940s, became the headquarters for recording the EXILE album. Dominique Tarlé's book *Exile - The Story of Exile on Main Street*, published in 2001, has some great photos which reflect the recording environment. The front door is at least 15 feet high and the building had tall ceilings with mirrored panelled doors and balconies opening on to palm tree gardens. Maybe it was an exotic venue but the locals wanted a piece of the action. Some were hired domestically and as security but generally there was resentment of the Stones, their lifestyle and the apparently freely-available drugs.
The property was like a hotel, with up to 30 people being accommodated and fed, including Keith Richards and Anita Pallenberg, with son Marlon. They adopted a normal family life, keen to keep to regular day and night hours and visiting local attractions to entertain Marlon. This went on for quite a few weeks. At different times during late spring and early summer other cast members arrived but the sessions did not commence until June, when the honeymoon period was over.
Attendees during the summer included - Mick Taylor and Rose Millar (with daughter Chloe), Rose's brother Robin Millar, Prince "Stash" Klossowski, Nicky Hopkins, "Spanish" Tony Sanchez and Madeleine D'Arcy, Marshall Chess, Ted Newman-Jones (Keith's new guitar roadie), photographer Dominique Tarlé, sometimes Gram Parsons and Gretchen, Jimmy Miller, Andy Johns, Bill Wyman, Charlie and Shirley Watts, Mick Jagger (Bianca was not seen often), Michael Cooper (at times), Michelle Breton (at times), Tommy Weber (good time cad) with wife Susan "Puss" (more than a good friend of Anita), Jim and Carol Price and child and Bobby Keys - even John Lennon, Yoko and Eric Clapton popped down for a while.
Some did not want to stay at the house and lived out of suitcases in rented houses and hotels. Bill and Astrid were in the hills in Grasse, where Nicky Hopkins often opted for the tranquillity rather than his allotted pitch with tearaways Jim Price and Bobby Keys. Charlie was keen to be removed from what he considered the falseness of the French Riviera and lived more than 130 miles away. This meant that he was more often a Monday to Friday session player, going back to the horse territory of the Camargue at weekends. The food was good on the Cote d'Azur, the wine flowed and drugs were abundant, with the sea port of gangland Marseille nearby. The most significant aspect of recording was that it was Keith who determined when and where and with whom. He was the band leader as Mick's mind was elsewhere with Bianca pregnant and he made no effort to join the entourage while she stayed in Paris. A rift of sorts developed between those who wanted to party and those who did not. Recording began, with some tracks being left over from previous sessions. *Loving Cup*, which was written prior to the 1969 Hyde Park concert and was performed there as *Give Me A Drink*, falls into that category, having been considered for recording at the Muscle Shoals sessions in December 1969.
The tone of the song is similar to *Torn And Frayed*. It does not follow the usual macho stance but deals compassionately with a guy who is unable to spill the beans with his girl - perhaps one of Keith's foibles as his current habits lay elsewhere? An extended six-and-a-half minute version from the same session, or from the overdubs at Sunset Sound, seems to have some rolls of steel-type drums played by Jimmy Miller - they are higher in the mix than the released version. It is Bill Wyman on bass and not Mick Taylor as suggested on the sleeve notes.
The female backing vocals of Clydie King and Venetta Fields are also more pronounced on the out-take version - these were certainly added at Sunset Sound. The song is driven by the intricate piano lines from Nicky Hopkins and, towards the end, by the trumpet of Jim Price. Engineer Jeremy (Bear) Gee was recruited by Ian Stewart to assist with the mobile unit. Later the same year, in December he took the unit to Montreux and played a successful role in capturing the sound of heavy rock merchants Deep Purple on their No. 1 album MACHINE HEAD.

528. I'M NOT SIGNIFYING (Jagger, Richard) 3.56
AKA: Ain't Gonna Lie, I Ain't Signifying, Mean Woman Blues, I Ain't Lying
7 June - October 1971; September - November; December 2009: Place: Rolling Stones Mobile, Nellcôte, France; One East Studio, New York, Henson Studios, Village Recording; Mix This!, Los Angeles, USA.
Rolling Stones with Nicky Hopkins, Bobby Keys, Jim Price.
Producer: Jimmy Miller, Don Was, The Glimmer Twins.
Engineer: Glyn Johns; Additional Engineering and Editing: Krish Sharma; Mixed by Bob Clearmountain.
Other Production: Andy Johns.
UK CD EXILE ON MAIN ST (EXTRA TRACKS): 17 May 2010: No. 1 - 10 weeks
USA CD EXILE ON MAIN ST (EXTRA TRACKS): 18 May 2010: No. 1 - 3 weeks

The track started life in the serenity of the English countryside at Stargroves and was known amongst other names as *Ain't Gonna Lie* (* a - 3.39). It is a slow 12-bar blues lightweight in content, featuring Mick Taylor on guitar. Another piano version of the track was recorded and released on the EXILE bonus disc, harmonica being added by Mick Jagger and the song enhanced with upbeat brass in the last minute. A version without harmonica and the brass also exists (* b - 3.46).
Don Was, the producer for the additional instrumentation, wanted to ensure that original musicians were used during the bonus tracks project. *I'm Not Signifying* has much more piano work than *Ain't Gonna Lie* while Mick Taylor's lead guitar stings its way through the 12-bar tune. Other out-takes from the sessions included

experiences from Nellcôte with *Head In The Toilet Blues, Labour Pains* and *Pommes de Terre*, as recalled by Keith Richards in *Life*. He also relates an unhappy visit to a go-kart track where he crashed and badly tore flesh on his back. A doctor said it was vital to keep the wound clean so every day a nurse visited Nellcôte to attend to it and administer a dose of morphine for the pain. Unfortunately, when this treatment was finished, other means of pain relief were sought in ever- increasing quantities.

529. PASS THE WINE (SOPHIA LOREN) (Jagger, Richard) 4.54
AKA: Sophia Loren
7 June - October 1971; September - November; December 2009: Place: Rolling Stones Mobile, Nellcôte, France; One East Studio, New York, Henson Studios, Village Recording; Mix This!, Los Angeles, USA.
Rolling Stones with Nicky Hopkins, Bobby Keys, Jim Price, Jimmy Miller, Lisa Fischer, Cindy Mizelle.
Producer: Jimmy Miller, Don Was, The Glimmer Twins.
Engineer: Glyn Johns; Additional Engineering and Editing: Krish Sharma; Mixed by Bob Clearmountain.
Other Production: Andy Johns.
UK CD EXILE ON MAIN ST (EXTRA TRACKS): 17 May 2010: No. 1 - 10 weeks
USA CD EXILE ON MAIN ST (EXTRA TRACKS): 18 May 2010: No. 1 - 3 weeks

One of the pleasures on the EXILE bonus disc is the track, much-fêted in bootleg history but never heard before, labelled *Sophia Loren*. Don Was, reflecting on the release, said: "that was a joy finding that". The re-work by Mick Jagger and Don Was is a real highlight, the original evidently centring around the piano and sax foundations from Nellcôte. It has a loose calypso groove to it and the newly-recorded vocals do not have a reference to Sophia Loren other than Mick dreaming: "So pass me the wine, baby, and let's make some love".
Sophia was a very desirable Italian film star, well known all over the world, but especially on the French and Italian Riviera. Mick said that the original cut was very long and had to be edited to its five-minute format as *Pass The Wine*. As well as Mick's distinctly modern vocal and harmonica input, Lisa Fischer and Cindy Mizelle overdubbed backing vocals in the period mode. Cindy had not recorded in the Stones' studio before but was involved as backing singer on the STEEL WHEELS tour. She had recorded a joint single with Lisa in 2008. Mick Taylor plays some great BB King-type licks and both he and Nicky Hopkins were great contributors to the song, just economically flicking in the notes as required.

530. VENTILATOR BLUES (Jagger, Richard, Taylor) 3.24
7 June - October; 30 November - 19 December 1971; 10 January - 28 March 1972: Place: Rolling Stones Mobile, Nellcôte, France; Sunset Sound Studios, LA, USA.
Played Live: 1972
Rolling Stones with Bobby Keys, Jim Price, Nicky Hopkins.
Producer: Jimmy Miller.
Engineer: Andy Johns, Glyn Johns, Joe Zagarino, Jeremy Gee.
UK LP EXILE ON MAIN ST: 12 May 1972: No. 1 - 16 weeks
USA LP EXILE ON MAIN ST: 22 May 1972: No. 1 - 17 weeks
UK CD EXILE ON MAIN ST (EXTRA TRACKS): 17 May 2010: No. 1 - 10 weeks
USA CD EXILE ON MAIN ST (EXTRA TRACKS): 18 May 2010: No. 1 - 3 weeks

As the title indicates, the song is a pondering blues track, inspired by the recording conditions in the humid basement where there was a lack of air - Andy Johns described it as 90 per cent humidity. The vents on the floor in the tiny one-fan room were shaped into Nazi swastikas but failed to create air. The guitars became out of tune after just one take and Mick Jagger was less than inspired by the cramped conditions. The song writing team includes for the second time (excluding out-takes) the merits of Mick Taylor - the first occasion on an officially-released album. The music publishing rights are not only credited to Cansel Ltd (as with most EXILE tracks) but also to Mick Taylor. This was due to the main guitar riff having been written by him.
The vocals are not sung in the usual blues mould and the horns contributed by the brass twins, Bobby Keys and Jimmy Price, do not exactly recreate a classic blues sound. However, towards the end, Nicky Hopkins is suitably carried away on the piano and Mick Taylor plays a worthy lead solo while Keith Richards is on slide guitar. In collaborative style, it was Bobby who suggested to Charlie Watts the 2/4 rhythm beat, which he illustrated to Charlie with claps. Keith Richards was pleased at the new dimension that the brass section gave to the Stones sound. He felt also, rather bizarrely, that: "Bobby Keys is the reincarnation of Brian Jones. It's very strange for us because he has these mannerisms. Just the things that he does, the things that he says and the way he is . . . he's very much like Brian. It's like having Brian back in the band again, you know. It's a strange thing." He described this to the Swedish interviewer Tommy Rander in the spring of 1971.

531. FRAGILE (Jagger, Richard)
7 June - October 1971: Place: Rolling Stones Mobile, Nellcôte, France.
Producer: Jimmy Miller.
Unavailable.

This recording has not been made available. It may be associated with the EXILE sessions because it was referred to within the *Cocksucker Blues* film project, when Mick sings a track with lyrics including "it's funny" (not the track on Voodoo Stew). There is even a segment which sounds like the beginnings of *Fool To Cry*.

532. SEPARATELY (Taylor, Richard) 4.18
7 June - October 1971; 25 November - 21 December 1972: Place: Rolling Stones Mobile, Nellcôte, France; Dynamic Sounds, Kingston, Jamaica.
Rolling Stones with Nicky Hopkins.
Producer: Jimmy Miller.
Bootleg only.

This track was recorded initially in Nellcôte. Mick Taylor had learned to play piano by listening to Nicky Hopkins during lulls in the session work. *Separately* is an instrumental which features Nicky on keyboards and the slightly echoed guitar of Mick Taylor, who wrote the track with Keith Richards. Mick Taylor recorded a version with vocals for inclusion on his intended second but unreleased, late 80s album SPECIAL.

533. TORN AND FRAYED (Jagger, Richard) 4.18
7 June - October; 30 November - 19 December 1971; 10 January - 28 March 1972: Place: Rolling Stones Mobile, Nellcôte, France; Sunset Sound Studios, LA, USA.
Played Live: 1972, 2002
Rolling Stones with Al Perkins, Jim Price, Nicky Hopkins.
Producer: Jimmy Miller.
Engineer: Andy Johns, Glyn Johns, Joe Zagarino, Jeremy Gee.
UK LP EXILE ON MAIN ST: 12 May 1972: No. 1 - 16 weeks
USA LP EXILE ON MAIN ST: 22 May 1972: No. 1 - 17 weeks
UK CD EXILE ON MAIN ST (EXTRA TRACKS): 17 May 2010: No. 1 - 10 weeks
USA CD EXILE ON MAIN ST (EXTRA TRACKS): 18 May 2010: No. 1 - 3 weeks

A country rock song, written by Keith Richards, which delves into the mythology of a touring band (a reckless, restless guitar player is hooked on codeine, prescribed by a doctor for a cough, his coat torn and frayed) given that this is a self-mocking display. It may have also portrayed Gram Parsons, who arrived at Nellcôte late in July with his wife Gretchen. He departed sometime at the end of the summer having worn out his welcome by consuming too much of Anita and Keith's drug supply. Keith claims to have written the song for the Olympic engineer Joe Zagarino who contributes the country acoustic. Mick Taylor and Jim Price put down their more familiar instruments to play bass and organ, respectively, while Al Perkins, a friend of Gram Parsons, is featured on steel guitar, a one-off contribution which was made when the album was mixed at Sunset Sound, Hollywood in the Fall of '71.
Al Perkins had a reputation for his steel guitar playing with other country artists such as Don Henley, although his career took off in 1972 when he worked with Stephen Stills and Manassas, The Flying Burrito Brothers, Gram Parsons and Joe Walsh. He brought along a relatively new guitar sold to him by Bakersfield steel player Tom Brunley. His overdub was recorded in the control room at the end of the console, direct into the desk, with Mick Jagger singing the lyrics live to give Al a live feel - his instruction was "do what you do".

534. ALL DOWN THE LINE (Jagger, Richard) 3.50
7 June - October; 30 November - 19 December 1971; 10 January - 28 March 1972: Place: Rolling Stones Mobile, Nellcôte, France; Sunset Sound Studios, LA, USA.
Played Live: 1972, 1973, 1975, 1977, 1978, 1981, 1994, 1995, 1998, 1999, 2002, 2003, 2005, 2006, 2007
Rolling Stones with Bobby Keys, Jim Price, Nicky Hopkins, Jimmy Miller, Kathi McDonald, Bill Plummer.
Producer: Jimmy Miller.
Engineer: Andy Johns, Glyn Johns, Joe Zagarino, Jeremy Gee.
UK LP EXILE ON MAIN ST: 12 May 1972: No. 1 - 16 weeks
USA LP EXILE ON MAIN ST: 22 May 1972: No. 1 - 17 weeks
USA B-side Happy: 14 July 1972
UK Compilation LP TIME WAITS FOR NO ONE - ANTHOLOGY 1971 - 1977: 1 June 1979
UK & USA Vinyl B-side Plundered My Soul (Radio Mix): 12 April 2010
UK e-Single Track Plundered My Soul (Radio Mix): 16 April 2010
UK CD EXILE ON MAIN ST (EXTRA TRACKS): 17 May 2010: No. 1 - 10 weeks
USA CD EXILE ON MAIN ST (EXTRA TRACKS): 18 May 2010: No. 1 - 3 weeks
UK CD box set THE SINGLES COLLECTION 1971-2006: 45 X 45s: 11 April 2011
USA CD box set THE SINGLES COLLECTION 1971-2006: 45 X 45s: 26 April 2011

One of the strong contenders on the album for a single release, it was considered at one time a stronger track than *Tumbling Dice* but it lost the battle and was displaced to the flip-side of *Happy*, a single which was only released in the States. This version is a different mix with an extended introduction and additional slide guitar solo three minutes in, which sounds quite different to the others (* a - 3.53). There is, also, an electric, instrumental version with sax (* b - 4.01) and a near complete mix with less guitar (* c - 3.47).
All Down The Line has since featured as a favourite on most Stones tours and it is easy to see why. It is an infectious, up-beat rocker in the vein of some of their previously successful singles. The sax twins open up the throttle and create the familiar *Brown Sugar* clash with the axe men, Keith Richards and Mick Taylor. Mick supplies the slide guitar licks, Keith plays the open chord chops and pulls. Bill Plummer helps out on double bass later, Bill Wyman plays electric bass, with Jimmy Miller on percussion and a newcomer to the Stones crew, Kathi McDonald, overdubs backing vocals. Kathi was one of Ike and Tina Turner's former Ikettes before playing with Janis Joplin's Big Brother & The Holding Company and Leon Russell before the EXILE session at Sunset Sound.
Bill Plummer overdubbed acoustic and upright bass on four EXILE tracks. Plummer, whose music pedigree was more mainstream jazz, was introduced by Jim Keltner, who played with him on a Basses International album that interested Mick Jagger. He listened to the four tracks and recorded them on a first-take each time for Joe Zagarino, telling John Perry this for his 2000 book *Classic Rock Albums* - Exile On Main St. It was one of the first tracks mixed and completed at Sunset Sound.

535. EXILE INSTRUMENTAL (Jagger, Richard) 7.12
7 June - October 1971: Place: Rolling Stones Mobile, Nellcôte, France.
Producer: Jimmy Miller.
Engineer: Glyn Johns, Andy Johns.
Bootleg only.

An out-take that emerged in 2011 and reported to be found with a bunch of other Exile period tracks that had different cuts of EXILE ON MAIN ST songs (all not available before). The tape had been given to Nicky Hopkins at the conclusion of the Nellcôte sessions. The instrumental has a slide guitar and a typical lead solo from Mick Taylor. There is a solid riff but most pronounced is a beautiful piano melody by Nicky Hopkins. Running at seven minutes it is a great, long-lost gem. Mick Taylor remarked that it was not unusual for just himself, Keith Richards, Jimmy Miller and Nicky to be alone recording and quite a few instrumentals were knocked out in that way.

536. FAST TALKING SLOW WALKING (Jagger, Richard) 6.34
7 June - October 1971; 30 November - 19 December 1971; 25 November - 21 December 1972: Place: Rolling Stones Mobile, Nellcôte, France; Dynamic Sound Studios, Kingston, Jamaica.
Rolling Stones with Billy Preston, Jim Price.
Producer: Jimmy Miller.
Engineer: Glyn Johns, Andy Johns.
Bootleg only.

The 1971 "Tropical Disease" sessions, as they became known due to the hot and sweaty inclement conditions, were in full flow. Mick Jagger advised the New Musical Express at the time that this was a provisional title for the album. The basement and outlying rooms had been temporarily converted into a studio and electronic wires led to the mobile recording unit stationed outside - and to the SNCF railway, where some national grid was used by the RSM generator due to the unreliability of the local facility. The Mobile could be run off one 13-amp 220/240 volt plug if needed.
All true, says Anita Pallenberg to John Perry in his 2000 book *Classic Rock Albums - Exile On Main St.* This simple but effective set-up created a unique laid-back atmosphere - the vin ordinaire (Châteauneuf Du Pape) and music flowed in voluminous quantities, although Mick Jagger felt that the dank conditions affected his voice. Keith Richards reckoned that he could restore some of the tonal qualities after a long session by using Jack Daniels.
The drink habit was costing £500 a week, as was the food to support such a household. Keith asked the band to give him £125 per week each for board and lodging but friends were free! It can't have been all bad because Jimmy Miller reports that, such was the quantity of material, that two double albums could have been created from the available tapes. This out-take, in an Elton John-type, honky tonk vein, was a good natured song that was worthy of release. It was re-recorded with Billy Preston on piano in Jamaica in 1972.

537. TURD ON THE RUN (Jagger, Richard) 2.38
7 June - October; 30 November - 19 December 1971; 10 January - 28 March 1972: Place: Rolling Stones Mobile, Nellcôte, France; Sunset Sound Studios, LA, USA.
Rolling Stones with Nicky Hopkins, Bill Plummer.
Producer: Jimmy Miller.
Engineer: Andy Johns, Glyn Johns, Joe Zagarino, Jeremy Gee.
UK LP EXILE ON MAIN ST: 12 May 1972: No. 1 - 16 weeks
USA LP EXILE ON MAIN ST: 22 May 1972: No. 1 - 17 weeks
UK CD EXILE ON MAIN ST (EXTRA TRACKS): 17 May 2010: No. 1 - 10 weeks
USA CD EXILE ON MAIN ST (EXTRA TRACKS): 18 May 2010: No. 1 - 3 weeks

The problems of recording in a family situation at the villa were evident. Tempers became frayed, the band being particularly annoyed when Keith Richards would disappear for hours as he put his son, Marlon, to bed. He would reappear in the early hours ready to record until dawn. Other band members, bored at the delay, would venture into the night life of either Nice or Monte Carlo. The frustrations were accentuated by Mick Jagger, who disappeared at regular intervals to visit his newly-wedded, mid-term pregnant wife Bianca in Paris. Keith was often upset by this, especially when, the previous night, the recording sessions were reaching new heights. It is surprising, in these circumstances, that such a cohesive album was created and Keith must take much of the early credit. *Turd On The Run* is a short country-style rocker, the upright bass being played by Bill Plummer (overdubbed at Sunset Sound) and the rebel yells at the end creating 50s images. The subject matter is the thematic jungle disease created by a lost relationship - "I lost a lot of love over you" - there were no takers for this bearing in mind the song title, which could have been a Keith jab at Mick.
Two out-takes illustrate the fast pace intended. It is a rockabilly number with Mick featured heavily on harmonica and Charlie Watts cruising tick-tack and hi-hat fashion. One wonders what influence the American band The Flamin' Groovies had over some of the 50s-type sounds on EXILE. The Stones were aware of the Flamin' Groovies because they said that TEENAGE HEAD, released in May 1971, was better than STICKY FINGERS. Certainly the Groovies had got off on the Stones sound on the excellent TEENAGE HEAD and had even used Jim Dickinson, from the Muscle Shoals sessions, to play piano on three numbers.

538. TUMBLING DICE (Jagger, Richard) 3.47
AKA: Good Time Women
7 June - October; 30 November - 19 December 1971; 10 January - 28 March 1972: Place: Rolling Stones Mobile, Nellcôte, France; Sunset Sound Studios, LA, USA.
Played Live: 1972, 1973, 1975, 1976, 1977, 1978, 1981, 1982, 1989, 1990, 1994, 1995, 1997, 1998, 1999, 2002, 2003, 2005, 2006, 2007
Rolling Stones with Bobby Keys, Jim Price, Nicky Hopkins, Clydie King, Venetta Fields, Merry Clayton, Jimmy Miller.
Producer: Jimmy Miller.
Engineer: Andy Johns, Glyn Johns, Joe Zagarino, Jeremy Gee.
Assistant Engineer: Robin Millar.
UK Single: 14 April 1972: No. 5 - 8 weeks
USA Single: 15 April 1972: No. 7 - 9 weeks
UK LP EXILE ON MAIN ST: 12 May 1972: No. 1 - 16 weeks
USA LP EXILE ON MAIN ST: 22 May 1972: No. 1 - 17 weeks
UK Compilation LP MADE IN THE SHADE: 6 June 1975: No. 14 - 12 weeks
USA Compilation LP MADE IN THE SHADE: 6 June 1975: No. 6 - 9 weeks
UK Compilation LP REWIND 1971-1984 (THE BEST OF THE ROLLING STONES): 29 June 1984: No. 45 - 5 weeks
USA Compilation LP REWIND 1971-1984 (THE BEST OF THE ROLLING STONES): 2 July 1984: No. 86 - 11 weeks
UK Compilation LP JUMP BACK THE BEST OF THE ROLLING STONES '71 - '93: 22 November 1993: No. 16 - 26 weeks
UK CD LP FORTY LICKS: 30 September 2002: No. 2 - 45 weeks
USA CD LP FORTY LICKS: 1 October 2002: No. 2 - 50 weeks

USA Compilation CD JUMP BACK THE BEST OF THE ROLLING STONES '71 - '93: 24 August 2004: No. 30 - 58 weeks
UK CD EXILE ON MAIN ST (EXTRA TRACKS): 17 May 2010: No. 1 - 10 weeks
USA CD EXILE ON MAIN ST (EXTRA TRACKS): 18 May 2010: No. 1 - 3 weeks
UK CD box set THE SINGLES COLLECTION 1971-2006: 45 X 45s: 11 April 2011
USA CD box set THE SINGLES COLLECTION 1971-2006: 45 X 45s: 26 April 2011

Tumbling Dice obtained Top 10 positions on both sides of the Atlantic but its spell in the charts was short-lived in comparison with the Stones' previous single successes. Although not a strong single release, *Tumbling Dice* is a convincing album track. Andy Johns does remember that it took more than two weeks to record and produced masses of tape - it may have seemed effortless and impromptu but in fact this was far from the truth. The single sleeve was designed by Ruby Mazur, who focussed on the mouth and tongue, based on John Pasche's initial design, but also included a distinctive two eyes, one winking.

The song rocks along in a relaxed manner but the tempo took ages to get right - Keith Richards plays effortless guitar licks, some Berryesque, and, on this occasion Mick Jagger, who took responsibility for the final mix, is complemented by Clydie King, Venetta Fields and Merry Clayton on backing vocals. Merry was simply credited as a "friend" on the sleeve. Mick contributes a guitar piece and Mick Taylor aids Bill Wyman on his bass lines. Charlie Watts does his firework opening at the beginning before settling back and letting the track roll. Jimmy Miller is also on drums and does the rock and roll climax at the end.

Keith wrote the riff in his front room above the studio and was able to immediately take it downstairs to record. Robin Millar, who was Rose Millar's 19-year-old brother, helped out with tape duties in what he describes as a chaotic recording situation. He was in the south of France for four months and specifically remembers recording *Tumbling Dice*. He was also a distraction to the girls at the house for their down-time!

Keith reckoned that it became his favourite song from EXILE - "I can play that song all night long." The lyrics were partly inspired by Mick's housekeeper in Los Angeles and friends who flew to Las Vegas for the weekend to gamble and play dice - so she knew some terminology. To ensure the mix and sound was radio friendly, they gave a version to KRLA (possibly to music friendly Dave Hull) and got in the car to listen to how it came across. The released version of *Tumbling Dice* is charmingly loose, a knack which was being perfected by another skilfully sloven British group, The Faces, who included Rod Stewart, a certain Ron Wood, and remnants of the Small Faces.

539. I JUST WANT TO SEE HIS FACE (Jagger, Richard) 2.53
AKA: Just Wanna
7 June - October; 30 November - 19 December 1971; 10 January - 28 March 1972: Place: Rolling Stones Mobile, Nellcôte, France; Sunset Sound Studios, LA, USA.
Rolling Stones with Bobby Whitlock, Bill Plummer, Jimmy Miller, Clydie King, Venetta Fields, Jesse Kirkland.
Producer: Jimmy Miller.
Engineer: Andy Johns, Glyn Johns, Joe Zagarino, Jeremy Gee.
UK LP EXILE ON MAIN ST: 12 May 1972: No. 1 - 16 weeks
USA LP EXILE ON MAIN ST: 22 May 1972: No. 1 - 17 weeks
UK CD EXILE ON MAIN ST (EXTRA TRACKS): 17 May 2010: No. 1 - 10 weeks
USA CD EXILE ON MAIN ST (EXTRA TRACKS): 18 May 2010: No. 1 - 3 weeks

Just Wanna (see inset of album cover) fades in from the remnants of *Ventilator Blues*. It is a gospel inspired song, complete with choralists - namely Clydie King, Venetta Fields and Jesse (not Jerry!) Kirkland, the latter a backing singer and songwriter with Billy Preston who had also worked with Quincy Jones. These backing vocals were included at the mixing stage, using the foundations of the initial track recorded at Nellcôte. The original surfaced with the unlikely Keith Richards delivering a haunting melody on a Wurlitzer electric piano and Mick Jagger improvising with some obscure chants, which gives it a real roots black-spell quality. The Wurlitzer could also have been played during overdubs by Bobby Whitlock, who was well known at the time for this electric piano type.

The normal rhythm section of Charlie Watts and Bill Wyman is replaced by the bass of Bill Plummer on acoustic and the electric bass of Mick Taylor. There is no other guitar work and Jimmy Miller plays African-style tom-tom percussion. The production is distinctly cloudy and mudzy giving it a steamy, swampy feel. Don Was was quick to point out that he did not touch the original EXILE album - that feel captured in *Just Wanna* was too precious. However, it was re-mastered (as all re-released albums are) to a certain degree by Stephen Marcussen and Stewart Whitmore. They did not re-master from the original finished product because somehow it did not exist. To authenticate their re-master they used pristine versions of a vinyl copy against the master tapes done for Virgin Records in 1993 and worked with those for the 2010 version. Ironically, Don Was says he assisted Bob Ludwig on the 1993 Virgin re-masters.

540. RIP THIS JOINT (Jagger, Richard) 2.22
7 June - October; 30 November - 19 December 1971; 10 January - 28 March 1972: Place: Rolling Stones Mobile, Nellcôte, France; Sunset Sound Studios, LA, USA.
Played Live: 1972, 1973, 1975, 1976, 1995, 2002, 2003
Rolling Stones with Bill Plummer, Bobby Keys, Jim Price, Nicky Hopkins.
Producer: Jimmy Miller.
Engineer: Andy Johns, Glyn Johns, Joe Zagarino, Jeremy Gee.
UK LP EXILE ON MAIN ST: 12 May 1972: No. 1 - 16 weeks
USA LP EXILE ON MAIN ST: 22 May 1972: No. 1 - 17 weeks
UK Compilation LP MADE IN THE SHADE: 6 June 1975: No. 14 - 12 weeks
USA Compilation LP MADE IN THE SHADE: 6 June 1975: No. 6 - 9 weeks
UK CD EXILE ON MAIN ST (EXTRA TRACKS): 17 May 2010: No. 1 - 10 weeks
USA CD EXILE ON MAIN ST (EXTRA TRACKS): 18 May 2010: No. 1 - 3 weeks

Kick ass and roll - the Stones shift their butts on this two-minute electric rock 'n' roller. Nicky Hopkins pounces on the black and white keys and the sax squeals in surprise, while Bill "winkle pickers Comet" Plummer plays the upright bass. The track's foundation, however, is the enraged guitar work of Keith Richards and the Route 66-type lyrics of Mick Jagger, which travel the States. Ah, let it rock, wham bam, round and round we go in a joint fog! Mention is made of the President, Richard Nixon, and the First Lady, Pat Nixon. It is classic Stones material.

An early unavailable out-take has Keith on vocals and is probably the original version recorded before the overdubs were made. You can also hear a great instrumental, full of slide guitar by Mick Taylor (* a - 2.32). At a tempo of "presto" or approximately 200 beats per minute it is a very fast song which Mick Jagger always considered too speedy.

541. HAPPY (Jagger, Richard) 3.05
7 June - October; 30 November - 19 December 1971; 10 January - 28 March 1972: Place: Rolling Stones Mobile, Nellcôte, France; Sunset Sound Studios, LA, USA.
Played Live: 1972, 1973, 1975, 1976, 1978, 1989, 1990, 1994, 1995, 2002, 2003, 2006, 2007
Rolling Stones with Bobby Keys, Jim Price, Nicky Hopkins, Jimmy Miller.
Producer: Jimmy Miller.
Engineer: Andy Johns, Glyn Johns, Joe Zagarino, Jeremy Gee.
UK LP EXILE ON MAIN ST: 12 May 1972: No. 1 - 16 weeks
USA LP EXILE ON MAIN ST: 22 May 1972: No. 1 - 17 weeks
USA Single: 14 July 1972: No. 22 - 4 weeks
UK Compilation LP MADE IN THE SHADE: 6 June 1975: No. 14 - 12 weeks
USA Compilation LP MADE IN THE SHADE: 6 June 1975: No. 6 - 9 weeks
UK CD LP FORTY LICKS: 30 September 2002: No. 2 - 45 weeks
USA CD LP FORTY LICKS: 1 October 2002: No. 2 - 50 weeks
UK CD EXILE ON MAIN ST (EXTRA TRACKS): 17 May 2010: No. 1 - 10 weeks
USA CD EXILE ON MAIN ST (EXTRA TRACKS): 18 May 2010: No. 1 - 3 weeks
UK CD box set THE SINGLES COLLECTION 1971-2006: 45 X 45s: 11 April 2011
USA CD box set THE SINGLES COLLECTION 1971-2006: 45 X 45s: 26 April 2011

Happy is a simply brilliant rock song, full of optimistic euphoria about having no money: "I need a love to keep me happy". Keith Richards had just been told by Anita Pallenberg that she was pregnant and so it reflects his mood. The song revolves around one of Keith's unique guitar riffs played on an open-G strung slide guitar. He also supplies an overdubbed rhythm guitar and the bass guitar part but, most noticeably, the lead vocal - the first occasion since *You Got The Silver*. Bobby Keys not only contributes some percussion work with Jimmy Miller, but also again teams up with Jim Price to sway some brass sounds and mesh them with Keith's guitar.
It was one of those tracks that fell into place effortlessly and with no apparent explanation. In his autobiography *Life*, Keith refers to it as one of his "incoming" moments. In Victor Bockris' book *Keith Richards*, Keith tells him that the track was recorded one afternoon in four hours, with just Jimmy Miller on drums and Bobby Keys on saxophone. It was a rough sketch that ended up on the album. According to Bill Wyman, the session took place in September, the song later providing the Stones with a Top 30 American hit in July 1972. It was the second US single to be released from the double album but Britain was granted, *Tumbling Dice. Happy* has since become a favourite on tours and, during a long set, it enabled Mick Jagger to rest and catch a quick malt liquor.

542. SOUL SURVIVOR (Jagger, Richard) 3.49
7 June - October; 30 November - 19 December 1971; 10 January - 28 March 1972: Place: Rolling Stones Mobile, Nellcôte, France; Sunset Sound Studios, LA, USA.
Rolling Stones with Nicky Hopkins.
Producer: Jimmy Miller.
Engineer: Andy Johns, Glyn Johns, Joe Zagarino, Jeremy Gee.
UK LP EXILE ON MAIN ST: 12 May 1972: No. 1 - 16 weeks
USA LP EXILE ON MAIN ST: 22 May 1972: No. 1 - 17 weeks
UK CD EXILE ON MAIN ST (EXTRA TRACKS): 17 May 2010: No. 1 - 10 weeks
USA CD EXILE ON MAIN ST (EXTRA TRACKS): 18 May 2010: No. 1 - 3 weeks

The true lead guitar of Mick Taylor resumes on *Soul Survivor* as he plays bottleneck slide. Keith Richards provides a rhythm back drop in open tune style and also lays down a bass line and a fuzzed-out lead. Nicky Hopkins is at the fore, taking a prime role on what is a very guitar and piano-orientated track. The band were in the bowels of the house, Mick Jagger at times recording in a toilet with Nicky's piano and organ set up in a room on the ground floor - not the most conducive of band arrangements. An early instrumental version also exists (* a - 4.02).
Hopkins was well used to the pressures of recording with the Stones but Mick Taylor, it is fair to say, did not settle so well, feeling intimidated by Mick Jagger, who sometimes taunted the younger man. The nomadic life was stretching Taylor's home situation and it was noticeable on EXILE that he was not as inspiring as on the forthcoming GOATS HEAD SOUP album. The song is about being a survivor of love on the high seas. Keith had a passion for the sea and had contemplated buying a boat - Errol Flynn's damaged yacht, which was awaiting a probate settlement, was in his sights. At Beaulieu harbour, when trying to buy another boat, as related in Tony Sanchez's book *Up And Down With The Rolling Stones* and Robert Greenfield's *A Season In Hell With The Rolling Stones*, an Italian couple managed to bump their Jaguar XJ6 into Keith's E-type Jaguar. Keith went ballistic and drew a knife on the husband. His ire was raised by a befuddled encounter Anita had with her friend Tommy Weber the previous night. The Italian, incensed by the mad Englishman, called in the harbour master, Keith grabbed one of Marlon's toy guns while the official took no risks and drew his own weapon, calling the police while a scuffle ensued. Tony Sanchez managed to throw the toy away and then legged it in the E-Type back to Nellcôte.
The lawyers were called and a story was concocted that Marlon had banged his head in a scuffle caused by the harbour master. A compromise was reached when Keith gave the police chief some signed albums. Somehow, Tony was convinced by Keith to take the blame for the incident and so he fled the country and, when the case came to court, Keith paid the fine. Keith eventually did buy a motor boat and then, when advised not to sail it back over mounting seas, ignored the advice. With Marlon and a few friends on board, he underestimated the swell and was saved by a fishing boat and the coast guard. Luckily not a soul survivor.

543. SOUL SURVIVOR - ALTERNATE TAKE (Jagger, Richard) 3.59
7 June - October; 30 November - 19 December 1971; September - November; December 2009: Place: Rolling Stones Mobile, Nellcôte, France; One East Studio, New York, Henson Studios, Village Recording; Mix This!, Los Angeles, USA.
Rolling Stones with Nicky Hopkins, Bobby Keys, Jim Price.
Producer: Jimmy Miller, Don Was, The Glimmer Twins.
Engineer: Glyn Johns; Additional Engineering and Editing: Krish Sharma; Mixed by Bob Clearmountain.
Other Production: Andy Johns.
UK CD EXILE ON MAIN ST (EXTRA TRACKS): 17 May 2010: No. 1 - 10 weeks
USA CD EXILE ON MAIN ST (EXTRA TRACKS): 18 May 2010: No. 1 - 3 weeks

This cut of *Soul Survivor* on the EXILE bonus disc excludes Mick Jagger's and the backing vocals, suggesting it was a Keith Richards original. Instead, Keith sings his own ad-libbed lyrics and, at the end, even adds "etcetera". There are alternative guitar parts and also a brass accompaniment which differs from the released version. Don Was thought it was sufficiently unusual to place on the new release in 2009 - he was right. The drum sound captured at Nellcôte by Jimmy Miller was essential to him as a percussionist and the overall feel. Mick Jagger felt the drum sound created was great after Charlie Watts' kit was moved from room to room to get the best sound - some had carpet laid on the walls by Ian Stewart to prevent echo.

544. ROCKS OFF (Jagger, Richard) 4.33
7 June - October; 30 November - 19 December 1971; 10 January - 28 March 1972: Place: Rolling Stones Mobile, Nellcôte, France; Sunset Sound Studios, LA, RCA Studios, LA, USA.
Played Live: 1972, 1975, 1994, 1995, 2002, 2003, 2005, 2006, 2007
Rolling Stones with Bobby Keys, Jim Price, Nicky Hopkins.
Producer: Jimmy Miller.
Engineer: Andy Johns, Glyn Johns, Joe Zagarino, Jeremy Gee.
UK LP EXILE ON MAIN ST: 12 May 1972: No. 1 - 16 weeks
USA LP EXILE ON MAIN ST: 22 May 1972: No. 1 - 17 weeks
UK CD EXILE ON MAIN ST (EXTRA TRACKS): 17 May 2010: No. 1 - 10 weeks
USA CD EXILE ON MAIN ST (EXTRA TRACKS): 18 May 2010: No. 1 - 3 weeks

Rocks Off is an arousing, sleazy song of sexual incapability, the exploits with a dancer friend being memorable. It is the opening cut on the first side of the double, a section that leaves the listener breathless. As such, *Rocks Off* sets the tone for the album without giving the whole game away. It starts with the guitars vying for attention, Keith Richards leading the way using his open tuned telecaster guitar through an Ampeg amplifier. Charlie Watts enters and Mick Jagger utters an "oh yeah" which signals the "we're back to business". The piano then comes in as the song ascends. By the first chorus, Bobby Keys and Jim Price drive hard around the familiar playing of Keith "Riffhard" then some echoes are added to the vocals as the song relaxes for a moment, before Mick utters the immortal lines "the sunshine bores the daylights out of me".
An instrumental mix of the released track has no studio extras but pounds along at a pace, with Nicky Hopkins in overdrive (* a - 4.33). Apparently the session finished as Keith crashed out but Andy Johns was called back at 5am, just as he had finished the 40-minute drive back to his accommodation. Keith wondered where everyone had gone and insisted that he record a second rhythm guitar part on his telecaster. This counterpointing of Keith's guitars made the track come alight in Andy Johns' opinion. Also, they used the echo of the basement rooms to bounce amplified sounds off walls and record the results.
In Robert Greenfield's book *A Season In Hell With The Rolling Stones*, Andy Johns said: "Two Telecasters, one on each side of the stereo, and it's absolutely brilliant. So I'm glad he got me back there." The Stones were aware that the release of a double album would inevitably lead to claims that there were weak tracks but it was agreed that all were worth releasing. Commercially, it sold relatively well despite costing more as a double. The cover was a collage of American images of troubadours, height-challenged individuals, a one-legged dancer, the human dog, the three marbles in the mouth picture and band images photographed by Robert Frank.
These images had been released in a book, *The Americans* (1959) and were selected by Charlie Watts. Jack Kerouac wrote the introduction to the book and quoted "that crazy feeling in America when the sun is hot on the streets and the music comes out of a jukebox or a funeral". Mick Jagger was trying to enter that world on EXILE. The pictures look like the type that were given away with cigarette packets in the 20s and 30s. Many fans and critics alike argue that EXILE is in fact the Stones' artistic peak but as Mick says it: " . . . bores the daylights out of me".

545. CASINO BOOGIE (Jagger, Richard) 3.34
7 June - October; 30 November - 19 December 1971; 10 January - 28 March 1972: Place: Rolling Stones Mobile, Nellcôte, France; Sunset Sound Studios, LA, USA.
Rolling Stones with Nicky Hopkins, Bobby Keys, Jim Price.
Producer: Jimmy Miller.
Engineer: Andy Johns, Glyn Johns, Joe Zagarino, Jeremy Gee.
UK LP EXILE ON MAIN ST: 12 May 1972: No. 1 - 16 weeks
USA LP EXILE ON MAIN ST: 22 May 1972: No. 1 - 17 weeks
UK CD EXILE ON MAIN ST (EXTRA TRACKS): 17 May 2010: No. 1 - 10 weeks
USA CD EXILE ON MAIN ST (EXTRA TRACKS): 18 May 2010: No. 1 - 3 weeks

A boogie song in classic blues tradition possibly played around with during the previous year. The music is more worthy than the clandestine, abstract "steaming heat" play on words in the lyrics - who plays suicidal Russian roulette these days? And as for kissing cunt in Cannes (which Keith on backing vocals tries to make more noticeable) that's not my style dear! The lyrics were achieved by cutting phrases out of newspaper pages and paper scraps, throwing them in the air and see what forms - a Brion Gysin and then William Burroughs cut-up literary technique copied by musicians to this date.
Mick Jagger delivers them by accentuating some words and muffling others, Keith Richards plays a hand of bass while Mick Taylor deals a mean lead. Nicky Hopkins is determined not to be forgotten and studies form in the corner. A full size roulette table, installed at Andy Johns villa, and the Monte Carlo casino had a lot for which to answer. As Mick fades out with "all right mama" the song develops into a jam, Keith's bass guitar sounding great as he shuffles dexterously to the lead guitar of Mick Taylor and the bar-room sounding piano.

546. PLUNDERED MY SOUL (Jagger, Richard) 3.58
7 June - October 1971; September - November; December 2009: Place: Rolling Stones Mobile, Nellcôte, France; London studio, One East Studio, New York, Henson Studios, Village Recording; Mix This!, Los Angeles, USA.
Rolling Stones with Nicky Hopkins, Lisa Fischer, Cindy Mizelle.
Producer: Jimmy Miller, Don Was, The Glimmer Twins.
Engineer: Glyn Johns; Additional Engineering and Editing: Krish Sharma; Mixed by Bob Clearmountain.
Other Production: Andy Johns.
UK CD EXILE ON MAIN ST (EXTRA TRACKS): 17 May 2010: No. 1 - 10 weeks
USA CD EXILE ON MAIN ST (EXTRA TRACKS): 18 May 2010: No. 1 - 3 weeks

547. PLUNDERED MY SOUL (RADIO MIX) (Jagger, Richard) 3.56
7 June - October 1971; September - November; December 2009: Place: Rolling Stones Mobile, Nellcôte, France; London studio, One East Studio, New York, Henson Studios, Village Recording; Mix This!, Los Angeles, USA.
Rolling Stones with Nicky Hopkins, Lisa Fischer, Cindy Mizelle.
Producer: Jimmy Miller, Don Was, The Glimmer Twins.
Engineer: Glyn Johns; Additional Engineering and Editing: Krish Sharma; Mixed by Bob Clearmountain.
Other Production: Andy Johns.
UK & USA Vinyl Single: 12 April 2010
UK e-Single: 16 April 2010

This was thought to be the stand-out track for single release from the EXILE bonus selection. Two were released since the mix was distinctly different on the single as opposed to the album which may have had the wrong version. The original tape from Nellcôte was purely an instrumental but more or less complete. However, there was little lead guitar so Mick Jagger worked on lyrics and asked Mick Taylor to add some licks in October 2009 in an unknown London studio. Backing vocals were overdubbed in the USA.

The end result is a good foretaste of the bonus tracks and certainly whetted the appetite. Mick Taylor proved that his guitar sound was intrinsic and, on the single mix, there is additional lead guitar mixed earlier on the song. The vocal mix is also a lot more upfront and the modern singing style recorded is much more pronounced and enunciated in Mick's phrasing, with notes being held longer too. The single was released on vinyl to celebrate the annual Record Store Day in a limited edition of 1,000 copies, the B-side being the normal album version of *All Down The Line*. A video produced by Jonas Odell accompanied the release with the album mix soundtrack. There was a clever collage, based on the album cover, with different windows opening to deliver footage from Robert Frank's Cocksucker Blues film and material shown in the *Stones In Exile* documentary which was premiered at the film festival in Cannes, France.

548. FOLLOWING THE RIVER (Jagger, Richard) 4.51
7 June - October 1971; October - November; December 2009: Place: Rolling Stones Mobile, Nellcôte, France; One East Studio, New York, Henson Studios, Village Recording; Mix This!, Los Angeles, USA.
Rolling Stones with Nicky Hopkins, Lisa Fischer, Cindy Mizelle.
Producer: Jimmy Miller, Don Was, The Glimmer Twins.
Engineer: Glyn Johns; Additional Engineering and Editing: Krish Sharma; Mixed by Bob Clearmountain.
Other Production: Andy Johns.
Strings Arrangement: David Campbell.
UK CD EXILE ON MAIN ST (EXTRA TRACKS): 17 May 2010: No. 1 - 10 weeks
USA CD EXILE ON MAIN ST (EXTRA TRACKS): 18 May 2010: No. 1 - 3 weeks
USA Promo CD Single: July 2010

Following The River stuck out to Don Was as one of the essential tracks to be worked on for the re-release but it was also the one that was most incomplete. It was mainly a beautiful piano refrain that was so typical of Nicky Hopkins. There was no melody line or lyrics and it was necessary to shorten the six-minute piano ballad and mix it with another very brief version to give the basis of the new track. This is what Mick Jagger worked on so there was a 38-year difference in styles as vocals, backing harmonies, percussion and strings were overlaid. As the new songs were mixed, it was important to Don Was to keep all the instrumentation at the same point in the left or right channels so it was consistent with the original album.

Following The River was almost a pensive eulogy to Nellcôte and how things used to be: "There's been some others in this room with me, we're really quite a crowd" but there was no pretence of Mick singing lyrics which were in the past. Don Was was proud of the overall outcome and saw himself as the designated driver of the Jimmy Miller role in his absence. There was a video to promote the song but no official single release other than on a promo where it was edited (* a - 4.01). The video was directed by Julian Gibbs and Julian House and is an evocative road and rail travelogue from Chicago to the cotton fields of the south and the Mississippi river's estuary. It uses old film images which are composited and coloured by hand.

549. LET IT LOOSE (Jagger, Richard) 5.18
AKA: Bedroom Blues
7 June - October; 30 November - 19 December 1971; 10 January - 28 March 1972: Place: Rolling Stones Mobile, Nellcôte, France; Sunset Sound Studios, LA, USA.
Rolling Stones with Nicky Hopkins, Bobby Keys, Jim Price, Tammi Lynn, Shirley Goodman, Mac Rebennack (Dr John), Venetta Fields, Clydie King, Joe Green.
Producer: Jimmy Miller
Engineer: Andy Johns, Glyn Johns, Joe Zagarino, Jeremy Gee.
UK LP EXILE ON MAIN ST: 12 May 1972: No. 1 - 16 weeks
USA LP EXILE ON MAIN ST: 22 May 1972: No. 1 - 17 weeks
UK CD EXILE ON MAIN ST (EXTRA TRACKS): 17 May 2010: No. 1 - 10 weeks
USA CD EXILE ON MAIN ST (EXTRA TRACKS): 18 May 2010: No. 1 - 3 weeks

Let It Loose, which came from an original Keith Richards idea, is an evocative "holier than thou" song, aided by an entourage of backing vocalists. Mick Jagger was determined to give the recording an authentic black gospel sound while Nicky Hopkins, on a quivery mellotron and beautiful underlying piano melody, shines for the first few verses until the Spanish-sounding horns of Jim Price take up the struggle halfway through. An extra guitar line and an additional saxophone break can be heard on a six-minute instrumental out-take (* a - 5.57). It sounds as though part of this was used when overdubs were made at Sunset Sound in Los Angeles. There are also the nine cuts from the Nellcôte sessions.

The Stones were aided and abetted by some very capable session singers. The backing vocal talents of Venetta Fields and Clydie King have since been used on the Stones' solo projects, such as Bill Wyman's STONE ALONE in 1975 and Ron Wood's 1234 in 1981. Dr John, alias Malcolm (Mac) Rebennack, was an influential keyboard player, who had worked with Professor Longhair. He recorded a solo album THE SUN MOON AND HERBS in the summer of 1970 for which Mick Jagger sang some backing vocals. When it was time to mix and overdub the EXILE sessions, Dr John was asked to provide some creole magic, so he summoned up his backing vocalists, Tammi Lynn and Shirley Goodman. Tammi had worked with Wilson Pickett and Bob Dylan while Shirley was a veteran performer, who worked with Leonard Lee as Shirley & Lee, their great success being the 1956 *Let The Good Times Roll*, plagiarised on the Stones' own *Good Times*. Joe Green had been part of the Quincy Jones contingent and, together, they all enhanced *Let It Loose* to anthem proportions. On one EXILE out-take, Mick asked Don "Sugercane" Harris, from the Frank Zappa band, to overlay some violin but the rest of the Stones thought this was just too much. The released cut of *Let It Loose* is a hidden gem on EXILE.

As the summer turned to autumn at Nellcôte, life was getting progressively more difficult. On 21 October 1971, Jade was born to Mick and Bianca, forcing the father to be away for a few weeks on parental leave. Perhaps this was just as well at a time when there were two burglaries, one of which resulted in all of Keith's guitars being stolen. It was more than likely an inside job by the local "cowboys". At around the same time, Anita Pallenberg thought it was a good idea to give the cook's daughter a special injection of heroin which she physically could not handle. The cook reported them to the authorities and the police took statements from everyone.

It was time to jump ship and mixing needed to be done in America. The police wanted some evidence of intent to return by Keith and Anita so they said they would continue to rent Nellcôte until charges came to court. On arrival in the United States an announcement was made that the Stones intended to tour in 1972. This time the tour was going to be run professionally with proper security, self-assembled mobile stages, hotels block-booked, private planes and bodyguards. The plans were drawn up as the last attentions to detail were given to the EXILE album. Once most overdubs were made, Andy Johns produced a completed mix of the album before the end of the year.

However, while he was finishing it, everyone was suggesting changes and, after much debate, Mick took responsibility for the album's conclusion and Andy Johns was not invited back after Christmas. Joe Zagarino worked on it but he could not better Andy's efforts. Eventually, Mick ate humble pie and Andy was called back, initially to Wally Heider's studios for two days, then to Sunset Sound where he mixed the album in a thirty-six hour marathon session. Still Marshall Chess felt it needed more work so further mixes were produced until the eventual agreement to go with Andy's earlier version.

550. I DON'T CARE (Jagger, Richard) 3.02
AKA: Sad Song
28 March 1972: Place: Sunset Sound Studios, Los Angeles, USA.
Producer: Jimmy Miller.
Bootleg only.

A track recorded while preparing the final pre-launch flexi disc. It features just Jagger on piano and vocals and is a sad song, expressing love for someone.

551. EXILE ON MAIN STREET BLUES (Jagger, Richard) 6.21
28 March 1972: Place: Sunset Sound Studios, Los Angeles, USA.
Producer: Jimmy Miller.
Week ending 29 April 1972: NME Flexi Disc: New Musical Express music magazine

Following the release of the *Tumbling Dice* single, the New Musical Express British weekly music paper provided the fans with a six-minute sampler of the album, which was to be released in two weeks. Mick Jagger, plus a piano accompaniment, is heard singing *Exile On Main Street Blues*, which incorporates ad-libbed lyrics from various song titles from the album. The flexi disc continues with excerpts of tracks featured are *All Down The Line*, *Tumbling Dice*, *Shine A Light* and *Happy*. The original one-and-a-half minute recording, minus the excerpts but with more lyrics, can be heard on bootleg (* a - 1.37). "Where's your ventilator baby?"

552. JOHN'S JAM (Nanker, Phelge) 3.34
17-21 May 1972: Place: Rialto Theatre, Montreux, Switzerland.
Bootleg only.

In early January 1972, London Records released a compilation double album HOT ROCKS 1964-1971. It became the Stones' most successful album ever, selling more than 12 million copies. In the UK, Decca released MILESTONES, which was much more of a lacklustre affair compared with HOT ROCKS. These releases could have jeopardised sales of EXILE but, with the album released, it was time to rehearse for the up and coming tour, due to commence on 4 June 1972.
The reasons for the location being Switzerland are complicated but it was there that Anita Pallenberg and Keith Richards went in late March in the final stages of her pregnancy - she tried to give up heroin and Keith entered detoxification treatment. Indeed, they liked Switzerland so much that they would later return. They stayed in the hills above Montreux and Dandelion (Angela) was born on 17 April 1972. Apparently, it was easier and kinder for the rest of the Stones to come to Keith to rehearse. *John's Jam* is an instrumental, kicked off by Charlie Watts' drums then the two guitarists drive solos past one another, Mick Taylor playing a funky riff while Keith's is much straighter.

553. LOVING CUP (Jagger, Richard) 6.51
17-21 May 1972: Place: Rialto Theatre, Montreux, Switzerland.
Bootleg only.

The backing band for the tour again comprised Nicky Hopkins, Bobby Keys and Jim Price and they can all be heard to great effect on this track. It was a song that they would only play on the first two dates. Perhaps that was because it was long and given a higher status than it deserved.

554. **SHAKE YOUR HIPS** (Moore) 3.42
17-21 May 1972: Place: Rialto Theatre, Montreux, Switzerland.
Producer: Michael Appleton
Engineer: Gregg Bailey
UK DVD Ladies & Gentlemen: 11 October 2010
USA DVD Ladies & Gentlemen: 12 October 2010

The rehearsal has the band close together with Charlie Watts and Keith Richards facing each other, giving Mick Taylor a prime view of Keith's licks, enabling him to take his solo cues easily. The two guitars are easily distinguished in the mix and it is a faithful copy of the released song, though *Shake Your Hips* was not used on the tour. The Rialto tracks originate from TV footage for The Old Grey Whistle Test (BBC) and the German Beat Club television programmes. Three tracks were given a video release when the film was transferred to DVD format in 2010 on the concert film *Ladies & Gentlemen*. The sound was probably captured by Gregg Bailey, who worked as location sound recordist for the BBC programme.

555. **TUMBLING DICE** (Jagger, Richard) 4.23
17-21 May 1972: Place: Rialto Theatre, Montreux, Switzerland.
Producer: Michael Appleton
Engineer: Gregg Bailey
UK DVD Ladies & Gentlemen: 11 October 2010
USA DVD Ladies & Gentlemen: 12 October 2010

Two versions of this track are available on bootleg (* a - 4.11). The recordings are unique as they capture the newness of the song. Which direction would it take? The open chords were important and the speed was slower than on the released cut. Mick Taylor's slide guitar was more pronounced, making it less of a rock and roll song but raw and loose nonetheless. There were no backing vocals - other than Keith Richards - or brass instrumentation, unlike the released recording.

556. **BLUESBERRY JAM** (Nanker, Phelge) 3.09
17-21 May 1972: Place: Rialto Theatre, Montreux, Switzerland.
Producer: Michael Appleton
Engineer: Gregg Bailey
UK DVD Ladies & Gentlemen: 11 October 2010
USA DVD Ladies & Gentlemen: 12 October 2010

A shuffle and roll blues song featuring Ian Stewart's piano and a whining electric lead guitar. The band seems perfectly relaxed and playing with eyes shut at times, Mick Jagger watching the action enthusiastically, toe tapping this instrumental. The tracks were recorded in a disused theatre, complete with the intended tour stage, under the direction of road/logistics manager Chip Monck and transport manager Alan Dunn.
The tour manager was Peter Rudge, who had handled the Who's 1970 and 1971 tours of America. He had a reputation for precision planning and the theatre rehearsals were clouded with security, just like a military campaign. The Stones returned to California and another rehearsal was held at Burbank in Los Angeles, with Jim Price and Bobby Keys, before they moved to Canada. A tape exists of 66 minutes of these preparations, including *Hip Shake, Can't You Hear Me Knocking, Rocks Off* and *Don't Lie To Me.*

557. **JUNGLE DISEASE** (Jagger, Richard) 3.56
23 June 1972: Place: Sumet-Burnet Studios, Dallas, Texas, USA.
Bootleg only.

The Stones' Rock And Roll Circus hit Northern America and Canada in the summer, commencing on the 3 June and performing to vast crowds and sell-out audiences at an average pop of $20. Rock and roll music was entering a professional age as the band themselves took 70 per cent of the ticket receipts. With Peter Rudge at the helm, the Who had led the way in 1971 Led Zeppelin, under Peter Grant's direction, had moved the action to large arena and stadium events in 1970, 1971 and 1972. The logistics of going from one USA state to another were awesome. Rudge masterminded the Stones tour hiring a private jet, with a lapping tongue logo, to travel in some style.
In 1972, the Stones and Led Zeppelin might easily have collided in the middle of the States in a gargantuan pile of rock excess. In June, Zeppelin went from east to west while the Stones travelled in the opposite direction, playing 39 dates and 48 shows in total with a tour doctor, tour make-up person and two accountants. Two shows were played at some events to satisfy the ticket demands, afternoon and evening shows contributing to the scale of the achievement. Chip Monck was in charge of stage production and, as the MC "voice of Woodstock" made the band introductions. To allow the crowd a better view, the PA was raised aloft rather than taking precedence on the stage.
Midway through the tour, the Stones wanted to sharpen their performance so, in between a far from smooth show in Kansas City and Fort Worth, where the cameras would be in position to record proceedings for a future film release, they decided to put in some extra work. The rehearsal result has been bootlegged and is known as the 1972 Dallas Rehearsals. This seems to consist of a laid-back two-and-a-bit hours practice session and hardly a full-blown tour rehearsal. There are about nine takes of *Let It Loose* (alias *Bedroom Blues*), and a couple each of *Ventilator Blues, Shake Your Hips* and *Torn And Frayed*. The rest is instrumental doodling, featuring piano and organ and guitar riffs, including jams around *Monkey Man, Gimme Shelter, Satisfaction* and *The Last Time*, as well as some Chuck Berry (*Memphis, Tennessee, Don't Lie To Me*).
There are not many discernible out-takes amongst the 30 or so ramblings which could be included in the Sessionography, (take the *Jungle Disease* sketching's and the blues of *Delta Slide* which is a bootleggers name for Elmore James licks) other than a passable, slow *Key To The Highway* with vocals which then runs into a Robert Johnson medley of *32-20 Blues* and *When You've Got A Good Friend*. There may be the formation of two new tracks, named *Whip's Crack* and *Tiger's Snarl*, at the end which seem to be heavier rock guitar riffs which evidently came to nothing.

558. **DELTA SLIDE** (Jagger, Richard) 2.50
23 June 1972: Place: Sumet-Burnet Studios, Dallas, Texas, USA.
Rolling Stones with Nicky Hopkins.
Bootleg only.

559. **32-20 BLUES** (Johnson) 1.41
23 June 1972: Place: Sumet-Burnet Studios, Dallas, Texas, USA.
Bootleg only.

560. **WHEN YOU GOT A GOOD FRIEND** (Johnson) 2.37
23 June 1972: Place: Sumet-Burnet Studios, Dallas, Texas, USA.
Bootleg only.

561. **KEY TO THE HIGHWAY** (Segar, Broonzy) 6.22
23 June 1972: Place: Sumet-Burnet Studios, Dallas, Texas, USA.
Rolling Stones with Nicky Hopkins.
Bootleg only.

562. **GIMME SHELTER** (Jagger, Richard) ✎ 4.49
24 June 1972: Place: Tarrant County Convention Centre, Fort Worth, Texas, USA. (Show One).
Rolling Stones with Nicky Hopkins, Bobby Keys, Jim Price.
Producer: Andy Johns.
Ladies And Gentlemen: The Rolling Stones Film: 14 April 1974
UK DVD Ladies & Gentlemen: 11 October 2010
USA DVD Ladies & Gentlemen: 12 October 2010

The Stones wanted to capture the tour on film and Robert Frank, who had worked on the EXILE sleeve, agreed to put together a documentary. The Fort Worth gigs were filmed for a future special concert film and the shows were recorded by Andy Johns on 16 tracks for a potential live album. To counter the unofficial demand for live material, a double album of the tour, including support artist Stevie Wonder, was planned. The source would be the concerts at Fort Worth and the Philadelphia Spectrum. Artwork was prepared for a sleeve design but the product never made the shops due to Decca Records' insistence that the new versions of old Stones numbers could not be released for a period of five years from the agreement. *Brown Sugar* and *Bitch* were specifically questioned.

Journalist Robert Greenfield was assigned to cover the tour on behalf of Rolling Stone magazine. He had befriended the Stones on the Goodbye Britain tour and had also interviewed Keith Richards in Nellcôte. He was trusted, even if his boss Truman Capote, said that he himself would take over the chore halfway through the tour. Robert wrote an article for Rolling Stone but, with his Stones Touring Party passes still valid for all access, decided to re-join the tour anyway. His accounts of the trip were published in the USA in 1974 under the title *S.T.P. A Journey Through America With The Rolling Stones*. This is the ultimate book of any rock tour, capturing the full flavour of lost times.

Security was very high on the agenda and Mick Jagger and Keith Richards, terrified that a gunman would shoot them, and carried .38 revolvers. Mick Jagger was quoted at the end of the tour: "Don't say I wasn't scared, man. I was scared shitless." The low-level stages from the last tour had been replaced by secured pits positioned between the higher walled stage. It was the first time the Stones had played in the States since Altamont and there were many rumours that the Hells Angels wanted revenge. Indeed, in New York, some representatives of the Angels contacted Peter Rudge and demanded the Stones play a benefit concert to help recoup legal fees. This hit a very raw nerve with the Stones and they delayed a decision until they were out of the country.

On the pretext of wanting an autograph, one attractive lady boarded the Stones jet and served papers by local Altamont residents, who were suing for damages to their properties during the free concert - this matter was eventually settled out of court. Riots were also a by-product of the tour. The kids were out on the streets going crazy and having fun and any opportunity by the authorities to control them with beatings and tear gas was used. The tour started in Vancouver, Canada before progressing through the States - Washington, a week in California, Arizona, New Mexico, Colorado, Minneapolis, Illinois, Kansas, then to Texas. This is where they recorded two nights at the Will Rogers Auditorium, Fort Worth and the Hofheinz Pavilion, Houston. *Brown Sugar* was the opening number for the tour after the band entered the stage to the strains of *2000 Light Years From Home*. *Bitch* and *Gimme Shelter* were the next numbers.

563. **DEAD FLOWERS** (Jagger, Richard) ✎ 4.09
24 June 1972: Place: Tarrant County Convention Centre, Fort Worth, Texas, USA. (Show One).
Rolling Stones with Nicky Hopkins, Bobby Keys, Jim Price.
Producer: Andy Johns.
Ladies And Gentlemen: The Rolling Stones Film: 14 April 1974
UK DVD Ladies & Gentlemen: 11 October 2010
USA DVD Ladies & Gentlemen: 12 October 2010

564. **SWEET BLACK ANGEL** (Jagger, Richard) ✎ 3.18
24 June 1972: Place: Tarrant County Convention Centre, Fort Worth, Texas, USA. (Show One).
Rolling Stones with Nicky Hopkins, Bobby Keys, Jim Price.
Bootleg only.

565. HAPPY (Jagger, Richard) ✏ 3.07
24 June 1972: Place: Tarrant County Convention Centre, Fort Worth, Texas, USA. (Show One).
Rolling Stones with Nicky Hopkins, Bobby Keys, Jim Price.
Producer: Andy Johns.
Ladies And Gentlemen: The Rolling Stones Film: 14 April 1974
UK DVD Ladies & Gentlemen: 11 October 2010
USA DVD Ladies & Gentlemen: 12 October 2010

566. SWEET VIRGINIA (Jagger, Richard) ✏ 4.30
24 June 1972: Place: Tarrant County Convention Centre, Fort Worth, Texas, USA. (Show One).
Rolling Stones with Nicky Hopkins, Bobby Keys, Jim Price.
Producer: Andy Johns.
Ladies And Gentlemen: The Rolling Stones Film: 14 April 1974
UK DVD Ladies & Gentlemen: 11 October 2010
USA DVD Ladies & Gentlemen: 12 October 2010

567. BITCH (Jagger, Richard) ✏ 4.44
24 June 1972: Place: Tarrant County Convention Centre, Fort Worth, Texas, USA. (Show Two).
Rolling Stones with Nicky Hopkins, Bobby Keys, Jim Price.
Producer: Andy Johns.
Ladies And Gentlemen: The Rolling Stones Film: 14 April 1974
UK DVD Ladies & Gentlemen: 11 October 2010
USA DVD Ladies & Gentlemen: 12 October 2010

568. DON'T LIE TO ME (Whittaker) ✏ 2.38
24 June 1972: Place: Tarrant County Convention Centre, Fort Worth, Texas, USA. (Show Two).
Rolling Stones with Nicky Hopkins, Bobby Keys, Jim Price.
Bootleg only.

569. RIP THIS JOINT (Jagger, Richard) ✏ 2.23
24 June 1972: Place: Tarrant County Convention Centre, Fort Worth, Texas, USA. (Show Two).
Rolling Stones with Nicky Hopkins, Bobby Keys, Jim Price.
Producer: Andy Johns.
Ladies And Gentlemen: The Rolling Stones Film: 14 April 1974
UK DVD Ladies & Gentlemen: 11 October 2010
USA DVD Ladies & Gentlemen: 12 October 2010

570. TUMBLING DICE (Jagger, Richard) ✏ 5.16
25 June 1972: Place: Hofheinz Pavilion, Houston, Texas, USA. (Show One).
Rolling Stones with Nicky Hopkins, Bobby Keys, Jim Price.
Producer: Andy Johns.
Ladies And Gentlemen: The Rolling Stones Film: 14 April 1974
UK DVD Ladies & Gentlemen: 11 October 2010
USA DVD Ladies & Gentlemen: 12 October 2010

571. LOVE IN VAIN (Payne) ✏ 6.35
25 June 1972: Place: Hofheinz Pavilion, Houston, Texas, USA. (Show One).
Rolling Stones with Nicky Hopkins, Bobby Keys, Jim Price.
Producer: Andy Johns.
Ladies And Gentlemen: The Rolling Stones Film: 14 April 1974
UK DVD Ladies & Gentlemen: 11 October 2010
USA DVD Ladies & Gentlemen: 12 October 2010

572. YOU CAN'T ALWAYS GET WHAT YOU WANT (Jagger, Richard) ✏ 7.22
25 June 1972: Place: Hofheinz Pavilion, Houston, Texas, USA. (Show One).
Rolling Stones with Nicky Hopkins, Bobby Keys, Jim Price.
Producer: Andy Johns.
Ladies And Gentlemen: The Rolling Stones Film: 14 April 1974
UK DVD Ladies & Gentlemen: 11 October 2010
USA DVD Ladies & Gentlemen: 12 October 2010

573. BYE BYE JOHNNY (Berry) ✎ 3.24
25 June 1972: Place: Hofheinz Pavilion, Houston, Texas, USA. (Show One).
Rolling Stones with Nicky Hopkins, Bobby Keys, Jim Price.
Producer: Andy Johns.
Ladies And Gentlemen: The Rolling Stones Film: 14 April 1974
UK DVD Ladies & Gentlemen: 11 October 2010
USA DVD Ladies & Gentlemen: 12 October 2010

574. JUMPING JACK FLASH (Jagger, Richard) ✎ 3.39
25 June 1972: Place: Hofheinz Pavilion, Houston, Texas, USA. (Show One).
Rolling Stones with Nicky Hopkins, Bobby Keys, Jim Price.
Producer: Andy Johns.
Ladies And Gentlemen: The Rolling Stones Film: 14 April 1974
UK DVD Ladies & Gentlemen: 11 October 2010
USA DVD Ladies & Gentlemen: 12 October 2010

575. BROWN SUGAR (Jagger, Richard) ✎ 4.23
25 June 1972: Place: Hofheinz Pavilion, Houston, Texas, USA. (Show Two).
Rolling Stones with Nicky Hopkins, Bobby Keys, Jim Price.
Producer: Andy Johns.
Ladies And Gentlemen: The Rolling Stones Film: 14 April 1974
UK DVD Ladies & Gentlemen: 11 October 2010
USA DVD Ladies & Gentlemen: 12 October 2010

576. ALL DOWN THE LINE (Jagger, Richard) ✎ 5.23
25 June 1972: Place: Hofheinz Pavilion, Houston, Texas, USA. (Show Two).
Rolling Stones with Nicky Hopkins, Bobby Keys, Jim Price.
Producer: Andy Johns.
Ladies And Gentlemen: The Rolling Stones Film: 14 April 1974
UK DVD Ladies & Gentlemen: 11 October 2010
USA DVD Ladies & Gentlemen: 12 October 2010

577. MIDNIGHT RAMBLER (Jagger, Richard) ✎ 12.42
25 June 1972: Place: Hofheinz Pavilion, Houston, Texas, USA. (Show Two).
Rolling Stones with Nicky Hopkins, Bobby Keys, Jim Price.
Producer: Andy Johns.
Ladies And Gentlemen: The Rolling Stones Film: 14 April 1974
UK DVD Ladies & Gentlemen: 11 October 2010
USA DVD Ladies & Gentlemen: 12 October 2010

578. STREET FIGHTING MAN (Jagger, Richard) ✎ 7.10
25 June 1972: Place: Hofheinz Pavilion, Houston, Texas, USA. (Show Two).
Rolling Stones with Nicky Hopkins, Bobby Keys, Jim Price.
Producer: Andy Johns.
Ladies And Gentlemen: The Rolling Stones Film: 14 April 1974
UK DVD Ladies & Gentlemen: 11 October 2010
USA DVD Ladies & Gentlemen: 12 October 2010

The pressure was beginning to take its toll, bubbling its way towards a make-or-break situation. Different allegiances were forming amongst the S.T.P. and that would boil over as they reached its conclusion in New York. Stevie Wonder's drummer Ollie Brown collapsed with exhaustion and his band failed to perform at Houston. Mick Jagger and Keith Richards were especially annoyed since this was a gig scheduled to be recorded - they had not "bottled" one show in their career, even when Brian was ill. However, the Texas dates which were filmed and put together for the *Ladies And Gentlemen* project, are of exceptional quality, both musically and historically.

All of the band members had reached a zenith for various reasons. Mick Taylor, for example, was so confident and inspirational, his bottleneck solo and then the lead on *Love In Vain* are exquisite. But he also contributed well to *Gimme Shelter*, *You Can't Always Get What You Want*, *All Down The Line*, *Midnight Rambler* and *Street Fighting Man*. Mick Jagger asks him to "play guitar boy" on *Dead Flowers* which allowed a fulsome and more rounded performance by Keith, who could concentrate on the song's structure to provide the rhythm and riffs. On film, he could be seen working with Charlie Watts with his back to the audience.

Bye Bye Johnny is another one of those timeless classic Berry covers that they got right playing it fast though the live version of *Don't Lie To Me*, which they originally recorded in 1964, was not so successful. It was specially introduced for the film crew and is best forgotten. Mick Jagger apologises to the audience for Stevie's no show - "expect he overslept". Keith has often commented that, during this period, he was like "a tiger unleashed on the audience" and is rousing on *Happy* and *Rip This Joint*. Robert Greenfield talks about this in his book, *S.T.P. A Journey Through America With The Rolling Stones*, commenting: "Some nights it was as though they brought Keith to the hall in a cage and his hour and a half on stage was the only freedom he was going to get . . . Keith was right there, all the time, playing for his life."

Mick takes musical performance to new heights on *Midnight Rambler*. His harmonica playing was not only subtle but, during the romping part, he was integral to the multiple instruments being featured. He plays with the audience (their input is now vital to the song), his belt comes off and he perfects his cock-rock role in true style, shouting "owwhh" as though his life did depend on it. His act was transformed on the larger USA stages as he ran from one side to another, his demonic maracas having been dropped in place of sheer fire and brimstone. Keith is great in the chug section of the "don't do that". As for the others, stalwarts like Bobby Keys, Nicky Hopkins and Bill Wyman - who is about as dependable and precise as you need - are completely on spot. Charlie, meanwhile, launches into rock and roll overdrive but not too flamboyantly, a conservative beat being sufficient.

Tumbling Dice has an arrangement where Mick slows it down and asks Charlie for some help, you got to roll me and rock is all about the "roll" as Keith fondly says. As far as the choice of set material was concerned, the new album was showcased with *Rocks Off, Tumbling Dice, Happy, Sweet Virginia, All Down The Line, Rip This Joint* being played consistently (in the States *Happy*, coupled with *All Down The Line*, was released as a single in July) while *Loving Cup, Ventilator Blues, Torn And Frayed* and *Sweet Black Angel* featured just the once, the latter to celebrate the release of black activist Angela Davis. The rest is made up of the aforementioned material. The period costume includes cowboy hat during *Bye Bye Johnny*, flares, scarves and bandanas, tongue t-shirt (worn by Taylor), blue velvet with white spots, white velvet with dark spots, denim tops, leg fringes, black leather, jump-suits alternated with slacks and tank-tops, Jagger's glitter on the forehead, a long mane and accentuated mascara eyes, Keith's skewed hair and the ultra violet light. Bill wears a suit! Chip Monck provided mirrors and bright white spotlights to give the stage much more of a lighted edge to it, although naturally rather meek in today's terms.

The show usually climaxed to *Jumping Jack Flash* and *Street Fighting Man*, when rose petals were thrown on the audience. A back stage joke was to hide various animal parts in the petals being thrown on to the audience only for one bloody liver to be thrown back on one occasion. From then on, the contents of the bucket were searched each night.

579. UPTIGHT / (I CAN'T GET NO) SATISFACTION (Moy, Cosby, Wonder and Jagger, Richard) ✐ 5.32
21 July 1972: Place: Spectrum Sports Arena, Philadelphia, USA.
Rolling Stones with Stevie Wonder, Nicky Hopkins, Bobby Keys, Jim Price.
Bootleg only.

580. BROWN SUGAR (Jagger, Richard) ✐ 1.48
25 July 1972: Place: Madison Square Garden, New York, USA.
Rolling Stones with Stevie Wonder, Nicky Hopkins, Bobby Keys, Jim Price.
USA DVD Dick Cavett Show: 16 August 2005

581. STREET FIGHTING MAN (Jagger, Richard) ✐ 1.44
25 July 1972: Place: Madison Square Garden, New York, USA.
Rolling Stones with Stevie Wonder, Nicky Hopkins, Bobby Keys, Jim Price.
USA DVD Dick Cavett Show: 16 August 2005

After Texas, the Stones moved on to Alabama, Tennessee, Washington DC, Virginia, North Carolina, Missouri, Ohio, Indiana, Michigan, back to Canada for Toronto and Quebec, then the Boston Garden, Philadelphia Spectrum, Pittsburgh PA before three nights at Madison Square Garden. What a turkey run! Still problems persisted - while a band truck, with speakers within, was parked outside the Montreal Forum, pro-French activists detonated some sticks of dynamite under it to promote their cause before a call came to say there were going to be three more! (But we are just a rock and roll band). Luckily nothing else happened and Jagger asked why they did not leave a note!

On the way back from Quebec, they were diverted from their next concert, Boston, to Warwick on Rhode Island because of fog. The band had to go through a check by customs and police staff who were not quite ready to deal with the STP. A photographer made a point of getting some snaps while the band were moving through the process and the bodyguards tried to prevent the exposure. A cat and mouse game unfurled until the photographer spotted Keith all alone. Never one to miss a photo opportunity, Keith swung a belt at the photographer and the police arrested him. Mick tried to explain that they were already late for a gig in Boston so they arrested him too, then the protesting Marshall Chess suffered a similar fate.

Tour security man Sam Moore (an ex-cop) put in his two penny worth and, to his embarrassment, also got nailed and so they all headed off to jail. Boston Mayor Kevin White, who had been hanging out at the Garden to ensure all was well, heard of the fiasco and, worried about the crowd finding out and rioting, ordered the Stones to be released and have a police escort to the "tea party". He told Boston the crowd what an up-standing member of the community he had been to get the Stones off the hook. Four hours later they arrived and played the Garden, exhausted but inspired by the ecstatic crowd. Robert Frank managed to film some of the goings-on but it was not included in his movie, entitled *Cocksucker Blues*.

The film was pretty lewd in places with X-rated content (albeit manufactured) of mile-high club activities in the Stones private jet, groupies injecting themselves and full frontal shots of both men and women, including Jagger feeling himself as he walked around a swimming pool in his shorts. There were some incomplete Stones live recordings from the tour and some out-take piano work of a song with "It's Funny" lyrics and referred to as *Fragile* - see EXILE sessions. In 1973, the Stones viewed the film and realised it was too hot for release, not commercial in nature but ultimately not enjoyable, although one bit of it did turn up on the compilation video *25 X 5*. This was when Bobby Keys and Keith Richards threw a television out of a hotel window. On the second night at the Boston Garden, the Stones were joined by Stevie Wonder for the first time on an encore which consisted of Stevie's *Uptight (Everything's Alright)* 1966 hit, which then segues into *Satisfaction*. This encore, with Jagger and Wonder singing on each other's track, was played almost every night for the remainder of the tour.

On 25 July 1972 at Madison Square Garden, *Brown Sugar* and *Street Fighting Man* were recorded by the Dick Cavett Show, which included very relaxed Mick Jagger and Bill Wyman interviews. Commenting on the audience Bill said: "Before, we used to hit the sort of 15 to 20s but now it is the 15 to 30s. The fans grew up and they are still coming and the younger ones are starting to come . . . we're not getting the mums and dads!" This was broadcast in August and two minutes of both these songs were released on DVD in 2005. Jagger refused to have the whole songs on DVD possibly for bootlegging reasons.

Watching these excerpts, you can tell that, at this point of the tour, the Stones were riding on helium. *Rip This Joint* was played even faster, *Jumping Jack Flash* featured reverb with Townshend-like guitar and *Street Fighting Man* provided the concert finale (remember this was a song banned in the States in 1968) enabling them to climax before the *Uptight* encore.

The last date of the tour was on Mick's 29th birthday, 26 July, and the crowd sang Happy Birthday with Charlie Watts kicking out the beat. Bianca came on stage and presented Mick with a panda bear and a birthday cake - cool man! Then hundreds of cream pies were handed out for an end of tour fight. The real party was over, except for the birthday bash, which was a star-studded affair that evening, complete with Count Basie (for Charlie, this was too good to be true) and Muddy Waters playing sets in honour of the Stones. What more can a poor boy do?

582. COMING DOWN AGAIN (Jagger, Richard) 5.55
25 November - 21 December 1972; 7 May - June 1973: Place: Dynamic Sounds, Kingston, Jamaica; Olympic Sound Studios, Island Studios, London, England.
Rolling Stones with Nicky Hopkins, Bobby Keys.
Producer: Jimmy Miller.
Engineer: Andy Johns.
Assistant Engineer: Carlton Lee, Howard Kilgour, Doug Bennett, Mikey Chung.
UK LP GOATS HEAD SOUP: 31 August 1973: No. 1 - 14 weeks
USA LP GOATS HEAD SOUP: 12 September 1973: No. 1 - 19 weeks

Following their most successful tour ever, both artistically and financially, the Stones disappeared to different corners of the globe. Keith Richards and Anita Pallenberg retreated back to the peace of Switzerland and entered an ever-deepening period of drug dependency. In September 1972, Mick Jagger recorded backing vocals with Carly Simon for her *You're So Vain* single at London's Trident Studios. Some 34 years later, Carly reflected that Mick had such confidence - he did not even ask to hear the play back. The song's subject matter is still debated but a clue was dropped by Carly. When re-recording it for 2010 release, she hinted to Uncut magazine that the name of the person was whispered in the song. There is a backward recording of the name "David" which leads to further speculation, with record company mogul David Geffen top of the suspect list.

A double compilation album, released in late 1972 by ABKCO, followed the success of HOT ROCKS - the album was titled MORE HOT ROCKS and mainly featured early songs, the latest being *No Expectations* and *Let It Bleed*. ABKCO wanted to release an album of unreleased material, provisionally called TRIDENT MIXES, originally recorded at Olympic in 1970. A Bell Sound Acetate was produced of these London studio mixes, which included *Jiving Sister Fanny, I'm Going Down, I Don't Know Why, Give Me A Hamburger To Go, Downtown Suzie, Blood Red Wine, Travelling Man, Family, Still A Fool, Family, Leather Jacket, Dancing In The Light, Potted Shrimp, Aladdin Story, And I Was A Country Boy, Who Am I?*, and *Untitled*.

It was a jump too far to release such rough mixes without overdubs though some did appear on METAMORPHOSIS in 1975. A copy of the vinyl acetate went missing, hence it appearing on bootleg. Mick joined Keith and Anita in Switzerland to talk and work on new songs for what would become GOATS HEAD SOUP, the album taking its name from a local Jamaican delicacy. It was a difficult period and the creative juices did not flow then, when a few ideas arrived, they had to decide on a studio. It couldn't be in the UK for tax reasons and France was ruled out because of potential drugs charges.

Ahmet Ertegun knew Byron Lee, who was one of Jamaica's leading exponents of West Indian music, who ran Dynamic Sounds, the Caribbean's top recording studio in Kingston. Byron had found fame by appearing in the James Bond film *Dr No*, which was shot in Kingston. This was the first time Jamaican calypso music had had such a high worldwide profile. Incidentally, one of the film's scenes in the Pussfeller Club has Chris Blackwell (later to be head of Island Records) dancing to the music of Byron Lee and The Dragonaires.

They went on to have hits with their ska music, which then progressed into the form labelled reggae. Both Byron Lee and Chris Blackwell helped to develop Bob Marley's music career, which was just about to take off internationally. Carlton Lee was an engineer for Bob Marley and had just recorded CATCH A FIRE with him. Keith, in particular, was intrigued by this music and so Jamaica was selected as it would be hospitable, quiet, warm and have a conducive atmosphere - they hoped. Jamaica also had a good reputation for recording rhythm songs well, an essential part of the Stones material. Keith later referred to the sessions as good for multi-ethnic music, with Guyanan percussion players and the Chinese Mikey "Mao" Chung assisting the engineering process.

Nicky Hopkins gently nestles his way into *Coming Down Again*, thereby starting the so-called "Goats Head Patties" sessions in late November 1972. He was the only additional musician present in Jamaica. The sessions lasted four weeks and were consolidated by Jimmy Miller to produce the GOATS HEAD SOUP album. Keith Richards wrote this soft country-style song and also featured in the singing role on various verses ("where are all my friends?" - eerily predictive of Gram Parsons' death). The song was full of pain and angst as the drug's high reduced to a low - a metaphor for the ups and downs of their lives. Mick was on backing vocals and sang the verses almost in duet style. Keith's wah-wah guitar effects helped to create a soft edge upon which Nicky Hopkins so instinctively thrived. Mick Taylor played bass on this track and a Bobby Keys sax solo was overdubbed later.

583. YOU SHOULD HAVE SEEN HER ASS (Jagger, Richard) 4.20
25 November - 21 December 1972: Place: Dynamic Sounds, Kingston, Jamaica.
Rolling Stones with Nicky Hopkins.
Producer: Jimmy Miller.
Bootleg only.

An up-tempo number which rocks and swings to a "tumbling dice" groove. The piano playing may even be Ian Stewart, since it has his bar-room style. Keith Richards wealds in some riff playing while Mick Jagger sings lyrics which are hard to distinguish.

584. WINTER (Jagger, Richard) 5.30
25 November - 21 December 1972; 7 May - June 1973: Place: Dynamic Sounds, Kingston, Jamaica; RSM Mobile, Newbury, Olympic Sound Studios, Island Studios, London, England.
Rolling Stones with Nicky Hopkins.
Producer: Jimmy Miller.
Engineer: Andy Johns.
Assistant Engineer: Carlton Lee, Howard Kilgour, Doug Bennett, Mikey Chung. String Arrangement: Nicky Harrison.
UK LP GOATS HEAD SOUP: 31 August 1973: No. 1 - 14 weeks
USA LP GOATS HEAD SOUP: 12 September 1973: No. 1 - 19 weeks

Winter is evocative of north winds and Christmas-tree lights, Nicky Harrison's strings escalating the song to an epic status. The track has Mick Jagger contributing a guitar line or two, which may have meant that Keith Richards was not involved. Jimmy Miller was not totally happy with the finished vocals, wanting something a little more powerful, but Mick, having laid down three or four takes, was called away from the studio by Bianca and the "magic" take was never made. Mick Taylor's unnerving lead guitar helps to make this one of the most powerful tracks, originating from what was dubbed the "Jamaican Patties" sessions. Andy Johns thought it was one of the best songs they had recorded. An alternate mix of the track can be found on bootleg. It sounds very similar to the released mix (* a - 5.25).

585. **DANCING WITH MR. D** (Jagger, Richard) 4.53
25 November - 21 December 1972; 27-30 January; 7 May - June 1973: Place: Dynamic Sounds, Kingston, Jamaica; Village Recorders, Los Angeles, USA; RSM Mobile, Newbury, Olympic Sound Studios, Island Studios, London, England.
Played Live: 1973
Rolling Stones with Pascal, Rebop, Nicky Hopkins.
Producer: Jimmy Miller.
Engineer: Andy Johns.
Assistant Engineer: Carlton Lee, Howard Kilgour, Doug Bennett, Mikey Chung.
UK LP GOATS HEAD SOUP: 31 August 1973: No. 1 - 14 weeks
USA LP GOATS HEAD SOUP: 12 September 1973: No. 1 - 19 weeks
USA B-side Doo Doo Doo Doo (Heartbreaker): 19 December 1973
UK Compilation LP TIME WAITS FOR NO ONE - ANTHOLOGY 1971 - 1977: 1 June 1979
UK CD box set THE SINGLES COLLECTION 1971-2006: 45 X 45s: 11 April 2011
USA CD box set THE SINGLES COLLECTION 1971-2006: 45 X 45s: 26 April 2011

About brushing and dicing with death, this is *Sympathy For The Devil* Part Two and the album's opening cut, which delves into the more day-to-day exploits of "Mister Fire and Brimstone". The tantalising dealings with Satan seemed to have a voodoo effect on the Stones' supporting cast. Anita Pallenberg herself, not unused to incantation, was getting involved with the Rasta mafia element of the Jamaican community, which was not going down well with the locals. Anita's home base was Tommy Steele's luxurious villa which Keith Richards was to buy later. Andy Johns had been ill prior to the sessions and was deteriorating and he missed the last few days due to his father being seriously ill. Jimmy Miller managed to hang on but also fell to the wayside and was not used again as a Stones producer. The doomsday images were heightened by the photographic artwork of David Bailey on the album cover, which featured the band in funereal mask poses. *Dancing* is one of the LP's few up-beat numbers, with additional percussion provided by Traffic member - his preferred instruments were timbales, bongos and conga. Pascal (Nik Pascal Raicevic) also played percussion. It was one of the album cuts that stood the test of time, being used as a single flip-side in America and also as fodder for subsequent tours.

An out-take exists which has a freer-flow approach, with Billy Preston's keyboard work, additional brass and a closing drum run (* a - 5.01). The backing track was used with live vocals for the Don Kirshner's Rock Concert programme, filmed by Michael Lindsay Hogg in July 1973 and broadcast 29 September that year. This same promo film and *Silver Train* were broadcast on the BBC TV's Old Grey Whistle Test to promote the release of GOATS HEAD SOUP.

586. **FIRST THING** (Jagger, Richard)
25 November - 21 December 1972: Place: Dynamic Sounds, Kingston, Jamaica.
Producer: Jimmy Miller.
Unavailable.

587. **AFTER MUDDY & CHARLIE** (Jagger, Richard)
25 November - 21 December 1972: Place: Dynamic Sounds, Kingston, Jamaica.
Producer: Jimmy Miller.
Unavailable.

588. **FOUR AND IN** (Jagger, Richard)
25 November - 21 December 1972: Place: Dynamic Sounds, Kingston, Jamaica.
Producer: Jimmy Miller.
Unavailable.

589. **ZABADOO** (Jagger, Richard)
25 November - 21 December 1972: Place: Dynamic Sounds, Kingston, Jamaica.
Producer: Jimmy Miller.
Unavailable.

590. **GIVE US A BREAK** (Jagger, Richard)
25 November - 21 December 1972: Place: Dynamic Sounds, Kingston, Jamaica.
Producer: Jimmy Miller.
Unavailable.

591. **JAMAICA** (Jagger, Richard)
25 November - 21 December 1972: Place: Dynamic Sounds, Kingston, Jamaica.
Producer: Jimmy Miller.
Unavailable.

592. **MIAMI** (Jagger, Richard)
25 November - 21 December 1972: Place: Dynamic Sounds, Kingston, Jamaica.
Producer: Jimmy Miller.
Unavailable.

The preceding tracks all marked as unavailable are merely talked about out-takes from the sessions. There is no proof of their identity.

593. CAN YOU HEAR THE MUSIC? (Jagger, Richard) 5.32
25 November - 21 December 1972; 7 May - June 1973: Place: Dynamic Sounds, Kingston, Jamaica; RSM Mobile, Newbury, Olympic Sound Studios, Island Studios, London, England.
Rolling Stones with Jimmy Miller, Pascal, Rebop, Nicky Hopkins, Jim Horn.
Producer: Jimmy Miller.
Engineer: Andy Johns.
Assistant Engineer: Carlton Lee, Howard Kilgour, Doug Bennett, Mikey Chung.
UK LP GOATS HEAD SOUP: 31 August 1973: No. 1 - 14 weeks
USA LP GOATS HEAD SOUP: 12 September 1973: No. 1 - 19 weeks
USA Track Promo EP Goats Head Soup: 14 September 1973

Percussion, bells, piano and the eerie flute playing of Jim Horn introduce this song. Horn was a session musician more renowned for his saxophone playing and had just released a solo album in 1972 under the guidance of Dave Hassinger, named THROUGH THE EYES OF A HORN. It included, amongst many others, Leon Russell, Rita Coolidge, Jim Keltner and Chuck Finley. *Can You Hear The Music?* is a strange, rhetorical, almost "psychedelia revisited" track which explores overdubbed, synthesised, vocal playbacks and wah-wah guitar.
There is a lot of instrumentation quietly going on in the depths of the song, much of it suggested by Mick Taylor and harking back to Brian Jones' experimentation. Jagger sings "can you hear the drums?" to which the bongos reply with a small flourish "can you hear the guitar?" The original guitar riff, written by Keith Richards, is almost lost in the track's unintended complexity and Keith almost failed to recognise the outcome. Mick Taylor contributes the bass and main guitar lines.

594. BROWN LEAVES (Jagger, Richard) 1.50
AKA: Dancing Girls
25 November - 21 December 1972; 5 January - 2 March 1978: Place: Dynamic Sounds, Kingston, Jamaica; EMI, Pathé Marconi, Paris, France.
Producer: Jimmy Miller, Chris Kimsey.
Bootleg only.

This track had a long life but was never officially released. It started off as an instrumental under the name of *Brown Leaves* in 1972 and another version was recorded in 1978. With vocals, it possibly appeared as the out-take *Dancing Girls*.

595. ANGIE (Jagger, Richard) 4.33
25 November - 21 December 1972; 7 May - June 1973: Place: Dynamic Sounds, Kingston, Jamaica; Olympic Sound Studios, Island Studios, London, England.
Played Live: 1973, 1975, 1976, 1982, 1989, 1990, 1994, 1995, 1998, 1999, 2002, 2003, 2005, 2006
Rolling Stones with Nicky Hopkins.
Producer: Jimmy Miller.
Engineer: Andy Johns.
Assistant Engineer: Carlton Lee, Howard Kilgour, Doug Bennett, Mikey Chung.
String arrangement: Nicky Harrison.
UK Single: 20 August 1973: No. 5 - 10 weeks
USA Single: 28 August 1973: No. 1 - 13 weeks
UK LP GOATS HEAD SOUP: 31 August 1973: No. 1 - 14 weeks
USA LP GOATS HEAD SOUP: 12 September 1973: No. 1 - 19 weeks
UK Compilation LP MADE IN THE SHADE: 6 June 1975: No. 14 - 12 weeks
USA Compilation LP MADE IN THE SHADE: 6 June 1975: No. 6 - 9 weeks
UK Compilation LP BY INVITATION ONLY: January 1976
UK Compilation LP TIME WAITS FOR NO ONE - ANTHOLOGY 1971 - 1977: 1 June 1979
UK Compilation LP REWIND 1971-1984 (THE BEST OF THE ROLLING STONES): 29 June 1984: No. 45 - 5 weeks
USA Compilation LP REWIND 1971-1984 (THE BEST OF THE ROLLING STONES): 2 July 1984: No. 86 - 11 weeks
UK Track 12-inch Single Almost Hear You Sigh: 18 June 1990
UK Compilation LP JUMP BACK THE BEST OF THE ROLLING STONES '71 - '93: 22 November 1993: No 16 - 26 weeks
UK CD LP FORTY LICKS: 30 September 2002: No 2 - 45 weeks
USA CD LP FORTY LICKS: 1 October 2002: No 2 - 50 weeks
USA Compilation CD JUMP BACK THE BEST OF THE ROLLING STONES '71 - '93: 24 August 2004: No 30 - 58 weeks
UK CD box set THE SINGLES COLLECTION 1971-2006: 45 X 45s: 11 April 2011
USA CD box set THE SINGLES COLLECTION 1971-2006: 45 X 45s: 26 April 2011

The gently strumming acoustic guitar, mainly played by Mick Taylor supported by Keith Richards, the soft piano touch of Nicky Hopkins (Nicky, especially enjoyed the song but not Kingston and left as soon as he could on 9 December) and the strings incorporated by Nicky Harrison, aided and abetted a worldwide hit single. Written by Keith who felt that, if you could not write a decent ballad, then rock 'n' roll songs would be even more difficult. *Angie* was the first ballad to be released as a single in Britain and the public, although at first shocked by the incongruous nature of the song, launched it to No. 5 in the UK. In the States and in other countries it became a mighty No. 1.
It must be remembered that at this time the Stones were contending for chart positions in Britain where the record-buying public favoured purchasing Donny Osmond, The Carpenters and Gary Glitter. In America, at least, they were still dealing with contemporary artists: Cher (whom they knocked off the top position) and Eddie Kendricks, formerly of The Temptations. Rumours abounded that the song was about David Bowie's wife, Angela, who had been seen socially in Jagger's company but, in fact, the song title was inspired by Keith's relationship with Anita Pallenberg and their recently born daughter, Dandelion - who was more commonly known by her middle name Angela.

In his autobiography *Life*, Keith explains that the first chords and song title were started early April when he did not know the name of his child. "In fact, Anita named her Dandelion. She was only given the name Angela because she was born in a Catholic hospital where they insisted that a proper name be added." She was brought up by Keith's mother in obscurity and still calls herself Angela and now lives (as does her mother) with Marlon, near Redlands.

A mix of *Angie* without strings was used for a new vocal cut by Mick in July 1973 and could be seen and heard on the Don Kirshner Rock Concert American TV programme in September (* a - 4.27). A short extract was shown on the 1990 *25 X 5 The Continuing Adventures Of The Rolling Stones* video with Mick Taylor at the piano. Two promotional films were made by Michael Lindsay Hogg and, as well as this one, another performance movie playback was made. This can be seen in full on *Video Rewind The Rolling Stones Great Video Hits* and is without the strings but does not have the revised vocal. The band are shown sitting on the stage edge resplendent in flared suits (except Charlie Watts) as they mime to the playback. Rose petals flutter down, creating a languid, inert atmosphere, Charlie and Bill seemingly nodding off at the end.

These promo films were now a standard policy and would continue for every single release, since they created maximum, worldwide television exposure with the minimum amount of travel involved. For some reason (maybe a simple error) ABKCO and Westminster Music hold the publishing rights to *Angie* as part of their extraction from Allen Klein, indicating the song was registered earlier.

596. 100 YEARS AGO (Jagger, Richard) 3.59
25 November - 21 December 1972; 7 May - June 1973: Place: Dynamic Sounds, Kingston, Jamaica; Olympic Sound Studios, Island Studios, London, England.
Played Live: 1973
Rolling Stones with Jimmy Miller, Nicky Hopkins, Billy Preston.
Producer: Jimmy Miller.
Engineer: Andy Johns.
Assistant Engineer: Carlton Lee, Howard Kilgour, Doug Bennett, Mikey Chung.
UK LP GOATS HEAD SOUP: 31 August 1973: No. 1 - 14 weeks
USA LP GOATS HEAD SOUP: 12 September 1973: No. 1 - 19 weeks
USA Track Promo EP Goats Head Soup: 14 September 1973

Written in the late 60s and early 70s by Mick Jagger, it has a wistful, reflective aura of times gone by. *100 Years Ago* was eventually recorded and released for the GOATS HEAD SOUP album. Billy Preston was invited to perform at one of the "Goat Patties" (a local delicacy made from road kill) sessions and this time he played the clavinet, which was probably overdubbed in London. The Stones were lucky to have a wealth of keyboard players to call upon. Keith Richards did not feature on the song.

As the lyrics near conclusion, Mick Taylor unpretentiously delivers his first solo, before the conclusion when Billy takes over in the "call me lazy bones" bridge before building the song up again as Charlie Watts increases the pace. Mick Jagger ad-libs "come ons" and "goodbyes" in his indomitable fashion, while Mick Taylor takes a winding and lengthy guitar solo using talents nurtured from his crusading days with John Mayall's Bluesbreakers. An out-take from an acetate has a slight extension at the end (* a - 4.07).

597. HIDE YOUR LOVE (Jagger, Richard) 4.12
25 November - 21 December 1972; 7 May - June 1973: Place: Dynamic Sounds, Kingston, Jamaica; RSM Mobile, Newbury, Olympic Sound Studios, Island Studios, London, England.
Rolling Stones with Jimmy Miller, Pascal, Rebop, Bobby Keys.
Producer: Jimmy Miller.
Engineer: Andy Johns.
Assistant Engineer: Carlton Lee, Howard Kilgour, Doug Bennett, Mikey Chung.
UK LP GOATS HEAD SOUP: 31 August 1973: No. 1 - 14 weeks
USA LP GOATS HEAD SOUP: 12 September 1973: No. 1 - 19 weeks
USA Track Promo EP Goats Head Soup: 14 September 1973

Hide Your Love is one of the weakest tracks recorded for GOATS HEAD SOUP and possibly originated from the summer 1970 sessions pre-EXILE. It includes Mick Jagger tampering in out-take manner on piano and Mick Taylor on lead blues guitar. Andy Johns liked the melody and insisted it was recorded and Mick Taylor again attempts to revive a flagging session with a blistering lead solo. The track has a poor ending, which served to underline an overall lack of depth and power, a criticism of the GOATS HEAD sessions. Indeed, at one time, the track *Criss Cross* was destined for the album but was replaced by this cut. An acetate out-take is available.

The up-tempo numbers such as *Star Star* and *Heartbreaker* are the gems while *Winter* and *Angie* are the only memorable slower tracks. The band's recent album successes demanded a consistent standard of work, which was not forthcoming on GOATS HEAD SOUP - Ian Stewart described it as insipid. The track was later worked on back in London and an out-take exists with the guitar higher in the mix (* a - 4.12). The GOATS HEAD sessions were interrupted in early December when the French authorities stated that they were going to issue the whole group with extradition warrants for using narcotics at the Nellcôte villa.

Mick Jagger, wanting to diffuse the problem so as not to cause potential visa problems for later tours, immediately flew to Nice with Bianca, Mick Taylor, Charlie Watts and Bill Wyman, to protest their innocence and provide written statements. These were accepted but, on 2 December, the French police issued a warrant for the arrest of Keith Richards, Anita Pallenberg and Bobby Keys who had been more cautious and stayed in Jamaica.

598. CRISS CROSS (Jagger, Richard, Taylor) 4.18
AKA: Save Me, Criss-Cross Man
25 November - 21 December 1972; June 1973: Place: Dynamic Sounds, Kingston, Jamaica; Island Recording Studios, London, England.
Rolling Stones with Jimmy Miller, Pascal, Rebop, Nicky Hopkins, Bobby Keys.
Producer: Jimmy Miller.
Bootleg only.

The up-tempo sound of *Criss Cross*, aka *Save Me* and *Criss-Cross Man*, produces a refreshing humorous song about drug taking, kissing lip to lip, tongue to tongue and blood transfusions. *Criss Cross* could have been considered suitable for release, although the band were conscious that too many rock numbers could have spoilt the album's balance (surely it was nothing to do with the Taylor song writing credit?)

Mick Taylor and Keith Richards play comfortably together, Mick doing the dexterous funky lead while Keith plays the rhythm chops. An acetate featuring the song was prepared and coupled with *Silver Train*. In hindsight, they may have reconsidered the decision not to release the track. There are three versions - one without saxophone (* a - 4.30) and two with (* b - 4.20, c - 4.46). The first just has sax at the song's end and the other throughout with a spoken studio moment at the very end: " . . . don't know what he was doing," says Jagger.

599. DOO DOO DOO DOO (HEARTBREAKER) (Jagger, Richard) 3.27
25 November - 21 December 1972; 27-30 January 1973; 7 May - June 1973: Place: Dynamic Sounds, Kingston, Jamaica; Village Recorders, Los Angeles, USA; RSM Mobile, Newbury, Olympic Sound Studios, Island Studios, London, England.
Played Live: 1973, 1975, 1994, 1995, 2003, 2005, 2007
Rolling Stones with Jimmy Miller, Pascal, Rebop, Billy Preston, Bobby Keys, Jim Price, Jim Horn, Chuck Finley.
Producer: Jimmy Miller.
Engineer: Andy Johns.
Assistant Engineer: Carlton Lee, Howard Kilgour, Doug Bennett, Mikey Chung.
UK LP GOATS HEAD SOUP: 31 August 1973: No. 1 - 14 weeks
USA LP GOATS HEAD SOUP: 12 September 1973: No. 1 - 19 weeks
USA Single: 19 December 1973: No. 15 - 6 weeks
UK Compilation LP MADE IN THE SHADE: 6 June 1975: No. 14 - 12 weeks
USA Compilation LP MADE IN THE SHADE: 6 June 1975: No. 6 - 9 weeks
USA Compilation CD REWIND 1971-1984 (THE BEST OF THE ROLLING STONES): 1 December 1986
UK CD box set THE SINGLES COLLECTION 1971-2006: 45 X 45s: 11 April 2011
USA CD box set THE SINGLES COLLECTION 1971-2006: 45 X 45s: 26 April 2011

A purposeful Mick Taylor "wah-wah" guitar and the clavinet keyboard work of Billy Preston blend together well to open the second American single to be taken from the album. Keith Richards rests his guitar and takes time out to play bass and the song is swept along by the horn arrangement, inspired by Jim Price while compatriot Chuck Finley plays the trumpet. The song's tempo is high during the chorus and slower while listening to the story, with Billy Preston responding accordingly.

The lyrics are vengeful, describing two incidents in the alleyways of New York - a boy shot by police in a case of mistaken identity and a 10-year-old girl's drug overdose on a street corner. There was no prescribed solution but one can be sure that the New York Police did not help to make it a No. 15 hit! An alternate take or part recording for the final mix was achieved in Los Angeles during rehearsals for the upcoming Australasia tour from January to February, 1973.

600. STAR STAR (Jagger, Richard) 4.25
AKA: Starfucker
25 November - 21 December 1972; 27-30 January 1973; 7 May - June 1973: Place: Dynamic Sounds, Kingston, Jamaica; Village Recorders, Los Angeles, USA; RSM Mobile, Newbury, Olympic Sound Studios, Island Studios, London, England.
Played Live: 1973, 1975, 1976, 1977, 1978, 1979, 1981, 1997, 1998, 2003
Rolling Stones with Bobby Keys, Jimmy Miller, Pascal, Rebop.
Producer: Jimmy Miller.
Engineer: Andy Johns.
Assistant Engineer: Carlton Lee, Howard Kilgour, Doug Bennett, Mikey Chung.
UK LP GOATS HEAD SOUP: 31 August 1973: No. 1 - 14 weeks
USA LP GOATS HEAD SOUP: 12 September 1973: No. 1 - 19 weeks
USA Track Promo EP Goats Head Soup: 14 September 1973
UK Compilation LP TIME WAITS FOR NO ONE - ANTHOLOGY 1971 - 1977: 1 June 1979

One of the final tracks recorded at the GOATS HEAD session, *Star Star* created a furore with Atlantic Records' late President Ahmet Ertegun. *Starfucker* hit too close to the belt for his liking and he insisted it was retitled to *Star Star* on the album's sleeve. The lyrics, such as "bet you keep your pussy clean" and "giving head to Steve McQueen", are certainly racy. In his defence, Mick Jagger said that he only wrote about what he saw and "star fuckers" are a way of life in the entertainment industry.

Ahmet died from injuries sustained at the Stones' New York City Beacon Theatre gig in 2006 when, as the band took the stage, he fell down a flight of stairs. In his respect to Ahmet, Mick said that he was very liberal in his thinking but he was fantastically sensitive to the market place and, in this case, women's issues. Atlantic Records were keen to disrupt the release of the album due to the inclusion of this track and told the Stones that Steve McQueen would sue. The band responded by sending McQueen a tape of the song and requesting his written permission to release it, which he simply did, not even minding the reference to his then partner Ali MacGraw.

The other problem was that the same verse contained the line "Yeah, I'm making bets that you gonna get John Wayne before he dies". Andy Johns was asked to blur the words John Wayne in the mix but listen hard to see if he did! It is fair to say, however, that Atlantic Records were conscious of anti-pornographic legislation passing through Congress and so the American version of *Star Star* was remixed to bludgeon out the reference to "pussy" and "John Wayne". Lyric sheets were also suitably altered and the chorus became "starbucker" (* a - 4.25)!

It was ironic that, for promotional purposes, a sampler EP of GOATS HEAD SOUP featuring four tracks, including the original mix of *Star Star* (side one, track one), was released with the full blessing of Atlantic. In Britain, the BBC banned the song from all air play. The music itself is basically the definitive rip-off of a Chuck Berry song that has never been written. Keith Richards' R 'n' B riff is lead guitar at its best and served to put the cream on top of an otherwise sagging album. Mick Taylor plays the rhythm track.

Chris Kimsey, Ron Wood at Sphere Studios in 2002 mixing the sound from Ron's Shepherds Bush Empire solo concert (December 2001)

Above and below courtesy of Chris Kimsey.

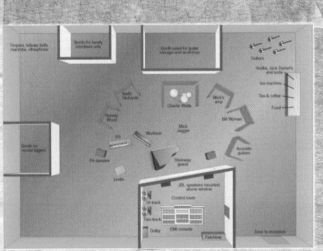

Pathe Marconi, Paris. Studio layout

MIC LINES

#	
#1	VOCAL (MICK) - U47
#2	BRASS D11
#5	GTR AMP (KEEF)
#6	GTR AMP (MICK)
#7	BRASS (AMP)
#8	— DO NOT USE-FAULTY
#9	SLIDE AMP (RONNIE)
#10	GTR AMP 37 (")
#11	BD
#12	SNR
#13	TOM (TOP)
#14	
#15	ROTO TOMS
#16	ROTO TOMS
#17	TOM (FLOOR)
#18	O/H - LIVE OR 20
#19	O/H - BACK
#23	GTR AMP (2002) (RONNIE)
#24	VOCAL - SHURE (MICK)

Microphone patch list at Pathe Marconi (Paris, 1977)

HOTEL CHATEAU FRONTENAC
54, Rue Pierre - Charron
75008 PARIS

MESSAGE TÉLÉPHONÉ

Par M R: MICK JAGGER.

Pour M _____ App' N° _____

REÇU

le _____
à _____ heures

AM AT THE GREAT AMERICAN DISASTER WITH WOODY & JO. TEL: 225. 0177.

CHRIS & CHUCK & BARRY ARE AT THE STUDIO

Jane Rose (Paris, 1977)

Chris Kimsey catching up at Pathé Marconi (Paris, 1977)

Keith's present to Barry Sage Gibson L6S (1977)

Sugar Blue (Paris, 1977)

Pierre "The Fiddler" (Paris, 1977)

Alan Dunn (Paris, 1977)

Chuch Magee relaxing (Paris, 1977)

Philippe (Paris, 1977)

Chris Kimsey at Pathé Marconi (Paris, 1977)

THE MARK III EMI TG DESK USED
AT PATHE MARCONI, PARIS

BARRY SAGE CHILLING.
(PARIS, 1977)

PHILIPPE AU VIN
(PARIS, 1977)

BARRY CHANNELLING THE
KEITH/RON INFLUENCE

CHRIS KIMSEY AT PATHE
MARCONI (PARIS, 1977)

MICK JAGGER, CHRIS KIMSEY
AT PATHE MARCONI (PARIS, 1977)

KEITH IN FLIGHT (1977)

BARRY SAGE IN THE ROLLING
STONES MOBILE (PARIS, 1980)

CHRIS KIMSEY AND MICHAEL BUTTERWORTH
MIXED EMOTIONS AT OLYMPIC STUDIOS, 1989

A N.B.

<u>NOTE</u>:— OLD GTRS. (1950 – 61-2) ARE USUALLY BETTER, IF IN GOOD NICK, BECAUSE THEY WERE MADE PRETTY MUCH BY HAND (WITH ALOT MORE PICK-UPS & HAND COILS)

ALTHOUGH, GIBSON AND FENDER, ARE BOTH GOING BACK TO SOME OF THEIR OLD AND BETTER WAYS.

P.S.
NONE OF THESE INSTRUMENTS WILL BE REASONABLY PRICED AS THE SKY IS DA LIMIT FOR GOOD CONDISH. 50s FENDERS AND GIBBYS!

BUT, SOMETIMES, EVERYBODY GETS LUCKY, AND HE MEET AN ABSOLUTE IDIOT WITH THIS "VERY OLD, OBSOLETE, FENDER CAN'T BE WORTH MUCH,- IF YOU GIVE ME £50 TO PAY MY RENT, YOU CAN HAVE IT. £45? IT'S CLUTTERED UP MY BROOM CUPBOARD FOR YEARS. £40? ALRIGHT, SOLD £35.........!!!!"

HAVE FAITH, BAROLO, THEY DO EXIST!!

THANKS,

& LIST OF GUITARS THAT ONE SHOULD ALWAYS BE ON THE LOOK-OUT FOR. (ESPECIALLY HAMBURG)

① GIBSON "MELODY MAKER" (EARLY '50's) USUALLY 1 PICK-UP, SUNBURST FINISH.

② GIBSON "LES PAUL, JNR." (EARLY '50'S) 1 PICK-UP; OFTEN A RED-MIDDLE '50'S WINE FINISH, BUT VARIOUS MODELS ARE TO BE FOUND.

③ FENDER "TELECASTER" (THROUGH-OUT '50'S) FOUND IN ANY FINISH. NO ALTHO '57?

④ FENDER "STRATOCASTER" (THROUGHOUT '50'S) MANY STYLES, FINISHES.

⑤ GIBSON "ES 125 ½ T" (EARLY-MID 50'S) SEMI-ACOUSTIC ¾ SIZE VERY LIGHT, 1 PICK-UP SUNBURST FINISH. TOPLE.

⑥ CERTAIN "RICKENBACKERS" (EARLY '60'S) TO FIND A GOOD ONE (ALWAYS WORTH TRYING OUT) IS SOMETIME A ODESSY (HERCULES- HEROIC FREAK DEMI-HOTER

⑦ FENDER "BROADCASTER" (VERY EARLY 50'S) NOT VERY C(IK)EY EVEN '49 BAROLO. BUT YOU CAN KEEP AN EYE OPEN

ACOUSTICS ARE BASICALLY DIVIDED: MARTIN' OR GIBSON.
THE BEST ACOUSTIC I'VE EVER HAD WAS A 'MARTIN D28' WHICH WAS MADE AROUND 1930. GIBSONS' BLACK "EVERY BROTHER" CUSTOM (SAME SHAPE, A LITTLE SMALLER THAN A JUMBO) IS A NICE GUITAR.

ACOUSTICS ARE MORE INDIVIDUAL THAN ELECTRIC ONE MAY STAIN AHEAD AND SHOULDERS ABOVE THE REST, ALTHOUGH IT LOOKS THE SAME.

ENJOY LITTLE BUGGERS P.T.O.?

REHEARSING AT PATHE MARCONI (PARIS, 1977)

IAN STEWART AT PATHE MARCONI (PARIS, 1977)

RON AND JO (PARIS, 1977)

JO AND RONNIE (PARIS, 1977)

KEITH, JO AND DAVE JORDAN AT PATHE MARCONI (PARIS, 1977)

Ron, Keith and Mick rehearsing at Pathe Marconi (Paris, 1977)

WOODY, BARRY, CHUCK
AT CHRISTMAS BREAK PARTY (PARIS, 1977)

Hi Barry — Rember 'em the good
times?!! — cheers Woody.
HOPE YOUR BACK SOON (HELP)
THE CHUCK

SESSIONS TO FOLLOW
—————————————

WORK THE NIGHT OF 29TH NOVEMBER AND START AGAIN

ON THE NIGHT OF 6TH DECEMBER.

FINISHING FOR XMAS AFTER THE NIGHT OF THE 15TH.

RESTART IN JANUARY ON THE 5TH IN STUDIO 3.

MOVING TO STUDIO 1 ON JANUARY 16TH UNTIL JANUARY 29TH.

601. **THROUGH THE LONELY NIGHTS** (Jagger, Richard) 4.13
25 November - 21 December 1972; 4 -27 May 1974: Place: Dynamic Sounds, Kingston, Jamaica; Olympic Studios, London, England.
Rolling Stones with Nicky Hopkins, Jimmy Page.
Producer: The Glimmer Twins.
Engineer: Keith Harwood, Glyn Johns.
UK B-side It's Only Rock 'N' Roll: 26 July 1974
USA B-side It's Only Rock 'N' Roll: 27 July 1974
USA CD LP ROLLING STONES RARITIES 1971-2003: 22 November 2005: No. 76 - 6 weeks
UK CD LP ROLLING STONES RARITIES 1971-2003: 28 November 2005
UK CD box set THE SINGLES COLLECTION 1971-2006: 45 X 45s: 11 April 2011
USA CD box set THE SINGLES COLLECTION 1971-2006: 45 X 45s: 26 April 2011

With the declining health of Andy Johns and Jimmy Miller, the Stones were left to officially try out their own production techniques on some out-takes and also two tracks, *Through The Lonely Nights* and *Tops*, which received belated official releases. Keith Harwood, who had been working with Led Zeppelin, stepped in to engineer these tracks. *Through The Lonely Nights* appeared as the flip side of the 1974 single, *It's Only Rock 'N' Roll* and, as such, is obviously a bonus issue - an indication that the Stones themselves wanted the track released.
It is an acoustic ballad and is said to feature guitarist Jimmy Page, a rumour which could easily be true since Keith Harwood, a Led Zeppelin engineer, was involved in the sessions. Page was known to the Stones, having previously played on demo material, notably the tracks available on the Decca-compiled METAMORPHOSIS album, and had also recorded at Mick Jagger's Stargroves house with the mobile unit. However, the lead guitar does sound like Mick Taylor.
The song was rehearsed but not played for the 1978 USA tour. It was released for the first time digitally in 2005 on the ROLLING STONES RARITIES 1971-2003 compilation. Keith Harwood had worked at Olympic and Island Recording (now known as Sarm) on Basing Street, with other Stones engineers Glyn Johns, Andy Johns, Eddie Kramer, Chris Kimsey, George Chkiantz, Phill Brown, Ron Nevison and Rod Thear. Everyone had great affection for him and Rod Thear described him thus: "He was a lovely guy who was very professional, very patient and vastly under-rated. He really got on well with people and to this day is sadly missed." Meanwhile, Keith Grant had built a family of talented individuals including many of the above over the years. There was no one-upmanship and studio hierarchy. Keith maintained that everything was shared to enhance everyone's technique. If the studio equipment was set up exactly the same way, one engineer would get a different sound from another by lending their personality to the recording.

602. **TOPS** (Jagger, Richards) 3.48
25 November - 21 December 1972; 27-30 January 1973; 25 June - 9 August, 30 August - October 1979: Place: Dynamic Sounds, Kingston, Jamaica; Village Recorders, Los Angeles, USA; EMI, Pathé Marconi, Paris, France.
Played Live: 1981
Rolling Stones with Mick Taylor, Nicky Hopkins.
Producer: The Glimmer Twins. Associate Producer: Chris Kimsey.
USA LP TATTOO YOU: 18 August 1981: No. 1 - 30 weeks
UK LP TATTOO YOU: 28 August 1981: No. 2 - 29 weeks

Tops resurfaced on the TATTOO YOU album eight to nine years later, much to Mick Taylor's annoyance since he had left the Stones. He sued them for royalties as there was no credit on the album cover to suggest he was playing and it was obvious the basis of the track was the one recorded back in Jamaica in 1972.
An instrumental out-take, which is longer than the released version, illustrates this (* a - 4.41). Taylor's guitar cannot be missed. Various overdubs may have been overlaid on to the original take but both Bill Wyman and Keith Richards have since indicated that very little alteration was made to the initial recording. Another out-take from Paris has Mick Jagger doing every vocal style imaginable, including falsetto.
On the TATTOO YOU version, the falsetto style was used for the backing vocals. It can be noted that, since *Tops* was released in 1981, Keith Richards is credited under his full name (i.e. with the "s"). And there is no reference to tops, just the top. Mick Taylor was working with Nicky Hopkins on his first solo album, recording four tracks for a title released in 1973 as THE TIN MAN WAS A DREAMER.

603. **SHORT AND CURLIES** (Jagger, Richard) 2.43
25 November - 21 December 1972; 12 April - 2 May; 4-27 May 1974: Place: Dynamic Sounds, Kingston, Jamaica; RSM, Stargroves, Newbury, England; Olympic Studios, London, England.
Rolling Stones with Ray Cooper.
Producer: The Glimmer Twins.
Engineer: Andy Johns, Keith Harwood.
Assistant Engineers: Tapani Tapanainen, Rod Thear, Howard Kilgour, Reinhold Mack, George Chkiantz.
UK LP IT'S ONLY ROCK 'N' ROLL: 16 October 1974: No. 2 - 9 weeks
USA LP IT'S ONLY ROCK 'N' ROLL: 18 October 1974: No. 1 - 11 weeks

The *Short And Curlies* track originated at the GOATS HEAD sessions and was completed in 1974, largely with Keith Richards at the helm and Mick Taylor opening on slide. Ian Stewart was a natural for the boogie-woogie bar-room piano display. He supplied the Stones' roll as opposed to the rock from the band. It is the shortest track on the IT'S ONLY ROCK 'N' ROLL album, lacking conviction and R 'n' B guts. The lyrics describe a woman's firm upper hand. Not Bianca surely?

604. **WAITING ON A FRIEND** (Jagger, Richards) 4.34
AKA: **Waiting For A Friend, Waiting On My Friend**
25 November - 21 December 1972; 22 January - 9 February 1975; 25 June - 9 August, 30 August - October 1979, 11 October - 12 November 1980; April - June 1981: Place: Dynamic Sound, Kingston, Jamaica; RSM, Rotterdam, Netherlands; EMI, Pathé Marconi, Paris, France, RS Mobile, Boulogne-Billancourt, Paris, France; Electric Ladyland, Atlantic Studio, New York, USA.
Played Live: 1981, 1997, 2003, 2005, 2007

Rolling Stones with Billy Preston, Sonny Rollins, Kasper Winding.
Producer: The Glimmer Twins. Associate Producer: Chris Kimsey.
Engineer: Chris Kimsey, Bob Clearmountain, Gary Lyons, Bob Ludwig.
USA LP TATTOO YOU: 18 August 1981: No. 1 - 30 weeks
UK LP TATTOO YOU: 28 August 1981: No. 2 - 29 weeks
UK Single: 17 November 1981: No. 50 - 6 weeks
USA Single: 30 November 1981: No. 13 - 12 weeks
UK Compilation LP REWIND 1971-1984 (THE BEST OF THE ROLLING STONES): 29 June 1984: No. 45 - 5 weeks
USA Compilation LP REWIND 1971-1984 (THE BEST OF THE ROLLING STONES): 2 July 1984: No. 86 - 11 weeks
UK Compilation LP JUMP BACK THE BEST OF THE ROLLING STONES '71 - '93: 22 November 1993: No. 16 - 26 weeks
USA Compilation CD JUMP BACK THE BEST OF THE ROLLING STONES '71 - '93: 24 August 2004: No. 30 - 58 weeks
UK CD box set THE SINGLES COLLECTION 1971-2006: 45 X 45s: 11 April 2011
USA CD box set THE SINGLES COLLECTION 1971-2006: 45 X 45s: 26 April 2011

Waiting On A Friend is another track, discovered by Chris Kimsey, that germinated at Sunset Sound in 1971 and was recorded in Jamaica but not released until 1981. As a result, it became one of his most favoured Stones songs - a true gem. An out-take from Dynamic Sound (*Waiting On My Friend*) shows that the foundation of the track was not significantly altered at all (* a - 3.20). The only requirement was for Mick Jagger to write some lyrics which relate to Mick's coming of age, where he is seeing a lady as a friend, "Making love and breaking hearts. It is a game for youth. But I'm not waiting on a lady. I'm just waiting on a friend."

Two other out-takes emanate from the Paris sessions. One lacks any sax but has the escalating high pitched "ooh-oohs" (* b - 4.19), the other has some sax which may be the work of Mel Collins or Bobby Keys (* c- 3.34). Acoustic guitars strum and the band warm to the song's laid-back character. The superb saxophone work of Sonny Rollins on the released version serves to complement the easy atmosphere. He had over-dubbed his sax, probably at the 1981 session. Rollins' musical background was jazz and he had played with all the greats - Miles Davis, Charlie Parker and Dizzy Gillespie to mention a few. Danish composer and drummer Kasper Winding is said to play percussion on an earlier version of the track. The natural, laid-back trait was used to good effect by Michael Lindsay-Hogg, who was back with the band to film a video to support a chart position.

Failing dismally in Britain, the song and the video were a great success in the States. Filmed on the boulevards of New York, it shows Mick and Keith Richards fraternising with street life. Keith, tobacco reefer in hand, joins Mick as they saunter to St Mark's Bar and Grill where the rest of the band can be found vertically aiding the bars' foundations. Bill Wyman and Charlie Watts lurk at the back on bar stools, while Mick sings the toon to bottle-toting Honest Ron. The film is available on the compilation video project, *Video Rewind The Rolling Stones Great Video Hits* with an edited version released on a promotional single in mono and stereo and the more recent 2011 SINGLES COLLECTION (* d - 3.35).

The GOATS HEAD sessions in Jamaica had concluded and the band headed back (with the exception of Anita) to the UK for Christmas, using up some of the precious days allowed out of tax exile. For Mick and Bianca Jagger, their peace in London was shattered on 23 December 1972 by three earthquakes which ripped through the heart of Managua, the capital of Nicaragua, killing 20,000 people and making 250,000 more homeless. Bianca's mother lived in Managua but all communication was cut off so they did not know what had happened to her. Jagger charted a private jet, complete with medical supplies, and, despite the chaos, they found the Bianca's mother and her family safe. While there, Mick decided that the Stones would do a fund-raising concert at the start of their tour in the USA.

605. IT'S ALL OVER NOW (Womack, Womack) ✏ 4.52
18 January 1973: Place: LA Forum, Inglewood, California, USA.
Rolling Stones with Bobby Keys, Jim Price.
Bootleg only.

The back end of 1972 had seen the re-election of Richard Nixon, with a promise that Henry Kissinger would seal an agreement to extricate America from Vietnam. At the beginning of 1973, a tour was due to commence in Honolulu on 21 January before proceeding to Japan for five sell-out concerts at the Tokyo Budokan Hall. But, at the last minute, the Japanese authorities refused to grant Mick Jagger a visa due to his drug conviction for possessing cannabis in 1967. Even the Australian government pontificated before agreeing to grant him a visa.

However, the planned benefit concert for the Managuan earthquake victims did take place at the LA Forum in Inglewood, California. Ticket prices were increased to ensure the maximum amount was raised, something that Jagger acknowledged to the crowd at the end of *It's All Over Now*: "I like to thank you all for shelling out so much bread, there's no band that's worth one hundred bucks really." The Stones played a long set of 19 numbers, which was very much based on the 1972 tour set-list, even still using the petals over the audience at the end of *Street Fighting Man*. There were no tracks from the forthcoming GOATS HEAD SOUP.

The surprise choice of *It's All Over Now* (described by Jagger at the start as definitely vintage) gave the audience the chance to see what Mick Taylor would do with it. Sure enough, he makes his mark on the song, along with the brass work of Bobby Keys and Jim Price. It was Taylor's last Stones USA gig. *No Expectations* was played for the first time since the Hyde Park 1969 concert while *It's All Over Now* had not been aired since 1965 and was very raunchy in comparison, featuring a Bobby Keys' saxophone. *Sweet Virginia* mentions California, of course, so that was a good choice, and *You Can't Always Get What You Want* included the conga player from the support group Santana.

The show raised $350,000 and, with other fund-raising activities, this amount was doubled. Jagger ensured that a trust would spend the money, since Nicaragua was in the hands of dictator Somoza. Other funds were "lost" and much of Managua, including the cathedral, was not rebuilt. Having done the warm-up concert, the tour started in Honolulu, followed by one date in New Zealand and nine Australian concerts in five cities.

In part of a ABC GTK interview by Juene Pritchard for Australian television in February, Mick Taylor revealed that, personally, the band did not offer him enough musical outlets: "No, there's lots of other things I'd like to do with other people and I will do when I get the opportunity. It is very satisfying playing with the group but it is frustrating on an individual level." He explained that it must be the same for everyone because, after all, a group is a collective entity.

During 1973, Taylor was approached in Jamaica by Free's Paul Rodgers and Simon Kirke at a time when their group had disbanded and they were about to form Bad Company but Mick felt committed to the Stones. The last gig, at the Royal race track in Sydney, Australia, was the last time Nicky Hopkins played live on the road with the band. Fittingly, in a bizarre rock royalty stage entrance they entered the arena in two white horse-drawn carriages.

606. WINDMILL (Jagger, Richard) 3.26
AKA: Wind Call
27-30 January 1973; 9-15 December 1974; 22 January - 9 February 1975: Place: Village Sound Recorders, Los Angeles, USA; Musicland Studios, Munich, Germany; RSM, De Doelen, Rotterdam, Netherlands.
Rolling Stones with Nicky Hopkins.
Producer: Jimmy Miller.
Engineer: Rob Fraboni, Baker Bigsby; Keith Harwood
Bootleg only.

The Stones started rehearsals for the upcoming tour in Los Angeles, with Nicky Hopkins, Jim Price and Bobby Keys, using the opportunity to record and work on some GOATS HEAD material such as *Dancing With Mr D, Doo Doo Doo Doo (Heartbreaker)* and *Star Star. Windmill* may have been a precursor to another out-take called *Wind Call*, which was recorded in 1974. Also, Keith Richards places the track as an EXILE out-take. It is an instrumental with Nicky Hopkins on piano, sounding as though there is something in there trying to get out - but it was not worked on again.
This session was the final one for producer Jimmy Miller, whose health had reached a very low ebb by now. Among the studio engineers was Rob Fraboni, who had worked with the Beach Boys and was just about to find fame by recording Bob Marley, The Band, Bob Dylan and Eric Clapton. Later, in 1997, he was to work on the production of BRIDGES TO BABYLON. The other engineer, Baker Bigsby, had worked with BB King, John Lee Hooker and Harvey Mandel. The Stones themselves would come across Mandel in 1974/75 in the great guitarist hunt.

607. BROWN SUGAR (Jagger, Richard) ✏ 3.56
17 October 1973 (Show One): Place: RSM, National Forest Arena, Brussels, Belgium.
Rolling Stones with Billy Preston, Jim Price, Trevor Lawrence, Steve Madaio.
Producer: The Glimmer Twins
Engineer: Recorded by: Andy Johns
Mixed by: Bob Clearmountain.
USA e-Album BRUSSELS AFFAIR 1973:16 November 2011
UK e-Album BRUSSELS AFFAIR 1973:17 November 2011

On the way back from Australasia in January and February 1973, Mick Jagger and Keith Richards went to their holiday homes in Jamaica. Plans were beginning to be made for a tour of Europe in September and October 1973 which would not involve Nicky Hopkins. He was involved with the release of his solo album but did not recall being asked to re-join the band. It was felt that Billy Preston could cover any keyboard songs.
While in London, Keith met Ronnie Wood through his wife Chrissie Wood and started to meet with him at his home in Wick. He also started a relationship - which was to last off and on for 18 months - with a German model, Uschi Obermaier, who he met at Ronnie's house. It was "off" when Keith had a call to say that Anita Pallenberg had been arrested for drug possession and that she was in a Jamaican jail awaiting trial. Keith wanted to go to her but felt that they may be setting a bait for him so he arranged for someone to pay the so-called bail money to get her out. Anita flew directly to London where it became apparent that she had been badly treated in jail. Later she went to recuperate in Switzerland.
On a return visit to London, in late May and until June 1973, the Stones completed recordings for GOATS HEAD SOUP at Olympic Studios. At the time, Keith's home in Cheyne Walk was raided and both he and Anita were arrested for drug possession and also having an illegal firearm. As well as a revolver, he had an antique shotgun which the police suggested was a sawn-off model. Could it get any worse? It did . . . their home at Redlands burned down at the end of July.
On 25 June, Mick Taylor played with Mike Oldfield, Steve Hillage and Kevin Ayers in a special performance of Tubular Bells at the Queen Elizabeth Hall in London. Rehearsals for the tour, using a mobile recording unit, began at the De Doelen concert hall, in Rotterdam, Netherlands on 18 August. There is a bootleg of some of these recordings and, though the sound quality is very poor, it was apparent that they were going to play some tracks from the newly-released album (*100 Years Ago, Hide Your Love, Angie, Star Star, Can You Hear The Music, Heartbreaker, Dancing With Mr. D* were all practised).
During the tour, the album went to No. 1 in both the UK and USA. Security man James Callaghan was recruited at the start of a 30-year career with the band. The support acts for the tour were Billy Preston, who played with the Stones on certain numbers, and Kracker (a Jimmy Miller-produced protégé, who were the first band signed to Rolling Stones Records), with whom Trevor Lawrence had played. At some concerts, Trevor would play alto sax with the Stones. The brass section had been extended to three, since it also included trumpeter Steve Madaio who, in 1972, recorded with BB King and on Stevie Wonder's classic INNERVISIONS album. Stevie was also associated with other past and future Stones session personnel - Jim Horn, Chuck Findley and Ernie Watts (all brass) and Dr John and Ollie Brown. Bobby Keys did not survive until the end of the tour as stories circulated that he was found in a bath of champagne with a groupie. He was sacked by Mick due to his excesses, although Bobby thought that the incident actually occurred in 1970. In his autobiography, *Every Night's A Saturday Night*, Keys said that the reason he left was due to his drug dependency and a need to rehabilitate. It was also fellow-Texan Jim Price's last performance for the band.
The tour commenced in Austria on 1 September and went to Germany before concentrating on the home countries. England and Scotland (a planned concert at Cardiff Castle, Wales was cancelled) were covered then it was back to Austria, Switzerland, Germany (again), Denmark, Sweden, Germany (again), the Netherlands and Belgium before ending in what was then West Berlin in West Germany.
During the tour, Mick Taylor played with Billy Preston's support band, sometimes disguised with a large afro-bush wig borrowed from Billy. The set list included Beatles songs which had been recorded during Billy's time with them in 1969, such as *Let It Be, Get Back* and even the earlier track *Day Tripper*. The results can be found on a 1974 album BILLY PRESTON'S LIVE EUROPEAN TOUR.

608. MIDNIGHT RAMBLER (Jagger, Richard) ✏ 12.53
17 October 1973 (Show One): Place: RSM, National Forest Arena, Brussels, Belgium.
Rolling Stones with Billy Preston, Jim Price, Trevor Lawrence, Steve Madaio.
Producer: The Glimmer Twins
Engineer: Recorded by: Andy Johns
Mixed by: Bob Clearmountain.
USA e-Album BRUSSELS AFFAIR 1973:16 November 2011
UK e-Album BRUSSELS AFFAIR 1973:17 November 2011

609. **STREET FIGHTING MAN** (Jagger, Richard) ✎ 3.27
17 October 1973 (Show One): Place: RSM, National Forest Arena, Brussels, Belgium.
Rolling Stones with Billy Preston, Jim Price, Trevor Lawrence, Steve Madaio.
Producer: The Glimmer Twins
Engineer: Recorded by: Andy Johns
Mixed by: Bob Clearmountain.
USA e-Album BRUSSELS AFFAIR 1973:16 November 2011
UK e-Album BRUSSELS AFFAIR 1973:17 November 2011

610. **GIMME SHELTER** (Jagger, Richard) ✎ 5.33
17 October 1973 (Show Two): Place: RSM, National Forest Arena, Brussels, Belgium.
Rolling Stones with Billy Preston, Jim Price, Trevor Lawrence, Steve Madaio.
Producer: The Glimmer Twins
Engineer: Recorded by: Andy Johns
Mixed by: Bob Clearmountain.
USA e-Album BRUSSELS AFFAIR 1973:16 November 2011
UK e-Album BRUSSELS AFFAIR 1973:17 November 2011

611. **HAPPY** (Jagger, Richard) ✎ 3.14
17 October 1973 (Show Two): Place: RSM, National Forest Arena, Brussels, Belgium.
Rolling Stones with Billy Preston, Jim Price, Trevor Lawrence, Steve Madaio.
Producer: The Glimmer Twins
Engineer: Recorded by: Andy Johns
Mixed by: Bob Clearmountain.
USA e-Album BRUSSELS AFFAIR 1973:16 November 2011
UK e-Album BRUSSELS AFFAIR 1973:17 November 2011

612. **TUMBLING DICE** (Jagger, Richard) ✎ 5.04
17 October 1973 (Show Two): Place: RSM, National Forest Arena, Brussels, Belgium.
Rolling Stones with Billy Preston, Jim Price, Trevor Lawrence, Steve Madaio.
Producer: The Glimmer Twins
Engineer: Recorded by: Andy Johns
Mixed by: Bob Clearmountain.
USA e-Album BRUSSELS AFFAIR 1973:16 November 2011
UK e-Album BRUSSELS AFFAIR 1973:17 November 2011

613. **STAR STAR** (Jagger, Richard) ✎ 4.16
17 October 1973 (Show Two): Place: RSM, National Forest Arena, Brussels, Belgium.
Rolling Stones with Billy Preston, Jim Price, Trevor Lawrence, Steve Madaio.
Producer: The Glimmer Twins
Engineer: Recorded by: Andy Johns
Mixed by: Bob Clearmountain.
USA e-Album BRUSSELS AFFAIR 1973:16 November 2011
UK e-Album BRUSSELS AFFAIR 1973:17 November 2011

614. **DANCING WITH MR. D** (Jagger, Richard) ✎ 4.37
17 October 1973 (Show Two): Place: RSM, National Forest Arena, Brussels, Belgium.
Rolling Stones with Billy Preston, Jim Price, Trevor Lawrence, Steve Madaio.
Producer: The Glimmer Twins
Engineer: Recorded by: Andy Johns
Mixed by: Bob Clearmountain.
USA e-Album BRUSSELS AFFAIR 1973:16 November 2011
UK e-Album BRUSSELS AFFAIR 1973:17 November 2011

615. **DOO DOO DOO DOO (HEARTBREAKER)** (Jagger, Richard) ✎ 5.03
17 October 1973 (Show Two): Place: RSM, National Forest Arena, Brussels, Belgium.
Rolling Stones with Billy Preston, Jim Price, Trevor Lawrence, Steve Madaio.
Producer: The Glimmer Twins
Engineer: Recorded by: Andy Johns
Mixed by: Bob Clearmountain.
USA e-Album BRUSSELS AFFAIR 1973:16 November 2011
UK e-Album BRUSSELS AFFAIR 1973:17 November 2011

616. **ANGIE** (Jagger, Richard) ✎ 5.15
17 October 1973 (Show Two): Place: RSM, National Forest Arena, Brussels, Belgium.
Rolling Stones with Billy Preston, Jim Price, Trevor Lawrence, Steve Madaio.
Producer: The Glimmer Twins
Engineer: Recorded by: Andy Johns
Mixed by: Bob Clearmountain.
USA e-Album BRUSSELS AFFAIR 1973:16 November 2011
UK e-Album BRUSSELS AFFAIR 1973:17 November 2011

617. **YOU CAN'T ALWAYS GET WHAT YOU WANT** (Jagger, Richard) ✎ 11.00
17 October 1973 (Show Two): Place: RSM, National Forest Arena, Brussels, Belgium.
Rolling Stones with Billy Preston, Jim Price, Trevor Lawrence, Steve Madaio.
Producer: The Glimmer Twins
Engineer: Recorded by: Andy Johns
Mixed by: Bob Clearmountain.
USA e-Album BRUSSELS AFFAIR 1973:16 November 2011
UK e-Album BRUSSELS AFFAIR 1973:17 November 2011

618. **HONKY TONK WOMEN** (Jagger, Richard) ✎ 3.11
17 October 1973 (Show Two): Place: RSM, National Forest Arena, Brussels, Belgium.
Rolling Stones with Billy Preston, Jim Price, Trevor Lawrence, Steve Madaio.
Producer: The Glimmer Twins
Engineer: Recorded by: Andy Johns
Mixed by: Bob Clearmountain.
USA e-Album BRUSSELS AFFAIR 1973:16 November 2011
UK e-Album BRUSSELS AFFAIR 1973:17 November 2011

619. **ALL DOWN THE LINE** (Jagger, Richard) ✎ 4.20
17 October 1973 (Show Two): Place: RSM, National Forest Arena, Brussels, Belgium.
Rolling Stones with Billy Preston, Jim Price, Trevor Lawrence, Steve Madaio.
Producer: The Glimmer Twins
Engineer: Recorded by: Andy Johns
Mixed by: Bob Clearmountain.
USA e-Album BRUSSELS AFFAIR 1973:16 November 2011
UK e-Album BRUSSELS AFFAIR 1973:17 November 2011

620. **RIP THIS JOINT** (Jagger, Richard) ✎ 2.25
17 October 1973 (Show Two): Place: RSM, National Forest Arena, Brussels, Belgium.
Rolling Stones with Billy Preston, Jim Price, Trevor Lawrence, Steve Madaio.
Producer: The Glimmer Twins
Engineer: Recorded by: Andy Johns
Mixed by: Bob Clearmountain.
USA e-Album BRUSSELS AFFAIR 1973:16 November 2011
UK e-Album BRUSSELS AFFAIR 1973:17 November 2011

621. **JUMPIN' JACK FLASH** (Jagger, Richard) ✎ 3.27
17 October 1973 (Show Two): Place: RSM, National Forest Arena, Brussels, Belgium.
Rolling Stones with Billy Preston, Jim Price, Trevor Lawrence, Steve Madaio.
Producer: The Glimmer Twins
Engineer: Recorded by: Andy Johns
Mixed by: Bob Clearmountain.
USA e-Album BRUSSELS AFFAIR 1973:16 November 2011
UK e-Album BRUSSELS AFFAIR 1973:17 November 2011

The tour heralded a new-found camp, glittery image, where make-up was lavish and Mick Jagger wore an array of zipped jump-suits particularly revealing at crutch level. The sound had reached a new tour de force where the tempo was maintained virtually throughout the set, although the performances were somewhat sporadic. The only quiet number most nights was *Angie*. The other GOATS HEAD SOUP songs played extensively were *Star Star*, *Heartbreaker* and *Dancing With Mr. D*. Mick Taylor was a revelation, his lead guitar work propelling the band together on a high musical plain, as can be heard on *Dancing*. His last concert with the Stones was on 19 October 1973, at the final show in Berlin.
Over the years, the most popular bootleg recordings of the Stones came from this tour, especially the Belgium and London concerts, due to a USA King Biscuit Flower Hour Radio Show, which was mixed and over-dubbed by Mick Jagger himself. It was recorded by Andy Johns using the well-travelled Rolling Stones Mobile van. Decca and ABKCO had prevented release of any of their material until 1976, making an official release unlikely. Music journalist Nick Kent wrote some inner-sleeve notes, having accompanied the Stones on the tour, but no release was made at the time.
However, in 2011, without much self-acclaim, a business link was established in the USA with the new Internet music download service from Google and a Brussels

recording was unveiled. It did not consist of the original broadcast, concentrating instead on the second show in the Forest Concert Arena and three songs from the afternoon event. The launch was made to the rest of the world with a potentially significant new web site, labelled Stones Archives.

An official statement claimed that, over the next year, five further live concerts would be made available. Bob Clearmountain had been asked to mix the tapes from the shows and his amazing work has at last done full justice to this much bootlegged and loved concert recording. His instrumental separation for the performers is supreme and Bill Wyman's bass has never been captured more perfectly. At last Mick Taylor had a live legacy which illustrated his lethal, potent force. The climax on *Street Fighting Man* with Jagger exhorting his primal urges, the guitars meshing and overflowing, the rhythm pounding and the swirling keyboard signalling a manic conclusion, is superb. Thank goodness the rusty vault doors had been truly oiled and greased and were at last open in such a non-assuming way.

The 1973 tour had not included France because of the warrant out for Keith's arrest. In October 1973, the French authorities fined Keith Richards, Anita Pallenberg and Bobby Keys and gave them a 12-month suspended sentence. Keith was also restricted from entering France for two years and he was back in court again on 24 October. Following the bust in June, Keith admitted, at Marlborough Street Magistrates Court, London, to having cannabis, a small amount of Chinese heroin, mandrax tablets, a revolver, a shotgun and 110 rounds of ammunition. The judge was incensed at the obvious sawn-off shotgun police "stitch-up" and only fined him a paltry total of £205. His solicitor fees were slightly more!

On a sad note, Gram Parsons died on 19 September 1973, apparently from a drug and alcohol overdose at the Joshua Tree Inn, near Palm Springs, Los Angeles. He had just completed his second solo album GRIEVOUS ANGEL and was enjoying a holiday in the Joshua Tree National Monument Park. Keith and Bobby sat in their hotel bar after a show in northern Austria and mulled over the loss but both continued on their own self-destructive course.

Before the funeral, Phil Kaufman (a previous minder for Jagger), who was the road manager and a general friend of Gram, stole his body from the mortuary, took it to the Joshua Tree Park and cremated it as he had apparently agreed to do in a pact with Gram. This might seem bizarre and weird but Gram did not want his body returned to his estranged family. Keith was very saddened by the death but Gram was just another cat seemingly destined to die young.

622. SLOW DOWN AND STOP (Jagger, Richard) 3.02
14-25 November 1973: Place: Musicland Studios, Munich, Germany.
Rolling Stones with Nicky Hopkins.
Producer: The Glimmer Twins
Engineer: Reinhold Mack.
Bootleg only.

Slow Down And Stop is an unpromising instrumental with Nicky Hopkins on piano. The Stones, minus Mick Taylor who was ill, went to Giorgio Moroder's Musicland Munchen Studios in late 1973 to perform material for an album planned for a quick release. Munich was an attraction due to the fact that Uschi Obermaier lived there, which appealed to Mick Jagger but, more importantly, to Keith Richards. The recording format was intended to be a return to the spontaneity captured in sessions such as BEGGARS BANQUET. Mick hoped to release some live material from the 1973 tour on one side of an album and new studio tracks on the other, early in 1974. He particularly wanted the new live arrangement of *You Can't Always Get What You Want* released but, because it was a Decca song, it was proving difficult to get their agreement. However, the use of Jimmy Miller as the band's producer was now at an amicable end, so Mick and Keith naturally drifted into producing themselves, hence the Glimmer Twins (a pseudonym for the duo coined by a woman in a bar who had asked the pair to "Give us a Glimmer" of their true identity) being credited with production.

The production team was enhanced by Andy Johns on a few of the session's earlier numbers but he was a spent Stones force and was also not seeing eye to eye with the band, so he jumped before being fired. In contrast, Keith Harwood, who had been recording with Humble Pie, Mott The Hoople, Wishbone Ash and Family, was becoming a very Stones-friendly engineer. Reinhold Mack, a local engineer who found considerable success later with Electric Light Orchestra and Queen, was strangely credited as Mac 'Munich' on the IT'S ONLY ROCK 'N' ROLL album.

623. AIN'T TOO PROUD TO BEG (Whitfield, Holland) 3.31
14-25 November 1973; 12 April - 2 May; 4-27 May 1974: Place: Musicland Studios, Munich, Germany; RSM, Stargroves, Newbury, England; Olympic Studios, London, England.
Played Live: 1975, 1976, 2002, 2003, 2005, 2006, 2007
Rolling Stones with Billy Preston, Ed Leach, Ray Cooper.
Producer: The Glimmer Twins.
Engineer: Andy Johns, Keith Harwood.
Assistant Engineers: Tapani Tapanainen, Rod Thear, Howard Kilgour, Reinhold Mack, George Chkiantz, Reinhold Mack.
UK LP IT'S ONLY ROCK 'N' ROLL: 16 October 1974: No. 2 - 9 weeks
USA LP IT'S ONLY ROCK 'N' ROLL: 18 October 1974: No. 1 - 11 weeks
USA Single: 25 October 1974: No. 17 - 7 weeks
UK CD box set THE SINGLES COLLECTION 1971-2006: 45 X 45s: 11 April 2011
USA CD box set THE SINGLES COLLECTION 1971-2006: 45 X 45s: 26 April 2011

Very occasionally, Tamla Motown tracks undoubtedly provided the band with inspiration, their copies of *Can I Get A Witness* and *Hitch Hike* instantly coming to mind. It is no surprise that they tackled this Temptations number, giving it the Stones treatment in their own unique manner, thereby allowing a new generation to steep themselves in Motown history. Billy Preston leads the band into the song on clavinet with a compressed wah-wah effect, promptly followed by Charlie Watts, who launches into the beat, kicking his foot pedals. The track also features Elton John's percussion man, Ray Cooper, on bongos and Eddie Leach rapping the cowbell. Keith Richards is inspirational, playing a particularly raw electric guitar. Also, his backing vocals, especially on the first verse, are quite memorable! Keith's guitar sound used a two amps technique. Andy Johns positioned a standard studio amp and one with an extension lead into a booth which caught a double guitar sound.

There is an out-take - a longer version with an extended outro but still with the pronounced echoed finish (* a - 3.51). *Ain't Too Proud To Beg* was edited (* b - 2.48) and released as a single in the States, just reaching the Billboard Top 20 - The Temptations version had previously peaked at No. 13 in November 1966. In June 1974, a promotional film was made by Michael Lindsay-Hogg with the backing track and live vocals. At the end, a garish blow-up inflatable (the first time an inflatable had been used in the rock arena) separated Mick Jagger from the band, who wore co-ordinated bright chiffon clothes. Mick would take this style to new levels on the 1975 American tour. The video was broadcast on Don Kirshner's Rock Concert programme in October 1974.

624. DRIFT AWAY (Williams) 4.10
14-25 November 1973, 20 February - 3 March; 12 April - 2 May 1974: Place: Musicland Studios, Munich, Germany; RSM, Stargroves, Newbury, England
Rolling Stones with Nicky Hopkins, Billy Preston, Ron Wood.
Producer: The Glimmer Twins.
Engineer: Andy Johns.
Reinhold Mack.
Bootleg only.

So you want to get lost in rock and roll? This is adequately achieved by the Stones on Dobie Gray's March 1973 No. 5 USA hit. Mick Jagger sings the lyrics with sparse accompaniment, apart from the piano and organ work of Nicky Hopkins and Billy Preston. Recorded live, it is a typical studio "run through" but very popular in out-take circles. There are two takes of the song (* a - 3.52). Andy Johns recalled Keith Richards listening incessantly to Dobie Gray's version and thought Ron Wood played on the session. The songwriter is hard to detect with some crediting Williams, as in the producer of Dobie Gray, Mentor Williams or just Chandler. The song was also covered on Rod Stewart's ATLANTIC CROSSING album in 1975. Mick Jagger intended to record a solo album, too, and had made his intentions well known to the band but they laughed it off because those plans never seemed to materialise as Stones projects took precedence.

625. IF YOU CAN'T ROCK ME (Jagger, Richard) 3.47
14-25 November 1973; 12 April - 2 May; 4-27 May 1974: Place: Musicland Studios, Munich, Germany; RSM, Stargroves, Newbury, England; Olympic Studios, London, England.
Played Live: 1975, 1976, 2002, 2003
Rolling Stones with Billy Preston, Ray Cooper.
Producer: The Glimmer Twins.
Engineer: Andy Johns, Keith Harwood.
Assistant Engineers: Tapani Tapanainen, Rod Thear, Howard Kilgour, Reinhold Mack, George Chkiantz.
UK LP IT'S ONLY ROCK 'N' ROLL: 16 October 1974: No. 2 - 9 weeks
USA LP IT'S ONLY ROCK 'N' ROLL: 18 October 1974: No. 1 - 11 weeks
UK Track CD Single Terrifying: 30 July 1990

If You Can't Rock Me, the opening cut, sets the tone for a non-revolutionary but competent album. The band's on stage and it's one of those nights - let's rock and roll. Charlie Watts' drum sound is more upfront, resonating like a machine gun, while Mick Taylor's guitar pierces the airwaves through Keith Richards' incessant riff machine deploying Andy John's two amps trick. There is a bass solo in the middle which is played by Keith, with Bill Wyman apparently missing from the session, and an alternate vocal mix, with an introductory plea from Jagger for the beat to be regular, as well as different ad-libs of "well" after the bass solo (* a - 3.49). The track's lyrics are sadly bitter and indicate a tiredness of not only the rock and roll lifestyle but also perhaps a personal dying relationship, as with Bianca.

626. FINGERPRINT FILE (Jagger, Richard) 6.33
14-25 November 1973; 12 April - 2 May; 4-27 May 1974: Place: Musicland Studios, Munich, Germany; RSM, Stargroves, Newbury, England; Olympic Studios, London, England.
Played Live: 1975, 1976
Rolling Stones with Billy Preston, Nicky Hopkins, Ray Cooper, Charlie Jolly.
Producer: The Glimmer Twins.
Engineer: Glyn Johns, Andy Johns, Keith Harwood.
Assistant Engineers: Tapani Tapanainen, Rod Thear, Howard Kilgour, Reinhold Mack, George Chkiantz.
UK LP IT'S ONLY ROCK 'N' ROLL: 16 October 1974: No. 2 - 9 weeks
USA LP IT'S ONLY ROCK 'N' ROLL: 18 October 1974: No. 1 - 11 weeks

Standing at six minutes and 40 seconds, *Fingerprint File* is the longest track on IT'S ONLY ROCK 'N' ROLL. *Fingerprint* describes the paranoia of an American society with Mick Jagger playing the role of a guy being followed by the FBI. The song was close to the truth since, in 1973, the Stones had been denied visas to work in the States due to the riots on the 1972 tour and their drug convictions. They would work hard to rescind this but it did explain the reason why they went to record in Munich. Jagger's vocals are the key to the theme of the song as he hustles the rhythm forward in rap manner.
Mick Jagger also takes up a guitar, joining the "slaves of rhythm", playing through a distorted Leslie amp, while Bill Wyman (possibly) and Mick Taylor experiment with Nicky Hopkins' Elka string synthesiser. Keith Richards plays the wah wah guitar effects which he over-dubbed later. Billy Preston is on the clavinet, Nicky on the piano and Mick Taylor also plays bass guitar. After the November sessions, Bill Wyman went to Los Angeles to record his first solo album, MONKEY GRIP, with producer Chris Kimsey - he was the first member to complete his own individual project. Obviously, a work permit was not a problem for him.
Mick also had plans to produce a solo album at this point since he had a number of songs unsuitable for the Stones. He had thought about recording with Billy Preston, Mick Taylor and Eric Clapton in 1974 - Taylor was also hoping to make a solo album in the same year. The tabla player on *Fingerprint File*, credited as Charlie Jolly, is in fact the Indian percussionist Jolly Kunjappu. The tabla is a term for two drums, the larger one being the tabla and the smaller copper one being the banya. Glyn Johns is credited solely with mixing the resultant track, his only contribution to the album. *Fingerprint File* is the ultimate studio track, using all available techniques to create a unique atmosphere.
A longer slower version of the song can be found on an out-take (* a - 7.05). This is the original intended cut which was speeded up by nearly 10 per cent for the released track, making Mick's vocals much more sultry and slurred. This was probably released by mistake on the SHM/SACD CD format of IT'S ONLY ROCK 'N' ROLL in Japan in 2011. The transfer was engineered by Mick McKenna, who was recruited by Ian Stewart to work on the Rolling Stones mobile and accompanied the band on their European tour in 1973.
After Munich, Bill and Mick went to Los Angeles and attended a session with John Lennon and Danny Kortchmar, also featuring Jesse Ed Davis (guitar), Bobby Keys and Trevor Lawrence (brass), Al Kooper (keyboards), Jack Bruce (bass - so no Bill), Jim Keltner (drums) and, on backing vocals, singer-songwriter Harry Nilsson. A track called *Too Many Cooks (Spoil The Soup)* was recorded and produced by John Lennon. An acetate was made and bootlegs circulated but it did not gain an official release until 2007, when it appeared on Mick Jagger's solo album THE VERY BEST OF MICK JAGGER. The sleeve notes said that Mick could not remember if John Lennon played guitar.

627. BLACK LIMOUSINE (Jagger, Richards, Wood) 3.33
AKA: Broken Head Blues
14-25 November 1973; 10 October - 29 November, 6 - 15 December 1977, 5 January - 2 March 1978, 25 June - 9 August, 30 August -
October 1979: Place: Musicland Studios, Munich, Germany; EMI, Pathé Marconi, Paris, France.
Played Live: 1981, 1982, 1995
Rolling Stones with Ronnie Wood.
Producer: The Glimmer Twins. Associate Producer: Chris Kimsey.
Engineer: Chris Kimsey, Bob Clearmountain, Gary Lyons, Bob Ludwig.
Reinhold Mack.
USA LP TATTOO YOU: 18 August 1981: No. 1 - 30 weeks
UK LP TATTOO YOU: 28 August 1981: No. 2 - 29 weeks
UK Compilation CD RONNIE WOOD ANTHOLOGY THE ESSENTIAL CROSSEXION: 26 June 2006
USA Compilation CD RONNIE WOOD ANTHOLOGY THE ESSENTIAL CROSSEXION: 26 September 2006

Black Limousine is possibly a Jagger, Richards song created in 1973 and offered to Ronnie Wood in exchange for his songwriting work on *It's Only Rock 'N' Roll* -
he then worked on the track which was reinvented in 1978 and 1979. Ronnie says it is a tribute to Muddy Waters or Jimmy Reed - it has an awkward timing like
a Reed song - and also attributes it to blues steel guitarist Harding 'Hop' (a derivation from harmonica/harp) Wilson. At that time, they were dabbling with the
Jimmy Reed songs *Shame Shame Shame* and *You Don't Have To Go.*
Broken Head Blues (a bootlegger's title) is an instrumental track with the same type of Muddy Waters/Jimmy Reed boogie approach but less harmonica. It was
recorded in November 1973 when Ronnie Wood attended for a day. *Black Limousine* was then laid down, with vocals, for both the SOME GIRLS and EMOTIONAL
RESCUE sessions - at least four out-takes show the song's progression. The lyrics were a lament by Mick to a lost babe.
The early out-takes have a 1-2-3 introduction and early lyrics seem optimistic about a relationship (* a - 4.13), while another has steel guitar and a more stilted
arrangement (* b - 3.26). The other two are both longer than the released take and have the well-crafted guitar solos - one which seems to be close to the finished
cut was made in 1978, except it has a longer intro to the vocals and the solo at the end is taken to its conclusion rather than fading out (* c - 4.06). It was edited
to a passable cut in 1979 and there is an out-take of this (* d - 3.39).
Black Limousine was a departure in style from the Stones' previously-recorded outings. A renewed vigour symbolised a return to basics but the guitar sound was
distinctly modern or, as Ian Stewart was heard to say, "bloody Status Quo music". It is, however, a good boogie song, complete with harp solos complementing
Ronnie's lead guitar solo work, and Ian Stewart does reluctantly join in on piano. *Black Limousine* was left off the SOME GIRLS and EMOTIONAL RESCUE albums
but thought suitable for the generally incohesive TATTOO YOU. Ron Wood is co-credited on his first Stones composition but I suspect that, after all these years, he
would have preferred the songwriting link to *It's Only Rock 'N' Roll.*

628. IT'S ONLY ROCK 'N' ROLL (BUT I LIKE IT) (Jagger, Richard) 5.07
2-7 December 1973; 12 April - 2 May; 4-27 May 1974: Place: The Wick Home Studios, London, England; RSM, Stargroves, Newbury, England;
Olympic Studios, London, England.
Played Live: 1975, 1976, 1977, 1989, 1990, 1994, 1995, 1997, 1998, 1999, 2002, 2003, 2005, 2006, 2007
Rolling Stones with Ron Wood, Ray Cooper, Kenny Jones, Willy Weeks, David Bowie.
Producer: The Glimmer Twins.
Engineer: George Chkiantz, Andy Johns, Keith Harwood.
Assistant Engineers: Tapani Tapanainen, Rod Thear, Howard Kilgour, Reinhold Mack.
UK Single: 26 July 1974: No. 10 - 7 weeks
USA Single: 27 July 1974: No. 16 - 7 weeks
UK LP IT'S ONLY ROCK 'N' ROLL: 16 October 1974: No. 2 - 9 weeks
USA LP IT'S ONLY ROCK 'N' ROLL: 18 October 1974: No. 1 - 11 weeks
UK Compilation LP MADE IN THE SHADE: 6 June 1975: No. 14 - 12 weeks
USA Compilation LP MADE IN THE SHADE: 6 June 1975: No. 6 - 9 weeks
UK Compilation LP BY INVITATION ONLY: January 1976
UK Compilation LP REWIND 1971-1984 (THE BEST OF THE ROLLING STONES): 29 June 1984: No. 45 - 5 weeks
USA Compilation CD REWIND 1971-1984 (THE BEST OF THE ROLLING STONES): 1 December 1986
UK Compilation LP JUMP BACK THE BEST OF THE ROLLING STONES '71 - '93: 22 November 1993: No. 16 - 26 weeks
UK CD LP FORTY LICKS: 30 September 2002: No. 2 - 45 weeks
USA CD LP FORTY LICKS: 1 October 2002: No. 2 - 50 weeks
USA Compilation CD JUMP BACK THE BEST OF THE ROLLING STONES '71 - '93: 24 August 2004: No. 30 - 58 weeks
UK CD box set THE SINGLES COLLECTION 1971-2006: 45 X 45s: 11 April 2011
USA CD box set THE SINGLES COLLECTION 1971-2006: 45 X 45s: 26 April 2011

The reason for such a strong personnel gathering on this record is mainly due to the inimitable Ron Wood. He had played for many years with Rod Stewart and
The Faces and, in late 1973 and early 1974, had started to record a solo project, belligerently titled I'VE GOT MY OWN ALBUM TO DO. Keith Richards, Mick Taylor
and Mick Jagger contributed quite extensively to this album and, one evening in December at The Wick, Ron's home in Richmond, *It's Only Rock And Roll* started
to evolve. Mick Jagger and Ron Wood were on guitars, Willie Weeks on bass guitar, Kenny Jones the drums and David Bowie took some backing vocals.
Bowie had just completed the recording of the DIAMOND DOGS album with Keith Harwood and Ronnie had played guitar on an out-take from PIN UPS called
Growing Up, written by Bruce Springsteen. Ron handed the end product of *It's Only Rock 'N' Roll* to Mick Jagger, who took the tape back to the group in a deal. In
exchange, Mick gave him *I Can Feel The Fire*, another Jagger, Wood collaboration, which became the opening track on his solo album, credited in his own name.
Ron Wood later described this incident in his 2007 biography *Ronnie*: "It was my apprenticeship".
The album cover credits Ronnie just for "inspiration" so he might have to wait a while before ending up on an album by his favourite band. Charlie Watts agreed
that there was no need to re-do the drums since he felt he could do no better. Willie Weeks had just completed sessions with Rod Stewart for his solo album SMILER

and was also Donny Hathaway's bass guitarist. Mick Taylor was in hospital during some of the Munich sessions and had missed one of the two major get-togethers. Perhaps this is why he made some rather jaded remarks concerning the song's forced rock and roll nature.

It was George Chkiantz who followed the song from Wick to the end result where the tapes were transferred and mixed at Olympic. Rod Thear, along with Tapani Tapanainen, was invited by Keith Harwood to join the Stones sessions which he was masterminding following Andy Johns' swift departure. Rod was involved with Keith's guitar overdub and they experimented with different locations. Olympic had three floors, with a reception and a garage on the ground, the main studio on the first, and the area used for cinematic soundtracks and a mezzanine above that.

Rod could not resist showing off his current day-work on a particularly gory film not realising Keith was squeamish on the sight of blood. He was quick to get back to the recording work which, for the guitar, was made from the garage workshop. The guitars were in the style of Chuck Berry and, when mixing, Ron's lead part was wiped by Keith, leaving just his acoustic 12-string, while the vocals were re-done and Ian Stewart supplied a piano melody. The original backing vocals of "I like it, like it, yes I do" from the Wick would have only been there in part due to microphone leakage, otherwise they were re-done. *It's Only Rock 'N' Roll* is not an out and out rocker - it is played mid-tempo with some acoustic parts.

Basically it is a riposte by Mick at some of the press who were predicting the band's demise, the pen in the heart single sleeve artwork confirms this. It seemed contrived at the time, particularly the "suicide on stage" lyrics, combating with mid-70s glam rock stars. But it has stood the test of time, being featured on most Stones tours since its release, though Mick Taylor later described it as "not real" and a parody.

The album was released in October 1974 only six months after the sessions had finished and received relatively good reviews, the record-buying public responding to create a lukewarm hit. An edited promotion single was released with a shorter version (* a - 4.46) and, on FORTY LICKS, it appeared with a fade (* b - 4.01). It remained in the charts for only nine weeks in the UK, becoming their least successful chart album.

It certainly signified a lean period for the Stones as 1974 was the first year since the start of their career during which they did not play a single concert. Keith, of course, wanted to tour but Mick argued against it. There remained problems with visas in the States and the two-year French ban was still in force.

629. IF YOU REALLY WANT TO BE MY FRIEND (Jagger, Richard) 6.16
AKA: Everyone Wants To Be My Friend
20 February - 3 March; 12 April - 2 May; 4-27 May 1974: Place: Musicland Studios, Munich, Germany; RSM, Stargroves, Newbury, England; Olympic Studios, London, England.
Rolling Stones with Nicky Hopkins, Ray Cooper, Blue Magic.
Producer: The Glimmer Twins.
Engineer: Andy Johns, Keith Harwood.
Assistant Engineers: Tapani Tapanainen, Rod Thear, Howard Kilgour, Reinhold Mack, George Chkiantz.
UK LP IT'S ONLY ROCK 'N' ROLL: 16 October 1974: No. 2 - 9 weeks
USA LP IT'S ONLY ROCK 'N' ROLL: 18 October 1974: No. 1 - 11 weeks

A slow, pleading gospel love song, it has some charm. Backing vocals are provided by acquaintances Blue Magic (Keith Beaton, Theodore Mills, Richard Pratt, Vernon Sawye, and Wendell Sawyer), along with Keith Richards and Mick Taylor, adding a certain distinctive quality, both playing through a Leslie amp. Blue Magic were a Philadelphia band well known for their vocal style and Mick Taylor responds accordingly with a nimble slide solo and acoustic guitar, but the track is again lightweight, not really tugging on the intended heart strings, but more forceful than *Till The Next Goodbye*. The solo was fitted on within the song's space and was never one that Mick Taylor was completely happy with.

630. TIME WAITS FOR NO ONE (Jagger, Richard) 6.38
20 February - 3 March; 12 April - 2 May; 4-27 May 1974: Place: Musicland Studios, Munich, Germany; RSM, Stargroves, Newbury, England; Olympic Studios, London, England.
Rolling Stones with Nicky Hopkins, Ray Cooper.
Producer: The Glimmer Twins.
Engineer: Andy Johns, Keith Harwood.
Assistant Engineers: Tapani Tapanainen, Rod Thear, Howard Kilgour, Reinhold Mack, George Chkiantz.
UK LP IT'S ONLY ROCK 'N' ROLL: 16 October 1974: No. 2 - 9 weeks
USA LP IT'S ONLY ROCK 'N' ROLL: 18 October 1974: No. 1 - 11 weeks
UK Compilation LP TIME WAITS FOR NO ONE - ANTHOLOGY 1971 - 1977: 1 June 1979
USA Compilation LP SUCKING IN THE SEVENTIES: 12 March 1981: No. 15 - 5 weeks
UK Compilation LP SUCKING IN THE SEVENTIES: 13 April 1981
If artefacts are required to immortalise an individual then the guitar virtuoso performance by Mick Taylor on *Time Waits For No One* is his vinyl piece de resistance (Carlos Santana has been trying to copy the style displayed ever since!). The Stones would later recognise this by releasing a compilation of works called TIME WAITS FOR NO ONE - ANTHOLOGY 1971-1977 in June 1979. *Time Waits For No One* took prime spot on side one and was the only track to come from the 1974 era, underlining its importance. In the 80s another compilation, SUCKING IN THE SEVENTIES, also included a version sacrilegiously edited by more than two minutes (* a - 4.25).

Charlie Watts was on metronome-style drums and Ray Cooper - most notably a member of the Elton John band - overdubbed percussion and tambourine at the Island Studios mixing sessions. Nicky Hopkins was also exceptional on this track as he helped to build up the song incrementally with single note harp-like progression. *Time Waits For No One* was a six-and-a-half minute Jagger, Taylor collaboration with the riff written by Keith Richards. Keith thought it was the best song Mick Taylor had contributed to.

Mick Jagger wrote the melody while Taylor concentrated on writing the instrumental break chords. Bill Wyman had his guitar treated through a just-released Synthi Hi-Fli synthesiser, which provided a little distortion and modulation to his sound. There is no credit to Mick Taylor and his frustration at the lack of credence given to his songwriting talents was beginning to show signs that the domination by Jagger and Richards was stultifying his ability. Music such as this song, despite some later competent solo albums and appearances with Jack Bruce and Bob Dylan, proved to be his zenith.

631. LUXURY (Jagger, Richard) 5.01
20 February - 3 March; 12 April - 2 May; 4-27 May 1974: Place: Musicland Studios, Munich, Germany; RSM, Stargroves, Newbury, England; Olympic Studios, London, England.
Played Live: 1975
Rolling Stones with Nicky Hopkins, Ray Cooper.
Producer: The Glimmer Twins.
Engineer: Andy Johns, Keith Harwood.
Assistant Engineers: Tapani Tapanainen, Rod Thear, Howard Kilgour, Reinhold Mack, George Chkiantz.
UK LP IT'S ONLY ROCK 'N' ROLL: 16 October 1974: No. 2 - 9 weeks
USA LP IT'S ONLY ROCK 'N' ROLL: 18 October 1974: No. 1 - 11 weeks

The engineering exploits of Keith Harwood and Co were well displayed on IT'S ONLY ROCK 'N' ROLL as more sophisticated studio electronics (the gimmick factors) played a more prominent role. The new credits on album covers underline this but Mick Taylor was more than disappointed when he saw the lack of songwriting "rewards" for him.
George Chkiantz, the Stones' affable over-dub engineer, was not new to the band as, at the instigation of Brian Jones in 1968, he had engineered the tapes recorded of the Marrakech Gnaoua'n musicians and had also assisted on the 1969 LET IT BLEED album. His engineering works also linked him with the 1973 Led Zeppelin album, HOUSES OF THE HOLY, hence the introduction to the band of his co-conspirator, Keith Harwood. Chkiantz had also worked with Blind Faith, Family, Humble Pie and David Bowie.
From that era Scottish band Nazareth, produced by Deep Purple's Roger Glover, paid tribute to the sound of the Stones when introducing the *Satisfaction* lick to their 1974 hit *Shanghai'd In Shanghai*. *Luxury* is a slick jibe (with a reggae beat) at all those who work so hard in offices to keep the wives back home in luxury. Keith Richards joins in on the middle-class theme, supporting Mick Jagger's vocals, while the band rock adequately on this mid-paced track. This was a slight change in direction and was indicative of things to come on BLACK AND BLUE. When the Virgin batch of CDs were released in 1994, *Luxury* had been extended by an extra 30 seconds (* a - 4.31).

632. LIVING IN THE HEART OF LOVE (Jagger, Richard) 2.37
20 February - 3 March 1974: Place: Musicland Studios, Munich, Germany
Rolling Stones with Nicky Hopkins.
Producer: The Glimmer Twins.
Engineer: Other Production: Reinhold Mack.
Bootleg only.

This track was possibly a forerunner, lyric-wise, for *Luxury*, using the theme of working hard. It is a classy number which certainly could have been worked on for release. The content is good enough.

633. LABOUR SWING (Jagger, Richard)
20 February - 3 March 1974: Place: Musicland Studios, Munich, Germany.
Producer: The Glimmer Twins.
Engineer: Other Production: Reinhold Mack.
Unavailable.

Bill Wyman specifically mentions this track in his book *Rolling With The Stones* but there is no bootlegged version.

634. DANCE LITTLE SISTER (Jagger, Richard) 4.11
20 February - 3 March; 12 April - 2 May; 4-27 May 1974: Place: Musicland Studios, Munich, Germany; RSM, Stargroves, Newbury, England; Olympic Studios, London, England.
Played Live: 1975, 1977
Rolling Stones with Ray Cooper.
Producer: The Glimmer Twins.
Engineer: Andy Johns, Keith Harwood.
Assistant Engineers: Tapani Tapanainen, Rod Thear, Howard Kilgour, Reinhold Mack, George Chkiantz.
UK LP IT'S ONLY ROCK 'N' ROLL: 16 October 1974: No. 2 - 9 weeks
USA LP IT'S ONLY ROCK 'N' ROLL: 18 October 1974: No. 1 - 11 weeks
USA B-side Ain't Too Proud To Beg: 25 October 1974
UK Compilation LP MADE IN THE SHADE: 6 June 1975: No. 14 - 12 weeks
USA Compilation LP MADE IN THE SHADE: 6 June 1975: No. 6 - 9 weeks
UK CD box set THE SINGLES COLLECTION 1971-2006: 45 X 45s: 11 April 2011
USA CD box set THE SINGLES COLLECTION 1971-2006: 45 X 45s: 26 April 2011

Ian Stewart confirms the song's rock 'n' roll origin, capturing a bar room piano feel. Mick and Bianca Jagger visited Trinidad in early 1974 where they watched cricket during the day and partied at night, as some of the lyrics refer to within *Dance Little Sister* - "On Saturday night, we don't go home, we bacchanal, ain't no dawn". There is a five-minute out-take version with a small guitar twill at the beginning and a different mix on the vocals (* a - 5.07). If the track had been on a previous album, then you could imagine Bobby Keys joining in on saxophone but, at this time, the Stones sound on IT'S ONLY ROCK 'N' ROLL lacks any brass sounds - which gave it a fresh feel. Bobby was kept busy recording with Carly Simon, John Lennon, Ringo Starr, Harry Nilsson and even Chris Jagger.
The American single featuring *Ain't Too Proud To Beg* and *Dance Little Sister*, released in October 1974, deserved to be credited as a double A side. They were both foot-tapping dance-orientated numbers. *Dance Little Sister* is a typical rocker, cruising at road-running pace with twin guitar riffs under the bonnet driven by the lead of Mick Taylor and the rhythm of Keith Richards. Keith's involvement on the album was really negligible compared to previous releases, though he did help

to produce the right mix for this single release.

It was at this time, in October, that, along with Rick Grech, Ron Wood and Jimmy Page, a small session evolved which created the song *Scarlet*. This was a Richards / Page-written song that was in the mould of folk but featuring reggae guitars.

635. TILL THE NEXT GOODBYE (Jagger, Richard) 4.36
20 February - 3 March; 12 April - 2 May; 4-27 May 1974: Place: Musicland, Studios Munich, Germany; RSM, Stargroves, Newbury, England; Olympic Studios, London, England.
Rolling Stones with Nicky Hopkins, Ray Cooper.
Producer: The Glimmer Twins.
Engineer: Andy Johns, Keith Harwood.
Assistant Engineers: Tapani Tapanainen, Rod Thear, Howard Kilgour, Reinhold Mack, George Chkiantz.
UK LP IT'S ONLY ROCK 'N' ROLL: 16 October 1974: No. 2 - 9 weeks
USA LP IT'S ONLY ROCK 'N' ROLL: 18 October 1974: No. 1 - 11 weeks

This is a country-sounding song featuring Jaggeresque, lilted vocals and bottleneck, steel guitar work by Keith Richards. It is reminiscent of earlier workings and may have originated from previous sessions, for instance, the EXILE ON MAIN STREET period. Nicky Hopkins contributes a piano line which is over-familiar and, in short, the song is adequate but is also on the verge of being a throw-away and is an anti-climax after the first three album numbers. An alternative mix is available on acetate (* a - 4.40).

It happened to be the final studio session and farewell track for Mick Taylor - again, he had contributed more than a few guitar pieces. Much later, in an interview with author Marc Spitz, Carly Simon claimed to have co-written the song with Mick Jagger but failed to get any recognition. In June 1974, a promotional film was made by Michael Lindsay-Hogg with the backing track and live vocals. It was filmed at London Weekend Television studios and was broadcast on Don Kirshner's Rock Concert TV programme in October 1974.

636. IT'S ONLY ROCK 'N' ROLL (BUT I LIKE IT) (Jagger, Richard) 4.44
1 June 1974: Place: ITV Studios, London, England.
Producer: The Glimmer Twins.
UK & USA VHS Video Rewind: The Rolling Stones Great Video Hits: November 1984

Before the release of the new album, the film *Ladies And Gentlemen* was at last released in April, with quadrophonic sound especially mixed for the USA cinema audience. To promote the single release at the end of July, which was a good ten weeks in advance of the album, a Michael Lindsay-Hogg film was shot at the London Weekend studios and was recorded with a uniquely different, looser arrangement, with changed backing vocals and guitars. It may have even been an earlier cut of the track, perhaps with an audible Mr Bowie.

The Stones, dressed in mock American Navy uniforms, entered a large inflated Perspex tent and performed the single. All was normal until foam bubbles started to enter the tent so quickly that they were soon shoulder high in them - not a problem until they realise that Charlie Watts, on the eve of his 33rd birthday, is still sitting at his drum kit. He is seen exiting stage right, not amused! The video can be seen on *Video Rewind: The Rolling Stones Great Video Hits*. In addition, *Till The Next Goodbye* and *Ain't Too Proud To Beg* were filmed to playbacks and promoted on Don Kirshner's US TV Show in October 1974.

637. ACT TOGETHER (Jagger, Richard) 4.48
AKA: We Got To Get Our Shit Together
9-15 December 1974; 22 January - 9 February 1975: Place: Musicland Studios, Munich, Germany; RSM, De Doelen, Rotterdam, Netherlands.
Rolling Stones with Nicky Hopkins.
Producer: The Glimmer Twins.
Engineer: Keith Harwood.
Other Production: Reinhold Mack.
Bootleg only.

Keith Richards played some concerts with Ronnie Wood's band in July 1974 which preceded the launch of the latter's solo album in September. The band consisted of Andy Newmark on drums, Willie Weeks (bass), Ian McLagan (piano), with Ron Wood and Keith Richards on guitar. Rod Stewart performed on a couple of songs as well, the band playing two nights at the London Kilburn Gaumont cinema in mid-July. Ian Stewart saw the gigs and felt Ron and Keith played very well together. Mick Jagger was working on the American visa situation and also went to Nicaragua to see how the proceeds of the fund-raising was being used. The next session was booked for Munich at the end of the year and, in the meantime, Mick had visited New York with Glyn Johns to help choose tracks for the intended BLACK BOX compilation set, due in 1975, and was asked whether he would consider coming back to record the band. Glyn wanted to produce the album and Mick was not keen. Eventually, though, a deal was struck but Glyn did not quite know what a mess he was heading for.

Mick Taylor was seriously considering his position and could not face another recording session and said as much to Jagger. He felt that the Stones had peaked musically on the European tour in 1973 and that he was beginning to find it difficult to express himself within the style of the group. He had already worked with jazz artiste Herbie Mann earlier that year. A band meeting in late October was held in Switzerland, where Keith was undergoing withdrawal treatment, to discuss future plans but a large warning bell sounded when Mick Taylor walked out.

Besides the musical differences and his mounting boredom, Taylor was frustrated and had missed the regularity of touring. Ron Wood was at Robert Stigwood's house at a party to celebrate Eric Clapton's Hammersmith concerts on 4 and 5 December when Mick Taylor said he wanted to play some different kind of music and told Mick Jagger. Mick turned to Ronnie, who was stood between them and said: "I think he is serious . . . what am I gonna do? Will you join?" Mick did not want to break up the Faces but said: "If I get desperate can I ring you?" Ronnie agreed and they shook hands on it.

On the 12 December, from the Musicland Studios, an official press release announced the departure of Mick Taylor. A contributory cause was certainly the songwriting upsets but, more importantly, Mick wanted to broaden his horizons and felt the band was limiting his artistic scope. The decision was helped by Andy Johns, who had produced Jack Bruce's 1974 album OUT OF THE STORM. During the sessions, he had suggested Taylor to Bruce as a possible collaborator and encouraged Mick to record and rehearse with the ex-Cream bass player. In late 1974, Taylor did just that and then joined the Jack Bruce Band during a full European tour in 1975. Many other tours followed, with Jack Bruce and Carla Olson, and also with Taylor's own band. He also had plenty of session work in subsequent years for Robin Millar, Tom Newman and Carla Olson. The period with Carla in the early 90s was an extremely satisfying one. Mick stated in one interview: "Carla is the most determined woman I know. She's got a lot of balls and yet always maintains her femininity. I have nothing but the utmost respect for her talents, as a player, a person and a friend."

On I'VE GOT MY OWN ALBUM TO DO, Mick Taylor provided guitar and there were two Jagger, Richard compositions, *Act Together* and *Sure The One You Need*. Neither featured Mick Jagger but had Keith Richards on vocals and guitar and were mainly written by him. *Act Together* was recorded in Munich and Keith plays electric piano, as he did on the Ron Wood album version. There are no vocals on this out-take which is played at a slower pace. All it needed was for Ronnie and Mick to walk in and play guitar and add the vocals. A great backing track was in the can.

638. I GOT A LETTER (Jagger, Richard) 4.26
9-15 December 1974; 22 January - 9 February 1975: Place: Musicland Studios, Munich, Germany; RSM, De Doelen, Rotterdam, Netherlands.
Rolling Stones with Nicky Hopkins.
Producer: The Glimmer Twins.
Engineer: Keith Harwood.
Other Production: Reinhold Mack.
Bootleg only.

The reggae roots learned in Jamaica were now surfacing rather more strongly than they had before. Two out-takes are around, one an instrumental (* a - 4.23) and another with Keith Richards who performs the vocals. He may have written the half-finished lyrics about Anita Pallenberg as he was happy to get a letter from his baby and honey. During the recording sessions for the Ron Wood album, Keith lived with Ron in the lodge at the bottom of his garden while Anita flitted between London and Switzerland. He was enjoying his freedom. The RSM is, of course, the Rolling Stones Mobile unit which they had used at the De Doelen concert hall while rehearsing for the 1973 European tour.

639. SOMETHING GOOD (Jagger, Richard)
9-15 December 1974: Place: Musicland Studios, Munich, Germany.
Rolling Stones with Nicky Hopkins.
Producer: The Glimmer Twins.
Engineer: Keith Harwood.
Other Production: Reinhold Mack.
Unavailable.

640. CABLE FROM MY BABY (Jagger, Richard)
9-15 December 1974: Place: Musicland Studios, Munich, Germany.
Rolling Stones with Nicky Hopkins.
Producer: The Glimmer Twins.
Engineer: Keith Harwood.
Other Production: Reinhold Mack.
Unavailable.

641. FOOL TO CRY (Jagger, Richard) 5.05
AKA: Daddy You're A Fool To Cry
12-15 December 1974, 25 March - 4 April; October-November 1975: Place: Musicland Studios, Munich, Germany; Casino, Montreux, Switzerland.
Played Live: 1976, 1977, 1995, 1997, 1998, 1999
Rolling Stones with Wayne Perkins, Nicky Hopkins.
Producer: The Glimmer Twins.
Engineer: Keith Harwood, Glyn Johns, Phil McDonald, Lew Hahn.
Assistant Engineer: Jeremy Gee, Dave Richards, Tapani Tapanainen, Steve Dowd, Gene Paul, Lee Hulko.
USA B-Side Hot Stuff: 8 April 1976
USA LP BLACK AND BLUE: 15 April 1976: No. 1 - 14 weeks
UK Single: 20 April 1976: No. 6 - 10 weeks
UK LP BLACK AND BLUE: 23 April 1976: No. 2 - 14 weeks
UK Compilation LP TIME WAITS FOR NO ONE - ANTHOLOGY 1971 - 1977: 1 June 1979
USA Compilation LP SUCKING IN THE SEVENTIES: 12 March 1981: No. 15 - 5 weeks
UK Compilation LP SUCKING IN THE SEVENTIES: 13 April 1981
UK Compilation LP REWIND 1971-1984 (THE BEST OF THE ROLLING STONES): 29 June 1984: No. 45 - 5 weeks
USA Compilation LP REWIND 1971-1984 (THE BEST OF THE ROLLING STONES): 2 July 1984: No. 86 - 11 weeks
UK Track 12-inch Single Almost Hear You Sigh: 18 June 1990
UK Compilation LP JUMP BACK THE BEST OF THE ROLLING STONES '71 - '93: 22 November 1993: No. 16 - 26 weeks
UK CD LP FORTY LICKS: 30 September 2002: No. 2 - 45 weeks
USA CD LP FORTY LICKS: 1 October 2002: No. 2 - 50 weeks
USA Compilation CD JUMP BACK THE BEST OF THE ROLLING STONES '71 - '93: 24 August 2004: No. 30 - 58 weeks
UK CD box set THE SINGLES COLLECTION 1971-2006: 45 X 45s: 11 April 2011
USA CD box set THE SINGLES COLLECTION 1971-2006: 45 X 45s: 26 April 2011

The band were left to find a replacement for Mick Taylor and the so-called "Great Guitarist Hunt" began. American Wayne Perkins was first to step into the breach on 12 December 1974. He may have been introduced by Bill Wyman, since Perkins plays on his solo album. Among others, he had recorded with Bob Marley on CATCH A FIRE and on Joni Mitchell's 1974 album COURT AND SPARK. The guitar lines that both he and Keith Richards play are understated and, on *Fool To Cry*, quite contrary to what Mick Taylor might have delivered.

Mick Jagger's accentuated, high-pitched vocals got to grips with the ballad *Fool To Cry* so much so that fans mimicked the high notes, betraying the song's touching sentiments of the tender feelings between children and a loved one. Ron Wood recollects that a very early version of the song was first aired to him by Mick in Ireland, in December 1972. It was known then, at a time when Mick's daughter Jade was just one year old, as *Daddy You're A Fool To Cry*.

His vocal delivery was classic Jagger, articulate and warm in an mock-American style and he claimed to have emulated the high-pitched sound from Don Covay's *Mercy Mercy*. Mick shares a convincing role on the electric piano with Nicky Hopkins (playing piano and string synthesiser), who was recording his last full session with the Stones. After eight years as an important band member, he managed to join the escape party with Mick Taylor, marking the end of a profound period. Charlie Watts' drumming is as precise and soft as required, the snare being tapped throughout the song while Bill Wyman's bass guitar simply had to maintain the tempo - and no more. An out-take has a different lyrical delivery in the ad-lib parts and no backing vocals, but is in the style of the released cut (* a - 6.04). Another out-take is obviously an early one with spoken vocals and unfinished lyrics; no falsetto twists and turns here (* b - 5.43). This time, though, the up-front lead guitar impressed, in the virtuoso vein of Mick Taylor.

The SUCKING IN THE SEVENTIES version is edited by a minute (* c - 4.06). A promotional film was made by Michael Lindsay-Hogg with new vocals to a playback of the track in May 1976. While the single reached a new audience, the regulars were a little stunned at this sentimental overdose. It was certainly Mick's creation but he was not convinced that it should have been a single release and wanted something more up-tempo.

Keith Richards preferred to humour its success, wryly recalling that he would fall asleep during the number when they toured with the BLACK AND BLUE set later in 1976. He was playing a wah-wah pedal guitar and, as he dropped off, his foot hit the pedal, causing a growl which Mick noticed, giving him the "St.evil eye".

642. CHERRY OH BABY (Donaldson) 3.57
15 December 1974; 22 January - 9 February; 25 March - 4 April; October-November 1975: Place: Musicland Studios, Munich, Germany; RSM, De Doelen, Rotterdam, Netherlands; Musicland Studios, Munich, Germany; Casino, Montreux, Switzerland.
Played Live: 1975, 1976
Rolling Stones with Nicky Hopkins, Ron Wood.
Producer: The Glimmer Twins.
Engineer: Keith Harwood, Glyn Johns, Phil McDonald, Lew Hahn.
Assistant Engineer: Jeremy Gee, Dave Richards, Tapani Tapanainen, Steve Dowd, Gene Paul, Lee Hulko.
USA LP BLACK AND BLUE: 15 April 1976: No. 1 - 14 weeks
UK LP BLACK AND BLUE: 23 April 1976: No. 2 - 14 weeks

A studio out-take version illustrates the problems associated with recording different music styles as reggae needs to be delivered with passion. On this occasion it lacks both the subtle rhythm and the required vocal graces. It is extended by an extra 30 seconds (* a - 4.32) and there is also a shorter out-take version (* b - 3.38). With better vocals on the released version and the danger of contrivance improved. Not many white artists could cross-over to this music-style although The Clash had satisfactorily tackled reggae in the late 70s. A call to Lee Byron in Jamaica might have been a wise move and it was strange that the album GOATS HEAD SOUP, recorded in the Caribbean, had no local music influences.

Reggae music in the mid-70s was beginning to capture the public's imagination, with such talents as Bob Marley and Peter Tosh emerging from Jamaica and leading the cross-over to chart compromise. It was natural that the Stones would try an odd delivery or two. The feigned deliverance of Eric Donaldson's 1971 hit *Cherry Oh Baby* unfortunately falls at the first hurdle. Guest guitarist Ron Wood's contribution is noted since it was his first official appearance with the Stones - his work on *It's Only Rock 'N' Roll* was not acknowledged by the band.

Keith Richards felt that it was obvious who was the right person for the gig, because "he played it by numbers" but was worried that his style was too close to his own. Mick Jagger and Ian Stewart persuaded him otherwise, with Mick stating: "It's either going to be Woody or no tour". There was the small issue of a pending Faces tour of the USA during 1975 but Ron must have been delighted to work with his old colleague Nicky Hopkins, from the Jeff Beck days.

Perhaps Ronnie and Nicky had found out the "truth" about rock at long last! He must have also been proud that his reggae song *I Can Feel The Fire*, with Mick on vocals and Keith on guitar, recorded for his solo album the previous year, was in fact a greater achievement of combining rock and reggae. Nicky's contribution to the album was minimal and his participation was not as emphatic as it had been. His health had diminished and his reliance on drink and drugs had reached a zenith and this was his final studio contribution. The eight-track version is shorter at three minutes (* c - 3.00).

643. HEAT WAVE (Holland, Dozier, Holland) 5.00
22 January - 9 February 1975: Place: RSM, De Doelen, Rotterdam, Netherlands.
Rolling Stones with Jeff Beck.
Producer: The Glimmer Twins.
Bootleg only.

The sessions for BLACK AND BLUE were split into three. The one prior to Christmas in Munich, which was to come to terms with Mick Taylor leaving, then a session in Rotterdam was used because it would save costs and enable the band to audition guitarists. The final March/April session took place back in Munich, where the concluding tracks for BLACK AND BLUE were recorded. The final mixing and overdubbing was done in Switzerland at the end of the year.
Heat Wave, a 1963 hit for Martha And The Vandellas, was recorded as an instrumental and featured Jeff Beck, who had finished recording his BLOW BY BLOW album and was being considered as a Stones guitarist. His music pedigree was with the Yardbirds in the 60s before forging a musical career in a jazz funk style. Later he was to guest on Mick Jagger's first two solo albums. During the period 1967-69 a young Ron Wood played with Jeff Beck, prior to joining The Small Faces and then instigating the formation of Rod Stewart and The Faces.

644. FREEWAY JAM (Middleton) 0.54
22 January - 9 February 1975: Place: RSM, De Doelen, Rotterdam, Netherlands.
Rolling Stones with Jeff Beck.
Producer: The Glimmer Twins.
Bootleg only.

Max Middleton was the keyboard player for the Jeff Beck Group and he wrote *Freeway Jam*, which was included on the March 1975 album BLOW BY BLOW. The album reached No. 4 in the USA in April. As a jam track, it allowed some free-flowing playing on the organ and guitar.

645. ENGLISH ROSE (Jagger, Richard) 1.27
22 January - 9 February 1975: Place: RSM, De Doelen, Rotterdam, Netherlands.
Rolling Stones with Jeff Beck.
Producer: The Glimmer Twins.
Engineer: Keith Harwood, Glyn Johns.
Bootleg only.

A slow song, with Jeff Beck playing guitar, along with Keith Richards. There are some vocals but the out-take is only a minute long so not a lot can be concluded.

646. SHAME, SHAME, SHAME (Robinson) 3.02
22 January - 9 February 1975: Place: RSM, De Doelen, Rotterdam, Netherlands.
Rolling Stones with Jeff Beck, Billy Preston.
Producer: The Glimmer Twins.
Engineer: Keith Harwood, Glyn Johns.
Bootleg only.

In February 1975, Shirley Goodman (an old Stones friend who played on *Let It Loose*) had a UK No. 6 hit and reached position 12 in the USA with *Shame, Shame, Shame*. She was the same Shirley from Shirley & Lee and registered a hit this time under the name of Shirley And Company - the songwriter was Shirley Robinson. The organ player is probably Billy Preston on an instrumental-only fun run-through with Jeff Beck on guitar.

647. MAN EATING WOMAN (Jagger, Richard) 3.45
22 January - 9 February 1975: Place: RSM, De Doelen, Rotterdam, Netherlands.
Rolling Stones with Jeff Beck
Producer: The Glimmer Twins.
Engineer: Keith Harwood, Glyn Johns.
Bootleg only.

Two guitarists can again be heard on this out-take and the track has a solid bass line with a jagged funky groove delivered by Jeff Beck. There are some Jagger vocals on seemingly unfinished lyrics - a true out-take. Glyn Johns had originally felt that the band without Mick Taylor and Nicky Hopkins had been pared back to their best days but, when the sessions resumed in Rotterdam, they became the most tedious ever.

648. CELLOPHANE TROUSERS (Jagger, Richard) 2.26
AKA: Cellophane Y-Fronts, Back To The Country
22 January - 9 February 1975; 25 March - 4 April 1975; 5 January - 29 January, February - 2 March 1978, 11 November - 16 December 1982: Place: RSM, De Doelen, Rotterdam, Netherlands; Musicland Studios, Munich, Germany; EMI, Pathé Marconi Studios, Paris, France.
Rolling Stones with Wayne Perkins.
Producer: The Glimmer Twins, Chris Kimsey.
Engineer: Keith Harwood, Barry Sage.
Bootleg only.

Opened with a Keith Richards riff, *Cellophane Trousers* is an upbeat, five-minute instrumental number with a Townshend-like *I Can't Explain* hook at the point of the imagined chorus. The other guitarist is likely to be Wayne Perkins. The riff was resurrected at the SOME GIRLS sessions in 1978 when Chris Kimsey (who knew the track as *Cellophane Y-Fronts*) felt it was good enough and should be worked upon further, hence its appearance on *Too Tough* on UNDERCOVER.

649. SLAVE (Jagger, Richards) 4.59
AKA: Black And Blue Jam, Vagina
22 January - 9 February 1975; 11 October - 12 November 1980; April - June 1981: Place: RSM, De Doelen, Rotterdam, Netherlands; RS Mobile, Boulogne-Billancourt, Paris, France; Atlantic Studios, New York, USA.
Rolling Stones with Ron Wood, Pete Townshend, Sonny Rollins, Billy Preston, Ollie Brown, Jeff Beck.
Producer: The Glimmer Twins.
Associate Producer: Chris Kimsey.
Engineer: Keith Harwood, Glyn Johns.
Other Production: Bob Clearmountain, Gary Lyons.
USA LP TATTOO YOU: 18 August 1981: No. 1 - 30 weeks
UK LP TATTOO YOU: 28 August 1981: No. 2 - 29 weeks

Slave is a BLACK AND BLUE session out-take, widely titled *Black And Blue Jam*. It was taken down from the shelves, dusted and remixed by Bob Clearmountain and Gary Lyons for inclusion on the 1981 TATTOO YOU album. Billy Preston plays organ and the illustrious sax talents of Sonny Rollins were over-dubbed later at the final session to formulate quite a loose composition of rhythm and funk. Pete Townshend performs backing vocals and Ollie Brown is on percussion.
The original *Black And Blue Jam* contains the guitar work of Jeff Beck (* a - 7.14) and Ron Wood's guitar was possibly over-dubbed later. There are no vocals, other than Jagger cajoling the jam of guitars and organ in a seven-minute controlled frenzy. Another rambling jam out-take comes with vocals (* b - 9.43), and two with saxophone and multiple spliced edits (* c - 8.20, d - 11.13), Mick's ad-lib lyrics getting close to the sort of jibe he would use on *Too Much Blood*.
The dusty shelves just mentioned were again seen in the November 2001 TV documentary, *Being Mick*, in which cans of tape can be distinctly seen with labels. This documentary was filmed by Mick Jagger's production company, Jagged Films, and was his first release. *Slave* was referred to under its original working title, *Vagina*, recorded in 1980. The other tracks were *Waiting On A Friend* and *Neighbours*. It could have been called the Sonny Rollins can of tape, since he appeared on all of these tracks.
The final cut was edited to five minutes and now had the production backing vocals and the three-line spoken mantra, which was the core of the lyric. The original album track is an edited version but, when the CDs were re-mastered for Virgin, *Slave* was allowed to roll for another one-and-a-half minutes (* e - 6.32).

650. WORRIED ABOUT YOU (Jagger, Richards) 5.16
AKA: Sometimes I Wonder Why
22 January - 9 February 1975; 25 June - 9 August, 30 August - October 1979: Place: RSM, De Doelen, Rotterdam, Netherlands; EMI, Pathé Marconi, Paris, France.
Played Live: 1977, 2002, 2003, 2006
Rolling Stones with Ron Wood, Wayne Perkins, Billy Preston Ollie Brown.
Producer: The Glimmer Twins.
Associate Producer: Chris Kimsey.
Engineer: Keith Harwood, Glyn Johns.
USA LP TATTOO YOU: 18 August 1981: No. 1 - 30 weeks
UK LP TATTOO YOU: 28 August 1981: No. 2 - 29 weeks

Provisionally, *Worried About You* was also lined up for the BLACK AND BLUE album. An out-take longer than the released version has Mick Jagger giving guidance to the others on scale changes (* a - 7.42). An edited version is also on bootleg (* b - 3.14). It was played live with Billy Preston at the El Mocambo in Toronto in 1977, well before its release, which was held over until the TATTOO YOU album. The track was not played live on the subsequent tour.
Worried About You is a soft, melodious venture into the *Fool To Cry* land of falsetto vocals (with the exception of Keith's backing), although the Jagger growl does explode later. He stated: "I like singing in falsetto, but just to be clear, I'm not really a fairy!" A piercing guitar solo is delivered mid-way through, an attempt by Wayne Perkins to gloss over the loss of Mick Taylor.
Apparently Keith was warming to Wayne's input, saying that he was a very good, melodic player, and he was becoming favourite to take the spare guitar place. The electric piano at the heart of the song is by Billy Preston. Another long version available as an out-take was recorded at the Pathé Marconi Studios in July-October 1979 and this was edited for TATTOO YOU (* c - 7.21). There is a Michael Lindsay-Hogg studio performance video that captures the band, supported by their Jack Daniels.

651. COME ON SUGAR (Jagger, Richard) 5.31
AKA: Let's Do It Right
22 January - 9 February 1975; April - June 1981: Place: RSM, De Doelen, Rotterdam, Netherlands; Atlantic Studios, New York, USA.
Rolling Stones with Jeff Beck.
Producer: The Glimmer Twins.
Engineer: Keith Harwood, Glyn Johns.
Bootleg only.

A more intense funk number, which was unfinished lyrically, provided Jeff Beck with the opportunity to groove again on the funk express. An extended version with an introductory pre-amble can be found on a Jeff Beck bootleg (* a - 6.19). During the sessions Glyn Johns had finally had enough and, after an argument with Keith Richards, left the sessions, never to return.
As a result, he failed to get the co-producer acknowledgement he had agreed. The argument was a petty one and involved the poor communication between the Stones mobile, parked outside the De Doelen Hall, and the band within. Keith had sauntered out to hear a particular take of a song but Glyn was unaware and the tapes were not rolling.

652. CRAZY MAMA (Jagger, Richard) 4.34
22 January - 9 February 1975; 29 March 1975; October-November 1975: Place: RSM, De Doelen, Rotterdam, Netherlands; Musicland Studios, Munich, Germany; Casino, Montreux, Switzerland.
Played Live: 1977, 1997, 1998
Rolling Stones with Billy Preston, Ollie Brown, Ron Wood.
Producer: The Glimmer Twins.
Engineer: Keith Harwood, Glyn Johns, Phil McDonald, Lew Hahn.
Assistant Engineer: Jeremy Gee, Dave Richards, Tapani Tapanainen, Steve Dowd, Gene Paul, Lee Hulko.
USA LP BLACK AND BLUE: 15 April 1976: No. 1 - 14 weeks
UK B-side Fool To Cry: 20 April 1976
USA Promo 12-inch Single: April 1976
UK LP BLACK AND BLUE: 23 April 1976: No. 2 - 14 weeks
UK Compilation LP TIME WAITS FOR NO ONE - ANTHOLOGY 1971 - 1977: 1 June 1979
USA Compilation LP SUCKING IN THE SEVENTIES: 12 March 1981: No. 15 - 5 weeks
UK Compilation LP SUCKING IN THE SEVENTIES: 13 April 1981
UK CD box set THE SINGLES COLLECTION 1971-2006: 45 X 45s: 11 April 2011
USA CD box set THE SINGLES COLLECTION 1971-2006: 45 X 45s: 26 April 2011

The extensive details on the inner cover of BLACK AND BLUE give a valuable insight into the make-up of a Rolling Stones track. It shows that Bill Wyman is removed from the line-up on *Crazy Mama* and that the lead and bass guitars are played by Keith Richards, with the exception of a rhythm piece by Mick Jagger and a rising and descending lead fill by Ron Wood. Keith also plays piano in the style of Ian Stewart with Ronnie and Billy Preston contributing backing vocals. Ollie Brown plays percussion, including the distinctive cow bell.
An early out-take has a sparse arrangement without the extra layers of guitar (* a - 4.04). *Crazy Mama* is a strong track in the mould of a typical sleaze rocker. It was featured on the British flip-side of *Fool To Cry*, the Americans preferring the funky *Hot Stuff*. A promotional film was made by Michael Lindsay-Hogg of the Stones running through the track on 1 May 1976, during the West German leg of the tour, though *Crazy Mama* was not actually played "live" on that trip. An edited version of the song was placed on a 12-inch promotional single in the USA and on the later compilation album SUCKING IN THE SEVENTIES (* b - 4.06).

653. I LOVE LADIES (Jagger, Richard) 4.31
AKA: Sexy Night, Lovely Lady
22 January - 9 February 1975: Place: RSM, De Doelen, Rotterdam, Netherlands.
Rolling Stones with Jeff Beck.
Producer: The Glimmer Twins.
Engineer: Keith Harwood, Glyn Johns.
Bootleg only.

I Love Ladies aka *Sexy Night* is an out-take in the vein of *Fool To Cry*, complete with Mick Jagger's high-pitched vocals. *Sexy Night* or *Lovely Lady* is a soft ballad which rises and falls in an unconvincing manner. A funky guitar accompanies the tune and this is provided by Jeff Beck, who (rumour has it) rejected the Stones because Bill Wyman and Charlie Watts could not funk it up (or Jeff could not rock it up!). He also had an album which had been released in March, BLOW BY BLOW, which needed promotion, so he described the situation as needing a flip of a coin.

654. MELODY (Jagger, Richard) 5.49
23 January 1975; January - February 1976: Place: RSM, De Doelen, Rotterdam, Netherlands; Atlantic Studios, New York, USA.
Played Live: 1977, 1999
Rolling Stones with Billy Preston.
Producer: The Glimmer Twins.
Engineer: Keith Harwood, Glyn Johns, Phil McDonald, Lew Hahn.
Assistant Engineer: Jeremy Gee, Dave Richards, Tapani Tapanainen, Steve Dowd, Gene Paul, Lee Hulko. Horns Arrangement: Arif Mardin.
USA LP BLACK AND BLUE: 15 April 1976: No 1 - 14 weeks
UK LP BLACK AND BLUE: 23 April 1976: No. 2 - 14 weeks

Inspired by and with the collaboration of Billy Preston, *Melody* is a pseudo-20s jazz song. *Do You Love Me?* was written in similar style by Billy Preston for the 1973 album EVERYBODY LIKES SOME KIND OF MUSIC. Bill Wyman and Charlie Watts are evidently familiar with and at home on jazz territory, Charlie gently taking the brushes to his drums.

After Bill left The Stones his troupe, The Rhythm Kings, often played *Melody* live and recorded it for his 1997 STRUTTIN' OUR STUFF album, with Georgie Fame taking the organ part, Dave Hartley the piano and Eric Clapton on lead guitar. Keith Richards exudes confidence, licks complementing the swing style of Billy Preston's piano and organ playing.

Billy also takes a strong vocal part, answering Mick's "Melody" and "It was her second name" in a New Orleans manner. Mick helps on percussion as he takes one of the 16 studio tracks just for his foot stomp. Horns were put on later at Atlantic and they were arranged by Arif Mardin. The long track is an inspired transgression and perhaps the album's most original and strongest cut.

655. MUNICH REGGAE (Jagger, Richard) 5.29
25 March - 4 April 1975; April - June 1981: Place: Musicland Studios, Munich, Germany; Atlantic Studios, New York, USA.
Producer: The Glimmer Twins.
Engineer: Keith Harwood.
Bootleg only.

The Faces toured the USA in 1975 and were in Los Angeles at the LA Forum in early March. They were tuning up when Mick Jagger wandered in and found the band with Bobby Womack In his autobiography *All The Rage*, it struck Ian McLagan that all three singers for the song *It's All Over Now* were in one room together. Doubtless, Mick was checking up on Ronnie again. *Munich Reggae* is another instrumental with a reggae tinge and may have been considered for the TATTOO YOU project, hence the track being worked on in 1981. A faded extract can be found on bootleg (* a - 2.02).

656. NEVER STOP (Jagger, Richard) 4.27
AKA: Start Me Up
25 March - 4 April 1975: Place: Musicland Studios, Munich, Germany.
Producer: The Glimmer Twins.
Engineer: Keith Harwood.
Bootleg only.

This is the infamous reggae take on *Start Me Up* and there is also an edited version (* a - 2.16). It's a track which is definitely "curio only" listening but it did illustrate Keith Richards' point that, if the original song was strong enough, then it should survive through tempo and melody changes. He was stretching a point on *Never Stop*. Mick Jagger sings guide vocals only of "Start It Up" and "Never Stop". During the many run-throughs, Keith and Charlie Watts improvised and created a rockier version and it was this that was found by Chris Kimsey amongst tape reels from the Stones' archives at their rehearsal room and warehouse in Bermondsey, South London. This resulted in the re-work of *Start Me Up*.

657. HAND OF FATE (Jagger, Richard) 4.27
25 March; October-November 1975: Place: Musicland Studios, Munich, Germany ; Casino, Montreux, Switzerland.
Played Live: 1976, 1977, 2002, 2003
Rolling Stones with Wayne Perkins, Ron Wood, Ollie Brown, Billy Preston.
Producer: The Glimmer Twins.
Engineer: Keith Harwood, Glyn Johns, Phil McDonald, Lew Hahn.
Assistant Engineer: Jeremy Gee, Dave Richards, Tapani Tapanainen, Steve Dowd, Gene Paul, Lee Hulko.
USA LP BLACK AND BLUE: 15 April 1976: No. 1 - 14 weeks
UK LP BLACK AND BLUE: 23 April 1976: No. 2 - 14 weeks
UK Compilation LP TIME WAITS FOR NO ONE - ANTHOLOGY 1971 - 1977: 1 June 1979

A return to a raunchy upbeat number, driven by Keith Richards' rhythm riff, *Hand Of Fate* rears its ugly head. Mick Jagger passionately relates a tale of a fugitive running out of luck from a crime of passion: "I shot that man and put him underground." Although a faster track, it is played in a confidently lazy, swaggering manner. The guitar solos are performed by Wayne Perkins, Ronnie Wood's role being restricted to backing vocals. Billy Preston plays the piano and Ollie Brown, formerly a Stevie Wonder side-kick, helps Charlie Watts on the percussion. There is a slightly longer out-take and a shorter fade-out with guide vocals (* a - 4.43, b - 3.46).

658. HOT STUFF (Jagger, Richard) 5.21
30 March 1975; October-November 1975: Place: Musicland Studios, Munich, Germany; Casino, Montreux, Switzerland.
Played Live: 1976, 1977, 1994, 2002
Rolling Stones with Harvey Mandel, Billy Preston, Ron Wood, Ollie Brown.
Producer: The Glimmer Twins.
Engineer: Keith Harwood, Glyn Johns, Phil McDonald, Lew Hahn.
Assistant Engineer: Jeremy Gee, Dave Richards, Tapani Tapanainen, Steve Dowd, Gene Paul, Lee Hulko.
USA Single: 8 April 1976: No. 10 - 7 weeks
USA LP BLACK AND BLUE: 15 April 1976: No. 1 - 14 weeks
UK LP BLACK AND BLUE: 23 April 1976: No. 2 - 14 weeks
USA Promo 12-inch Single: April 1976
USA Compilation LP SUCKING IN THE SEVENTIES: 12 March 1981: No. 15 - 5 weeks
UK Compilation LP SUCKING IN THE SEVENTIES: 13 April 1981
UK Compilation LP JUMP BACK THE BEST OF THE ROLLING STONES '71 - '93: 22 November 1993: No. 16 - 26 weeks

USA Compilation CD JUMP BACK THE BEST OF THE ROLLING STONES '71 - '93: 24 August 2004: No 30 - 58 weeks
UK CD box set THE SINGLES COLLECTION 1971-2006: 45 X 45s: 11 April 2011
USA CD box set THE SINGLES COLLECTION 1971-2006: 45 X 45s: 26 April 2011

Hot Stuff is one of the two tracks on which noted American virtuoso Harvey Mandel, from Canned Heat, played lead guitar. His solo guitar work on *Hot Stuff* is certainly vigorous and unlike any previous Stones sound and probably owed Billy Preston a credit for inspiration. It was Mick Jagger's idea to bring Harvey Mandel in and produce a style different to Wayne Perkins. The track encircles the disco format of funk, so was contemporary at the time.
Bill Wyman plucks the rhythm which drives the song forward, Keith Richards does support licks and a wah-wah piece while Billy is on piano and background vocals. Mick lays down some rap jive, popularising the track into an underground clubland hit, the probable reason for its American single release. It was initially the A-side until *Fool To Cry* received more radio plays.
Charlie Watts (with Ollie Brown, Bill, Mick and even Ian Stewart on percussion) concludes the track unexpectedly with two sharp beats. *Hot Stuff* was, at one time, a working title for the album. A rough out-take version with limited vocals is in existence (* a - 4.52). The track was filmed for promotion purposes by Michael Lindsay-Hogg in May 1976. The SUCKING IN THE SEVENTIES take edited by almost two minutes, an exercise originally undertaken for a promotional single (* b - 3.30).

659.   MEMORY MOTEL (Jagger, Richard) 7.09
31 March; October-November 1975: Place: Musicland Studios, Munich, Germany; Casino, Montreux, Switzerland.
Played Live: 1994, 1995, 1997, 1998, 1999, 2006
Rolling Stones with Wayne Perkins, Harvey Mandel, Billy Preston, Ron Wood.
Producer: The Glimmer Twins.
Engineer: Keith Harwood, Glyn Johns, Phil McDonald, Lew Hahn.
Assistant Engineer: Jeremy Gee, Dave Richards, Tapani Tapanainen, Steve Dowd, Gene Paul, Lee Hulko.
USA LP BLACK AND BLUE: 15 April 1976: No. 1 - 14 weeks
UK LP BLACK AND BLUE: 23 April 1976: No. 2 - 14 weeks

With the formidable keyboard line-up of Mick Jagger on concert piano (Nicky Hopkins now not a part of the set-up), Keith Richards performing electric piano and Billy Preston on the string synthesiser, *Memory Motel* is a lengthy sojourn with reminiscences into life on the road. There is a shortened instrumental out-take version available (* a - 4.14). Keith Richards is featured heavily on harmony vocals in a brotherly duet with Mick, leaving the acoustic guitar to Wayne Perkins and the electric to Harvey Mandel. It is a slow meandering song that has stood the test of time.
At the end of the sessions, Marshall Chess decided that he had had enough and resigned, totally burnt out - he walked quite simply before he was carried out. *Memory Motel* was cut again in one of Mick Jagger's solo sessions for PRIMITIVE COOL with Dave Stewart. It was recorded for the rock movie soundtrack BEYOND THE GROOVE which starred Bob Geldof, Dave Stewart and Annie Lennox.

660.   HEY NEGRITA (Jagger, Richard) 4.59
2 April 1975; January - February 1976: Place: Musicland Studios, Munich, Germany; Atlantic Studios, New York, USA.
Played Live: 1976
Rolling Stones with Ron Wood, Billy Preston, Ollie Brown.
Producer: The Glimmer Twins.
Engineer: Keith Harwood, Glyn Johns, Phil McDonald, Lew Hahn.
Assistant Engineer: Jeremy Gee, Dave Richards, Tapani Tapanainen, Steve Dowd, Gene Paul, Lee Hulko.
USA LP BLACK AND BLUE: 15 April 1976: No. 1 - 14 weeks
UK LP BLACK AND BLUE: 23 April 1976: No. 2 - 14 weeks

Fittingly from the BLACK AND BLUE sessions, the last guitar "audition" was reserved for Ronnie Wood but it must be emphasised that he was still a committed member of The Faces and did not intend to let Rod Stewart down. Despite this, it seems that, above all the other guitarists, he was most suited to the spare axe position and most at ease with the Stones' ambience, prepared to inter-weave guitars - and he was English! Little did Ronnie know that, in 1969, shortly after Brian Jones left the group, Ian Stewart rang the studio where The Small Faces were recording and asked if Woody would want to join the Stones. Ronnie Lane answered "no", not even giving Ron Wood the chance to answer for himself.
Other stories relate that Ian called the studio, asked to speak to Ronnie and Ronnie Lane believed they meant him and said he did not feel he was suited to be considered as the Stones' spare guitarist. In *Rock On Wood* by Terry Rawlings, Ron said that Mick Jagger phoned him himself but he thought someone was messing around and he replied that he was busy. In 1975, the only other serious contender was Wayne Perkins but, for various reasons, his signing was not agreed. This was probably because his style was too similar to Mick Taylor.
If you believe certain sources (some are confirmed sightings), the merits of Rory Gallagher, Shuggie Otis, Chris Spedding (who had known Jagger since the late 60s when he supported the Stones at Hyde Park with Battered Ornaments), Peter Frampton, Mick Ronson, Jeff Beck, Nils Lofgren, Robert A Johnson, Steve Marriott, Paul Kossoff, Jimmy Page, Wilko Johnson, Bobby Tench, Hank Marvin and Harvey Mandel were considered, though some were not even invited to an audition and others were just rumoured by the New Musical Express. Pete Townshend managed to keep a low profile and avoided inclusion on the hit list. It was a fee-free way of getting session musicians on the album.
Most of them are essentially lead guitarists when a return to the dual rhythm thrust of the early Richards/Jones days was needed, hence Keith Richards' natural choice of honest mate and current landlord, Ron Wood, despite favouring Steve Marriott at the outset. The final shortlist consisted of Jeff Beck, Eric Clapton and Ron Wood. While Ronnie was recording in Munich, a press release stated he was involved with the Stones and that Keith Richards was staying with him. Dutifully, the British police swooped and arrested Chrissie Wood and a friend for possession of small quantities of cocaine.
Ron managed to play with both the Faces and the Stones in 1975 and his position in the band was not formally confirmed in the press until December following the break-up of The Faces when Rod Stewart decided to go solo.
Hey Negrita ran the risk of upsetting racial harmony. Mick Jagger thought of it more as a compliment and heard others fondly call Bianca "Negrita" and she thought it would make a good song title. The lyrics also contain other Hispanic words, somewhat lost in translation. Further risk was taken when the album was

released - posters with a sado-masochistic streak displayed a girl, roped and beaten, sitting on an enlarged album cover. The caption read: "I'm black and blue with the Rolling Stones and I love it." The cover also confirmed Ron Wood's position as a Stones henchman, as he was pictured with the rest of the band, although his guitar had only featured on two tracks.

Hey Negrita is a mid-tempo funky rock song that has a distinctive groove fuelled by the guitar of Ron Wood. In his audition, he said he wanted them to cut a song he had partly written and Charlie Watts, quoted in Ronnie's biography, said: "He's only just walked in and he's bossing us around". Ron did not mind not getting a credit because he disliked the Spanish, slightly misogynist lyrics. A 30-second longer out-take has different experimental lead solos and no organ (* a - 5.30); this cut was also edited (* b - 4.38).

A promotional film was made by Michael Lindsay-Hogg of the Stones and Billy Preston, all wearing sunglasses and performing the track, in May 1976. The basis of the album was there but it could not be released in time for the Tour Of The Americas, which was due to start in June 1975. In April, it was announced that Ron had agreed to be the stand-in guitarist for the tour.

Mick had to use all his diplomacy skills to obtain a USA visa for Keith Richards, since he had a heroin conviction. A blood test was taken to detect drug use and it was rumoured that Richards had had a transfusion to slowly replace all the blood in his body - radical measures indeed but maybe a little exaggerated. A visa was granted and the tour was on, although the Stones learned that President Richard Nixon himself had been adverse to them visiting again - but he resigned in August 1974 in the wake of "Watergate", making the path slightly clearer.

661. SURE THE ONE YOU NEED (Jagger, Richard) ✎ 4.48
6 June 1975: Place: Arrowhead Stadium, Kansas City, USA.
Rolling Stones with Ron Wood, Billy Preston, Ollie Brown.
Bootleg only.

The Rolling Stones released a compilation album MADE IN THE SHADE to promote the forthcoming tour - it covered the period from 1970 to 1974. Decca and ABKCO released METAMORPHOSIS on the same day, greeted by derisory comments from the Stones, despite the album being agreed in the ABKCO settlement. The tour announcement was officially made on 1 May 1975 by an unusual method, a flat-bed truck being hired and driven up 5th Avenue in New York City. The press were at the pre-arranged hotel rendezvous, while outside the Stones were on the back of a truck playing *Brown Sugar*. It was midday in the pouring rain and the band provided great entertainment for the office workers as they came out for an early lunch. This was the first time that Ron Wood had played live with the band. The flat-bed was an idea of Charlie Watts, who was aware that black jazz artists from Harlem would use them around other parts of New York to increase audience awareness of their music.

While playing *Brown Sugar*, a billboard showing the tour dates was unfurled on Broadway. More than one million tickets were put on sale, of which 80 per cent had been sold by 8pm. Billed as the Tour Of The Americas, it was due to finish in Caracas, Venezuela, on 31 August after taking in Mexico and Brazil on the way - a total of 58 concerts were planned. However, the South America part of the tour had to be cancelled for financial reasons and a one-off gig on Easter Island, nearly 3,000 miles west of Chile in the South Pacific, was considered but the authorities thought better of it. This did not matter too much as the Stones would play to nearly two million people and gross $11 million. At one point during 1975, Mick Jagger wanted to organise a huge rock event with the Faces and Led Zeppelin also appearing with the Stones. All three bands did manage large, successful USA tours in that year but independently of each other.

A luxurious Boeing 720 jet called Starship, used previously by Led Zeppelin, Bob Dylan and Deep Purple, flew the Stones to their destinations and 12 trucks carried the gear, Peter Rudge again masterminding the operation, with Alan Dunn efficiently handling band logistics. It was designed to zigzag from east coast to west as opposed to the more common reverse route. Tour rehearsals were at Stewart Airport, Newburgh, New York, in mid-May where Ron learned a catalogue of 45 numbers. Two different size stages had been designed, a 10-tonne lightweight one for general purpose touring and a heavier 25-tonne version to be used in the big cities of New York, Chicago and Los Angeles. The lighting and sound systems were hung from a frame suspended above the stage which was designed to give the crowd maximum viewing ability. A few weeks later the tour commenced on 1 June at Louisiana State University in Baton Rouge - fittingly, it was Ronnie's birthday.

One contentious matter for the authorities to consider, particularly at more provincial venues, was an inflatable phallus that was to be ridden by Mick Jagger during *Star Star*. A few days before, in San Antonio, the police said that Mick would be arrested if it was used so it stayed limp at their second and third concerts. For most of the tour the Stones were supported by The Meters, a funk group from New Orleans led by Art Neville, his brother Cyril and Joseph "Ziggy" Modeliste.

Depending on the venue, other support groups included reggae artists The Wailers, country rock group The Eagles, southern country rock boogie from The Charlie Daniels Band, gospel from The Mighty Clouds Of Joy, blues artist Furry Lewis, heavy rock from Montrose and Trapeze, Caribbean and calypso from The Steel Band Association Of America, the soul and funk of Rufus and The Tower Of Power, jazz from The Crusaders, the soul repertoire of The Commodores, and rock and roll with a tad of rhythm and blues from the excellent J. Geils Band.

Guest artists who played with the Stones included Eric Clapton, Carlos Santana and Elton John. *Sure The One You Need* was played on two dates only (the other one being Milwaukee on 8 June) and is introduced by Mick as a tune written by Keith Richards and Ronnie. This was the only recording by the full Stones line-up and was always intended to be an integral part of the set list of the 1975 USA tour. It was only played twice, though, due to a lack of crowd response and promptly replaced by *Happy*. Keith took lead vocals and Ron backed him up.

The track, mostly written by Keith, originates from the September 1974 Ron Wood album I'VE GOT MY OWN ALBUM TO DO. As the tour progressed, many of the shows were recorded for potential future release.

662. FINGERPRINT FILE (Jagger, Richard) ✎ 5.17
17 June 1975: Place: Maple Leaf Gardens, Toronto, Ontario, Canada.
Rolling Stones with Ron Wood, Billy Preston, Ollie Brown.
Producer: The Glimmer Twins.
Engineer: Keith Harwood, Eddie Kramer, Ron Nevison, Dave Jordan, Jimmy Douglass.
Assistant Producer: Mick McKenna, Tom Heid, Randy Hason, Bobby Warner, Lew Hahn, Tapani Tapanainen, Lee Hulko.
USA LP LOVE YOU LIVE: 15 September 1977: No. 5 - 7 weeks
UK LP LOVE YOU LIVE: 16 September 1977: No. 3 - 8 weeks

663. **IT'S ONLY ROCK 'N' ROLL** (Jagger, Richard) ✏ 4.26
17 June 1975: Place: Maple Leaf Gardens, Toronto, Ontario, Canada.
Rolling Stones with Ron Wood, Billy Preston, Ollie Brown.
Producer: The Glimmer Twins.
Engineer: Keith Harwood, Eddie Kramer, Ron Nevison, Dave Jordan, Jimmy Douglass.
Assistant Producer: Mick McKenna, Tom Heid, Randy Hason, Bobby Warner, Lew Hahn, Tapani Tapanainen, Lee Hulko.
USA LP LOVE YOU LIVE: 15 September 1977: No. 5 - 7 weeks
UK LP LOVE YOU LIVE: 16 September 1977: No. 3 - 8 weeks

The Maple Leaf Gardens in Toronto provided the venue for two tracks for the LOVE YOU LIVE album.

664. **CARNIVAL TO RIO** (Clapton) 1.43
AKA: Carnival
25 - 28 June 1975: Place: Electric Ladyland Studios, New York, USA.
Rolling Stones with Eric Clapton, Ron Wood, George Terry, Billy Preston, Dick Sims, Ollie Brown, Yvonne Elliman, Marcy Levy.
Bootleg only.

On 22 June, the show arrived in Madison Square Garden, New York, for six nights, which provided a new challenge for Mick Jagger and Keith Richards. Keith thought it was somewhat disorientating, not journeying every day, while Mick said it reminded him of a summer residency. The show's encore number was *Sympathy For The Devil* with the support act, The Steel Band Association Of America, joining in on percussion. Eric Clapton was in town and guested with the band for the encore. Carlos Santana was to do the same for the final night at MSG. All of the band, Billy Preston and Ollie Brown reciprocated for Eric's performance by attending a recording session at Electric Ladyland.
Carnival is an up tempo number with Mick Jagger very prominent on vocals. It was intended for Eric Clapton's next studio album NO REASON TO CRY. Due to contractual reasons it was re-recorded by Eric and appeared as *Carnival*. Another Mick contribution was to Leslie West's 1975 album, THE GREAT FATSBY, on which he co-wrote and played guitar on *High Roller*, a reference to the Stones and the sound of *Brown Sugar*.

665. **SYMPATHY FOR THE DEVIL** (Jagger, Richard) ✏ 7.57
9 July 1975: Place: LA Forum, Inglewood, California, USA.
Rolling Stones with Ron Wood, Billy Preston, Ollie Brown, Steel Band Association of America.
Producer: The Glimmer Twins.
Engineer: Keith Harwood, Eddie Kramer, Ron Nevison, Dave Jordan, Jimmy Douglass.
Assistant Producer: Mick McKenna, Tom Heid, Randy Hason, Bobby Warner, Lew Hahn, Tapani Tapanainen, Lee Hulko.
USA LP LOVE YOU LIVE: 15 September 1977: No. 5 - 7 weeks
UK LP LOVE YOU LIVE: 16 September 1977: No. 3 - 8 weeks

666. **HONKY TONK WOMEN** (Jagger, Richard) ✏ 5.29
13 July 1975: Place: Record Plant Mobile, LA Forum, Inglewood, California, USA.
Rolling Stones with Ron Wood, Billy Preston, Ollie Brown.
Engineer: Ron Nevison.
Remixed & Remastered: Bob Clearmountain.
USA e-Album L.A. FRIDAY (LIVE 1975): 2 April 2012
UK e-Album L.A. FRIDAY (LIVE 1975): 3 April 2012

The Los Angeles Forum was the base for five consecutive "summer season" concerts from 9 July. The personnel of Ron Wood, Billy Preston and Ollie Brown were supplemented sparingly by the brass players of Bobby Keys, Trevor Lawrence and Steve Madaio during certain numbers for the LA leg. The final concert was released in its entirety in April 2012 as part of the bootleg series of live official recordings remastered by Bob Clearmountain from a recording made by Ron Nevison on Record Plant's 16-track mobile. The shows had been recorded with the intention of a live album release and a soundboard had been bootlegged widely under the titles of *LA Confidential* and *LA Friday*; the latter actually being Sunday's show. The Friday show was filmed professionally and has also been bootlegged and a number of videos were made available on the Stones official YouTube website pages in April 2012.
The concert shows a Chinese dragon entering the back of the arena before proceeding towards the stage ahead of the strains of Aaron Copeland's *Fanfare For The Common Man* filling the PA. As the fanfare subsides the crown-shaped stage unfurls mechanically, like a lotus petal flower, revealing Mick Jagger holding on to the highest position of a petal until it drops slowly and the rest of the band are revealed and the opening riffs of *Honky Tonk Women* belch forward for Mick to commence the bar-room inspired lyrics.

667. **ALL DOWN THE LINE** (Jagger, Richard) ✏ 4.05
13 July 1975: Place: Record Plant Mobile, LA Forum, Inglewood, California, USA.
Rolling Stones with Ron Wood, Billy Preston, Ollie Brown.
Engineer: Ron Nevison.
Remixed & Remastered: Bob Clearmountain.
USA e-Album L.A. FRIDAY (LIVE 1975): 2 April 2012
UK e-Album L.A. FRIDAY (LIVE 1975): 3 April 2012

668. **IF YOU CAN'T ROCK ME** (Jagger, Richard) 🖉 3.24
13 July 1975: Place: Record Plant Mobile, LA Forum, Inglewood, California, USA.
Rolling Stones with Ron Wood, Billy Preston, Ollie Brown.
Engineer: Ron Nevison.
Remixed & Remastered: Bob Clearmountain.
USA e-Album L.A. FRIDAY (LIVE 1975): 2 April 2012
UK e-Album L.A. FRIDAY (LIVE 1975): 3 April 2012

669. **GET OFF MY CLOUD** (Jagger, Richard) 🖉 4.02
13 July 1975: Place: Record Plant Mobile, LA Forum, Inglewood, California, USA.
Rolling Stones with Ron Wood, Billy Preston, Ollie Brown.
Engineer: Ron Nevison.
Remixed & Remastered: Bob Clearmountain.
USA e-Album L.A. FRIDAY (LIVE 1975): 2 April 2012
UK e-Album L.A. FRIDAY (LIVE 1975): 3 April 2012

670. **STAR STAR** (Jagger, Richard) 🖉 4.45
13 July 1975: Place: Record Plant Mobile, LA Forum, Inglewood, California, USA.
Rolling Stones with Ron Wood, Billy Preston, Ollie Brown.
Engineer: Ron Nevison.
Remixed & Remastered: Bob Clearmountain.
USA e-Album L.A. FRIDAY (LIVE 1975): 2 April 2012
UK e-Album L.A. FRIDAY (LIVE 1975): 3 April 2012

671. **GIMME SHELTER** (Jagger, Richard) 🖉 6.12
13 July 1975: Place: Record Plant Mobile, LA Forum, Inglewood, California, USA.
Rolling Stones with Ron Wood, Billy Preston, Ollie Brown.
Engineer: Ron Nevison.
Remixed & Remastered: Bob Clearmountain.
USA e-Album L.A. FRIDAY (LIVE 1975): 2 April 2012
UK e-Album L.A. FRIDAY (LIVE 1975): 3 April 2012

672. **AIN'T TOO PROUD TO BEG** (Jagger, Richard) 🖉 4.24
13 July 1975: Place: Record Plant Mobile, LA Forum, Inglewood, California, USA.
Rolling Stones with Ron Wood, Billy Preston, Ollie Brown.
Engineer: Ron Nevison.
Remixed & Remastered: Bob Clearmountain.
USA e-Album L.A. FRIDAY (LIVE 1975): 2 April 2012
UK e-Album L.A. FRIDAY (LIVE 1975): 3 April 2012

673. **YOU GOTTA MOVE** (McDowell, Davis) 🖉 4.32
13 July 1975: Place: Record Plant Mobile, LA Forum, Inglewood, California, USA.
Rolling Stones with Ron Wood, Billy Preston, Ollie Brown.
Engineer: Ron Nevison.
Remixed & Remastered: Bob Clearmountain.
USA e-Album L.A. FRIDAY (LIVE 1975): 2 April 2012
UK e-Album L.A. FRIDAY (LIVE 1975): 3 April 2012

674. **YOU CAN'T ALWAYS GET WHAT YOU WANT** (Jagger, Richard) 🖉 15.23
13 July 1975: Place: Record Plant Mobile, LA Forum, Inglewood, California, USA.
Rolling Stones with Ron Wood, Billy Preston, Trevor Lawrence, Ollie Brown.
Engineer: Ron Nevison.
Remixed & Remastered: Bob Clearmountain.
USA e-Album L.A. FRIDAY (LIVE 1975): 2 April 2012
UK e-Album L.A. FRIDAY (LIVE 1975): 3 April 2012

675. **HAPPY** (Jagger, Richard) 🖉 2.45
13 July 1975: Place: Record Plant Mobile, LA Forum, Inglewood, California, USA.
Rolling Stones with Ron Wood, Billy Preston, Ollie Brown.
Engineer: Ron Nevison.
Remixed & Remastered: Bob Clearmountain.
USA e-Album L.A. FRIDAY (LIVE 1975): 2 April 2012
UK e-Album L.A. FRIDAY (LIVE 1975): 3 April 2012

676. TUMBLING DICE (Jagger, Richard) ✎ 5.23
13 July 1975: Place: Record Plant Mobile, LA Forum, Inglewood, California, USA.
Rolling Stones with Ron Wood, Billy Preston, Ollie Brown.
Engineer: Ron Nevison.
Remixed & Remastered: Bob Clearmountain.
USA e-Album L.A. FRIDAY (LIVE 1975): 2 April 2012
UK e-Album L.A. FRIDAY (LIVE 1975): 3 April 2012

677. IT'S ONLY ROCK 'N' ROLL (Jagger, Richard) ✎ 6.04
13 July 1975: Place: Record Plant Mobile, LA Forum, Inglewood, California, USA.
Rolling Stones with Ron Wood, Billy Preston, Ollie Brown.
Engineer: Ron Nevison.
Remixed & Remastered: Bob Clearmountain.
USA e-Album L.A. FRIDAY (LIVE 1975): 2 April 2012
UK e-Album L.A. FRIDAY (LIVE 1975): 3 April 2012

678. DOO DOO DOO DOO (HEARTBREAKER) (Jagger, Richard) ✎ 4.22
13 July 1975: Place: Record Plant Mobile, LA Forum, Inglewood, California, USA.
Rolling Stones with Ron Wood, Billy Preston, Ollie Brown.
Engineer: Ron Nevison.
Remixed & Remastered: Bob Clearmountain.
USA e-Album L.A. FRIDAY (LIVE 1975): 2 April 2012
UK e-Album L.A. FRIDAY (LIVE 1975): 3 April 2012

679. FINGERPRINT FILE (Jagger, Richard) ✎ 8.43
13 July 1975: Place: Record Plant Mobile, LA Forum, Inglewood, California, USA.
Rolling Stones with Ron Wood, Billy Preston, Ollie Brown.
Engineer: Ron Nevison.
Remixed & Remastered: Bob Clearmountain.
USA e-Album L.A. FRIDAY (LIVE 1975): 2 April 2012
UK e-Album L.A. FRIDAY (LIVE 1975): 3 April 2012

680. ANGIE (Jagger, Richard) ✎ 5.18
13 July 1975: Place: Record Plant Mobile, LA Forum, Inglewood, California, USA.
Rolling Stones with Ron Wood, Billy Preston, Ollie Brown.
Engineer: Ron Nevison.
Remixed & Remastered: Bob Clearmountain.
USA e-Album L.A. FRIDAY (LIVE 1975): 2 April 2012
UK e-Album L.A. FRIDAY (LIVE 1975): 3 April 2012

681. WILD HORSES (Jagger, Richard) ✎ 7.25
13 July 1975: Place: Record Plant Mobile, LA Forum, Inglewood, California, USA.
Rolling Stones with Ron Wood, Billy Preston, Ollie Brown.
Engineer: Ron Nevison.
Remixed & Remastered: Bob Clearmountain.
USA e-Album L.A. FRIDAY (LIVE 1975): 2 April 2012
UK e-Album L.A. FRIDAY (LIVE 1975): 3 April 2012

682. THAT'S LIFE (Preston) ✎ 3.17
13 July 1975: Place: Record Plant Mobile, LA Forum, Inglewood, California, USA.
Rolling Stones with Ron Wood, Billy Preston, Ollie Brown.
Engineer: Ron Nevison.
Remixed & Remastered: Bob Clearmountain.
USA e-Album L.A. FRIDAY (LIVE 1975): 2 April 2012
UK e-Album L.A. FRIDAY (LIVE 1975): 3 April 2012

683. OUTA-SPACE (Greene, Preston) ✎ 4.04
13 July 1975: Place: Record Plant Mobile, LA Forum, Inglewood, California, USA.
Rolling Stones with Ron Wood, Billy Preston, Ollie Brown.
Engineer: Ron Nevison.
Remixed & Remastered: Bob Clearmountain.
USA e-Album L.A. FRIDAY (LIVE 1975): 2 April 2012
UK e-Album L.A. FRIDAY (LIVE 1975): 3 April 2012

684. BROWN SUGAR (Jagger, Richard) ✏ 4.15
13 July 1975: Place: Record Plant Mobile, LA Forum, Inglewood, California, USA.
Rolling Stones with Ron Wood, Billy Preston, Bobby Keys, Ollie Brown.
Engineer: Ron Nevison.
Remixed & Remastered: Bob Clearmountain.
USA e-Album L.A. FRIDAY (LIVE 1975): 2 April 2012
UK e-Album L.A. FRIDAY (LIVE 1975): 3 April 2012

685. MIDNIGHT RAMBLER (Jagger, Richard) ✏ 15.15
13 July 1975: Place: Record Plant Mobile, LA Forum, Inglewood, California, USA.
Rolling Stones with Ron Wood, Billy Preston, Ollie Brown.
Engineer: Ron Nevison.
Remixed & Remastered: Bob Clearmountain.
USA e-Album L.A. FRIDAY (LIVE 1975): 2 April 2012
UK e-Album L.A. FRIDAY (LIVE 1975): 3 April 2012

686. RIP THIS JOINT (Jagger, Richard) ✏ 2.06
13 July 1975: Place: Record Plant Mobile, LA Forum, Inglewood, California, USA.
Rolling Stones with Ron Wood, Billy Preston, Trevor Lawrence, Bobby Keys, Steve Madaio, Ollie Brown.
Engineer: Ron Nevison.
Remixed & Remastered: Bob Clearmountain.
USA e-Album L.A. FRIDAY (LIVE 1975): 2 April 2012
UK e-Album L.A. FRIDAY (LIVE 1975): 3 April 2012

687. STREET FIGHTING MAN (Jagger, Richard) ✏ 4.05
13 July 1975: Place: Record Plant Mobile, LA Forum, Inglewood, California, USA.
Rolling Stones with Ron Wood, Billy Preston, Trevor Lawrence, Bobby Keys, Steve Madaio, Ollie Brown.
Engineer: Ron Nevison.
Remixed & Remastered: Bob Clearmountain.
USA e-Album L.A. FRIDAY (LIVE 1975): 2 April 2012
UK e-Album L.A. FRIDAY (LIVE 1975): 3 April 2012

688. JUMPING JACK FLASH (Jagger, Richard) ✏ 6.57
13 July 1975: Place: Record Plant Mobile, LA Forum, Inglewood, California, USA.
Rolling Stones with Ron Wood, Billy Preston, Ollie Brown.
Engineer: Ron Nevison.
Remixed & Remastered: Bob Clearmountain.
USA e-Album L.A. FRIDAY (LIVE 1975): 2 April 2012
UK e-Album L.A. FRIDAY (LIVE 1975): 3 April 2012

689. SYMPATHY FOR THE DEVIL (Jagger, Richard) ✏ 10.21
13 July 1975: Place: Record Plant Mobile, LA Forum, Inglewood, California, USA.
Rolling Stones with Ron Wood, Jesse Ed Davis, Billy Preston, Ollie Brown.
Engineer: Ron Nevison.
Remixed & Remastered: Bob Clearmountain.
USA e-Album L.A. FRIDAY (LIVE 1975): 2 April 2012
UK e-Album L.A. FRIDAY (LIVE 1975): 3 April 2012

The rest of the gig commenced with *All Down The Line*, followed by *If You Can't Rock Me* which seems to breathe new life, as it segues into *Get Off My Cloud*, Jagger playing off Billy Preston's vocals. The "problematic" blow-up cock rose during *Star Star* for Mick Jagger to mount and taunt the audience before the older *Gimme Shelter* rippled its familiar tones. The concert mid-section portrayed another song from the last album, namely *Ain't Too Proud To Beg*, before the 60s songs - an almost acapella version of *You Gotta Move* and a very long 15-minute *You Can't Always Get What You Want*. That provided Trevor Lawrence with a sax solo and enabled Ron Wood to illustrate his lead guitar solo capabilities. Keith Richards is brought to the front of the stage to perform *Happy* with Mick whipping the audience up alongside. *Tumbling Dice* and *It's Only Rock 'n' Roll* follow before the band namecheck where Ron Wood was introduced as a member of The Faces. *Heartbreaker* swirls into action next before *Fingerprint File* - a song only played in the States - with Ron Wood swapping to bass while Bill Wyman played the synthesiser and Mick on guitar.
A slower section of *Angie* and *Wild Horses* continue before Billy Preston is showcased with two numbers featuring a synthesiser. *That's Life* was taken from his new album IT'S MY PLEASURE, released that year and the jam-like *Outa-Space* from the 1971 album, I WROTE A SIMPLE SONG. His songs were augmented by the band line-up, except for Ollie Brown swapping the percussion for the drums. The two songs gave Mick Jagger a partial rest before the show's climax, although he did prance and dance with Billy.
It is said that he also found time to take the drugs that were freely available on the stage amplifiers, which were hidden from the audience by drapes. Certainly, his vocal output suffered because much of his delivery was shouted and sounded hoarse. The final flourish incorporated old favourites *Brown Sugar* - with Bobby Keys - *Midnight Rambler, Rip This Joint, Street Fighting Man* and a theatrical *Jumping Jack Flash*, with a confetti spewing, blow-up phallic dragon, and Billy freed from the keyboard with a mobile clavinet. A superb encore of *Sympathy For The Devil* ensued, during a time when that song had been attempted consistently on

tour since the fatal Altamont incident. For the last concert encore, Jesse Ed Davis, who had last played with the Stones at the *Rock 'N' Roll Circus* event in 1968 with the Taj Mahal band, was also featured on lead guitar. The song provided Ron and Keith with a chance to trade guitar solos like long lost brothers and was a deliberate ploy to try and produce a fast climax, due to the increased set list.

The brass sounds were only used in full on a couple of numbers, which uncluttered the show's look, and the stage costumes, designed especially for the Stones, became increasingly elaborate. Even Bill Wyman wore a silver suit, Mick camp and fey in Russian-style trousers, silk shirts and harem pants. Ron Wood had begun to learn how the band worked on stage; there was a lot of non-verbal contact and eye-to-eye looks, which evidently meant something. If Ron felt the tempo needed to be faster he had to first nod at Keith to gain his agreement, then they both caught Charlie's attention to up the beat. Keith got arrested twice on tour, first in Fordyce, Arkansas - along with Ronnie Wood and security man Jim Callaghan (JC) - for possession of an offensive weapon (a pen-knife and, having found this, the police did not look for any stash which was hidden in a door panel).

The tour concluded on 8 August 1975, in Buffalo, New York, where they played to a crowd of 70,000. Bill Wyman started sessions for his second solo album as did Ronnie Wood, in between touring with The Faces in the United States from August until the end of October. This was the acrimonious conclusion of The Faces, after Rod Stewart finally decided to go solo. It must be remembered that, when on tour, Ron Wood was not used to the dual guitar role. His American gigs with the Stones were the first time that he had attempted this and Keith said that he adapted and fitted in remarkably well.

In December 1975, it was agreed that Ron would join the Stones and a tentative announcement was made by Mick that the former Faces man had been working on a new album and that he would tour Europe with them.

Rolling Stones Mach III was on the runway and taking off. Ron brought with him two backline technical support personnel in the shape of Russell Schlagbaum and Royden "Chuch" Magee from Detroit. They had met in the early 70s at a gig and ended up joining The Faces entourage before hitching a long ride with the Stones. November 1975 saw the release of a UK double album by Decca named ROLLED GOLD, in the form of a true 60s document of hits and album tracks from *Come On* to *Gimme Shelter*. It remained in the UK charts for a year. Originally, it was intended to be a more extensive three LP box set entitled THE HISTORY OF THE ROLLING STONES and test pressings were created. Keith Richards was trying to renew his relationship with Anita Pallenberg, with the result that she became pregnant. Meanwhile, the drugs were taking their toll on both of them. Mick and Bianca retreated to Ireland before the Stones started work on the conclusion of the BLACK AND BLUE album.

690. IF YOU CAN'T ROCK ME (Jagger, Richard) ✏ 1.27
27 May 1976: Place: Earl's Court, London, England.
Rolling Stones with Billy Preston, Ollie Brown.
Producer: The Glimmer Twins.
Engineer: Keith Harwood, Eddie Kramer, Ron Nevison, Dave Jordan, Jimmy Douglass.
Assistant Producer: Mick McKenna, Tom Heid, Randy Hason, Bobby Warner, Lew Hahn, Tapani Tapanainen, Lee Hulko.
USA LP LOVE YOU LIVE: 15 September 1977: No. 5 - 7 weeks
UK LP LOVE YOU LIVE: 16 September 1977: No. 3 - 8 weeks
UK Compilation LP TIME WAITS FOR NO ONE - ANTHOLOGY 1971 - 1977: 1 June 1979

691. GET OFF MY CLOUD (Jagger, Richard) ✏ 3.34
27 May 1976: Place: Earl's Court, London, England.
Rolling Stones with Billy Preston, Ollie Brown.
Producer: The Glimmer Twins.
Engineer: Keith Harwood, Eddie Kramer, Ron Nevison, Dave Jordan, Jimmy Douglass.
Assistant Producer: Mick McKenna, Tom Heid, Randy Hason, Bobby Warner, Lew Hahn, Tapani Tapanainen, Lee Hulko.
USA LP LOVE YOU LIVE: 15 September 1977: No. 5 - 7 weeks
UK LP LOVE YOU LIVE: 16 September 1977: No. 3 - 8 weeks
UK Compilation LP TIME WAITS FOR NO ONE - ANTHOLOGY 1971 - 1977: 1 June 1979

There was a long break of eight months between the American and European tours. Rehearsals started mid-April in France before the band moved to Frankfurt for the first concert date. BLACK AND BLUE was released on 26 April 1976 and *Fool To Cry* was high in the charts. Ron Wood's solo album NOW LOOK came out and Bill Wyman also had MONKEY GRIP available, both being advertised in the tour programme. The demand for the Stones as a performing group was now at a peak and the heavy schedule of a three-month tour of America in 1975 was followed by a three-month jaunt around Europe in April, May and June, 1976, calling at countries never toured before. Places visited included Germany, Belgium, Scotland, England, Netherlands, France, Switzerland, Spain, Yugoslavia and Austria, though a request to play in the USSR was denied.

When the British leg of the tour was announced, a cool one million postal applications were received at an average request of four tickets each. So an estimated four million Britons wanted to see a performance by the greatest rock and roll band in the world! Many would be disappointed since only 15 shows at small venues were performed in the UK. One ticket tout offered £1,000 for 100 tickets for each of the six nights at Earls Court. The Stones declined the offer.

The concerts at London's Earl's Court were played to mixed reviews, some critics panning them for the awful sound, fans loving them. It depended where you were in the hall; further back gave echoes from the steel arena structure, while up close the sound was directed from the PA. Keith Richards thought the concerts were some of the best of the tour and the band were indeed very tight. Backstage at one of the London shows, Mick Jagger met Jerry Hall, while she was still dating Bryan Ferry.

692. HONKY TONK WOMEN (Jagger, Richard) ✏ 3.20
5 June 1976: Place: Aux Abattoirs, Paris, France.
Rolling Stones with Billy Preston, Ollie Brown.
Producer: The Glimmer Twins.
Engineer: Keith Harwood, Eddie Kramer, Ron Nevison, Dave Jordan, Jimmy Douglass.
Assistant Producer: Mick McKenna, Tom Heid, Randy Hason, Bobby Warner, Lew Hahn, Tapani Tapanainen, Lee Hulko.
USA LP LOVE YOU LIVE: 15 September 1977: No. 5 - 7 weeks
UK LP LOVE YOU LIVE: 16 September 1977: No. 3 - 8 weeks

693. YOU GOTTA MOVE (McDowell) ⟋ 4.19
5 June 1976: Place: Aux Abattoirs, Paris, France.
Rolling Stones with Billy Preston, Ollie Brown.
Producer: The Glimmer Twins.
Engineer: Keith Harwood, Eddie Kramer, Ron Nevison, Dave Jordan, Jimmy Douglass.
Assistant Producer: Mick McKenna, Tom Heid, Randy Hason, Bobby Warner, Lew Hahn, Tapani Tapanainen, Lee Hulko.
USA LP LOVE YOU LIVE: 15 September 1977: No. 5 - 7 weeks
UK LP LOVE YOU LIVE: 16 September 1977: No. 3 - 8 weeks

694. HAPPY (Jagger, Richard) ⟋ 2.54
5 June 1976: Place: Aux Abattoirs, Paris, France.
Rolling Stones with Billy Preston, Ollie Brown.
Producer: The Glimmer Twins.
Engineer: Keith Harwood, Eddie Kramer, Ron Nevison, Dave Jordan, Jimmy Douglass.
Assistant Producer: Mick McKenna, Tom Heid, Randy Hason, Bobby Warner, Lew Hahn, Tapani Tapanainen, Lee Hulko.
USA LP LOVE YOU LIVE: 15 September 1977: No. 5 - 7 weeks
UK LP LOVE YOU LIVE: 16 September 1977: No. 3 - 8 weeks

695. HOT STUFF (Jagger, Richard) ⟋ 4.36
6 June 1976: Place: Aux Abattoirs, Paris, France.
Rolling Stones with Billy Preston, Ollie Brown.
Producer: The Glimmer Twins.
Engineer: Keith Harwood, Eddie Kramer, Ron Nevison, Dave Jordan, Jimmy Douglass.
Assistant Producer: Mick McKenna, Tom Heid, Randy Hason, Bobby Warner, Lew Hahn, Tapani Tapanainen, Lee Hulko.
USA LP LOVE YOU LIVE: 15 September 1977: No. 5 - 7 weeks
UK LP LOVE YOU LIVE: 16 September 1977: No. 3 - 8 weeks

696. STAR STAR (Jagger, Richard) ⟋ 4.10
6 June 1976: Place: Aux Abattoirs, Paris, France.
Rolling Stones with Billy Preston, Ollie Brown.
Producer: The Glimmer Twins.
Engineer: Keith Harwood, Eddie Kramer, Ron Nevison, Dave Jordan, Jimmy Douglass.
Assistant Producer: Mick McKenna, Tom Heid, Randy Hason, Bobby Warner, Lew Hahn, Tapani Tapanainen, Lee Hulko.
USA LP LOVE YOU LIVE: 15 September 1977: No. 5 - 7 weeks
UK LP LOVE YOU LIVE: 16 September 1977: No. 3 - 8 weeks

697. BROWN SUGAR (Jagger, Richard) ⟋ 3.11
6 June 1976: Place: Aux Abattoirs, Paris, France.
Rolling Stones with Billy Preston, Ollie Brown.
Producer: The Glimmer Twins.
Engineer: Keith Harwood, Eddie Kramer, Ron Nevison, Dave Jordan, Jimmy Douglass.
Assistant Producer: Mick McKenna, Tom Heid, Randy Hason, Bobby Warner, Lew Hahn, Tapani Tapanainen, Lee Hulko.
USA LP LOVE YOU LIVE: 15 September 1977: No. 5 - 7 weeks
UK LP LOVE YOU LIVE: 16 September 1977: No. 3 - 8 weeks

698. JUMPIN' JACK FLASH (Jagger, Richard) ⟋ 3.57
6 June 1976: Place: Aux Abattoirs, Paris, France.
Rolling Stones with Billy Preston, Ollie Brown.
Producer: The Glimmer Twins.
Engineer: Keith Harwood, Eddie Kramer, Ron Nevison, Dave Jordan, Jimmy Douglass.
Assistant Producer: Mick McKenna, Tom Heid, Randy Hason, Bobby Warner, Lew Hahn, Tapani Tapanainen, Lee Hulko.
USA LP LOVE YOU LIVE: 15 September 1977: No. 5 - 7 weeks
UK LP LOVE YOU LIVE: 16 September 1977: No. 3 - 8 weeks

699. YOU CAN'T ALWAYS GET WHAT YOU WANT (Jagger, Richard) ⟋ 7.44
7 June 1976: Place: Aux Abattoirs, Paris, France.
Rolling Stones with Billy Preston, Ollie Brown.
Producer: The Glimmer Twins.
Engineer: Keith Harwood, Eddie Kramer, Ron Nevison, Dave Jordan, Jimmy Douglass.
Assistant Producer: Mick McKenna, Tom Heid, Randy Hason, Bobby Warner, Lew Hahn, Tapani Tapanainen, Lee Hulko.
USA LP LOVE YOU LIVE: 15 September 1977: No. 5 - 7 weeks
UK LP LOVE YOU LIVE: 16 September 1977: No. 3 - 8 weeks

700. TUMBLING DICE (Jagger, Richard) ✐ 3.59
7 June 1976: Place: Aux Abattoirs, Paris, France.
Rolling Stones with Billy Preston, Ollie Brown.
Producer: The Glimmer Twins.
Engineer: Keith Harwood, Eddie Kramer, Ron Nevison, Dave Jordan, Jimmy Douglass.
Assistant Producer: Mick McKenna, Tom Heid, Randy Hason, Bobby Warner, Lew Hahn, Tapani Tapanainen, Lee Hulko.
USA LP LOVE YOU LIVE: 15 September 1977: No. 5 - 7 weeks
UK LP LOVE YOU LIVE: 16 September 1977: No. 3 - 8 weeks

701. NOTHING FROM NOTHING (Greene, Preston) ✐ 2.50
7 June 1976: Place: Aux Abattoirs, Paris, France.
Rolling Stones with Billy Preston, Ollie Brown.
Producer: The Glimmer Twins.
Engineer: Keith Harwood, Eddie Kramer, Ron Nevison, Dave Jordan, Jimmy Douglass.
Assistant Producer: Mick McKenna, Tom Heid, Randy Hason, Bobby Warner, Lew Hahn, Tapani Tapanainen, Lee Hulko.
Bootleg only.

A prerequisite of the tour was that the Stones would put on an unequalled performance so the unique stage set was transported from America. It covered 500 square yards, using a variety of theatrical gimmicks. Clowns and bongo drummers roamed the auditorium enhancing the atmosphere. Due to the album release of BLACK AND BLUE, the set included *Hand Of Fate, Hey Negrita, Hot Stuff* and *Fool To Cry*. The exception to this was *Cherry Oh Baby*, which was played a couple of times in New York.

Unlike the USA, there were no horns on the tour, which gave Keith Richards more guitar freedom, not restricting him totally to the rhythm. The screeching synthesiser and clavinet sounds were not so pronounced on the European leg maybe illustrating why many of the LOVE YOU LIVE tunes were from the European section. In Paris, the lyrics to *Honky Tonk Women* contained the reference to the French capital city instead of New York.

Unusually, in a complete one-off, Eric Clapton guested on Big Bill Broonzy's *Key To The Highway* in Leicester, England, while *Nothing From Nothing* replaced *That's Life* in the Preston two-song spot. More seriously, Keith crashed his car in a field after a gig at Stafford, in England. He had fallen asleep at the wheel and, despite discarding his normal stash, police found traces of substances on him, including LSD, which he did not use. Later, in 1977, he was found guilty only of possession of cocaine and fined. On 6 June, his two-month-old baby daughter Tara was the victim of a cot death in Geneva. Distraught, he still performed at that evening's Paris concert, apparently playing an even more intense set.

The LOVE YOU LIVE double album, recorded by Keith Harwood, captured the atmosphere of this Paris show on a few tracks and French TV also broadcast highlights of the concert. Overall, the album of the tour, which is on three vinyl sides, is a little subdued compared to the "real thing". The quality is high but the vision of Jagger shimmying with Billy Preston and swinging on ropes in *Outa-Space*, riding a blow-up phallic shape during *Star Star* and dousing fans with buckets of water at the show's end are lost forever.

An EP was produced for promotional purposes in the States. It contained *If You Can't Rock Me, Get Off My Cloud, Hot Stuff, Brown Sugar* and *Jumping Jack Flash* (note the added "g" to the latter, unlike the 1968 original). LOVE YOU LIVE was dedicated to the memory of Keith Harwood, who died in a car accident in September 1977, following a recording session with Keith Richards and John Phillips. The album cover was designed by Andy Warhol from original photographs of Mick pretending to bite his daughter Jade. The outline was repeated and traced sketch-like. It was based on some similar artwork that Warhol produced of Mick in 1975. The double-fold inside cover has similar poses by the other band members. Andy Warhol was none too happy when he saw the final product, which had Mick's yellow etched pen with the band name and album title scrawled over his sketch.

702. WILD HORSES (Jagger, Richard) ✐ 5.56
21 August 1976: Place: Knebworth, England.
Rolling Stones with Billy Preston, Ollie Brown.
Producer: Michael Lindsay-Hogg
Assistant TV Director: David Crossman.
UK e-EP Video Track Wild Horses: 20 November 2009

An all-day rock festival enabled the Stones to thank British fans for their past support and, hopefully, compensate those who could not get tickets for the arena shows and the bad sound quality at Earl's Court. More than one hundred thousand troops responded and witnessed a day of rock and blues set in the illustrious Knebworth country estate. The concert was promoted by Freddie Bannister, who had a great tradition of organising festivals at Bath and Knebworth, as well as being a well-known 60s entrepreneur, who had booked the Stones before.

It was Bannister's third concert at Knebworth, having already promoted The Allman Brothers and Pink Floyd as headliners. Having set up Led Zeppelin's first outdoor show in Bath in 1969, his final Knebworth promotion ten years later was the band's last concert in Britain. The support act in 1979 were Ron Wood's New Barbarians, of which we shall hear more later.

In 1976, Led Zeppelin and Queen had originally been approached for the event; the former declined, while the latter accepted. However, the Stones were also deliberating an offer and Mick Jagger finally said the band were prepared to play so Bannister had to tell Queen's manager John Reid that he favoured the Stones over Queen.

Reid felt that the only band Queen would have been bounced for was the Rolling Stones. Instead they used the same tent stage for their own free Hyde Park show on 18 September. One condition was placed on the Stones event - that it was not first advertised in the music press. Promotions for the event started with leaflets dropped in central London by clowns, fire eaters and jugglers during the last weekend in June. At the Wimbledon tennis championships, national TV cameras captured the sight of two clowns invading Centre Court during the men's singles final, carrying placards stating: "Stones at Knebworth". Mick was sat in the crowd and must have been proud of the stunt.

Two topless girls did the same at a televised Sussex county cricket match on the day after and, finally, banners were placed at strategic points overnight in London. The Stones performance at Knebworth was put in jeopardy the day before when Keith accidentally sliced his playing finger with a razor but he was patched up, even if he did bleed during the performance. The Don Harrison Band (with the rhythm players from Creedence Clearwater Revival), Hot Tuna, Todd Rundgren's Utopia (who got the first encore of the day with the Move's *Do Ya*), Lynyrd Skynyrd and 10cc were the support acts.

Late afternoon, Lynyrd Skynyrd took the stage and introduced to England a set of magical, southern blues boogie. *Freebird* was one of the most inspired musical performances ever seen on a British rock stage, even if the band did encroach on the protruded tongue part of the stage, reportedly against Mick's express instruction. The crowd, some perched precariously in oak trees, were ecstatic, rebel flags waving furiously. 10cc had a hard job to follow this and there was a two-hour delay (allegedly Keith Richards needed to rest from the day's excess and, in order to delay things, the Stones roadies cut the power cable) before they hit the stage before a by now sour, sun-blistered crowd.

The Stones were unable to recapture the atmosphere created by Lynyrd Skynyrd. The tongue-shaped stage had been especially built for the appearance and extended into the crowd, although this was not apparent until inflatables at the front pursed their lips just before the band went on. For the first time at a Stones gig, walkways extended to the left and right for Jagger to be able to move between more people. This design was a taste of what was to come.

The Stones went on late at night, when the warmth of the day had evaporated, and performed a lengthy set of more than two-and-a-half hours, drawing a fine mixture of material from the 60s and 70s. The set included *Satisfaction*, *Get Off My Cloud*, *Around And Around*, *Little Red Rooster*, *Let's Spend The Night Together*, *Route 66*, *Stray Cat Blues*, *You Can't Always Get What You Want*, *Honky Tonk Women* (with a snatch of *Country Honk* at the end in which Mick teases Ron - "did you play on that?"), *Midnight Rambler*, *Jumpin' Jack Flash*, *Street Fighting Man*, *Star Star*, *You Gotta Move*, *Dead Flowers*, *Wild Horses*, *Tumbling Dice*, *Happy*, *Brown Sugar* and *Rip This Joint*. There was also some more up-to-date material, including *Ain't Too Proud To Beg*, *If You Can't Rock Me*, *Hand Of Fate*, *Hey Negrita*, *Hot Stuff*, *Fool To Cry* and *It's Only Rock 'n' Roll*.

There were also the two Billy Preston numbers, *Nothing From Nothing* and *Outa-Space*. In all, it was a gargantuan 28 number set list marred by technical sound difficulties but fully appreciated as ground breaking and risk taking. The concert was filmed by Michael Lindsay-Hogg for London Weekend Television and soundboard recordings are available but, regretfully, no legitimate releases have been made of either, other than the video of *Wild Horses*, which was released in 2009 as an EP with the STICKY FINGERS version and the 1995 STRIPPED studio take. Knebworth proved to be a day that was a mark of respect to hippiedom, but the tide was turning.

703. AROUND AND AROUND (Berry) ✏ 4.07
4/5 March 1977: Place: El Mocambo, Toronto, Canada.
Rolling Stones with Billy Preston, Ollie Brown.
Producer: The Glimmer Twins.
Engineer: Keith Harwood, Eddie Kramer, Ron Nevison, Dave Jordan, Jimmy Douglass.
Assistant Producer: Mick McKenna, Tom Heid, Randy Hason, Bobby Warner, Lew Hahn, Tapani Tapanainen, Lee Hulko.
USA LP LOVE YOU LIVE: 15 September 1977: No. 5 - 7 weeks
UK LP LOVE YOU LIVE: 16 September 1977: No. 3 - 8 weeks

Following the Knebworth concert Mick Jagger, Ron Wood and Ollie Brown became involved in a recording project with John Phillips of Mamas And Papas fame. Mick Taylor had been working with Phillips on an unreleased soundtrack for *The Man Who Fell To Earth* film and so was also present. Chris Spedding was the other guitarist since Ron provided bass and, before long, Keith Richards could not resist joining in. On one track, *Zulu Warrior*, Mick Taylor and Keith linked arms together, John Phillips describing Taylor's playing as "12-bar ballet".

Another track, *Just 14*, was purported to be about John's child film-star daughter, Mackenzie Phillips, who was allegedly caught in her locked bedroom with Mick Jagger, although, in 2009, she confessed to an incestuous relationship with her father. The album took shape over many years but most of the recording was done in London, in September 1976. It was proposed that it would be released on the Rolling Stones label.

The photographs from the sessions show an emaciated Keith and the heroin was clearly taking a severe grip on his spirit. This is supported by comments made by people such as New Musical Express writer Nick Kent. In 1974, he had famously labelled Keith in the as "The World's Most Elegantly Wasted Human Being". The John Phillips album, PAY PACK AND FOLLOW, produced by The Glimmer Twins, was posthumously released in 2001. Late in November 1976, Decca released a UK-only double vinyl compilation of their 60s singles, ROLLED GOLD.

Early in 1977, plans were well underway for the double LOVE YOU LIVE album, with most of it being taken from the Paris concerts, recorded by Mick McKenna. At the end of February, the Stones signed a four-album contract with WEA (Warner, Elektra, Atlantic) in North America and EMI for the rest of the world, for $14 million. For a short, two-week period they were in the same "stable" as the Sex Pistols, until EMI lost patience with them - in Mick's view, the record company was short-sighted and told them so.

At that time, both the British and American music scene was evolving fast as the Woodstock fashion styles of flares, flowers and flowing clothes were being discarded for a harsher, back-to-the-roots music. There had always been an underground hard-core rock and roll following (The Seeds, MC5, The Flamin' Groovies, The Stooges, The Strangeloves, The Standells, The Electric Prunes - all genuine nugget territory) but with fast riffs and short, sharp melodies, a new revolution of taste was growing. In America, The Ramones, Patti Smith (a Keith fanatic), Blondie and Television were gaining exposure led by their protégés, The New York Dolls (who had the Jagger-like David Johansen as their singer).

In Britain, there were just as excellent R 'n' B sounds emanating from the likes of Dr Feelgood and Eddie And The Hotrods. In 1976 Johnny Rotten (John Lydon), from the Sex Pistols, said of the Stones, " . . . they are established and just do not mean anything to anyone". Malcolm McLaren (whom Jerry Hall knew well from his Kings Road Sex clothes shop, which he ran with designer Vivienne Westwood) had already launched his band, The Sex Pistols, on the scene. Keith acknowledged later that the attitude of the Sex Pistols shook them up.

Malcolm was an Andrew Oldham entrepreneur, who knew the face of rock and roll was about to change and he would be manipulating the publicity machine just as Andrew and Brian Epstein had done in the 60s. Mick always had a feel for contemporary music and suggested that The Rolling Stones return to their roots and record some songs in a club, just like the old days in Windsor, Maidenhead and Richmond. He was also involved in negotiating the next Stones recording contract and a venue was needed within commuter distance of New York.

After research, the small (circa 500) El Mocambo club in Toronto was booked because Canada did not require an entry visa, an important factor as, of course, Keith had been charged and fined for possession of cocaine following his motorway crash and arrest the previous year in England. Tickets were distributed to a select few by a two-week charity competition on a local radio rock show (CHUM FM). The headliners were April Wine, supported by the Cockroaches, for two nights only. April Wine were there for a week to record a LIVE AT THE EL MOCAMBO album, produced by Myles Goodwyn and recorded and engineered by Eddie Kramer.

704. LITTLE RED ROOSTER (Dixon) ✏ 4.39
4/5 March 1977: Place: El Mocambo, Toronto, Canada.
Rolling Stones with Billy Preston, Ollie Brown.
Producer: The Glimmer Twins.
Engineer: Keith Harwood, Eddie Kramer, Ron Nevison, Dave Jordan, Jimmy Douglass.
Assistant Producer: Mick McKenna, Tom Heid, Randy Hason, Bobby Warner, Lew Hahn, Tapani Tapanainen, Lee Hulko.
USA LP LOVE YOU LIVE: 15 September 1977: No. 5 - 7 weeks
UK LP LOVE YOU LIVE: 16 September 1977: No. 3 - 8 weeks

705. MANNISH BOY (London, McDaniel, Morganfield) ✏ 6.29
4/5 March 1977: Place: El Mocambo, Toronto, Canada.
Rolling Stones with Billy Preston, Ollie Brown.
Producer: The Glimmer Twins.
Engineer: Keith Harwood, Eddie Kramer, Ron Nevison, Dave Jordan, Jimmy Douglass.
Assistant Producer: Mick McKenna, Tom Heid, Randy Hason, Bobby Warner, Lew Hahn, Tapani Tapanainen, Lee Hulko.

USA LP LOVE YOU LIVE: 15 September 1977: No. 5 - 7 weeks
UK LP LOVE YOU LIVE: 16 September 1977: No. 3 - 8 weeks
USA Compilation LP SUCKING IN THE SEVENTIES: 12 March 1981: No. 15 - 5 weeks
UK Compilation LP SUCKING IN THE SEVENTIES: 13 April 1981
USA CD LP ROLLING STONES RARITIES 1971-2003: 22 November 2005: No. 76 - 6 weeks
UK CD LP ROLLING STONES RARITIES 1971-2003: 28 November 2005

706. CRACKIN' UP (McDaniel) ⟋ 5.40
4/5 March 1977: Place: El Mocambo, Toronto, Canada.
Rolling Stones with Billy Preston, Ollie Brown.
Producer: The Glimmer Twins.
Engineer: Keith Harwood, Eddie Kramer, Ron Nevison, Dave Jordan, Jimmy Douglass.
Assistant Producer: Mick McKenna, Tom Heid, Randy Hason, Bobby Warner, Lew Hahn, Tapani Tapanainen, Lee Hulko.
USA LP LOVE YOU LIVE: 15 September 1977: No. 5 - 7 weeks
UK LP LOVE YOU LIVE: 16 September 1977: No. 3 - 8 weeks

A quiet stay in Toronto was planned, the intention being to record five gigs at the snug El Mocambo Club and place some of the tracks on the forthcoming live double album. Keith Richards was eventually persuaded to join the band in Canada after a series of pleading phone calls, coupled with threatening telegrams. On arrival at the airport, Anita Pallenberg, Keith and son Marlon had their bags searched, hashish and traces of heroin being found. Anita was arrested and later fined for the offence.

Plans were further disrupted on 27 February when the Mounties visited Keith's suite at the Harbour Castle Hotel. It was a well-co-ordinated plan, in the early hours of the morning, with undercover cops dressed as hotel employees and even as waiters. Search and arrest warrants in hand, they discovered a bountiful supply of hallucinogens. Keith, who had to be woken up before the arrest could be made (not an easy task), was charged with possession of cocaine and, more seriously, intent to traffic. The potential consequences were grave as trafficking in Canada carried a life sentence.

Meanwhile, brave Ronnie Wood was seen on the boulevard cavorting with the Prime Minister's bohemian young wife, Margaret Trudeau. The intended quiet stay in Canada became a major incident and the world's press loved it. Margaret's alleged escapades at the El Mocambo Club and various hotel suites prompted the press to launch an attack on the credibility of the Canadian Government, while Keith's future jeopardised the Stones' very existence.

Despite these events, the band set about rehearsing for a reduced run of two gigs at the El Mocambo Club, where Keith likened the cosy atmosphere to the Crawdaddy in Richmond. The crowd were excited and in awe at seeing the Stones in such intimate circumstances - the normal house rules went out the window. The band were inspired and performed two electrifying sets, the second night outstripping the first.

Both concerts were recorded by Eddie Kramer - a full release of the original concert soundboards would be welcome! All cuts on the album were edited and some tracks would have had vocal, harmonica and guitar overdubs on them. *Mannish Boy* was further edited by almost two minutes for the SUCKING IN THE SEVENTIES album. *Crackin' Up*, a Bo Diddley number, was recalled from the murky depths and at last given an official release following the January 1963 IBC sessions. *Hand Of Fate* rips and snarls faster than the original and *Route 66* keeps up the pace. *Worried About You* was played before it had appeared officially. *Around And Around*, with Mick's humorous introduction (all right Margaret!), has Keith flawlessly riff-playing. It would have made a perfect single release in late 1977 amid the furore about the punk music scene emanating from Britain. "No more, Elvis, Beatles or Rolling Stones in 1977" cried angry Joe Strummer, ironically.

707. SING ME BACK HOME (Haggard) 4.17
12/13 March 1977: Place: Sounds Interchange, Toronto, Canada.
Keith Richards, Ian Stewart.
Bootleg only.

708. APARTMENT NO. 9 (Austin, Owen, Paycheck) 3.44
12/13 March 1977: Place: Sounds Interchange, Toronto, Canada.
Keith Richards, Ian Stewart.
Bootleg only.

709. WORRIED LIFE BLUES (Merriweather) 2.15
12/13 March 1977: Place: Sounds Interchange, Toronto, Canada.
Keith Richards, Ian Stewart.
Bootleg only.

Technically these are not real Stones' sessions and should not be included within the sessionography but they are mentioned for their historical interest. These gems were recorded while Keith was technically detained on bail in Canada, pending a decision on the charges following the drugs bust. One by one, the band had left him to go their separate ways and each departure must have felt like a physical punch. Jagger's priority was to secure a new recording contract, which he did with the band's' consent. The session vocals are a shade rusty but, for pure authenticity, they are great collectors' items.

In 1979, there were plans to release the tapes officially, with the title of BAD LUCK. Backed by Ian Stewart and, unusually, with Anita Pallenberg in the studio, Keith sings his heart out about his current dilemma - "my friends have all left me". The following night, Keith added some overdubs to the recordings. *Worried Life Blues*, a traditional standard, was originally performed by the king of Chicago blues piano, Big Maceo Merriweather.

Apartment No. 9, a Tammy Wynette song, was re-recorded in 1981 but failed to capture the poignancy of the Toronto session. When Keith appeared with the New Barbarians - Ron Wood's touring band - *Apartment No. 9* was a stage favourite. The Merle Haggard song *Sing Me Back Home* was brought to Keith's attention by Gram Parsons. On 14 March, Richards was ordered to return on 27 June for a court appearance but, in the meantime, he was free to go - but who would have him? As it turned out, the United States allowed the family to enter the country but only for drug treatment - and that is what happened for the whole of April 1977, Keith being surprised but very grateful to get this medical visa from the USA. That summer, recuperation continued while LOVE YOU LIVE was finally put to bed, following overdubs at the Plaza hotel in New York, before its release in September. Since Billy Preston had played on all of the tracks he wanted a cut of the royalties and, much to Jagger's annoyance, this was agreed.

Having received positive news, Keith put a lot of effort into compiling the live tracks for LOVE YOU LIVE, something that Mick had grown accustomed to. They disagreed about the track selection and, at one point, the project almost became two live albums, one selected by Mick and the other by Keith, featuring the tracks from Mocambo. There was also a plan to celebrate an era of Mick Taylor, with a proposal that one side should be live tracks featuring him. Arguably this could have delivered a punch in the teeth from 1973.

Now that Keith had taken a decisive step towards being clean, along with the bonus of having a new European contract with EMI (LOVE YOU LIVE was the first release in September) and a renewed deal with Atlantic in the States, the time was right for him to enter the studio again.

710. MUNICH HILTON (Jagger, Richards) 10.35

10 October - 29 November, 6 - 15 December 1977; 18 January - 12 February 1979; 11 November - 16 December 1982: Place: EMI, Pathé Marconi Studios, Paris, France; Compass Point Studios, Nassau, Bahamas, USA; EMI, Pathé Marconi Studios, Paris, France.
Rolling Stones with Ian McLagan.
Producer: The Glimmer Twins.
Engineer: Chris Kimsey, Barry Sage.
Bootleg only.

"The No More Fast Numbers" sessions (as they soon became known) produced a plentiful crop of songs, requiring a wily selection process to cut them down to the standard single album format of ten tracks. The sessions lasted until early March 1978 with a break for Christmas. The Pathé Marconi venue, the official EMI studios in Paris, had an olde-world charm and atmosphere and the soundboard desk produced a clear but earthy taint.

The actual area used by the Stones was a rehearsal room rather than a normal studio but was large enough to have a bar in a corner to help make the sessions free and easy. The engineer aiding and abetting the Glimmer Twins was Chris Kimsey, for his aptly-named production company Wonderknob Ltd. He had been an assistant engineer to Andy Johns back in late 1969 and 1970 for most of the STICKY FINGERS material. He was good friends with Glyn Johns and, through him, Ian Stewart - and it was Ian who approached him to come and work with the band. It was a last-minute arrangement but one that would stick for many years.

Ironically, The Beatles visited Pathé Marconi on 29 January 1964 when they re-recorded German vocals onto a backing track for *I Want To Hold Your Hand*. They also recorded a brand new German version of *She Loves You* and an English-vocalised *Can't Buy Me Love* at Marconi, with a few overdubs later at Abbey Road. Such was the Stones' love affair with the studios that they continued to record there until 1985. Chris Kimsey was particularly fond of the studio but he did have a little contretemps when, after a few weeks of recording, Mick Jagger announced that he was ready to move next door to the larger studio.

Chris convinced him that the smaller room suited them better and Keith Richards agreed, refusing to move. *Munich Hilton* was inspired by the 1974/75 Munchen recording period and the town's Hilton Hotel. When in a hotel on tour, Mick would place a note on the bathroom mirror to remind him where he was. *Munich Hilton* is a lengthy number centred around one of Keith Richards' guitar riffs and Ronnie Wood is also believed to have co-written the music.

Similar in style to *Tumbling Dice*, it raunches and rolls. Charlie Watts' percussion, cymbals and hi-hat are very distinctive in the mix. There are three versions - the longest is an instrumental lasting more than 10 minutes; there's a seven-minute effort with a Mick opening comment (* a - 6.57) and another with a slightly faster pace (* b - 5.41). It is possible that Ian McLagan, who was invited to play on some of the sessions one weekend because of his friendship with Ron Wood, played organ on the instrumental.

Ron's guitar sound is very low on the fret board and provides the hallmark of the SOME GIRLS sessions. *Munich Hilton* evidently played on Keith's imagination because it was included on an unofficial album featuring his solo electric guitar work recorded during rehearsals for the 1981 US tour. It was worked on again in 1979, when guide vocals were added (* c - 7.39) and again in 1982, with a reggae beat and guitar licks similar to *Golden Caddy* - but it still remains an out-take (* d - 5.29).

711. EVERYTHING IS TURNING TO GOLD (Jagger, Richards, Wood) 4.06
AKA: Time To Go
10 October - 29 November, 6 - 15 December 1977, 5 January - 2 March 1978: Place: EMI, Pathé Marconi Studios, Paris, France.
Rolling Stones with Mel Collins.
Producer: The Glimmer Twins.
Engineer: Chris Kimsey, Barry Sage.
USA B-side Shattered: 29 November 1978
USA Compilation LP SUCKING IN THE SEVENTIES: 12 March 1981: No. 15 - 5 weeks
UK Compilation LP SUCKING IN THE SEVENTIES: 13 April 1981
USA CD FLASHPOINT (COLLECTIBLES): 20 May 1991
UK Compilation CD RONNIE WOOD ANTHOLOGY THE ESSENTIAL CROSSEXION: 26 June 2006
USA Compilation CD RONNIE WOOD ANTHOLOGY THE ESSENTIAL CROSSEXION: 26 September 2006
UK CD box set THE SINGLES COLLECTION 1971-2006: 45 X 45s: 11 April 2011
USA CD box set THE SINGLES COLLECTION 1971-2006: 45 X 45s: 26 April 2011

The band performed as a unit on SOME GIRLS and session players were kept to a minimum, though there was a separate booth for family and guests. The Paris location assisted this anonymity. Chris Kimsey set up the small £200-a-day studio in a semi-circle with the EMI TG 16-track control booth opposite, a line-up originally designed for Abbey Road Studios. He listened to the playbacks with JBL wall-mounted speakers and, due to a slant of the walls, the left one was closer to the right. It was all a little quirky but, for all that, the sound was amazing. From left to right, Kimsey positioned the keyboards then timpani, Ron Wood, Keith Richards, Charlie Watts' Gretsch kit, Mick Jagger plus amp in the floor centre, Bill Wyman, an acoustic guitar station and finally a bar complete with ice machine. Screens divided each performer's work station to prevent too much leakage and a Shure PA was used to convey Mick's vocals and Charlie's snare and kick drums to the rest of the band.

It was a golden rule not to use headphones unless absolutely necessary to encourage a live band environment. The floor was graphite and there were horrible orange hessian cushions on the walls to counter the reverb. A good atmosphere was created and most tracks were, therefore, Jagger, Richards compositions just involving the five instrumentalists. Ron was co-composer on *Everything Is Turning To Gold* - he wrote the melody and chorus while Mick took care of the verses. The song came about as a direct result of the birth of his first son, Jesse James Wood who was born on 1 November 1976, in Los Angeles. The birth was long and required a caesarean to complete. Mick was in the car that took Krissie Wood to hospital and stayed for more than 20 hours supporting both parents. The track evaded album recognition, the Mel Collins saxophone work again being destined only to appear as a single flip-side (like his contribution on *I Think I'm Going Mad*). Mel Collins was the sax player for King Crimson but also a session artist for Bad Company, Humble Pie, Alexis Korner, Bryan Ferry and Eric Clapton, amongst others. He was introduced to the band by his friend Chris Kimsey, who remembered him being particularly nervous for the session. In Britain, the track was not released until the 1981 collection of 70s material, SUCKING IN THE SEVENTIES. A longer ten-minute out-take (without sax) from the session was titled *Time To Go* (* a - 9.51) and there is also an extended version of the released cut (* b - 4.28).

712. LIES (Jagger, Richards) 3.11
10 October - 29 November, 6 - 15 December 1977, 5 January - 29 January, February - 2 March 1978: Place: EMI, Pathé Marconi Studios, Paris, France.
Played Live: 1978
Producer: The Glimmer Twins.
Engineer: Chris Kimsey.
Assistant Engineer: Barry Sage, Dave Jordan, Ben King, Philippe. Mixed by Chris Kimsey.
UK LP SOME GIRLS: 9 June 1978: No 2 - 25 weeks
USA LP SOME GIRLS: 17 June 1978: No. 1 - 32 weeks
UK CD SOME GIRLS: 21 November 2011: No. 57 - 1 week
USA CD SOME GIRLS: 21 November 2011: No. 46 - 2 weeks

SOME GIRLS was predominantly an album conceived and inspired by Mick Jagger. Another working title for the album was "Lies" which illustrates the importance of this track written mostly by Mick. It was a subject he evidently wanted to get off his chest but who could the "dirty jezebel" be? Mick was very conscious of the young British bands springing up in "Garage Land" and was inspired by the refreshing punk rock scene. As Charlie Watts said they were: "Trying to be Johnny Rotten, who was trying to be us, was fine with me. It's really all the same thing. Writing those songs is the difficult part."

Mick seemed to want to prove that he, too, could relive his past and sing in an "angry young man" stance but could he persuade the band to join in on a derivative musical thrash? Evidently *Lies* is in this turion mould, but the Stones' R 'n' B formula was not easily forgotten; the pace quickened but the end product was distinctively The Rolling Stones.

An extended version highlights Jagger's fervour as he whips the band into a rock and roller coaster, his guitar work, as tutored by Ron Wood, becoming more than just a few rhythm chords (* a - 3.50). The only problem was Mick's guitar was always played live so a Neumann mic was used to soften it. One out-take has an affected "one, two, tray, four" intro with Mick on early lyrics, shouting "why" and "whoo" at the top of his voice (* b - 4.13).

Barry Sage suggested that one of the reasons for the success of the SOME GIRLS album was the guitar-orientated edge delivered by Mick. As an inexperienced player he had a raw and rough edge quality, contemporary to the era. Barry joined the sessions after a few weeks since Chris Kimsey needed further assistance and to help spread the load of the language issue with local engineers. He had worked with Chris before at his employer's Basing Street Studios, a venue Chris tended to use when Olympic was full.

713. I LOVE YOU TOO MUCH (Jagger, Richards) 3.10
AKA: I Can't Help It, Love You Too Much, Shaved Stone, And I Know
10 October - 29 November, 6 - 15 December 1977, 5 January - 29 January, February - 2 March 1978; 11 November - 16 December 1982; August - September 2011: Place: EMI, Pathé Marconi Studios, Paris, France; La Fourchette Home Studio, Fourchette, Tours, France, Electric Lady, New York, Berkeley St., Mix This!, Los Angeles, USA.
Producer: Chris Kimsey, Don Was, The Glimmer Twins.
Engineer: Chris Kimsey, Barry Sage.
Overdubs recorded by: Krish Sharma, Matt Clifford. Assisted by Phil Joly. Mixed by Bob Clearmountain. Assisted by Brandon Duncan.
Mastered by Stephen Marcussen. Digital editing by Stewart Whitmore.
UK CD SOME GIRLS BONUS DISC: 21 November 2011: No. 57 - 1 week
USA CD SOME GIRLS BONUS DISC: 21 November 2011: No. 46 - 2 weeks

The track was re-done for the SOME GIRLS re-issue project in 2011. Keith Richards added some piano, harmony vocals and perhaps some guitar while Mick Jagger overdubbed lead vocals with some new lyrics written during late summer 2011. References to a "sniff of the crotch" and a "martini lunch" did not resonate too well with the punk style. At least current tracks like *Rough Justice*, from 2005, were done with tongue-in-cheek humour.

The original from 1977 was naturally more raw, Mick's vocals being a touch too much like Johnny Rotten in delivery - really snarling and venomous. The band were also stripped to the bare essentials and sounded as if they were recording in a back street garage. Both Mick and Keith had visited the country, blue-grass and blues club (CBGBs) which had provided a venue for cut-back raw music such as the Voidoids, Dead Boys, Television, Ramones and the Dictators - even AC/DC of whom their lead singer Bon Scott hung out at the Paris studios for a few days as a friend of Ron Wood and the band.

The line had to be drawn and Keith, determined to keep the Stones within their own well-found limits, argued with Mick about the character and tempo of some of the session material. As Barbara Charone confirms, Keith put it a little more bluntly: "What the fuck do we need to try and sound like the Sex Pistols for?" *I Can't Help It*, alias *Shaved Stone*, remained on the cutting room floor, Keith Richards ensuring a diplomatic compromise (* a - 4.22).

The song was written by Keith about his love for Anita. Other versions, obviously in his preferred style, include a slower take with a Ron Wood lead guitar solo (* b - 2.32). There is an instrumental version as well (* c - 3.24). Another slower cut has Keith on backing vocals and Mick singing the song with additional lyrics (* d - 4.08), with Ron playing a steel slide. It was also re-visited as an instrumental in 1982 (* e - 3.25).

Keith admitted in 2011 that the punks had given the band a kick up the arse, even if most couldn't play. It was a realisation, too, that the Stones had now moved on to a later generation. It was necessary to strip down the band and make a good record full of attitude and energy just like the punk bands but done in their own inimitable style.

714. BEFORE THEY MAKE ME RUN (Jagger, Richards) 3.25
AKA: Rotten Roll
10 October - 29 November, 6 - 15 December 1977, February - 2 March 1978: Place: EMI, Pathé Marconi Studios, Paris, France.
Played Live: 1989, 1990, 1994, 1995, 1999, 2002, 2003, 2006, 2007
Producer: The Glimmer Twins.
Engineer: Dave Jordan. Mixed by Chris Kimsey.
UK LP SOME GIRLS: 9 June 1978: No. 2 - 25 weeks
USA LP SOME GIRLS: 17 June 1978: No. 1 - 32 weeks
USA Promo Single: June 1978
UK & USA eSingle Track No Spare Parts: 14 November 2011
UK CD SOME GIRLS: 21 November 2011: No. 57 - 1 week
USA CD SOME GIRLS: 21 November 2011: No. 46 - 2 weeks
UK & USA Vinyl B-side No Spare Parts: 25 November 2011

Not since *Happy* was recorded in 1971 had Keith Richards sung the lead vocals on an album cut. *Before They Make Me Run*, a Richards-penned track, autobiographical in lyrical message (he was still waiting the trial date - would they let him free to walk or have to run?), was recorded while Mick Jagger was away from the Paris sessions in March 1978 and had to meet with his approval when he returned and over-dubbed some backing vocals. He may have recognised the basis of the song from an out-take, *Rotten Roll*, recorded late in 1977 with different lyrics.
There are various out-takes that are longer in length (* a - 4.40 and b - 4.51). Lyrics such as "Well it's another goodbye to another good friend" while self-deprecating may have been mourning the loss of the likes of Gram Parsons - or perhaps his own freedom. *Before They Make Me Run* was engineered by Dave Jordan, the only time on the album when Chris Kimsey was not at the control desk. Dave had engineered the LOVE YOU LIVE album. Chris recalled that Dave and Keith disappeared into the mixing room for a non-stop, five-day session which stretched everyone. Keith likened the studio to the shelter a church offered and he felt safe to write freely.
Dave Jordan and Barry Sage finally left the studio after four days and Keith passed out under the mixing desk, only to wake and find a police band listening to a playback of their latest masterpiece. So engrossed were they that Keith managed to recover his narcotic paraphernalia and escape from the marathon session. In 2011, celebrating the re-issue, he referred back to the incident: "Yeah, my engineer nearly died. He got a medal for that one."
Before They Make Me Run is a high-energy rock 'n' roller played in a classic open-G style, proving that Keith's unique guitar technique was "almost grown". He plays bass and acoustic guitar while Ron Wood works on the pedal steel and electric slide. Barry Sage knew that Keith was inwardly worried about his impending sentence, even though the studio provided a release - he had been recording several solo numbers with a prison theme, such as *Apartment No. 9*. Keith was listening a lot to artists like George Jones and Gram Parsons. Along with other tracks like *Run Rudolph Run* and *You Win Again*, Keith intended that it would be released should he be sent to jail.

715. BEFORE THEY MAKE ME RUN (BOB CLEARMOUNTAIN REMIX) (Jagger, Richards) 3.14
10 October - 29 November, 6 - 15 December 1977, February - 2 March 1978: Place: EMI, Pathé Marconi Studios, Paris, France, Power Station Studio, New York, USA.
Producer: The Glimmer Twins.
Engineer: Dave Jordan.
USA Promo Single: June 1978

A US stereo and mono single promo release re-mixed by Bob Clearmountain differs slightly from the album version, including minor lyrical changes such as "give me a kiss and you can cum" and with lines switched around at the end. It was a more punchy version which Keith Richards initiated with Bob Clearmountain. Anne Liebovitz's excellent colour sleeve for this single is frameable! And so the Paris sessions finally expired in early March 1978, having produced some good sounds and a highly respectable album, which was mixed at Atlantic in New York later that month. The whole process had taken just over six months, which was a real return to basics.

716. SILVER COATED RAILS (Jagger, Richards) 3.18
AKA: Tall & Slender Blondes
10 October - 29 November, 6 - 15 December 1977, 5 January - 29 January, February - 2 March 1978: Place: EMI, Pathé Marconi Studios, Paris, France.
Producer: The Glimmer Twins.
Engineer: Chris Kimsey, Barry Sage.
Bootleg only.

An instrumental track with a happy refrain, slightly reggae in nature.

717. WHEN THE WHIP COMES DOWN (Jagger, Richards) 4.20
10 October - 29 November, 6 - 15 December 1977, 5 January - 29 January, February - 2 March 1978: Place: EMI, Pathé Marconi Studios, Paris, France.
Played Live: 1978, 1979, 1981, 1982, 1997, 1998, 1999, 2002, 2003
Producer: The Glimmer Twins.
Engineer: Chris Kimsey.
Assistant Engineer: Barry Sage, Ben King, Philippe. Mixed by Chris Kimsey.
UK LP SOME GIRLS: 9 June 1978: No. 2 - 25 weeks
USA LP SOME GIRLS: 17 June 1978: No. 1 - 32 weeks
USA B-side Beast Of Burden: 28 August 1978

UK B-side Respectable: 15 September 1978
UK CD box set THE SINGLES COLLECTION 1971-2006: 45 X 45s: 11 April 2011
USA CD box set THE SINGLES COLLECTION 1971-2006: 45 X 45s: 26 April 2011
UK CD SOME GIRLS: 21 November 2011: No. 57 - 1 week
USA CD SOME GIRLS: 21 November 2011: No. 46 - 2 weeks
UK & USA B-side Vinyl Beast Of Burden: 21 November 2011

This is a harsh song about a gay learning the ropes in New York City, having moved from a more liberal Los Angeles. The music is a punishing, raunchy, hard driving, no nonsense boogie. The guitars thrash and writhe, Jagger's included, while Ron Wood can be heard on the pedal steel. Barry Sage thought the session on 4 November was riveting, helped by an appearance from Keith Moon, who entered the studio and tried to entice the band to come to Le Crazy-Horse review show. The band and crew stayed in the studio but Keith disappeared and returned a few hours later with a crowd of exotic dancers. Mick Jagger worked best when he could focus his singing on a person or in this case a gaggle of ladies and produced an amazing performance to seal his vocal take. Keith Moon went back to the Paris Ritz Hotel, where management called the police and he was arrested for unruly behaviour. Stones lawyers extricated him on the condition that he was escorted to the airport for a one-way flight. What a night!

The track, coupled with *Respectable* in Britain, provided a double slice of hard rock 'n' roll. An out-take version obtainable on bootleg is a lengthy 10-minute rendition without backing vocals (* a - 9.56). The tempo changes two or three times, simmering down before boisterously building up again, the three guitars and Bill Wyman's bass literally panting for attention. There is also an extended take of the released album version (* b - 6.19) and an edited cut of the long out-take (* c - 7.22).

The riff was written by Keith Richards but the song structure was Mick Jagger's. In his autobiography *Life*, Keith revealed: "Mick wrote it and I looked around and said, shit, he's finally written a rock and roll song. By himself!" Ian McLagan recalls that he listened to a playback with Keith and mentioned he had just recorded with the Rich Kids, featuring Midge Ure, Steve New, Rusty Egan and ex-Sex Pistols' Glen Matlock on bass. Keith was keen to hear and learn more about the punk scene despite his press speak.

The sonic sound created by Chris Kimsey was due to a small PA being set up in the studio so all the Stones could hear the music and play together like a live band without headphones interfering. Charlie Watts did have headphones, though, and much of the hard-hitting sound came from his rhythmic crashing snare. His drums were recorded with six mics (bass drum, snare, two rototoms and two for toms, high and one on the floor) creating a stereo effect.

It was a technique Chris Kimsey had learnt from Glyn Johns, who usually used four balanced microphones to record the drums. In all, out of the 24 channels, most songs required 17 to record - Keith was on number nine. An extra technique was used as Barry Sage explained: "Chris employed a further speaker fed from the PA of Charlie's snare, which got sent to a passage way, which we mic'ed up separately to get that distinctive natural reverb sound on the snare."

According to Chris, the other mark of the SOME GIRLS sound is the band were playing live with a great element of leakage from the vocalist's microphone. "Leakage actually creates a sound and an atmosphere that you can hear. When a band is all playing in the same room with the vocals, then everything is going down that vocal mic. During gaps in the verses the band pops in to the sound. Forget separate booths, just a big room with lots of screens." Chris was a little disappointed that the re-mastered studio album sounded a little thin and compressed compared to his original. Compression is a technique used by engineers to narrow the sound so that there are not so many peaks and troughs; supposedly to make it more palatable to the ear but critics said it lacked a real feel.

718. LOS TRIOS GUITAROS (Jagger, Richards) 3.22

10 October - 29 November, 6 - 15 December 1977, 5 January - 29 January, February - 2 March 1978: Place: EMI, Pathé Marconi Studios, Paris, France.
Producer: The Glimmer Twins.
Engineer: Chris Kimsey, Barry Sage.
Bootleg only.

The song title is taken from the three guitars and is instrumental and similar in nature to *Silver Coated Rails*. There is a shimmering synthesiser-type noise, which may have been created by Bill Wyman or was it a guitar pedal effect? Perhaps *Los Trios Guitaros* gave them an opportunity to experiment with different guitar sounds. Ron Wood was at the forefront of the song and may have written it.

719. RESPECTABLE (Jagger, Richards) 3.07

10 October - 29 November, 6 - 15 December 1977, 5 January - 29 January, February - 2 March 1978: Place: EMI, Pathé Marconi Studios, Paris, France.
Played Live: 1978, 1979, 1995, 1997, 1998, 1999, 2003, 2006, 2007
Producer: The Glimmer Twins.
Engineer: Chris Kimsey.
Assistant Engineer: Barry Sage, Ben King, Philippe. Mixed by Chris Kimsey.
UK LP SOME GIRLS: 9 June 1978: No. 2 - 25 weeks
USA LP SOME GIRLS: 17 June 1978: No. 1 - 32 weeks
UK Single: 15 September 1978: No. 23 - 9 weeks
UK Compilation LP REWIND 1971-1984 (THE BEST OF THE ROLLING STONES): 29 June 1984: No. 45 - 5 weeks
UK Compilation LP JUMP BACK THE BEST OF THE ROLLING STONES '71 - '93: 22 November 1993: No. 16 - 26 weeks
USA Compilation CD JUMP BACK THE BEST OF THE ROLLING STONES '71 - '93: 24 August 2004: No. 30 - 58 weeks
UK CD SOME GIRLS: 21 November 2011: No. 57 - 1 week
USA CD SOME GIRLS: 21 November 2011: No. 46 - 2 weeks
UK & USA DVD Some Girls De-Luxe: 21 November 2011

Viewed by fans as a tongue-in-cheek prod at their own social status, *Respectable* streaks along at an energetic pace. Reference in the lyrics is made to Bianca's attraction with the then President's son, Jack Ford, at the White House: "We're talking heroin with the President!" and "You're the easiest lay on the White House lawn". A more prickly target may have been Margaret Trudeau, who had brief liaisons with both Mick Jagger and Ron Wood during 1977.

Keith Richards and Ronnie lay claim to another volume in their guitar solo autobiography as they weave their way in and out. Keith provided the Chuck Berry solo while Ronnie was very comfortable during his first official sessions as a band member and contributed some lyrics to the song. Mick also plays guitar, ensuring the electric rock and roll dynamics were high on the agenda and extending his musical credibility - as Keith said: "he's had a good teacher".

Bill Wyman contributes an effective Fender Mustang bass melody. *Respectable* was released as the second single from the SOME GIRLS album in Britain, but it failed to make a strong impact, only charting at No. 23. An out-take (the motherfucker version) can be heard with Mick issuing instructions to the rest of the band on tempo and guitar breaks - "solos anybody?" - as the boys jumped in for a line or two (* a - 3.52).

The "talking heroin with the President" is repeated for a second verse but becomes "taking heroin with the Duke of Kent" and instead of "go take my wife", there is "don't fuck my wife". As the Sex Pistols said in the same silver jubilee year: "God Save The Queen, we mean it maan". Good mother-mocking fun. There is also another extended version but this is similar to the released track (* b - 3.57). In May 1978, a very punk-like Michael Lindsay-Hogg promotional film was made in New York City with overdubbed vocals to the soundtrack. This can be seen on the extras part of the 2011 release.

720. FAR AWAY EYES (Jagger, Richards) 4.23
AKA: Girl With The Faraway Eyes, Truckdriver Blues
10 October - 29 November, 6 - 15 December 1977, 5 January - 29 January, February - 2 March 1978: Place: EMI, Pathé Marconi Studios, Paris, France.
Played Live: 1978, 1994, 1995, 1997, 2002, 2006
Producer: The Glimmer Twins.
Engineer: Chris Kimsey.
Assistant Engineer: Barry Sage, Ben King, Philippe. Mixed by Chris Kimsey.
UK B-side Miss You (Edit): 19 May 1978
USA B-side Miss You (Edit): 19 May 1978
UK LP SOME GIRLS: 9 June 1978: No. 2 - 25 weeks
USA LP SOME GIRLS: 17 June 1978: No. 1 - 32 weeks
UK CD box set THE SINGLES COLLECTION 1971-2006: 45 X 45s: 11 April 2011
USA CD box set THE SINGLES COLLECTION 1971-2006: 45 X 45s: 26 April 2011
UK CD SOME GIRLS: 21 November 2011: No. 57 - 1 week
USA CD SOME GIRLS: 21 November 2011: No. 46 - 2 weeks
UK & USA DVD Some Girls De Luxe: 21 November 2011

Mick Jagger, Stetson in hand, turns on a Bakersfield accent and preaches the optimistic teachings of the Sacred Bleeding Heart of Jesus. Bakersfield is a town in California and the musical environs allowed Capitol Music to exploit the country music populated by the sappier Nashville. The Byrds and later the Flying Burrito Brothers were an illustration of this as was one of Keith Richards' and Mick's favourites - Merle Haggard.

The lyrics are perhaps the best, certainly the most humorous, on the album and Mick's delivery is convincingly staged. Keith thought the final take was too affected, preferring a straighter approach with just a touch of satirical flavour. Ron Wood is featured on pedal steel guitar, which illustrated the renewed return to the basics of the five-piece band, pared down and certainly creatively sharpened. Both Keith and Mick contribute on the piano. There is an out-take with an extended piano introduction which has a different pedal steel solo and extra bars between the verses which lengthens the song to just over five minutes (* a - 5.17).

The edited release on the flipside of *Miss You* preceded the album release (* b - 3.43). A Michael Lindsay-Hogg promotional film, with the band performing in front of EXILE photos, was made in May 1978 and belatedly released in 2011. In Britain, due to significant radio air-play, it became a double A-side and at one stage was credited in the charts as *Far Away Eyes*, taking over from its flip, the disco-orientated *Miss You*.

Far Away Eyes along with *Miss You* had the distinction of being the first Stones release on a new marketing phenomenon - the 12 inch single - notwithstanding that its appearance on 2 June 1978 was a limited edition in gaudy pink vinyl. Collectors can still find the product in backstreet second-hand shops fetching rather more than the original cost.

721. SHATTERED (Jagger, Richards) 3.46
10 October - 29 November, 6 - 15 December 1977, 5 January - 29 January, February - 2 March 1978: Place: EMI, Pathé Marconi Studios, Paris, France.
Played Live: 1978, 1979, 1981, 1982, 1989, 1994, 1995, 1999, 2002, 2005, 2006, 2007
Rolling Stones with Ian McLagan, Simon Kirke, 1 Moroccan, 1 Jew, 1 Wasp. (Moroccan, Jane Rose, Ron Wood)
Producer: The Glimmer Twins.
Engineer: Chris Kimsey.
Assistant Engineer: Barry Sage, Ben King, Philippe. Mixed by Chris Kimsey.
UK LP SOME GIRLS: 9 June 1978: No. 2 - 25 weeks
USA LP SOME GIRLS: 17 June 1978: No. 1 - 32 weeks
USA Single: 29 November 1978: No. 31 - 4 weeks
USA Promo Single: 29 November 1978
USA Compilation LP SUCKING IN THE SEVENTIES: 12 March 1981: No. 15 - 5 weeks
UK Compilation LP SUCKING IN THE SEVENTIES: 13 April 1981
UK Track CD Single Terrifying: 30 July 1990
UK CD LP FORTY LICKS: 30 September 2002: No. 2 - 45 weeks
USA CD LP FORTY LICKS: 1 October 2002: No. 2 - 50 weeks
UK CD box set THE SINGLES COLLECTION 1971-2006: 45 X 45s: 11 April 2011
USA CD box set THE SINGLES COLLECTION 1971-2006: 45 X 45s: 26 April 2011
UK CD SOME GIRLS: 21 November 2011: No. 57 - 1 week
USA CD SOME GIRLS: 21 November 2011: No. 46 - 2 weeks

Apparently a long time in the making with many overdubs, *Shattered* is a percussive assault on the senses about the seediness of New York. It was written against the background of a cash-strapped city, loaned to the hilt, with Mick Jagger explaining: "This town's been wearin' tatters". This was reflected in July 1977 when New York had seen overnight looting, vandalism and arson over many neighbourhoods during a power failure caused by lightning strikes. More than 3,000 arrests were made in the battered city.

Two stripped-down instrumental out-takes reveal the song in its formative stages (* a - 3.46, b - 3.01). Bill Wyman takes no part again, Ron Wood (modesty forbid) performing on bass, pedal, steel guitar, bass-drum and backing vocals. Other percussive sounds are made by a foreign legion of Moroccans, Jews and Wasps. Ian McLagan's book *All The Rage* reveals that Simon Kirke, the ex-Free and Bad Company drummer was playing congas, with Ian McLagan on Hammond organ and Ian Stewart piano. McLagan thought he was not on the released version but felt the band were fresh and great on this number.

Barry Sage recalled that, quite often when extra percussion and hand-claps were required, whoever was in the studio would get roped in. "Certainly, one was Jane Rose and I remember that a Moroccan stayed with Chuck Magee and myself for a week or so and would accompany us to the studio. The tongue-in-cheek credits were Mick and Keith's nod to New York." Jane Rose confirmed this was the case and the "Wasp" (NYC street slang) was in fact Ronnie Wood.

Subtle guitar weaves its way through the song, one solo during the clapping session is distinctively that of Keith Richards and the pedal steel belongs to Ronnie. Other guitars are over-dubbed and twilled into the mix. Keith used a guitar phaser 100, made by Dunlop MXR, to give the tracks on SOME GIRLS a reverb-echo effect which was prominent in contemporary music of the day. It was a new sound for the band and elevated the overall texture on the faster numbers.

A different version of *Shattered* was released on 8-track only and also on a promotional single titled 'short version' (* c - 2.43). Released as a single in the States, it struggled up the charts. Mick's vocals and incredible lyrics: "love and sex and hopes and dreams" illustrated optimism and saved the bacon of an otherwise over-baked number - "I'm feeling ShiDooBee down - shit, shat and shattered."

722. A DIFFERENT KIND (Jagger, Richards) 6.01
AKA: Thinking About You, Nanker Phelge
10 October - 29 November, 6 - 15 December 1977, 5 January - 29 January, February - 2 March 1978: Place: EMI, Pathé Marconi Studios, Paris, France.
Producer: The Glimmer Twins.
Engineer: Chris Kimsey, Barry Sage.
Bootleg only.

A slow tempo song over six minutes in length. It is mainly an instrumental although there are some spoken Jagger vocals performed in a guide style. The prominent sound is the Hawaiian steel guitar or bottleneck dobro played by Ron Wood.

723. BEAST OF BURDEN (Jagger, Richards) 4.25
10 October - 29 November, 6 - 15 December 1977, 5 January - 29 January, February - 2 March 1978: Place: EMI, Pathé Marconi Studios, Paris, France.
Played Live: 1978, 1979, 1981, 1982, 1994, 1995, 2002, 2005, 2007
Producer: The Glimmer Twins.
Engineer: Chris Kimsey.
Assistant Engineer: Barry Sage, Ben King, Philippe. Mixed by Chris Kimsey.
UK LP SOME GIRLS: 9 June 1978: No. 2 - 25 weeks
USA LP SOME GIRLS: 17 June 1978: No. 1 - 32 weeks
USA Single: 28 August 1978: No. 8 - 9 weeks
USA Compilation LP SUCKING IN THE SEVENTIES: 12 March 1981: No. 15 - 5 weeks
UK Compilation LP SUCKING IN THE SEVENTIES: 13 April 1981
UK Compilation LP REWIND 1971-1984 (THE BEST OF THE ROLLING STONES): 29 June 1984: No. 45 - 5 weeks
USA Compilation LP REWIND 1971-1984 (THE BEST OF THE ROLLING STONES): 2 July 1984: No. 86 - 11 weeks
UK B-side 12-inch Single Almost Hear You Sigh: 18 June 1990
UK Compilation LP JUMP BACK THE BEST OF THE ROLLING STONES '71 - '93: 22 November 1993: No. 16 - 26 weeks
UK CD LP FORTY LICKS: 30 September 2002: No. 2 - 45 weeks
USA CD LP FORTY LICKS: 1 October 2002: No. 2 - 50 weeks
USA Compilation CD JUMP BACK THE BEST OF THE ROLLING STONES '71 - '93: 24 August 2004: No. 30 - 58 weeks
UK CD box set THE SINGLES COLLECTION 1971-2006: 45 X 45s: 11 April 2011
USA CD box set THE SINGLES COLLECTION 1971-2006: 45 X 45s: 26 April 2011
UK CD SOME GIRLS: 21 November 2011: No. 57 - 1 week
USA CD SOME GIRLS: 21 November 2011: No. 46 - 2 weeks
UK & USA Vinyl Single: 21 November 2011

The spirits invoked on numbers such as *Under My Thumb* winced at the imagery of *Beast of Burden*. "I've walked miles for your loving and my feet are hurting", was the picture painted. Jagger obviously thought hard before singing the vocals true to their context in solemn tones. Bootlegged out-takes suggest that high falsetto vocals were also attempted but these would have given a soft, wry edge to the track (* a - 5.34, b - 4.05).

Ron Wood and Keith Richards, who was the principal writer, lay down an acoustic tracking and overdubbed electric guitars. Their lead solos, which require an attentive ear, are particularly pleasing and prove the new Stones format was a convincing one. This was originally intended as a more upbeat and funkier number until it mellowed into a slower groove. Selected as the second American single, it charted in September 1978, obtaining a very respectable No. 8 position. Ian McLagan recollects cutting a part for *Beast Of Burden* with Keith which he believed was going to be an alternate single version but it was never released. It is likely that this mix would have been made by Bob Clearmountain.

Mick wanted the song to be unveiled in the UK as the second single but EMI wanted the far more upbeat *Respectable*, which seemed to fit better with the guitar-motivated punk rock scene. The JUMP BACK version is an edited single as is the one on SUCKING IN THE SEVENTIES. Another rare take, with different lyrics and extended by a minute, was released on the old eight-track format (* c - 5.20). There is also an instrumental dub version but this seems to be the result of a Keith Richards solo session or Keith as a guest of a Black Uhuru session (* d - 5.49). The single version, certainly a completely different recording and not a mix, was edited by a minute (* e - 3.20). The original USA picture sleeve was a possible EXILE album cover but was withdrawn. It represented "a lion sitting on a woman" - who's your beast of burden?

It finally saw the light of day in 2011 as part of the SOME GIRLS DE-LUXE package. In March 1984, Bette Midler did a cover, which was a minor hit for her, Mick having a cameo role in the video. In 1990, a 12-inch single was released which featured just the ballads, *Almost Hear You Sigh, Beast Of Burden, Angie* and *Fool To Cry*. Later, British band The Kooks incorporated *Burden* into a medley with *Sweet Jane* in their live shows. The band supported the Stones in 2006 on their BIGGER BANG tour and, in 2010, Georgia Jagger dated their lead singer and co-guitarist Luke Pritchard. On reflection, when interviewed for the album re-issue, Keith commented that the song was as much a response to him wanting to take more of the band burden that had befallen Mick during his hazy heroin days. At the time, he still had to prove that it had been dealt with.

724. COVERED IN BRUISES (Jagger, Richards, Wood)
AKA: 1-2-3-4
10 October - 29 November, 6 - 15 December 1977, 5 January - 29 January, February - 2 March 1978: Place: EMI, Pathé Marconi Studios, Paris, France.
Producer: The Glimmer Twins.
Engineer: Chris Kimsey, Barry Sage.
Unavailable.

An early version of Ron Wood's track *1-2-3-4* released on his 1981 solo album of the same name.

725. ONCE YOU START (Jagger, Richards, Wood)
10 October - 29 November, 6 - 15 December 1977, 5 January - 29 January, February - 2 March 1978: Place: EMI, Pathé Marconi Studios, Paris, France.
Producer: The Glimmer Twins.
Engineer: Chris Kimsey, Barry Sage.
Unavailable.

A track that has not been bootlegged. Ron Wood mentions it on the inside cover of his GIMME SOME NECK album, saying he wrote the music while Mick Jagger provided the words. In his biography Ronnie Wood fondly recalls that period as one of the best and that, to this day, SOME GIRLS is a favourite album. It helped that he had just moved into a Parisian apartment with English model Jo Karslake, and was madly in love, starting what would be a 20-year relationship. He also enjoyed the interplay with Mick Jagger and was learning from him. "We were building the foundations of our lifelong relationship, through music, wine and song." Perhaps the alternative title for SOME GIRLS of "Don't Steal My Girlfriend" was a warning to Mick.

726. SOME GIRLS (Jagger, Richards) 4.36
AKA: Some More Girls
10 October - 29 November, 6 - 15 December 1977, 5 January - 29 January, February - 2 March 1978: Place: EMI, Pathé Marconi Studios, Paris, France.
Played Live: 1999, 2006, 2007
Rolling Stones with Sugar Blue.
Producer: The Glimmer Twins.
Engineer: Chris Kimsey.
Assistant Engineer: Barry Sage, Ben King, Philippe. Mixed by Chris Kimsey.
UK LP SOME GIRLS: 9 June 1978: No. 2 - 25 weeks
USA LP SOME GIRLS: 17 June 1978: No. 1 - 32 weeks
UK CD SOME GIRLS: 21 November 2011: No. 57 - 1 week
USA CD SOME GIRLS: 21 November 2011: No. 46 - 2 weeks

Some Girls, the album's essential title track, was written by Mick Jagger and featured the harmonica work of Sugar Blue, which inspired the almost sardonic working title for the album of Sugar Blue And His Fabulous Rolling Stones. Sugar Blue (James Whiting), a well-known harmonica session player from New York, was living in France at the time. Earl McGrath, the new President of Rolling Stones Records, was present at his first recording sessions and knew of Sugar Blue, the harmonica player preferring the Paris metro for busking rather than the New York subway, which was much dirtier. The recording session was also Jane Rose's first with the Stones and, apart from overdubs and mixing for LOVE YOU LIVE, she remembered being transfixed at the performance the band gave on this song.

Jane has performed management duties for the Stones, first directly for Mick and latterly, to this day, for Keith Richards. *Some Girls* also featured Bill Wyman, who shed his bass guitar for the synthesiser, with Keith stepping in. A slightly longer out-take has an extended harp solo before the vocals commence and the last verse has some longer, repeated verses (* a - 5.12) . Another long out-take (six-and-a-half minutes) has a more aggressive lead guitar playing and Mick almost speaking the last verse and lyrics relating to "I don't want your mother, she's too goddamn old" (* b - 6.29).

Chris Kimsey said there was also an original 23-minute version, which was massively edited. It took him hours to pick the best verses and edit it down to a standard four-minute album cut. Mick felt that this was one song where the creative juices kept flowing - there was plenty of "jam". The lyrics would come back to haunt Jagger, for example: "some girls give me children I never asked them for" and "some girls give me children I only made love to her once".

He also referred to Bob Dylan's divorce to Sarah, which was finalised in June 1977, where part of the settlement was his house in Zuma Beach, Malibu, California, and "half of what he owes". Salutary stuff for the future but, at this point, final efforts were being made to save his marriage with Bianca in London, while Jerry Hall was very much on the scene in Paris. *Some Girls* also became a contentious number due to a one-liner proclaiming that black girls have athletic, nocturnal sexual habits. Reverend Jesse Jackson complained to Atlantic Records and the Stones saying, "It is an insult to our race and degrading to our women." Atlantic tried to have the line rewritten but the band refused and the consequence was that, when released, it did not become a radio hit. When playing the song live, the lyrics were gradually changed and reflected Mick's feelings on his latest relationship. The concept and design of the album cover by Peter Corriston (he had devised Led Zeppelin's PHYSICAL GRAFFITI sleeve) also created problems. It was loosely copied from a mail catalogue order for "Permanently Styled S-T-R-E-T-C-H wigs", featuring a 1973 advertisement for Valmor Wigs of Chicago, from a Jet Magazine. Prices were from $6.99 each.

Some of the girls depicted on Peter Corriston's artwork were from the celebrity world and were less than happy at being on the front of a Rolling Stones album, with rouged lips advertising wigs and bras on the back cover, together with the Stones in drag. Lucille Ball's legal action, not long after the album's release, forced a change to the sleeve work as images were coloured out. Raquel Welch and Farrah Fawcett also objected to the photos, as did the estates of Judy Garland (through Liza Minnelli) and Marilyn Monroe. Surely, Raquel Welch and Brigitte Bardot, with faux red make-up, must have seen the funny side . . .

The message "Pardon Our Appearance - Cover Under Re-Construction" was used on the second version. With all of this, no wonder the original covers became collectors' items. There were two designs featuring the photos, one was lighter in colour and another garish green, yellow, blue and pink. A final, third one was produced with sketched faces to disguise everything further for subsequent re-releases.

727. MISS YOU (12 INCH VERSION) (Jagger, Richards) 8.26
AKA: Miss You (Dance Version)
10 October - 29 November, 6 - 15 December 1977, 5 January - 29 January, February - 2 March 1978: Place: EMI, Pathé Marconi Studios, Paris, France, Power Station Studio, New York, USA.
Rolling Stones with Ian McLagan, Sugar Blue.
Producer: The Glimmer Twins.
Engineer: Chris Kimsey.
Assistant Engineer: Barry Sage, Ben King, Philippe.
Extended Mix: Bob Clearmountain.
UK 12-inch Single: 19 May 1978: No. 3 - 13 weeks
USA 12-inch Single: 20 May 1978: No. 1 - 20 weeks
USA CD FLASHPOINT (COLLECTIBLES): 20 May 1991
UK Single Track Don't Stop (New Rock Mix): 16 December 2002
USA CD LP ROLLING STONES RARITIES 1971-2003: 22 November 2005: No. 76 - 6 weeks
UK CD LP ROLLING STONES RARITIES 1971-2003: 28 November 2005
UK CD box set THE SINGLES COLLECTION 1971-2006: 45 X 45s: 11 April 2011
USA CD box set THE SINGLES COLLECTION 1971-2006: 45 X 45s: 26 April 2011

728. MISS YOU (EDIT) (Jagger, Richards) 3.34
10 October - 29 November, 6 - 15 December 1977, 5 January - 29 January, February - 2 March 1978: Place: EMI, Pathé Marconi Studios, Paris, France, Power Station Studio, New York, USA.
Rolling Stones with Ian McLagan, Mel Collins, Sugar Blue.
Producer: The Glimmer Twins.
Engineer: Chris Kimsey.
Assistant Engineer: Barry Sage, Ben King, Philippe.
Mix: Bob Clearmountain.
UK Single: 19 May 1978: No. 3 - 13 weeks
USA Single: 20 May 1978: No. 1 - 20 weeks
USA B-side Too Tough: 3 July 1984
UK Compilation LP JUMP BACK THE BEST OF THE ROLLING STONES '71 - '93: 22 November 1993: No. 16 - 26 weeks
UK CD LP FORTY LICKS: 30 September 2002: No. 2 - 45 weeks
USA CD LP FORTY LICKS: 1 October 2002: No. 2 - 50 weeks
USA Compilation CD JUMP BACK THE BEST OF THE ROLLING STONES '71 - '93: 24 August 2004: No. 30 - 58 weeks
UK CD box set THE SINGLES COLLECTION 1971-2006: 45 X 45s: 11 April 2011
USA CD box set THE SINGLES COLLECTION 1971-2006: 45 X 45s: 26 April 2011

729. MISS YOU (DR DRE REMIX 2002) (Jagger, Richards) 3.42
10 October - 29 November, 6 - 15 December 1977, 5 January - 29 January, February - 2 March 1978; May - June 2002: Place: EMI, Pathé Marconi Studios, Paris, France; Encore Studios, Burbank, California, USA.
Rolling Stones with Ian McLagan, Mel Collins, Sugar Blue.
Producer: The Glimmer Twins, Dr Dre, Mike Elizondo.
Engineer: Chris Kimsey.
Assistant Engineer: Barry Sage, Ben King, Philippe.
USA CD AUSTIN POWERS GOLDMEMBER [SOUNDTRACK]: 16 July 2002
UK CD AUSTIN POWERS GOLDMEMBER [SOUNDTRACK]: 21 July 2002
USA DVD Four Flicks: 11 November 2003
UK DVD Four Flicks: 17 November 2003

730. MISS YOU (Jagger, Richards) 4.49
AKA: I Miss You
10 October - 29 November, 6 - 15 December 1977, 5 January - 29 January, February - 2 March 1978: Place: EMI, Pathé Marconi Studios, Paris, France.
Played Live: 1978, 1979, 1981, 1982, 1989, 1990, 1994, 1995, 1997, 1998, 2002, 2003, 2005, 2006, 2007
Rolling Stones with Ian McLagan, Mel Collins, Sugar Blue.
Producer: The Glimmer Twins.
Engineer: Chris Kimsey.
Assistant Engineer: Barry Sage, Ben King, Philippe.
Mixed by Chris Kimsey.
UK LP SOME GIRLS: 9 June 1978: No. 2 - 25 weeks
USA LP SOME GIRLS: 17 June 1978: No. 1 - 32 weeks
UK Compilation LP REWIND 1971-1984 (THE BEST OF THE ROLLING STONES): 29 June 1984: No. 45 - 5 weeks
USA Compilation LP REWIND 1971-1984 (THE BEST OF THE ROLLING STONES): 2 July 1984: No. 86 - 11 weeks
UK CD SOME GIRLS: 21 November 2011: No. 57 - 1 week
USA CD SOME GIRLS: 21 November 2011: No. 46 - 2 weeks
UK & USA DVD SOME GIRLS DE LUXE: 21 November 2011

The disco-entrenched four-on-the-floor disco beat of *Miss You*, more than any other 70s track, opened up avenues only Mick Jagger had ever thought the band were capable of exploring. Music at New York's recently-opened Studio 54 was playing heavily-orientated disco funk music, including Chic, Rose Royce, Heatwave and KC & The Sunshine Band. The atmosphere was charged with celebrities, drugs and sexual voyeurism.

Mick and Bianca were regular attendees, as were Andy Warhol, Liza Minnelli, Cher and Brooke Shields, all sat behind private, velvet-roped areas. Mick did not fail to see the exotic dance floor moves of a certain young Texan. Jerry Hall recounts in her book, *Life In Pictures*, that she met Mick in May 1977 at a dinner party. She saw him again soon after when he took her to the Bottom Line, where they saw Lou Reed, before moving on to the dance grooves of Disco 54.

Indeed, the song's lyrics are said to be about Jerry Hall, who was by now not-so-secretly dating him. *Miss You* was a song that was recorded to appease Mick's love for this "chic" music but even Keith Richards was forced to admit that they did not live in a vacuum, they were influenced by what was around them and the beat was kind of interesting, just as he had felt on *Hot Stuff*. Charlie Watts also liked the groove it created and even he was not a stranger to the odd disco nightclub or two that he attended with Bill Wyman in Paris. It provided the Stones with their most contemporary and distinctive sound since the chart-topping *Brown Sugar*. In the States, it became their most successful No. 1 ever, even out-pacing the monumental *Honky Tonk Women*. The latter had a run of 14 weeks in the charts while the media-catapulted *Miss You* ran for 20 weeks. Time was certainly on the Stones' side though, reflecting back, Mick had not considered that some critics and fans would view it in the same light as Bob Dylan going electric. The single release was made in the usual seven-inch format but edited and also produced for the first time on glorious 12-inch, where an extended version was mixed by Bob Clearmountain to eight-and-a-half minutes long - it does not have the sax and harmonica backing but has early lyrics and great driving guitars.

The jazz rap vocals on these are very innovative. An out-take with different, early lyrics and more improvised rapping, clocking in at nearly 12 minutes long, with sax and harp, has surfaced on bootleg (* a - 11.40). In that earlier take, those Puerto Rican girls always turn out to be a man! Keith described an early version as being far more sophisticated and bluesy. The eight-track release was longer than the album version by a minute (* b - 5.43). Listen carefully to the final cut because it is possible to hear Mick's guide vocals from the PA bleed.

The finished article was an inspired and calculated attempt to reach a new audience, helping significantly to promote the SOME GIRLS album, although Mick had some doubt about its inclusion. Joining the band on the album version were harpist Sugar Blue, who was in his awe playing with the idols, Mac on Wurlitzer electric piano and saxophonist Mel Collins. The sax was only on the album and 8-track versions, Bob Clearmountain choosing not to use that instrument for the dance track.

The harp was just featured on the album and 12-inch releases but not the eight-track. Chris Kimsey remarked: "Bob's and my mixes were so very close, there were a few times when I listened to what I thought was his mix and it turned out to be mine. I was driving down LA's Pacific Coast Highway after SOME GIRLS had been released and hearing *Miss You* on the radio. In his version of the mix, Bob had edited out the sax solo and this was what I thought I was listening to on my hire car's great stereo system. I was thinking, 'Wow, this sounds amazing. Bob really is a genius!' But then the sax solo came on and I nearly left the road. I couldn't believe it. That taught me to not get too hasty about my own work."

Ian McLagan's trademark was the "Wurly" sound which he had used on *Tin Soldier* and *Stay With Me*.

He visited Paris for a weekend of non-stop session work and did not touch his bed. He knew the band well and also Ronnie Wood's guitar technician, Chuch Magee from the very early days of The Faces. Chuch had visited London for a brief stopover and Ian and him ended up on a "bender" where he proceeded to cut his hair very short before he returned to Paris. Charlie remarked that Chuch must have ended up being arrested and "clinked up" but Chuch explained it was Mac's fault. The outcome was a phone call to Ian for him to join the sessions to cut a couple of numbers that required organ.

Ian's studio take with *Miss You* was a live recording of the song, which he was very happy with. Finally, since those distant days at the Crawdaddy, he had played with his favourite band. The next day he was back in London recording with Steve Marriott, having been paid 120 francs in cash from Mick's small change. The bass line by Bill Wyman on his custom-made Travis Bean TB2000 was impressive. It was improvised by him after visiting Paris discotheques and studying the bass beat and also listening to Billy Preston, who suggested playing octave riffs.

Early attempts of the song had been worked upon by Billy and Mick during the 1976 tour and also a year later in Toronto, where he bashed the disco drum beat at the El Mocambo. A dull video, released for the BBC's Top Of The Pops programme, featured an edited version of the track that was also shown in part on the *Video Rewind* VHS tape and in full on the *Some Girls* re-issue DVD. It was produced by promo stalwart Michael Lindsay-Hogg, the Stones miming to the lyrics while Charlie Watts showed off his new GI-style hair crop (* c - 3.55).

So the Stones, an R 'n' B-originated band, were enjoying a new disco success and Chicago blues guitarist Phil Guy (and brother of Keith's sparring partner, Buddy) used it in 1988-89 to close his totally blues act! In May/June 2002, The dance version was released on a single package with *Don't Stop* in 2002 and edited for the RARITIES album (* d - 7.33). Dr Dre remixed *Miss You* for the new Austin Powers movie soundtrack, featuring 70s music. Two minutes were used for the HBO broadcast introduction of the Madison Square Garden concert in 2003.

731. EVERLASTING IS MY LOVE (Jagger, Richards) 5.00
10 October - 29 November, 6 - 15 December 1977, 5 January - 29 January, February - 2 March 1978: Place: EMI, Pathé Marconi Studios, Paris, France.
Producer: The Glimmer Twins.
Engineer: Chris Kimsey, Barry Sage.
Bootleg only.

The Stones perform a country ballad and show the softer side of life in a studio. Many out-takes from the Paris sessions for SOME GIRLS were in this mould, yielding a prodigious crop of material. Some are unavailable, such as *Once You Start* and *Covered With Bruises*, the latter being tried a number of times before being re-recorded as *1-2-3-4* for Ron Wood's solo album.
There is an acoustic version, with pedal steel guitar, and a falsetto vocal take with an electric slide (* a - 3.54). Another cut does not have the falsetto vocals (* b - 4.14). It is apparent that much of this type of session work involved Mick Jagger, Ron Wood and the rest of the band, Keith not contributing so extensively. He had postponed his Canadian trial visit until December 1977 so that was looming over his head.

732. JUST MY IMAGINATION (RUNNING AWAY WITH ME) (Whitfield, Strong) 4.38
10 October - 29 November, 6 - 15 December 1977, 5 January - 29 January, February - 2 March 1978: Place: EMI, Pathé Marconi Studios, Paris, France.
Played Live: 1978, 1979, 1981, 1982, 1995, 1997, 1999, 2006
Rolling Stones with Ian McLagan.
Producer: The Glimmer Twins.
Engineer: Chris Kimsey.
Assistant Engineer: Barry Sage, Ben King, Philippe. Mixed by Chris Kimsey.
UK LP SOME GIRLS: 9 June 1978: No. 2 - 25 weeks
USA LP SOME GIRLS: 9 June 1978: No. 1 - 32 weeks
UK CD SOME GIRLS: 21 November 2011: No. 57 - 1 week
USA CD SOME GIRLS: 21 November 2011: No. 46 - 2 weeks

Definitely a highlight of the album, this 1971 Motown No. 1 USA hit for the Temptations, was moulded into the Stones slick R 'n' B forma, and the band cruise along - after all, "Papa was a Rolling Stone". Mick Jagger massaged the original lyrics and subject matter to suit his phrasing and noticeably mentioned New York in the first verse keeping in tone with a re-occurring album theme.
Ron Wood epitomized a new-found freshness in the Stones' studio performance. He helped to inspire Mick Jagger to play guitar on a number of tracks and moulded a contemporary rock sound. He had become an integral addition to the band, blending the partnership and mediating where necessary. Even Bill Wyman commented on how much he enjoyed the SOME GIRLS recordings, due to Ronnie's presence. The ultimate accolade, however, is the camaraderie he instinctively struck with Keef the Riff, as if he was his long lost younger brother.
The guitar rhapsody charge, which synchronises with Charlie Watts' beat during the last few minutes ("runs away with me") is a highlight. The six-minute, 40-second out-take provides a chance to enjoy the three charging guitars for longer (* a - 6.46). *Just My Imagination* should have been a single! Ian McLagan is in the background on the Hammond organ.
Chris Kimsey recollected inviting pianist Tim Hinkley to play on the sessions. In the middle of a tour with Elkie Brooks, he attended a 12-hour, drug-laced session, where his fee was forfeited due to his expensive habit and no chords made it to disc. As well as Chris Kimsey, other engineers included colleagues from Olympic Sound, Barry Sage and Ben King, and the local Marconi man, Philippe.

733. MUCK SPREADING DUB (Jagger, Richards) 3.23
10 October - 29 November, 6 - 15 December 1977; 18 January - 12 February 1979: Place: EMI, Pathé Marconi Studios, Paris, France; Compass Point Studios, Nassau, Bahamas, USA.
Producer: The Glimmer Twins.
Engineer: Chris Kimsey, Barry Sage.
Bootleg only.

An instrumental track with a pronounced guitar riff.

734. JAH IS WONDERFUL (Jagger, Richards)
AKA: Jah Wonderful, Guitar Wonderful
November 1977, 5 January - 29 January, February - 2 March 1978: Place: EMI, Pathé Marconi Studios, Paris, France.
Producer: The Glimmer Twins.
Engineer: Chris Kimsey, Barry Sage.
Unavailable.

The track may have originated from the BLACK AND BLUE sessions in Munich and is not available as an out-take. A humorous story, courtesy of journalist Barbara Charone, indicates that a 50-minute version was recorded. The winsome reggae sounds of *Jah Is Wonderful* emanated powerfully onto the Marconi hi-fi. With their new recording stars having just signed to them for a six-album deal outside North America, two senior EMI executives arrived to hear how the new album was progressing. Mick Jagger, in buoyantly mischievous mood, played them the track in its entirety, seriously insisting that *Jah* was the album, though offering that it could be cut down to the usual 45- minute album format. Exit two worried execs.

735. CLAUDINE (Jagger, Richards) 3.42
November 1977, 5 January - 29 January, February - 2 March 1978; August - September 2011: Place: EMI, Pathé Marconi Studios, Paris, France; La Fourchette Home Studio, Fourchette, Tours, France, Electric Lady, New York, Berkeley St., Mix This!, Los Angeles, USA.
Producer: Chris Kimsey, Don Was, The Glimmer Twins.
Engineer: Chris Kimsey, Barry Sage.
Overdubs recorded by: Krish Sharma, Matt Clifford. Assisted by Phil Joly. Mixed by Bob Clearmountain. Assisted by Brandon Duncan.
Mastered by Stephen Marcussen.
Digital editing by Stewart Whitmore.
UK CD SOME GIRLS BONUS DISC: 21 November 2011: No. 57 - 1 week
USA CD SOME GIRLS BONUS DISC: 21 November 2011: No. 46 - 2 weeks

This is an instantaneous, up-tempo country track which relates the tale of actress and singer Claudine Longet, former wife of celebrity Andy Williams, who had covered *Let's Spend The Night Together* with her trademark soft, erotic tones. She was convicted of manslaughter following the accidental death of her lover, the professional skier Vladimir 'Spider' Sabich, in March 1976. He had been showing her how to use a gun when the safety catch failed and she shot him in the stomach. Rumours that both were using alcohol and cocaine were not brought out during the trial. The one-month sentence was moderated to allow her family rights during the week meaning she was only imprisoned at weekends. There is the more common electric bootleg version of the song (* a - 3.31) and two acoustic takes - a short one (* b - 3.33) and a long one (* c - 7.33), which also has electric guitar pickings. Mick Jagger's vocals are stated in his usual ironic way with the lyrics having a resemblance to Jack Scott's 1958 song *Leroy*.
The guitars, which included Mick, are played in classic country and roll style. At the chorus stage, the song rocks and is a contrast to the quieter pieces. The electric version is more rock and roll and is played at a striking pace, governed by an Ian Stewart-type boogie piano player. It fades in and fades out, indicating there was a longer version. Ian McLagan was played the track on first arrival in Paris and thought it sounded really good, especially Mick's live vocal, which was perfect. On leaving the session, Keith gave him a tape of the acoustic version without piano. Although worthy of future album release, *Claudine* was not included on EMOTIONAL RESCUE due to the threat of litigation, the lyrics including the words: "The prettiest girl I ever seen, I saw you on the movie screen, hope you don't try to make a sacrifice of me, Claudine" and "Don't get trigger happy with me, don't wave a gun at me, Claudine."
In 2011, all the controversy was forgotten when the track was selected for a re-appraisal of SOME GIRLS-era works in a retrospective re-master and re-issue. The re-master was achieved at Stephen Marcussen's studios, 11 other tracks being chosen for the re-opening of the vaults. The same process as EXILE was adopted, with Don Was by now well versed at delving into the "sweetie shop" to pick potential tracks for Mick and Keith to evaluate for inclusion.
The cleaned-up track is still vibrant and has only been partially polished with new backing vocals. Chris Kimsey thought it was not a surprise that the best vocal on the re-issue was a true original: "Some of the lyrics and vocals on the extra tracks sound stuck on top, nothing like the original feel of the guide vocal." On reflection, Chris and Barry Sage both remembered Claudine affectionately and felt it was a solid number very close to being included on the original release but, due to the need for written clearance, it would have delayed the album's appearance.

736. START ME UP (Jagger, Richards) 3.33
AKA: Start It Up
November 1977, 5 January - 29 January, February - 2 March 1978, 25 June - 9 August, 30 August - October 1979; 11 October - 12 November 1980; April - June 1981: Place: EMI, Pathé Marconi Studios, Paris, France; RS Mobile, Boulogne-Billancourt, Paris, France; Atlantic Studio, New York, USA.
Played Live: 1981, 1982, 1989, 1990, 1994, 1995, 1997, 1998, 1999, 2002, 2003, 2005, 2006, 2007
Rolling Stones with Chris Kimsey, Barry Sage
Producer: The Glimmer Twins. Associate Producer: Chris Kimsey.
Engineer: Chris Kimsey, Barry Sage, Bob Clearmountain, Gary Lyons, Bob Ludwig.
USA Single: 6 August 1981: No. 2 - 18 weeks
UK Single: 17 August 1981: No. 7 - 9 weeks
USA LP TATTOO YOU: 18 August 1981: No. 1 - 30 weeks
UK LP TATTOO YOU: 28 August 1981: No. 2 - 29 weeks
UK Compilation LP REWIND 1971-1984 (THE BEST OF THE ROLLING STONES): 29 June 1984: No. 45 - 5 weeks
USA Compilation LP REWIND 1971-1984 (THE BEST OF THE ROLLING STONES): 2 July 1984: No. 86 - 11 weeks
UK Track CD Single Terrifying: 30 July 1990
UK Compilation LP JUMP BACK THE BEST OF THE ROLLING STONES '71 - '93: 22 November 1993: No. 16 - 26 weeks
UK CD LP FORTY LICKS: 30 September 2002: No. 2 - 45 weeks
USA CD LP FORTY LICKS: 1 October 2002: No. 2 - 50 weeks
USA Compilation CD JUMP BACK THE BEST OF THE ROLLING STONES '71 - '93: 24 August 2004: No. 30 - 58 weeks
UK CD box set THE SINGLES COLLECTION 1971-2006: 45 X 45s: 11 April 2011
USA CD box set THE SINGLES COLLECTION 1971-2006: 45 X 45s: 26 April 2011

The sound and feel of *Start Me Up*, right from the slightly echoed opening open tuned guitar chords, is instantaneous and proved the Stones' mettle was not broken. Originally recorded during the 1975 Munich sessions as a reggae number, it was re-recorded as a rock song in Paris in 1978 (a Paris out-take has unfinished lyrics (* a - 3.44)) and additional overdubs in 1979 and 1980 before final re-mixing, from April to June 1981, for the TATTOO YOU album at the Power Station, New York. It was the killer opening track. Keith Richards lays down another classic Stones riff, reminiscent of some of their hottest singles, which fits with Mick Jagger's strident vocal charge. He added as many car metaphors as he could think of and also performed very Keith-like backing vocals. Charlie Watts is a co-conspirator in the track's attack, his drum sound supported by claps inducing the infectious head-banging syndrome.
The production team joined in with these handclaps in 1980 (body percussion as registered with the Phonographic Performance Ltd), ensuring their claim to performance rights. *Start Me Up* certainly reaffirmed the Stones' chart presence, becoming their biggest chart topper of the 80s on both sides of the Atlantic, receiving great airplay despite its lyrical ending. It was promoted by a Michael Lindsay-Hogg video, with Mick giving his best characterisation of himself strutting and hand-clapping so often copied by mimics.

Such has been the song's popularity that in stage shows it has been included in finale material with the likes of *Brown Sugar, Jumpin' Jack Flash, Street Fighting Man* and *Satisfaction*. Keith never quite liked the final version, thinking it sounded like Spirit and Jay Ferguson, from Jo Jo Gunne, who recorded *Thunder Island* in 1978. Keith was so unsure he even asked Chris Kimsey to bin it but Chris persisted. Chris put it down to the fact that perhaps Keith always saw the reggae in it as he had originally intended.

Take a good listen, both the songs' intros sound very similar. When it was first re-modelled from the reggae original in 1977, Ian McLagan was present and worked on an early cut. Looking back on it, Keith recognised the quality of the riff: "It became a sports anthem . . . and I gave it a good whack." When releasing their software product Windows 95, Microsoft chased Prince Lowenstein and the Stones around the globe to snatch *Start Me Up* as its signature tune.

Mick Jagger did not want to hurt the bands "artistic purity" since their products had not been used in any television commercials but Keith could see the financial reward so a deal was struck. The delivered snippet was a live version of *Start Me Up*, which would result in higher royalties for the Glimmer Twins, rather than the studio version, which would be shared by other musicians. Microsoft refused to play ball, though, and eventually the studio recording was produced.

737. DON'T BE A STRANGER (Jagger, Richards) 4.06
AKA: Lucky In Love, Feel No Pain No More, Do You Get Enough?
5 January - 29 January, February - 2 March 1978; August - September 2011: Place: EMI, Pathé Marconi Studios, Paris, France; La Fourchette Home Studio, Fourchette, Tours, France, Electric Lady, New York, Berkeley St., Mix This!, Los Angeles, USA.
Rolling Stones with Sugar Blue, Don Was, Matt Clifford.
Producer: Chris Kimsey, Don Was, The Glimmer Twins.
Engineer: Chris Kimsey, Barry Sage.
Overdubs recorded by: Krish Sharma, Matt Clifford. Assisted by Phil Joly. Mixed by Bob Clearmountain. Assisted by Brandon Duncan.
Mastered by Stephen Marcussen. Digital editing by Stewart Whitmore.
UK CD SOME GIRLS BONUS DISC: 21 November 2011: No. 57 - 1 week
USA CD SOME GIRLS BONUS DISC: 21 November 2011: No. 46 - 2 weeks

Keith Richards attended a hearing in Toronto on 2 December when a trial date was set for 6 February 1978 - the trafficking charge would not be dropped. Chris Kimsey noted the pressure that the band were under, due to the impending decision, especially Mick Jagger, who could be left to pick up the pieces. Mick tried not to show this and professionally went about his business. Keith spent Christmas with Anita as the relationship began to implode more rapidly while, at this stage, Mick was seeing more and more of Jerry Hall.

Two versions from 1978 can be found on bootleg (* a - 5.20, b - 4.18). The out-take title was used for a track on Mick's solo album SHE'S THE BOSS. It was re-vamped by him in 2011 and given a new title, *Don't Be A Stranger,* with added Latin percussion from Matt Clifford and a new set of lyrics and vocals. At first Mick did not feel he could do anything with the song since it had no melody or lyrics but it did eventually build up. Keith is also likely to have provided some guitar and percussion. It still commenced with Sugar Blue's by now familiar low-pitch harmonica, supported by a bass track from Don Was as Bill Wyman had been engaged on the marimba. The track has a good summery feel but does not quite fit the mould created on the original album. The slightly lecherous lyrics and reference to a girl's "swatch" are quite bizarre. But certainly we can agree, "the south of Spain just ain't the same anymore."

738. I NEED YOU (Jagger, Richards) 3.43
5 January - 29 January, February - 2 March 1978,: Place: EMI, Pathé Marconi Studios, Paris, France.
Rolling Stones with Ian McLagan.
Producer: The Glimmer Twins.
Engineer: Chris Kimsey, Barry Sage.
Bootleg only.

I Need You was in an early stage but the country steel guitar shines through, while Jagger struggles with improvised lyrics as he promises not to fuck her too much! Keith is featured prominently on vocals. All had a good time on this jaunty song that had some potential. The song is very close melody-wise to *I Can't Help It* albeit in a different style. There is an edited version available too (* a - 2.41).

739. HANG FIRE (Jagger, Richards) 2.20
AKA: Lazy Bitch
5 January - 29 January, February - 2 March 1978, 25 June - 9 August, 30 August - October 1979: Place: EMI, Pathé Marconi Studios, Paris, France.
Played Live: 1981, 1982
Producer: The Glimmer Twins. Associate Producer: Chris Kimsey.
Engineer: Chris Kimsey, Barry Sage, Bob Clearmountain, Gary Lyons, Bob Ludwig.
USA LP TATTOO YOU: 18 August 1981: No 1 - 30 weeks
UK LP TATTOO YOU: 28 August 1981: No. 2 - 29 weeks
USA Single: 4 March 1982: No. 20 - 6 weeks
USA Compilation LP REWIND 1971-1984 (THE BEST OF THE ROLLING STONES): 2 July 1984: No. 86 - 11 weeks
UK Compilation CD REWIND 1971-1984 (THE BEST OF THE ROLLING STONES): 27 November 1986
UK CD box set THE SINGLES COLLECTION 1971-2006: 45 X 45s: 11 April 2011
USA CD box set THE SINGLES COLLECTION 1971-2006: 45 X 45s: 26 April 2011

A band favourite, this song is characterised by innocent-sounding harmony vocals. The track portrays the depressing state of a country racked by unemployment and poverty. It has a cynical ring since the people described seem content to remain at the bottom of the social pile - the working title (*Lazy Bitch*) confirms these suspicions. "The country dear friends is one where I used to come from" sings Jagger.

The single release was only made in the States, the insinuations perhaps too strong for an upfront appearance on home territory. *Hang Fire*'s mood is up tempo, yet another fast number, and, since the SOME GIRLS quota was full, it was not released until the TATTOO YOU album. It was recorded originally at the Paris More

Girls sessions under the title *Lazy Bitch*, due to its alternative lyrics. An out-take from those sessions lasts for six minutes and is a true guitar opus as Keith Richards and Ron Wood take it in turns to solo in between Ian Stewart's piano work (* a - 6.22). It is essential collector material.

Another, even more accelerated, six-minute out-take exists (* b - 6.06). Two others have the "doo-doo-doo" harmony vocals and are consistent in length and style with the final two-minute released version (* c - 2.28). One of these has Mick "ooh-oohing" in falsetto tones (* d - 2.26). Mick can be seen in flares and knitted jumper (so very 80s) on a Michael Lindsay-Hogg performance video, with the band in front of TATTOO YOU cover illustrations.

740. KEEP UP BLUES (Jagger, Richards) 4.20
AKA: Some People Tell Me
5 January - 29 January, February - 2 March 1978; August - September 2011: Place: EMI, Pathé Marconi Studios, Paris, France; La Fourchette Home Studio, Fourchette, Tours, France, Electric Lady, New York, Berkeley St., Mix This!, Los Angeles, USA.
Producer: Chris Kimsey, Don Was, The Glimmer Twins.
Engineer: Chris Kimsey, Barry Sage.
Overdubs recorded by: Krish Sharma, Matt Clifford. Assisted by Phil Joly. Mixed by Bob Clearmountain. Assisted by Brandon Duncan.
Mastered by Stephen Marcussen. Digital editing by Stewart Whitmore.
UK CD SOME GIRLS BONUS DISC: 21 November 2011: No. 57 - 1 week
USA CD SOME GIRLS BONUS DISC: 21 November 2011: No. 46 - 2 weeks

The notion of keeping up with the times was humorously plied in 2011 on this upbeat blues number, by taking the original backing track from 1978 (* a - 4.54). Originally, *Some People Tell Me* was a track that Mick Jagger growled the lyrics to. One of the two guitarists plays a funky blues lick and another solos furiously in the background. New lyrics and vocals were delivered by Mick in addition to a good harmonica line. This was recorded by Matt Clifford and Krish Sharma at Mick's home studio for the SOME GIRLS re-issue. The concluding line, "well that's it" is retained to simply finish it.

741. DO YOU THINK I REALLY CARE? (Jagger, Richards, Wood) 4.22
AKA: Yellow Cab
5 January - 29 January, February - 2 March 1978; August - September 2011: Place: EMI, Pathé Marconi Studios, Paris, France; La Fourchette Home Studio, Fourchette, Tours, France, Electric Lady, New York, Berkeley St., Mix This!, Los Angeles, USA.
Producer: Chris Kimsey, Don Was, The Glimmer Twins.
Engineer: Chris Kimsey, Barry Sage.
Overdubs recorded by: Krish Sharma, Matt Clifford. Assisted by Phil Joly. Mixed by Bob Clearmountain. Assisted by Brandon Duncan.
Mastered by Stephen Marcussen. Digital editing by Stewart Whitmore.
UK CD SOME GIRLS BONUS DISC: 21 November 2011: No. 57 - 1 week
USA CD SOME GIRLS BONUS DISC: 21 November 2011: No. 46 - 2 weeks

Some gems can be dug up from the past and this one passes muster with a great new vocal delivery and additional lyrics despite a dubious "put an umbrella up your arse, baby" reference at the end. It is also known as *Yellow Cab* and features a pedal steel slide (almost Hawaiian-sounding), country guitar and the great piano playing of Ian Stewart. As an out-take it was a six-minute country rock song with lilted and growled vocals by Mick Jagger (* a - 6.09). Other out-takes from 1978 exist but these are edited versions of the first one with a count in (* b - 3.02) and another faded, passable cut (* c - 4.26). After ending a verse with the words "yellow cab" he would also shout "Ronnie".

The vocals were re-done and new verses added but it retained the New York references to the "subway D-train", "yellow cab", "Long island", "57th Broadway", "Max's Kansas City" and the "Giants games". Not exactly the usual location for a country rock song. On the artwork cover of GIMME SOME NECK, Ronnie Wood wrote a little passage labelled The Stack House where he states he supplied words for the song *Do You Think I Really Care?* but there was no acknowledgement of this in 2011.

742. FIJI GIN (Jagger, Richards) 4.01
AKA: Fiji Jim
5 January - 29 January, February - 2 March 1978: Place: EMI, Pathé Marconi Studios, Paris, France.
Producer: The Glimmer Twins.
Engineer: Chris Kimsey, Barry Sage.
Bootleg only.

There are two versions of *Fiji Gin*. The first is a clean, distilled one where Keith's favourite Scotty Moore guitar riffs are extracted from the all-time rock 'n' roll soundtrack of guitar breaks and used on a pseudo 50s rocker with a country connection. The other version has more of a rock style, with key prompts, the band being literally propelled forward on a collision course with their favourite blend of Pacific Gin - South Pacific Distilleries Booth's or Regal Gin (* a - 3.26). Ronnie Wood lays claim to have written one verse for this track - possibly a self-reference within the lines, "Come on and bring your wah-wah pedal, then let's go on stage. Ronnie brought about 50,000 kids and then slipped out in the rain." Mick Jagger could get really inspired and when he vocalised ad-libbed lyrics, sometimes he was simply at his best, according to Chris Kimsey.

743. MISTY ROADS (Jagger, Richards) 4.28
AKA: The Way She Held Me Tight
5 January - 29 January, February - 2 March 1978: Place: EMI, Pathé Marconi Studios, Paris, France.
Producer: The Glimmer Twins.
Engineer: Chris Kimsey, Barry Sage.
Bootleg only.

Another excursion into the Nashville land of tinkling piano (probably Ian Stewart) and country rock guitar licks. Mick Jagger's vocals use the ever popular falsetto "ooh-ooh-oohs".

744. SUMMER ROMANCE (Jagger, Richards) 3.16
5 January - 29 January, February - 2 March; 23 August - 7 September 1978; 25 June - 9 August, 30 August - October 1979: Place: EMI, Pathé Marconi Studios, Paris, France; Wally Heider (RCA) Studios, Hollywood, USA; EMI, Pathé Marconi Studios, Paris, France.
Producer: The Glimmer Twins. Associate Producer: Chris Kimsey.
Engineer: Barry Sage, Sean Fullan, Brad Samuelsohn, 'Snake' Reynolds, Jon Smith, Michael Carnavale.
UK LP EMOTIONAL RESCUE: 20 June 1980: No. 1 - 18 weeks
USA LP EMOTIONAL RESCUE: 23 June 1980: No. 1 - 20 weeks

Another pacey number with Ian Stewart accompanying the band as they strain to recollect those "Butlins Holiday Romances". Keith Richards and Ron Wood intuitively wind up their guitars to produce a number which is essentially lead-orientated. A guitar-picking sound fills in when the lead fades out. Original acetates of the album had *Summer Romance* as the opening lead track instead of *Dance*.
Initially laid down in Paris and Hollywood, it was re-recorded a year later for the EMOTIONAL RESCUE album in the French capital. Earlier versions have different lyrics and the guitars are more aggressive, the first with count-in (* a - 4.42, b - 5.37). Both are led by great bass rumbles, with guitars swinging from speaker to speaker. There is another extended version (* c - 5.11). The out-take from the RCA session shows Mick Jagger had almost completed the lyrics and it is near to the released cut (* d - 5.32).

745. DANCING GIRLS (Jagger, Richards) 2.52
AKA: Brown Leaves
5 January - 29 January, February - 2 March 1978; 18 January - 12 February 1979: Place: EMI, Pathé Marconi Studios, Paris, France; Compass Point Studios, Nassau, Bahamas, USA.
Producer: The Glimmer Twins.
Engineer: Chris Kimsey, Barry Sage.
Bootleg only.

With unfinished lyrics, *Dancing Girls* lacks any spark. It is one of those tracks that has no identity but is reminiscent of others. It has a *She's So Cold* introduction, a riff from *Brown Leaves* and guitar sounds from *Just My Imagination*. Ian Stewart contributes piano. Two versions exist, recorded at the SOME GIRLS and the EMOTIONAL RESCUE sessions (* a - 4.08). The latter is more than a minute longer than the first. As an instrumental, the track was also known as *Brown Leaves*.

746. SHAME, SHAME, SHAME (Reed) 4.01
5 January - 29 January, February - 2 March 1978: Place: EMI, Pathé Marconi Studios, Paris, France.
Played Live: 1963, 1997
Producer: The Glimmer Twins.
Engineer: Chris Kimsey, Barry Sage.
Bootleg only.

Shame, Shame, Shame is the Jimmy Reed song which Keith Richards opens with a delicate riff. A boogie then follows with Ian Stewart on the piano and Mick Jagger on vocals and harmonica.

747. PIANO INSTRUMENTAL (Jagger, Richards) 4.37
5 January - 29 January, February - 2 March 1978: Place: EMI, Pathé Marconi Studios, Paris, France.
Producer: The Glimmer Twins.
Engineer: Chris Kimsey, Barry Sage.
Bootleg only.

A piano instrumental with marimba sounds accompanying.

748. PETROL BLUES (Jagger, Richards) 1.35
AKA: Petrol Gang, Petrol
5 January - 29 January, February - 2 March 1978; August - September 2011: Place: EMI, Pathé Marconi Studios, Paris, France; La Fourchette Home Studio, Fourchette, Tours, France, Electric Lady, New York, Berkeley St., Mix This!, Los Angeles, USA.
Producer: Chris Kimsey, Don Was, The Glimmer Twins.
Engineer: Chris Kimsey, Barry Sage.
Overdubs recorded by: Krish Sharma, Matt Clifford. Assisted by Phil Joly. Mixed by Bob Clearmountain. Assisted by Brandon Duncan. Mastered by Stephen Marcussen.
Digital editing by Stewart Whitmore.
UK CD SOME GIRLS BONUS DISC: 21 November 2011: No. 57 - 1 week
USA CD SOME GIRLS BONUS DISC: 21 November 2011: No. 46 - 2 weeks

The delicate subject of the 1973 Arab oil embargo, due to the USA and Western European involvement in supplying arms to Israel for the short Arab-Israeli war, was tackled in 1978. Oil and petrol was rationed by the USA and gas-guzzling cars were considered non-chic. The latter was the lyrical message that Mick Jagger satirically picked upon. He asked Mr President for help since he does not want to sell his new Cadillac which he had just paid for. There is also mention of oil companies and magnates Texaco, Standard Oil and the Getty organisation.
The only instrumentation is the piano supplied by Ian Stewart, although the 2011 credits mention Mick Jagger. This short version is very much a cut-and-paste job of the original, which clearly has Mick asking Ian Stewart to keep pace at one point with his vocal delivery (* a - 3.41). Taking into account this politically correct modern age, Don Was apparently did not want to offend any Arabs - either the old-style leaders or those from the Arab Spring conflicts of 2011.

749. **GOLDEN CADDY** (Jagger, Richards) 1.58
AKA: Golden Mile
5 January - 29 January, February - 2 March 1978, 11 November - 16 December 1982: Place: EMI, Pathé Marconi Studios, Paris, France.
Rolling Stones with Chuck Leavell.
Producer: The Glimmer Twins.
Engineer: Chris Kimsey, Barry Sage.
Bootleg only.

This went around the Stones recording mill in 1982 when it was worked on again for potential release on the UNDERCOVER album. There are two out-takes from 1978, a short and longer instrumental (* a - 3.18). It was hard to see where this track was leading with its dual repetitive riffs. It was tried with less lead guitar and with more keyboard and mellotron sounds in 1982, where there are two other out-takes (* b - 6.15). The last, a lengthy nine-minute take, has a few spoken words by Mick Jagger and a Spanish sounding guitar (* c - 8.56).

750. **BROKEN TOE** (Jagger, Richards) 1.55
AKA: Broken Wrist
5 January - 29 January, February - 2 March 1978: Place: EMI, Pathé Marconi Studios, Paris, France.
Producer: The Glimmer Twins.
Engineer: Chris Kimsey, Barry Sage.
Bootleg only.

One of Keith Richards' riffs is the main feature of this hard-edged instrumental. A background lead guitar solo is played by Ron Wood.

751. **IT'S A LIE** (Jagger, Richards) 4.36
5 January - 29 January, February - 2 March 1978: Place: EMI, Pathé Marconi Studios, Paris, France.
Producer: The Glimmer Twins.
Engineer: Chris Kimsey, Barry Sage.
Bootleg only.

A satisfactory mid-tempo country rock song, with harmonica and Keith Richards providing some vocals.

752. **REMEMBER THESE DAYS** (Jagger, Richards) 4.16
5 January - 29 January, February - 2 March 1978: Place: EMI, Pathé Marconi Studios, Paris, France.
Producer: The Glimmer Twins.
Engineer: Chris Kimsey, Barry Sage.
Bootleg only.

An instrumental with a slow tremolo guitar effect and electric piano.

753. **FOLLOW YOU** (Jagger, Richards) 1.30
5 January - 29 January, February - 2 March 1978: Place: EMI, Pathé Marconi Studios, Paris, France.
Producer: The Glimmer Twins.
Engineer: Chris Kimsey, Barry Sage.
Bootleg only.

With a funky Shirley & Company, *Shame Shame Shame* tempo, *Follow You* is a short instrumental out-take.

754. **SHEEP DIP BLUES** (Jagger, Richards) 0.37
5 January - 29 January, February - 2 March 1978: Place: EMI, Pathé Marconi Studios, Paris, France.
Producer: The Glimmer Twins.
Engineer: Chris Kimsey, Barry Sage.
Bootleg only.

A very short segment of harmonica and slow piano blues with a distinctive guitar by Keith Richards.

755. **ARMPIT BLUES** (Jagger, Richards) 2.39
5 January - 29 January, February - 2 March 1978: Place: EMI, Pathé Marconi Studios, Paris, France.
Producer: The Glimmer Twins.
Engineer: Chris Kimsey, Barry Sage.
Bootleg only.

A blues track, as the title suggests, with a sweet-sounding harmonica, Ian Stewart's inimitable piano and an authentic electric lead guitar, all taking it in turn to go solo.

756. **AFTER HOURS** (Parrish) 5.04
5 January - 29 January, February - 2 March 1978: Place: EMI, Pathé Marconi Studios, Paris, France.
Producer: The Glimmer Twins.
Engineer: Chris Kimsey, Barry Sage.
Bootleg only.

Another Ian Stewart-inspired tune with wailing Larry Adler-sounding harmonica. The original, written by pianist Avery Parrish, was a jazzy blues favourite from the 40s.

757. IT'S ALL WRONG (Jagger, Richards) 3.37
5 January - 29 January, February - 2 March 1978: Place: EMI, Pathé Marconi Studios, Paris, France.
Producer: The Glimmer Twins.
Engineer: Chris Kimsey, Barry Sage.
Bootleg only.

It's All Wrong is a return to *Respectable* territory but with harsher rock guitars and more punk vocals. Chris Kimsey denied that on the faster numbers there was ever an intention to sound "punk" but felt that, because there was a minimum of other instrumentation such as brass and due to the band being recorded live, it would obviously sound more guitar-orientated and thrustful. Chris decried the often heard thought that SOME GIRLS is disco or punk. "The reason for the new dynamic was simply that Mick Jagger picked up an electric guitar and his spirit gave it that fresh punk style."
One other visitor to the studio was a member of the Monty Python comedian team, Eric Idle. Together with Mick and Bianca Jagger and Ron Wood they were concluding arrangements for the cinematic release in March 1978 of *All You Need Is Cash* featuring a fictitious spoof pop-act The Rutles from Liverpool. Ron played the part of a Hell's Angel while Bianca acted and Mick was interviewed as himself.

758. NO SPARE PARTS (Jagger, Richards) 4.30
AKA: Got No Spare Parts, Got No Oil To Change
5 January - 29 January, February - 2 March 1978; August - September 2011: Place: EMI, Pathé Marconi Studios, Paris, France; La Fourchette Home Studio, Fourchette, Tours, France, Electric Lady, New York, Berkeley St., Mix This!, Los Angeles, USA.
Producer: Chris Kimsey, Don Was, The Glimmer Twins.
Engineer: Chris Kimsey, Barry Sage.
Overdubs recorded by: Krish Sharma, Matt Clifford. Assisted by Phil Joly. Mixed by Bob Clearmountain. Assisted by Brandon Duncan.
Mastered by Stephen Marcussen. Digital editing by Stewart Whitmore.
UK & USA e-Single: 14 November 2011
UK CD SOME GIRLS BONUS DISC: 21 November 2011: No. 57 - 1 week
USA CD SOME GIRLS BONUS DISC: 21 November 2011: No. 46 - 2 weeks
UK & USA Vinyl Single: 25 November 2011

This is a worthwhile country rock song, with Ron Wood's pedal steel accompanying an electric piano track by Mick Jagger who, on the out-take's does a country-hick drawl to the juice-laden, lonely heart sentiments (* a - 5.01, b - 6.06). The 2011 version may have some fresh steel parts. The new vocal delivery is stilted and accentuated as Mick enunciates particular words. Chris Kimsey always thought that Mick tackled country songs very well and could have created a killer country album, especially with his brother Chris Jagger, who, in his own right, was a great songwriter. Indeed, the BONUS DISC release of SOME GIRLS goes some way to achieving this, since many tracks were in that country rock vein.
The original 1978 lyrics on *No Spare Parts* seem complete and take the listener on a journey through San Antone to return to Dallas for Thanksgiving with a turkey in hand. It is still a road trip, albeit one which meanders around Southern California and Texas, heading for Los Angeles to meet a girl, apparently relating a true tale for Mick.
The new lyrics mention the Marfa lights atmospheric phenomenon in Texas. This was absent from the original and the warm reference to taking turkey and booze for a Thanksgiving celebration was also changed. It was released as an electronic single download in advance of the album and was accompanied by a promotional video, directed by Mat Whitecross.

759. WHEN YOU'RE GONE (Jagger, Richards, Wood) 3.51
AKA: Redeyes
5 January - 29 January, February - 2 March 1978; August - September 2011: Place: EMI, Pathé Marconi Studios, Paris, France; La Fourchette Home Studio, Fourchette, Tours, France, Electric Lady, New York, Berkeley St., Mix This!, Los Angeles, USA.
Producer: Chris Kimsey, Don Was, The Glimmer Twins.
Engineer: Chris Kimsey, Barry Sage.
Overdubs recorded by: Krish Sharma, Matt Clifford. Assisted by Phil Joly. Mixed by Bob Clearmountain. Assisted by Brandon Duncan.
Mastered by Stephen Marcussen. Digital editing by Stewart Whitmore.
UK CD SOME GIRLS BONUS DISC: 21 November 2011: No. 57 - 1 week
USA CD SOME GIRLS BONUS DISC: 21 November 2011: No. 46 - 2 weeks

Ron Wood was making the most of the time in Paris, recording his next solo album at the same studios, with Charlie Watts on drums, Mick Jagger (backing vocals), Keith Richards (guitar), Robert "Pops" Popwell (Crusaders and Swamp Dogg) on bass and Jerry Williams (also from The Swamp Dogg band) on keyboards. The last two were also part of Irma Thomas's backing band in the early 60s. Inevitably, there was some cross-pollination and this was one track that remained with Ron until 1981 when it was released without vocals as *Redeyes*.
When You're Gone was a slow boogie, with a pronounced bass-sounding guitar by Ron, and a lead guitar further back in the mix (* a - 3.58). The track was resurrected by Don Was for the SOME GIRLS re-master and extras disc with a co-credit to Ron Wood. Mick added lyrics to those on the original, which were sung for guide purposes. He also overdubbed a harmonica. The track becomes a worthy boogie blues number.

760. ANGELINE (Jagger, Richards)
5 January - 29 January, February - 2 March 1978: Place: EMI, Pathé Marconi Studios, Paris, France.
Producer: The Glimmer Twins.
Engineer: Chris Kimsey, Barry Sage.
Unavailable.

A track only rumoured to have been recorded.

761. DISCO MUSIK (Jagger, Richards) 5.55
5 January - 29 January, February - 2 March 1978: Place: EMI, Pathé Marconi Studios, Paris, France.
Producer: The Glimmer Twins.
Engineer: Chris Kimsey, Barry Sage.
Bootleg only.

With *Miss You* under their belts, a more audacious attempt at disco was tried on this track. Slightly synthesised vocals are used by Mick Jagger as he hand-claps and stomps around the bass rhythm to a funk guitar. Jagger asks, "tell me what you want" - no more disco musik!

762. IT WON'T BE LONG (Jagger, Richards) 2.38
5 January - 29 January, February - 2 March 1978; 18 January - 12 February 1979: Place: EMI, Pathé Marconi Studios, Paris, France; Compass Point Studios, Nassau, Bahamas, USA.
Producer: The Glimmer Twins.
Engineer: Chris Kimsey, Barry Sage.
Bootleg only.

Two versions recorded year on year in 1978 (* a - 2.33) and 1979. Mick Jagger and Keith Richards share some unfinished vocals. The second was prepared for EMOTIONAL RESCUE and has a reggae tinge and additional keyboards, with a xylophone.

763. NEVER MAKE ME CRY (Jagger, Richards) 4.01
AKA: Never Make You Cry
5 January - 29 January, February - 2 March 1978: Place: EMI, Pathé Marconi Studios, Paris, France.
Producer: The Glimmer Twins.
Engineer: Chris Kimsey, Barry Sage.
Bootleg only.

A soft rock song which is uneventful.

764. LIGHT UP (Jagger, Richards) 4.44
5 January - 29 January, February - 2 March 1978: Place: EMI, Pathé Marconi Studios, Paris, France.
Producer: The Glimmer Twins.
Engineer: Chris Kimsey, Barry Sage.
Bootleg only.

The pedal steel guitar trait on SOME GIRLS, courtesy of Ron Wood, appears again on the instrumental *Light Up*, giving it a country feel. At the time, Ronnie was still coming to terms with the instrument, experimenting with the metal tone bars on the fret and the pedal positioning. And still the out-takes kept coming.

765. NEVER LET HER GO (Jagger, Richards) 4.51
5 January - 29 January, February - 2 March 1978: Place: EMI, Pathé Marconi Studios, Paris, France.
Producer: The Glimmer Twins.
Engineer: Chris Kimsey, Barry Sage.
Bootleg only.

The soft ripples of piano from Ian Stewart, with a lazy atmosphere accentuated by Mick Jagger's sloven vocals, suggest this song could have been worked upon.

766. NOT THE WAY TO GO (Jagger, Richards) 9.39
5 January - 29 January, February - 2 March 1978; 23 August - 7 September 1978: Place: EMI, Pathé Marconi Studios, Paris, France; Wally Heider (RCA) Studios, Hollywood, USA.
Rolling Stones with Ian McLagan.
Producer: The Glimmer Twins.
Engineer: Chris Kimsey, Barry Sage.
Bootleg only.

A lively number with some West Indian influences. The organ rocks on a memorable chorus. After the American tour it was worked upon again. Two out-takes exist, one is faster than the other and has guide vocals on key changes (* a - 7.10).

767. STAY WHERE YOU ARE (Jagger, Richards) 1.43
AKA: Sunshine Glance
5 January - 29 January, February - 2 March 1978: Place: EMI, Pathé Marconi Studios, Paris, France.
Producer: The Glimmer Twins.
Engineer: Chris Kimsey, Barry Sage.
Bootleg only.

An instrumental track, which has a nice rhythm lick played by Keith Richards.

768. UP AGAINST THE WALL (Jagger, Richards) 6.24
AKA: On Our Knees
5 January - 29 January, February - 2 March 1978: Place: EMI, Pathé Marconi Studios, Paris, France.
Producer: The Glimmer Twins.
Engineer: Chris Kimsey, Barry Sage.
Bootleg only.

An instrumental with harmonica and an introduction reminiscent of *Ventilator Blues*. Keith Richards is at the forefront of the mix while Ron Wood can hardly be heard in the background.

769. BROKEN HEAD BLUES (Jagger, Richards) 2.12
AKA: Biscuit Blues
5 January - 29 January, February - 2 March 1978: Place: EMI, Pathé Marconi Studios, Paris, France.
Producer: The Glimmer Twins.
Engineer: Chris Kimsey, Barry Sage.
Bootleg only.

A pre-cursor to *Black Limousine* and similar to the Jimmy Reed song *You Don't Have To Go*, with no harmonica or lyrics.

770. YOU DON'T HAVE TO GO (Reed) 2.16
AKA: Broken Head Blues
5 January - 29 January, February - 2 March 1978: Place: EMI, Pathé Marconi Studios, Paris, France.
Producer: The Glimmer Twins.
Engineer: Chris Kimsey, Barry Sage.
Bootleg only.

A Jimmy Reed song played in guitar boogie fashion with shrill harmonica. A lead guitar weaves for the song's duration in Eric Clapton style. There are two versions, one with vocals and the other a shortened instrumental. The track has similarities to what was attempted on *Black Limousine* as out-takes of that song and an early one known as *Broken Head Blues*, demonstrate. Ron Wood was very keen on the boogie and rhythm style influences of Jimmy Reed.

771. SO YOUNG (1994 VERSION) (Jagger, Richards) 3.25
5 January - 29 January, February - 2 March 1978; 15 January - April 1994: Place: EMI, Pathé Marconi Studios, Paris, France; Don Was' Studio and A&M Studios, Los Angeles, USA.
Rolling Stones with Chuck Leavell.
Producer: Chris Kimsey, The Glimmer Twins.
Engineer: Barry Sage.
CD Single Track Love Is Strong: 5 July 1994
UK CD box set THE SINGLES COLLECTION 1971-2006: 45 X 45s: 11 April 2011
USA CD box set THE SINGLES COLLECTION 1971-2006: 45 X 45s: 26 April 2011

A good-time song that waited 16 years for an official release on the *Love Is Strong* single. Produced by Chris Kimsey in 1978, with some overdubs made in 1994 including Chuck Leavell's piano. Chris confirmed that the SOME GIRLS sessions produced more than 150 reels of tapes. They were all filed away and logged by Barry Sage but, unfortunately, when Ian Stewart cleared the studio on completion of the sessions, somehow these logs were lost. On the other hand, Chris believed the written records were destroyed in a flood at the Stones' archive facilities in London. This was "back in the day" when Ian drove from Paris to England with all the studio tapes in the back of the vehicle. Apparently, it was necessary to have to distract customs' inspectors with records and other freebies to prevent the session tapes from being held for investigation.
The vocal chorus is very similar to *The Storm* which has a "so long" refrain. That is track two on the 1994 CD single while *So Young* is track three - an interesting juxtaposition. Charlie Watts crashes into the song and Mick Jagger immediately joins on vocals, worried that she will steal his heart and that he needs to put his dick on a leash. Surely not a problem to anyone in the band?
The guitars rock well together and there is an opportunity to solo in rock and roll manner, not only for them but also Ian Stewart on piano. A different take from the original sessions has a sloppier approach lead guitar solo (* a - 2.57). The released version has a completely different set of lyrics and Ian Stewart is more pronounced in the mix.

772. SO YOUNG (PIANO VERSION) (Jagger, Richards) 2.55
5 January - 29 January, February - 2 March 1978; 15 January - April 1994; August - September 2011: Place: EMI, Pathé Marconi Studios, Paris, France; Don Was' Studio and A&M Studios, Los Angeles, USA; La Fourchette Home Studio, Fourchette, Tours, France, Electric Lady, New York, Berkeley St., Mix This!, Los Angeles, USA.
Rolling Stones with Chuck Leavell.
Producer: Chris Kimsey, The Glimmer Twins.
Engineer: Barry Sage.
Overdubs recorded by: Krish Sharma, Matt Clifford. Assisted by Phil Joly. Mixed by Bob Clearmountain. Assisted by Brandon Duncan.
Mastered by Stephen Marcussen. Digital editing by Stewart Whitmore.
UK e-Download: 21 November 2011

Don Was took the original 1994 version and re-mixed it to produce more of an acoustic piano romp; the guitar channels are turned down which accentuates Bill Wyman's driving bass. It was released in 2011 when it could be digitally downloaded for a limited period as part of the SOME GIRLS re-issue and physically available on disc as part of the Japanese release of the BONUS DISC album.

773. SO YOUNG (2011 VERSION) (Jagger, Richards) 3.18
5 January - 29 January, February - 2 March 1978; 15 January - April 1994; August - September 2011: Place: EMI, Pathé Marconi Studios, Paris, France; Don Was' Studio and A&M Studios, Los Angeles, USA; La Fourchette Home Studio, Fourchette, Tours, France, Electric Lady, New York, Berkeley St., Mix This!, Los Angeles, USA.
Rolling Stones with Chuck Leavell.
Producer: Chris Kimsey, Don Was, The Glimmer Twins.
Engineer: Chris Kimsey, Barry Sage.
Overdubs recorded by: Krish Sharma, Matt Clifford. Assisted by Phil Joly. Mixed by Bob Clearmountain. Assisted by Brandon Duncan.
Mastered by Stephen Marcussen. Digital editing by Stewart Whitmore.
UK e-Single: 9 November 2011
UK CD SOME GIRLS BONUS DISC: 21 November 2011: No. 57 - 1 week
USA CD SOME GIRLS BONUS DISC: 21 November 2011: No. 46 - 2 weeks

The first release as part of the 2011 SOME GIRLS re-issue was a strange version of *So Young*. Minor lead and new harmony vocals had been added by Mick Jagger but, in many ways, the track was no different to the 1978 version re-done by Don Was in 1994. One wonders if the Stones were aware that it had just been released in April 2011, although admittedly on an expensive box set singles compilation.

774. YOU WIN AGAIN (Williams) 3.00
5 January - 29 January, February - 2 March 1978; August - September 2011: Place: EMI, Pathé Marconi Studios, Paris, France; La Fourchette Home Studio, Fourchette, Tours, France, Electric Lady, New York, Berkeley St., Mix This!, Los Angeles, USA.
Producer: Chris Kimsey, Don Was, The Glimmer Twins.
Engineer: Chris Kimsey, Barry Sage.
Overdubs recorded by: Krish Sharma, Matt Clifford. Assisted by Phil Joly. Mixed by Bob Clearmountain. Assisted by Brandon Duncan.
Mastered by Stephen Marcussen. Digital editing by Stewart Whitmore.
UK CD SOME GIRLS BONUS DISC: 21 November 2011: No. 57 - 1 week
USA CD SOME GIRLS BONUS DISC: 21 November 2011: No. 46 - 2 weeks

The short, five-year career of Hank Williams produced some notorious country records. *You Win Again* was a hit for him in 1952 before he died on his way to a concert on 1 January 1953, aged only 29. The Stones originally attempted a sloppy, drunken version with Keith Richards on piano and the unlikely sound of marimbas can be heard played by Bill Wyman or Ian Stewart (* a - 3.20). Ian was not very fond of country and western, preferring boogie-woogie. Ron Wood plays the pedal steel guitar. Mick Jagger and Keith are on vocals, gently sending up the song during the long held notes, particularly on the unreleased version. It did not need much work in 2011 and Mick stated in Mojo magazine: "My goal is always to keep the spirit of the thing. I imagine everything was recorded last week and I just had to come in and finish them - a line here or a line there." He recorded some new vocals for the track to give it a more reverential feel.

775. WHERE THE BOYS GO (Jagger, Richards) 3.29
AKA: Where The Boys All Go
5 January - 29 January, February - 2 March; 23 August - 7 September 1978; 25 June - 9 August, 30 August - October 1979: Place: EMI, Pathé Marconi Studios, Paris, France; Wally Heider (RCA) Studios, Hollywood, USA; EMI, Pathé Marconi Studios, Paris, France.
Rolling Stones with Ian McLagan, Jerry Hall, Jo Karslake.
Producer: The Glimmer Twins.
Associate Producer: Chris Kimsey.
Engineer: Sean Fullan, Brad Samuelsohn, David 'Snake' Reynolds, Jon Smith.
UK LP EMOTIONAL RESCUE: 20 June 1980: No. 1 - 18 weeks
USA LP EMOTIONAL RESCUE: 23 June 1980: No. 1 - 20 weeks

This was one track that was revised later and worked on again and again. The original five-minute take from the early Paris sessions is a thunderous, boisterous version (* a - 5.15). *Where The Boys All Go* was hung over for use on the next studio album, EMOTIONAL RESCUE. It is an up-tempo Saturday-night-out-rocker which Mick Jagger described as a parody of youth. The band sounded tight. Charlie Watts' drum sounds just right, Ian Stewart seems at home and Mick Jagger is particularly wry on spoken cockney vocals.
There were typical British references to "see me down the pub" and "I piss away my money", "a Saturday night piece of arse" and "I'll see you around the back". Keith Richards and Ron Wood delivered the lead solos and a third guitar was added by Mick. Later on, neither Keith nor Ron could agree on who actually did the lead solo. Ian Stewart boogies on piano, Bill Wyman's simple but effective bass rumbles and Chris Kimsey confirms that none other than Jerry Hall and Jo Karslake add to the atmosphere by joining in on Travolta/Newton-John-type backing vocals at the song's climax, replying with "where the girls all go".
Two early out-takes have different lyrics and additional piano, with Keith starting off the second take, and there is also a brief intro segment (* b - 3.48, c - 3.52, d - 0.35). A lesser known thermo graphic video was made by Adam Friedman using a slightly different recorded mix. The sessions concluded on the same day that Keith Moon died back in Mayfair, London, aged 32.

776. SUMMERTIME BLUES (Cochran, Capeheart) 1.49
19 May - 9 June 1978: Place: Todd Rundgren's Bearsville Studio, Woodstock, New York, USA.
Bootleg only.

With work completed in Paris, Mick Jagger busied himself signing Peter Tosh to Rolling Stones Records and, as a consequence, he became an opening act for most of the tour. A base was needed for rehearsals and Mick rented Todd Rundgren's house and studio in Woodstock, New York. He moved in with Jerry Hall and was filed for divorce by Bianca in May 1878. Keith Richards was invited by Mick to Woodstock to stay there for a period and it was here that he underwent heroin withdrawal self-treatment, although there was apparently plenty of coke about. Anita failed to join him on the trip, hence another reason for their incompatibility. At this time he met Liz Wergilis, a Swedish friend of Jo Karslake, who took up the slack created by the loss of the fix. Keith helped out Peter Tosh on a couple of

tracks for his forthcoming album BUSH DOCTOR, which was re-mixed at the Bearsville Studios in the month before the tour. Mick provided backing vocals to Peter Tosh's track *(You've Gotta Walk) Don't Look Back* which was written by Motown artists Robinson/White. They also acted as the album producers.
The studios were used to rehearse material for the up and coming United States tour. These rehearsals were taped and provide a unique musical account of the Stones' late 70s period. Continuing the SOME GIRLS theme, the band was a tight and unified "sixsome", the sixth member was Ian Stewart.
As in Europe, 1976, there was to be no brass on the tour. In rehearsal, the Stones enjoyed playing numbers from the past such as *Sweet Little Sixteen, High Heeled Sneakers, Beautiful Delilah, Got My Mojo Working, The Fat Man, Crackin' Up* and Eddie Cochran numbers *Somethin' Else, C'mon Everybody* and *Summertime Blues.* Mick's vocal delivery on *Summertime Blues* was in his own dialect of Cockney southern drawl. Only *Sweet Little Sixteen* would be played on the tour.

777. COCKSUCKER BLUES (Jagger, Richard) 6.49
AKA: Schoolboy's Blues, Lonesome Schoolboy
19 May - 9 June 1978: Place: Todd Rundgren's Bearsville Studio, Woodstock, New York, USA.
Bootleg only.

Another track recorded at Bearsville was an extraordinary electric version of *Cocksucker Blues*, with organ, harmonica and lead guitar, which extended the track to almost seven minutes. A raunchy *Crazy Mama* was rehearsed, as was *Star Star, Memory Motel, Hot Stuff*, even *Tell Me* and *Play With Fire, No Expectations, All Down The Line, Brown Sugar, It's Only Rock 'n' Roll, Jumping Jack Flash, Gimme Shelter, Love In Vain, Honky Tonk Women, Let's Spend The Night Together, Hip Shake, Cherry Oh Baby, Let It Rock* and of course SOME GIRLS material, including the out-take *Claudine*. There was still a need for another keyboards player but thoughts of sharing Peter Tosh's man, Bernard "Touter" Harvey, were soon dropped.
At the very last minute, a call was made to England for Ian McLagan to join the band and, after touring with The Rich Kids, he jumped at the chance to appear with his contemporaries and idols. He arrived 48 hours before the tour was due to commence. Some rehearsal - he timed it at about three hours! He quickly worked out with Ian Stewart which tracks he would take a prominent role on and those which Stewart would not perform such as *Miss You*. McLagan found Stewart to be incredibly friendly and, as well as his piano duties, he acted as Charlie Watts drum kit technician.

778. SWEET LITTLE SIXTEEN (Berry) ✎ 2.58
14 June 1978: Place: Capitol Theatre, Passaic, New Jersey, USA.
Rolling Stones with Ian McLagan.
Bootleg only.

779. HOUND DOG (Leiber, Stoller) ✎ 2.00
28 June 1978: Place: Mid-South Coliseum, Memphis, Tennessee, USA.
Rolling Stones with Ian McLagan.
Bootleg only.

780. WHEN THE WHIP COMES DOWN (Jagger, Richards) ✎ 4.25
6 July 1978: Place: Masonic Hall, Detroit, Michigan, USA.
Rolling Stones with Ian McLagan.
USA Compilation LP SUCKING IN THE SEVENTIES: 12 March 1981: No. 15 - 5 weeks
UK Compilation LP SUCKING IN THE SEVENTIES: 13 April 1981

The tour, promoted by Bill Graham, was small by recent comparisons with a short, 25-date list, lasting more than six weeks and being played in stadiums and smaller theatre venues. The stadiums demanded a larger stage, with a 20-metre walkway either side of a large tongue facade and a rectangular tongue protruding into the crowd. A mass release of balloons announced the Stones' arrival and fireworks their departure. It was also the first tour where wireless connectors were used for guitar and microphone, allowing Mick to wander away from the main stage still maintaining vocal contact.
Essentially it was a promotion for the SOME GIRLS album which was released a day before the first gig, on 10 June 1978. *When The Whip Comes Down* originated from a stereo FM recording and was released without any explanation of its origin except for the track title (live version) on the tongue-twisting 1981 compilation SUCKING IN THE SEVENTIES. During a visit to Chicago on 9 July the band went to see Muddy Waters and Willie Dixon with Ronnie Wood, Mick Jagger and Keith Richards guesting on a few numbers.

781. LET IT ROCK (Anderson) ✎ 2.12
18 July 1978: Place: Will Rogers Memorial Center, Fort Worth, Texas, USA.
Rolling Stones with Ian McLagan.
Producer: Jack Calmes.
Engineer: Sound recording 1978: BJ Schiller.
Audio mix by Bob Clearmountain. Assisted by Brandon Duncan.
Audio mastered by Mazen Murad.
UK CD, DVD SOME GIRLS - LIVE IN TEXAS '78: 21 November 2011
USA CD, DVD SOME GIRLS - LIVE IN TEXAS '78: 22 November 2011

The line-up for the tour was stripped back to the minimum and Ian McLagan was the only support player. At Keith Richards' insistence Etta James, who had fallen on poor times, was asked to support the band on a few dates and he also teamed up with Lil Wergelis for a crazy 18-month shindig. The late Etta had been a Chess Records artist and was a colourful character, who also sang backing vocals for Chuck Berry. The tour poster reflected a Chinese propaganda campaign which rallied workers but also depicted smoke-laden, belching American factories and cars.

782. ALL DOWN THE LINE (Jagger, Richard) ✎ 3.56
18 July 1978: Place: Will Rogers Memorial Center, Fort Worth, Texas, USA.
Rolling Stones with Ian McLagan.
Producer: Jack Calmes.
Engineer: Sound recording 1978: BJ Schiller.
Audio mix by Bob Clearmountain. Assisted by Brandon Duncan.
Audio mastered by Mazen Murad.
UK CD, DVD SOME GIRLS - LIVE IN TEXAS '78: 21 November 2011
USA CD, DVD SOME GIRLS - LIVE IN TEXAS '78: 22 November 2011

783. HONKY TONK WOMEN (Jagger, Richard) ✎ 3.38
18 July 1978: Place: Will Rogers Memorial Center, Fort Worth, Texas, USA.
Rolling Stones with Ian McLagan.
Producer: Jack Calmes.
Engineer: Sound recording 1978: BJ Schiller.
Audio mix by Bob Clearmountain. Assisted by Brandon Duncan. Audio mastered by Mazen Murad.
UK CD, DVD SOME GIRLS - LIVE IN TEXAS '78: 21 November 2011
USA CD, DVD SOME GIRLS - LIVE IN TEXAS '78: 22 November 2011

784. STAR STAR (Jagger, Richard) ✎ 3.47
18 July 1978: Place: Will Rogers Memorial Center, Fort Worth, Texas, USA.
Rolling Stones with Ian McLagan.
Producer: Jack Calmes.
Engineer: Sound recording 1978: BJ Schiller.
Audio mix by Bob Clearmountain. Assisted by Brandon Duncan. Audio mastered by Mazen Murad.
UK CD, DVD SOME GIRLS - LIVE IN TEXAS '78: 21 November 2011
USA CD, DVD SOME GIRLS - LIVE IN TEXAS '78: 22 November 2011

785. WHEN THE WHIP COMES DOWN (Jagger, Richards) ✎ 5.13
18 July 1978: Place: Will Rogers Memorial Center, Fort Worth, Texas, USA.
Rolling Stones with Ian McLagan.
Producer: Jack Calmes.
Engineer: Sound recording 1978: BJ Schiller.
Audio mix by Bob Clearmountain. Assisted by Brandon Duncan. Audio mastered by Mazen Murad.
UK CD, DVD SOME GIRLS - LIVE IN TEXAS '78: 21 November 2011
USA CD, DVD SOME GIRLS - LIVE IN TEXAS '78: 22 November 2011

786. BEAST OF BURDEN (Jagger, Richards) ✎ 6.28
18 July 1978: Place: Will Rogers Memorial Center, Fort Worth, Texas, USA.
Rolling Stones with Ian McLagan.
Producer: Jack Calmes.
Engineer: Sound recording 1978: BJ Schiller.
Audio mix by Bob Clearmountain. Assisted by Brandon Duncan. Audio mastered by Mazen Murad.
UK CD, DVD SOME GIRLS - LIVE IN TEXAS '78: 21 November 2011
USA CD, DVD SOME GIRLS - LIVE IN TEXAS '78: 22 November 2011

787. MISS YOU (Jagger, Richards) ✎ 8.35
18 July 1978: Place: Will Rogers Memorial Center, Fort Worth, Texas, USA.
Rolling Stones with Ian McLagan.
Producer: Jack Calmes.
Engineer: Sound recording 1978: BJ Schiller.
Audio mix by Bob Clearmountain. Assisted by Brandon Duncan. Audio mastered by Mazen Murad.
UK CD, DVD SOME GIRLS - LIVE IN TEXAS '78: 21 November 2011
USA CD, DVD SOME GIRLS - LIVE IN TEXAS '78: 22 November 2011

788. JUST MY IMAGINATION (RUNNING AWAY WITH ME) (Barrett, Norman) ✎ 6.40
18 July 1978: Place: Will Rogers Memorial Center, Fort Worth, Texas, USA.
Rolling Stones with Ian McLagan.
Producer: Jack Calmes.
Engineer: Sound recording 1978: BJ Schiller.
Audio mix by Bob Clearmountain. Assisted by Brandon Duncan. Audio mastered by Mazen Murad.
UK CD, DVD SOME GIRLS - LIVE IN TEXAS '78: 21 November 2011
USA CD, DVD SOME GIRLS - LIVE IN TEXAS '78: 22 November 2011

789. SHATTERED (Jagger, Richards) ⟋ 4.44
18 July 1978: Place: Will Rogers Memorial Center, Fort Worth, Texas, USA.
Rolling Stones with Ian McLagan.
Producer: Jack Calmes.
Engineer: Sound recording 1978: BJ Schiller.
Audio mix by Bob Clearmountain. Assisted by Brandon Duncan. Audio mastered by Mazen Murad.
UK CD, DVD SOME GIRLS - LIVE IN TEXAS '78: 21 November 2011
USA CD, DVD SOME GIRLS - LIVE IN TEXAS '78: 22 November 2011

790. RESPECTABLE (Jagger, Richards) ⟋ 3.23
18 July 1978: Place: Will Rogers Memorial Center, Fort Worth, Texas, USA.
Rolling Stones with Ian McLagan.
Producer: Jack Calmes.
Engineer: Sound recording 1978: BJ Schiller.
Audio mix by Bob Clearmountain. Assisted by Brandon Duncan. Audio mastered by Mazen Murad.
UK CD, DVD SOME GIRLS - LIVE IN TEXAS '78: 21 November 2011
USA CD, DVD SOME GIRLS - LIVE IN TEXAS '78: 22 November 2011

791. FAR AWAY EYES (Jagger, Richards) ⟋ 5.51
18 July 1978: Place: Will Rogers Memorial Center, Fort Worth, Texas, USA.
Rolling Stones with Ian McLagan, Doug Kershaw.
Producer: Jack Calmes.
Engineer: Sound recording 1978: BJ Schiller.
Audio mix by Bob Clearmountain. Assisted by Brandon Duncan. Audio mastered by Mazen Murad.
UK CD, DVD SOME GIRLS - LIVE IN TEXAS '78: 21 November 2011
USA CD, DVD SOME GIRLS - LIVE IN TEXAS '78: 22 November 2011

792. LOVE IN VAIN (Payne) ⟋ 4.53
18 July 1978: Place: Will Rogers Memorial Center, Fort Worth, Texas, USA.
Rolling Stones with Ian McLagan, Doug Kershaw.
Producer: Jack Calmes.
Engineer: Sound recording 1978: BJ Schiller.
Audio mix by Bob Clearmountain. Assisted by Brandon Duncan. Audio mastered by Mazen Murad.
UK CD, DVD SOME GIRLS - LIVE IN TEXAS '78: 21 November 2011
USA CD, DVD SOME GIRLS - LIVE IN TEXAS '78: 22 November 2011

793. TUMBLING DICE (Jagger, Richard) ⟋ 4.38
18 July 1978: Place: Will Rogers Memorial Center, Fort Worth, Texas, USA.
Rolling Stones with Ian McLagan.
Producer: Jack Calmes.
Engineer: Sound recording 1978: BJ Schiller.
Audio mix by Bob Clearmountain. Assisted by Brandon Duncan. Audio mastered by Mazen Murad.
UK CD, DVD SOME GIRLS - LIVE IN TEXAS '78: 21 November 2011
USA CD, DVD SOME GIRLS - LIVE IN TEXAS '78: 22 November 2011

794. HAPPY (Jagger, Richard) ⟋ 3.12
18 July 1978: Place: Will Rogers Memorial Center, Fort Worth, Texas, USA.
Rolling Stones with Ian McLagan.
Producer: Jack Calmes.
Engineer: Sound recording 1978: BJ Schiller.
Audio mix by Bob Clearmountain. Assisted by Brandon Duncan. Audio mastered by Mazen Murad.
UK CD, DVD SOME GIRLS - LIVE IN TEXAS '78: 21 November 2011
USA CD, DVD SOME GIRLS - LIVE IN TEXAS '78: 22 November 2011

795. SWEET LITTLE SIXTEEN (Berry) ⟋ 3.11
18 July 1978: Place: Will Rogers Memorial Center, Fort Worth, Texas, USA.
Rolling Stones with Ian McLagan.
Producer: Jack Calmes.
Engineer: Sound recording 1978: BJ Schiller.
Audio mix by Bob Clearmountain. Assisted by Brandon Duncan. Audio mastered by Mazen Murad.
UK CD, DVD SOME GIRLS - LIVE IN TEXAS '78: 21 November 2011
USA CD, DVD SOME GIRLS - LIVE IN TEXAS '78: 22 November 2011

796. BROWN SUGAR (Jagger, Richard) ✏ 3.14
18 July 1978: Place: Will Rogers Memorial Center, Fort Worth, Texas, USA.
Rolling Stones with Ian McLagan.
Producer: Jack Calmes.
Engineer: Sound recording 1978: BJ Schiller.
Audio mix by Bob Clearmountain. Assisted by Brandon Duncan.
Audio mastered by Mazen Murad.
UK CD, DVD SOME GIRLS - LIVE IN TEXAS '78: 21 November 2011
USA CD, DVD SOME GIRLS - LIVE IN TEXAS '78: 22 November 2011

797. JUMPIN' JACK FLASH (Jagger, Richard) ✏ 6.14
18 July 1978: Place: Will Rogers Memorial Center, Fort Worth, Texas, USA.
Rolling Stones with Ian McLagan.
Producer: Jack Calmes.
Engineer: Sound recording 1978: BJ Schiller.
Audio mix by Bob Clearmountain. Assisted by Brandon Duncan.
Audio mastered by Mazen Murad.
UK CD, DVD SOME GIRLS - LIVE IN TEXAS '78: 21 November 2011
USA CD, DVD SOME GIRLS - LIVE IN TEXAS '78: 22 November 2011

The tour did not immediately spur any releases until, belatedly in 2011, when, in conjunction with the re-release of SOME GIRLS with extra tracks, the summer of 1978 was fully remembered with a film, video and audio disc of the Fort Worth Texan gig. Prior to this, the audio had been heard on radio and hence bootlegged. The King Biscuit Flower Hour (KBFH) recorded some concerts from the 1978 tour; four such numbers were on a CD, made in 1987, of a few tracks from Brussels 1973 and the 1981 tour.

The show's name was derived from the influential blues radio show King Biscuit Time, which was sponsored by the King Biscuit Flour Company. The programme was broadcast on Sunday nights from 1973 until 1993. It was a syndicated rock show with broadcasts of live concerts, hosted by Bill Minkin, and was taken by 300 radio stations throughout the US. Shows were initially distributed by reels but progressed to vinyl and also later CD, hence its wide availability. Fort Worth was widely bootlegged as "Handsome Girls". For many years it provided an outstanding legacy of the 1978 tour.

It was a last-minute decision for Mick Jagger to work with Jack Calmes, who was the owner of Showco, who hired sound and lighting for rock concerts, even doing this with the Stones on more recent tours. Jack believed a film of the Stones in a Texas concert arena would make unique viewing and that the SOME GIRLS album was a very good release. His 24-track recording rig would be in sync with the film cameramen directed by his then wife Lynn Lenau. A handshake agreement was reached just six hours from show time.

The Stones set was sharp and concise (there were no *You Can't Always Get What You Want*, *Sympathy For The Devil* or *Midnight Ramblers* on this tour) and commenced with *Let It Rock*, *All Down The Line*, *Honky Tonk Women* and *Star Star*. Then followed a brave seven numbers from SOME GIRLS - the only ones not being attempted were *Lies*, *Some Girls* and *Before They Make Me Run*. The concluding numbers were *Love In Vain*, *Tumbling Dice*, *Happy*, *Sweet Little Sixteen*, *Brown Sugar* and *Jumpin' Jack Flash*.

Some nights *Street Fighting Man* was an added bonus and, occasionally, *Lies* was performed in addition mid-set. Collectors will be interested in the detours from the standard set, such as the salute in Memphis with *Hound Dog* and Linda Ronstadt guesting on *Tumbling Dice* in Arizona. Linda had recorded her own version of *Tumbling Dice* in 1977 and Mick Jagger sang backing vocals, just as he did on Carly Simon's *You're So Vain*. Mick had told Linda that she needed to sing more rock at her concerts and the film reflects what a cut back Stones performance can deliver.

The camera lands on the only additional band members, in the shape of Ian McLagan and Ian Stewart, captured in his own inimitable, hunched piano pose. Bashfully, country's own Louisiana Man, Doug Kershaw played fiddle on *Far Away Eyes*. Mick is thrust forward not just to sing but play guitar in the SOME GIRLS section. *When The Whip Comes Down* has him confident, yet arrogant, dressed in a Vivienne Westwood and Malcolm McLaren "destroy" t-shirt with cock-hugging red leathers.

He is caught tip-toeing through *Miss You*, vocalising in different styles on *Just My Imagination*. *Shattered* comes to life and delivered its album promise as his pouch probed outrageously. On *Respectable* he adopted his cross-pond drawl. The show climaxed with a rocking *Sweet Little Sixteen* before the two numbers taken from the late 60s. Nicky Hopkins and Bobby Keys joined the band for the final concerts in Anaheim and on Jagger's birthday in Oakland.

The Fort Worth sound recording, initially laid down by Showco's BJ Schiller, was re-mastered in 2011 by Bob Clearmountain. His job was to fine tune the sound quality and to set the relative levels from track to track to ensure the concert sound flowed. The entire performance illustrated great youthful exhilaration and it was a shame it would not stretch to the rest of the world. It was not released at the time because Mick was not happy that more concert film footage would not cover up any mistakes and, at 35 years of age, he felt he no longer looked youthful.

798. WHAT GIVES YOU THE RIGHT (Jagger, Richards) 5.03
AKA: The Right To Think
23 August - 7 September 1978: Place: Wally Heider (RCA) Studios, Hollywood, USA.
Rolling Stones with Ian McLagan.
Producer: The Glimmer Twins.
Engineer: Michael Carnavale.
Bootleg only.

At the end of the tour, the band stayed together to complete some Paris session material (*Summer Romance* was worked upon) in the RCA studios and also to record a few new numbers. It was as though Keith Richards wanted to concentrate on music rather than the impending Canadian trial and was a useful means of stockpiling songs should the worse happen. There are two out-takes. The first one has a count-in, with an up-front piano and guitar and clear vocals, while the other out-take is more keyboard based and has softer vocals (* a - 5.23). It is a passable ballad.

799. WHAT AM I LIVING FOR? (Harris, Jacobson) 9.35
AKA: If Not For You
23 August - 7 September 1978: Place: Wally Heider (RCA) Studios, Hollywood, USA.
Rolling Stones with Ian McLagan
Producer: The Glimmer Twins.
Engineer: Michael Carnavale.
Bootleg only.

This song, made popular by Chuck Willis in the late 50s, was also covered by Carl Perkins and The Animals. It is played with some irony as Keith awaited his fate. An electric organ accompanies Mick Jagger's plaintiff lyrics and there's a stinging guitar on this slow, calypso-style cruiser. An out-take is also available (* a - 7.05).

800. BLUES WITH A FEELING (Jacobs) 3.12
23 August - 7 September 1978: Place: Wally Heider (RCA) Studios, Hollywood, USA.
Producer: The Glimmer Twins.
Engineer: Michael Carnavale.
Bootleg only.

Little Walter (Marion Walter Jacobs) had toured with the Stones in Britain during 1964. He wrote music and was a virtuoso on the harmonica, playing with the Muddy Waters band before having single success in his own right. This has Jagger conservatively emulating his hero on a short harp solo, his role being more auspicious on vocals. Ian Stewart and Keith Richards play with feeling, recording authentic blues unlike anything they had done for many years.

801. MY FIRST PLEA (Reed, Reed) 4.14
23 August - 7 September 1978: Place: Wally Heider (RCA) Studios, Hollywood, USA.
Producer: The Glimmer Twins.
Engineer: Michael Carnavale.
Bootleg only.

Another one for the "Prison" album, Keith Richards sings vocals on this Jimmy and Mary Reed slow blues while Mick Jagger is on the harmonica. Ian McLagan asked Keith how to play it and Keith responded on the piano by playing "a death march". Four versions were recorded (* a - 4.50, b - 5.16, c - 3.50).

802. YOUR ANGEL STEPS OUT OF HEAVEN (Ripley) 3.05
23 August - 7 September 1978: Place: Wally Heider (RCA) Studios, Hollywood, USA.
Rolling Stones with Ian McLagan.
Producer: The Glimmer Twins.
Engineer: Michael Carnavale.
Bootleg only.

Songwriter Jack Ripley was, for many a year, a cohort of George Jones, who recorded this track as Elvis Costello also did later. It had come to Keith Richards' attention from Gram Parsons, who did a version with The Flying Burrito Brothers. Ronnie Wood plays pedal steel and Keith not only does the vocals (and over-dubbed backing vocals) but also probably the piano as well. Ian McLagan plays a very slow organ.

803. ONE NIGHT (Bartholomew, King) 2.50
23 August - 7 September 1978: Place: Wally Heider (RCA) Studios, Hollywood, USA.
Producer: The Glimmer Twins.
Engineer: Michael Carnavale.
Bootleg only.

A cover of Elvis Presley's hit. Some strident Ian Stewart piano opens the track and is followed by the guitars working themselves into the action. Mick Jagger's vocals were captured off mic' so can hardly be heard.

804. BACK IN THE USA (Berry) 2.05
23 August - 7 September 1978: Place: Wally Heider (RCA) Studios, Hollywood, USA.
Played Live: 1962
Producer: The Glimmer Twins.
Engineer: Michael Carnavale.
Bootleg only.

A quick jog around the USA on this version of the Chuck Berry song previously unrecorded by the Stones. It is likely that the piano player is Ian Stewart rather than Ian McLagan.

805. TALLAHASSEE LASSIE (Slay, Crewe, Picariello) 2.37
23 August - 7 September 1978; August - September 2011: Place: Wally Heider (RCA) Studios, Hollywood, USA; La Fourchette Home Studio, Fourchette, Tours, France, Electric Lady, New York, Berkeley St., Mix This!, Los Angeles, USA.
Rolling Stones with John Fogerty, Don Was.
Producer: Chris Kimsey, Don Was, The Glimmer Twins.
Engineer: Michael Carnavale. Recorded by Chris Kimsey.

Overdubs recorded by: Krish Sharma, Matt Clifford. Assisted by Phil Joly. Mixed by Bob Clearmountain. Assisted by Brandon Duncan. Mastered by Stephen Marcussen. Digital editing by Stewart Whitmore.

UK CD SOME GIRLS BONUS DISC: 21 November 2011: No. 57 - 1 week
USA CD SOME GIRLS BONUS DISC: 21 November 2011: No. 46 - 2 weeks

The classic Freddy Cannon (alias Frederico Anthony Picariello) song *Tallahassee Lassie* was covered by the Stones (* a - 2.37). The great Flamin' Groovies released a version in 1972 which Keith Richards would have been aware of, being a fan of their work. Many of the songs recorded at the RCA sessions were covers, which suggests they were played for loose enjoyment rather than any serious intention of them being recorded for an album. Barry Sage recalls the fun they had; he happened to be in the studio, but not this time in the capacity of an engineer, since he was a guest of Keith Richards and the band. He hung out for a few days, principally with Keith.

The sessions were lively and *Tallahassee Lassie* was worthy of the late release in 2011, having been selected by Don Was and Mick Jagger. For some reason, he thought it sounded like it had been done in a wind tunnel. However, it turned out really well with great 50s guitar, vocals and a driving rhythm complemented by Ian Stewart's rockabilly honky tonk. Additional overdubs of handclaps were made at Apogee's studios in Santa Monica's Berkeley Street. In the studio at the time was John Fogerty, who was recording one of his rare studio albums - so he joined in too.

806. I'LL LET YOU KNOW (Jagger, Richards) 6.55
23 August - 7 September 1978: Place: Wally Heider (RCA) Studios, Hollywood, USA.

Rolling Stones with Ian McLagan.
Producer: The Glimmer Twins.
Engineer: Michael Carnavale.
Bootleg only.

I'll Let You Know is an instrumental which looked as though it could have been worked on further. It has Ron Wood on bass and pedal steel, Ian McLagan on organ and Mick Jagger playing the electric piano. Keith Richards does a hook and riff that confirms the song's country rock-influenced potential. Ian McLagan recalls that he was about to record some vocals to the track when he fell asleep at the microphone and, when he awoke, the lyrics had vanished from his head.

807. I AIN'T SUPERSTITIOUS (Dixon) 4.21
23 August - 7 September 1978: Place: Wally Heider (RCA) Studios, Hollywood, USA.

Producer: The Glimmer Twins.
Engineer: Michael Carnavale.
Bootleg only.

Written by Willie Dixon, *I Ain't Superstitious* was most notably recorded by Howlin' Wolf. It had also been covered by Jeff Beck. Bill Wyman and Charlie Watts would have remembered playing the song with Howlin' Wolf for the 1971 album THE LONDON HOWLIN' WOLF SESSIONS, which also featured Eric Clapton and Steve Winwood. The Stones play it very straight without frills.

808. JIMMY REED BLUES JAM (Reed) 6.50
23 August - 7 September 1978: Place: Wally Heider (RCA) Studios, Hollywood, USA.

Rolling Stones with Ian McLagan.
Producer: The Glimmer Twins.
Engineer: Michael Carnavale.
Bootleg only.

Mick Jagger rasps on the harmonica throughout this blues jam. Ian Stewart and Ian McLagan perform the piano and organ roles respectively. The session was a success but none of it was released commercially as Ian McLagan remarked ruefully in his book *All The Rage* - a session fee had to be extracted like pulling teeth, painfully and slowly.

809. SERIOUS LOVE (Dunbar) 1.38
23 August - 7 September 1978: Place: Wally Heider (RCA) Studios, Hollywood, USA.

Rolling Stones with Ian McLagan.
Producer: The Glimmer Twins.
Engineer: Michael Carnavale.
Bootleg only.

A short out-take recorded by Ronnie Wood and Keith Richards with Sly Dunbar, the producer and percussionist for Peter Tosh's band. Naturally it is in the reggae style and has Keith doing the vocals.

810. THE HARDER THEY COME (Cliff) 3.47
23 August - 7 September 1978: Place: Wally Heider (RCA) Studios, Hollywood, USA.

Rolling Stones with Ian McLagan.
Producer: The Glimmer Twins.
Engineer: Michael Carnavale.
USA B-Side Run Rudolph Run: 12 December 1978

Keith Richards' favourite reggae song from the period was Jimmy Cliff's *The Harder They Come*. This recording was released with *Run Rudolph Run* as Keith's first solo single in December 1978. *Run Rudolph Run* was originally recorded on 10 December 1976 at Island Studios (aptly-named Fallout Shelter) in London with session drummer, Mike Driscoll and Ian Stewart. An out-take from this session has Mick Jagger on backing vocals (* a - 3.39).

811. **KNEE TREMBLER** (Jagger, Richards) 5.35
23 August - 7 September 1978: Place: Wally Heider (RCA) Studios, Hollywood, USA.
Rolling Stones with Ian McLagan, Bobby Keys.
Producer: The Glimmer Twins.
Engineer: Michael Carnavale.
Bootleg only.

It had been a while since Bobby Keys had appeared as a session player. This five minute, 30 second instrumental, with a heavy organ underneath, is a jazz funk number with a strong bass line.

812. **SUMMER ROMANCE** (Jagger, Richards) 6.25
6 October 1978: Place: NBC TV Studios, New York, USA.
Rolling Stones with Ian McLagan.
Producer: Lorne Michaels
Bootleg only.

813. **BEAST OF BURDEN** (Jagger, Richards) 5.13
7 October 1978: Place: NBC TV Studios, New York, USA.
Rolling Stones with Ian McLagan.
Producer: Lorne Michaels
UK & USA DVD Some Girls: De Luxe: 21 November 2011

814. **RESPECTABLE** (Jagger, Richards) 3.13
7 October 1978: Place: NBC TV Studios, New York, USA.
Rolling Stones with Ian McLagan.
Producer: Lorne Michaels
UK & USA DVD Some Girls: De Luxe: 21 November 2011

815. **SHATTERED** (Jagger, Richards) 4.15
7 October 1978: Place: NBC TV Studios, New York, USA.
Rolling Stones with Ian McLagan.
Producer: Lorne Michaels
UK & USA DVD Some Girls: De Luxe: 21 November 2011

At the end of August, the *Beast Of Burden* single was released in the USA while, in the UK, *Respectable* was about to go Top 30 late September 1978. To promote these events the Stones were booked on the first Saturday Night Live TV programme of the new series on 7 October 1978, for the princely sum of $350. The live musical extracts were released on the DVD part of the SOME GIRLS: DE LUXE album released in 2011. The programme included John Belushi, Bill Murray, Jane Curtin, Garrett Morris, Gilda Radner, Laraine Newman and Dan Aykroyd.

The format was sketches, live music and interviews and the band hosted the show. One sketch that was cut was a mock interview where Keith Richards was asked if he was doing a gig in February. He replied that every February he goes to Switzerland to get his blood changed! The three songs performed live were *Beast Of Burden*, *Respectable* and *Shattered*. They are marred by Mick Jagger's vocals as he had lost his voice during rehearsal. They are the closest he gets in intonation to Keith!

Memorably, on an impulse, Mick kisses Ronnie full on the lips. Rehearsals can also be captured on bootleg and that is the source of the reggae or calypso version of *Summer Romance*. Ronnie holds up proceedings up at one point as he is literally "out of sight". He is reminded by Jagger that he is one of the group. A version of *Respectable* comes crashing to an abrupt stop during Ron's solo as the band leap forward in different directions. Just like making wine, sums up Keith, except we miss out the fermenting part.

They played up to the faster punk sound with Mick wearing a ripped Beast t-shirt, orange tight trousers and sneakers while Keith was in leather jacket with tight striped tie. From a personal stance things were getting better for Keith, he was off heroin and, in advance of his trial, lawyers had negotiated the reduced charges of possessing heroin, not trafficking. So, on 23 October, Keith went to face the music. The sentence a day later was one year's probation, to continue his drug treatment and to play a benefit concert for the Canadian Institute for the Blind within six months.

This unusual demand was in part due to a blind girl fan, who personally went to the judge's house to plead for him not to be imprisoned and also because of the quality of Keith's lawyer and plea bargaining. Keith referred to the fan as the "blind angel". He had protected her when she followed the Stones on the 1978 tour by ensuring that she was looked after at concerts. He feared she would get run over. In the video *25 X 5*, there is an emotional interview in which Keith tells this story.

Jane Rose, Keith's personal manager, concluded that the blind girl's intervention probably saved the cat's ninth life. Naturally, Keith was delighted at the compassion showed. He later acknowledged that the Canadians had been very kind to him, which was true as, from then on, the cops drove him to the office (a concert performance) and took him back home again.

On the 25 October, Keith celebrated his freedom and joined Dave Edmunds and Nick Lowe with their band Rockpile at the Bottom Line in New York. It was thought the Stones might follow up their '78 tour with a European itinerary but this did not happen. Keith related in early 1979 that a gig at the small Paris Le Palais Theatre was booked but somehow the press leaked the news and the band cancelled it. Originally, in an Atlantic press release in May 1978, they planned to undertake a whirlwind detour from the USA to Europe for one concert each in a British, French and West German city.

816. IT'S COLD DOWN THERE (Jagger, Richards) 3.37
18 January - 12 February 1979: Place: Compass Point Studios, Nassau, Bahamas, USA.
Producer: The Glimmer Twins. Associate Producer: Chris Kimsey.
Engineer: Chris Kimsey.
Bootleg only.

The first sessions for the EMOTIONAL RESCUE album were in January 1979. The choice this time was the beautifully-located beachside Compass Point Studios, near Nassau, in the Bahamas. They were founded by the owner of Island Records, Chris Blackwell in 1977. Chris Kimsey was with the band to assist the recording process. A repetitive reggae, calypso beat played on guitar and the cymbal work of Charlie Watts are the sounds that assault you on this number. Another guitar enters the track and Mick Jagger joins in with "la-la's" on unfinished lyrics. A shorter version also exists (* a - 1.36).

817. I THINK I'M GOING MAD (Jagger, Richards) 4.12
AKA: *Think I'm Going Mad*
18 January - 12 February 1979; 11 November - 16 December 1982; June - July 1983: Place: Compass Point Studios, Nassau, Bahamas, USA; EMI, Pathé Marconi Studios, Paris, France; The Hit Factory, New York, USA.
Rolling Stones with Mel Collins.
Producer: The Glimmer Twins.
Engineer: Bob Clearmountain.
Recorded by: Chris Kimsey.
UK B-side She Was Hot: 24 January 1984
USA B-side She Was Hot: 24 January 1984
UK Promo Single She Was Hot (DJ Version): 24 January 1984
UK CD box set THE SINGLES COLLECTION 1971-2006: 45 X 45s: 11 April 2011
USA CD box set THE SINGLES COLLECTION 1971-2006: 45 X 45s: 26 April 2011

At first it was considered for the EMOTIONAL RESCUE album but *Going Mad* was finally released in 1984 as the flip-side of *She Was Hot*, having been re-mixed at the Hit Factory Studios in New York. Not considered strong enough for the album, it was a slow, self-ridiculing number and a welcome change from the usual "B-side from the album" rip off. It started life in 1979 at Nassau, where there is an out-take without sax and some falsetto vocals (* a - 6.49). It was completed in 1983 with final overdubs.
Mel Collins, who also played on *Miss You*, is the saxophone player, although Ron Wood is also said to have recorded the tenor sax for another extended version of the original version (* b - 5.47). Some copies of these were heard on American radio stations when the official version was released. Along with the sax, the country steel guitars by Ron Wood and the Ian Stewart piano are, again, the track's prominent instruments. The song had frustrated Chris Kimsey since he felt it needed more at the end, hence the contact with Mel Collins during the UNDERCOVER sessions, asking him to supply the sax. Keith Richards is on backing vocals.
In 1982, a 15-minute sax version was re-recorded with Keith on vocals (* c - 14.57). Due to the recordings stretching over a number of years, the brass saxophone credits differ. Along with Mel Collins, David Sanborn or even Steve Madaio are often credited as playing on this song. It may have been considered for the EMOTIONAL RESCUE album and also the RARITIES album in 2005 but the master tape could not be located.

818. SWEET HOME CHICAGO (Johnson) 4.49
18 January - 12 February 1979: Place: Compass Point Studios, Nassau, Bahamas, USA.
Producer: The Glimmer Twins. Associate Producer: Chris Kimsey.
Engineer: Chris Kimsey.
Bootleg only.

A slow Robert Johnson blues song, also credited to Woody Payne, which the band seem to enjoy. Keith is at home meandering along the fret-board. Well worth a listen!

819. STILL IN LOVE (Jagger, Richards) 5.22
18 January - 12 February 1979; 11 November - 16 December 1982: Place: Compass Point Studios, Nassau, Bahamas, USA; EMI, Pathé Marconi Studios, Paris, France.
Producer: The Glimmer Twins.
Associate Producer: Chris Kimsey.
Engineer: Chris Kimsey.
Bootleg only.

Still In Love was worked on over two sessions, ending up as a possibility for the UNDERCOVER album. The Compass out-take is a guitar version with vocals including falsetto (* a - 1.45), while two out-takes from Paris are instrumentals, the longer one having ghost vocals (* b - 7.29). It seemed to be a Keith Richards melody which worked slightly better on a piano version, rather than just electric guitar. The out-take from UNDERCOVER is again an instrumental (* c - 5.38). Chris Kimsey thought it was actually a beautiful melody that could have been worked on further. For the Paris sessions, Ron Wood played a country style guitar. It may also have been re-cut in 2002, when recording the extra tracks for FORTY LICKS, illustrating its potential.

820. SANDS OF TIME (Jagger, Richards)
18 January - 12 February 1979: Place: Compass Point Studios, Nassau, Bahamas, USA.
Producer: The Glimmer Twins.
Associate Producer: Chris Kimsey.
Engineer: Chris Kimsey.
Unavailable.

Rumoured to have been recorded at the session but unavailable.

821. **LONELY AT THE TOP** (Jagger, Richards) 4.40
18 January - 12 February 1979: Place: Compass Point Studios, Nassau, Bahamas, USA.
Producer: The Glimmer Twins.
Associate Producer: Chris Kimsey. Engineer: Chris Kimsey.
Bootleg only.

Mick Jagger was evidently fond of this song since he re-recorded it with Jeff Beck and Pete Townsend on his 1985 solo album SHE'S THE BOSS. The lyrics were altered and generally it was given an uplift compared with this duller version.

822. **GUITAR LESSON** (Jagger, Richards) 4.06
AKA: **Again And Again And Again**
18 January - 12 February 1979: Place: Compass Point Studios, Nassau, Bahamas, USA.
Producer: The Glimmer Twins.
Associate Producer: Chris Kimsey. Engineer: Chris Kimsey.
Bootleg only.

An instrumental mainly featuring a repetitive riff and Ron Wood on a Dick Dale sounding fast-picked surf guitar. The Beach Boys were heavily influenced by the guitar of Dick Dale.

823. **NEVER TOO INTO** (Jagger, Richards) 5.04
18 January - 12 February 1979: Place: Compass Point Studios, Nassau, Bahamas, USA.
Producer: The Glimmer Twins.
Associate Producer: Chris Kimsey. Engineer: Chris Kimsey.
Bootleg only.

A guitar work-out which probably includes Mick Jagger. There is a fast soloing guitar, Keith's rhythm and a picking boogie rhythm guitar. Mick sings some catchy escalating "ooh-ooh-ooh's" to some unfinished lyrics.

824. **LET'S GO STEADY AGAIN** (Alexander) 2.51
AKA: **She Left Me, Let's Go Steady**
18 January - 12 February 1979: Place: Compass Point Studios, Nassau, Bahamas, USA.
Rolling Stones with Kristi Kimsey.
Producer: The Glimmer Twins.
Associate Producer: Chris Kimsey. Engineer: Chris Kimsey.
Bootleg only.

A classic out-take featuring a duet between Keith Richards and Kristi Kimsey on this 1959 James Alexander-penned Sam Cooke tune, which was the B-side to *Only Sixteen*. Neil Sedaka later covered it in 1963 and enjoyed a single chart entry with it. Keith knew that Kristi was a vocalist, having seen her recording with Crystal Grass in the next door Pathé Marconi Studio, Paris, for a 1978 European disco concept album LOVE TRAIN.
On one occasion in Nassau, when Keith was working late, he called her in the middle of the night and asked if she could pop down to the studio. Explaining that she might not give her best vocal performance she agreed to meet up the next day. She walked in to the studio and listened to the backing track recorded the previous night, with Ron Wood on saxophone. Then, with Keith, she took to the stage - much to husband Chris Kimsey's surprise - and improvised the duet, not even agreeing which lines they would sing. Kristi recalled that, for some reason, the control room was full of onlookers but together the cut was made. It is a splendid ballad full of soulful ramblings. Chris was very proud that she did such a fantastic performance on it. The studio track has never been released. Later that year it would be played live as part of the New Barbarians' set list.
The Stones recorded in Nassau principally because the Bahamas did not have the same tax restraints as the USA but it benefitted Keith because he loved the sun. The session was the first since Keith's court appearance, Chris Kimsey describing it as happy and playful. Keith was particularly triumphal and also in love, being in the middle of a relationship with Scandinavian Lil Wergilis.

825. **JAH IS NOT DEAD** (Jagger, Richards) 10.47
18 January - 12 February 1979: Place: Compass Point Studios, Nassau, Bahamas, USA.
Rolling Stones with Max Romeo, Boz Scaggs.
Producer: The Glimmer Twins.
Associate Producer: Chris Kimsey. Engineer: Chris Kimsey.
Bootleg only.

Jah Is Not Dead may have been inspired by the 1978 film *Rockers*, which was about Jamaican life and featured local reggae artists. One of these was Winston Rodney, who was the man behind the band Burning Spear. *Jah No Dead* was sung by him on a beach acapella-style, with the noise of the surf lapping, to teach another cast member the power of religion within Jah. Keith Richards and Ron Wood were clearly influenced by the sound of reggae. It was about this time that Keith recorded with Black Uhuru, which had been formed by Robbie Shakespeare, Keith Sterling and Sly Dunbar, from the Peter Tosh band.
The Stones recorded *Jah Is Not Dead* with the help of reggae singer Max Romeo and Boz Scaggs (ex of Steve Miller Band and now a solo recording artist in his own right) on vocals. It is obviously set to a reggae beat and has some raging guitar work. Chris Kimsey was not present when Max and Boz recorded their parts. Mick Jagger performs the vocals for the first part of the song before solo reggae artist Max takes up the lyrics - about 2,000 years of Christianity - before ending with Mick and Max skanking and chanting together "Jah Is Not Dead" on this near 11-minute epic.

826. **BLUES JAM** (Jagger, Richards) 3.05
18 January - 12 February 1979: Place: Compass Point Studios, Nassau, Bahamas, USA.
Producer: The Glimmer Twins.
Associate Producer: Chris Kimsey. Engineer: Chris Kimsey.
Bootleg only.

Two blues out-takes from Nassau (* a - 1.40).

827. **GUESS I SHOULD KNOW** (Jagger, Richards) 4.06
18 January - 12 February 1979: Place: Compass Point Studios, Nassau, Bahamas, USA.
Producer: The Glimmer Twins.
Associate Producer: Chris Kimsey. Engineer: Chris Kimsey.
Bootleg only.

A slow number with a prominent lead guitar. There are some rough vocals at the start. Definitely an out-take.

828. **YOU LEFT ME** (Jagger, Richards)
18 January - 12 February 1979: Place: Compass Point Studios, Nassau, Bahamas, USA.
Producer: The Glimmer Twins.
Associate Producer: Chris Kimsey. Engineer: Chris Kimsey.
Unavailable.

Bill Wyman, in his *Rolling With The Stones* book, quotes *You Left Me* as being considered for album inclusion in March 1980. Since it may have been near completion and has not appeared on bootleg, it may have been another out-take under a different name or even a later track such as *Pretty Beat Up*.

829. **YOU'RE SO BEAUTIFUL** (Jagger, Richards)
18 January - 12 February 1979: Place: Compass Point Studios, Nassau, Bahamas, USA.
Producer: The Glimmer Twins.
Associate Producer: Chris Kimsey. Engineer: Chris Kimsey.
Unavailable.

An unverified out-take.

830. **BREAK AWAY** (Jagger, Richards) 4.30
AKA: Chain Reaction Groove
18 January - 12 February 1979: Place: Compass Point Studios, Nassau, Bahamas, USA.
Producer: The Glimmer Twins.
Associate Producer: Chris Kimsey. Engineer: Chris Kimsey.
Bootleg only.

A song played with the raunch and pace of *Tumbling Dice*. Mick Jagger's vocals are not understandable.

831. **SHE'S SO COLD** (Jagger, Richards) 4.13
AKA: Stuck In The Cold, She's So Cold (God Damn Version)
18 January - 12 February; 25 June - 9 August, 30 August - October 1979: Place: Compass Point Studios, Nassau, Bahamas, USA; EMI, Pathé Marconi Studios, Paris, France.
Played Live: 1981, 1982, 2005, 2006, 2007
Rolling Stones with Bobby Keys.
Producer: The Glimmer Twins.
Associate Producer: Chris Kimsey.
Engineer: Sean Fullan, Brad Samuelsohn, David 'Snake' Reynolds, Jon Smith.
UK LP EMOTIONAL RESCUE: 20 June 1980: No. 1 - 18 weeks
USA LP EMOTIONAL RESCUE: 23 June 1980: No. 1 - 20 weeks
USA Single: 10 September 1980: No. 26 - 5 weeks
USA Promo Single: 10 September 1980
UK Single: 22 September 1980: No. 33 - 6 weeks
UK Compilation LP REWIND 1971-1984 (THE BEST OF THE ROLLING STONES): 2 July 1984: No. 45 - 5 weeks
UK CD box set THE SINGLES COLLECTION 1971-2006: 45 X 45s: 11 April 2011
USA CD box set THE SINGLES COLLECTION 1971-2006: 45 X 45s: 26 April 2011

A mid-tempo rocker reminiscent of *Shattered* and written by Mick Jagger, where the rhythm guitars of Keith Richards and Ron Wood jostle for attention. The guitar effect for the rockabilly sound is dampened tape delay. They hardly break sweat, playing on the dexterity of their string-driven fingers. Ron Wood felt quite at ease in this situation, where neither was labelled as lead guitarist. It was not constrictive and allowed the band to free-flow around the song's main structure. Some better than average material was needed now on which to work.
Jagger was "hot, hot, hot", up and erupting for it, in more ways than one but the young girl in question was just not interested or ready. An early, seven-minute out-take with piano and guide vocals but missing the understated sax on the released cut, is available (* a - 6.51). *She's So Cold* (to paraphrase "frigid like a refrigerator") was the second single from the album, a Jagger favourite and was unsuccessful.

In Britain it was their worst chart position (No. 33) ever, remaining there for a very cool six weeks. Dave Mallet's humorous video, which was partly shot in an ice compartment, did nothing to assist the defrosted music. It was also known as *Stuck In The Cold* and was even recorded as such, presumably with different lyrics. A promo version was released for radio stations in the United States, minus a reference to the Arctic girl being "goddamn cold" (* b - 4.06).

The frozen tongue that adorned the single sleeve was created by John Pasche who was the original red tongue designer. John Pasche has since been a cover designer for many bands including some great artwork for Budgie plus the memorable branding of Judas Priest, Whitesnake and Jeff Wayne. He even worked with the Stones on the album cover for GOATS HEAD SOUP. The promo single was coupled with *She's So Cold (God Damn Version)* which was the album cut.

832. ALL ABOUT YOU (Jagger, Richards) 4.18
AKA: The Train Song, Tram Song
18 January - 12 February; November - December 1979: Place: Compass Point Studios, Nassau, Bahamas, USA; Electric Lady Studios, New York, USA.
Played Live: 1997, 1998, 1999
Rolling Stones with Bobby Keys.
Producer: The Glimmer Twins.
Associate Producer: Chris Kimsey. Engineer: Sean Fullan, Brad Samuelsohn, David 'Snake' Reynolds, Jon Smith.
UK LP EMOTIONAL RESCUE: 20 June 1980: No. 1 - 18 weeks
USA LP EMOTIONAL RESCUE: 23 June 1980: No. 1 - 20 weeks

Written by Keith Richards, the album release was delayed until he was convinced that the track had not been subconsciously copied from another artist. Keith performs as lead vocalist, a velvet balladeer, on some fine lyrics. He provided most of the instrumentation, including bass guitar and piano. Charlie Watts enjoyed playing it and especially liked the song, later calling it a classic. It was a bitter sweet romantic song, expressing Keith's anger with "lies and deceit and jerks like you", but ending with a conciliatory "so how come I'm still in love with you?" Do they purport to be about Keith's failed relationship with Anita Pallenberg or actually, more likely, the strains of life with Mick?

In reality on release, it became a song about everyone when they first heard it, even Keith's children. The song was recorded especially because he wanted *Dance* to remain as an instrumental rather than Mick Jagger's vocal version. Eventually, Keith had to relent but the rift had ensured that, from this album onwards, there was always a "Keith track". On closing the last bars of the song, Keith grabbed his Jack Daniels bottle to exit the studio and cut himself, poetically leaving a blood trail across the floor for what was EMOTIONAL RESCUE's last take. It is a pity the record company never pressed Keith to release the promised solo album.

Works such as this and the rejected *Let's Go Steady*, would have formed a good basis for an individual album. When the Stones renewed their worldwide record company deals, the only solo guaranteed project was that of Mick Jagger. Keith was unaware of this arrangement. He thought (perhaps wisely) that solo projects could only disrupt the direction of the Stones and he was not going to be the first (well, second after Bill Wyman) to do so. However, he did tour with Ronnie Wood's New Barbarians in April, May and August, which Mick was not particularly happy with.

833. LINDA LU (Sharpe) 4.34
18 January - 12 February 1979: Place: Compass Point Studios, Nassau, Bahamas, USA.
Producer: The Glimmer Twins.
Associate Producer: Chris Kimsey.
Engineer: Chris Kimsey.
Bootleg only.

The Stones recorded approximately 40 songs during 1979 for the EMOTIONAL RESCUE album but only 25 were of an acceptable standard. The creative juices had dried up a little and the Mick Jagger and Keith Richards dynamics were still finding their legs, now that Keith wanted to contribute more. It was the least satisfying of Chris Kimsey's work with them but he did find that the winter's sun went some way to energise the band and compensate somewhat.

During leisure times, Keith worshipped the sun and Chris enjoyed accompanying Ian Stewart to go snorkeling and diving in the warm seas. *Linda Lu* is one which did not make the mastering stage. It is a soft rock and roll, almost a rockabilly number, on which Ron Wood and Keith are kept conservatively employed - but only just! Mick ad-libs the lyrics at the end singing, ". . . had a real bad dream last night, she went and fucked Ronnie". The song was a hit for Texan blues player Ray Sharpe and was covered by Bobby Vee in 1963. Perhaps Bobby Keys introduced the song to the band.

834. WHAT'S THE MATTER? (Jagger, Richards) 4.44
18 January - 12 February 1979: Place: Compass Point Studios, Nassau, Bahamas, USA.
Producer: The Glimmer Twins.
Associate Producer: Chris Kimsey.
Engineer: Chris Kimsey.
Bootleg only.

What's The Matter? is acceptable as an out-take. The guitar work is bluesy and accompanied by presumably an over-dubbed harp and an Ian Stewart Nashville piano. Mick Jagger can be heard prompting the band on scale changes.

835. BULLDOG (Jagger, Richards) 3.50
AKA: Little T & A
18 January - 12 February 1979: Place: Compass Point Studios, Nassau, Bahamas, USA.
Producer: The Glimmer Twins.
Associate Producer: Chris Kimsey.
Engineer: Chris Kimsey.
Bootleg only.

836. **LITTLE T & A** (Jagger, Richards) 3.23
AKA: Bulldog
18 January - 12 February 1979: Place: Compass Point Studios, Nassau, Bahamas, USA.
Played Live: 1981, 1982, 2006, 2007
Producer: The Glimmer Twins. Associate Producer: Chris Kimsey.
Engineer: Chris Kimsey, Bob Clearmountain, Gary Lyons, Bob Ludwig.
USA LP TATTOO YOU: 18 August 1981: No. 1 - 30 weeks
UK LP TATTOO YOU: 28 August 1981: No. 2 - 29 weeks
USA B-side Waiting On A Friend: 17 November 1981
UK B-side Waiting On A Friend: 30 November 1981
UK CD box set THE SINGLES COLLECTION 1971-2006: 45 X 45s: 11 April 2011
USA CD box set THE SINGLES COLLECTION 1971-2006: 45 X 45s: 26 April 2011

Mick Jagger's frustrations on *She's So Cold* were satisfied by Keith Richards' "bitch who keeps bitching", "the snitcher who keeps snitching" and "the juice that keeps pumping". He also acknowledged that the dealers were squealing as he was off heroin. Prices must have nose-dived! The classic line "the pool's in but the patio ain't dry" is a reference to Lenny Bruce's 20-minute routine, "The Palladium" about the comedian's manager, who states, "the pool isn't in yet but the patio's dry". Keith had read the book, *The Essential Lenny Bruce*, which quotes the 1958 skit. Was Keith's interpretation due to the lure of an underage bitch with soul? Keith takes the lead vocals on what was initially a song labelled *Bulldog*. The instrumental out-take has a *She's So Cold*-style opening and pronounced pedal steel slide guitar played by Ron Wood. It is very different to the end product, a clean digital cassette version showing it off with wonderful sound. There are longer out-takes with unfinished lyrics but with the guitar riff opening (* a - 3.41, b - 4.13).

The track was recorded at the EMOTIONAL RESCUE sessions and intended for that album but put aside until it was remixed in 1981 by Bob Clearmountain and Gary Lyons for the rush job of the album TATTOO YOU. The Stones wanted an album with which to tour but did not have sufficient time or inclination to record a full LP's worth of material, hence the tracks being pulled from anywhere. Chris Kimsey realised that there would be many tapes with hidden gems that could be used to compile a new album. He found some from GOATS HEAD SOUP, BLACK AND BLUE, SOME GIRLS and EMOTIONAL RESCUE.

From the opening guitar chords *Little T & A* is full of excitement. Guitar riffs and lead breaks courtesy of Keith abound while he twists his tongue around the vocal slang - T & A standing for "tits and ass". Mick joins in on backing vocals. *Little T & A* was released as the B-side of *Waiting On A Friend*. Incidentally, The Bulldogs was a pseudonym later used by the band when mixing the UNDERCOVER album in 1983. It is not a song often played live but was heard on the A BIGGER BANG tour in 2006 and captured on BIGGEST BANG. Keith fondly relates the song now to his daughters, Theodora and Alexandra, so maybe his wife Patti has relented from her original distaste for it.

837. **BEFORE THEY MAKE ME RUN** (Jagger, Richards) ✗ 3.10
22 April 1979: Place: Oshawa Civic Auditorium, Toronto, Canada.
Bootleg only.

In late February 1979, Mick Jagger and Keith Richards returned to New York from Nassau. Mick was served divorce papers from Bianca Jagger. He was still visiting the Studio 54 nightclub but Keith was not as impressed with the venue, though he still attended with his comedian pal John Belushi. He reckoned they ruined a good theatre by turning it into a place full of "faggots in boxing shorts waving champagne bottles in front of your face." One night, while out with John Phillips and being chased by Britt Ekland, Keith called in to Studio 54.

Coincidentally, model Patti Hansen was there celebrating her 23rd birthday and Keith soon became besotted, though he would not meet her again until his own birthday, in December. Meanwhile, Mick Jagger put forward a submission to embassy officials as to why the Rolling Stones should play in China. If they agreed, then maybe a tour could be mounted but Mick was not hopeful. Back in the UK, elections were held in May, following which Margaret Thatcher, the "iron lady" became Prime Minister.

838. **PRODIGAL SON** (Wilkins) ✗ 3.06
22 April 1979: Place: Oshawa Civic Auditorium, Toronto, Canada.
Bootleg only.

The time had come for Keith Richards' fracas with the Canadian authorities to be put to rest. Among other conditions set by the authorities, he had to play in Toronto in aid of the Canadian National Institute for The Blind. Ron Wood had formed a touring band for his solo album GIMME SOME NECK, named The New Barbarians by Neil Young. It consisted of Keith as special guest guitarist, Bobby Keys (sax), Ian McLagan (keyboards), Stanley Clarke (bass) and Joseph "Zigaboo" Modeliste (drums). They provided the basis for the free concert held on 22 April 1979.

Before They Make Me Run and *Prodigal Son* had apt titles and were the climax of the two sets the Barbarians performed that day - with Keith on vocals and a sparse, acoustic duet by Mick Jagger and Keith. Then at the end came the full Rolling Stones line-up on stage, a surprise to the ecstatic Canadian crowd. They opened with *Let It Rock* before continuing with nine songs, consisting of *Respectable*, *Star Star*, *Beast Of Burden*, *Just My Imagination*, *When The Whip Comes Down*, *Shattered*, *Miss You* and *Jumping Jack Flash*. Mick told the audience that Keith was delighted to appear here in such a worthwhile event. This was the last time the Stones played together until 1981.

In April and May, The Barbarians' tour travelled around the United States without the rest of the Stones, a time when Keith began to slip back into his old habits. In July, as previously related, a young male friend staying with Anita Pallenberg was fatally injured in a tragic shooting incident. The event also provided the death knell of Keith's and Anita's relationship, especially as Keith was happy with his new girl in his life, Lil Wergilis, who he described later as a breath of fresh air. During the summer, the Stones continued recording in Paris. The sessions were spent mainly touching up EMOTIONAL RESCUE material but a few new recordings were made. In August 1979, Ronnie and Keith combined again for a one-off UK concert at Knebworth, where Led Zeppelin were headlining two huge concerts, one weekend after another. These turned out to be the last Led Zeppelin concerts on British soil. The New Barbarians could only make one of the dates, on 11 August.

839. DANCE (INSTRUMENTAL) (Jagger, Richards, Wood) 4.37
25 June - 9 August, 30 August - October; November - December 1979: Place: EMI, Pathé Marconi Studios, Paris, France; Electric Lady Studios, New York, USA.
Rolling Stones with Bobby Keys, Michael Shrieve, Max Romeo.
Producer: The Glimmer Twins. Associate Producer: Chris Kimsey.
Engineer: Sean Fullan, Brad Samuelsohn, David 'Snake' Reynolds, Jon Smith.
USA Promo 12-inch Track If I Was A Dancer (Dance Part Two): March 1981

This version is a rare promotional only (RSR / DMD 253) instrumental issue made as the flip side of *If I Was A Dancer (Dance Part Two)*, which was released to coincide with the SUCKING IN THE SEVENTIES album. Keith Richards wanted the track to remain as an instrumental but Mick Jagger insisted on the addition of vocals.

840. IF I WAS A DANCER (DANCE PART TWO) (Jagger, Richards, Wood) 5.50
25 June - 9 August, 30 August - October; November - December 1979; 25 November - December 1980: Place: EMI, Pathé Marconi Studios, Paris, France; Electric Lady Studios, New York, USA; EMI, Pathé Marconi Studios, Paris, France
Rolling Stones with Bobby Keys, Michael Shrieve, Max Romeo.
Producer: The Glimmer Twins. Associate Producer: Chris Kimsey.
Engineer: Sean Fullan, Brad Samuelsohn, David 'Snake' Reynolds, Jon Smith.
USA Compilation LP SUCKING IN THE SEVENTIES: 12 March 1981: No. 15 - 5 weeks
USA Promo 12-inch Single: March 1981
UK Compilation LP SUCKING IN THE SEVENTIES: 13 April 1981
USA CD LP ROLLING STONES RARITIES 1971-2003: 22 November 2005: No. 76 - 6 weeks
UK CD LP ROLLING STONES RARITIES 1971-2003: 28 November 2005

841. DANCE (Jagger, Richards, Wood) 4.23
25 June - 9 August, 30 August - October; November - December 1979: Place: EMI, Pathé Marconi Studios, Paris, France; Electric Lady Studios, New York, USA.
Played Live: 2002, 2003
Rolling Stones with Bobby Keys, Michael Shrieve, Max Romeo.
Producer: The Glimmer Twins. Associate Producer: Chris Kimsey.
Engineer: Sean Fullan, Brad Samuelsohn, David 'Snake' Reynolds, Jon Smith.
UK LP EMOTIONAL RESCUE: 20 June 1980: No. 1 - 18 weeks
USA LP EMOTIONAL RESCUE: 23 June 1980: No. 1 - 20 weeks

Here we have three variations on a theme of rhythmic mayhem instigated by Santana drummer, Michael Shrieve, on percussion and the monkey-like back-up vocals of reggae artist Max Romeo. The Electric Ladyland Studios were used just for album over-dubs. This would have included vocals, since the lyrics feature the Electric Lady location. Texan expatriate Bobby Keys, ever loyal to the Stones, supports the cause on saxophone.
Ron Wood, practiced at the art of deception, is credited as a co-songwriter with Jagger and Richards, mostly written by Ronnie, but with help from Mick Jagger and guitar parts by Keith Richards. Mick wrote the verbose lyrics. The first version, *Dance*, was recorded in one take and was subsequently released on the EMOTIONAL RESCUE album, its beat laced with funk. It was a great track and typical of the disco dance era. Chris Kimsey reflected: *"Dance is actually ahead of its time, quite innovative."* Different lyrics on top of a different mix of *Dance* continue the story on *If I Was A Dancer*, a mix which remained unreleased for almost a year until the appearance of the compilation SUCKING IN THE SEVENTIES. Prior to this, *If I Was A Dancer* had been widely bootlegged. Mick intended that *Dance* would be the second single, coupled with *If I Was A Dancer*. There are at least three long early out-takes of *Dance*, with different lyrics and openings (* a - 6.54, b - 7.40, c - 8.04). The released album versions combined would have produced a worthwhile 12-inch single. It opened the new album and the disco beat was an attempt at contemporary appeal but, but as Mick said: "it is time to get into something new".

842. WE HAD IT ALL (Seals, Fritts) 2.54
25 June - 9 August, 30 August - October 1979; August - September 2011: Place: EMI, Pathé Marconi Studios, Paris, France; La Fourchette Home Studio, Fourchette, Tours, France, Electric Lady, New York, Berkeley St., Mix This!, Los Angeles, USA.
Rolling Stones with Sugar Blue.
Producer: Chris Kimsey, Don Was, The Glimmer Twins.
Engineer: Recorded by: Chris Kimsey
Overdubs recorded by: Krish Sharma, Matt Clifford. Assisted by Phil Joly. Mixed by Bob Clearmountain. Assisted by Brandon Duncan. Mastered by Stephen Marcussen. Digital editing by Stewart Whitmore.
UK & USA CD SOME GIRLS BONUS DISC: 21 November 2011

We Had It All is a Troy Seals and Donnie Fritts composition. Green On Red covered it to good effect on their 1988 album HERE COME THE SNAKES, with Jim Dickinson of Muscles Shoals fame. Mick Jagger, for the SOME GIRLS retrospective, assumed that Keith Richards may have listened to it through Waylon Jennings, from his HONKY TONK HEROES album with *"Crazy Arms"* Ralph Mooney on steel guitar. Apparently Waylon always said: "Hell, there's only one steel guitar player, and it's Ralph Mooney." *We Had It All* was taken from it and charted at No. 28 in the USA in 1974. With Keith taking the piano and lead vocals, his gold-labelled voice glides competently over what is quite a sentimental song. There is some gentle harmonica work by Sugar Blue. This is not on a couple of out-takes (* a - 2.55, b - 2.55). The song was included within The New Barbarians' set list, Sugar Blue playing with the band at Knebworth. Ron Wood adds an excellent pedal steel guitar but the moment belongs to Keith.
There were no cover songs on the EMOTIONAL RESCUE album, which may be why this passable cut was not released until the SOME GIRLS re-issue project in 2011. Mick Jagger had to ask Don Was whether it was a Keith penned tune when he was first heard it again. The instrumentation is mainly unchanged but there seems to be a new vocal track and maybe an acoustic by Keith that was probably completed at Electric Lady Studios in New York.

843. **EMOTIONAL RESCUE** (Jagger, Richards) 5.39
25 June - 9 August, 30 August - October; November - December 1979: Place: EMI, Pathé Marconi Studios, Paris, France; Electric Lady Studios, New York, USA.
Rolling Stones with Bobby Keys, Max Romeo.
Producer: The Glimmer Twins.
Associate Producer: Chris Kimsey.
Engineer: Sean Fullan, Brad Samuelsohn, David 'Snake' Reynolds, Jon Smith.
UK Single: 20 June 1980: No. 9 - 8 weeks
USA Single: 20 June 1980: No. 3 - 14 weeks
USA 12-inch Promo Single: 20 June 1980
UK LP EMOTIONAL RESCUE: 20 June 1980: No. 1 - 18 weeks
USA LP EMOTIONAL RESCUE: 23 June 1980: No. 1 - 20 weeks
USA Compilation LP REWIND 1971-1984 (THE BEST OF THE ROLLING STONES): 3 July 1984: No. 86 - 11 weeks
UK Compilation CD REWIND 1971-1984 (THE BEST OF THE ROLLING STONES): 27 November 1986
UK Compilation LP JUMP BACK THE BEST OF THE ROLLING STONES '71 - '93: 22 November 1993: No. 16 - 26 weeks
UK CD LP FORTY LICKS: 30 September 2002: No. 2 - 45 weeks
USA CD LP FORTY LICKS: 1 October 2002: No. 2 - 50 weeks
USA Compilation CD JUMP BACK THE BEST OF THE ROLLING STONES '71 - '93: 24 August 2004: No. 30 - 58 weeks
UK CD box set THE SINGLES COLLECTION 1971-2006: 45 X 45s: 11 April 2011
USA CD box set THE SINGLES COLLECTION 1971-2006: 45 X 45s: 26 April 2011

This is the album title track and another number formulated in the disco mould, reminiscent of the hit single *Miss You* (remember the falsetto vocals?) Mick Jagger takes centre stage, performing different vocalising styles which unfurl, rap-style, with a message of chivalry, rescuing the screwed-up chick during the percussion and bass bridge. Written by Mick on the electric piano, the initial backing track was recorded simply by him with Ron Wood on bass and Charlie Watts on drums. The saxophone was added by Bobby Keys and guitar parts overlaid at the mixing stage. Bill Wyman plays a squeaky synthesiser noise in the background and apparently, due to his contribution, could have claimed songwriting credit status. Ian Stewart is also on electric piano. Mick, who had an interest in electronic keyboard music, saw Jean Michel Jarre performing to an audience of more than a million at the Place de la Concorde, in Paris, on Bastille Day, 14 July 1979. There was talk of Jean playing with the Stones on the album but he was committed to a tour while they were recording in Paris.

Keith Richards' part was small as the track was not a favourite of his though Mick was in the ascendancy at that point in their career and felt the song was a highlight of the album. A longer, seven-minute dub version of the song was apparently mixed, however Chris Kimsey could not recall this. A short cut was released on an American promo single (* a - 4.18) and an edited version of the album was placed on FORTY LICKS (* b - 3.42). There is a longer extended out-take (* c - 6.58). *Emotional Rescue* did not exactly emulate the success of *Miss You* but consolidated the Stones' contemporary position, as they again achieved Top 10 positions and entered yet another decade, the 80s, in chart form. To accompany the single, a video was produced by Adam Friedman. The film, in parts, uses the same techniques of heat-image camera work that appeared on the front and rear sleeves of the album and also the freebie inner poster of 15 similar works. Roy Adzak inspired this thermo graphic idea and took the photos. Peter Corriston designed the album cover based on these images.

The video, as a piece of imagery, was a step up from the previous *Miss You* promotion. There is also a band playback version, with Bobby Keys filmed performance style by David Mallet. He was a new producer who, through the next decade, would direct some video greats such as David Bowie's Ashes To Ashes, Queen's Radio Ga Ga and AC/DC's Thunderstruck, complete with a guitar-cam technique which Ronnie would later use in 2002. Michael Lindsay-Hogg was offered the shoot but gave the impression he was not keen on the song and, after 15 years, another red card was issued.

844. **GANGSTER'S MOLL** (Jagger, Richards) 2.20
25 June - 9 August, 30 August - October 1979: Place: EMI, Pathé Marconi Studios, Paris, France.
Producer: The Glimmer Twins.
Associate Producer: Chris Kimsey.
Bootleg only.

Mick Jagger can be heard directing *Gangster's Moll*, uttering the different scales for the band to play before a proper vocal take, something you would never hear Keith Richards doing. He would have got there intuitively. It has quite a catchy country lick and could have made the grade to an official release - "You can see the whole wide world as a gangster's mistress moll." Ron Wood can be heard in the background on pedal steel. It was not forgotten as Mick Jagger recorded a seven-minute version with Jeff Beck during his PRIMITIVE COOL sessions in 1986. Bill Wyman did not attend every session and at the time was considering his future with the band. Martin Gordon from The Radio Stars who was working at another studio in Paris was taking advantage of the refreshments during a couple of evenings and stepped in to play bass. He recalled, "We thrashed through a number of up-tempo tunes, and then some faster ones."

845. **DOWN IN THE HOLE** (Jagger, Richards) 3.57
25 June - 9 August, 30 August - October 1979: Place: EMI, Pathé Marconi Studios, Paris, France.
Rolling Stones with Sugar Blue.
Producer: The Glimmer Twins.
Associate Producer: Chris Kimsey.
Engineer: Sean Fullan, Brad Samuelsohn, David 'Snake' Reynolds, Jon Smith.
UK B-side Emotional Rescue: 20 June 1980
USA B-side Emotional Rescue: 20 June 1980
UK LP EMOTIONAL RESCUE: 20 June 1980: No. 1 - 18 weeks
USA LP EMOTIONAL RESCUE: 23 June 1980: No. 1 - 20 weeks
UK CD box set THE SINGLES COLLECTION 1971-2006: 45 X 45s: 11 April 2011
USA CD box set THE SINGLES COLLECTION 1971-2006: 45 X 45s: 26 April 2011

Something of a surprise to fans, the Stones produced a spontaneous work of the blues! The blues had always been a foundation for the Stones' soul, but the style was revered to the extent that very few attempts were made at recording a modern-day song. As Mick Jagger said: "writing good blues is very difficult". Progression in sound had always been a strong theme; not to progress musically would have stopped them in their tracks in the mid-60s. The story is based on Mick's post-war austerity and subsequent travels to the American zones in Austria and Berlin.

A wailing Sugar Blue harmonica opens the track as the song fades in and it continues throughout. Mick laid down some passionately wrenched vocals. Derivative in sound, the lyrics were modern in contrast and incompatible - as such, *Down In The Hole* misses the mark. An earlier out-take has different lyrics (* a - 3.56). Ron Wood was a major influence on the song's structure but is not credited and was not concerned, due to the incongruous lyrics.

846. INDIAN GIRL (Jagger, Richards) 4.23
25 June - 9 August, 30 August - October; November - December 1979: Place: EMI, Pathé Marconi Studios, Paris, France; Electric Lady Studios, New York, USA.
Rolling Stones with Nicky Hopkins, Max Romeo.
Producer: The Glimmer Twins.
Associate Producer: Chris Kimsey.
Engineer: Sean Fullan, Brad Samuelsohn, David 'Snake' Reynolds, Jon Smith. Horns Arrangement: Jack Nitzsche. Horns directed: Arif Mardin.
UK LP EMOTIONAL RESCUE: 20 June 1980: No. 1 - 18 weeks
USA LP EMOTIONAL RESCUE: 23 June 1980: No. 1 - 20 weeks

The country-styled guitars of Keith Richards and Ron Wood glide their way into this song about a country's strife against external influences. *Indian Girl* is a ravaged tale of the individual's mother and father fighting a war of liberation. The Castro-backed Sandinistas, fighting their way through the streets of Masaya, Nicaragua, are mentioned along with the Angolan guerrilla war of the nationalist MPLA, backed by Cuba and Russia.

The Stones were incongruously trying to make their voices heard on the international scene through Cuba. The pessimism of the message contrasted sharply with the optimistic tone of the Latin Mexican horns arranged by long-lost associate, Jack Nitzsche, who had worked with the Stones in 1965 and 1966 when he was the arranger at RCA's studios in Los Angeles. Arif Mardin, who conducted the horns on *Melody* in January 1975, revisits the Stones to do the same on *Indian Girl* with unknown mariachi horn players. Max Romeo plays the marimba to enhance the song's percussion.

There is a longer extended version of the release track (* a - 6.05). The EMOTIONAL RESCUE album credits Nicky Hopkins with piano, a contribution which was over-dubbed at Electric Lady studios late in 1979. He had met Mick Jagger, having just completed recording for Graham Parker's THE UP ESCALATOR album. Along with *Send It To Me* and *No Use In Crying*, this completed his 13 years tenure with the band. In 2011, Chris Kimsey summed up that he found Nicky to be a calm, placid, lovely man, who gave the band a sense of rhythm with his orchestral, keyboard genius.

847. SEND IT TO ME (Jagger, Richards) 3.43
25 June - 9 August, 30 August - October; November - December 1979: Place: EMI, Pathé Marconi Studios, Paris, France; Electric Lady Studios, New York, USA.
Rolling Stones with Nicky Hopkins, Bobby Keys, Sugar Blue, Max Romeo.
Producer: The Glimmer Twins.
Associate Producer: Chris Kimsey.
Engineer: Sean Fullan, Brad Samuelsohn, David 'Snake' Reynolds, Jon Smith.
UK LP EMOTIONAL RESCUE: 20 June 1980: No. 1 - 18 weeks
USA LP EMOTIONAL RESCUE: 23 June 1980: No. 1 - 20 weeks
USA B-side She's So Cold: 10 September 1980
UK B-side She's So Cold: 22 September 1980
UK CD box set THE SINGLES COLLECTION 1971-2006: 45 X 45s: 11 April 2011
USA CD box set THE SINGLES COLLECTION 1971-2006: 45 X 45s: 26 April 2011

Played with a reggae beat, *Send It To Me* is one of the weakest tracks included on the album. The sessions produced more than 40 numbers, of which approximately two dozen were shaped and recorded for possible release. Many were reclaimed from the Paris shelves but only a lucky ten were mastered for the album. An out-take of *Send It To Me* is lengthened and features Sugar Blue's harmonica work more prominently.

It had up to about 20 verses which were edited together to produce the final edited version (* a - 6.15). The humoristic lyrics, with an interesting delivery, pertain to a request for a girl in what would today be an on-line dating website. Send me a blonde or brunette Rumanian, or a Bulgarian (a parentage mixture of Bulgaria and Rumania), Albanian, Hungarian, Ukrainian or even Australian or even an alien. Nicky Hopkins was on the synthesiser.

848. LET ME GO (Jagger, Richards) 3.51
25 June - 9 August, 30 August - October 1979: Place: EMI, Pathé Marconi Studios, Paris, France.
Played Live: 1981, 1982
Rolling Stones with Bobby Keys.
Producer: The Glimmer Twins.
Associate Producer: Chris Kimsey.
Engineer: Sean Fullan, Brad Samuelsohn, David 'Snake' Reynolds, Jon Smith.
UK LP EMOTIONAL RESCUE: 20 June 1980: No. 1 - 18 weeks
USA LP EMOTIONAL RESCUE: 23 June 1980: No. 1 - 20 weeks

A typical Keith Richards rocker on which Ron Wood also snatches a country guitar line or two. Ian Stewart is the pianist while Bobby Keys' sax only enters on the fade out. There is also a version without sax (* a - 3.52). Keith is the convincing partner, his boot-laced tie retrieved from the remnants of Stones' rock 'n' roll acts of the past. The song, fast in pace, surges forward against the backbone of the rhythm, with Charlie Watts' frenetic hi-hat in good form. The song proclaimed to a lover: "Can't you get it through your thick head, this affair is as dead as a door-nail, hey baby won't you let me go." Although not a classic, it became a popular stage favourite on the World Tour of 1981/82.

849. NO USE IN CRYING (Jagger, Richards, Wood) 3.25
AKA: Ain't No Use In Crying
25 June - 9 August, 30 August - October 1979: Place: EMI, Pathé Marconi Studios, Paris, France.
Rolling Stones with Nicky Hopkins.
Producer: The Glimmer Twins.
Associate Producer: Chris Kimsey.
Engineer: Chris Kimsey, Bob Clearmountain, Gary Lyons, Bob Ludwig.
USA B-side Start Me Up: 6 August 1981
UK B-side Start Me Up: 17 August 1981
USA LP TATTOO YOU: 18 August 1981: No. 1 - 30 weeks
UK LP TATTOO YOU: 28 August 1981: No. 2 - 29 weeks
UK CD box set THE SINGLES COLLECTION 1971-2006: 45 X 45s: 11 April 2011
USA CD box set THE SINGLES COLLECTION 1971-2006: 45 X 45s: 26 April 2011

Ain't No Use In Crying is the kind of track that the Stones could regularly turn out at a session. Ron Wood gains another songwriting credit, having helped Mick Jagger out when Mick was living at Linda Ronstadt's house (Linda was an ex-flame). It is a slow song, fuelled both by a piano and an organ, played possibly by Nicky Hopkins. Mick's vocals are mixed from one channel to another which results occasionally in the odd echo diminishing the vocal line at verse end.
Although veneered in typical Stones mould it is not a classic. Recorded originally at the Pathé Marconi studios in summer 1979, it was re-mixed for the TATTOO YOU album. There are at least four out-takes of the track, three of which are a minute longer than the released one. The differences between them are small, more backing vocals, more piano, more use of echo on the lead vocal (* a - 3.35, b - 4.28, c - 4.26). However, there is one without piano (* d - 4.28).
Mixing started at the end of the year for the EMOTIONAL RESCUE album, for which this track was considered, and was completed in April 1980. A long gap then followed until the Stones reunited in Paris. At his birthday party in December 1979, Keith Richards again met Patricia Hansen and love blossomed immediately. Patti managed to fend off some of the drug hounds and a significant relationship developed. Away from the road or recording studio, Keith was like a tiger in a cage. Mick was waiting for the appropriate time to return so, for Keith, Patti was a calming influence during the lay-off.

850. HEAVEN (Jagger, Richards) 4.22
11 October - 12 November, 25 November - December 1980; April - June 1981: Place: EMI, Pathé Marconi Studios, Paris, France; RS Mobile, Boulogne-Billancourt, Paris, France; Electric Ladyland, Atlantic Studio, New York, USA.
Rolling Stones with Chris Kimsey.
Producer: The Glimmer Twins.
Associate Producer: Chris Kimsey.
Engineer: Chris Kimsey, Bob Clearmountain, Gary Lyons, Bob Ludwig.
Assistant Engineer: Barry Sage.
USA LP TATTOO YOU: 18 August 1981: No. 1 - 30 weeks
UK LP TATTOO YOU: 28 August 1981: No. 2 - 29 weeks

The group did get back together in Paris in October, with Chris Kimsey at the helm again. The purpose was to complete the work necessary for TATTOO YOU. Much of this was for vocal overdubs. The sessions were mainly done in a very cheap fashion next to a rehearsal warehouse on the western Paris Périphérique ring road. The Rolling Stones Mobile was parked outside and Chris Kimsey found that it was freezing working there. He had to wait for Mick Jagger to show up, usually after a social engagement, to record on a stage used by French singer Sylvie Vartan to rehearse her arena shows during the day.
Despite the low budget he brought in some industrial heaters to stay warm and still has nightmares about those particular sessions. "It was diabolical and so cold that Mick's breath could clearly be seen in the icy conditions." Another night, while waiting for the band minus Keith Richards (who had returned to the USA) to arrive, Mick Jagger was playing some guitar chords which Chris accompanied on the piano. He was just doodling but Mick liked it and, as such, his contribution was not planned. The other early arrivals were naturally Charlie Watts and Bill Wyman and they continued to work on the track, Bill playing synthesiser as well as bass. Before they knew it the track, enhanced by the studio techniques of Chris Kimsey and Barry Sage, began to feel good. The song's backbone is founded on whispering jangles and Charlie Watts' percussion work. Mick's vocals caress the sensual lyrics in superb style. Given a head start, the track surprisingly becomes lost in the mire of TATTOO YOU's general non-collectiveness and is now relatively unheard. Two out-takes are available, swirling in a trance-like manner (* a - 5.17, b - 5.24). On the back of *Start Me Up*, the album did very well and became their second biggest seller after SOME GIRLS.

851. NEIGHBOURS (Jagger, Richards) 3.33
11 October - 12 November, 25 November - December 1980; April - June 1981: Place: EMI, Pathé Marconi Studios, Paris, France; RS Mobile, Boulogne-Billancourt, Paris, France; Electric Ladyland, Atlantic Studio, New York, USA.
Played Live: 1981, 1982, 2002, 2003
Rolling Stones with Sonny Rollins, Jennifer McLean, Susan McLean.
Producer: The Glimmer Twins.
Associate Producer: Chris Kimsey.
Engineer: Chris Kimsey, Bob Clearmountain, Gary Lyons, Bob Ludwig. Assistant Engineer: Barry Sage.
USA LP TATTOO YOU: 18 August 1981: No. 1 - 30 weeks
UK LP TATTOO YOU: 28 August 1981: No. 2 - 29 weeks
USA B-side Hang Fire: 4 March 1982
UK CD box set THE SINGLES COLLECTION 1971-2006: 45 X 45s: 11 April 2011
USA CD box set THE SINGLES COLLECTION 1971-2006: 45 X 45s: 26 April 2011

Everybody can, at times, do without neighbours and the Michael Lindsay-Hogg video of apartment life portrays the seedy side of neighbours (note the English spelling - the album sleeve states Neighbors). There are, for example, the silk-laced copulating couples and the gory hacksaw disintegration of a missing wife. Both figure in an unforgiving manner in the footage, which can be found on *Video Rewind*. The song ponders the subject by leaps and bounds, under the twin thrust of guitars and saxophone, the latter again protagonised by jazz musician Sonny Rollins, a performance over-dubbed at the second session.

In the Rolling Stones Mobile, Barry Sage added backing vocals to the track in the cold suburbs of Paris. These were achieved by friends of his who were more well-known in the fashion world as The McLean Twins. The video, including the lace-dressed prostitute and the be-devilled murder, was banned by the American network MTV. It is said it was filmed in one of Mick Jagger's New York apartments and was written about Keith Richards, who was the most disruptive Stone - especially for close neighbours - and had been evicted from one property.

The subject matter was inspired by Keith, having been evicted by his landlord for unsociable behaviour. Bill Wyman, when asked if he had ever shared a room with Keith, replied: "No, but I once tried to sleep in the same hotel!" Ron Wood also joined the bad boys when he was arrested, along with Jo Karslake (his girlfriend for the past three years), for cocaine possession in February 1980. They were released uncharged as he continued to fight drug demons and financial problems. He had even sold his royalty rights to EMOTIONAL RESCUE.

The music is rocky and raucous and was included on subsequent tours. An out-take without the saxophone solo is available; there seems to be more guitar, higher in the mix and Charlie's pounding drum beat is not as clear. It also lacks the fade-out piano solo by Ian Stewart (* a - 3.26). The sessions were not as extensive nor as fruitful as had been hoped and there was a general lack of material for the next album. As a result, Chris Kimsey and Mick waded as far back through old material to BLACK AND BLUE to find enough for an album. TATTOO YOU proved to be a very successful LP, even outselling SOME GIRLS. It was an album of two parts, side one of fast songs and the second slower.

The sleeve featured the third consecutive design by "Shakey" Peter Corriston for which he won a Grammy for best album cover. The album title came from a series of photographs, given to Mick Jagger, with etched black line face paintings and was provisionally just called TATTOO. Oddly there were no credits on the album cover, something that obviously disguised some of the guest contributors. Some of these were the golden McLean Twins, Jennifer and Susan, who hung out with the band for a three-week period in 1980.

They provided very subtle vocals too: "Is it any wonder that they fuss and fight neighbours". The twins released *Wooly Bully* as a single under the name Attila's Brides, in 1981. To put the Sessionography in context, as *Neighbours* concluded 1980, John Lennon was murdered on 8 December, when he was just over 40 years old. Mick Jagger lived in the next building to him. Paranoia had become a thing of the present.

852. MUNICH HILTON (Jagger, Richards) 8.32
August - 14 September 1981: Place: Long View Farm, Brookfield, Massachusetts, USA.
Keith Richards and his Rolling Stones!
Bootleg only.

The year 1981 started with Mick Jagger becoming briefly involved in a film project called *Fitzcarraldo* but he withdrew when the shooting over ran. In late 1980, he also supervised the unremarkable spring 1981 release of the compilation album SUCKING IN THE SEVENTIES, with Chris Kimsey and Barry Sage - it included largely edited versions of already released tracks. Ron Wood continued to work on his next solo project 1-2-3-4 and Bill Wyman became a true pop star when his self-penned and promoted single *(Si Si) Je Suis Un Rock Star* became a No. 14 hit in the UK in July. It is still the most successful chart single by a solo member, despite Mick's many attempts.

Keith played on and produced Max Romeo's new album HOLDING OUT MY LOVE TO YOU. Charlie Watts and Ian Stewart teamed up to create an album with Ian's touring band Rocket 88. Meanwhile Mick was convinced that, after the release of TATTOO YOU, there should be a world tour. Bill Graham took over as tour director from Peter Rudge and another period of travelling began to be planned, sponsored by cosmetics company Jovan.

Graham was famous for promoting bands at the Fillmore and, in 1972, had handled the Californian leg of the Stones tour for Peter Rudge. He was also responsible for the 1985 American Live Aid concert in Philadelphia. It was the first time in six years that a long tour had been contemplated and it was decided that stadiums would be the main venues and, where possible, they would play the same venue twice to maximise profit. The logistics were immense, with 35 juggernaut trucks and four stage systems, but Bill Graham's experience ensured success.

The press speculated that every gig was the penultimate one, stating that the middle-aged band (thankfully there were no visible signs of middle-age, apart from Charlie Watts' receding hair line!) was about to break up - they were not far from the truth. A recording studio at Long View Farm was suggested by Peter Wolf, of the J. Geils Band, as the rehearsal venue for the tour. A bootlegged album has just Keith Richards playing solo riffs on lead guitar; it includes Stones' numbers *Brown Sugar, Tumbling Dice, Start Me Up, Cherry Oh Baby, Honky Tonk Women* and *Munich Hilton*.

A version of Hoagy Carmichael's *Nearness Of You* was recorded during the visit to Long View and that prompted a congratulatory call from the songwriter himself. Apparently, the phone rang and someone said: "it's Hoagy for you Keith!" Hoagy Carmichael died a few months later, in December 1981, and Keith felt honoured to have received such a phone call. The tour personnel were carefully selected. Mick wanted it to be drugs free and even Ron Wood's position was scrutinised due to his bust in the Caribbean.

Also, Ron was in an extremely embarrassing financial position so a money-spinning tour was most welcome. Ian McLagan and Bobby Keys were invited but warned about using drugs, as was Ronnie Wood. Ironically it was Keith Richards who was on Ronnie's case and there was a big bust-up at one point. Bobby was called in for the last half of the tour.

The first three dates did not have any brass and then the late Lee Allen (New Orleans tenor sax player for Fats Domino) was recruited for the next three but he had his mind blown by the size of the gigs and so Ernie Watts was invited to join the team. It was Quincy Jones who helped Mick select Ernie for the San Diego show. He had a jazz musical pedigree having played with the Buddy Rich band, as well as recording with Thelonious Monk.

853. TOPS (Jagger, Richards) ⬀ 3.58
25 September 1981: Place: JFK Stadium, Philadelphia, USA.
Producer: The Glimmer Twins.
Bootleg only.

854. DOWN THE ROAD APIECE (Raye) ⬀ 2.11
26 September 1981: Place: JFK Stadium, Philadelphia, USA.
Producer: The Glimmer Twins.
Bootleg only.

855. MONA (McDaniel) ◹ 4.01
26 September 1981: Place: JFK Stadium, Philadelphia, USA.
Producer: The Glimmer Twins.
Bootleg only.

The tour was announced by Mick Jagger at a press conference at the JFK Stadium, Philadelphia. The first gig, on 14 September 1981, was a very small warm-up affair at Sir Morgan's Cove in Worcester, Massachusetts, where the Stones were billed as Blue Sunday and The Cockroaches. Then the real tour started at the JFK Stadium where they played for two nerve-wracking, consecutive nights. The sets continued to have material from SOME GIRLS but drew also on the last two albums. The only songs taken from EMOTIONAL RESCUE were *She's So Cold* and *Let Me Go*. From TATTOO YOU, *Tops* was played only a few times, while slow material was left out, except for *Waiting On A Friend*. Faster tracks included *Hang Fire*, *Little T & A*, *Black Limousine* and *Neighbours*.
Start Me Up was one song that, as the tour progressed, worked its way nearer and nearer to the top of the set list. In the rock and roll covers section, *Down The Road Apiece* appeared a few times early on in the tour, as did *Mona*. Eddie Cochran's *Twenty Flight Rock*, however, was a real pleaser that stayed for the duration, as did Smokey Robinson's *Going To A Go Go*. Support acts changed from venue to venue. The regular ones included The J. Geils Band, George Thorogood, The Fabulous Thunderbirds, ZZ Top, Tina Turner, The Stray Cats and Bobby Womack. AC/DC were reportedly offered one million dollars to play as support for just one large city venue but they reluctantly declined since their own headlining American tour was due to commence in November.
One act that did not last the course was Prince who, in his provocative stage wear and tunes like *Jack-U-Off*, was pelted off the stage. Charlie Watts had promoted his inclusion stating to the rest of the band that he would become big and so was disappointed that he did not play more shows. The support acts certainly had no nod to the punk era as that had run its course, as had "new wave", the attention now being on the modern romantics and hip hop. The only artists which Keith Richards acknowledged that had stayed the course and matured in their mould was The Clash. They were also a band well respected by Mick Jagger and Charlie, perhaps due to their fusion of rock, dance and jazz sounds.

856. UNDER MY THUMB (Jagger, Richard) ◹ 4.18
5 November 1981: Place: Brendan Byrne Arena, The Meadowlands, New Jersey, USA.
Rolling Stones with Ian McLagan, Ernie Watts.
Producer: The Glimmer Twins.
Engineer: Malcolm Pollack, Barry Bongiovi, Larry Alexander, Phil Gitomer, Kooster McAllister, David Brown, Bob Ludwig.
Recorded by: Bob Clearmountain, David Hewitt.
UK LP STILL LIFE: 1 June 1982: No. 4 - 18 weeks
USA LP STILL LIFE: 1 June 1982: No. 5 - 10 weeks
UK B-side 12-inch Single Time Is On My Side: 13 September 1982
UK CD box set THE SINGLES COLLECTION 1971-2006: 45 X 45s: 11 April 2011
USA CD box set THE SINGLES COLLECTION 1971-2006: 45 X 45s: 26 April 2011

857. GOING TO A GO-GO (Robinson, Moore, Johnson, Rogers) ◹ 3.23
5-6 November 1981: Place: Brendan Byrne Arena, The Meadowlands, New Jersey, USA.
Rolling Stones with Ian McLagan, Ernie Watts.
Producer: The Glimmer Twins, Ronald L Schwary. Director: Hal Ashby.
Recorded by: David Hewitt. Mixed by Bob Clearmountain.
UK & USA Video Let's Spend The Night Together: 1983

858. YOU CAN'T ALWAYS GET WHAT YOU WANT (Jagger, Richard) ◹ 5.57
5-6 November 1981: Place: Brendan Byrne Arena, The Meadowlands, New Jersey, USA.
Rolling Stones with Ian McLagan, Ernie Watts.
Producer: The Glimmer Twins, Ronald L Schwary. Director: Hal Ashby.
Recorded by: David Hewitt. Mixed by Bob Clearmountain.
UK & USA Video Let's Spend The Night Together: 1983

859. LITTLE T&A (Jagger, Richards) ◹ 2.13
5-6 November 1981: Place: Brendan Byrne Arena, The Meadowlands, New Jersey, USA.
Rolling Stones with Ian McLagan, Ernie Watts.
Producer: The Glimmer Twins, Ronald L Schwary. Director: Hal Ashby.
Recorded by: David Hewitt. Mixed by Bob Clearmountain.
UK & USA Video Let's Spend The Night Together: 1983

860. TUMBLING DICE (Jagger, Richard) ◹ 2.27
5-6 November 1981: Place: Brendan Byrne Arena, The Meadowlands, New Jersey, USA.
Rolling Stones with Ian McLagan, Ernie Watts.
Producer: The Glimmer Twins, Ronald L Schwary. Director: Hal Ashby.
Recorded by: David Hewitt. Mixed by Bob Clearmountain.
UK & USA Video Let's Spend The Night Together: 1983

861. **SHE'S SO COLD** (Jagger, Richards) ✎ 3.20
5-6 November 1981: Place: Brendan Byrne Arena, The Meadowlands, New Jersey, USA.
Rolling Stones with Ian McLagan, Ernie Watts.
Producer: The Glimmer Twins, Ronald L Schwary. Director: Hal Ashby.
Recorded by: David Hewitt. Mixed by Bob Clearmountain.
UK & USA Video Let's Spend The Night Together: 1983

862. **ALL DOWN THE LINE** (Jagger, Richard) ✎ 3.03
5-6 November 1981: Place: Brendan Byrne Arena, The Meadowlands, New Jersey, USA.
Rolling Stones with Ian McLagan, Ernie Watts.
Producer: The Glimmer Twins, Ronald L Schwary. Director: Hal Ashby.
Recorded by: David Hewitt. Mixed by Bob Clearmountain.
UK & USA Video Let's Spend The Night Together: 1983

863. **HANG FIRE** (Jagger, Richards) ✎ 2.07
5-6 November 1981: Place: Brendan Byrne Arena, The Meadowlands, New Jersey, USA.
Rolling Stones with Ian McLagan, Ernie Watts.
Producer: The Glimmer Twins, Ronald L Schwary. Director: Hal Ashby.
Recorded by: David Hewitt. Mixed by Bob Clearmountain.
UK & USA Video Let's Spend The Night Together: 1983

864. **MISS YOU** (Jagger, Richards) ✎ 4.04
5-6 November 1981: Place: Brendan Byrne Arena, The Meadowlands, New Jersey, USA.
Rolling Stones with Ian McLagan, Ernie Watts.
Producer: The Glimmer Twins, Ronald L Schwary. Director: Hal Ashby.
Recorded by: David Hewitt. Mixed by Bob Clearmountain.
UK & USA Video Let's Spend The Night Together: 1983

865. **LET IT BLEED** (Jagger, Richard) ✎ 2.57
5-6 November 1981: Place: Brendan Byrne Arena, The Meadowlands, New Jersey, USA.
Rolling Stones with Ian McLagan, Ernie Watts, Bobby Keys.
Producer: The Glimmer Twins, Ronald L Schwary. Director: Hal Ashby.
Recorded by: David Hewitt. Mixed by Bob Clearmountain.
UK & USA Video Let's Spend The Night Together: 1983

866. **START ME UP** (Jagger, Richards) ✎ 2.34
5-6 November 1981: Place: Brendan Byrne Arena, The Meadowlands, New Jersey, USA.
Rolling Stones with Ian McLagan, Ernie Watts.
Producer: The Glimmer Twins, Ronald L Schwary. Director: Hal Ashby.
Recorded by: David Hewitt. Mixed by Bob Clearmountain.
UK & USA Video Let's Spend The Night Together: 1983

867. **BROWN SUGAR** (Jagger, Richard) ✎ 2.09
5-6 November 1981: Place: Brendan Byrne Arena, The Meadowlands, New Jersey, USA.
Rolling Stones with Ian McLagan, Ernie Watts, Bobby Keys.
Producer: The Glimmer Twins, Ronald L Schwary. Director: Hal Ashby.
Recorded by: David Hewitt. Mixed by Bob Clearmountain.
UK & USA Video Let's Spend The Night Together: 1983

868. **(I CAN'T GET NO) SATISFACTION** (Jagger, Richard) ✎ 3.05
5-6 November 1981: Place: Brendan Byrne Arena, The Meadowlands, New Jersey, USA.
Rolling Stones with Ian McLagan, Ernie Watts.
Producer: The Glimmer Twins, Ronald L Schwary. Director: Hal Ashby.
Recorded by: David Hewitt. Mixed by Bob Clearmountain.
UK & USA Video Let's Spend The Night Together: 1983

869. **BEAST OF BURDEN** (Jagger, Richards) ✎ 4.38
25 November 1981: Place: Rosemont Horizon, Chicago, Illinois, USA.
Rolling Stones with Ian McLagan, Ernie Watts.
Producer: The Glimmer Twins.
Engineer: Malcolm Pollack, Barry Bongiovi, Larry Alexander, Phil Gitomer, Kooster McAllister, David Brown, Bob Ludwig.
Recorded by: Bob Clearmountain, David Hewitt.
UK B-side Going To A Go-Go: 1 June 1982
USA B-side Going To A Go-Go: 1 June 1982
USA CD FLASHPOINT (COLLECTIBLES): 20 May 1991

USA CD LP ROLLING STONES RARITIES 1971-2003: 22 November 2005: No. 76 - 6 weeks
UK CD LP ROLLING STONES RARITIES 1971-2003: 28 November 2005
UK CD box set THE SINGLES COLLECTION 1971-2006: 45 X 45s: 11 April 2011
USA CD box set THE SINGLES COLLECTION 1971-2006: 45 X 45s: 26 April 2011

870. START ME UP (Jagger, Richards) ⁄ 4.21
25 November 1981: Place: Rosemont Horizon, Chicago, Illinois, USA.
Rolling Stones with Ian McLagan, Ernie Watts.
Producer: The Glimmer Twins.
Engineer: Malcolm Pollack, Barry Bongiovi, Larry Alexander, Phil Gitomer, Kooster McAllister, David Brown, Bob Ludwig.
Recorded by: Bob Clearmountain, David Hewitt.
UK LP STILL LIFE: 1 June 1982: No. 4 - 18 weeks
USA LP STILL LIFE: 1 June 1982: No. 5 - 10 weeks

871. LET ME GO (Jagger, Richards) ⁄ 3.32
8 December 1981: Place: Capital Center, Largo, Washington, USA.
Rolling Stones with Ian McLagan, Ernie Watts.
Producer: The Glimmer Twins.
Engineer: Malcolm Pollack, Barry Bongiovi, Larry Alexander, Phil Gitomer, Kooster McAllister, David Brown, Bob Ludwig.
Recorded by: Bob Clearmountain, David Hewitt.
UK LP STILL LIFE: 1 June 1982: No. 4 - 18 weeks
USA LP STILL LIFE: 1 June 1982: No. 5 - 10 weeks

872. TWENTY FLIGHT ROCK (Fairchild, Cochran) ⁄ 1.51
9 December 1981: Place: Capital Center, Largo, Washington. USA.
Rolling Stones with Ian McLagan, Ernie Watts.
Producer: The Glimmer Twins.
Engineer: Malcolm Pollack, Barry Bongiovi, Larry Alexander, Phil Gitomer, Kooster McAllister, David Brown, Bob Ludwig.
Recorded by: Bob Clearmountain, David Hewitt.
UK LP STILL LIFE: 1 June 1982: No. 4 - 18 weeks
USA LP STILL LIFE: 1 June 1982: No. 5 - 10 weeks
UK B-side Time Is On My Side: 13 September 1982
USA B-side Time Is On My Side: 13 September 1982
UK CD box set THE SINGLES COLLECTION 1971-2006: 45 X 45s: 11 April 2011
USA CD box set THE SINGLES COLLECTION 1971-2006: 45 X 45s: 26 April 2011

873. GOING TO A GO-GO (Robinson, Moore, Johnson, Rogers) ⁄ 3.23
9 December 1981: Place: Capital Center, Largo, Washington, USA.
Rolling Stones with Ian McLagan, Ernie Watts.
Producer: The Glimmer Twins.
Engineer: Malcolm Pollack, Barry Bongiovi, Larry Alexander, Phil Gitomer, Kooster McAllister, David Brown, Bob Ludwig.
Recorded by: Bob Clearmountain, David Hewitt.
UK Single: 1 June 1982: No. 26 - 6 weeks
USA Single: 1 June 1982: No. 25 - 5 weeks
UK LP STILL LIFE: 1 June 1982: No. 4 - 18 weeks
USA LP STILL LIFE: 1 June 1982: No. 5 - 10 weeks
UK CD box set THE SINGLES COLLECTION 1971-2006: 45 X 45s: 11 April 2011
USA CD box set THE SINGLES COLLECTION 1971-2006: 45 X 45s: 26 April 2011

874. UNDER MY THUMB (Jagger, Richard) ⁄ 3.45
13 December 1981: Place: Sun Devil Stadium, Tempe, Arizona, USA.
Rolling Stones with Ian McLagan, Ernie Watts.
Producer: The Glimmer Twins, Ronald L Schwary. Director: Hal Ashby.
Recorded by: David Hewitt. Mixed by Bob Clearmountain.
UK & USA Video Let's Spend The Night Together: 1983

875. LET'S SPEND THE NIGHT TOGETHER (Jagger, Richard) ⁄ 2.59
13 December 1981: Place: Sun Devil Stadium, Tempe, Arizona, USA.
Rolling Stones with Ian McLagan, Ernie Watts.
Producer: The Glimmer Twins, Ronald L Schwary. Director: Hal Ashby.
Recorded by: David Hewitt. Mixed by Bob Clearmountain.
UK & USA Video Let's Spend The Night Together: 1983

876. **SHATTERED** (Jagger, Richards) ✎ 3.31
13 December 1981: Place: Sun Devil Stadium, Tempe, Arizona, USA.
Rolling Stones with Ian McLagan, Ernie Watts.
Producer: The Glimmer Twins, Ronald L Schwary. Director: Hal Ashby. Recorded by: David Hewitt. Mixed by Bob Clearmountain.
UK & USA Video Let's Spend The Night Together: 1983

877. **NEIGHBOURS** (Jagger, Richards) ✎ 3.03
13 December 1981: Place: Sun Devil Stadium, Tempe, Arizona, USA.
Rolling Stones with Ian McLagan, Ernie Watts.
Producer: The Glimmer Twins, Ronald L Schwary. Director: Hal Ashby.
Recorded by: David Hewitt. Mixed by Bob Clearmountain.
UK & USA Video Let's Spend The Night Together: 1983

878. **BLACK LIMOUSINE** (Jagger, Richards, Wood) ✎ 3.10
13 December 1981: Place: Sun Devil Stadium, Tempe, Arizona, USA.
Rolling Stones with Ian McLagan, Ernie Watts.
Producer: The Glimmer Twins, Ronald L Schwary. Director: Hal Ashby.
Recorded by: David Hewitt. Mixed by Bob Clearmountain.
UK & USA Video Let's Spend The Night Together: 1983

879. **JUST MY IMAGINATION (RUNNING AWAY WITH ME)** (Jagger, Richard) ✎ 5.45
13 December 1981: Place: Sun Devil Stadium, Tempe, Arizona, USA.
Rolling Stones with Ian McLagan, Ernie Watts.
Producer: The Glimmer Twins, Ronald L Schwary. Director: Hal Ashby.
Recorded by: David Hewitt. Mixed by Bob Clearmountain.
UK & USA Video Let's Spend The Night Together: 1983

880. **TWENTY FLIGHT ROCK** (Fairchild, Cochran) ✎ 1.41
13 December 1981: Place: Sun Devil Stadium, Tempe, Arizona, USA.
Rolling Stones with Ian McLagan, Ernie Watts.
Producer: The Glimmer Twins, Ronald L Schwary. Director: Hal Ashby.
Recorded by: David Hewitt. Mixed by Bob Clearmountain.
UK & USA Video Let's Spend The Night Together: 1983

881. **LET ME GO** (Jagger, Richards) ✎ 2.47
13 December 1981: Place: Sun Devil Stadium, Tempe, Arizona, USA.
Rolling Stones with Ian McLagan, Ernie Watts.
Producer: The Glimmer Twins, Ronald L Schwary. Director: Hal Ashby.
Recorded by: David Hewitt. Mixed by Bob Clearmountain.
UK & USA Video Let's Spend The Night Together: 1983

882. **TIME IS ON MY SIDE** (Ragovoy, Norman) ✎ 3.26
13 December 1981: Place: Sun Devil Stadium, Tempe, Arizona, USA.
Rolling Stones with Ian McLagan, Ernie Watts.
Producer: The Glimmer Twins, Ronald L Schwary. Director: Hal Ashby.
Recorded by: David Hewitt. Mixed by Bob Clearmountain.
UK & USA Video Let's Spend The Night Together: 1983

883. **BEAST OF BURDEN** (Jagger, Richards) ✎ 4.38
13 December 1981: Place: Sun Devil Stadium, Tempe, Arizona, USA.
Rolling Stones with Ian McLagan, Ernie Watts.
Producer: The Glimmer Twins, Ronald L Schwary. Director: Hal Ashby.
Recorded by: David Hewitt. Mixed by Bob Clearmountain.
UK & USA Video Let's Spend The Night Together: 1983

884. **WAITING ON A FRIEND** (Jagger, Richards) ✎ 2.56
13 December 1981: Place: Sun Devil Stadium, Tempe, Arizona, USA.
Rolling Stones with Ian McLagan, Ernie Watts.
Producer: The Glimmer Twins, Ronald L Schwary. Director: Hal Ashby.
Recorded by: David Hewitt. Mixed by Bob Clearmountain.
UK & USA Video Let's Spend The Night Together: 1983

885. **HONKY TONK WOMEN** (Jagger, Richard) ✎ 3.24
13 December 1981: Place: Sun Devil Stadium, Tempe, Arizona, USA.
Rolling Stones with Ian McLagan, Ernie Watts.

Producer: The Glimmer Twins, Ronald L Schwary. Director: Hal Ashby.
Recorded by: David Hewitt. Mixed by Bob Clearmountain.
UK & USA Video Let's Spend The Night Together: 1983

886. JUMPING JACK FLASH (Jagger, Richard) ∦ 3.43
13 December 1981: Place: Sun Devil Stadium, Tempe, Arizona, USA.
Rolling Stones with Ian McLagan, Ernie Watts.
Producer: The Glimmer Twins, Ronald L Schwary. Director: Hal Ashby.
Recorded by: David Hewitt. Mixed by Bob Clearmountain.
UK & USA Video Let's Spend The Night Together: 1983

887. (I CAN'T GET NO) SATISFACTION (Jagger, Richard) ∦ 4.24
13 December 1981: Place: Sun Devil Stadium, Tempe, Arizona, USA.
Rolling Stones with Ian McLagan, Ernie Watts.
Producer: The Glimmer Twins. Engineer: Malcolm Pollack, Barry Bongiovi, Larry Alexander, Phil Gitomer, Kooster McAllister, David Brown, Bob Ludwig.
Recorded by: Bob Clearmountain, David Hewitt.
UK LP STILL LIFE: 1 June 1982: No. 4 - 18 weeks
USA LP STILL LIFE: 1 June 1982: No. 5 - 10 weeks

888. UNDER MY THUMB (Jagger, Richard) ∦ 5.04
18 December 1981: Place: Hampton Roads Coliseum, Hampton, Virginia, USA.
Rolling Stones with Ian McLagan, Ernie Watts.
Producer: The Glimmer Twins.
Recorded by: Bob Clearmountain, David Hewitt. Remixed & Remastered: Bob Clearmountain.
USA e-Album HAMPTON COLISEUM: LIVE 1981: 31 January 2012
UK e-Album HAMPTON COLISEUM: LIVE 1981: 1 February 2012

889. WHEN THE WHIP COMES DOWN (Jagger, Richards) ∦ 5.06
18 December 1981: Place: Hampton Roads Coliseum, Hampton, Virginia, USA.
Rolling Stones with Ian McLagan, Ernie Watts.
Producer: The Glimmer Twins.
Recorded by: Bob Clearmountain, David Hewitt. Remixed & Remastered: Bob Clearmountain.
USA e-Album HAMPTON COLISEUM: LIVE 1981: 31 January 2012
UK e-Album HAMPTON COLISEUM: LIVE 1981: 1 February 2012

890. LET'S SPEND THE NIGHT TOGETHER (Jagger, Richard) ∦ 4.32
18 December 1981: Place: Hampton Roads Coliseum, Hampton, Virginia, USA.
Rolling Stones with Ian McLagan, Ernie Watts.
Producer: The Glimmer Twins.
Engineer: Malcolm Pollack, Barry Bongiovi, Larry Alexander, Phil Gitomer, Kooster McAllister, David Brown, Bob Ludwig.
Recorded by: Bob Clearmountain, David Hewitt. Remixed & Remastered: Bob Clearmountain.
UK LP STILL LIFE: 1 June 1982: No. 4 - 18 weeks
USA LP STILL LIFE: 1 June 1982: No. 5 - 10 weeks
USA e-Album HAMPTON COLISEUM: LIVE 1981: 31 January 2012
UK e-Album HAMPTON COLISEUM: LIVE 1981: 1 February 2012

891. SHATTERED (Jagger, Richard) ∦ 4.50
18 December 1981: Place: Hampton Roads Coliseum, Hampton, Virginia, USA.
Rolling Stones with Ian McLagan, Ernie Watts.
Producer: The Glimmer Twins.
Engineer: Malcolm Pollack, Barry Bongiovi, Larry Alexander, Phil Gitomer, Kooster McAllister, David Brown, Bob Ludwig.
Recorded by: Bob Clearmountain, David Hewitt. Remixed & Remastered: Bob Clearmountain.
UK LP STILL LIFE: 1 June 1982: No. 4 - 18 weeks
USA LP STILL LIFE: 1 June 1982: No. 5 - 10 weeks
USA e-Album HAMPTON COLISEUM: LIVE 1981: 31 January 2012
UK e-Album HAMPTON COLISEUM: LIVE 1981: 1 February 2012

892. NEIGHBOURS (Jagger, Richards) ∦ 4.23
18 December 1981: Place: Hampton Roads Coliseum, Hampton, Virginia, USA.
Rolling Stones with Ian McLagan, Ernie Watts.
Producer: The Glimmer Twins.
Recorded by: Bob Clearmountain, David Hewitt. Remixed & Remastered: Bob Clearmountain.
USA e-Album HAMPTON COLISEUM: LIVE 1981: 31 January 2012
UK e-Album HAMPTON COLISEUM: LIVE 1981: 1 February 2012

893. BLACK LIMOUSINE (Jagger, Richards, Wood) ✎ 3.28
18 December 1981: Place: Hampton Roads Coliseum, Hampton, Virginia, USA.
Rolling Stones with Ian McLagan, Ernie Watts.
Producer: The Glimmer Twins.
Recorded by: Bob Clearmountain, David Hewitt. Remixed & Remastered: Bob Clearmountain.
USA e-Album HAMPTON COLISEUM: LIVE 1981: 31 January 2012
UK e-Album HAMPTON COLISEUM: LIVE 1981: 1 February 2012
UK DVD Muddy Waters & The Rolling Stones Live At The Checkerboard Lounge, Chicago 1981: 9 July 2012
USA DVD Muddy Waters & The Rolling Stones Live At The Checkerboard Lounge, Chicago 1981: 10 July 2012

894. JUST MY IMAGINATION (RUNNING AWAY WITH ME) (Jagger, Richards, Wood) ✎ 9.46
18 December 1981: Place: Hampton Roads Coliseum, Hampton, Virginia, USA.
Rolling Stones with Ian McLagan, Ernie Watts.
Producer: The Glimmer Twins.
Recorded by: Bob Clearmountain, David Hewitt. Remixed & Remastered: Bob Clearmountain.
USA e-Album HAMPTON COLISEUM: LIVE 1981: 31 January 2012
UK e-Album HAMPTON COLISEUM: LIVE 1981: 1 February 2012

895. TWENTY FLIGHT ROCK (Fairchild, Cochran) ✎ 1.47
18 December 1981: Place: Hampton Roads Coliseum, Hampton, Virginia, USA.
Rolling Stones with Ian McLagan, Ernie Watts.
Producer: The Glimmer Twins.
Recorded by: Bob Clearmountain, David Hewitt. Remixed & Remastered: Bob Clearmountain.
USA e-Album HAMPTON COLISEUM: LIVE 1981: 31 January 2012
UK e-Album HAMPTON COLISEUM: LIVE 1981: 1 February 2012

896. GOING TO A GO-GO (Robinson, Moore, Johnson, Rogers) ✎ 4.03
18 December 1981: Place: Hampton Roads Coliseum, Hampton, Virginia, USA.
Rolling Stones with Ian McLagan, Ernie Watts.
Producer: The Glimmer Twins.
Recorded by: Bob Clearmountain, David Hewitt. Remixed & Remastered: Bob Clearmountain.
USA e-Album HAMPTON COLISEUM: LIVE 1981: 31 January 2012
UK e-Album HAMPTON COLISEUM: LIVE 1981: 1 February 2012

897. LET ME GO (Jagger, Richards) ✎ 5.25
18 December 1981: Place: Hampton Roads Coliseum, Hampton, Virginia, USA.
Rolling Stones with Ian McLagan, Ernie Watts.
Producer: The Glimmer Twins.
Recorded by: Bob Clearmountain, David Hewitt. Remixed & Remastered: Bob Clearmountain.
USA e-Album HAMPTON COLISEUM: LIVE 1981: 31 January 2012
UK e-Album HAMPTON COLISEUM: LIVE 1981: 1 February 2012

898. TIME IS ON MY SIDE (Meade, Norman) ✎ 4.13
18 December 1981: Place: Hampton Roads Coliseum, Hampton, Virginia, USA.
Rolling Stones with Ian McLagan, Ernie Watts.
Producer: The Glimmer Twins.
Engineer: Malcolm Pollack, Barry Bongiovi, Larry Alexander, Phil Gitomer, Kooster McAllister, David Brown, Bob Ludwig.
Recorded by: Bob Clearmountain, David Hewitt. Remixed & Remastered: Bob Clearmountain.
UK LP STILL LIFE: 1 June 1982: No. 4 - 18 weeks
USA LP STILL LIFE: 1 June 1982: No. 5 - 10 weeks
UK Single, 12-inch Single: 13 September 1982: No. 62 - 2 weeks
USA Single: 13 September 1982
UK CD box set THE SINGLES COLLECTION 1971-2006: 45 X 45s: 11 April 2011
USA CD box set THE SINGLES COLLECTION 1971-2006: 45 X 45s: 26 April 2011
USA e-Album HAMPTON COLISEUM: LIVE 1981: 31 January 2012
UK e-Album HAMPTON COLISEUM: LIVE 1981: 1 February 2012

899. BEAST OF BURDEN (Jagger, Richards) ✎ 7.24
18 December 1981: Place: Hampton Roads Coliseum, Hampton, Virginia, USA.
Rolling Stones with Ian McLagan, Ernie Watts.
Producer: The Glimmer Twins.
Recorded by: Bob Clearmountain, David Hewitt. Remixed & Remastered: Bob Clearmountain.
USA e-Album HAMPTON COLISEUM: LIVE 1981: 31 January 2012
UK e-Album HAMPTON COLISEUM: LIVE 1981: 1 February 2012

900. **WAITING ON A FRIEND** (Jagger, Richards) ✎ 5.55
18 December 1981: Place: Hampton Roads Coliseum, Hampton, Virginia, USA.
Rolling Stones with Ian McLagan, Ernie Watts.
Producer: The Glimmer Twins.
Recorded by: Bob Clearmountain, David Hewitt. Remixed & Remastered: Bob Clearmountain.
USA e-Album HAMPTON COLISEUM: LIVE 1981: 31 January 2012
UK e-Album HAMPTON COLISEUM: LIVE 1981: 1 February 2012

901. **LET IT BLEED** (Jagger, Richard) ✎ 6.58
18 December 1981: Place: Hampton Roads Coliseum, Hampton, Virginia, USA.
Rolling Stones with Ian McLagan, Ernie Watts.
Producer: The Glimmer Twins.
Recorded by: Bob Clearmountain, David Hewitt. Remixed & Remastered: Bob Clearmountain.
USA e-Album HAMPTON COLISEUM: LIVE 1981: 31 January 2012
UK e-Album HAMPTON COLISEUM: LIVE 1981: 1 February 2012

902. **YOU CAN'T ALWAYS GET WHAT YOU WANT** (Jagger, Richard) ✎ 9.35
18 December 1981: Place: Hampton Roads Coliseum, Hampton, Virginia, USA.
Rolling Stones with Ian McLagan, Ernie Watts.
Producer: The Glimmer Twins.
Recorded by: Bob Clearmountain, David Hewitt. Remixed & Remastered: Bob Clearmountain.
USA e-Album HAMPTON COLISEUM: LIVE 1981: 31 January 2012
UK e-Album HAMPTON COLISEUM: LIVE 1981: 1 February 2012

903. **LITTLE T&A** (Jagger, Richards) ✎ 3.58
18 December 1981: Place: Hampton Roads Coliseum, Hampton, Virginia, USA.
Rolling Stones with Ian McLagan, Ernie Watts.
Producer: The Glimmer Twins.
Recorded by: Bob Clearmountain, David Hewitt. Remixed & Remastered: Bob Clearmountain.
USA e-Album HAMPTON COLISEUM: LIVE 1981: 31 January 2012
UK e-Album HAMPTON COLISEUM: LIVE 1981: 1 February 2012

904. **TUMBLING DICE** (Jagger, Richard) ✎ 4.48
18 December 1981: Place: Hampton Roads Coliseum, Hampton, Virginia, USA.
Rolling Stones with Ian McLagan, Ernie Watts.
Producer: The Glimmer Twins.
Recorded by: Bob Clearmountain, David Hewitt. Remixed & Remastered: Bob Clearmountain.
USA e-Album HAMPTON COLISEUM: LIVE 1981: 31 January 2012
UK e-Album HAMPTON COLISEUM: LIVE 1981: 1 February 2012

905. **SHE'S SO COLD** (Jagger, Richards) ✎ 4.25
18 December 1981: Place: Hampton Roads Coliseum, Hampton, Virginia, USA.
Rolling Stones with Ian McLagan, Ernie Watts.
Producer: The Glimmer Twins.
Recorded by: Bob Clearmountain, David Hewitt. Remixed & Remastered: Bob Clearmountain.
USA e-Album HAMPTON COLISEUM: LIVE 1981: 31 January 2012
UK e-Album HAMPTON COLISEUM: LIVE 1981: 1 February 2012

906. **HANG FIRE** (Jagger, Richards) ✎ 2.40
18 December 1981: Place: Hampton Roads Coliseum, Hampton, Virginia, USA.
Rolling Stones with Ian McLagan, Ernie Watts.
Producer: The Glimmer Twins.
Recorded by: Bob Clearmountain, David Hewitt. Remixed & Remastered: Bob Clearmountain.
USA e-Album HAMPTON COLISEUM: LIVE 1981: 31 January 2012
UK e-Album HAMPTON COLISEUM: LIVE 1981: 1 February 2012

907. **MISS YOU** (Jagger, Richards) ✎ 7.46
18 December 1981: Place: Hampton Roads Coliseum, Hampton, Virginia, USA.
Rolling Stones with Ian McLagan, Ernie Watts.
Producer: The Glimmer Twins.
Recorded by: Bob Clearmountain, David Hewitt. Remixed & Remastered: Bob Clearmountain.
USA e-Album HAMPTON COLISEUM: LIVE 1981: 31 January 2012
UK e-Album HAMPTON COLISEUM: LIVE 1981: 1 February 2012

908. HONKY TONK WOMEN (Jagger, Richard) ✎ 3.42
18 December 1981: Place: Hampton Roads Coliseum, Hampton, Virginia, USA.
Rolling Stones with Ian McLagan, Ernie Watts, Bobby Keys.
Producer: The Glimmer Twins.
Recorded by: Bob Clearmountain, David Hewitt. Remixed & Remastered: Bob Clearmountain.
USA e-Album HAMPTON COLISEUM: LIVE 1981: 31 January 2012
UK e-Album HAMPTON COLISEUM: LIVE 1981: 1 February 2012

909. BROWN SUGAR (Jagger, Richard) ✎ 3.39
18 December 1981: Place: Hampton Roads Coliseum, Hampton, Virginia, USA.
Rolling Stones with Ian McLagan, Ernie Watts, Bobby Keys.
Producer: The Glimmer Twins.
Recorded by: Bob Clearmountain, David Hewitt. Remixed & Remastered: Bob Clearmountain.
USA e-Album HAMPTON COLISEUM: LIVE 1981: 31 January 2012
UK e-Album HAMPTON COLISEUM: LIVE 1981: 1 February 2012

910. START ME UP (Jagger, Richards) ✎ 5.06
18 December 1981: Place: Hampton Roads Coliseum, Hampton, Virginia, USA.
Rolling Stones with Ian McLagan, Ernie Watts.
Producer: The Glimmer Twins.
Recorded by: Bob Clearmountain, David Hewitt. Remixed & Remastered: Bob Clearmountain.
USA e-Album HAMPTON COLISEUM: LIVE 1981: 31 January 2012
UK e-Album HAMPTON COLISEUM: LIVE 1981: 1 February 2012

911. JUMPIN' JACK FLASH (Jagger, Richard) ✎ 8.43
18 December 1981: Place: Hampton Roads Coliseum, Hampton, Virginia, USA.
Rolling Stones with Ian McLagan, Ernie Watts.
Producer: The Glimmer Twins.
Recorded by: Bob Clearmountain, David Hewitt. Remixed & Remastered: Bob Clearmountain.
USA e-Album HAMPTON COLISEUM: LIVE 1981: 31 January 2012
UK e-Album HAMPTON COLISEUM: LIVE 1981: 1 February 2012

912. (I CAN'T GET NO) SATISFACTION (Jagger, Richard) ✎ 7.28
18 December 1981: Place: Hampton Roads Coliseum, Hampton, Virginia, USA.
Rolling Stones with Ian McLagan, Ernie Watts.
Producer: The Glimmer Twins.
Recorded by: Bob Clearmountain, David Hewitt. Remixed & Remastered: Bob Clearmountain.
USA e-Album HAMPTON COLISEUM: LIVE 1981: 31 January 2012
UK e-Album HAMPTON COLISEUM: LIVE 1981: 1 February 2012

913. JUST MY IMAGINATION (RUNNING AWAY WITH ME) (Whitfield, Strong) ✎ 5.23
19 December 1981: Place: Hampton Roads Coliseum, Hampton, Virginia, USA.
Rolling Stones with Ian McLagan, Ernie Watts.
Producer: The Glimmer Twins.
Engineer: Malcolm Pollack, Barry Bongiovi, Larry Alexander, Phil Gitomer, Kooster McAllister, David Brown, Bob Ludwig. Recorded by: Bob Clearmountain, David Hewitt.
UK LP STILL LIFE: 1 June 1982: No. 4 - 18 weeks
USA LP STILL LIFE: 1 June 1982: No. 5 - 10 weeks

The USA tour included 51 dates, vamping its way across the States much more professionally than before. One date in Kansas unexpectedly allowed Mick Taylor to join the stage for half a dozen numbers. It was filmed and a full-length motion movie, produced by Hal Ashby, was released by Embassy Pictures in early 1983. Its original title was ROCKS OFF, despite the song not being in the set list. By that time, Hal's career had already featured *Harold And Maude*, *Shampoo*, *Bound For Glory*, *Coming Home* and *Being There*. Keith Richards was the only band member who vehemently objected to the idea, claiming that it was not practical to make a Hollywood feature film of the band on stage because it would be impossible to do justice to both the camera and the audience.
He wanted the film to be interspersed with rare small club footage. The film was mainly recorded at three different concerts, two of them at Meadowlands arena on 5 and 6 November and a gig at Sun Devil Stadium on 13 December 1981. The film opens with the stadium gig, where walkways are used to maximum effect by Jagger. The use of radio microphones enabled the group to move around the stage even if, due to the distance between them, they occasionally forgot where they were in the song. The backdrop consisted of large cloth graphics including phallic guitar images designed by a Japanese painter. They stretched the width of the stadium or arena and met for the stage curtain. There were shots from helicopters and from the back of the auditorium. Technology was advancing and there was even a small neon advertising board at the centre of the stage flashing "Jagger" and "Stones" intermittently.
For tracks like *Time Is On My Side*, a montage of other footage is segued into the film. This included Ed Sullivan material and backstage film of the Brian Jones era. Mick was dressed in crotch-tight American football pants, t-shirts, football tops, smart jacket and dapper hats. Keith had boots, jeans and rip-like t-shirts, skull ring and leopard skin jacket and was perfecting his wildcat-like crouches.
As the first arena footage starts with *Going To A Go-Go*, there are speeded up images of the stage being built and the crowd entering until the audience is shown real-time with shots of *You Can't Always Get What You Want*. New material such as *She's So Cold*, *Let Me Go*, *Neighbours* and *Hang Fire* are played at a frantic pace,

Charlie Watts accommodating the beat powerfully. A vodka-fuelled Ron Wood buffoons around but his guitar playing is usually spot on. Bill Wyman is as stoic as ever but nonetheless fashion-conscious in a yellow suit.

Hal Ashby's recording technique showed Charlie occasionally but both Ian McLagan and Ian Stewart were kept well hidden from the camera. Ian McLagan related that he viewed the tour in two parts. Up until the gigs in Candlestick Park, San Francisco, the backline was much more together as a band but, after then, it moved further to the left (from a viewing perspective) and this required separate monitors for the keyboard players - it never sounded as good for him from there onwards. For *Honky Tonk Women*, the Stones wheeled out dozens of women dressed in bordello costumes along the cat-walks. Some of these beautiful belles can be identified as Jerry Hall, Patti Hansen, Jo Wood and Shirley Watts.

Keith ensured this was not a permanent tour feature. During *Jumping Jack Flash*, a cherry picker grabbed Mick and swung him over the audience. For the encore *Satisfaction*, Mick wore a Union Jack and Stars and Stripes combined cape as balloons and confetti wafted down on the audience. At Kansas City in December, Mick Taylor, while on a tour with Alvin Lee, joined the Stones on stage for most of the show.

The tour ended with two shows at the Hampton Roads Coliseum in Virginia, the first on Keith's birthday and the second on 19 December 1981. This was the first concert recorded for TV as a pay-per-view event. Special walkways were built, extending half-way around the arena in an increasing fashion, eventually appearing to be at one with the crowd. The band were smokin' and gave a tremendous rockin' performance. For the first time on the tour, Bobby Keys came out of the shadows and guested on two numbers.

The concert is memorable for Keith's axe-handling technique - during *Satisfaction* and amidst all the balloons falling, he catches a fan running at Mick. No punches are pulled but instead he smashes his Fender Telecaster on the individual's head. Asked later why he did it, he said that, "the guy was on his turf, he could have been a nutter, I was defending my friends". So he chopped the "mother" down and claimed not to miss a beat doing it. Apparently Charlie was upset because the guy was knocked across his drum kit.

This Hampton concert was finally released as an electronic download in January/February 2012. Footage of four videos were released on YouTube by the band - *Black Limousine, Little T&A, She's So Cold, (I Can't Get No) Satisfaction*. The 1981 on-the-tour experience was enhanced by an appearance at the Checkerboard Lounge with Muddy Waters, Buddy Guy and Junior Wells when Mick Jagger, Keith Richards, Ian Stewart and Ron Wood performed with the blues Buddha on numbers, *Baby Please Don't Go, Hoochie Coochie Man, Long Distance Call, Mannish Boy* and *Champagne And Reefer*. The show sticks out to Jane Rose as a precious Stones moment and her favourite live experience and in July 2012, to illustrate its historic significance, the concert was released on DVD and CD.

914. CHANTILLY LACE (Richardson) ⟋ 4.17
25 June 1982: Place: Wembley Stadium, London, England.
Rolling Stones with Chuck Leavell, Bobby Keys, Gene Barge.
Bootleg only.

Unlike America, the European section of the tour was not such a great money-spinner, something that Mick Jagger was well aware of. For the first time, the Stones used Bill Graham in Europe since he had gained trust with the band following the USA tour. It lasted from 26 May to 25 July and, for the first time, consisted mainly of outdoor football stadium events, helping to promote not only the last LP, TATTOO YOU, but also the release of a live album culled by Bob Clearmountain from vast amounts of tape of the American tour.

It became a single album live souvenir of both the tour and the film. It was mixed and over-dubbed in March and April 1982 at the Hit Factory in New York. The album, titled STILL LIFE, was perhaps the Stones' best live project to date, recorded by Bob Clearmountain and David Hewitt (first of a long relationship), capturing perfectly the excitement of the occasion. It has to be admitted, though, that there were some wasted opportunities on the 1972, 1973 and 1978 tours, when the band were cooking on gas.

Two previously unrecorded tracks were included on the album, the good-time Smokey Robinson Motown song *Going To A Go-Go* and an "untouched by The Who" Eddie Cochran rock 'n' roll standard, *Twenty Flight Rock*. The former was released in June 1982 as the band's next single, obtaining a modest chart entry. In Britain, demand for tickets was so great that the Stones performed for the first time in one of the bastions of English fortification, the giant Wembley football arena. When Keith Richards was asked how he would approach this formidable gig he shrugged and muttered "from Heathrow".

On Friday and Saturday 25 and 26 June 1982, more than 145,000 witnessed the spectacle, those at the back visually aided by huge video screens. A film recording of the Saturday show was made by the tour crew. It includes the half circle of balloons above the stage, Bill Wyman in a blue suit with white headband, the cherry picker being used for the encore *Satisfaction* and a slightly subdued performance by the band. Mick Jagger gave an athletic performance but tensions were running high. Ronnie Wood was not at his best, his playing at times was cumbersome, and both Keith Richards and Mick were annoyed that he was not doing as well as he could. The tour package included the prestigious American R 'n' B artists The J. Geils Band and true rhythm exponents Sly Dunbar and Robbie Shakespeare, in their Jamaican band Black Uhuru. (They were later to offer their talents on the 1983 UNDERCOVER album). The show was watched by an audience whose age-span took in the original protagonists from the 1960s (now in their 40s) and teenage newcomers. Smaller British venues included the football stadiums in Bristol and Newcastle, which were also used to good advantage during a provincial excursion of the heartland including, for once, a sizable Scottish section.

Bootlegs of both the film soundtrack and various venues showed that the only significant change to the set list was the inclusion of The Big Bopper's *Chantilly Lace* but the performance was stilted. The tour personnel changed for the European gigs; Ian Stewart was still present on piano but Ian McLagan was replaced by ex-Allman Brothers, Chuck Leavell. Ian had commitments to record with Bonnie Raitt on her album GREEN LIGHTS while Chuck had been introduced to the band in America and guested at a concert. Ian Stewart felt Chuck was well suited to the band and became very friendly with him, teaching boogie-woogie music. Chuck also succeeded Nicky Hopkins with studio duties. It was the start of a strong relationship that has lasted to this day.

He was a great fan of Nicky's playing and, for live concerts, would study Nicky's studio versions to ensure he produced a worthy performance. The saxophone players were again Bobby Keys and Gene Barge, who replaced Ernie Watts. Gene was one of the renowned artists who played on many a Chess Studio classic in the 60s. The tour visited Scotland for some small warm-up gigs in May and the 100 Club in London to coincide with the album release.

There followed the Netherlands, Germany, France, Sweden, Spain, Italy, Switzerland and Ireland before returning to England to play Newcastle and Bristol. Keith remembered the Newcastle gig to be special as it rained and the crowd were really up for it. Back to Europe, they completed the tour in July with gigs at Slane Castle, in Dublin, and Leeds' Roundhay Park.

The tour support acts were the aforementioned J. Geils Band and Black Uhuru. In France only, Telephone, UB40 and George Thorogood appeared. It was rumoured that R 'n' B guitarist George Thorogood was asked to rehearse Stones numbers in case Ronnie succumbed to the strain. The tour was followed in September by the release of the live *Time Is On My Side*, with *Twenty Flight Rock* and *Under My Thumb* on the 12-inch single.

915. WANNA HOLD YOU (Jagger, Richards) 3.52
AKA: I Wanna Hold You
October; 11 November - 16 December 1982; April; May - July 1983: Place: Unknown studio, Paris, France; EMI Pathé Marconi Studios, Paris, France; Compass Point, Nassau, Bahamas; The Hit Factory, New York, USA.
Played Live: 1997, 1998, 2007
Producer: The Glimmer Twins, Chris Kimsey.
Engineer: Brian McGee, Rod Thear, Steve Lipson, Bobby Cohen, Benji Armbrister.
UK LP UNDERCOVER: 7 November 1983: No. 3 - 18 weeks
USA LP UNDERCOVER: 7 November 1983: No. 4 - 12 weeks

In anticipation of the sessions to be held for the next album, Mick Jagger and Keith Richards worked in a small basement studio in Paris, with eight-track recording facilities. They shared recent ideas and wrote and performed in the old style. One of the first recordings was written by Keith Richards and performed almost exclusively by him. *I Wanna Hold You* is a warm, uplifting number reminiscent of the optimistic *Happy*, also sung by Keith.
The released cassette track and subsequent CBS CD re-releases, include an additional 35 seconds of the song with an extra verse. The lyrics are about love and friendship and were inspired by Keith's love for Patti Hansen, although working with Mick at close hand could have helped. Several worthwhile tracks originated out of the early basement recordings, of which this is one. The original demo has Mick on drums, Ron Wood on bass, while Keith bashes out the lead guitar and adds his rough-textured vocals.
Keith has been heard to say that the song is akin to the spirit of a pop song such as the Beatles' *I Wanna Hold Your Hand*. In other words, it could have been a classic! An early out-take has a country- sounding lead guitar from Ronnie with early lyrics (* a - 6.28), another with completed lyrics sounds close to the finished take (* b - 3.22), but the preferred out-take is a seven-minute rough cut with Keith singing early lyrics and playing an extended lead solo (* c - 6.57). An edit was made on earlier copies of the album (* d - 3.15).

916. CAN'T FIND LOVE (Jagger, Richards)
October 1982: Place: Unknown studio, Paris, France.
Producer: The Glimmer Twins
Unavailable.

917. YOU KEEP IT COOL (Jagger, Richards)
October 1982: Place: Unknown studio, Paris, France.
Producer: The Glimmer Twins
Unavailable.

918. CHRISTINE (Jagger, Richards)
October 1982: Place: Unknown studio, Paris, France.
Producer: The Glimmer Twins
Unavailable.

Other tracks were worked on that may have ended up with different working titles.

919. SLIDE ON (Jagger, Richards) 5.49
11 November - 16 December 1982: Place: EMI Pathé Marconi Studios, Paris, France.
Producer: The Glimmer Twins, Chris Kimsey.
Bootleg only.

The full band returned to the territory of the EMI-owned Pathé Marconi Studios in late 1982. Chris Kimsey was asked by Rupert Lowenstein's office to produce the sessions, which he agreed to do warily. The warm familiarity with the Paris-based studios, which had started in 1977 with the SOME GIRLS sessions, had continued on every album recorded to date. The Stones simply felt no pressure recording in Paris, enjoying the French lifestyle.
However, the sessions proved to be fractious and Mick Jagger and Keith Richards rarely recorded together. They would turn up at different times and ask what the other had done and then dismiss each other's input. EMI also allowed the Stones to record "time gratis" as opposed to the studios of competitors who would charge by the hour. *Slide On* is a slow blues instrumental featuring piano and a lead guitar with strains of Eric Clapton. A shorter version is also available (* a - 4.15).

920. PRETTY BEAT UP (Jagger, Richards, Wood) 4.05
AKA: Dog Shit, XXX, Ronnie's Idea
11 November - 16 December 1982; April; May - July 1983: Place: EMI Pathé Marconi Studios, Paris, France; Compass Point, Nassau, Bahamas; The Hit Factory, New York, USA.
Rolling Stones with David Sanborn, Moustapha Cisse, Brahms Coundoul, Martin Ditcham, Sly Dunbar, Robbie Shakespeare, Chuck Leavell.
Producer: The Glimmer Twins, Chris Kimsey.
Engineer: Brian McGee, Rod Thear, Steve Lipson, Bobby Cohen, Benji Armbrister.

UK LP UNDERCOVER: 7 November 1983: No. 3 - 18 weeks
USA LP UNDERCOVER: 7 November 1983: No. 4 - 12 weeks

Bill Wyman had good cause to remember *Pretty Beat Up* since he assists Chuck Leavell in the keyboards role by playing the Yamaha piano. Is this why he recollected the working title of the track so vividly? Roles were reversed as Keith Richards grabs the bass guitar while the sweet saxophone is performed by new sax recruit, David Sanborn - Bobby Keys and Ernie Watts were ousted for the moment. David had played with Stevie Wonder on the 1972 tour.

Ronnie Wood wrote the song with some support from Jagger and Richards - his only co-composition on the album - chipping in with the Bo Diddley rhythm. An early take of the song, with different X-rated lyrics, was called *XXX* (* a). There are also two instrumental cuts, one of which at six minutes has a real groove (* b - 6.08, c - 4.28). Mick Jagger may have played guitar on the song. Ron also takes the lead guitar role but *Pretty Beat Up* is an average album contribution, the subject material by now having a familiar, sardonic ring. Ron played the song on his SLIDE ON LIVE tour album from 1993 with Ian McLagan and Bernard Fowler.

921. ALL MIXED UP (Traditional) 6.36
11 November - 16 December 1982: Place: EMI Pathé Marconi Studios, Paris, France.
Producer: The Glimmer Twins, Chris Kimsey.
Bootleg only.

Continuing with the blues theme, this traditional song was recorded twice, once as an instrumental (* a - 2.38) and then with some Mick Jagger vocals.

922. ALL THE WAY DOWN (Jagger, Richards) 3.14
11 November - 16 December 1982; April; May - July 1983: Place: EMI Pathé Marconi Studios, Paris, France; Compass Point, Nassau, Bahamas; The Hit Factory, New York, USA.
Rolling Stones with Jim Barber, Chuck Leavell.
Producer: The Glimmer Twins, Chris Kimsey.
Engineer: Brian McGee, Rod Thear, Steve Lipson, Bobby Cohen, Benji Armbrister.
UK B-side Undercover Of The Night: 1 November 1983
USA B-side Undercover Of The Night: 1 November 1983
UK LP UNDERCOVER: 7 November 1983: No. 3 - 18 weeks
USA LP UNDERCOVER: 7 November 1983: No. 4 - 12 weeks
UK CD box set THE SINGLES COLLECTION 1971-2006: 45 X 45s: 11 April 2011
USA CD box set THE SINGLES COLLECTION 1971-2006: 45 X 45s: 26 April 2011

"Don't want to hear it from the beginning, just drop us in", cried Keith Richards on the studio's intercom and so the band respond on what is a mediocre rocker, having left out the proposed intro to the song on Chris Kimsey's advice. A ragged out-take exists with early lyrics (* a - 3.43). The rather wry-sounding vocals of Mick Jagger are quite aesthetic and there are also some nice guitar lines, including an acoustic piece when the vocals are slowed down, down, down.

It was reputedly about one of Mick's conquests when he was aged 21 and she went . . . all the way down. Released as the flipside of the seven-inch version of *Undercover Of The Night*, it was a foretaste of what was to come on. This was a pity, since it is one of the album's weaker tracks. The production team were amused at the phrase "just drop us in" with Brian McGee and Chris creating a five-minute comedy sample of the phrase for Keith.

Steve Lipson, who joined the session initially, left after two weeks not fully appreciating the lengthy process the Stones adopted for recording. He decided to work with an incarnation of Yes on another album, named 90125. Ian Stewart recalled the work Rod Thear did back in 1974 and phoned him to join the sessions. Thear had also worked with Chris with Spooky Tooth in 1973.

923. SHE WAS HOT (Jagger, Richards) 4.42
11 November - 16 December 1982; April; May - July 1983: Place: EMI Pathé Marconi Studios, Paris, France; Compass Point, Nassau, Bahamas; The Hit Factory, New York, USA.
Played Live: 2006, 2007
Rolling Stones with Chuck Leavell.
Producer: The Glimmer Twins, Chris Kimsey.
Engineer: Brian McGee, Rod Thear, Steve Lipson, Bobby Cohen, Benji Armbrister.
UK LP UNDERCOVER: 7 November 1983: No. 3 - 18 weeks
USA LP UNDERCOVER: 7 November 1983: No. 4 - 12 weeks
UK Single: 24 January 1984: No. 42 - 4 weeks
USA Single: 24 January 1984
UK CD box set THE SINGLES COLLECTION 1971-2006: 45 X 45s: 11 April 2011
USA CD box set THE SINGLES COLLECTION 1971-2006: 45 X 45s: 26 April 2011

Released as the follow up to the *Undercover* single, *She Was Hot*, with politics forgotten, is a guitar-laden boogie-woogie (Ian Stewart's forte and one of his last studio recordings) song with more than a tinge of typical Jagger humour. This was evidently portrayed on the video, directed by Julien Temple, at a Mexican location. Anita Morris is the red-headed girl with heated aspirations. Employed by the Stones, she seduces Mick Jagger in the first verse in a cold and damp New York then her attentions turn to Keith Richards in smoky, grey Detroit.

Still not defused, Anita is then thrust into a scene with the whole band, which is a rip-off of the Jayne Mansfield film, *The Girl Can't Help It*, complete with instruments hanging from the ceiling. Other choice moments in the video include Charlie Watts convincingly playing a showbiz agent and Bill Wyman and Jo Karslake (Ron Wood's confidante) made up like hillbilly geriatrics, being deluged by gallons of water. There was a phone number in the background, which unfortunately turned out to be that of a real household. The Stones paid for it to be changed.

Four "company executives", who are watching Anita Morris pose provocatively, cannot control themselves on the video and buttons burst on one man's trousers. This shot resulted in the video being banned on the American MTV network, a by now familiar fate. It was later re-edited to MTV's satisfaction. Keith Richards worried that video would kill rock 'n' roll, a bit like people coming out of the cinema and saying, "I preferred the book".

A strong song could be ruined by a bad video but Mick enjoyed this alternative music format. Julien Temple respected the fact that the band had been doing this for 20 years where most artists could not survive a week. The music is a mid-tempo rocker and evidently a cousin of *She's So Cold*. An early version is much more country-like and played at a slower pace (* a - 6.44).

A long, almost 10-minute out-take is sung straight with extra piano and, when the vocals finish, continues with the two guitars playing country fashion, unlike the rock of the released version (* b - 9.27). Some radio stations played this extended cut, albeit edited, which somehow leaked out of Atlantic records. In the UK, a DJ version was made available (* c - 3.59).

On the *Rewind* video, the song is extended and includes sound effects and an additional verse (* d - 4.58). Chuck Leavell plays keyboards and Ian tinkles in boogie fashion on the piano. Chuck's piano refrain, when the music slows down, is much appreciated. Keith and Ronnie Wood's guitars flash angrily as they play rhythm riffs - solos asunder. Rod Thear thought that Chuck fitted in perfectly to the Stones camp. He blended particularly well with Ian Stewart and was well received by the band because of his general good humour. *She Was Hot* was resurrected to great success on the A BIGGER BANG tour.

924. COOKIN' UP (Jagger, Richards) 4.01
AKA: Chainsaw Rocker
11 November - 16 December 1982: Place: EMI Pathé Marconi Studios, Paris, France.
Rolling Stones with Chuck Leavell.
Producer: The Glimmer Twins, Chris Kimsey.
Bootleg only.

A real rocker that smacks along fortified by some boogie piano. Mick Jagger's vocals can be heard in the background. A longer, earlier version can also be heard (* a - 5.57).

925. TIE YOU UP (THE PAIN OF LOVE) (Jagger, Richards) 4.16
11 November - 16 December 1982; April; May - July 1983: Place: EMI Pathé Marconi Studios, Paris, France; Compass Point, Nassau, Bahamas; The Hit Factory, New York, USA.
Rolling Stones with Moustapha Cisse, Brahms Coundoul, Martin Ditcham, Sly Dunbar, Chuck Leavell.
Producer: The Glimmer Twins, Chris Kimsey.
Engineer: Brian McGee, Rod Thear, Steve Lipson, Bobby Cohen, Benji Armbrister.
UK LP UNDERCOVER: 7 November 1983: No. 3 - 18 weeks
USA LP UNDERCOVER: 7 November 1983: No. 4 - 12 weeks

One of Mick Jagger's favourites on the album. After it was recorded, Mick reckoned that it reminded him of blues artist Lowell Fulson, due to the way Keith Richards played on it. The lyrics are certainly provocative if taken at face value "feel the hot cum dripping on your thigh" - Mick sings them in a tough brogue while the guitar solos, dropped from *She Was Hot*, are laced to good effect on *Tie You Up*.
Ron Wood plays bass and Chuck Leavell the organ while Keith delivers the guitar message in a combined blues funk-rock style. After a few verses the rhythm simmers down to allow a nifty percussive passage. Charlie Watts' drums are positively featured by Chris Kimsey, making the song's overall sound almost funky. The percussion is supported by Senegalese artists Moustapha Cisse and Brahms Coundoul, Martin Ditcham, from the Chris Rea band, and Black Uhurus' Sly Dunbar. Just how many tracks they played percussion on is unclear but the tight rhythms were certainly a feature of the UNDERCOVER album, helping to make it contemporary. On this occasion, the disco beat hits its mark. The groove extended for 11 minutes on an early out-take (* a - 10.48).

926. STOP THAT (Jagger, Richards) 5.40
AKA: In Your Hand
11 November - 16 December 1982: Place: EMI Pathé Marconi Studios, Paris, France.
Producer: The Glimmer Twins, Chris Kimsey.
Bootleg only.

Stop That is a fast, six-minute number with piano by Ian Stewart. It builds up to quite a crescendo. Like *Cookin' Up,* the vocals are not distinct due to them being recorded off microphone.

927. LOOKING FOR TROUBLE (Taylor) 3.03
11 November - 16 December 1982: Place: EMI Pathé Marconi Studios, Paris, France.
Producer: The Glimmer Twins, Chris Kimsey.
Bootleg only.

Just to illustrate their knowledge of the blues, this Eddie Taylor cover was recorded. Eddie was a contemporary and friend of Jimmy Reed. It is standard blues fare with Ian Stewart on piano.

928. TOO TOUGH (Jagger, Richards) 3.51
11 November - 16 December 1982; April; May - July 1983: Place: EMI Pathé Marconi Studios, Paris, France; Compass Point, Nassau, Bahamas; The Hit Factory, New York, USA.
Rolling Stones with Chuck Leavell, Sly Dunbar.
Producer: The Glimmer Twins, Chris Kimsey.
Engineer: Brian McGee, Rod Thear, Steve Lipson, Bobby Cohen, Benji Armbrister.
UK LP UNDERCOVER: 7 November 1983: No. 3 - 18 weeks
USA LP UNDERCOVER: 7 November 1983: No. 4 - 12 weeks
USA Single: 3 July 1984
UK CD box set THE SINGLES COLLECTION 1971-2006: 45 X 45s: 11 April 2011
USA CD box set THE SINGLES COLLECTION 1971-2006: 45 X 45s: 26 April 2011

Too Tough seemed to have the promise of a classic rocker in the mould of a *Brown Sugar*. The guitar riff was certainly a contributory factor to this but, alas, the song's potential was somehow lost. Some of it is reminiscent of the out-take *Cellophane Trousers* but the necessary raw edge on *Too Tough* was lacking and it remains as no more than an album filler.

Ron Wood plays a mighty heavy rock guitar solo and Mick Jagger also features on guitar, with Keith Richards on slide. The vocals belong to Mick though an extended out-take, with unfinished lyrics, has Keith singing the bridge to the song on three occasions (* a - 5.24).

The bridge on the released version is sung ensemble with slightly echoed fazed vocals. Sly Dunbar supported the percussion on Simmons electronic drums. In July 1984, *Too Tough*, mixed by Chris Kimsey, was mysteriously released as an American single to promote the REWIND compilation album but predictably failed to chart.

929. COOK COOK BLUES (Jagger, Richards) 4.11
11 November - 16 December 1982; 15 May - 29 June 1989: Place: EMI Pathé Marconi Studios, Paris, France; Olympic Sound Studios, London, England.
Rolling Stones with Chuck Leavell.
Producer: Chris Kimsey, The Glimmer Twins.
Engineer: Christopher Marc Potter, Rupert Coulson.
UK & USA B-side Rock And A Hard Place: 13 November 1989
UK CD Track Rock And A Hard Place (Dance Mix): 13 November 1989
USA CD FLASHPOINT (COLLECTIBLES): 20 May 1991
UK CD box set THE SINGLES COLLECTION 1971-2006: 45 X 45s: 11 April 2011
USA CD box set THE SINGLES COLLECTION 1971-2006: 45 X 45s: 26 April 2011

Cook Cook Blues sounds as though it was used at the beginning of a session to create a mood for subsequent recording. It started life during the UNDERCOVER sessions, where quite a few takes were made of blues tunes, with Ian Stewart and Chuck Leavell attempting to outdo each other, and was completed at the STEEL WHEELS sessions. It is a fine boogie and stroll tune which gently fades in and doubtless would have remained on the cutting room floor if a flip side to the single had not been required. At least the Stones were no longer releasing tracks from the album as the B-side.

930. IT MUST BE HELL (Jagger, Richards) 5.04
11 November - 16 December 1982; April; May - July 1983: Place: EMI Pathé Marconi Studios, Paris, France; Compass Point, Nassau, Bahamas; The Hit Factory, New York, USA.
Rolling Stones with Moustapha Cisse, Brahms Coundoul, Martin Ditcham, Sly Dunbar, Chuck Leavell.
Producer: The Glimmer Twins, Chris Kimsey.
Engineer: Brian McGee, Rod Thear, Steve Lipson, Bobby Cohen, Benji Armbrister.
UK LP UNDERCOVER: 7 November 1983: No. 3 - 18 weeks
USA LP UNDERCOVER: 7 November 1983: No. 4 - 12 weeks

Keith Richards rated the lyrics written by Mick Jagger on UNDERCOVER as some of his best since the 1969-72 period. Some, as on *It Must Be Hell*, are full of bleak pessimism. Mick acknowledged that the album had perhaps more social commentary than their usual efforts.

The problems associated with over-dominant, one-leadership states in the eastern world are tackled. On this song, Mick wanted to show the east had more problems than the west. Mick would have also had thoughts on the recent Falklands war, earlier in the year, where Britain defended the sovereignty of the islands in the Southern Atlantic, battling against the Argentinian invasion until their surrender.

Keith Richards opens with a riff then plays a chord sequence, reminding one in parts *Honky Tonk Women* and *Soul Survivor*, before it ferments into an archetypal Stones rocker. Bill Wyman ably supports the rhythm and Ronnie Wood delivers the lead solo as Mick gives the "whoo who" echoed salute. A six-minute out-take does not disguise the additional percussion (* a -5.45).

931. TRIED TO TALK HER INTO IT (Jagger, Richards) 3.19
11 November - 16 December 1982: Place: EMI Pathé Marconi Studios, Paris, France.
Rolling Stones with Chuck Leavell.
Producer: The Glimmer Twins, Chris Kimsey.
Bootleg only.

A country rock song with jangly Byrds-like guitars and piano, Jagger can be heard offering chord changes. There is a quiet passage where Mick rhetorically asks: "What would you do if you give her money and she refuses?" Was that before or after you tried to talk her into it?

932. CRAZY ARMS (Mooney, Seals) 1.30
11 November - 16 December 1982: Place: EMI Pathé Marconi Studios, Paris, France.
Producer: The Glimmer Twins, Chris Kimsey.
Bootleg only.

A song with just Keith Richards on piano, vocals and a country steel guitar. It was simply a sketch or a practice cut. It is a country and western standard by Ralph Mooney and Charles Seals, which was covered by Patsy Cline, Merle Haggard, Chuck Berry, Jerry Lee Lewis, Waylon Jennings and, of course, The Flying Burrito Brothers - to mention just a few. Unusually, the album UNDERCOVER had no cover versions.

933. HIDEAWAY (King)
11 November - 16 December 1982: Place: EMI Pathé Marconi Studios, Paris, France.
Producer: The Glimmer Twins, Chris Kimsey.
Unavailable.

A Freddie King instrumental.

934. ELIZA UPCHINK (Jagger, Richards)
11 November - 16 December 1982: Place: EMI Pathé Marconi Studios, Paris, France.
Producer: The Glimmer Twins, Chris Kimsey.
Unavailable.

935. DANCE MR. K (Jagger, Richards)
11 November - 16 December 1982: Place: EMI Pathé Marconi Studios, Paris, France.
Producer: The Glimmer Twins, Chris Kimsey.
Unavailable.

936. PULLOVER (Jagger, Richards)
11 November - 16 December 1982: Place: EMI Pathé Marconi Studios, Paris, France.
Producer: The Glimmer Twins, Chris Kimsey.
Unavailable.

937. SHOW ME A WOMAN (Jagger, Richards)
11 November - 16 December 1982: Place: EMI Pathé Marconi Studios, Paris, France.
Producer: The Glimmer Twins, Chris Kimsey.
Unavailable.

938. IDENTIFICATION (Jagger, Richards)
11 November - 16 December 1982: Place: EMI Pathé Marconi Studios, Paris, France.
Producer: The Glimmer Twins, Chris Kimsey.
Unavailable.

939. PINK PICK (Jagger, Richards)
11 November - 16 December 1982: Place: EMI Pathé Marconi Studios, Paris, France.
Producer: The Glimmer Twins, Chris Kimsey.
Unavailable.

940. CHRISTMAS ISSUE (Jagger, Richards)
11 November - 16 December 1982: Place: EMI Pathé Marconi Studios, Paris, France.
Producer: The Glimmer Twins, Chris Kimsey.
Unavailable.

941. STIFF (Jagger, Richards)
11 November - 16 December 1982: Place: EMI Pathé Marconi Studios, Paris, France.
Producer: The Glimmer Twins, Chris Kimsey.
Unavailable.

942. HEARTBEAT (Jagger, Richards)
11 November - 16 December 1982: Place: EMI Pathé Marconi Studios, Paris, France.
Producer: The Glimmer Twins, Chris Kimsey.
Unavailable.

943. MELLOBAR (Jagger, Richards)
11 November - 16 December 1982: Place: EMI Pathé Marconi Studios, Paris, France.
Producer: The Glimmer Twins, Chris Kimsey.
Unavailable.

In Bill Wyman's book *Rolling With The Stones*, he mentions a number of tracks for the UNDERCOVER sessions. Some may be working titles for known songs and all are unavailable. UNDERCOVER was unusual since most of the tracks were new and not resurrected from previous sessions.
The album cover was again designed by Peter Corriston, with artwork by Hubert Kretzschmar. It was an image of a naked lady with strategic stickers placed on the rude bits. The rear cover with song titles, of course, had a naked cheeky bum. The sticker idea was a costly option since each had to be applied individually so this was only available for a limited edition before the body parts were covered permanently. Hubert had worked with Peter Corriston on the artwork for SOME GIRLS, EMOTIONAL RESCUE and also TATTOO YOU but was not credited.

944. TOO MUCH BLOOD (DUB VERSION) (Jagger, Richards) 8.00
11 November - 16 December 1982; April; May - July 1983: Place: EMI Pathé Marconi Studios, Paris, France; Compass Point, Nassau, Bahamas; The Hit Factory, New York, USA.
Rolling Stones with Moustapha Cisse, Brahms Coundoul, Martin Ditcham, Sly Dunbar, Chuck Leavell, Jim Barber, Chops.
Producer: The Glimmer Twins, Chris Kimsey.
Engineer: Brian McGee, Rod Thear, Steve Lipson, Bobby Cohen, Benji Armbrister.
USA B-side 12-inch Single Too Much Blood (Dance Version): December 1984

945. TOO MUCH BLOOD (DANCE VERSION) (Jagger, Richards) 12.33
11 November - 16 December 1982; April; May - July 1983: Place: EMI Pathé Marconi Studios, Paris, France; Compass Point, Nassau, Bahamas; The Hit Factory, New York, USA.
Rolling Stones with Moustapha Cisse, Brahms Coundoul, Martin Ditcham, Sly Dunbar, Chuck Leavell, Jim Barber, Chops.
Producer: The Glimmer Twins, Chris Kimsey.
Engineer: Brian McGee, Rod Thear, Steve Lipson, Bobby Cohen, Benji Armbrister.
USA 12-inch Single: December 1984
UK Track CD Single Sad Sad Sad: 13 August 1990

946. TOO MUCH BLOOD (Jagger, Richards) 6.25
11 November - 16 December 1982; April; May - July 1983: Place: EMI Pathé Marconi Studios, Paris, France; Compass Point, Nassau, Bahamas; The Hit Factory, New York, USA.
Rolling Stones with Moustapha Cisse, Brahms Coundoul, Martin Ditcham, Sly Dunbar, Chuck Leavell, Jim Barber, Chops.
Producer: The Glimmer Twins, Chris Kimsey.
Engineer: Brian McGee, Rod Thear, Steve Lipson, Bobby Cohen, Benji Armbrister.
UK LP UNDERCOVER: 7 November 1983: No. 3 - 18 weeks
USA LP UNDERCOVER: 7 November 1983: No. 4 - 12 weeks
USA B-side 12-inch Single Too Much Blood (Dance Version): December 1984

The musical and lyrical repertoires of the Stones and their crew of friends culminate on *Too Much Blood*, the undisputed high point of the UNDERCOVER album. The riff played on the horns by the Sugarhill brass section Chops - namely Darryl Dixon and Dave Watson (over-dubbed at a later stage in New York) - is inspirational and lifts the track to epic proportions. They were asked by Mick Jagger to work on this instrumental and provide a melody for it.

Mick's lyrics, added later as the song gained potential and power, are uncompromising and savagely vivid; Jagger's intertwined tang of humour is first class. The rap sequences, suitably X-rated, are especially good, with Mick's vocal delivery quite superb. Rod Thear was particularly impressed with the apparent ad-libs. With the help of his notebook, Mick had a great knack for combining ad-hoc phrases.

The track, formulated by Mick, was started when Keith was away. It began with Mick rapping away with just Charlie Watts and Bill Wyman present. The main guitar piece is taken by Stones equipment specialist and sometime session musician, Jim Barber, who puts down another, line filling out the rhythm of Keith's Jesselli and Ronnie Wood's electric fender. Chris Kimsey had to use all his diplomacy skills to get any participation for this track by Keith because he hated it, especially the lyrical psychosis.

He gave Keith an instrumental-only version and he then over-dubbed the rhythm. Charlie's drum sound strives at the grandmaster of funk, while even Bill's short-necked bass has an opportunity to shine and he delivers a solo passage or two. The late-night movie script conjured up by *Too Much Blood* ensured it could not be officially released as a single without getting savagely edited. Instead, in 1984, at Mick's instigation, *Too Much Blood* was re-cut by the Latin Rascals, Albert Cabrera and Tony Moran.

Arthur Baker, famous for his mixes on the 12-inch single format, reworked the track for a release which was principally intended for night clubs. Stones collectors have since fought to get the product in import shops. The culmination of the project is a gargantuan 20-minute product, which includes a dance and club version of the song. The Stones were brought into the computerised, technological age by the syncopated control room boys. Arthur Baker's unique production style added a further dimension to *Too Much Blood* but Mick did not agree with some of the ideas. Baker worked better on a free production rein which Mick was reluctant to give.

The Cadets, an American rock and roll act from the 1950s, would have been proud of Mick because, while recording further vocal tracks on *Too Much Blood*, he quoted their infamous line "Meanwhile, back in the jungle". Other vocals used in the different mixes by Arthur Baker include a humorous dialogue about Michael Jackson's Thriller video - "How does a werewolf make fucking love anyway"' and Mick calling in desperation to his only mate "Keith!" The censors were put to work again in January, 1984.

After the recording of the *She Was Hot* video, Julien Temple filmed the Stones in Mexico for a possible *Too Much Blood* follow-up. This became fact when it was announced in 1984 that a home video cassette of Stones videos, entitled *Rewind*, would be released and include the gory number, *Too Much Blood*. The compilation was inspired and compiled by Bill Wyman. In the *Too Much Blood* video, Keith and Ron can be seen rampaging with electric saws and there is also the crazy scene involving a body in the refrigerator.

These are included due to the two rap sequences, in which Mick tells the story of Renee Hartwelt, who disappeared on 12 June 1981. A man was spotted dumping two suitcases containing parts of her body in the Bois de Boulogne. The luggage was traced to Issei Sagawa, a Japanese man who had apparently cannibalised her - more parts were found in his kitchen and refrigerator.

The other rap was about the 1974 film *Texas Chainsaw Massacre* based on a crazed set of brothers who hone their butchery skills on the local community, one wearing a human skin mask. On an out-take, Mick is heard giving chord changes and much of the rap speak was obviously already written (* a - 6.26).

A similar extract can also be found (* b - 2.51), the beginning of which has bongo drums, not unlike *Sympathy For The Devil*. At one stage Mick is heard to say: "What do you say to a one legged woman - open your leg" and he continues "at least it made Bill laugh". This particular part was changed to "dancing with a one-legged woman". There is another version with the Chops horns playing in an even more manic fashion.

947. FEEL ON BABY (Jagger, Richards) 5.07
31 January - 9 February, 15 February - March; April; May - July 1983: Place: EMI Pathé Marconi Studios, Paris, France; Compass Point, Nassau, Bahamas; The Hit Factory, New York, USA.
Rolling Stones with Moustapha Cisse, Brahms Coundoul, Martin Ditcham, Sly Dunbar, Robbie Shakespeare, Chuck Leavell.
Producer: The Glimmer Twins, Chris Kimsey.
Engineer: Brian McGee, Rod Thear, Steve Lipson, Bobby Cohen, Benji Armbrister.
UK LP UNDERCOVER: 7 November 1983: No. 3 - 18 weeks
USA LP UNDERCOVER: 7 November 1983: No. 4 - 12 weeks

948. FEEL ON BABY (INSTRUMENTAL MIX) (Jagger, Richards) 6.31
AKA: Feel On Baby (Instrumental Dub)
31 January - 9 February, 15 February - March; April; May - July 1983: Place: EMI Pathé Marconi Studios, Paris, France; Compass Point, Nassau, Bahamas; The Hit Factory, New York, USA.
Rolling Stones with Moustapha Cisse, Brahms Coundoul, Martin Ditcham, Sly Dunbar, Robbie Shakespeare, Chuck Leavell.
Producer: The Glimmer Twins, Chris Kimsey.
Engineer: Brian McGee, Rod Thear, Steve Lipson, Bobby Cohen, Benji Armbrister.
UK B-side 12-inch Single: Undercover Of The Night: 1 November 1983
USA B-side 12-inch Single: Undercover Of The Night: 1 November 1983
UK CD box set THE SINGLES COLLECTION 1971-2006: 45 X 45s: 11 April 2011
USA CD box set THE SINGLES COLLECTION 1971-2006: 45 X 45s: 26 April 2011

When Keith Richards dutifully appeared on BBC's radio programme My Top Ten in 1986, he cited Jamaica as a major musical influence, especially reggae exponents Max Romeo and Gregory Isaacs. The sound of reggae emerged on Stones albums in a hesitant manner - they preferred not to dupe the music form. In its two forms, *Feel On Baby* tackles the rhythm and a remixed dub version. The latter appeared on a 12-inch extended single vinyl format which was mixed by Chris Kimsey, assisted by Brian McGee, at the Hit Factory, New York City.

The Stones were joined in the UNDERCOVER sessions by Jamaican rhythm heroes Sly Dunbar and Robbie Shakespeare. They fronted the Black Uhuru band but were principally noted for their overall involvement in the reggae scene. Such was their esteem, that they were now crossing frontiers and being asked to perform on "white man's" rock music. They were paying back Keith's contribution to their album. *Feel On Baby* was written mostly by Keith and he contributes what could be described as "bouncing vocals".

He recalls that the percussion on the track is enhanced by Senegalese musicians, who played some amazing village instruments. These can be plainly heard on the track, interspersed by Chuck Leavell's organ playing and Charlie Watts' "slave to the rhythm" drums. Keith introduces the track with a skank "Feel on baby" before the organ gently comes in to Mick Jagger's vocals sung straight, not attempting any Jamaican dialect. A mouth organ is also used to good effect as the song enters its dub phase.

The album was complete but it received a lukewarm reception, despite the radio banning of certain material, which in itself usually creates interest and curiosity. The promotional videos of *Undercover*, *She Was Hot* and *Too Much Blood* received some exposure (the latter two being recorded in Mexico City, in January 1984). Mick's decision not to tour so soon after the 1981/82 escapade reduced further sales potential. Mick informed Keith that, in 1984, he planned to take time out to work on other projects, which included the video for Bette Midler's *Beast Of Burden*, where he had a pie thrown in his face, and a Michael Jackson collaboration on a single labelled *State Of Shock*. He could also be heard on *Pretty Lady*, a track featured on Peter Wolf's solo album.

One successful Stones project involved Mick and Bill Wyman working on the *Rewind* video collection, featuring videos from the 70s and 80s, including three from UNDERCOVER. The videos were interspersed with sketches in a rock and roll museum and rare interview footage. It sold extremely well and was supported by a retrospective album of tracks pulled together from 1971 to 1984 and released in July 1984. The UK version had two bonus tracks.

In August 1983, the band signed a $28 million worldwide deal with CBS for four albums and rights to the back catalogue. Keith did not appreciate that this also included one Jagger solo album. This was, perhaps, the most significant event for Mick Jagger and resulted in a one-year sabbatical from the Stones. He first started writing songs for a solo album in March 1984 while relaxing on holiday in the Caribbean. This was the sticking point. Of course a precedent had been set by Bill Wyman but Keith viewed the Glimmer Twins in the same light as the Three Musketeers. All for one and one for all! So instead of working, he decided to get married for the first time, on his 40th birthday (18 December 1983), to Patti Hansen, the girl who had been his soul mate.

949. UNDERCOVER OF THE NIGHT (DUB VERSION) (Jagger, Richards) 6.21
AKA: Undercover Of The Night (Extended Cheeky Version), Undercover Of The Night (Special Dance Remix)
31 January - 9 February, 15 February - March; April; May - July 1983: Place: EMI Pathé Marconi Studios, Paris, France; Compass Point, Nassau, Bahamas; The Hit Factory, New York, USA.
Rolling Stones with Moustapha Cisse, Brahms Coundoul, Martin Ditcham, Sly Dunbar, Robbie Shakespeare, Chuck Leavell.
Producer: The Glimmer Twins, Chris Kimsey.
Engineer: Brian McGee, Rod Thear, Steve Lipson, Bobby Cohen, Benji Armbrister.
UK 12-inch Single: 1 November 1983: No. 11 - 9 weeks
USA 12-inch Single: 1 November 1983: No. 9 - 10 weeks
UK CD box set THE SINGLES COLLECTION 1971-2006: 45 X 45s: 11 April 2011
USA CD box set THE SINGLES COLLECTION 1971-2006: 45 X 45s: 26 April 2011

950. UNDERCOVER OF THE NIGHT (Jagger, Richards) 4.33
31 January - 9 February, 15 February - March; April; May - July 1983: Place: EMI Pathé Marconi Studios, Paris, France; Compass Point, Nassau, Bahamas; The Hit Factory, New York, USA.
Played Live: 1989, 1994, 1999, 2002, 2006
Rolling Stones with Moustapha Cisse, Brahms Coundoul, Martin Ditcham, Sly Dunbar, Robbie Shakespeare, Chuck Leavell.
Producer: The Glimmer Twins, Chris Kimsey.
Engineer: Brian McGee, Rod Thear, Steve Lipson, Bobby Cohen, Benji Armbrister.
UK Single: 1 November 1983: No. 11 - 9 weeks
USA Single: 1 November 1983: No. 9 - 10 weeks
USA Promo Single: 1 November 1983: No. 9 - 10 weeks
USA B-side 12-inch Promo B-side Undercover Of The Night (Dub Version): 1 November 1983
UK LP UNDERCOVER: 7 November 1983: No. 3 - 18 weeks
USA LP UNDERCOVER: 7 November 1983: No. 4 - 12 weeks

UK Compilation LP REWIND 1971-1984 (THE BEST OF THE ROLLING STONES): 29 June 1984: No. 45 - 5 weeks
USA Compilation LP REWIND 1971-1984 (THE BEST OF THE ROLLING STONES): 2 July 1984: No. 86 - 11 weeks
UK Compilation LP JUMP BACK THE BEST OF THE ROLLING STONES '71 - '93: 22 November 1993: No. 16 - 26 weeks
UK CD LP FORTY LICKS: 30 September 2002: No. 2 - 45 weeks
USA CD LP FORTY LICKS: 1 October 2002: No. 2 - 50 weeks
USA Compilation CD JUMP BACK THE BEST OF THE ROLLING STONES '71 - '93: 24 August 2004: No. 30 - 58 weeks
UK CD box set THE SINGLES COLLECTION 1971-2006: 45 X 45s: 11 April 2011
USA CD box set THE SINGLES COLLECTION 1971-2006: 45 X 45s: 26 April 2011

The first single taken from the album was released in October 1983 and provides the title and opening track. It was mixed especially as a single and was so good that it replaced the intended album version. For an American 12-inch promotional single, a different, extended 'dub' or 'cheeky' version was released. There are also two edited takes, slightly different in length, one of which appeared on the 2011 singles collection (* a - 4.13).

Undercover was recorded in 1983, a few months after the first session. In May, Compass Point was also used to re-work some tracks before final mixing occurred at the Hit Factory in the summer. The song was influenced by William Burroughs' *Cities Of The Red Night*, a story about South American political problems and totalitarianism states. Significantly, the song is shaped around a harsh upfront drum sound moulded by Charlie Watts' percussion 'kettledrum' bash.

At first it was simply an acoustic with piano. Early out-takes of the song show how the percussion was built up - one out-take is exclusively a timpani percussion for four minutes until the guitar enters briefly (* b - 4.26). Another has a percussion opening followed by guitar (* c - 3.54) and a third take has a guitar opening with almost spoken vocals (* d - 4.48).

A fourth is getting closer to the final take, with clean guitar stabs using vibrato but without organ (* e - 4.53). Mick Jagger wrote the song on the guitar with a little assistance from Ron Wood. Chuck Leavell applies an electric organ track while, at the controls, Chris Kimsey deploys phasing techniques on guitar and drums with Sly and Robbie, which gives the song its unique rhythmic qualities. On reflection, he reckoned that this track was where he made the biggest contribution of all his career with the band.

One of his skills was to draw a song to its conclusion. If left to the band, then there would be always be another attempt to produce a final cut. One thing was certain, once Keith Richards left the studio, the session was over. Kimsey found that even Mick Jagger was reluctant to leave before Keith. Bill Wyman's bass sound was a vital part of the track, being economically effective. It took Chris a week to innovatively mix the track with different ideas, including backwards, upside down and tape playing with delay. This trick is exaggerated on the 12-inch dub version, alias an extended cheeky mix of *Undercover*. The track is coupled with the single version.

A very rare promo single version is shrunk to just four minutes (* f - 4.02). The essential ingredient is, however, the menacing lyrics of political repression written by Mick Jagger; these were vividly brought to life in the video. Produced by Michael Hamlin and directed by Julien Temple, it was shot in two stages. The first part, recorded on 18 October 1983, filmed the Stones on stage at a Paris club, the Bain-Douches, in front of a bunch of extras while they mimed to the song's lyrics.

The next week the story line was concluded in Mexico City, featuring the "terrorist" antics of Keith and "journalist" Mick, who was tracking a kidnap victim. The mini epic, supposedly set in El Salvador, showed Jagger being held by arch-villain Keith and his motley crew of gun-laden masked activists.

The two talking points of the video were the shooting at close range of the kidnap victim with a paper bag over his head and an ensuing gun battle in a church. These vivid images resulted in the video being banned on British television, although the more adventurous Channel 4 programme, The Tube, showed it with the camera moving away for a reaction shot of Mick and Julien Temple being interviewed at the vital blood-soaked moments.

The pair defended the video during the interview, stating it was no worse than some late-night films. As a safety measure, another version of the video, using more of the Bain-Douches scenes, ensured a screening on Top of The Pops and a healthy No. 11 hit followed. In the United States it went into the top ten and became the biggest selling single there since *Start Me Up*.

951. ONE HIT (TO THE BODY) (LONDON MIX) (Jagger, Richards, Wood) 7.00
12 January - 3 March, 8 April - 17 June; 16 July - 17 August, 10 September - 15 October; 15 November - 5 December 1985: Place: EMI Pathé Marconi Studios, Paris, France, France; RPM Studios, New York, USA; Right Track Studios, New York, USA.
Rolling Stones with Chuck Leavell, Kirsty MacColl, Patti Scialfa, Beverly D'Angelo, Bobby Womack, Don Covay, Jimmy Page.
Producer: Steve Lillywhite, The Glimmer Twins.
Engineer: Dave Jerden, Steve Parker, Tim Crich, Mike Krewick.
Re-mix Engineer: Alan Douglas.
UK 12-inch Single: 19 May 1986
USA 12-inch Single: 20 May 1986
UK CD box set THE SINGLES COLLECTION 1971-2006: 45 X 45s: 11 April 2011
USA CD box set THE SINGLES COLLECTION 1971-2006: 45 X 45s: 26 April 2011

952. ONE HIT (TO THE BODY) (Jagger, Richards, Wood) 4.44
AKA: One More From Your Body
12 January - 3 March, 8 April - 17 June; 16 July - 17 August, 10 September - 15 October; 15 November - 5 December 1985: Place: EMI Pathé Marconi Studios, Paris, France; RPM Studios, New York, USA; Right Track Studios, New York, USA.
Played Live: 1989
Rolling Stones with Chuck Leavell, Kirsty MacColl, Patti Scialfa, Beverly D'Angelo, Bobby Womack, Don Covay, Jimmy Page.
Producer: Steve Lillywhite, The Glimmer Twins.
Engineer: Dave Jerden, Steve Parker, Tim Crich, Mike Krewick.
UK LP DIRTY WORK: 24 March 1986: No. 4 - 10 weeks
USA LP DIRTY WORK: 24 March 1986: No. 4 - 15 weeks
UK Single: 19 May 1986
USA Single: 20 May 1986: No. 28 - 4 weeks
USA 12-inch Single: 20 May 1986

UK CD box set THE SINGLES COLLECTION 1971-2006: 45 X 45s: 11 April 2011
USA CD box set THE SINGLES COLLECTION 1971-2006: 45 X 45s: 26 April 2011

After Jerry Hall gave birth to his daughter, Elizabeth, in March 1984, Mick Jagger worked on more solo projects, including a single release with Michael Jackson called *State Of Shock*. The big production sound captured was used partly as an inspiration for HYSTERIA, an album recorded by Def Leppard in 1987. In May 1984, Mick teamed up with an array of guest musicians, including Nile Rodgers, Jeff Beck, Pete Townshend, Carlos Alomar, Eddie Martinez, Herbie Hancock, Michael Shrieve, Chuck Leavell, Bernard Fowler (backing vocals), Bill Laswell, Ray Cooper, Sly and Robbie, Paul Buckmaster and John Bundrick for a solo album SHE'S THE BOSS.

Bernard, recommended to join the recording by Bill Laswell, did overdubs in London and, in true Jagger fashion, didn't get paid - though it did prove to be a career-investing decision for him. The rest of the group members pursued other activities. The solo work put paid to rumours that the Stones might open the 1984 Olympics Opening Ceremony in Los Angeles in July. Ronnie did some re-hab in a clinic in Devon, England, following the birth of his new son, Tyrone, before recording with Bob Dylan. Charlie Watts and Ian Stewart revived Rocket 88 as a tribute to the death of Alexis Korner. Bill Wyman, not to be out-done by Jagger, formed Willie And The Poor Boys, which featured Andy Fairweather-Low, Paul Rodgers, Jimmy Page, Ray Cooper, Chris Rea, Terry Williams, Geraint Watkins, Henry Spinetti, Kenney Jones and even Charlie Watts on certain tracks. An album was released in April 1985.

A summit meeting was held in October 1984 to decide the group's next step. It was a fractious affair and included the notorious Jagger/Watts argument. This occurred after some late night drinking when Mick, worse for wear, knocked on Charlie's hotel door and asked for his drummer to come downstairs. Charlie got dressed, marched into the breakfast area and punched the living daylights out of him, following up with a verbal right-hook: "I am not your drummer, you are my singer." For Ron Wood, 1985 got off to a rousing start as he married Jo Karslake, with Charlie Watts and Keith Richards as co-best men. Meanwhile, in an incredulous move, EMI had renovated the recording facility that the Stones used in Paris, turning it into an archive area, just leaving the main studios available. After Keith had checked things out and decided he was happy to use them, the Stones went there in January to start work on the next album.

The sessions were not the most rewarding. The DIRTY WORK album only had three Jagger/Richards tunes. Four were by Richards and Wood although Jagger was added to the credits and there was one collaboration with Chuck Leavell. Unusually, there were also two covers. One of the early songs recorded was *One Hit*, a raw and tough song where the artistic direction was controlled, as it was on much of the album, by Keith Richards and Ron Wood.

It was one of Mick's favourites to be unveiled as a single but the more commercial *Harlem Shuffle* was released before it. The guitar sound is outstanding on *One Hit*. From the opening acoustic patter by Ronnie, the song leaps forward to a clash of lead and rhythm thrusts. Jimmy Page is featured on lead, his two solos being added in New York, but, for contractual reasons, he was not credited on the sleeve notes or even paid. He added his performance while on the way back from the Live Aid concert where Led Zeppelin had temporarily re-formed.

Because of the acoustic guitar, critics were fast to point out the similarity with the anthemic *Street Fighting Man*. The backing vocals give the song a Stateside feel but, when released as a single, it failed to achieve high chart positions, remaining in the low 40s in the UK. An early acoustic guitar jam version, with Keith Richards and Mick Jagger, can be heard via an out-take (* a - 7.51). Keith is helping Mick out with the vocal arrangement.

There is also an instrumental-only (* b - 4.59) and an early piano version without backing vocals but with Mick ad-libbing and giving key changes (* c - 4.57). A similar out-take, without the piano bridge but still with Mick giving key changes, shows some aggression, Mick's vocals obviously getting into gear (* d - 4.41). Another out-take, probably at the time of vocal overdubs in the USA, features Kirsty MacColl (Steve Lillywhite's wife) and Patti Scialfa (* e - 4.44). Patti was one of Bruce Springsteen's backing vocalists (and future wife), "The Boss" being on a European and USA tour to promote the BORN IN THE USA album.

The recording was made when the tour hit the United States. Her contribution to the sessions fuelled wild stories of possible guest guitar appearances by the Springsteen on the album, none of which would be confirmed. Beverly D'Angelo, a session singer, also performs backing vocals with Bobby Womack and Don "Goodtimer" Covay. A remix by Alan Douglas and Steve Lillywhite for the 12-inch single market is interesting but not essential. The track was edited for the single release (* f - 4.12). A promotional video to accompany it failed to assist. Filmed by young producer Russell Mulcahy at London's Elstree Studios, the video is sparse and angry as the guys work out.

Mick and Keith can be seen sparring with each other. Images of fights are pushed at the viewer as the Stones explore back street gutter land. It shows that they knew the negative energy and public perception could be turned positive by a bit of self-parody. Charlie appears bored by it all, a suspicion confirmed by a documentary, filmed by BBC TV's Old Grey Whistle Test, which captures the shooting of the video on 1 May 1986. As an epitaph, Charlie wisely concluded to presenter David Hepworth that the Stones' life had been spent "five years working, 20 years hanging around!"

953. THESE ARMS OF MINE (Redding)
12 January - 3 March 1985: Place: EMI Pathé Marconi Studios, Paris, France.
Rolling Stones with Chuck Leavell.
Producer: The Glimmer Twins.
Engineer: Dave Jerden.
Unavailable.

At the January sessions, some of the recordings just involve Mick Jagger and Keith Richards in a studio playing old standards around the piano, presumably to warm up and get some ideas. This Otis Redding song was covered in this manner. Steve Lillywhite had been selected by Mick as the new producer but initial work was started by Dave Jerden.

Chris Kimsey was quite happy to have a rest from the band after the tensions of the last album. Rod Thear did not feel any friction at the UNDERCOVER sessions and thought that everyone worked well together but acknowledged he was not at the fore of proceedings like Chris. He was asked by Ian Stewart to join the sessions but had other commitments at the time.

Mick wanted to find an "in" and "current" producer. Steve was aged 29 at the time, having started his career helping to discover the band Ultravox before enjoying his first chart success with Siouxsie and The Banshees. He came to fame working with U2 for their first three albums, BOY, OCTOBER and WAR.

954. MEXICAN DIVORCE (Bacharach, Hilliard) 3.31
AKA: Broken Hearts For Me And You
12 January - 3 March 1985: Place: EMI Pathé Marconi Studios, Paris, France.
Producer: The Glimmer Twins.
Engineer: Dave Jerden.
Bootleg only.

Keith Richards leads this incomplete version of the Burt Bacharach song on acoustic guitar. Bootleggers named the track *Broken Hearts For Me And You*. At the end, Keith admits that this is "so far, so good".

955. THIRTY NINE AND HOLDING (Williamson) 6.26
12 January - 3 March 1985: Place: EMI Pathé Marconi Studios, Paris, France.
Rolling Stones with Chuck Leavell.
Producer: The Glimmer Twins.
Engineer: Dave Jerden.
Bootleg only.

The Sonny Boy Williamson song *Thirty Nine And Holding* was covered with electric piano, possibly played by Chuck Leavell or Keith Richards. Mick Jagger and Keith duet together.

956. DON'T BE CRUEL (Blackwell, Presley) 4.49
12 January - 3 March 1985: Place: EMI Pathé Marconi Studios, Paris, France.
Rolling Stones with Chuck Leavell.
Producer: The Glimmer Twins.
Engineer: Dave Jerden.
Bootleg only.

The session was flowing along and this Elvis Presley number again features Keith Richards and Mick Jagger dueting in drink-sodden, slurred fashion to a piano backing.

957. WHAT AM I GONNA DO WITH YOUR LOVE? (Jagger, Richards) 5.29
AKA: What Are You Gonna Do With My Love?, Your Love
12 January - 3 March, 8 April - 17 June; 16 July - 17 August 1985: Place: EMI Pathé Marconi Studios, Paris, France; RPM Studios, New York, USA.
Rolling Stones with Tom Waits, Kirsty MacColl, Patti Scialfa, Don Covay, Bobby Womack.
Producer: Steve Lillywhite, The Glimmer Twins.
Engineer: Dave Jerden.
Bootleg only.

A very early Paris out-take constructs the song with various slices of cover tracks thrown in (* a - 14.38). In New York, the band are joined on this gospel track by some guest artists, who perform a credible, vocal-orientated song. Mick Jagger takes the lead with Keith Richards on backing vocals. Kirsty MacColl, Patti Scialfa, Don Covay and Bobby Womack provide the gospel invocation of "your love".
Tom Waits possibly plays the piano at the session in New York. He was recording his next album RAIN DOGS in the city at the same time as the Stones and Keith took time out to play on a couple of tracks. *What Am I Gonna Do With Your Love?* started life in Paris under the title *Your Love*, with Chuck Leavell (or possibly one of the Glimmers) on electric piano. Keith directs the vocals and the song's tempo is worked on by Mick.

958. BABY, YOU'RE TOO MUCH I (Jagger, Richards) 5.13
AKA: You're Too Much
12 January - 3 March, 8 April - 17 June; 16 July - 17 August 1985: Place: EMI Pathé Marconi Studios, Paris, France; RPM Studios, New York, USA.
Rolling Stones with Chuck Leavell, Kirsty MacColl, Patti Scialfa, Beverly D'Angelo, Bobby Womack, Don Covay.
Producer: The Glimmer Twins, Steve Lillywhite.
Engineer: Dave Jerden.
Bootleg only.

Another chance for Keith Richards to show his vocal talents. The DIRTY WORK sessions demonstrated the freshness and maturity of Keith's songwriting approach. A very early acoustic guitar version, with incomplete lyrics, was recorded in Paris (* a - 1.39). By the time the song had evolved in New York, it had been transformed into a very worthwhile Keith number. His electric lead guitar was also in fine form.
You're Too Much uses a gathering of backing vocalists who perform the song in gospel style. They may be the same singers as used on *One Hit*. This style was to be featured extensively on Keith Richards' solo album TALK IS CHEAP, released in October 1988. It would also be tried again on *Sleep Tonight*.

959. CRUSHED PEARL (Jagger, Richards) 3.17
12 January - 3 March, 8 April - 17 June 1985: Place: EMI Pathé Marconi Studios, Paris, France.
Rolling Stones with Chuck Leavell.
Producer: The Glimmer Twins, Steve Lillywhite.
Engineer: Dave Jerden.
Bootleg only.

Crushed Pearl is a slow number with Keith Richards on vocals. The lead guitar is again sharp, supported by a funky guitar with a pronounced bass guitar pattern.

960. IF I DON'T HAVE YOU (Isaacs) 3.14
AKA: I Want Nobody Else
12 January - 3 March, 8 April - 17 June 1985: Place: EMI Pathé Marconi Studios, Paris, France.
Rolling Stones with Chuck Leavell.
Producer: The Glimmer Twins, Steve Lillywhite.
Engineer: Dave Jerden.
Bootleg only.

Three attempts were made at getting this song together but it clearly was not taking shape, Mick Jagger and Keith Richards suggesting different ways of tackling it (* a - 2.41, b - 4.23). *If I Don't Have You*, aka. *I Want Nobody Else*, was a Gregory Isaacs cover tried many times over the months but didn't make it to the USA. It has a piano base and Mick Jagger and Keith Richards are the co-vocalists. Under the name *I Want Nobody Else* two longer versions were cut (* c - 7.07, d - 7.23).

961. PUTTY (IN YOUR HANDS) (Patton, Rogers)
12 January - 3 March 1985: Place: EMI Pathé Marconi Studios, Paris, France.
Rolling Stones with Chuck Leavell.
Producer: The Glimmer Twins.
Engineer: Dave Jerden.
Unavailable.

A very brief segment is available of this Shirelles and Yardbirds cover from the early 60s. There were many run-throughs of covers, as stated in Bill Wyman's *Rolling With The Stones*. They included Fats Domino's *Blue Monday* and *I'm Ready*, the Beatles' *Bungalow Bill*, Chuck Berry's *Betty Jean* and *Carol*, The Everly Brothers' *Claudette*, Elmore James' *Dust My Broom*, Ricky Nelson's *Hello Mary-Lou*, George Jones' *I'm Gonna Tear Your Playhouse Down*, Buddy Holly's *It's So Easy* and *True Love Ways*, Muddy Waters' *Louisiana Blues*, Howlin' Wolf's *Moanin' At Midnight* and *Spoonful*, Hoagy Carmichael's *Nearness Of You*, The Ventures' *Perfidia*, Santo and Johnny's *Sleepwalk*, Sam Cooke's *Soothe Me*, Bobby Darin's *Splish Splash*, The Supremes' *Stop In The Name Of Love* and Hank Williams' *Your Cheatin' Heart*.

962. BACK ON THE STREETS AGAIN (Jackson, Ward) 5.21
12 January - 3 March 1985: Place: EMI Pathé Marconi Studios, Paris, France.
Rolling Stones with Chuck Leavell.
Producer: The Glimmer Twins.
Engineer: Dave Jerden.
Bootleg only.

Both Mick Jagger and Keith Richards sing on this slow piano boogie with acoustic guitar. It is played in jam-like fashion. The songwriter is not known but is likely to be George "Memphis" Jackson and John Ward or even Lee Hazlewood.

963. YOU CAN'T CUT THE MUSTARD (Jagger, Richards, Wood) 3.26
AKA: Had It With You
8 April - 17 June 1985: Place: EMI Pathé Marconi Studios, Paris, France.
Rolling Stones with Chuck Leavell.
Producer: Steve Lillywhite, The Glimmer Twins.
Engineer: Dave Jerden.
Bootleg only.

The sessions were split after the initial get-together in January. Dave Jerden was one of the engineers at the sessions, as he had been for Jagger's album. The release SHE'S THE BOSS in February 1985, although not a surprise to the band since it was a negotiated settlement of the Stones' CBS contract, did prove to be a troublesome element during the recording of DIRTY WORK.
As a result, Mick hardly brought any songs to the table. He pointed out that he had been the last member of the band to do a solo project but Keith Richards openly said that he thought it the timing totally inappropriate - "it could have at least been an album of Irish folk songs or summat!" Mick's energies were spent in promotion work for his album in March, while Keith returned to New York to be present at the birth of his daughter, Theodora.
The band reconvened in April to work on more tracks for DIRTY WORK. *You Can't Cut The Mustard* is a Keith Richards and Ron Wood affair and is a precursor to *Had It With You*. It is very much a rock and roll song, with Berry-style guitar riffs and gyrating piano.
There are two versions, both with Keith Richards on vocals, supported by Ronnie Wood. The first one just mentions the title track while the second begins to refer to *Had It With You* (* a - 2.55). The lyrics are totally different to the released *Had It With You*. Ron Wood had now secured the services of lawyer Nick Cowan as his manager and he was busy trying to unravel the guitarist's financial affairs and, more importantly, change his role from hired hand to being a shared member of the band. His 22-year partnership with Ron is recorded in Nick's book *Fifty Tea Bags And A Bottle Of Rum*.

964. HAD IT WITH YOU (Jagger, Richards, Wood) 3.20
8 April - 17 June; 16 July - 17 August, 10 September - 15 October; 15 November - 5 December 1985: Place: EMI Pathé Marconi Studios, Paris, France; RPM Studios, New York, USA; Right Track Studios, New York, USA.
Producer: Steve Lillywhite, The Glimmer Twins.
Engineer: Dave Jerden, Steve Parker, Tim Crich, Mike Krewick.
UK B-side Harlem Shuffle: 10 March 1986
USA B-side Harlem Shuffle: 10 March 1986
UK LP DIRTY WORK: 24 March 1986: No. 4 - 10 weeks
USA LP DIRTY WORK: 24 March 1986: No. 4 - 15 weeks

UK CD box set THE SINGLES COLLECTION 1971-2006: 45 X 45s: 11 April 2011
USA CD box set THE SINGLES COLLECTION 1971-2006: 45 X 45s: 26 April 2011

Keith Richards got together with Ronnie at Wood's rented house in London. *Had It With You* is a very basic rocker in veritable R 'n' B tradition. Various bass guitars were tried, including an upright bass, but these takes sounded a little too ordinary - "Oh it's the Stones at work again". To avoid this type of sound, the bass and piano were left off so that only Charlie Watts and Keith provided the main instrumentation. It was recorded in just a couple of takes, Mick providing a real live harmonica.

The song was known jokingly at one stage as "I've Haddock It With You". There is an out-take which starts at a slow pace with Mick Jagger on vocals - it speeds up when the lyrics start. This take again has unfinished lyrics and is with harmonica (* a - 2.55). The final lyrics can, of course, be interpreted as an attack on Mick by Keith but Mick went along with it and probably even helped write a song which was about an incestuous sister and brother affair.

At a later date, in order to fill out the song, Ronnie Wood offered a track of whispering tenor sax. On the record, at the track's end, production controller Steve Lillywhite can be heard switching on the studio intercom. Asked later what his role was for the Stones, he likened it to Henry Kissinger's peace-making efforts; as opposed to the last album, which required Chris Kimsey's diplomacy, this one required a peace-maker for war-mongers!

Those surprised to find Ronnie on sax may be interested to learn his brass talents were also used on a 1985 Bill Wyman And His All Stars video and album package titled WILLIE AND THE POOR BOYS, a charity project in aid of multiple sclerosis. The music was in the good time *Had It With You* style. Bill Wyman recounted that other Ronnie titles were *Golden Opportunity*, *Hard To Carry On* and *Right Now* - all unavailable.

965. HIGH TEMPERATURE (Jacobs, Cohen) 5.23
8 April - 17 June 1985: Place: EMI Pathé Marconi Studios, Paris, France.
Rolling Stones with Chuck Leavell.
Producer: Steve Lillywhite, The Glimmer Twins.
Engineer: Dave Jerden.
Bootleg only.

Little Walter (Marion Walter Jacobs) was the inspiration for this cover, a slow blues which has a shrill harmonica, a bass and lead guitar. Keith Richards supplies the vocals.

966. TOO RUDE (Roberts) 3.13
AKA: Girl, You're Too Rude, Winsome
8 April - 17 June; 16 July - 17 August, 10 September - 15 October; 15 November - 5 December 1985: Place: EMI Pathé Marconi Studios, Paris, France; RPM Studios, New York, USA; Right Track Studios, New York, USA.
Rolling Stones with Jimmy Cliff, Chuck Leavell.
Producer: Steve Lillywhite, The Glimmer Twins.
Engineer: Dave Jerden, Steve Parker, Tim Crich, Mike Krewick.
UK LP DIRTY WORK: 24 March 1986: No. 4 - 10 weeks
USA LP DIRTY WORK: 24 March 1986: No. 4 - 15 weeks

Steve Lillywhite had an excellent pedigree, his most recent production successes being with the Irish rock band, U2 for Chris Blackwell's Island label in the mid-70s. He had also produced British reggae band Steel Pulse and his experience in that field allowed him to step comfortably into the world of dub mixes and tackle *Too Rude*. It was written by Jamaican Lindon Roberts, who released it as his second single under his artist name Half Pint and the song title *Winsome*.

The Stones had attempted the reggae format before but this is their most noteworthy performance. Keith Richards' vocals are used to good effect. Although suitably tempered and layered by Steve Lillywhite, they sound almost too good to be Keith's. Lots of echo tracks are used, particularly on bass and drums, confirming the belief that all good reggae tracks are in the mix. Jimmy Cliff, a well-known reggae artist, assisted in this respect, having supported Keith on the vocals.

There is an out-take which has no backing vocals (* a -3.34) and a ten-minute slower, more organ-orientated take (* b - 10.21). *Too Rude* was provisionally a title of the new album, until DIRTY WORK was selected. *Too Rude* was covered by Keith's X-pensive Winos when they performed it live in 1988.

967. MY BABY LEFT ME (Jagger, Richards) 3.20
8 April - 17 June 1985: Place: EMI Pathé Marconi Studios, Paris, France.
Rolling Stones with Chuck Leavell.
Producer: Steve Lillywhite, The Glimmer Twins.
Engineer: Dave Jerden.
Bootleg only.

A song sung by Keith Richards - distinctly an out-take.

968. SHE NEVER LISTENS TO ME (Jagger, Richards) 7.34
8 April - 17 June 1985: Place: EMI Pathé Marconi Studios, Paris, France.
Rolling Stones with Chuck Leavell.
Producer: Steve Lillywhite, The Glimmer Twins.
Engineer: Dave Jerden.
Bootleg only.

A reggae song that has a choppy organ, echoed percussion and the trademark reggae guitar of Keith Richards, who also performs vocals. Don't apologise for this one.

969. FIGHT (Jagger, Richards, Wood) 3.10
AKA: I Wanna Fight
8 April - 17 June; 16 July - 17 August, 10 September - 15 October; 15 November - 5 December 1985: Place: EMI Pathé Marconi Studios, Paris, France; RPM Studios, New York, USA; Right Track Studios, New York, USA.
Rolling Stones with Janice Pendarvis, Dolette MacDonald, Chuck Leavell.
Producer: Steve Lillywhite, The Glimmer Twins. Engineer: Dave Jerden, Steve Parker, Tim Crich, Mike Krewick.
UK LP DIRTY WORK: 24 March 1986: No. 4 - 10 weeks
USA LP DIRTY WORK: 24 March 1986: No. 4 - 15 weeks
UK B-side One Hit (To The Body) (London Mix): 19 May 1986
UK 12-inch Track One Hit (To The Body): 19 May 1986
USA B-side One Hit (To The Body): 20 May 1986
USA 12-inch Track One Hit (To The Body) (London Mix): 20 May 1986
UK CD box set THE SINGLES COLLECTION 1971-2006: 45 X 45s: 11 April 2011
USA CD box set THE SINGLES COLLECTION 1971-2006: 45 X 45s: 26 April 2011

Bill Wyman confirmed that Steve Lillywhite was able to add a new recording element, particularly to the trademark drum sound, without over-complicating the issue. Charlie Watts' work on *Fight* supports this. Being at work in Paris with new-waver Steve Lillywhite, the Stones attracted some modern-day pop stars, including members of Duran Duran, who were invited to the studio by Mick Jagger and Ronnie Wood. They were startled to find the Stones being recorded as an ensemble with overdubs and re-tracking kept to a bare minimum. Keith Richards retorted that this is what playing music is all about and called them "deranged, deranged"! The song's tone, as the title suggests, is angry and vitriolic, which is conveyed expressively in Mick's vocals "slash you with a razor". Keith Richards mercilessly attacks the victim with his axe. Steve Lillywhite confirmed later to the AV Club: "You need a good tailwind to make a great record, and there wasn't a great tailwind with the Stones at that point. There was too much bitterness. It was the bad end of the drug-taking. It was just messy, but I had to do it. I learned a lot more from them than they learned from me, that's all I can say about that experience."
An out-take with early lyrics is a wild affair, the guitars solo (and it sounds like three of them) in an aggressive non-Stones manner (* a - 3.59). The released cut is quite sedate in contrast. There is an instrumental out-take with the organ, bass and drums higher in the mix (* b - 3.03). The circumstances which led to the song's recording are recalled by Keith, who remembers it happened when the band broke up after a less than fruitful day's recording.
A sparse arrangement has Keith formulating the song (* c - 4.57). Frustrated and angry, he took hold of his guitar and proceeded to conjure up an instantaneous "Jumping Jack" lick. Ron Wood joined in on pedal steel and the guitar roadie, Alan Rogan, plugged in a bass. However, the final version did not include his bass which was re-recorded by Ron Wood. Rogan was "lent" to the Stones by Pete Townshend during the 1981/82 tour and Alan decided to stay!

970. KNOCK YOUR TEETH OUT (Wood, Fowler, Lloyd)
8 April - 17 June 1985: Place: EMI Pathé Marconi Studios, Paris, France.
Producer: Steve Lillywhite, The Glimmer Twins.
Engineer: Dave Jerden.
Unavailable.

One Ron Wood track, worked upon with Keith Richards, that did not appear as an out-take but was certainly in the spirit of the DIRTY WORK sessions - it was named *Knock Your Teeth Out*. It eventually appeared on his 1992 album SLIDE ON THIS but credited with co-writers Bernard Fowler and Julian Lloyd. TALK IS CHEAP was the title of Keith's debut solo album and said to be recorded at the DIRTY WORK sessions, again reflecting again their mood.

971. TREAT ME LIKE A FOOL (Jagger, Richards) 6.40
8 April - 17 June 1985: Place: EMI Pathé Marconi Studios, Paris, France.
Rolling Stones with Chuck Leavell.
Producer: Steve Lillywhite, The Glimmer Twins.
Engineer: Dave Jerden.
Bootleg only.

Ironically, it was Keith Richards who seemed to be acquiring masses of solo material from the DIRTY WORK sessions. This is another vocal performance by him, a little more up-tempo than some of his gospel ballads. The song was cut on a few occasions (* a - 5.06, b - 3.10, c - 1.52).

972. WHAT ARE YOU GONNA TELL YOUR BOYFRIEND? (Jagger, Richards) 5.13
AKA: What You're Gonna Do With Your Boyfriend
8 April - 17 June 1985: Place: EMI Pathé Marconi Studios, Paris, France.
Rolling Stones with Chuck Leavell.
Producer: Steve Lillywhite, The Glimmer Twins.
Engineer: Dave Jerden.
Bootleg only.

Reminiscent of *Sleep Tonight*, Keith Richards again takes the vocals on a slow rock track with a strong guitar and piano presence.

973. DON'T GET MAD (Jagger, Richards) 0.58
8 April - 17 June 1985: Place: EMI Pathé Marconi Studios, Paris, France.
Producer: Steve Lillywhite, The Glimmer Twins. Engineer: Dave Jerden.
Bootleg only.

A short, end of session, out-take featuring Keith Richards and Ron Wood.

974. WHO'S SHAGGING WHO? (Jagger, Richards) 2.04
8 April - 17 June 1985: Place: EMI Pathé Marconi Studios, Paris, France.
Producer: Steve Lillywhite, The Glimmer Twins.
Engineer: Dave Jerden.
Bootleg only.

Definitely an improvised out-take with studio chat, it is hardly worth a mention.

975. CUT YOUR THROAT (Jagger, Richards) 5.59
8 April - 17 June 1985: Place: EMI Pathé Marconi Studios, Paris, France.
Rolling Stones with Chuck Leavell.
Producer: Steve Lillywhite, The Glimmer Twins.
Engineer: Dave Jerden.
Bootleg only.

A Keith Richards vocal on a boogie rock and roller. Other Keith tracks laid down but not available include *I Don't Wanna Hurt You, I Got A Hard-On For You Baby* and *My Kind Of Rubbish*. At one point an attempt was made to burgle Keith's car and a security person literally pulled a knife on the would-be robber.

976. YOU GOT IT (Jagger, Richards) 2.56
8 April - 17 June 1985: Place: EMI Pathé Marconi Studios, Paris, France.
Rolling Stones with Chuck Leavell.
Producer: Steve Lillywhite, The Glimmer Twins.
Engineer: Dave Jerden.
Bootleg only.

An incomplete Keith Richards track.

977. SOME OF US ARE ON OUR KNEES (Jagger, Richards) 5.38
8 April - 17 June 1985: Place: EMI Pathé Marconi Studios, Paris, France.
Rolling Stones with Chuck Leavell.
Producer: Steve Lillywhite, The Glimmer Twins.
Engineer: Dave Jerden.
Bootleg only.

A slow rocking track led by Keith Richards on guitar and vocals. Some of the ideas gained from such tracks were used for *Sleep Tonight*.

978. BREAKIN' (Jagger, Richards) 2.55
8 April - 17 June 1985: Place: EMI Pathé Marconi Studios, Paris, France.
Rolling Stones with Chuck Leavell.
Producer: Steve Lillywhite, The Glimmer Twins.
Engineer: Dave Jerden.
Bootleg only.

Two versions of *Breakin'* were recorded, one with Mick Jagger on vocals (* a) and another with Keith Richards. Keith liked the song since, when he capitulated and went for a solo album in 1987, *Breakin'* was considered as a possibility.

979. STRICTLY MEMPHIS (Jagger, Richards) 3.41
AKA: Step On It
8 April - 17 June, 16 July - 17 August 1985: Place: EMI Pathé Marconi Studios, Paris, France; RPM Studios, New York, USA.
Rolling Stones with Bobby Womack, Chuck Leavell.
Producer: Steve Lillywhite, The Glimmer Twins.
Engineer: Dave Jerden.
Bootleg only.

The final version of this song is a great funky duet with Mick Jagger and Bobby Womack on vocals (* a - 3.22). Other vocalists kept Mick on his toes and this example of a DIRTY WORK out-take proves how useful this tactic could be. The track is likely to have originated from the BLACK AND BLUE sessions as an instrumental. The first DIRTY WORK out-take has earlier lyrics and Mick guides the song along in an eight-minute version without Bobby Womack (* b - 8.15). Titles of other Mick Jagger led tracks were *Darker Side Of Me, In Love, I Need Your Love* and *Nobody's Perfect*. Bobby Womack certainly saw some of the divide during this period when he received a call from Mick to work on a track for the album and another from Keith Richards in another studio asking him to come along.

980. DIRTY WORK (Jagger, Richards, Wood) 3.53
AKA: Let Some Fucker Do The Dirty Work
8 April - 17 June; 16 July - 17 August, 10 September - 15 October; 15 November - 5 December 1985: Place: EMI Pathé Marconi Studios, Paris, France; RPM Studios, New York, USA; Right Track Studios, New York, USA.
Rolling Stones with Chuck Leavell.
Producer: Steve Lillywhite, The Glimmer Twins.
Engineer: Dave Jerden, Steve Parker, Tim Crich, Mike Krewick.
UK LP DIRTY WORK: 24 March 1986: No. 4 - 10 weeks
USA LP DIRTY WORK: 24 March 1986: No. 4 - 15 weeks

The title track of the album, the sleeve for which featured, for the first time in 20 years, all of the band photographed together on a cover, Annie Liebovitz capturing them slouching undramatically on a sofa. The song itself also languishes, not really realising its own expectations. It is, however, more of a "brunch" than a sandwich filler. The track, musically and lyrically, is a grower with overdosed guitars. Ron Wood again receives a songwriting credit. Mick Jagger was very grateful that Ron brought so many songs to the studio, since his worth was being used on his solo album.

Two guitars are understood to be on the original track and then a further two were dubbed on. This enabled solos to continue indefinitely as one stepped on to another and the rock 'n' roll riffs returned. Chuck Leavell, meanwhile, was integral to the song, feeding the rhythm. An out-take continues the pace throughout and does not have the softer end with echoed vocals (* a - 4.19).

Sales were again not aided by the usual album/tour format, it being one of their least satisfactory albums. Rumours continued to circulate that all was not well with the Jagger, Richards relationship. Indeed both Dave Jerden and Steve Lillywhite and the band themselves likened the atmosphere to World War III. The album working title was 19 Stitches due to the comings and goings and what was needed to just keep things just afloat.

When Dave Jerden joined the project at Mick's request, Keith said that he would give him a week. Dave duly survived and earned a cuddle from Keith and a "welcome to the Rolling Stones". The recording process was like crawling for two miles on rusty razorblades and much of it being achieved during winter in Paris, Dave recalled. Of course, Keith wanted to go on the road with the album but Mick was unwilling.

He was thinking about stepping out of the Stones' mould to concentrate on his solo project. Mick was bored, thought the music on DIRTY WORK was not up to scratch and that the band could not sustain a tour physically as they were just not getting on well enough ("it would have been a nightmare"), even though there was some mutual thawing when the recording moved to New York. He recorded a comical promotional video with the much tempered down lines, "OK you dirty mothers, get out and sell your butt, get down and do the dirty work!" On reflection, Steve Lillywhite was heard to say, "I produced the worst-ever Rolling Stones album. Until the one after, that is." He acknowledged he learnt a lot, though, saying: "A real man would never turn down the chance of working with them."

981. HARLEM SHUFFLE (LONDON MIX) (Relf, Nelson) 6.19
16 July - 17 August, 10 September - 15 October; 15 November - 5 December 1985: Place: RPM Studios, New York, USA; Right Track Studios, New York, USA.
Rolling Stones with Chuck Leavell, Ivan Neville, Bobby Womack, Don Covay, Tom Waits.
Producer: Steve Lillywhite, The Glimmer Twins.
Engineer: Dave Jerden, Steve Parker, Tim Crich, Mike Krewick.
Remix Engineers: Steve Thompson, Michael Barbiero.
UK B-side 12-inch Single Harlem Shuffle (NY Mix): 10 March 1986
USA B-side 12-inch Single Harlem Shuffle (NY Mix): 10 March 1986
UK 12-inch Track Terrifying: 30 July 1990
USA CD FLASHPOINT (COLLECTIBLES): 20 May 1991
UK CD box set THE SINGLES COLLECTION 1971-2006: 45 X 45s: 11 April 2011
USA CD box set THE SINGLES COLLECTION 1971-2006: 45 X 45s: 26 April 2011

982. HARLEM SHUFFLE (NY MIX) (Relf, Nelson) 6.36
16 July - 17 August, 10 September - 15 October; 15 November - 5 December 1985: Place: RPM Studios, New York, USA; Right Track Studios, New York, USA.
Rolling Stones with Chuck Leavell, Ivan Neville, Bobby Womack, Don Covay, Tom Waits.
Producer: Steve Lillywhite, The Glimmer Twins.
Engineer: Dave Jerden, Steve Parker, Tim Crich, Mike Krewick.
Remix Engineers: Steve Thompson, Michael Barbiero.
UK 12-inch Single: 10 March 1986: No. 13 - 7 weeks
USA 12-inch Single: 10 March 1986: No. 5 - 10 weeks
USA CD LP ROLLING STONES RARITIES 1971-2003: 22 November 2005: No. 76 - 6 weeks
UK CD LP ROLLING STONES RARITIES 1971-2003: 28 November 2005

While most fans welcomed the release on the ROLLING STONES RARITIES 1971-2003 compilation in 2005, it was shortened by just under a minute (* a - 5.49).

983. HARLEM SHUFFLE (Relf, Nelson) 3.26
16 July - 17 August, 10 September - 15 October; 15 November - 5 December 1985: Place: RPM Studios, New York, USA; Right Track Studios, New York, USA.
Played Live: 1986, 1989, 1990
Rolling Stones with Chuck Leavell, Ivan Neville, Bobby Womack, Don Covay, Tom Waits.
Producer: Steve Lillywhite, The Glimmer Twins.
Engineer: Dave Jerden, Steve Parker, Tim Crich, Mike Krewick.
UK Single: 10 March 1986: No. 13 - 7 weeks
USA Single: 10 March 1986: No. 5 - 10 weeks
UK LP DIRTY WORK: 24 March 1986: No. 4 - 10 weeks
USA LP DIRTY WORK: 24 March 1986: No. 4 - 15 weeks
UK Track CD Single Terrifying (Seven Inch Remix Edit): 30 July 1990
UK Compilation LP JUMP BACK THE BEST OF THE ROLLING STONES '71 - '93: 22 November 1993: No. 16 - 26 weeks
USA Compilation CD JUMP BACK THE BEST OF THE ROLLING STONES '71 - '93: 24 August 2004: No. 30 - 58 weeks
UK CD box set THE SINGLES COLLECTION 1971-2006: 45 X 45s: 11 April 2011
USA CD box set THE SINGLES COLLECTION 1971-2006: 45 X 45s: 26 April 2011

In March 1986, *Harlem Shuffle* was released as a single, the first time since the recalcitrant days of the early 60s for a non-Jagger/Richards track. Indeed, ironically it was the first since the No. 1 hit *It's All Over Now* which the Stones had recorded back in 1964. Bobby Womack co-wrote *It's All Over Now* and also performed on *Harlem Shuffle*, which had originally been a Top 10 hit in the UK for Bob and Earl (Bobby Relf and Earl Nelson), during the spring of 1969. In the United States it was a No. 44 hit in 1964.

Keith Richards, when preparing compilation tapes for his travels, often found that he had included the catchy *Harlem Shuffle*. In anticipation that the Stones might record it, Keith would often copy the song on a tape for Mick Jagger, thinking Mick would be a natural for the vocals. The bait was not taken until one night the band ran through the track in rehearsal for the new album. Mick walked into the sessions, heard the number and put down a vocal track.

To enhance the vocals along the lines of the original duo, Bob and Earl, the Stones employed a mate of Ronnie Wood's, Bobby Womack, as well as an old soulster, Don Covay. It is thought that Tom Waits is on backing vocals. There are three production out-takes (* a - 4.09, b - 3.45). One has Bobby and Mick jiving at the end, grooving and uttering ad libs until the fade out (* c - 5.35). They mention Sylvia's Restaurant in Harlem where you can still find the 'Queen Of Soul Food'. These out-takes have the organ introduction, Bobby's entrance followed by Mick's "whooo" used on the final cut.

The opening chords of *Harlem Shuffle* use some deft acoustic strumming which Keith claimed to have learned from recent trips to Mexico. The technique is lifted from the Mexican fandango guitar players. Either Chuck Leavell or Ivan Neville play keyboards and it is this instrument that replaces the horns used so predominantly on the Bob and Earl arrangement. The organ can be heard much more to the fore on the extended mix versions. Ivan was Aaron Neville's son and was to contribute extensively to Keith's solo work.

The track was amongst the first completed for the album and Dave Jerden, the sound engineer, said it was recorded in two takes. The single's success was enhanced by a simple but effective video by animation expert Ralph Bakshi and John Kricfalusi, which mixed cartoon characters (one of whom resembles a dishevelled Ron Wood) and the band performing on stage at the Kool Kat Club. It was premiered on MTV on 6 March.

Keith Richards looks particularly distinguished in gangster trilby, posing ridiculously at the video's end. The Stones were back in the charts again, attaining respectable Top 20 positions. Steve Lillywhite commented that he witnessed snippets of the Stones magic and this was one example. "Occasionally, I just got this little glimpse of how a great band operated . . . on *Harlem Shuffle* they just clicked; just imagine cogs . . . if they are not all aligned nothing works but then all of a sudden it just goes 'click' . . . that's how the Rolling Stones worked, 99% of the time it was the worst pub band you had ever heard and then there is this little magical thing happens".

984. **INVITATION** (Jagger, Richards) 15.52
AKA: You Don't Tell Me, Sending Out An Invitation
16 July - 17 August 1985: Place: RPM Studios, New York, USA.
Rolling Stones with Bobby Womack, Don Covay, Chuck Leavell, Dollette McDonald, Dan Collette, Janice Pendarvis, Alan Rogan, John Regan.
Producer: The Glimmer Twins.
Engineer: Dave Jerden.
Bootleg only.

The DIRTY WORK sessions featured a galaxy of recording artists. In Paris, members of Duran Duran, were meant to have jammed with the Stones while, in New York, there are artists credited on the album cover without it being clear which tracks they played on. Charlie Drayton, drummer and bass guitarist, played some percussion. Steve Jordan, another drummer recommended by Charlie Watts, participated in the sessions.

Charlie remembered him from the Saturday Night shows where he was in the house band. He had also been in the Blues Brothers. Charlie was not present at all at the sessions, due to his own drugs and mid-life issues. Even Keith Richards pointed out to Charlie that drugs like heroin were "shit" but he felt that Charlie only dabbled with them and none of the Stones liked to participate in "finger wagging".

Invitation is a track that was led by Ronnie Wood possibly as a solo collaboration with Bobby Womack. Other contributors were vocalist Dollette McDonald, trumpet player Dan Collette, singer Janice Pendarvis, guitarist Alan Rogan (Keith's technician) and John Regan, the bass guitarist. John recorded the single *Dancing In The Street* with Mick Jagger and David Bowie for the Live Aid concert and Charlie Drayton later appeared on Keith's solo album.

Sly Stone is rumoured to have sung on *Invitation* but it is more likely to be Bobby Womack and Don Covay. The track is an incredible, 16-minute soulful exchange of organ, piano and the dueting vocals of Bobby and Don. It is very unlikely that the songwriters are Jagger/Richards, more likely to be a jazz soul scriber.

985. **DEEP LOVE** (Jagger, Richards) 4.11
16 July - 17 August 1985: Place: RPM Studios, New York, USA.
Producer: The Glimmer Twins.
Engineer: Dave Jerden.
Bootleg only.

A rock number on which Keith Richards took the lead vocal. The riff is strong and the two guitars mesh well making it a very passable out-take. In fact, at one point, it was scheduled to be on the album. Keith reckoned the second side should start with *Fight*, then *Winning Ugly* before *Deep Love*. On 13 July 1985, Bob Geldof's Live Aid project provided an unique opportunity for the Stones to play live again.

The irony is that the full band were together for the recording sessions but Mick Jagger and Keith declined the show. Various rumours circulated about their non-appearance but possible explanations include Mick's split with Keith, the latter's distrust of charity events, the studio commitments of DIRTY WORK or was it the intimidating line-up at Wembley?

Once the Stones officially declined to appear, Mick was asked to perform with David Bowie. Instead of a joint performance, they decided to record a cover of *Dancing In The Street* and, within a 24-hour period, also filmed a video for worldwide broadcast during the finale of the UK 'Live Aid' night. The Martha and The Vandellas hit was later released by Bowie and Jagger, the proceeds going to African famine relief. It became a gigantic hit on both sides of the Atlantic, entering the British charts at No. 1. Mick, without full Stones support, performed in Philadelphia on the American Live Aid show, playing a rousing set backed by the Hall and Oates band. The numbers were *Lonely At The Top, Just Another Night* and *Miss You*. He was then joined by Tina Turner for two memorable numbers, *State Of Shock* and *It's Only Rock 'n' Roll*, during which Tina's skirt got ripped off to reveal modest lingerie underneath.

The latter three songs and the video appeared on a compilation box set DVD finally released in 2005, The other Stones remained silent, although Keith and Ron Wood made fools of themselves when they accompanied Bob Dylan on a disastrous acoustic set at the Live Aid finale. Keith was cajoled into appearing by Ronnie and they later blamed the poor result on the atrocious sound quality, as can be heard in the concluding song, *We Are The World*. Dylan, in his belligerent style, also played totally different songs than were rehearsed, which did not help matters.

986. BACK TO ZERO (Jagger, Richards, Leavell) 4.00
16 July - 17 August, 10 September - 15 October; 15 November - 5 December 1985: Place: RPM Studios, New York, USA; Right Track Studios, New York, USA.
Rolling Stones with Chuck Leavell, Bobby Womack, Anton Fig, Dan Collette.
Producer: Steve Lillywhite, The Glimmer Twins.
Engineer: Dave Jerden, Steve Parker, Tim Crich, Mike Krewick.
UK LP DIRTY WORK: 24 March 1986: No. 4 - 10 weeks
USA LP DIRTY WORK: 24 March 1986: No. 4 - 15 weeks

Chuck Leavell, who worked with Mick Jagger on his solo project, co-wrote this song with Jagger and Richards. This was an honour only previously bestowed on official Stones members, Ron Wood and Mick Taylor. It signified the adoption of a freer, more natural approach to the rigours of collating an album. *Back To Zero* is a funky number, full of rhythmic guitar passages (supplied by Bobby Womack) and, of course, the synthesised organ work of Chuck.
Anton Fig, who had worked with Mick on his solo album, plays additional percussion. On a pared back out-take additional shakers can clearly be heard (* a - 4.17). Ron Wood probably plays bass guitar and Bill Wyman helps out on keyboard synthesiser. There is a shrill burst of trumpet by Dan Collette at the end of the song. The anti-nuclear lyrics herald the two-nation race to world destruction.
However, times were-a-changing and, in March 1985, the old communist war horse Chernenko was replaced by Mikhail Gorbachev, bringing a thaw in attitudes. Again, the Stones were singing angrily, determined not to dodge their perceived responsibilities.

987. LOVING YOU IS SWEETER THAN EVER (Hunter, Wonder) 6.20
16 July - 17 August 1985: Place: RPM Studios, New York, USA.
Rolling Stones with Chuck Leavell.
Producer: The Glimmer Twins.
Engineer: Dave Jerden.
Bootleg only.

Loving You Is Sweeter Than Ever was written by George (Ivy) Hunter and Stevie Wonder. It was popularised in July 1966 by The Four Tops, when it achieved a No. 21 hit with it in the UK. The Stones' version is loose, principally led by the piano, Jagger's vocals and a couple of guitars, one of which is that of Ron Wood.

988. WINNING UGLY (NY MIX) (Jagger, Richards) 7.03
16 July - 17 August, 10 September - 15 October; 15 November - 5 December 1985: Place: RPM Studios, New York, USA; Right Track Studios, New York, USA.
Rolling Stones with Chuck Leavell, Janice Pendarvis, Dolette MacDonald.
Producer: Steve Lillywhite, The Glimmer Twins.
Engineer: Dave Jerden, Steve Parker, Tim Crich, Mike Krewick. Re-mix by Francois Kevorkian.
Canadian 12-inch B Side Winning Ugly (London Mix): November 1986

989. WINNING UGLY (LONDON MIX) (Jagger, Richards) 7.55
16 July - 17 August, 10 September - 15 October; 15 November - 5 December 1985: Place: RPM Studios, New York, USA; Right Track Studios, New York, USA.
Rolling Stones with Chuck Leavell, Janice Pendarvis, Dolette MacDonald.
Producer: Steve Lillywhite, The Glimmer Twins.
Engineer: Dave Jerden, Steve Parker, Tim Crich, Mike Krewick.
Canadian 12-inch Single: November 1986
USA CD FLASHPOINT (COLLECTIBLES): 20 May 1991
UK Track CD Single Ruby Tuesday: 24 May 1991
UK CD box set THE SINGLES COLLECTION 1971-2006: 45 X 45s: 11 April 2011
USA CD box set THE SINGLES COLLECTION 1971-2006: 45 X 45s: 26 April 2011

990. WINNING UGLY (Jagger, Richards) 4.33
16 July - 17 August, 10 September - 15 October; 15 November - 5 December 1985: Place: RPM Studios, New York, USA; Right Track Studios, New York, USA.
Rolling Stones with Chuck Leavell, Janice Pendarvis, Dolette MacDonald.
Producer: Steve Lillywhite, The Glimmer Twins.
Engineer: Dave Jerden, Steve Parker, Tim Crich, Mike Krewick.
UK LP DIRTY WORK: 24 March 1986: No. 4 - 10 weeks
USA LP DIRTY WORK: 24 March 1986: No. 4 - 15 weeks

Opened by Charlie Watts and Bill Wyman, *Winning Ugly* is essentially a lead guitarist's song. Keith Richards and Ronnie Wood create an overload of lead solos which charge in and out of the mix. They are centred on and controlled by one of Keith's prestigious rock riffs, nicked from the Motown catalogue. An out-take with different lyrics, no backing vocals and Jagger guiding the band through the different breaks, is available (* a - 4.55).
The song is about the increasing ugliness of life in the early 80s with Ronald Reagan and Margaret Thatcher holding the capitalist court: "I wanna be on top, forever on the up, and damn the competition, I never play it fair, I never turn a hair, just like the politicians, I wrap my conscience up." A Canadian 12-inch single of *Winning Ugly* includes extended London and New York mixes. The mix features acoustic guitar and a slowed down piece, where the boogie guitar scratches and burns with a vibrato lead. Mick's vocals are enhanced by female backing artistes, two of whom are mentioned on the album sleeve - Janis (Janice) Pendarvis and Dolette MacDonald.

991. **HOLD BACK** (Jagger, Richards) 3.53
16 July - 17 August, 10 September - 15 October; 15 November - 5 December 1985: Place: RPM Studios, New York, USA; Right Track Studios, New York, USA.
Rolling Stones with Chuck Leavell, Ivan Neville, Bobby Womack.
Producer: Steve Lillywhite, The Glimmer Twins.
Engineer: Dave Jerden, Steve Parker, Tim Crich, Mike Krewick.
UK LP DIRTY WORK: 24 March 1986: No. 4 - 10 weeks
USA LP DIRTY WORK: 24 March 1986: No. 4 - 15 weeks

One of only three Jagger, Richards contributions on the album, a fact which would set the Glimmer Inc into a stocks 'n' shares bear market! It replaced *Deep Love* as an album cut. *Hold Back* was a track originally thought to be nothing better than an out-take. It was salvaged on a play-back when the band decided that the drum sound was too good to waste. To polish it off, Ivan Neville was asked to re-do a funky bass line and so the track ended up on the album as a sandwich spread. The song is a rocker right from Charlie Watts' opening whack on the drums. Ronnie Wood tries to redeem the song with a good lead solo and Bobby Womack also takes a guitar part. Mick Jagger sings, or rather shouts, the lengthy verse. The message is there in the lyrics; trust your instinct, go for it.
Dave Jerden was impressed with the band despite their tensions and reasoned that they still existed because of Mick's business mind and Keith's soul. "I could name some that thought they were really tough ass mother fuckers but they don't even come close to the Stones. As far as being stressful a gig, I don't know if I would want to do it again but you know something it was an experience in hindsight that I wouldn't miss for the world because I was actually in the centre of an amazing creative duo. Unfortunately they were not gelling so well on this one . . . they have this umbrella of understanding that can make great records . . . very rarely do you run into the real thing and I was fortunate enough to do that."

992. **SLEEP TONIGHT** (Jagger, Richards) 5.14
16 July - 17 August, 10 September - 15 October; 15 November - 5 December 1985: Place: RPM Studios, New York, USA; Right Track Studios, New York, USA.
Rolling Stones with Tom Waits, Janice Pendarvis, Dolette MacDonald.
Producer: Steve Lillywhite, The Glimmer Twins.
Engineer: Dave Jerden, Steve Parker, Tim Crich, Mike Krewick.
UK LP DIRTY WORK: 24 March 1986: No. 4 - 10 weeks
USA LP DIRTY WORK: 24 March 1986: No. 4 - 15 weeks

Keith Richards' repartee with other artists reached a zenith during the DIRTY WORK period. He performed on a Nona Hendryx solo album and, along with Ron Wood, played with Bono on a U2 song, *Silver And Gold*, for an apartheid cause. Keith was also involved with one track on the PHANTOM, ROCKER AND SLICK album and contributed an outstanding three tracks to the new Tom Waits album RAIN DOGS. This particular input was reciprocated by Tom Waits when he, allegedly, performed on *Sleep Tonight*, perhaps on backing vocals. It is unlikely he played piano since Keith would have taken that role.
The outcome is a beautiful country rock ballad. Keith uses open Nashville tuning on an acoustic and delivers a sincere passage on electric guitar. Ron Wood supplements the action playing the drums for a change - Charlie Watts admitted he could not have done better. This may have happened when Charlie broke his leg, confining him to his home in Devon, England. Keith's singing graces the track, his second vocal outing on the album. Gospel vocals assist in the background. A seven-minute version with no backing vocals was recorded at the RPM Studio, New York, where the album was mixed, allowing a few extra guitar licks (* a - 6.50). Keith really enjoys the song, ad-libbing "baby's" and even laughing at one stage. The song probably started its life back in Paris but was perfected in New York. In December 1985, after the completion of the new album, Ian Stewart, who with Brian Jones was one of the band's founder members, tragically died of a heart attack while waiting to see his specialist in London's Harley Street.
The sessionography has always included his contribution within the description, Rolling Stones "Personnel", since he had played a major role in forming the band's overall groove. The Sixth Stone, the official Stones' Company Secretary, Desperate Dan or plain Stu, was a musicians' musician and one of the greatest exponents of boogie and blues as his own band, Rocket 88, testifies. Among the mourners at the funeral, on 20 December 1985, were the Stones, Eric Clapton and Astrid Lundstrom (Bill Wyman's girlfriend). Albert Ammons' warm tones of Boogie Woogie Dream reflected the sad day. As a tribute, on the DIRTY WORK album, a final 30 second fragment of *Key To The Highway* by Ian was added to complete the release.
Charlie was heard to say: "Who's going to tell us off now?" In February 1986, at the 100 Club in London, the band played a private gig as a memorial to the boogie man. It was a night of uncompromising R 'n' B. Celebrity contributions were made by Pete Townshend, Eric Clapton and Jeff Beck, who were all old mates of Ian Stewart. There are no recordings of the concert, however Paul McCartney was in the audience and is rumoured to have taped it. Bill German, who wrote the *Beggars Banquet* fan club newsletter, summed up the impromptu concert in his book *Under Their Thumb*.
He described that, after a set by Rocket 88, the Stones started without Charlie - Simon Kirke filled in. They played *Route 66, Down The Road Apiece, Key To The Highway* with Eric, *Confessin' The Blues, I'm A Man, Bye Bye Johnny* with Jeff Beck, *Harlem Shuffle* with Pete Townshend and *Little Red Rooster*. Charlie then went on stage for *Down In The Bottom, Dust My Broom* and finally *Little Queenie*. This 1986 stage tribute was how Ian could best be remembered and a good night was had by all.

993. **HANG ON TONIGHT** (Jagger)
AKA: **Hang On To Me Tonight**
January - 23 March 1989: Place: Blue Wave Studios, Barbados, USA.
Producer: The Glimmer Twins.
Unavailable.

The band spent the early part of 1986, from March to May, promoting the album and singles released. Mick Jagger made it clear to the rest of the band that he did not want to tour that year. Ron Wood and his manager Nick Cowan were devastated at the financial implication of this and Keith Richards also was totally frustrated at the decision. So for the rest of the year they went their own ways.

Mick worked on the soundtrack of RUTHLESS PEOPLE, with Dave Stewart and Darryl Hall, and played at The Prince's Trust concert with David Bowie, performing a rendition of *Dancing In The Street*. He also started writing songs for his next solo album. Charlie Watts created a big band orchestra and recorded an album LIVE AT FULHAM TOWN HALL. Ron Wood played with every star he could - Prince, Tom Petty, Bob Dylan, Jerry Lee Lewis, Chuck Berry and at a ramshackle Faces reunion at Wembley Stadium, London, with Bill Wyman on bass guitar.

In June, Keith and Steve Jordan recorded *Jumping Jack Flash* with Aretha Franklin and Ron Wood and *Miss You* with his favourite lady, Etta James. Another daughter was added to the family, Alexandra. From June, Keith started a major project, recording Chuck Berry for a full-length concert film and video entitled *Hail! Hail! Rock 'n' Roll*.

This was easier said than done, Keith remarking that Chuck was even more difficult to work with than Mick! The concert took place on 18 October and contributions were made by Bobby Keys, Chuck Leavell (both of Stones fame), Eric Clapton, Robert Cray, Etta James, Julian Lennon, Linda Ronstadt, Joe Walsh, Joey Spamianato, Ingrid Berry and the legendary Johnnie Johnson, who prompted Keith to recall the piano playing of departed mate, Stu. Putting a band together for Chuck inspired Keith to think that it could also be done for a solo album.

Meanwhile, 1987 started with both Mick and Ron in the studio for their next individual projects. Ron teamed up with Keith to work on an unknown British outfit, The Dirty Strangers, who had played a few years back at Ronnie and Jo Wood's wedding. The producer was Keith's 60s buddy, Prince 'Stash' Klossowski, and the music was good time rock - the two Stones' members contributed to a large number of tracks for the self-titled album, which featured guitarist Paul Fox (ex of The Ruts) and band founder Alan Clayton.

He had met Keith through work as a nightclub bouncer with the late Joe Seabrook, who was Keith's security man. Mick's album PRIMITIVE COOL, recorded with Dave Stewart, was released in September 1987. Stewart acted as co-producer and guest artists were restricted to - oh, just a handful, but principally: Jeff Beck, Simon Phillips, Doug Wimbish, G E Smith, Phil Ashley and Richard Cottle. This second solo album provoked rumours that the band was about to split.

Keith believes that, if he had forced the issue with Mick, it could have done so. Instead, he relented and signed a deal with Virgin for two solo albums. He and Steve Jordan began to write songs and collaborated with Feargal Sharkey (an ex-Undertone) on his solo album, along with Waddy Wachtel (a Warren Zevon band member and producer). Keith played on one number, *More Love*. Meanwhile Charlie took his orchestra to the United States and Bill Wyman and Terry Taylor worked on a movie soundtrack.

Ron Wood started a unique partnership with Bo Diddley and toured the States with him during November 1987. A live album and video were recorded at the New York Ritz for future release, the tour reaching Europe in 1988. While Keith was working on the completion of his album, he realised that Mick was preparing to tour in his own right, promoted by Bill Graham. He was not happy, especially when he found out the large number of Stones tracks being rehearsed.

Despite this, in May 1988, Mick and Keith began to talk about the possibility of recording again the next year. Ron and Bo visited Japan in March 1988, coincidentally at the same time as Mick - their tours overlapped by a few days. Mick's tour reached Australia in September and October, the nucleus of the band being Joe Satriani and Jimmy Rip on guitars, Doug Wimbish bass, Simon Phillips drums, Phil Ashley keyboards and Bernard Fowler on backing vocals.

Mick found that Bernard and his harmonies were just what he required, hence his invite on the tour. Keith desperately wanted to avoid recording solo since he felt it was an admission that he had failed to keep the band together. He was very sensitive about the possibility of a band break-up and it was only after working with Steve Jordan on the Aretha Franklin and Chuck Berry enterprises, that he could summon sufficient nerve to record an album.

He did so with Steve Jordan on drums, Charley Drayton on bass (although sometimes Steve and Charley swapped roles) and Waddy Wachtel on guitar. Guest appearances were made by Mick Taylor, Bootsy Collins, Chuck Leavell, Bobby Keys, Maceo Parker, Ivan Neville, Patti Scialfa, Willie Mitchell, Joey Spaminato, Sarah Dash, Memphis Horns, Bernie Worrell, Michael Doucet and Stanley "Buckwheat" Dural.

The main band became known as the X-Pensive Winos due to their consumption of costly Lafite-Rothschild wines. Keith's album, TALK IS CHEAP, finally appeared in October 1988. All the tracks were co-written with Steve Jordan, who had worked on the DIRTY WORK album and the Chuck Berry project. At the end of 1988, Keith took the band on a tour of the USA where the critics were very positive about TALK IS CHEAP. Both Glimmers had exorcised some demons.

While both men had extended their boundaries, only Mick had realised his limits. It was agreed that Mick and Keith, encouraged by Ron, would meet each other in late 1988 and then, in 1989, at Eddie Grant's Blue Wave Studios in Barbados, to discuss how they might work with each other again. It was not a very subtle idea to bring Keith to the studio used by Mick for his solo album but the island's ambience was pleasing.

Before Keith departed for Barbados, he told his "old lady" Patti, that he would be gone either for a few weeks or for a few days. Happily after a few days, Mick and Keith agreed to start working again with each other for the first time in three years. The resulting session was only briefly interrupted when they returned to the States on 18 January for The Rolling Stones to be inducted into the Rock And Roll Hall Of Fame. The presenter, Pete Townshend, described them as giant artists - "guys, don't try and grow old gracefully - it wouldn't suit you".

Mick's acceptance speech acknowledged the contribution of Ian Stewart and Brian Jones while Mick Taylor joined Mick, Keith and Ron to play some Stones numbers with the other inductees - the first occasion the Glimmers had played together on stage since 1982. During the remainder of the 70s, Mick Taylor had not achieved much until his first solo, self-titled, album was released in 1979.

The 80s were fairly quiet, too, until tours with John Mayall, and a golden era with Bob Dylan, recording INFIDELS in 1983 and then touring with him. Finally, he went out on the road in his own right during the last years of the decade and much of the next. A first-rate album, with an acknowledgement to his past, A

STONES THROW was released in 1998. Back at the Hall Of Fame, in 1988, The Beatles, The Beach Boys and Bob Dylan were inducted (again the Beatles were ahead of the Stones).

Mick Jagger sang on the finale, with George Harrison and Bruce Springsteen, amongst many others, performing *I Saw Her Standing There*. Mick and Keith recharged and resumed the sessions in February, writing around 50 songs, hooks and riffs. Most were unfinished but 16 were considered strong enough for the team to be called in - first Charlie joined them in Bridgetown in February, then Ron and Bill followed in March.

The tapes from the STEEL WHEELS sessions were kept very close to their chests but, in 2008, a few extra tracks escaped. This still unavailable track was one that had been worked on by Mick and was left over for his next solo project, WANDERING SPIRIT, under the title *Hang On To Me Tonight*. The same was true of another Jagger composition, *Sweet Thing*.

994. HELLHOUND ON MY TRAIL (Johnson) 1.15
January - 23 March 1989: Place: Blue Wave Studios, Barbados, USA.
Producer: The Glimmer Twins.
Bootleg only.

A Robert Johnson cover that was recorded during filming of the documentary *25 X 5: The Continuing Adventures Of The Rolling Stones*. It was not included in the final video.

995. WISH I'D NEVER MET YOU (Jagger, Richards) 4.42
9 - 23 March; 29 March - 2 May; 15 May - 29 June 1989: Place: Blue Wave Studios, Barbados, USA; Air Studios, Montserrat; Olympic Sound Studios, London, England.
Rolling Stones with Chuck Leavell
Producer: The Glimmer Twins.
Engineer: Christopher Marc Potter, Rupert Coulson Michael H Brauer.
Re-mix: Chris Kimsey.
UK B-side Almost Hear You Sigh: 18 June 1990
UK Track CD Single Almost Hear You Sigh: 18 June 1990
UK Track CD Single Terrifying: 30 July 1990
USA CD FLASHPOINT (COLLECTIBLES): 20 May 1991
USA CD LP ROLLING STONES RARITIES 1971-2003: 22 November 2005: No. 76 - 6 weeks
UK CD LP ROLLING STONES RARITIES 1971-2003: 28 November 2005
UK CD box set THE SINGLES COLLECTION 1971-2006: 45 X 45s: 11 April 2011
USA CD box set THE SINGLES COLLECTION 1971-2006: 45 X 45s: 26 April 2011

Thought to have been started at the DIRTY WORK sessions, *Wish I'd Never Met You* is a slow blues. The piano is boogie-woogie and so, if the track was originally recorded in Paris in 1985, then it may have been Ian Stewart. There are two blues lead guitars jostling for attention with Mick's wailing blues vocals. The track was released on two singles as their B-sides in 1990. The first was a normal single, while the release on *Terrifying* was a special three-inch CD.

996. MIXED EMOTIONS (CHRIS KIMSEY'S TWELVE-INCH) (Jagger, Richards) 6.13
9 - 23 March; 29 March - 2 May; 15 May - 29 June 1989: Place: Blue Wave Studios, Barbados, USA; Air Studios, Montserrat; Hit Factory, New York, USA, Olympic Sound Studios, London, England.
Rolling Stones with Chuck Leavell, Luis Jardin, Sarah Dash, Lisa Fischer, Bernard Fowler, Kick Horns
Producer: Chris Kimsey, The Glimmer Twins.
Engineer: Christopher Marc Potter, Rupert Coulson, Michael H Brauer
Remix Engineer: Chris Kimsey. Assistant Engineer: Michael Butterworth, Al Stone.
UK 12-inch Single: 21 August 1989: No. 36 - 5 weeks
USA 12-inch Single: 21 August 1989: No. 5 - 12 weeks
USA CD FLASHPOINT (COLLECTIBLES): 20 May 1991
USA CD LP ROLLING STONES RARITIES 1971-2003: 22 November 2005: No. 76 - 6 weeks
UK CD LP ROLLING STONES RARITIES 1971-2003: 28 November 2005

997. MIXED EMOTIONS (Jagger, Richards) 4.38
9 - 23 March; 29 March - 2 May; 15 May - 29 June 1989: Place: Blue Wave Studios, Barbados, USA; Air Studios, Montserrat; Hit Factory, New York, USA, Olympic Sound Studios, London, England.
Played Live: 1989, 1990
Rolling Stones with Chuck Leavell, Luis Jardin, Sarah Dash, Lisa Fischer, Bernard Fowler, Kick Horns
Producer: Chris Kimsey, The Glimmer Twins.
Engineer: Christopher Marc Potter, Rupert Coulson. Assistant Engineer: Michael Butterworth, Al Stone.
UK Single: 21 August 1989: No. 36 - 5 weeks
USA Single: 21 August 1989: No. 5 - 12 weeks
USA LP STEEL WHEELS: 28 August 1989: No. 3 - 20 weeks
UK LP STEEL WHEELS: 29 August 1989: No. 2 - 20 weeks
UK Track 12-inch Single Almost Hear You Sigh: 18 June 1990
UK Track CD Single Almost Hear You Sigh: 18 June 1990
UK Compilation LP JUMP BACK THE BEST OF THE ROLLING STONES '71 - '93: 22 November 1993: No. 16 - 26 weeks

UK CD LP FORTY LICKS: 30 September 2002: No. 2 - 45 weeks
USA CD LP FORTY LICKS: 1 October 2002: No. 2 - 50 weeks
USA Compilation CD JUMP BACK THE BEST OF THE ROLLING STONES '71 - '93: 24 August 2004: No. 30 - 58 weeks
UK CD box set THE SINGLES COLLECTION 1971-2006: 45 X 45s: 11 April 2011
USA CD box set THE SINGLES COLLECTION 1971-2006: 45 X 45s: 26 April 2011

Chris Kimsey, who had last worked with the Stones on the UNDERCOVER album, was asked by Mick Jagger, in December 1988, to produce the Stones' album. He agreed on the condition that the album was recorded over only a few months. He did not want it to deteriorate into a lengthy UNDERCOVER-type album, at the end of which he had sworn he would not work again with the Stones' ramblings. This suited Mick, who wanted the album to be released late summer and for a States tour to commence in the autumn - a schedule more reminiscent of the 60s.

While the Stones wrote songs in Barbados, Chris was working with Yes, in the guise of Jon Anderson, Bill Bruford, Rick Wakeman and Steve Howe, at George Martin's Air Studios, 300 miles away in Montserrat. Suitably, in a tax haven, this was to be the studio where all the Stones would gather to commence recording and was also, in part, the venue for Keith Richards' solo album. Chris would fly over occasionally to comment on the progress of the material and was pleased to find The Glimmer Twins in such fine fettle - the hatchet had definitely been buried.

It was his intention to make a slick and graphic album that leapt out at you sonically, as well as being contemporary. If things went right, then the one after would be dirty and raw but that opportunity would never arise. An early version of *Mixed Emotions* struts along with quite a groove and Mick utters guide breaks (* a - 6.44). It is nearly seven minutes long, an engineer saying at the end, "great guys, very good". A more complete version has the backing vocals overdubbed (* b - 6.36). The album was mixed at Olympic in London in June 1989, the first time these studios had been used by the Stones since December 1970.

In response to Keith Richards' *You Don't Move Me*, Mick Jagger wrote the autobiographical lyrics of *Mixed Emotions*. It is an introspective song and, while the rousing chorus gives it a rock appeal, the verses are much more profound and romantic. *Mixed Emotions* heralded a return by the Stones to recording. More importantly it was a desperately-needed antibody to the wound inflicted by The Glimmer Twins, which had been open ever since the release of DIRTY WORK - due to Mick's solo projects. Keith was often taunted that the song was really Mick's Demotion. Mick was determined to contribute more on STEEL WHEELS. *Mixed Emotions* was composed by Keith during one weekend. It has a strong hook line but lacked a distinctive quality for it to be a huge hit. Columbia Record Company executives Clifford Burnstein and Peter Mensch visited the studio and heard a playback of the song's opening. Peter reckoned that it would sound better if they chopped some of the playing and cut to the chorus quicker.

Chris Kimsey looked around the studio, studying their reactions, and saw Keith grab his bag, pull out a knife and throw it between Mensch's feet, saying: "Listen sonny, no-one tells the Rolling Stones how to write a song, now fuck off." They were not seen again at the sessions. The 12-inch version of *Mixed Emotions* was mixed in Olympic by Michael H Brauer and then remixed by Chris Kimsey at the Hit Factory in New York.

It was something he wanted to do and just presented the end result to the band. The Stones were so pleased with his work that the 12-inch includes his name in the song title in brackets. The album version was edited for normal single release (* c - 4.00). Mick plays the distinctive up and down guitar strum on *Mixed Emotions* and also performs strongly on vocals. Chuck Leavell is featured on piano and a Hammond organ while Luis Jardin, whose credits appear with ABC, Frankie Goes to Hollywood and Dave Gilmour, assists with percussion. Bernard Fowler, Lisa Fischer and Sarah Dash (a former Labelle member, who has also performed with Sir Ronald of Wood and on Keith's solo album) contribute backing vocals. Brass is supplied by a four-piece entitled Kick Horns.

The production is deliberately up front for single exposure and, for once, the 12-inch has a groove which gives it a far more enjoyable edge than the shorter, four-minute single edit. Chuck's newly-revived Hammond organ sound is much more audible in the extended mix and the band's guitars jangle effectively. The track especially comes alive towards the end of the six minutes when the horns, organ and vocals are accompanied by the strong percussive back drop - then the guitar's riff is menacingly introduced.

A South American single version, entitled *Mixed Emotions (New Mix)* (* d - 4.37), was made available. The video to accompany the single release was shot by Jim Signorelli and directed by Crescenzo Notarile in August 1989 during tour rehearsals at an ex-girls school, Wykeham Rise, near Washington, Connecticut. The video is simply a run through of the song in rehearsal but cuts to black and white film of the Montserrat Studio sessions, including shots of Chris Kimsey's mixing desk and the Stones relaxing - Ronnie playing pool and a photo session mastered by Dimo Safari. The video *25 X 5: The Continuing Adventures Of The Rolling Stones* has rehearsal footage of the recording of this song, Jagger and Richards feeding off each other.

998. ROCK AND A HARD PLACE (DANCE MIX) (Jagger, Richards) 6.54
9 - 23 March; 29 March - 2 May; 15 May - 29 June 1989: Place: Blue Wave Studios, Barbados, USA; Air Studios, Montserrat; Olympic Sound Studios, London, England.
Rolling Stones with Chuck Leavell, Matt Clifford, Sarah Dash, Lisa Fischer, Bernard Fowler, Kick Horns
Producer: Chris Kimsey, The Glimmer Twins.
Engineer: Christopher Marc Potter, Rupert Coulson, Michael H Brauer.
Remixed by Don Was and Michael Brauer.
UK 12-inch Single: 13 November 1989: No. 63 - 1 week
USA 12-inch Single: 13 November 1989: No. 23 - 13 weeks
USA Single: 13 November 1989: No. 23 - 13 weeks
UK 12-inch Track Terrifying: 30 July 1990
UK CD box set THE SINGLES COLLECTION 1971-2006: 45 X 45s: 11 April 2011
USA CD box set THE SINGLES COLLECTION 1971-2006: 45 X 45s: 26 April 2011

999. ROCK AND A HARD PLACE (BONUS BEATS MIX) (Jagger, Richards) 4.08
9 - 23 March; 29 March - 2 May; 15 May - 29 June 1989: Place: Blue Wave Studios, Barbados, USA; Air Studios, Montserrat; Olympic Sound Studios, London, England.
Rolling Stones with Chuck Leavell, Matt Clifford, Sarah Dash, Lisa Fischer, Bernard Fowler, Kick Horns
Producer: Chris Kimsey, The Glimmer Twins.
Engineer: Christopher Marc Potter, Rupert Coulson, Michael H Brauer.
Remixed by Don Was and David McMurray.

UK CD Track Rock And A Hard Place (Michael Brauer Mix): 13 November 1989
USA CD Track Rock And A Hard Place (Dance Mix): 13 November 1989
UK CD box set THE SINGLES COLLECTION 1971-2006: 45 X 45s: 11 April 2011
USA CD box set THE SINGLES COLLECTION 1971-2006: 45 X 45s: 26 April 2011

1000. ROCK AND A HARD PLACE (OH-OH HARD DUB MIX) (Jagger, Richards) 6.54
9 - 23 March; 29 March - 2 May; 15 May - 29 June 1989: Place: Blue Wave Studios, Barbados, USA; Air Studios, Montserrat; Olympic Sound Studios, London, England.
Rolling Stones with Chuck Leavell, Matt Clifford, Sarah Dash, Lisa Fischer, Bernard Fowler, Kick Horns
Producer: Chris Kimsey, The Glimmer Twins.
Engineer: Christopher Marc Potter, Rupert Coulson, Michael H Brauer.
Remixed by Don Was and Michael Brauer. Edits by Omar Santana.
UK CD Track Rock And A Hard Place (Dance Mix): 13 November 1989
USA CD Track Rock And A Hard Place (Dance Mix): 13 November 1989
USA B-side 12-inch Rock And A Hard Place (Dance Mix): 13 November 1989
UK CD box set THE SINGLES COLLECTION 1971-2006: 45 X 45s: 11 April 2011
USA CD box set THE SINGLES COLLECTION 1971-2006: 45 X 45s: 26 April 2011

1001. ROCK AND A HARD PLACE (ROCK MIX EDIT) (Jagger, Richards) 5.39
9 - 23 March; 29 March - 2 May; 15 May - 29 June 1989: Place: Blue Wave Studios, Barbados, USA; Air Studios, Montserrat; Olympic Sound Studios, London, England.
Rolling Stones with Chuck Leavell, Matt Clifford, Sarah Dash, Lisa Fischer, Bernard Fowler, Kick Horns
Producer: Chris Kimsey, The Glimmer Twins.
Engineer: Christopher Marc Potter, Rupert Coulson, Michael H Brauer.
Remixed by Don Was and Michael Brauer. Edits by Mike Corbett.
USA Promo CD Track Terrifying: February 1990

A very rare promotional-only mix released for the radio station Columbia CSK 1897. Only 25 copies are said to exist.

1002. ROCK AND A HARD PLACE (MICHAEL BRAUER MIX) (Jagger, Richards) 7.05
9 - 23 March; 29 March - 2 May; 15 May - 29 June 1989: Place: Blue Wave Studios, Barbados, USA; Air Studios, Montserrat; Olympic Sound Studios, London, England.
Rolling Stones with Chuck Leavell, Matt Clifford, Sarah Dash, Lisa Fischer, Bernard Fowler, Kick Horns
Producer: Chris Kimsey, The Glimmer Twins.
Engineer: Christopher Marc Potter, Rupert Coulson, Michael H Brauer.
Remixed by Michael Brauer.
USA 12-inch Track Rock And A Hard Place (Dance Mix): 13 November 1989
UK 12-inch Single: 13 November 1989: No. 63 - 1 week
USA CD FLASHPOINT (COLLECTIBLES): 20 May 1991
UK CD box set THE SINGLES COLLECTION 1971-2006: 45 X 45s: 11 April 2011
USA CD box set THE SINGLES COLLECTION 1971-2006: 45 X 45s: 26 April 2011

1003. ROCK AND A HARD PLACE (Jagger, Richards) 5.25
AKA: Steel Wheels, Between A Rock (And A Hard Place)
9 - 23 March; 29 March - 2 May; 15 May - 29 June 1989: Place: Blue Wave Studios, Barbados, USA; Air Studios, Montserrat; Olympic Sound Studios, London, England.
Played Live: 1989, 1990, 1995, 1997, 2002
Rolling Stones with Chuck Leavell, Matt Clifford, Sarah Dash, Lisa Fischer, Bernard Fowler, Kick Horns
Producer: Chris Kimsey, The Glimmer Twins.
Engineer: Christopher Marc Potter, Rupert Coulson Michael H Brauer. Mixed: Michael H Brauer.
USA LP STEEL WHEELS: 28 August 1989: No. 3 - 20 weeks
UK LP STEEL WHEELS: 29 August 1989: No. 2 - 20 weeks
USA Single: 13 November 1989: No. 23 - 13 weeks
UK Single: 13 November 1989: No. 63 - 1 week
USA CD Track Rock And A Hard Place (Dance Mix): 13 November 1989
UK CD Single Track Terrifying (Seven Inch Remix Edit):30 July 1990
UK Compilation LP JUMP BACK THE BEST OF THE ROLLING STONES '71 - '93: 22 November 1993: No. 16 - 26 weeks
USA Compilation CD JUMP BACK THE BEST OF THE ROLLING STONES '71 - '93: 24 August 2004: No. 30 - 58 weeks
UK CD box set THE SINGLES COLLECTION 1971-2006: 45 X 45s: 11 April 2011
USA CD box set THE SINGLES COLLECTION 1971-2006: 45 X 45s: 26 April 2011

When the songwriting team had completed the ground work on the 16 feasible tunes, Mick Jagger and Keith Richards went to Air Studios in March. Ronnie Wood confirmed that they had deliberately left Mick and Keith together to settle their differences and recreate some of the old magic. At about the same time, Matt Clifford joined the band - apparently hijacked from the Yes camp where he had just finished recording with Chris Kimsey, Christopher Marc Potter and Rupert Coulson on the album ANDERSON-BRUFORD-WAKEMAN-HOWE.

Matt was a former Gloucestershire chorister who specialised on the keyboard and synthesiser and was a good friend of Steve Howe and Jon Anderson. The sessions were the first time that Chris Kimsey concentrated on production alone, thus giving him more freedom, while he left the recording to Chris Potter. It was the first album he had recorded digitally with the band.

There is an out-take version of *Rock And A Hard Place* which has a count-in and Mick directing break changes. It is heavily synthesised and has electronic drums. The production team were to play a fundamental part in creating the revitalised, contemporary Stones sound. *Rock And A Hard Place* was one of the first tracks to be recorded at the sessions and was known as *Steel Wheels* - there is a near complete out-take labelled as such (* a - 5.49). Another early version, with a Mick count-in and pronounced keyboards, can be found (* b - 5.52).

It is a funky, guitar-laden song, Bill's Wal bass as peppery and fiery as ever. Several solos abound and the brass and female vocals are used extensively. The track was released as the second single from the album and it became a popular FM Stereo favourite on both sides of the Atlantic. The single edition was a shortened version of the album cut (* c - 4.10) - the 12-inch single and compact disc formats gave the marketing profession plenty of scope for different mixes, which were undertaken by Don Was, David McMurray and Michael Brauer.

David and Michael had worked with Don Was on his Was Not Was projects. The re-mixes do not come up to the standard of the *Too Much Blood* dance and dub ones. A video shot by Wayne Isham was filmed at a concert on the Steel Wheels tour. Layered on top of the video are transparent logos, lyrics and letters from the song. Another version on *25 X 5* has concert film and the band, shot within scaffolding, miming to the song.

1004. ALMOST HEAR YOU SIGH (Jagger, Richards, Jordan) 4.37
9 - 23 March; 29 March - 2 May; 15 May - 29 June 1989: Place: Blue Wave Studios, Barbados, USA; Air Studios, Montserrat; Olympic Sound Studios, London, England.
Played Live: 1989, 1990

Rolling Stones with Chuck Leavell, Matt Clifford, Luis Jardim, Sarah Dash, Lisa Fischer, Bernard Fowler, Kick Horns
Producer: Chris Kimsey, The Glimmer Twins.
Engineer: Christopher Marc Potter, Rupert Coulson, Michael H Brauer.
Literary Editor: Chris Jagger.
USA LP STEEL WHEELS: 28 August 1989: No. 3 - 20 weeks
UK LP STEEL WHEELS: 29 August 1989: No. 2 - 20 weeks
USA Promo CD Track Almost Hear You Sigh (Remix): January 1990
USA Single: January 1990: No. 50
USA Promo CD Single: January 1990
UK Single: 18 June 1990: No. 31 - 5 weeks
UK CD box set THE SINGLES COLLECTION 1971-2006: 45 X 45s: 11 April 2011
USA CD box set THE SINGLES COLLECTION 1971-2006: 45 X 45s: 26 April 2011

Almost Hear You Sigh (a cousin of *Beast Of Burden*, which Keith Richards christened in the studio), is a classic Stones ballad and was written by Keith and Steve Jordan during recording for the former's solo album, TALK IS CHEAP. The album was generally cohesive, sometimes soulful, and turned out to be a trump card for reuniting the Stones. Just as Keith was beginning to promote its release, Mick Jagger phoned and suggested getting the band back together, Keith jokingly retorting "what are you trying to screw me up for?"

In Barbados, Keith told Mick that he had this *Beast Of Burden*-type song which would be great for his vocals. There are two longer out-take versions sung by Keith, one earlier ad-libbing cut (* a - 5.22) and another with more vocals (* b - 4.52). The lyrics were just for guideline purposes but the song title, tempo and sentiment were kept by Mick in the released version.

Keith used a classical guitar, while Matt Clifford and Chuck Leavell played on piano/keyboards. Chuck's contribution was over-dubbed later in London, as were the backing vocals. Mick had adjusted some of the lyrics and Keith was a little unhappy about the line "feeling your tongue on mine" instead of the less seductive "lips". Chris Jagger was credited with being the literary editor on the song.

At different times in 1990, it was released as a single in the USA and UK, where it was timed to coincide with the Urban Jungle tour. A shorter track than the original was offered as a rare promotional-only single in USA, with a Columbia records matrix of CSK73093 (* c - 4.06). The black and white video of them performing the song was filmed by Jake Scott (then an up-and-coming video director).

1005. SAD SAD SAD (Jagger, Richards) 3.35
9 - 23 March; 29 March - 2 May; 15 May - 29 June 1989: Place: Blue Wave Studios, Barbados, USA; Air Studios, Montserrat; Olympic Sound Studios, London, England.
Played Live: 1989, 1990, 1994, 2002

Rolling Stones with Chuck Leavell, Bernard Fowler, Kick Horns, Simon Clarke, Roddy Lorimer, Tim Sanders, Paul Spong
Producer: Chris Kimsey, The Glimmer Twins.
Engineer: Christopher Marc Potter, Rupert Coulson Michael H Brauer.
Mixed: Michael H Brauer.
USA LP STEEL WHEELS: 28 August 1989: No. 3 - 20 weeks
UK LP STEEL WHEELS: 29 August 1989: No. 2 - 20 weeks
UK CD Single: 13 August 1990

Sad Sad Sad is a typical Stones' belter. It opens with an open-tuned electric guitar by Mick Jagger, then Keith Richards at the end of the riff, followed by Ronnie Wood, all drawing fire from one to the other. Mick spouts the "now you're down then you're up" lyrics. Horns were added, which enabled parallels to be drawn with other Stones garage tunes, *Bitch* and *Rocks Off*.

The brass was selected by Chris Kimsey and arranged by the troupe Kick Horns and the quad sound of Simon Clarke, Roddy Lorimer, Tim Sanders (all from Dave Gilmour's 1984 band) and Paul Spong, who had appeared with pop duo Wham. There is a version without brass, which has earlier lyrics and is slightly extended (* a - 3.58) while another, with finished lyrics, is counted in and rocks like no other (* b - 3.53). *Sad Sad Sad* was written by Mick with the assistance of Charlie Watts.

They wanted to produce a rocker for the album without it falling into a Stones cliché. Mick played rhythm guitar with good technique, which left Keith to play the lead and take the spotlight on the solo. Bill Wyman was absent from the session which produced *Sad Sad Sad* - his bass role was taken by Ron Wood. Ron tended to play the bass in a much more frenzied manner, strumming it as opposed to Bill's plucking style.

Bill's absence was due to having been sent by the band to Antigua for a press conference following the announcement of his engagement to Mandy Smith, who he planned to marry in June. Bill's association with Mandy had consistently attracted major press attention ever since stories circulated of under-age sexual encounters with her at the time of the DIRTY WORK sessions when she was just 13-years-old. Mick summed up the situation when he shrugged and said, "well, that's lurve in the rock and roll world". Meanwhile, Bill made some men jealous by confirming that Mandy gave him youth and made him feel younger.

1006. HEARTS FOR SALE (Jagger, Richards) 4.41
9 - 23 March; 29 March - 2 May; 15 May - 29 June 1989: Place: Blue Wave Studios, Barbados, USA; Air Studios, Montserrat; Olympic Sound Studios, London, England.
Rolling Stones with Matt Clifford, Bernard Fowler
Producer: Chris Kimsey, The Glimmer Twins.
Engineer: Christopher Marc Potter, Rupert Coulson Michael H Brauer.
Mixed: Michael H Brauer.
USA LP STEEL WHEELS: 28 August 1989: No. 3 - 20 weeks
UK LP STEEL WHEELS: 29 August 1989: No. 2 - 20 weeks

STEEL WHEELS was acclaimed by the rock press as a very strong album and *Hearts For Sale* is typical of the album's depth, proving it was not just the Rolling Stones rehashing the past. The guitar sound is strong, from Mick Jagger's opening speaker-distorted feedback to the Latin strumming. Mick also adds a burning harmonica and one of Keith Richards' Fenders. Bernard Fowler can be clearly heard on backing vocals. The lyrics deal with the opposites of contentment with life and the loss of willpower for love, hence the heart being up for sale.

An out-take without Bernard's vocals and the harmonica at the song's end can be heard (* a - 4.30) - there is also a more finished version that has a great lead solo by Ron Wood (* b - 4.35). Chris Kimsey paid tribute to Mick's harmonica playing when he said that the front man managed to sound like all those old harp players, "real breathy, the gaps were just as important as the sound".

Similarly, Keith also pointed out in interviews that, as a musician, your canvas is silence and what you do is play around with that silence - "that's what rhythm is all about". The song that really turned him on to this concept many years earlier was Elvis Presley's Heartbreak Hotel, where there was a juxtaposition between Scotty Moore's guitar and the rhythmic gaps of silence: "Don't obliterate the silence, use it as part of the depth of the canvas."

Mick's extensive contribution was to play guitar on two-thirds of the album, a significant increase - Woody's lessons had obviously paid off. Ron later cracked that the STEEL WHEELS sessions had allowed the "L" plates to be taken off Mick's plectrum. Unlike DIRTY WORK, where Mick was hardly in evidence, STEEL WHEELS was very much a Glimmer Twin production. The location must have helped: it was not so easy to get out of Montserrat as it was Paris, the venue for the previous album.

1007. HOLD ON TO YOUR HAT (Jagger, Richards) 3.32
AKA: Hold On To Yourself
9 - 23 March; 29 March - 2 May; 15 May - 29 June 1989: Place: Blue Wave Studios, Barbados, USA; Air Studios, Montserrat; Olympic Sound Studios, London, England.
Producer: Chris Kimsey, The Glimmer Twins.
Engineer: Christopher Marc Potter, Rupert Coulson Michael H Brauer.
Mixed: Michael H Brauer.
USA LP STEEL WHEELS: 28 August 1989: No. 3 - 20 weeks
UK LP STEEL WHEELS: 29 August 1989: No. 2 - 20 weeks

It is surprising that the two out-and-out rockers on STEEL WHEELS combine the guitar work of Keith Richards and rhythm of Mick Jagger. Originally, it had Chuck Leavell with a rocking bar-room piano; this can be heard on an excellent out-take (* a - 4.10). At the end of the cut, Chris Kimsey shouts "fucking great" and Mick responds "good, good, good; can we hear it". Arguably, this should have been the version released but Chris Kimsey was quick to point out that the band (Mick and Keith) chose which one was the final cut.

There is also a version with false starts and laughter (* b - 4.07). Ron Wood was playing the bass again but loses no power. Guitar licks are traded and meshed as well, as on any Richards/Wood outing. The track was written by Charlie Watts and Mick, confirming that Charlie's low profile belies his actual contribution. Chris Kimsey was worried that recording the band digitally might harm the Stones' furrow, everything might sound too clean, especially Charlie's drum sound. These worries were unfounded, Chris agreeing that every nuance of Charlie's playing was perfectly captured.

Keith, recalling the sessions, remembers particularly the drive and determination shown by Charlie, "he was at those sessions working a solid 12 hours a day". In more ways than one, Charlie had been a foundation stone to the band's reunion. Keith thought that Charlie might have had something to prove to him - how dare Keith work with another drummer, alias Steve Jordan!

1008. SLIPPING AWAY (Jagger, Richards) 4.29
9 - 23 March; 29 March - 2 May; 15 May - 29 June 1989: Place: Blue Wave Studios, Barbados, USA; Air Studios, Montserrat; Olympic Sound Studios, London, England.
Played Live: 1995, 2002, 2003, 2005, 2006, 2007
Rolling Stones with Chuck Leavell, Matt Clifford, Bernard Fowler, Kick Horns, Sarah Dash, Lisa Fischer
Producer: Chris Kimsey, The Glimmer Twins.
Engineer: Christopher Marc Potter, Rupert Coulson Michael H Brauer. Mixed: Michael H Brauer.
USA LP STEEL WHEELS: 28 August 1989: No. 3 - 20 weeks
UK LP STEEL WHEELS: 29 August 1989: No. 2 - 20 weeks

An early instrumental illustrates the way the song was founded (* a - 5.25). Keith Richards is featured on vocals on *Slipping Away*. His performance is a la Al Green on this plaintive ballad. The chorus line "first the sun and then the moon, one of them will be round soon" is an inspired piece of imagery. Kristi Kimsey was naturally around for the sessions and one evening, after the filming for the studio footage of the *Mixed Emotions* video, suggested the song's vocal bridge to Keith. Kristi felt the sessions were very family orientated and relaxed.

They took evening meals together and sometimes went socialising in the main town of Plymouth, which was later destroyed in the volcano eruption of 1995. Generally the recording was done from 9 to 5 and the weekends were held over for the family. It was quite a common occurrence to find the band sat around the pool as about 12 children commandeered the water and Keith tended the barbecue. As well as the SOME GIRLS sessions, Chris Kimsey felt that the STEEL WHEELS sessions were the most enjoyable and creative time for him. Thinking about those times now, Chris thought they had a bizarre Fellini, dream-like quality; perhaps, as it turned out, they were too good to last.

On *Slipping Away,* Matt Clifford provides synthesised strings and also plays an electric piano, while Chuck Leavell plays organ and piano. Mick Jagger hides away, supporting Keith on backing vocals. The overall effect is to allow the album to wistfully fade away. However, it has been well received during Keith's spot mid-set on later tours and that quintessential line with the full moon aloft provides a great concert moment.

Out-takes from STEEL WHEELS surfaced in 2008 - one of which was the afore-mentioned instrumental of *Slipping Away* and another has vocals and backing singers (* b - 5.38). The out-take tracks originated from a family member of a Stones employee who had passed away; they were not sure of the origins of the two digital cassette tapes. Gradually they circulated into collectors' hands. One had early unfinished versions, some probably from Barbados, and another was entering the final mix stages, presumably at Montserrat before finally being completed by Keith, Mick and Chris Kimsey in London.

1009. FOR YOUR PRECIOUS LOVE (Brooks, Brooks, Butler) 6.39
AKA: Precious Love
9 - 23 March; 29 March - 2 May 1989: Place: Blue Wave Studios, Barbados, USA; Air Studios, Montserrat.
Rolling Stones with Chuck Leavell, Bernard Fowler, Lisa Fischer, Sarah Dash
Producer: Chris Kimsey, The Glimmer Twins.
Engineer: Christopher Marc Potter.
Bootleg only.

A Jerry Butler and Arthur and Richard Brooks song which was an original top 20 USA hit for Jerry and Curtis Mayfield's band, The Impressions, in 1958. Other lesser known acts who covered the song and attained USA chart positions were Garnet Mimms and The Enchanters and Oscar Toney Junior.
The Stones took the opportunity to record it during the sessions and, as a cover, it was certainly worth releasing as a B-side but probably not suitable for the Jagger, Richards-written STEEL WHEELS album. Mick's vocals are particularly good. There are two versions both over six minutes. The original cut is sparse with less keyboards and no backing vocals (* a - 6.21).

1010. GIVING IT UP (Jagger, Richards) 5.32
9 - 23 March; 29 March - 2 May 1989: Place: Blue Wave Studios, Barbados, USA; Air Studios, Montserrat.
Rolling Stones with Chuck Leavell
Producer: Chris Kimsey, The Glimmer Twins.
Engineer: Christopher Marc Potter.
Bootleg only.

A five-and-a-half minute out-take of a soft rock ballad with a keyboard intro reminiscent of Bruce Hornsby & The Range's *The Way It Is*. The track then mellows into a groove but fails to evolve further. Other tracks said to come from the sessions include *Hot Line, Sweet Thing, Three Oceans, When I Get To Thinking* and *You've Got Some Nerve. Sweet Thing* was recorded in 1992 by Mick Jagger for his WANDERING SPIRIT album.

1011. READY YOURSELF (Jagger, Richards) 3.37
9 - 23 March; 29 March - 2 May 1989: Place: Blue Wave Studios, Barbados, USA; Air Studios, Montserrat.
Rolling Stones with Chuck Leavell
Producer: Chris Kimsey, The Glimmer Twins.
Engineer: Christopher Marc Potter.
Bootleg only.

Two versions of this out-take can be found. It is a mid-tempo song with an ungainly piano riff. Originally it was recorded as an instrumental (* a - 3.45) but there is also a Keith Richards vocal version, with Keith ad-libbing the song title.

1012. CAN'T BE SEEN (Jagger, Richards) 4.10
AKA: I Just Can't Be Seen
9 - 23 March; 29 March - 2 May; 15 May - 29 June 1989: Place: Blue Wave Studios, Barbados, USA; Air Studios, Montserrat; Olympic Sound Studios, London, England.
Played Live: 1989, 1990
Rolling Stones with Chuck Leavell, Matt Clifford, Bernard Fowler, Luis Jardim
Producer: Chris Kimsey, The Glimmer Twins.
Engineer: Christopher Marc Potter, Rupert Coulson Michael H Brauer. Mixed: Michael H Brauer.
USA LP STEEL WHEELS: 28 August 1989: No. 3 - 20 weeks
UK LP STEEL WHEELS: 29 August 1989: No. 2 - 20 weeks

Can't Be Seen is another vehicle for Keith Richards' vocals - the track likely to have been a TALK IS CHEAP out-take and was recorded in what turned out to be a long, protracted session. There is a five-minute out-take that exists, which has a one-minute guitar-led outro (* a - 5.14) and another more complete mix with more pronounced organ work (* b - 5.25).

The vocals are very un-Stone like - since when did a Stone worry about another woman being married? - their music was indeed growing up. A Wurlitzer-type organ by Chuck Leavell announces the track's start and then it is immediately powered forward by Bill Wyman's bass and the percussion work of Charlie Watts and Luis Jardim. Ronnie Wood's guitar also takes an opportunity to shine.

Bernard Fowler provides great background vocals, as he does on most of the album, helping to keep it consistent. He recalls that most of the tracks brought to London were complete songs ready for overdub. He also had to win over Keith, having arrived from Mick's solo entourage. Eventually Keith gave Bernard a brother's handshake and said he was cool. Matt Clifford contributes clavinet on what is, musician-wise, a good track - song-wise, though, it is a little thin.

1013. BREAK THE SPELL (Jagger, Richards) 3.07
AKA: Call Girl Blues
9 - 23 March; 29 March - 2 May; 15 May - 29 June 1989: Place: Blue Wave Studios, Barbados, USA; Air Studios, Montserrat; Olympic Sound Studios, London, England.
Rolling Stones with Matt Clifford
Producer: Chris Kimsey, The Glimmer Twins.
Engineer: Christopher Marc Potter, Rupert Coulson Michael H Brauer.
Mixed: Michael H Brauer.
USA LP STEEL WHEELS: 28 August 1989: No. 3 - 20 weeks
UK LP STEEL WHEELS: 29 August 1989: No. 2 - 20 weeks
USA B-side Almost Hear You Sigh: January 1990
UK CD box set THE SINGLES COLLECTION 1971-2006: 45 X 45s: 11 April 2011
USA CD box set THE SINGLES COLLECTION 1971-2006: 45 X 45s: 26 April 2011

Ron Wood stepped into the breach again substituting for Bill Wyman's bass steps. The track is an adventurous journey into the land of Tom Waits' blues, hence the aka *Call Girl Blues*. It features the Little Walter-harp playing of Mick Jagger, Matt Clifford on keyboards and Ron Wood on steel dobro. Keith Richards picks a mean guitar while Mick's vocals are suitably affected, in a Tom Waits' vein, by the production team.

The lyrics contain some interesting imagery of a lost love. An early version has Mick gently proffering some lyrics under the aka title (* a - 3.36). Another one has more distinct vocals and instrumentation (* b - 3.50). Chris Kimsey felt that the sessions illustrated by this song produced a rich sound, with a cinematic wide-screen appeal, and he was well pleased that he was working with a joined-up band again.

1014. BLINDED BY LOVE (Jagger, Richards) 4.36
9 - 23 March; 29 March - 2 May; 15 May - 29 June 1989: Place: Blue Wave Studios, Barbados, USA; Air Studios, Montserrat; Olympic Sound Studios, London, England.
Played Live: 1990
Rolling Stones with Chuck Leavell, Matt Clifford, Bernard Fowler, Phil Beer, Luis Jardim
Producer: Chris Kimsey, The Glimmer Twins.
Engineer: Christopher Marc Potter, Rupert Coulson Michael H Brauer.
Mixed: Michael H Brauer.
USA LP STEEL WHEELS: 28 August 1989: No. 3 - 20 weeks
UK LP STEEL WHEELS: 29 August 1989: No. 2 - 20 weeks
UK Track CD Single Sad Sad Sad: 13 August 1990

The strange marriage of tex-mex, country and western music and the lyrics of women's undoing of men through the centuries is bizarre. The Stones always liked the extraneous world of country but this particular example is contrived. The music sounds like a Mick Jagger solo out-take (Mick is on acoustic). Technically it is good, the use of Phil Beer on fiddle and mandolin being interesting, but overall it is not a patch on the humorous offerings of *Far Away Eyes*.

On first hearing it, some Americans commented that the lyrics relating to the Prince of Wales giving up his crown might offend, not realising it was not about the present incumbent! Chris Jagger is puzzlingly credited as literary editor on *Blinded By Love*.

He must have provided the historic references to Cleopatra and Mark Antony, Samson and Delilah, King Edward VIII and Wallis Simpson. A longer out-take version, counted in by Keith Richards, is very much a straightforward Spanish acoustic song, Keith booming out on backing vocals (* a - 5.20). There is another out-take with the fiddle (* b- 5.07).

1015. TERRIFYING (TWELVE INCH RE-MIX) (Jagger, Richards) 6.56
9 - 23 March; 29 March - 2 May; 15 May - 29 June 1989: Place: Blue Wave Studios, Barbados, USA; Air Studios, Montserrat; Olympic Sound Studios, London, England.
Rolling Stones with Chuck Leavell, Matt Clifford, Roddy Lorimer, Lisa Fischer
Producer: Chris Kimsey, The Glimmer Twins.
Engineer: Christopher Marc Potter, Rupert Coulson, Michael H Brauer. Mixing and Additional Production: Steve Thompson, Michael Barbiero.
UK 12-inch Single: 30 July 1990
UK Track CD Single Terrifying (7 Inch Remix Edit): 30 July 1990
UK CD box set THE SINGLES COLLECTION 1971-2006: 45 X 45s: 11 April 2011
USA CD box set THE SINGLES COLLECTION 1971-2006: 45 X 45s: 26 April 2011

1016. **TERRIFYING** (Jagger, Richards) 4.53
9 - 23 March; 29 March - 2 May; 15 May - 29 June 1989: Place: Blue Wave Studios, Barbados, USA; Air Studios, Montserrat; Olympic Sound Studios, London, England.
Played Live: 1989, 1990
Rolling Stones with Chuck Leavell, Matt Clifford, Roddy Lorimer, Lisa Fischer
Producer: Chris Kimsey, The Glimmer Twins.
Engineer: Christopher Marc Potter, Rupert Coulson Michael H Brauer.
Mixed: Michael H Brauer.
USA LP STEEL WHEELS: 28 August 1989: No. 3 - 20 weeks
UK LP STEEL WHEELS: 29 August 1989: No. 2 - 20 weeks
USA Promo CD Single: February 1990
UK 12-inch Single: 30 July 1990
UK CD Single: 30 July 1990
UK CD box set THE SINGLES COLLECTION 1971-2006: 45 X 45s: 11 April 2011
USA CD box set THE SINGLES COLLECTION 1971-2006: 45 X 45s: 26 April 2011

The whole team burns on this excellent funk number. The rhythm section of Charlie Watts and Bill Wyman provide a great back beat - Charlie tick tacks wonderfully almost in jazz fashion. Chris Kimsey thought that Michael Brauer, the mixing engineer, really got the best results from Bill's bass - Michael was good at the bottom end. Chris also shared a laugh with Michael as one young recording assistant bore the brunt of their humour.

Somehow, he was always out of the studio when a master fader "Louis", who apparently wore a mysterious black glove, was hired specifically to provide the highly technical work of a final fade to a track. Check the album credits, courtesy of Keith Richards who arranged - Fades & Stops: Louis Bagadonuts! Mick Jagger's vocals are used to terrific effect, the lyrics being full of animal similes, with the "strange, strange desires" chorus impressive. A version has incomplete lyrics and introduced by Keith Richards telling someone to shut up in the studio in no uncertain terms (* a - 5.09).

This version already has the tinkling keyboard chimes from Matt Clifford. Another out-take comes from Montserrat (* b - 5.40). Roddy Lorimer, from Kick Horns, provides a bar or two of trumpet and Matt Clifford and Chuck Leavell are again used on keyboards and organ respectively. It was edited and released as a single to promote the Urban Jungle tour in the summer of 1990 (* c - 4.10).

A longer version, mixed by Steve Thompson and Michael Barbiero, who did the *Dancing In The Street* and *Harlem Shuffle* re-mixes, was also released in the UK in July 1990. It was called the *Twelve Inch Re-mix* in honour of that vinyl format but, increasingly, vinyl was for collectors only while the digitised Compact Disc format became the media norm. The re-mix cut the sound back even more and, as a result, Roddy's trumpet, Bill's bass guitar, the percussion, the organ, Mick's vocals and the guitar all take it in turns to be featured. Julien Temple filmed the video for this track with the band playing live and included other footage from their North American tour.

1017. **FANCYMAN BLUES** (Jagger, Richards) 5.12
AKA: **Fancy Man Blues**
9 - 23 March; 29 March - 2 May; 15 May - 29 June 1989: Place: Blue Wave Studios, Barbados, USA; Air Studios, Montserrat; Olympic Sound Studios, London, England.
Rolling Stones with Chuck Leavell
Producer: Chris Kimsey, The Glimmer Twins.
Engineer: Christopher Marc Potter, Rupert Coulson Michael H Brauer..
Mixed: Michael H Brauer.
UK & USA B-side Mixed Emotions: 21 August 1989
USA CD FLASHPOINT (COLLECTIBLES): 20 May 1991
USA CD LP ROLLING STONES RARITIES 1971-2003: 22 November 2005: No. 76 - 6 weeks
UK CD LP ROLLING STONES RARITIES 1971-2003: 28 November 2005
UK CD box set THE SINGLES COLLECTION 1971-2006: 45 X 45s: 11 April 2011
USA CD box set THE SINGLES COLLECTION 1971-2006: 45 X 45s: 26 April 2011

As if to prove the Stones were again in fine form, *Fancyman Blues* (the UK title but otherwise *Fancy Man Blues*), which was the flip-side of *Mixed Emotions*, is a barnstormer of a Jimmy Reed-type blues track. Chris Kimsey found that very often, to relieve the recording process, the band would dissolve into playing blues numbers - it was a release for them but it did mean that sometimes he was unsure whether the track was a blues standard or, in this case, a self-penned number. Played in a strictly pedestrian manner with an atypical blues-style piano and the compulsory wailing harmonica, it was never intended to be an album cut. There is a slightly longer out-take available with early lyrics (* a - 5.48) and another extended version to just under seven minutes (* b - 6.46).

While the Stones toured the States in September 1989, hurricane Hugo swept through the Caribbean and devastated the island of Montserrat. George Martin organised a compilation album to help raise funds for the storm's victims, it was called AFTER THE HURRICANE, the Stones contributing *Fancyman Blues*. It was originally mixed in June 1989 by Chris Kimsey and The Glimmer Twins at Olympic Studios in London. In May 1989, Bill Wyman opened his Sticky Fingers restaurant in Kensington, London, upsetting the other band members after failing to get permission to use the name.

This did not stop them joining him for his wedding on 2 June. At Olympic, they pinned up a cartoon on the wall from an English tabloid newspaper, the Daily Mirror, depicting the band fumbling their way down the aisle for Bill and Mandy Smith's wedding. The cartoon was doubtless inspired by Spike Milligan's gift to Bill of a walking frame! Eric Clapton bought a pair of silk pyjamas saying that, at Bill's age, he might need something to keep him warm in bed! Dignity had at last arrived but as Mick Jagger was quick to quip, "a dignified rock band is a contradiction in terms".

1018. **CONTINENTAL DRIFT** (Jagger, Richards) 5.15
AKA: Speed Of Light
9 - 23 March; 29 March - 2 May; 15 May - 29 June 1989; (16 - 17 June): Place: Blue Wave Studios, Barbados, USA; Air Studios, Montserrat;
Olympic Sound Studios, London, England; (The Palace Of Ben Abbou, Tangier, Morocco).
Rolling Stones with Matt Clifford, Master Musicians of Jajouka, Bachir Attar, Bernard Fowler, Sarah Dash, Lisa Fischer, Sonia Morgan, Tessa Niles, Farafina
Producer: Chris Kimsey, The Glimmer Twins.
Engineer: Christopher Marc Potter.
Arranged by: Mick Jagger, Matt Clifford.
USA LP STEEL WHEELS: 28 August 1989: No. 3 - 20 weeks
UK LP STEEL WHEELS: 29 August 1989: No. 2 - 20 weeks
USA B-side 12-inch Almost Hear You Sigh: January 1990

Experimenting had always been one of the Stones' strengths but a degree of conservatism had crept into the Stones' sound since the mid-70s. *Continental Drift* was an attempt to renounce this. It was written by Mick Jagger when he was experimenting with a drum machine and a Korg synthesiser. Matt Clifford helped to programme the synthesiser and was very enthusiastic about the track, hence his credit on the album cover as co-arranger.

An instrumental six-minute plus out-take (* a - 6.21) illustrates that the broad brush riff from the keyboards and the percussive rhythm was retained but speeded up as another one illustrates with lead vocals (* b - 6.22). As the song developed, it was apparent that it had a North African or Eastern feel to it (*Paint It Black* revisited). At one stage, Mick felt that the Burundi drummers should be approached to add percussion but a sequence of events during which history repeated itself dictated otherwise. Brian Jones had recorded the G'naous and the Maalimin of Jajouka in 1968. Now Bachir Attar, the son of the then chief, had written to the Stones inviting them to Morocco to record. It seemed a perfect opportunity to take the backing track to Tangier and record the musicians of Jajouka - their music was a rhythmic incantation which featured the ahaita, a high-pitched instrument, and the tebel drums. Keith Richards was not so sure it was such a good idea to emulate the past. It was impossible to record the locals at their village, due to the lack of basic amenities like electricity, so they were brought to the beautiful Palace Ben Abbou at the Casbah, near Tangier.

It was a very social gathering at the palace and there were a lot of old acquaintances who passed by, turning it into a real event. The night before the musicians turned up, Chris Kimsey suffered a bout of food poisoning and so was not a 100 per cent. He did recall that it was incredibly difficult to get the rhythm and speed exactly right as they enthusiastically contributed their part. A BBC documentary, as part of the Rhythms of the World series, captured the recording process.

The musicians were still going full tilt even when the original basis for *Continental Drift* had finished. As F'dall, one of the musicians confirmed, *Continental Drift* is "big music". Mick hoped that, because of the Moroccan connection the Stones, they would not be accused of traipsing the New World music made popular by the likes of Peter Gabriel. Charlie Watts later overdubbed drums, Ron Wood an electric bass and Keith an acoustic guitar. The rhythmic troupe, Farafina, also overdubbed their African percussive instruments. When the song was originally written in Barbados, Keith had the idea of humanising the programming of Mick and Matt by incorporating the reverberations of a bicycle wheel.

As it spun around, Keith hit the spokes with a stick, brush, spoon and knife - the quite audible effect can be heard early on in the track. The stress of Keith's enthusiasm caused the bike to buckle. *Speed Of Light* is a masterpiece of recording and has become a Stones classic. In just under six months, the band had recorded and mixed an album of 12 songs - a remarkable feat for post-60s times. Without further delay, STEEL WHEELS was released at the end of August 1989.

1019. **ROCK AND A HARD PLACE** (Jagger, Richards) ✏ 4.52
AKA: Steel Wheels
25 November 1989: Place: The Gator Bowl, Jacksonville, Florida, USA.
Rolling Stones with Matt Clifford, Chuck Leavell, Bobby Keys, The Uptown Horns, Bernard Fowler, Lisa Fischer, Cindy Mizelle.
Producer: Chris Kimsey, The Glimmer Twins.
Engineer: Bob Ludwig, Richard Sullivan, Spencer May.
Mixed by: Christopher Marc Potter. Recorded by Bob Clearmountain, David Hewitt, Cedric Beatty, Harry Braun, Dierk.
USA LP FLASHPOINT: 2 April 1991: No. 16 - 5 weeks
UK LP FLASHPOINT: 8 April 1991: No. 6 - 7 weeks
UK Track 12-inch Single: Ruby Tuesday: 21 May 1991
UK CD box set THE SINGLES COLLECTION 1971-2006: 45 X 45s: 11 April 2011
USA CD box set THE SINGLES COLLECTION 1971-2006: 45 X 45s: 26 April 2011

A press conference was held on 11 July 1989 at Grand Central Station, New York, to announce the North American tour, the group arriving on board a private train. Mick Jagger denied the tour was a farewell of greatest hits or retrospective and played the new single *Mixed Emotions*. He wanted it to be contemporary for "love, fame and fortune" and, as Keith Richards added, "for the glory".

Nick Cowan had negotiated for Ron Wood a contract with Prince Lowenstein that ensured a share of the tour profits. The tour was named after the album, whose logo cover depicted steel wheels designed by John Warwicker. The "steel rolling" wheels were also a reference to a DJ scratch turntable. Budweiser sponsorship helped pay for the tour, which was the beginning of even bigger business deals. The band's publicist for 15 years, Paul Wasserman, was not hired as they used the huge corporate Rogers & Cowan, who are still used to this day.

Michael Cohl was selected as promoter instead of Bill Graham (who died in a helicopter accident in October 1991). Apparently the deal Michael Cohl offered was too big to refuse. He had promoted Canadian gigs and also directed Michael Jackson's Thriller tour. Of course, his $65-70 million up front States tour contract was an offer not to be refuted, but Mick Jagger was quick to point out publically that, if money was the sole concern, the European tour would have been long since booked. Before confirming this, they wanted to ensure the magic was still there. Unlike the ramblings of The Who, who played in the States and Britain in 1989, the Stones were proving they were not in it for the money alone - a point which even Pete Townshend acknowledged. Within a week from finishing the mixing in London, they started rehearsals in July at a girl's boarding school in Wykeham Rise, Connecticut. Pre-tour press interviews took place in the headmistresses' office.

At a venue called Toad's Place Bar near local university Yale on 12 August, they played an unannounced short introductory concert as a warm-up (only 55 more to go, Mick said). The set opened with *Start Me Up*, followed with *Bitch* - two new songs were practised - *Sad, Sad, Sad* and *Mixed Emotions*, plus a piano-heavy rendition of *Little Red Rooster*. Five more songs were played before concluding with *Jumping Jack Flash* (at the end Mick said that they were going to go home to work on some [song] bridges!) They did this at the Nassau Coliseum, New York, where they were able to do a full production stadium rehearsal for the whole month of August. Chuck Leavell's role was elevated to help with these arrangements and also to work on a compilation of set lists with Mick.

After seven years away from the stage, designer Mark Fisher (of "The Wall" fame), in conjunction with the band, had constructed a steel monstrosity which Mark likened to "guerrilla architecture". It was designed to convey the message that the Stones were back. This was an awe-inspiring construction of cat walks, 130-feet tall at its highest point, giant orange girders and steel shafts representing a decayed urban scene of long-lost steel factories or abandoned docklands.

Two sets were built so that the tour could leap-frog its way across America. Just as much effort was placed on the lighting for the show, designed by Patrick Woodroffe. Pyrotechnics were also used, including the notorious *Start Me Up* wall of fire. The tour was the first to enter the computer age. Because the lighting was pre-programmed, all the songs were strictly choreographed and rehearsed. There were occasional lapses but the tour was designed to be totally professional with the rock and roll shining through, even though the stage did appear over-crowded at times.

The supporting cast featured: Chuck Leavell and Matt Clifford on keyboards and synthesiser, Bobby Keys (saxophone), the Uptown Horns quartet of Crispin Cioe (saxophone), Arno Hecht (tenor saxophone), Paul "Hollywood" Litteral (trumpet) and Robert Funk (trombone) with Bernard Fowler, Lisa Fischer and Cindy Mizelle the backing vocalists. Bernard, who was a young musician at the time, was quite blown away at the size of the tour. The Uptown Horns were old mates of Chris Kimsey, having worked with him on Joan Jett's 1984 album GLORIOUS RESULTS OF A MISPENT YOUTH and he introduced them to Mick.

They could not get over the amount of crew necessary for the tour - the Stones did not do a tour of cities, but rather brought their city to the people. Initially, the saxophone role was intended to be covered by the Uptown Horns but Keith brought Bobby Keys back into the equation, insisting that, if Mick could hire Matt Clifford, then he could recruit Bobby. The Steel Wheels tour kicked off ironically for the veteran group at the Veterans' Stadium in Philadelphia, on 31 August 1989.

The support act was the hard rockers' Living Colour, with whom Mick had worked previously, playing on and producing three tracks on their 1988 VIVID album. During the third number, *Shattered*, the sound system broke down when a generator blew. Mick ran off immediately, leaving some puzzled faces, until the rest of the band followed. Superstitions ensured that *Shattered* would not be played again during the tour which moved from state to state and into Canada, often criss-crossing on itself. Many stadiums were played two or three times to maximise the effort put into the building of the stage backdrop. Once the tour had built up momentum, some shows were recorded to provide a live album of the tour.

1020.   YOU CAN'T ALWAYS GET WHAT YOU WANT (Jagger, Richard) ⟋ 7.26
25 November 1989: Place: The Gator Bowl, Jacksonville, Florida, USA.
Rolling Stones with Matt Clifford, Chuck Leavell, Bernard Fowler, Lisa Fischer, Cindy Mizelle.
Producer: Chris Kimsey, The Glimmer Twins.
Engineer: Bob Ludwig, Richard Sullivan, Spencer May.
Mixed by: Christopher Marc Potter. Recorded by Bob Clearmountain, David Hewitt, Cedric Beatty, Harry Braun, Dierk.
USA LP FLASHPOINT: 2 April 1991: No. 16 - 5 weeks
UK LP FLASHPOINT: 8 April 1991: No. 6 - 7 weeks
UK Track CD Single Ruby Tuesday: 24 May 1991
UK CD box set THE SINGLES COLLECTION 1971-2006: 45 X 45s: 11 April 2011
USA CD box set THE SINGLES COLLECTION 1971-2006: 45 X 45s: 26 April 2011

1021.   MISS YOU (Jagger, Richard) ⟋ 5.55
25 November 1989: Place: The Gator Bowl, Jacksonville, Florida, USA.
Rolling Stones with Matt Clifford, Chuck Leavell, Bobby Keys, Bernard Fowler, Lisa Fischer, Cindy Mizelle.
Producer: Chris Kimsey, The Glimmer Twins.
Engineer: Bob Ludwig, Richard Sullivan, Spencer May.
Mixed by: Christopher Marc Potter. Recorded by Bob Clearmountain, David Hewitt, Cedric Beatty, Harry Braun, Dierk.
USA LP FLASHPOINT: 2 April 1991: No. 16 - 5 weeks
UK LP FLASHPOINT: 8 April 1991: No. 6 - 7 weeks

1022.   START ME UP (Jagger, Richards) ⟋ 3.54
26 November 1989: Place: Death Valley Stadium, Clemson, South Carolina, USA.
Rolling Stones with Matt Clifford, Chuck Leavell.
Producer: Chris Kimsey, The Glimmer Twins.
Engineer: Bob Ludwig, Richard Sullivan, Spencer May.
Mixed by: Christopher Marc Potter. Recorded by Bob Clearmountain, David Hewitt, Cedric Beatty, Harry Braun, Dierk.
USA LP FLASHPOINT: 2 April 1991: No. 16 - 5 weeks
UK LP FLASHPOINT: 8 April 1991: No. 6 - 7 weeks

1023.   (I CAN'T GET NO) SATISFACTION (Jagger, Richard) ⟋ 6.09
26 November 1989: Place: Death Valley Stadium, Clemson, South Carolina, USA.
Rolling Stones with Matt Clifford, Chuck Leavell, Bobby Keys, The Uptown Horns, Bernard Fowler, Lisa Fischer, Cindy Mizelle.
Producer: Chris Kimsey, The Glimmer Twins.
Engineer: Bob Ludwig, Richard Sullivan, Spencer May.
Mixed by: Christopher Marc Potter. Recorded by Bob Clearmountain, David Hewitt, Cedric Beatty, Harry Braun, Dierk.
USA LP FLASHPOINT: 2 April 1991: No. 16 - 5 weeks
UK LP FLASHPOINT: 8 April 1991: No. 6 - 7 weeks

1024.   PLAY WITH FIRE (Jagger, Richard) ⟋ 3.46
26 November 1989: Place: Death Valley Stadium, Clemson, South Carolina, USA.
Rolling Stones with Matt Clifford, Chuck Leavell.
Producer: Chris Kimsey, The Glimmer Twins.
Engineer: Bob Ludwig, Richard Sullivan, Spencer May.
Mixed by: Christopher Marc Potter. Recorded by Bob Clearmountain, David Hewitt, Cedric Beatty, Harry Braun, Dierk.
UK Track CD Single Highwire: 21 March 1991
UK B-side Single Ruby Tuesday: 24 May 1991
UK B-side 12-inch Single Ruby Tuesday: 24 May 1991
UK Track CD Single Ruby Tuesday: 24 May 1991
UK CD box set THE SINGLES COLLECTION 1971-2006: 45 X 45s: 11 April 2011
USA CD box set THE SINGLES COLLECTION 1971-2006: 45 X 45s: 26 April 2011

1025.   CAN'T BE SEEN (Jagger, Richards) ⟋ 4.17
26 November 1989: Place: Death Valley Stadium, Clemson, South Carolina, USA.
Rolling Stones with Matt Clifford, Chuck Leavell, Bobby Keys, The Uptown Horns, Bernard Fowler, Lisa Fischer, Cindy Mizelle.
Producer: Chris Kimsey, The Glimmer Twins.
Engineer: Bob Ludwig, Richard Sullivan, Spencer May.
Mixed by: Christopher Marc Potter. Recorded by Bob Clearmountain, David Hewitt, Cedric Beatty, Harry Braun, Dierk.
USA CD FLASHPOINT: 2 April 1991: No. 16 - 5 weeks
UK CD FLASHPOINT: 8 April 1991: No. 6 - 7 weeks

1026.   GIMME SHELTER (Jagger, Richard) ⟋ 4.54
26 November 1989: Place: Death Valley Stadium, Clemson, South Carolina, USA.
Rolling Stones with Matt Clifford, Chuck Leavell, Bernard Fowler, Lisa Fischer, Cindy Mizelle.
Producer: Chris Kimsey, The Glimmer Twins.
Engineer: Bob Ludwig, Richard Sullivan, Spencer May.
Special thanks to: Sherry Daly and Sarah at Munro Sounds.
UK Cassette Single: 13 April 1993.

1027.   BITCH (Jagger, Richard) ⟋ 3.41
19 December 1989: Place: Atlantic City Convention Center, Atlantic City, New Jersey, USA.
Rolling Stones with Matt Clifford, Chuck Leavell, Bobby Keys, The Uptown Horns, Bernard Fowler, Lisa Fischer, Cindy Mizelle.
Music Mix: Bob Clearmountain.
Bootleg only.

1028.   SAD SAD SAD (Jagger, Richards) ⟋ 3.33
19 December 1989: Place: Atlantic City Convention Center, Atlantic City, New Jersey, USA.
Rolling Stones with Matt Clifford, Chuck Leavell, Bobby Keys.
Producer: Chris Kimsey, The Glimmer Twins.
Engineer: Bob Ludwig, Richard Sullivan, Spencer May.
Mixed by: Christopher Marc Potter. Recorded by Bob Clearmountain, David Hewitt, Cedric Beatty, Harry Braun, Dierk.
USA LP FLASHPOINT: 2 April 1991: No. 16 - 5 weeks
UK LP FLASHPOINT: 8 April 1991: No. 6 - 7 weeks

1029.   UNDERCOVER OF THE NIGHT (Jagger, Richards) ⟋ 3.54
19 December 1989: Place: Atlantic City Convention Center, Atlantic City, New Jersey, USA.
Rolling Stones with Matt Clifford, Chuck Leavell, Bernard Fowler, Lisa Fischer, Cindy Mizelle.
Producer: Chris Kimsey, The Glimmer Twins.
Engineer: Bob Ludwig, Richard Sullivan, Spencer May.
Mixed by: Christopher Marc Potter. Recorded by Bob Clearmountain, David Hewitt, Cedric Beatty, Harry Braun, Dierk.
UK Track CD Single Ruby Tuesday: 24 May 1991
Japan Track CD Sex Drive (Club Version): 18 July 1991
USA B-side Sex Drive (Single Edit): August 1991
UK CD box set THE SINGLES COLLECTION 1971-2006: 45 X 45s: 11 April 2011
USA CD box set THE SINGLES COLLECTION 1971-2006: 45 X 45s: 26 April 2011

1030.   TERRIFYING (Jagger, Richards) ⟋ 5.20
19 December 1989: Place: Atlantic City Convention Center, Atlantic City, New Jersey, USA.
Rolling Stones with Matt Clifford, Chuck Leavell, Bernard Fowler, Lisa Fischer, Cindy Mizelle.
Music Mix: Bob Clearmountain.
Bootleg only.

1031. SALT OF THE EARTH (Jagger, Richard) ✏ 5.05
19 December 1989: Place: Atlantic City Convention Center, Atlantic City, New Jersey, USA.
Rolling Stones with Axl Rose, Izzy Stradlin, Matt Clifford, Chuck Leavell, Bobby Keys, The Uptown Horns, Bernard Fowler, Lisa Fischer, Cindy Mizelle.
Music Mix: Bob Clearmountain.
Bootleg only.

1032. MIXED EMOTIONS (Jagger, Richards) ✏ 5.32
19 December 1989: Place: Atlantic City Convention Center, Atlantic City, New Jersey, USA.
Rolling Stones with Matt Clifford, Chuck Leavell, Bobby Keys, The Uptown Horns, Bernard Fowler, Lisa Fischer, Cindy Mizelle.
Music Mix: Bob Clearmountain.
Bootleg only.

1033. HONKY TONK WOMEN (Jagger, Richard) ✏ 5.14
19 December 1989: Place: Atlantic City Convention Center, Atlantic City, New Jersey, USA.
Rolling Stones with Matt Clifford, Chuck Leavell, Bobby Keys, The Uptown Horns, Bernard Fowler, Lisa Fischer, Cindy Mizelle.
Music Mix: Bob Clearmountain.
Bootleg only.

1034. MIDNIGHT RAMBLER (Jagger, Richard) ✏ 10.46
19 December 1989: Place: Atlantic City Convention Center, Atlantic City, New Jersey, USA.
Rolling Stones with Matt Clifford, Chuck Leavell.
Music Mix: Bob Clearmountain.
Bootleg only.

1035. LITTLE RED ROOSTER (Dixon) ✏ 5.15
19 December 1989: Place: Atlantic City Convention Center, Atlantic City, New Jersey, USA.
Rolling Stones with Eric Clapton, Matt Clifford, Chuck Leavell.
Producer: Chris Kimsey, The Glimmer Twins.
Engineer: Bob Ludwig, Richard Sullivan, Spencer May.
Mixed by: Christopher Marc Potter. Recorded by Bob Clearmountain, David Hewitt, Cedric Beatty, Harry Braun, Dierk.
USA LP FLASHPOINT: 2 April 1991: No. 16 - 5 weeks
UK LP FLASHPOINT: 8 April 1991: No. 6 - 7 weeks

1036. BOOGIE CHILLEN' (Hooker, Besman) ✏ 5.32
19 December 1989: Place: Atlantic City Convention Center, Atlantic City, New Jersey, USA.
Rolling Stones with John Lee Hooker, Eric Clapton, Matt Clifford, Chuck Leavell.
Producer: Chris Kimsey, The Glimmer Twins.
Music Mix: Bob Clearmountain.
USA Compilation DVD John Lee Hooker - Come And See About Me: 1 June 2004

1037. HAPPY (Jagger, Richard) ✏ 4.37
19 December 1989: Place: Atlantic City Convention Center, Atlantic City, New Jersey, USA.
Rolling Stones with Matt Clifford, Chuck Leavell, Bobby Keys, The Uptown Horns, Bernard Fowler, Lisa Fischer, Cindy Mizelle.
Music Mix: Bob Clearmountain.
Bootleg only.

1038. IT'S ONLY ROCK 'N' ROLL (Jagger, Richards) ✏ 4.48
19 December 1989: Place: Atlantic City Convention Center, Atlantic City, New Jersey, USA.
Rolling Stones with Matt Clifford, Chuck Leavell, Bernard Fowler, Lisa Fischer, Cindy Mizelle.
Music Mix: Bob Clearmountain.
Bootleg only.

The available musical output from the USA tour is staggering, with the live album FLASHPOINT ensuring eight tracks. Other odd tracks became available through inclusion on 12-inch and CD singles, even one (*Gimme Shelter*) was released just on a cassette single. Bob Clearmountain and David Hewitt were again involved recording the concerts, as they had been on STILL LIFE. David Hewitt felt there was nothing better than recording on the road with the buzz of the show and all the technical issues to be sorted. He continues to work on live Stones work, with his Remote Recording Services.

The penultimate concert date was at the cosy 16,000 capacity Atlantic City Convention Center (the second of three shows there) with the whole gig being broadcast live on pay-per-view television under the title, *Terrifying*. After the rhythmic, pre-recorded *Continental Drift* introduction, the band burst on to a stage lit by huge roman candles which span the full width. *Start Me Up* is the opening number which is then followed by a sharp *Bitch*.

Keith Richards takes a solo at the end watched by Bill Wyman in dark red jacket and boot-laced tie. *Sad Sad Sad* sounds great as Jagger straps on his guitar to extend the guitar noise. *Undercover* (still with Mick on guitar) and *Harlem Shuffle* illustrate the well-rehearsed nature of the show as the brass and backing vocals become integral to the arrangements. *Tumbling Dice* continues as the keyboards and brass warm up for an extended *Miss You*. *Terrifying* was played for the first time on the tour at a faster pace than the album version, again the organ of Chuck Leavell and the keyboards of Matt Clifford give the song an instantaneous appeal. Chuck's piano and Matt's flute (aka synthesised keyboard) are the mainstay of instrumentation for the hit from the past, *Ruby Tuesday*. Guns 'n' Roses opened for the Stones in Los Angeles and Axl Rose and Izzy Stradlin were invited to select and perform on a song at Atlantic City. Ticket prices for the smaller Donald Trump convention centre venue were extraordinarily high, even for Steel Wheels. The pair chose *Salt Of The Earth* and, while Izzy played rhythm guitar, after Keith and Mick Jagger in turn opened the first two verses, Axl (in a skeleton leather jacket and backwards baseball cap) sang a few verses himself and also backing vocals. The arrangement was completed by Ron Wood's slide guitar, the organ and female backing vocals. It was the first time the song had been played in concert and the outcome was satisfactory. *Rock And A Hard Place*, with Mick on guitar, and *Mixed Emotions* followed - Mick stating that they needed to play some new material, "we can't keep re-cycling old songs". Such variance was not the tour standard though. The whole band were very tight and professional and Ronnie said that you could not afford to miss your cue or lengthen the guitar solo, if only by a few bars.

Keith, however, felt that if he dropped a vital riff, then Charlie would disguise the fact, turn it around and hand it back again. This discipline gave the set a polished quality which some fans felt was "over the top". But what Mick, in particular, wanted to achieve was to return to the original arrangements and see if they could replicate them in concert. He wanted the audience to hear the hits as they were on record and Keith battled to incorporate new and improvised songs. During *Honky Tonk Women*, two large buxom inflatables, named affectionately Angie and Ruby, arose provocatively stage left and right. Mick had time during the song to run to both sides and give both girls a tweak.

They inflated in 30 seconds and disappeared in a puff at the song's end. *Midnight Rambler* did not fare quite as well - less piano and a crowd-pleasing middle section would have helped. As usual, the audience was encouraged to sing along to *You Can't Always Get What You Want* and the introduction even included Matt on French horn. The song segued into the blues of *Little Red Rooster* at which point Eric Clapton, Keith's blood brother, walked on to ecstatic applause.

This version is on the FLASHPOINT album; Clapton's exquisite two lead solos recorded permanently, even Mick was impressed as can be witnessed by his glances at Eric. As one legend finished, another one entered for John Lee Hooker joined the Stones to sing his song, *Boogie Chillen*. Eric stayed on stage to perform on this track as well. By the end of these two songs the crowd had just enjoyed a glorious 10 minutes during which five guitarists played some unadulterated blues. Modest John Lee did not stop for applause or acknowledgement.

Then Keith celebrated his recent birthday with *Can't Be Seen*, from STEEL WHEELS, and *Happy. Can't Be Seen* was recorded at Clemson and ended up on the CD-only version of FLASHPOINT, which had three extra tracks compared with the vinyl release. The 60s were revived with the next four songs, *Paint It Black, 2000 Light Years From Home, Sympathy For The Devil* and *Gimme Shelter. Paint It Black* had an acoustic opening (albeit with one of Keith's electrics) and a swirling keyboard backing, with a hypnotic Latin climax. As the strains ebbed away, the theatrics of *2000 Light Years* commenced. Never attempted on stage before, it became a tour favourite as the lighting effects and strobes backed Mick performing a specially choreographed, trippy dance.

At the end, the synthesisers and keyboards continued giving Mick sufficient time to change costume and catch a lift to the top of one of the towers with a precarious vantage point, from where he began the well-trusted *Sympathy*, with an explosive pyrotechnic opening (only in Stadiums). He did not use a radio microphone up there in case of failure and, as one gig in Germany, the mike malfunctioned and he had to travel all the way back down before starting the vocals! It was a good thing that they now used a recorded synthesised percussion backing track to open the song.

At Atlantic City, Bill was encouraged to move from his spot and do some "ooh oohs" with Lisa and Cindy. *Gimme Shelter* became an opportunity for Lisa Fischer to take the spotlight and share the vocals with Mick. At one point, she takes the lead role, just as Merry Clayton had done before. The show climaxes with *It's Only Rock 'n' Roll*, where the large screens depict images of Elvis Presley and Buddy Holly, then *Brown Sugar* and *Satisfaction*. The encore is *Jumping Jack Flash*. On the last night, the stage was decorated with a Christmas theme and Santa hats were worn. The performances on the tour were far flung from the one at Toad's Place, Yale, New Haven, Connecticut, but the Stones had proved that they could up their ante, divide and conquer.

1039. SYMPATHY FOR THE DEVIL (Jagger, Richard) ∕ 5.35
26 February 1990: Place: Korakuen Dome, Tokyo, Japan.
Rolling Stones with Matt Clifford, Chuck Leavell, Bernard Fowler, Lisa Fischer, Cindy Mizelle.
Producer: Chris Kimsey, The Glimmer Twins.
Engineer: Bob Ludwig, Richard Sullivan, Spencer May.
Mixed by: Christopher Marc Potter. Recorded by Bob Clearmountain, David Hewitt, Cedric Beatty, Harry Braun. Audio mix by Bob Clearmountain.
UK Track CD Single: Highwire: 21 March 1991
UK Track 12-inch Single: Highwire: 21 March 1991
USA LP FLASHPOINT: 2 April 1991: No. 16 - 5 weeks
UK LP FLASHPOINT: 8 April 1991: No. 6 - 7 weeks
UK CD box set THE SINGLES COLLECTION 1971-2006: 45 X 45s: 11 April 2011
USA CD box set THE SINGLES COLLECTION 1971-2006: 45 X 45s: 26 April 2011
USA e-Album LIVE AT THE TOKYO DOME: 10 July 2012
UK e-Album LIVE AT THE TOKYO DOME: 11 July 2012

When released in 2012, the track was the full un-edited version (* a - 7.58).

1040. RUBY TUESDAY (Jagger, Richard) ∕ 3.33
27 February 1990: Place: Korakuen Dome, Tokyo, Japan.
Rolling Stones with Matt Clifford, Chuck Leavell.
Producer: Chris Kimsey, The Glimmer Twins.
Engineer: Bob Ludwig, Richard Sullivan, Spencer May.
Mixed by: Christopher Marc Potter. Recorded by Bob Clearmountain, David Hewitt, Cedric Beatty, Harry Braun.
USA LP FLASHPOINT: 2 April 1991: No. 16 - 5 weeks
UK LP FLASHPOINT: 8 April 1991: No. 6 - 7 weeks
UK 12-inch Single: 24 May 1991: No. 59 - 2 weeks
UK CD Single: 24 May 1991: No. 59 - 2 weeks
UK CD box set THE SINGLES COLLECTION 1971-2006: 45 X 45s: 11 April 2011
USA CD box set THE SINGLES COLLECTION 1971-2006: 45 X 45s: 26 April 2011

1041. JUMPING JACK FLASH (Jagger, Richard) ✎ 5.00
27 February 1990: Place: Korakuen Dome, Tokyo, Japan.
Rolling Stones with Matt Clifford, Chuck Leavell, Bobby Keys, The Uptown Horns, Bernard Fowler, Lisa Fischer, Cindy Mizelle.
Producer: Chris Kimsey, The Glimmer Twins.
Engineer: Bob Ludwig, Richard Sullivan, Spencer May.
Mixed by: Christopher Marc Potter. Recorded by Bob Clearmountain, David Hewitt, Cedric Beatty, Harry Braun.
USA LP FLASHPOINT: 2 April 1991: No. 16 - 5 weeks
UK LP FLASHPOINT: 8 April 1991: No. 6 - 7 weeks
UK Single: 29 November 1991
UK CD Single: 29 November 1991

The Steel Wheels set was flown to Japan and assembled at the Korakuen Dome in Tokyo for a 10-night stint from 14 to 27 February 1990. The erection of the stage, which normally took a week, had to be achieved in two days due to a world heavyweight title fight between Mike Tyson and Buster Douglas on 11 February. This was achieved and the Stones played their first ever concerts on Japanese soil to a sell-out 50,000 fans every night. Mick Jagger and Bernard Fowler had played Japan a couple of years earlier so had some idea of the audience and fan reaction. The shows were recorded and three tracks were featured on FLASHPOINT and in July 2012 the entire night of the 26 February, 1990 was released in the archive series of official bootlegs, labelled LIVE AT THE TOKYO DOME. That night was also professionally filmed and was seen, partly edited, on Japanese television.
Mick Jagger, in attempting to cross cultural barriers (as he often did when visiting different countries), learnt a few words of Japanese to thank the fans. For the Japanese dates, *Almost Hear You Sigh* was aired for the first time and *Play With Fire* resumed its place in the set list. Afterwards, in March, the Stones announced details of the European section of their World Tour in the summer of 1990. In order to make the show more exciting for the Stones and the audience, as well as to make allowance for smaller stages and reduce costs, a new set called the Urban Jungle was designed by Mark Fisher.

1042. HARLEM SHUFFLE (Relf, Nelson) ✎ 4.05
27 February 1990: Place: Korakuen Dome, Tokyo, Japan.
Rolling Stones with Matt Clifford, Chuck Leavell, Bobby Keys, The Uptown Horns, Bernard Fowler, Lisa Fischer, Cindy Mizelle.
Producer: Chris Kimsey, The Glimmer Twins.
Engineer: Bob Ludwig, Richard Sullivan, Spencer May.
Mixed by: Christopher Marc Potter. Recorded by Bob Clearmountain, David Hewitt, Cedric Beatty, Harry Braun.
UK Track CD Single: Ruby Tuesday: 24 May 1991
UK CD box set THE SINGLES COLLECTION 1971-2006: 45 X 45s: 11 April 2011
USA CD box set THE SINGLES COLLECTION 1971-2006: 45 X 45s: 26 April 2011

1043. PAINT IT BLACK (Jagger, Richard) ✎ 4.02
14 June 1990: Place: Olympic Stadium, Barcelona, Spain.
Rolling Stones with Matt Clifford, Chuck Leavell, Bernard Fowler.
Producer: Chris Kimsey, The Glimmer Twins.
Engineer: Bob Ludwig, Richard Sullivan, Spencer May.
Mixed by: Christopher Marc Potter. Recorded by Bob Clearmountain, David Hewitt, Cedric Beatty, Harry Braun.
USA LP FLASHPOINT: 2 April 1991: No. 16 - 5 weeks
UK LP FLASHPOINT: 8 April 1991: No. 6 - 7 weeks

1044. 2000 LIGHT YEARS FROM HOME (Jagger, Richard) ✎ 3.27
14 June 1990: Place: Olympic Stadium, Barcelona, Spain.
Rolling Stones with Matt Clifford, Chuck Leavell, Bernard Fowler, Lorelei McBroom, Sophia Jones.
Producer: Chris Kimsey, The Glimmer Twins.
Engineer: Bob Ludwig, Richard Sullivan, Spencer May.
Mixed by: Christopher Marc Potter. Recorded by Bob Clearmountain, David Hewitt, Cedric Beatty, Harry Braun.
UK Track CD Single Highwire: 21 March 1991
UK Track 12-inch Single Highwire: 21 March 1991
UK CD box set THE SINGLES COLLECTION 1971-2006: 45 X 45s: 11 April 2011
USA CD box set THE SINGLES COLLECTION 1971-2006: 45 X 45s: 26 April 2011

1045. FACTORY GIRL (Jagger, Richard) ✎ 2.47
6 July 1990: Place: Wembley Stadium, London, England.
Rolling Stones with Matt Clifford, Chuck Leavell.
Producer: Chris Kimsey, The Glimmer Twins.
Engineer: Bob Ludwig, Richard Sullivan, Spencer May.
Mixed by: Christopher Marc Potter. Recorded by Bob Clearmountain, David Hewitt, Cedric Beatty, Harry Braun.
UK Track CD Single Highwire: 21 March 1991
USA LP FLASHPOINT: 2 April 1991: No. 16 - 5 weeks
UK LP FLASHPOINT: 8 April 1991: No. 6 - 7 weeks
UK CD box set THE SINGLES COLLECTION 1971-2006: 45 X 45s: 11 April 2011
USA CD box set THE SINGLES COLLECTION 1971-2006: 45 X 45s: 26 April 2011

1046.   I JUST WANT TO MAKE LOVE TO YOU (Dixon) ✏ 4.07
6 July 1990: Place: Wembley Stadium, London, England.
Rolling Stones with Matt Clifford, Chuck Leavell.
Producer: Chris Kimsey, The Glimmer Twins.
Engineer: Bob Ludwig, Richard Sullivan, Spencer May.
Mixed by: Christopher Marc Potter. Recorded by Bob Clearmountain, David Hewitt, Cedric Beatty, Harry Braun.
UK Track CD Single Highwire: 21 March 1991
UK Track 12-inch Single Highwire: 21 March 1991
USA CD LP ROLLING STONES RARITIES 1971-2003: 22 November 2005: No. 76 - 6 weeks
UK CD LP ROLLING STONES RARITIES 1971-2003: 28 November 2005
UK CD box set THE SINGLES COLLECTION 1971-2006: 45 X 45s: 11 April 2011
USA CD box set THE SINGLES COLLECTION 1971-2006: 45 X 45s: 26 April 2011

1047.   SAD SAD SAD (Jagger, Richards) ✏ 3.21
28 July 1990: Place: Stadio Delle Alpi, Turin, Italy.
Rolling Stones with Matt Clifford, Chuck Leavell, Bobby Keys, The Uptown Horns, Bernard Fowler, Lorelei McBroom, Sophia Jones.
Producer: Chris Kimsey, The Glimmer Twins.
Engineer: Paul Massey, Michael H Brauer.
Executive Producers: Michael Cohl, Andre Picard, Creative Consultant: Julien Temple, Location Directors: Roman Kroitor, David Douglas, Noel Archambault.
UK, USA Video, DVD: At The Max: 25 October 1991

1048.   ROCK AND A HARD PLACE (Jagger, Richards) ✏ 4.57
28 July 1990: Place: Stadio Delle Alpi, Turin, Italy.
Rolling Stones with Matt Clifford, Chuck Leavell, Bobby Keys, The Uptown Horns, Bernard Fowler, Lorelei McBroom, Sophia Jones.
Producer: Chris Kimsey, The Glimmer Twins.
Engineer: Paul Massey, Michael H Brauer.
Executive Producers: Michael Cohl, Andre Picard, Creative Consultant: Julien Temple, Location Directors: Roman Kroitor, David Douglas, Noel Archambault.
UK, USA Video, DVD: At The Max: 25 October 1991

1049.   HONKY TONK WOMEN (Jagger, Richard) ✏ 5.02
28 July 1990: Place: Stadio Delle Alpi, Turin, Italy.
Rolling Stones with Matt Clifford, Chuck Leavell, Bobby Keys, The Uptown Horns, Bernard Fowler, Lorelei McBroom, Sophia Jones.
Producer: Chris Kimsey, The Glimmer Twins.
Engineer: Paul Massey, Michael H Brauer.
Executive Producers: Michael Cohl, Andre Picard, Creative Consultant: Julien Temple, Location Directors: Roman Kroitor, David Douglas, Noel Archambault.
UK, USA Video, DVD: At The Max: 25 October 1991

1050.   PAINT IT BLACK (Jagger, Richard) ✏ 4.18
28 July 1990: Place: Stadio Delle Alpi, Turin, Italy.
Rolling Stones with Matt Clifford, Chuck Leavell, Bernard Fowler.
Producer: Chris Kimsey, The Glimmer Twins.
Engineer: Paul Massey, Michael H Brauer.
Executive Producers: Michael Cohl, Andre Picard, Creative Consultant: Julien Temple, Location Directors: Roman Kroitor, David Douglas, Noel Archambault.
UK, USA Video, DVD: At The Max: 25 October 1991

1051.   2000 LIGHT YEARS FROM HOME (Jagger, Richard) ✏ 5.41
28 July 1990: Place: Stadio Delle Alpi, Turin, Italy.
Rolling Stones with Matt Clifford, Chuck Leavell, Bernard Fowler, Lorelei McBroom, Sophia Jones.
Producer: Chris Kimsey, The Glimmer Twins.
Engineer: Paul Massey, Michael H Brauer.
Executive Producers: Michael Cohl, Andre Picard, Creative Consultant: Julien Temple, Location Directors: Roman Kroitor, David Douglas, Noel Archambault.
UK, USA Video, DVD: At The Max: 25 October 1991

1052.   BROWN SUGAR (Jagger, Richard) ✏ 4.45
28 July 1990: Place: Stadio Delle Alpi, Turin, Italy.
Rolling Stones with Matt Clifford, Chuck Leavell, Bobby Keys, The Uptown Horns, Bernard Fowler, Lorelei McBroom, Sophia Jones.
Producer: Chris Kimsey, The Glimmer Twins.
Engineer: Bob Ludwig, Richard Sullivan, Spencer May.
Mixed by: Christopher Marc Potter. Recorded by Bob Clearmountain, David Hewitt, Cedric Beatty, Harry Braun.
USA LP FLASHPOINT: 2 April 1991: No. 16 - 5 weeks
UK LP FLASHPOINT: 8 April 1991: No. 6 - 7 weeks

1053. HAPPY (Jagger, Richard) ✎ 4.20
14 August 1990: Place: Weisensee, Berlin, Germany.
Rolling Stones with Matt Clifford, Chuck Leavell, Bobby Keys, The Uptown Horns, Bernard Fowler, Lorelei McBroom, Sophia Jones.
Producer: Chris Kimsey, The Glimmer Twins.
Engineer: Paul Massey, Michael H Brauer.
Executive Producers: Michael Cohl, Andre Picard, Creative Consultant: Julien Temple, Location Directors: Roman Kroitor, David Douglas, Noel Archambault.
UK, USA Video, DVD: At The Max: 25 October 1991

1054. IT'S ONLY ROCK 'N' ROLL (Jagger, Richard) ✎ 5.00
14 August 1990: Place: Weisensee, Berlin, Germany.
Rolling Stones with Matt Clifford, Chuck Leavell, Bernard Fowler, Lorelei McBroom, Sophia Jones.
Producer: Chris Kimsey, The Glimmer Twins.
Engineer: Paul Massey, Michael H Brauer.
Executive Producers: Michael Cohl, Andre Picard, Creative Consultant: Julien Temple, Location Directors: Roman Kroitor, David Douglas, Noel Archambault.
UK, USA Video, DVD: At The Max: 25 October 1991

1055. START ME UP (Jagger, Richards) ✎ 4.03
24 August 1990: Place: Wembley Stadium, London, England.
Rolling Stones with Matt Clifford, Chuck Leavell.
Producer: Chris Kimsey, The Glimmer Twins.
Engineer: Paul Massey, Michael H Brauer.
Executive Producers: Michael Cohl, Andre Picard, Creative Consultant: Julien Temple, Location Directors: Roman Kroitor, David Douglas, Noel Archambault.
UK, USA Video, DVD: At The Max: 25 October 1991

1056. TUMBLING DICE (Jagger, Richards) ✎ 4.22
24 August 1990: Place: Wembley Stadium, London, England.
Rolling Stones with Matt Clifford, Chuck Leavell, Bobby Keys, The Uptown Horns, Bernard Fowler, Lorelei McBroom, Sophia Jones.
Producer: Chris Kimsey, The Glimmer Twins.
Engineer: Bob Ludwig, Richard Sullivan, Spencer May.
Mixed by: Christopher Marc Potter. Recorded by Bob Clearmountain, David Hewitt, Cedric Beatty, Harry Braun.
UK, USA Video, DVD: At The Max: 25 October 1991
UK B-side Single Jumping Jack Flash: 29 November 1991
UK Track CD Single Jumping Jack Flash: 29 November 1991

1057. SYMPATHY FOR THE DEVIL (Jagger, Richard) ✎ 6.38
24 August 1990: Place: Wembley Stadium, London, England.
Rolling Stones with Matt Clifford, Chuck Leavell, Bernard Fowler, Lorelei McBroom, Sophia Jones.
Producer: Chris Kimsey, The Glimmer Twins.
Engineer: Paul Massey, Michael H Brauer.
Executive Producers: Michael Cohl, Andre Picard, Creative Consultant: Julien Temple, Location Directors: Roman Kroitor, David Douglas, Noel Archambault.
UK, USA Video, DVD: At The Max: 25 October 1991

1058. (I CAN'T GET NO) SATISFACTION (Jagger, Richard) ✎ 8.32
24 August 1990: Place: Wembley Stadium, London, England.
Rolling Stones with Matt Clifford, Chuck Leavell, Bobby Keys, The Uptown Horns, Bernard Fowler, Lorelei McBroom, Sophia Jones.
Producer: Chris Kimsey, The Glimmer Twins.
Engineer: Paul Massey, Michael H Brauer.
Executive Producers: Michael Cohl, Andre Picard, Creative Consultant: Julien Temple, Location Directors: Roman Kroitor, David Douglas, Noel Archambault.
UK, USA Video, DVD: At The Max: 25 October 1991

1059. RUBY TUESDAY (Jagger, Richard) ✎ 3.46
25 August 1990: Place: Wembley Stadium, London, England.
Rolling Stones with Matt Clifford, Chuck Leavell.
Producer: Chris Kimsey, The Glimmer Twins.
Engineer: Paul Massey, Michael H Brauer.
Executive Producers: Michael Cohl, Andre Picard, Creative Consultant: Julien Temple, Location Directors: Roman Kroitor, David Douglas, Noel Archambault.
UK, USA Video, DVD: At The Max: 25 October 1991

1060. YOU CAN'T ALWAYS GET WHAT YOU WANT (Jagger, Richard) ✎ 7.18
25 August 1990: Place: Wembley Stadium, London, England.
Rolling Stones with Matt Clifford, Chuck Leavell, Bernard Fowler, Lorelei McBroom, Sophia Jones.
Producer: Chris Kimsey, The Glimmer Twins.
Engineer: Paul Massey, Michael H Brauer.
Executive Producers: Michael Cohl, Andre Picard, Creative Consultant: Julien Temple, Location Directors: Roman Kroitor, David Douglas, Noel Archambault.
UK, USA Video, DVD: At The Max: 25 October 1991

1061. STREET FIGHTING MAN (Jagger, Richard) ✎ 6.05
25 August 1990: Place: Wembley Stadium, London, England.
Rolling Stones with Matt Clifford, Chuck Leavell, Bernard Fowler.
Producer: Chris Kimsey, The Glimmer Twins.
Engineer: Bob Ludwig, Richard Sullivan, Spencer May.
Mixed by: Christopher Marc Potter. Recorded by Bob Clearmountain, David Hewitt, Cedric Beatty, Harry Braun.
UK, USA Video, DVD: At The Max: 25 October 1991
UK Track CD Single Jumping Jack Flash: 29 November 1991

1062. BROWN SUGAR (Jagger, Richard) ✎ 4.45
25 August 1990: Place: Wembley Stadium, London, England.
Rolling Stones with Matt Clifford, Chuck Leavell, Bobby Keys, Bernard Fowler, Lorelei McBroom, Sophia Jones.
Producer: Chris Kimsey, The Glimmer Twins.
Engineer: Paul Massey, Michael H Brauer.
Executive Producers: Michael Cohl, Andre Picard, Creative Consultant: Julien Temple, Location Directors: Roman Kroitor, David Douglas, Noel Archambault.
UK, USA Video, DVD: At The Max: 25 October 1991

Mark Fisher was asked to design a new set to take advantage of the lighter European summer evenings, as well as making it easier to transport and quicker to erect. So the behemoth of Steel Wheels designed for bright lights, was replaced by the more colourful Urban Jungle set. Some new artwork intended to be included were jungle animals and foliage - images of this can be seen within the European tour programme. The theme was abandoned at the last minute for a twirly yellow, orange and purple approach.

Centre stage was the Urban Jungle, a crazed, dog-like beast with claws and fangs, which had been selected as the logo for the tour. Rehearsals commenced in Paris during April when Lorelei McBroom and Sophia Jones replaced Lisa Fischer and Cindy Mizelle (due to other commitments, working with Luther Vandross and the recording of Lisa's first solo album). The tour played mainstream European countries; there had been an uprising of civil unrest in Eastern Europe, starting with Poland in early 1989 and the fall of communism continued with Hungary, East Germany, Bulgaria, Czechoslovakia and Romania.

The Stones made some inroads at new venues, playing Berlin for the first time since the demolition of the Berlin Wall on 9 November 1989. (East and West Germany finally came together in 1990.) As special guests of newly-elected President Vaclav Havel, they played a huge stadium gig to more than 100,000 people in Prague, where Czechoslovakia was celebrating freedom from the communist government, which had resigned in November 1989.

The fans were assisted by Havel, who allowed border guards to admit anyone with a Stones ticket into the country without a visa. Many fans could not afford the cost of admission. While some gained access free, Bernard Fowler recalled buying tickets and giving them away. The atmosphere was simply amazing, rock 'n' roll truly transcending politics. The tour posters read, "Tanks are rolling out, The Stones are rolling in". The Stones reached a wider public through the Wembley concert on Saturday 7 July being broadcast on BBC radio, while the Barcelona gig, on the 13 June, was recorded for a later screening on European television.

The Berlin, Turin and August London shows were also filmed for wide-screen IMAX at Michael Cohl's suggestion, shots of *Ruby Tuesday* being used for single promotion purposes. To ensure maximum film impact, the Steel Wheels set was especially constructed at these shows. Ten concerts were played in Britain, five of which were at Wembley Stadium. Collectively, this was the biggest audience the Stones had ever played to in Britain. On 4 July 1990, the Stones performed at Wembley while the English national football team were playing in the same Turin stadium as the band would later. When considering the tour schedule, Mick Jagger would never have thought that a huge clash of interests would be created by England reaching the World Cup semi-finals against West Germany on the same night.

BBC presenter Des Lynam said half of Britain was watching the match and he wondered what the other half were doing; some 70,000 were desperately following the proceedings from within the national stadium. After 59 minutes, England were 1-0 down in Turin but, when Gary Lineker equalised in the 80th minute, there was an eruption among the Wembley fans during Ronnie Wood's guitar solo on *Almost Hear You Sigh*. Ron incorrectly thought the cheers were for him, much to Mick's amusement. The band were unable to delay the concert until the match had finished but were intrigued to find most of the crowd equipped with radio ear pieces, listening to the match.

People in the crowd would then relay the news to others. The match went to extra time and then penalties. Each kick was cheered with boos (if Germany scored) and cheers at England's penalties. At 3-3 each, Stuart Pearce failed to score and so did Chris Waddle, prompting the inevitable groans. To continue the World Cup theme, Angie (now with jogging bottoms) and Ruby were kitted out with football and boots for the Urban Jungle tour. After that Wembley gig, Keith Richards injured his hand in Glasgow and, as a result, two further London shows were postponed. They were re-scheduled for late August 1990.

Notable tracks covered on the tour were *Almost Hear You Sigh* (the current single in Europe), *Factory Girl* and a slowed down version of *I Just Want To Make Love To You*, played just once at Wembley. *Street Fighting Man* was added to the climax of the set and this enabled further inflatables to be brought onto the stage. They were angry dogs named Top Dog, Kennel Dog, Skippy and Shagger. The last dog had jaws within which Mick disappeared, having just made it angry by hitting its private parts with a stick. The inflatables, made by Air Artists of Suffolk, England, have since become a tour feature - the company have also made Eddie for Iron Maiden, the pig and teacher for Roger Waters' Berlin Wall in 1990 and Rosie for AC/DC.

The IMAX film captures the show vividly - the medium requires huge video cameras, carried on rail tracks. The sound captured by Chris Kimsey and his crew on *At The Max* is well defined. The film focusses on the stage, apart from glimpses backstage as *Continental Drift* warms the audience up. You can also see Keith being told to have a good show, Charlie Watts doing a little dance to psyche himself up and Mick holding his ears as the fireworks illuminate the stage. Angie and Ruby return to their bordello clothes, football long forgotten, although Ruby accidentally boots Mick's head when he approaches.

Other moments include a close-up of Ronnie Wood's face when he takes the solo on *You Can't Always Get What You Want* and his steel guitar on *Happy*. In Italy, the crowd did the *Paint It Black* vocal shuffle at the song's end. On the FLASHPOINT album, the famous crowd shout for "Paint It Black you devil" was dubbed into the album. Chris Kimsey wanted to do this as testimony to the singular voice heard on GET YER YA YA'S OUT, since no solo, crowd, voice had made such an impact on a record before. Keith solos on *Sympathy*. Bill Wyman was lifted on Matt Clifford's shoulders during *Before They Make Me Run* to try and put Keith off - either Keith did not see or chose not to notice.

The encore was *Satisfaction* which heralded another firework explosion and, at the conclusion, there were cascading showers of flame followed by glitter shrouds raining on the band. Bill's bow at the end was his last on English soil with the band he joined in 1962. It was an excellent tour, by far exceeding all expectations. The STEEL WHEELS album had been the sticking plaster, the American tour the tourniquet and, following the Urban Jungle tour, the wound had been truly cauterized.

1063. HIGHWIRE (Jagger, Richards) 4.45
7-18 January 1991: Place: Hit Factory Studio, London, England.
Rolling Stones with Bernard Fowler.
Producer: Chris Kimsey, The Glimmer Twins.
Engineer: Mark Stent, Charlie Smith.
Mix: Chris Kimsey.
USA Single: 5 March 1991: No. 57 - 7 weeks
USA CD 12-inch Single: 5 March 1991: No. 57 - 7 weeks
UK Single: 11 March 1991: No. 29 - 4 weeks
UK CD 12-inch Single: 11 March 1991: No. 29 - 4 weeks
USA LP FLASHPOINT: 2 April 1991: No. 16 - 5 weeks
UK LP FLASHPOINT: 8 April 1991: No. 6 - 7 weeks
UK CD box set THE SINGLES COLLECTION 1971-2006: 45 X 45s: 11 April 2011
USA CD box set THE SINGLES COLLECTION 1971-2006: 45 X 45s: 26 April 2011

During October and November 1990, the FLASHPOINT album was mixed at Olympic Studios, London. Selecting the tracks for inclusion were a nightmare and Chris Kimsey spent many an hour listening to the first four or five from each show, until it became apparent whether or not the concert was a good one. He believes the Turin, Barcelona and Wembley gigs to be spot on performances. The task was especially difficult since Michael Cohl wanted the outcome to be compatible with IMAX.

The IMAX technical staff wanted each instrument to be on a separate channel, which exacerbated the long process so much so that Michael Brauer completed the work. During this time, Ron Wood had both legs broken after an horrendous car smash on the M4 west of London. Mick Jagger took Jerry Hall to Bali, Indonesia and, on 21 November, a priest performed the Hindu marriage rites, which included an exchange of gold rings, painting of hands and feet and the Ghari Puja where food grains are exchanged.

The ceremony was witnessed by their children and Alan Dunn. In the autumn of 1990, Bill Wyman released his first book *Stone Alone*, written with Ray Coleman. The launch took place at his Sticky Fingers restaurant, which had been opened the previous year. *Stone Alone* concentrated on the early days of the band's career, up to the point of Brian's death and Altamont. Bill's views were treated as authoritative as he had kept meticulous diaries and collected documents for future reference, including a record of bank statements. Personally, Bill had made it known to the other band members that he was thinking of quitting, but they told him to wait and see, since there were no planned commitments in 1991.

Meanwhile, tensions were high in the Middle East due to the Iraqi invasion of Kuwait in August 1990. The Rolling Stones thought the resulting war ironic and so, in January 1991, they recorded *Highwire*, an attack on the undercover politics that permitted sales of arms to countries like Iraq and Iran - the build them up, knock them down, syndrome. The result was demands for the BBC to ban the single and, on Top Of The Pops, the video was shown without the first verse.

An arms-to-Iraq inquiry followed the First Gulf War in 1992, which culminated in a new bill designed to close the loopholes and only served to further prompt the fall of Conservative Prime Minister John Major. The lyrics on *Highwire* explain the band's thoughts a year before this. "We sell them missiles, we sell them tanks . . . we act so greedy it makes me sick, sick sick." The music is up-tempo and without any frills, the only support being Bernard Fowler on backing vocals. Mick is probably on guitar, since Ron Wood was missing from most of the sessions. The song's structure seems to have come from a Mick and Jeff Beck 1987 out-take from PRIMITIVE COOL called *Danger Up Ahead*, especially the chorus refrain "hot, hot night" in lieu of *Highwire*'s "hot guns and cold, cold lies".

The lyrics opened with, "Are the lawyers gonna rape you while the cops all stare?" On 1 March, the band, without Bill, met on Pier 3 near Brooklyn Bridge, New York, to tape a video for the promotion of the single. The shooting took place during a cold night session. Julien Temple was the director and the imagery from Steel Wheels is repeated with gangways, chain pulleys, ladders, explosions and searchlights. Charlie Watts sits through it all at his drum stool dressed in a suit, while Mick, Keith and Ron cavort around him.

Such was the potency of the song, that it was included on the FLASHPOINT album, released with new record company Virgin, who had signed the band for a purported $40 million. An edited version of the track was released on single in March and just made the UK top 30 (* a - 3.41). Later, in May 1991, a live version of *Ruby Tuesday* was released from the album and, as with the *Highwire* single, this allowed additional release of non-album live material.

1064. SEXDRIVE (DIRTY HANDS MIX) (Jagger, Richards) 4.27
7-18 January 1991: Place: Hit Factory Studio, London, England.
Rolling Stones with Katie Kissoon, Tessa Niles, Kick Horns.
Producer: Chris Kimsey, The Glimmer Twins.
Engineer: Mark Stent, Charlie Smith.
Mix: Chris Kimsey. Additional Production and Remix by Michael Brauer. Assistant engineer: Chris Theis.
UK Track 12-inch Single Sexdrive (Club Version): 19 August 1991
Netherlands B-side Sexdrive (Single Edit): 19 August 1991

1065. SEXDRIVE (CLUB VERSION) (Jagger, Richards) 6.18
7-18 January 1991: Place: Hit Factory Studio, London, England.
Rolling Stones with Katie Kissoon, Tessa Niles, Kick Horns.
Producer: Chris Kimsey, The Glimmer Twins.
Engineer: Mark Stent, Charlie Smith.
Mix: Chris Kimsey. Additional Production and Remix by Michael Brauer. Assistant engineer: Chris Theis.
Japan CD Single: 18 July 1991
UK 12-inch Single: 19 August 1991

There is an edit of this track (* a - 4.33).

1066. **SEX DRIVE** (Jagger, Richards) 5.07
7-18 January 1991: Place: Hit Factory Studio, London, England.
Rolling Stones with Katie Kissoon, Tessa Niles, Kick Horns.
Producer: Chris Kimsey, The Glimmer Twins.
Engineer: Mark Stent, Charlie Smith.
Mix: Chris Kimsey.
USA LP FLASHPOINT: 2 April 1991: No. 16 - 5 weeks
UK LP FLASHPOINT: 8 April 1991: No. 6 - 7 weeks
Japan Track CD Sexdrive (Club Version): 18 July 1991
Netherlands Single: 19 August 1991
UK Track 12-inch Sexdrive (Club Version): 19 August 1991
USA Single: August 1991
UK CD box set THE SINGLES COLLECTION 1971-2006: 45 X 45s: 11 April 2011
USA CD box set THE SINGLES COLLECTION 1971-2006: 45 X 45s: 26 April 2011

The funky *Sex Drive* was worked on at the same time as the recording for *Highwire* took place. It is a retro-funk number with memories of *Hot Stuff* and James Brown. The song may have started its writing process in Tokyo in February 1990. Katie Kissoon and Tessa Niles, both very well respected session singers, were on backing vocals and the four-piece Kick Horns added the brass. They were probably there to record some over-dubbing for the FLASHPOINT album. Julien Temple directed the video at the Shepperton Studios, Twickenham, London, in May 1991. Bill Wyman made an appearance but was missing from the *Highwire* video filmed in New York. This time a psychiatrist's chair was used in a Freudian way for some sex therapy, with scantily-clad girls swarming around in see-through, plastic dresses. Charlie Watts did the spoof diagnosis of Mick's problems. The three girls come to Mick's aid from behind a stage curtain but Ronnie and Keith encourage them to return, the latter closes the curtain at the end. Singer, actress and sultry model Lisa Barbuscia, who played the lead minx in a G-string and see through mac, dated Mick briefly. This video was for late night viewing only, prompting a re-cut to allow some daytime screening on MTV and other stations.
The song was re-mixed by Michael Brauer in various formats which were made available on European and Japanese-only releases. The track also ended up on the mainly live album FLASHPOINT and apparently displaced a version of *Undercover*. There is also a single with a count in (* a - 4.28). It marked the end of Chris Kimsey's direct production credits. All told, his six-album tenure had helped to shift more than 15 million copies, making him the best-selling Stones producer.

1067. **THRU AND THRU** (Jagger, Richards) 6.15
20 April - May; 9 July - 6 August & September; 3 November - 16 December 1993; 15 January - April 1994: Place: Blue Wave Studios, Barbados; Ron Wood's Home, Dublin, Ireland; Windmill Lane Studios, Dublin, Ireland; Don Was' Studio & A&M Studios, Los Angeles, USA.
Played Live: 2002, 2003
Rolling Stones with Darryl Jones, Pierre de Beauport, Bernard Fowler, Ivan Neville.
Producer: Don Was, The Glimmer Twins.
Engineer: Don Smith, Dan Bosworth, Alastair McMillan.
UK LP VOODOO LOUNGE: 11 July 1994: No. 1 - 24 weeks
USA LP VOODOO LOUNGE: 12 July 1994: No. 2 - 17 weeks

Mick Jagger started work on a new film, *Freejack*, directed by Geoff Murphy, in early 1991. As a futuristic bounty hunter, he wants to take over the body of a modern day racing driver, Emilio Estevez, whom he has projected 20 years into the future. A chase follows, in which the driver meets his girlfriend from 20 years previously. She is working for a huge corporation headed by Anthony Hopkins. Despite the pace and explosive atmosphere, Mick was not convincing as a villain. After the film was released in 1992, Keith Richards returned to music and helped John Lee Hooker with a track for his new album, MR. LUCKY.
Bernard Fowler worked with Keith Richards on two tracks for the 1991 Johnnie Johnson album JOHNNIE B. BAD, *Tanqueray* (jointly a Johnnie and Keith composition) and *Key To The Highway*, proving Bernard felt that he was not solely "a Mick person". Steve Jordan was instrumental in arranging the collaboration. Johnnie was songster and pianist for Chuck Berry - Keith reckoned that Johnnie did far more for Chuck than play the piano and wrote most of the melodies for the legend's tunes without gaining a credit or royalty.
Charlie Watts also returned to his jazz band and released a box set with a re-print of his 1964 book *Ode To A High Flying Bird* and a CD of Charlie Parker's tunes. The band, with Bernard featuring, visited London, New York and Tokyo during the year. Ron Wood started work on his next solo album at his home in Ireland in the summer of 1991. It was called SLIDE ON THIS and he was partnered by Bernard Fowler, Doug Wimbish, Simon Phillips, Wayne Sheehy, Ian McLagan, Chuck Leavell, The Edge from U2 and Joe Elliott from Def Leppard - even Charlie played on one track.
Not to be outdone by all this solo activity, Mick played around with some songs and Keith also started writing. During October, Keith and the Winos visited Seville in Spain as part of the forthcoming Expo 92 celebrations and contributed some songs for the Guitar Legends Show. He played *Shake Rattle And Roll* with Bob Dylan (would Keith never learn?) and then, with the X-Pensive Winos, *I'm Going Down* (the Freddie King version, not the Stones'), Eddie Cochran's *Somethin' Else* and the Winos' favourite Stones number, *Connection*, before a finale song *I Can't Turn You Loose* with Dave Edmunds, Bob, Chuck Leavell, Simon Phillips, Ray Cooper and the Miami Horns (Bruce Springsteen and Southside Johnny's horn section). Jack Bruce was on bass and sang the vocals with Keith.
It was the perfect promotion for the unveiling in December of a live album and the video release from his 1988 tour, *Live At The Hollywood Palladium*. The IMAX film was also released but, because of its technical requirements, could only be viewed in special cinemas. Mick, Keith, Charlie and Ron also found time to follow Keith's footsteps and sign with Richard Branson's Virgin. This was approximately for $40 million and included three new albums and the rights to re-release the post-Klein back catalogue from STICKY FINGERS. Notably Bill Wyman did not sign as he felt that his time had been exhausted with the Stones.
As a team, the Stones were not active in 1992 but they were busy individually. When Mick arrived in Japan to promote his film *Freejack*, he was refused entry due to his previous drugs' conviction. Eventually he was given a temporary visa. Mick, Charlie and Ronnie all played solo sets in the UK on the 28 June and came together for two numbers to celebrate National Music Day. Charlie toured with his Quintet in South America and visited New York, Philadelphia and Chicago in July. Ron Wood's new solo album SLIDE ON THIS was released in September and was followed by a tour of North America. Again Bernard Fowler was involved, co-writing eight songs with Ronnie.
This came about as result of the great camaraderie of touring with the band members. Bernard's black and white nomad portrait - the original of which remains with Ronnie - was included within the album cover artwork. Bill got back on the road with Willie And The Poor Boys and a solo album STUFF was released in Japan

only. Keith's next solo album, MAIN OFFENDER, was released in October and featured Bernard on eight tracks. Being a vocalist, he found it natural to work with Keith, Ronnie and Charlie.

The album was supported by a few dates in Argentina before a tour of Europe. His final concert was at the Town and Country club, London, on his birthday. This was then followed by a North American stretch during January and February 1993. Ron also visited Japan with his band before recording an MTV unplugged session with Rod Stewart, in Los Angeles, in February. A one-off Faces reunion was arranged for the Brits Awards and, as previously, Bill filled in on bass guitar. Mick's album WANDERING SPIRIT was released in February 1993 and one concert date was played. All solo activity had ceased by April and, as agreed the previous year, Mick and Keith arrived in Barbados to do some pre-recording for the Rolling Stones.

First they sat down in Mick's kitchen with a glass of wine to discuss the direction they wanted to take and who would be the replacement bass guitarist, since Bill had announced his resignation on 6 January 1993. He had felt the previous tour was a perfect climax on which to exit after 30 years as he wanted to undertake his own projects. He preferred to return to music like Willie & The Poor Boys - good time blues, R 'n' B and rock and roll.

He modestly thought that leaving the band would not have disastrous consequences. Charlie, who had always disliked the rock and roll shenanigans, was closer to Keith's heart. Guitar and drums were the basis, while the bass just filled in, as testified by Charlie's powerhouse contribution to the recent albums. As before, the Glimmer Twins used Eddy Grant's studio to write songs and bounce ideas off each other. Charlie joined them on 30 April. Don Smith was responsible for the gear used for the session and he reckoned about 75 songs were written in various states, of which 32 were put onto tape. *Thru And Thru* was written by Keith after one of his "incoming" moments following an evening out "on the piss" with Pierre De Beauport (Keith's guitar technician, who was present in Barbados).

He insisted on recording his thoughts and two out-takes of him gently strumming a short riff and singing the vocals are early poignant material recorded in Barbados (* a - 4.45, b - 3.11). The strange riff was improvised on a Jimmy Reed technique. The second version has more complete lyrics and repeats the line about "now I get those fucking blues". Another rehearsal out-take has additional percussion in the form of shakers and scratchers, where he can be heard attempting to get the sound right (* c - 11.49). Pierre De Beauport is also on acoustic guitar - he did not realise this would be kept on the final take and was delighted when Keith said it would be.

The song builds slowly and climactically until Charlie's thump, thump enters, his drum sound reverberating like a thunder storm as it was literally recorded three floors down in a stairwell near reception. Sometimes, bizarre suggestions can be inspirational and *Thru And Thru* certainly was one of the more distinctive sounds on VOODOO LOUNGE. Keith reckoned this saved the song from ambling nowhere.

Darryl Jones commented that they were more like a jazz band, due to their improvisation, than some of those with whom he had played. Another out-take has a sweeping synthesised organ, possibly played by Ivan Neville, and the background vocals of Bernard Fowler and Neville (* d - 4.11). An eight-minute extended version has the same swirling, synthesised sounds (* e - 8.32). There is a mainly acoustic instrumental with just Pierre, Charlie and Keith (* f - 8.26) and, finally, an eight-minute out-take very close to the final cut, with over-layered backing vocals, but without the electric piano (* g - 8.23).

The final take also has Mick on backing vocals. Darryl Jones played bass as he did on most of the VOODOO LOUNGE album. He arrived via Mick through his exploits with Miles Davis, Sting, Lionel Ritchie and Eric Clapton. He had first met Mick in 1985 through Sting and, when he heard Bill had left the group, sent a message to the Stones' management, indicating that he was interested in auditioning. The organ/electric piano sound is used sparingly on the final version and on the sleeve notes is credited to Keith.

It was a sparse, powerful Keith track unusual in its delivery and highly creative. Slash, from Guns 'n' Roses, who was present at a mixing session for *Thru And Thru*, said that he could overdub a couple of mean guitar licks but Keith made it quite clear that no-one was getting close to his baby.

1068. RANDY WHORE (Jagger, Richards) 7.57
20 April - May 1993: Place: Blue Wave Studios, Barbados.
Producer: The Glimmer Twins.
Bootleg only.

The VOODOO sessions are exceptionally well documented by a series of bootleg releases with professional packaging and sleeve notes. The recording quality is first class and highly recommended to collectors. Indeed it is so high that there were rumours that the tapes were deliberately leaked from insiders within Sandymount. Ron Wood was reportedly furious when he found out the source. Mick Jagger would ensure recording tapes were much more closely guarded in future, however "to him that will, ways are not wanting".

They provide a unique historical background to the recording of the album. Two versions of *Randy Whore* exist - a long one with Keith Richards on vocals and electric guitar, Charlie Watts on drums and Mick Jagger on backing vocals sung guide style. The other, half its former length, is with just Mick on guide vocals (* a - 3.58). It is a slow rock number with a strong hook.

1069. DISPOSITION BOOGIE (Jagger, Richards) 1.32
20 April - May 1993: Place: Blue Wave Studios, Barbados.
Producer: The Glimmer Twins.
Bootleg only.

Keith Richards and Charlie Watts on a medium tempo guitar boogie.

1070. ALTERATION BOOGIE (Jagger, Richards) 4.45
20 April - May 1993: Place: Blue Wave Studios, Barbados.
Producer: The Glimmer Twins.
Bootleg only.

Keith Richards' boogie lament for Charlie Watts' dress sense. You know it don't hang right. A fun ad-lib on shirts and double-breasted suits. The title was jokingly suggested by Mick Jagger at the song's end.

1071. GET YOUR HANDS OFF (Jagger, Richards) 3.41
20 April - May 1993: Place: Blue Wave Studios, Barbados.
Producer: The Glimmer Twins.
Bootleg only.

The twin guitarists are Mick Jagger and Keith Richards. Mick sings vocals off-mike on one version and on another out-take Keith sings the "give me a lotta lovin" lyrics, joined later by Mick as they alternate verses on this longer version (* a - 6.38).

1072. MY LOVE IS MY LOVE (Jagger, Richards) 9.20
20 April - May 1993: Place: Blue Wave Studios, Barbados.
Producer: The Glimmer Twins.
Bootleg only.

A stop and start run-through - again Mick Jagger and Keith Richards share vocals. Charlie Watts metronomes his drum beat, waiting for the song to evolve. Mick tries keyboards to see if they help.

1073. GLIMMER TWINS BOOGIE (Jagger, Richards) 1.36
20 April - May 1993: Place: Blue Wave Studios, Barbados.
Producer: The Glimmer Twins.
Bootleg only.

It's all in the title - slow pace - no drums - short.

1074. SLIPS AWAY (Jagger, Richards) 16.01
20 April - May 1993: Place: Blue Wave Studios, Barbados.
Producer: The Glimmer Twins.
Bootleg only.

A slow whispering acoustic and gentle (off-mike) vocal by Keith Richards. Not even in Barbados would you break sweat on this one. A studio ramble follows before another attempt is made. Then a boogie passage is needed before another attempt at the beautiful chord surrounding the basis of the song. There are 16 minutes in all, Keith's acoustic putting paint on the canvas bit by bit.

1075. GOODBYE TO LOVE (Shapiro, Mann) 2.29
20 April - May 1993: Place: Blue Wave Studios, Barbados.
Producer: The Glimmer Twins.
Bootleg only.

Written by Barry Mann and Joe Shapiro and recorded by the Chantels and the Marcels in the early 'sixties. Mick Jagger and Keith Richards combine on vocals and guitars. Pierre De Beauport is asked to answer the phone by Mick near the end. Mick and Keith reminisce that *Goodbye To Love* is the B-side to the Marcels hit *Blue Moon*. Keith thought *Blue Moon* was bloody awful but the B-side was a killer. The song is attempted twice more, just by Keith on a long solo recording of mainly covers and riffs.
Amongst others, he covers *Salty Dog*, *Cocaine* (written in the 1890s, Keith reckons, although he learnt it from The Rambling Jack Elliott version at art school, not realising what cocaine was), some Bob Dylan and the Beatles' *Please Please Me*. On a good stereo it sounds terrific and, with a strong imagination, you can believe that he is in the same room, his hand clearly heard on the fret board, with the evening crickets chirping outside, the ice in the glass chinking, the cigarette lighter flicking and the puff and exhale clearly heard. Absolute magic! The stories and tales brim forth. Room service - another bottle of JD required.

1076. IVY LEAGUE (Jagger, Richards) 3.13
20 April - May; 9 July - 6 August & September; 3 November - 16 December 1993: Place: Blue Wave Studios, Barbados, Ron Wood's Sandymount Studios, Kildare, Ireland; Windmill Lane Studios, Dublin, Ireland.
Rolling Stones with Chuck Leavell.
Producer: Don Was, The Glimmer Twins.
Bootleg only.

One of the working songs that went from Barbados to Ireland. Both out-takes have brief guide vocals by Mick Jagger, with the second having additional guitar and keyboards. It has an interesting hook to it and is similar in style to *Moon Is Up*. One evening at the sessions, Keith Richards was running from the house to the studio in a tropical rain storm when he stumbled upon a bedraggled kitten, which he named Voodoo. In his studio work space, the amps already had a label on them saying "Doc's Office" to which he added "and Voodoo's Lounge".
So all through the sessions on top of the amps it read "Doc's Office and Voodoo's Lounge". When it came to giving the album a name, Mick looked at the amp and suggested VOODOO LOUNGE. The cat was taken back to Connecticut and became a permanent addition to the Richards' household as well as to Stones folklore.

1077. YELLOW JACKET (Jagger, Richards) 2.05
20 April - May 1993: Place: Blue Wave Studios, Barbados.
Producer: The Glimmer Twins.
Bootleg only.

A short instrumental with a Bo Diddley riff and a percussive bottle tapper.

1078. HE LOVES YOU SO (Jagger, Richards) 5.54
20 April - May 1993: Place: Blue Wave Studios, Barbados.
Producer: The Glimmer Twins.
Bootleg only.

The sessions were producing a number of soft love songs. Keith Richards takes up the vocals and Mick Jagger plays piano, giving it his Irish folk lilt on guide vocals.

1079. WHY YOU RUNNIN'? (Jagger, Richards) 4.54
20 April - May 1993: Place: Blue Wave Studios, Barbados.
Producer: The Glimmer Twins.
Bootleg only.

In its infancy *Why You Runnin'?* has Mick Jagger on vocals and guitar. Charlie Watts joins in halfway through.

1080. YOU GOT AWAY WITH MURDER (Jagger, Richards) 4.42
20 April - May 1993: Place: Blue Wave Studios, Barbados.
Producer: The Glimmer Twins.
Bootleg only.

Keith Richards and Mick Jagger work together on one of Keith's ideas. The studio chat has Keith saying it has definite possibilities and is a pretty song. With some re-working it could have turned into *Anyway You Look At It* or Keith Richards' solo track *Make No Mistake*.

1081. ALRIGHT CHARLIE (Jagger, Richards) 4.09
20 April - May; 9 July - 6 August & September; 3 November - 16 December 1993: Place: Blue Wave Studios, Barbados; Ron Wood's Sandymount Studios, Kildare, Ireland; Windmill Lane Studios, Dublin, Ireland.
Rolling Stones with Darryl Jones.
Producer: Don Was, The Glimmer Twins.
Bootleg only.

As the title suggests, Charlie Watts and other percussion are prominent on this upbeat track. Near the end it becomes quite percussive with additional bongo drums, possibly played by Mick Jagger. One version has a piano base and guide vocals while the second, with a full band, is more guitar laden without piano (* a - 5.04). There is an additional, shorter out-take similar to the second (* b - 3.09).

1082. KEITH'S BLUES (Jagger, Richards) 3.33
20 April - May 1993: Place: Blue Wave Studios, Barbados.
Producer: The Glimmer Twins.
Bootleg only.

A solo effort by Keith Richards - just an acoustic blues jam.

1083. I'M FALLIN' (Jagger, Richards) 6.35
20 April - May 1993: Place: Blue Wave Studios, Barbados.
Producer: The Glimmer Twins.
Bootleg only.

The Mick Jagger and Charlie Watts duo knock out a slow tempo number. It was possibly the fore-runner of *Low Down*, which was destined for their next album.

1084. MAKE IT NOW (Jagger, Richards) 4.29
20 April - May; 9 July - 6 August & September; 3 November - 16 December 1993: Place: Blue Wave Studios, Barbados; Ron Wood's Sandymount Studios, Kildare, Ireland; Windmill Lane Studios, Dublin, Ireland.
Rolling Stones with Darryl Jones, Chuck Leavell.
Producer: Don Was, The Glimmer Twins.
Bootleg only.

Recorded initially in Barbados, *Make It Now* is a delicate, acoustic Keith Richards' instrumental number including Chuck Leavell on piano (* a - 9.15). It had potential, as proved by a second out-take from Ireland which has Jagger's faint vocals (* b - 7.35). The third out-take allowed Keith Richards to come up with some lyrics and Chuck switched to organ and electric piano to accompany him. Don Was felt Keith was in a very creative period, ready to experiment and not being regimented in his views. He had a vibrant character, unlike the Spinal Tap-like image painted by some journalists.

1085. LOOK OUT BABY (Jagger, Richards) 10.23
20 April - May 1993: Place: Blue Wave Studios, Barbados.
Producer: The Glimmer Twins.
Bootleg only.

Experimenting on the keyboard combines a blues vocal style with an eastern synthesised riff, bringing back memories of *Continental Drift*. It was a lengthy excursion aided by a drum machine.

1086. VOODOO RESIDUE - UNTITLED #1 (Jagger, Richards) 6.57
20 April - May 1993: Place: Blue Wave Studios, Barbados.
Producer: The Glimmer Twins.
Bootleg only.

The electric piano, guitar and percussion strive to work out a song from somewhere. It is untitled, hence the song name above.

1087. VOODOO RESIDUE - UNTITLED #2 (Jagger, Richards) 1.51
20 April - May 1993: Place: Blue Wave Studios, Barbados.
Producer: The Glimmer Twins.
Bootleg only.

Another untitled out-take with Mick Jagger on piano and guide vocals. Keith Richards is on acoustic.

1088. IT'S FUNNY (Jagger, Richards) 4.36
20 April - May; 9 July - 6 August & September; 3 November - 16 December 1993: Place: Blue Wave Studios, Barbados; Ron Wood's Home, Dublin, Ireland; Windmill Lane Studios, Dublin, Ireland.
Rolling Stones with Darryl Jones, Chuck Leavell.
Producer: Don Was, The Glimmer Twins.
Bootleg only.

It's Funny has a catchy melody that ensured it would be worked upon throughout the sessions. Mick Jagger wondered whether some of the chords could be used to enhance *You Got Away With Murder*. At first it was recorded with an acoustic guitar and Mick Jagger on bass but later, with Darryl Jones and possibly Chuck Leavell on piano. The band recorded three versions - the earlier Barbados ad-libbed take (* a - 2.38), a later instrumental (* b - 6.24) and the one with Keith's vocals.

1089. ANYTHING FOR YOU (Jagger, Richards) 8.14
20 April - May; 9 July - 6 August & September; 3 November - 16 December 1993: Place: Blue Wave Studios, Barbados; Ron Wood's Sandymount Studios, Kildare, Ireland; Windmill Lane Studios, Dublin, Ireland.
Rolling Stones with Darryl Jones.
Producer: Don Was, The Glimmer Twins.
Bootleg only.

A slow instrumental captured at over eight minutes. It has a ghost vocal by Keith Richards and shakers supporting the percussion throughout the song. Parts of it sound like *Almost Hear You Sigh*. An early jammed version with Mick Jagger in the background and Keith commenting that he felt there was something in there (the piano chords) (* a - 5.49).

1090. SUCK ON THE JUGULAR (Jagger, Richards) 4.28
AKA: Holetown Prison
20 April - May; 9 July - 6 August & September; 3 November - 16 December 1993; 15 January - April 1994: Place: Blue Wave Studios, Barbados; Ron Wood's Home, Dublin, Ireland; Windmill Lane Studios, Dublin, Ireland; Don Was' Studio & A&M Studios, Los Angeles, USA.
Rolling Stones with Darryl Jones, David McMurray, Mark Isham, Ivan Neville, Luis Jardim, Lenny Castro, Bernard Fowler.
Producer: Don Was, The Glimmer Twins.
Engineer: Don Smith, Dan Bosworth, Alastair McMillan.
UK CD LP VOODOO LOUNGE: 11 July 1994: No. 1 - 24 weeks
USA CD LP VOODOO LOUNGE: 12 July 1994: No. 2 - 17 weeks

Barbados' oldest settlement, Holetown, was halfway up the west coast and the location of an old military prison. It was the inspiration for this Mick Jagger-led guitar funk song played with wah-wah, a harmonica and the percussive attack of Charlie Watts. Mick Jagger likened his mouth organ sound to a trumpet. Charlie was asked by Keith Richards to keep the demanding beat up for several minutes. He said that was no problem, later agreeing that he liked these kind of groove tracks, rather than the slower ballads.
There is a six-minute extended out-take (* a - 5.47) with vocals, prominent organ and horns and an instrumental with distant guide vocal (* b - 5.50). The final take includes Was Not Was band members David McMurray and Mark Isham on brass, the Hammond organ of Ivan Neville and added percussion. The backing vocals are used for a repeated response to Mick's chorus. These were recorded in New York and California, along with the other overdubs.

1091. LOVE IS STRONG (BOB CLEARMOUNTAIN REMIX) (Jagger, Richards) 3.49
9 July - 6 August & September; 3 November - 16 December 1993; 15 January - April 1994: Place: Ron Wood's Sandymount Studios, Kildare, Ireland; Windmill Lane Studios, Dublin, Ireland; Don Was' Studio & A&M Studios, Los Angeles, USA.
Rolling Stones with Darryl Jones, Chuck Leavell, Bernard Fowler, Ivan Neville.
Producer: Don Was, The Glimmer Twins.
Engineer: Don Smith, Dan Bosworth, Alastair McMillan.
UK CD Track Single Love Is Strong: 5 July 1994
UK CD box set THE SINGLES COLLECTION 1971-2006: 45 X 45s: 11 April 2011
USA CD box set THE SINGLES COLLECTION 1971-2006: 45 X 45s: 26 April 2011

1092. LOVE IS STRONG (TEDDY RILEY RADIO REMIX) (Jagger, Richards) 4.08
9 July - 6 August & September; 3 November - 16 December 1993; 15 January - April 1994: Place: Ron Wood's Sandymount Studios, Kildare, Ireland; Windmill Lane Studios, Dublin, Ireland; Don Was' Studio & A&M Studios, Los Angeles, USA.
Rolling Stones with Darryl Jones, Chuck Leavell, Bernard Fowler, Ivan Neville.
Producer: Don Was, The Glimmer Twins.
Engineer: Don Smith, Dan Bosworth, Alastair McMillan.
Remix: Teddy Riley, Sprague Williams. Remix Engineer: John Hanes, George Mayers, Serban Ghenea.
UK CD Single: 5 July 1994: No 14 - 5 weeks
UK CD box set THE SINGLES COLLECTION 1971-2006: 45 X 45s: 11 April 2011
USA CD box set THE SINGLES COLLECTION 1971-2006: 45 X 45s: 26 April 2011

1093. LOVE IS STRONG (TEDDY RILEY EXTENDED REMIX) (Jagger, Richards) 5.04
9 July - 6 August & September; 3 November - 16 December 1993; 15 January - April 1994: Place: Ron Wood's Sandymount Studios, Kildare, Ireland; Windmill Lane Studios, Dublin, Ireland; Don Was' Studio & A&M Studios, Los Angeles, USA.
Rolling Stones with Darryl Jones, Chuck Leavell, Bernard Fowler, Ivan Neville.
Producer: Don Was, The Glimmer Twins.
Engineer: Don Smith, Dan Bosworth, Alastair McMillan.
Remix: Teddy Riley, Sprague Williams. Remix Engineer: John Hanes, George Mayers, Serban Ghenea.
UK Track CD Single Love Is Strong (Teddy Riley Radio Remix): 5 July 1994
UK CD box set THE SINGLES COLLECTION 1971-2006: 45 X 45s: 11 April 2011
USA CD box set THE SINGLES COLLECTION 1971-2006: 45 X 45s: 26 April 2011

1094. LOVE IS STRONG (TEDDY RILEY EXTENDED ROCK REMIX) (Jagger, Richards) 4.48
9 July - 6 August & September; 3 November - 16 December 1993; 15 January - April 1994: Place: Ron Wood's Sandymount Studios, Kildare, Ireland; Windmill Lane Studios, Dublin, Ireland; Don Was' Studio & A&M Studios, Los Angeles, USA.
Rolling Stones with Darryl Jones, Chuck Leavell, Bernard Fowler, Ivan Neville.
Producer: Don Was, The Glimmer Twins.
Engineer: Don Smith, Dan Bosworth, Alastair McMillan.
Remix: Teddy Riley, Sprague Williams.
Remix Engineer: John Hanes, George Mayers, Serban Ghenea.
UK Track CD Single Love Is Strong (Teddy Riley Radio Remix): 5 July 1994
UK CD box set THE SINGLES COLLECTION 1971-2006: 45 X 45s: 11 April 2011
USA CD box set THE SINGLES COLLECTION 1971-2006: 45 X 45s: 26 April 2011

1095. LOVE IS STRONG (TEDDY RILEY DUB REMIX) (Jagger, Richards) 4.07
9 July - 6 August & September; 3 November - 16 December 1993; 15 January - April 1994: Place: Ron Wood's Sandymount Studios, Kildare, Ireland; Windmill Lane Studios, Dublin, Ireland; Don Was' Studio & A&M Studios, Los Angeles, USA.
Rolling Stones with Darryl Jones, Chuck Leavell, Bernard Fowler, Ivan Neville.
Producer: Don Was, The Glimmer Twins.
Engineer: Don Smith, Dan Bosworth, Alastair McMillan.
Remix: Teddy Riley, Sprague Williams.
Remix Engineer: John Hanes, George Mayers, Serban Ghenea.
UK Track CD Single Love Is Strong (Teddy Riley Radio Remix): 5 July 1994
UK CD box set THE SINGLES COLLECTION 1971-2006: 45 X 45s: 11 April 2011
USA CD box set THE SINGLES COLLECTION 1971-2006: 45 X 45s: 26 April 2011

1096. LOVE IS STRONG (TEDDY RILEY INSTRUMENTAL) (Jagger, Richards) 4.46
9 July - 6 August & September; 3 November - 16 December 1993; 15 January - April 1994: Place: Ron Wood's Sandymount Studios, Kildare, Ireland; Windmill Lane Studios, Dublin, Ireland; Don Was' Studio & A&M Studios, Los Angeles, USA.
Rolling Stones with Darryl Jones, Chuck Leavell, Bernard Fowler, Ivan Neville.
Producer: Don Was, The Glimmer Twins.
Engineer: Don Smith, Dan Bosworth, Alastair McMillan.
Remix: Teddy Riley, Sprague Williams.
Remix Engineer: John Hanes, George Mayers, Serban Ghenea.
UK Track CD Single Love Is Strong (Teddy Riley Radio Remix): 5 July 1994
UK CD box set THE SINGLES COLLECTION 1971-2006: 45 X 45s: 11 April 2011
USA CD box set THE SINGLES COLLECTION 1971-2006: 45 X 45s: 26 April 2011

1097. LOVE IS STRONG (JOE THE BUTCHER CLUB MIX) (Jagger, Richards) 5.25
9 July - 6 August & September; 3 November - 16 December 1993; 15 January - April 1994: Place: Ron Wood's Sandymount Studios, Kildare, Ireland; Windmill Lane Studios, Dublin, Ireland; Don Was' Studio & A&M Studios, Los Angeles, USA.
Rolling Stones with Darryl Jones, Chuck Leavell, Bernard Fowler, Ivan Neville.
Producer: Don Was, The Glimmer Twins.
Engineer: Don Smith, Dan Bosworth, Alastair McMillan. Remix: Joe 'The Butcher' Nicolo. Remix Engineer: Joe Nicolo, Phil Nicolo.

UK Track CD Single Love Is Strong (Teddy Riley Radio Remix): 5 July 1994
UK CD box set THE SINGLES COLLECTION 1971-2006: 45 X 45s: 11 April 2011
USA CD box set THE SINGLES COLLECTION 1971-2006: 45 X 45s: 26 April 2011

1098. LOVE IS STRONG (Jagger, Richards) 3.50
9 July - 6 August & September; 3 November - 16 December 1993; 15 January - April 1994: Place: Ron Wood's Sandymount Studios, Kildare, Ireland; Windmill Lane Studios, Dublin, Ireland; Don Was' Studio & A&M Studios, Los Angeles, USA.
Played Live: 1994, 1995, 1998, 2006, 2007
Rolling Stones with Darryl Jones, Chuck Leavell, Bernard Fowler, Ivan Neville.
Producer: Don Was, The Glimmer Twins.
Engineer: Don Smith, Dan Bosworth, Alastair McMillan.
UK Single: 5 July 1994: No. 14 - 5 weeks
USA Single: 5 July 1994: No. 91 - 5 weeks
UK LP VOODOO LOUNGE: 11 July 1994: No. 1 - 24 weeks
USA LP VOODOO LOUNGE: 12 July 1994: No. 2 - 17 weeks
UK CD LP FORTY LICKS: 30 September 2002: No. 2 - 45 weeks
USA CD LP FORTY LICKS: 1 October 2002: No. 2 - 50 weeks
UK CD box set THE SINGLES COLLECTION 1971-2006: 45 X 45s: 11 April 2011
USA CD box set THE SINGLES COLLECTION 1971-2006: 45 X 45s: 26 April 2011

The choice of Ireland was inspired for it provided a relaxed and peaceful environment. The trio in Barbados became a foursome in Ireland as Ron Wood's house and studio became a focal point for more writing and rehearsals. This approach proved that the Jagger/Richards relationship was strong and in love. There was no hurry in selecting a bass player and, between them, they took on the duties until recording began in earnest at Windmill Lane, from 1 November until 16 December. There they worked on reducing the brew to something more like a stew. Don Was took on the producer role and joined up with engineer Don Smith. He had worked for, amongst others, the Eurythmics, Tom Petty, Roy Orbison and on both of Keith's solo albums. He was well respected by Keith, who reckoned he was the best person to record the Stones as a band, playing in a single room together. Don Was had re-mixed *Rock And A Hard Place* but this was his first full production credit with the Stones. He liked to work directly with the band and was often found in the recording area itself, nurturing the sounds, rather than at the controls. He wanted to ensure that they did not fall into self-imitation but made the kind of album with which they felt comfortable.

He was respected because he was also a successful musician in his own right. Keith Richards reckoned he provided the most significant input since Jimmy Miller. *Love Is Strong* was the first single and opening number on the album. Keith was the key writer of the song and likened it to *Wicked As It Seems* which was on his MAIN OFFENDER album. Mick Jagger had complimented Keith on his album, especially liking *Wicked As It Seems*.

It has the same guitar sound and tempo. An instrumental out-take has Mick helping the band by advising when the bridge to the song should take place (* a - 5.47). Obviously Mick's main contribution on the song is the gutsy harmonica. It gives *Love Is Strong* a clearly defined edge and is not normally the type of song on which you would find a harmonica. As the instrumentation is low-key on this out-take, Chuck Leavell's contribution on the Wurlitzer piano can be closely studied. A five-minute second out-take with vocals ended with a crash landing (* b - 5.41). There is also a nearly six-minute out-take with Keith on vocals singing early lyrics, evidently enjoying himself with sinister "ha ha" laughs (* c - 5.42).

This was possibly the original version, in which Mick over-dubbed his first harmonica playing. Ron Wood assists him on acoustic and electric rhythm guitar. All of this was condensed to a four-minute powerful single cut for the album. The song is Mick's even if the guitars shine, with Keith combining acoustic and electric himself, the backing vocals of Bernard Fowler and Ivan Neville helping to make a beautiful team. The lyrics are re-written to a dream-like chase for love . . . "out on the street . . . I followed you through swirling seas, down darkened woods, with silent trees."

The imagery is quite strong and the delivery is unique, Mick adopting a vocal that was recorded on the harmonica microphone and delivered at an octave lower than he would normally sing, to give it a breathy, sexy tone. On the play-back everyone just nodded and acknowledged that no tweaking was necessary.

Consistent with the idea of re-mixing multiple versions for single release, Teddy Riley of Michael Jackson *Danger* notoriety, mixed five different versions, adding brass horns. Rapper Joe The Butcher was also asked to re-mix a version as was the more conventional Bob Clearmountain. The video to accompany the song played on the dreamy imagery, with the band seen walking like giants through the streets of New York. It was filmed by David Fincher, who was used to special effects, having worked on *Star Wars* and *Indiana Jones* movies.

1099. VOODOO BREW - UNTITLED #1 (Jagger, Richards) 6.19
9 July - 6 August & September; 3 November - 16 December 1993: Place: Ron Wood's Sandymount Studios, Kildare, Ireland; Windmill Lane Studios, Dublin, Ireland.
Rolling Stones with Darryl Jones, Chuck Leavell.
Producer: Don Was, The Glimmer Twins.
Bootleg only.

The *Love Is Strong* harmonica sound was used again for this untitled track. The harmonica riff is one that Mick Jagger would remember since he repeated it for the track *Lucky Day* on his 2001 solo album GODDESS IN THE DOORWAY. Mick Jagger can also be heard on faint vocals. This technique of providing ad-libbed vocals is called "vowel movement". It is a slow tempo song with keyboards.

1100. VOODOO BREW - UNTITLED #2 (Jagger, Richards) 3.51
AKA: Track With No Name
9 July - 6 August & September; 3 November - 16 December 1993: Place: Ron Wood's Sandymount Studios, Kildare, Ireland; Windmill Lane Studios, Dublin, Ireland.
Rolling Stones with Darryl Jones, Chuck Leavell.
Producer: Don Was, The Glimmer Twins.
Bootleg only.

Another untitled instrumental number, with acoustic, electric guitars and the organ, hence its aka. There are suggestions of where the verse and chorus should be. The melody is catchy, if a bit soft rock, and the riff sounds familiar. An earlier version was labelled *Untitled #2* (* a - 5.57).

1101. VOODOO BREW - UNTITLED #3 (Jagger, Richards) 5.47
9 July - 6 August & September; 3 November - 16 December 1993: Place: Ron Wood's Sandymount Studios, Kildare, Ireland; Windmill Lane Studios, Dublin, Ireland.
Rolling Stones with Darryl Jones, Chuck Leavell.
Producer: Don Was, The Glimmer Twins.
Bootleg only.

This has a distinctive keyboard melody, a funky guitar riff that replies to it and a strong bass line that suggests it could have been worked upon further. Mick Jagger can be heard on distant "all the time" vocals. Darryl Jones was shaping up to be the one player with whom the Stones felt comfortable. He had auditioned for the band in New York in June 1993 and was asked to join them during October to work on some album tracks.
Also in the frame was Pino Palladino and Doug Wimbish, from Living Colour. Keith Richards remarked that he felt Bill Wyman had bowed out gracefully - the Stones required 100 per cent commitment. At the end of the VOODOO rehearsals, Charlie was asked to choose the next bass player because, as Keith Richards put it, he wanted "reciprocating engines" in the rhythm section. The thoughts were on a tour to promote the album.

1102. VOODOO BREW - UNTITLED #4 (Jagger, Richards) 3.50
9 July - 6 August & September; 3 November - 16 December 1993: Place: Ron Wood's Sandymount Studios, Kildare, Ireland; Windmill Lane Studios, Dublin, Ireland.
Rolling Stones with Darryl Jones.
Producer: Don Was, The Glimmer Twins.
Bootleg only.

Back to reggae calypso for this untitled song. Another ghost vocal and Chuck Leavell on the organ on this skip and a hop fun number.

1103. BABY, YOU'RE TOO MUCH II (Jagger, Richards) 5.24
AKA: Voodoo Brew - Untitled #5
9 July - 6 August & September; 3 November - 16 December 1993; 13 March - July 1997: Place: Ron Wood's Sandymount Studios, Kildare, Ireland; Windmill Lane Studios, Dublin, Ireland; Ocean Way Recording Studios, Hollywood, California, USA.
Rolling Stones with Darryl Jones, Chuck Leavell.
Producer: Don Was, The Glimmer Twins.
Bootleg only.

A slow instrumental focussing in on piano and guitars. It was worked upon again during the BRIDGES TO BABYLON sessions and is a different track to the 1985 version.

1104. BUMP AND RIDE (Jagger, Richards) 5.48
9 July - 6 August & September; 3 November - 16 December 1993: Place: Ron Wood's Sandymount Studios, Kildare, Ireland; Windmill Lane Studios, Dublin, Ireland.
Rolling Stones with Chuck Leavell.
Producer: Don Was, The Glimmer Twins.
Bootleg only.

On what sounds like an improvised vocal, *Bump And Ride* is a six-minute jazz funk number with background organ.

1105. ZIP MOUTH ANGEL (Jagger, Richards) 3.33
9 July - 6 August & September; 3 November - 16 December 1993: Place: Ron Wood's Sandymount Studios, Kildare, Ireland; Windmill Lane Studios, Dublin, Ireland.
Producer: Don Was, The Glimmer Twins.
Bootleg only.

Zip Mouth Angel has well worked upon lyrics. It is a pretty soft rock song which features Mick Jagger on vocals and acoustic guitar. Charlie Watts is on drums while any contribution that Keith Richards provides is on shaker and/or organ.

1106. ZULU (Jagger, Richards) 4.37
9 July - 6 August & September; 3 November - 16 December 1993: Place: Ron Wood's Sandymount Studios, Kildare, Ireland; Windmill Lane Studios, Dublin, Ireland.
Producer: Don Was, The Glimmer Twins.
Bootleg only.

Zulu has a Caribbean feel to it with Ron Wood playing the pedal steel guitar. Don Was encouraged him to play the steel guitar and, if he suggested it, then the band went along with it. There are two versions - one with guide vocals and the second on which Mick Jagger, from the studio talk, agrees to provide additional percussion. The second cut runs straight on from the first and has Keith Richards singing some "you better believe it" vocals (* a - 4.11).

1107. IT'S ALRIGHT (Jagger, Richards) 4.00
9 July - 6 August & September; 3 November - 16 December 1993: Place: Ron Wood's Sandymount Studios, Kildare, Ireland; Windmill Lane Studios, Dublin, Ireland.
Rolling Stones with Darryl Jones, Chuck Leavell.
Producer: Don Was, The Glimmer Twins.
Bootleg only.

It's Alright thumps along with stereotypical twin electric guitars. Mick Jagger can be heard on ghost vocals but the main contributor is Chuck Leavell's eddying organ.

1108. BLINDED BY RAINBOWS (Jagger, Richards) 4.33
9 July - 6 August & September; 3 November - 16 December 1993; 15 January - April 1994: Place: Ron Wood's Sandymount Studios, Kildare, Ireland; Windmill Lane Studios, Dublin, Ireland; Don Was' Studio & A&M Studios, Los Angeles, USA.
Rolling Stones with Darryl Jones, Benmont Tench, Lenny Castro.
Producer: Don Was, The Glimmer Twins.
Engineer: Don Smith, Dan Bosworth, Alastair McMillan.
UK CD LP VOODOO LOUNGE: 11 July 1994: No. 1 - 24 weeks
USA CD LP VOODOO LOUNGE: 12 July 1994: No. 2 - 17 weeks

Benmont Tench (from the Tom Petty Band) and Lenny Castro had worked with Mick Jagger on his WANDERING SPIRIT album, from which *Blinded By Rainbows* was a left-over. Keith Richards thought it sounded like *Lady Jane* and suggested the keyboard sound to accompany it. Benmont plays a haunting Hammond organ and piano while Lenny, a renowned session musician, worked on percussion. Ron Wood plays the lead solo. An early out-take has unfinished lyrics and indicates that originally the tune was in the mode of a love song (* a - 6.55).
With changed lyrics, it had a powerful message as Mick wondered if terrorists slept at night and was their conscience clear as the war in Northern Ireland dragged on and on? He had to take a swipe at the situation in divided Ireland even though he knew his views would have no effect. Mick can also be heard on tremolo guitar. Keith Richards plays acoustic and Ron Wood takes the lead solo on electric guitar. There is an instrumental out-take with ghost vocals (* b - 4.42) and another with finished lyrics but without additional instrumental over-dubs (* c - 4.34).

1109. MOON IS UP (Jagger, Richards) 3.42
AKA: If (Moon Is Up)
9 July - 6 August & September; 3 November - 16 December 1993; 15 January - April 1994: Place: Ron Wood's Sandymount Studios, Kildare, Ireland; Windmill Lane Studios, Dublin, Ireland; Don Was' Studio & A&M Studios, Los Angeles, USA.
Played Live: 1999
Rolling Stones with Darryl Jones, Chuck Leavell, Benmont Tench, Bernard Fowler, Bobby Womack.
Producer: Don Was, The Glimmer Twins.
Engineer: Don Smith, Dan Bosworth, Alastair McMillan.
UK CD LP VOODOO LOUNGE: 11 July 1994: No. 1 - 24 weeks
USA CD LP VOODOO LOUNGE: 12 July 1994: No. 2 - 17 weeks

Keith Richards can be heard introducing an out-take, "this is a new song I've written, *If*". Keith performs the vocals and the acoustic guitar while Darryl Jones is on bass, Ron Wood the pedal steel and Charlie Watts the drums on this early version (* a - 5.04). The combined instruments on the final version of *Moon Is Up* are considerable and give the song a sophisticated but warm quality. Right from the opening squealing wah-wah pedal steel, the purposeful acoustic guitar from Keith Richards played through a Leslie amp, the harmonium from Chuck Leavell, the accordion from Benmont Tench and the castanets and harmonica from Mick Jagger - they all contribute on this track.
Mick also sang through the harmonica microphone to give it an additional phased nuance, just as he did with *Love Is Strong*. The drum sound was improvised - on the sleeve notes Charlie Watts was credited with playing a mystery drum. This he did by experimenting and hitting a metallic garbage bin with sticks and brushes at the top of a four-flight stairwell. Mick acknowledged that, if the album had been more of a 10-track than a 15-track venture, then *Moon Is Up* may not have appeared.
The longer format was due to the availability of CD, while the vinyl version had to become a double album and, even then, *Mean Disposition* was missed off the vinyl edition, despite there being sufficient room for it. One out-take is a ghost vocal instrumental version (* a - 5.03), while another is almost complete but without backing vocals by Bernard Fowler and Bobby Womack or the castanets from Mick (* b - 4.18).
On the final cut, Keith can be heard doing one of his "ha ha's" early on and there is some studio chat at the drum fade-out. Perhaps Don Was tried to capture the relaxed atmosphere within the studio. It was certainly one of the most creative songs on the album. He likened the songwriting process, particularly with Keith, as moulding putty, constantly kneading it and building until the clay began to set.

1110. THE WORST (Jagger, Richards) 2.24
9 July - 6 August & September; 3 November - 16 December 1993; 15 January - April 1994: Place: Ron Wood's Sandymount Studios, Kildare, Ireland; Windmill Lane Studios, Dublin, Ireland; Don Was' Studio & A&M Studios, Los Angeles, USA.
Played Live: 1994, 1995, 2002, 2003, 2005
Rolling Stones, Darryl Jones, Chuck Leavell, Frankie Gavin.
Producer: Don Was, The Glimmer Twins.
Engineer: Don Smith, Dan Bosworth, Alastair McMillan.
UK CD LP VOODOO LOUNGE: 11 July 1994: No. 1 - 24 weeks
USA CD LP VOODOO LOUNGE: 12 July 1994: No. 2 - 17 weeks

The Worst was claimed to be written by Keith Richards in a kitchen at the Blue Wave studios in Barbados. They were located on the Bayleys plantation, in the St. Philip Parish, at the old slavery Great House now owned by Eddy Grant. When the song was recorded in Ireland, it took on a traditional country feel with an Irish leaning, due to the use of a fiddle by Frankie Gavin. Ron Wood accompanies the two-minute track on pedal steel and Chuck Leavell is on piano. The steel was used because Jerry Lee Lewis had popped by and Keith wanted to hear him play some country music. They duly got together, having found Ronnie's pedal steel. Later, that same guitar was used for *The Worst*. Keith played his Gibson Robert Johnson acoustic. Mick Jagger took second stage on backing vocals, prompting him to state that he felt his delivery was unusual and he did not recognise himself. Three out-takes exist - one with a different arrangement and slightly altered lyrics (* a - 3.08) and another with complete lyrics and no backing vocal (* b - 2.26). A third has distinctly separated stereo instrumentation (* c - 2.27).

The sweet little chord structure at the end on the out-takes was performed more notably by the guitar while, on the album, the fiddle is more to the fore. The lyrics stated, "I said from the first I am the worst kind of guy for you to be around". Keith told interviewer Bruna Lombardi in 1993 that inspiration for songs came from his demons within: "I write songs from some of the conversations I have with my demon and some that I have with my angel and then some that I have with my daughters and some that I have with my wife and some that I have with old girlfriends and some with old friends and some people I don't know who I'm talking to - maybe my ancestors, I don't know."

1111. POSSESSES ME (Jagger, Richards) 7.37
9 July - 6 August & September; 3 November - 16 December 1993: Place: Ron Wood's Sandymount Studios, Kildare, Ireland; Windmill Lane Studios, Dublin, Ireland.
Rolling Stones with Chuck Leavell.
Producer: Don Was, The Glimmer Twins.
Bootleg only.

A Keith Richards composition on which he also performs vocals. It is a rough, ad-libbed song with a BB King-style blues guitar. Keith often commented that there was only one song written and that was by Adam and Eve - every other song was a variation on a theme.

1112. I GOT A HOLD ON YOU (Jagger, Richards) 4.37
AKA: Hold On You
9 July - 6 August & September; 3 November - 16 December 1993: Place: Ron Wood's Sandymount Studios, Kildare, Ireland; Windmill Lane Studios, Dublin, Ireland.
Rolling Stones with Darryl Jones, Chuck Leavell.
Producer: Don Was, The Glimmer Twins.
Bootleg only.

Spliced on to the end of *It's Alright*, this track has some hard guitar sounds. Mick Jagger is just off microphone and can be heard faintly on this up-beat number from Ireland. You can just catch the "hold on you" line. The guitar bridge sounds unusual and not quintessential Stones.

1113. MONSOON RAGOON (Jagger, Richards) 4.36
9 July - 6 August & September; 3 November - 16 December 1993: Place: Ron Wood's Sandymount Studios, Kildare, Ireland; Windmill Lane Studios, Dublin, Ireland.
Rolling Stones with Chuck Leavell.
Producer: Don Was, The Glimmer Twins.
Bootleg only.

An out-take from Barbados that was worked on again in Ireland. It has a pre-programmed orchestral tape that Chuck Leavell integrates with a piano piece. Mick Jagger provides some guide vocals.

1114. MEAN DISPOSITION (Jagger, Richards) 4.07
9 July - 6 August & September; 3 November - 16 December 1993; 15 January - April 1994: Place: Ron Wood's Sandymount Studios, Kildare, Ireland; Windmill Lane Studios, Dublin, Ireland; Don Was' Studio & A&M Studios, Los Angeles, USA.
Rolling Stones with Darryl Jones, Chuck Leavell.
Producer: Don Was, The Glimmer Twins.
Engineer: Don Smith, Dan Bosworth, Alastair McMillan.
UK CD VOODOO LOUNGE: 11 July 1994: No. 1 - 24 weeks
USA CD VOODOO LOUNGE: 12 July 1994: No. 2 - 17 weeks

Mean Disposition was the final track on the CD album and did not appear on the vinyl double edition. It is a fast, often over-looked number. An instrumental-only out-take, including acoustic guitar, demonstrates the fast pace, with Chuck Leavell tinkering boogie style on the piano (* a - 4.13). A second out-take has additional guitar and lead vocals by Mick Jagger (* b - 3.14). It fades out soon after the last verse. The riff is not a Keef classic but, as usual he and Ron Wood augment each other well, particularly as the final verse ceases and the band flow freely and for longer on the final cut.

With all the additional musicians used on the album, *Mean Disposition* was just the six-piece working comfortably together, Darryl Jones' strong line on his acoustic fretless bass ensuring his permanent position in the band. The song is no relation to the Muddy Waters or Kinks songs, although the former may have inspired the title. Mick Jagger was particularly wary initially that engineer Don Smith would try to recreate the sound from earlier classic albums and not embrace new technology. This was the old Mick and Keith battle. Don Smith said in an interview in December 1994 within Sound On Sound: "It just ain't right. It's like half the echo's gone, the bottom's gone, the 400 cycles have gone, and it's very frustrating. The only advantage I can attribute to digital is that I can bring a DAT home and listen to it at the right speed. But the rest of it, they can use for boat anchors as far as I'm concerned!" Many critics felt that VOODOO LOUNGE did have many sound pointers towards EXILE ON MAIN ST but was that such a bad thing?

1115. ANOTHER CR (Jagger, Richards) 9.46
9 July - 6 August & September; 3 November - 16 December 1993: Place: Ron Wood's Sandymount Studios, Kildare, Ireland; Windmill Lane Studios, Dublin, Ireland.
Rolling Stones with Chuck Leavell.
Producer: Don Was, The Glimmer Twins.
Bootleg only.

Another CR is a nine-minute jam featuring the drums of Charlie Watts on his riser. It starts off with Ronnie Wood improvising on pedal steel then Charlie starts what is essentially a drum solo - something not normally associated with The Rolling Stones. At the end of the solo, a heavier electric guitar joins the jam, an organ also enters and Mick Jagger chips in with a quick vocal line, "sitting and thinking which way to go". Charlie's roots had always been in jazz, which created a swing rather than a rock and roll beat.
Another CR may have inspired Charlie in the future - could it have been a pre-cursor for the excellent and innovative 2000 CHARLIE WATTS JIM KELTNER PROJECT collaboration? This album, which received some very favourable reviews, was an electronic, techno percussive jazz opus, paying homage to great jazz drummers, each track being named after one.

1116. YOU GOT ME ROCKING (Jagger, Richards) 3.35
9 July - 6 August & September; 3 November - 16 December 1993; 15 January - April 1994: Place: Ron Wood's Sandymount Studios, Kildare, Ireland; Windmill Lane Studios, Dublin, Ireland; Don Was' Studio & A&M Studios, Los Angeles, USA.
Played Live: 1994, 1995, 1997, 1998, 1999, 2002, 2003, 2005, 2006, 2007
Rolling Stones with Darryl Jones, Chuck Leavell, Bernard Fowler, Ivan Neville.
Producer: Don Was, The Glimmer Twins.
Engineer: Don Smith, Dan Bosworth, Alastair McMillan.
UK CD LP VOODOO LOUNGE: 11 July 1994: No. 1 - 24 weeks
USA CD LP VOODOO LOUNGE: 12 July 1994: No. 2 - 17 weeks
UK Single: 26 September 1994: No. 23 - 3 weeks
USA Track CD, 12-inch Single You Got Me Rocking (Perfecto Mix): 3 January 1995
UK CD LP FORTY LICKS: 30 September 2002: No. 2 - 45 weeks
USA CD LP FORTY LICKS: 1 October 2002: No. 2 - 50 weeks
UK CD box set THE SINGLES COLLECTION 1971-2006: 45 X 45s: 11 April 2011
USA CD box set THE SINGLES COLLECTION 1971-2006: 45 X 45s: 26 April 2011

This is the barnstormer on the album. It is about taking a grip on your life and seizing the moment: "I was the boxer who can't get in the ring, I was a hooker losing her looks". From the intense opening drum beat and almost simultaneous riff, the song rocks forcefully. The track was written by Keith Richards who, on an 11-minute early slower version, guides it forward with a heavy organ (* a - 10.58). The piano is also an important part of the song's direction, although the pace was a lot slower than the final version.
Indeed, the original melody was written on the piano and it was eventually transferred to the rocking guitar. Mick Jagger is co-vocalist to Keith but more often in a backing role. Due to the length of the out-take, this version soon disintegrates. The song has alternative vocals just like a second out-take, in which Mick is on vocals with no backing vocal accompaniment from Bernard Fowler or Ivan Neville (* b - 4.11).
Due to the track lasting an additional 30 or 40 seconds, an extended Ron Wood blistering slide guitar solo can be heard. Charlie Watts' drums were again recorded in the stairwell. It was never one of Mick's favourite songs but it was to grow on him. Keith had quite a job convincing Mick to even record the song. Another similar instrumental out-take has Mick on maracas and Keith laughing in the background at the end (* c - 4.13).
There is a short extract that precedes this cut (* d - 1.13). Finally a fifth out-take, with extra guitar overdubs and backing vocals more upfront in the mix, can be heard (* e - 4.05). Keith is credited with "mystery guitar" on the sleeve notes - that turned out to be a dobro played with a stick from Ronnie's garden. Don Was seemed keen for each song to have something extra and unique to make it distinctive. The track was released as the second single but there was an additional three-month wait before a USA issue.
The track was re-mixed three times by Paul Oakenfield and Steve Osborne. They used additional percussion by Steve Sidelnyk (no stranger to the Stones due to his re-mixing on the Soup Dragons' single *I'm Free*) and vocals by Anita Jarrett. The re-mixed vocals sounded similar to those which featured on *Too Much Blood*. Incidentally, the three producers on the album, Don Was, Don Smith and Dan Bosworth, were fondly known as the 3 Ds! The promotional video for the single was a collage of live shots from the 1994 tour.

1117. YOU GOT ME ROCKING (PERFECTO MIX) (Jagger, Richards) 5.04
9 July - 6 August & September; 3 November - 16 December 1993; 15 January - April 1994: Place: Ron Wood's Sandymount Studios, Kildare, Ireland; Windmill Lane Studios, Dublin, Ireland; Don Was' Studio & A&M Studios, Los Angeles, USA.
Rolling Stones with Darryl Jones, Chuck Leavell, Bernard Fowler, Ivan Neville, Anita Jarrett, Steve Sidelnyk.
Producer: Don Was, The Glimmer Twins.
Engineer: Don Smith, Dan Bosworth, Alastair McMillan. Production and Remix: Paul Oakenfold, Steve Osborne.
UK Track CD Single You Got Me Rocking: 26 September 1994
UK 12-inch Single: 26 September 1994
USA Promo CD Single: January 1995
USA Track 12-inch You Got Me Rocking: January 1995
USA Track CD Single You Got Me Rocking: January 1995
UK CD box set THE SINGLES COLLECTION 1971-2006: 45 X 45s: 11 April 2011
USA CD box set THE SINGLES COLLECTION 1971-2006: 45 X 45s: 26 April 2011

An edited version was released on a promo single (* a - 3.49).

1118. YOU GOT ME ROCKING (SEXY DISCO DUB MIX) (Jagger, Richards) 6.18
9 July - 6 August & September; 3 November - 16 December 1993; 15 January - April 1994: Place: Ron Wood's Sandymount Studios, Kildare, Ireland; Windmill Lane Studios, Dublin, Ireland; Don Was' Studio & A&M Studios, Los Angeles, USA.
Rolling Stones with Darryl Jones, Chuck Leavell, Bernard Fowler, Ivan Neville, Anita Jarrett, Steve Sidelnyk.
Producer: Don Was, The Glimmer Twins.
Engineer: Don Smith, Dan Bosworth, Alastair McMillan. Production and Remix: Paul Oakenfold, Steve Osborne.
UK Track CD Single You Got Me Rocking: 26 September 1994
UK B-side 12-inch Single You Got Me Rocking (Perfecto Mix): 26 September 1994
USA Track 12-inch You Got Me Rocking: January 1995
USA Track CD Single You Got Me Rocking: January 1995
UK CD box set THE SINGLES COLLECTION 1971-2006: 45 X 45s: 11 April 2011
USA CD box set THE SINGLES COLLECTION 1971-2006: 45 X 45s: 26 April 2011

1119. YOU GOT ME ROCKING (TRANCE MIX) (Jagger, Richards) 5.00
9 July - 6 August & September; 3 November - 16 December 1993; 15 January - April 1994: Place: Ron Wood's Sandymount Studios, Kildare, Ireland; Windmill Lane Studios, Dublin, Ireland; Don Was' Studio & A&M Studios, Los Angeles, USA.
Rolling Stones with Darryl Jones, Chuck Leavell, Bernard Fowler, Ivan Neville, Anita Jarrett, Steve Sidelnyk.
Producer: Don Was, The Glimmer Twins.
Engineer: Don Smith, Dan Bosworth, Alastair McMillan. Production and Remix: Paul Oakenfold, Steve Osborne.
UK B-side 12-inch Single You Got Me Rocking (Perfecto Mix): 26 September 1994
USA Track 12-inch You Got Me Rocking: January 1995
USA Track CD Single You Got Me Rocking: January 1995
UK CD box set THE SINGLES COLLECTION 1971-2006: 45 X 45s: 11 April 2011
USA CD box set THE SINGLES COLLECTION 1971-2006: 45 X 45s: 26 April 2011

1120. HONEST MAN (Jagger, Richards) 4.28
9 July - 6 August & September; 3 November - 16 December 1993: Place: Ron Wood's Sandymount Studios, Kildare, Ireland; Windmill Lane Studios, Dublin, Ireland.
Producer: Don Was, The Glimmer Twins.
Bootleg only.

One of the best out-takes from the sessions. Mick Jagger uses the harmonica but in a stronger blues style; the background music is up front rock and roll with a real duck and diving riff. The vocals sound as if they are finished and Mick may be on guitar. Two out-take versions can be heard and are very similar to one another (* a - 4.23).

1121. SAMBA (Jagger, Richards) 3.42
9 July - 6 August & September; 3 November - 16 December 1993: Place: Ron Wood's Sandymount Studios, Kildare, Ireland; Windmill Lane Studios, Dublin, Ireland.
Producer: Don Was, The Glimmer Twins.
Bootleg only.

This out-take probably has Mick Jagger on electric piano and congas with Charlie Watts on drums. After the album was released, Mick commented that many of the groove and African influences were not encouraged by Don Was, which Mick thought was a mistake. "He tried to remake EXILE ON MAIN ST." But he did consider the end result was very much of the time and place.

1122. THE STORM (Jagger, Richards) 2.49
9 July - 6 August & September; 3 November - 16 December 1993; 15 January - April 1994: Place: Ron Wood's Sandymount Studios, Kildare, Ireland; Windmill Lane Studios, Dublin, Ireland; Don Was' Studio & A&M Studios, Los Angeles, USA.
Rolling Stones with Darryl Jones, Chuck Leavell, Bernard Fowler, Ivan Neville.
Producer: Don Was, The Glimmer Twins.
Engineer: Don Smith, Dan Bosworth, Alastair McMillan.
UK B-side Love Is Strong: 5 July 1994
USA B-side Love Is Strong: 5 July 1994
UK CD box set THE SINGLES COLLECTION 1971-2006: 45 X 45s: 11 April 2011
USA CD box set THE SINGLES COLLECTION 1971-2006: 45 X 45s: 26 April 2011

The VOODOO LOUNGE album became their most popular since EMOTIONAL RESCUE in 1980, selling more than two million in the USA. This is characterised by a "focus" that Mick Jagger and Keith Richards were determined to capture. As Keith put it, they both wanted to be looking down the same telescope, so there were intellectual conversations to decide the album's direction. Keith and Don Was wanted to produce an album that would be musically amongst their top three. However, Mick and Charlie Watts wanted a more rhythmic and less retro outcome but they did not fight the issue. *The Storm* illustrates this as much as anything else. Although not on the album, it was a re-visit to those *No Expectations* blues so perfectly captured before. An exquisite moment is the ten-minute working version, with Ron Wood on slide acoustic guitar, ending with Charlie Watts wondering if the song would be better off in mono (* a - 9.56).
A second (much shorter) version has an echoed vocal and harmonica (* b - 3.19). A third has Keith on backing vocals and Mick on harp again (* c - 3.17). The final take, with Keith on backing vocals and Mick on harmonica and a gold-plated Dobro (Ronnie's guitar), was regrettably only released as a single flip side. Bernard Fowler felt the album was a special one for him because he was involved from the ground-floor up, helping them to formulate many of the tracks rather than just overdubbing vocals once the song was recorded.

1123. YOU GOT IT MADE (Jagger, Richards) 5.01
AKA: Get It Made
9 July - 6 August & September; 3 November - 16 December 1993: Place: Ron Wood's Sandymount Studios, Kildare, Ireland; Windmill Lane Studios, Dublin, Ireland.
Rolling Stones with Darryl Jones, Pierre de Beauport, Chuck Leavell.
Producer: Don Was, The Glimmer Twins.
Bootleg only.

Pierre De Beauport assists the band on this Keith Richards number. The first out-take is mainly instrumental with Mick Jagger on faint vocals and a pretty piano melody (* a - 4.27). The second is more accomplished with Keith taking lead and backing vocals, as well as the other guitar parts. Chuck Leavell swaps the piano for the organ. Another unique insight into the Ron Wood and Keith relationship is heard during a 17-minute excerpt of a playback where they add backing vocals and agree who does what and which words to use (* b - 17.16). Keith says, "It's a tall order for two queers" and, when Ron gets confused between using the word "while" or "time", Keith sagely retorts, "time is money, while is forever". When Ron asks Don Was to tell them what to do, Keith says that he is calling the shots . . . he truly was the leader and big brother.

1124. NEW FACES (Jagger, Richards) 2.52
9 July - 6 August & September; 3 November - 16 December 1993; 15 January - April 1994: Place: Ron Wood's Sandymount Studios, Kildare, Ireland; Windmill Lane Studios, Dublin, Ireland; Don Was' Studio & A&M Studios, Los Angeles, USA.
Rolling Stones with Darryl Jones, Chuck Leavell, Luis Jardim, Frankie Gavin.
Producer: Don Was, The Glimmer Twins.
Engineer: Don Smith, Dan Bosworth, Alastair McMillan.
UK CD LP VOODOO LOUNGE: 11 July 1994: No. 1 - 24 weeks
USA CD LP VOODOO LOUNGE: 12 July 1994: No. 2 - 17 weeks

An instrumental out-take labelled the "unplugged penny whistle mix" features both Keith and Mick Jagger on acoustic guitar, Darryl Jones' bass, Chuck Leavell on harpsichord sounds created by a synthesiser and Luis Jardim on the shaker. The flute - not the aforementioned pennywhistle - is played by Celtic man, Frankie Gavin (* a - 2.54).
On a second out-take, Frankie reverts to the penny whistle, which gives it less of a retro feel, more Irish in tone, while Chuck plays the harmonium (* b - 2.47). Charlie Watts only needs to tap the tambourine on this quiet number for the percussion. On the final version, Keith also sings on harmony backing vocals.

1125. TEASE ME (Jagger, Richards) 4.21
9 July - 6 August & September; 3 November - 16 December 1993: Place: Ron Wood's Sandymount Studios, Kildare, Ireland; Windmill Lane Studios, Dublin, Ireland.
Producer: Don Was, The Glimmer Twins.
Bootleg only.

A Keith Richards tune with partially completed lyrics and a guitar chord structure that went up and down the fret board.

1126. SPARKS WILL FLY (Jagger, Richards) 3.16
9 July - 6 August & September; 3 November - 16 December 1993; 15 January - April 1994: Place: Ron Wood's Sandymount Studios, Kildare, Ireland; Windmill Lane Studios, Dublin, Ireland; Don Was' Studio & A&M Studios, Los Angeles, USA.
Played Live: 1994, 1995
Rolling Stones with Darryl Jones, Bernard Fowler.
Producer: Don Was, The Glimmer Twins.
Engineer: Don Smith, Dan Bosworth, Alastair McMillan.
UK CD LP VOODOO LOUNGE: 11 July 1994: No. 1 - 24 weeks
USA CD LP VOODOO LOUNGE: 12 July 1994: No. 2 - 17 weeks
UK Track CD Single Out Of Tears: 28 November 1994
UK CD box set THE SINGLES COLLECTION 1971-2006: 45 X 45s: 11 April 2011
USA CD box set THE SINGLES COLLECTION 1971-2006: 45 X 45s: 26 April 2011

Everyday moments sometimes inspire a song. A log fire was burning in Ron Wood's garden and, as Keith Richards chucked some logs on it and sparks flared, he had one of his moments of inspiration. Straight away he went into the basement studio with Charlie Watts and worked on the important rhythm and drum track. Mick Jagger soon joined them and dove-tailed the link to the verse. No-one else played on it until the three of them had cemented the rhythm.
From an early out-take, the opening few bars were supplied by Charlie's drum before Keith's guitar enters the mix (* a - 3.20). Keith is heard on the vocals. A unique, 14-minute audio extract from the studio has Keith working on a Nashville tuned acoustic guitar borrowed from Ron (* b - 14.33). A conversation evolves during which Ron and Jo Wood talk about Christmas presents. Keith gave Ron a guitar case and, when he excitedly opened it, he found a cardboard guitar cut-out. Ron called it the "ruddock".
Jo remembered being given an unlicensed gun from Keith which she had to leave behind for fear of travelling through customs with it. In between strumming, Keith comments that he is not sure whether there is a guitar part for Ronnie on *Sparks Will Fly*, although he had thought of a place where a fill-in may be required. A second out-take has Keith still on lead and over-dubbed backing vocals with improvised lyrics, and Ron playing a B-Bender guitar trying to find the right fill moment (* c - 3.16). Another out-take has Mick in the studio doing scratch vocals (* d - 3.19).
A fourth is getting close to the final arrangement, with the same match sound at the beginning, and Mick unveils the words he had written for the song (* e - 3.15). Both Keith and Charlie were surprised at the "hot" lyrics - "did he say that?" It was all about a desire to get back to an old girlfriend and, despite sniffing around old hunting grounds, Mick had never found a woman so hot. The line, "I want to kiss your sweet ass", resulted in an airplay ban and was altered by Don Was in the *Radio Clean* edit (* f - 3.15).

Mick was encouraged by Don Was to record his vocals free style on the faster numbers and was not restricted to one position. He could roam the room as he did in live performances to give it that bit of extra passion. The December 1994 Sound On Sound interview provides a fascinating insight to Don Was' enthusiasm for the band. "He'd give it the full stage bit and, in fact, it was so awesome I had to keep looking down at the console, because I didn't want to be wowed too much! I mean, I used to wait in line overnight to get tickets to see these guys, just for some shitty seats. And now I had them about five feet in front of me, on the other side of the glass, and I didn't want to be biased in my assessment of his vocal. So, I had to look down and just listen to make sure it was working, because otherwise I could have lost my objectivity."

1127. OUT OF TEARS (DON WAS EDIT) (Jagger, Richards) 4.22
9 July - 6 August & September; 3 November - 16 December 1993; 15 January - April 1994: Place: Ron Wood's Sandymount Studios, Kildare, Ireland; Windmill Lane Studios, Dublin, Ireland; Don Was' Studio & A&M Studios, Los Angeles, USA.
Rolling Stones with Darryl Jones, Chuck Leavell, Lenny Castro, Benmont Tench, David Campbell.
Producer: Don Was, The Glimmer Twins.
Engineer: Don Smith, Dan Bosworth, Alastair McMillan.
UK Single: 28 November 1994: No. 36 - 4 weeks
USA Single: 28 November 1994: No. 60 - 15 weeks
UK CD box set THE SINGLES COLLECTION 1971-2006: 45 X 45s: 11 April 2011
USA CD box set THE SINGLES COLLECTION 1971-2006: 45 X 45s: 26 April 2011

1128. OUT OF TEARS (BOB CLEARMOUNTAIN REMIX EDIT) (Jagger, Richards) 4.21
9 July - 6 August & September; 3 November - 16 December 1993; 15 January - April 1994: Place: Ron Wood's Sandymount Studios, Kildare, Ireland; Windmill Lane Studios, Dublin, Ireland; Don Was' Studio & A&M Studios, Los Angeles, USA.
Rolling Stones with Darryl Jones, Chuck Leavell, Lenny Castro, Benmont Tench, David Campbell.
Producer: Don Was, The Glimmer Twins.
Engineer: Don Smith, Dan Bosworth, Alastair McMillan.
Remix: Bob Clearmountain.
UK Track CD Single Out Of Tears (Don Was Edit): 28 November 1994
UK CD box set THE SINGLES COLLECTION 1971-2006: 45 X 45s: 11 April 2011
USA CD box set THE SINGLES COLLECTION 1971-2006: 45 X 45s: 26 April 2011

1129. OUT OF TEARS (Jagger, Richards) 5.27
9 July - 6 August & September; 3 November - 16 December 1993; 15 January - April 1994: Place: Ron Wood's Sandymount Studios, Kildare, Ireland; Windmill Lane Studios, Dublin, Ireland; Don Was' Studio & A&M Studios, Los Angeles, USA.
Played Live: 1994, 1995
Rolling Stones with Darryl Jones, Chuck Leavell, Lenny Castro, Benmont Tench, David Campbell.
Producer: Don Was, The Glimmer Twins.
Engineer: Don Smith, Dan Bosworth, Alastair McMillan.
UK CD LP VOODOO LOUNGE: 11 July 1994: No. 1 - 24 weeks
USA CD LP VOODOO LOUNGE: 12 July 1994: No. 2 - 17 weeks

The song reflected past loves and eras and had similarities to *Angie*. It was one of Mick Jagger's favourites from the album and, on one early out-take, he is performing on piano with a Charlie Watts drum beat. Usually the guitar was the main method for writing but keyboards inevitably gave the song a different feel. On this occasion the guitar was added afterwards. A very sparse drum, piano and vocal version is available (* a - 4.23).
On an instrumental out-take there are more over-dubbed guitar tracks than on the final cut - a vocal is just audible (* b - 5.29). Mick also plays acoustic and Ron Wood an excellent slide guitar. Chuck Leavell plays the piano on the last cut. The final version breathes with added organ from Benmont Tench, percussion from Lenny Castro and strings arranged by David Campbell. An out-take without backing vocals, Benmont's organ and the full string arrangement can also be heard (* c - 5.24).
Out Of Tears builds up and down on the piano, Mick as plaintive as he can be until the emotive slide guitar enters. Mick then does another sad passage until Charlie's percussion enters before the final chorus. Keith Richards was later to acknowledge that the quality of Mick's vocals on the album was superb - there was no indolent air, just high passion and energy. Back at the A&M studios, Don Was experimented with enhancing the sound by giving the tape some echo, just as Phil Spector had achieved on John Lennon's IMAGINE album.
In November 1994, the track was released as an edited single in the UK, cut by a minute by Don Was. It was the third single from the album. Another version was edited by Bob Clearmountain and was an extra track on the CD single. As a single vinyl release, *Out Of Tears* had a distinctive tear-shaped disc. A video by Jake Scott was filmed on the streets of Cleveland and in a bar and a hotel room, each Stone captured in a different location.

1130. MIDDLE OF THE SEA (Jagger, Richards) 3.42
9 July - 6 August & September; 3 November - 16 December 1993: Place: Ron Wood's Sandymount Studios, Kildare, Ireland; Windmill Lane Studios, Dublin, Ireland.
Producer: Don Was, The Glimmer Twins.
Bootleg only.

A funky guitar number with Mick Jagger on vocals and harmonica. Mick's phobias of ocean monsters obviously came to the fore on this one.

1131.   JUMP ON TOP OF ME (Jagger, Richards) 4.24

9 July - 6 August & September; 3 November - 16 December 1993; 15 January - April 1994: Place: Ron Wood's Sandymount Studios, Kildare, Ireland;& Windmill Lane Studios, Dublin, Ireland; Don Was' Studio & A&M Studios, Los Angeles, USA.

Played Live: 1995

Rolling Stones with Darryl Jones, Chuck Leavell, Frankie Gavin.

Producer: Don Was, The Glimmer Twins.

Engineer: Don Smith, Dan Bosworth, Alastair McMillan.

Remix: Bob Clearmountain.

UK B-Side You Got Me Rocking: 26 September 1994

UK Track CD Single You Got Me Rocking: 26 September 1994

USA Compilation CD ROBERT ALTMAN'S PRET-A-PORTER (READY TO WEAR): 6 December 1994

UK CD box set THE SINGLES COLLECTION 1971-2006: 45 X 45s: 11 April 2011

USA CD box set THE SINGLES COLLECTION 1971-2006: 45 X 45s: 26 April 2011

Jump On Top Of Me has the same images as *Sparks Will Fly* with the "I want to get laid" approach. An instrumental out-take shapes this boogie song with slide guitar, a distant vocal, a shrill harmonica and a fiddle played by Frankie Gavin (* a - 5.03). It was released as the B-side to *You Got Me Rocking* and also on the film soundtrack to *Prêt-à-Porter*. Many tracks were recorded ensemble in a semi-circle, with Charlie Watts positioned in the middle. It was a small room sound that harked back to the Chess Studios.

Don Was gave Don Smith freedom to capture this. "He did an incredible job, the record sounds very natural and intimate. Sometimes, just given the nature of the technology, you almost have to create an illusion of smallness. Maybe a room is larger than you want it to be and the sound is too big, so to get it tighter requires some manoeuvring and this is not as simple as it appears to be." Don Smith died in 2009 and Keith Richards sent a tribute to his funeral, showing all those years later what a recording force he was.

1132.   I'M GONNA DRIVE (Jagger, Richards) 3.42

9 July - 6 August & September; 3 November - 16 December 1993; 15 January - April 1994: Place: Ron Wood's Sandymount Studios, Kildare, Ireland; Windmill Lane Studios, Dublin, Ireland; Don Was' Studio & A&M Studios, Los Angeles, USA.

Rolling Stones with Darryl Jones, Chuck Leavell.

Producer: Don Was, The Glimmer Twins.

Engineer: Don Smith, Dan Bosworth, Alastair McMillan.

Remix: Bob Clearmountain.

UK Track CD Single Out Of Tears: 28 November 1994

UK CD box set THE SINGLES COLLECTION 1971-2006: 45 X 45s: 11 April 2011

USA CD box set THE SINGLES COLLECTION 1971-2006: 45 X 45s: 26 April 2011

In a similar musical vein to *Jump On Top Of Me* but with less boogie, *I'm Gonna Drive* again has Ron Wood on slide guitar. Mick Jagger, using all his vocal repertoire; spoken, slurred, affected, drawled, whoops and growls that he wants to escape to the edge of the world, away from the dirty lies. There is a five-minute instrumental out-take available from the sessions (* a - 5.27).

1133.   BABY BREAK IT DOWN (Jagger, Richards) 4.09

9 July - 6 August & September; 3 November - 16 December 1993; 15 January - April 1994: Place: Ron Wood's Sandymount Studios, Kildare, Ireland; Windmill Lane Studios, Dublin, Ireland; Don Was' Studio & A&M Studios, Los Angeles, USA.

Rolling Stones with Darryl Jones, Ivan Neville, Bernard Fowler.

Producer: Don Was, The Glimmer Twins.

Engineer: Don Smith, Dan Bosworth, Alastair McMillan.

UK CD LP VOODOO LOUNGE: 11 July 1994: No. 1 - 24 weeks

USA CD LP VOODOO LOUNGE: 12 July 1994: No. 2 - 17 weeks

This may be considered filler material for the extended album. It has a nice rhythmic groove, interesting guitar lines from Keith Richards and the instantly recognisable pedal steel work of Ron Wood. A Keith vocal out-take also has him tinkering on piano (* a - 6.02). It was half-written by Keith and Mick Jagger helped to finish it off. For the final version this was appended by the Hammond B3 organ playing of Ivan Neville. This is clearly heard on an instrumental only out-take (* b - 5.56). There is a Mick Jagger vocal version without backing vocals and with more up-front pedal steel (* c - 4.11). A fourth is much closer to the final take but two minutes longer (* d - 5.59). Bernard Fowler is also on backing vocals. The album cover was put together by the 4i Group, who started work with the band on STEEL WHEELS. For that album they asked the question, "How do you put cheek in a tongue?" The answer is, by giving it a jagged edge.

That became the tongue motif for that tour as well as the STEEL WHEELS cover. They also designed the Urban Jungle dog while, for VOODOO LOUNGE, made things even sharper by introducing the spiked tongue and the Leopard Voodoo doll used on the cover and designed by Mark Norton. The inside sleeve, not unlike BEGGARS BANQUET, was Satan's Play Room extracted from *Satan's Daily Life In The 19th Century* by photographer Jac Remise. These images were starkly used for the *You Got Me Rocking* single cover. All this album artwork, motifs and stage design were principally approved by Mick and Charlie.

1134.   BRAND NEW CAR (Jagger, Richards) 4.15

9 July - 6 August & September; 3 November - 16 December 1993; 15 January - April 1994: Place: Ron Wood's Sandymount Studios, Kildare, Ireland; Windmill Lane Studios, Dublin, Ireland; Don Was' Studio & A&M Studios, Los Angeles, USA.

Played Live: 1994, 1999, 2002

Rolling Stones with Chuck Leavell, David McMurray, Mark Isham, Lenny Castro, Luis Jardim, Ivan Neville.

Producer: Don Was, The Glimmer Twins.

Engineer: Don Smith, Dan Bosworth, Alastair McMillan.

UK CD LP VOODOO LOUNGE: 11 July 1994: No. 1 - 24 weeks

USA CD LP VOODOO LOUNGE: 12 July 1994: No. 2 - 17 weeks

This is drawn from material not used for Mick Jagger's solo album WANDERING SPIRIT. The subject matter on *Brand New Car* can be taken in two ways - either for a car or a lover. Mick sings, "check if her oil smells good . . . touch her on the seat . . . I drive her in the dark". Can't imagine Jagger giving it some polish and stick although, in 1973, he did admit to dicing with death at 120mph on the German autobahns. An early out-take with count-in just has the four main personnel (* a - 5.29) while a second with ghost vocals plods along hardly breaking sweat to get on the motorway (* b - 5.05).

It is not until the guest artists join in that the track rises above anonymity to become worthwhile but it is certainly not a classic. The band are joined by Don Was contacts at Was Not Was, in David McMurray (saxophone) and Mark Isham (trumpet) playing the quizzical refrain. The percussion is assisted by Luis Jardim and Lenny Castro. Keith Richards plays bass, wah-wah and electric guitar. The backing vocalists are Ivan Neville and Keith. On a near final out-take, Keith plays more of a co-vocalist role (* c - 5.04).

1135. SWEETHEARTS TOGETHER (Jagger, Richards) 4.45
9 July - 6 August & September; 3 November - 16 December 1993; 15 January - April 1994: Place: Ron Wood's Sandymount Studios, Kildare, Ireland; Windmill Lane Studios, Dublin, Ireland; Don Was' Studio & A&M Studios, Los Angeles, USA.
Rolling Stones with Chuck Leavell, Flaco Jimenez, Max Baca, Luis Jardim, Bernard Fowler, Ivan Neville.
Producer: Don Was, The Glimmer Twins.
Engineer: Don Smith, Dan Bosworth, Alastair McMillan.
UK CD LP VOODOO LOUNGE: 11 July 1994: No. 1 - 24 weeks
USA CD LP VOODOO LOUNGE: 12 July 1994: No. 2 - 17 weeks

This is probably a track which originated in Barbados and is one of the more widely covered out-takes (six in all). Two early ones, accompanied by a slowly strumming acoustic guitar, have both Keith Richards and Mick Jagger on vocals (* a - 3.39, b - 5.58). The first has studio chat and Mick enquiring whether the acoustic is a Martin. There is an instrumental with Mick also on acoustic guitar and percussion with Luis Jardim (* c - 5.54). *Sweethearts* evolved again as guest musicians joined in. On one take there is the fiddle work of Frankie Gavin and Chuck Leavell on B3 Organ (* d - 5.48). There is also a Keith Richards out-take with the combination of Frankie and Chuck, as Keith delivers some rough guide vocals (* e - 5.56). Frank Gavin was not on the final take. Ron Wood does his lap steel thing with pedals. This is the almost six-minute "Chihuahua" mix where Keith sings the word near the end. Chihuahua is the biggest state in Mexico and possibly inspired the next recruits for *Sweethearts Together* - Tex-Mex button accordion player Flaco Jimenez and the bajo sexto guitar of Max Baca. A final out-take has Mick and Keith dueting on vocals (* f - 5.51).

Don Was encouraged them to play acoustic guitars in an isolation booth and sing facing slightly away from each other into two microphones, something they had not done for some time. People who had worked with the Stones for a while couldn't believe it was happening! For Don Was, that moment epitomised the collaboration which characterises the whole album. "I think that's why it's a better record than others they've done in recent years." Ron said that, whenever a row brewed, they would say that they had better sing *Sweethearts Together* to soothe it away.

1136. I GO WILD (SCOTT LITT REMIX) (Jagger, Richards) 4.39
9 July - 6 August & September; 3 November - 16 December 1993; April 1994: Place: Ron Wood's Sandymount Studios, Kildare, Ireland; Windmill Lane Studios, Dublin, Ireland; Right Track Studios, New York, USA.
Rolling Stones with Darryl Jones, Chuck Leavell, Phil Jones, Bernard Fowler, Ivan Neville.
Producer: Don Was, The Glimmer Twins.
Engineer: Bob Clearmountain, Jennifer Monnar.
Remixed by Scott Litt at Louie's Clubhouse, Los Angeles, California, USA.
USA CD Track Single: I Go Wild (Album Version): 4 April 1995
UK CD Track Single: I Go Wild (Album Version): 7 July 1995
UK CD box set THE SINGLES COLLECTION 1971-2006: 45 X 45s: 11 April 2011
USA CD box set THE SINGLES COLLECTION 1971-2006: 45 X 45s: 26 April 2011

1137. I GO WILD (LUIS RESTO STRAIGHT VOCAL MIX) (Jagger, Richards) 5.40
9 July - 6 August & September; 3 November - 16 December 1993; April 1994: Place: Ron Wood's Sandymount Studios, Kildare, Ireland; Windmill Lane Studios, Dublin, Ireland; Right Track Studios, New York, USA.
Rolling Stones with Darryl Jones, Chuck Leavell, Phil Jones, Bernard Fowler, Ivan Neville.
Producer: Don Was, The Glimmer Twins.
Engineer: Bob Clearmountain, Jennifer Monnar.
Remix and additional production by Luis Resto. Mixed and played by Luis Resto.
Recorded at Chomsky Ranch, Los Angeles, California, USA.
USA CD Track Single: I Go Wild (Album Version): 4 April 1995
UK CD Track Single: I Go Wild (Album Version): 7 July 1995
UK CD box set THE SINGLES COLLECTION 1971-2006: 45 X 45s: 11 April 2011
USA CD box set THE SINGLES COLLECTION 1971-2006: 45 X 45s: 26 April 2011

1138. I GO WILD (Jagger, Richards) 4.23
9 July - 6 August & September; 3 November - 16 December 1993; April 1994: Place: Ron Wood's Sandymount Studios, Kildare, Ireland; Windmill Lane Studios, Dublin, Ireland; Right Track Studios, New York, USA.
Played Live: 1994, 1995
Rolling Stones with Darryl Jones, Chuck Leavell, Phil Jones, Bernard Fowler, Ivan Neville.
Producer: Don Was, The Glimmer Twins.
Engineer: Bob Clearmountain, Jennifer Monnar.

UK CD LP VOODOO LOUNGE: 11 July 1994: No. 1 - 24 weeks
USA CD LP VOODOO LOUNGE: 12 July 1994: No. 2 - 17 weeks
USA Single: 4 April 1995
UK Single: 7 July 1995: No. 29 - 3 weeks
UK CD box set THE SINGLES COLLECTION 1971-2006: 45 X 45s: 11 April 2011
USA CD box set THE SINGLES COLLECTION 1971-2006: 45 X 45s: 26 April 2011

I Go Wild was written by Mick Jagger in collaboration with Charlie Watts. The theme is back to rock and roll and the three guitarists provide a heavy battery of electric strings. Ron Wood uses the B-Bender again on his Telecaster creating that unique stretched sound. Clarence White invented the technique which provides a pedal steel effect with a bit of slide, pulling the b-note down. Mick is on rhythm guitar while Keith Richards looks after the riff. An angry, five-minute out-take just has Mick, Keith, Charlie and Darryl Jones running through the song (* a - 5.33).

Phil Jones was probably introduced to the band by Benmont Tench (from their times playing with Tom Petty) and he assists with percussion. There is another near five-minute out-take with vocals but without backing singers (* b - 4.40). Harsh imagery is used for the subject matter of the lyrics. There is a line about "waitresses with broken noses" supposedly included because Ronnie knew every waitress in Dublin.

There are also references to the garish, alcoholic wives of politicians who make sex difficult for their husbands. Bob Clearmountain mixed the album track instead of Don Was. *I Go Wild* was released as a single a year after the album to promote it for their 1995 European tour. Additional mixes were carried out by Scott Litt (of Nirvana and REM fame) at Louie's Clubhouse in Los Angeles - where he used more guitar licks - and Luis Resto, who did an extended re-mix in a disco style. The video was shot in Mexico City and featured spoof live playing of the track. Keith felt the album would be good played live and most tracks were ready for it. *I Go Wild* became a tour favourite during 1994/95. With the last track in the can in April 1994, it was expected that the album would be promoted by a tour, especially since the vibes surrounding the band felt so good. Mark Fisher was called to see if he could come up with something even more impressive than the Steel Wheels extravaganza.

1139. THE ROCKY ROAD TO DUBLIN (Trad Arranger: Paddy Moloney) 5.03
30 September - 1 October 1993: Place: Windmill Lane Studios, Dublin, Ireland.
Rolling Stones with Darryl Jones, Martin Fay, Sean Keane, Kevin Conneff, Matt Molloy, Paddy Moloney, Derek Bell, Colin James, James Blennerhassett, Brian Masterson, Jean Butler.
Producer: Paddy Moloney and Chris Kimsey.
Engineer: Chris Kimsey.
Assisted by Alistair McMillan.
UK LP THE CHIEFTAINS: THE LONG BLACK VEIL: 19 February 1995: No. 17 - 9 weeks
USA LP THE CHIEFTAINS: THE LONG BLACK VEIL: 19 February 1995: No. 22 - 19 weeks
USA CD THE WIDE WORLD OVER: A 40 YEAR CELEBRATION: 5 March 2002
UK CD THE WIDE WORLD OVER: A 40 YEAR CELEBRATION: 7 January 2003

The album THE LONG BLACK VEIL was a collaboration by the Chieftains with other artists. Chris Kimsey was the producer and was asked by Paddy Maloney to see if he could get the Stones to play. Luckily the Stones were in town so Paddy and Chris drove down to Ronnie's house to get their agreement. Other artists featured on the Chieftains album were Sting, Van Morrison, Sinead O'Connor, Mark Knopfler, Tom Jones, Ry Cooder and Marianne Faithfull. Mick Jagger and Darryl Jones played on the chilling *The Long Black Veil*.

All the band played on *The Rocky Road To Dublin* which, as Paddy describes it in the sleeve notes, was an "ad-lib hooley - at one time I thought I was in control. Clearly I wasn't. Each time I tried to end the session, the song just went on and on, with our friends in the studio getting up to dance. Jean Butler is credited for the Irish dancing and her steps can be clearly heard on the track. After the second verse and chorus, a distinctive lead guitar reproduces a slow *Satisfaction* riff and a quick jam circles around for some seconds before the third verse.

Again, after the next chorus, some *Satisfaction* frills are used alongside the fiddles. It was Paddy's idea to include this hint of the Stones involvement. The song lasts for five minutes so it was a good job that the usual five verses on this 19th-century song were cut to just three. As Paddy testifies, it was "perhaps the most enjoyable of our recording sessions." Chris Kimsey was credited as producer alongside Paddy for both contributions. It was edited for release on their 2002 THE WIDE WORLD OVER 40 year career collection (* a - 4.17).

1140. TROUBLE MAN (Gaye) 4.00
3 November - 16 December 1993: Place: Windmill Lane Studios, Dublin, Ireland.
Producer: Don Was, The Glimmer Twins.
Bootleg only.

During late November, the sessions had got to the point of over-dubbing backing vocals and play-backs. Ron Wood said that there were a lot of firsts with the album and one of those was Charlie Watts attending play-backs! *Trouble Man* is a real session out-take in so far as it is just Mick Jagger on piano and vocals warming up before proper recording. During a second version Keith Richards joins in on guitar (* a - 4.43).

Other tracks recorded during the lull in the proceedings were a minute and a bit of *It Takes A Lot To Laugh* (Dylan), *We Shall Overcome* (Horton, Hamilton, Carawan, Seeger), and Keith's favourite *Nearness Of You* (Carmichael, Washington). Keith was solo on *We Shall Overcome*; it was a song that he covered on his 1995 Jamaican project, which produced the album WINGLESS ANGELS on his own Mindless Records label. The album was recorded by Rob Fraboni in a stripped down fashion, with just five microphones, to get an authentic Jamaican feel. Most was recorded naturally in his living room at his tropical house named Point Of View in Jamaica.

1141. CAN'T GET NEXT TO YOU (Holland, Dozier, Holland) ⚡ 5.45
19 July 1994: Place: RPM Club, Toronto, Canada.
Rolling Stones with Jeff Healey, Darryl Jones, Chuck Leavell, Lisa Fischer, Bernard Fowler, Bobby Keys.
Bootleg only

At the end of the recording of VOODOO LOUNGE, Charlie Watts released a jazz-flavoured album, recorded with Bernard Fowler and titled WARM AND TENDER. The Stones' first album for Virgin, released in November 1993, was a compilation of hits from 1971 to 1989 labelled JUMP BACK. The success was partly due to the recordings being re-done with 20-bit technology, a treatment that was planned for eight other post-1970s albums, which would be given original artwork in a limited edition. In February, Keith Richards recorded three tracks with Jack Jones - *Say It's Not You* appeared on the album THE BRADLEY BARN SESSIONS.

On 3 May 1994, the Stones hired the Honey Fitz boat (an ex-Presidential yacht) and went down the Hudson River in New York to Pier 60 where 400 journalists were gathered for the announcement of the VOODOO LOUNGE album and tour. They also confirmed that the bass position would be filled by Darryl Jones. At least Ronnie Wood was happy that, after 19 years, he was no longer the new boy. The tour would start in the States and Canada in 1994 and proceed to Mexico and, for the first time, to South America in January and February 1995. South Africa would be visited for the first time in February, followed by an extensive Japanese tour in March and Australia and New Zealand in late March and early April.

Another first for a rock band was a 20-minute live Internet stream of their concert in Dallas, Texas, which was seen by only a few, due to the low quality and high bandwidth required - but the exercise showed that Jagger was being as innovative as ever. The European section would be during the summer of 1995. The tour rehearsals were at a school in Toronto in mid-June (flip-charts surrounded the band to build a set list for the tour). An aircraft hangar was hired at Toronto International Airport to put the stadium stage through its paces.

The RPM Club, in Toronto, provided the band with a venue for a warm-up gig. The $5 cover charge for entrance was re-distributed to support the plight of kids living on the streets. It was Darryl Jones' first gig with the band (only 100 more to do on the tour, Jagger quipped), although the seasoned professionals of Chuck Leavell, Lisa Fischer, Bernard Fowler and Bobby Keys were present. The Stones performed some new numbers strongly - *You Got Me Rocking, Sparks Will Fly, Love Is Strong, Brand New Car* and *I Go Wild. Live With Me, No Expectations* (Mick played guitar) and *Monkey Man* (with Lisa as co-vocalist) were resurrected from the past. The warm-up showed that *Monkey Man*, which had never before been tried live, needed some further work to its ending, as did *Love Is Strong* at the beginning. When Mick announced the band before *Street Fighting Man* he forgot to mention Charlie Watts during introductions but made amends at the start of the song. The support act for the gig was Canada's own blind blues guitarist, Jeff Healey. He was asked to guest with the band on the encore number, which was a 1969 Temptations' cover *Can't Get Next To You.*

Played by the Stones and the slide guitar of Jeff Healey that night, it was more of a blues affair rather than a soul number. In interviews afterwards, Chuck Leavell said that it was the best club gig he had ever done with a band. Ron Wood made a point of telling Bill Wyman that he was missing some great scenery, with reference to the bra-throwing that accompanied some numbers. Keith remarked that touching base with such a small crowd was much better than walking out on a stadium, which would be a bit dry. Mick Jagger thought that one show like the RPM was worth two weeks of rehearsal. Darryl Jones just beamed at being on stage with such a great band and was so looking forward to the impending tour. On 1 August 1994, with the warm-up completed, the opening show of the new tour at Robert F Kennedy Memorial Stadium, in Washington, beckoned.

1142. NOT FADE AWAY (Petty, Hardin) ✏ 2.39
14 August 1994: Place: Giants Stadium, The Meadowlands, New Jersey, USA.
Rolling Stones with Darryl Jones, Chuck Leavell, Lisa Fischer, Bernard Fowler, Bobby Keys, Michael Davis, Kent Smith, Andy Snitzer.
Producer: Eric Liekefet.
Director: Jim Gable, Executive Producer: Michael Cohl.
UK, USA Video Live Voodoo Live 94/95: September 1994

1143. TUMBLING DICE (Jagger, Richard) ✏ 4.02
14 August 1994: Place: Giants Stadium, The Meadowlands, New Jersey, USA.
Rolling Stones with Darryl Jones, Chuck Leavell, Lisa Fischer, Bernard Fowler, Bobby Keys, Michael Davis, Kent Smith, Andy Snitzer.
Producer: Eric Liekefet.
Director: Jim Gable, Executive Producer: Michael Cohl.
UK, USA Video Live Voodoo Live 94/95: September 1994

1144. YOU GOT ME ROCKING (Jagger, Richards) ✏ 3.45
14 August 1994: Place: Giants Stadium, The Meadowlands, New Jersey, USA.
Rolling Stones with Darryl Jones, Chuck Leavell, Lisa Fischer, Bernard Fowler, Bobby Keys, Michael Davis, Kent Smith, Andy Snitzer.
Producer: Eric Liekefet.
Director: Jim Gable, Executive Producer: Michael Cohl.
UK, USA Video Live Voodoo Live 94/95: September 1994

1145. SHATTERED (Jagger, Richards) ✏ 4.08
14 August 1994: Place: Giants Stadium, The Meadowlands, New Jersey, USA.
Rolling Stones with Darryl Jones, Chuck Leavell, Lisa Fischer, Bernard Fowler, Bobby Keys, Michael Davis, Kent Smith, Andy Snitzer.
Producer: Eric Liekefet.
Director: Jim Gable, Executive Producer: Michael Cohl.
UK, USA Video Live Voodoo Live 94/95: September 1994

1146. ROCKS OFF (Jagger, Richard) ✏ 5.05
14 August 1994: Place: Giants Stadium, The Meadowlands, New Jersey, USA.
Rolling Stones with Darryl Jones, Chuck Leavell, Lisa Fischer, Bernard Fowler, Bobby Keys, Michael Davis, Kent Smith, Andy Snitzer.
Producer: Eric Liekefet.
Director: Jim Gable, Executive Producer: Michael Cohl.
UK, USA Video Live Voodoo Live 94/95: September 1994

1147. SPARKS WILL FLY (Jagger, Richards) ✎ 4.29
14 August 1994: Place: Giants Stadium, The Meadowlands, New Jersey, USA.
Rolling Stones with Darryl Jones, Chuck Leavell, Lisa Fischer, Bernard Fowler, Bobby Keys, Michael Davis, Kent Smith, Andy Snitzer.
Producer: Eric Liekefet.
Director: Jim Gable, Executive Producer: Michael Cohl.
UK, USA Video Live Voodoo Live 94/95: September 1994

1148. (I CAN'T GET NO) SATISFACTION (Jagger, Richard) ✎ 5.28
14 August 1994: Place: Giants Stadium, The Meadowlands, New Jersey, USA.
Rolling Stones with Darryl Jones, Chuck Leavell, Lisa Fischer, Bernard Fowler, Bobby Keys, Michael Davis, Kent Smith, Andy Snitzer.
Producer: Eric Liekefet.
Director: Jim Gable, Executive Producer: Michael Cohl.
UK, USA Video Live Voodoo Live 94/95: September 1994

1149. OUT OF TEARS (Jagger, Richards) ✎ 5.33
14 August 1994: Place: Giants Stadium, The Meadowlands, New Jersey, USA.
Rolling Stones with Darryl Jones, Chuck Leavell, Lisa Fischer, Bernard Fowler, Bobby Keys, Michael Davis, Kent Smith, Andy Snitzer.
Producer: Eric Liekefet.
Director: Jim Gable, Executive Producer: Michael Cohl.
UK, USA Video Live Voodoo Live 94/95: September 1994

1150. MISS YOU (Jagger, Richards) ✎ 6.40
14 August 1994: Place: Giants Stadium, The Meadowlands, New Jersey, USA.
Rolling Stones with Darryl Jones, Chuck Leavell, Lisa Fischer, Bernard Fowler, Bobby Keys, Michael Davis, Kent Smith, Andy Snitzer.
Producer: Eric Liekefet.
Director: Jim Gable, Executive Producer: Michael Cohl.
UK, USA Video Live Voodoo Live 94/95: September 1994

1151. HONKY TONK WOMEN (Jagger, Richard) ✎ 4.48
14 August 1994: Place: Giants Stadium, The Meadowlands, New Jersey, USA.
Rolling Stones with Darryl Jones, Chuck Leavell, Lisa Fischer, Bernard Fowler, Bobby Keys, Michael Davis, Kent Smith, Andy Snitzer.
Producer: Eric Liekefet.
Director: Jim Gable, Executive Producer: Michael Cohl.
UK, USA Video Live Voodoo Live 94/95: September 1994

1152. THE WORST (Jagger, Richards) ✎ 2.49
14 August 1994: Place: Giants Stadium, The Meadowlands, New Jersey, USA.
Rolling Stones with Darryl Jones, Chuck Leavell, Lisa Fischer, Bernard Fowler, Bobby Keys, Michael Davis, Kent Smith, Andy Snitzer.
Producer: Eric Liekefet.
Director: Jim Gable, Executive Producer: Michael Cohl.
UK, USA Video Live Voodoo Live 94/95: September 1994

1153. MONKEY MAN (Jagger, Richard) ✎ 4.25
14 August 1994: Place: Giants Stadium, The Meadowlands, New Jersey, USA.
Rolling Stones with Darryl Jones, Chuck Leavell, Lisa Fischer, Bernard Fowler, Bobby Keys, Michael Davis, Kent Smith, Andy Snitzer.
Producer: Eric Liekefet.
Director: Jim Gable, Executive Producer: Michael Cohl.
UK, USA Video Live Voodoo Live 94/95: September 1994

1154. START ME UP (Jagger, Richards) ✎ 4.02
14 August 1994: Place: Giants Stadium, The Meadowlands, New Jersey, USA.
Rolling Stones with Darryl Jones, Chuck Leavell, Lisa Fischer, Bernard Fowler, Bobby Keys, Michael Davis, Kent Smith, Andy Snitzer.
Producer: Eric Liekefet.
Director: Jim Gable, Executive Producer: Michael Cohl.
UK, USA Video Live Voodoo Live 94/95: September 1994

1155. IT'S ONLY ROCK 'N' ROLL (Jagger, Richard) ✎ 4.49
14 August 1994: Place: Giants Stadium, The Meadowlands, New Jersey, USA.
Rolling Stones with Darryl Jones, Chuck Leavell, Lisa Fischer, Bernard Fowler, Bobby Keys, Michael Davis, Kent Smith, Andy Snitzer.
Producer: Eric Liekefet.
Director: Jim Gable, Executive Producer: Michael Cohl.
UK, USA Video Live Voodoo Live 94/95: September 1994

1156. STREET FIGHTING MAN (Jagger, Richard) ✏ 5.13
14 August 1994: Place: Giants Stadium, The Meadowlands, New Jersey, USA.
Rolling Stones with Darryl Jones, Chuck Leavell, Lisa Fischer, Bernard Fowler, Bobby Keys, Michael Davis, Kent Smith, Andy Snitzer.
Producer: Eric Liekefet.
Director: Jim Gable, Executive Producer: Michael Cohl.
UK, USA Video Live Voodoo Live 94/95: September 1994

1157. BROWN SUGAR (Jagger, Richard) ✏ 5.47
14 August 1994: Place: Giants Stadium, The Meadowlands, New Jersey, USA.
Rolling Stones with Darryl Jones, Chuck Leavell, Lisa Fischer, Bernard Fowler, Bobby Keys, Michael Davis, Kent Smith, Andy Snitzer.
Producer: Eric Liekefet.
Director: Jim Gable, Executive Producer: Michael Cohl.
UK, USA Video Live Voodoo Live 94/95: September 1994

1158. JUMPING JACK FLASH (Jagger, Richard) ✏ 5.49
14 August 1994: Place: Giants Stadium, The Meadowlands, New Jersey, USA.
Rolling Stones with Darryl Jones, Chuck Leavell, Lisa Fischer, Bernard Fowler, Bobby Keys, Michael Davis, Kent Smith, Andy Snitzer.
Producer: Eric Liekefet.
Director: Jim Gable, Executive Producer: Michael Cohl.
UK, USA Video Live Voodoo Live 94/95: September 1994

The tour logistics did not get any easier. The briefing from Mick Jagger for Mark Fisher was to make the set reflect a city of the future with an invisible flow of information. Mark Fisher and Jonathan Park created a set huge in scale and one that Mark hoped Prince Charles would hate architecturally. It was made from aluminium and stainless steel, flowing and curving, rather than without any square-edges. The result was a $4 million set, 100 metres wide and, at its peak, 27 meters high. The foundations were a sub-structure of steel and the huge Cobra steel shape was supported by a counter-weight of 45 tons of water.
It took 250 people four days to set up - this time three crews leap-frogged across the world. No wonder 56 trailers, nine buses and a Boeing 727 were needed to transport the entourage. Two huge towers supported the sound system as well as providing walkways which linked different parts of the stage. The web hanging from every corner of the set became a sea of lights computerised and synchronized to the music when the show came near to the climax. The "Jumbotron", the largest video screen ever used up to then, was an integral part of the set.
Images of the band six metres tall meshed into the background to contribute to the light show. When the Stones played four nights at Giants Stadium, in New Jersey, part of the show on a damp, wet, Sunday night was filmed, the resultant video being released for sale in September at the tour's merchandise shops. It opened with a roadie waking up and finding himself late for work, having slept with a girl and after having told her that he was Ronnie - when she discovered the truth, a sharp exit was required to the arena! The video was a great souvenir of the concert show. The actual film of *You Got Me Rocking* was used for promotional purposes on TV.
The tour progressed but, on 6 September, was hit by tragic news of the death of Nicky Hopkins at the age of 50. He had died as a result of surgery linked to Crohn's disease, which had troubled him for most of his life. In the latter stages of treatment, the Stones had paid for some of his hospital bills. Perhaps there was some guilt that being a session player for the Stones was hardly a lucrative career. Nicky felt he was short-changed not only financially but also because he attained no songwriting credits. It was a familiar tale that Nicky's friend Chuck Leavell could relate to.
Musician Julian Dawson who wrote an excellent biography titled *And On Piano . . . Nicky Hopkins* recorded a track with Nicky that became *You're Listening Now* from Julian's 1995 TRAVEL ON album. The last verse said it all, "It seems to me that dying has set you free somehow, and I know you're out there somewhere, and you're listening now." A short time after Nicky's death, on 22 October, Jimmy Miller also passed away, aged 52. His last successful project was with Primal Scream on their ground-breaking SCREAMADELICA album, which won a Mercury Prize in 1992.

1159. NOT FADE AWAY (Petty, Hardin) ✏ 2.54
25 November 1994: Place: Joe Robbie Stadium, Miami, Florida, USA.
Rolling Stones with Darryl Jones, Chuck Leavell.
Producer: David Hewitt.
Engineer: Mixed by: Bob Clearmountain.
Director: David Mallet, Producer: Rocky Oldham, Executive Producer: Michael Cohl.
UK, USA Video, DVD Voodoo Lounge: 21 November 1995

1160. TUMBLING DICE (Jagger, Richard) ✏ 4.01
25 November 1994: Place: Joe Robbie Stadium, Miami, Florida, USA.
Rolling Stones with Darryl Jones, Chuck Leavell, Lisa Fischer, Bernard Fowler, Bobby Keys, Michael Davis, Kent Smith, Andy Snitzer.
Producer: David Hewitt.
Engineer: Mixed by: Bob Clearmountain.
Director: David Mallet, Producer: Rocky Oldham, Executive Producer: Michael Cohl.
UK, USA Video, DVD Voodoo Lounge: 21 November 1995

1161. YOU GOT ME ROCKING (Jagger, Richards) ✏ 3.15
25 November 1994: Place: Joe Robbie Stadium, Miami, Florida, USA.
Rolling Stones with Darryl Jones, Chuck Leavell, Lisa Fischer, Bernard Fowler.
Producer: David Hewitt.
Engineer: Mixed by: Bob Clearmountain. Director: David Mallet, Producer: Rocky Oldham, Executive Producer: Michael Cohl.
UK, USA Video, DVD Voodoo Lounge: 21 November 1995

1162. ROCKS OFF (Jagger, Richard) ✏ 5.02
25 November 1994: Place: Joe Robbie Stadium, Miami, Florida, USA.
Rolling Stones with Darryl Jones, Chuck Leavell, Lisa Fischer, Bernard Fowler, Bobby Keys, Michael Davis, Kent Smith, Andy Snitzer.
Producer: David Hewitt.
Engineer: Mixed by: Bob Clearmountain. Director: David Mallet, Producer: Rocky Oldham, Executive Producer: Michael Cohl.
Bootleg only.

1163. SPARKS WILL FLY (Jagger, Richards) ✏ 4.19
25 November 1994: Place: Joe Robbie Stadium, Miami, Florida, USA.
Rolling Stones with Darryl Jones, Chuck Leavell, Lisa Fischer, Bernard Fowler.
Producer: David Hewitt.
Engineer: Mixed by: Bob Clearmountain.
Director: David Mallet, Producer: Rocky Oldham, Executive Producer: Michael Cohl.
Bootleg only.

1164. LIVE WITH ME (Jagger, Richard) ✏ 4.31
25 November 1994: Place: Joe Robbie Stadium, Miami, Florida, USA.
Rolling Stones, Darryl Jones, Chuck Leavell, Lisa Fischer, Bernard Fowler, Cheryl Crow, Bobby Keys.
Producer: David Hewitt.
Engineer: Mixed by: Bob Clearmountain.
Director: David Mallet, Producer: Rocky Oldham, Executive Producer: Michael Cohl.
Bootleg only.

1165. (I CAN'T GET NO) SATISFACTION (Jagger, Richard) ✏ 5.28
25 November 1994: Place: Joe Robbie Stadium, Miami, Florida, USA.
Rolling Stones, Darryl Jones, Chuck Leavell, Lisa Fischer, Bernard Fowler.
Producer: David Hewitt.
Engineer: Mixed by: Bob Clearmountain.
Director: David Mallet, Producer: Rocky Oldham, Executive Producer: Michael Cohl.
UK, USA Video, DVD Voodoo Lounge: 21 November 1995

1166. BEAST OF BURDEN (Jagger, Richards) ✏ 5.48
25 November 1994: Place: Joe Robbie Stadium, Miami, Florida, USA.
Rolling Stones with Darryl Jones, Chuck Leavell, Lisa Fischer, Bernard Fowler.
Producer: David Hewitt.
Engineer: Mixed by: Bob Clearmountain.
Director: David Mallet, Producer: Rocky Oldham, Executive Producer: Michael Cohl.
Bootleg only.

1167. ANGIE (Jagger, Richard) ✏ 3.30
25 November 1994: Place: Joe Robbie Stadium, Miami, Florida, USA.
Rolling Stones with Darryl Jones, Chuck Leavell.
Producer: David Hewitt.
Engineer: Mixed by: Bob Clearmountain.
Director: David Mallet, Producer: Rocky Oldham, Executive Producer: Michael Cohl.
UK, USA Video, DVD Voodoo Lounge: 21 November 1995

1168. DEAD FLOWERS (Jagger, Richard) ✏ 4.23
25 November 1994: Place: Joe Robbie Stadium, Miami, Florida, USA.
Rolling Stones with Darryl Jones, Chuck Leavell.
Producer: David Hewitt.
Engineer: Mixed by: Bob Clearmountain.
Director: David Mallet, Producer: Rocky Oldham, Executive Producer: Michael Cohl.
Bootleg only.

1169. SWEET VIRGINIA (Jagger, Richard) ✏ 4.34
25 November 1994: Place: Joe Robbie Stadium, Miami, Florida, USA.
Rolling Stones with Darryl Jones, Whoopi Goldberg, Chuck Leavell, Lisa Fischer, Bernard Fowler, Bobby Keys.
Producer: David Hewitt.
Engineer: Mixed by: Bob Clearmountain.
Director: David Mallet, Producer: Rocky Oldham, Executive Producer: Michael Cohl.
UK, USA Video, DVD Voodoo Lounge: 21 November 1995

1170.   DOO DOO DOO DOO (HEARTBREAKER) (Jagger, Richard) ⤩ 3.57
25 November 1994: Place: Joe Robbie Stadium, Miami, Florida, USA.
Rolling Stones with Darryl Jones, Chuck Leavell, Lisa Fischer, Bernard Fowler, Bobby Keys, Michael Davis, Kent Smith, Andy Snitzer.
Producer: David Hewitt.
Engineer: Mixed by: Bob Clearmountain.
Director: David Mallet, Producer: Rocky Oldham, Executive Producer: Michael Cohl.
Bootleg only.

1171.   IT'S ALL OVER NOW (Womack, Womack) ⤩ 3.32
25 November 1994: Place: Joe Robbie Stadium, Miami, Florida, USA.
Rolling Stones with Darryl Jones, Chuck Leavell, Lisa Fischer, Bernard Fowler.
Producer: David Hewitt.
Engineer: Mixed by: Bob Clearmountain.
Director: David Mallet, Producer: Rocky Oldham, Executive Producer: Michael Cohl.
UK, USA Video, DVD Voodoo Lounge: 21 November 1995

1172.   STOP BREAKING DOWN (Johnson) ⤩ 4.20
25 November 1994: Place: Joe Robbie Stadium, Miami, Florida, USA.
Rolling Stones with Darryl Jones, Robert Cray, Chuck Leavell.
Producer: David Hewitt.
Engineer: Mixed by: Bob Clearmountain.
Director: David Mallet, Producer: Rocky Oldham, Executive Producer: Michael Cohl.
UK, USA Video, DVD Voodoo Lounge: 21 November 1995

1173.   WHO DO YOU LOVE (McDaniel) ⤩ 3.59
25 November 1994: Place: Joe Robbie Stadium, Miami, Florida, USA.
Rolling Stones with Darryl Jones, Bo Diddley, Chuck Leavell.
Producer: David Hewitt.
Engineer: Mixed by: Bob Clearmountain.
Director: David Mallet, Producer: Rocky Oldham, Executive Producer: Michael Cohl.
UK, USA Video, DVD Voodoo Lounge: 21 November 1995

1174.   I GO WILD (Jagger, Richards) ⤩ 6.30
25 November 1994: Place: Joe Robbie Stadium, Miami, Florida, USA.
Rolling Stones with Chuck Leavell, Lisa Fischer, Bernard Fowler.
Producer: David Hewitt.
Engineer: Mixed by: Bob Clearmountain.
UK CD Track Single: I Go Wild (Album Version): 4 April 1995
USA CD Track Single: I Go Wild (Album Version): 15 May 1995
UK CD box set THE SINGLES COLLECTION 1971-2006: 45 X 45s: 11 April 2011
USA CD box set THE SINGLES COLLECTION 1971-2006: 45 X 45s: 26 April 2011

1175.   MISS YOU (Jagger, Richards) ⤩ 9.27
25 November 1994: Place: Joe Robbie Stadium, Miami, Florida, USA.
Rolling Stones with Darryl Jones, Chuck Leavell, Lisa Fischer, Bernard Fowler, Bobby Keys.
Producer: David Hewitt.
Engineer: Mixed by: Bob Clearmountain.
Director: David Mallet, Producer: Rocky Oldham, Executive Producer: Michael Cohl.
UK, USA Video, DVD Voodoo Lounge: 21 November 1995

1176.   HONKY TONK WOMEN (Jagger, Richard) ⤩ 4.13
25 November 1994: Place: Joe Robbie Stadium, Miami, Florida, USA.
Rolling Stones with Darryl Jones, Chuck Leavell, Lisa Fischer, Bernard Fowler, Bobby Keys, Michael Davis, Kent Smith, Andy Snitzer.
Producer: David Hewitt. Engineer: Mixed by: Bob Clearmountain.
Director: David Mallet, Producer: Rocky Oldham, Executive Producer: Michael Cohl.
UK, USA Video, DVD Voodoo Lounge: 21 November 1995

1177.   BEFORE THEY MAKE ME RUN (Jagger, Richard) ⤩ 4.12
25 November 1994: Place: Joe Robbie Stadium, Miami, Florida, USA.
Rolling Stones with Darryl Jones, Chuck Leavell, Lisa Fischer, Bernard Fowler, Bobby Keys.
Producer: David Hewitt. Engineer: Mixed by: Bob Clearmountain.
Director: David Mallet, Producer: Rocky Oldham, Executive Producer: Michael Cohl.
Bootleg only.

1178. THE WORST (Jagger, Richards) ✎ 2.35
25 November 1994: Place: Joe Robbie Stadium, Miami, Florida, USA.
Rolling Stones with Darryl Jones, Chuck Leavell.
Producer: David Hewitt.
Engineer: Mixed by: Bob Clearmountain.
Director: David Mallet, Producer: Rocky Oldham, Executive Producer: Michael Cohl.
UK, USA Video, DVD Voodoo Lounge: 21 November 1995

1179. SYMPATHY FOR THE DEVIL (Jagger, Richard) ✎ 5.57
25 November 1994: Place: Joe Robbie Stadium, Miami, Florida, USA.
Rolling Stones with Darryl Jones, Chuck Leavell, Lisa Fischer, Bernard Fowler.
Producer: David Hewitt.
Engineer: Mixed by: Bob Clearmountain.
Director: David Mallet, Producer: Rocky Oldham, Executive Producer: Michael Cohl.
UK, USA Video, DVD Voodoo Lounge: 21 November 1995

1180. MONKEY MAN (Jagger, Richard) ✎ 4.22
25 November 1994: Place: Joe Robbie Stadium, Miami, Florida, USA.
Rolling Stones with Darryl Jones, Chuck Leavell, Lisa Fischer, Bernard Fowler.
Producer: David Hewitt.
Engineer: Mixed by: Bob Clearmountain.
Director: David Mallet, Producer: Rocky Oldham, Executive Producer: Michael Cohl.
Bootleg only.

1181. STREET FIGHTING MAN (Jagger, Richard) ✎ 5.12
25 November 1994: Place: Joe Robbie Stadium, Miami, Florida, USA.
Rolling Stones with Darryl Jones, Chuck Leavell, Lisa Fischer, Bernard Fowler.
Producer: David Hewitt.
Engineer: Mixed by: Bob Clearmountain.
Director: David Mallet, Producer: Rocky Oldham, Executive Producer: Michael Cohl.
Bootleg only.

1182. START ME UP (Jagger, Richards) ✎ 3.56
25 November 1994: Place: Joe Robbie Stadium, Miami, Florida, USA.
Rolling Stones with Darryl Jones, Chuck Leavell, Lisa Fischer, Bernard Fowler.
Producer: David Hewitt.
Engineer: Mixed by: Bob Clearmountain.
Director: David Mallet, Producer: Rocky Oldham, Executive Producer: Michael Cohl.
UK, USA Video, DVD Voodoo Lounge: 21 November 1995

1183. IT'S ONLY ROCK 'N' ROLL (Jagger, Richard) ✎ 4.57
25 November 1994: Place: Joe Robbie Stadium, Miami, Florida, USA.
Rolling Stones with Darryl Jones, Chuck Leavell, Lisa Fischer, Bernard Fowler.
Producer: David Hewitt.
Engineer: Mixed by: Bob Clearmountain.
Director: David Mallet, Producer: Rocky Oldham, Executive Producer: Michael Cohl.
UK, USA Video, DVD Voodoo Lounge: 21 November 1995

1184. BROWN SUGAR (Jagger, Richard) ✎ 5.40
25 November 1994: Place: Joe Robbie Stadium, Miami, Florida, USA.
Rolling Stones with Darryl Jones, Chuck Leavell, Lisa Fischer, Bernard Fowler, Bobby Keys.
Producer: David Hewitt.
Engineer: Mixed by: Bob Clearmountain.
Director: David Mallet, Producer: Rocky Oldham, Executive Producer: Michael Cohl.
UK, USA Video, DVD Voodoo Lounge: 21 November 1995

1185. JUMPIN' JACK FLASH (Jagger, Richard) ✎ 5.35
25 November 1994: Place: Joe Robbie Stadium, Miami, Florida, USA.
Rolling Stones with Darryl Jones, Whoopi Goldberg, Chuck Leavell, Lisa Fischer, Bernard Fowler, Bobby Keys, Michael Davis, Kent Smith, Andy Snitzer.
Producer: David Hewitt.
Engineer: Mixed by: Bob Clearmountain.
Director: David Mallet, Producer: Rocky Oldham, Executive Producer: Michael Cohl.
UK, USA Video, DVD Voodoo Lounge: 21 November 1995

The VOODOO LOUNGE tour gimmicks opened with the Cobra, a huge curved semi-arch overshadowing the stage. Lights gradually flashed on from the tail to the head, from which flames spewed out, giving a feeling of impending doom. Rhythmic drums whooped out of the PA, Charlie Watts picking up the beat and creating the Diddley shuffle. A lift brought Mick Jagger up from below to the point at the front a smoke-ridden stage, where he opened with *Not Fade Away*. This entrance was dropped by the time the tour reached Miami when Mick simply strolled out from stage right before the rest of the band assembled.

Still the song climaxed with fireworks stage left and right. The concert from the Joe Robbie Stadium was chosen for a pay-per-view TV event introduced by Whoopi Goldberg. During *Tumbling Dice*, the band were joined by their supporting musicians, the number of which Keith had been keen to reduce from the large entourage used on the Steel Wheels tour. He did not want the band to have to rely too much on the support of others. On the VOODOO LOUNGE tour, there were Lisa Fischer and Bernard Fowler, who appeared on the left during *Tumbling Dice* next to Ron Wood and Mick.

The brass sounds by Bobby Keys, Michael Davis, Kent Smith and Andy Snitzer went to Keith's right on one of the hanging gantries. The large jumbo videotron was also used to supply computerised images for tracks like *You Got Me Rocking* and *Sparks Will Fly*. On the pay-per-view event, Sheryl Crow joined Mick to sing co-vocals on *Live With Me*. She looked a little awkward following behind Mick's strutting. *Satisfaction* was followed by the slower *Beast Of Burden*. An innovation at the Miami concert was a mini stage, complete with drum kit, keyboards and stools.

This was the beginning of the concept of a B-stage for, as *Angie* opened, the stage moved out into the crowd, who were a few feet away and started throwing clothing and scarves to the band in an attempt to make eye contact. U2 were the inspiration for this as they had used a B-Stage on their Zoo TV Tour, for an acoustic set mid-audience, in 1992/93. *Dead Flowers* and *Sweet Virginia* finished this small-stage landmark in Stones' touring history. During *Sweet Virginia*, the sax and backing vocals were played on the main stage as there was no room for everybody.

The event returned to the main stage and continued with *Heartbreaker* and *It's All Over Now* (the video screen changing to a scratchy black and white to emphasise the age of the song). Another guest, Robert Cray, came on to sing co-vocals and play blues lead guitar on EXILE's *Stop Breaking Down*. The great Bo Diddley, with his square guitar, rocked up a rhythm with *Who Do You Love* before the band went wild, Mick on guitar for *I Go Wild* - this enabled the four guitarists to go head-banging (some poetic licence here!) together at the front of the stage.

This track was one of the few to become available on CD. Darryl Jones' turn came on *Miss You* as he vented the 70s bass beat, Lisa vamped herself around the stage and Ronnie sidled and looned with Bobby on his gantry during the sax solo. The Voodoo video women perform on the jumbotron during *Honky Tonk Women* and Keith delivers a mock piano solo on Chuck Leavell's keyboard. Mick introduced the Honky Tonk Man for *Before They Make Me Run* and *The Worst*, where Ron is featured on a Hawaiian table steel.

A short Voodoo animation film follows before the samba beat of *Sympathy* opens and Mick appears from the lift dressed as a Voodoo witch doctor. At this point, the look of the stage is changed by the use of blow-up images of the Virgin Mary, a Voodoo doctor, a Goat's head, a cobra, a Hindu goddess, the cult western "young" Elvis and a Shiva-like Indian goddess. Keyboards announce *Monkey Man* and Lisa duets with Mick on a song which was a permanent tour feature.

The set picked up a head of steam with *Street Fighting Man* as the lights were used to create a visual bomb blast display. The pyrotechnics exploded for *Start Me Up* and white light and smoke was everywhere - the inflatables disappeared. *It's Only Rock And Roll* and *Brown Sugar* concluded the show as the ringed neck of the cobra became erect.

The encore was *Jumping Jack Flash*, which gave Keith an opportunity to slap hands with the crowd in the pit. Fireworks concluded the event as usual. A video released in 1995 and simply titled *Voodoo Lounge*, had 17 of the 27 Miami tracks played on it. It won a TEC award for Bob Clearmountain's monitor set-up. The show, titled *Hoodoo U Voodoo*, was broadcast in full for pay-per-view television. Overall the tour was musically looser than STEEL WHEELS, the set lists were varied, which demonstrated overall confidence and the overblown keyboards, horns and vocal sections were cut back to create more of a band than a show band.

1186. OUT OF TEARS (Jagger, Richards) ✏ 5.23
25 February 1995: Place: Ellis Park, Johannesburg, South Africa.
Rolling Stones with Darryl Jones, Chuck Leavell, Lisa Fischer, Bernard Fowler.
Bootleg only.

South Africa had always been blacklisted by the band in the past due to the government's racial discrimination and apartheid legislation. However, there were signs of change as Nelson Mandela was freed on 11 February 1990, which led to the first non-racial election during April 1994 and a 63 per cent vote victory for the ANC. In May 1994, Mandela was inaugurated as the new South African president and this paved the way for the Stones to visit in 1995 for two concerts at Ellis Park Stadium, in Johannesburg. As Keith Richards said before the concert, "the time is right", though to date, they have not ventured back.

Whitney Houston had set the pace in 1994 but security was a huge issue and many people were mugged. The concerts of 1995 started in January with Roxette, February for the Stones and March for Phil Collins. Ten days before the concert season began, the police were still unaware of the security arrangements. Pro-tect International were chosen for internal stadium and VIP security and the Roxette concert proceeded with limited disruption - so they would be hired for the Stones concert, too. The Stones had just finished another "first" with a tumultuous welcome to the South American leg of the tour in Brazil, Argentina and Chile. Jane Rose recalled that, particularly the five Argentinian concerts at the River Plate Stadium, were quite extraordinary for the crowd reaction and the most incredible she had ever witnessed. Then, using a container ship and four jumbo jets, the Stones took their massive stage set-up for their first concert on the African continent. Mick Jagger was brief as usual during the introductions simply saying - welcome to the Voodoo Lounge and that Johannesburg would give you a nice welcome. He asked if there was anyone from out of town such as Pretoria, Durban and Cape Town.

The whole concert was broadcast on television and radio by SABC. The set list was similar to other shows and, after an uproarious *Satisfaction*, they slowed it down for older members of the audience (Mick's words) with *Out Of Tears* and *Angie*. *Out Of Tears* was opened delicately by Chuck Leavell on piano and had Mick on electric guitar. The solo was performed by Ronnie Wood on bottleneck slide guitar. During the introductions, Ron referred to Mick as the "Dartford diablo", Darryl Jones did a show of brotherhood by clenching his arm poignantly and Keith claimed it was "good to be in Africa, 30 years and I walked all the way!" For Bernard Fowler it was an emotional visit and he likened it to being back home for the first time.

1187. PARACHUTE WOMAN (Jagger, Richard)
3 - 4 March 1995: Place: Toshiba-EMI Studios, Tokyo, Japan.
Rolling Stones with Darryl Jones, Chuck Leavell.
Producer: Don Was, The Glimmer Twins.
Engineer: Ed Cherney.
Unavailable.

After their concerts in South Africa, the Stones arrived in Tokyo and recorded tracks at EMI for a new album, combining studio tracks and live performances. The idea from the Toronto "school" rehearsal was to show another side of the Stones. There had been talk of them doing an Unplugged recording and this was their way of achieving something similar, stripped back to the quick. Chuck Leavell had experience of the format when he recorded with Eric Clapton for his 1992 UNPLUGGED album. When approached by MTV, Mick Jagger declined the invite saying it would have been scheduled during the European leg of the tour. He would have also realised that the format had been going since 1989. A number of tracks were not released, some surfaced as unofficial out-takes while others like *Parachute Woman* are not available. However, if you wanted to put a marker up as the type of tracks to play, then this was one such number.

Don Was and Ed Cherney (invited by Don) recorded the session and were very pleased with the performance and production. They had just finished attending the Grammys in Los Angeles, where they were both presented with production and engineer awards for Bonnie Raitt's LONGING IN THEIR HEARTS. They travelled overnight to Tokyo where the band were waiting for them in the studio.

1188. NO EXPECTATIONS (Jagger, Richard) 5.01
3 - 4 March 1995: Place: Toshiba-EMI Studios, Tokyo, Japan.
Rolling Stones with Darryl Jones, Chuck Leavell.
Producer: Don Was, The Glimmer Twins.
Engineer: Ed Cherney.
Bootleg only.

It was a pleasure for Ronnie Wood to play on tracks like *No Expectations* in the studio. He played slide guitar, a role Brian Jones had performed before. Like *Honest I Do*, *No Expectations* is an excellent out-take.

1189. LET IT BLEED (Jagger, Richard) 1.05
3 - 4 March 1995: Place: Toshiba-EMI Studios, Tokyo, Japan.
Rolling Stones with Darryl Jones, Chuck Leavell.
Producer: Don Was, The Glimmer Twins.
Engineer: Ed Cherney.
Bootleg only.

Only a snatch of the first verse is heard on this one minute out-take. Ronnie Wood plays slide guitar and there is a piano accompaniment.

1190. BEAST OF BURDEN (Jagger, Richards) 3.30
3 - 4 March 1995: Place: Toshiba-EMI Studios, Tokyo, Japan.
Rolling Stones with Darryl Jones, Chuck Leavell.
Producer: Don Was, The Glimmer Twins.
Engineer: Ed Cherney.
Bootleg only.

Soft, gentle acoustic guitars and the organ accompany the vocals of Mick Jagger. He changes some of the lyrics as he recollects the song.

1191. MEMORY MOTEL (Jagger, Richards) 6.21
3 - 4 March 1995: Place: Toshiba-EMI Studios, Tokyo, Japan.
Rolling Stones with Darryl Jones, Chuck Leavell.
Producer: Don Was, The Glimmer Twins.
Engineer: Ed Cherney.
Bootleg only.

The soft tones of the piano introduce *Memory Motel* from the BLACK AND BLUE album. Mick Jagger played with the lyrics - there was no mention of the peachy kind of girl or her nose being slightly curved. Keith Richards performs backing vocals and, as in the original, also contributes his couple of lines but repeating the same one as if they did not have the lyrics or a prompter in front of them. The mood is country flavoured, a similar theme to that on STRIPPED.

1192. THE WORST (Jagger, Richards)
3 - 4 March 1995: Place: Toshiba-EMI Studios, Tokyo, Japan.
Rolling Stones with Darryl Jones, Chuck Leavell.
Producer: Don Was, The Glimmer Twins.
Engineer: Ed Cherney.
Unavailable

Some of the tracks are distinctly Keith Richards led. Another that has not surfaced from the sessions.

1193. LOVE IN VAIN (Payne Adapted by Jagger, Richards) 5.31
3 - 4 March 1995: Place: Toshiba-EMI Studios, Tokyo, Japan.
Rolling Stones with Darryl Jones, Chuck Leavell.
Producer: Don Was, The Glimmer Twins.
Engineer: Peter Brandt, Henk Van Helvoirt, Sander Nagel, Rene Suydendorp, Ronnie Rivera, Masaaki Ugajih, Kazuaki Fujita.
Recorded by: Ed Cherney. Mixed by: Bob Clearmountain. Assisted by: Ryan Freeland. Mastered by: Stephen Marcussen. Digitally edited by: Ron Boustead.
UK CD LP STRIPPED: 13 November 1995: No. 9 - 11 weeks
USA CD LP STRIPPED: 13 November 1995: No. 9 - 19 weeks

The Stones always loved to play with the arrangements of a song, throwing it around and seeing what happened. Keith Richards said at the end of VOODOO LOUNGE that it was not until you got the song on the road that it would take on other qualities. Some of the studio scenes were recorded for a promotional film, including conversations. At the beginning of *Love In Vain*, they announced "basher" Watts as he arrived.

During the documentary, Mick Jagger recites the line "when the train comes in the station" and Keith replies in his mock English accent, "Paddington, or is that Waterloo or Blackfriars, Charing Cross?" Talking of trains, while in Tokyo playing their gigs, on 20 March, there was a domestic terrorist attack using Sarin gas on the Tokyo Subway, aimed at government employees and causing 13 deaths and many casualties.

Love In Vain has a false start due to Keith missing the right note. Only a band totally comfortable with their profession would allow a mistake to be recorded in such a way. The first verse has just Keith and Mick until the drums roll in. The bottleneck dobro slide guitar was played by Ronnie Wood and there was a different studio arrangement with the inclusion of keyboards and mouth organ.

1194. SLIPPING AWAY (Jagger, Richards) 4.55
3 - 4 March 1995: Place: Toshiba-EMI Studios, Tokyo, Japan.
Rolling Stones with Darryl Jones, Chuck Leavell, Bernard Fowler, Lisa Fischer, Bobby Keys, Andy Snitzer, Michael Davis, Kent Smith.
Producer: Don Was, The Glimmer Twins.
Engineer: Peter Brandt, Henk Van Helvoirt, Sander Nagel, Rene Suydendorp, Ronnie Rivera, Masaaki Ugajih, Kazuaki Fujita.
Recorded by: Ed Cherney. Mixed by: Bob Clearmountain. Assisted by: Ryan Freeland. Mastered by: Stephen Marcussen. Digitally edited by: Ron Boustead.
UK CD LP STRIPPED: 13 November 1995: No. 9 - 11 weeks
USA CD LP STRIPPED: 13 November 1995: No. 9 - 19 weeks

Keith Richards was encouraged by the rest of the band to record *Slipping Away* because it was one of those album cuts which, at that point, had not been covered live and was in danger of disappearing. The New West Horns enjoyed playing on the track and Lisa Fischer joined Keith on the vocal. The result was, as he says at the end, "sweet".

1195. HONEST I DO (Reed) 3.57
3 - 4 March 1995: Place: Toshiba-EMI Studios, Tokyo, Japan.
Rolling Stones with Darryl Jones, Chuck Leavell, Bernard Fowler.
Producer: Don Was, The Glimmer Twins.
Compilation USA CD: HOPE FLOATS: 7 April 1998.

One of the joys of the STRIPPED sessions was to hear the band in the studio recording authentic blues; it made fans want a whole album of such tunes. The sessions were captured live as the whole band played together, which created a pure atmosphere. On *Honest I Do*, the electric and acoustic guitars blend perfectly and equally, each being as important as the other. Mick Jagger plays mouth organ and Chuck Leavell piano. This track would only be available on a bootleg recording if it had not been for a soundtrack album featuring country-influenced artists. HOPE FLOATS was a compilation to support the film of the same name and was released in 1998.

1196. THE SPIDER AND THE FLY (Jagger, Richard) 3.28
3 - 4 March 1995: Place: Toshiba-EMI Studios, Tokyo, Japan.
Rolling Stones with Chuck Leavell.
Producer: Don Was, The Glimmer Twins.
Engineer: Peter Brandt, Henk Van Helvoirt, Sander Nagel, Rene Suydendorp, Ronnie Rivera, Masaaki Ugajih, Kazuaki Fujita.
Recorded by: Ed Cherney. Mixed by: Bob Clearmountain. Assisted by: Ryan Freeland. Mastered by: Stephen Marcussen. Digitally edited by: Ron Boustead.
UK CD LP STRIPPED: 13 November 1995: No. 9 - 11 weeks
USA CD LP STRIPPED: 13 November 1995: No. 9 - 19 weeks

The Spider And The Fly was a track that had only been released in the UK as a B-side to *Satisfaction* and on a dodgy compilation album, STONE AGE. The song had not been played by the Stones for 30 years. Mick Jagger said that it was like a terrible Rolling Stones' game show where you try and guess the lyrics. So, with acoustics strapped on, Charlie Watts on the brushes and a piano, they tackled the track again, Mick describing the experience as being like stuck in a time warp. Mick changed the lyrics slightly to suit his preferred delivery and the original 30-year-old girl with whom he had considered running away became 50.

1197. WILD HORSES (Jagger, Richard) 5.09
3 - 4 March 1995: Place: Toshiba-EMI Studios, Tokyo, Japan.
Rolling Stones with Darryl Jones, Chuck Leavell.
Producer: Don Was, The Glimmer Twins.
Engineer: Peter Brandt, Henk Van Helvoirt, Sander Nagel, Rene Suydendorp, Ronnie Rivera, Masaaki Ugajih, Kazuaki Fujita.
Recorded by: Ed Cherney. Mixed by: Bob Clearmountain. Assisted by: Ryan Freeland. Mastered by: Stephen Marcussen. Digitally edited by: Ron Boustead.
UK CD LP STRIPPED: 13 November 1995: No. 9 - 11 weeks
USA CD LP STRIPPED: 13 November 1995: No. 9 - 19 weeks
UK CD Single: 11 March 1996
USA CD LP ROLLING STONES RARITIES 1971-2003: 22 November 2005: No. 76 - 6 weeks
UK CD LP ROLLING STONES RARITIES 1971-2003: 28 November 2005
e-EP Track Wild Horses: 20 November 2009

Wild Horses had recently been added to the tour repertoire. They tried it in the studio and Keith Richards enjoyed being able to add some harmony vocals which were not on the original. It was a lighter and freer version creating space for the guitars. The track was cut by a minute for a promotional single including *I'm Free* from the album and also the non-edited take (* a - 4.07). The full version was released as a single in 1996, with three live songs from the tour not available before (*Live With Me*, *Tumbling Dice* and *Gimme Shelter*).

1198. **LET'S SPEND THE NIGHT TOGETHER** (Jagger, Richard) 3.20
3 - 4 March 1995: Place: Toshiba-EMI Studios, Tokyo, Japan.
Rolling Stones with Darryl Jones, Chuck Leavell.
Producer: Don Was, The Glimmer Twins.
Engineer: Ed Cherney.
Bootleg only.

Some tracks, like *Let's Spend The Night Together*, were etched so well in the memory that they did not need a reminder of how they went. This arrangement, played at a slower pace, has an acoustic guitar base, the normal piano and Keith Richards' vocals are heard well up in the mix. It does not have the normal harmony "ba ba ba bap" vocals.

1199. **THE LAST TIME** (Jagger, Richard)
3 - 4 March 1995: Place: Toshiba-EMI Studios, Tokyo, Japan.
Rolling Stones with Darryl Jones, Chuck Leavell.
Producer: Don Was, The Glimmer Twins.
Engineer: Ed Cherney.
Unavailable.

1200. **ANGIE** (Jagger, Richard)
3 - 4 March 1995: Place: Toshiba-EMI Studios, Tokyo, Japan.
Rolling Stones with Darryl Jones, Chuck Leavell.
Producer: Don Was, The Glimmer Twins.
Engineer: Ed Cherney.
Unavailable.

1201. **MAKE NO MISTAKE** (Richards, Jordan)
3 - 4 March 1995: Place: Toshiba-EMI Studios, Tokyo, Japan.
Rolling Stones with Darryl Jones, Chuck Leavell, Bernard Fowler.
Producer: Don Was, The Glimmer Twins.
Engineer: Ed Cherney.
Unavailable.

1202. **HEARTBEAT** (Montgomery, Petty)
3 - 4 March 1995: Place: Toshiba-EMI Studios, Tokyo, Japan.
Rolling Stones with Darryl Jones, Chuck Leavell, Bernard Fowler.
Producer: Don Was, The Glimmer Twins.
Engineer: Ed Cherney.
Unavailable.

One can assume that some tracks were made while Mick Jagger was out of the studio - certainly it can be said for the last two numbers, *Make No Mistake* being from Keith Richards' solo album TALK IS CHEAP.

1203. **LITTLE BABY** (Dixon) 4.00
3 - 4 March 1995: Place: Toshiba-EMI Studios, Tokyo, Japan.
Rolling Stones with Darryl Jones, Chuck Leavell.
Producer: Don Was, The Glimmer Twins.
Engineer: Peter Brandt, Henk Van Helvoirt, Sander Nagel, Rene Suydendorp, Ronnie Rivera, Masaaki Ugajih, Kazuaki Fujita.
Recorded by: Ed Cherney. Mixed by: Bob Clearmountain. Assisted by: Ryan Freeland. Mastered by: Stephen Marcussen. Digitally edited by: Ron Boustead.
UK CD LP STRIPPED: 13 November 1995: No. 9 - 11 weeks
USA CD LP STRIPPED: 13 November 1995: No. 9 - 19 weeks

The boys swing on this Howlin' Wolf number written by Willie Dixon. It was Mick Jagger's idea to tackle it as it had never been captured before in the studio. They recorded it in one take. Electric guitars and the solid bass guitar of Darryl Jones flinch together as Charlie Watts drum beat rides for attention with Mick Jagger's vocals. Both guitars solo in classic style to Chuck Leavell's tinkering piano. The fade-out is a little unrehearsed but nonetheless sweet for that.

1204. **I'M LEFT, YOU'RE RIGHT, SHE'S GONE** (Kesler, Taylor)
3 - 4 March 1995: Place: Toshiba-EMI Studios, Tokyo, Japan.
Rolling Stones with Darryl Jones, Chuck Leavell, Bernard Fowler.
Producer: Don Was, The Glimmer Twins.
Engineer: Ed Cherney.
Unavailable.

The conclusion of the session and a well-known song, notably from Elvis Presley's Sun Sessions, recorded in March 1955. Mick Jagger and Keith Richards had first played it under their first incarnation of Little Boy Blue & The Blue Boys. Stan Kesler was a Sun session guitarist while Bill Taylor was a Sun trumpeter and vocalist in his own right. The session, recorded by Ed Cherney, was a great success and seven tracks were released. Video was also made which appeared on a STRIPPED documentary. There was an idea of a special, featuring just the Tokyo sessions but Mick Jagger rejected it as it would make "the dullest TV ever . . . without an audience".

1205.   ANGIE (Jagger, Richard) ✎ 3.52
6 March 1995: Place: Tokyo Dome, Tokyo, Japan.
Rolling Stones with Darryl Jones, Chuck Leavell.
Producer: Don Was, The Glimmer Twins.
Engineer: Ed Cherney.
Japan CD BRIDGES TO BABYLON: 27 September 1997

Angie was recorded at the first concert in Japan and, due to its popularity, was included as a bonus track on the next studio album BRIDGES TO BABYLON.

1206.   NOT FADE AWAY (Petty, Hardin) ✎ 2.50
12 March 1995: Place: Tokyo Dome, Tokyo, Japan.
Rolling Stones with Darryl Jones, Chuck Leavell.
Producer: Yasumi Takeuch, Kazuo Dobashi.
Engineer: Benji Lefevre, Satoru Fujii, Yoshiyasu Kumada.
Japan Video Voodoo Lounge In Japan: September 1995

In total, nine concerts were played in Japan, seven at the Tokyo Dome baseball stadium and two at the Fukuoka Dome. The Tokyo Dome (Tokyo's Big-Egg) capacity was 55,000, so almost half a million people witnessed these gigs. During the concert, Keith Richards told the audience, "I don't see you often but when I do, I see a lot of you." Not quite as many as Michael Jackson who, in the Dome's inaugural year, had played it nine times over the 1998 Christmas period. The Stones' March 12 concert was filmed and broadcast on Japanese Television. It was released in Japan on video later that year.

1207.   TUMBLING DICE (Jagger, Richard) ✎ 4.03
12 March 1995: Place: Tokyo Dome, Tokyo, Japan.
Rolling Stones with Darryl Jones, Chuck Leavell, Lisa Fischer, Bernard Fowler, Bobby Keys, Michael Davis, Kent Smith, Andy Snitzer.
Producer: Yasumi Takeuch, Kazuo Dobashi.
Engineer: Benji Lefevre, Satoru Fujii, Yoshiyasu Kumada.
Japan Video Voodoo Lounge In Japan: September 1995

1208.   YOU GOT ME ROCKING (Jagger, Richards) ✎ 3.23
12 March 1995: Place: Tokyo Dome, Tokyo, Japan.
Rolling Stones with Darryl Jones, Chuck Leavell, Lisa Fischer, Bernard Fowler.
Producer: Yasumi Takeuch, Kazuo Dobashi.
Engineer: Benji Lefevre, Satoru Fujii, Yoshiyasu Kumada.
Japan Video Voodoo Lounge In Japan: September 1995

1209.   LIVE WITH ME (Jagger, Richard) ✎ 3.52
12 March 1995: Place: Tokyo Dome, Tokyo, Japan.
Rolling Stones with Darryl Jones, Chuck Leavell, Lisa Fischer, Bernard Fowler, Bobby Keys.
Producer: Yasumi Takeuch, Kazuo Dobashi.
Engineer: Benji Lefevre, Satoru Fujii, Yoshiyasu Kumada.
Japan Video Voodoo Lounge In Japan: September 1995

1210.   ROCKS OFF (Jagger, Richard) ✎ 4.44
12 March 1995: Place: Tokyo Dome, Tokyo, Japan.
Rolling Stones with Darryl Jones, Chuck Leavell, Lisa Fischer, Bernard Fowler, Bobby Keys, Michael Davis, Kent Smith, Andy Snitzer.
Producer: Yasumi Takeuch, Kazuo Dobashi.
Engineer: Benji Lefevre, Satoru Fujii, Yoshiyasu Kumada.
Japan Video Voodoo Lounge In Japan: September 1995

1211.   SPARKS WILL FLY (Jagger, Richards) ✎ 3.58
12 March 1995: Place: Tokyo Dome, Tokyo, Japan.
Rolling Stones with Darryl Jones, Chuck Leavell, Lisa Fischer, Bernard Fowler.
Producer: Yasumi Takeuch, Kazuo Dobashi.
Engineer: Benji Lefevre, Satoru Fujii, Yoshiyasu Kumada.
Japan Video Voodoo Lounge In Japan: September 1995

1212.   (I CAN'T GET NO) SATISFACTION (Jagger, Richard) ✎ 5.50
12 March 1995: Place: Tokyo Dome, Tokyo, Japan.
Rolling Stones with Darryl Jones, Chuck Leavell, Lisa Fischer, Bernard Fowler.
Producer: Yasumi Takeuch, Kazuo Dobashi.
Engineer: Benji Lefevre, Satoru Fujii, Yoshiyasu Kumada.
Japan Video Voodoo Lounge In Japan: September 1995

1213. ANGIE (Jagger, Richard) ✏ 3.35
12 March 1995: Place: Tokyo Dome, Tokyo, Japan.
Rolling Stones with Darryl Jones.
Producer: Yasumi Takeuch, Kazuo Dobashi.
Engineer: Benji Lefevre, Satoru Fujii, Yoshiyasu Kumada.
Japan Video Voodoo Lounge In Japan: September 1995

1214. SWEET VIRGINIA (Jagger, Richard) ✏ 4.22
12 March 1995: Place: Tokyo Dome, Tokyo, Japan.
Rolling Stones with Darryl Jones, Chuck Leavell, Lisa Fischer, Bernard Fowler, Bobby Keys.
Producer: Yasumi Takeuch, Kazuo Dobashi.
Engineer: Benji Lefevre, Satoru Fujii, Yoshiyasu Kumada.
Japan Video Voodoo Lounge In Japan: September 1995

1215. ROCK AND A HARD PLACE (Jagger, Richards) ✏ 4.46
12 March 1995: Place: Tokyo Dome, Tokyo, Japan.
Rolling Stones with Darryl Jones, Chuck Leavell, Lisa Fischer, Bernard Fowler, Bobby Keys, Michael Davis, Kent Smith, Andy Snitzer.
Producer: Yasumi Takeuch, Kazuo Dobashi.
Engineer: Benji Lefevre, Satoru Fujii, Yoshiyasu Kumada.
Japan Video Voodoo Lounge In Japan: September 1995

1216. LOVE IS STRONG (Jagger, Richards) ✏ 5.02
12 March 1995: Place: Tokyo Dome, Tokyo, Japan.
Rolling Stones with Darryl Jones, Chuck Leavell, Lisa Fischer, Bernard Fowler.
Producer: Yasumi Takeuch, Kazuo Dobashi.
Engineer: Benji Lefevre, Satoru Fujii, Yoshiyasu Kumada.
Japan Video Voodoo Lounge In Japan: September 1995

1217. I GO WILD (Jagger, Richards) ✏ 5.59
12 March 1995: Place: Tokyo Dome, Tokyo, Japan.
Rolling Stones with Darryl Jones, Chuck Leavell, Lisa Fischer, Bernard Fowler.
Producer: Yasumi Takeuch, Kazuo Dobashi.
Engineer: Benji Lefevre, Satoru Fujii, Yoshiyasu Kumada.
Japan Video Voodoo Lounge In Japan: September 1995

1218. MISS YOU (Jagger, Richards) ✏ 9.37
12 March 1995: Place: Tokyo Dome, Tokyo, Japan.
Rolling Stones with Darryl Jones, Chuck Leavell, Lisa Fischer, Bernard Fowler, Bobby Keys.
Producer: Yasumi Takeuch, Kazuo Dobashi.
Engineer: Benji Lefevre, Satoru Fujii, Yoshiyasu Kumada.
Japan Video Voodoo Lounge In Japan: September 1995

1219. HONKY TONK WOMEN (Jagger, Richards) ✏ 4.24
12 March 1995: Place: Tokyo Dome, Tokyo, Japan.
Rolling Stones with Darryl Jones, Chuck Leavell, Lisa Fischer, Bernard Fowler, Bobby Keys, Michael Davis, Kent Smith, Andy Snitzer.
Producer: Yasumi Takeuch, Kazuo Dobashi.
Engineer: Benji Lefevre, Satoru Fujii, Yoshiyasu Kumada.
Japan Video Voodoo Lounge In Japan: September 1995

1220. BEFORE THEY MAKE ME RUN (Jagger, Richards) ✏ 3.36
12 March 1995: Place: Tokyo Dome, Tokyo, Japan.
Rolling Stones with Darryl Jones, Chuck Leavell, Lisa Fischer, Bernard Fowler, Bobby Keys.
Producer: Yasumi Takeuch, Kazuo Dobashi.
Engineer: Benji Lefevre, Satoru Fujii, Yoshiyasu Kumada.
Japan Video Voodoo Lounge In Japan: September 1995

1221. SLIPPING AWAY (Jagger, Richards) ✏ 5.05
12 March 1995: Place: Tokyo Dome, Tokyo, Japan.
Rolling Stones with Darryl Jones, Chuck Leavell, Lisa Fischer, Bernard Fowler, Bobby Keys, Michael Davis, Kent Smith, Andy Snitzer.
Producer: Yasumi Takeuch, Kazuo Dobashi.
Engineer: Benji Lefevre, Satoru Fujii, Yoshiyasu Kumada.
Japan Video Voodoo Lounge In Japan: September 1995

1222.   SYMPATHY FOR THE DEVIL (Jagger, Richards) ✎ 5.53
12 March 1995: Place: Tokyo Dome, Tokyo, Japan.
Rolling Stones with Darryl Jones, Chuck Leavell, Lisa Fischer, Bernard Fowler.
Producer: Yasumi Takeuch, Kazuo Dobashi.
Engineer: Benji Lefevre, Satoru Fujii, Yoshiyasu Kumada.
Japan Video Voodoo Lounge In Japan: September 1995

1223.   MONKEY MAN (Jagger, Richards) ✎ 4.04
12 March 1995: Place: Tokyo Dome, Tokyo, Japan.
Rolling Stones with Darryl Jones, Chuck Leavell, Lisa Fischer, Bernard Fowler, Bobby Keys, Michael Davis, Kent Smith, Andy Snitzer.
Producer: Yasumi Takeuch, Kazuo Dobashi.
Engineer: Benji Lefevre, Satoru Fujii, Yoshiyasu Kumada.
Japan Video Voodoo Lounge In Japan: September 1995

1224.   STREET FIGHTING MAN (Jagger, Richard) ✎ 5.41
12 March 1995: Place: Tokyo Dome, Tokyo, Japan.
Rolling Stones with Darryl Jones, Chuck Leavell, Lisa Fischer, Bernard Fowler.
Producer: Yasumi Takeuch, Kazuo Dobashi.
Engineer: Benji Lefevre, Satoru Fujii, Yoshiyasu Kumada.
Japan Video Voodoo Lounge In Japan: September 1995

1225.   START ME UP (Jagger, Richards) ✎ 4.03
12 March 1995: Place: Tokyo Dome, Tokyo, Japan.
Rolling Stones with Darryl Jones, Chuck Leavell, Lisa Fischer, Bernard Fowler.
Producer: Yasumi Takeuch, Kazuo Dobashi.
Engineer: Benji Lefevre, Satoru Fujii, Yoshiyasu Kumada.
Japan Video Voodoo Lounge In Japan: September 1995

1226.   IT'S ONLY ROCK 'N' ROLL (Jagger, Richard) ✎ 4.50
12 March 1995: Place: Tokyo Dome, Tokyo, Japan.
Rolling Stones with Darryl Jones, Chuck Leavell, Lisa Fischer, Bernard Fowler.
Producer: Yasumi Takeuch, Kazuo Dobashi.
Engineer: Benji Lefevre, Satoru Fujii, Yoshiyasu Kumada.
Japan Video Voodoo Lounge In Japan: September 1995

1227.   BROWN SUGAR (Jagger, Richard) ✎ 6.10
12 March 1995: Place: Tokyo Dome, Tokyo, Japan.
Rolling Stones with Darryl Jones, Chuck Leavell, Lisa Fischer, Bernard Fowler, Bobby Keys, Michael Davis, Kent Smith, Andy Snitzer.
Producer: Yasumi Takeuch, Kazuo Dobashi.
Engineer: Benji Lefevre, Satoru Fujii, Yoshiyasu Kumada.
Japan Video Voodoo Lounge In Japan: September 1995

1228.   JUMPIN' JACK FLASH (Jagger, Richard) ✎ 6.02
12 March 1995: Place: Tokyo Dome, Tokyo, Japan.
Rolling Stones with Darryl Jones, Chuck Leavell, Lisa Fischer, Bernard Fowler, Bobby Keys, Michael Davis, Kent Smith, Andy Snitzer.
Producer: Yasumi Takeuch, Kazuo Dobashi.
Engineer: Benji Lefevre, Satoru Fujii, Yoshiyasu Kumada.
Japan Video Voodoo Lounge In Japan: September 1995

The structure of the concert did not vary greatly from the 1994 set list. The two acoustic slow numbers were changed regularly. In Tokyo they played *Angie, Sweet Virginia, Love In Vain, Dead Flowers, No Expectations, Let It Bleed, Beast Of Burden, Out Of Tears* and *Memory Motel*. The band then journeyed onwards to take in Australia and New Zealand before they took a month-long break.

1229.   GIMME SHELTER (Jagger, Richard) ✎ 6.53
26 May 1995: Place: The Paradiso, Amsterdam, Netherlands.
Rolling Stones with Darryl Jones, Chuck Leavell, Bernard Fowler, Lisa Fischer.
Producer: Don Was, The Glimmer Twins.
Engineer: Peter Brandt, Henk Van Helvoirt, Sander Nagel, Rene Suydendorp, Ronnie Rivera, Masaaki Ugajih, Kazuaki Fujita.
Recorded by: Ed Cherney. Mixed by: Bob Clearmountain. Assisted by: Ryan Freeland. Mastered by: Stephen Marcussen. Digitally edited by: Ron Boustead.
UK CD Track Single Wild Horses: 11 March 1996
UK CD Track Single Saint Of Me (Radio Edit): 26 January 1998
USA CD Track Single Saint Of Me (Radio Edit): 26 January 1998
UK CD box set THE SINGLES COLLECTION 1971-2006: 45 X 45s: 11 April 2011
USA CD box set THE SINGLES COLLECTION 1971-2006: 45 X 45s: 26 April 2011

1230. STREET FIGHTING MAN (Jagger, Richard) ✎ 3.40
26 May 1995: Place: The Paradiso, Amsterdam, Netherlands.
Rolling Stones with Darryl Jones, Chuck Leavell, Bernard Fowler..
Producer: Don Was, The Glimmer Twins.
Engineer: Peter Brandt, Henk Van Helvoirt, Sander Nagel, Rene Suydendorp, Ronnie Rivera, Masaaki Ugajih, Kazuaki Fujita.
Recorded by: Ed Cherney. Mixed by: Bob Clearmountain. Assisted by: Ryan Freeland. Mastered by: Stephen Marcussen. Digitally edited by: Ron Boustead.
UK CD LP STRIPPED: 13 November 1995: No. 9 - 11 weeks
USA CD LP STRIPPED: 13 November 1995: No. 9 - 19 weeks

1231. IT'S ALL OVER NOW (Womack, Womack) ✎ 3.34
27 May 1995: Place: The Paradiso, Amsterdam, Netherlands.
Rolling Stones with Darryl Jones, Chuck Leavell, Bernard Fowler, Lisa Fischer, Bobby Keys, Andy Snitzer, Michael Davis, Kent Smith.
Producer: Don Was, The Glimmer Twins.
Recorded by: Ed Cherney.
UK & USA e-Single Track Neighbours: November 2004

This is the only official recording of this track which was released electronically to coincide with the release of LIVE LICKS and the lead track *Neighbours*.

1232. DEAD FLOWERS (Jagger, Richard) ✎ 4.11
27 May 1995: Place: The Paradiso, Amsterdam, Netherlands.
Rolling Stones with Darryl Jones, Chuck Leavell, Bernard Fowler.
Producer: Don Was, The Glimmer Twins.
Engineer: Ed Cherney.
Bootleg only.

1233. STILL A FOOL (Morganfield) ✎ 5.37
AKA: Two Trains Running
27 May 1995: Place: The Paradiso, Amsterdam, Netherlands.
Rolling Stones with Darryl Jones, Chuck Leavell.
Producer: Don Was, The Glimmer Twins.
Engineer: Ed Cherney.
Bootleg only.

1234. DOWN IN THE BOTTOM (Dixon) ✎ 5.08
27 May 1995: Place: The Paradiso, Amsterdam, Netherlands.
Rolling Stones with Darryl Jones, Chuck Leavell.
Producer: Don Was, The Glimmer Twins.
Engineer: Ed Cherney.
Bootleg only.

1235. SHINE A LIGHT (Jagger, Richard) ✎ 4.56
27 May 1995: Place: The Paradiso, Amsterdam, Netherlands.
Rolling Stones with Darryl Jones, Chuck Leavell, Don Was, Bernard Fowler, Lisa Fischer.
Producer: Don Was, The Glimmer Twins.
Engineer: Ed Cherney.
Bootleg only.

1236. JUMP ON TOP OF ME (Jagger, Richards) ✎ 4.15
27 May 1995: Place: The Paradiso, Amsterdam, Netherlands.
Rolling Stones with Darryl Jones, Chuck Leavell, Bernard Fowler, Lisa Fischer, Bobby Keys, Andy Snitzer, Michael Davis, Kent Smith.
Producer: Don Was, The Glimmer Twins.
Engineer: Ed Cherney.
Bootleg only.

1237. CAN'T GET NEXT TO YOU (Holland, Dozier, Holland) ✎ 5.22
27 May 1995: Place: The Paradiso, Amsterdam, Netherlands.
Rolling Stones with Darryl Jones, Chuck Leavell, Bernard Fowler, Lisa Fischer, Bobby Keys, Andy Snitzer, Michael Davis, Kent Smith.
Producer: Don Was, The Glimmer Twins.
Engineer: Ed Cherney.
Bootleg only.

1238. ALL DOWN THE LINE (Jagger, Richard) ✎ 4.22
27 May 1995: Place: The Paradiso, Amsterdam, Netherlands.
Rolling Stones with Darryl Jones, Chuck Leavell, Bernard Fowler, Lisa Fischer, Bobby Keys, Andy Snitzer, Michael Davis, Kent Smith.
Producer: Don Was, The Glimmer Twins.

Engineer: Peter Brandt, Henk Van Helvoirt, Sander Nagel, Rene Suydendorp, Ronnie Rivera, Masaaki Ugajih, Kazuaki Fujita.
Recorded by: Ed Cherney. Mixed by: Bob Clearmountain. Assisted by: Ryan Freeland. Mastered by: Stephen Marcussen. Digitally edited by: Ron Boustead.
UK CD Track Single Like A Rolling Stone: 30 October 1995
UK CD box set THE SINGLES COLLECTION 1971-2006: 45 X 45s: 11 April 2011
USA CD box set THE SINGLES COLLECTION 1971-2006: 45 X 45s: 26 April 2011

As a warm-up to the European section of the tour after Australasia, the Stones played a monster two nights at the small (700 capacity) Paradiso Club in Amsterdam, Netherlands. The Stones' banner for the gig was The Foot Tappers And Wheel Shunters Club Gig. Relay screens were set up in Amsterdam for a further 40,000 people to watch the two shows which were recorded visually and in audio. Attractive, young women were picked off the streets and given wrist bands and escorted to the front of stage for the cameras' eye candy.

This overt technique would be used on a few more occasions. The Paradiso gigs were musically notable because of the variation to the setlists and the opportunity to play non-standard material. *The Spider And The Fly*, recorded a few months earlier, was played live for the first time. Another first was the inclusion of Bob Dylan's *Like A Rolling Stone*, which Mick Jagger said Bob had especially written for them! *Jump On Top Of Me* was also played live for the first time.

If that was not enough, there was Muddy Waters' *Still A Fool* and Willie Dixon's *Down In The Bottom*, both studio out-takes not previously recorded live. In keeping with the acoustic atmosphere, *Dead Flowers* allowed Jagger to adopt his country lilt even at the song's conclusion - "well thaank you". The gospel track *Shine A Light* had never been played before and featured Don Was on organ and Chuck Leavell on piano. *Can't Get Next To You* was played for the first time in Europe. More standard fare that ended up on releases were *All Down The Line*, *Gimme Shelter* (both only appeared as CD tracks on a single), a download only release of *It's All Over Now* and *Street Fighting Man*.

The latter was played both nights, once as an encore and as the finale on the second gig, before the encore. The version is a classic, energised by those acoustic guitars, Bernard Fowler's shakers plus Chuck Leavell's piano, which seeps through the mix, and the marching, charging vocal delivery by Mick. After so many years of the song being played electrically, it was refreshing for it to return to the original recording format, even though it was incongruous to see Keith sitting down during the performance.

1239. NOT FADE AWAY (Petty, Hardin) ✏ 2.58
3 June 1995: Place: Olympic Stadium, Stockholm, Sweden.
Rolling Stones with Darryl Jones, Chuck Leavell.
Producer: Michael Cohl.
Engineer: Benji Lefevre.
Bootleg only.

1240. YOU GOT ME ROCKING (Jagger, Richards) ✏ 3.13
3 June 1995: Place: Olympic Stadium, Stockholm, Sweden.
Rolling Stones with Darryl Jones, Chuck Leavell, Lisa Fischer, Bernard Fowler.
Producer: Michael Cohl.
Engineer: Benji Lefevre.
Bootleg only.

1241. I GO WILD (Jagger, Richards) ✏ 5.51
3 June 1995: Place: Olympic Stadium, Stockholm, Sweden.
Rolling Stones with Darryl Jones, Chuck Leavell, Lisa Fischer, Bernard Fowler.
Producer: Michael Cohl.
Engineer: Benji Lefevre.
Bootleg only.

The support acts for the tour varied greatly but, in Europe, Robert Cray opened for the early dates while others included: The Tragically Hip, Bon Jovi, Del Amitri, The Black Crowes, Bob Dylan, Andrew Strong and Big Country. The first stadium show was in Stockholm, Sweden, where the gig was recorded for TV promotional purposes to boost sales for the European leg. *Not Fade Away*, *You Got Me Rocking* and *I Go Wild* were broadcast in full during the 45-minute special.

1242. TUMBLING DICE (Jagger, Richard) ✏ 4.08
3 July 1995: Place: Olympia Theatre, Paris, France.
Rolling Stones with Darryl Jones, Chuck Leavell, Bernard Fowler, Lisa Fischer, Bobby Keys, Andy Snitzer, Michael Davis, Kent Smith.
Producer: Don Was, The Glimmer Twins.
Engineer: Ed Cherney.
UK CD Track Single Wild Horses: 11 March 1996
USA CD LP ROLLING STONES RARITIES 1971-2003: 22 November 2005: No. 76 - 6 weeks
UK CD LP ROLLING STONES RARITIES 1971-2003: 28 November 2005

1243. LET IT BLEED (Jagger, Richard) ✏ 4.15
3 July 1995: Place: Olympia Theatre, Paris, France.
Rolling Stones with Darryl Jones, Chuck Leavell, Bernard Fowler, Lisa Fischer.
Producer: Don Was, The Glimmer Twins.
Engineer: Peter Brandt, Henk Van Helvoirt, Sander Nagel, Rene Suydendorp, Ronnie Rivera, Masaaki Ugajih, Kazuaki Fujita.
Recorded by: Ed Cherney. Mixed by: Bob Clearmountain. Assisted by: Ryan Freeland. Mastered by: Stephen Marcussen. Digitally edited by: Ron Boustead.
UK CD LP STRIPPED: 13 November 1995: No. 9 - 11 weeks
USA CD LP STRIPPED: 13 November 1995: No. 9 - 19 weeks

1244. ANGIE (Jagger, Richard) ✏ 3.28
3 July 1995: Place: Olympia Theatre, Paris, France.
Rolling Stones with Darryl Jones, Chuck Leavell.
Producer: Don Was, The Glimmer Twins.
Engineer: Peter Brandt, Henk Van Helvoirt, Sander Nagel, Rene Suydendorp, Ronnie Rivera, Masaaki Ugajih, Kazuaki Fujita.
Recorded by: Ed Cherney. Mixed by: Bob Clearmountain. Assisted by: Ryan Freeland. Mastered by: Stephen Marcussen. Digitally edited by: Ron Boustead.
UK CD LP STRIPPED: 13 November 1995: No. 9 - 11 weeks
USA CD LP STRIPPED: 13 November 1995: No. 9 - 19 weeks

1245. SHINE A LIGHT (Jagger, Richard) ✏ 4.38
3 July 1995: Place: Olympia Theatre, Paris, France.
Rolling Stones with Darryl Jones, Chuck Leavell, Don Was, Bernard Fowler, Lisa Fischer.
Producer: Don Was, The Glimmer Twins.
Engineer: Peter Brandt, Henk Van Helvoirt, Sander Nagel, Rene Suydendorp, Ronnie Rivera, Masaaki Ugajih, Kazuaki Fujita.
Recorded by: Ed Cherney. Mixed by: Bob Clearmountain. Assisted by: Ryan Freeland. Mastered by: Stephen Marcussen. Digitally edited by: Ron Boustead.
UK CD LP STRIPPED: 13 November 1995: No. 9 - 11 weeks
USA CD LP STRIPPED: 13 November 1995: No. 9 - 19 weeks

The Olympia Theatre in Paris, which had been used by the band on previous trips in 1965/1966, was another venue where recording took place for the STRIPPED album - three songs and a track for a CD single. The atmosphere was terrific, which was typical with all club gigs. *Angie* was sung to a backdrop of lighters flickering in the audience, *Shine A Light* was another opportunity for Don Was to play organ to Chuck Leavell's piano and there was an excellent Ron Wood solo electric guitar as Keith Richards sat on a stool with an acoustic guitar.

Mick Jagger was particularly surprised when the crowd sang along to the chorus to what he thought was an unusual song. *Angie* was recorded on a live album for the first time. *Let It Bleed* was also a pleasure, Ronnie's performance on the slide confirming that he was having a golden period with the Stones. *Tumbling Dice* was used as a warm-up before the gig and the recording of this can be seen on the video before it segues into the live performance. In the audience, Jack Nicholson joined Jerry Hall in the balcony and commented on the promotional TV documentary for STRIPPED that, just after one show, his pulse was racing and he had to lie down.

1246. LIVE WITH ME (Jagger, Richard) ✏ 3.52
19 July 1995: Place: Brixton Academy, Brixton, London, England.
Rolling Stones with Darryl Jones, Chuck Leavell, Bernard Fowler, Bobby Keys.
Producer: Don Was, The Glimmer Twins.
Recorded by: Chris Kimsey.
UK CD Track Single Wild Horses: 11 March 1996
USA CD LP ROLLING STONES RARITIES 1971-2003: 22 November 2005: No. 76 - 6 weeks
UK CD LP ROLLING STONES RARITIES 1971-2003: 28 November 2005

1247. BLACK LIMOUSINE (Jagger, Richards, Wood) ✏ 3.30
19 July 1995: Place: Brixton Academy, Brixton, London, England.
Rolling Stones with Darryl Jones, Chuck Leavell, Bernard Fowler, Lisa Fischer.
Producer: Don Was, The Glimmer Twins.
Engineer: Peter Brandt, Henk Van Helvoirt, Sander Nagel, Rene Suydendorp, Ronnie Rivera, Masaaki Ugajih, Kazuaki Fujita.
Recorded by: Chris Kimsey. Mixed by: Bob Clearmountain. Assisted by: Ryan Freeland. Mastered by: Stephen Marcussen. Digitally edited by: Ron Boustead.
UK CD Track Single: Like A Rolling Stone: 30 October 1995
UK CD box set THE SINGLES COLLECTION 1971-2006: 45 X 45s: 11 April 2011
USA CD box set THE SINGLES COLLECTION 1971-2006: 45 X 45s: 26 April 2011

1248. DEAD FLOWERS (Jagger, Richard) ✏ 4.13
19 July 1995: Place: Brixton Academy, Brixton, London, England.
Rolling Stones with Darryl Jones, Chuck Leavell, Bernard Fowler, Lisa Fischer.
Producer: Don Was, The Glimmer Twins.
Engineer: Peter Brandt, Henk Van Helvoirt, Sander Nagel, Rene Suydendorp, Ronnie Rivera, Masaaki Ugajih, Kazuaki Fujita.
Recorded by: Chris Kimsey. Mixed by: Bob Clearmountain. Assisted by: Ryan Freeland. Mastered by: Stephen Marcussen. Digitally edited by: Ron Boustead.
UK CD LP STRIPPED: 13 November 1995: No. 9 - 11 weeks
USA CD LP STRIPPED: 13 November 1995: No. 9 - 19 weeks

1249. SWEET VIRGINIA (Jagger, Richard) ✏ 4.05
19 July 1995: Place: Brixton Academy, Brixton, London, England.
Rolling Stones with Darryl Jones, Chuck Leavell, Bernard Fowler, Lisa Fischer, Bobby Keys.
Producer: Don Was, The Glimmer Twins. Recorded by: Chris Kimsey.
Bootleg only.

1250. FAR AWAY EYES (Jagger, Richards) ✏ 4.43
19 July 1995: Place: Brixton Academy, Brixton, London, England.
Rolling Stones with Darryl Jones, Chuck Leavell, Bernard Fowler, Lisa Fischer.
Producer: Don Was, The Glimmer Twins. Recorded by: Chris Kimsey.
Bootleg only.

1251. LIKE A ROLLING STONE (Dylan) ✎ 5.38
19 July 1995: Place: Brixton Academy, Brixton, London, England.
Rolling Stones with Darryl Jones, Chuck Leavell.
Producer: Don Was, The Glimmer Twins.
Engineer: Peter Brandt, Henk Van Helvoirt, Sander Nagel, Rene Suydendorp, Ronnie Rivera, Masaaki Ugajih, Kazuaki Fujita.
Recorded by: Chris Kimsey. Mixed by: Bob Clearmountain. Assisted by: Ryan Freeland.
Mastered by: Stephen Marcussen. Digitally edited by: Ron Boustead.
UK CD Single: 30 October 1995: No. 12 - 5 weeks
UK CD LP STRIPPED: 13 November 1995: No. 9 - 11 weeks
USA CD LP STRIPPED: 13 November 1995: No. 9 - 19 weeks
UK CD box set THE SINGLES COLLECTION 1971-2006: 45 X 45s: 11 April 2011
USA CD box set THE SINGLES COLLECTION 1971-2006: 45 X 45s: 26 April 2011

The track had been destined to be recorded and released as a single due to the enormous potential of Bob Dylan's hook line and it had also been receiving more and more attention in live European concerts. In 1995, Mick Jagger told Jann Wenner, from Rolling Stone magazine, what appealed to him about the song: "Well, melodically I quite like it. It's very well put together; it's got a proper three sections to it, real good choruses and a good middle bit, and great lyrics. It's a really well-constructed pop song, in my opinion." It was also a number where Mick enjoyed playing the harmonica.
The released version was recorded from the Brixton Academy show and attained a respectable No. 12 position in the UK. An edited version was also produced (* a - 4.20). Chris Kimsey was asked to record the concert using the Eurosound Mobile, since Ed Cherney could not make the date. Pierre de Beauport believed that the whole concert recorded by Chris was a fantastic mix and cherishes his copy of it. The released tracks of *Black Limousine* and *Live With Me* prove the point. On 25 September 1995, at Bagley's warehouse in King's Cross, London, a promotional video film was shot to support the single.
It was produced by Michel Gondry who was well known for his camera wizardry. The video incorporated "bullet-time" technology, where images stand still as though in a dream sequence as life continues normally. Mick Jagger referred to the method as the chewing gum effect. The technique was used for the film *The Matrix*. *Like A Rolling Stone* was one of the first videos Gondry produced and he progressed to many others, including feature films. There were many run-throughs of the track but at least an impromptu concert of 14 songs was held with *Little Baby* and Keith Richards performing *You Got The Silver* and an instrumental *Street Fighting Man*. About 150 guests went home very happy as the band mingled with the audience.

1252. CONNECTION (Jagger, Richard) ✎ 3.48
19 July 1995: Place: Brixton Academy, Brixton, London, England.
Rolling Stones with Darryl Jones, Chuck Leavell, Bernard Fowler, Lisa Fischer.
Producer: Don Was, The Glimmer Twins.
Recorded by: Chris Kimsey.
Bootleg only.

1253. RIP THIS JOINT (Jagger, Richard) ✎ 2.32
19 July 1995: Place: Brixton Academy, Brixton, London, England.
Rolling Stones with Darryl Jones, Chuck Leavell, Bernard Fowler, Lisa Fischer, Bobby Keys, Andy Snitzer, Michael Davis, Kent Smith.
Producer: Don Was, The Glimmer Twins.
Recorded by: Chris Kimsey.
Bootleg only.

As with the Steel Wheels and Urban Jungle tours, careful consideration had been given to the optimum number of shows, keeping in mind the number of set erections and break-downs. In June 1995, Sweden, Finland, Norway, Denmark, the Netherlands, Germany, Belgium and France were played before the homeland was reached. Italy was omitted because of the poor turn-out by fans in some cities on the Urban Jungle tour. Generally, the venues and audiences were large, especially at festival sites such as Nijmigen and Landgraaf in the Netherlands, Werchter in Belgium and Longchamps in Paris. Just these seven concerts saw upwards of half a million in attendance. The Landgraaf site saw such a large, wild crowd at the stage front, that there were genuine fears that the stage would collapse into a large sinkhole. The new Don Valley Stadium, in Sheffield, was the venue for the start of the English (not British this time) leg of the tour.
Three concerts were played at Wembley Stadium in Charlie Watts' Middlesex, one on the Wednesday and then the weekend of 15, 16 July 1995, bringing Stones fever to the city of London that week. Bill Wyman, with his new wife Suzanne Accosta, saw the band perform at Wembley and met Darryl Jones for the first time. They enjoyed the show from the vantage point of the Royal Box . The set list for the European tour of fields, arenas and stadiums was changed marginally. *Like A Rolling Stone* had become a permanent feature but, during the Keith Richards' section, *Connection* and *Slipping Away* were added and *Let It Bleed* was also performed occasionally.
As Mick Jagger left the stage on the Sunday night at Wembley he said, "See you in Brixton." confirming rumours of a small gig there just as they had done in Amsterdam and Paris. The venue was the Academy, one of Britain's premier live venues and one of the oldest, starting life in 1929. Its famous feature is the arch, based on the Rialto Bridge. The floor, as with all old seated venues also used for films is sloped to aid the viewing from the rear. On a hot, humid night - 19 July 1995 - the Stones played a changed set to 3,000 fans, with another 800 guests in the balcony.
Four tracks ended up on official releases. Early on, *Live With Me* was played as the heat was beginning to take its toll on the band and the crowd. To emphasise the point, Mick mopped Keith's brow. One of Ron Wood's favourites, *Black Limousine*, was tackled and three country songs followed in a row - *Dead Flowers*, *Sweet Virginia* and, for the first time on the tour, *Far Away Eyes*. A highlight was the performance of *Like A Rolling Stone*, a natural song for the band to play. It was used frequently during session warm-ups but they considered it was such a cliché that they had refused to record it.
This policy had changed in Amsterdam and the Brixton recording appeared as a single. When released in November 1995, it became their biggest single hit in the UK since *Undercover* in 1983. Later on the tour, Bob Dylan joined the Stones at their Lyon, France concert for a rendition. Not sure how the band would deliver the chorus, Dylan asked Ronnie and was told - "just follow the crowd!" There was a prior occasion when Mick Jagger sang *Like A Rolling Stone* with Bob Dylan at the Rock 'n' Roll Hall of Fame ceremony, in February 1988.

At the Paradiso in Amsterdam, *Connection* became part of Keith's set - sometimes it was performed with Mick on co-vocals and at others, such as in Brixton, by himself. Just as in Paris, *Midnight Rambler* was also included as part of the club gig set-list. This was followed by a glowing *Rip This Joint* with Darryl Jones on upright bass, as can be witnessed by some shots in the video. Given the show's variety and quality of sound, it is a shame that MTV did not buy the video rights. MTV were probably disappointed that the Stones had not agreed to an Unplugged performance. Frustratingly, as with other professionally-shot films, they lurk in someone's library/garage.

1254. **NOT FADE AWAY** (Petty, Hardin) 3.06
25-26 July 1995: Place: Estudios Valentim De Carvalho, Lisbon, Portugal.
Rolling Stones with Darryl Jones, Chuck Leavell, Bernard Fowler.
Producer: Don Was, The Glimmer Twins.
Engineer: Peter Brandt, Henk Van Helvoirt, Sander Nagel, Rene Suydendorp, Ronnie Rivera, Masaaki Ugajih, Kazuaki Fujita.
Recorded by: Ed Cherney. Mixed by: Bob Clearmountain. Assisted by: Ryan Freeland. Mastered by: Stephen Marcussen. Digitally edited by: Ron Boustead.
UK CD LP STRIPPED: 13 November 1995: No. 9 - 11 weeks
USA CD LP STRIPPED: 13 November 1995: No. 9 - 19 weeks

Brixton was followed by performances in Gijon, Spain and Lisbon, Portugal on 22, 24 July respectively. After the concert in Lisbon, the Stones used the well-established musical complex, Estudios Number 1-2 Valentim De Carvalho to record some more tracks. *Not Fade Away* was recorded with a new treatment; they would have been familiar with the tune, having played it on every tour opener.
The style change starts with a strange percussive opening, slightly echoed and electronically enhanced, using the rims of the drums. The acoustic guitar is followed by a harmonica in the familiar shuffle beat. Then, once Mick Jagger starts the vocals, Chuck Leavell strolls in on organ. The backing vocals paid homage to the original by Buddy Holly's Crickets, with the Bo Diddley style "bom, bom, bom bomp" chirps.

1255. **I'M FREE** (Jagger, Richard) 3.12
25-26 July 1995: Place: Estudios Valentim De Carvalho, Lisbon, Portugal.
Rolling Stones with Darryl Jones, Chuck Leavell, Bernard Fowler, Lisa Fischer.
Producer: Don Was, The Glimmer Twins.
Engineer: Peter Brandt, Henk Van Helvoirt, Sander Nagel, Rene Suydendorp, Ronnie Rivera, Masaaki Ugajih, Kazuaki Fujita.
Recorded by: Ed Cherney. Mixed by: Bob Clearmountain. Assisted by: Ryan Freeland. Mastered by: Stephen Marcussen. Digitally edited by: Ron Boustead.
UK CD LP STRIPPED: 13 November 1995: No. 9 - 11 weeks
USA CD LP STRIPPED: 13 November 1995: No. 9 - 19 weeks
UK Promo CD Single B-Side Wild Horses: 11 March 1996

The British Soup Dragons had a No. 5 cover version hit with *I'm Free* in 1990. Keith Richards remembers hearing it a few years later but did not take much notice, apart from being proud that someone had taken the time to record one of their songs. Keith and Chuck Leavell were jamming with a few sounds and started to play *Tracks Of My Tears*. Keith asked Chuck if he could remember the Stones doing a similar 60s soul thing and, between them, up popped *I'm Free*. A very different version from the original, it takes on new pastel shades with the organ and Lisa Fischer's backing vocals.

1256. **SWEET VIRGINIA** (Jagger, Richard) 4.15
25-26 July 1995: Place: Estudios Valentim De Carvalho, Lisbon, Portugal.
Rolling Stones with Darryl Jones, Chuck Leavell, Bernard Fowler, Lisa Fischer, Bobby Keys.
Producer: Don Was, The Glimmer Twins.
Engineer: Peter Brandt, Henk Van Helvoirt, Sander Nagel, Rene Suydendorp, Ronnie Rivera, Masaaki Ugajih, Kazuaki Fujita.
Recorded by: Ed Cherney. Mixed by: Bob Clearmountain. Assisted by: Ryan Freeland. Mastered by: Stephen Marcussen. Digitally edited by: Ron Boustead.
UK CD LP STRIPPED: 13 November 1995: No. 9 - 11 weeks
USA CD LP STRIPPED: 13 November 1995: No. 9 - 19 weeks

Bob Dylan would have been proud of this re-take of *Sweet Virginia*. It is played with live, loose, gay abandon; drums, acoustic guitars, piano, harmonica, saxophone and country hick vocals, all attempting to devour the speed off the bottom of the shoes, mentioned in the lyrics. France, Switzerland, Austria, Germany, Czechoslovakia, Hungary, Germany again, Luxembourg and the Netherlands concluded the 39-date tour of Europe on 30 August 1995, 13 months after they set off. It followed the 60-plus dates of the American tour.
The final session for STRIPPED was in Portugal and Bernard Fowler felt that the Japan and Portugal recordings were very special. To complete the STRIPPED album, other live shots and effects were recorded when they met at the Bagley's Warehouse, London, on 21 September 1995. Ed Cherney and Steve Marcussen found that they interacted well: "In the mastering process Steve will make changes in levels between songs, if needed, and apply overall equalisation and compression to make it sound and feel fabulous." said Ed.
Released in November 1995, it became a unique feature in the Stones' catalogue of albums. It included interactive bonus video tracks (incomplete *Tumbling Dice*, *Shattered* and *Like A Rolling Stone*) and band interviews, another first for the band. The technology was enhanced by an interactive CD ROM for the PC which enabled purchasers to tour the Voodoo Lounge, creating their own video backgrounds, conversing with security, going to the boys' and girls' rooms and entering the backstage area as the band went on stage.

1257. PAYING THE COST TO BE THE BOSS (King) 3.34
13 March - April 1997: Place: Ocean Way Recording Studios, Hollywood, Cherokee Recording Studios, Los Angeles, California, USA.
Rolling Stones with B B King, Darryl Jones, Tommy Eyre, Joe Sublett, Darrell Leonard.
Producer: John Porter.
Engineer: Joe McGrath.
Mixed by Chris Lord-Alge.
USA CD DEUCES WILD: 4 November 1997: No. 73 - 30 weeks.
UK CD DEUCES WILD: 3 January 1998

The rest of 1995 and most of 1996 past off uneventfully, although Charlie Watts recorded and released a solo album titled LONG AGO & FAR AWAY with Bernard Fowler on vocals. He followed this up with a short promotional tour in America while the continued promotion of STRIPPED allowed further solo projects. Keith Richards and Ron Wood played on the Bo Diddley album, A MAN AMONGST MEN, which was recorded late 1995. Keith also worked on tracks with the Winos. In the summer of 1996 they both recorded with Scotty Moore on different tracks. Keith sung a duet with Levon Helm backed by Rick Danko, Scotty Moore and D.J. Fontana named *Deuce And A Quarter* which was released on ALL THE KING'S MEN. Meanwhile, Ron worked with Jeff Beck on one track, *Unsung Heroes*. Mick Jagger became involved in a Jimmy Rip album and the recording of a soundtrack for a film project, BENT, in which he plays a gay Nazi prisoner thrown into a concentration camp. At his studios in Dublin, Ronnie worked with Bob Dylan preparing him for his new album TIME OUT OF MY MIND. Ronnie also joined forces with Bernard Fowler on a great version of Little Richard's classic soul ballad *I Don't Know What You've Got*, the original of which had Don Covay on vocals - it was his composition and had Jimi Hendrix on guitar, when he was a session musician in 1964/65. In October 1996, a CD and video of the long-hidden THE ROLLING STONES ROCK AND ROLL CIRCUS was finally released.

The footage had disappeared for many years until following Ian Stewart's death, it was found in his country house by his widow Cynthia. ABKCO had won the rights to the product as part of their settlement with the band and Allen Klein was determined that one day it would see the light of the day. The year concluded in November and December with the commencement of recording for the next Stones album. Tracks were sketched at Keith's home studio in Connecticut before formal recording sessions in 1997.

Paying The Cost To Be The Boss was originally released in 1968 on B B King's album BLUES ON TOP OF BLUES. He re-recorded it in 1997 with The Rolling Stones while they were working on the BRIDGES TO BABYLON album. The track was part recorded at Ocean Way and then the old MGM Studios, which had been renamed Cherokee. Joe Sublett and Darrell Leonard, who were involved in the Stones album, also provided saxophone and trumpet respectively on this and other cuts. The late Tommy Eyre played the rocking keyboards. His talents are evident all over the music scene, but in particular with Joe Cocker, Dan McCafferty, Alex Harvey, John Martyn, Greg Lake, Gary Moore, Wham, Ian Gillan, Gerry Rafferty and John Mayall. Mick Jagger shares the vocals with B B King and also plays the harmonica, taking the song to the fade-out. The guitars are used sparingly although there is a nice Keith Richards solo before the signature virtuoso by B B King.

1258. PRECIOUS LIPS (Jagger, Richards)
13 March - July 1997: Place: Ocean Way Recording Studios, Hollywood, California, USA.
Producer: Don Was, The Glimmer Twins.
Unavailable.

In November 1996, Mick Jagger and Keith Richards entered Dangerous Music Studios in the East Village of New York, which had views over the city. There, they contemplated the direction of the next album and wrote and recorded some demos. Mick brought some material he was planning for a solo album, which he thought might be suitable for the Stones. They continued working in New York after Christmas when Charlie Watts joined the Glimmer Twins and, early in February, the recording sessions moved to London, at Trevor Horn's Sarm West Studios and also the Westside Studios, in Holland Park.

Finally, the sessions proper started at Ocean Way with Don Was. After the VOODOO LOUNGE studio bootlegs, the out-takes from the sessions were carefully protected and are unavailable. Rumoured tracks include *Precious Lips, Don't Apologise, Ever Changing World, Feeling Now, High Or Low, I'm Cured, Smooth Stuff* and *Young Enough*.

1259. MIGHT AS WELL GET JUICED (Jagger, Richards) 5.23
13 March - July 1997: Place: Ocean Way Recording Studios, Hollywood, California, USA.
Played Live: 1998
Rolling Stones with Waddy Wachtel, Doug Wimbish.
Producer: The Dust Brothers, The Glimmer Twins.
Engineer: The Dust Brothers, Ed Cherney, Dan Bosworth.
Assistant Engineers: Alan Sanderson, Charles Gooden. Mixed by Danny Saber, Rich Lowe.
UK LP BRIDGES TO BABYLON: 29 September 1997: No. 6 - 6 weeks
USA LP BRIDGES TO BABYLON: 29 September 1997: No. 3 - 27 weeks

The earlier sessions did not produce a cohesive edge to the album content and BRIDGES TO BABYLON went off in different directions as Keith Richards recorded a number of songs with Don Was, while Mick Jagger and Charlie Watts worked with The Dust Brothers and Danny Saber. It was a deliberate decision to try to find different, fresh ideas. Charlie enjoyed working with different musicians and producers who Mick brought to the sessions.

Mick and Keith agreed to let each other work in their own particular way. Keith ensured the retention of Don Was as Executive Producer to oversee the overall direction and control of the album. One of the first songs recorded was *Might As Well Get Juiced*. Keith recorded a raw blues version (unavailable) which was then handed to Mick and he thought it was right for the Dust Brothers to work on.

Ed Cherney was involved for the first five weeks of the sessions before he moved to another project that he was booked and committed to. He did not recall an early blues version of the song but said that Mick was happy with the flange effect achieved on his vocals. He was called back to complete this track, as he was with *Always Suffering*, the Dust Brothers and Danny Saber engineering and mixing *Might As Well Get Juiced*. John King and Mike Simpson are the Dust Brothers, who were most influenced by electronics and re-mixing.

They had come to the fore when producing and mixing for The Beastie Boys and then Beck's highly successful 1996 album, ODELAY. When Mike Simpson first met Mick he was upfront and said that he was not too familiar with all their works, which Mick thought was great since there would be a fresh, funky approach. Don Was told the Dust Brothers how it would work. First you record Mick's vocals and keyboard overdubs then Charlie and finally Keith and the bass which was an unusual process. On this track, the bass was played by Doug Wimbish, from the Sugarhill Records houseband.

It was well known that Keith was not entirely happy with The Dust Brothers' techniques and thought that the synthesised parts detracted from the Stones sound. He was not always as communicative with them as he could be and mumbled his way through some of the takes. Mick was trying to add a cutting edge, which would compare well with that of current artists and, in this respect he succeeded. Some compromise was reached since the final cut was mixed by Danny Saber, a musician and producer. He recorded with Shaun Ryder's Black Grape - a spin-off group from The Happy Mondays.

The lyrics are about a middle life crisis, where consolation for uncertainty is sought in alcohol. The synthesised keyboard sound of Mick opens the song and Charlie's swaggering drum beat lurches the song into a groove. They wanted Charlie to hit the hi-hat on time with the snare but the drummer retorted, "I don't do that", although he did give it a try. As with *Love Is Strong*, the harmonica was used to good effect on a track not normally associated with that instrument.

A series of re-mixes appeared on two bootlegged albums. It is difficult to establish the origin of these but they seem to be authentic. One of is sub-titled *Keith's Revenge Re-mix* (* a - 10.50) which might imply that Keith would have preferred a different mix, probably more in a blues style without the synthesisers. The other is labelled *Cult-Club* (* b - 7.21). The guitars on the track include Ron Wood on slide and Keith on electric, joined by Waddy Wachtel from the X-Pensive Winos.

1260. LOW DOWN (Jagger, Richards) 4.25
13 March - July 1997: Place: Ocean Way Recording Studios, Hollywood, California, USA.
Played Live: 1998
Rolling Stones with Jim Keltner, Waddy Wachtel, Darrell Leonard, Joe Sublett, Bernard Fowler, Blondie Chaplin.
Producer: Don Was, The Glimmer Twins.
Engineer: Rob Fraboni, Dan Bosworth.
Assistant Engineers: Alan Sanderson, John Sorenson. Mixed by Tom Lord-Alge, assisted by Mauricio Riagorri.
UK LP BRIDGES TO BABYLON: 29 September 1997: No. 6 - 6 weeks
USA LP BRIDGES TO BABYLON: 29 September 1997: No. 3 - 27 weeks

One of the first songs written for BRIDGES TO BABYLON, *Low Down* starts optimistically with a Keef riff and progresses lazily into a medium-tempo rocker that does not sustain the original beat. Rob Fraboni was Keith Richards' favoured producer and he worked on all of the Keith tracks. He had briefly helped out with the band back in 1973 when he worked at the Village Recorder studios, his credits including Bob Dylan, The Band, Eric Clapton, The Beach Boys and Bonnie Raitt.

He revealed that Keith wanted the album to be recorded sparsely in true rock and roll style but this idea fragmented when a mixture of producers and engineers became involved. A 12-inch edit bootleg and remix can be obtained (* b - 6.21, c - 6.04). The BRIDGES TO BABYLON title originated from the stage design, the concept of a "bridge" being discussed early on. One of Mick Jagger's friends suggested the word Babylon and it seemed to fit.

There were more than a few instances of the alliteration of the B words for album titles. And so the album and tour name became BRIDGES TO BABYLON. The name Babylon originated as the "gate of god", an ancient city whose citizens revered the lion as an icon of power, hence the lion (dubbed Simba) on the front cover. Keith may have thought about the link with reggae society and the "Lion of Judah". Other tour themed images taken from Babylon included the Tower Of Babel.

1261. ANYBODY SEEN MY BABY? (Jagger, Richards, Lang, Mink) 4.31
13 March - July 1997: Place: Ocean Way Recording Studios, Hollywood, California, USA.
Played Live: 1997, 1998
Rolling Stones with Waddy Wachtel, Don Was, Jamie Muhoberac, Bernard Fowler, Blondie Chaplin.
Producer: Don Was, The Dust Brothers, The Glimmer Twins.
Engineer: The Dust Brothers, Dan Bosworth.
Assistant Engineers: Alan Sanderson, Charles Gooden. Mixed by Tom Lord-Alge, assisted by Mauricio Riagorri.
UK Track CD Single Anybody Seen My Baby (LP Edit): 22 September 1997
UK LP BRIDGES TO BABYLON: 29 September 1997: No. 6 - 6 weeks
USA LP BRIDGES TO BABYLON: 29 September 1997: No. 3 - 27 weeks
UK CD box set THE SINGLES COLLECTION 1971-2006: 45 X 45s: 11 April 2011
USA CD box set THE SINGLES COLLECTION 1971-2006: 45 X 45s: 26 April 2011

Anybody Seen My Baby was written by Mick Jagger and the Dust Brothers saw the single potential in the song. As Darryl Jones was not present, the bass sound, so prominent in the mix, was delivered by session musician Jamie Muhoberac, who was more famous for his keyboard work, which he also contributes to the track. Don Was plays keyboards as well and Waddy Wachtel electric and acoustic guitar. The backing vocals that enhance the electronic feel to the track are supplied by Blondie Chaplin (contributor of guitar, vocals and percussion to The Band and The Beach Boys). In the album's final stages of production, Keith Richards, at home with Angela, listened to a playback and she heard k.d. lang's 1992 *Constant Craving* in the song.

It was checked out and *Anybody Seen My Baby* had a small passing similarity to *Constant Craving*. In the song-writing process all sorts of references are sucked in and this time they had unintentionally strayed across the permissible boundary by copying some chords. Mick denies that he had ever heard the lang song. The problem was quickly resolved by k.d. lang agreeing that her and Ben Mink would be appended as songwriters - an unusual and overly dramatic way of being credited as a co-writer on a Rolling Stones single.

In the video to accompany the single, directed by Samuel Mayer, Ron Wood introduced a girl in a tacky strip joint with, "Welcome to the Sleaze Ball Lounge and I'm the biggest sleaze of them all!" She dances to the track watched by the band and, as she leaves the stage, Mick follows her. The video continues in the New

York streets where Mick chases the girl. Along the boulevards, she is revealed as the very attractive Angelina Jolie, dressed in a gold, conically-shaped bosom basque and mackintosh. There are images of Keith on The Chrysler Building's devil gargoyle, beggars begging, subway journeys (during which Mick uses the tannoy to ask "Has anybody seen my baby?") and taxi rides - but she evades all his attempts to find her.

Mick was quite fixated with Angelina and, it is claimed, started a brief affair with her. Three principal re-mixes were made by renowned DJ and producer, Armand Van Helden (who used the line "Just in my imagination"), Soul Solution (Bobbie Guy and Ernie Lake) and Phil Jones. A (*Call Out Hook*) chorus version on the Single EP lasts nine seconds and was designed for radio station jingles only (* a - 0.09). A multitude of mixes appeared on single releases. Two Arman mixes were not released (* b - 9.32, c - 13.37).

1262. ANYBODY SEEN MY BABY? (ARMAND'S ROLLING STEELO MIX) (Jagger, Richards, Lang, Mink) 10.30
13 March - July 1997: Place: Ocean Way Recording Studios, Hollywood, California, USA.
Rolling Stones with Waddy Wachtel, Don Was, Jamie Muhoberac, Bernard Fowler, Blondie Chaplin.
Producer: Don Was, The Dust Brothers, The Glimmer Twins. Additional Production And Remix by Armand Van Helden.
Engineer: The Dust Brothers, Dan Bosworth.
Assistant Engineers: Alan Sanderson, Charles Gooden.
Mixed by Tom Lord-Alge, assisted by Mauricio Riagorri.
UK Track CD Single Anybody Seen My Baby? (LP Edit): 22 September 1997
USA Track CD Single Anybody Seen My Baby? (LP Edit): 22 September 1997
Europe Promo CD Single: 22 September 1997
USA Promo Vinyl Single: September 1997
UK CD box set THE SINGLES COLLECTION 1971-2006: 45 X 45s: 11 April 2011
USA CD box set THE SINGLES COLLECTION 1971-2006: 45 X 45s: 26 April 2011

1263. ANYBODY SEEN MY BABY? (SOUL SOLUTION REMIX EDIT) (Jagger, Richards, Lang, Mink) 4.20
13 March - July 1997: Place: Ocean Way Recording Studios, Hollywood, California, USA.
Rolling Stones with Waddy Wachtel, Don Was, Jamie Muhoberac, Bernard Fowler, Blondie Chaplin.
Producer: Don Was, The Dust Brothers, The Glimmer Twins. Additional Production And Remix by Soul Solution (Bobby Guy, Ernie Lake).
Engineer: The Dust Brothers, Dan Bosworth.
Assistant Engineers: Alan Sanderson, Charles Gooden.
Mixed by Tom Lord-Alge, assisted by Mauricio Riagorri.
UK Track Vinyl Single Anybody Seen My Baby? ((LP/Single Edit):22 September 1997
UK CD box set THE SINGLES COLLECTION 1971-2006: 45 X 45s: 11 April 2011
USA CD box set THE SINGLES COLLECTION 1971-2006: 45 X 45s: 26 April 2011

1264. ANYBODY SEEN MY BABY? (SOUL SOLUTION VOCAL DUB) (Jagger, Richards, Lang, Mink) 3.44
13 March - July 1997: Place: Ocean Way Recording Studios, Hollywood, California, USA.
Rolling Stones with Waddy Wachtel, Don Was, Jamie Muhoberac, Bernard Fowler, Blondie Chaplin.
Producer: Don Was, The Dust Brothers, The Glimmer Twins. Additional Production And Remix by Soul Solution (Bobby Guy, Ernie Lake).
Engineer: The Dust Brothers, Dan Bosworth.
Assistant Engineers: Alan Sanderson, Charles Gooden.
Mixed by Tom Lord-Alge, assisted by Mauricio Riagorri.
USA Track Promo Vinyl Single Anybody Seen My Baby? (Armand's Rolling Steelo Mix): September 1997

1265. ANYBODY SEEN MY BABY? (SOUL SOLUTION REMIX) (Jagger, Richards, Lang, Mink) 9.31
13 March - July 1997: Place: Ocean Way Recording Studios, Hollywood, California, USA.
Rolling Stones with Waddy Wachtel, Don Was, Jamie Muhoberac, Bernard Fowler, Blondie Chaplin.
Producer: Don Was, The Dust Brothers, The Glimmer Twins. Additional Production And Remix by Soul Solution (Bobby Guy, Ernie Lake).
Engineer: The Dust Brothers, Dan Bosworth.
Assistant Engineers: Alan Sanderson, Charles Gooden. Mixed by Tom Lord-Alge, assisted by Mauricio Riagorri.
UK Track CD Single Anybody Seen My Baby? (LP Edit): 22 September 1997
USA Track CD Single Anybody Seen My Baby? (LP Edit): 22 September 1997
Europe Track Promo CD Single Anybody Seen My Baby (Armand's Rolling Steelo Mix): 22 September 1997
UK CD box set THE SINGLES COLLECTION 1971-2006: 45 X 45s: 11 April 2011
USA CD box set THE SINGLES COLLECTION 1971-2006: 45 X 45s: 26 April 2011

1266. ANYBODY SEEN MY BABY? (BONUS ROLL MIX) (Jagger, Richards, Lang, Mink) 6.04
13 March - July 1997: Place: Ocean Way Recording Studios, Hollywood, California, USA.
Rolling Stones with Waddy Wachtel, Don Was, Jamie Muhoberac, Bernard Fowler, Blondie Chaplin.
Producer: Don Was, The Dust Brothers, The Glimmer Twins.
Engineer: The Dust Brothers, Dan Bosworth.
Assistant Engineers: Alan Sanderson, Charles Gooden. Mixed by Tom Lord-Alge, assisted by Mauricio Riagorri.
Europe Track Promo CD Single Anybody Seen My Baby (Armand's Rolling Steelo Mix): 22 September 1997
UK CD box set THE SINGLES COLLECTION 1971-2006: 45 X 45s: 11 April 2011
USA CD box set THE SINGLES COLLECTION 1971-2006: 45 X 45s: 26 April 2011

1267.   ANYBODY SEEN MY BABY? (LP/SINGLE EDIT) (Jagger, Richards, Lang, Mink) 4.07
13 March - July 1997: Place: Ocean Way Recording Studios, Hollywood, California, USA.
Rolling Stones with Waddy Wachtel, Don Was, Jamie Muhoberac, Bernard Fowler, Blondie Chaplin.
Producer: Don Was, The Dust Brothers, The Glimmer Twins.
Engineer: The Dust Brothers, Dan Bosworth.
Assistant Engineers: Alan Sanderson, Charles Gooden. Mixed by Tom Lord-Alge, assisted by Mauricio Riagorri.
UK Single: 22 September 1997: No. 22 - 3 weeks
USA Single: 22 September 1997
USA Promo CD Single: September 1997
UK CD LP FORTY LICKS: 30 September 2002: No. 2 - 45 weeks
USA CD LP FORTY LICKS: 1 October 2002: No. 2 - 50 weeks
UK CD box set THE SINGLES COLLECTION 1971-2006: 45 X 45s: 11 April 2011
USA CD box set THE SINGLES COLLECTION 1971-2006: 45 X 45s: 26 April 2011

1268.   ANYBODY SEEN MY BABY? (DON WAS RADIO REMIX) (Jagger, Richards, Lang, Mink) 3.45
13 March - July 1997: Place: Ocean Way Recording Studios, Hollywood, California, USA.
Rolling Stones with Waddy Wachtel, Don Was, Jamie Muhoberac, Bernard Fowler, Blondie Chaplin.
Producer: Don Was, The Dust Brothers, The Glimmer Twins.
Engineer: The Dust Brothers, Dan Bosworth.
Assistant Engineers: Alan Sanderson, Charles Gooden. Mixed by Tom Lord-Alge, assisted by Mauricio Riagorri. Remix by Don Was.
UK Track CD Single Anybody Seen My Baby? (LP Edit): 22 September 1997
USA Track CD Single Anybody Seen My Baby? (LP Edit): 22 September 1997
USA Track Promo CD Anybody Seen My Baby? (LP/Single Edit): September 1997

1269.   ANYBODY SEEN MY BABY? (NO BIZ EDIT) (Jagger, Richards, Lang, Mink) 4.03
13 March - July 1997: Place: Ocean Way Recording Studios, Hollywood, California, USA.
Rolling Stones with Waddy Wachtel, Don Was, Jamie Muhoberac, Bernard Fowler, Blondie Chaplin.
Producer: Don Was, The Dust Brothers, The Glimmer Twins.
Engineer: The Dust Brothers, Dan Bosworth.
Assistant Engineers: Alan Sanderson, Charles Gooden. Mixed by Tom Lord-Alge, assisted by Mauricio Riagorri.
UK Track CD Single Anybody Seen My Baby? (LP Edit): 22 September 1997
USA Track CD Single Anybody Seen My Baby? (LP Edit): 22 September 1997
USA Track Promo CD Anybody Seen My Baby? (LP/Single Edit): September 1997

1270.   ANYBODY SEEN MY BABY? (PHIL JONES REMIX) (Jagger, Richards, Lang, Mink) 4.30
13 March - July 1997: Place: Ocean Way Recording Studios, Hollywood, California, USA.
Rolling Stones with Waddy Wachtel, Don Was, Jamie Muhoberac, Bernard Fowler, Blondie Chaplin.
Producer: Don Was, The Dust Brothers, The Glimmer Twins.
Engineer: The Dust Brothers, Dan Bosworth.
Assistant Engineers: Alan Sanderson, Charles Gooden. Mixed by Tom Lord-Alge, assisted by Mauricio Riagorri. Remix by Phil Jones.
UK Track CD Single Saint Of Me: 26 January 1998
USA Track CD Single Saint Of Me: 26 January 1998
UK CD box set THE SINGLES COLLECTION 1971-2006: 45 X 45s: 11 April 2011
USA CD box set THE SINGLES COLLECTION 1971-2006: 45 X 45s: 26 April 2011

1271.   ANYBODY SEEN MY BABY? (CASANOVA NEW VOCAL REMIX) (Jagger, Richards, Lang, Mink) 6.33
13 March - July 1997: Place: Ocean Way Recording Studios, Hollywood, California, USA.
Rolling Stones with Waddy Wachtel, Don Was, Jamie Muhoberac, Bernard Fowler, Blondie Chaplin.
Producer: Don Was, The Dust Brothers, The Glimmer Twins.
Engineer: The Dust Brothers, Dan Bosworth.
Assistant Engineers: Alan Sanderson, Charles Gooden. Mixed by Tom Lord-Alge, assisted by Mauricio Riagorri. Remix by Phil Jones.
USA Track Promo Vinyl Single Anybody Seen My Baby? (Armand's Rolling Steelo Mix): September 1997

1272.   FLIP THE SWITCH (Jagger, Richards) 3.27
13 March - July 1997: Place: Ocean Way Recording Studios, Hollywood, California, USA.
Played Live: 1997, 1998
Rolling Stones with Waddy Wachtel, Jim Keltner, Jeff Sarli, Joe Sublett, Bernard Fowler, Blondie Chaplin.
Producer: Don Was, The Glimmer Twins.
Engineer: Rob Fraboni, Dan Bosworth.
Assistant Engineers: Alan Sanderson, John Sorenson. Mixed by Tom Lord-Alge, assisted by Mauricio Riagorri.
UK LP BRIDGES TO BABYLON: 29 September 1997: No. 6 - 6 weeks
USA LP BRIDGES TO BABYLON: 29 September 1997: No. 3 - 27 weeks
UK & USA Promo Single: December 1997

Claimed by Mick Jagger to be faster than *Rip This Joint*, *Flip The Switch* lifts off the flight deck like no other Stones song. The momentum propels it forward until it runs out of gas, a little quicker than you would expect. The bass (an upright acoustic) slot this time is taken by a relatively unknown session player, Jeff Sarli - it produced a wider, fatter sound that Keith Richards loved in a rock and roll record. Waddy Wachtel is featured again on electric guitar and Jim Keltner on percussion. He formulated the fast rhythm, with Charlie Watts on a long percussive out-take.

It was suggested that Jim play a couple of percussive pieces on the album and he ended up being on it all. Both Ron Wood and Keith were inspired by the freshness of Charlie's playing. *On Flip The Switch*, Keith had a hook that he placed on top of the mix and it sure kicked ass. A baritone saxophone is played by Joe Sublett. In the No.134 Q magazine article by David Sinclair, Mick Jagger says that the mass suicide by the Heaven's Gate cult was anticipated by him. On 26 March 1997, 39 of the cult members committed suicide en masse (with a bizarre uniform and a shaving kit). As Mick says in the lyrics written 10 days before the incident in San Diego, "I got my money, my ticket, all that shit, I even got myself a little shaving kit". The song is about being on death row . . . chill me, freeze me, it's in my blood, flip the switch.

It was edited without the word "shit" to make it more radio friendly (* a - 3.28) and, on the same promotional CD, the call out hooks were featured (* b - 0.13, c - 0.14). On a bootleg hyper mix, the pace of the song was no slower but more keyboard orientated unlike the original (* d - 5.59). *Flip The Switch* was at one time a working title for the album, as was *Blessed Poison*. Ronnie Wood owned a racing horse named *Flip The Switch*, which raced in the late 90s and produced a winning performance.

1273. ALWAYS SUFFERING (Jagger, Richards) 4.43
13 March - July 1997: Place: Ocean Way Recording Studios, Hollywood, California, USA.
Rolling Stones with Darryl Jones, Waddy Wachtel, Jim Keltner, Benmont Tench, Bernard Fowler, Doug Wimbish, Blondie Chaplin.
Producer: Don Was, Pierre De Beauport, The Glimmer Twins.
Engineer: Ed Cherney, Dan Bosworth.
Assistant Engineer: Alan Sanderson. Mixed by Ed Cherney, assisted by Stewart Brawley.
UK LP BRIDGES TO BABYLON: 29 September 1997: No. 6 - 6 weeks
USA LP BRIDGES TO BABYLON: 29 September 1997: No. 3 - 27 weeks

As can already be seen by the personnel on the album, the closeness of VOODOO LOUNGE in terms of guest artists was sacrificed for more variety and diversity on BRIDGES. Mick Jagger wanted it to be a change of direction - as well as vocals he plays guitar on *Always Suffering*. It is a slow tempo song and does not quite meet the mark - it is an obvious Jagger-penned song.

Waddy Wachtel plays acoustic guitar, Benmont Tench a Hammond B-3 organ and piano and Jim Keltner is on percussion. The backing vocals include Keith Richards, Waddy Wachtel, Benmont Tench, Bernard Fowler, Doug Wimbish, Blondie Chaplin and do we believe the sleeve notes that say Charlie Watts also contributed vocals? For one of the few times on BRIDGES, Darryl Jones plays his white bass guitar. A bootleg remix can be obtained (* a - 9.22).

1274. THIEF IN THE NIGHT (Jagger, Richards, De Beauport) 5.15
13 March - July 1997: Place: Ocean Way Recording Studios, Hollywood, California, USA.
Played Live: 1998, 2003
Rolling Stones with Darryl Jones, Pierre De Beauport, Jim Keltner, Waddy Wachtel, Darrell Leonard, Joe Sublett, Bernard Fowler, Blondie Chaplin.
Producer: Don Was, The Glimmer Twins.
Engineer: Rob Fraboni, Dan Bosworth.
Assistant Engineers: Alan Sanderson. Mixed by Rob Fraboni, assisted by George Fullan.
UK LP BRIDGES TO BABYLON: 29 September 1997: No. 6 - 6 weeks
USA LP BRIDGES TO BABYLON: 29 September 1997: No. 3 - 27 weeks

The last two tracks on the BRIDGES TO BABYLON album are both slow Keith Richards compositions, one rolls into another. As the biblical book of Peter said, "But the day of the Lord will come as a thief in the night" which is how Keith came upon the song title. The waspish soul of *Thief In The Night* has a wash-over of percussion by Jim Keltner riding throughout the song and silky backing vocals by Bernard Fowler and Blondie Chaplin.

As Keith introduced the song on tour he said, "this is a new song about an old story" concerning a lost love. In fact it was about Keith's journey through his relationships from Dartford, touching upon an early love and then Ronnie Spector, Anita and Patti. Pierre De Beauport is given a songwriting credit by creating the original riff and plays a suitcase Fender Rhodes piano and a classic Wurlitzer, while Keith is on a standard piano. The Dust Brothers noted that Pierre played a major role with the band not just musically but also made the engineer's job easier by setting up microphones and other equipment just the way the band liked it.

Mick Jagger felt that *Thief In The Night* was one of the weaker tracks on the album and apparently did not do a convincing vocal. Keith re-did it with Bernard Fowler and Blondie Chaplin. This version was mysteriously lost as master tapes were produced for the released product. Keith, now back home in Connecticut, went to a studio on Long Island and, along with Pierre, helped to remix it again. This tape was sent back to Don Was for inclusion on the album and with a note that, in no uncertain terms, this was the final cut. It was not to be messed with.

Apparently, part of the problem was that this would give Keith three solo vocal tracks on one album, something which Mick was not happy with. It was Don Was that tactically suggested to Mick that the last two tracks on the album by Keith would segue into each other like a song medley. Keith was surprised that Mick allowed Pierre a songwriting credit. However, the delay caused the band to commence the tour without a released product.

1275. SAINT OF ME (Jagger, Richards) 5.14
13 March - July 1997: Place: Ocean Way Recording Studios, Hollywood, California, USA.
Played Live: 1997, 1998, 1999, 2003
Rolling Stones with Me'Shell Ndegeocello, Billy Preston, Pierre De Beauport, Waddy Wachtel, Jamie Muhoberac, Bernard Fowler, Blondie Chaplin.
Producer: The Dust Brothers, The Glimmer Twins.
Engineer: The Dust Brothers, Dan Bosworth.
Assistant Engineers: Alan Sanderson, Charles Gooden. Mixed by Tom Lord-Alge, assisted by Mauricio Riagorri.
UK LP BRIDGES TO BABYLON: 29 September 1997: No. 6 - 6 weeks
USA LP BRIDGES TO BABYLON: 29 September 1997: No. 3 - 27 weeks

UK Single: 26 January 1998: No. 26 - 2 weeks
USA Single: 26 January 1998: No. 94 - 4 weeks
USA CD Promo Edit Single: January 1998
UK CD box set THE SINGLES COLLECTION 1971-2006: 45 X 45s: 11 April 2011
USA CD box set THE SINGLES COLLECTION 1971-2006: 45 X 45s: 26 April 2011

Saint Of Me was written by Mick Jagger and took shape over a number of different sessions with the Dust Brothers at their PCP Labs studio in Silverlake, Los Angeles, before he got together with Keith Richards. He played around with the track on keyboards and acoustic guitar, trying to get to grips with the composition.
The religious lyrics tell stories of the persecuted and betrayed: Saul, who became St Paul when converted; Salome, who demanded that Herod should serve John the Baptist's head on a plate. The outcome is a passionate discourse (listen to Mick on "I thought I heard an angel cry") and became a high spot of the album. The religious tones are complemented by Billy Preston's Hammond organ playing - Chuck Leavell was missing from the sessions.
The bass guitar was a combination of Me'Shell Ndegeocello and Pierre De Beauport on six-string bass. Keith was conspicuous by his absence on the track, Waddy Wachtel and Ron Wood fulfilling the guitar roles. The excellent catchy chorus was used to good effect during live shows and became a sing-a-long moment. In January 1998, it was released as a single during the American tour and was subjected to a number of re-mixes by the Dust Brothers and Todd Terry.
The video, set in a wash-room, has an angel floating a foot above the floor (surely nothing to do with angel dust?), John The Baptist's head is also shown on the dinner plate. The video finishes with a halo over Mick's head . . . silly . . . Saint Mick, a consecration that was a title too far even for him. Again a multitude of mixes are available some bootlegs. The one labelled *Alternate* and *Detroit Floor* are bootlegs (* a - 5.13, b - 12.42). A *Call Out Hook Version* (* c - 0.12). The single release was edited (* d - 4.11).

1276.   SAINT OF ME (TODD TERRY EXTENDED MIX) (Jagger, Richards) 6.03
13 March - July 1997: Place: Ocean Way Recording Studios, Hollywood, California, USA.
Rolling Stones with Me'Shell Ndegeocello, Billy Preston, Pierre De Beauport, Waddy Wachtel, Jamie Muhoberac, Bernard Fowler, Blondie Chaplin.
Producer: The Dust Brothers, The Glimmer Twins.
Engineer: The Dust Brothers, Dan Bosworth.
Assistant Engineers: Alan Sanderson, Charles Gooden. Mixed by Tom Lord-Alge, assisted by Mauricio Riagorri.
Promo 12-inch Track Saint Of Me (Deep Dish Club Mix Part One): January 1998
UK CD box set THE SINGLES COLLECTION 1971-2006: 45 X 45s: 11 April 2011
USA CD box set THE SINGLES COLLECTION 1971-2006: 45 X 45s: 26 April 2011

1277.   SAINT OF ME (TODD TERRY FADE) (Jagger, Richards) 3.32
13 March - July 1997: Place: Ocean Way Recording Studios, Hollywood, California, USA.
Rolling Stones with Me'Shell Ndegeocello, Billy Preston, Pierre De Beauport, Waddy Wachtel, Jamie Muhoberac, Bernard Fowler, Blondie Chaplin.
Producer: The Dust Brothers, The Glimmer Twins.
Engineer: The Dust Brothers, Dan Bosworth.
Assistant Engineers: Alan Sanderson, Charles Gooden. Mixed by Tom Lord-Alge, assisted by Mauricio Riagorri.
Promo 12-inch Track Saint Of Me (Deep Dish Club Mix Part One): January 1998.

1278.   SAINT OF ME (TODD TERRY TEE'S FREEZE DUB) (Jagger, Richards) 7.43
13 March - July 1997: Place: Ocean Way Recording Studios, Hollywood, California, USA.
Rolling Stones with Me'Shell Ndegeocello, Billy Preston, Pierre De Beauport, Waddy Wachtel, Jamie Muhoberac, Bernard Fowler, Blondie Chaplin.
Producer: The Dust Brothers, The Glimmer Twins.
Engineer: The Dust Brothers, Dan Bosworth.
Assistant Engineers: Alan Sanderson, Charles Gooden. Mixed by Tom Lord-Alge, assisted by Mauricio Riagorri.
Promo 12-inch Track Saint Of Me (Deep Dish Club Mix Part One): January 1998.

1279.   SAINT OF ME (TODD TERRY DUB NO. 2) (Jagger, Richards) 7.40
13 March - July 1997: Place: Ocean Way Recording Studios, Hollywood, California, USA.
Rolling Stones with Me'Shell Ndegeocello, Billy Preston, Pierre De Beauport, Waddy Wachtel, Jamie Muhoberac, Bernard Fowler, Blondie Chaplin.
Producer: The Dust Brothers, The Glimmer Twins.
Engineer: The Dust Brothers, Dan Bosworth.
Assistant Engineers: Alan Sanderson, Charles Gooden. Mixed by Tom Lord-Alge, assisted by Mauricio Riagorri.
Promo 12-inch Track Saint Of Me (Deep Dish Club Mix Part One): January 1998.

1280.   SAINT OF ME (DEEP DISH CLUB MIX PART ONE) (Jagger, Richards) 7.35
13 March - July 1997: Place: Ocean Way Recording Studios, Hollywood, California, USA.
Rolling Stones with Me'Shell Ndegeocello, Billy Preston, Pierre De Beauport, Waddy Wachtel, Jamie Muhoberac, Bernard Fowler, Blondie Chaplin.
Producer: The Dust Brothers, The Glimmer Twins.
Engineer: The Dust Brothers, Dan Bosworth.
Assistant Engineers: Alan Sanderson, Charles Gooden. Mixed by Tom Lord-Alge, assisted by Mauricio Riagorri. Remix by Dubfire & Sharam.
UK Track CD Single Saint Of Me (Radio Edit): 26 January 1998
USA Track CD Single Saint Of Me (Radio Edit): 26 January 1998
Promo 12-inch Single: January 1998
UK CD box set THE SINGLES COLLECTION 1971-2006: 45 X 45s: 11 April 2011
USA CD box set THE SINGLES COLLECTION 1971-2006: 45 X 45s: 26 April 2011

1281. SAINT OF ME (DEEP DISH ROLLING DUB) (Jagger, Richards) 7.12
13 March - July 1997: Place: Ocean Way Recording Studios, Hollywood, California, USA.
Rolling Stones with Me'Shell Ndegeocello, Billy Preston, Pierre De Beauport, Waddy Wachtel, Jamie Muhoberac, Bernard Fowler, Blondie Chaplin.
Producer: The Dust Brothers, The Glimmer Twins.
Engineer: The Dust Brothers, Dan Bosworth.
Assistant Engineers: Alan Sanderson, Charles Gooden. Mixed by Tom Lord-Alge, assisted by Mauricio Riagorri. Remix by Dubfire & Sharam.
Promo 12-inch Single Saint Of Me (Deep Dish Club Mix Part One): January 1998
UK CD box set THE SINGLES COLLECTION 1971-2006: 45 X 45s: 11 April 2011
USA CD box set THE SINGLES COLLECTION 1971-2006: 45 X 45s: 26 April 2011

1282. SAINT OF ME (DEEP DISH GRUNGE GARAGE DUB) (Jagger, Richards) 7.25
13 March - July 1997: Place: Ocean Way Recording Studios, Hollywood, California, USA.
Rolling Stones with Me'Shell Ndegeocello, Billy Preston, Pierre De Beauport, Waddy Wachtel, Jamie Muhoberac, Bernard Fowler, Blondie Chaplin.
Producer: The Dust Brothers, The Glimmer Twins.
Engineer: The Dust Brothers, Dan Bosworth.
Assistant Engineers: Alan Sanderson, Charles Gooden. Mixed by Tom Lord-Alge, assisted by Mauricio Riagorri. Remix by Dubfire & Sharam.
UK Track CD Single Saint Of Me (Radio Edit): 26 January 1998
USA Track CD Single Saint Of Me (Radio Edit): 26 January 1998
Promo 12-inch Single Saint Of Me (Deep Dish Club Mix Part One): January 1998
UK CD box set THE SINGLES COLLECTION 1971-2006: 45 X 45s: 11 April 2011
USA CD box set THE SINGLES COLLECTION 1971-2006: 45 X 45s: 26 April 2011

1283. SAINT OF ME (DEEP DISH GRUNGE GARAGE REMIX EDIT) (Jagger, Richards) 3.22
13 March - July 1997: Place: Ocean Way Recording Studios, Hollywood, California, USA.
Rolling Stones with Me'Shell Ndegeocello, Billy Preston, Pierre De Beauport, Waddy Wachtel, Jamie Muhoberac, Bernard Fowler, Blondie Chaplin.
Producer: The Dust Brothers, The Glimmer Twins.
Engineer: The Dust Brothers, Dan Bosworth.
Assistant Engineers: Alan Sanderson, Charles Gooden. Mixed by Tom Lord-Alge, assisted by Mauricio Riagorri. Remix by Dubfire & Sharam.
USA Promo CD Single: February 1998

1284. SAINT OF ME (DEEP DISH GRUNGE GARAGE REMIX) (Jagger, Richards) 14.08
AKA: Saint Of Me (Deep Dish Grunge Garage Remix Parts 1 & 2)
13 March - July 1997: Place: Ocean Way Recording Studios, Hollywood, California, USA.
Rolling Stones with Me'Shell Ndegeocello, Billy Preston, Pierre De Beauport, Waddy Wachtel, Jamie Muhoberac, Bernard Fowler, Blondie Chaplin.
Producer: The Dust Brothers, The Glimmer Twins.
Engineer: The Dust Brothers, Dan Bosworth.
Assistant Engineers: Alan Sanderson, Charles Gooden. Mixed by Tom Lord-Alge, assisted by Mauricio Riagorri. Remix by Dubfire & Sharam.
UK Track CD Single Saint Of Me (Radio Edit): 26 January 1998
USA Track CD Single Saint Of Me (Radio Edit): 26 January 1998
UK CD box set THE SINGLES COLLECTION 1971-2006: 45 X 45s: 11 April 2011
USA CD box set THE SINGLES COLLECTION 1971-2006: 45 X 45s: 26 April 2011

1285. YOU DON'T HAVE TO MEAN IT (Jagger, Richards) 3.44
13 March - July 1997: Place: Ocean Way Recording Studios, Hollywood, California, USA.
Played Live: 1997, 1998, 1999, 2002, 2003
Rolling Stones with Darryl Jones, Clinton Clifford, Jim Keltner, Darrell Leonard, Joe Sublett, Bernard Fowler, Blondie Chaplin.
Producer: Don Was, Rob Fraboni, The Glimmer Twins.
Engineer: Rob Fraboni, Dan Bosworth.
Assistant Engineers: Alan Sanderson. Mixed by Rob Fraboni. Mix Engineer: John Sorenson, assisted by Robi Banerji.
UK LP BRIDGES TO BABYLON: 29 September 1997: No. 6 - 6 weeks
USA LP BRIDGES TO BABYLON: 29 September 1997: No. 3 - 27 weeks

Clinton Clifford opens *You Don't Have To Mean It* with a flourish on the B-3 organ and the piano. It is a reggae song that swings along effectively with brass sounds by Darrell Leonard and Joe Sublett. The beat is unusual, which was confirmed by Mick Jagger, since it started life with Mick on drums, giving it a Buddy Holly backbeat. It then evolved into a reggae tune. Keith Richards is lead vocalist, backed by Bernard Fowler and Blondie Chaplin.
Darryl Jones provides bass on one of his three tracks for the album. Originally it was written in a Jamaican bar of ill-repute in Barbados. Keith hired a room with a bevy of bikini-clad women to drink, talk and play guitar - not their usual gig. They were snoozing and Keith popped questions at them, which contributed to the song's lyrics. One of them was: "What do you talk about to the gentlemen?" The answer was: "Anything - you don't have to mean it".

1286. ALREADY OVER ME (Jagger, Richards) 5.24
13 March - July 1997: Place: Ocean Way Recording Studios, Hollywood, California, USA.
Played Live: 1998
Rolling Stones with Jim Keltner, Don Was, Benmont Tench, Kenny Aronoff, Blondie Chaplin, Bernard Fowler.
Producer: Don Was, The Glimmer Twins.

Engineer: John X Volaitis, Dan Bosworth.

Assistant Engineers: Alan Sanderson, John Sorenson. Mixed by Bob Clearmountain, assisted by Ryan Freeland.

UK LP BRIDGES TO BABYLON: 29 September 1997: No. 6 - 6 weeks
USA LP BRIDGES TO BABYLON: 29 September 1997: No. 3 - 27 weeks

As well as the Dust Brothers, Mick Jagger also wanted to use the talents of Ken "Babyface" Edmonds to overdub and mix tracks. Babyface was very complimentary about *Already Over Me* and worked on a version. The outcome was not to Mick's liking; he just knew it was not right and later agreed that Babyface should have worked on another track. There were no compromises and Don Was agreed that it had to be re-recorded in a more traditional Stones' style.

This was done with Mick on acoustic, Keith Richards' lead guitar, Don Was on bass, piano by Blondie Chaplin, organ by Benmont Tench, mysteriously a bucket by percussionist Kenny Aronoff and also Jim Keltner on percussion. The feel of the track was enhanced by the guitar playing of Ron Wood, who contributed a dobro steel and a warm baritone guitar. The escalating guitar chords were the hook for an ambient mix depicting a defining contribution to the track. Engineer John X Volaitis was from the Danny Saber camp, having also worked with Black Grape. Two longer, ambient mixes appeared on a bootleg (* a - 9.04, b - 9.13).

1287. TOO TIGHT (Jagger, Richards) 3.37
13 March - July 1997: Place: Ocean Way Recording Studios, Hollywood, California, USA.
Rolling Stones with Jeff Sarli, Jim Keltner, Waddy Wachtel, Bernard Fowler, Blondie Chaplin.
Producer: Don Was, The Glimmer Twins.
Engineer: Rob Fraboni, Dan Bosworth, Jim Scott.
Assistant Engineers: Alan Sanderson, John Sorenson. Mixed by Tom Lord-Alge, assisted by Mauricio Riagorri.
UK LP BRIDGES TO BABYLON: 29 September 1997: No. 6 - 6 weeks
USA LP BRIDGES TO BABYLON: 29 September 1997: No. 3 - 27 weeks

From a dextrous, 15-second tranquil entrance by Keith Richards and Ron Wood, *Too Tight* soon emerges from the starting blocks fired by the song's riff. It is standard rocker fare with three guitarists including Keith, Ron (pedal steel and electric) and Waddy Wachtel. Acoustic bass and piano are played rock and roll style by Jeff Sarli and Blondie Chaplin respectively. The song was not played live on the subsequent tour which, perhaps, indicates its low importance.

1288. GUNFACE (Jagger, Richards) 5.02
13 March - July 1997: Place: Ocean Way Recording Studios, Hollywood, California, USA.
Rolling Stones with Jim Keltner, Danny Saber.
Producer: Danny Saber, The Glimmer Twins.
Engineer: John X Volaitis.
Assistant Engineers: John Sorenson, Alan Sanderson. Mixed by John X Volaitis.
UK LP BRIDGES TO BABYLON: 29 September 1997: No. 6 - 6 weeks
USA LP BRIDGES TO BABYLON: 29 September 1997: No. 3 - 27 weeks

The Black Grape production team (Danny Saber and John Volaitis) led this guitar orientated rock/funk number. Danny Saber even played the synthesised keyboards, bass and electric guitar. Three studios within the same building were used to record, which concentrated the mind and speeded up the recording process. Mick Jagger would be in one studio on piano while Keith Richards would be over-dubbing guitar in another.

On *Gunface*, additional guitar pieces were played by Mick, Keith and Ron Wood, who was on a heavy slide. Charlie Watts plays drums and Jim Keltner assists on percussion. It has a decidedly fresh yet menacing sound and raises its head above some of the other album cuts. The lyrics relate to a guy who wants to put a gun in the face of his girlfriend's lover - "make him and then her, obsolete" and "I'm gonna teach her how to scream". An extended re-mix is available on bootleg (* a - 6.17).

1289. ANYWAY YOU LOOK AT IT (Jagger, Richards) 4.20
13 March - July 1997: Place: Ocean Way Recording Studios, Hollywood, California, USA.
Producer: Don Was, The Glimmer Twins.
UK Track CD Single Saint Of Me (Radio Edit): 26 January 1998
USA Track CD Single Saint Of Me (Radio Edit): 26 January 1998
USA Track 12-Inch Single Saint Of Me (Deep Dish Club Mix): 9 February 1998
USA CD LP ROLLING STONES RARITIES 1971-2003: 22 November 2005: No. 76 - 6 weeks
UK CD LP ROLLING STONES RARITIES 1971-2003: 28 November 2005
UK CD box set THE SINGLES COLLECTION 1971-2006: 45 X 45s: 11 April 2011
USA CD box set THE SINGLES COLLECTION 1971-2006: 45 X 45s: 26 April 2011

A soft ballad featuring violin and acoustic guitars. The violin (even if electronic) is certainly not an instrument that one normally associates with the Stones. The track is a quiet number without any distinct percussion - Mick Jagger almost speaks the lyrics and Keith Richards contributes a one-liner. *Anyway You Look At It* was not released on the album but appeared on the *Saint Of Me* single.

1290. OUT OF CONTROL (IN HAND WITH FLUKE) (Jagger, Richards) 8.28
13 March - July 1997: Place: Ocean Way Recording Studios, Hollywood, California, USA.
Rolling Stones with Jim Keltner, Waddy Wachtel, Don Was, Jamie Muhoberac, Danny Saber, Bernard Fowler, Blondie Chaplin.
Producer: Don Was, The Glimmer Twins.
Engineer: John X Volaitis, Dan Bosworth.
Assistant Engineers: John Sorenson, Alan Sanderson. Mixed by Wally Gagel, assisted by Alan Sanderson. Remixed by Fluke.
UK Track CD Single Out Of Control (Album Radio Edit): 17 August 1998
UK CD box set THE SINGLES COLLECTION 1971-2006: 45 X 45s: 11 April 2011
USA CD box set THE SINGLES COLLECTION 1971-2006: 45 X 45s: 26 April 2011

1291. OUT OF CONTROL (IN HAND WITH FLUKE - RADIO EDIT) (Jagger, Richards) 4.32
13 March - July 1997: Place: Ocean Way Recording Studios, Hollywood, California, USA.
Rolling Stones with Jim Keltner, Waddy Wachtel, Don Was, Jamie Muhoberac, Danny Saber, Bernard Fowler, Blondie Chaplin.
Producer: Don Was, The Glimmer Twins.
Engineer: John X Volaitis, Dan Bosworth.
Assistant Engineers: John Sorenson, Alan Sanderson. Mixed by Wally Gagel, assisted by Alan Sanderson. Remixed by Fluke.
UK B-side Single Out Of Control (Album Radio Edit): 17 August 1998
UK CD box set THE SINGLES COLLECTION 1971-2006: 45 X 45s: 11 April 2011
USA CD box set THE SINGLES COLLECTION 1971-2006: 45 X 45s: 26 April 2011

1292. OUT OF CONTROL (IN HAND WITH FLUKE INSTRUMENTAL) (Jagger, Richards) 5.55
13 March - July 1997: Place: Ocean Way Recording Studios, Hollywood, California, USA.
Rolling Stones with Jim Keltner, Waddy Wachtel, Don Was, Jamie Muhoberac, Danny Saber, Bernard Fowler, Blondie Chaplin.
Producer: Don Was, The Glimmer Twins.
Engineer: John X Volaitis, Dan Bosworth.
Assistant Engineers: John Sorenson, Alan Sanderson. Mixed by Wally Gagel, assisted by Alan Sanderson. Remixed by Fluke.
UK Track CD Single Out Of Control (Album Radio Edit): 17 August 1998
UK CD box set THE SINGLES COLLECTION 1971-2006: 45 X 45s: 11 April 2011
USA CD box set THE SINGLES COLLECTION 1971-2006: 45 X 45s: 26 April 2011

1293. OUT OF CONTROL (SABER MASTER WITH FADE) (Jagger, Richards) 4.42
13 March - July 1997: Place: Ocean Way Recording Studios, Hollywood, California, USA.
Rolling Stones with Jim Keltner, Waddy Wachtel, Don Was, Jamie Muhoberac, Danny Saber, Bernard Fowler, Blondie Chaplin.
Producer: Don Was, The Glimmer Twins.
Engineer: John X Volaitis, Dan Bosworth.
Assistant Engineers: John Sorenson, Alan Sanderson. Mixed by Wally Gagel, assisted by Alan Sanderson. Remixed by Danny Saber.
Promo CD Single: June 1998

This same mix was extended by an extra minute with no fade and that was titled - *Out Of Control 'Danny Saber's Demo'* (* a - 5.39). This was released on in-house Virgin Records Promo CDR's containing ten unreleased tracks. These mixes include *Bi-Polar Horns Of Control* (* b - 5.09), *Bi-Polar Fat Controller Mix (Percussive Version)* (* c - 5.24), *S.D.S. Mix* (* d - 4.23), *S.D.S. Mix (No Samples)* (* e - 4.22), *S.D.S. Dub Mix* (* f - 4.51), *Fluke Vocal 12-inch* (* g - 6.36), *Fluke Instrumental* (* h - 5.36), *Fluke Vocal 12-inch #2* (* i - 6.51) and *Fluke Vocal 7-inch #2* (* j - 4.10).

1294. OUT OF CONTROL (SABER FINAL MIX) (Jagger, Richards) 5.45
13 March - July 1997: Place: Ocean Way Recording Studios, Hollywood, California, USA.
Rolling Stones with Jim Keltner, Waddy Wachtel, Don Was, Jamie Muhoberac, Danny Saber, Bernard Fowler, Blondie Chaplin.
Producer: Don Was, The Glimmer Twins.
Engineer: John X Volaitis, Dan Bosworth.
Assistant Engineers: John Sorenson, Alan Sanderson. Mixed by Wally Gagel, assisted by Alan Sanderson. Remixed by Danny Saber.
UK CD Single: 17 August 1998: No. 51 - 1 week
UK CD box set THE SINGLES COLLECTION 1971-2006: 45 X 45s: 11 April 2011
USA CD box set THE SINGLES COLLECTION 1971-2006: 45 X 45s: 26 April 2011

1295. OUT OF CONTROL (BI-POLAR AT THE CONTROLS) (Jagger, Richards) 5.12
13 March - July 1997: Place: Ocean Way Recording Studios, Hollywood, California, USA.
Rolling Stones with Jim Keltner, Waddy Wachtel, Don Was, Jamie Muhoberac, Danny Saber, Bernard Fowler, Blondie Chaplin.
Producer: Don Was, The Glimmer Twins.
Engineer: John X Volaitis, Dan Bosworth.
Assistant Engineers: John Sorenson, Alan Sanderson. Mixed by Wally Gagel, assisted by Alan Sanderson. Remixed by Fluke.
UK Promo Single: August 1998
UK Track CD Single Out Of Control (Saber Final Mix): 17 August 1998
UK CD box set THE SINGLES COLLECTION 1971-2006: 45 X 45s: 11 April 2011
USA CD box set THE SINGLES COLLECTION 1971-2006: 45 X 45s: 26 April 2011

1296. OUT OF CONTROL (BI-POLAR'S OUTER VERSION) (Jagger, Richards) 5.09
13 March - July 1997: Place: Ocean Way Recording Studios, Hollywood, California, USA.
Rolling Stones with Jim Keltner, Waddy Wachtel, Don Was, Jamie Muhoberac, Danny Saber, Bernard Fowler, Blondie Chaplin.
Producer: Don Was, The Glimmer Twins.
Engineer: John X Volaitis, Dan Bosworth.
Assistant Engineers: John Sorenson, Alan Sanderson. Mixed by Wally Gagel, assisted by Alan Sanderson. Remixed by Fluke.
UK Promo B-side Single Out Of Control (Bi-Polar At The Controls): August 1998
UK CD box set THE SINGLES COLLECTION 1971-2006: 45 X 45s: 11 April 2011
USA CD box set THE SINGLES COLLECTION 1971-2006: 45 X 45s: 26 April 2011

1297. OUT OF CONTROL (BI-POLAR'S FAT CONTROLLER MIX) (Jagger, Richards) 5.24
13 March - July 1997: Place: Ocean Way Recording Studios, Hollywood, California, USA.
Rolling Stones with Jim Keltner, Waddy Wachtel, Don Was, Jamie Muhoberac, Danny Saber, Bernard Fowler, Blondie Chaplin.
Producer: Don Was, The Glimmer Twins.
Engineer: John X Volaitis, Dan Bosworth.
Assistant Engineers: John Sorenson, Alan Sanderson. Mixed by Wally Gagel, assisted by Alan Sanderson. Remixed by Fluke.
UK Track CD Single Out Of Control (Saber Final Mix): 17 August 1998
UK CD box set THE SINGLES COLLECTION 1971-2006: 45 X 45s: 11 April 2011
USA CD box set THE SINGLES COLLECTION 1971-2006: 45 X 45s: 26 April 2011

1298. OUT OF CONTROL (Jagger, Richards) 4.43
13 March - July 1997: Place: Ocean Way Recording Studios, Hollywood, California, USA.
Played Live: 1997, 1998, 1999, 2003, 2005
Rolling Stones with Jim Keltner, Waddy Wachtel, Don Was, Jamie Muhoberac, Danny Saber, Bernard Fowler, Blondie Chaplin.
Producer: Don Was, The Glimmer Twins.
Engineer: John X Volaitis, Dan Bosworth.
Assistant Engineers: John Sorenson, Alan Sanderson. Mixed by Wally Gagel, assisted by Alan Sanderson.
UK LP BRIDGES TO BABYLON: 29 September 1997: No. 6 - 6 weeks
USA LP BRIDGES TO BABYLON: 29 September 1997: No. 3 - 27 weeks
UK Single: 17 August 1998: No. 51 - 1 week
UK CD box set THE SINGLES COLLECTION 1971-2006: 45 X 45s: 11 April 2011
USA CD box set THE SINGLES COLLECTION 1971-2006: 45 X 45s: 26 April 2011

The highlight of the album is *Out Of Control* and no expense was spared on the guest musicians. It is a subtle track that is quiet during the verse and builds up to the chorus, crashes and rolls, then simmers down before boiling over again. The harmonica is used with good effect as the song grooves along. Mick Jagger wrote the basis of the song and also plays a wah-wah guitar; other guitars include Keith Richards, Waddy Wachtel, Ron Wood and Danny Saber on bass. The keyboards of Jamie Muhoberac and Don Was add to the colour, as well as Danny on the clavinet.
It was Blondie Chaplin's idea to add the Wurlitzer piano, just two notes on the first two beats of a bar. This made the tapestry of the song richer. Percussion again features Charlie Watts and Jim Keltner. The backing vocals are sung by Keith, Bernard Fowler and Blondie. The bass line has a riff that is very similar to the Temptations' *Papa Was A Rolling Stone*.
This similarity was extended by the re-mixers, especially on the recommended 10-minute bootleg mix, which includes samples from the Temptations (* a - 10.21). An equally diverse re-mix has reggae overtones, hence its bracketed title (* b - 5.09). Fluke, an acid-house troupe, did a trippy dance orientated mix for CD single. Danny also engineered a worthwhile re-mix for a CD single release, which naturally featured his punchy clavinet keyboard work. It was edited for single purposes (* c - 4.00) and there is a *Call Out Hook* version (* d - 0.18). In addition to the official mixes there are various bootleg cuts including an *Old School Mix* (* e - 8.58),

1299. YOUNG LOVE (Jagger, Richards)
13 March - July 1997: Place: Ocean Way Recording Studios, Hollywood, California, USA.
Rolling Stones with Bernard Fowler, Blondie Chaplin, Waddy Wachtel, Don Was.
Producer: Don Was, The Glimmer Twins.
Unavailable.

The session tapes were closely guarded on this occasion after the VOODOO LOUNGE proliferation of available out-takes. However, Bernard Fowler confirms the existence of this track, which he remembers well since he is featured on vocals. The percussion is probably provided by Jim Keltner. Most of the out-takes were very Keith Richards-influenced and may have been considered for an X-pensive Winos release. Other unverified tracks are *Don't Apologise, High Or Low, Feeling Now, Ever Changing World, Smooth Stuff, Hide My Love* and *I'm Cured*, These were likely to be recorded by Keith with Rob Fraboni.

1300. HOW CAN I STOP (Jagger, Richards) 6.54
13 March - July 1997: Place: Ocean Way Recording Studios, Hollywood, California, USA.
Played Live: 1998
Rolling Stones with Don Was, Jeff Sarli, Waddy Wachtel, Jim Keltner, Blondie Chaplin, Bernard Fowler, Wayne Shorter.
Producer: Don Was, The Glimmer Twins.
Engineer: Rob Fraboni (including mix). Assistant Engineers: Alan Sanderson, John Sorenson. Mixed by John Sorenson, assisted by Robi Banerji.
UK LP BRIDGES TO BABYLON: 29 September 1997: No. 6 - 6 weeks
USA LP BRIDGES TO BABYLON: 29 September 1997: No. 3 - 27 weeks

The final track on the album and one of the last to be recorded as well. It has distinct jazz and soul undertones and was one of Charlie Watts' favourites, proved by the drum flourish at the end as the piano precedes the entrance of Wayne Shorter on soprano saxophone. He is one of the most influential saxophone players in modern day jazz, recording with Miles Davis, Herbie Hancock, Art Blakey and Weather Report - he also performed a jazz composer role.
Don Was produces the song and lets it flow naturally - some laughter is captured at one point and at the end Jim Keltner is allowed to continue on percussion before a fade-out. Don also contributes the Wurlitzer while Blondie Chaplin plays piano. The guitar lines include Ronnie Wood, Waddy Wachtel and, of course, Keith Richards who wrote the song and also performs vocals. Jeff Sarli again plays the acoustic bass enabling the song truly to breathe. Charlie Watts often said that rock 'n' roll is very restricting while jazz breathes.
The very effective backing vocals are intrinsic to the soul nature of the song. Bernard Fowler and Blondie Chaplin got on very well together and played a very effective part in the entire recording of BRIDGES TO BABYLON - both on Mick's and Keith's songs. Bernard remembers it was one of the few songs that he was there

for, from the writing to the recording. *How Can I Stop* is a classic, commendable track and naturally concludes the album. Apparently, Don Was remembers that after Charlie's last cymbal brush he went straight from the studio to catch a plane back to the UK, his job finished for the time being. Don Was remembers thinking how fitting a song it would be to finish their career with - and in such a fantastic session. At that point, he did not imagine the band recording again.

1301. SHAME, SHAME, SHAME (Reed) ∕ 3.59
18 September 1997: Place: The Double Door Club, Chicago, USA.

Rolling Stones with Darryl Jones, Chuck Leavell, Bernard Fowler, Lisa Fischer, Blondie Chaplin, Bobby Keys, Andy Snitzer, Michael Davis, Kent Smith.
Producer: The Glimmer Twins.
Bootleg only.

The album was concluded and finally put to bed on the same day as the BRIDGES TO BABYLON North American tour was announced. The Egyptian flavoured lion on the album cover was designed by Jay Bryan. It was on 18 August 1997 when the band, with Mick Jagger at the wheel, drove across the Brooklyn Bridge, in New York, in a red Cadillac flanked by a police escort to the press conference. With only a month to go, the announcement was nearer the start date than for other tours and it was the first for which tickets were available on the Internet.
Mick jokingly joined the press to say "I've always wanted to do this . . . Is this going to be your last tour?" Keith Richards replied: "Yes, this and the next five!" The tour rehearsals were at the Mosanic Temple theatre in Toronto, Canada. There were the same band members as for the VOODOO LOUNGE tour, plus Blondie Chaplin. Some of the rehearsals are captured on an excellent quality bootleg. Two warm-up gigs were played, the first at the Horseshoe Tavern in Toronto, and a second at the Double Door Club, in Chicago.
Both the sets took off with rousing *Little Queenies*, while *19th Nervous Breakdown* was tried out, complete with authentic backing vocals. *Under My Thumb* and *Little Red Rooster* were tackled in Toronto, while *Let It Bleed* and *Crazy Mama* were sung in Chicago. In both cities, *The Last Time* was on the set list. New songs from the forthcoming album included *Anybody Seen My Baby?* and *Out Of Control*, the latter sounding plausible and rousing while *Anybody* was still rusty.
The Jimmy Reed song *Shame Shame Shame* is a standard boogie song with guitars, harmonica and piano but noteworthy for its first live performance in many years. *Honky Tonk Women*, *Start Me Up*, *Jumping Jack Flash* and *Brown Sugar* concluded the hot and sweaty show.

1302. GIMME SHELTER (Jagger, Richard) ∕ 6.22
25 October 1997: Place: Capitol Theatre, Port Chester, New York, USA.

Rolling Stones with Darryl Jones, Chuck Leavell, Bernard Fowler, Lisa Fischer, Blondie Chaplin.
Producer: The Glimmer Twins. Production Co-ordination: Pierre De Beauport.
Engineer: Ed Cherney, John Harris. Assistant Engineers: Adam Blackburn, Hardi Kamsani, Jerry Hall.
Additional Production and Mix: Chris Potter.
UK CD LP NO SECURITY: 9 November 1998: No. 67 - 1 week
USA CD LP NO SECURITY: 16 November 1998: No. 34 - 8 weeks
UK Promo CD Single: November 1998

From the Cobra of 94/95 to the Lion of this tour, The Rolling Stones man and beast were unleashed, the cages opened and they were ready to maim and maul during their BRIDGES TO BABYLON concerts. This tour would test their stamina to the limits as the dates stretched inexorably ahead of them for months (even years!) The first gig kicked off five days after their Double Door appearance and was at the Soldier Field Stadium in Chicago.
As usual the stadium package was well-rehearsed with a mixture of new album cuts, numbers pulled from the past and the standard greatest hits. The tour sprinted through Canada and the United States in its efficient manner, playing mostly in stadiums but occasionally turning up in arena and club venues such as Madison Square Garden, the Capitol Theatre in New York and the MGM Grand Garden, in Las Vegas. It was planned to play smaller arenas but advantage was taken of the bigger outdoor stadiums while the weather was still warm.
The band felt that the performances kept getting better and better and the show remained interesting by varying it from venue to venue. This was achieved by changing the set list by up to four numbers each night and using the alternative small stage, which became known as the B-stage. At this point the audience, who were in the middle of the stadium, became the focus of attention as the band congregated to play club-style, surrounded by fans on all four sides.
A concert was recorded by MTV for their Live From 10 Spot programme in the smaller venue of the Capitol Theatre. *Gimme Shelter* appeared on the live album, NO SECURITY, and was also released edited as a European promo single (* a - 4.16). The version features Lisa Fischer strongly in the vocal spotlight. Amusingly, Jerry Hall is quoted as engineer on this track.

1303. (I CAN'T GET NO) SATISFACTION (Jagger, Richard) ∕ 5.09
12 December 1997: Place: TWA Dome, St Louis, USA.

Rolling Stones with Darryl Jones, Chuck Leavell.
Producer: The Glimmer Twins. Production Co-ordination: Pierre De Beauport.
Engineer: Recorded and Mixed: Ed Cherney.
Assisted by: Dan Thompson, Peter Doell.
UK, USA, Video, DVD Bridges To Babylon 1998: 8 June 1998

1304. LET'S SPEND THE NIGHT TOGETHER (Jagger, Richard) ∕ 4.26
12 December 1997: Place: TWA Dome, St Louis, USA.

Rolling Stones with Darryl Jones, Chuck Leavell, Bernard Fowler, Lisa Fischer, Blondie Chaplin.
Producer: The Glimmer Twins. Production Co-ordination: Pierre De Beauport.
Engineer: Recorded and Mixed: Ed Cherney.
Assisted by: Dan Thompson, Peter Doell.
UK, USA, Video, DVD Bridges To Babylon 1998: 8 June 1998

1305. FLIP THE SWITCH (Jagger, Richards) ✎ 4.09
12 December 1997: Place: TWA Dome, St Louis, USA.
Rolling Stones with Darryl Jones, Chuck Leavell, Bernard Fowler, Lisa Fischer, Blondie Chaplin, Bobby Keys.
Producer: The Glimmer Twins. Production Co-ordination: Pierre De Beauport.
Engineer: Recorded and Mixed: Ed Cherney.
Assisted by: Dan Thompson, Peter Doell.
UK, USA, Video, DVD Bridges To Babylon 1998: 8 June 1998

1306. GIMME SHELTER (Jagger, Richard) ✎ 6.34
12 December 1997: Place: TWA Dome, St Louis, USA.
Rolling Stones with Darryl Jones, Chuck Leavell, Bernard Fowler, Lisa Fischer.
Producer: The Glimmer Twins. Production Co-ordination: Pierre De Beauport.
Engineer: Recorded and Mixed: Ed Cherney.
Assisted by: Dan Thompson, Peter Doell.
UK, USA, Video, DVD Bridges To Babylon 1998: 8 June 1998

1307. WILD HORSES (Jagger, Richard) ✎ 5.59
12 December 1997: Place: TWA Dome, St Louis, USA.
Rolling Stones with Darryl Jones, Dave Matthews, Chuck Leavell, Bernard Fowler, Lisa Fischer.
Producer: The Glimmer Twins. Production Co-ordination: Pierre De Beauport.
Engineer: Recorded and Mixed: Ed Cherney.
Assisted by: Dan Thompson, Peter Doell.
UK, USA, Video, DVD Bridges To Babylon 1998: 8 June 1998

1308. ANYBODY SEEN MY BABY? (Jagger, Richards, Mink, Lang) ✎ 4.47
12 December 1997: Place: TWA Dome, St Louis, USA.
Rolling Stones with Darryl Jones, Chuck Leavell, Bernard Fowler, Lisa Fischer, Blondie Chaplin.
Producer: The Glimmer Twins. Production Co-ordination: Pierre De Beauport.
Engineer: Recorded and Mixed: Ed Cherney.
Assisted by: Dan Thompson, Peter Doell.
Bootleg only.

1309. SAINT OF ME (Jagger, Richards) ✎ 5.20
12 December 1997: Place: TWA Dome, St Louis, USA.
Rolling Stones with Darryl Jones, Chuck Leavell, Bernard Fowler, Lisa Fischer, Blondie Chaplin, Bobby Keys, Andy Snitzer, Michael Davis, Kent Smith.
Producer: The Glimmer Twins. Production Co-ordination: Pierre De Beauport.
Engineer: Recorded and Mixed: Ed Cherney.
Assisted by: Dan Thompson, Peter Doell.
UK, USA, Video, DVD Bridges To Babylon 1998: 8 June 1998

1310. CORRINA (Mahal, Davis) ✎ 4.17
12 December 1997: Place: TWA Dome, St Louis, USA.
Rolling Stones with Darryl Jones, Taj Mahal, Chuck Leavell.
Producer: The Glimmer Twins. Production Co-ordination: Pierre De Beauport.
Engineer: Ed Cherney, Dave Hewitt. Assistant Engineers: Daryl Borstein, Skip Kent, Ryan Hewitt.
Additional Production and Mix: Chris Potter.
UK CD LP NO SECURITY: 9 November 1998: No. 67 - 1 week
USA CD LP NO SECURITY: 16 November 1998: No. 34 - 8 weeks

1311. OUT OF CONTROL (Jagger, Richards) ✎ 8.01
12 December 1997: Place: TWA Dome, St Louis, USA.
Rolling Stones with Darryl Jones, Chuck Leavell, Bernard Fowler, Lisa Fischer, Blondie Chaplin, Michael Davis.
Producer: The Glimmer Twins. Production Co-ordination: Pierre De Beauport.
Engineer: Recorded and Mixed: Ed Cherney.
Assisted by: Dan Thompson, Peter Doell.
UK, USA, Video, DVD Bridges To Babylon 1998: 8 June 1998

1312. WAITING ON A FRIEND (Jagger, Richard) ✎ 5.02
12 December 1997: Place: TWA Dome, St Louis, USA.
Rolling Stones with Darryl Jones, Joshua Redman, Chuck Leavell, Bernard Fowler, Lisa Fischer.
Producer: The Glimmer Twins. Production Co-ordination: Pierre De Beauport.
Engineer: Ed Cherney, Dave Hewitt. Assistant Engineers: Daryl Borstein, Skip Kent, Ryan Hewitt.
Additional Production and Mix: Chris Potter.

UK CD LP NO SECURITY: 9 November 1998: No. 67 - 1 week
USA CD LP NO SECURITY: 16 November 1998: No. 34 - 8 weeks
UK, USA, Video, DVD Bridges To Babylon 1998: 8 June 1998

1313. MISS YOU (Jagger, Richards) ✎ 9.15
12 December 1997: Place: TWA Dome, St Louis, USA.
Rolling Stones with Darryl Jones, Chuck Leavell, Bernard Fowler, Lisa Fischer, Bobby Keys, Andy Snitzer, Michael Davis, Kent Smith.
Producer: The Glimmer Twins. Production Co-ordination: Pierre De Beauport.
Engineer: Recorded and Mixed: Ed Cherney.
Assisted by: Dan Thompson, Peter Doell.
UK, USA, Video, DVD Bridges To Babylon 1998: 8 June 1998

1314. ALL ABOUT YOU (Jagger, Richards) ✎ 4.45
12 December 1997: Place: TWA Dome, St Louis, USA.
Rolling Stones with Darryl Jones, Chuck Leavell, Bernard Fowler, Lisa Fischer, Blondie Chaplin, Bobby Keys, Andy Snitzer, Michael Davis, Kent Smith.
Producer: The Glimmer Twins. Production Co-ordination: Pierre De Beauport.
Engineer: Recorded and Mixed: Ed Cherney.
Assisted by: Dan Thompson, Peter Doell.
Bootleg only.

1315. WANNA HOLD YOU (Jagger, Richards) ✎ 4.51
12 December 1997: Place: TWA Dome, St Louis, USA.
Rolling Stones with Darryl Jones, Chuck Leavell, Bernard Fowler, Lisa Fischer, Blondie Chaplin, Bobby Keys, Andy Snitzer, Michael Davis, Kent Smith.
Producer: The Glimmer Twins. Production Co-ordination: Pierre De Beauport.
Engineer: Recorded and Mixed: Ed Cherney.
Assisted by: Dan Thompson, Peter Doell.
UK, USA, Video, DVD Bridges To Babylon 1998: 8 June 1998

1316. IT'S ONLY ROCK 'N' ROLL (Jagger, Richard) ✎ 4.46
12 December 1997: Place: TWA Dome, St Louis, USA.
Rolling Stones with Darryl Jones, Chuck Leavell.
Producer: The Glimmer Twins. Production Co-ordination: Pierre De Beauport.
Engineer: Recorded and Mixed: Ed Cherney.
Assisted by: Dan Thompson, Peter Doell.
UK, USA, Video, DVD Bridges To Babylon 1998: 8 June 1998

1317. THE LAST TIME (Jagger, Richard) ✎ 4.47
12 December 1997: Place: TWA Dome, St Louis, USA.
Rolling Stones with Darryl Jones, Chuck Leavell.
Producer: The Glimmer Twins. Production Co-ordination: Pierre De Beauport.
Engineer: Ed Cherney, Dave Hewitt. Assistant Engineers: Daryl Borstein, Skip Kent, Ryan Hewitt.
Additional Production and Mix: Chris Potter.
UK CD LP NO SECURITY: 9 November 1998: No. 67 - 1 week
USA CD LP NO SECURITY: 16 November 1998: No. 34 - 8 weeks

1318. LIKE A ROLLING STONE (Dylan) ✎ 5.26
12 December 1997: Place: TWA Dome, St Louis, USA.
Rolling Stones with Darryl Jones, Chuck Leavell.
Producer: The Glimmer Twins. Production Co-ordination: Pierre De Beauport.
Engineer: Recorded and Mixed: Ed Cherney.
Assisted by: Dan Thompson, Peter Doell.
UK, USA, Video, DVD Bridges To Babylon 1998: 8 June 1998

1319. SYMPATHY FOR THE DEVIL (Jagger, Richard) ✎ 8.00
12 December 1997: Place: TWA Dome, St Louis, USA.
Rolling Stones with Darryl Jones, Chuck Leavell, Bernard Fowler, Lisa Fischer, Blondie Chaplin.
Producer: The Glimmer Twins. Production Co-ordination: Pierre De Beauport.
Engineer: Recorded and Mixed: Ed Cherney.
Assisted by: Dan Thompson, Peter Doell.
UK, USA, Video, DVD Bridges To Babylon 1998: 8 June 1998

1320. TUMBLING DICE (Jagger, Richard) ✎ 5.31
12 December 1997: Place: TWA Dome, St Louis, USA.
Rolling Stones with Darryl Jones, Chuck Leavell, Bernard Fowler, Lisa Fischer, Blondie Chaplin, Bobby Keys, Andy Snitzer, Michael Davis, Kent Smith.
Producer: The Glimmer Twins. Production Co-ordination: Pierre De Beauport.
Engineer: Recorded and Mixed: Ed Cherney.
Assisted by: Dan Thompson, Peter Doell.
UK, USA, Video, DVD Bridges To Babylon 1998: 8 June 1998

1321. HONKY TONK WOMEN (Jagger, Richard) ✎ 5.02
12 December 1997: Place: TWA Dome, St Louis, USA.
Rolling Stones with Darryl Jones, Chuck Leavell, Bernard Fowler, Lisa Fischer, Blondie Chaplin, Bobby Keys, Andy Snitzer, Michael Davis, Kent Smith.
Producer: The Glimmer Twins. Production Co-ordination: Pierre De Beauport.
Engineer: Recorded and Mixed: Ed Cherney.
Assisted by: Dan Thompson, Peter Doell.
UK, USA, Video, DVD Bridges To Babylon 1998: 8 June 1998

1322. START ME UP (Jagger, Richards) ✎ 4.37
12 December 1997: Place: TWA Dome, St Louis, USA.
Rolling Stones with Darryl Jones, Chuck Leavell, Bernard Fowler, Lisa Fischer, Blondie Chaplin, Bobby Keys, Andy Snitzer, Michael Davis, Kent Smith.
Producer: The Glimmer Twins. Production Co-ordination: Pierre De Beauport.
Engineer: Recorded and Mixed: Ed Cherney.
Assisted by: Dan Thompson, Peter Doell.
UK, USA, Video, DVD Bridges To Babylon 1998: 8 June 1998

1323. JUMPING JACK FLASH (Jagger, Richard) ✎ 7.02
12 December 1997: Place: TWA Dome, St Louis, USA.
Rolling Stones with Darryl Jones, Chuck Leavell, Bernard Fowler, Lisa Fischer, Blondie Chaplin, Bobby Keys, Andy Snitzer, Michael Davis, Kent Smith.
Producer: The Glimmer Twins. Production Co-ordination: Pierre De Beauport.
Engineer: Recorded and Mixed: Ed Cherney.
Assisted by: Dan Thompson, Peter Doell.
UK, USA, Video, DVD Bridges To Babylon 1998: 8 June 1998

1324. YOU CAN'T ALWAYS GET WHAT YOU WANT (Jagger, Richard) ✎ 5.37
12 December 1997: Place: TWA Dome, St Louis, USA.
Rolling Stones with Darryl Jones, Chuck Leavell, Bernard Fowler, Lisa Fischer, Blondie Chaplin, Kent Smith.
Producer: The Glimmer Twins. Production Co-ordination: Pierre De Beauport.
Engineer: Recorded and Mixed: Ed Cherney.
Assisted by: Dan Thompson, Peter Doell.
UK, USA, Video, DVD Bridges To Babylon 1998: 8 June 1998

1325. BROWN SUGAR (Jagger, Richard) ✎ 6.23
12 December 1997: Place: TWA Dome, St Louis, USA.
Rolling Stones with Darryl Jones, Chuck Leavell, Bernard Fowler, Lisa Fischer, Blondie Chaplin, Bobby Keys.
Producer: The Glimmer Twins. Production Co-ordination: Pierre De Beauport.
Engineer: Recorded and Mixed: Ed Cherney.
Assisted by: Dan Thompson, Peter Doell.
UK, USA, Video, DVD Bridges To Babylon 1998: 8 June 1998

On 12 December 1997, the show at the TWA Dome in St Louis was recorded in full by Ed Cherney and broadcast on pay-per-view. It was released in June 1998 to help promote the European leg of the tour. The set and lights were again designed by tour guru veterans, Mark Fisher and Patrick Woodroffe. Mick gave them a briefing and the concept of several bridges was discussed as they also had for the VOODOO LOUNGE tour, when it had been decided that, technically, it was not possible. The stage set did not have as many effects to distract from the performance but was used gradually to reveal or close certain aspects.
At first the stage was clothed in huge curtains to obscure most of the set. On either side stood the two speaker towers, shaped like huge goblets and connected to the stage beneath through a curved archway. This time the jumbotron was circular in shape and surrounded by lights. When the screen was revealed, it was bathed in blue and, to a background of primeval music, a distant star was seen hurtling towards earth. The comet smashes through the screen and pyrotechnics explode at the same time as Keith Richards appears on the stage dressed in a full floor-length leopard coat and playing the opening bars of *Satisfaction* - some entrance. Although the Stones were not keen on the song, the guitar only arrangement worked well. *Let's Spend The Night Together* was played traditionally, the scrawny bum of Jagger that Charlie Watts so fondly talks about appeared in *Flip The Switch* through some choreographed moves. There is some great guitar work from Keith as he also contributes on *Gimme Shelter*. Lisa Fischer is co-vocalist and has her moment during the "rape and murder" scene. On *Wild Horses*, another co-vocalist, Dave Matthews, was used his smooth vocals definitely being an acquired taste. By now, the arrangement of *Anybody Seen My Baby?* was improved and Blondie Chaplin indicated that they were here to rock St Louis in the rap section. *Saint Of Me* followed as some of the draped curtains were removed to reveal more golden towers.
Two nude Babylonian inflatables fondly named Cindy (the reclining one) and Xanthe (in slave chains) had a part in the tour but one got singed by a fire and did not appear again. Mick played acoustic guitar in part and Ron took the lead solo. The song's character was beginning to unfurl and would evolve even more strongly

TH
ROLLING

13 & 14 October 1973, Ahoy, Rotterdam, Netherlands.

Courtesy of Graham Wiltshire, FRPS.

14 October 1973, Dancing With Mr. D, Ahoy, Rotterdam, Netherlands.

23 December 1974, Keith backstage before appearing with The Faces,
Kilburn Gaumont Theatre, London, England.
Courtesy of Graham Wiltshire, FRPS.

26 June 1975, Madison Square Gardens, New York, USA.

Alexis, Bobbie Korner, Bill Wyman backstage.

27 June 1975, Madison Square Gardens, New York, USA.
Stones with Steel Association.

27 June 1975, Unknown, Pete Rudge and Mick, Madison Square Gardens, New York, USA.

22 May 1976, Earls Court, London, England.

14 May 1976, Granby Hall, Leicester, England.

26 May 1976, You Gotta Move with Ollie Brown and Billy Preston, Earls Court, London, England.

26 May 1976, Earls Court, London, England.

21 August 1976, Ian Stewart, Unknown,
Charlie Watts, Knebworth, England.

27 May 1976, Earls Court, London, England. 30 May 1976, Den Haag (Zuiderpark), The Hague, Netherlands.

Courtesy of Graham Wiltshire, FRPS.

27 May 1976, Earls Court, London, England.

27 June 1982, Ashton Gate, Bristol, England.

20 September 2003, Twickenham, London, England.

29 August 2006. Millennium Stadium, Cardiff, Wales.
Courtesy of Graham Wiltshire, FRPS.

on the South American and European legs of the tour. Taj Mahal, who had not been seen on a Stones stage since 1968, joined the band to perform vocals and dobro guitar for *Corinne Corinna*. The track, written by Taj and Jesse Ed Davis, was released on the live album, NO SECURITY, and was so popular it was one of the first to be selected.

The bass and percussion opening to *Out Of Control* belies the hidden menace within as the song explodes three times to a barrage of strobe white light. Michael Davis plays an excellent trombone, giving it a certain jazz quality, and Ron uses a wah-wah-enhanced guitar, while Keith riffs mercilessly. It was destined to become a tour classic. A new innovation was the cyber vote conducted on the tour website to enable fans to vote from a prepared list for their track. But sometimes the vote was ignored if the song was not representative of the gig. Nor would they risk a guest appearance to please web voters, since the choice that night was *Waiting On A Friend*, where Joshua Redman played an eloquent saxophone.

Miss You took on an extended quiet bass section while Mick and the demure Lisa flirted with each other, then Bobby's sax and Ronnie's lead solo are featured. After the introductions, Keith's solo spot took on the soft touch of *All About You* and the lengthy big brass "rock it up" of *Wanna Hold You*. At this point the stage darkens and two twin red lights pierce the front as the ratchets wheel 70 metres of bridge, linking the main stage to the B-stage.

This certainly bridged a gap between themselves and the audience, turning the back row into the front row. However, at the first show in Chicago, the mechanism was not ready and so the band walked to the centre. Once the bridge is in place two metres above the crowd, the band saunter over to huge applause to the sound of *The Sticks* by Julian Adderley - a sight to behold. The bridge retracts during the first number and the small stage lowers to be head height among the fans. For those at the shows near the B-stage, the show changes quality at this point. Songs like *It's Only Rock 'n' Roll* and *The Last Time* were almost transformed back to their original identity, although the latter sounds a little strained. The B-stage performance was concluded with *Like A Rolling Stone*. As the band, minus Mick, return to the main stage the percussive notes of *Sympathy* commence.

This gave Mick a chance to put on an elaborate wizard's gown (his "fantasy coat", designed by the Malakapour sisters) before he too uses the walkway to return and join the rest of the group for *Sympathy*. *Tumbling Dice* is the home-straight starter with a camera giving a view from Ronnie's guitar neck and sweeping spotlights backlighting the stage. The riff of *Honky Tonk* strains forth and the cowbell is supplied by Blondie.

Keith joined Chuck Leavell for a few stage-managed piano bars. Andy Snitzer plays keyboards and fills the sound out with Chuck on *Start Me Up*. *Jumping Jack Flash* concluded with fireworks exploding across the width of the stage, fire breathing from the towers and the spotlights circling the set, stage, stadium and sky. The encore was *You Can't Always Get What You Want*, followed by *Brown Sugar*, during which a blizzard of silver and gold paper descended upon the crowd. The finale was marked by another round of explosions and fireworks as the band took their well-deserved bows.

1326. **OUT OF CONTROL (DON WAS LIVE REMIX)** (Jagger, Richards) ✐ 6.54
16 January 1998: Place: Madison Square Garden, New York, USA.
Rolling Stones with Darryl Jones, Chuck Leavell, Bernard Fowler, Lisa Fischer, Blondie Chaplin, Michael Davis.
Producer: The Glimmer Twins. Production Co-ordination: Pierre De Beauport.
Engineer: Ed Cherney, Dave Hewitt. Assistant Engineers: Ryan Hewitt, Phil Giromer, Sean McClintock.
Additional Production and Mix: Chris Potter.
USA Promo Track CD Out Of Control: July 1998

After a couple weeks of rest over Christmas the tour recommenced in the USA, playing a few arenas in January 1998. The format was different due to the smaller stages and it was labelled NO SECURITY in line with the just-released live album and had the familiar yellow and black security tape moniker. The stage used a circular rear walkway and was open to allow 360-degree seating. The show's introduction utilised a promotional film purporting to be the band walking from the dressing room to the stage in the stark, metallic world of a stadium behind the scenes and was directed by Dick Carruthers. It served to heighten the crowd's pre-show anticipation.

The only personnel change was Tim Ries, who replaced Andy Snitzer for the rest of the tour. There were three shows at Madison Square Garden (re-arranged from just before Christmas '97). In the first Mick Jagger was recovering from a cold but, by the second and third nights, the Stones were blistering. This version of *Out Of Control* was recorded at the second, Friday night show. Bob Dylan was due to play *Like A Rolling Stone* on the Saturday but pulled out at the last minute when he realised that he would have to go to the B-stage to perform.

Maybe he was put off by the world champion bra-throwing contest which took place - some women had no shame! Following the MSG shows, the band flew to Hawaii for three concerts - one, in a tent, paid for by Pepsi, to celebrate their 100th anniversary. The other two were at the Aloha Stadium the first time they had played there for 25 years. Canada and Mexico followed with some further US dates thrown in. The second leg of the tour finished at a small club gig, The Joint in Las Vegas, on 15 February 1998.

1327. **SAINT OF ME** (Jagger, Richards) ✐ 5.25
4 April 1998: Place: River Plate, Buenos Aires, Argentina.
Rolling Stones with Darryl Jones, Chuck Leavell, Bernard Fowler, Lisa Fischer, Blondie Chaplin, Bobby Keys, Andy Snitzer, Michael Davis, Kent Smith.
Producer: The Glimmer Twins. Production Co-ordination: Pierre De Beauport.
Engineer: Ed Cherney, Dave Hewitt. Assistant Engineers: Ryan Hewitt, Phil Giromer, Sean McClintock.
Additional Production and Mix: Chris Potter.
UK CD LP NO SECURITY: 9 November 1998: No. 67 - 1 week
USA CD LP NO SECURITY: 16 November 1998: No. 34 - 8 weeks

1328. **OUT OF CONTROL** (Jagger, Richards) ✐ 7.59
4 April 1998: Place: River Plate, Buenos Aires, Argentina.
Rolling Stones with Darryl Jones, Johnny Starbuck, Chuck Leavell, Bernard Fowler, Lisa Fischer, Blondie Chaplin, Michael Davis.
Producer: The Glimmer Twins. Production Co-ordination: Pierre De Beauport.
Engineer: Ed Cherney, Dave Hewitt. Assistant Engineers: Ryan Hewitt, Phil Giromer, Sean McClintock.
Additional Production and Mix: Chris Potter.
UK CD LP NO SECURITY: 9 November 1998: No. 67 - 1 week
USA CD LP NO SECURITY: 16 November 1998: No. 34 - 8 weeks

Six dates were played in Japan during March 1998 before a historical five nights at the River Plate Stadium, Argentina. Those gigs attracted a level of sheer fan excitement and over-exuberance not seen for many years, the sort of atmosphere created by fervent football followers. Meredith Brooks, the support artist, had to dodge bottles and rocks such was the crowd's disapproval and impatience for the Stones. Bob Dylan was the support act at one gig (well he performed first!) and, for some of his set, Mick Jagger, Charlie Watts and Ronnie Wood watched from the sides.

There were no decent remote recording trucks in Argentina that Ed Cherney could locate so he constructed an improvised unit from equipment shipped in especially. He recalled he was in the bowels of the stadium below and behind the stage. He did not get a chance to sound check with a full PA and it resonated so badly from the sub-woofers that they could not hear what they were recording - "We were trapped in a big bass cabinet but could not leave our station. We adjusted the levels as appropriate and hoped for the best."

The next night he brought in more speakers to hear better and put up foam. The same thing happened again, the acoustic treatment came flying off the walls and all the speakers were blown. The recording captured on NO SECURITY by Ed Cherney ended up being great. "I have to say that The Stones at River Plate is always amazing. The crowds there are off the hook. Incredible fans and certainly the loudest anywhere." The result on *Saint Of Me* and *Out Of Control* speaks for itself as the crowd participation goes up a notch.

Head road crew man and lead guitar technician, Johnny Starbuck, contributed shakers to *Out Of Control*. In 1976, he joined the band as Billy Preston's technical assistant and has remained with the Stones' backline staff to this day. During *Like A Rolling Stone*, Bob Dylan joined the band but his vocal phrasing made the duet sound quite strange and he struggled to recall his own lyrics. However, Ed Cherney felt that, "the performance was mind-blowingly exciting."

1329. LIKE A ROLLING STONE (Dylan) ✎ 6.22
11 April 1998: Place: Praça da Apoteose, Rio De Janeiro, Brazil.
Rolling Stones with Bob Dylan, Darryl Jones, Chuck Leavell, Blondie Chaplin.
Bootleg only.

1330. LITTLE QUEENIE (Berry) ✎ 4.27
11 April 1998: Place: Praça da Apoteose, Rio De Janeiro, Brazil.
Rolling Stones with Darryl Jones, Chuck Leavell.
Bootleg only.

There were a few days to enable some rest before two gigs in Brazil. Keith Richards and Ron Wood went to some islands off the coast. Ronnie took a pleasure trip but things went awry when the boat's engine caught fire and the passengers had to be rescued by a boat of pursuing "undercover" journalists. A few days later and Bob Dylan was in attendance again in Brazil and guested on his *Like A Rolling Stone*. Mick Jagger again introduced it as a song that Bob wrote for us! Bob, sporting a white cowboy hat, sang the first verse until Mick Jagger helped him out with the chorus and the next verse. Bob was totally out of tune and at odds with Mick but the crowd were no less enthusiastic than Argentina.

One of the staple numbers played during the B-stage set list was *Little Queenie*. Quite often this would have Keith Richards in exciting form. For Keith, the guitar solo on Chuck's version was the best recorded and, together with Chuck Leavell, the sound was truly authentic late 60s and early 70s. The show was broadcast on Brazilian Vivo Television. The Rio and Sao Paulo shows completed this section of the American tour before they returned for a handful of gigs in Canada and the United States.

1331. THIEF IN THE NIGHT (Jagger, Richards, De Beauport) ✎ 5.37
13 June 1998: Place: Zeppelinfield, Nuremburg, Germany.
Rolling Stones with Darryl Jones, Pierre de Beauport, Leah Wood, Chuck Leavell, Bernard Fowler, Lisa Fischer, Blondie Chaplin, Bobby Keys, Andy Snitzer, Michael Davis, Kent Smith.
Producer: The Glimmer Twins. Production Co-ordination: Pierre De Beauport.
Engineer: Ed Cherney, Peter Brandt. Assistant Engineer: Tiemen Boelens, Henk van Helvoirt.
Additional Production and Mix: Chris Potter.
UK CD LP NO SECURITY: 9 November 1998: No. 67 - 1 week
USA CD LP NO SECURITY: 16 November 1998: No. 34 - 8 weeks

The European section of the BRIDGES TO BABYLON tour was subject to unparalleled problems. On 17 March 1998, the British government announced that any "foreign earnings" would be subject to full tax if the tax payer returned to the UK for any length of time and earned UK income within the same tax year. Previously there had been a 62-day allowance of which the Stones had taken advantage. Now there was a potential bill for the band and their crew of £12 million. They thought it was unfair to impose the tax retrospectively because the tour had already started and European dates had been booked.

So the Stones' management caused a big controversy by announcing their withdrawal from the five-date UK section of the tour. A Treasury spokesperson said: "We are not going to be lectured on tax affairs by tax exiles." Some press and fans thought the Stones could have borne the cost themselves but they maintained it affected every member of the UK personnel on the tour and would have negated their earnings from months of hard work. The result was the Stones did not tour the UK until 1999, 10 months later. To make things worse in early May, Keith Richards fell from a step ladder in his library while attempting to retrieve a book and broke a couple of ribs.

As a result, the European tour had to be postponed from 22 May 1998 until he had recovered, just before the scheduled Nuremburg concert on the 13 June 1998. At a press conference dealing with the tax situation and the fall, Mick Jagger said that he would make it up to the British fans by playing provincial dates in smaller venues. He was to regret this promise since he failed to fulfil it. Keith announced that he was fit enough to start the belated European tour and revealed that the volume which caused him to fall was Leonardo Da Vinci's Book On Anatomy!

Seven concerts were re-scheduled and the first night of the tour was in Germany on 13 June 1998. Introducing *Thief In The Night*, Keith Richards said: "I'm sorry I'm late - everybody cocks up once in a while . . . hey it's great to be back, it's great to be here, it's great to be anywhere" (apart from the apology, the latter was a standard phrase used on most dates). *Thief In The Night* was recorded at Zeppelinfield and was released on the NO SECURITY album; it included Pierre De Beauport on Wurlitzer piano and Leah Wood performed backing vocals.

1332. I JUST WANT TO MAKE LOVE TO YOU (Dixon) ✎ 5.19
1 July 1998: Place: Arena, Amsterdam, Netherlands.
Rolling Stones with Darryl Jones, Chuck Leavell, Bernard Fowler, Lisa Fischer, Blondie Chaplin.
Producer: The Glimmer Twins. Production Co-ordination: Pierre De Beauport.
Engineer: Ed Cherney, Ulli Poesselt. Assistant Engineer: Peter Brandt, Tiemen Boelens, Henk van Helvoirt.
Additional Production and Mix: Chris Potter.
Japan CD LP NO SECURITY: 21 November 1998

1333. FLIP THE SWITCH (Jagger, Richards) ✎ 4.12
1 July 1998: Place: Arena, Amsterdam, Netherlands.
Rolling Stones with Darryl Jones, Chuck Leavell, Bernard Fowler, Lisa Fischer, Blondie Chaplin, Bobby Keys.
Producer: The Glimmer Twins. Production Co-ordination: Pierre De Beauport.
Engineer: Ed Cherney, Ulli Poesselt. Assistant Engineer: Peter Brandt, Tiemen Boelens, Henk van Helvoirt.
Additional Production and Mix: Chris Potter.
UK CD LP NO SECURITY: 9 November 1998: No. 67 - 1 week
USA CD LP NO SECURITY: 16 November 1998: No. 34 - 8 weeks

1334. LIVE WITH ME (Jagger, Richard) ✎ 3.54
1 July 1998: Place: Arena, Amsterdam, Netherlands.
Rolling Stones with Darryl Jones, Chuck Leavell, Bernard Fowler, Lisa Fischer, Blondie Chaplin, Bobby Keys.
Producer: The Glimmer Twins. Production Co-ordination: Pierre De Beauport.
Engineer: Ed Cherney, Ulli Poesselt. Assistant Engineer: Peter Brandt, Tiemen Boelens, Henk van Helvoirt.
Additional Production and Mix: Chris Potter.
UK CD LP NO SECURITY: 9 November 1998: No. 67 - 1 week
USA CD LP NO SECURITY: 16 November 1998: No. 34 - 8 weeks

1335. MEMORY MOTEL (Jagger, Richard) ✎ 6.05
5 July 1998: Place: Arena, Amsterdam, Netherlands.
Rolling Stones with Darryl Jones, Dave Matthews, Chuck Leavell, Bernard Fowler, Lisa Fischer, Blondie Chaplin.
Producer: The Glimmer Twins. Production Co-ordination: Pierre De Beauport.
Engineer: Ed Cherney, Ulli Poesselt. Assistant Engineer: Peter Brandt, Tiemen Boelens, Henk van Helvoirt.
Additional Production and Mix: Chris Potter.
UK CD LP NO SECURITY: 9 November 1998: No. 67 - 1 week
USA CD LP NO SECURITY: 16 November 1998: No. 34 - 8 weeks
UK CD Single: 1999

The track was edited and released as a promo single (* a - 4.45) with a call out hook (* b - 0.15).

1336. RESPECTABLE (Jagger, Richard) ✎ 3.35
5 July 1998: Place: Arena, Amsterdam, Netherlands.
Rolling Stones with Darryl Jones, Chuck Leavell, Bernard Fowler, Lisa Fischer, Blondie Chaplin.
Producer: The Glimmer Twins. Production Co-ordination: Pierre De Beauport.
Engineer: Ed Cherney, Ulli Poesselt. Assistant Engineer: Peter Brandt, Tiemen Boelens, Henk van Helvoirt.
Additional Production and Mix: Chris Potter.
UK CD LP NO SECURITY: 9 November 1998: No. 67 - 1 week
USA CD LP NO SECURITY: 16 November 1998: No. 34 - 8 weeks

1337. YOU GOT ME ROCKING (Jagger, Richards) ✎ 3.25
6 July 1998: Place: Arena, Amsterdam, Netherlands.
Rolling Stones with Darryl Jones, Chuck Leavell, Bernard Fowler, Lisa Fischer, Blondie Chaplin.
Producer: The Glimmer Twins. Production Co-ordination: Pierre De Beauport.
Engineer: Ed Cherney, Ulli Poesselt. Assistant Engineer: Peter Brandt, Tiemen Boelens, Henk van Helvoirt.
Additional Production and Mix: Chris Potter.
UK CD LP NO SECURITY: 9 November 1998: No. 67 - 1 week
USA CD LP NO SECURITY: 16 November 1998: No. 34 - 8 weeks

1338. SISTER MORPHINE (Jagger, Richard, Faithfull) ✎ 6.16
6 July 1998: Place: Arena, Amsterdam, Netherlands.
Rolling Stones with Darryl Jones, Chuck Leavell.
Producer: The Glimmer Twins. Production Co-ordination: Pierre De Beauport.
Engineer: Ed Cherney, Ulli Poesselt. Assistant Engineer: Peter Brandt, Tiemen Boelens, Henk van Helvoirt.
Additional Production and Mix: Chris Potter.
UK CD LP NO SECURITY: 9 November 1998: No. 67 - 1 week
USA CD LP NO SECURITY: 16 November 1998: No. 34 - 8 weeks

The tour continued through June to September, visiting old and new venues. The countries included, Belgium, Germany, Netherlands, Switzerland, Austria, Spain, France, Denmark, Sweden, Norway, Finland, Estonia, Russia (a first for the band), Poland, Croatia, Czech Republic, more dates in the Netherlands, Germany, Sweden and Greece, before another first, Turkey, on 19 September. The Russian date gave the band the chance to have photos taken in Red Square. It was the first time they had played the Estonia singing festival fields of Tallinn too.

Five dates were played at the Amsterdam Arena and seven songs ended up on releases because the arena had a roof, enabling the sound to better controlled. *I Just Want To Make Love To You* was only made available on the Japanese version of NO SECURITY. *Memory Motel* was released as a single featuring Dave Matthews on co-lead vocals. The album reached distributors in November 1998 balancing unreleased, old tracks with new. *Respectable* took on a new lease of life and *You Got Me Rocking* climbed among the greats.

There were four new tracks from the recent album, while the oldest played was *The Last Time* (which ironically Ron Wood starts, not having been there for the original), *Live With Me* and *Sister Morphine*, for which Marianne Faithfull was credited with the songwriting. The running order was not disguised as being from a show - it was a straight selection made by taking the set list and comparing tracks not before released on a live album, although *Live With Me* was on YA YA's. It was also decided to include other vocals to spread the sound.

There were no over-dubs or touch-ups apart from some introductions. The album cover was very distinctive with black and yellow security tape used as the border and a photo of two fans within the golden circle waiting for the show, with stage curtains closed. The idea was to take a number of shots of typical couples before the show. The shot on the cover, of a long-haired rocker and a tattooed lady, was chosen by Mick Jagger. There is a story that he was a security person who took off his t-shirt to have the photo taken; hence there was "no security" and the album title was selected.

1339. MIDNIGHT RAMBLER (Jagger, Richard) ✏ 10.02
11 February 1999: Place: The Arrowhead Pond, Anaheim, California.
Rolling Stones with Darryl Jones, Chuck Leavell.
Bootleg only.

Potential dates for 1999 were discussed in the summer of 1998. The UK section of the tour had been re-arranged for May and June but consideration was also being given to a further USA tour of arenas. On 16 November 1998, it was announced that the NO SECURITY arena tour would be from January to April 1999, which meant the band would play live in the USA three years in a row. At a show in Chicago on 12 April 1999, Chris Evans interviewed the band for a revealing UK TV documentary shown as a C4 TFI special to help promote the European tour.

Ronnie Wood admitted to having four or five pints of Guinness and a shot of vodka before hitting the stage - having just got up before the show, it constituted his breakfast! Keith Richards had chains woven into his hair and joked, "Should I see a doctor?" He explained that the "ancient form of weaving" was not about splitting solos up but bringing the song together. He thought the band were getting so hot that they could not afford (financially or artistically?) to stop.

On tour, the main stage was decked in yellow and black "no security" with a walkway to a B-stage. The opening was to the strains of *Might As Well Get Juiced*, during which the band appears back-stage on a black and white video making their way towards the audience, a technique used by other acts but still very exciting. The first night, the highlight of the show was Keith doing *You Got The Silver* and *Midnight Rambler* returned to the set as the first encore before it was moved to the B-stage.

A weird gimmick was used for *Out Of Control* in which Mick opened in a cage before escaping, Houdini-like, to the stage at the song's climax. This routine was only used for three performances. The more intimate nature of the NO SECURITY shows made them a big success with audiences totalling more than a half a million during the four months.

1340. MELODY (Jagger, Richard) ✏ 5.06
8 June 1999: Place: Shepherds Bush Empire, London, England.
Rolling Stones with Darryl Jones, Chuck Leavell, Lisa Fischer, Bernard Fowler, Bobby Keys, Blondie Chaplin, Tim Ries, Michael Davis, Kent Smith.
Bootleg only.

The final leg of the BRIDGES TO BABYLON tour consisted of 11 dates in Europe, five were in the UK - one each at Edinburgh and Sheffield and three in London. Tour rehearsals started in Amsterdam from 17 to 24 May. Internet reports about the contents whetted the appetite and indicated that some new tunes would be played. *Brand New Car, One Hit, Moon Is Up* and *Salt Of The Earth* were possibilities. The first show, in Stuttgart, Germany, confirmed that the set was similar to the NO SECURITY tour and that the band were in the mood for an excellent finale.

A field in Imst, Austria, was next before Groningen in the Netherlands. Here the set list did change when the encore, *Sympathy For The Devil* (complete with the NO SECURITY horns), dropped down the set and was replaced by *Satisfaction* - not altogether a popular choice but one that stayed for the rest of the tour. The Murrayfield rugby ground in Edinburgh, Scotland, came next, then Sheffield where a feature of the European tour returned - the rain. Sheryl Crow joined Mick Jagger to sing on *Honky Tonk Women*.

Rumours of a club gig in London were high and the grapevine of mobile phones, Stones' fan web-sites, Stones' mailing lists, e-mail and Sunday paper stories confirmed that tickets would be sold Monday morning in London. It was strange to see Stones' fans leaving Sheffield before the encore in order to be first in line for the club gig tickets. The queue started outside Tower Records, Piccadilly, London in the early hours of the morning.

For some, their arrival in the queue included early morning car rides from all corners of Britain, a late-night busker who just happened to be in the right place at the right time, taxis bringing people straight from Heathrow and listeners to the Chris Evan's breakfast show, which announced the concert officially. By late morning, around 1,000 people had secured their tickets and wrist-bands for the Shepherds Bush Empire.

1341. BRAND NEW CAR (Jagger, Richards) ✏ 4.30
8 June 1999: Place: Shepherds Bush Empire, London, England.
Rolling Stones with Darryl Jones, Chuck Leavell, Lisa Fischer, Bernard Fowler, Bobby Keys, Blondie Chaplin, Tim Ries, Michael Davis, Kent Smith.
Bootleg only.

1342. MOON IS UP (Jagger, Richards) ⟋ 4.58
8 June 1999: Place: Shepherds Bush Empire, London, England.
Rolling Stones with Darryl Jones, Chuck Leavell.
Bootleg only.

The Shepherds Bush Empire had been a variety hall for 50 years from 1903 until the BBC bought it as a studio theatre before selling it to the current concert promoters in 1994. The capacity for the gig was 2,000 with most on the general admission floor and guests on the upper balcony. After the warm-up by Sheryl Crow, an announcer plainly said, "Ladies and gentlemen please welcome the Rolling Stones". The opening number was *Shattered*, which indicated that a varied club set list might be in order. Two standard numbers, *It's Only Rock 'n' Roll* and *Respectable*, followed before the alternative *All Down The Line*.

Mick Jagger, despite being restricted by the space of the stage, showed he was more than capable of projecting himself in a club, arena or stadium - he just did not have to run so far. The *Some Girls* lyrics were altered to be more politically correct with white girls instead of those black girls. The lyric that some girls gave him children, "even though I only made love to them once", was apt due to his affair with Luciana Morad, which was the final nail in his much-hammered coffin, signalling the demise of his relationship with Jerry Hall. Mick said that they had never performed *Melody* before, forgetting El Mocambo 22 years before.

Nevertheless, it was a pleasure to hear, with Lisa Fischer on co-vocals. *I Got The Blues* and *Brand New Car* continued the new song section before they played *Moon Is Up* for the first time. The lack of rehearsals resulted in Mick not realising he should be on harmonica. The set returned to the more familiar with *Saint Of Me*, the crowd being interrupted when doing the end of song sing-a-long by the guitar chords of *Honky Tonk Women*, which featured Sheryl Crow. Bar stools were brought on for Keith Richards' spot with *You Got The Silver* (Keith improvised the lyrics), which was just right for such an intimate event.

Before They Make Me Run was next before *Route 66*, *You Got Me Rocking*, *Tumbling Dice*, *Brown Sugar* and an encore of *Jumping Jack Flash* concluded a fantastic gig. Mick invited those who wanted to hear the familiar tunes, to go up the road at the weekend where the twin towers of Wembley welcomed fans to two great rock and roll shows, including an electrifying *Midnight Rambler*. After Britain the tour went to Santiago de Compostela, Spain, Landgraaf, Netherlands and lastly Cologne, Germany, on 20 June 1999. Finally, after 22 months, 150 shows, seen by more than 5,000,000 fans, it was time for cold turkey!

1343. LOSING MY TOUCH (Jagger, Richards) 5.06
13 May - 8 June 2002: Place: Studio Guillaume Tell, Paris, France; Mix This! Studios, Los Angeles, USA.
Rolling Stones with Darryl Jones, Chuck Leavell.
Producer: Don Was, The Glimmer Twins.
Engineer: Ed Cherney.
Mixed by: Bob Clearmountain.
UK CD LP FORTY LICKS: 30 September 2002: No. 2 - 45 weeks
USA CD LP FORTY LICKS: 1 October 2002: No. 2 - 50 weeks
USA Promo EP Four New Flicks: October 2002

Much needed rest and recuperation followed such a lengthy tour - finally everyone had escaped from the "communal village" that, during such a lengthy tour, had witnessed births, marriages and divorces. Keith Richards did get back on stage on 14 September 1999 to perform with Sheryl Crow for her live album, SHERYL CROW AND FRIENDS LIVE FROM CENTRAL PARK. He sang lead vocals on *Happy* and also performed *Sweet Little Rock 'n' Roller. Happy* was the track released on the album in 1999. At the end of the year Mick Jagger and Keith recorded for the charity, Children's Promise, providing some guitar and vocal parts.

This was for a re-recorded track, *It's Only Rock 'N' Roll*, which had a huge galaxy of guest artists (who offered a vocal-only contribution) including Kid Rock, Jon Bon Jovi, Iggy Pop, Joe Cocker, Jackson Browne, Womack & Womack, Status Quo, Annie Lennox and Chrissie Hynde. Next, in 2000, Mick worked on a new film, *Enigma*, based on the World War II electronic machine which de-scrambled German encrypted code - Mick even owned an original machine. Charlie Watts oversaw the release of his percussion project with Jim Keltner.

During 2001, Keith played on the track *You Win Again* for a forthcoming tribute album to Hank Williams. He also formed a band with Steve Jordan for a one-off concert to promote the Rainforest Alliance. Ron Wood threatened to record a joint album with Rod Stewart which did not materialise and also started work on a solo album. Mick began work on his new solo album with Matt Clifford, Lenny Kravitz and Rob Thomas, which was completed in July. Matt had become a long-term friend and confidant to Mick since the STEEL WHEELS album and tour; Mick respected his musical production. In June, Charlie and his Tentet had an almost two-week residency at Ronnie Scott's club in London.

The tragic events of September 11 initiated a charity concert organised by Paul McCartney at which Mick and Keith performed a rousing *Salt Of The Earth* and *Miss You* on behalf of New York - the event raised $14 million for the Robin Hood fund, who were committed to ending poverty in the city. Later Charlie visited Japan and then New York with his Tentet. Mick's album GODDESS IN THE DOORWAY was released in November 2001; it was one of his better solo projects.

This was followed by a TV documentary called "Being Mick" which was a lively, warm film about the making of his solo album, topical social events and the confirmation of a meeting in 2001, at which the Stones discussed activities for 2002. Mick took a lead role in a film, *The Man From Elysian Fields*, which depicted him as a failed novelist now running a high-class escort agency for rich women. Ronnie's album NOT FOR BEGINNERS also emerged in November.

It was an uncomplicated album and probably his best to date. He promoted it with a short tour which included an unlikely guitar partnership with Slash, ex of Guns 'n' Roses. During March 2002, at Keith's home in Jamaica, Mick and Keith started writing and swapping ideas for new tracks which they recorded in Paris during May and June. *Losing My Touch*, described by Mick as "very slow" is a ballad written and sung by Keith originating from autumn 2001. Darryl Jones contributes an acoustic bass and Chuck Leavell piano while Ron Wood supports Keith acoustic on a pedal steel.

1344. KEYS TO YOUR LOVE (Jagger, Richards) 4.12
13 May - 8 June 2002: Place: Studio Guillaume Tell, Paris, France; Mix This! Studios, Los Angeles, USA.
Producer: Don Was, The Glimmer Twins.
Engineer: Ed Cherney.
Mixed by: Bob Clearmountain.
UK CD LP FORTY LICKS: 30 September 2002: No. 2 - 45 weeks
USA CD LP FORTY LICKS: 1 October 2002: No. 2 - 50 weeks
USA Promo EP Four New Flicks: October 2002

Each of the Stones tours had been announced to obtain maximum publicity . . . 1975 the Stones arrived on the back of a flat-bed truck playing *Brown Sugar* . . . 1978 was more discreet . . . 1981 was proclaimed at JFK Stadium, Philadelphia . . . for the 1989 STEEL WHEELS they rode on a train to the conference at Grand Central railway station, New York . . . 1994 and VOODOO LOUNGE was down the Hudson on a boat to a quay in New York . . . and, for the 1997 BRIDGES TO BABYLON, a Cadillac took them to Brooklyn Bridge, New York. No surprise then that New York was again the venue for the announcement of their 2002/2003 tour on 7 May 2002. Mick Jagger referring to "the media capital of the United States", before being corrected by Ron Wood: "the media capital of the World." This time the mode of transport had been leaked over the Internet by those who had sighted test-flights of a yellow Blimp aircraft with a huge Stones tongue on either side. The tour was not launched with a name, despite the obvious banners of the "40th Anniversary Tour". Mick Jagger said: "The concept for the tour is a rock band playing guitars." And there was a re-assurance that Ronnie would be playing one of those guitars despite rumours that he would be axed due to his alcohol and drug-related problems being a bit more than "recreational". An ultimatum had been given by his family and Mick with the result that he entered a re-hab clinic for some weeks in April and early May.

At the conference he was on top-form and very much looked the young man of the band. The Blimp descended into the Van Cortlandt Park, New York, and the group walked to the marquees erected for the news media. Charlie Watts wobbled a bit, apparently not enjoying his "one time [blimp flight] experience". Mick Jagger stated that the tour would include stadium, arena and selected club/theatre gigs to allow them to create different set-lists for each type of show. There would also be a retrospective double CD release of their Greatest Hits for the first time, spanning the ten-year Decca and London period (with ABKCO's permission) as well as the last 30 years. This CD would also include some new releases - they had not been recorded then, but the bandana-wearing Keith Richards thought

that was a "minor problem". Mick confirmed that tour rehearsals would be in Toronto. Asked why they were touring Mick said, "well, either we stay at home and become pillars of the community or we go out and tour and we couldn't really find any communities that still needed pillars!"

News of the worldwide concerts was broken weeks before the official conference by the Stones' Internet community. Following the conference the band journeyed to Paris where they recorded for the first time at the Studio Guillaume Tell. Producer Don Was confirmed that recordings from the May sessions were fruitful and could reach a full album-worth. Ed Cherney, who was the engineer, was also pleased with the ambience of the sessions and felt that the recordings were made in one of the best-sounding rooms he had ever used. In all, about 28 to 30 songs were recorded, although some were just ideas and riffs.

At first, Mick conservatively thought that two would be included on the Greatest Hits album but this was expanded to four when the sessions proved more fruitful. Only four or five were actually mixed from the sessions but the band gave clues that some of the remaining material may turn up on an album released after the tour. While not fully following through on this hint, some may have been released on *Four Flicks. Keys To Your Love* is an up-beat ballad which Mick thought was like The Impressions. Keith likened it to *Beast Of Burden*. It has a warm soul feel to it and it gently grooves along with Mick's vocals ranging from straight to falsetto.

1345. STEALING MY HEART (Jagger, Richards) 3.42
13 May - 8 June 2002: Place: Studio Guillaume Tell, Paris, France; Mix This! Studios, Los Angeles, USA.
Producer: Don Was, The Glimmer Twins.
Engineer: Ed Cherney. Mixed by: Bob Clearmountain.
UK CD LP FORTY LICKS: 30 September 2002: No. 2 - 45 weeks
USA CD LP FORTY LICKS: 1 October 2002: No. 2 - 50 weeks
USA Promo EP Four New Flicks: October 2002

As well as the Greatest Hits project titled FORTY LICKS, there were rumours and suggestions from the band that there would also be a live compilation of material, an album of BBC sessions and a box set package including out-takes but, at that time, the Stones did not have a great reputation for expunging their past, much preferring to concentrate on the future. However, other releases were due to hit the shops in advance of the tour. ABKCO intended to re-release 22 of the UK and USA formatted albums under their control for the new Sony/Philips developed DSD technology and SACD/CD dual format, some "tender loving care" re-mastering attempting to reclaim some of ABKCO's lost credibility over the years.

A condition made by the Stones was that the artistic integrity of the original album must be maintained so, apart from changes to include any original stereo mixes and replacing any reprocessed stereo mixes back to mono, additional tracks located could not be added, apart from on the compilation releases. ABKCO's Chief Audio Engineer and Teri Landi enlisted help from Jane Byrne and Mick McKenna to research the Stones archives. Jody Klein (ABKCO's CEO and Restoration Producer) oversaw the production whilst Steve Rosenthal conducted the excellent sound restoration and final mastering was applied by Bob Ludwig.

Steve Rosenthal had won a Grammy for his restoration and archival work of Alan Lomax recordings of folk music with the American Library of Congress. He wanted to ensure the original graininess of the analogue recording was retained thereby maintaining its historical integrity. ABKCO were responsible for editing and transferring from analogue tape to DSD/SACD in separate album packages. It then took him four months to master the 22 albums and down sample them for the usual PCM CD format. This involved comparing them to the original vinyl and the original 1986 digital versions.

Normally he would have worked straight from the analogue tapes but this would have been impractical and ultimately time constrained. SACD authoring was conducted by Hiroyuki Komuro. One man missing from the credits was Allen Klein, who originated the ABKCO label, although a certain Lenne Allik was credited with "concept". Even the sleeve notes for the project were maintained exactly as the original packaging. Gus Skinas who, as a Sony product manager in the 1980s, had been one of the leaders in promoting PCM digital recording technology, was the DSD expert and he was assisted by Sony's Representative Andrew Demery in setting up the transfer system.

This took place in a specially-created room at Steve Rosenthal's Magic Shop studios in New York in 2001 and is where the bulk of the tape transfers were carried out. Together with Steve they extracted every last nuance they could from the original analogue recordings before converting them to digital DSD format. Jody Klein brought a quarter-inch master tape that was used to cut an acetate of *Satisfaction* back in 1965 and that was the first track they chose to listen to and convert. ABKCO had the majority of the recordings but the Rolling Stones also lent several first-generation masters to the project. The FORTY LICKS album from the same era was not in SACD format but was the first significant occasion when ABKCO and Rolling Stones Records finally joined together. The idea for such a project had been talked about as long ago as 1998 as time thawed the previous rift between the organisations.

On the 16 June 2002, it was announced that Mick Jagger would become a United Kingdom "knight of the realm". He was to become Sir Michael Philip Jagger - arise Sir Michael of Jagger. Keith had been previously heard to say that, "I don't want Her to come near me with a sword . . . much too sharp!" In an interview, Mick described *Stealing My Heart*, "It is more like garage rock with a hook." Written by Mick, it is a catchy, swaggering number with guitars breathing fire into the song.

1346. DON'T STOP (Jagger, Richards) 3.58
AKA: Don't Know How To Stop
13 May - 8 June 2002: Place: Studio Guillaume Tell, Paris, France; Mix This! Studios, Los Angeles, USA.
Played Live: 2002, 2003
Rolling Stones with Chuck Leavell, Darryl Jones.
Producer: Don Was, The Glimmer Twins.
Engineer: Ed Cherney. Mixed by: Bob Clearmountain.
UK CD LP FORTY LICKS: 30 September 2002: No. 2 - 45 weeks
USA Promo CD Track Don't Stop (Edit): September 2002
USA CD LP FORTY LICKS: 1 October 2002: No. 2 - 50 weeks
UK Single: 7 October 2002: No. 36 - 2 weeks
USA Single: 8 October 2002
USA Promo EP Four New Flicks: October 2002
UK Single: 16 December 2002
UK CD box set THE SINGLES COLLECTION 1971-2006: 45 X 45s: 11 April 2011
USA CD box set THE SINGLES COLLECTION 1971-2006: 45 X 45s: 26 April 2011

Keith Richards' electric guitar opens the ironically-named *Don't Stop* and Charlie Watts' drums enter the arena in a mid-tempo rock song, which is clearly designed to be a single. It is a straightforward pop song with no great twists and turns but played in a relaxed manner. The lyrics relate to a lost love who has twisted in the knife - is that you Jerry? They also include throw back references to *Highwire* with the "cold, cold" refrain. Mick Jagger doesn't rely on an atypical affected enunciation but rather sings the song plain and simply. Ron Wood takes the initiative from Keith and supplants the lead solo which is very clean and radio friendly. A third guitar, an acoustic, sits back in the mix.

As Keith said to Guitar World in the mid-90s: "When in doubt, if something doesn't sound right, just brush on an acoustic guitar and see what happens. What it does, if you're recording a band, is fill the air between the cymbals and all the electric instruments. It's like a wash in painting. Just a magical thing. If something sounds a little dry or heavy or tight, put on an acoustic, or maybe just a few notes of piano-another acoustic instrument. Somehow it will just add that extra glue." In essence Mick Jagger told Bob Clearmountain his thoughts: "It's a band, not a fuckin' metronome." Perhaps this technique was used for *Don't Stop*. There are no backing vocals or any detectable backing instrumentation such as Chuck Leavell's organ. It is the band making a statement that they are back and that they intend to rock. In the documentary *Tip Of The Tongue*, Mick did not want any country lilts to the song, it should be a sinewy and snaky rock effort. As well as the album version, there is a *Radio Edit* friendly take (* a - 3.32) a *Call Out Hook* (* b - 0.13) and a slightly rockier mix by Jack Joseph Puig from Ocean Way Studios, all available on the single. Of the new songs it was the only one to be played live on the tour.

1347. DON'T STOP (NEW ROCK MIX) (Jagger, Richards) 4.01
13 May - 8 June 2002: Place: Studio Guillaume Tell, Paris, France; Mix This! Studios, Ocean Way, Los Angeles, USA.
Rolling Stones with Chuck Leavell, Darryl Jones.
Producer: Don Was, The Glimmer Twins.
Engineer: Ed Cherney. Assistant: Chris Steffen.
Mixed by: Jack Joseph Puig.
Mastered by: Stephen Marcussen.
USA Promo EP Four New Flicks: October 2002
European CD Single Track Don't Stop:21 October 2002
UK Single Track Don't Stop (New Rock Mix): 16 December 2002
UK CD box set THE SINGLES COLLECTION 1971-2006: 45 X 45s: 11 April 2011
USA CD box set THE SINGLES COLLECTION 1971-2006: 45 X 45s: 26 April 2011

1348. EXTREME WESTERN GRIP (Jagger, Richards) 3.05
13 May - 8 June 2002: Place: Studio Guillaume Tell, Paris, France.
Rolling Stones with Darryl Jones, Chuck Leavell.
Producer: Don Was, The Glimmer Twins.
Engineer: Ed Cherney.
USA DVD Four Flicks: 11 November 2003
UK DVD Four Flicks: 17 November 2003

The *Four Flicks* DVD revealed some bonus tracks recorded at the same time, including the filming of the May/June session. *Extreme Western Grip* is an instrumental blues in the "don't do that" rambler style complete with mouth harp and Chuck Leavell organ. Ron Wood's lead guitar adds to the rambler vibe. Keith Richards reveals the song title at the end. World events were escalating in Afghanistan where the USA and their allies were retaliating for the 9/11 monstrosity against the Taliban, toppling them and insurgents from power and installing a western pro-democracy acting president.

1349. WELL WELL (Jagger, Richards) 3.01
13 May - 8 June 2002: Place: Studio Guillaume Tell, Paris, France.
Rolling Stones with Darryl Jones, Chuck Leavell.
Producer: Don Was, The Glimmer Twins.
Engineer: Ed Cherney.
USA DVD Four Flicks: 11 November 2003
UK DVD Four Flicks: 17 November 2003

Well Well is an out-take recorded on another day for the DVD but more funked up by Chuck Leavell and Darryl Jones' bass line. Don Was studies the task in hand sat cross-legged on the floor. The vocals are ad-libbed hence the "well well" title. It was a pleasure to see the band perform both of these tracks on film even if they were jam run throughs. Another song covered during the sessions was a version of Buddy Guy's *Leave My Guy Alone*, which is partly featured on the *Four Flicks, Tip Of The Tongue* documentary. The film was produced by Victoria Pearman, who was head of Mick Jagger's Jagged Films production company and had worked on the film *Enigma* and the documentary, *Being Mick*. Other tracks hinted at, with song titles seen in *Four Flicks*, are *Smooth 180, I Only Found* and *Still In Love* . . . which may have been the older *Still In Love* track.

1350. HURRICANE (Jagger, Richards) 1.25
AKA: 9/11 Hurricane
13 May - 8 June 2002: Place: Studio Guillaume Tell, Paris, France.
Keith Richards
Producer: Don Was, The Glimmer Twins.
Engineer: Ed Cherney.
USA Charity CD Single: November 2005
UK CD VINTAGE VINOS: 25 October 2010
USA CD VINTAGE VINOS: 2 November 2010

Written about the 9/11 disaster approaching its first anniversary, *Hurricane* is a very short acoustic number sung and played by Keith Richards with acoustic slide from Ronnie Wood. It described the impact of a huge catastrophe in the shape of a hurricane or a flood. It was not meant to be political, more a short country song. It would probably have remained stored in the library but for the vengeful Hurricane Katrina which devastated Florida and the southern States of Mississippi and Louisiana but principally the city of New Orleans, in August 2005. The flood defences were breached and the area became a disaster site. As a result, the track was released as a one-sided single to raise money for a donation to the victims of Katrina. This was distributed during A BIGGER BANG tour when the Californian leg was reached in November 2005.

1351. I CAN'T TURN YOU LOOSE (Redding) ⟋ 4.49
16 August 2002: Place: Palais Royale, Toronto, Canada.
Rolling Stones with Darryl Jones, Chuck Leavell, Lisa Fischer, Bernard Fowler, Bobby Keys, Blondie Chaplin, Tim Ries, Michael Davis, Kent Smith.
Bootleg only.

Rehearsals started in Toronto, on 16 July 2002, for the dates formerly known as "The War Horse Tour". With only a few nights under their belts during the 18 July rehearsal, Royden "Chuch" Magee collapsed and died of a heart attack at the age of 54. He had been Ron Wood's guitar technician in the early 70s but stayed with the Stones after being introduced into the camp by Ron. He was a much loved man and the band were deeply affected by his loss.
It brought home to them their own mortal coil. Keith Richards said that the Stones were looking for five people to replace Chuch and acknowledged that it was ironic that he died " . . . behind the amplifiers where he's always worked, where he's always taken care of business." Ron Wood had to go into a clinic to dry out and intended to remain sober for the entire tour. Mick Jagger had warned him in no uncertain terms that this was a requirement for him joining the tour.
He needed the money desperately, too, receiving a tour advance to help with his debts. News began to filter around the world of the material covered at the sessions and it was clear the Stones were dusting off some of the old repertoire, which Ronnie especially enjoyed. Songs such as *She Smiled Sweetly*, *If You Can't Rock Me*, *That's How Strong My Love Is*, *I'm A Hog For You Baby*, *Sway*, *Cherry Oh Baby*, *Worried About You*, *Torn And Frayed*, *Loving Cup*, *Hand Of Fate*, *Hot Stuff*, *Heart Of Stone*, *Dance*, *Mannish Boy* and, above all, *Can't You Hear Me Knocking*, were getting special treatment. After a month the band played their usual warm-up club gig at the Palais Royale in Toronto. The performance was a relaxed affair and, despite some first night nerves, it provided some great moments.
The Otis Redding song *I Can't Turn You Loose*, which was a UK hit in 1966, reaching No. 29, was one of the highlights of the evening with its epochal brass riff. Sometimes, covering other material does not quite work but on this occasion the song had been "nailed" to quote some fans who attended. The full set list was *It's Only Rock 'n' Roll*, *Sad Sad Sad*, *If You Can't Rock Me* (the first time it had been played complete live), *Stray Cat Blues*, *Hot Stuff*, *Don't Stop* (the new single but played with organ and brass, very unlike the studio version), *Honky Tonk Women*, *Torn and Frayed* (not for the first time, as Jagger claimed on the night), *Wild Horses*, *Happy*, *I Can't Turn You Loose*, *Heart Of Stone* (Keith enjoyed digging this one up), *Can't You Hear Me Knocking* (oh yes, live for the first time ever!), *Jumping Jack Flash* and the encore *Brown Sugar*.

1352. CAN'T YOU HEAR ME KNOCKING (Jagger, Richard) ⟋ 8.48
3 September 2002: Place: Fleet Center, Boston, Massachusetts, USA.
Rolling Stones with Darryl Jones, Chuck Leavell, Lisa Fischer, Bernard Fowler, Bobby Keys, Blondie Chaplin, Tim Ries, Michael Davis, Kent Smith.
Bootleg only.

The period between May and September is documented by Eileen Gregory in memory of Chuch Magee for the DVD *Four Flicks*. As well as the recording process, it takes in the band backstage at the Palais Royale, rehearsals at a very cold Foxboro stadium and onwards to the Fleet Center. Eileen Gregory's previous work, *Honest*, had been a black comedy film starring individuals from All Saints. The producer and possible link was musician and film maker Dave Stewart. Boston was the first city where a trinity of gigs took place; the theme of the LICKS tour, as it became named, was to play theatres, arenas and stadiums, with a plan to vary and change the set list accordingly, not to mention the stage, which was again designed by Mark Fisher.
Keith Richards described it as "The Underwear Tour" as in small, medium or large! The Fleet Center was a 15,000 capacity arena and, two days later, they played the 68,000 Gillette stadium in Foxboro. The last gig of the three came two days later at the Boston Orpheum theatre, which housed just over 2,500. At the arena, supported by the Pretenders, they performed *Street Fighting Man* as the opening number and followed with a section of old and the new, including an as yet unreleased *Don't Stop*. There followed a bold four-section song set from EXILE, comprising *Loving Cup*, *Rocks Off*, *Rip This Joint* and *Tumbling Dice*.
After Keith Richards' set they resumed with a soulful version of the O'Jays *Love Train*, which had Mick Jagger wearing a top hat and white coat. The backing vocalists - Lisa Fischer, Bernard Fowler and Blondie Chaplin - were an essential part of this act and encouraged a sing-a-long and a reprise section. *Can't You Hear Me Knocking* looked as though it would be included as a showpiece and one of the significant songs of the tour. From the opening dramatic riff, it relaxed into a jam with Bobby Keys weaving with the guitar boys, Mick Jagger jamming on harmonica and Ronnie Wood proving his guitar aptitude. After some war horses (well-known songs) the band took to the B-stage travelator as it journeyed to the arena's floor end where *Mannish Boy*, *Neighbours* and a sparse *Brown Sugar*, with just Bobby Keys guesting. The band then disappeared as the show ended.
However, two songs were encored back at the main stage, the 22-number set concluding with *Jumping Jack Flash*. Certainly, it was an unusual format. At the Gillette Stadium, a further 13 new songs were played and the theatre provided nine more alternatives. Between the three shows, an incredible total of 44 songs were played. Only six numbers were played on every night - *It's Only Rock 'n' Roll*, *Tumbling Dice*, Keith's *Slipping Away*, *Honky Tonk Women*, *Brown Sugar* and *Jumping Jack Flash*. Buddy Guy was the guest act at the Orpheum and he also performed on *Rock Me Baby*, while *Parachute Woman* and *Brand New Car* were afforded immense, once-only tour performances.
This showcase of Stones material was unlike any seen before and was repeated in cities Chicago, Philadelphia and New York. The theatre gigs were the must-catch for all fans as they paid for multiple internet fan club memberships to gain magical passcodes that would lead to the ultimate Stones ticket - a club gig. The set lists for such events always allowed some of those rarer tracks to creep in and this tour was not one to disappoint. *Hot Stuff* was played at the Tower Theatre, Philadelphia, with BLACK AND BLUE's *Hand Of Fate*. At the Aragon Ballroom in Chicago, *Don't Look Back* was played the one and only time and U2's Bono came on and contributed to *It's Only Rock 'n' Roll*, improvising during a *Going To A Go-Go* segment, even saying he loved Keith and Sir Mick! Having worked up the crowd, Dr John followed with *I Just Want To Make Love To You* - and so they marched onwards.
New York welcomed them at the aptly-named Giants' (American football) Stadium and the legendary Madison Square Garden where spell-binding performances of *Can't You Hear Me Knocking* and *Mannish Boy* were played - even *Thru And Thru* was debuted by Keith. The stadium unveiled a new poster back drop, especially designed by Jeff Koons, replacing a photo of his Licks work, named by the entourage as "corn and panties". The yellow theme was removed to make way for more

multi-colour but the artwork still included underwear, red lips and an inflatable Scooby Doo look-a-like. The Roseland Ballroom in New York was definitely the hardest gig for celebrities and fans to attend due to the huge demand for tickets. They were honoured by a one-off performance of *She Smiled Sweetly* and the support artist Jonny Lang (aged 22) played guitar on *Rock Me Baby*.

1353. BEAST OF BURDEN (Jagger, Richards) ✎ 5.19
4 November 2002: Place: Wiltern Theatre, Los Angeles, USA.
Rolling Stones with Darryl Jones, Chuck Leavell, Blondie Chaplin, Bernard Fowler.
Producer: DVD: Marty Callner, Randall Gladstein. CD: The Glimmer Twins, Don Was.
Engineer: Ed Cherney. CD: Assisted Mike Butler.
Other Production: DVD: Don Was, Mastered: Stephen Marcussen. CD: Peter Brandt, David Hewitt.
Mix: Bob Clearmountain, Kevin Horn. Mastered: Stephen Marcussen.
USA DVD Four Flicks: 11 November 2003
UK DVD Four Flicks: 17 November 2003
UK CD LP LIVE LICKS: 1 November 2004: No. 38 - 4 weeks
USA CD LP LIVE LICKS: 1 November 2004: No. 50 - 2 weeks

A mixture of arenas and stadiums were played for the next three weeks until the band landed in Los Angeles, where another trio of performances was witnessed at the Staples Center, Edison Field and the Wiltern Theatre. The latter show (capacity 2,300) was recorded by Ed Cherney for the *Four Flicks* DVD released only a year later in 2003. Cherney had first recorded the Stones on the STRIPPED album and every subsequent live work up to SHINE A LIGHT. He first worked with Don Was when they produced and engineered the Grammy Award-winning Bonnie Raitt's album NICK OF TIME. The *Four Flicks* project would include a DVD from T.O.A.S.T. a tour of arenas, stadiums and theatres.
The Wiltern may have been the preferred location for the theatre DVD release but the outcome is murky compared with Paris Olympia, the camera work being very different. *Beast Of Burden* shows perfectly the intimacy of the lyrics and how the song was used perfectly for B-stage endings as Mick engages with the audience. The twin guitars have their roles too, Ronnie Wood bending and soloing while Keith Richards uses his pick on the guitar neck with Blondie Chaplin in the background giving acoustic support. Keith reckoned that their live interpretation of this song improved upon the original.

1354. EVERYBODY NEEDS SOMEBODY TO LOVE (Berns, Burke, Wexler) ✎ 6.34
4 November 2002: Place: Wiltern Theatre, Los Angeles, USA.
Rolling Stones with Solomon Burke, Solomon Burke Jnr, Darryl Jones, Chuck Leavell, Blondie Chaplin, Lisa Fischer, Bernard Fowler, Bobby Keys, Tim Ries, Michael Davis, Kent Smith.
Producer: The Glimmer Twins, Don Was.
Engineer: Ed Cherney, Mike Butler.
Other Production: Peter Brandt, David Hewitt.
Mix: Bob Clearmountain, Kevin Horn. Mastered: Stephen Marcussen.
UK CD LP LIVE LICKS: 1 November 2004: No. 38 - 4 weeks
USA CD LP LIVE LICKS: 1 November 2004: No. 50 - 2 weeks

Solomon Burke was the support artist for the gig and guested on his own number, *Everybody Needs Somebody To Love*. During the duet Solomon Burke anointed Mick Jagger "Ladies and Gentlemen, the crowned kings of rock 'n' roll", Burke Junior placing Solomon's trademark gold inner and purple outer cape over Mick's shoulders. By now it was more enlarged than when he first started wearing it in the 80s and Mick admitted later he did not understand what was going on, while Keith Richards and Ron Wood sniggered in the background. He took it off and tried to hand it back but Solomon denied him. "I crowned the Rolling Stones 'The True Kings of Rock 'n' Roll' when I gave Mick the golden cloak", says Burke. "Several institutions, including the Smithsonian and the R&B Foundation, have been after it for years, but I wanted to pass it on to the Stones. They have been spreading the word and awareness of black artists throughout the world for nearly forty years now."
Embarrassed by the gesture Mick said at the song climax, "Thank you Solomon Burke, that was a moment. Blimey that's some big cloak." While on a solo tour in October 2010, as Solomon landed at Schippol Airport in Amsterdam, he unfortunately collapsed and died. He had provided the Rolling Stones and many others with such great tunes but this one was played extensively on the Licks tour. The footage of the performance did not end up on the Bootleg section of the *Four Flicks* DVD but the audio was received well on the LIVE LICKS CD. Mick paid tribute to him at the time but also at the Grammy awards in 2011, where Raphael Saadiq and his band performed the trademark song.

1355. YOU DON'T HAVE TO MEAN IT (Jagger, Richards) ✎ 4.34
4 November 2002: Place: Wiltern Theatre, Los Angeles, USA.
Rolling Stones with Darryl Jones, Chuck Leavell, Blondie Chaplin, Lisa Fischer, Bernard Fowler, Bobby Keys, Tim Ries, Michael Davis, Kent Smith.
Producer: DVD: Marty Callner, Randall Gladstein. CD: The Glimmer Twins, Don Was.
Engineer: Ed Cherney. CD: Assisted Mike Butler.
Other Production: DVD: Don Was, Mastered: Stephen Marcussen. CD: Peter Brandt, David Hewitt. Mix: Bob Clearmountain, Kevin Horn. Mastered: Stephen Marcussen.
USA DVD Four Flicks: 11 November 2003
UK DVD Four Flicks: 17 November 2003
UK CD LP LIVE LICKS: 1 November 2004: No. 38 - 4 weeks
USA CD LP LIVE LICKS: 1 November 2004: No. 50 - 2 weeks

It was on the Licks tour that, during Keith Richards', set he would not combine vocals and guitar but instead concentrate on just one at any time. Blondie Chaplin, who now also played electric guitar, gave him the freedom to do this. On this number, Ronnie Wood played the chopsy organ while the suitably-dreadlocked Bernard Fowler and Lisa Fischer provided great backing vocals. The reggae horns really lift the atmosphere and the song grinds along well. It was used sparingly by Keith within his set but they played it a few days later in Oakland.

1356. ROCK ME BABY (King, Bihari) ✎ 3.50
4 November 2002: Place: Wiltern Theatre, Los Angeles, USA.
Rolling Stones with Darryl Jones, Chuck Leavell, Blondie Chaplin, Lisa Fischer, Bernard Fowler, Bobby Keys, Tim Ries, Michael Davis, Kent Smith.
Producer: DVD: Marty Callner, Randall Gladstein. CD: The Glimmer Twins, Don Was.
Engineer: Ed Cherney. CD: Assisted Mike Butler.
Other Production: DVD: Don Was, Mastered: Stephen Marcussen. CD: Peter Brandt, David Hewitt.
Mix: Bob Clearmountain, Kevin Horn. Mastered: Stephen Marcussen.
USA DVD Four Flicks: 11 November 2003
UK DVD Four Flicks: 17 November 2003
UK CD LP LIVE LICKS: 1 November 2004: No. 38 - 4 weeks
USA CD LP LIVE LICKS: 1 November 2004: No. 50 - 2 weeks

Rock Me Baby was used at different times on the tour but played on four occasions at theatre gigs. Usually a guest artist would appear, as Jonny Lang did at New York's Roseland Ballroom but this time it is restricted to the tightness of just the tour band, with Ron Wood and Keith Richards riffing and soloing together proficiently. By now, the tour head of steam was really rocking and stadium shows and arenas also captured a great band who were really immersed, enjoying their music and playing like a slick, well-oiled machine.
Bernard Fowler endorsed this when, in June 2008, he described the Licks performance, format and tour: "on the day, it was the best, it just didn't get any better than this" - quite an accolade considering his tour appearances since 1989. He was also pleased at the multiple-song repertoire which kept everything fresh. Chuck Leavell was researching each venue and checking set lists for the last time they played in any particular city to ensure the local crowd enjoyed a mixture of numbers. He would pass the recommendations to Mick Jagger for final approval. There are not many bands that had the luxury of the Stones catalogue.

1357. CAN'T YOU HEAR ME KNOCKING (Jagger, Richard) ✎ 10.02
4 November 2002: Place: Wiltern Theatre, Los Angeles, USA.
Rolling Stones with Darryl Jones, Jim Keltner, Chuck Leavell, Blondie Chaplin, Lisa Fischer, Bernard Fowler, Bobby Keys, Tim Ries, Michael Davis, Kent Smith.
Producer: The Glimmer Twins, Don Was.
Engineer: Ed Cherney, Mike Butler.
Other Production: Peter Brandt, David Hewitt.
Mix: Bob Clearmountain, Kevin Horn. Mastered: Stephen Marcussen.
UK CD LP LIVE LICKS: 1 November 2004: No. 38 - 4 weeks
USA CD LP LIVE LICKS: 1 November 2004: No. 50 - 2 weeks

Many concluded that this track was a tour classic moment as it really captured every band nuance from backing brass, vocals, guitars and percussion. On this occasion, the latter was ably assisted by guest Jim Keltner. On the right night, which was most, it was mesmerising and hypnotic. The song was re-interpreted, the opening riff by Keith Richards almost instantly followed by the lightning strike of Charlie's drums and Darryl Jones' bass - then Mick Jagger's "yeahh". There were no meanderings here. Only ten seconds into the song, the band's rhythmic assault is already with us. The sound diminishes as the riffs introduce the first verse "you got Chinese boots, you got cocaine eyes" and the two guitars "interlock like teeth in a zipper" (I quote Jon Wilde of Uncut magazine, who reviewed LIVE LICKS). Keith and Ronnie provided the teeth but Ed Cherney created the zipper, enabling each taught ripple to be heard and spliced together. By three-quarters-of-a-minute in, the chorus and backing singers join with Mick on the repeated song title one-liner. This continues with the organ flowing and swirling in the background for the second and last verse. At just over two-and-a-half minutes, the main song structure is over until you expect to hear the union with Mick Taylor's superb guitar improvisation of old. Not attempting to copy the original, the arrangement did gradually embellish as the tour progressed but essentially it was to an agreed structure.
First, the percussion of Charlie and Jim in Los Angeles started their brief tale before Bobby Keys provided the wow factor, emulating his very own signature chords. All the time the organ was churning continuously around Bobby until his jazz-flavoured pips squeak out having doubled the song length so far. Next it is the talents of Mick on harmonica who takes on the pips until wailing a blues lament for just under a couple of minutes. Ronnie's background guitar work comes more to the fore and poses his rhetoric refrains before leading the riff through the guitar and saxophone finale chant and concluding the song at 10 minutes, three quarters of which is an instrumental trip.

1358. BITCH (Jagger, Richard) ✎ 4.00
4 November 2002: Place: Wiltern Theatre, Los Angeles, USA.
Rolling Stones with Darryl Jones, Chuck Leavell, Blondie Chaplin, Lisa Fischer, Bernard Fowler, Bobby Keys, Tim Ries, Michael Davis, Kent Smith.
Producer: Marty Callner, Randall Gladstein.
Engineer: Ed Cherney.
Other Production: Don Was, Mastered: Stephen Marcussen. Recorded by: Peter Brandt, David Hewitt.
Mix: Bob Clearmountain, Kevin Horn.
USA DVD Four Flicks: 11 November 2003
UK DVD Four Flicks: 17 November 2003

Bitch is the final cut made available from the Wiltern recordings, while *Tumbling Dice* unusually closed the night there. The tour moved north from here, playing Seattle, Sheryl Crow joining the tour as the opener but also sang on *Wild Horses*. She played back in California in San Francisco on *Honky Tonk Women* and *Wild Horses* on different nights at the Pacific Bell Park. Frankie Gavin played fiddle on *Sweet Virginia* in Oakland and Sheryl was back dueting *Honky Tonk Women*. At first Sheryl found it strange being on stage without a guitar but soon raunched and rolled with Mick Jagger, even competing with his jive.
The last Californian gig was in warmer San Diego where again Sheryl performed and played on *Honky Tonk Women*. Corporate rock was confirmed when the band named their price and earned $7 million to play a private gig for Texan David Bonderman to celebrate his 60th birthday with friends at the Joint, Las Vegas. A stadium set list of 17 numbers was supplied. After a couple of more arenas they were back in Las Vegas for another Joint appearance - this time the public paying up to $1,000 a head - but also at the MGM Grand, where they concluded the first tour segment. There followed a five-week break for Christmas.

1359. STREET FIGHTING MAN (Jagger, Richard) ✎ 4.20
18 January 2003: Place: Madison Square Garden, New York, USA.
Rolling Stones with Darryl Jones, Chuck Leavell.
Producer: Marty Callner, Randall Gladstein.
Engineer: Ed Cherney.
Other Production: Don Was, Mastered: Stephen Marcussen. Recorded by: Peter Brandt, David Hewitt.
Mix: Bob Clearmountain, Kevin Horn.
USA DVD Four Flicks: 11 November 2003
UK DVD Four Flicks: 17 November 2003

1360. START ME UP (Jagger, Richards) ✎ 4.02
18 January 2003: Place: Madison Square Garden, New York, USA.
Rolling Stones with Darryl Jones, Chuck Leavell.
Producer: The Glimmer Twins, Don Was.
Engineer: Ed Cherney, Mike Butler.
Other Production: Peter Brandt, David Hewitt. Mix: Bob Clearmountain, Kevin Horn. Mastered: Stephen Marcussen.
UK CD LP LIVE LICKS: 1 November 2004: No. 38 - 4 weeks
USA CD LP LIVE LICKS: 1 November 2004: No. 50 - 2 weeks

1361. IF YOU CAN'T ROCK ME (Jagger, Richard) ✎ 4.06
18 January 2003: Place: Madison Square Garden, New York, USA.
Rolling Stones with Darryl Jones, Chuck Leavell.
Producer: DVD: Marty Callner, Randall Gladstein. CD: The Glimmer Twins, Don Was.
Engineer: Ed Cherney. CD: Assisted Mike Butler.
Other Production: DVD: Don Was, Mastered: Stephen Marcussen. CD: Peter Brandt, David Hewitt.
Mix: Bob Clearmountain, Kevin Horn. Mastered: Stephen Marcussen.
USA DVD Four Flicks: 11 November 2003
UK DVD Four Flicks: 17 November 2003
Japan CD LIVE LICKS: 1 November 2004

1362. DON'T STOP (Jagger, Richards) ✎ 4.58
18 January 2003: Place: Madison Square Garden, New York, USA.
Rolling Stones with Darryl Jones, Chuck Leavell.
Producer: Marty Callner, Randall Gladstein.
Engineer: Ed Cherney.
Other Production: Don Was, Mastered: Stephen Marcussen. Recorded by: Peter Brandt, David Hewitt. Mix: Bob Clearmountain, Kevin Horn.
USA DVD Four Flicks: 11 November 2003
UK DVD Four Flicks: 17 November 2003

1363. MONKEY MAN (Jagger, Richard) ✎ 4.04
18 January 2003: Place: Madison Square Garden, New York USA.
Rolling Stones with Darryl Jones, Chuck Leavell, Blondie Chaplin, Bernard Fowler, Bobby Keys.
Producer: DVD: Marty Callner, Randall Gladstein. CD: The Glimmer Twins, Don Was.
Engineer: Ed Cherney. CD: Assisted Mike Butler.
Other Production: DVD: Don Was, Mastered: Stephen Marcussen. CD: Peter Brandt, David Hewitt.
Mix: Bob Clearmountain, Kevin Horn. Mastered: Stephen Marcussen.
USA DVD Four Flicks: 11 November 2003
UK DVD Four Flicks: 17 November 2003
UK CD LP LIVE LICKS: 1 November 2004: No. 38 - 4 weeks
USA CD LP LIVE LICKS: 1 November 2004: No. 50 - 2 weeks

1364. ANGIE (Jagger, Richard) ✎ 3.29
18 January 2003: Place: Madison Square Garden, New York USA.
Rolling Stones with Darryl Jones, Chuck Leavell, Tim Ries.
Producer: DVD: Marty Callner, Randall Gladstein. CD: The Glimmer Twins, Don Was.
Engineer: Ed Cherney. CD: Assisted Mike Butler.
Other Production: DVD: Don Was, Mastered: Stephen Marcussen. CD: Peter Brandt, David Hewitt.
Mix: Bob Clearmountain, Kevin Horn. Mastered: Stephen Marcussen.
USA DVD Four Flicks: 11 November 2003
UK DVD Four Flicks: 17 November 2003
UK CD LP LIVE LICKS: 1 November 2004: No. 38 - 4 weeks
USA CD LP LIVE LICKS: 1 November 2004: No. 50 - 2 weeks

1365. LET IT BLEED (Jagger, Richard) ✕ 4.59
18 January 2003: Place: Madison Square Garden, New York USA.
Rolling Stones with Darryl Jones, Chuck Leavell, Bernard Fowler.
Producer: Marty Callner, Randall Gladstein.
Engineer: Ed Cherney.
Other Production: Don Was, Mastered: Stephen Marcussen. Recorded by: Peter Brandt, David Hewitt.
Mix: Bob Clearmountain, Kevin Horn.
USA DVD Four Flicks: 11 November 2003
UK DVD Four Flicks: 17 November 2003

1366. MIDNIGHT RAMBLER (Jagger, Richard) ✕ 12.25
18 January 2003: Place: Madison Square Garden, New York USA.
Rolling Stones with Darryl Jones, Chuck Leavell.
Producer: Marty Callner, Randall Gladstein.
Engineer: Ed Cherney.
Other Production: Don Was, Mastered: Stephen Marcussen. Recorded by: Peter Brandt, David Hewitt.
Mix: Bob Clearmountain, Kevin Horn.
USA DVD Four Flicks: 11 November 2003
UK DVD Four Flicks: 17 November 2003

1367. THRU AND THRU (Jagger, Richards) ✕ 7.12
18 January 2003: Place: Madison Square Garden, New York USA.
Rolling Stones with Darryl Jones, Chuck Leavell, Blondie Chaplin, Lisa Fischer, Bernard Fowler, Bobby Keys, Tim Ries, Michael Davis, Kent Smith.
Producer: Marty Callner, Randall Gladstein.
Engineer: Ed Cherney.
Other Production: Don Was, Mastered: Stephen Marcussen. Recorded by: Peter Brandt, David Hewitt.
Mix: Bob Clearmountain, Kevin Horn.
USA DVD Four Flicks: 11 November 2003
UK DVD Four Flicks: 17 November 2003
USA CD LP ROLLING STONES RARITIES 1971-2003: 22 November 2005: No. 76 - 6 weeks
UK CD LP ROLLING STONES RARITIES 1971-2003: 28 November 2005

1368. HAPPY (Jagger, Richard) ✕ 3.37
18 January 2003: Place: Madison Square Garden, New York USA.
Rolling Stones with Darryl Jones, Chuck Leavell, Blondie Chaplin, Lisa Fischer, Bernard Fowler, Bobby Keys, Tim Ries, Michael Davis, Kent Smith.
Producer: DVD: Marty Callner, Randall Gladstein. CD: The Glimmer Twins, Don Was.
Engineer: Ed Cherney. CD: Assisted Mike Butler.
Other Production: DVD: Don Was, Mastered: Stephen Marcussen. CD: Peter Brandt, David Hewitt.
Mix: Bob Clearmountain, Kevin Horn. Mastered: Stephen Marcussen.
USA DVD Four Flicks: 11 November 2003
UK DVD Four Flicks: 17 November 2003
UK CD LP LIVE LICKS: 1 November 2004: No. 38 - 4 weeks
USA CD LP LIVE LICKS: 1 November 2004: No. 50 - 2 weeks

1369. GIMME SHELTER (Jagger, Richard) ✕ 6.50
18 January 2003: Place: Madison Square Garden, New York USA.
Rolling Stones with Darryl Jones, Chuck Leavell, Blondie Chaplin, Lisa Fischer, Bernard Fowler, Bobby Keys, Tim Ries, Michael Davis, Kent Smith.
Producer: The Glimmer Twins, Don Was.
Engineer: Ed Cherney, Mike Butler.
Other Production: Peter Brandt, David Hewitt. Mix: Bob Clearmountain, Kevin Horn. Mastered: Stephen Marcussen.
UK CD LP LIVE LICKS: 1 November 2004: No. 38 - 4 weeks
USA CD LP LIVE LICKS: 1 November 2004: No. 50 - 2 weeks

1370. YOU GOT ME ROCKING (Jagger, Richards) ✕ 3.56
18 January 2003: Place: Madison Square Garden, New York USA.
Rolling Stones with Darryl Jones, Chuck Leavell, Blondie Chaplin, Lisa Fischer, Bernard Fowler, Bobby Keys, Tim Ries, Michael Davis, Kent Smith.
Producer: Marty Callner, Randall Gladstein.
Engineer: Ed Cherney.
Other Production: Don Was, Mastered: Stephen Marcussen. Recorded by: Peter Brandt, David Hewitt.
Mix: Bob Clearmountain, Kevin Horn.
USA DVD Four Flicks: 11 November 2003
UK DVD Four Flicks: 17 November 2003

1371. CAN'T YOU HEAR ME KNOCKING (Jagger, Richard) ✎ 11.19
18 January 2003: Place: Madison Square Garden, New York USA.
Rolling Stones with Darryl Jones, Chuck Leavell, Blondie Chaplin, Lisa Fischer, Bernard Fowler, Bobby Keys.
Producer: Marty Callner, Randall Gladstein.
Engineer: Ed Cherney.
Other Production: Don Was, Mastered: Stephen Marcussen. Recorded by: Peter Brandt, David Hewitt.
Mix: Bob Clearmountain, Kevin Horn.
USA DVD Four Flicks: 11 November 2003
UK DVD Four Flicks: 17 November 2003

1372. HONKY TONK WOMEN (Jagger, Richard) ✎ 3.24
18 January 2003: Place: Madison Square Garden, New York USA.
Rolling Stones with Darryl Jones, Sheryl Crow, Chuck Leavell, Blondie Chaplin, Lisa Fischer, Bernard Fowler, Bobby Keys, Tim Ries, Michael Davis, Kent Smith.
Producer: DVD: Marty Callner, Randall Gladstein. CD: The Glimmer Twins, Don Was.
Engineer: Ed Cherney. CD: Assisted Mike Butler.
Other Production: DVD: Don Was, Mastered: Stephen Marcussen. CD: Peter Brandt, David Hewitt.
Mix: Bob Clearmountain, Kevin Horn. Mastered: Stephen Marcussen.
USA DVD Four Flicks: 11 November 2003
UK DVD Four Flicks: 17 November 2003
USA CD Promo Four Flicks Audio Sampler: November 2003
UK CD LP LIVE LICKS: 1 November 2004: No. 38 - 4 weeks
USA CD LP LIVE LICKS: 1 November 2004: No. 50 - 2 weeks

1373. (I CAN'T GET NO) SATISFACTION (Jagger, Richard) ✎ 7.33
18 January 2003: Place: Madison Square Garden, New York USA.
Rolling Stones with Darryl Jones, Chuck Leavell, Blondie Chaplin, Lisa Fischer, Bernard Fowler.
Producer: DVD: Marty Callner, Randall Gladstein. CD: The Glimmer Twins, Don Was.
Engineer: Ed Cherney. CD: Assisted Mike Butler.
Other Production: DVD: Don Was, Mastered: Stephen Marcussen. CD: Peter Brandt, David Hewitt.
Mix: Bob Clearmountain, Kevin Horn. Mastered: Stephen Marcussen.
USA DVD Four Flicks: 11 November 2003
UK DVD Four Flicks: 17 November 2003
UK CD LP LIVE LICKS: 1 November 2004: No. 38 - 4 weeks
USA CD LP LIVE LICKS: 1 November 2004: No. 50 - 2 weeks

1374. IT'S ONLY ROCK 'N' ROLL (Jagger, Richard) ✎ 4.54
18 January 2003: Place: Madison Square Garden, New York USA.
Rolling Stones with Darryl Jones, Chuck Leavell.
Producer: DVD: Marty Callner, Randall Gladstein. CD: The Glimmer Twins, Don Was.
Engineer: Ed Cherney. CD: Assisted Mike Butler.
Other Production: DVD: Don Was, Mastered: Stephen Marcussen. CD: Peter Brandt, David Hewitt.
Mix: Bob Clearmountain, Kevin Horn. Mastered: Stephen Marcussen.
USA DVD Four Flicks: 11 November 2003
UK DVD Four Flicks: 17 November 2003
UK CD LP LIVE LICKS: 1 November 2004: No. 38 - 4 weeks
USA CD LP LIVE LICKS: 1 November 2004: No. 50 - 2 weeks

1375. WHEN THE WHIP COMES DOWN (Jagger, Richards) ✎ 4.28
18 January 2003: Place: Madison Square Garden, New York USA.
Rolling Stones with Darryl Jones, Chuck Leavell.
Producer: DVD: Marty Callner, Randall Gladstein. CD: The Glimmer Twins, Don Was.
Engineer: Ed Cherney. CD: Assisted Mike Butler.
Other Production: DVD: Don Was, Mastered: Stephen Marcussen. CD: Peter Brandt, David Hewitt.
Mix: Bob Clearmountain, Kevin Horn. Mastered: Stephen Marcussen.
USA DVD Four Flicks: 11 November 2003
UK DVD Four Flicks: 17 November 2003
UK CD LP LIVE LICKS: 1 November 2004: No. 38 - 4 weeks
USA CD LP LIVE LICKS: 1 November 2004: No. 50 - 2 weeks

1376. BROWN SUGAR (Jagger, Richard) ✎ 3.50
18 January 2003: Place: Madison Square Garden, New York USA.
Rolling Stones with Darryl Jones, Chuck Leavell, Bobby Keys.
Producer: DVD: Marty Callner, Randall Gladstein. CD: The Glimmer Twins, Don Was.
Engineer: Ed Cherney. CD: Assisted Mike Butler.
Other Production: DVD: Don Was, Mastered: Stephen Marcussen. CD: Peter Brandt, David Hewitt.
Mix: Bob Clearmountain, Kevin Horn. Mastered: Stephen Marcussen.
USA DVD Four Flicks: 11 November 2003
UK DVD Four Flicks: 17 November 2003
UK CD LP LIVE LICKS: 1 November 2004: No. 38 - 4 weeks
USA CD LP LIVE LICKS: 1 November 2004: No. 50 - 2 weeks

1377. SYMPATHY FOR THE DEVIL (Jagger, Richard) ✎ 6.15
18 January 2003: Place: Madison Square Garden, New York USA.
Rolling Stones with Darryl Jones, Chuck Leavell, Blondie Chaplin, Lisa Fischer, Bernard Fowler.
Producer: Marty Callner, Randall Gladstein.
Engineer: Ed Cherney.
Bootleg only.

1378. JUMPIN' JACK FLASH (Jagger, Richard) ✎ 5.55
18 January 2003: Place: Madison Square Garden, New York USA.
Rolling Stones with Darryl Jones, Chuck Leavell, Blondie Chaplin, Lisa Fischer, Bernard Fowler, Bobby Keys, Tim Ries, Michael Davis, Kent Smith.
Producer: Marty Callner, Randall Gladstein.
Engineer: Ed Cherney.
Other Production: Don Was, Mastered: Stephen Marcussen. Recorded by: Peter Brandt, David Hewitt.
Mix: Bob Clearmountain, Kevin Horn.
USA DVD Four Flicks: 11 November 2003
UK DVD Four Flicks: 17 November 2003
USA CD Promo Four Flicks Audio Sampler: November 2003

The second leg of the tour, focussed on arenas because of the time of year, commenced in Montreal on 8 January. Three dates were played before the Madison Square Garden magic was attempted again. A midweek gig took place, with Hubert Sumlin joining the band on *Let It Bleed* and also a Saturday show, which was being filmed for a live HBO transmission. Ed Cherney, who recorded the sound as he did for most of the tour, was nominated for an Emmy. Marty Callner and Randy Gladstein handled the live HBO feed but also the *Four Flicks* DVD production as this event was chosen for the arena gig.

A collage of American events, including historic film of the Stones, introduced the HBO broadcast. The film journeyed through the 60s, taking in the Nixon and eras Clinton before the present surfaced with music from Dr Dre's re-mix of *Miss You* as the band supposedly arrived at the Garden. JC took them from their cars to the back stage area until live film of the African drum chant intro and the chords of *Street Fighting Man* started the show. *Start Me Up* was not on the DVD but is available on the LIVE LICKS CD. *If You Can't Rock Me* displayed Ronnie Wood's guitar prowess, his lead solos very low on the Fender Strat's neck. The effect of riding with Ronnie's guitar neck via his guitar-cam was used on *Don't Stop* and Mick Jagger also strapped on an electric.

The jumbotron showed images of Ronnie jigging during his solo and also some luscious red lips animation. *Monkey Man* features Ronnie again on his old reliable Zemaitis slide and *Angie* has Keith Richards on acoustic as the mood softens, leading into the LET IT BLEED segment of *Let It Bleed* and *Midnight Rambler*, with a freeway video of traffic flowing. As usual, a real groove started on *Rambler*, the three guitarists lined up as Darryl Jones played in front of Charlie Watts. Ronnie played his trusted "doozy" Duesenberg and Keith Richards his Fender Telecaster Sunburst "Sonny". The song presented the band as a tough, compact smiling unit, clearly enjoying themselves indulging in playing great blues, boogie and rock. Keith's set continued with *Thru And Thru* and *Happy*, the stage now full with all the backing entourage. On the Licks tour some of the backing band did play and sing, even though they were not present on stage; this was to embellish the songs and provide fill to the overall sound. *Thru And Thru* was not released on CD until RARITIES appeared in 2005.

Ironically, it was the only true rarity on the disappointing RARITIES. *Gimme Shelter* was not on the DVD but appeared on LIVE LICKS. It was a shame not to capture the lovely Lisa Fischer vocal performance and see her ripping the lyrics, with Mick seemingly entranced. Ronnie slid his way through a rousing *You Got Me Rocking*. Mick confirmed that, despite what was in that day's newspaper, this would not be the last time at MSG. The jazzy tones of *Can't You Hear Me Knocking* followed, a performance made more ethereal with some back screen psychedelic images. *Honky Tonk Women* used some animation of a topless lady riding a tongue, legs astride holding on to the honky tongue ride and designed by a Japanese animation artist. Sheryl Crow did not lower the raunchiness as she entered to sing with Mick in tight stars and stripes hipsters.

Bernard kept a firm eye on her as the tongue devoured the dominatrix, spitting out her black high-heels at the song's conclusion - "bye Sheryl". *Satisfaction* allowed the house lights to show the crowd and Keith wandered to the raised side platform to salute the audience on both sides. It was played with no brass instrumentation. First Mick, then Charlie, walked down the narrow raised platform to the B-Stage. This was the unusual show climax for the arena performance. It allowed the far end of the crowd to participate up front at their very own concert.

Also, at the end of *Honky Tonk*, seasoned fans would make their way to the B-stage, heading for a prime spot as one-off attendees failed to see the impending small club crowd swamping the area. It allowed for some rock 'n' roll and the Garden had *It's Only Rock 'n' Roll*, *When The Whip Comes Down* and *Brown Sugar*. The seven performed a bow at the end of *Brown Sugar* whereupon they left the stage through the crowd flanked by security until disappearing under the seating to return to the front of house for the two-song encore. *Sympathy For The Devil* was on the HBO broadcast but was not released on DVD or CD by the Stones.

The last song was *Jumpin' Jack Flash*, which deluged the crowd in red confetti. At the end, a Union Jack was thrown on the stage and Mick placed it on the bass drum before the final bow. Despite the recent lay-off the Stones had recaptured their previous form. The camera crew followed the band to the cars and they drove off, concluding the HBO broadcast.

1379. I CAN'T TURN YOU LOOSE (Redding) ∕ 7.13
8 June 2003: Place: Circus Krone, Munich, Germany.
Rolling Stones with Darryl Jones, Chuck Leavell, Blondie Chaplin, Lisa Fischer, Bernard Fowler, Bobby Keys, Tim Ries, Michael Davis, Kent Smith.
Producer: Marty Callner, Randall Gladstein.
Engineer: Ed Cherney.
Other Production: Don Was, Mastered: Stephen Marcussen. Recorded by: Peter Brandt, David Hewitt. Mix: Bob Clearmountain, Kevin Horn.
USA DVD Four Flicks: 11 November 2003
UK DVD Four Flicks: 17 November 2003

The rest of January and February 2003 allowed more arena shows but also a stadium in Texas where pianist Johnnie Johnson guested on *Honky Tonk Women*. The Staples Center in Los Angeles hosted a benefit for NRDC, an organisation which funded climate change projects. Bill Clinton (rent-a-guest) was invited to introduce the Stones and promote the cause. Percussionist Remi Kabaka joined them for a couple of songs. The final concert of the second American tour leg ended at another MGM Grand concert finale in Las Vegas. A week later the band were in Australia to perform there ahead of Far East countries. Returning to a smaller venue, they opened at the Enmore Theatre in Sydney.

They included *Midnight Rambler* as the opening number and Otis Redding's *I Can't Turn You Loose* followed by other club classics, *Everybody Needs Somebody To Love*, a great *That's How Strong My Love Is* and *Going To A Go-Go*. *Rock Me Baby* enabled the guitarists from AC/DC, Malcolm and Angus Young, to duel with the Stones, which was the first occasion they had met their heroes. The Rolling Stones' official website showed the band performing the number, Angus duck-walking across the stage in Berry fashion. Arenas were performed in mainstream Sydney, Melbourne and Brisbane but no west coast dates. Six Japanese gigs were played, including the smaller non-seated Budokan floor arena, where the locals and travellers were treated to a theatre set list. Whilst playing Osaka, the USA and UK allies invaded Iraq with the support of the Kurds in order to evict President Hussein from power and secure Saudi Arabian and Kuwaiti oil in the second Gulf War. On tour, Singapore was next and then India for the very first time. The concert in the Bangalore Palace Gardens was played in a monsoon, the show recorded by Ed Cherney and filmed for television. The performance was amazing as they and Ed Cherney's sound engineers contended with the elements. "I was in a tent backstage, used a spare PA mixing board and a rack of mic pre-amps we were carrying," he recalled. "I had condenser microphones scattered around to capture the audience and took a split from the normal stage mics. As the rain came down, I kept hearing fizzing and pops as mic after mic failed after the rain fell on them. That show required a lot of editing."

The weather was so bad that Mick Jagger was wearing a large white cowboy mac, complete with Stetson hat, during a rousing *Midnight Rambler*. To prove his fortitude, Keith Richards left his position by the drum riser on more than one occasion to venture into the downpour. Planned concerts in Hong Kong and China were cancelled, due to a World Health Organisation warning. They advised against travel to these countries due to the SARS influenza illness, which cost many lives worldwide. Another concert in Thailand suffered logistic problems and was cancelled too. Jim Callaghan (JC), the Stones' Head of Security, much loved by the fans, suffered a heart attack in Mumbai, India, but recovered well. The Far East leg concluded in Mumbai on 7 April. The first stage of the Allied military invasion was over as Baghdad fell. Keith felt this part of the tour was between war and pestilence.

A planned rest followed for the Stones until the end of May when the much-anticipated European leg commenced with a trio of concerts in Munich along the T.O.A.S.T format that was last tested in Sydney and Tokyo. *I Can't Turn You Loose* was largely performed at the smaller theatre gig, appearing for the sixth time in Europe at the Circus Krone, the home of the old Bavarian circus and a beautiful venue. Keith was no stranger to the track having played it live in Seville, Spain, in 1990. The Krone version, unusually, was used as the show encore and it was evident that the last thing they wanted to do was stop playing; reprise after reprise ensued, Mick whipping the audience into a frenzy in an already smouldering atmosphere.

It was no wonder the recording was used for the *Four Flicks* DVD as one of the "bootleg" tracks in what Mick described as the hottest gig. The show proved to be one of the strongest theatre gigs with *Worried About You*, *Stray Cat Blues*, *Dance Pt. 1* and a new Keith number, a cover of *The Nearness Of You*. In Germany police investigated the sale of VIP "meet and greet" passes. It was established that JC, in a modern-day Robin Hood guise, had been selling tickets for his own gain to genuine fans and agreed to leave the tour.

1380. ROCK ME BABY (Josea, King) ∕ 7.02
20 June 2003: Place: Festwiese, Leipzig, Germany.
Rolling Stones with Darryl Jones, Angus Young, Malcolm Young, Chuck Leavell.
Producer: Marty Callner, Randall Gladstein, Rocky Oldham.
Engineer: Ed Cherney.
Other Production: Don Was, Mastered: Stephen Marcussen. Recorded by: Peter Brandt, David Hewitt. Mix: Bob Clearmountain, Kevin Horn.
USA DVD AC/DC Plug Me In: 16 October 2007
UK DVD AC/DC Plug Me In: 22 October 2007

Four stadium gigs followed in Italy, Germany and Austria before another return to Germany for the Leipzig concert in the heart of Saxony. *Rock Me Baby*, with Angus and Malcolm Young, was released on AC/DC's DVD *Plug Me In*. The diminutive Angus took the first solo, Keith Richards looking decidedly tall against him, but what he lacked in height he made up for with his strong methodical guitar playing.

Angus and Ron Wood were rewarded with a resounding cheer when they both duck-walked during the second solo, while Keith Richards sparred with Malcolm. AC/DC had guested for the Stones earlier, earning a million dollars each for their three German field shows. The other support act, The Pretenders, permitted Chrissie Hynde to sing on *Honky Tonk Women*. This line-up continued for the Hockenheim Ring racetrack gig a few days later when the hot summer started.

1381. START ME UP (Jagger, Richard) ∕ 4.34
11 July 2003: Place: Olympia Theatre, Paris, France.
Rolling Stones with Darryl Jones, Chuck Leavell.
Producer: Marty Callner, Randall Gladstein.
Engineer: Ed Cherney.
Other Production: Don Was, Mastered: Stephen Marcussen. Recorded by: Peter Brandt, David Hewitt. Mix: Bob Clearmountain, Kevin Horn.
USA DVD Four Flicks: 11 November 2003
UK DVD Four Flicks: 17 November 2003

1382.   LIVE WITH ME (Jagger, Richard) ✐ 4.41
11 July 2003: Place: Olympia Theatre, Paris, France.
Rolling Stones with Darryl Jones, Chuck Leavell, Blondie Chaplin, Bernard Fowler, Bobby Keys.
Producer: Marty Callner, Randall Gladstein.
Engineer: Ed Cherney.
Other Production: Don Was, Mastered: Stephen Marcussen. Recorded by: Peter Brandt, David Hewitt. Mix: Bob Clearmountain, Kevin Horn.
USA DVD Four Flicks: 11 November 2003
UK DVD Four Flicks: 17 November 2003

1383.   NEIGHBOURS (Jagger, Richards) ✐ 3.40
11 July 2003: Place: Olympia Theatre, Paris, France.
Rolling Stones with Darryl Jones, Chuck Leavell, Blondie Chaplin, Lisa Fischer, Bernard Fowler, Tim Ries.
Producer: DVD: Marty Callner, Randall Gladstein. CD: The Glimmer Twins, Don Was.
Engineer: Ed Cherney. CD: Assisted Mike Butler.
Other Production: DVD: Don Was, Mastered: Stephen Marcussen. CD: Peter Brandt, David Hewitt. Mix: Bob Clearmountain, Kevin Horn. Mastered: Stephen Marcussen.
USA DVD Four Flicks: 11 November 2003
UK DVD Four Flicks: 17 November 2003
UK CD LP LIVE LICKS: 1 November 2004: No. 38 - 4 weeks
USA CD LP LIVE LICKS: 1 November 2004: No. 50 - 2 weeks
UK & USA e-Single: November 2004

(* a - 4.05)

1384.   HAND OF FATE (Jagger, Richard) ✐ 4.32
11 July 2003: Place: Olympia Theatre, Paris, France.
Rolling Stones with Darryl Jones, Chuck Leavell, Blondie Chaplin, Lisa Fischer, Bernard Fowler.
Producer: Marty Callner, Randall Gladstein.
Engineer: Ed Cherney.
Other Production: Don Was, Mastered: Stephen Marcussen. Recorded by: Peter Brandt, David Hewitt. Mix: Bob Clearmountain, Kevin Horn.
USA DVD Four Flicks: 11 November 2003
UK DVD Four Flicks: 17 November 2003
UK Vinyl B-Side Single Biggest Mistake; 21 August 2006
USA Vinyl B-Side Single Biggest Mistake; 22 August 2006
UK CD box set THE SINGLES COLLECTION 1971-2006: 45 X 45s: 11 April 2011
USA CD box set THE SINGLES COLLECTION 1971-2006: 45 X 45s: 26 April 2011

1385.   NO EXPECTATIONS (Jagger, Richard) ✐ 4.50
11 July 2003: Place: Olympia Theatre, Paris, France.
Rolling Stones with Darryl Jones, Chuck Leavell.
Producer: Marty Callner, Randall Gladstein.
Engineer: Ed Cherney.
Other Production: Don Was, Mastered: Stephen Marcussen. Recorded by: Peter Brandt, David Hewitt. Mix: Bob Clearmountain, Kevin Horn.
USA DVD Four Flicks: 11 November 2003
UK DVD Four Flicks: 17 November 2003

1386.   WORRIED ABOUT YOU (Jagger, Richard) ✐ 6.00
11 July 2003: Place: Olympia Theatre, Paris, France.
Rolling Stones with Darryl Jones, Chuck Leavell, Blondie Chaplin, Lisa Fischer, Bernard Fowler.
Producer: DVD: Marty Callner, Randall Gladstein. CD: The Glimmer Twins, Don Was.
Engineer: Ed Cherney. CD: Assisted Mike Butler.
Other Production: DVD: Don Was, Mastered: Stephen Marcussen. CD: Peter Brandt, David Hewitt. Mix: Bob Clearmountain, Kevin Horn. Mastered: Stephen Marcussen.
USA DVD Four Flicks: 11 November 2003
UK DVD Four Flicks: 17 November 2003
UK CD LP LIVE LICKS: 1 November 2004: No. 38 - 4 weeks
USA CD LP LIVE LICKS: 1 November 2004: No. 50 - 2 weeks

1387.   DOO DOO DOO DOO (HEARTBREAKER) (Jagger, Richard) ✐ 4.07
11 July 2003: Place: Olympia Theatre, Paris, France.
Rolling Stones with Darryl Jones, Chuck Leavell, Blondie Chaplin, Lisa Fischer, Bernard Fowler, Bobby Keys, Tim Ries, Michael Davis, Kent Smith.
Producer: Marty Callner, Randall Gladstein.
Engineer: Ed Cherney.
Other Production: Don Was, Mastered: Stephen Marcussen. Recorded by: Peter Brandt, David Hewitt. Mix: Bob Clearmountain, Kevin Horn.
USA DVD Four Flicks: 11 November 2003
UK DVD Four Flicks: 17 November 2003

1388.   STRAY CAT BLUES (Jagger, Richard) ⟋ 5.06
11 July 2003: Place: Olympia Theatre, Paris, France.
Rolling Stones with Darryl Jones, Chuck Leavell, Blondie Chaplin, Lisa Fischer, Bernard Fowler, Tim Ries.
Producer: Marty Callner, Randall Gladstein.
Engineer: Ed Cherney.
Other Production: Don Was, Mastered: Stephen Marcussen. Recorded by: Peter Brandt, David Hewitt. Mix: Bob Clearmountain, Kevin Horn.
USA DVD Four Flicks: 11 November 2003
UK DVD Four Flicks: 17 November 2003
USA CD Promo Four Flicks Audio Sampler: November 2003

1389.   DANCE (PT. 1) (Jagger, Richards) ⟋ 6.13
11 July 2003: Place: Olympia Theatre, Paris, France.
Rolling Stones with Darryl Jones, Chuck Leavell, Blondie Chaplin, Lisa Fischer, Bernard Fowler, Bobby Keys, Tim Ries, Michael Davis, Kent Smith.
Producer: Marty Callner, Randall Gladstein.
Engineer: Ed Cherney.
Other Production: Don Was, Mastered: Stephen Marcussen. Recorded by: Peter Brandt, David Hewitt. Mix: Bob Clearmountain, Kevin Horn.
USA DVD Four Flicks: 11 November 2003
UK DVD Four Flicks: 17 November 2003
UK CD Track Single Biggest Mistake; 21 August 2006
USA CD Track Single Biggest Mistake; 22 August 2006
UK CD box set THE SINGLES COLLECTION 1971-2006: 45 X 45s: 11 April 2011
USA CD box set THE SINGLES COLLECTION 1971-2006: 45 X 45s: 26 April 2011

1390.   EVERYBODY NEEDS SOMEBODY TO LOVE (Burns, Burke, Wexler) ⟋ 5.48
11 July 2003: Place: Olympia Theatre, Paris, France.
Rolling Stones with Darryl Jones, Chuck Leavell, Blondie Chaplin, Lisa Fischer, Bernard Fowler, Bobby Keys, Tim Ries, Michael Davis, Kent Smith.
Producer: Marty Callner, Randall Gladstein.
Engineer: Ed Cherney.
Other Production: Don Was, Mastered: Stephen Marcussen. Recorded by: Peter Brandt, David Hewitt. Mix: Bob Clearmountain, Kevin Horn.
USA DVD Four Flicks: 11 November 2003
UK DVD Four Flicks: 17 November 2003

1391.   THAT'S HOW STRONG MY LOVE IS (Jamison) ⟋ 5.09
11 July 2003: Place: Olympia Theatre, Paris, France.
Rolling Stones with Darryl Jones, Chuck Leavell, Bobby Keys, Tim Ries, Michael Davis, Kent Smith.
Producer: DVD: Marty Callner, Randall Gladstein. CD: The Glimmer Twins, Don Was.
Engineer: Ed Cherney. CD: Assisted Mike Butler.
Other Production: DVD: Don Was, Mastered: Stephen Marcussen. CD: Peter Brandt, David Hewitt. Mix: Bob Clearmountain, Kevin Horn. Mastered: Stephen Marcussen.
USA DVD Four Flicks: 11 November 2003
UK DVD Four Flicks: 17 November 2003
UK CD LP LIVE LICKS: 1 November 2004: No. 38 - 4 weeks
USA CD LP LIVE LICKS: 1 November 2004: No. 50 - 2 weeks

1392.   GOING TO A GO-GO (Moore, Robinson, Rogers, Tarplin) ⟋ 7.49
11 July 2003: Place: Olympia Theatre, Paris, France.
Rolling Stones with Darryl Jones, Chuck Leavell, Blondie Chaplin, Lisa Fischer, Bernard Fowler, Bobby Keys, Tim Ries, Michael Davis, Kent Smith.
Producer: Marty Callner, Randall Gladstein.
Engineer: Ed Cherney.
Other Production: Don Was, Mastered: Stephen Marcussen. Recorded by: Peter Brandt, David Hewitt. Mix: Bob Clearmountain, Kevin Horn.
USA DVD Four Flicks: 11 November 2003
UK DVD Four Flicks: 17 November 2003

1393.   THE NEARNESS OF YOU (Carmichael, Washington) ⟋ 4.34
11 July 2003: Place: Olympia Theatre, Paris, France.
Rolling Stones with Darryl Jones, Chuck Leavell, Blondie Chaplin, Lisa Fischer, Bernard Fowler, Bobby Keys, Tim Ries, Michael Davis, Kent Smith.
Producer: DVD: Marty Callner, Randall Gladstein. CD: The Glimmer Twins, Don Was.
Engineer: Ed Cherney. CD: Assisted Mike Butler.
Other Production: DVD: Don Was, Mastered: Stephen Marcussen. CD: Peter Brandt, David Hewitt. Mix: Bob Clearmountain, Kevin Horn. Mastered: Stephen Marcussen.
USA DVD Four Flicks: 11 November 2003
UK DVD Four Flicks: 17 November 2003
UK CD LP LIVE LICKS: 1 November 2004: No. 38 - 4 weeks
USA CD LP LIVE LICKS: 1 November 2004: No. 50 - 2 weeks

1394. BEFORE THEY MAKE ME RUN (Jagger, Richards) ✏ 4.00
11 July 2003: Place: Olympia Theatre, Paris, France.
Rolling Stones with Darryl Jones, Chuck Leavell, Blondie Chaplin, Lisa Fischer, Bernard Fowler, Bobby Keys, Tim Ries, Michael Davis, Kent Smith.
Producer: Marty Callner, Randall Gladstein.
Engineer: Ed Cherney.
Other Production: Don Was, Mastered: Stephen Marcussen. Recorded by: Peter Brandt, David Hewitt. Mix: Bob Clearmountain, Kevin Horn.
USA DVD Four Flicks: 11 November 2003
UK DVD Four Flicks: 17 November 2003
UK CD Track Single Biggest Mistake; 21 August 2006
USA CD Track Single Biggest Mistake; 22 August 2006
UK CD box set THE SINGLES COLLECTION 1971-2006: 45 X 45s: 11 April 2011
USA CD box set THE SINGLES COLLECTION 1971-2006: 45 X 45s: 26 April 2011

1395. LOVE TRAIN (Gamble, Huff) ✏ 6.03
11 July 2003: Place: Olympia Theatre, Paris, France.
Rolling Stones with Darryl Jones, Chuck Leavell, Blondie Chaplin, Lisa Fischer, Bernard Fowler, Bobby Keys, Tim Ries, Michael Davis, Kent Smith.
Producer: Marty Callner, Randall Gladstein.
Engineer: Ed Cherney.
Other Production: Don Was, Mastered: Stephen Marcussen. Recorded by: Peter Brandt, David Hewitt. Mix: Bob Clearmountain, Kevin Horn.
USA DVD Four Flicks: 11 November 2003
UK DVD Four Flicks: 17 November 2003

1396. RESPECTABLE (Jagger, Richards) ✏ 3.03
11 July 2003: Place: Olympia Theatre, Paris, France.
Rolling Stones with Darryl Jones, Chuck Leavell, Blondie Chaplin, Lisa Fischer, Bernard Fowler.
Producer: Marty Callner, Randall Gladstein.
Engineer: Ed Cherney.
Other Production: Don Was, Mastered: Stephen Marcussen. Recorded by: Peter Brandt, David Hewitt. Mix: Bob Clearmountain, Kevin Horn.
USA DVD Four Flicks: 11 November 2003
UK DVD Four Flicks: 17 November 2003

1397. HONKY TONK WOMEN (Jagger, Richard) ✏ 4.22
11 July 2003: Place: Olympia Theatre, Paris, France.
Rolling Stones with Darryl Jones, Chuck Leavell, Blondie Chaplin, Lisa Fischer, Bernard Fowler, Bobby Keys, Tim Ries, Michael Davis, Kent Smith.
Producer: Marty Callner, Randall Gladstein.
Engineer: Ed Cherney.
Other Production: Don Was, Mastered: Stephen Marcussen. Recorded by: Peter Brandt, David Hewitt. Mix: Bob Clearmountain, Kevin Horn.
USA DVD Four Flicks: 11 November 2003
UK DVD Four Flicks: 17 November 2003

1398. BROWN SUGAR (Jagger, Richard) ✏ 6.30
11 July 2003: Place: Olympia Theatre, Paris, France.
Rolling Stones with Darryl Jones, Chuck Leavell, Blondie Chaplin, Lisa Fischer, Bernard Fowler, Bobby Keys, Tim Ries, Michael Davis, Kent Smith.
Producer: Marty Callner, Randall Gladstein.
Engineer: Ed Cherney.
Other Production: Don Was, Mastered: Stephen Marcussen. Recorded by: Peter Brandt, David Hewitt. Mix: Bob Clearmountain, Kevin Horn.
USA DVD Four Flicks: 11 November 2003
UK DVD Four Flicks: 17 November 2003

1399. JUMPIN' JACK FLASH (Jagger, Richard) ✏ 7.07
11 July 2003: Place: Olympia Theatre, Paris, France.
Rolling Stones with Darryl Jones, Chuck Leavell, Blondie Chaplin, Lisa Fischer, Bernard Fowler, Bobby Keys, Tim Ries, Michael Davis, Kent Smith.
Producer: Marty Callner, Randall Gladstein.
Engineer: Ed Cherney.
Other Production: Don Was, Mastered: Stephen Marcussen. Recorded by: Peter Brandt, David Hewitt. Mix: Bob Clearmountain, Kevin Horn.
USA DVD Four Flicks: 11 November 2003
UK DVD Four Flicks: 17 November 2003
USA CD Promo Four Flicks Audio Sampler: November 2003

After a series of hot-hot Spanish concerts, which reminded them of the reception they got in South America, and a concert in Marseille, France, another trio of concerts followed in Paris. The Bercy Arena and the large Stade de France stadium, where the full moon was a great back-drop for the lyrics of Keith Richards' *Slipping Away*, played host to the big shows The smaller Olympia, dedicated to Bruno Coquatrix, had played host to many of the greats, including Marlene Dietrich, Edith Piaf, Frank Sinatra, Bill Haley, Johnny Hallyday and The Beatles. The Stones played there for the first time on 20 October 1964 but, on his return in 2003, Mick Jagger did not need the bar stool he used back then! That was given to Ron Wood, who used it for playing the lap steel Weisenborn for a knock-out *No Expectations*.

After this slower number the concert was a sweaty dash through some lesser known material. As Mick Jagger said after playing *Neighbours* - it only appeared twice during the whole tour - they were the type of songs the band didn't know that well. *Hand Of Fate* was received enthusiastically for the first time on the European tour, given an airing for the first occasion since September 2002.

The DVD did not reflect the entire gig; old standards like *It's Only Rock 'n' Roll* and *Tumbling Dice* were not included while, surprisingly, a great version of *Rip This Joint* was also not released. They did not appear as tracks on the album LIVE LICKS or as bonus extras on other releases. Such was the show quality that four tracks (*Neighbours, Worried About You,* a plaintive *That's How Strong My Love Is* and *The Nearness Of You*) were not only on the DVD but also received a CD release for the 2004 compilation of the tour LIVE LICKS. An unedited version of *Neighbours* appeared as part of a download single in 2004.

Darryl Jones now had an extended bass part in *Stray Cat Blues* and *Dance*, which was musically tight with a brief percussion interlude contributed by Bernard Fowler on whistle and hand drum and Blondie Chaplin (shaker and tambourine). Keith's set allowed Mick to rehydrate, coiffeur his hair and change into a purple shirt and jacket with white fedora hat. This heralded *Love Train*, with Lisa Fischer and Bernard Fowler joining Mick on the small, extended stage jetty to sing the refrain. Mick captured the *Honky Tonk* moment crowd scenes with a hand-held camera and they were spliced into the video tape release. Mick, c'est encore moi!

1400. START ME UP (Jagger, Richards) ✎ 5.19
30 July 2003: Place: Downsview Park, Toronto, Canada.
Rolling Stones with Darryl Jones, Chuck Leavell.
Producer: Executive: Michael Cohl: Production: Stephen Howard, David Kines, Randall Gladstein, Fred Nicolaidis
Engineer: Ed Cherney, David Hewitt, Doug Middlement, Todd Farracia
Other Production: Directors: Marty Callner, Dave Russell
USA Compilation DVD Toronto Rocks: 28 June 2004
UK Compilation DVD Toronto Rocks: 5 July 2004

The tour departed for Scandinavia where The Hives and Hellacopters were the support acts and played Denmark, Finland (where ZZ Top supported the band) and Sweden where another three shows were played at a stadium, arena and theatre. As a venue, Stockholm Olympic Stadium is beautiful with a stone facade and turret towers. It was a hot, steamy day and evening that lasted forever, not really turning into night but, sadly, the band did not seem fully charged. At the Globen, matters improved and a rousing four consecutive songs were played from EXILE in the album slot.

Thru And Thru made a last appearance on the tour and *When The Whip Comes Down* was heard for the first time on the European leg. Rest days saw different band members going towards the Archipelago and Baltic Sea on water taxis during late afternoon and evening, taking advantage of the stunning Scandinavian weather. The gig at the Cirkus was similar to Paris Olympia in content, just swapping *Ain't Too Proud To Beg* for *Dance* and *I Can't Turn You Loose* for *Love Train*. It was filmed and recorded as back-up for the Paris footage but no track has been made available. *Jumpin' Jack Flash* was on the set list but as an either/or with *Sympathy For The Devil* and the latter made an appearance as a dramatic encore while a thunderstorm raged fittingly outside.

There were a couple of shows after Sweden in Germany and Czech Republic where they performed the large Letenska Plan Park. The night before Mick Jagger celebrated his 60th birthday at a private party with Vaclav Havel, the Czech president. Havel introduced the band at the park, which had been used as a rallying point for the Czech people, who demonstrated in 1989 so it was a poignant scene. The tour then took a peculiar deviation to Toronto, Canada.

1401. RUBY TUESDAY (Jagger, Richard) ✎ 3.19
30 July 2003: Place: Downsview Park, Toronto, Canada.
Rolling Stones with Darryl Jones.
Producer: Executive: Michael Cohl: Production: Stephen Howard, David Kines, Randall Gladstein, Fred Nicolaidis
Engineer: Ed Cherney, David Hewitt, Doug Middlement, Todd Farracia
Other Production: Directors: Marty Callner, Dave Russell
USA Compilation DVD Toronto Rocks: 28 June 2004
UK Compilation DVD Toronto Rocks: 5 July 2004

1402. MISS YOU (Jagger, Richards) ✎ 6.22
30 July 2003: Place: Downsview Park, Toronto, Canada.
Rolling Stones with Darryl Jones, Justin Timberlake, Chuck Leavell, Blondie Chaplin, Lisa Fischer, Bernard Fowler, Bobby Keys, Tim Ries, Michael Davis, Kent Smith.
Producer: Executive: Michael Cohl: Production: Stephen Howard, David Kines, Randall Gladstein, Fred Nicolaidis
Engineer: Ed Cherney, David Hewitt, Doug Middlement, Todd Farracia
Other Production: Directors: Marty Callner, Dave Russell
USA Compilation DVD Toronto Rocks: 28 June 2004
UK Compilation DVD Toronto Rocks: 5 July 2004

1403. ROCK ME BABY (Josea, King) ✎ 6.49
30 July 2003: Place: Downsview Park, Toronto, Canada.
Rolling Stones with Darryl Jones, Angus Young, Malcolm Young, Chuck Leavell.
Producer: Executive: Michael Cohl: Production: Stephen Howard, David Kines, Randall Gladstein, Fred Nicolaidis
Engineer: Ed Cherney, David Hewitt, Doug Middlement, Todd Farracia
Other Production: Directors: Marty Callner, Dave Russell
USA Compilation DVD Toronto Rocks: 28 June 2004
UK Compilation DVD Toronto Rocks: 5 July 2004

1404. **(I CAN'T GET NO) SATISFACTION** (Jagger, Richard) ✎ 9.09
30 July 2003: Place: Downsview Park, Toronto, Canada.
Rolling Stones with Darryl Jones, Chuck Leavell, Blondie Chaplin, Lisa Fischer, Bernard Fowler, Bobby Keys, Tim Ries, Michael Davis, Kent Smith.
Producer: Executive: Michael Cohl: Production: Stephen Howard, David Kines, Randall Gladstein, Fred Nicolaidis
Engineer: Ed Cherney, David Hewitt, Doug Middlement, Todd Farracia
Other Production: Directors: Marty Callner, Dave Russell
USA Compilation DVD Toronto Rocks: 28 June 2004
UK Compilation DVD Toronto Rocks: 5 July 2004

1405. **JUMPIN' JACK FLASH** (Jagger, Richard) ✎ 6.27
30 July 2003: Place: Downsview Park, Toronto, Canada.
Rolling Stones with Darryl Jones, Chuck Leavell, Blondie Chaplin, Lisa Fischer, Bernard Fowler, Bobby Keys, Tim Ries, Michael Davis, Kent Smith.
Producer: Executive: Michael Cohl: Production: Stephen Howard, David Kines, Randall Gladstein, Fred Nicolaidis
Engineer: Ed Cherney, David Hewitt, Doug Middlement, Todd Farracia
Other Production: Directors: Marty Callner, Dave Russell
USA Compilation DVD Toronto Rocks: 28 June 2004
UK Compilation DVD Toronto Rocks: 5 July 2004

The SARS epidemic had damaged many people's lives and Toronto was one of the biggest cities affected, with travellers wary of paying a visit. The Stones had particular affection for the Canadian city so agreed to perform an all-day and all-ticket charity concert there to promote a "business as usual" message - despite the fact that they were in the middle of a European tour. Many bands performed but the main concert featured locals like Sam Roberts, Jim Belushi with Dan Aykroyd, Sass Jordan with Jeff Healey, Blue Rodeo, The Flaming Lips, The Isley Brothers, Justin Timberlake, Guess Who (another reunion), Rush (who interspersed *The Spirit Of Radio* with *Paint It Black*), and AC/DC before the Stones performed a shortened, 16 song set in front of a reportedly 500,000-strong crowd. The concert was filmed for a video release and these six numbers ended up on the 2004 DVD released by Michael Cohl's film company. Justin Timberlake proved to be a strange choice amongst all the other acts and received a rough time from the crowd, plastic bottles being thrown on stage. This also happened when he performed with the band on *Miss You*. Keith Richards was incensed enough to berate the trouble makers. After the show he said, "the main point is I do not want to get hit and I do not want Charlie Watts getting hit or Mick. If they've got a good aim, they can hit Justin, he's not in my band!" Justin himself said that, if he had come to see AC/DC, he would not probably want to see himself. Being a favourite of Keith, AC/DC performed at the behest of the Stones as they had at the German field concerts.
The Stones set included the slower sing-along *Ruby Tuesday* but essentially theirs was a hits package with the aforementioned *Miss You*. *Rock Me Baby* appeased the AC/DC faithful, most of which had moved back to allow the Stones' fans to come forward. The set was purpose-built for all the acts and had two giant jumbotrons either side, at least three relay screens and the band's moniker was present above all the acts. Additionally, another first for the band and crew in Toronto, was Clear Channel (tour promoters), who had a fast Wireless Local Area Network (WLAN) installed for the rest of the tour, enabling communication with loved ones by email and general internet use to ensure good morale. It was also used when needed to download updated software drivers for faulty equipment and, perhaps more importantly, it enabled Mick Jagger and Charlie Watts to watch the Cricket World Cup over the internet when they were in Singapore. If you brought a laptop to the gig it was possible to join the WLAN since the network at that time was deliberately not secured - but no file sharing was permitted.

1406. **BROWN SUGAR** (Jagger, Richard) ✎ 4.08
24 August 2003: Place: Twickenham Stadium, London, England.
Rolling Stones with Darryl Jones, Chuck Leavell, Bobby Keys.
Producer: Marty Callner, Randall Gladstein.
Engineer: Ed Cherney.
Other Production: Don Was, Mastered: Stephen Marcussen. Recorded by: Peter Brandt, David Hewitt. Mix: Bob Clearmountain, Kevin Horn.
USA DVD Four Flicks: 11 November 2003
UK DVD Four Flicks: 17 November 2003

The Stones journeyed straight back to Europe where a concert they were due to play in Benidorm, on the Spanish Costa Blanca on 6 August, was postponed due to Mick Jagger being ill. The trans-Atlantic haul must have had some impact and taken its toll. However, it did provide band and crew with a week's worth of rest even if they did build the Benidorm stage, only for it to be dismantled when the show was deferred with little or no notice. Many sound checks before the gigs were achieved with Bernard Fowler on vocals in order to rest Mick. He found it a great honour to sing for the band on behalf of Mick.
Another return to the never-satiated Germans was next before a week long run in the Netherlands. First, two dates at the Rotterdam Feyenoord football arena where the set list added the yet unplayed *Paint It Black* and a B-stage of *Star Star*, *Little Red Rooster* and *Street Fighting Man* on the first night. The Ahoy provided the arena choice and a day later (which was very unusual) they performed the much smaller Utrecht Vredenburg club, 25 miles from Rotterdam. There were a few surprises when the old BRIDGES TO BABYLON sing-a-long *Saint Of Me* was performed for the first time on this tour.
Before his set, Keith Richards said that the room was great and he wanted to wrap it up and take it with him. Then came a unique delivery of *Thief In The Night*, with co-writer Pierre de Beauport on keyboards, before the more familiar *Happy*. The four-song conclusion really rocked powerfully even if *Brown Sugar* did falter at the start. Two dates were meant to be played at Amsterdam Arena but the second was postponed because Mick was still suffering a Toronto hangover. The cost to travelling fans of these postponements could not be under-estimated but everyone wanted him better for the London gigs. The postponement was also a problem for the filming of the intended video release since both Amsterdam dates were scheduled for this purpose, as was Twickenham.
One of the two dates at Twickenham was also put off that weekend so the first one at the international rugby ground west of London turned out to be on Sunday 24 August. Wembley Stadium had been demolished to make way for a brand new stadium and was not available. Twickenham had chairs installed to maximise ticket prices, unlike other European stadiums which had a pitch standing area. Welcome back to the USA ticket pricing strategy, a move which restricted the capacity to 55,000. The film crew joined from Amsterdam and the event would end up on the forthcoming video release later that year. Ed Cherney recorded many Licks shows for the eventual release.

He said: "Sometimes I brought in a remote truck, sometimes I just did it guerrilla style and brought in some gear and set up wherever I could. It was always challenging, exciting and usually scary, although it typically worked out and I never missed a single note of music. I would take a split from the stage and take my own feed. I would always run mics and get as much audience coverage and response as was humanly possible. I wasn't often consulted about the venue . . . I would usually get a call from Mick telling me when and where, I would get the equipment and crew we needed and go to work. We recorded many more venues and shows than ended up on the final DVD."

1407. YOU GOT ME ROCKING (Jagger, Richards) ⚡ 4.10
24 August 2003: Place: Twickenham Stadium, London, England.
Rolling Stones with Darryl Jones, Chuck Leavell.
Producer: Marty Callner, Randall Gladstein.
Engineer: Ed Cherney.
Other Production: Don Was, Mastered: Stephen Marcussen. Recorded by: Peter Brandt, David Hewitt.
Mix: Bob Clearmountain, Kevin Horn.
USA DVD Four Flicks: 11 November 2003
UK DVD Four Flicks: 17 November 2003

1408. ROCKS OFF (Jagger, Richard) ⚡ 3.41
24 August 2003: Place: Twickenham Stadium, London, England.
Rolling Stones with Darryl Jones, Chuck Leavell, Blondie Chaplin, Lisa Fischer, Bernard Fowler, Bobby Keys, Tim Ries, Michael Davis, Kent Smith.
Producer: DVD: Marty Callner, Randall Gladstein. CD: The Glimmer Twins, Don Was.
Engineer: Ed Cherney. CD: Assisted Mike Butler.
Other Production: DVD: Don Was, Mastered: Stephen Marcussen. CD: Peter Brandt, David Hewitt.
Mix: Bob Clearmountain, Kevin Horn.
Mastered: Stephen Marcussen.
USA DVD Four Flicks: 11 November 2003
UK DVD Four Flicks: 17 November 2003
UK CD LP LIVE LICKS: 1 November 2004: No. 38 - 4 weeks
USA CD LP LIVE LICKS: 1 November 2004: No. 50 - 2 weeks

1409. WILD HORSES (Jagger, Richard) ⚡ 5.04
24 August 2003: Place: Twickenham Stadium, London, England.
Rolling Stones with Darryl Jones, Chuck Leavell, Blondie Chaplin, Lisa Fischer, Bernard Fowler.
Producer: Marty Callner, Randall Gladstein.
Engineer: Ed Cherney.
Other Production: Don Was, Mastered: Stephen Marcussen. Recorded by: Peter Brandt, David Hewitt.
Mix: Bob Clearmountain, Kevin Horn.
USA DVD Four Flicks: 11 November 2003
UK DVD Four Flicks: 17 November 2003

1410. YOU CAN'T ALWAYS GET WHAT YOU WANT (Jagger, Richard) ⚡ 6.45
24 August 2003: Place: Twickenham Stadium, London, England.
Rolling Stones with Darryl Jones, Chuck Leavell, Blondie Chaplin, Lisa Fischer, Bernard Fowler, Tim Ries, Michael Davis.
Producer: DVD: Marty Callner, Randall Gladstein. CD: The Glimmer Twins, Don Was.
Engineer: Ed Cherney. CD: Assisted Mike Butler.
Other Production: DVD: Don Was, Mastered: Stephen Marcussen. CD: Peter Brandt, David Hewitt.
Mix: Bob Clearmountain, Kevin Horn.
Mastered: Stephen Marcussen.
USA DVD Four Flicks: 11 November 2003
UK DVD Four Flicks: 17 November 2003
UK CD LP LIVE LICKS: 1 November 2004: No. 38 - 4 weeks
USA CD LP LIVE LICKS: 1 November 2004: No. 50 - 2 weeks

1411. PAINT IT BLACK (Jagger, Richard) ⚡ 4.44
24 August 2003: Place: Twickenham Stadium, London, England.
Rolling Stones with Darryl Jones, Chuck Leavell, Bernard Fowler.
Producer: Marty Callner, Randall Gladstein.
Engineer: Ed Cherney.
Other Production: Don Was, Mastered: Stephen Marcussen. Recorded by: Peter Brandt, David Hewitt.
Mix: Bob Clearmountain, Kevin Horn.
USA DVD Four Flicks: 11 November 2003
UK DVD Four Flicks: 17 November 2003

1412. TUMBLING DICE (Jagger, Richard) *✕* 5.38
24 August 2003: Place: Twickenham Stadium, London, England.
Rolling Stones with Darryl Jones, Chuck Leavell, Blondie Chaplin, Lisa Fischer, Bernard Fowler, Bobby Keys, Tim Ries, Michael Davis, Kent Smith.
Producer: Marty Callner, Randall Gladstein.
Engineer: Ed Cherney.
Other Production: Don Was, Mastered: Stephen Marcussen. Recorded by: Peter Brandt, David Hewitt.
Mix: Bob Clearmountain, Kevin Horn.
USA DVD Four Flicks: 11 November 2003
UK DVD Four Flicks: 17 November 2003

1413. SLIPPING AWAY (Jagger, Richards) *✕* 5.54
24 August 2003: Place: Twickenham Stadium, London, England.
Rolling Stones with Darryl Jones, Chuck Leavell, Blondie Chaplin, Lisa Fischer, Bernard Fowler, Bobby Keys, Tim Ries, Michael Davis, Kent Smith.
Producer: Marty Callner, Randall Gladstein.
Engineer: Ed Cherney.
Other Production: Don Was, Mastered: Stephen Marcussen. Recorded by: Peter Brandt, David Hewitt.
Mix: Bob Clearmountain, Kevin Horn.
USA DVD Four Flicks: 11 November 2003
UK DVD Four Flicks: 17 November 2003

1414. SYMPATHY FOR THE DEVIL (Jagger, Richard) *✕* 9.54
24 August 2003: Place: Twickenham Stadium, London, England.
Rolling Stones with Darryl Jones, Chuck Leavell, Blondie Chaplin, Lisa Fischer, Bernard Fowler.
Producer: Marty Callner, Randall Gladstein.
Engineer: Ed Cherney.
Other Production: Don Was, Mastered: Stephen Marcussen. Recorded by: Peter Brandt, David Hewitt.
Mix: Bob Clearmountain, Kevin Horn.
USA DVD Four Flicks: 11 November 2003
UK DVD Four Flicks: 17 November 2003

1415. STAR STAR (Jagger, Richards) *✕* 4.08
24 August 2003: Place: Twickenham Stadium, London, England.
Rolling Stones with Darryl Jones, Chuck Leavell.
Producer: Marty Callner, Randall Gladstein.
Engineer: Ed Cherney.
Other Production: Don Was, Mastered: Stephen Marcussen.
Recorded by: Peter Brandt, David Hewitt.
Mix: Bob Clearmountain, Kevin Horn.
USA DVD Four Flicks: 11 November 2003
UK DVD Four Flicks: 17 November 2003

1416. I JUST WANT TO MAKE LOVE TO YOU (Dixon) *✕* 4.52
24 August 2003: Place: Twickenham Stadium, London, England.
Rolling Stones with Darryl Jones, Chuck Leavell.
Producer: Marty Callner, Randall Gladstein.
Engineer: Ed Cherney.
Other Production: Don Was, Mastered: Stephen Marcussen.
Recorded by: Peter Brandt, David Hewitt.
Mix: Bob Clearmountain, Kevin Horn.
USA DVD Four Flicks: 11 November 2003
UK DVD Four Flicks: 17 November 2003

1417. STREET FIGHTING MAN (Jagger, Richard) *✕* 3.43
24 August 2003: Place: Twickenham Stadium, London, England.
Rolling Stones with Darryl Jones, Chuck Leavell.
Producer: DVD: Marty Callner, Randall Gladstein. CD: The Glimmer Twins, Don Was.
Engineer: Ed Cherney. CD: Assisted Mike Butler.
Other Production: DVD: Don Was, Mastered: Stephen Marcussen. CD: Peter Brandt, David Hewitt.
Mix: Bob Clearmountain, Kevin Horn. Mastered: Stephen Marcussen.
USA DVD Four Flicks: 11 November 2003
UK DVD Four Flicks: 17 November 2003
UK CD LP LIVE LICKS: 1 November 2004: No. 38 - 4 weeks
USA CD LP LIVE LICKS: 1 November 2004: No. 50 - 2 weeks

1418. **GIMME SHELTER** (Jagger, Richard) 🖉 9.00
24 August 2003: Place: Twickenham Stadium, London, England.
Rolling Stones with Darryl Jones, Chuck Leavell, Blondie Chaplin, Lisa Fischer, Bernard Fowler, Bobby Keys, Tim Ries, Michael Davis, Kent Smith.
Producer: Marty Callner, Randall Gladstein.
Engineer: Ed Cherney.
Other Production: Don Was, Mastered: Stephen Marcussen.
USA DVD Four Flicks: 11 November 2003
UK DVD Four Flicks: 17 November 2003

1419. **HONKY TONK WOMEN** (Jagger, Richard) 🖉 4.38
24 August 2003: Place: Twickenham Stadium, London, England.
Rolling Stones with Darryl Jones, Chuck Leavell, Blondie Chaplin, Lisa Fischer, Bernard Fowler, Bobby Keys, Tim Ries, Michael Davis, Kent Smith.
Producer: Marty Callner, Randall Gladstein.
Engineer: Ed Cherney.
Other Production: Don Was, Mastered: Stephen Marcussen.
USA DVD Four Flicks: 11 November 2003
UK DVD Four Flicks: 17 November 2003

1420. **(I CAN'T GET NO) SATISFACTION** (Jagger, Richard) 🖉 8.14
24 August 2003: Place: Twickenham Stadium, London, England.
Rolling Stones with Darryl Jones, Chuck Leavell, Blondie Chaplin, Lisa Fischer, Bernard Fowler, Bobby Keys, Tim Ries, Michael Davis, Kent Smith.
Producer: Marty Callner, Randall Gladstein.
Engineer: Ed Cherney.
Other Production: Don Was, Mastered: Stephen Marcussen.
USA DVD Four Flicks: 11 November 2003
UK DVD Four Flicks: 17 November 2003

1421. **JUMPIN' JACK FLASH** (Jagger, Richard) 🖉 7.39
24 August 2003: Place: Twickenham Stadium, London, England.
Rolling Stones with Darryl Jones, Chuck Leavell, Blondie Chaplin, Lisa Fischer, Bernard Fowler, Bobby Keys, Tim Ries, Michael Davis, Kent Smith.
Producer: Marty Callner, Randall Gladstein.
Engineer: Ed Cherney.
Other Production: Don Was, Mastered: Stephen Marcussen.
USA DVD Four Flicks: 11 November 2003
UK DVD Four Flicks: 17 November 2003
USA CD Promo Four Flicks Audio Sampler: November 2003

London is a mecca for travelling fans and they started arriving mid-week for the series of concerts. The internet was the co-ordination vehicle for this and Shidoobees, from the USA, joined European fanatics from IORR and Rocks Off with other fans descending from all over the world. Discounted hotels, social engagements, watering holes and Thames boat trips were arranged. French fans had led the way with trips on the Seine. *The Four Flicks* film of the stadium gig at Twickenham starts with a collection of London moments as fans travel to the gig. Opening with the pared back *Brown Sugar* minus support players - except of course for Bobby Keys - the stage backdrop is displayed and the crowd salute the ensemble for their British homecoming.

"It is nice of you to come," says Mick Jagger, dressed in his three-quarter-length gold coat with matching red and gold tongue t-shirt, both styled by Maryam Malakapour. Immediately it is apparent that the 25 cameras are interspersing shots filmed at Amsterdam Arena with those from Twickenham. There was some continuity in clothing, Charlie Watts having to wear his Dutch orange t-shirt. Mick is intent on working the crowd having now almost recovered from his throat problems and, by the time *Rocks Off* arrives, he is already at the stage wings and front approach to the B-stage. *Don't Stop, Happy* or *Start Me Up* were not in the released film. Before *Wild Horses*, Mick comments that it is their first concert at Twickenham rugby ground and how they used to play in Richmond Athletic Club many years ago - not far from here to there.

The four screens above the stage show cascading sparks during the softer acoustic number. The concert builds momentum and the sound achieved in such a large ground was excellent. The Amsterdam Arena had not coped so well. The introductions allowed Charlie a brief stroll backstage before he was announced as the Wembley whammer. The opening notes from *Sympathy For The Devil* gained a fabulous crowd roar and the huge flames that leapt from the set roof physically warmed the crowd even more. The Patrick Woodruffe lights were now coming to the fore as dusk turned into night. *Star Star* was the first song on the B-stage, as it was for Rotterdam and the Amsterdam Arena. These were its only tour appearances. One 90-year-old senior citizen at the secondary stage was Mick's very proud father Joe.

The blues of Muddy Waters' *I Just Want To Make Love To You* and the rock of *Street Fighting Man* in far from sleepy old London town concluded the small stage. Lisa Fischer serenaded them back to the main stage now backed by "Liberace drapes" for *Gimme Shelter* and her pièce de résistance. Then the final section, with red confetti raining down for *Satisfaction*, Mick running the width of the Twickenham stage and the encore where he was able to Jump, Jack and Flash with the stage seeming to explode as pyrotechnics, flames and fireworks illuminated his dance. Mick's teasing "see you on Wednesday" was a little worrying for the small Astoria theatre, scene of the next London concert.

At the now defunct theatre on Charing Cross Street, close to Soho and Covent Garden, expectations were high and Mick Taylor was in town, prompting rumours that he might make an appearance. He did attend the gig but the planned contribution did not happen on *Rock Me Baby*. Apparently he missed the rehearsal and, because of an 11.30 curfew on the night, he did not play. After a hurried *I Can't Turn You Loose*, the band went straight into *Honky Tonk Women*, despite *Rock Me Baby* being on the set list.

Another four classics were performed in what was by then a standard theatre conclusion. Somehow an opportunity had been lost to play a spectacular show but it was a great pleasure to see the band performing in such a small, fun venue on home territory. Four arena shows continued at Wembley and Scotland's Glasgow

SECC before moving on to the Manchester Evening Arena. There was a return to real form as the band gelled in these arenas.

A re-arranged field gig at Werchter, Belgium, took place before a return to Ireland and two further dates at Wembley Arena. The smaller Point venue, where two concerts were played, was a great choice and the band were truly energised. Andrea Corr dueted with Mick on *Wild Horses* and Keith Richards took the Irish contingent on a quick rendition of *It's A Long Way To Tipperary* just as he had in Scotland with *I'll Take The High Road*. To conclude the UK section, two more dates were set for Wembley Arena and another rearranged for Twickenham.

1422. SALT OF THE EARTH (Jagger, Richard) ✏ 4.51
20 September 2003: Place: Twickenham Stadium, London, England.
Rolling Stones with Darryl Jones, Chuck Leavell, Blondie Chaplin, Lisa Fischer, Bernard Fowler, Tim Ries, Michael Davis, Kent Smith.
Bootleg only.

After two lively arena concerts at Wembley, Tim Ries took to front of stage for the first number at Twickenham, deputising for an ill Bobby Keys, and honked his way through *Brown Sugar*, even adding a little chord twirl finale. The crew and entourage gave him a resounding pat on the back as he exited the stage. *It's Only Rock 'n' Roll* continued the thrust as the audience were decidedly upbeat, realising that this concert, which was set to be the first of the series in August, became the last a month later. Mick Jagger apologised for messing up any holiday plans before *Don't Stop* started. The hits continued with *Miss You*, which Tim also contributed to.

Then Mick said: "So anyway, we thought we'd try a song we haven't done for a long while here tonight." The acoustic guitar rang out and Keith Richards sang the first verse to the song not played as a band since December 1989 and for only the second time ever. Those who listened to the sound check earlier that afternoon would have heard the same unfamiliar notes of *Salt Of The Earth*. It was a mark of thanks to the British fans and perhaps, more importantly, those from further away, who changed their travel and hotel arrangements to come back to London. Afterwards, two guests joined them for *Rock Me Baby* - Angus and Malcolm Young, who had been in a London recording studio at the time.

Angus and Keith Richards used the stage wings to show off their licks and incite the crowd more. At Ronnie's persuasion, Malcolm even ventured from his normal position in the background and did a solo at the front. The blues continued with *Midnight Rambler* - what a fantastic three song segment. The up-tempo songs carried on coming and they managed to keep to the stadium curfew, finishing at 10.30 pm. Local residents had been invited to the show for free as compensation for the noise and disruption caused. More rearranged dates were performed back at Amsterdam Arena and Benidorm's Foites Stadium then there was one gig each in Portugal and Spain before the last Euro concert in the heat of Letzigrund Stadium, Zurich, Switzerland.

It was an excellent extended summer but the tour was not finished because there were more commitments a month later in Hong Kong. Unusually, the Tamar festival site became the last two Licks gigs and coincided with the release of both the live album and the DVD. LIVE LICKS contained some poor editing (overseen by Don Was), especially during *Rocks Off*, when it went into the famous "the sunshine bores the daylights out of me". Indeed the hatchet job undermined the release as about ten tracks were edited by over 30 seconds, particularly *Street Fighting Man*, *Honky Tonk Women* and *Satisfaction*. There were two sides to the release, one featured the hits and another the more rare and perhaps not so well known tracks. Depending on how you liked a *Honky Tonk* dominatrix CD cover supplied, either with a bra top or topless. However the CD and DVD were their best representation of a tour so far and proved the theatrical and musical high the FORTY LICKS tour achieved with their unique format.

1423. RAIN FALL DOWN (Jagger, Richards) 4.53
June, November - December 2004, January, March - April; June 2005: Place: La Fourchette Home Studio, Fourchette, Tours, France & St. Vincent's Home Studio, West Indies; Ocean Way Studio & Henson Studios, Hollywood, California, USA.
Played Live: 2005, 2006
Rolling Stones with Darryl Jones, Matt Clifford.
Producer: Don Was, The Glimmer Twins.
Engineer: Krish Sharma, Germán Villacorta
Pre-production: Matt Clifford
UK CD LP A BIGGER BANG: 5 September 2005: No. 2 - 4 weeks
USA CD LP A BIGGER BANG: 6 September 2005: No. 3 - 19 weeks
UK & USA CD/DVD A BIGGER BANG: 18 November 2005

On 12 December 2003, Mick Jagger bowed in front of Prince Charles who, on behalf of Queen Elizabeth II was to honour him as a Knight Bachelor. He was accompanied by his father, Joe Jagger, and daughters, Karis and Elizabeth. Charlie Watts performed a two-week residency at Ronnie Scott's club in London in April 2004 with his Tentet. A double CD was released later in the year, including an interpretation of *Satisfaction* called *Faction*. At the same time in April, Mick collaborated with Dave Stewart on a soundtrack for a new version of the 60s classic film *Alfie*. The album was released in October to coincide with the film release, which starred Jude Law in the Michael Caine role. Back in the early summer Mick and Keith Richards agreed to look at working on songs for the next album.

The era of digital recordings, with tools such as the Apple (TM) and Windows (TM), compatible Pro Tools reached prominence in 1997 with its 24 and 48-track ability version. Much of A BIGGER BANG was recorded in this way using home studios, in France and the West Indies. Recordings could be sent electronically using the internet or via courier to other world studios for additional work. Some of Ron Wood's guitar parts may have been achieved in this way, via his studio in Ireland. The songwriting process started in June at Mick's chateau in the Loire region, France. Keith Richards joined him in what was a very conducive atmosphere.

This was partly broken by the news that Charlie had been diagnosed with throat cancer and was receiving treatment so obviously could not join them. Should they continue? They agreed they would write songs and send them to Charlie for comment so things started slowly but constructively in their beautiful surroundings. Mick was a respected part of the community and supported the local economy. The locals protected him and affectionately called him Sir Mick, le pape du rock, Sir Jagger, Mick de Fourchette, Dr Jagger, sexy papy Briton, le père Mick, Le Seigneur de Fourchette and Mister Mick.

Charlie did join them in November when he received his first "cancer clear" message and that is when Don Was and Krish Sharma recorded the band. A couple of Mick's small adjoining rooms were chosen, with Charlie in one and Mick and Keith, both usually on guitar, in another. Pierre de Beauport gave Keith and Mick help with their guitars and keyboard set-up. The technique, while not used recently, was not totally unusual. Ronnie, who was not needed until November, was in guitar action for Rod Stewart, a Ronnie Lane memorial, the Stereophonics, Ian McLagan, the Charlatans, Jeff Beck, Bob Dylan, his brother Art Wood and the Hothouse Flowers.

He also attended the Strat celebration in autumn 2004 at Wembley arena and played with the Crickets, Albert Lee and Brian May on *That'll Be The Day* before an all-star finale on *Stay With Me*. Keith put in a worthy Wiltern Theatre appearance with Willie Nelson. It was filmed for USA television and *We Had It All* was released on a CD. Following his return from France in July, he played with Norah Jones on *Love Hurts* at a Gram Parsons tribute concert. *Rain Fall Down* was based on a funk, jangling guitar riff played by Mick. There were some disco and perfunctory rap-like vocals reminiscent of the old Chic style and Stereo MCs. It was probably written on the keyboard by Mick and Matt Clifford, who plays on the vastly over-dubbed final cut. Somewhere in there is an acoustic guitar and background vocals by Keith Richards.

The prophetic phrase "the bankers are wankers" pre-empted the economic credit crunch collapse of the west and Japan which commenced in 2007. Over-lending by USA mortgage companies started the descent as governments acted to shore up similar collapsing financial institutions all over the world. The reference to "feel like we're living in a battleground, everybody's jazzed" was written about London and how the capital had deteriorated into a city with armed police patrolling the streets. Britain hit a new low following the terrorist suicide bombings, in London, on 7 July 2005.

In all its different guises, *Rain Fall Down* was released as the single from the album. The principal single re-mix was by will.i.am, of the Black Eyed Peas, while Britain's Ashley Beedle also produced a "heavy disco" version, including a small orchestra extract not on the original. The video to promote the song was a steamy encounter of girls kissing and a couple making out in a down and out room with the rain pouring down outside. Naturally a wild party is going on as a stockbroker finds his way home after dark, doubtless on a Thursday night. The band perform individually but never knowingly near the "jazzed" action directed by Jonas Akerlund and Shawn Tolleson.

1424. RAIN FALL DOWN (RADIO RE-EDIT) (Jagger, Richards) 4.02
June, November - December 2004, January, March - April; June 2005: Place: La Fourchette Home Studio, Fourchette, Tours, France & St. Vincent's Home Studio, West Indies; Ocean Way Studio & Henson Studios, Hollywood, California, USA.
Rolling Stones with Darryl Jones, Matt Clifford.
Producer: Don Was, The Glimmer Twins.
Engineer: Krish Sharma, Germ n Villacorta
Pre-production: Matt Clifford
UK CD/Vinyl Track Rain Fall Down (will.i.am remix): 5 December 2005
UK CD box set THE SINGLES COLLECTION 1971-2006: 45 X 45s: 11 April 2011
USA CD box set THE SINGLES COLLECTION 1971-2006: 45 X 45s: 26 April 2011

1425. RAIN FALL DOWN (WILL.I.AM REMIX) (Jagger, Richards) 4.05
June, November - December 2004, January, March - April; June 2005: Place: La Fourchette Home Studio, Fourchette, Tours, France & St. Vincent's Home Studio, West Indies; Ocean Way Studio & Henson Studios, Hollywood, California, USA.
Rolling Stones with Darryl Jones, Matt Clifford.
Producer: Don Was, The Glimmer Twins.
Engineer: Krish Sharma, Germ n Villacorta
Pre-production: Matt Clifford; Re-mix by will.i.am
UK CD/Vinyl Single: 5 December 2005: No. 33 - 2 weeks
UK CD box set THE SINGLES COLLECTION 1971-2006: 45 X 45s: 11 April 2011
USA CD box set THE SINGLES COLLECTION 1971-2006: 45 X 45s: 26 April 2011

1426. RAIN FALL DOWN (WILL.I.AM INSTRUMENTAL) (Jagger, Richards) 4.05
June, November - December 2004, January, March - April; June 2005: Place: La Fourchette Home Studio, Fourchette, Tours, France & St. Vincent's Home Studio, West Indies; Ocean Way Studio & Henson Studios, Hollywood, California, USA.
Rolling Stones with Darryl Jones, Matt Clifford.
Producer: Don Was, The Glimmer Twins.
Engineer: Krish Sharma, Germ n Villacorta
Pre-production: Matt Clifford; Re-mix by will.i.am
UK CD/Vinyl Track Rain Fall Down (willi.i.am remix): 5 December 2005

1427. RAIN FALL DOWN (ASHLEY BEEDLE'S 'HEAVY DISCO' VOCAL RE-EDIT) (Jagger, Richards) 6.13
June, November - December 2004, January, March - April; June 2005: Place: La Fourchette Home Studio, Fourchette, Tours, France & St. Vincent's Home Studio, West Indies; Ocean Way Studio & Henson Studios, Hollywood, California, USA.
Rolling Stones with Darryl Jones, Matt Clifford.
Producer: Don Was, The Glimmer Twins.
Engineer: Krish Sharma, Germ n Villacorta
Pre-production: Matt Clifford; Re-mix by Ashley Beedle
UK & USA CD/DVD A BIGGER BANG: 18 November 2005
UK CD/Vinyl Track Rain Fall Down (willi.i.am remix): 5 December 2005
UK CD box set THE SINGLES COLLECTION 1971-2006: 45 X 45s: 11 April 2011
USA CD box set THE SINGLES COLLECTION 1971-2006: 45 X 45s: 26 April 2011

1428. RAIN FALL DOWN (ASHLEY BEEDLE'S 'HEAVY DISCO' DUB RE-EDIT) (Jagger, Richards) 6.07
June, November - December 2004, January, March - April; June 2005: Place: La Fourchette Home Studio, Fourchette, Tours, France & St. Vincent's Home Studio, West Indies; Ocean Way Studio & Henson Studios, Hollywood, California, USA.
Rolling Stones with Darryl Jones, Matt Clifford.
Producer: Don Was, The Glimmer Twins.
Engineer: Krish Sharma, Germ n Villacorta
Pre-production: Matt Clifford; Re-mix by Ashley Beedle
UK CD/Vinyl Track Rain Fall Down (willi.i.am remix): 5 December 2005

1429. RAIN FALL DOWN (ASHLEY BEEDLE'S 'HEAVY DISCO' RADIO RE-EDIT) (Jagger, Richards) 4.06
June, November - December 2004, January, March - April; June 2005: Place: La Fourchette Home Studio, Fourchette, Tours, France & St. Vincent's Home Studio, West Indies; Ocean Way Studio & Henson Studios, Hollywood, California, USA.
Rolling Stones with Darryl Jones, Matt Clifford.
Producer: Don Was, The Glimmer Twins.
Engineer: Krish Sharma, Germ n Villacorta
Pre-production: Matt Clifford; Re-mix by Ashley Beedle
UK CD/Vinyl Track Rain Fall Down (willi.i.am remix): 5 December 2005
UK CD box set THE SINGLES COLLECTION 1971-2006: 45 X 45s: 11 April 2011
USA CD box set THE SINGLES COLLECTION 1971-2006: 45 X 45s: 26 April 2011

1430. LET ME DOWN SLOW (Jagger, Richards) 4.16
AKA: Take Me Down Slowly
June, November - December 2004, January, March - April; June 2005: Place: La Fourchette Home Studio, Fourchette, Tours, France & St. Vincent's Home Studio, West Indies; Ocean Way Studio & Henson Studios, Hollywood, California, USA.
Rolling Stones with Darryl Jones.
Producer: Don Was, The Glimmer Twins.
Engineer: Krish Sharma, Jack Joseph Puig, Dean Nelson
UK CD LP A BIGGER BANG: 5 September 2005: No. 2 - 4 weeks
USA CD LP A BIGGER BANG: 6 September 2005: No. 3 - 19 weeks
UK & USA CD/DVD A BIGGER BANG: 18 November 2005

Ron Wood embellishes this Mick Jagger song well with some "west coast" slide guitar. He recorded all his guitar parts in a ten-day stint, often not needing more than one or two takes. The contrary verse and chorus was Keith Richards' idea, using a descending major on the chorus designed to grab attention and not to make the song sound too samey. He also performs the open-tuned guitar and has a purposeful solo. The song describes a relationship ending as a couple nestle in the afterglow. For some reason, the song empathises enough with Keith to refer to it in his autobiography *Life* when telling a tale of the only time he slept with Marianne Faithfull. Three out-takes can be obtained that seem very similar or have a tad rougher mix than the released one (* a - 4.17, b - 4.16, c - 4.17).

1431. STREETS OF LOVE (Jagger, Richards) 5.10
June, November - December 2004, January, March - April; June 2005: Place: La Fourchette Home Studio, Fourchette, Tours, France & St. Vincent's Home Studio, West Indies; Ocean Way Studio & Henson Studios, Hollywood, California, USA.
Played Live: 2006, 2007
Rolling Stones with Darryl Jones, Chuck Leavell, Matt Clifford.
Producer: Don Was, The Glimmer Twins, Matt Clifford.
Engineer: Krish Sharma, Jack Joseph Puig, Dean Nelson
UK CD/Vinyl Single: 22 August 2005; No. 15 - 4 weeks
USA CD/Vinyl Single: c/w Rough Justice 23 August 2005
UK CD LP A BIGGER BANG: 5 September 2005: No. 2 - 4 weeks
USA CD LP A BIGGER BANG: 6 September 2005: No. 3 - 19 weeks
UK & USA CD/DVD A BIGGER BANG: 18 November 2005
UK CD box set THE SINGLES COLLECTION 1971-2006: 45 X 45s: 11 April 2011
USA CD box set THE SINGLES COLLECTION 1971-2006: 45 X 45s: 26 April 2011

Possibly because of a surfeit of material from the ALFIE project, on which he worked with Matt Clifford, this was another Mick Jagger song. The vocal style is distinctly the enunciated Jagger but the song does have a flow that gave it a movie soundtrack quality. This is due to its repetitive structure and the much edited (in length) version is perhaps the best way to hear it. Matt Clifford uses orchestral flourishes to extend this feeling and it merges well with Ron Wood's lead solo. The literary phrasing encapsulated by "cross the Rubicon" is again typical Mick as he reaches the point of no return of another ending relationship. He must have been in a dark, reflective mood.
The chorus of never-ending falsetto "ayehh, ayehh, ayehh" naturally made it the catchy single choice from the album. Keith Richards enjoyed the retro feel of the song. It has shades of Mick Jagger's solo song *Brand New Set Of Rules*. It was released as the A BIGGER BANG tour commenced and, while on tour in Canada on 29 August, Jake Nava directed a couple of promotional films to accompany it. These were shot with an audience at the intimate Zaphod Beeblebrox night club in Ottawa.
It portrays the band performing live and at ease, albeit to a playback. Canadian actor Tan Arcade sees his girl in the club but she reluctantly avoids him. Another edit has more narrative shots of Tan Arcade in the streets of Ottawa before he gets knocked over by a car. A standard playback performance version is in full colour mode and filmed in Toronto. Both the latter videos were released on the A BIGGER BANG DVD extra disc to appeal to the younger female audience. Two further versions at production and mix stage are available (* a - 5.10, b - 5.09). There is a *Radio Edit Version* which appeared on the single (* c - 4.04).

1432. IT WON'T TAKE LONG (Jagger, Richards) 3.54
June, November - December 2004, January, March - April; June 2005: Place: La Fourchette Home Studio, Fourchette, Tours, France & St. Vincent's Home Studio, West Indies; Ocean Way Studio & Henson Studios, Hollywood, California, USA.
Played Live: 2005
Rolling Stones with Darryl Jones, Chuck Leavell.
Producer: Don Was, The Glimmer Twins.
Engineer: Krish Sharma, Jack Joseph Puig, Dean Nelson
UK CD LP A BIGGER BANG: 5 September 2005: No. 2 - 4 weeks
USA CD LP A BIGGER BANG: 6 September 2005: No. 3 - 19 weeks
UK & USA CD/DVD A BIGGER BANG: 18 November 2005

At a heavier tempo, *It Won't Take Long* rocks from the initial Keith Richards guitar riff but it is evident that this is a standard tune that fails to lead anywhere. It was originally tried in a soul vein until the harder tempo was attempted. The lead guitars are produced high and combined they do give it a swagger that could have provided the sandwich filler for any Stones album. It starts to fade after three-and-a-half minutes. Again, two out-takes of slightly longer length are available (* a - 4.12, b - 4.12). It was played just once on tour, at the Hollywood Bowl in Los Angeles.

1433. BACK OF MY HAND (Jagger, Richards) 3.32
June, November - December 2004, January, March - April; June 2005: Place: La Fourchette Home Studio, Fourchette, Tours, France & St. Vincent's Home Studio, West Indies; Ocean Way Studio & Henson Studios, Hollywood, California, USA.
Played Live: 2005, 2006
Producer: Don Was, The Glimmer Twins.
Engineer: Krish Sharma, Germ n Villacorta
UK CD LP A BIGGER BANG: 5 September 2005: No. 2 - 4 weeks
USA CD LP A BIGGER BANG: 6 September 2005: No. 3 - 19 weeks
UK & USA CD/DVD A BIGGER BANG: 18 November 2005

The album style is pessimistic and bleak, perhaps created by Charlie Watts' initial absence at the songwriting process but also reflecting the perceived loss of strong values prevalent in Britain at the time. This track cuts way back to the authentic blues past of their masters. In interviews, Keith Richards remembered when he first heard Mick Jagger improvising the song and strumming blues chords; he knew it had possibilities. Mick had an old Silvertone guitar which sounded particularly good when played in slide style.

On hearing Mick play it, Keith was impressed. His LV (lead vocalist) was quite a proficient master - and why not? By now, with his pedigree and long hair, he was a true blues professor! He felt it sounded like a track they could have cut as long ago as the Chess studio session in 1964. The band could not have been more sparse, as Mick contributed vocals and wonderfully authentic slide guitar but also percussion and a caustic harmonica.

The result was a great work of homage with a bar room slow stomp bass beat sometimes created with a foot on the floor. On first hearing it, fans raved at the genuine bravura result that came out of the delta, bringing the ghost of Muddy Waters and Little Walter with it, whom Keith described as being among their friends. During live performances on the tour, an extra verse was sometimes added. The song has been covered by the British blues duo, Sisters In Grease.

1434. SHE SAW ME COMING (Jagger, Richards) 3.12
June, November - December 2004, January, March - April; June 2005: Place: La Fourchette Home Studio, Fourchette, Tours, France & St. Vincent's Home Studio, West Indies; Ocean Way Studio & Henson Studios, Hollywood, California, USA.

Rolling Stones with Blondie Chaplin.
Producer: Don Was, The Glimmer Twins.
Engineer: Krish Sharma, Jack Joseph Puig, Dean Nelson
UK CD LP A BIGGER BANG: 5 September 2005: No. 2 - 4 weeks
USA CD LP A BIGGER BANG: 6 September 2005: No. 3 - 19 weeks
UK & USA CD/DVD A BIGGER BANG: 18 November 2005

While songwriting was being completed in 2005, Mick Jagger played at the annual blues festival at Basil's Bar in Mustique, West Indies, in February. He also joined Ron Wood on stage to perform *Dance*, at a London gig in March. The principal engineer chosen by Don Was for A BIGGER BANG was Krish Sharma; he was normally associated with heavier guitar rock music but had worked with many different music styles, including with the Stones on VOODOO LOUNGE. This track may have been written either in France or the West Indies but Don Was and Krish Sharma recorded it in a live take. Ron Wood was keen to work live in the studio more because, to him, this track sounded spontaneous and fresh.

However, there were overdubs, with Mick Jagger playing bass on the backing track, Ron on slide and Keith Richards on lead. Charlie Watts' characteristic lively, undamped snare adds to the ring. There is plenty of chord and lyrical repetition as Mick relates the standard "she ripped me off" vocal that we had seen before. His explanatory vocals describe the ladies' ills while the band and Blondie Chaplin give added shout to the title. The result is the sound of American east coast rock. A slightly longer out-take is available (* a - 3.22).

1435. DANGEROUS BEAUTY (Jagger, Richards) 3.48
June, November - December 2004, January, March - April; June 2005: Place: La Fourchette Home Studio, Fourchette, Tours, France & St. Vincent's Home Studio, West Indies; Ocean Way Studio & Henson Studios, Hollywood, California, USA.

Producer: Don Was, The Glimmer Twins.
Engineer: Krish Sharma, Jack Joseph Puig, Dean Nelson
UK CD LP A BIGGER BANG: 5 September 2005: No. 2 - 4 weeks
USA CD LP A BIGGER BANG: 6 September 2005: No. 3 - 19 weeks
UK & USA CD/DVD A BIGGER BANG: 18 November 2005

Bang in the middle of working on the album, photos began to emerge of the inhumane treatment of Iraqi prisoners of war by American soldiers in Baghdad's Abu Ghraib prison. The Mick Jagger lyrics to *Dangerous Beauty* are not evasive or veiled but pointed and thought-provoking just as they were intended. The striking photo of a soldier holding a leash to a prisoner cowering on the floor in Iraq became an iconic image and the song's focal point.

Punishments were meted out in 2005 after the leaked photographs had flooded the world media and rightly created a backlash against the Americans and their allies. As reported in August 2005, Mick was worried that the over-reaching imperialism would take the west to a place where it would all collapse. The track itself is sparse with just Charlie Watts and Mick on bass playing rhythm around a heavy valve guitar riff by Keith Richards. Two slightly longer out-take mixes are available (* a - 4.14, b - 4.15).

1436. DON'T WANNA GO HOME (Jagger, Richards) 3.34
AKA: We Don't Wanna Go Home
June, November - December 2004, January, March - April; June 2005: Place: La Fourchette Home Studio, Fourchette, Tours, France & St. Vincent's Home Studio, West Indies; Ocean Way Studio & Henson Studios, Hollywood, California, USA.

Rolling Stones with Darryl Jones.
Producer: Don Was, The Glimmer Twins.
Engineer: Krish Sharma.
UK & USA DVD A Bigger Bang: 18 November 2005

The out-takes from A BIGGER BANG emerged on the internet and were allegedly found by an "internal person" on a server in a folder marked "Rolling Stones". They were converted to MP3 and distributed via the web to thousands after the album release. *Don't Wanna Go Home* has three alternative versions all sounding very similar but are a minute longer than the released cut (* a - 4.33, b - 4.32, c - 4.33).

It is apparent that all the out-takes are in this vein, though they are not truly different or early takes - they have simply not been faded earlier or have a slight mix tweak. *Don't Wanna Go Home* was only released officially on the A BIGGER BANG extras DVD which was sold as a special edition. It is only an audio despite being on a DVD and has completed vocals, less than unique lyrics and would have been considered for the album or as an alternative track on a single.

1437. OH NO, NOT YOU AGAIN (Jagger, Richards) 3.46
June, November - December 2004, January, March - April; June 2005: Place: La Fourchette Home Studio, Fourchette, Tours, France & St. Vincent's Home Studio, West Indies; Ocean Way Studio & Henson Studios, Hollywood, California, USA.
Played Live: 2005, 2006, 2007
Rolling Stones with Darryl Jones.
Producer: Don Was, The Glimmer Twins.
Engineer: Krish Sharma, Jack Joseph Puig, Dean Nelson

UK CD LP A BIGGER BANG: 5 September 2005: No. 2 - 4 weeks
USA CD LP A BIGGER BANG: 6 September 2005: No. 3 - 19 weeks
USA CD Promo Single Track Oh No Not You Again (Clean Mix); October 2005
UK & USA CD/DVD A BIGGER BANG: 18 November 2005

The lyrics for *Oh No Not You Again* were a humorous attempt at self-analysis of Mick Jagger's own 1998 affair with Brazilian model Luciana Gimenez Morad in New York. The affair produced a son named Lucas in 1999 and this was the final denouement in Mick's marriage with Jerry Hall. Mick has done the honourable deed, paying a settlement and meeting Lucas since. The lyrics work well for any situation where you meet someone and go out with them, then go your separate ways - but later bump into them again. It worked well also for the next tour when fans met each other again.

Charlie Watts suggested that it could have been the tour title. The song structure sees two of verse and two of chorus, with changing 2nd, 3rd and 4th lines in the chorus together with the classic guitar solo bridge. This continues for some 13 stanzas; the last "oh no not you again" chorus being repeated three times. The lyrics were patched together after soliciting ideas and rhymes from the band. The song must have been a nightmare to remember when on the world tour since it was a commonly played song from the album.

It was previewed when the band promoted the launch of their tour for the press. The references to "fucking up my life" and "staring down your tits" ensured the necessity of an edited "clean" version for use on a promo single and for airplay (* a - 3.49). It is a pounding harmony rocker that Mick thought sounded a bit punk-like as three guitars, including his, thrash around amid the Charlie Watts combination of throbbing bass drum and snare. There is also an alternative, unreleased mix (* b - 3.48).

1438. THIS PLACE IS EMPTY (Jagger, Richards) 3.16
June, November - December 2004, January, March - April; June 2005: Place: La Fourchette Home Studio, Fourchette, Tours, France & St. Vincent's Home Studio, West Indies; Ocean Way Studio & Henson Studios, Hollywood, California, USA.
Played Live: 2006
Rolling Stones with Don Was.
Producer: Don Was, The Glimmer Twins.
Engineer: Krish Sharma, Jack Joseph Puig, Dean Nelson
UK CD LP A BIGGER BANG: 5 September 2005: No. 2 - 4 weeks
USA CD LP A BIGGER BANG: 6 September 2005: No. 3 - 19 weeks
UK & USA CD/DVD A BIGGER BANG: 18 November 2005

A three-minute song and an ode to Patti Hansen, Keith Richards' wife, written one evening when she was out. Keith knew at the time it was one of those "within that moment that had to be grabbed before it disappeared". It seems to be recorded live with two pianos, played by Keith and Don Was. Keith also sings the low, raspy vocals and Mick Jagger supplies the backing to a retro, jazzy, smoky, sensual ballad number.

Keith also injects some humour, "come on honey, bare your breasts" and "come on, simmer down". In an article by Jon Wilde in Loaded magazine's November 1995 edition, Keith said: "There's nothing more beautiful than a great-looking chick removing her clothes. In fact, the only thing better is a great looking chick removing mine!" Keith was much more into writing about the body and soul than politics but somehow he felt the album nicely combined the two with some funk.

1439. UNDER THE RADAR (Jagger, Richards) 4.36
June, November - December 2004, January, March - April; June 2005: Place: La Fourchette Home Studio, Fourchette, Tours, France & St. Vincent's Home Studio, West Indies; Ocean Way Studio & Henson Studios, Hollywood, California, USA.
Rolling Stones with Darryl Jones.
Producer: Don Was, The Glimmer Twins.
Engineer: Krish Sharma.
UK & USA DVD A Bigger Bang: 18 November 2005

Plenty of action in the shape of a Ronnie Wood slide, Keith Richards' rhythm and Mick Jagger shaping the song riff in what became a very guitar-orientated, no frills approach for Mick, perhaps encapsulating the relaxed air of the French Loire. To his credit, Don Was did little to provide massive overdubs at the conclusion in Los Angeles. An out-take to this DVD-only released audio track has an extended 30-second finish (* a - 5.09).

1440. DRIVING TOO FAST (Jagger, Richards) 3.56
June, November - December 2004, January, March - April; June 2005: Place: La Fourchette Home Studio, Fourchette, Tours, France & St. Vincent's Home Studio, West Indies; Ocean Way Studio & Henson Studios, Hollywood, California, USA.
Rolling Stones with Darryl Jones, Chuck Leavell.
Producer: Don Was, The Glimmer Twins.
Engineer: Krish Sharma, Jack Joseph Puig, Dean Nelson
UK CD LP A BIGGER BANG: 5 September 2005: No. 2 - 4 weeks
USA CD LP A BIGGER BANG: 6 September 2005: No. 3 - 19 weeks
UK & USA CD/DVD A BIGGER BANG: 18 November 2005

One of the more mediocre efforts on the album, *Driving Too Fast* is an upbeat four-minute track that careers down the highway. It is extended by a further 30 seconds in an out-take (* a - 4.29). It was not played live on the A BIGGER BANG TOUR.

1441. BIGGEST MISTAKE (Jagger, Richards) 4.06
June, November - December 2004, January, March - April; June 2005: Place: La Fourchette Home Studio, Fourchette, Tours, France &
St. Vincent's Home Studio, West Indies; Ocean Way Studio & Henson Studios, Hollywood, California, USA.
Rolling Stones with Darryl Jones, Chuck Leavell.
Producer: Don Was, The Glimmer Twins.
Engineer: Krish Sharma, Jack Joseph Puig, Dean Nelson
UK CD LP A BIGGER BANG: 5 September 2005: No. 2 - 4 weeks
USA CD LP A BIGGER BANG: 6 September 2005: No. 3 - 19 weeks
UK & USA CD/DVD A BIGGER BANG: 18 November 2005
UK CD/Vinyl Single; 21 August 2006; No. 51 - 1 week
UK CD box set THE SINGLES COLLECTION 1971-2006: 45 X 45s: 11 April 2011
USA CD box set THE SINGLES COLLECTION 1971-2006: 45 X 45s: 26 April 2011

There are immediate comparisons for those involved in the failure of successful love partnerships which leads to regret and self-pity. Jerry Hall was the instant source of the song lyrics of "biggest mistake of my life". Keith Richards had encouraged the cathartic approach to opening up and delivering these lyrics. Acoustic guitars, Chuck Leavell's organ and Ronnie Wood's slide flood the aura and the soft rock tones lament what has been with Mick Jagger's "ooh, ooh, ooh" falsetto harmonies. As he explained to a magazine in 2010: "You can't give into temptation all your life, otherwise you'd have no through line; you'd never get anything finished. But it's absolutely no fun at all unless you give into temptation some of your life. If you never do, you're really boring and dull."
Certainly the song outcome was a bold statement for his girlfriend L'Wren Scott to swallow but their relationship was strong and stable. It was edited and released as the third single in the UK, charting for one week despite receiving support from BBC Radio 2. Unlike the edited and album version, the out-take concludes the song a minute later, without fade-out (* a - 4.53). An edited version was released for single release (* b - 3.33) and also an instrumental (* c - 4.09).

1442. LAUGH, I NEARLY DIED (Jagger, Richards) 4.54
June, November - December 2004, January, March - April; June 2005: Place: La Fourchette Home Studio, Fourchette, Tours, France &
St. Vincent's Home Studio, West Indies; Ocean Way Studio & Henson Studios, Hollywood, California, USA.
Rolling Stones with Darryl Jones.
Producer: Don Was, The Glimmer Twins.
Engineer: Krish Sharma, Germ n Villacorta
UK CD LP A BIGGER BANG: 5 September 2005: No. 2 - 4 weeks
USA CD LP A BIGGER BANG: 6 September 2005: No. 3 - 19 weeks
UK & USA CD/DVD A BIGGER BANG: 18 November 2005

This was written by Mick Jagger during the ALFIE solo sessions. It was a mournful work of self-analysis and accusation that traces roots of the past. The song is simplistic but well-constructed, the Keith Richards guitars delivering a great refrain. To enhance the black roots atmosphere the vocal, claps and backing vocals without instrumentation give a gospel feel.

1443. INFAMY (Jagger, Richards) 3.48
June, November - December 2004, January, March - April; June 2005: Place: La Fourchette Home Studio, Fourchette, Tours, France &
St. Vincent's Home Studio, West Indies; Ocean Way Studio & Henson Studios, Hollywood, California, USA.
Played Live: 2005
Rolling Stones with Blondie Chaplin.
Producer: Don Was, The Glimmer Twins.
Engineer: Krish Sharma, Germ n Villacorta
UK CD LP A BIGGER BANG: 5 September 2005: No. 2 - 4 weeks
USA CD LP A BIGGER BANG: 6 September 2005: No. 3 - 19 weeks
UK & USA CD/DVD A BIGGER BANG: 18 November 2005

Looking at the personnel credits on *Infamy* gives you an idea of the contribution level and togetherness of Mick Jagger and Keith Richards on A BIGGER BANG. Primarily, it was unusual for Keith to sing vocals on a song with so much participation by Mick. They both played guitar, keyboards and percussion while Keith also contributed bass guitar. The chorus backing vocals were sung not just by Keith but also by Mick and Blondie Chaplin. With a few electronic repeated keyboard notes the song opens to a powerful phased twang riff and an acoustic guitar.
Just before the first chorus of the play on words "you've got it in for me" Mick starts a distinctive, wailing harmonica. Keith sings about a lady with a bad reputation trying to knock him off his perch and convict him. The A BIGGER BANG album cover was designed by photographer Nick Knight who was more commonly known for his fashion shots in Vanity Fair and Vogue. It depicts the band almost obscured, staring from a darkened background into a table top-reflected abyss of bright flash lights and supposed apocalypse as the world was created.
Mick is pictured laughing demonically invoking images of the late 60s. Slightly different poses are shown in the reflection, Mick arms high in rejoice and Keith's guitar is now thrust forward. The picture is very reminiscent of Paul McCartney's 1979 Wings album cover for BACK TO THE EGG taken by John Shaw for Hipgnosis. Nick Knight also designed the neon and metallic Stones lips used for the album inner cover, singles and subsequent tour.

1444. LOOK WHAT THE CAT DRAGGED IN (Jagger, Richards) 3.57
June, November - December 2004, January, March - April; June 2005: Place: La Fourchette Home Studio, Fourchette, Tours, France &
St. Vincent's Home Studio, West Indies; Ocean Way Studio & Henson Studios, Hollywood, California, USA.
Rolling Stones with Darryl Jones, Lenny Castro.
Producer: Don Was, The Glimmer Twins.
Engineer: Krish Sharma, Germ n Villacorta

UK CD LP A BIGGER BANG: 5 September 2005: No. 2 - 4 weeks
USA CD LP A BIGGER BANG: 6 September 2005: No. 3 - 19 weeks
UK & USA CD/DVD A BIGGER BANG: 18 November 2005

A dance beat drives *Look What The Cat Dragged* In with a Tim Farriss (Inxs) guitar-sounding riff exhortation by Ronnie Wood. Lenny Castro, who had worked on Mick Jagger solo projects and VOODOO LOUNGE, plays bongo percussion on this Jagger-penned track. Mick plays guitar and bass as does Darryl Jones. The tale of a girl in a mess strangely refers to the parody of a leper dressed as Sgt Pepper and, in another verse, to the Syrian occupation of Lebanon. It was not a strong album cut and not going to be a "new sensation".

1445. SWEET NEOCON (Jagger, Richards) 4.33
June, November - December 2004, January, March - April; June 2005: Place: La Fourchette Home Studio, Fourchette, Tours, France & St. Vincent's Home Studio, West Indies; Ocean Way Studio & Henson Studios, Hollywood, California, USA.
Rolling Stones with Darryl Jones, Lenny Castro.
Producer: Don Was, The Glimmer Twins.
Engineer: Krish Sharma, Germán Villacorta
UK CD LP A BIGGER BANG: 5 September 2005: No. 2 - 4 weeks
USA CD LP A BIGGER BANG: 6 September 2005: No. 3 - 19 weeks
UK & USA CD/DVD A BIGGER BANG: 18 November 2005

Sweet Neocon is a political song that caused a minor stir even before the album release. The neo-con terminology was reference to the conservatives from the Pentagon and White House who had promoted the national crusade against Iraq by USA in 2003. The song is heavy on irony as reference is made to the oil services conglomerate Halliburton and its subsidiary Kellogg, Brown & Root (both Halliburton and Brown & Root are mentioned in the lyrics) and juxtaposes the claim to be a Christian with a hypocrite and a crock full of shit.

This was due to illicit payments for contracts. The "sweet" guy possibly referred to is either the more obvious Republican President George W Bush or Dick Cheney, who was Chief Executive of Halliburton and Vice-President at the White House. There was no hiding from the social comment within the lyrical content, a voice that had never daunted the Stones previously. Mick Jagger promotes the song by contributing the lyrics but also a guitar, bass and harmonica. Keith Richards was concerned that, due to American patriotism, *Sweet Neocon* could it detract from the other songs but, since Mick felt strongly about the matter, he supported him. It emphasised the album's general cohesiveness and compactness, even Ronnie Wood did not gain many credits on the album. Mick referred to this as getting back to the emotional core of the band. Don Was said: "It was clear from the first day of recording that the Rolling Stones - the band rather than the individuals who comprise it - came into focus on this album." Despite press speculation, *Sweet Neocon* was not played on the USA stage of the next tour. The album's recording was generally complete on conclusion of Keith Richards, Charlie Watts and Mick's stay in France. Keith relates in his auto-biography *Life* that Mick now felt that it was time to take the songs and record them properly in a big studio. Keith and Charlie apparently pointed out that, in their mind, the near finished product was on the tapes.

As a result a few overdubs and some new recordings were made in California to conclude the album. Two studios were used by Don Was and Krish Sharma for final recordings and mixes. Jack Puig and Dean Nelson chose Ocean Way, while Germán Villacorta used the historic Chaplin and A&M (Herb Alpert and Jerry Moss) studios now owned by Jim Henson. The last time the Stones had used that studio was with Don Was on VOODOO LOUNGE, while Ocean Way was the venue for BRIDGES TO BABYLON.

1446. ROUGH JUSTICE (Jagger, Richards) 3.13
June, November - December 2004, January, March - April; June 2005: Place: La Fourchette Home Studio, Fourchette, Tours, France & St. Vincent's Home Studio, West Indies; Village Recorder, Los Angeles, USA.
Played Live: 2005, 2006, 2007
Rolling Stones with Darryl Jones, Chuck Leavell.
Producer: Don Was, The Glimmer Twins.
Engineer: Krish Sharma, Dave Sardy, Ryan Castle, Andy Brohard.
UK CD/Vinyl Single c/w Streets Of Love: 22 August 2005; No. 15 - 4 weeks
USA CD/Vinyl Single c/w Streets Of Love: 23 August 2005
UK CD LP A BIGGER BANG: 5 September 2005: No. 2 - 4 weeks
USA CD LP A BIGGER BANG: 6 September 2005: No. 3 - 19 weeks
UK CD Track Single Biggest Mistake (Radio Edit); 21 August 2006
USA CD Track Single Biggest Mistake (Radio Edit); 22 August 2006
UK & USA CD/DVD A BIGGER BANG: 18 November 2005
UK CD box set THE SINGLES COLLECTION 1971-2006: 45 X 45s: 11 April 2011
USA CD box set THE SINGLES COLLECTION 1971-2006: 45 X 45s: 26 April 2011

Rough Justice was the last recorded cut for the album and Village Recorder (of GOATS HEAD SOUP production) provided the studio space for mixing. The engineers Dave Sardy, Ryan Castle and Andy Brohard specified in the credits had just completed recording for Oasis' DON'T BELIEVE THE TRUTH. The result is an out and out direct three-minute rocker, the riff for which came to Keith Richards in his dreams after which he grabbed his guitar. Ron Wood plays Zemaitis slide guitar on what was his album highlight. It was a blast from the past.

On first listen, the lyrics seem childish but were actually humorous and naturally turned the song into single material - "And once upon a time I was your little rooster, am I just one of your cocks?" It was coupled with *Streets Of Love* enabling the radio listener to hear different Stones facets in advance of the album release. The video is a stage performance with playback filmed in a Toronto studio, as was *Streets Of Love*, and is also on the album's extra DVD disc. It became one of the most played tunes on the American tour leg and was well represented, too, in Europe and afield.

1447.   BROWN SUGAR (Jagger, Richard) 3.46
9 May 2005: Place: S.I.R. Studios, New York, USA.
Rolling Stones with Darryl Jones.
Bootleg only

1448.   OH NO, NOT YOU AGAIN (Jagger, Richards) 3.51
9 May 2005: Place: S.I.R. Studios, New York, USA.
Rolling Stones with Darryl Jones.
Bootleg only

1449.   START ME UP (Jagger, Richards) ✎ 4.47
10 May 2005: Place: Julliard School Of Music, New York, USA.
Rolling Stones with Darryl Jones, Chuck Leavell.
Bootleg only

1450.   OH NO, NOT YOU AGAIN (Jagger, Richards) ✎ 4.25
10 May 2005: Place: Julliard School Of Music, New York, USA.
Rolling Stones with Darryl Jones, Chuck Leavell.
Bootleg only

1451.   BROWN SUGAR (Jagger, Richard) ✎ 5.32
10 May 2005: Place: Julliard School Of Music, New York, USA.
Rolling Stones with Darryl Jones, Chuck Leavell.
Bootleg only

The album was not yet fully complete but the tour was announced on 10 May 2005, at the Julliard School of Music in New York. Usually the tour was announced via a different means of transport. They considered their options and even thought about using the Queen Mary II, which was due to dock in New York at the end of April until 4 May, but agreed that they should do what the tour is all about and play live. The band performed three numbers for the press and a crowd of students and fans at this open-air event.
Start Me Up, Oh No, Not You Again, from the forthcoming album, and *Brown Sugar* were played by the four band members, along with Darryl Jones and Chuck Leavell. Even Bobby Keys was absent for a raw version of *Brown Sugar*. They had rehearsed the previous day for the performance at the SIR studios in New York and the short, sharp versions of *Brown Sugar* and *Oh No, Not You Again* could be seen on the Rolling Stones official web-site. The guitars reflected and jarred against each other in an off-the-cuff manner.
At the Julliard, Mick Jagger commented after the unveiling of the new number, "I think the examiners at Julliard might have us come back and re-take that one!" The stage had a Stones tongue with a baseball design and curiously the words "on stage" underneath and this became the tour label. Tour director Michael Cohl made plans for a year-long schedule consisting of baseball stadiums and other worldwide venues. The band were then interviewed by the press and Mick said the stadium gigs would feature a new element of fans somehow appearing on stage with them. In answer to the obligatory question of "will this be the last time?" Charlie Watts uttered his one-word conference statement: "Yes".

1452.   BACK OF MY HAND (Jagger, Richards) ✎ 4.13
10 August 2005: Place: Phoenix Concert Theatre, Toronto, Canada.
Rolling Stones with Darryl Jones, Chuck Leavell.
Producer: The Rolling Stones
Engineer: Music Mix: Bob Clearmountain; Music Production: Ed Cherney; Additional Mixes / Engineer: Brandon Duncan; FOH Sound Engineer: Dave Natale.
Executive Producer: Michael Cohl, Director: Hamish Hamilton.
USA DVD The Biggest Bang: 23 June 2007
UK DVD The Biggest Bang: 5 August 2007

From mid-July, the band gathered in Toronto for tour rehearsals at a college and were joined in August by the familiar supporting cast to fine tune arrangements. Bernard Fowler could not wait to receive the call from Keith Richards, to drop everything and join the band: "that call is always such a privilege for me". Charlie Watts was still recovering from his cancer treatment and claimed to be about 50 per cent fit so clearly it was a tall order to get everyone ready for the impending year of activity. He did so, though, with his own determination and the help of Mick Jagger's physio Torje Eike. The Live 8 day of 2 July 2005, organised by Bob Geldof, was clearly out of the question despite Michael Cohl organising the Canadian event north of Toronto in Barrie. An airport hangar in Toronto was used by the crew to practise the set-up of the arena and stadium stages. It was designed by the Mark Fisher Studio to be scalable depending on the venue size. The stadium gigs required more personnel and two more trucks.

1453.   GET UP, STAND UP (Marley, Tosh) ✎ 5.53
10 August 2005: Place: Phoenix Concert Theatre, Toronto, Canada.
Rolling Stones with Darryl Jones, Chuck Leavell, Bobby Keys, Lisa Fischer, Bernard Fowler, Blondie Chaplin, Tim Ries, Michael Davis, Kent Smith.
Producer: The Rolling Stones
Engineer: Music Mix: Bob Clearmountain; Music Production: Ed Cherney, Dave Natale; Additional Mixes / Engineer: Brandon Duncan; FOH Sound Engineer: Dave Natale.
Executive Producer: Michael Cohl, Director: Hamish Hamilton.
USA DVD The Biggest Bang: 23 June 2007
UK DVD The Biggest Bang: 5 August 2007

1454. MR. PITIFUL (Cropper, Redding) ✐ 3.18
10 August 2005: Place: Phoenix Concert Theatre, Toronto, Canada.
Rolling Stones with Darryl Jones, Chuck Leavell, Bobby Keys, Tim Ries, Michael Davis, Kent Smith.
Producer: The Rolling Stones
Engineer: Music Mix: Bob Clearmountain; Music Production: Ed Cherney; Additional Mixes / Engineer: Brandon Duncan; FOH Sound Engineer: Dave Natale.
Executive Producer: Michael Cohl, Director: Hamish Hamilton.
USA DVD The Biggest Bang: 23 June 2007
UK DVD The Biggest Bang: 5 August 2007

Toronto was privileged to pay host to its fourth pre-tour warm-up gig on 10 August 2005. The day before, Pulse 24 the local radio station, leaked the news that a concert would occur but no venue was confirmed. By deduction, it was guessed that the small Phoenix Theatre would be the venue with a capacity of 1,100. Rumours swept the Internet boards and queues started to form outside the venue 24 hours before show time. On the day, about 300 tickets and wristbands were handed out for $10 and a further 50 regulars at the rehearsal venue also received tickets. The remainder were distributed to the band's family and friends, VIP's and music industry insiders. The concert was a short, sharp, frenetic work-out. New numbers were played, commencing with the concert opener *Rough Justice,* with Mick Jagger on slide guitar, *Back Of My Hand,* Keith Richards' seven-minute *Infamy* and *Oh No Not You Again. Back Of My Hand* had an extended verse with a woman on a corner and children drawing in the sand, "And someone offers to read my fortune. I can read it like the back of my hand." The concert was filmed and two tracks were released on *The Biggest Bang* DVD and an almost complete *Back Of My Hand* which is in the A Bigger Bang Tour Documentary of the DVD. Rarer Phoenix songs played were a slowed down, new arrangement of *19th Nervous Breakdown, She's So Cold, Dead Flowers* and *Ain't Too Proud To Beg.* As well as rock, country and blues, *Get Up, Stand Up* was a rousing cover of a Bob Marley song; Mick and Keith wanted to perform a reggae tune and Mick contributes guitar and a convincing Jamaican patois, stirring the crowd to sing along. The soul genre made an appearance, too, in the shape of Otis Redding's *Mr. Pitiful,* which had also not been played before. It proved that they still wanted to extend their repartee and, after 14 numbers and one-and-a-half hours, the show was completed. The video footage on the DVD illustrates how small the venue was and how enjoyable a show it was for band and crowd alike. The fuse had been lit for the A BIGGER BANG Tour and the show would be considered in 2012 for the official live bootleg series.

1455. SHATTERED (Jagger, Richards) ✐ 4.44
21 August 2005: Place: Fenway Park, Boston, Massachusetts, USA.
Rolling Stones with Darryl Jones, Chuck Leavell.
Producer: Jake Cohl, Anthony Green
Engineer: FOH Sound Engineer: Dave Natale.
Bootleg only.

1456. BACK OF MY HAND (Jagger, Richards) ✐ 5.18
21 August 2005: Place: Fenway Park, Boston, Massachusetts, USA.
Rolling Stones with Darryl Jones, Chuck Leavell.
Producer: Jake Cohl, Anthony Green
Engineer: FOH Sound Engineer: Dave Natale.
Bootleg only.

The production team moved from Toronto to Boston for the start of the tour at Fenway Park, home of the Boston Red Sox baseball team, on 21 and 23 August (it was unusual on this tour to play two dates in one city). Generally the baseball stadiums were smaller than the larger football venues and theoretically a better target for sales. It was the first chance to see the huge stage, designed by Mark Fisher and Patrick Woodroffe, with pens resembling theatre boxes on tiers either side of the stage above the band. Tickets for the 400 "on stage" viewing points cost $500 each.
In reality, many of these elevated ticket holders amongst the stage structure were upgraded or special guests since, while a novelty, the price was a little prohibitive for many. Certainly they provided a different perspective for those perched amongst the artistic stage backdrop, overseeing the Stones' rears. Opening night is always very special and two tracks were shown in full at the official rollingstones.com website and enticed everyone with what was on offer. Before *Shattered,* Mick Jagger explained why they had selected Boston - because it was a champion city.
The Patriots had won the football Super Bowl and the Red Sox were the baseball World Series champions. Mick also made mention of hitting a ball over the Green Monster - the painted wall that housed the scoreboard. Jake Cohl and Anthony Green were the hand-held camera makers who produced tour material for the Stones official website. They also included professional film footage sometimes used for the stage jumbotron and helped to make *The Biggest Bang* tour DVD and documentary *Salt Of The Earth.*
Back Of My Hand was one of the four new album tracks played on opening night. *Rough Justice, Infamy* and *Oh No, Not You Again* were the others. Ron Wood was an additional guitarist for the live version, giving the song a more electric blues feel. Before the song, Mick said that, for opening night, many people had travelled far and wide, with some coming from England, New York and California. He made a mocking welcome to the then Governor of California, Arnold Schwarzenegger, who was fundraising for his electoral campaign by selling concert tickets for his own personal box. Mick quipped: "As a matter of fact, he was seen out in front of Fenway Park scalping tee-shirts and tickets."

1457. WILD HORSES (Jagger, Richard) ✐ 4.47
28 September 2005: Place: PNC Park, Pittsburgh, Pennsylvania, USA.
Rolling Stones with Eddie Vedder, Darryl Jones, Chuck Leavell.
Producer: The Rolling Stones
Engineer: Music Mix: Bob Clearmountain; Music Production: Ed Cherney; Additional Mixes / Engineer: Brandon Duncan; FOH Sound Engineer: Dave Natale.
Executive Producer: Michael Cohl, Director: Hamish Hamilton.
USA DVD The Biggest Bang: 23 June 2007
UK DVD The Biggest Bang: 5 August 2007

The first leg of the tour, from August until December, took in 42 dates and visited the USA and four Canadian venues, including one in the western territory of Calgary. Late in August, Hurricane Katrina wreaked its havoc on the coastline of south eastern United States, even breaking the levee in New Orleans. The circumstances were such that a national emergency was called as hundreds lost their lives and billions of dollars damage were done. As a small compensation, the Stones played *Waiting On A Friend* on 8 September during a very subdued performance in Milwaukee for subsequent broadcast and a music relief concert on national television two days later.

Buddy Guy was guest guitarist during a cover of Ray Charles' *Night Time Is The Right Time*, which was an alternative for *I'll Go Crazy*. They had also rehearsed Ray Charles' *Lonely Avenue*. A few weeks later, at the Nationwide Arena, Columbus, they also used Otis Redding's *Mr. Pitiful* in the same slot and this show, on 24 September, also saw a one-off performance of *Sway*. On 28 September, Pearl Jam supported the band in Pittsburgh and Eddie Vedder took to the stage to sing vocals on the second verse then dueted with Mick Jagger, the result appearing on *The Biggest Bang*. On 6 October, in Charlottesville, Virginia, just before Keith Richards' set, an unusual evacuation took place after a telephoned bomb threat to the stage area.

There was a 45-minute delay while police with sniffer dogs searched the area and, after the all-clear, the Stones re-commenced with *Miss You*. One of the biggest crowd pleasers that night was, of course, *Sweet Virginia* (or Sweet Vagina as Ron Wood called it in rehearsals). New songs from the album *Rain Fall Down* appeared in Philadelphia and *It Won't Take Long* at the prestigious, smaller Hollywood Bowl in Los Angeles. This second night at the Bowl also produced a set at the front of the stage where *As Tears Go By* was surprisingly played. California featured on the Stones' website with *Sympathy For The Devil*, from the first Hollywood show, and *Midnight Rambler* selected from San Diego's Petco Park. On arrival in Houston on 29 November, after the Dallas show, the European summer tour announcement was made.

The band were in mischievous form nearing the completion of the first leg of the tour. With Michael Cohl, they were waiting for different satellite feeds from various European countries. Short live sections of *Jumpin' Jack Flash* and *Rain Fall Down* were issued for potential transmission. The "on stage" name was dropped for A Bigger Bang and American Express took over the sponsor role from Ameriquest Mortgage. Mick Jagger announced some of the more unusual venues like St. Petersburg, Belgrade and Zagreb on a list which would culminate in Cardiff, in August.

After concerts at Houston and Memphis on 3 December, the band took a break until resumption in January 2006. During 2005, not only was A BIGGER BANG released, but also another ABKCO singles box set (from 1968 to 1971) was produced in February. It included a four-track DVD of rarer material featuring an Ed Sullivan transmission of *Time Is On My Side*, the promo versions of *Have You Seen Your Mother, Baby* and *Jumpin' Jack Flash*, together with the video of Neptune's Remix *Sympathy For The Devil*. In May, Tim Ries released an enjoyable CD, THE TIM RIES PROJECT, featuring Charlie Watts and Darryl Jones, with performances by Keith Richards and Ron Wood. In November, Virgin Records released a RARITIES 1971-2003 album.

It had poor sleeve notes and, despicably, a cover shot of the band in the 1978 video for *Respectable*, with Bill Wyman air-brushed out, despite the full photo being used within FORTY LICKS and him contributing to all but four tracks. The CD tracks were nothing more than obscure B-sides and shortened versions of released remixes, although to be fair some were from vinyl and UK-only compilations, released for the first time in digital format.

1458. START ME UP (Jagger, Richards) ⟋ 3.44
5 February 2006: Place: Ford Field, Detroit, Michigan, USA.
Rolling Stones with Darryl Jones, Chuck Leavell.
Producer: Don Mischer Productions.
Engineer: Don Was; FOH Sound Engineer: Dave Natale.
USA DVD NFL Super Bowl XL - Pittsburgh Steelers Championship: 28 February 2006
USA DVD NFL Super Bowl I-XL Collector's Set: 8 August 2006

1459. ROUGH JUSTICE (Jagger, Richards) ⟋ 2.49
5 February 2006: Place: Ford Field, Detroit, Michigan, USA.
Rolling Stones with Darryl Jones, Chuck Leavell.
Producer: Don Mischer Productions.
Engineer: Don Was; FOH Sound Engineer: Dave Natale.
USA DVD NFL Super Bowl XL - Pittsburgh Steelers Championship: 28 February 2006
USA DVD NFL Super Bowl I-XL Collector's Set: 8 August 2006

1460. (I CAN'T GET NO) SATISFACTION (Jagger, Richard) ⟋ 5.25
5 February 2006: Place: Ford Field, Detroit, Michigan, USA.
Rolling Stones with Darryl Jones, Chuck Leavell.
Producer: Don Mischer Productions.
Engineer: Don Was; FOH Sound Engineer: Dave Natale.
USA DVD NFL Super Bowl XL - Pittsburgh Steelers Championship: 28 February 2006
USA DVD NFL Super Bowl I-XL Collector's Set: 8 August 2006

The tour resumed in Montreal, Canada, on 10 January 2006, after more than a month off. Additional songs (from the album *This Place Is Empty*) were added to the set list as the Stones returned to places already played in the USA for a short, seven-city arena tour leg. One commitment that they were keen to fulfil was a performance at the NFL Super Bowl half-time show, which had previously showcased Gloria Estefan, Michael Jackson, Diana Ross, U2 and, the year previously, Paul McCartney. The venue was Detroit's Ford Field and the date Sunday 5 February for the Pittsburgh Steelers versus Seattle Seahawks showdown.

The stage had to be assembled during half-time on the pitch area and a tongue-shaped design was chosen, with an open mouth in the middle, where a small crowd would be able to watch. This had to be wheeled into position in different segments and 350 volunteers were recruited a month earlier for this task with a commitment to attend two days of rehearsals. In a press conference, the Stones were cannily asked whether they had moved closer to the USA mainstream culture or had the culture moved closer to them since the first Super Bowl in 1967? Diplomatically, Mick Jagger replied "both", explaining that a lot had changed and hopefully they both had their core values still intact. Exactly 40 years before, the Stones had appeared on the Ed Sullivan show the same night as the first Super Bowl and, in 2006, they were still subject to censoring!

The band, together with lighting, sound, dry ice, pyrotechnics, guitars, amplifiers and essential backstage staff, were placed in position in five-and-a-half minutes. A large drape covered the middle section until this was peeled back at the beginning of *Start Me Up* revealing the crowd. Without hesitating, this was followed by *Rough Justice* after which Mick said that the next song could have been performed at Super Bowl number one - it was, of course, a rapid fire *Satisfaction*. After 13 minutes, the show was dismantled and moved back into the bowels of the stadium. Don Was lived in Detroit and recorded the show, enabling Ed Cherney to have some down time.

1461. JUMPIN' JACK FLASH (Jagger, Richard) ✎ 3.53
18 February 2006: Place: Copacabana Beach, Rio De Janeiro, Brazil.
Rolling Stones with Darryl Jones, Chuck Leavell, Blondie Chaplin.
Producer: The Rolling Stones, Marty Callner, Randall Gladstein.
Engineer: Music Mix: Bob Clearmountain; Music Production: Ed Cherney, Kooster McAllister; Additional Mixes / Engineer: Brandon Duncan; FOH Sound Engineer: Dave Natale.
Executive Producer: Michael Cohl, Director: J.B. De Oliveira.
USA DVD The Biggest Bang: 23 June 2007
UK DVD The Biggest Bang: 5 August 2007

The North American leg was concluded at Philips Arena, Atlanta, before they hopped off to the Caribbean island of Puerto Rico for an inaugural concert there. The venue was the state-of-the-art Coliseum in San Juan, dedicated to entertainer Jos' Miguel Agrelot. Next they skipped down for a short, five-date stint in South America. The first concert was a small beach party on Rio de Janeiro's Copacabana glowing sands. This had been used for rock events before and was the scene for a bash by Rod Stewart on New Year's Eve 1994. More than three million had partied that evening.

The Stones were expecting a large crowd, too, for the show was free and the stage scaffolding was built more than a week before the touring production crew arrived from Puerto Rico to assemble the stage in 35-degree heat. There were also the normal beach distractions of Latin "bunda" and cooling waves in the shadow of Sugar Loaf mountain. Some of the backline crew (Mike Cormier, Dave Rouze, Philip de Beauport and Alan Clayton plus Bernard "shidoob" Fowler) played gigs on the tour and sound-checked some songs during the heat of the day.

The normal A Bigger Bang towers and platforms could not be used due to the construction having to be made on shifting sands so Mark Fisher designed a lightweight one, with red and black arrowed chevrons which was named "Latin America". Even the 25-metre high stage was built precariously close to its weight limits as Charlie Watts' drum riser initially cracked the temporary floor.

Electrical cables had to be fed under the sand to power the gig and 16 relay towers served sound, video and music over two-and-a-half kilometres of the beach length, not to mention construction of the B-stage and travelator. The Stones stayed in the Copacabana Palace hotel, which had a prime location looking over the venue and the promoters built an extravagant platform walkway to take the band personnel to the stage. Mick Jagger later said that he would have been quite happy to use a people carrier. Much of the band's entourage had seaward hotel vantage points, which welcomed the beach dwellers and flotilla of boats.

They could see the atmosphere and expectation build as they peeked from behind the bedroom curtains. About five hours before the group were unleashed, Michael Cohl predicted there were 100,000 in attendance but this quickly swelled as the day's heat turned into the evening's afterglow, with fans and arriving from the bars. Police estimated the final crowd size at one-and-a-quarter million, which was a little nerve-wracking even for the likes of Mick Jagger. Keith Richards did not find he got nervous but tended to lose his appetite before a gig and could get some icy feelings.

1462. IT'S ONLY ROCK 'N' ROLL (Jagger, Richard) ✎ 4.32
18 February 2006: Place: Copacabana Beach, Rio De Janeiro, Brazil.
Rolling Stones with Darryl Jones, Chuck Leavell, Blondie Chaplin, Lisa Fischer.
Producer: The Rolling Stones, Marty Callner, Randall Gladstein.
Engineer: Music Mix: Bob Clearmountain; Music Production: Ed Cherney, Kooster McAllister; Additional Mixes / Engineer: Brandon Duncan; FOH Sound Engineer: Dave Natale.
Executive Producer: Michael Cohl, Director: J.B. De Oliveira.
USA DVD The Biggest Bang: 23 June 2007
UK DVD The Biggest Bang: 5 August 2007

1463. YOU GOT ME ROCKING (Jagger, Richards) ✎ 3.17
18 February 2006: Place: Copacabana Beach, Rio De Janeiro, Brazil.
Rolling Stones with Darryl Jones, Chuck Leavell, Blondie Chaplin.
Producer: The Rolling Stones, Marty Callner, Randall Gladstein.
Engineer: Music Mix: Bob Clearmountain; Music Production: Ed Cherney, Kooster McAllister; Additional Mixes / Engineer: Brandon Duncan; FOH Sound Engineer: Dave Natale.
Executive Producer: Michael Cohl, Director: J.B. De Oliveira.
USA DVD The Biggest Bang: 23 June 2007
UK DVD The Biggest Bang: 5 August 2007

1464. TUMBLING DICE (Jagger, Richard) ✎ 4.19
18 February 2006: Place: Copacabana Beach, Rio De Janeiro, Brazil.
Rolling Stones with Darryl Jones, Chuck Leavell, Bobby Keys, Lisa Fischer, Bernard Fowler, Blondie Chaplin, Tim Ries, Michael Davis, Kent Smith
Producer: The Rolling Stones, Marty Callner, Randall Gladstein.
Engineer: Music Mix: Bob Clearmountain; Music Production: Ed Cherney, Kooster McAllister; Additional Mixes / Engineer: Brandon Duncan; FOH Sound Engineer: Dave Natale.
Executive Producer: Michael Cohl, Director: J.B. De Oliveira.
Bootleg only.

1465.   OH NO, NOT YOU AGAIN (Jagger, Richards) ✎ 4.01
18 February 2006: Place: Copacabana Beach, Rio De Janeiro, Brazil.
Rolling Stones with Darryl Jones, Chuck Leavell, Lisa Fischer, Bernard Fowler, Blondie Chaplin.
Producer: The Rolling Stones, Marty Callner, Randall Gladstein.
Engineer: Music Mix: Bob Clearmountain; Music Production: Ed Cherney, Kooster McAllister; Additional Mixes / Engineer: Brandon Duncan; FOH Sound Engineer: Dave Natale.
Executive Producer: Michael Cohl, Director: J.B. De Oliveira.
Bootleg only.

1466.   WILD HORSES (Jagger, Richard) ✎ 5.24
18 February 2006: Place: Copacabana Beach, Rio De Janeiro, Brazil.
Rolling Stones with Darryl Jones, Chuck Leavell, Lisa Fischer, Bernard Fowler, Blondie Chaplin, Tim Ries.
Producer: The Rolling Stones, Marty Callner, Randall Gladstein.
Engineer: Music Mix: Bob Clearmountain; Music Production: Ed Cherney, Kooster McAllister; Additional Mixes / Engineer: Brandon Duncan; FOH Sound Engineer: Dave Natale.
Executive Producer: Michael Cohl, Director: J.B. De Oliveira.
USA DVD The Biggest Bang: 23 June 2007
UK DVD The Biggest Bang: 5 August 2007

1467.   RAIN FALL DOWN (Jagger, Richards) ✎ 5.45
18 February 2006: Place: Copacabana Beach, Rio De Janeiro, Brazil.
Rolling Stones with Darryl Jones, Chuck Leavell, Lisa Fischer, Bernard Fowler, Blondie Chaplin.
Producer: The Rolling Stones, Marty Callner, Randall Gladstein.
Engineer: Music Mix: Bob Clearmountain; Music Production: Ed Cherney, Kooster McAllister; Additional Mixes / Engineer: Brandon Duncan; FOH Sound Engineer: Dave Natale.
Executive Producer: Michael Cohl, Director: J.B. De Oliveira.
USA DVD The Biggest Bang: 23 June 2007
UK DVD The Biggest Bang: 5 August 2007

1468.   MIDNIGHT RAMBLER (Jagger, Richard) ✎ 11.53
18 February 2006: Place: Copacabana Beach, Rio De Janeiro, Brazil.
Rolling Stones with Darryl Jones, Chuck Leavell.
Producer: The Rolling Stones, Marty Callner, Randall Gladstein.
Engineer: Music Mix: Bob Clearmountain; Music Production: Ed Cherney, Kooster McAllister; Additional Mixes / Engineer: Brandon Duncan; FOH Sound Engineer: Dave Natale.
Executive Producer: Michael Cohl, Director: J.B. De Oliveira.
USA DVD The Biggest Bang: 23 June 2007
UK DVD The Biggest Bang: 5 August 2007

1469.   NIGHT TIME IS THE RIGHT TIME (Herman) ✎ 8.38
18 February 2006: Place: Copacabana Beach, Rio De Janeiro, Brazil.
Rolling Stones with Darryl Jones, Chuck Leavell, Bobby Keys, Lisa Fischer, Bernard Fowler, Blondie Chaplin, Tim Ries, Michael Davis, Kent Smith
Producer: The Rolling Stones, Marty Callner, Randall Gladstein.
Engineer: Music Mix: Bob Clearmountain; Music Production: Ed Cherney, Kooster McAllister; Additional Mixes / Engineer: Brandon Duncan; FOH Sound Engineer: Dave Natale.
Executive Producer: Michael Cohl, Director: J.B. De Oliveira.
USA DVD The Biggest Bang: 23 June 2007
UK DVD The Biggest Bang: 5 August 2007

1470.   THIS PLACE IS EMPTY (Jagger, Richards) ✎ 3.34
18 February 2006: Place: Copacabana Beach, Rio De Janeiro, Brazil.
Rolling Stones with Darryl Jones, Chuck Leavell, Bobby Keys, Lisa Fischer, Bernard Fowler, Blondie Chaplin, Tim Ries, Michael Davis, Kent Smith
Producer: The Rolling Stones, Marty Callner, Randall Gladstein.
Engineer: Music Mix: Bob Clearmountain; Music Production: Ed Cherney, Kooster McAllister; Additional Mixes / Engineer: Brandon Duncan; FOH Sound Engineer: Dave Natale.
Executive Producer: Michael Cohl, Director: J.B. De Oliveira.
Bootleg only.

1471.   HAPPY (Jagger, Richard) ✎ 3.36
18 February 2006: Place: Copacabana Beach, Rio De Janeiro, Brazil.
Rolling Stones with Darryl Jones, Chuck Leavell, Bobby Keys, Lisa Fischer, Bernard Fowler, Blondie Chaplin, Tim Ries, Michael Davis, Kent Smith
Producer: The Rolling Stones, Marty Callner, Randall Gladstein.
Engineer: Music Mix: Bob Clearmountain; Music Production: Ed Cherney, Kooster McAllister; Additional Mixes / Engineer: Brandon Duncan; FOH Sound Engineer: Dave Natale.
Executive Producer: Michael Cohl, Director: J.B. De Oliveira.
USA DVD The Biggest Bang: 23 June 2007
UK DVD The Biggest Bang: 5 August 2007

1472. MISS YOU (Jagger, Richards) ∕ 5.38
18 February 2006: Place: Copacabana Beach, Rio De Janeiro, Brazil.
Rolling Stones with Darryl Jones, Chuck Leavell, Lisa Fischer, Bernard Fowler, Blondie Chaplin.
Producer: The Rolling Stones, Marty Callner, Randall Gladstein.
Engineer: Music Mix: Bob Clearmountain; Music Production: Ed Cherney, Kooster McAllister; Additional Mixes / Engineer: Brandon Duncan; FOH Sound Engineer: Dave Natale.
Executive Producer: Michael Cohl, Director: J.B. De Oliveira.
USA DVD The Biggest Bang: 23 June 2007
UK DVD The Biggest Bang: 5 August 2007

1473. ROUGH JUSTICE (Jagger, Richards) ∕ 3.18
18 February 2006: Place: Copacabana Beach, Rio De Janeiro, Brazil.
Rolling Stones with Darryl Jones, Chuck Leavell.
Producer: The Rolling Stones, Marty Callner, Randall Gladstein.
Engineer: Music Mix: Bob Clearmountain; Music Production: Ed Cherney, Kooster McAllister; Additional Mixes / Engineer: Brandon Duncan; FOH Sound Engineer: Dave Natale.
Executive Producer: Michael Cohl, Director: J.B. De Oliveira.
USA DVD The Biggest Bang: 23 June 2007
UK DVD The Biggest Bang: 5 August 2007

1474. GET OFF MY CLOUD (Jagger, Richard) ∕ 3.17
18 February 2006: Place: Copacabana Beach, Rio De Janeiro, Brazil.
Rolling Stones with Darryl Jones, Chuck Leavell, Lisa Fischer.
Producer: The Rolling Stones, Marty Callner, Randall Gladstein.
Engineer: Music Mix: Bob Clearmountain; Music Production: Ed Cherney, Kooster McAllister; Additional Mixes / Engineer: Brandon Duncan; FOH Sound Engineer: Dave Natale.
Executive Producer: Michael Cohl, Director: J.B. De Oliveira.
USA DVD The Biggest Bang: 23 June 2007
UK DVD The Biggest Bang: 5 August 2007

1475. HONKY TONK WOMEN (Jagger, Richard) ∕ 4.11
18 February 2006: Place: Copacabana Beach, Rio De Janeiro, Brazil.
Rolling Stones with Darryl Jones, Chuck Leavell, Bobby Keys, Lisa Fischer, Bernard Fowler, Blondie Chaplin, Tim Ries, Michael Davis, Kent Smith.
Producer: The Rolling Stones, Marty Callner, Randall Gladstein.
Engineer: Music Mix: Bob Clearmountain; Music Production: Ed Cherney, Kooster McAllister; Additional Mixes / Engineer: Brandon Duncan; FOH Sound Engineer: Dave Natale.
Executive Producer: Michael Cohl, Director: J.B. De Oliveira.
USA DVD The Biggest Bang: 23 June 2007
UK DVD The Biggest Bang: 5 August 2007

1476. SYMPATHY FOR THE DEVIL (Jagger, Richard) ∕ 7.51
18 February 2006: Place: Copacabana Beach, Rio De Janeiro, Brazil.
Rolling Stones with Darryl Jones, Chuck Leavell, Lisa Fischer, Bernard Fowler, Blondie Chaplin.
Producer: The Rolling Stones, Marty Callner, Randall Gladstein.
Engineer: Music Mix: Bob Clearmountain; Music Production: Ed Cherney, Kooster McAllister; Additional Mixes / Engineer: Brandon Duncan; FOH Sound Engineer: Dave Natale.
Executive Producer: Michael Cohl, Director: J.B. De Oliveira.
Bootleg only.

1477. START ME UP (Jagger, Richards) ∕ 3.59
18 February 2006: Place: Copacabana Beach, Rio De Janeiro, Brazil.
Rolling Stones with Darryl Jones, Chuck Leavell, Lisa Fischer, Bernard Fowler, Blondie Chaplin.
Producer: The Rolling Stones, Marty Callner, Randall Gladstein.
Engineer: Music Mix: Bob Clearmountain; Music Production: Ed Cherney, Kooster McAllister; Additional Mixes / Engineer: Brandon Duncan; FOH Sound Engineer: Dave Natale.
Executive Producer: Michael Cohl, Director: J.B. De Oliveira.
USA DVD The Biggest Bang: 23 June 2007
UK DVD The Biggest Bang: 5 August 2007

1478. BROWN SUGAR (Jagger, Richard) ∕ 6.37
18 February 2006: Place: Copacabana Beach, Rio De Janeiro, Brazil.
Rolling Stones with Darryl Jones, Chuck Leavell, Bobby Keys, Lisa Fischer, Bernard Fowler, Blondie Chaplin, Tim Ries, Michael Davis, Kent Smith
Producer: The Rolling Stones, Marty Callner, Randall Gladstein.
Engineer: Music Mix: Bob Clearmountain; Music Production: Ed Cherney, Kooster McAllister; Additional Mixes / Engineer: Brandon Duncan; FOH Sound Engineer: Dave Natale.
Executive Producer: Michael Cohl, Director: J.B. De Oliveira.
USA DVD The Biggest Bang: 23 June 2007
UK DVD The Biggest Bang: 5 August 2007

1479.   YOU CAN'T ALWAYS GET WHAT YOU WANT (Jagger, Richard) ✏ 7.10
18 February 2006: Place: Copacabana Beach, Rio De Janeiro, Brazil.
Rolling Stones with Darryl Jones, Chuck Leavell, Lisa Fischer, Bernard Fowler, Blondie Chaplin, Tim Ries.
Producer: The Rolling Stones, Marty Callner, Randall Gladstein.
Engineer: Music Mix: Bob Clearmountain; Music Production: Ed Cherney, Kooster McAllister; Additional Mixes / Engineer: Brandon Duncan; FOH Sound Engineer: Dave Natale.
Executive Producer: Michael Cohl, Director: J.B. De Oliveira.
USA DVD The Biggest Bang: 23 June 2007
UK DVD The Biggest Bang: 5 August 2007

1480.   (I CAN'T GET NO) SATISFACTION (Jagger, Richard) ✏ 8.18
18 February 2006: Place: Copacabana Beach, Rio De Janeiro, Brazil.
Rolling Stones with Darryl Jones, Chuck Leavell, Bobby Keys, Lisa Fischer, Bernard Fowler, Blondie Chaplin, Tim Ries, Michael Davis, Kent Smith
Producer: The Rolling Stones, Marty Callner, Randall Gladstein.
Engineer: Music Mix: Bob Clearmountain; Music Production: Ed Cherney, Kooster McAllister; Additional Mixes / Engineer: Brandon Duncan; FOH Sound Engineer: Dave Natale.
Executive Producer: Michael Cohl, Director: J.B. De Oliveira.
USA DVD The Biggest Bang: 23 June 2007
UK DVD The Biggest Bang: 5 August 2007

Just before ten o'clock, as darkness encroached the vast spectacle, they ventured across the bridge to the temporary sand castle and held back the tide for two hours with their own power of rock and Canute. With concentration etched on their faces, they powered into *Jumpin' Jack Flash* and *It's Only Rock 'n' Roll* as the crowd came to terms with what was happening before them. As well as the throng, there were also live television feeds to Canada, USA and Mexico and the investment in extra cameras for the eventual worldwide video release.

It was not until the mid-section of *Midnight Rambler* and the blues interpretation of *Night Time Is The Right Time*, giving Lisa Fischer her tour spotlight, that the atmosphere accelerated. The trip to the B-stage seemed to take them deeper into potentially tricky territory, away from the VIP section, as the crowd's density and vocal levels soared. During *Honky Tonk Women*, the final song before the return to the mother stage, t-shirts were being waved frantically in a circular motion. For the two-song encore, Mick Jagger wore a Brazilian national t-shirt to enhance the frenzy. Due to safety issues, there were no fireworks to signify the show's end, though Patrick Woodroffe was asked to replace them with a barrage of lights, which equated to Brazil's own bigger bang.

Guitar technician Johnny Starbuck summed up the event afterwards, describing the audience as an endless mass of people but shrugged and said he regarded his job in the same way whether it be for an audience of one-and-a-half million or in a small theatre. For such a large gig, it was incredibly well-managed and was testament to the power of the Stones, their management and crew, Rio and the Brazilian nation. Certainly it will sustain its rightful place in Stones folklore as theirs and the world's biggest rock concert ever - apart from those on a New Year's Eve.

1481.   WORRIED ABOUT YOU (Jagger, Richards) ✏ 6.20
21 February 2006: Place: River Plate Stadium, Buenos Aires, Argentina.
Rolling Stones with Darryl Jones, Chuck Leavell, Lisa Fischer, Bernard Fowler, Blondie Chaplin, Tim Ries.
Producer: The Rolling Stones, Marty Callner, Randall Gladstein.
Engineer: Music Mix: Bob Clearmountain; Music Production: Ed Cherney, Kooster McAllister; Additional Mixes / Engineer: Brandon Duncan; FOH Sound Engineer: Dave Natale.
Executive Producer: Michael Cohl, Director: Fernando Rolon.
USA DVD The Biggest Bang: 23 June 2007
UK DVD The Biggest Bang: 5 August 2007

1482.   HAPPY (Jagger, Richard) ✏ 4.05
21 February 2006: Place: River Plate Stadium, Buenos Aires, Argentina.
Rolling Stones with Darryl Jones, Chuck Leavell, Bobby Keys, Lisa Fischer, Bernard Fowler, Blondie Chaplin, Tim Ries, Michael Davis, Kent Smith
Producer: The Rolling Stones, Marty Callner, Randall Gladstein.
Engineer: Music Mix: Bob Clearmountain; Music Production: Ed Cherney, Kooster McAllister; Additional Mixes / Engineer: Brandon Duncan; FOH Sound Engineer: Dave Natale.
Executive Producer: Michael Cohl, Director: Fernando Rolon.
USA DVD The Biggest Bang: 23 June 2007
UK DVD The Biggest Bang: 5 August 2007

1483.   MISS YOU (Jagger, Richards) ✏ 6.49
21 February 2006: Place: River Plate Stadium, Buenos Aires, Argentina.
Rolling Stones with Darryl Jones, Chuck Leavell, Lisa Fischer, Bernard Fowler, Blondie Chaplin.
Producer: The Rolling Stones, Marty Callner, Randall Gladstein.
Engineer: Music Mix: Bob Clearmountain; Music Production: Ed Cherney, Kooster McAllister; Additional Mixes / Engineer: Brandon Duncan; FOH Sound Engineer: Dave Natale.
Executive Producer: Michael Cohl, Director: Fernando Rolon.
USA DVD The Biggest Bang: 23 June 2007
UK DVD The Biggest Bang: 5 August 2007

1484. PAINT IT BLACK (Jagger, Richard) ⤳ 4.26
21 February 2006: Place: River Plate Stadium, Buenos Aires, Argentina.
Rolling Stones with Darryl Jones, Chuck Leavell, Lisa Fischer, Bernard Fowler, Blondie Chaplin.
Producer: The Rolling Stones, Marty Callner, Randall Gladstein.
Engineer: Music Mix: Bob Clearmountain; Music Production: Ed Cherney, Kooster McAllister; Additional Mixes / Engineer: Brandon Duncan; FOH Sound Engineer: Dave Natale.
Executive Producer: Michael Cohl, Director: Fernando Rolon.
USA DVD The Biggest Bang: 23 June 2007
UK DVD The Biggest Bang: 5 August 2007

1485. (I CAN'T GET NO) SATISFACTION (Jagger, Richard) ⤳ 8.25
21 February 2006: Place: River Plate Stadium, Buenos Aires, Argentina.
Rolling Stones with Darryl Jones, Chuck Leavell, Bobby Keys, Lisa Fischer, Bernard Fowler, Blondie Chaplin, Tim Ries, Michael Davis, Kent Smith
Producer: The Rolling Stones, Marty Callner, Randall Gladstein.
Engineer: Music Mix: Bob Clearmountain; Music Production: Ed Cherney, Kooster McAllister; Additional Mixes / Engineer: Brandon Duncan; FOH Sound Engineer: Dave Natale.
Executive Producer: Michael Cohl, Director: Fernando Rolon.
USA DVD The Biggest Bang: 23 June 2007
UK DVD The Biggest Bang: 5 August 2007

The band had some expectation of what might greet them in Buenos Aires but even they must have been surprised that, over the ensuing years, the fan fervour had not diminished. The Argentinians were in a different league - "absolutely insane" said Charlie Watts; "the most amazing, energetic, enthusiastic audience anybody could ask for", said Keith Richards. They used the same stage design as Rio but it was very much scaled back for just an intimate 50,000 crowd for two nights. The second evening was wet so the footage and recordings from the first concert were used for inclusion on *The Biggest Bang* world tour disc.
Kooster McAllister, from Record Plant Remote, was selected by Ed Cherney to record the Rio and Buenos Aires shows. The travel to the B-stage during *Miss You* saw the crowd moving like shoal fish following their prize food. The small stage floor resembled a day's end at the sales with clothes and undergarments scattered on the floor. *Paint It Black* was particularly favoured by the Latin crowd and, during *Satisfaction*, the torsos looked like a churning, bacchanalian sea. The whole show was professionally filmed and broadcast on national television. The end result was a great coming together of band and crowd reaction.
Twenty fans were injured and dozens arrested on the second night, when violence broke out as fans without tickets battled against police outside the River Plate stadium. Police retaliated with water cannons, clubs and rubber bullets to hold back the crowd. Two dates in the relative quiet of Mexico ensued and then a very brief five-date visit to the USA. The last commitment was at Radio City Music Hall, a smaller gig in New York in aid of the Robin Hood Foundation poverty charity. More than 11 million dollars was raised and Mick Jagger indicated that the audience was their wealthiest ever - and they had probably had the most marriages too. *Shattered* was played to all the Big Apple types and this concluded their USA shows for the time being.

1486. LET'S SPEND THE NIGHT TOGETHER (Jagger, Richard) ⤳ 4.02
2 April 2006: Place: Saitama Super Arena, Saitama, Japan.
Rolling Stones with Darryl Jones, Chuck Leavell, Lisa Fischer, Bernard Fowler, Blondie Chaplin.
Producer: The Rolling Stones
Engineer: Music Mix: Bob Clearmountain; Music Production: Ed Cherney; Additional Mixes / Engineer: Brandon Duncan; FOH Sound Engineer: Dave Natale.
Executive Producer: Michael Cohl, Director: Toru Uehara.
USA DVD The Biggest Bang: 23 June 2007
UK DVD The Biggest Bang: 5 August 2007
USA Blu-Ray DVD The Biggest Bang: 16 June 2009
UK Blu-Ray DVD The Biggest Bang: 29 June 2009

1487. RAIN FALL DOWN (Jagger, Richards) ⤳ 5.45
2 April 2006: Place: Saitama Super Arena, Saitama, Japan.
Rolling Stones with Darryl Jones, Chuck Leavell, Lisa Fischer, Bernard Fowler, Blondie Chaplin.
Producer: The Rolling Stones
Engineer: Music Mix: Bob Clearmountain; Music Production: Ed Cherney; Additional Mixes / Engineer: Brandon Duncan; FOH Sound Engineer: Dave Natale.
Executive Producer: Michael Cohl, Director: Toru Uehara.
USA DVD The Biggest Bang: 23 June 2007
UK DVD The Biggest Bang: 5 August 2007
USA Blu-Ray DVD The Biggest Bang: 16 June 2009
UK Blu-Ray DVD The Biggest Bang: 29 June 2009

1488. ROUGH JUSTICE (Jagger, Richards) ⤳ 3.25
2 April 2006: Place: Saitama Super Arena, Saitama, Japan.
Rolling Stones with Darryl Jones, Chuck Leavell.
Producer: The Rolling Stones
Engineer: Music Mix: Bob Clearmountain; Music Production: Ed Cherney; Additional Mixes / Engineer: Brandon Duncan; FOH Sound Engineer: Dave Natale.
Executive Producer: Michael Cohl, Director: Toru Uehara.
USA DVD The Biggest Bang: 23 June 2007
UK DVD The Biggest Bang: 5 August 2007
USA Blu-Ray DVD The Biggest Bang: 16 June 2009
UK Blu-Ray DVD The Biggest Bang: 29 June 2009

A wider than usual five-date tour of the treasure island of Japan was next, following on a week later. In a press call, Michael Cohl said that they were about to play to their one millionth customer since 1990. As well as two Tokyo Dome concerts, they performed in a cold Sapporo on the northern island, Saitama and Nagoya, closer to Tokyo. Saitama was the smallest venue and the one chosen for audio and video recording. *Rain Fall Down* was growing into the arena set list as the backing singers took it to heart and Darryl Jones gained the spotlight for his bass solo. Dave Natale was credited for his part in the sound production, though his role for the whole tour was as the Stones' front of house sound mixer.

1489.   BITCH (Jagger, Richard) ✏ 4.38
8 April 2006: Place: The Grand Stage, Shanghai, China.
Rolling Stones with Darryl Jones, Chuck Leavell, Bobby Keys, Bernard Fowler, Tim Ries, Michael Davis, Kent Smith
Producer: The Rolling Stones
Engineer: Music Mix: Bob Clearmountain; Music Production: Ed Cherney; Additional Mixes / Engineer: Brandon Duncan; FOH Sound Engineer: Dave Natale.
Executive Producer: Michael Cohl, Director: Mr. Wang Xianshen.
USA DVD The Biggest Bang: 23 June 2007
UK DVD The Biggest Bang: 5 August 2007

1490.   WILD HORSES (Jagger, Richard) ✏ 5.16
8 April 2006: Place: The Grand Stage, Shanghai, China.
Rolling Stones with Cui Jian, Darryl Jones, Chuck Leavell, Bobby Keys, Lisa Fischer, Bernard Fowler, Blondie Chaplin, Tim Ries, Michael Davis, Kent Smith
Producer: The Rolling Stones
Engineer: Music Mix: Bob Clearmountain; Music Production: Ed Cherney; Additional Mixes / Engineer: Brandon Duncan; FOH Sound Engineer: Dave Natale.
Executive Producer: Michael Cohl, Director: Mr. Wang Xianshen.
USA DVD The Biggest Bang: 23 June 2007
UK DVD The Biggest Bang: 5 August 2007

1491.   MIDNIGHT RAMBLER (Jagger, Richard) ✏ 7.43
8 April 2006: Place: The Grand Stage, Shanghai, China.
Rolling Stones with Darryl Jones, Chuck Leavell.
Producer: The Rolling Stones
Engineer: Music Mix: Bob Clearmountain; Music Production: Ed Cherney; Additional Mixes / Engineer: Brandon Duncan; FOH Sound Engineer: Dave Natale.
Executive Producer: Michael Cohl, Director: Mr. Wang Xianshen.
USA DVD The Biggest Bang: 23 June 2007
UK DVD The Biggest Bang: 5 August 2007

1492.   GIMME SHELTER (Jagger, Richard) ✏ 6.18
8 April 2006: Place: The Grand Stage, Shanghai, China.
Rolling Stones with Darryl Jones, Chuck Leavell, Lisa Fischer, Bernard Fowler, Blondie Chaplin.
Producer: The Rolling Stones
Engineer: Music Mix: Bob Clearmountain; Music Production: Ed Cherney; Additional Mixes / Engineer: Brandon Duncan; FOH Sound Engineer: Dave Natale.
Executive Producer: Michael Cohl, Director: Mr. Wang Xianshen.
USA DVD The Biggest Bang: 23 June 2007
UK DVD The Biggest Bang: 5 August 2007

1493.   THIS PLACE IS EMPTY (Jagger, Richards) ✏ 3.23
8 April 2006: Place: The Grand Stage, Shanghai, China.
Rolling Stones with Darryl Jones, Chuck Leavell, Bobby Keys, Lisa Fischer, Bernard Fowler, Blondie Chaplin, Tim Ries, Michael Davis, Kent Smith
Producer: The Rolling Stones
Engineer: Music Mix: Bob Clearmountain; Music Production: Ed Cherney; Additional Mixes / Engineer: Brandon Duncan; FOH Sound Engineer: Dave Natale.
Executive Producer: Michael Cohl, Director: Mr. Wang Xianshen.
USA DVD The Biggest Bang: 23 June 2007
UK DVD The Biggest Bang: 5 August 2007

1494.   IT'S ONLY ROCK 'N' ROLL (Jagger, Richard) ✏ 4.32
8 April 2006: Place: The Grand Stage, Shanghai, China.
Rolling Stones with Darryl Jones, Chuck Leavell, Lisa Fischer, Bernard Fowler, Blondie Chaplin.
Producer: The Rolling Stones
Engineer: Music Mix: Bob Clearmountain; Music Production: Ed Cherney; Additional Mixes / Engineer: Brandon Duncan; FOH Sound Engineer: Dave Natale.
Executive Producer: Michael Cohl, Director: Mr. Wang Xianshen.
USA DVD The Biggest Bang: 23 June 2007
UK DVD The Biggest Bang: 5 August 2007

The concert, in the smog of Shanghai in mainland China, had been a long time coming. They had tried to gain access to the country during the VOODOO LOUNGE 1995 tour but were labelled then as "cultural pollution". Censorship and control were very much part of the Chinese Government administration but approval of a Stones visit represented a proffered olive branch and a thaw in what had been a cold relationship. The group were all genuinely excited about visiting and playing the eastern coast city of Shanghai. Western rock music was not encouraged but a movement which empathised with students had been born in 1984 and culminated during the oppression of Tiananmen Square in 1989.

The so-called instigator and father of Chinese rock was Cui Jian. He was given permission to support the Stones during the Licks tour when SARS had prevented the concert taking place. The complete ban of Cui Jian playing in China was only removed during 2005. A list was provided by the authorities of the songs that the Stones were not permitted to play, such as *Beast Of Burden* and *Honky Tonk Women*. However, they could make a "dead man cum" and "bitch" all they want, which they duly did at the Grand Stage! The aforementioned Cui Jian slowly approached the already-started *Wild Horses* and joined Mick Jagger to sing a chorus and verse and also play acoustic strums.

At the end, he celebrated 20 years of Chinese rock. From the video tape, it was clear that the first rows were kept for seated dignitaries and local authorities but the odd ex-pat could be seen, along with more enthusiastic concert goers and overseas visitors a little further back. Another landmark and touring notch had been achieved, Keith Richards admitting it was not often that these days he achieved a "first" experience. The remaining part of the tour took in two short dates in Australia and two stadiums in New Zealand before a six week lay-off and the start of the already announced European stretch. That would start in Barcelona on 27 May and was due to finish at Cardiff 's Millennium Stadium on 29 August 2006.

So they went their separate ways, Charlie Watts and Mick Jagger returning to Europe, while Ron Wood and Keith Richards flew 1,600 miles north to the private island of Wakaya, a short distance east of Fiji for a tropical holiday with their wives. Just over a week later, on 28 April, reports started to emanate from news sources that Keith had suffered a head injury and was being taken to Suva hospital on the Fiji mainland. A day later, on Sunday, newspapers in Australia were reporting that this occurred on Thursday 26th when he was examined and then flown the same day to hospital in Auckland, New Zealand.

Apparently Keith had fallen from a palm tree causing a serious head injury. A Stones spokesperson confirmed that he suffered mild concussion and was flown to hospital for observation but was unaware how the incident had happened. Newspaper reports on 8 May stated he had a subdural haematoma brain operation at some point and was in recovery, causing the tour to be delayed. Keith was discharged on 11 May and returned to his home in USA by 22 May, thankfully making a full recovery.

The tour was officially re-scheduled and shortened, recommencing on 11 July in Milan, Italy and concluding on 3 September in Denmark. The postponed shows would be rearranged, leading to speculation that maybe this would take place the following year since fans were advised to hold on to their tickets or apply for a refund. In July, it was also announced that there would be a Fall tour the of USA.

1495. I CAN'T BE SATISFIED (McKinley, Morganfield) 3.32
6-8 July 2006: Place: Discotheque Alcatraz, Milan, Italy.
Rolling Stones with Darryl Jones.
Producer: The Rolling Stones.
Engineer: Music Mix: Bob Clearmountain; Music Production: Ed Cherney; Additional Mixes / Engineer: Brandon Duncan; FOH Sound Engineer: Dave Natale.
Executive Producer: Michael Cohl, Director: Hamish Hamilton.
USA DVD The Biggest Bang: 23 June 2007
UK DVD The Biggest Bang: 5 August 2007

Everyone was back together in Italy for the first reconvened stadium show. Keith Richards was rested and ready to be road tested as Charlie Watts had been a year before. Rumours of Keith and Ron Wood drunkenly climbing palm trees for coconuts in Fiji was a fabrication. However, not to undo such a good story, denials were not vehemently made. Keith would talk about falling off his perch and eventually that it was no more than a "gnarled tree" or shrub that he had climbed on to dry off after a swim and from which he accidentally fell. They arrived in Milan on 6 July and rehearsed at the Discotheque Alcatraz music club, where one episode is filmed and later included in *The Biggest Bang* DVD.

An impromptu moment has Charlie Watts enquiring whether Mick Jagger can remember *I Can't Be Satisfied*. Mick plays a few notes with his slide until he gets the right chords and then launches into the song they last covered in 1964. Charlie looks pleased and impressed and joins in with the rhythm and Keith Richards and Ron Wood play along too as Mick recalls the lyrics for a three-minute rendition. Within an accompanying interview, Charlie is heard to say that it is rare to record a cover better than the original but felt they had done some different, but still good, versions in their time.

1496. CON LE MIE LACRIME (Jagger, Richard, Oldham) ✗ 3.38
AKA: As Tears Go By
11 July 2006: Place: Stadio Giuseppe Meazza, San Siro, Milan, Italy.
Rolling Stones with Darryl Jones, Chuck Leavell, Lisa Fischer, Bernard Fowler, Blondie Chaplin.
Bootleg only.

One effect of Keith Richards' accident was that it provided some more weeks to rest and relax for the others. Charlie Watts could not return to Britain for tax reasons so enjoyed a sedate tour of European cities visiting tourist sites and museums, purchasing clothes as he needed them. On 6 June their old friend Billy Preston passed away, much to everyone's sadness. The first gig in Milan came just two days after the World Cup Final, between Italy and France, held in Berlin, Germany. England had lost their quarter final against Portugal on penalties, a match which Mick Jagger attended. The final also produced a penalty shoot-out after a 1-1 draw. Italy had previously had problems themselves with taking penalties and had not won by in three preceding attempts.

On this occasion they clinched an overall 5-3 victory. Fabio Grosso scored the winning penalty and Pirlo, Materazzi, Daniele de Rossi, Alessandro del Piero all converted theirs too. They had won the World Cup four times and Italy would have been a country jumping for joy as the band rehearsed. This fever continued well into the Stones appearance at the San Siro stadium on a sweltering hot evening. The band debuted *Streets Of Love* before a stool was brought out for Keith Richards at the stage front to play an acoustic guitar. Mick joined them and they launched into *As Tears Go By* except Mick was singing the lyrics in Italian, as he had done 40 years previously. Of course it was very well received. Just before the encore, on the big screen, they showed the Materazzi goal that secured the World Cup final draw and then the winning penalties, which whipped everyone into a frenzy. Marco Materazzi and Alessandro del Piero came on stage during the final bow to receive their plaudits and also to conduct a crowd sing-a-long in a fitting conclusion.

Everyone was a winner but no more so than Keith Richards, who had managed to get fit for the tour just six weeks after an injury which most doctors would say should take six months in recovery. Dr Andrew Law helped Keith with the recovery process and attended the Milan concert. He relates in Keith's autobiography *Life* that everyone was nervous at the potential reaction while he was performing but "he came off the stage euphoric because he'd proved he could do it".

1497.   ONLY FOUND OUT YESTERDAY (Richards) 1.57
AKA: I Only Found Out Yesterday
11 September 2006: Place: Palmdale Studios, California, USA.
Soundtrack DVD Pirates Of The Caribbean: At Worlds End: 24 May 2007

The tour progressed through Europe with excursions to Austria, Germany, France, Netherlands, Switzerland, Portugal, Great Britain, Norway and Denmark. Most countries only witnessed one event, usually at a large stadium, but Germany and Britain hosted five concerts and France two. After the Portuguese concert, where Mick Jagger seemed to be in vocal discomfort, they were due to play two dates in Spain but both were cancelled at very short notice following doctor's advice - Mick had developed laryngitis, causing him throat problems.

In Britain, the Twickenham Rugby ground again was the selected stadium, since Wembley was still not complete. Mick said, "I think it will be ready for the farewell tour of the Arctic Monkeys!" Sheffield's Don Valley stadium received a rain-soaked show, Cardiff's Millennium Stadium in Wales and Scotland's Hampden Park were the other UK dates. The smallest tour venue was a fantastic fjord location, situated within the town walls in, Bergen, Norway. The overpriced "on stage" experience continued for a while but disappeared in Britain as the show dropped to 19 songs from 20. The stilted tour concluded on 3 September, allowing a break until the planned USA and Canada tour, from 20 September 2006.

The short period was used by Keith Richards to fulfil a contract to film a cameo part for the Disney film *Pirates Of The Caribbean, At World's End*. He plays Captain Teague, the father of Johnny Depp's character Jack Sparrow, the scene depicting him writing a song for an impending birth of a baby. "Aye," he laughs, "It's hardly as worthy as gold and myrrh, but it'll have to make do. Thinking of calling it, 'Only Found Out Yesterday'. Been working on it since you told me, after all. Just having some trouble sorting it all out."

In reality, it was probably written a few years before and the dialogue gave it the song title. It is an acoustic, romantic, song in Spanish guitar style and turned up on release of the film *Shine A Light* during the credits. "No, no worries. Just don't tell anyone that ol' Teague's gone soft. It'd be the end of me," Keith's character chuckled. The song was played and filmed with Keith sat solitary on stage during a rehearsal for the 29 October Beacon Theatre concert, along with a short harmonica-inspired version of *Wild Horses*.

1498.   LET IT BLEED (Jagger, Richard) ✐ 5.11
17 October 2006: Place: Qwest Field, Seattle, Washington, USA.
Rolling Stones with Dave Matthews, Darryl Jones, Chuck Leavell, Lisa Fischer, Bernard Fowler, Blondie Chaplin.
Producer: The Rolling Stones
Engineer: Music Mix: Bob Clearmountain; Music Production: Ed Cherney; Additional Mixes / Engineer: Brandon Duncan; FOH Sound Engineer: Dave Natale.
Executive Producer: Michael Cohl, Director: Hamish Hamilton.
USA DVD The Biggest Bang: 23 June 2007
UK DVD The Biggest Bang: 5 August 2007

There were constant changes to the schedule as dates changed and were then rearranged. There were indications that they would play a small charity concert in New York but details were not released until a month before. It would be in aid of the Bill Clinton Foundation and take place on 29 October at the aforementioned Beacon Theatre. Commencing in Boston, they then moved to a wet Canada in Halifax, Nova Scotia. They performed on the Churchill Downs racetrack in Louisville, Kentucky, and received a cheer for the "Kentucky derby day" line in *Dead Flowers* and did a chorus of Glen Campbell's *Wichita Lineman* in Wichita, Kansas.

Two dates were played in the agricultural plains of Regina, Saskatchewan, in Canada, until they returned to the city of Chicago and then Qwest Field in Seattle. It was here that Dave Matthews joined them for a duet on *Let It Bleed*, much to the appreciation of the audience. He was in awe of the Stones and commented that it was an honour to play with the devil and all his majesty. The recording was an extra on *The Biggest Bang* DVD. *She Was Hot* was included in Seattle, having been played in Chicago. Still the band marched on, filling venues with slightly reduced ticket prices. The next was in El Paso, Texas, where Dave Matthews performed the opening set and was with them on *Let It Bleed*.

1499.   YOU GOT ME ROCKING (Jagger, Richards) ✐ 3.35
22 October 2006: Place: Zilker Park, Austin, Texas, USA.
Rolling Stones with Darryl Jones, Chuck Leavell, Lisa Fischer, Bernard Fowler, Blondie Chaplin.
Producer: The Rolling Stones
Engineer: Music Mix: Bob Clearmountain; Music Production: Ed Cherney, David Hewitt; Additional Mixes / Engineer: Brandon Duncan; FOH Sound Engineer: Dave Natale.
Executive Producer: Michael Cohl, Director: Hamish Hamilton.
USA DVD The Biggest Bang: 23 June 2007
UK DVD The Biggest Bang: 5 August 2007
USA Blu-Ray DVD The Biggest Bang: 16 June 2009
UK Blu-Ray DVD The Biggest Bang: 29 June 2009

Next stop was the self-proclaimed "Live Music Capital of the World", Austin, in central Texas. The show in Zilker Park was recorded for a digital video release and this was announced before the performance to the crowd by director Hamish Hamilton. It captured the A Bigger Bang stadium experience for history. There is a short documentary that accompanies the release filmed in Austin. The band are seen rehearsing two new numbers they intended to cover. Another documentary made by Chris Jagger, called *I Got The Blues*, is a blues excursion to Austin, interviewing Muddy Waters pianist Pinetop Perkins, Hubert Sumlin of Chuck Berry and Howlin' Wolf fame and guitarist Jimmy Vaughan. Tommy Shannon, Chris Layton, Joe Ely, Miss Lavelle White and Lucas Martin are also included.

The final 15 minutes cover Joe Willie "Pinetop" Perkins' arrival with Chris Jagger backstage as guests of the band. At that time he was aged 93 and was filmed sat at a piano with Chuck Leavell. He could not play the blues for religious reasons because it was a Sunday. Mick visited Pinetop and asked him to reminisce about his heroes, an exercise which produced a who's who of the piano world, even extending to Aaron Copland and Big Maceo Merriweather. Chris Jagger gave his brother a white Stetson and Mick remarked that there was a song in the set list perfect for wearing it with. Ian McLagan's band, who lived in Texas and advocated their local music scene, opened the show. He had offered his services to be the opener, an invitation which was eagerly accepted. He felt it was a huge honour and was thrilled to play with the Stones in Austin.

The show's opening montage was a galactic flight through the creation of stars and planets until the traveller approaches earth and lands at the Stones' latest rock venue. When viewed from a distance, the huge five-storey stage with horizontal strips of lighting resembled an airport terminus building. Three layers could house a crowd for the "on stage" close encounter and the two below were reserved for the performers, the second allowing Mick Jagger to traverse above fellow band members on the ground floor. The jumbotron screen divided those on the left tiers from the right sections. Open-G licks from Keith Richards' "micawber" blonde Telecaster guitar, with a revised lap guitar pick-up, opened the event and, in Austin, it was for the guitar feast of *You Got Me Rocking.*

1500. **LET'S SPEND THE NIGHT TOGETHER** (Jagger, Richard) ⚋ 4.22
22 October 2006: Place: Zilker Park, Austin, Texas, USA.
Rolling Stones with Darryl Jones, Chuck Leavell, Lisa Fischer, Bernard Fowler, Blondie Chaplin.
Producer: The Rolling Stones
Engineer: Music Mix: Bob Clearmountain; Music Production: Ed Cherney, David Hewitt; Additional Mixes / Engineer: Brandon Duncan; FOH Sound Engineer: Dave Natale.
Executive Producer: Michael Cohl, Director: Hamish Hamilton.
USA DVD The Biggest Bang: 23 June 2007
UK DVD The Biggest Bang: 5 August 2007
USA Blu-Ray DVD The Biggest Bang: 16 June 2009
UK Blu-Ray DVD The Biggest Bang: 29 June 2009

1501. **SHE'S SO COLD** (Jagger, Richards) ⚋ 4.39
22 October 2006: Place: Zilker Park, Austin, Texas, USA.
Rolling Stones with Darryl Jones, Chuck Leavell, Lisa Fischer, Bernard Fowler, Blondie Chaplin.
Producer: The Rolling Stones
Engineer: Music Mix: Bob Clearmountain; Music Production: Ed Cherney, David Hewitt; Additional Mixes / Engineer: Brandon Duncan; FOH Sound Engineer: Dave Natale.
Executive Producer: Michael Cohl, Director: Hamish Hamilton.
USA DVD The Biggest Bang: 23 June 2007
UK DVD The Biggest Bang: 5 August 2007
USA Blu-Ray DVD The Biggest Bang: 16 June 2009
UK Blu-Ray DVD The Biggest Bang: 29 June 2009

1502. **OH NO, NOT YOU AGAIN** (Jagger, Richards) ⚋ 4.00
22 October 2006: Place: Zilker Park, Austin, Texas, USA.
Rolling Stones with Darryl Jones, Chuck Leavell, Lisa Fischer, Bernard Fowler, Blondie Chaplin.
Producer: The Rolling Stones
Engineer: Music Mix: Bob Clearmountain; Music Production: Ed Cherney, David Hewitt; Additional Mixes / Engineer: Brandon Duncan; FOH Sound Engineer: Dave Natale.
Executive Producer: Michael Cohl, Director: Hamish Hamilton.
USA DVD The Biggest Bang: 23 June 2007
UK DVD The Biggest Bang: 5 August 2007
USA Blu-Ray DVD The Biggest Bang: 16 June 2009
UK Blu-Ray DVD The Biggest Bang: 29 June 2009

1503. **SWAY** (Jagger, Richard) ⚋ 3.45
22 October 2006: Place: Zilker Park, Austin, Texas, USA.
Rolling Stones with Darryl Jones, Chuck Leavell, Lisa Fischer, Bernard Fowler, Blondie Chaplin.
Producer: The Rolling Stones
Engineer: Music Mix: Bob Clearmountain; Music Production: Ed Cherney, David Hewitt; Additional Mixes / Engineer: Brandon Duncan; FOH Sound Engineer: Dave Natale.
Executive Producer: Michael Cohl, Director: Hamish Hamilton.
USA DVD The Biggest Bang: 23 June 2007
UK DVD The Biggest Bang: 5 August 2007
USA Blu-Ray DVD The Biggest Bang: 16 June 2009
UK Blu-Ray DVD The Biggest Bang: 29 June 2009

1504. **BOB WILLS IS STILL KING** (Jennings) ⚋ 3.34
22 October 2006: Place: Zilker Park, Austin, Texas, USA.
Rolling Stones with Darryl Jones, Chuck Leavell, Lisa Fischer, Bernard Fowler, Blondie Chaplin.
Producer: The Rolling Stones
Engineer: Music Mix: Bob Clearmountain; Music Production: Ed Cherney, David Hewitt; Additional Mixes / Engineer: Brandon Duncan; FOH Sound Engineer: Dave Natale.
Executive Producer: Michael Cohl, Director: Hamish Hamilton.
USA DVD The Biggest Bang: 23 June 2007
UK DVD The Biggest Bang: 5 August 2007
USA Blu-Ray DVD The Biggest Bang: 16 June 2009
UK Blu-Ray DVD The Biggest Bang: 29 June 2009

1505. STREETS OF LOVE (Jagger, Richards) ✎ 5.25
22 October 2006: Place: Zilker Park, Austin, Texas, USA.
Rolling Stones with Darryl Jones, Chuck Leavell, Lisa Fischer, Bernard Fowler, Blondie Chaplin.
Producer: The Rolling Stones
Engineer: Music Mix: Bob Clearmountain; Music Production: Ed Cherney, David Hewitt; Additional Mixes / Engineer: Brandon Duncan; FOH Sound Engineer: Dave Natale.
Executive Producer: Michael Cohl, Director: Hamish Hamilton.
USA DVD The Biggest Bang: 23 June 2007
UK DVD The Biggest Bang: 5 August 2007
USA Blu-Ray DVD The Biggest Bang: 16 June 2009
UK Blu-Ray DVD The Biggest Bang: 29 June 2009

1506. AIN'T TOO PROUD TO BEG (Whitfield, Holland) ✎ 5.06
22 October 2006: Place: Zilker Park, Austin, Texas, USA.
Rolling Stones with Darryl Jones, Chuck Leavell, Bobby Keys, Lisa Fischer, Bernard Fowler, Blondie Chaplin, Tim Ries, Michael Davis, Kent Smith.
Producer: The Rolling Stones
Engineer: Music Mix: Bob Clearmountain; Music Production: Ed Cherney, David Hewitt; Additional Mixes / Engineer: Brandon Duncan; FOH Sound Engineer: Dave Natale.
Executive Producer: Michael Cohl, Director: Hamish Hamilton.
USA DVD The Biggest Bang: 23 June 2007
UK DVD The Biggest Bang: 5 August 2007
USA Blu-Ray DVD The Biggest Bang: 16 June 2009
UK Blu-Ray DVD The Biggest Bang: 29 June 2009

1507. BITCH (Jagger, Richard) ✎ 3.03
22 October 2006: Place: Zilker Park, Austin, Texas, USA.
Rolling Stones with Darryl Jones, Chuck Leavell, Bobby Keys, Lisa Fischer, Bernard Fowler, Blondie Chaplin, Tim Ries, Michael Davis, Kent Smith.
Producer: The Rolling Stones
Engineer: Music Mix: Bob Clearmountain; Music Production: Ed Cherney, David Hewitt; Additional Mixes / Engineer: Brandon Duncan; FOH Sound Engineer: Dave Natale.
Executive Producer: Michael Cohl, Director: Hamish Hamilton.
USA DVD The Biggest Bang: 23 June 2007
UK DVD The Biggest Bang: 5 August 2007
USA Blu-Ray DVD The Biggest Bang: 16 June 2009
UK Blu-Ray DVD The Biggest Bang: 29 June 2009

1508. TUMBLING DICE (Jagger, Richard) ✎ 7.55
22 October 2006: Place: Zilker Park, Austin, Texas, USA.
Rolling Stones with Darryl Jones, Chuck Leavell, Bobby Keys, Lisa Fischer, Bernard Fowler, Blondie Chaplin, Tim Ries, Michael Davis, Kent Smith.
Producer: The Rolling Stones
Engineer: Music Mix: Bob Clearmountain; Music Production: Ed Cherney, David Hewitt; Additional Mixes / Engineer: Brandon Duncan; FOH Sound Engineer: Dave Natale.
Executive Producer: Michael Cohl, Director: Hamish Hamilton.
USA DVD The Biggest Bang: 23 June 2007
UK DVD The Biggest Bang: 5 August 2007
USA Blu-Ray DVD The Biggest Bang: 16 June 2009
UK Blu-Ray DVD The Biggest Bang: 29 June 2009

1509. LEARNING THE GAME (Holly) ✎ 3.15
22 October 2006: Place: Zilker Park, Austin, Texas, USA.
Rolling Stones with Darryl Jones, Chuck Leavell, Blondie Chaplin.
Producer: The Rolling Stones
Engineer: Music Mix: Bob Clearmountain; Music Production: Ed Cherney, David Hewitt; Additional Mixes / Engineer: Brandon Duncan; FOH Sound Engineer: Dave Natale.
Executive Producer: Michael Cohl, Director: Hamish Hamilton.
USA DVD The Biggest Bang: 23 June 2007
UK DVD The Biggest Bang: 5 August 2007
USA Blu-Ray DVD The Biggest Bang: 16 June 2009
UK Blu-Ray DVD The Biggest Bang: 29 June 2009

1510. LITTLE T&A (Jagger, Richards) ✎ 3.47
22 October 2006: Place: Zilker Park, Austin, Texas, USA.
Rolling Stones with Darryl Jones, Chuck Leavell, Bobby Keys, Lisa Fischer, Bernard Fowler, Blondie Chaplin, Tim Ries, Michael Davis, Kent Smith.
Producer: The Rolling Stones
Engineer: Music Mix: Bob Clearmountain; Music Production: Ed Cherney, David Hewitt; Additional Mixes / Engineer: Brandon Duncan; FOH Sound Engineer: Dave Natale.
Executive Producer: Michael Cohl, Director: Hamish Hamilton.
USA DVD The Biggest Bang: 23 June 2007
UK DVD The Biggest Bang: 5 August 2007
USA Blu-Ray DVD The Biggest Bang: 16 June 2009
UK Blu-Ray DVD The Biggest Bang: 29 June 2009

1511. UNDER MY THUMB (Jagger, Richard) ✏ 5.18
22 October 2006: Place: Zilker Park, Austin, Texas, USA.
Rolling Stones with Darryl Jones, Chuck Leavell.
Producer: The Rolling Stones
Engineer: Music Mix: Bob Clearmountain; Music Production: Ed Cherney, David Hewitt; Additional Mixes / Engineer: Brandon Duncan; FOH Sound Engineer: Dave Natale.
Executive Producer: Michael Cohl, Director: Hamish Hamilton.
USA DVD The Biggest Bang: 23 June 2007
UK DVD The Biggest Bang: 5 August 2007
USA Blu-Ray DVD The Biggest Bang: 16 June 2009
UK Blu-Ray DVD The Biggest Bang: 29 June 2009

1512. GET OFF MY CLOUD (Jagger, Richard) ✏ 3.10
22 October 2006: Place: Zilker Park, Austin, Texas, USA.
Rolling Stones with Darryl Jones, Chuck Leavell, Lisa Fischer, Bernard Fowler.
Producer: The Rolling Stones
Engineer: Music Mix: Bob Clearmountain; Music Production: Ed Cherney, David Hewitt; Additional Mixes / Engineer: Brandon Duncan; FOH Sound Engineer: Dave Natale.
Executive Producer: Michael Cohl, Director: Hamish Hamilton.
USA DVD The Biggest Bang: 23 June 2007
UK DVD The Biggest Bang: 5 August 2007
USA Blu-Ray DVD The Biggest Bang: 16 June 2009
UK Blu-Ray DVD The Biggest Bang: 29 June 2009

1513. HONKY TONK WOMEN (Jagger, Richard) ✏ 4.07
22 October 2006: Place: Zilker Park, Austin, Texas, USA.
Rolling Stones with Darryl Jones, Chuck Leavell, Bobby Keys, Lisa Fischer, Bernard Fowler, Blondie Chaplin, Tim Ries, Michael Davis, Kent Smith
Producer: The Rolling Stones
Engineer: Music Mix: Bob Clearmountain; Music Production: Ed Cherney, David Hewitt; Additional Mixes / Engineer: Brandon Duncan; FOH Sound Engineer: Dave Natale.
Executive Producer: Michael Cohl, Director: Hamish Hamilton.
USA DVD The Biggest Bang: 23 June 2007
UK DVD The Biggest Bang: 5 August 2007
USA Blu-Ray DVD The Biggest Bang: 16 June 2009
UK Blu-Ray DVD The Biggest Bang: 29 June 2009

1514. SYMPATHY FOR THE DEVIL (Jagger, Richard) ✏ 7.36
22 October 2006: Place: Zilker Park, Austin, Texas, USA.
Rolling Stones with Darryl Jones, Chuck Leavell, Lisa Fischer, Bernard Fowler, Blondie Chaplin.
Producer: The Rolling Stones
Engineer: Music Mix: Bob Clearmountain; Music Production: Ed Cherney, David Hewitt; Additional Mixes / Engineer: Brandon Duncan; FOH Sound Engineer: Dave Natale.
Executive Producer: Michael Cohl, Director: Hamish Hamilton.
USA DVD The Biggest Bang: 23 June 2007
UK DVD The Biggest Bang: 5 August 2007
USA Blu-Ray DVD The Biggest Bang: 16 June 2009
UK Blu-Ray DVD The Biggest Bang: 29 June 2009

1515. JUMPIN' JACK FLASH (Jagger, Richard) ✏ 4.11
22 October 2006: Place: Zilker Park, Austin, Texas, USA.
Rolling Stones with Darryl Jones, Chuck Leavell, Lisa Fischer, Bernard Fowler, Blondie Chaplin.
Producer: The Rolling Stones
Engineer: Music Mix: Bob Clearmountain; Music Production: Ed Cherney, David Hewitt; Additional Mixes / Engineer: Brandon Duncan; FOH Sound Engineer: Dave Natale.
Executive Producer: Michael Cohl, Director: Hamish Hamilton.
USA DVD The Biggest Bang: 23 June 2007
UK DVD The Biggest Bang: 5 August 2007
USA Blu-Ray DVD The Biggest Bang: 16 June 2009
UK Blu-Ray DVD The Biggest Bang: 29 June 2009

1516. (I CAN'T GET NO) SATISFACTION (Jagger, Richard) ✏ 6.10
22 October 2006: Place: Zilker Park, Austin, Texas, USA.
Rolling Stones with Darryl Jones, Chuck Leavell, Bobby Keys, Lisa Fischer, Bernard Fowler, Blondie Chaplin, Tim Ries, Michael Davis, Kent Smith.
Producer: The Rolling Stones
Engineer: Music Mix: Bob Clearmountain; Music Production: Ed Cherney, David Hewitt; Additional Mixes / Engineer: Brandon Duncan; FOH Sound Engineer: Dave Natale.
Executive Producer: Michael Cohl, Director: Hamish Hamilton.
USA DVD The Biggest Bang: 23 June 2007
UK DVD The Biggest Bang: 5 August 2007
USA Blu-Ray DVD The Biggest Bang: 16 June 2009
UK Blu-Ray DVD The Biggest Bang: 29 June 2009

1517. BROWN SUGAR (Jagger, Richard) ⟋ 6.11
22 October 2006: Place: Zilker Park, Austin, Texas, USA.
Rolling Stones with Darryl Jones, Chuck Leavell, Bobby Keys, Lisa Fischer, Bernard Fowler, Blondie Chaplin, Tim Ries, Michael Davis, Kent Smith.
Producer: The Rolling Stones
Engineer: Music Mix: Bob Clearmountain; Music Production: Ed Cherney, David Hewitt; Additional Mixes / Engineer: Brandon Duncan; FOH Sound Engineer: Dave Natale.
Executive Producer: Michael Cohl, Director: Hamish Hamilton.
USA DVD The Biggest Bang: 23 June 2007
UK DVD The Biggest Bang: 5 August 2007
USA Blu-Ray DVD The Biggest Bang: 16 June 2009
UK Blu-Ray DVD The Biggest Bang: 29 June 2009

The 60s song *Let's Spend The Night Together* was often played in the second tour slot after which Mick Jagger announced the band as "virgins of Austin". Hamish Hamilton was determined to provide some unusual concert shots and, while the aerial film of *She's So Cold* was not unique, other footage included audience close-ups as the camera work darted on and off stage. The dance rock tempo continued with *Oh No Not You Again* and the slower tones of *Sway*, featuring Ronnie Wood on slide then lead guitar. As hinted in the rehearsal, they performed a much-appreciated Waylon Jennings country song that proffered *Bob Wills Is Still King*.
A Buddy Emmons lap steel accompanied an acoustic from Mick, who did not wear the promised white Stetson, even though it was placed on a stage monitor. For a brief moment, the slower *Streets Of Love* gave a purplish and green hue with more tranquil settings before the brass quad sound joined them for *Ain't Too Proud To Beg*. Mick starts to use the stage wings and introduced some nifty foot work. The camera shots have the backing singers filmed in profile, with Lisa Fischer showing off a revealing gangster suit and trilby. Only the soundtrack of *Bitch* is heard on the credits of the video release and the following number, *Tumbling Dice*, has Keith Richards playing the lead solo from wide on the left wing. Another surprise debut is within Keith's set as another Texan, Buddy Holly, is covered on *Learning The Game*. *Little T&A* has a great camera shot of Keith with his black Gibson in stage side profile but guitar to the fore, with a Zilker Park floodlit oak tree silhouetted behind him.
During the vocals, Keith is assisted by Blondie Chaplin's electric guitar. Darryl Jones' bass and Chuck Leavell's organ introduced another 60s classic with an authentic *Under My Thumb* as the B-stage train pulled out and extended towards the central park destination. Four rows of stacked delay speaker towers take the sound to the rear. From the same era, *Get Off My Cloud* is performed to an ecstatic local crowd, who can't quite believe that the Stones are actually playing before them right now. *Start Me Up* is not revealed on the DVD but *Honky Tonk Women* shows the return journey to the main stage with underwear being thrown towards Mick. As they approach, the stage is transformed with inflatable lips and a protruding tongue as individual lights on the tiers now welcome them back on - "Mick it's me again" says one banner.
As the stage darkens, the tongue collapses and voodoo images with red lighting accompany the percussive start of *Sympathy For The Devil*. On the second floor, directly in front of the jumbotron, Mick (dressed in red and black leopard pattern coat with matching hat) opens the "woah woah" and the first verse. The lyrical phrase "Pleased to meet you" beckons flames of fire either side of the stage ceiling. Keith is dressed for the cold of the night, wearing a red and white scarf and a camouflage woollen jacket, as he starts the first lead guitar solo. Yet more pyrotechnics are launched for the introduction of *Jumpin' Jack Flash*.
Satisfaction concluded the show before the encore of *You Can't Always Get What You Want* and *Brown Sugar*, the former not making it to the video. Mick is dressed in a silver waistcoat and long coat which he discarded for a run to the B-stage and back. A "no expense spared" barrage of fireworks signal the final conclusion and the blasting of 30-metre trivera ribbons fired from 36 pneumatic cannons from the width of the stage towers. The centre screen is adorned with a lapping Stones tongue as the band made its final exit.
Clair Brothers were the chosen company for the work of providing the tour public address and the front of house engineer was the much respected independent recording expert, Dave Natale - hence his credit on *The Biggest Bang* along with the recording team of Ed Cherney and Dave Hewitt. Clair Brothers were a vast worldwide sound business, who had not worked with the Stones since the Tour Of America in 1975. On the A Bigger Bang tour it took 10 of their technical staff to mix and engineer the FOH sound. Many overdubs were made particularly to the guitar sound to enable the film release.

1518. I'M FREE (Jagger, Richard) ⟋ 3.30
29 October 2006: Place: Beacon Theatre, New York, USA.
Rolling Stones with Darryl Jones, Chuck Leavell, Lisa Fischer, Bernard Fowler, Blondie Chaplin.
Producer: Michael Cohl, Zane Weiner, Steve Bing, Victoria Pearman.
Engineer: Mixing Editor: Bob Clearmountain; Re-Recording Mixer: Tom Fleischman; Music Recording Engineers: David Hewitt, Phil Gitomer, Bob Clearmountain; Digital Editing: Brandon Duncan; Mastered: Steve Marcussen.
Director: Martin Scorsese; Executive Producer: The Rolling Stones; Co-Executive Producer: Jane Rose.
USA CD SHINE A LIGHT: 1 April 2008: No. 11 - 7weeks
UK CD SHINE A LIGHT: 7 April 2008: No. 2 - 7 weeks
USA DVD Shine A Light: 29 July 2008
UK DVD Shine A Light: 3 November 2008

The planned concert in Atlanta City, on 27 October, was cancelled due to Mick Jagger suffering from laryngitis and so the much-anticipated Beacon Theatre concerts were next on the schedule a week later. There were two events planned on 29 and 31 October. The concerts were to be directed by the great Martin Scorsese for a cinematic feature film and, for that reason, both dates were needed. He was a lifelong Stones fan and had used much of their work within scores of his films. Who can forget the impact of *Paint It Black* in the film credits of *Full Metal Jacket*, *Satisfaction* during *Apocalypse Now* or *Jumpin' Jack Flash* in *Mean Streets*? Originally Mick Jagger wanted Scorsese to film a large, cinematic event such as the Rio concert or Amsterdam Arena, rather than a small one. In March 2006, however, Marty persuaded him that he was more suited to recording in a more intimate environment where a personal connection could be made between the audience and the band.
He suggested also that New York was a special place for the Stones to play in and that the I-Max camera format was an option. The relatively new 3D technique was discussed too. The first show was held to celebrate Bill Clinton's 60th birthday and also to raise money for the former US president's charitable foundation. Tickets were hard to find, especially for the first evening. Scorsese employed only the best camera operators, who were Grammy winners in their own right, but also asked for a young, predominantly female audience to be recruited for the first couple of rows to perform concert eye-candy duties.

Volunteers, including fans and would-be actors, were specifically auditioned for this purpose and naturally only the best were selected. Ultimately, this did not make for a convincing rock 'n' roll show audience. A featurette on the DVD gives some background to the rehearsals showing the film entourage to be hundreds strong. Other segments have film maker Albert Maysles talking to Keith Richards and Ron Wood, Mick on the phone to Martin Scorsese about the filming logistics on stage, Bill Clinton introducing his family to the group and rehearsal clips of *Wild Horses*, played with guitars and a mouth organ, three acoustics on *Factory Girl*. "What a bunch of hillbillies", shouts Keith. Only four tracks from the concert ended up on the *Shine A Light* film. These are included as bonus songs within a DVD of the film. The reason for this is likely to be the tight impositions on the band, crew and audience by the film entourage. Even band assistants were heard to mutter about the constraints and the attitude of the film makers. The guitar technicians and usual back line crew were kept to a minimum. During *I'm Free*, the group of front-of-stage extras seemed to resemble a birthday tea party rather than an impassioned rock concert.

1519. UNDERCOVER OF THE NIGHT (Jagger, Richards) ✏ 4.24
29 October 2006: Place: Beacon Theatre, New York, USA.
Rolling Stones with Darryl Jones, Chuck Leavell, Lisa Fischer, Bernard Fowler, Blondie Chaplin.
Producer: Michael Cohl, Zane Weiner, Steve Bing, Victoria Pearman.
Engineer: Mixing Editor: Bob Clearmountain; Re-Recording Mixer: Tom Fleischman; Music Recording Engineers: David Hewitt, Phil Gitomer, Bob Clearmountain; Digital Editing: Brandon Duncan; Mastered: Steve Marcussen.
Director: Martin Scorsese; Executive Producer: The Rolling Stones; Co-Executive Producer: Jane Rose.
Japan CD SHINE A LIGHT: 9 April 2008
USA DVD SHINE A LIGHT: 29 July 2008
UK DVD Shine A Light: 3 November 2008

1520. SHINE A LIGHT (Jagger, Richard) ✏ 4.05
29 October 2006: Place: Beacon Theatre, New York, USA.
Rolling Stones with Darryl Jones, Chuck Leavell, Lisa Fischer, Bernard Fowler, Blondie Chaplin.
Producer: Michael Cohl, Zane Weiner, Steve Bing, Victoria Pearman.
Engineer: Mixing Editor: Bob Clearmountain; Re-Recording Mixer: Tom Fleischman; Music Recording Engineers: David Hewitt, Phil Gitomer, Bob Clearmountain; Digital Editing: Brandon Duncan; Mastered: Steve Marcussen.
Executive Producer: The Rolling Stones; Co-Executive Producer: Jane Rose.
USA CD SHINE A LIGHT: 1 April 2008: No. 11 - 7weeks
UK CD SHINE A LIGHT: 7 April 2008: No. 2 - 7 weeks

1521. LITTLE T&A (Jagger, Richards) ✏ 4.09
29 October 2006: Place: Beacon Theatre, New York, USA.
Rolling Stones with Darryl Jones, Chuck Leavell, Bobby Keys, Lisa Fischer, Bernard Fowler, Blondie Chaplin, Tim Ries, Michael Davis, Kent Smith
Producer: Michael Cohl, Zane Weiner, Steve Bing, Victoria Pearman.
Engineer: Mixing Editor: Bob Clearmountain; Re-Recording Mixer: Tom Fleischman; Music Recording Engineers: David Hewitt, Phil Gitomer, Bob Clearmountain; Digital Editing: Brandon Duncan; Mastered: Steve Marcussen.
Director: Martin Scorsese; Executive Producer: The Rolling Stones; Co-Executive Producer: Jane Rose.
USA CD SHINE A LIGHT: 1 April 2008: No. 11 - 7weeks
UK CD SHINE A LIGHT: 7 April 2008: No. 2 - 7 weeks
USA DVD Shine A Light: 29 July 2008
UK DVD Shine A Light: 3 November 2008

1522. PAINT IT BLACK (Jagger, Richard) ✏ 4.28
29 October 2006: Place: Beacon Theatre, New York, USA.
Rolling Stones with Darryl Jones, Chuck Leavell, Lisa Fischer, Bernard Fowler, Blondie Chaplin, Tim Ries.
Producer: Michael Cohl, Zane Weiner, Steve Bing, Victoria Pearman.
Engineer: Mixing Editor: Bob Clearmountain; Re-Recording Mixer: Tom Fleischman; Music Recording Engineers: David Hewitt, Phil Gitomer, Bob Clearmountain; Digital Editing: Brandon Duncan; Mastered: Steve Marcussen.
Director: Martin Scorsese; Executive Producer: The Rolling Stones; Co-Executive Producer: Jane Rose.
USA CD SHINE A LIGHT: 1 April 2008: No. 11 - 7weeks
UK CD SHINE A LIGHT: 7 April 2008: No. 2 - 7 weeks
USA DVD Shine A Light: 29 July 2008
UK DVD Shine A Light: 3 November 2008

The theatre was a beautiful piece of 1920s neo-Grecian art decor and had three tiers originally designed for film and stage productions. It was not until the late 60s that it became used for rock and roll purposes. Buddy Guy was the opening act for the show and Bill Clinton provided a short speech before the group took the stage for the first concert. The stage was designed by Mark Fisher with input from Martin Scorsese and Mick Jagger. The set list is best described as part of the film but the recordings available on CD and DVD have the band in good musical form, no surprise considering that this was towards the end of a long tour.
I'm Free had been used recently in TV advertisements and so would have been more well known. *Undercover Of The Night* was also a track not played during the tour and so the funk tones and Keith Richards' guitar licks were refreshing. It matched the vibrancy of the filming and lighting which was largely bright white, casting halos over the heads of the band. *Undercover* appeared on CD as a bonus track for the Japanese version of the SHINE A LIGHT. *Shine A Light*, with a fine Ronnie guitar solo, was just on the same CD release.
Darryl Jones had a bass solo in the chugging rock and roll part of *Little T&A*, the stage cramped as the brass section had joined the band. Keith commented during his set that the concert was for "birthdays and shit". *Paint It Black* really rocked as Ron Wood again showed how enjoyable an experience he found the concert.

Certainly there were no theatrical re-takes and it was staged as a proper concert, despite restricted views in the balconies and the boom cameras swinging in front of band members. Even Mick Jagger said that, for a proper view, you would need to see the DVD. He even expressed concern to Bill Clinton about how the crowd would react with all the cameras present.

1523.   JUMPIN' JACK FLASH (Jagger, Richard) ⤢ 4.22
1 November 2006: Place: Beacon Theatre, New York, USA.
Rolling Stones with Darryl Jones, Chuck Leavell, Lisa Fischer, Bernard Fowler.
Producer: Michael Cohl, Zane Weiner, Steve Bing, Victoria Pearman.
Engineer: Mixing Editor: Bob Clearmountain; Re-Recording Mixer: Tom Fleischman; Music Recording Engineers: David Hewitt, Phil Gitomer, Bob Clearmountain; Digital Editing: Brandon Duncan; Mastered: Steve Marcussen.
Director: Martin Scorsese; Executive Producer: The Rolling Stones; Co-Executive Producer: Jane Rose.
USA CD SHINE A LIGHT: 1 April 2008: No. 11 - 7weeks
UK CD SHINE A LIGHT: 7 April 2008: No. 2 - 7 weeks
USA DVD Shine A Light: 29 July 2008
UK DVD Shine A Light: 3 November 2008

1524.   SHATTERED (Jagger, Richards) ⤢ 4.06
1 November 2006: Place: Beacon Theatre, New York, USA.
Rolling Stones with Darryl Jones, Chuck Leavell, Lisa Fischer, Bernard Fowler.
Producer: Michael Cohl, Zane Weiner, Steve Bing, Victoria Pearman.
Engineer: Mixing Editor: Bob Clearmountain; Re-Recording Mixer: Tom Fleischman; Music Recording Engineers: David Hewitt, Phil Gitomer, Bob Clearmountain; Digital Editing: Brandon Duncan; Mastered: Steve Marcussen.
Director: Martin Scorsese; Executive Producer: The Rolling Stones; Co-Executive Producer: Jane Rose.
USA CD SHINE A LIGHT: 1 April 2008: No. 11 - 7weeks
UK CD SHINE A LIGHT: 7 April 2008: No. 2 - 7 weeks
USA DVD Shine A Light: 29 July 2008
UK DVD Shine A Light: 3 November 2008

1525.   SHE WAS HOT (Jagger, Richards) ⤢ 4.44
1 November 2006: Place: Beacon Theatre, New York, USA.
Rolling Stones with Darryl Jones, Chuck Leavell, Lisa Fischer, Bernard Fowler, Blondie Chaplin, Tim Ries.
Producer: Michael Cohl, Zane Weiner, Steve Bing, Victoria Pearman.
Engineer: Mixing Editor: Bob Clearmountain; Re-Recording Mixer: Tom Fleischman; Music Recording Engineers: David Hewitt, Phil Gitomer, Bob Clearmountain; Digital Editing: Brandon Duncan; Mastered: Steve Marcussen.
Director: Martin Scorsese; Executive Producer: The Rolling Stones; Co-Executive Producer: Jane Rose.
USA CD SHINE A LIGHT: 1 April 2008: No. 11 - 7weeks
UK CD SHINE A LIGHT: 7 April 2008: No. 2 - 7 weeks
USA DVD Shine A Light: 29 July 2008
UK DVD Shine A Light: 3 November 2008

1526.   ALL DOWN THE LINE (Jagger, Richard) ⤢ 4.35
1 November 2006: Place: Beacon Theatre, New York, USA.
Rolling Stones with Darryl Jones, Chuck Leavell, Bobby Keys, Lisa Fischer, Bernard Fowler, Blondie Chaplin, Tim Ries, Michael Davis, Kent Smith.
Producer: Michael Cohl, Zane Weiner, Steve Bing, Victoria Pearman.
Engineer: Mixing Editor: Bob Clearmountain; Re-Recording Mixer: Tom Fleischman; Music Recording Engineers: David Hewitt, Phil Gitomer, Bob Clearmountain; Digital Editing: Brandon Duncan; Mastered: Steve Marcussen.
Director: Martin Scorsese; Executive Producer: The Rolling Stones; Co-Executive Producer: Jane Rose.
USA CD SHINE A LIGHT: 1 April 2008: No. 11 - 7weeks
UK CD SHINE A LIGHT: 7 April 2008: No. 2 - 7 weeks
USA DVD Shine A Light: 29 July 2008
UK DVD Shine A Light: 3 November 2008

1527.   LOVING CUP (Jagger, Richard) ⤢ 4.02
1 November 2006: Place: Beacon Theatre, New York, USA.
Rolling Stones with Jack White, Darryl Jones, Chuck Leavell, Bobby Keys, Lisa Fischer, Bernard Fowler, Blondie Chaplin, Tim Ries, Michael Davis, Kent Smith.
Producer: Michael Cohl, Zane Weiner, Steve Bing, Victoria Pearman.
Engineer: Mixing Editor: Bob Clearmountain; Re-Recording Mixer: Tom Fleischman; Music Recording Engineers: David Hewitt, Phil Gitomer, Bob Clearmountain; Digital Editing: Brandon Duncan; Mastered: Steve Marcussen.
Director: Martin Scorsese; Executive Producer: The Rolling Stones; Co-Executive Producer: Jane Rose.
USA CD SHINE A LIGHT: 1 April 2008: No. 11 - 7weeks
UK CD SHINE A LIGHT: 7 April 2008: No. 2 - 7 weeks
USA DVD Shine A Light: 29 July 2008
UK DVD Shine A Light: 3 November 2008

1528. AS TEARS GO BY (Jagger, Richard, Oldham) ✐ 3.31
1 November 2006: Place: Beacon Theatre, New York, USA.
Rolling Stones with Darryl Jones, Chuck Leavell, Tim Ries.
Producer: Michael Cohl, Zane Weiner, Steve Bing, Victoria Pearman.
Engineer: Mixing Editor: Bob Clearmountain; Re-Recording Mixer: Tom Fleischman; Music Recording Engineers: David Hewitt, Phil Gitomer, Bob Clearmountain; Digital Editing: Brandon Duncan; Mastered: Steve Marcussen.
Director: Martin Scorsese; Executive Producer: The Rolling Stones; Co-Executive Producer: Jane Rose.
USA CD SHINE A LIGHT: 1 April 2008: No. 11 - 7weeks
UK CD SHINE A LIGHT: 7 April 2008: No. 2 - 7 weeks
USA DVD Shine A Light: 29 July 2008
UK DVD Shine A Light: 3 November 2008

1529. SOME GIRLS (Jagger, Richards) ✐ 4.19
1 November 2006: Place: Beacon Theatre, New York, USA.
Rolling Stones with Darryl Jones, Chuck Leavell, Bernard Fowler.
Producer: Michael Cohl, Zane Weiner, Steve Bing, Victoria Pearman.
Engineer: Mixing Editor: Bob Clearmountain; Re-Recording Mixer: Tom Fleischman; Music Recording Engineers: David Hewitt, Phil Gitomer, Bob Clearmountain; Digital Editing: Brandon Duncan; Mastered: Steve Marcussen.
Director: Martin Scorsese; Executive Producer: The Rolling Stones; Co-Executive Producer: Jane Rose.
USA CD SHINE A LIGHT: 1 April 2008: No. 11 - 7weeks
UK CD SHINE A LIGHT: 7 April 2008: No. 2 - 7 weeks
USA DVD Shine A Light: 29 July 2008
UK DVD Shine A Light: 3 November 2008

1530. JUST MY IMAGINATION (RUNNING AWAY WITH ME) (Barrett, Norman) ✐ 6.39
1 November 2006: Place: Beacon Theatre, New York, USA.
Rolling Stones with Darryl Jones, Chuck Leavell, Bobby Keys, Lisa Fischer, Bernard Fowler, Tim Ries, Michael Davis, Kent Smith.
Producer: Michael Cohl, Zane Weiner, Steve Bing, Victoria Pearman.
Engineer: Mixing Editor: Bob Clearmountain; Re-Recording Mixer: Tom Fleischman; Music Recording Engineers: David Hewitt, Phil Gitomer, Bob Clearmountain; Digital Editing: Brandon Duncan; Mastered: Steve Marcussen.
Director: Martin Scorsese; Executive Producer: The Rolling Stones; Co-Executive Producer: Jane Rose.
USA CD SHINE A LIGHT: 1 April 2008: No. 11 - 7weeks
UK CD SHINE A LIGHT: 7 April 2008: No. 2 - 7 weeks
USA DVD Shine A Light: 29 July 2008
UK DVD Shine A Light: 3 November 2008

1531. FAR AWAY EYES (Jagger, Richards) ✐ 4.37
1 November 2006: Place: Beacon Theatre, New York, USA.
Rolling Stones with Darryl Jones, Chuck Leavell, Lisa Fischer, Bernard Fowler, Blondie Chaplin.
Producer: Michael Cohl, Zane Weiner, Steve Bing, Victoria Pearman.
Engineer: Mixing Editor: Bob Clearmountain; Re-Recording Mixer: Tom Fleischman; Music Recording Engineers: David Hewitt, Phil Gitomer, Bob Clearmountain; Digital Editing: Brandon Duncan; Mastered: Steve Marcussen.
Director: Martin Scorsese; Executive Producer: The Rolling Stones; Co-Executive Producer: Jane Rose.
USA CD SHINE A LIGHT: 1 April 2008: No. 11 - 7weeks
UK CD SHINE A LIGHT: 7 April 2008: No. 2 - 7 weeks
USA DVD Shine A Light: 29 July 2008
UK DVD Shine A Light: 3 November 2008

1532. CHAMPAGNE & REEFER (Morganfield with Guy) ✐ 5.58
1 November 2006: Place: Beacon Theatre, New York, USA.
Rolling Stones with Buddy Guy, Darryl Jones, Chuck Leavell.
Producer: Michael Cohl, Zane Weiner, Steve Bing, Victoria Pearman.
Engineer: Mixing Editor: Bob Clearmountain; Re-Recording Mixer: Tom Fleischman; Music Recording Engineers: David Hewitt, Phil Gitomer, Bob Clearmountain; Digital Editing: Brandon Duncan; Mastered: Steve Marcussen.
Director: Martin Scorsese; Executive Producer: The Rolling Stones; Co-Executive Producer: Jane Rose.
USA CD SHINE A LIGHT: 1 April 2008: No. 11 - 7weeks
UK CD SHINE A LIGHT: 7 April 2008: No. 2 - 7 weeks
USA DVD Shine A Light: 29 July 2008
UK DVD Shine A Light: 3 November 2008

1533. TUMBLING DICE (Jagger, Richards) ⟋ 4.24
1 November 2006: Place: Beacon Theatre, New York, USA.
Rolling Stones with Darryl Jones, Chuck Leavell, Bobby Keys, Lisa Fischer, Bernard Fowler, Blondie Chaplin, Tim Ries, Michael Davis, Kent Smith.
Producer: Michael Cohl, Zane Weiner, Steve Bing, Victoria Pearman.
Engineer: Mixing Editor: Bob Clearmountain; Re-Recording Mixer: Tom Fleischman; Music Recording Engineers: David Hewitt, Phil Gitomer, Bob Clearmountain; Digital Editing: Brandon Duncan; Mastered: Steve Marcussen.
Director: Martin Scorsese; Executive Producer: The Rolling Stones; Co-Executive Producer: Jane Rose.
USA CD SHINE A LIGHT: 1 April 2008: No. 11 - 7weeks
UK CD SHINE A LIGHT: 7 April 2008: No. 2 - 7 weeks
USA DVD Shine A Light: 29 July 2008
UK DVD Shine A Light: 3 November 2008

1534. YOU GOT THE SILVER (Jagger, Richards) ⟋ 3.21
1 November 2006: Place: Beacon Theatre, New York, USA.
Rolling Stones with Darryl Jones, Chuck Leavell, Blondie Chaplin.
Producer: Michael Cohl, Zane Weiner, Steve Bing, Victoria Pearman.
Engineer: Mixing Editor: Bob Clearmountain; Re-Recording Mixer: Tom Fleischman; Music Recording Engineers: David Hewitt, Phil Gitomer, Bob Clearmountain; Digital Editing: Brandon Duncan; Mastered: Steve Marcussen.
Director: Martin Scorsese; Executive Producer: The Rolling Stones; Co-Executive Producer: Jane Rose.
USA CD SHINE A LIGHT: 1 April 2008: No. 11 - 7weeks
UK CD SHINE A LIGHT: 7 April 2008: No. 2 - 7 weeks
USA DVD Shine A Light: 29 July 2008
UK DVD Shine A Light: 3 November 2008

1535. CONNECTION (Jagger, Richard) ⟋ 3.30
1 November 2006: Place: Beacon Theatre, New York, USA.
Rolling Stones with Darryl Jones, Chuck Leavell, Bobby Keys, Lisa Fischer, Bernard Fowler, Blondie Chaplin, Tim Ries, Michael Davis, Kent Smith
Producer: Michael Cohl, Zane Weiner, Steve Bing, Victoria Pearman.
Engineer: Mixing Editor: Bob Clearmountain; Re-Recording Mixer: Tom Fleischman; Music Recording Engineers: David Hewitt, Phil Gitomer, Bob Clearmountain; Digital Editing: Brandon Duncan; Mastered: Steve Marcussen.
Director: Martin Scorsese; Executive Producer: The Rolling Stones; Co-Executive Producer: Jane Rose.
USA CD SHINE A LIGHT: 1 April 2008: No. 11 - 7weeks
UK CD SHINE A LIGHT: 7 April 2008: No. 2 - 7 weeks
USA DVD Shine A Light: 29 July 2008
UK DVD Shine A Light: 3 November 2008

1536. SYMPATHY FOR THE DEVIL (Jagger, Richard) ⟋ 5.56
1 November 2006: Place: Beacon Theatre, New York, USA.
Rolling Stones with Darryl Jones, Chuck Leavell, Lisa Fischer, Bernard Fowler, Blondie Chaplin.
Producer: Michael Cohl, Zane Weiner, Steve Bing, Victoria Pearman.
Engineer: Mixing Editor: Bob Clearmountain; Re-Recording Mixer: Tom Fleischman; Music Recording Engineers: David Hewitt, Phil Gitomer, Bob Clearmountain; Digital Editing: Brandon Duncan; Mastered: Steve Marcussen.
Director: Martin Scorsese; Executive Producer: The Rolling Stones; Co-Executive Producer: Jane Rose.
USA CD SHINE A LIGHT: 1 April 2008: No. 11 - 7weeks
UK CD SHINE A LIGHT: 7 April 2008: No. 2 - 7 weeks
USA DVD Shine A Light: 29 July 2008
UK DVD Shine A Light: 3 November 2008

1537. LIVE WITH ME (Jagger, Richards) ⟋ 3.54
1 November 2006: Place: Beacon Theatre, New York, USA.
Rolling Stones with Christina Aguilera, Darryl Jones, Chuck Leavell, Bobby Keys, Lisa Fischer, Bernard Fowler, Blondie Chaplin.
Producer: Michael Cohl, Zane Weiner, Steve Bing, Victoria Pearman.
Engineer: Mixing Editor: Bob Clearmountain; Re-Recording Mixer: Tom Fleischman; Music Recording Engineers: David Hewitt, Phil Gitomer, Bob Clearmountain; Digital Editing: Brandon Duncan; Mastered: Steve Marcussen.
Director: Martin Scorsese; Executive Producer: The Rolling Stones; Co-Executive Producer: Jane Rose.
USA CD SHINE A LIGHT: 1 April 2008: No. 11 - 7weeks
UK CD SHINE A LIGHT: 7 April 2008: No. 2 - 7 weeks
USA DVD Shine A Light: 29 July 2008
UK DVD Shine A Light: 3 November 2008

1538. START ME UP (Jagger, Richard) ✗ 4.05
1 November 2006: Place: Beacon Theatre, New York, USA.
Rolling Stones with Darryl Jones, Chuck Leavell, Lisa Fischer, Bernard Fowler, Blondie Chaplin.
Producer: Michael Cohl, Zane Weiner, Steve Bing, Victoria Pearman.
Engineer: Mixing Editor: Bob Clearmountain; Re-Recording Mixer: Tom Fleischman; Music Recording Engineers: David Hewitt, Phil Gitomer, Bob Clearmountain; Digital Editing:
Brandon Duncan; Mastered: Steve Marcussen.
Director: Martin Scorsese; Executive Producer: The Rolling Stones; Co-Executive Producer: Jane Rose.
USA CD SHINE A LIGHT: 1 April 2008: No. 11 - 7weeks
UK CD SHINE A LIGHT: 7 April 2008: No. 2 - 7 weeks
USA DVD Shine A Light: 29 July 2008
UK DVD Shine A Light: 3 November 2008

1539. BROWN SUGAR (Jagger, Richard) ✗ 5.25
1 November 2006: Place: Beacon Theatre, New York, USA.
Rolling Stones with Darryl Jones, Chuck Leavell, Bobby Keys, Lisa Fischer, Bernard Fowler, Blondie Chaplin, Tim Ries, Michael Davis, Kent Smith.
Producer: Michael Cohl, Zane Weiner, Steve Bing, Victoria Pearman.
Engineer: Mixing Editor: Bob Clearmountain; Re-Recording Mixer: Tom Fleischman; Music Recording Engineers: David Hewitt, Phil Gitomer, Bob Clearmountain; Digital Editing:
Brandon Duncan; Mastered: Steve Marcussen.
Director: Martin Scorsese; Executive Producer: The Rolling Stones; Co-Executive Producer: Jane Rose.
USA CD SHINE A LIGHT: 1 April 2008: No. 11 - 7weeks
UK CD SHINE A LIGHT: 7 April 2008: No. 2 - 7 weeks
USA DVD Shine A Light: 29 July 2008
UK DVD Shine A Light: 3 November 2008

1540. (I CAN'T GET NO) SATISFACTION (Jagger, Richard) ✗ 5.37
1 November 2006: Place: Beacon Theatre, New York, USA.
Rolling Stones with Darryl Jones, Chuck Leavell, Bobby Keys, Lisa Fischer, Bernard Fowler, Blondie Chaplin, Tim Ries, Michael Davis, Kent Smith.
Producer: Michael Cohl, Zane Weiner, Steve Bing, Victoria Pearman.
Engineer: Mixing Editor: Bob Clearmountain; Re-Recording Mixer: Tom Fleischman; Music Recording Engineers: David Hewitt, Phil Gitomer, Bob Clearmountain; Digital Editing:
Brandon Duncan; Mastered: Steve Marcussen.
Director: Martin Scorsese; Executive Producer: The Rolling Stones; Co-Executive Producer: Jane Rose.
USA CD SHINE A LIGHT: 1 April 2008: No. 11 - 7weeks
UK CD SHINE A LIGHT: 7 April 2008: No. 2 - 7 weeks
USA DVD Shine A Light: 29 July 2008
UK DVD Shine A Light: 3 November 2008

The second concert was originally planned for Halloween, 31 October, but Mick Jagger's recurring throat problems delayed the show by a day. The final film commences with planning dialogue held during their tour at various concert venues. Scorsese suggested to Mick Jagger various songs that they could play like *Sitting On A Fence* and *Take It Or Leave It* while Mick was coming up with some different, unplayed material such as *Down The Road Apiece, Tell Me, Country Honk, Winter, Moonlight Mile* or even the funk cover of *Live It Up* by the Isley Brothers. Tracks considered from the latest album were *Biggest Mistake, Sweet Neocon* and *Laugh I Nearly Died.*

Scorsese was preparing individual tracks for camera shots so the set list was of major concern to him, something that Mick appeared to find funny and joked he would give Marty the final version an hour before the show, something that the film played up to. The final list arrived and the opening number was Marty's favourite, *Jumpin' Jack Flash* - "ok let's get ready to go". The banks of white neon lights illuminated not just the band but also the crowd at the front, which this time resembled a rock audience, albeit a young, predominantly female one. The show falls into line with the first night's set list as the New York-dominated *Shattered* followed.

The Big Apple theme is continued with *She Was Hot* and the backing group are now visible - Tim Ries playing keyboards with Chuck Leavell and the vocalists Lisa Fischer and Bernard Fowler, Blondie Chaplin on electric guitar. *All Down The Line* ensued and, to save space, both vocalists and the brass section are vertically placed on the stage as opposed to the more normal "in line" formation. Short cameo interviews intersperse some of the songs on the film release. Jack White, with his distinctive vocals, was the guest for a duet with Mick on *Loving Cup* and they both played acoustic guitar as well. White was given the choice of this song, *Let It Bleed* or *Some Girls*. His band The White Stripes had played *Stop Breaking Down* on their first self-titled album.

For *As Tears Go By*, Tim Ries unusually plays piano and, within the film, there is an orchestral backing track to the soft romantic song that Mick described as embarrassing when they first wrote it - ain't it lovely now? A three guitar-orientated *Some Girls* is next and Mick's vocal treatment bent and twisted the lyrics ironically as ever. More attention was made to the girls in New York with *Just My Imagination* where again Mick joined in on guitar, extending the song to seven minutes. The great *Far Away Eyes* was a change to the previous concert and Ronnie sat at his lap steel as Mick played up to the country drawl.

The moment when Keith clasped Mick with his arms when singing with him was captured by a defining, close-up shot. It was a pre-meditated moment which had been dreamed up back in March of that year. Marty wanted to capture the intimacy of the two guys who had been entwined since 1962. Buddy Guy is featured on a real blues highlight, *Champagne And Reefer*. Mick adjusts the lyrics to include and respect Buddy Guy's name and so inspired was Keith, that he presented his black Gibson to their special guest at the end of the song. The reverse cameras gave more of a perspective of the audience and the balconies on *Tumbling Dice* and an atmosphere of "a concert" was reached the further back and higher up they went.

A short-lived band introduction phase was captured before Keith's set of *You Got The Silver* - included at Marty's behest but not featuring Keith on guitar - and a rocked-up *Connection*. Afterwards Keith said that this was a departure for him and he felt liberated just singing and not playing. The film intermingled interview extracts but *Connection* showed them during the performance. The familiar red pastel lights and jungle percussive rhythm commenced the "woah woahs" within the audience until Mick joined off stage before suddenly arriving through the rear left audience door, resplendent in a backdrop of white light.

Security lined the gangway to ensure a safe walk to the stage, while his finger pointed aloft, silhouetted against the powerful wall of lights. This was an entrance planned by Scorsese since he agreed to act as the film maker. He was warned that if Mick stayed in the lights for more than 15 seconds then he would burn. Comically on film, Marty said, "We cannot burn Mick Jagger!" Once on stage, the lyrics begin and the white neon lights are used in place of the usual pyrotechnics. By now the crowd realised they were witnessing the denouement of the act and adjusted accordingly. Another microphone stand heralded the arrival of another guest in the curvaceous shape of Christina Aguilera. She sang, sidled up to Mick and shrilled her lungs off to *Live With Me*. In an interview, Charlie Watts suggested he introduced the others to the likes of Jack White and Christina.

Finally the anthems of *Honky Tonk Women* and *Start Me Up* continued before the band returned to perform *Brown Sugar* and *Satisfaction* and conclude the show. The Stones left the stage and, in the film, a camera morphs into Mick Jagger to exit the theatre and disappear over the city lights and the moon above New York, which mutates into a Stones tongue. Scorsese is seen providing a trademark acting cameo. The soundtrack, recorded by Dave Hewitt, Phil Gitomer and Bob Clearmountain (Ed Cherney was on family duties), was a credit to them all. Bob Clearmountain had to create separate mixes for theatrical film release, Imax, DVD 5.1 surround sound and normal DVD stereo, plus an entirely separate CD stereo version. He ended up mixing the material up to 15 times from a master of 80 channels, taking two years in total.

Each instrument was perfectly audible and mixed and blended to a superb live band sound. Marty wanted to hear Ronnie's guitar high in the middle of the mix when he saw a film image of him bending a note. It was if you were stood on stage next to the performer on screen. Of course, this was not the case for the CD version. The result could not be compared to other gigs at smaller venues where the audience was a lot more enthused, but it was still another career highlight. Martin Scorsese did justice to the concert and interlinked camera shots seamlessly, capturing winks, nods and nuances never normally witnessed at a concert.

One sad event that accompanied the Beacon show was that Ahmet Ertegun (president and co-founder of Atlantic Records), who was a guest backstage, was injured during a fall on the night of the first show on 29 October. At first he was stable in hospital but died on 14 December and so the film was dedicated to his memory. In France, two extra DVDs were included within the package, the first an interview with rock critic Philippe Manoeuvre and the second a documentary film, Vers l'Olympe, by Philippe Puicouyoul.

The latter was a series of interviews from fans from all over the world, concentrating primarily on the significance of the Paris Olympia theatre played during the Licks tour. The soundtrack of Martin Scorsese's film appeared as the first release on the Stones' new Universal label. The public first saw the film when it was shown at the Berlin Music Festival on 7 February 2008. It was debuted later in London, on 2 April 2008. Commenting in February 2008 for the sleeve notes of the impending release, Marty enthusiastically recalled the concert: "They stopped time, lifted us all up and delivered us into a world of pure beauty."

1541. SHINE A LIGHT (Jagger, Richard) ✏ 4.22
25 November 2006: Place: BC Place Arena, Vancouver, British Columbia, Canada.
Rolling Stones with Bonnie Raitt, Darryl Jones, Chuck Leavell, Lisa Fischer, Bernard Fowler, Blondie Chaplin.
Producer: The Rolling Stones
Engineer: Music Mix: Bob Clearmountain; Music Production: Ed Cherney; Additional Mixes / Engineer: Brandon Duncan.
Executive Producer: Michael Cohl, Director: Hamish Hamilton.
USA DVD The Biggest Bang: 23 June 2007
UK DVD The Biggest Bang: 5 August 2007

After the concert and the celebratory parties, the band jetted off to San Francisco, as the lyrics had reflected in the last performance of *Honky Tonk Women*. Over the Bay Bridge they went to Oakland for another stadium show where the encore was reduced to one number. After a concert in Arizona, Mick Jagger flew back to London to see his father, Joe Jagger, who had suffered a fall a week earlier. He found him improving and loyally jetted back to the tour for the next day's concert in Las Vegas, where unfortunately he learnt that his father had passed away that day.

However, Mick still performed at the MGM Grand that evening, proving gig cancellations were a last resort. He would also have been aware that the tour leg was about to conclude and, according to reports, all of the band jumped up another notch. The last gig was in Canada at the British Columbia Arena, in the western provinces. It was a fitting stadium to perform in and they delivered a hot show, made hotter by *Shine A Light*.

In rehearsal, Mick struggled to remember the chords on a piano; the song was a favourite of Bonnie Raitt who supported them that evening and sang with them on *Dead Flowers*, a few days earlier in Los Angeles. She was a big fan and had followed them on their 1969 tour after dropping out of college and starting a music career. It was a highlight for her to perform with the Stones and sing the vocals duet-style. The show was noticeable, too, for a rare three-song set by Keith Richards. The recordings were complete for *The Biggest Bang* DVD release and the song *Shine A Light* appeared as a bonus extra.

1542. START ME UP (Jagger, Richards) ✏ 3.49
10 June 2007: Place: Isle Of Wight Festival, Isle Of Wight, England.
Rolling Stones with Darryl Jones, Chuck Leavell.
Producer: The Rolling Stones
Director: Matt Askem.
Bootleg only.

1543. AIN'T TOO PROUD TO BEG (Whitfield, Holland) ✏ 4.01
10 June 2007: Place: Isle Of Wight Festival, Isle Of Wight, England.
Rolling Stones with Amy Winehouse, Darryl Jones, Chuck Leavell, Bobby Keys, Lisa Fischer, Bernard Fowler, Tim Ries, Michael Davis, Kent Smith.
Producer: The Rolling Stones
Director: Matt Askem.
Bootleg only.

The year 2006 had been busy, in keeping with the Stones' high profile across the world. As well as the Stones World Tour, Keith Richards had contended with a much-publicised, serious medical condition but had also appeared on various other projects. He was on a compilation disc of mainly religious folk songs, a family venture for his sister-in-law, Marsha Hansen. This included *Rock In Jerusalem*, *I Want Jesus To Walk With Me* and *Been In The Storm So Long*, on which Blondie Chaplin also guested.

There was the bit part filming of *Pirates Of The Caribbean* and contribution to one song on a Jerry Lee Lewis CD LAST MAN STANDING, which also included *Evening Gown*, with parts by Mick Jagger and Ron Wood. Ronnie had a compilation double album of solo material released ANTHOLOGY THE ESSENTIAL CROSSEXION, which included two Stones tracks, *Black Limousine* and *Everything Is Turning To Gold*, plus release of a New Barbarians live concert from 1979 BURIED ALIVE: LIVE IN MARYLAND. For all the band, the first five months of 2007 were an important time to prepare for more summer shows in Europe that had come about through cancellations the preceding year but also a genuine willingness to play live again.

The three-month tour was announced in March at the Grosvenor Hotel in London by a live webcast internet interview with Mick Jagger, hosted by Russ Williams. He confirmed the release of a four-DVD package of the Bigger Bang tour in May or June. They would kick off 27 dates at Werchter Park, in Belgium, on 6 June and conclude at London's O2 Arena on 21 August. There was also to be one other UK gig on the Isle Of White, climaxing the three-day festival on 10 June. Why did they choose the Isle Of Wight for their first UK festival in 30 years since Knebworth? Mick replied, "Because we were asked. It's like being asked to a party." This may have been a veiled question as to why they had selected that one above Glastonbury though, it has to be said, that the Stones had not performed at many festivals during their long career.

The conversation did not address the fact that the Stones' European booking agent was John Giddings, who was also promoting the Isle Of Wight event. Previously, the Stones had appeared at the Green Festival in Zurich in 1998 and, before that, the Richmond Jazz Festivals in 1963 and 1964. In the USA, they had played the West Palm Beach festival in 1969. Rehearsal for the tour started in Brussels on 26 May and lasted just over a week. For the first concert in Werchter, they introduced *Can't You Hear Me Knocking* back into the set list and only performed one track from the album. This continued at another park in the Netherlands, where Van Morrison provided the support, before moving across The Solent, from the location of Keith's West Wittering home to the Seaclose Park site, in Newport, Isle Of Wight.

The festival had witnessed Snow Patrol headlining on the Friday and Muse on the Saturday. Other support acts included Amy Winehouse and Paolo Nutini, Keane, Fratellis and Ash. The Stones set list was curtailed due to an 11pm Sunday curfew. It was a greatest hits package that relied on their core repertoire, something that the shows had now resorted to. To keep in touch, Paolo Nutini joined them for *Love In Vain* while the late, great Amy Winehouse mugged along to *Ain't Too Proud To Beg*.

Film footage of the concert was made and was broadcast during a 90-minute highlights show on Channel 4 television in the UK. Later that year, the Isle of Wight event won the award "Best Major Festival" at the UK Festival Awards. Acts such as Muse and The Rolling Stones were a major influence. As well as this, John Giddings won the award for "Outstanding Contribution to UK Festivals". In 2002, he had brought the historic festival back into the limelight after a 32-year gap. It was a one-man crusade, concentrating on the old-style, one-stage event instead of multi-stages as found at many other festivals.

1544. SHE WAS HOT (Jagger, Richards) ✏ 4.51
26 August 2007: Place: O2 Arena, London, England.
Rolling Stones with Darryl Jones, Chuck Leavell, Lisa Fischer, Bernard Fowler, Blondie Chaplin.
Bootleg only.

The tour moved along to Germany, two dates in France, two in northern Spain and over to Portugal before returning for another two frenetic concerts in Madrid and Almeria's El Ejido stadium. Regrettably in Madrid, two riggers were killed in a tragic accident when dismantling the stage. There was an unusually small but enthusiastic crowd at the Olympic Stadium in Rome before the beach of Jaz, near Budva, in Montenegro, was given the Stones treatment. The country had gained its independence from parts of the Socialist Federal Republic of Yugoslavia in 2006 and a formal President had yet to be elected. As ever, the Stones liked to be at the forefront of new territories.

The venue was constructed back from the sands in a beautiful natural arena, overshadowed by the "black mountains" and the Stones played a relaxed but shortened set in one of Europe's smallest countries. A few days later, the set list was even smaller when they played for a private party numbering some 700. Deutsche Bank paid a throw-away five million euros for the privilege, the gig taking place in the classic Sala Oval of the Palau Nacional, in Barcelona, Spain. *Rain Fall Down* was not promoted despite Mick Jagger making some financial jibes. The venues got bigger as they navigated the River Danube, taking in the capital cities of Serbia, Rumania and Hungary in an Eastern European heat wave. Next was Brno, in the Czech Republic, where *Love Is Strong* was returned to the set list. The Stones moved on to Warsaw, Poland and then the romantic setting of the iconic Palace Square of St Petersburg, where they accomplished the "perfect uprising" by playing *Sympathy For The Devil* and this time Anastasia, the last Russian Czar and his ministers, were spared from execution.

The four Scandinavian countries were next in the lands of the almost never setting sun. More traditional touring countries of Switzerland and two cities in Germany started the last few weeks of the trip. The final dates were left to Slane Castle in Dublin, Ireland, and three indoor gigs at the O2 Arena in London, England. The Stones were now firmly back at the centre of Greenwich mean time. The entourage swelled as the band, children and now grandchildren visited to see them on their final tour dates.

1545. I'LL GO CRAZY (Brown) ✏ 3.20
26 August 2007: Place: O2 Arena, London, England.
Rolling Stones with Darryl Jones, Chuck Leavell, Lisa Fischer, Bernard Fowler, Blondie Chaplin.
Bootleg only.

For the final night and what remains as their last ever concert, the children joined the band for *Sympathy For The Devil* and sang along with Blondie Chaplin, Bernard Fowler and Lisa Fischer on the "woohs". Keith Richards thought the sound and atmosphere at the O2 Dome was a great experience. For the last date, Bill Wyman was in attendance but did not join them on stage. The band were determined to provide a great show and, having played three dates on the Tuesday, Thursday and Sunday at the same venue, expectations were high. The set list was consistent, except from song five until eight, when it was varied every night.

The first gig had the slower *Let It Bleed* and *Beast Of Burden*, while the second had *She's So Cold* and *Shine A Light*. The final night featured *Ain't Too Proud To Beg* and, for only the third time that year (and ever live), *She Was Hot* was included. The latter appeared as a video on rollingstones.com. Mick remarked that it had taken 40 years to get them from their origins in Richmond to Greenwich and Keith Richards said that the tour had been a long haul. It had commenced two years earlier and amounted to nearly 150 shows. The confetti that rained down that evening made for an extremely poignant moment when *Brown Sugar* concluded proceedings. *I'll Go Crazy* was a James Brown song that was featured on the 2007 European leg and therefore was not released on any media. It was from James Brown's 1960 album THINK! and was a showcase for Lisa Fischer.

There was speculation that the tour would re-commence in spring 2008 to accompany the release of the *Shine A Light* movie. However, Keith's plans were suddenly devastated when Patti Hansen developed cancer and their time was devoted to her recovery. Mick had one more release in 2007, a solo collection titled THE VERY BEST OF MICK JAGGER. There was a Decca re-release on the back of the ABKCO re-masters ROLLED GOLD with a + appendage, since 12 additional tracks were released in November.

As well as the 10, there were two extra tracks not on the original release - *Brown Sugar* and *Wild Horses* - in their attempt to release a complete as possible greatest hits and B-sides from the 60s. Ronnie Wood oversaw the release of a recording of his 1974 solo concert with Keith, that spawned the New Barbarians concept. The album was titled LIVE FROM KILBURN. Keith released a download single of his *Run Rudolph Run* song, this time coupled with the recent version of *Pressure Drop* that he did with Toots & The Maytals for their 2005 album TRUE LOVE. On 7 February 2008, the Stones joined Martin Scorsese at the Berlin Film Festival for the premiere of the *Shine A Light* concert documentary film of the Beacon Theatre shows.

Their public welcome at the press conference in Berlin was very enthusiastic, which visibly surprised them. To summarise why they were so popular, Mick put on his best London mockney accent: "I'd say the defining thing about the Rolling Stones is that we're very British. It's very British rock 'n' roll." Further promotions and premieres occurred in New York on 24 March and 2 April in London while the soundtrack was released at the same time on a one-album contract with Universal. The Stones formally left EMI Records on 25 July, after their contract expired in May, to permanently sign up with Universal Music Group.

Their catalogue since the 70s issue of STICKY FINGERS went with them. Strangely, Decca Records was now a subsidiary of Universal, so a full circle had been achieved. *You Can't Always Get What You Want* received a new, digital download release, re-mixed by the Belgium Dewaele Brothers (known as Soulwax) for the 2008 film *21*. Keith Richards had a 1994 track, *Burn Your House Down*, recorded with George Jones, released on the album BURN YOUR PLAYHOUSE DOWN: THE UNRELEASED DUETS. He also saw the release of the Merle Haggard-penned *Sing Me Back Home*, recorded late in 2007 with Marianne Faithfull, on her new album EASY COME EASY GO. In October, he performed with the Crickets on *That'll Be The Day*, *Not Fade Away* and *Peggy Sue* at the Rock 'n' Roll Hall Of Fame.

Ronnie Wood and Rod Stewart were talking promisingly about a Faces reunion in 2009. Ronnie had also become besotted by drink again and by a Russian good-time waitress named Ekaterina, whom he had met in an escort bar. In the summer, he left his wife Jo to set up house with Ekaterina at his Irish home in County Kildare. During that year, drummer Carlo Little, who had played off and on with the Stones in the very early days, had a posthumous album of cover songs released. Ronnie played on three tracks on CARLO LITTLE ALLSTARS, which had been recorded in 2001.

Ronnie based himself in Los Angeles and used the early part of 2009 to demo and record some new songs for a solo release and also to attend a session for Jerry Lee Lewis. Along with Keith, he appeared on the new Dirty Strangers album WEST 12 TO WITTERING (ANOTHER WESTSIDE STORY). Their extensive contribution, where Keith played piano, guitar and co-wrote two songs, was made in 2007 after the A Bigger Bang tour. Alan Clayton was the band songwriter who, as a friend of Keith, had joined the Stones on tour as part of the guitar technical backline.

1546. WATCHING THE RIVER FLOW (Dylan) 5.09
1-5 February; February; 21 October; November 2010: Place: Helicon Mountain Studio, Blackheath, London; Chapel Studios, London; One East Studios, New York, USA; La Fourchette Home Studio, Fourchette, Tours, France.
Rolling Stones with Bill Wyman, Ben Waters, Tom Waters, Jools Holland, Willy Garnet, Don Weller, Alex Garnet, Dave Swift
Producer: Ben Waters. Assistant Producer: Glyn Johns, Mick McKenna
Engineer: Charles Reeves, Mick McKenna, Head, Mike Hallet, Steven Williams, Matt Clifford, Matt Wells. Mixed: Glyn Johns.
Executive Producer: Sherry Daly
UK CD BOOGIE 4 STU: 18 April 2011

Charlie Watts started touring in April 2009 with a new outfit labelled The ABC of Boogie Woogie band, including Axel Zwingenberger and Ben Watts on piano. Axel was a known German solo artist and had contributed to Bill Wyman's 2005 JUST FOR A THRILL album. Ben Waters was a pianist whose family were friends of Ian Stewart. While at a family party aged just eight, Ben witnessed Ian Stewart playing and that inspired him to follow a career in music. Ian Stewart also sent back cine-film reels of his favourite piano players to the family from America when on tour with the Stones - he had filmed the likes of Albert Ammons, Pete Johnson and Meade Lux Lewis.

Ben studied these films and, such was his mastery of the Stewart style, that he was subsequently asked to play with Rocket 88 following Ian's death. The catalogue of stars he has played for include royalty, Mick Jagger and the likes of Chuck Berry, Jools Holland, Dave Gilmour and Shirley Bassey, to name a few. The music was mostly unashamed authentic piano-based boogie woogie, inspired by Amos Milburn and Fats Domino. Dave Green, the double bass exponent from the original Rocket 88 band and childhood friend of Charlie, later joined them - so they became the ABC and D of Boogie Woogie band.

The Faces reunion did not happen but, with Mick Hucknall as vocalist, there was a one-off charity gig where Ron Wood and Bill Wyman joined Ian McLagan and Kenney Jones as the Faces. Don Was had started work on the re-issue of the EXILE ON MAIN ST album, that would include bonus tracks. He sifted through material converted from reel-to-reel tape to the digital format in order to come up with a shortlist of additional tracks recorded in that era. He found that many were incomplete and lacked any vocals so, in the autumn, Mick Jagger, with Keith Richards' input, worked out the detail for adding these, as well as recording backing vocals, percussion and some guitar. Mick Taylor was asked to go into a London studio with Mick to add some guitar for *Plundered My Soul* and Keith Richards also supplied some guitar parts, in particular for *So Divine*.

The move to include Mick Taylor was a gracious one and acknowledged what a strong part he had played in that Stone Age of the late 60s and early 70s. In late October, Mick Jagger went on stage with U2 in New York to sing *Gimme Shelter* and *Stuck In A Moment* for the 25th anniversary of the Rock and Roll Hall of Fame - the songs were included on a compilation CD in November. Charlie continued work with the ABC and D Band and Ronnie legally separated from Jo Wood, only to find his new relationship on the rocks by the end of the year.

The year 2009 also marked the passing away of Tom Keylock, a stalwart Stones employee from the 60s and Allen Klein, of ABKCO. In late 2009, the Stones confirmed the re-release of EXILE, with bonus tracks, for the following year. In January 2010, a press statement revealed that there would be no tour that year. Ben Waters was keen to follow a personal aspiration to record a tribute album in aid of the British Heart Foundation for Ian Stewart, just over 25 years after his death. The natural approach was to ask Charlie, with whom he was playing, for his view and he said he would gladly help and contribute to the recording.

Ben also knew Jools Holland, who offered up his Helicon Mountain studio free of charge to record the album, as more people agreed to play in honour of Ian. Studio time was booked for the first week of February. The week in London was a very friendly, family affair, literally and musically as Ben's son Tom also performed on *Watching The River Flow* - Ben's mother Ann, who is also his manager, was in attendance. Ben approached old friends Willy Garnet (Alex is Willy's son) and Don Weller from Rocket 88. Dave Swift was a musician for the Jools Holland band and supported with bass and percussion. Hamish Maxwell, who also knew Ian and was best man at his wedding, was a guest vocalist.

After the foundations of the recordings were made in two days, Ben phoned Sherry Daly at the Stones office to update her. Ronnie Wood happened to be in the office and offered to come in on the third day to participate. Sherry Daly then thought it appropriate that Ben write to Bill Wyman, Keith and Mick to let them know. They also wanted to offer their services. Bill Wyman overdubbed three album cuts in London. The 11 tracks recorded that would appear on the album, together with two original Rocket 88 live songs, featured seven by Charlie. One of these, *Kidney Stew*, was only released in Japan as a bonus. The principal Stones-related numbers were *Rooming House Boogie* (Keith on guitar and Bill on bass), *Worried Life Blues* (Ronnie on vocals and guitar, Charlie drums and Keith vocals), *Roll 'Em Pete* (Charlie and Bill) and *Watching The River Flow*.

The latter track was recorded via three or four different sources. The band and Ronnie did their parts first at Helicon, while Bill overdubbed his bass at Chapel Studios, Keith went to a New York studio and Mick added his harmonica and vocals at home in France. *Watching The River Flow* was selected by Ben because he knew it was the only piano-based one by Dylan that Ian liked (it featured Leon Russell). Ben Waters flew to New York and met Keith Richards at the One East Studios on 21 October. The original intention was that Keith wanted to contribute to Amos Milburn's *Rooming House Boogie* since he liked the song but, in a seven-hour session, he did much more. On *Worried Life Blues*, he asked if he could do a guitar part and vocals. Ronnie had already done vocals but Ben suggested a compromise and shared, alternate verses, were recorded. Quite accidentally, he also chose to play guitar on *Watching The River Flow* - Ben confirmed it was not by design. Ben really enjoyed his time with Keith, describing him as a humorous, warm, true gentleman.

Later in the year, Mick finalised the track by recording his vocal and harp in La Fourchette, engineered by Matt Clifford. Originally Ben was going to do a vocal but, as soon as Mick agreed, that was fine by him! The result became a genuine, full-band contribution by the Stones and, musically, reunited them with Bill Wyman for the first time since 1991. The only non-cover was written by Ben with Jools Holland and it became the album title, BOOGIE 4 STU. This was similar to the name of the song - Boogie With Stu - that Ian had recorded with Led Zeppelin for their PHYSICAL GRAFFITI album. Ian Stewart's friends Glyn Johns, who was the Stones first producer, and Mick McKenna (Stones recording engineer) helped Ben out with album production.

Ben Waters' cousin, solo artiste PJ Harvey, was on vocals for one track and the album was completed by material from a Rocket 88 gig at the 1984 Montreux Jazz Festival. The artwork for the album was provided by Stones fan Sir Peter Blake, with a great water colour portrait of Ian.

STILL ROLLING . . .

Activities continued in the Stones camp with the long-awaited appearance of the extras on the re-issue of EXILE ON MAIN ST preceded by the single release of *Plundered My Soul*. To prove the commercial worth of this venture, the album went to number one in the UK and USA, the first time this had happened since EMOTIONAL RESCUE. Following the Ian Stewart tribute album in April 2010, the *Stones In Exile* film was released, produced for the BBC by Stephen Kijak and premiered in Cannes, France, on 19 May. It contained archive and unseen footage but also current interviews at Stargroves and Olympic Studios and with guests, including Don Was. It came out on DVD in July. Keith released the second Wingless Angels album in August, WINGLESS ANGELS II. It had been recorded over many years and overdubbed for release by Steve Jordan, Bernard Fowler and Lisa Fischer. Keith's much-awaited biography *Life* appeared in the shops in October, the subject providing maximum exposure, with interviews and book releases in the USA and Europe.

The content was written by reputable Fleet Street journalist James Fox, who interviewed Keith extensively and researched contacts vigorously. He managed to articulate Keith's style and manner very plausibly. Mick was given advance access to some extracts before publication but did not see it all. On release, he found some topics were a little close to the knuckle which upset the relationship between them both. Of course, some extracts were sensationalised but overall the book was well received and leapt to the best sellers' number one position. It was refreshingly honest and made much of the music.

By August 2011, the book had amassed more than one million sales and much credit must go to Keith and James Fox. Surely the success of *Life* would awaken Mick's literary urges? Ron Wood started a regular radio show for UK Absolute Radio and received critical acclaim when he was presented with the Sony "best newcomer" award for national radio in 2011. He did three gigs with the Faces, featuring Glen Matlock on bass and a very worthy rock-sounding Mick Hucknall on vocals, delivering the pitches that Rod Stewart admitted he could no longer reach. There was one outdoor festival gig as headliners at the Goodwood Vintage Festival on 13 August, preceded a few days earlier by a very small press concert at the O2 Bubble. They also played in Denmark at a small indoor venue for just over 1,000 people.

In September, there was an official release in cinemas of the Stones' *Ladies & Gentlemen* film from the 1972 USA tour, followed by a DVD in November. This release, the EXILE extras disc and other film projects demonstrated a renewed enthusiasm for the wealth of material available in the vaults. The special edition format, with replica scarf and poster from the 1974 cinematic release, included the *Stones In Exile* film and The Dick Cavett interviews from 1973, with performance extracts. Ronnie Wood's recordings from 2009 materialised in a solo album I FEEL LIKE PLAYING, following on from his "I Feel Like Painting" art exhibitions.

He described it as therapeutic and "like washing your underwear in public". A whole host of session player luminaries had participated on another creditable Ronnie album - Slash, Billy Gibbons, Bob Rock, Bobby Womack, Waddy Wachtel, Ian McLagan, Ivan Neville, Flea (Red Hot Chilli Peppers) on bass, Steve Ferrone (drums), Jim Keltner, Blondie Chaplin and Darryl Jones. A month later, he played a one-off gig, performing the entire album at the Ambassadors Theatre in London on 19 October. The dates were recorded and the second show in its entirety appeared in March 2011 on a double live vinyl-only album produced by Stones fan, collector and aficionado Matt Lee. Matt was also credited for archive artefacts within the EXILE and SOME GIRLS re-releases. Ron played alongside Mick Taylor in the Steven Dale Petit All Stars band, with Dick Taylor on bass, Jack Greenwood on drums and the great all-star himself, Chris Barber, on trombone. Keith Richards also had a release of the best of his solo recordings VINTAGE WINOS. It included a version of the Stones' *Too Rude*, played live by the X-Pensive Winos.

The ABC and D of Boogie Woogie continued to tour in France and Italy, during September. Mick attended the annual Grammy awards on 13 February and performed with guitarist Raphael Saadiq and his band on *Everybody Needs Somebody To Love*, a tribute to Solomon Burke. He had also commenced recordings with performers Dave Stewart, Joss Stone, Damian Marley and A R Rahman in an eclectic outfit named SuperHeavy. The reggae-influenced *Miracle Worker* proved to be a hit at summer festivals. Their album SUPERHEAVY was released in September 2011. Charlie commenced a European tour with the ABC and D Band, which took in a gig at the Ambassadors Theatre, London, with two different sets. It was a very special evening, hosted by Jools Holland, who also performed. The backing band was Charlie Watts and Bill Wyman, Willy Garnet, Don Weller and Tom Waters all on sax, Martyn Hope (Shakin' Stevens Band) on guitar and, at different times, Hamish Maxwell and Shakin' Stevens contributing vocals. The show lived up to all expectations when Ron Wood and Mick Taylor joined the proceedings too. Rumours that Mick and Keith would play were unfounded. In April 2011, an ambitious Universal project to release 45 Rolling Stones singles was achieved - 45 X 5 THE SINGLES COLLECTION: 1971-2006 - with the help of Bill Wyman. While not claiming to be a complete recount of their single catalogue, including mixes and B-sides since *Brown Sugar*, it was unfortunate that a full set of this work was not achieved.

Ron's enthusiasm could not be extinguished - he was performing with the Charlatans, Hothouse Flowers and, in the summer of 2011, with Rod Stewart for a couple of numbers in London. The new Faces band got back together again in July, performing at the Cornbury Festival, near Oxford, in Belgium, Netherlands, at Kenney Jones' polo club and also at the Japanese Fuji Festival. Mick Jagger was at the top of the USA charts at least in name when Maroon 5 charted at No. 1 with a single featuring Christine Aguilera - *Moves Like Jagger*. He also guested on a will.i.am and Jennifer Lopez December single release, which reached No. 3 in February 2012. A completely mad-cap string of Stones releases followed in November when, not only was SOME GIRLS re-issued with bonus tracks, but an official release was also made of the 1978 USA Fort Worth show, in both DVD and CD formats. Finally, the Brussels 1973 show, with Mick Taylor, completed the classic output available from a new, official "archive" download website. To provide an indication of possible future work, the band got together at Jeremy Stacey's Snake Ranch Studio, Chelsea, London from 6-9 December 2011 simply to jam together. It was Charlie's idea to use Jeremy's studio which was out of the way next door to the 606 Jazz Club. Bill Wyman was invited to sit in on bass and Ben Waters on piano, while reportedly Mick turned up during the last day. Mick Taylor was also invited but was prevented from attending by family commitments abroad. Further "bootleg" albums from the archives were released of the 1981 Hampton concert in January 2012 and, in April 2012, from the 1975 North America's Tour a concert was released from the L.A. Forum.

In February, Mick appeared at the White House for President Obama's Blues Night and Keith played at the "black house", namely the Harlem Apollo, with Eric Clapton and James Cotton. Late March saw Ron busy appearing with Kelly Jones, Roger Daltrey and Paul McCartney during their performances in London for a Cancer Trust charity. He also recorded a solo track, *Coming Together*, on 25 March at Kore Studios in London with Mick Taylor and Kelly Jones, which was produced by Chris Kimsey and mixed later at Olympic Studios. At the Rock and Roll Hall of Fame awards in April he picked up a second nomination for inauguration and the Faces and Small Faces joined his "other" band in being inducted too. He commented that this inauguration he remembered, since he was completely sober, unlike the first one in 1989. During the same month, he performed a great set-list of solo tracks, Faces and Stones' songs in Atlantic City with Bernard Fowler, Chuck Leavell, Willy Weeks, Steve Jordan and Andy Wallace. The ABC and D of Boogie Woogie continued to tour in March and Mick Taylor was an invited special guest at several gigs. The band met again in New York for a few days from 1 May 2012 where the four main members jammed again with Chuck Leavell and Don Was on bass and talked about future plans. On the last day they were filmed by Brett Morgen for a documentary celebrating the group's anniversary due for release in the autumn. On the 19 May, Mick hosted, acted and performed on the end of season Saturday Night Live programme in New York. The three musical interludes were with the Foo Fighters (*19th Nervous Breakdown* and *It's Only Rock 'n' Roll*), then Jeff Beck (a new song: *Tea Party*) and Arcade Fire (*The Last Time* and *Ruby Tuesday*). Quite a statement, since he had only played a few weeks earlier with his main band. Another Ron Wood gig along with Mick Taylor and Bill Wyman celebrated the history of Chess Records at London's Hammersmith Apollo on 30 June. It was announced in June that Keith contributed guitar and co-produced with Don Was on Aaron Neville's new album due for autumn release. The A B C & D of Boogie Woogie featuring Charlie Watts released their first album LIVE IN PARIS in late June 2012 and another archive release in the second week of July produced the full Tokyo Dome concert of 26 February, 1990. The same week there was a release from 1981 of the Muddy Waters with Buddy Guy and Junior Wells concert which included guest spots by Mick Jagger, Keith Richards, Ron Wood and Ian Stewart. The sound was newly mixed by Bob Clearmountain for CD and DVD format.

While this hiatus of activities continued, the 50th anniversary of the Stones' creation in 1962 crept up on 12 July, 2012 and during the month another band meeting took place in London. They also conducted picture calls and interviews to coincide with their anniversary date and attended a photo exhibition at Somerset House, London, which celebrated their 50-year career and the release of their book *The Rolling Stones 50* made in conjunction with The Daily Mirror newspaper. Mick Jagger at Somerset House gave a promise to one news agency stating: ". . . 50 years seems an awfully long time but seems to have gone very, very quickly" and to the inevitable question whether the band would appear again: "definitely later on, later on this year, on stage ok." Keith argued that this was the anniversary of the conception when Jagger, Jones and Richards first played live as the Rollin' Stones at the Marquee. But the anniversary can stretch until 2013, since the birth of the band took place on 12 January, 1963 at Ealing Jazz club when, finally, Charlie and Bill joined their concert line-up.

There may be plans to venture into the studio and record again but, to date, no tour has been announced on the back of any release; the summer of 2012 was busy enough with The Queen's Golden Jubilee celebrations and the London Olympic Games. If and when another tour does happen, don't expect the old format, as it's likely that just a few big cities or festivals around the world would be strategically selected for a number of concerts. Would they end up by playing an English final show at Knebworth or Glastonbury in 2013?

Keith Richards has said that, "The Rolling Stones are bigger and better than any of the single parts - there is nothing that will surpass what the band can do together." They have progressed in rock 'n' roll from beyond youth, gathered maturity and achieved the status of senior rock statesmen to a position of just growing old gracefully - as opposed to disgracefully. Individually, they have proved that there is something beyond the enigma of the Rolling Stones. One thing is for certain, millions of fans, old and new, continue rocking to the phenomenon that is The Rolling Stones. Their star and legend will not be eclipsed even if the sun is setting and a new lunar crescent rises to illuminate their achievements.

SESSION TRACKS INDEX

(Available as a file on stonessessions.com)
* Not Officially Released Tracks

1962

January - March 1962 Bexleyheath, Kent, England.
1. **Around And Around (Little Boy Blue & The Blue Boys)** (Time: 1.21) *
2. **Little Queenie (Little Boy Blue & The Blue Boys)** (Time: 4.32) *
   (a) Alternative Take - (4.11)
3. **Beautiful Delilah (Little Boy Blue & The Blue Boys)** (Time: 2.58) *
   (a) Alternative Take - (2.18)
4. **La Bamba (Little Boy Blue & The Blue Boys)** (Time: 0.18) *
5. **Go On To School (Little Boy Blue & The Blue Boys)** (Time: 2.02) *
6. **You're Right, I'm Left, She's Gone (Little Boy Blue & The Blue Boys)** (Time: 2.31) *
7. **Down The Road Apiece (Little Boy Blue & The Blue Boys)** (Time: 2.12) *
8. **Don't Want No Woman (Little Boy Blue & The Blue Boys)** (Time: 2.30) *
9. **I Ain't Got You (Little Boy Blue & The Blue Boys)** (Time: 2.00) *
10. **Johnny B. Goode (Little Boy Blue & The Blue Boys)** (Time: 2.24) *
11. **Reelin' And A Rockin' (Little Boy Blue & The Blue Boys)** *
12. **Bright Lights, Big City (Little Boy Blue & The Blue Boys)** *

27 October 1962 Curly Clayton Sound Studios, Highbury, London, England.
13. **You Can't Judge A Book By The Cover** (Time: 0.36) *
14. **Soon Forgotten** *
15. **Close Together** *

1963

11 March 1963 IBC Studios, London, England.
16. **Diddley Daddy** (Time: 2.38) *
17. **Road Runner** (Time: 3.02) *
18. **I Want To Be Loved** (Time: 1.53) *
19. **Baby, What's Wrong?** (Time: 3.24) *
20. **Bright Lights, Big City** (Time: 2.25) *

20 April 1963 R G Jones Studio, Morden, Surrey, England.
21. **Pretty Thing** *
22. **It's All Right Babe** *

23 April 1963 BBC Radio, London, England.
23. **I'm Moving On** *
24. **I'm A Hog For You Baby** *

10 May 1963 Olympic Studios, Carton St, London, England.
25. **Come On** (Time: 1.50)
26. **I Want To Be Loved** (Time: 1.51)

9 July 1963 Decca, West Hampstead, London, England.
27. **Fortune Teller** (Time: 2.18)
   (a) Alternative Take - (2.06)

15 July 1963 Decca, West Hampstead, London, England.
28. **Poison Ivy** (Time: 2.30)

8 August 1963 Decca, West Hampstead, London, England.
29. **You Better Move On** (Time: 2.40)
30. **Bye Bye Johnny** (Time: 2.12)
31. **Money** (Time: 2.34)

23 September 1963 BBC Maida Vale Studios, London, England.
32. **Money** *
33. **I'm Talkin' About You** *
34. **Come On** (Time: 2.02) *
35. **Memphis Tennessee** (Time: 2.20) *
36. **Roll Over Beethoven** (Time: 2.17) *

7 October 1963 De Lane Lea Studios, Kingsway, London, England.
37. **I Wanna Be Your Man** (Time: 1.43) *
38. **Stoned** (Time: 2.09)

14-15 November 1963 Decca, West Hampstead, London, England.
39. **Go Home Girl** (Time: 2.26) *
40. **I'm Talkin' About You** *
41. **Poison Ivy** (Time: 2.09)

20-21 November 1963 Regent Sound Studios, London, England.
43. **Shang A Doo Lang** (Time: 0.10) *
44. **My Only Girl** (Time: 2.01) *
45. **That Girl Belongs To Yesterday** *
46. **Leave Me Alone** (Time: 1.57) *

20-21 November, 7 December 1963 Regent Sound Studios, London, England.
42. **Will You Be My Lover Tonight?** *
47. **Sure I Do** *
48. **So Much In Love** (Time: 0.11) *
49. **Give Me Your Hand** (Time: 0.06) *
50. **I Want You To Know** (Time: 0.11) *
51. **When A Girl Loves A Boy** (Time: 0.21) *
52. **You Must Be The One** (Time: 0.16) *
53. **It Should Be You** (Time: 1.45) *
54. **Tell Me (You're Coming Back) (Early Version)** (Time: 2.47)
   (a) Alternative Take - (3.02)

1964

2 January 1964 Regent Sound Studios, London, England.
55. **To Know Him Is To Love Him** (Time: 3.09)
56. **There Are But Five Rolling Stones** (Time: 2.23)

3 January 1964 Regent Sound Studios, London, England.
57. **Route 66** (Time: 2.23)
58. **Mona (I Need You Baby)** (Time: 3.35)
59. **Carol** (Time: 2.35)

10 January Regent Sound Studios, London, England.
61. **(Walkin' Thru The) Sleepy City** (Time: 2.52)
62. **Each And Everyday Of The Year** (Time: 2.49)

10, 28 January, 4 February 1964 Regent Sound Studios, London, England.
60. **Not Fade Away** (Time: 1.49)
   (a) Take 1 - (1.49)

28 January, 24-25 February 1964 Regent Sound Studios, London, England.
63. **I Just Want To Make Love To You** (Time: 2.19)
64. **Honest I Do** (Time: 2.12)
65. **I'm A King Bee** (Time: 2.37)
66. **You Can Make It If You Try** (Time: 2.03)
67. **Walking The Dog** (Time: 3.11)
68. **Tell Me (You're Coming Back)** (Time: 3.49)
   (a) Long Cut - (4.05)

January 1964 Regent Sound Studios, London, England.
69. **Oh I Do Like To See Me On The B-Side** (Time: 2.24) J
70. **365 Rolling Stones (One For Each Day Of The Year)** (Time: 2.01)

3 February 1964 BBC Maida Vale Studios, London, England.
71. **Don't Lie To Me** (Time: 1.43) *
72. **Mona** (Time: 2.11) *
73. **Walking The Dog** (Time: 2.35) *

380

74. Bye Bye Johnny (Time: 2.11) *
75. I Wanna Be Your Man (Time: 1.49) *
76. You Better Move On (Time: 2.35) *

4 February 1964 Regent Sound Studios, London, England.
77. Andrew's Blues (Time: 3.03) *
78. Mr Spector And Mr Pitney Came Too (Time: 2.47) *
79. Little By Little (Time: 2.41)
80. Can I Get A Witness (Time: 2.58)
81. Now I've Got A Witness (Like Uncle Phil and Uncle Gene)
   (Time: 2.32)

6 February 1964 Star Sound Studios, London, England.
82. Wake Up In The Morning (Time: 0.27) *

24-25 February 1964 Regent Sound Studios, London, England.
85. Good Times, Bad Times (Time: 2.30)
86. Over You *

March 1964 Olympic Studios, Carton St, London, England.
43. Shang A Doo Lang (Time: 0.10) *

8-14 March 1964 De Lane Lea Studios, Kingsway, Olympic, London, England.
87. As Time Goes By (Time: 2.13) *

8-14 March 1964 De Lane Lea Studios, Kingsway, London, England.
88. No One Knows (Time: 0.09) *
89. Come And Dance With Me *

18 March 1964 Regent Sound Studios or IBC Studios, London, England.
90. Look What You've Done *

13 April 1964 BBC Maida Vale Studios, London, England.
100. Not Fade Away (Time: 2.07) *
101. Walking The Dog (Time: 3.00) *
102. I Just Want To Make Love To You (Time: 2.11) *
103. Beautiful Delilah (Time: 2.18) *
104. High Heeled Sneakers (Time: 2.34) *
105. Carol (Time: 2.30) *

20 April 1964 ITV TV Ready Steady Go!, Montreux, Switzerland.
106. Mona *
107. Route 66 *
108. Not Fade Away *

12 May 1964 Regent Sound Studios, London, England.
115. Don't Lie To Me (Time: 2.02)

12 May, 24-26 June 1964 Regent Sound Studios, London, England.
116. Congratulations (Time: 2.29)

25 May 1964 BBC Broadcasting House, London, England.
117. Down In The Bottom (Time: 2.46) *
118. You Can Make It If You Try (Time: 2.13) *
119. Route 66 (Time: 2.27) *
120. Confessin' The Blues (Time: 3.00) *
121. Down The Road Apiece (Time: 2.05) *

3 June 1964 Hollywood Palace TV Show, Los Angeles, California, USA.
122. Not Fade Away (Time: 1.55) *
123. I Just Want To Make Love To You (Time: 1.12) *

10 June 1964 Chess Studios, Chicago, USA.
124. Stewed and Keefed (Time: 4.12) *
125. I Can't Be Satisfied (Time: 3.26)
126. Time Is On My Side (Time: 2.56)
127. It's All Over Now (Time: 3.28)
   (a) USA Edit Version - (2.48)

10-11 June 1964 Chess Studios, Chicago, USA.
128. Reelin' And A Rockin' (Time: 3.32) *

11 June 1964 Chess Studios, Chicago, USA.
129. If You Need Me (Time: 2.05)
130. Empty Heart (Time: 2.38)
131. 2120 South Michigan Avenue (Time: 2.38)
   (a) Extended Version - (3.39)
132. Confessin' The Blues (Time: 2.48)
133. Around And Around (3.04)
134. High Heeled Sneakers (Time: 2.59) *
135. Tell Me Baby (Time: 1.57)
136. Down In The Bottom (Time: 2.43) *
137. Down The Road Apiece (Time: 2.51)
138. Look What You've Done (Time: 2.16)

18 June 1964 Mike Douglas Show, Cleveland, Ohio, USA.
139. Carol (Time: 2.49) *
140. Tell Me (You're Coming Back) (Time: 2.35) *
141. Not Fade Away (Time: 2.00)

24-26 June 1964 Regent Sound Studios, London, England.
142. Time Is On My Side (Time: 2.52)
143. You've Just Made My Day (Time: 0.38) *
144. Off The Hook (Time: 2.34)
145. You Can't Catch Me (Time: 3.30)

1-10 July 1964 Greenford Studios, Greenford, Regent Sound Studios, Decca,
West Hampstead, London, England.
146. Godzi *
147. Memphis Tennessee (Time: 2.28)
148. Some Things Just Stick In Your Mind (Time: 2.27)
149. We're Wastin' Time (Time: 2.44)
   (a) Take 1 - (2.53)
150. Blue Turns To Grey (Time: 2.29) *
151. Try A Little Harder (Time: 2.19)

1-10 July 1964, 31 August 1964 - 4 September 1964 Greenford Studios,
Greenford, Decca, West Hampstead, Regent Sound, London, England.
61. (Walkin' Thru The) Sleepy City (Time: 2.52)
62. Each And Everyday Of The Year (Time: 2.49)

17 July 1964 Playhouse Theatre, London, England.
152. It's All Over Now (Time: 3.29) *
153. If You Need Me (Time: 2.01) *
154. Confessin' The Blues (Time: 3.00) *
155. Carol (Time: 2.38) *
156. Mona (Time: 2.58) *
157. Around And Around (Time: 2.45) *
158. If You Need Me (Time: 2.02) *
159. I Can't Be Satisfied (Time: 2.30) *
160. Crackin' Up (Time: 2.14) *

21 July-August 1964 Regent Sound Studios, Decca, West Hampstead, London,
England.
161. Heart Of Stone (Time: 3.48) *
   (a) Alternative Mix - (4.11)

31 August 1964 - 4 September 1964 Greenford Studios, Greenford, Decca, West
Hampstead, Regent Sound, London, England.
149. We're Wastin' Time (Time: 2.44)
150. Blue Turns To Grey (Time: 2.29) *

31 August 1964 - 4 September 1964 Regent Sound Studios, Decca, West
Hampstead, London, England.
162. Hear It (Time: 3.04) *

1 September 1964 Regent Sound Studios, London, England.
163. Da Doo Ron Ron (Time: 2.21)

2 September 1964 Regent Sound Studios, London, England.
164. Under The Boardwalk (Time: 2.46)

2-3 September 1964 Regent Sound Studios, London, England.
166. Little Red Rooster (Time: 3.06)

28-29 September 1964 Regent Sound Studios, London, England.
145. You Can't Catch Me (Time: 3.30)
167. I'm Relying On You (Time: 0.24) *
168. We Were Falling In Love (Time: 1.20) *
169. Grown Up Wrong (Time: 1.59)
170. Susie Q (Time: 1.48)
171. Surprise, Surprise (Time: 2.31)

8 October 1964 Playhouse Theatre, London, England.
172. Dust My Pyramids *
173. If You Need Me *
174. Around And Around *
175. Ain't That Lovin' You Baby (Time: 1.54) *
176. I'm A Love You *
177. Mona *
178. 2120 South Michigan Avenue (Time: 3.46) *

25 October 1964 Ed Sullivan TV Show, CBS Studio 50, New York, USA.
179. Around And Around (Time: 2.23)
180. Time Is On My Side (Time: 2.44)

2 November 1964 RCA Studios, Hollywood, USA.
187. Down Home Girl (Time: 4.08)
188. Everybody Needs Somebody To Love (Time: 5.00)
     (a) Short Version - (2.57)
189. Pain In My Heart (Time: 2.05)
190. Heart Of Stone (Time: 2.51)
     (a) Stereo Version - (2.59)
191. Hitch Hike (Time: 2.26)
192. Oh, Baby (We Got A Good Thing Going) (Time: 2.09)

8 November 1964 Chess Studios, Chicago, USA.
193. Little Red Rooster *
194. Key To The Highway (Time: 3.25) *
195. Goodbye Girl (Time: 2.14) *
196. What A Shame (Time: 2.59)
197. Mercy Mercy (Time: 2.44) *

20 November 1964 Ready, Steady, Go! TV Studio, London, England.
198. Off The Hook (Time: 2.30)
199. Little Red Rooster (Time: 2.58)

1965
11-12; 17-18 January, 18 February 1965 De Lane Lea Studios, Kingsway, London, England; RCA, Hollywood, USA.
200. The Last Time (Time: 3.42)
201. Play With Fire (Time: 2.15)

24 - 28 February 1965 Decca Studios, West Hampstead, London, England.
202. I'd Much Rather Be With The Boys (Time: 2.12)

1 March 1965 Playhouse Theatre, London, England.
203. Down The Road Apiece (Time: 2.05) *
204. Everybody Needs Somebody To Love (Time: 3.31) *
205. The Last Time (Time: 3.07) *
206. If You Need Me *

9 April 1965 Ready, Steady, Goes Live, ITV Studio One, Wembley, London, England.
213. Everybody Needs Somebody To Love (Time: 2.33) *
214. Pain In My Heart (Time: 2.01) *
215. I'm Alright (Time: 3.28) *
216. The Last Time (Time: 2.59) *

2 May 1965 Ed Sullivan TV Show, CBS Studio 50, New York, USA.
223. The Last Time (Time: 3.12)
224. Little Red Rooster (Time: 2.34)
225. Everybody Needs Somebody To Love (Time: 2.18)
226. 2120 South Michigan Avenue (Time: 1.34)

3 May 1965 Clay Cole TV Show, New York, USA.
227. Little Red Rooster *

10-11 May 1965 Chess Studios, Chicago, USA.
228. Mercy Mercy (Time: 2.46)
229. Try Me (Time: 2.25) *
230. The Under Assistant West Coast Promotion Man (Time: 3.07)
     (a) Long Version - (3.20)
231. That's How Strong My Love Is (Time: 2.25)
232. (I Can't Get No) Satisfaction (Time: 3.53) *

12-13 May 1965 RCA Studios, Hollywood, USA.
233. (I Can't Get No) Satisfaction (Time: 3.44)
     (a) Instrumental - (3.44)
234. The Spider And The Fly (Time: 3.39)
235. One More Try (Time: 1.58)
236. Good Times (Time: 1.59)
237. Cry To Me (Time: 3.10)
238. I've Been Loving You Too Long (Time: 2.57)
239. My Girl (Time: 2.39)

18 May 1965 RCA Studios, Hollywood, USA.
240. Little Red Rooster (Time: 3.04) *
241. The Last Time (Time: 3.04) *
242. Play With Fire (Time: 2.09) *

20 May 1965 Shindig ABC TV Studios, Hollywood, Los Angeles, USA.
243. Down The Road Apiece (Time: 1.04) *
244. (I Can't Get No) Satisfaction (Time: 2.43) *

28 July 1965 Twickenham Studios, London, England.
245. Mercy Mercy *
246. Hitch Hike *
247. That's How Strong My Love Is *
248. (I Can't Get No) Satisfaction *

20 August 1965 BBC Maida Vale Studios, London, England.
249. Mercy Mercy (Time: 2.51) *
250. Oh, Baby (We Got A Good Thing Going) (Time: 1.54) *
251. (I Can't Get No) Satisfaction (Time: 3.52) *
252. The Spider And The Fly (Time: 3.26) *
253. Cry To Me (Time: 3.06) *
254. Fanny Mae (Time: 2.11) *

2 September 1965 Ready, Steady, Go! TV Show, Wembley, London, England.
255. Oh, Baby (We Got A Good Thing Goin') (Time: 1.21) *
256. That's How Strong My Love Is (Time: 1.56) *
257. (I Can't Get No) Satisfaction (Time: 4.17)

3-4 September 1965 Adelphi Theatre, Dublin, Eire or ABC Theatre, Belfast, N Ireland.
258. Charlie Is My Darling (Time: 3.16)

5 September 1965 RCA Studios, Hollywood, USA.
259. Get Off My Cloud (Time: 2.56)

6 September 1965 RCA Studios, Hollywood, USA.
260. Blue Turns To Grey (Time: 2.29)
261. She Said Yeah (Time: 1.35)
262. Gotta Get Away (Time: 2.07)
263. Talkin' 'Bout You (Time: 2.32)
264. I'm Free (Time: 2.24)
270. Looking Tired (Time: 2.15) *

271. The Singer Not The Song (Time: 2.23)

22 October 1965 Ready, Steady, Go! TV Studio, Wembley, London, England.
272. Cry To Me (Time: 2.46) *
273. She Said Yeah (Time: 2.13) *
274. Get Off My Cloud (Time: 2.29) *

26 October 1965 IBC Studios, London, England.
275. As Tears Go By (Time: 2.46)

11 November 1965 Hullabaloo TV, NBC Studios, New York, USA.
276. She Said Yeah (Time: 1.41)

8 December 1965 RCA Studios, Hollywood, USA.
277. 19th Nervous Breakdown (Time: 3.57)
   (a) Take 1 - (4.03)

8-10 December 1965 RCA Studios, Hollywood, USA.
270. Looking Tired (Time: 2.15)
278. Mother's Little Helper (Time: 2.45)
279. Doncha Bother Me (Time: 2.41)
280. Goin' Home (Time: 11.14)
281. Take It Or Leave It (Time: 2.47)
282. Think (Time: 3.09)
283. Ride On Baby (Time: 2.53)
284. Sittin' On A Fence (Time: 3.02)
285. Sad Day (Time: 3.02)

1966
13 February 1966 Ed Sullivan TV Show, CBS Studio 50, New York, USA.
286. (I Can't Get No) Satisfaction (Time: 2.36)
287. As Tears Go By (Time: 2.18)
288. 19th Nervous Breakdown (Time: 4.11)

6-9 March 1966 RCA Studios, Hollywood, USA.
289. Out Of Time (Time: 5.37)
   (a) Edited Version - (3.42)
   (b) No Lead Vocals - (4.58)
290. Lady Jane (Time: 3.08)
291. It's Not Easy (Time: 2.56)
292. Stupid Girl (Time: 2.56)
293. Paint It, Black (Time: 3.20)
   (a) Instrumental - (2.22)
   (b) Album Version - (3.45)
   (c) Stereo Version - (3.24)
   (d) Alternative Take - (2.22)
294. Long Long While (Time: 3.01)
295. Under My Thumb (Time: 3.41)
296. High And Dry (Time: 3.08)
297. Flight 505 (Time: 3.27)
298. I Am Waiting (Time: 3.11)
299. What To Do (Time: 2.32)

15 March 1966 IBC Studios, London, England.
300. Con Le Mie Lacrime (Time: 2.44)
   (a) No Harpsichord - (2.59)

27-30 April, 6 May 1966 Pye Studios, London, England.
301. Out Of Time (Time: 3.22)

12 May 1966 BBC TV, London, England.
302. Paint It Black (Time: 2.13) *

3-11 August 1966 RCA Studios, Hollywood, USA.
146. Godzi *
304. Panama Powder Room *
305. Who's Driving Your Plane? (Time: 3.13)

3-11 August; 8 November - 6 December 1966 RCA Studios, Hollywood, USA;
Olympic Sound Studios, Barnes, London, England.
306. Get Yourself Together (Time: 3.10) *
307. My Obsession (Time: 3.18)
   (a) Instrumental - (4.08)
308. All Sold Out (Time: 2.18)
   (a) Take 1 - (2.48)
309. She Smiled Sweetly (Time: 2.45)
310. Yesterday's Papers (Time: 2.05)
   (a) Take 1 - (2.06)
   (b) Take 2 - (2.12)
   (c) Extended Backing Track - (3.08)
311. Please Go Home (Time: 3.18)
   (a) Instrumental - (3.20)
312. Miss Amanda Jones (Time: 2.48)
313. Back Street Girl (Time: 3.28)
314. Cool, Calm And Collected (Time: 4.19)
315. Something Happened To Me Yesterday (Time: 4.55)
316. Who's Been Sleeping Here? (Time: 3.57)
317. Complicated (Time: 3.16)
   (a) Instrumental - (3.25)
318. Connection (Time: 2.10)

3-11 August; 31 August; 8 September 1966 RCA Studios, Hollywood, USA; IBC
Studios, London, England; RCA Hollywood, USA.
**319. Have You Seen Your Mother, Baby, Standing In The
    Shadow?** (Time: 2.36)
   (a) Take 1 - (2.29)
   (b) No Lead Vocal - (2.33)
   (c) Stereo Version - (2.36)

31 August-2 September 1966 IBC Studios, London, England.
239. My Girl (Time: 2.39)
305. Who's Driving Your Plane? (Time: 3.13)

9 September 1966 Ed Sullivan TV Show, CBS Studio 50, New York, USA.
320. Paint It Black (Time: 2.17)
321. Lady Jane (Time: 3.07)
322. Have You Seen Your Mother, Baby, Standing In The Shadow?
(Time: 2.28)

4 October 1966 Ready, Steady, Go!, Wembley TV Studio, London, England.
**327. Have You Seen Your Mother, Baby, Standing In The
    Shadow?** (Time: 2.27) *

11-20 October 1966 IBC Studios, London, England.
333. Fortune Teller (Time: 1.56)
334. I've Been Loving You Too Long (Time: 2.54)

8 November - 6 December 1966 Olympic Sound Studios, Barnes,
London, England.
335. English Summer *
336. Trouble In Mind (Time: 3.43) *
337. Sometimes Happy, Sometimes Blue (Time: 2.05) *
338. Dandelion (Time: 3.33)
339. If You Let Me (Time: 3.18)

16 November - 6 December 1966 Olympic Sound Studios, Barnes,
London, England.
340. Ruby Tuesday (Time: 3.11)
   (a) Take 1 - (3.25)
   (b) Alt Mix - (3.17)
341. Let's Spend The Night Together (Time: 3.39)
   (a) No Lead Vocal - (3.56)
   (b) Instrumental - (3.46)
   (c) Single Version - (3.26)
   (d) Stereo Version - (3.37)

1967

15 January 1967 Ed Sullivan TV Show, CBS Studio 50, New York, USA.
342. Ruby Tuesday (Time: 3.19)
343. Let's Spend Some Time Together (Time: 3.03)

20 January 1967 Olympic Sound Studios, London, England.
344. Connection (Time: 2.25) *
345. Ruby Tuesday (Time: 3.17) *
346. It's All Over Now (Time: 3.18) *
347. Let's Spend The Night Together (Time: 2.44) *

5 February 1967 Eamonn Andrews Show, ATV Studios, London, England.
348. She Smiled Sweetly *

11 February 1967 Olympic Sound Studios, London, England.
349. Blues 1 *

11 February, 7-22 July, 10 August - 7 September 1967 Olympic Sound Studios, London, England.
350. 2000 Light Years From Home (Time: 4.45)
    (a) Early Take - (2.05)
    (b) Many Alternative Cuts - (30.32)
    (c) Single Version - (3.27)
    (d) Edited Version - (2.51)

11 February, 13-22 July 1967 Olympic Sound Studios, London, England.
351. In Another Land (Time: 3.15)
    (a) Takes 1-19 - (8.34)
    (b) Alternative Takes 1-14 - (12.54)

16-20 May, 12-13 June 1967 Olympic Sound Studios, London, England.
352. She's A Rainbow (Time: 4.35)
    (a) Promo Only Version - (2.51)
    (b) Cut 1 - (4.10)
    (c) Takes 1 - 7 - (12.15)

16-20 May 1967 Olympic Sound Studios, London, England.
353. Telstar II *
354. Manhole Cover *

9 June, 7-22 July, 10 August - 7 September 1967 Olympic Sound Studios, London, England.
355. Citadel (Time: 2.50)
    (a) Alternative Instrumental Takes - (25.21)

13, 21 June, 2, 19 July 1967 Olympic Sound Studios, London, England.
356. We Love You (Time: 4.21)
    (a) Instrumental Alternative Take - (3.02)
    (b) Instrumental Takes - (9.52)

7-22 July, 5 August 1967 Olympic Sound Studios, London, England.
362. Gomper (Time: 5.08)
    (a) Cut 1 - (8.50)
    (b) Cut 2 - (8.56)
    (c) Many Alternative Cuts - (6.49)
370. The Lantern (Time: 4.23)
    (a) Many Alternative Takes - (26.45)

7-22 July, 10 August - 7 September 1967 Olympic Sound Studios, London, England.
357. She's Doing Her Thing *
358. Blow Me Mama *
359. Bathroom *
360. Sing This All Together (Time: 3.46)
361. Sing This All Together (See What Happens) (Time: 7.52)
    (a) Un-edited Cut - (14.54)
363. Majesties Honky Tonk (Time: 2.28) *
    (a) Various Takes - (20.41)

364. 5 Part Jam (Time: 3.33) *
    (a) Many Takes - (25.51)
366. Title 15 (Time: 4.05) *
    (a) Take 1 - (4.08)
367. Title 5 (Time: 1.47)
368. Satanic Organ Jam (Time: 1.44) *
369. Soul Blues (Time: 3.53) *
    (a) Take 1 - (1.46)
    (b) Take 2 - (2.05)
371. Blues No. 3 (Time: 3.02) *
    (a) Multiple Alternative Takes - (19.21)
372. Jam One (Time: 4.05) *
    (a) More Alternative Takes - (6.20)
373. Gold Painted Fingernails (Time: 5.00) *
    (a) Multiple Various Takes - (31.56)

7-22 July, 5 August, 2-5 October 1967 Olympic Sound Studios, London, England.
374. On With The Show (Time: 3.39)
    (a) 10 Various Takes - (25.21)

7-22 July, 5 August, 16, 21, 23 October 1967 Olympic Sound Studios, London, England.
365. 2000 Man (Time: 3.07)
    (a) Takes 1 - 15 - (38.53)

7-22 July, 16, 21, 23 October 1967 Olympic Sound Studios, London, England.
375. Child Of The Moon (Time: 3.12)
    (a) Early Cuts - (9.57)
    (b) Acoustic Cut - (4.16)

16, 21, 23 October 1967 Olympic Sound Studios, London, England.
376. Cosmic Christmas (Time: 0.40)

1968

21 February - 14 March 1968 RG Jones Studios, Morden, Surrey, England.
377. My Home Is A Prison (Time: 2.43) *
378. Hold On I'm Coming (Time: 4.08) *
379. Rock Me Baby (Time: 0.41) *

February - 14 March; 17-31 March 1968 Rolling Stones Mobile, Redlands, Sussex, England; Olympic Sound Studios, London, England.
380. Pay Your Dues (Time: 3.05) *

1-14, 17-31 March; 13-18 May, 4-10 June 1968 RG Jones Studios, Morden, Surrey, England; Olympic Sound Studios, London, England.
381. No Expectations (Time: 3.56)
    (a) Alternative Take - (4.20)
382. Stray Cat Blues (Time: 4.37)
    (a) Take 1 - (4.17)

23-29 March 1968 Olympic Sound Studios, London, England.
375. Child Of The Moon (Time: 3.12)
    (c) Alt Mix - (3.11)
    (d) No Lead Vocals - (3.11)

12-13; 23-29 March 1968 RG Jones Studios, Morden, Surrey, England; Olympic Sound Studios, London, England.
383. Jumpin' Jack Flash (Time: 3.41)
    (a) Early Guitar Riff - (2.17)
    (b) Take 1 - (3.25)
    (c) No Lead Vocals - (3.52)
    (d) USA Single Edit Version - (2.42)
    (e) Promotional Film - (3.58)

17-31 March; 6-25 July 1968 Olympic Sound Studios, London, England; Sunset Sound Studios, Los Angeles, California, USA.
384. Jigsaw Puzzle (Time: 6.06)
    (a) Take 1 - (6.07)
    (b) Many Alternative Cuts - (53.35)

17-31 March 1968 Olympic Sound Studios, London, England.
385. Parachute Woman (Time: 2.20)
   (a) Take 1 - (2.15)

17-31 March 1968 Mobile at Redlands, Sussex, England.
386. Highway Child (Time: 5.02) *

March-September 1968 Olympic Sound Studios, London, England.
387. Natural Magic (Time: 1.39)

9-10, 13-18 May; 6-25 July 1968 Olympic Sound Studios, London, England; Sunset Sound Studios, Los Angeles, California, USA.
388. Salt Of The Earth (Time: 4.47)
   (a) Take 1 - (4.48)

13-18 May 1968 Olympic Sound Studios, London, England.
391. Street Fighting Man (Time: 3.16)
   (a) USA Single Version - (3.10)
392. Dear Doctor (Time: 3.22)
   (a) Take 1 - (3.28)
   (b) Take 2 - (3.24)
394. Give Me A Hamburger To Go (Time: 3.25) *
396. Factory Girl (Time: 2.09)
399. Blood Red Wine (Time: 5.20) *

13-18 May, 24 June 1968 Olympic Sound Studios, London, England.
393. Prodigal Son (Time: 2.52)

13-18 May, 28 June 1968 Olympic Sound Studios, London, England.
395. Family (Time: 4.06)
   (a) Acoustic - (4.13)
   (b) Take 1 - (4.01)

13 May - June 1968 Olympic Sound Studios, London, England.
397. Sister Morphine (Time: 5.34)

13-18 May; 26-30 June 1968 Mobile at Redlands, Sussex, Olympic Sound Studios, London, England.
399. Still A Fool (Time: 6.43) *
   (a) Extended Slow - (9.48)

4-10 June 1968 Olympic Sound Studios, London, England.
400. Lady (Time: 1.32) *
401. The Devil Is My Name *
402. Sympathy For The Devil (Time: 6.18)
   (a) Take 1 - (6.23)
   (b) Edited Cut - (5.57)

September-October 1968 Olympic Sound Studios, London, England.
409. Memo From Turner (Time: 4.03)
   (a) Organ Cut - (3.54)

16-17 November 1968 Morgan Studios, London, Olympic Sound Studios, London, England.
410. You Can't Always Get What You Want (Time: 7.28)

17 November 1968 Olympic Sound Studios, London, England.
412. Memo From Turner (Time: 2.46)
   (a) Take 1 - (2.49)

30 November 1968 David Frost LWT TV Show, London, England.
413. Sympathy For The Devil (Time: 5.30)

10-11 December 1968 Intertel Studios, Stonebridge, London, England.
414. Route 66 *
415. Confessin' The Blues *
416. Look On Yonder Wall *
417. Walkin' Blues *
418. Jumping Jack Flash (Time: 3.35)

419. Parachute Woman (Time: 2.58)
420. No Expectations (Time: 4.13)
421. You Can't Always Get What You Want (Time: 4.24)
422. Sympathy For The Devil (Time: 8.38)
423. Salt Of The Earth (Time: 5.07)

1969

9-10 February, 10-11 March, 16 May; 18 October - 3 November 1969 Olympic Sound Studios, London, England; Sunset Sound Studios, Elektra Studios, Los Angeles, USA.
424. Midnight Rambler (Time: 6.52)

9-18 February 1969 Olympic Sound Studios, London, England.
425. You Got The Silver (Time: 2.50)
   (a) MJ Vocal - (2.51)

9 February-31 March 1969 Olympic Sound Studios, London, England.
426. Love In Vain (Time: 4.19)
   (a) Promo Only

15 March; April - May 1969. Olympic Sound Studios, London, England; CBS Studios, New York, USA.
410. You Can't Always Get What You Want (Time: 7.28)
   (a) Single Edit Version - (4.52)

23-25 February, 15 March - 23 April 1969 Olympic Sound Studios, London, England.
427. Downtown Suzie (Time: 3.53)
   (a) Take 1 - (3.45)

22-31 March 1969 Olympic Sound Studios, London, England.
397. Sister Morphine (Time: 5.34)
   (a) Marianne Faithfull Version - (5.29)
   (b) Early Take - (5.35)

23-25 February, 15 March; 18 October - 3 November 1969 Olympic Sound Studios, London, England; Sunset Sound Studios, Elektra Studios, Los Angeles, USA.
428. Gimmie Shelter (Time: 4.30)
   (a) Early Take - (4.22)
   (b) KR Vocal - (4.31)

22-23 March 1969 Olympic Sound Studios, London, England.
429. The Jimmy Miller Show *

23 March 1969 Olympic Sound Studios, London, England.
430. I'm A Country Boy (Time: 4.30) *

31 March 1969 Olympic Sound Studios, London, England.
431. Get A Line On You *

March 1969 Olympic Sound Studios, London, England.
432. So Divine (Aladdin Story) (Time: 4.32)

17-22 April, 5 June - 3 July; 18 October - 3 November 1969 Olympic Sound Studios, London, England; Sunset Sound Studios, Elektra Studios, Los Angeles, USA.
433. Monkey Man (Time: 4.11)

12 May - 8 June 1969 Olympic Sound Studios, London, England.
434. Honky Tonk Women (Time: 3.01)
   (a) Early Take 1 - (3.06)
   (b) Take 2 - (2.52)
   (c) Single Version - (3.02)

12-31 May; 18 October - 3 November 1969 Olympic Sound Studios, London, England; Sunset Sound Studios, Elektra Studios, Los Angeles, USA.
435. Live With Me (Time: 3.33)

12 May, 5 June - 3 July; 18 October - 3 November 1969 Olympic Sound Studios, London, England; Sunset Sound Studios, Elektra Studios, Los Angeles, USA.
436. Country Honk (Time: 3.07)
   (a) Early Take - (3.04)

5 June - 3 July 1969 Olympic Sound Studios, London, England.
437. Give Me A Drink (Time: 6.39) *
438. Loving Cup - Alternate Take (Time: 5.26)
439. Let It Bleed (Time: 5.27)
441. Jiving Sister Fanny (Time: 3.25)
   (a) Take 1 - (3.24)
442. All Down The Line (Acoustic) (Time: 4.22) *

5 June - 3 July; 18 October - 3 November 1969 Olympic Sound Studios,
London, England; Sunset Sound Studios, Elektra Studios, Los Angeles, USA.
440. I'm Going Down (Time: 2.52)
   (a) Take 1 - (3.04)

29-30 June - 3 July 1969 Olympic Sound Studios, London, England.
443. I Don't Know Why (Time: 3.02)

July - August 1969 Elektra Studios, Los Angeles, USA.
387. Natural Magic (Time: 1.39)

18 October - 3 November 1969 Sunset Sound Studios, Elektra Studios,
Los Angeles, USA.
458. I Don't Know The Reason Why (Time: 11.29) *
   (a) Cut 1 - (5.57)

18 November 1969 Ed Sullivan TV Show, CBS Studios, Los Angeles, USA.
459. Gimme Shelter (Time: 3.51)
460. Love In Vain (Time: 3.30)
461. Honky Tonk Women (Time: 2.57)

2-4 December; 15 December 1969 Muscle Shoals, Alabama, USA; Rolling
Stones Mobile, Stargroves, Newbury.
482. You Gotta Move (Time: 2.34)
   (a) Take 1 - (2.35)

3-4 December; 14 December 1969 Muscle Shoals, Alabama, USA; Olympic
Sound Studios, London, England.
483. Brown Sugar (Time: 3.49)
   (a) Muscle Shoals Take 1 - (3.43)
   (b) Muscle Shoals Take 2 - (3.49)

3-4 December; 15 December 1969 Muscle Shoals, Alabama, USA; Olympic
Sound Studios, London, England.
484. Wild Horses (Time: 5.42)
   (a) Pedal Steel - Pete Kleinow - (5.22)

15 December 1969, 24 April 1970 Olympic Sound Studios, London, England.
489. Dead Flowers (Time: 4.05)

1970
March - May 1970 Rolling Stones Mobile, Stargroves, Newbury, Olympic Sound
Studios, London, England.
490. Rock It *
491. Travelling Tiger *
492. As Now *
482. You Gotta Move (Time: 2.34)
495. Can't You Hear Me Knocking (Time: 7.15)
493. Moonlight Mile (Time: 5.56)
497. Dancing In The Light (Time: 4.22)
   (a) Take 1 - (2.44)

24 April, December 1970 Olympic Sound Studios, London, England.
483. Brown Sugar (Time: 3.49)
   (c) Multiple Cut Segments
   (d) Olympic Take 3 (Hot Rocks Version) - (3.48)
   (e) Olympic Take 4 - (3.52)
   (f) Olympic Alternate Mix - (3.54)

17 February, August 1970 Olympic Sound Studios, Trident Studios, London,
England.
484. Wild Horses (Time: 5.42)
   (b) Short Promo Version - (3.26)
   (c) Alternative Take - (5.45)
   (d) Billy Preston (Organ) Take - (5.43)

March - May; 21 -31 October 1970. Rolling Stones Mobile, Stargroves,
Newbury, Olympic Sound Studios, London, England.
496. Good Time Women (Time: 3.21)
   (a) Cut 1 - (3.17)

March - May 1970; 14-15 July 1970 Rolling Stones Mobile, Stargroves,
Newbury, England; Olympic Sound Studios, London, England.
498. Who Am I? (Time: 3.49) *

May 1970 Rolling Stones Mobile, Stargroves, Newbury, Olympic Sound Studios,
London, England.
499. Cocksucker Blues (Time: 3.28)
   (a) Electric Take - (5.05)

16 June - 27 July 1970 Olympic Sound Studios, London, England.
500. Candlewick Bedspread *

14 - 15 July 1970 Olympic Sound Studios, London, England.
440. I'm Going Down (Time: 2.52)
   (a) Take 1 - (3.04)

16 June - 27 July 1970 Olympic Sound Studios, London, England.
501. Hey Mama *
503. Leather Jacket (Time: 3.31) *

16 June - 27 July, 21 - 31 October 1970 Olympic Sound Studios,
London, England.
502. Stop Breaking Down (Time: 4.34)
504. All Down The Line (Electric) (Time: 4.09)

30 June, 20 July, 21 - 31 October 1970 Olympic Sound Studios,
London, England.
505. Sweet Virginia (Time: 4.26)
   (a) Take 1 - (4.23)

23 July 1970 Olympic Sound Studios, London, England.
506. Shine A Light (Time: 4.17)

21 - 31 October 1970 Olympic Sound Studios, London.
432. So Divine (Aladdin Story) (Time: 4.32)
511. Shake Your Hips (Time: 2.59)
512. Travellin' Man (Time: 5.58) *
513. Potted Shrimps (Time: 4.12) *
514. Trident Jam (Time: 3.43) *
515. Silver Train (Time: 4.26)

21 October - November 1970 Rolling Stones Mobile, Stargroves, Newbury,
Olympic Sound Studios, London, England.
508. Red House *
509. Bitch (Time: 3.37)
   (a) Take 1 - (3.39)
   (b) Take 2 - (2.24)
   (c) Single Version - (3.42)
510. Sweet Black Angel (Time: 2.58)

21 October - November 1970; January 1971 Rolling Stones Mobile,
Stargroves, Newbury, Olympic Sound Studios; Island Studios, Trident
Studios, London, England.
516. Sway (Time: 3.52)
   (a) Single Version - (3.33)
18 December 1970 Olympic Sound Studios, London, England.
517. Brown Sugar (Time: 4.05) *

1971

7 June - October; 30 November - 19 December 1971; 10 January - 28 March 1972 Rolling Stones Mobile, Nellcôte, France; Sunset Sound Studios, LA, USA.
502. Stop Breaking Down (Time: 4.34)
505. Sweet Virginia (Time: 4.26)
   (a) Alternative Mix - (4.32)
506. Shine A Light (Time: 4.17)
510. Sweet Black Angel (Time: 2.58)
   (a) Instrumental Cut - (3.00)
511. Shake Your Hips (Time: 2.59)
   (a) Alternative Take - (4.11)
527. Loving Cup (Time: 4.25)
530. Ventilator Blues (Time: 3.24)
533. Torn And Frayed (Time: 4.18)
534. All Down The Line (Time: 3.50)
   (a) Take 1 - (3.53)
   (b) Instrumental Take 1 - (4.01)
   (c) Take 2 - (3.47)
537. Turd On The Run (Time: 2.38)
538. Tumbling Dice (Time: 3.47)
539. I Just Want To See His Face (Time: 2.53)
540. Rip This Joint (Time: 2.22)
   (a) Instrumental Take - (2.32)
541. Happy (Time: 3.05)
542. Soul Survivor (Time: 3.49)
   (a) Early Take - (4.02)
543. Soul Survivor - Alternate Take (Time: 3.59)
544. Rocks Off (Time: 4.33)
   (a) Instrumental Mix - (4.33)
545. Casino Boogie (Time: 3.34)
549. Let It Loose (Time: 5.18)
   (a) Instrumental Take - (5.57)

7 June - October 1971 Rolling Stones Mobile, Nellcôte, France.
528. I'm Not Signifying (Time: 3.56)
   (a) Early Take - (3.39)
   (b) Take 2 (Piano) - (3.46)
529. Pass The Wine (Sophia Loren) (Time: 4.54)
531. Fragile *
532. Separately (Time: 4.18) *
535. Exile Instrumental (Time: 7.12) *
536. Fast Talking Slow Walking (Time: 6.34) *
546. Plundered My Soul (Time: 3.58)
548. Following The River (Time: 4.51)

1972-1973

28 March 1972 Sunset Sound Studios, Los Angeles, USA.
550. I Don't Care (Time: 3.02) *
551. Exile On Main Street Blues (Time: 6.21)
   (a) Original Cut - (1.37)

17-21 May 1972 Rialto Theatre, Montreux, Switzerland.
552. John's Jam (Time: 3.34) *
553. Loving Cup (Time: 6.51) *
554. Shake Your Hips (Time: 3.42)
555. Tumbling Dice (Time: 4.23)
   (a) Alternative Take (4.11)
556. Bluesberry Jam (Time: 3.09)

23 June 1972 Sumet-Burnet Studios, Dallas, Texas, USA.
557. Jungle Disease (Time: 3.56) *
558. Delta Slide (Time: 2.50) *
559. 32-20 Blues (Time: 1.41) *
560. When You Got A Good Friend (Time: 2.37) *
561. Key To The Highway (Time: 6.22) *

25 November - 21 December 1972; 7 May - June 1973 Dynamic Sounds, Kingston, Jamaica; Olympic Sound Studios, Island Studios, London, England.
515. Silver Train (Time: 4.26)
   (a) Early Take 1 - (3.36)
   (b) Take 2 - (4.36)
582. Coming Down Again (Time: 5.55)
584. Winter (Time: 5.30)
   (a) Take 1 - (5.25)
593. Can You Hear The Music? (Time: 5.32)
595. Angie (Time: 4.33)
   (a) No Strings Alternative Take - (4.27)
596. 100 Years Ago (Time: 3.59)
   (a) Take 1 - (4.07)
597. Hide Your Love (Time: 4.12)
   (a) Take 1 - (4.12)

25 November - 21 December 1972 Dynamic Sounds, Kingston, Jamaica.
532. Separately (Time: 4.18) *
583. You Should Have Seen Her Ass (Time: 4.20) *
586. First Thing *
587. After Muddy & Charlie *
588. Four And In *
589. Zabadoo *
590. Give Us A Break *
591. Jamaica *
592. Miami *
594. Brown Leaves (Time: 1.50) *
601. Through The Lonely Nights (Time: 4.13)
603. Short And Curlies (Time: 2.43)
604. Waiting On A Friend (Time: 4.34)
   (a) Early Take 1 - (3.20)

25 November - 21 December 1972; 27-30 January; 7 May - June 1973 Dynamic Sounds, Kingston, Jamaica; Village Recorders, Los Angeles, USA; RSM Mobile, Newbury, Olympic Sound Studios, Island Studios, London, England.
585. Dancing With Mr. D (Time: 4.53)
   (a) Take 1 - (5.01)
598. Criss Cross (Time: 4.18) *
   (a) Take 1 - No Sax - (4.30)
   (b) Take 2 - (4.20)
   (c) Take 3 - (4.46)
599. Doo Doo Doo Doo (Heartbreaker) (Time: 3.27)
600. Star Star (Time: 4.25)
   (a) Censored Version - (4.25)
602. Tops (Time: 3.48)
   (a) Instrumental - (4.41)

1973-1974

27-30 January 1973 Village Sound Recorders, Los Angeles, USA.
606. Windmill (Time: 3.26) *

14-25 November 1973 Musicland Studios, Munich, Germany.
622. Slow Down And Stop (Time: 3.02) *
627. Black Limousine (Time: 3.33)

14-25 November 1973; 12 April - 2 May; 4-27 May 1974 Musicland Studios, Munich, Germany; RSM, Stargroves, Newbury, England; Olympic Studios, London, England.
623. Ain't Too Proud To Beg (Time: 3.31)
   (a) Alternative Mix - (3.51)
   (b) Edited Single Version - (2.48)
625. If You Can't Rock Me (Time: 3.47)
   (a) Alternative Mix - (3.49)
626. Fingerprint File (Time: 6.33)
   (a) Original Speed Version - (7.05)

14-25 November 1973, 20 February - 3 March; 12 April - 2 May 1974 Musicland Studios, Munich, Germany; RSM, Stargroves, Newbury, England.
624. Drift Away (Time: 4.10) *
   (a) Alternative Take - (3.52)

2-7 December 1973; 12 April - 2 May; 4-27 May 1974 The Wick Home Studios, London, England; RSM, Stargroves, Newbury, England; Olympic Studios, London, England.
628. It's Only Rock 'N' Roll (But I Like It) (Time: 5.07)
  (a) Edited Version 1 - (4.46)
  (b) Edited Version 2 - (4.01)

1974
20 February - 3 March 1974 Musicland Studios, Munich, Germany.
632. Living In The Heart Of Love (Time: 2.37) *
633. Labour Swing *

12 April - 2 May; 4-27 May 1974 RSM, Stargroves, Newbury, England; Olympic Studios, London, England.
603. Short And Curlies (Time: 2.43)

20 February - 3 March; 12 April - 2 May; 4-27 May 1974 Musicland Studios, Munich, Germany; RSM, Stargroves, Newbury, England; Olympic Studios, London, England.
629. If You Really Want To Be My Friend (Time: 6.16)
630. Time Waits For No One (Time: 6.38)
  (a) Edited Version - (4.25)
631. Luxury (Time: 5.01)
  (a) Edited Original Release - (4.31)
634. Dance Little Sister (Time: 4.11)
  (a) Take 1 - (5.07)
635. Till The Next Goodbye (Time: 4.36)
  (a) Alternative Mix - (4.40)

4 - 27 May 1974 Olympic Studios, London, England.
601. Through The Lonely Nights (Time: 4.13)

1 June 1974 ITV Studios, London, England.
636. It's Only Rock 'N' Roll (But I Like It) (Time: 4.44)

9-15 December 1974 Musicland Studios, Munich, Germany.
639. Something Good *
640. Cable From My Baby *

1974-1975
9-15 December 1974; 22 January - 9 February 1975 Musicland Studios, Munich, Germany; RSM, De Doelen, Rotterdam, Netherlands.
606. Windmill (Time: 3.26) *
637. Act Together (Time: 4.48) *
638. I Got A Letter (Time: 4.26) *
  (a) Instrumental Take - (4.23)

12-15 December 1974, 25 March - 4 April; October-November 1975 Musicland Studios, Munich, Germany; Casino, Montreux, Switzerland.
641. Fool To Cry (Time: 5.05)
  (a) Take 1 - (6.04)
  (b) Take 2 - (5.43)
  (c) Edited Version - (4.06)

15 December 1974; 22 January - 9 February; 25 March - 4 April; October-November 1975 Musicland Studios, Munich, Germany; RSM, De Doelen, Rotterdam, Netherlands; Musicland Studios, Munich, Germany; Casino, Montreux, Switzerland.
642. Cherry Oh Baby (Time: 3.57)
  (a) Take 1 - (4.32)
  (b) Take 2 - (3.38)
  (c) 8 Track Version - (3.00)

1975
22 January - 9 February 1975 RSM, De Doelen, Rotterdam, Netherlands.
604. Waiting On A Friend (Time: 4.34)
643. Heat Wave (Time: 5.00) *
644. Freeway Jam (Time: 0.54) *
645. English Rose (Time: 1.27) *
646. Shame, Shame, Shame (Time: 3.02) *
647. Man Eating Woman (Time: 3.45) *

648. Cellophane Trousers (Time: 2.26) *
649. Slave (Time: 4.59)
  (a) Take 1 - (7.14)
  (b) Take 2 - (9.43)
  (c) Take 3 - Sax - (8.20)
  (d) Take 4 - Sax - (11.13)
  (e) Extended Version - (6.32)
650. Worried About You (Time: 5.16)
651. Come On Sugar (Time: 5.31) *
653. I Love Ladies (Time: 4.31) *
654. Melody (Time: 5.49)

22 January - 9 February 1975; 29 March 1975; October-November 1975 RSM, De Doelen, Rotterdam, Netherlands; Musicland Studios, Munich, Germany; Casino, Montreux, Switzerland.
652. Crazy Mama (Time: 4.34)
  (a) Early Take 1 - (4.04)
  (b) Edited Version - (4.06)

25 March - 4 April 1975 Musicland Studios, Munich, Germany.
655. Munich Reggae (Time: 5.29) *
  (a) Edited Cut - (2.02)
656. Never Stop (Time: 4.27) *

March; October-November 1975 Musicland Studios, Munich, Germany ; Casino, Montreux, Switzerland.
657. Hand Of Fate (Time: 4.27)
  (a) Take 1 - (4.43)
  (b) Take 2 - (3.46)
658. Hot Stuff (Time: 5.21)
  (a) Take 1 - (4.52)
  (b) Special Edited Single Version - (3.30)
659. Memory Motel (Time: 7.09)
  (a) Instrumental - (4.14)

2 April 1975; January - February 1976 Musicland Studios, Munich, Germany; Atlantic Studios, New York, USA.
660. Hey Negrita (Time: 4.59)
  (a) Take 1 - (5.30)
  (b) Edited Take 1 - (4.38)

25 - 28 June 1975 Electric Ladyland Studios, New York, USA.
664. Carnival To Rio (Time: 1.43) *

1976
654. Melody (Time: 5.49) January - February 1976 Atlantic Studios, New York, USA.

1977
12/13 March 1977 Sounds Interchange, Toronto, Canada.
707. Sing Me Back Home (Time: 4.17) *
708. Apartment No. 9 (Time: 3.44) *
709. Worried Life Blues (Time: 2.15) *

1977-1978
10 October - 29 November, 6 - 15 December 1977 EMI, Pathé Marconi Studios, Paris, France.
733. Muck Spreading Dub (Time: 3.23) *

10 October - 29 November, 6 - 15 December 1977, 5 January - 2 March 1978 EMI, Pathé Marconi, Paris, France.
627. Black Limousine (Time: 3.33)
710. Munich Hilton (Time: 10.35) *
  (a) Take 1 - (6.57)
  (b) Take 2 - (5.41)
  (c) Take 3 Vocals - (7.39)
  (d) Take 4 - (5.29)
711. Everything Is Turning To Gold (Time: 4.06)
  (a) Take 1 - (9.51)

(b) Extended Take 2 - (4.28)
712. Lies (Time: 3.11)
  (a) Take 1 - (3.50)
  (b) Take 2 - (4.13)
713. I Love You Too Much (Time: 3.10)
  (a) Take 1 - (4.22)
  (b) Take 2 - (2.32)
  (c) Instrumental Take 3 - (3.24)
  (d) Take 4 - (4.08)
  (e) Instrumental Take 5 - (3.25)
714. Before They Make Me Run (Time: 3.25)
  (a) Take 1 - (4.40)
  (b) Take 2 - (4.51)
716. Silver Coated Rails (Time: 3.18) *
717. When The Whip Comes Down (Time: 4.20)
  (a) Take 1 - (9.56)
  (b) Extended Take 2 - (6.19)
  (c) Edited Extended Take 1 - (7.22)
718. Los Trios Guitaros (Time: 3.22) *
719. Respectable (Time: 3.07)
  (a) Take 1 - (3.52)
  (b) Take 2 - (3.57)
720. Far Away Eyes (Time: 4.23)
  (a) Take 1 - (5.17)
  (b) Edited Version - (3.43)
721. Shattered (Time: 3.46)
  (a) Take 1 - (3.46)
  (b) Take 2 - (3.01)
  (c) Short Version - (2.43)
722. A Different Kind (Time: 6.01) *
723. Beast Of Burden (Time: 4.25)
  (a) Take 1 - (5.34)
  (b) Take 2 - (4.05)
  (c) 8 Track Version - (5.20)
  (d) Instrumental Dub Cut - (5.49)
  (e) Single Edit Version - (3.20)
724. Covered In Bruises *
725. Once You Start *
726. Some Girls (Time: 4.36)
  (a) Take 1 - (5.12)
  (b) Take 2 - (6.29)
730. Miss You (Time: 4.49)
  (a) Take 1 - (11.40)
  (b) 8 Track Version - (5.43)
  (c) Video Version - (3.55)
731. Everlasting Is My Love (Time: 5.00) *
  (a) Acoustic Take 1 - (3.54)
  (b) Take 2 - (4.14)
732. Just My Imagination (Running Away With Me) (Time: 4.38)
  (a) Alternative Take - (6.46)
734. Jah Is Wonderful *
735. Claudine (Time: 3.42)
  (a) Take 1 - (3.31)
  (b) Acoustic Take 1 - (3.33)
  (c) Acoustic Take 2 - (7.33)
736. Start Me Up (Time: 3.33)

1978
5 January - 2 March 1978 EMI, Pathé Marconi, Paris, France.
594. Brown Leaves (Time: 1.50) *
648. Cellophane Trousers (Time: 2.26) *
737. Don't Be A Stranger (Time: 4.06)
  (a) Take 1 - (5.20)
  (b) Take 2 - (4.18)
738. I Need You (Time: 3.43) *
  (a) Edited Cut - (2.41)
739. Hang Fire (Time: 2.20)
  (a) Take 1 - Lazy Bitch - (6.22)
  (b) Take 2 - Lazy Bitch - (6.06)

740. Keep Up Blues (Time: 4.20)
  (a) Some People Tell Me - (4.54)
741. Do You Think I Really Care? (Time: 4.22)
  (a) Take 1 - (6.09)
  (b) Edited Take 1 - (3.02)
  (c) Edited Take 1 - (4.26)
742. Fiji Gin (Time: 4.01) *
  (a) Alternative Take - (3.26)
743. Misty Roads (Time: 4.28) *
744. Summer Romance (Time: 3.16)
744. Dancing Girls (Time: 2.52) *
  (a) Alternative Take - (4.08)
746. Shame, Shame, Shame (Time: 4.01) *
747. Piano Instrumental (Time: 4.37) *
748. Petrol Blues (Time: 1.35)
  (a) Alternative Take - (3.41)
749. Golden Caddy (Time: 1.58) *
  (a) Take 1 - (3.18)
  (b) Take 2 - (6.15)
  (c) Take 3 - (8.56)
750. Broken Toe (Time: 1.55) *
751. It's A Lie (Time: 4.36) *
752. Remember These Days (Time: 4.16) *
753. Follow You (Time: 1.30) *
754. Sheep Dip Blues (Time: 0.37) *
755. Armpit Blues (Time: 2.39) *
756. After Hours (Time: 5.04) *
757. It's All Wrong (Time: 3.37) *
758. No Spare Parts (Time: 4.30)
  (a) Take 1 - (5.01)
  (b) Take 2 - (6.06)
759. When You're Gone (Time: 3.51)
  (a) Alternative Take - (3.58)
760. Angeline *
761. Disco Musik (Time: 5.55) *
762. It Won't Be Long (Time: 2.38) *
  (a) Take 1 - (2.33)
763. Never Make Me Cry (Time: 4.01) *
764. Light Up (Time: 4.44) *
765. Never Let Her Go (Time: 4.51) *
766. Not The Way To Go (Time: 9.39) *
  (a) Alternative Take - (7.10)
767. Stay Where You Are (Time: 1.43) *
768. Up Against The Wall (Time: 6.24) *
769. Broken Head Blues (Time: 2.12) *
770. You Don't Have To Go (Time: 2.16) *
771. So Young (Time: 3.25)
  (a) Original Take - (2.57)
774. You Win Again (Time: 3.00)
  (a) Alternative Take - (3.20)
775. Where The Boys Go (Time: 3.29)
  (a) Early Take 1 - (5.15)
  (b) Take 2 - (3.48)
  (c) Take 3 - (3.52)
  (d) Intro Segment - (0.35)

February - March 1978 Power Station Studio, New York, USA.
715. Before They Make Me Run (Bob Clearmountain Remix) (Time: 3.14)
727. Miss You (12 Inch Version) (Time: 8.26)
  (a) Remix Edit Version - (7.33)
728. Miss You (Edit) (Time: 3.34)

19 May - 9 June 1978 Todd Rundgren's Bearsville Studio, Woodstock, New York, USA.
776. Summertime Blues (Time: 1.49) *
777. Cocksucker Blues (Time: 6.49) *

23 August - 7 September 1978 Wally Heider (RCA) Studios, Hollywood, USA.
744. Summer Romance (Time: 3.16)

(a) Take 1 - (4.42)
(b) Take 2 - (5.37)
(c) Take 3 - (5.11)
(d) Take 4 - (5.32)
766. Not The Way To Go (Time: 9.39) *
775. Where The Boys Go (Time: 3.29)
798. What Gives You The Right (Time: 5.03) *
(a) Alternative Take - (5.23)
799. What Am I Living For? (Time: 9.35) *
800. Blues With A Feeling (Time: 3.12) *
801. My First Plea (Time: 4.14) *
(a) Take 1 - (4.50)
(b) Take 2 - (5.16)
(c) Take 3 - (3.50)
802. Your Angel Steps Out Of Heaven (Time: 3.05) *
803. One Night (Time: 2.50) *
804. Back In The USA (Time: 2.05) *
805. Tallahassee Lassie (Time: 2.37)
(a) Original Cut - (2.37)
806. I'll Let You Know (Time: 6.55) *
807. I Ain't Superstitious (Time: 4.21) *
808. Jimmy Reed Blues Jam (Time: 6.50) *
809. Serious Love (Time: 1.38) *
810. The Harder They Come (Time: 3.47)
(a) Alternative Take - (3.39)
811. Knee Trembler (Time: 5.35) *

6 October 1978 NBC TV Studios, New York, USA.
812. Summer Romance (Time: 6.25) *

7 October 1978 NBC TV Studios, New York, USA.
813. Beast Of Burden (Time: 5.13)
814. Respectable (Time: 3.13)
815. Shattered (Time: 4.15)

1979
18 January - 12 February 1979 Compass Point Studios, Nassau, Bahamas, USA.
733. Muck Spreading Dub (Time: 3.23) *
745. Dancing Girls (Time: 2.52) *
761. It Won't Be Long (Time: 2.38) *
816. It's Cold Down There (Time: 3.37) *
(a) Alternative Cut - (1.36)
817. I Think I'm Going Mad (Time: 4.12)
(a) No Sax - (6.49)
818. Sweet Home Chicago (Time: 4.49) *
819. Still In Love (Time: 5.22) *
(a) Early Take 1 - (1.45)
(b) Take 2 - (7.29)
(c) Take 3 - (5.38)
820. Sands Of Time *
821. Lonely At The Top (Time: 4.40) *
822. Guitar Lesson (Time: 4.06) *
823. Never Too Into (Time: 5.04) *
824. Let's Go Steady Again (Time: 2.51) *
825. Jah Is Not Dead (Time: 10.47) *
826. Blues Jam (Time: 3.05) *
(a) Alternative Take - (1.40)
827. Guess I Should Know (Time: 4.06) *
828. You Left Me *
829. You're So Beautiful *
830. Break Away (Time: 4.30) *
831. She's So Cold (Time: 4.13)
832. All About You (Time: 4.18)
833. Linda Lu (Time: 4.34) *
834. What's The Matter? (Time: 4.44) *
835. Bulldog (Time: 3.50) *
836. Little T & A (Time: 3.23)
(a) Take 1 - (3.41)
(b) Take 2 - (4.13)

25 June - 9 August, 30 August - October 1979 EMI, Pathé Marconi, Paris, France.
602. Tops (Time: 3.48)
(a) Instrumental - (4.41)
604. Waiting On A Friend (Time: 4.34)
(b) Take 2 - No Sax - (4.19)
627. Black Limousine (Time: 3.33)
(a) Take 1 - (4.13)
(b) Take 2 - (3.26)
(c) Take 3 - (4.06)
(d) Edit Take 3 - (3.39)
650. Worried About You (Time: 5.16)
(a) Take 1 - (7.42)
(b) Edited Take 1 - (3.14)
(c) Long Take 2 - (7.21)
736. Start Me Up (Time: 3.33)
(a) Alternative Take - (3.44)
739. Hang Fire (Time: 2.20)
(c) Take 1 - (2.28)
(d) Take 2 - (2.26)
744. Summer Romance (Time: 3.16)
(a) Take 1 - (4.42)
(b) Take 2 - (5.37)
(c) Take 3 - (5.11)
(d) Take 4 - (5.32)
775. Where The Boys Go (Time: 3.29)
809. She's So Cold (Time: 4.13)
(a) Alternative Take - (6.51)
(b) Cleaned Up Version - (4.06)
842. We Had It All (Time: 2.54)
(a) Take 1 - (2.55)
(b) Take 2 - (2.55)
844. Gangster's Moll (Time: 2.20) *
845. Down In The Hole (Time: 3.57)
(a) Early Take - (3.56)
848. Let Me Go (Time: 3.51)
(a) Without Sax - (3.52)
849. No Use In Crying (Time: 3.25)
(a) Take 1 - (3.35)
(b) Take 2 - (4.28)
(c) Take 3 - (4.26)
(d) Take 4 - (4.28)

25 June - 9 August, 30 August - October; November - December 1979 EMI, Pathé Marconi Studios, Paris, France; Electric Lady Studios, New York, USA.
839. Dance (Instrumental) (Time: 4.37)
840. If I Was A Dancer (Dance Part Two) (Time: 5.50)
841. Dance (Time: 4.23)
(a) Take 1 - (6.54)
(b) Take 2 - (7.40)
(c) Take 3 - (8.04)
843. Emotional Rescue (Time: 5.39)
(a) Short Promo Version - (4.18)
(b) Forty Licks Edit Version - (3.42)
(c) Alternative Take - (6.58)
846. Indian Girl (Time: 4.23)
(a) Long Take - (6.05)
847. Send It To Me (Time: 3.43)
(a) Long Take - (6.15)

November - December 1979 Electric Lady Studios, New York, USA.
832. All About You (Time: 4.18)

1980-1981
11 October - 12 November 1980; April - June 1981 RS Mobile, Boulogne-Billancourt, Paris, France; Electric Ladyland, Atlantic Studio, New York, USA.
604. Waiting On A Friend (Time: 4.34)
(c) Take 3 - Sax - (3.34)
(d) Edited Version - (3.35)

649. Slave (Time: 4.59)
  (a) Take 1 - (7.14)
  (b) Take 2 - (9.43)
  (c) Take 3 - Sax - (8.20)
  (d) Take 4 - Sax - (11.13)
  (e) Extended Version - (6.32)
850. Heaven (Time: 4.22)
  (a) Take 1 - (5.17)
  (b) Take 2 - (5.24)
851. Neighbours (Time: 3.33)
  (a) Alternative Take - (3.26)
736. Start Me Up (Time: 3.33)
  (a) Alternative Take - (3.44)

1981
April - June 1981 Atlantic Studios, New York, USA.
651. Come On Sugar (Time: 5.31) *
  (a) Take 1 - (6.19)
655. Munich Reggae (Time: 5.29) *
  (a) Edited Cut - (2.02)

August - 14 September 1981 Long View Farm, Brookfield, Massachusetts, USA.
852. Munich Hilton (Time: 8.32) *

1982
October 1982 Unknown studio, Paris, France.
916. Can't Find Love *
917. You Keep It Cool *
918. Christine *

11 November - 16 December 1982 EMI, Pathé Marconi Studios, Paris, France.
648. Cellophane Trousers (Time: 2.26) *
713. I Love You Too Much (Time: 3.10)
749. Golden Caddy (Time: 1.58) *
819. Still In Love (Time: 5.22) *
919. Slide On (Time: 5.49) *
  (a) Short Take - (4.15)
921. All Mixed Up (Time: 6.36) *
  (a) Instrumental Take - (2.38)
924. Cookin' Up (Time: 4.01) *
  (a) Early Take - (5.57)
926. Stop That (Time: 5.40) *
927. Looking For Trouble (Time: 3.03) *
929. Cook Cook Blues (Time: 4.11)
931. Tried To Talk Her Into It (Time: 3.19) *
932. Crazy Arms (Time: 1.30) *
933. Hideaway *
934. Eliza Upchink *
935. Dance Mr. K *
936. Pullover *
937. Show Me A Woman *
938. Identification *
939. Pink Pick *
940. Christmas Issue *
941. Stiff *
942. Heartbeat *
943. Mellobar *

1982-1983
October; 11 November - 16 December 1982; April; May - July 1983 Unknown studio, Paris, France; EMI Pathé Marconi Studios, Paris, France; Compass Point, Nassau, Bahamas; The Hit Factory, New York, USA.
915. Wanna Hold You (Time: 3.52)
  (a) Take 1 - (6.28)
  (b) Take 2 - (3.22)
  (c) Take 3 - (6.57)
  (d) Edited Version - (3.15)

11 November - 16 December 1982; June - July 1983 EMI, Pathé Marconi Studios, Paris, France; The Hit Factory, New York, USA.
817. I Think I'm Going Mad (Time: 4.12)
  (b) Alternative Take - (5.47)
  (c) Alternative KR Vocal - (14.57)

11 November - 16 December 1982; April; May - July 1983 EMI Pathé Marconi Studios, Paris, France; Compass Point, Nassau, Bahamas; The Hit Factory, New York, USA.
920. Pretty Beat Up (Time: 4.05)
  (a) XXX Take
  (b) Instrumental Take 1 - (6.08)
  (c) Instrumental Take 2 - (4.28)
922. All The Way Down (Time: 3.14)
  (a) Early Take - (3.43)
923. She Was Hot (Time: 4.42)
  (a) Early Take - (6.44)
  (b) Long Take - (9.27)
  (c) Single Promo Version - (3.59)
  (d) Video Version - (4.58)
925. Tie You Up (The Pain Of Love) (Time: 4.16)
  (a) Early Take - (10.48)
928. Too Tough (Time: 3.51)
  (a) Early Take - (5.24)
930. It Must Be Hell (Time: 5.04)
  (a) Early Take - (5.45)

1983
31 January - 9 February, 15 February - March; April; May - July 1983 EMI Pathé Marconi Studios, Paris, France; Compass Point, Nassau, Bahamas; The Hit Factory, New York, USA.
944. Too Much Blood (Dub Version) (Time: 8.00)
945. Too Much Blood (Dance Version) (Time: 12.33)
  (a) Early Take - (6.26)
  (b) Extract Take - (2.51)
947. Feel On Baby (Time: 5.07)
948. Feel On Baby (Instrumental Mix) (Time: 6.31)
949. Undercover Of The Night (Dub Version) (Time: 6.21)
950. Undercover Of The Night (Time: 4.33)
  (a) Single Edit Version - (4.13)
  (b) Take 1 - (4.26)
  (c) Take 2 - (3.54)
  (d) Take 3 - (4.48)
  (e) Take 4 - (4.53)
  (f) Promo Single Version - (4.02)

June - July 1983 The Hit Factory, New York, USA.
817. I Think I'm Going Mad (Time: 4.12)

1985
12 January - 3 March 1985 EMI Pathé Marconi Studios, Paris, France.
953. These Arms Of Mine *
954. Mexican Divorce (Time: 3.31) *
955. Thirty Nine And Holding (Time: 6.26) *
956. Don't Be Cruel (Time: 4.49) *
961. Putty (In Your Hands) *
962. Back On The Streets Again (Time: 5.21) *

12 January - 3 March, 8 April - 17 June; 16 July - 17 August, 10 September - 15 October; 15 November - 5 December 1985 EMI Pathé Marconi Studios, Paris, France, France; RPM Studios, New York, USA; Right Track Studios, New York, USA.
951. One Hit (To The Body) (London Mix) (Time: 7.00)
952. One Hit (To The Body) (Time: 4.44)
  (a) Early Take - (7.51)
  (b) Instrumental Take - (4.59)
  (c) Take 3 - (4.57)
  (d) Take 4 - (4.41)
  (e) Take 5 - (4.44)
  (f) Edit 12 Inch Single - (4.12)

12 January - 3 March, 8 April - 17 June; 16 July - 17 August 1985 EMI Pathé Marconi Studios, Paris, France; RPM Studios, New York, USA.
957. What Am I Gonna Do With Your Love? (Time: 5.29) *
   (a) Early Take - (14.38)

958. Baby, You're Too Much ! (Time: 5.13) *
   (a) Early Take - (1.39)

12 January - 3 March, 8 April - 17 June 1985 EMI Pathé Marconi Studios, Paris, France.
959. Crushed Pearl (Time: 3.17) *
960. If I Don't Have You (Time: 3.14) *
   (a) Take 1 - (2.41)
   (b) Take 2 - (4.23)
   (c) Take 3 - (7.07)
   (d) Take 4 - (7.23)

8 April - 17 June 1985 EMI Pathé Marconi Studios, Paris, France.
963. You Can't Cut The Mustard (Time: 3.26) *
   (a) Early Take - (2.55)
965. High Temperature (Time: 5.23) *
967. My Baby Left Me (Time: 3.20) *
968. She Never Listens To Me (Time: 7.34) *
970. Knock Your Teeth Out *
971. Treat Me Like A Fool (Time: 6.40) *
   (a) Take 1 - (5.06)
   (b) Take 2 - (3.10)
   (c) Take 3 - (1.52)
972. What Are You Gonna Tell Your Boyfriend? (Time: 5.13) *
973. Don't Get Mad (Time: 0.58) *
974. Who's Shagging Who? (Time: 2.04) *
975. Cut Your Throat (Time: 5.59) *
976. You Got It (Time: 2.56) *
977. Some Of Us Are On Our Knees (Time: 5.38) *
978. Breakin' (Time: 2.55) *
   (a) MJ Take

8 April - 17 June; 16 July - 17 August 1985 EMI Pathé Marconi Studios, Paris, France; RPM Studios, New York, USA.
979. Strictly Memphis (Time: 3.41) *
   (a) Take 1 - (3.22)
   (b) Take 2 - (8.15)

8 April - 17 June; 16 July - 17 August, 10 September - 15 October; 15 November - 5 December 1985 EMI Pathé Marconi Studios, Paris, France; RPM Studios, New York, USA; Right Track Studios, New York, USA.
964. Had It With You (Time: 3.20)
   (a) Early Take - (2.55)
966. Too Rude (Time: 3.13)
   (a) Take 1 - (3.34)
   (b) Take 2 - (10.21)
959. Fight (Time: 3.10)
   (a) Take 1 - (3.59)
   (b) Instrumental Take 2 - (3.03)
   (c) Take 3 - (4.57)
980. Dirty Work (Time: 3.53)
   (a) Early Take - (4.19)

16 July - 17 August, 10 September - 15 October; 15 November - 5 December 1985 RPM Studios, New York, USA; Right Track Studios, New York, USA.
981. Harlem Shuffle (London Mix) (Time: 6.19)
982. Harlem Shuffle (NY Mix) (Time: 6.36)
   (a) NY Mix Edit Version - (5.49)
983. Harlem Shuffle (Time: 3.26)
   (a) Take 1 - (4.09)
   (b) Take 2 - (3.45)
   (c) Take 3 - (5.35)
986. Back To Zero (Time: 4.00)
   (a) Early Take - (4.17)

988. Winning Ugly (NY Mix) (Time: 7.03)
989. Winning Ugly (London Mix) (Time: 7.55)
990. Winning Ugly (Time: 4.33)
   (a) Early Take - (4.55)
991. Hold Back (Time: 3.53)
992. Sleep Tonight (Time: 5.14)
   (a) Early Take - (6.50)

16 July - 17 August 1985 RPM Studios, New York, USA.
984. Invitation (Time: 15.52) *
985. Deep Love (Time: 4.11) *
987. Loving You Is Sweeter Than Ever (Time: 6.20) *

1989
January - 23 March 1989 Blue Wave Studios, Barbados, USA.
993. Hang On Tonight *
994. Hellhound On My Trail (Time: 1.15) *

9 - 23 March; 29 March - 2 May 1989 Blue Wave Studios, Barbados, USA; Air Studios, Montserrat.
1009. For Your Precious Love (Time: 6.39) *
   (a) Take 1 - (6.21)
1010. Giving It Up (Time: 5.32) *
1011. Ready Yourself (Time: 3.37) *

15 May - 29 June 1989 Olympic Sound Studios, London, England.
929. Cook Cook Blues (Time: 4.11)

9 - 23 March; 29 March - 2 May; 15 May - 29 June 1989 Blue Wave Studios, Barbados, USA; Air Studios, Montserrat; Olympic Sound Studios, London, England.
995. Wish I'd Never Met You (Time: 4.42)
996. Mixed Emotions (Chris Kimsey's Twelve-Inch) (Time: 6.13)
997. Mixed Emotions (Time: 4.38)
   (a) Take 1 - (6.44)
   (b) Take 2 - (6.36)
   (c) Edited Single Version - (4.00)
   (d) New Mix Version - (4.37)
998. Rock And A Hard Place (Dance Mix) (Time: 6.54)
999. Rock And A Hard Place (Bonus Beats Mix) (Time: 4.08)
1000. Rock And A Hard Place (Oh-Oh Hard Dub Mix) (Time: 6.54)
1001. Rock And A Hard Place (Rock Mix Edit) (Time: 5.39)
1002. Rock And A Hard Place (Michael Brauer Mix) (Time: 7.05)
1003. Rock And A Hard Place (Time: 5.25)
   (a) Early Take 1 - (5.49)
   (b) Take 2 - (5.52)
   (c) Edited Single Version - (4.10)
1004. Almost Hear You Sigh (Time: 4.37)
   (a) Take 1 - (5.22)
   (b) Take 2 - (4.52)
   (c) Remix Version - (4.06)
1005. Sad Sad Sad (Time: 3.35)
   (a) Take 1 - (3.58)
   (b) Take 2 - (3.53)
1006. Hearts For Sale (Time: 4.41)
   (a) Take 1 - (4.30)
   (b) Take 2 - (4.35)
1007. Hold On To Your Hat (Time: 3.32)
   (a) Take 1 - (4.10)
   (b) Take 2 - (4.07)
1008. Slipping Away (Time: 4.29)
   (a) Early Take 1 - (5.25)
   (b) Take 2 - (5.38)
1012. Can't Be Seen (Time: 4.10)
   (a) Take 1 - (5.14)
   (b) Take 2 - (5.25)
1013. Break The Spell (Time: 3.07)
   (a) Take 1 - (3.36)
   (b) Take 2 - (3.50)

1014. Blinded By Love (Time: 4.36)
   (a) Take 1 - (5.20)
   (b) Take 2 - (5.07)
1015. Terrifying (Twelve Inch Re-mix) (Time: 6.56)
1016. Terrifying (Time: 4.53)
   (a) Take 1 - (5.09)
   (b) Take 2 - (5.40)
   (c) Seven-Inch Re-Mix Edit - (4.10)
1017. Fancyman Blues (Time: 5.12)
   (a) Take 1 - (5.48)
   (b) Take 2 - (6.46)

9 - 23 March; 29 March - 2 May; 15 May - 29 June 1989; (16 - 17 June) Blue Wave Studios, Barbados, USA; Air Studios, Montserrat; Olympic Sound Studios, London, England; (The Palace Of Ben Abbou, Tangier, Morocco.)
1018. Continental Drift (Time: 5.15)
   (a) Instrumental Take 1 - (6.21)
   (b) Take 2 - (6.22)

1991
7-18 January 1991 Hit Factory Studio, London, England.
1063. Highwire (Time: 4.45)
   (a) Edited Single Version - (3.41)
1064. Sexdrive (Dirty Hands Mix) (Time: 4.27)
1065. Sexdrive (Club Version) (Time: 6.18)
   (a) Edited Club Version - (4.33)
1066. Sex Drive (Time: 5.07)

1993
20 April - May 1993 Blue Wave Studios, Barbados.
1068. Randy Whore (Time: 7.57) *
   (a) Take 1 - (3.58)
1069. Disposition Boogie (Time: 1.32) *
1070. Alteration Boogie (Time: 4.45) *
1071. Get Your Hands Off (Time: 3.41) *
   (a) Take 1 - (6.38)
1072. My Love Is My Love (Time: 9.20) *
1073. Glimmer Twins Boogie (Time: 1.36) *
1074. Slips Away (Time: 16.01) *
1075. Goodbye To Love (Time: 2.29) *
1077. Yellow Jacket (Time: 2.05) *
1078. He Loves You So (Time: 5.54) *
1079. Why You Runnin'? (Time: 4.54) *
1080. You Got Away With Murder (Time: 4.42) *
1082. Keith's Blues (Time: 3.33) *
1083. I'm Fallin' (Time: 6.35) *
1085. Look Out Baby (Time: 10.23) *
1086. Voodoo Residue - Untitled #1 (Time: 6.57) *
1087. Voodoo Residue - Untitled #2 (Time: 1.51) *

20 April - May; 9 July - 6 August & September; 3 November - 16 December 1993 Blue Wave Studios, Barbados, Ron Wood's Sandymount Studios, Kildare, Ireland; Windmill Lane Studios, Dublin, Ireland.
1076. Ivy League (Time: 3.13) *
1081. Alright Charlie (Time: 4.09) *
   (a) Take 1 - (5.04)
   (b) Take 2 - (3.09)
1084. Make It Now (Time: 4.29) *
   (a) Take 1 - (9.15)
   (b) Take 2 - (7.35)
1088. It's Funny (Time: 4.36) *
   (a) Early Take 1 - (2.38)
   (b) Take 2 - (6.24)
1089. Anything For You (Time: 8.14) *
   (a) Take 1 - (5.49)

9 July - 6 August & September; 3 November - 16 December 1993 Ron Wood's Sandymount Studios, Kildare, Ireland; Windmill Lane Studios, Dublin, Ireland.
1099. Voodoo Brew - Untitled #1 (Time: 6.19) *

1100. Voodoo Brew - Untitled #2 (Time: 3.51) *
   (a) Take 1 - (5.57)
1101. Voodoo Brew - Untitled #3 (Time: 5.47) *
1102. Voodoo Brew - Untitled #4 (Time: 3.50) *
1103. Baby, You're Too Much II (Time: 5.24) *
1104. Bump And Ride (Time: 5.48) *
1105. Zip Mouth Angel (Time: 3.33) *
1106. Zulu (Time: 4.37) *
   (a) Take 1 - (4.11)
1107. It's Alright (Time: 4.00) *
1111. Possesses Me (Time: 7.37) *
1112. I Got A Hold On You (Time: 4.37) *
1113. Monsoon Ragoon (Time: 4.36) *
1115. Another CR (Time: 9.46) *
1120. Honest Man (Time: 4.28) *
   (a) Take 1 - (4.23)
1121. Samba (Time: 3.42) *
1123. You Got It Made (Time: 5.01) *
   (a) Take 1 - (4.27)
   (b) Take 2 & Conversation - (17.16)
1125. Tease Me (Time: 4.21) *
1130. Middle Of The Sea (Time: 3.42) *

30 September - 1 October 1993 Windmill Lane Studios, Dublin, Ireland.
1139. The Rocky Road To Dublin (Time: 5.03) *
   (a) Edited Version - (4.17)

3 November - 16 December 1993 Windmill Lane Studios, Dublin, Ireland.
1140. Trouble Man (Time: 4.00) *
   (a) Take 1 - (4.43)

1993-1994
20 April - May; 9 July - 6 August & September; 3 November - 16 December 1993; 15 January - April 1994 Blue Wave Studios, Barbados; Ron Wood's Home, Dublin, Ireland; Windmill Lane Studios, Dublin, Ireland; Don Was' Studio & A&M Studios, Los Angeles, USA.
1067. Thru And Thru (Time: 6.15)
   (a) Early Take 1 - (4.45)
   (b) Early Take 2 - (3.11)
   (c) Take 3 - (11.49)
   (d) Take 4 - (4.11)
   (e) Take 5 - (8.32)
   (f) Take 6 - (8.26)
   (g) Take 7 - (8.23)
1090. Suck On The Jugular (Time: 4.28)
   (a) Take 1 - (5.47)
   (b) Take 2 - (5.50)

9 July - 6 August & September; 3 November - 16 December 1993; 15 January - April 1994 Ron Wood's Sandymount Studios, Kildare, Ireland; Windmill Lane Studios, Dublin, Ireland; Don Was' Studio & A&M Studios, Los Angeles, USA.
1098. Love Is Strong (Time: 3.50)
   (a) Take 1 - (5.47)
   (b) Take 2 - (5.41)
   (c) Take 3 - (5.42)
1108. Blinded By Rainbows (Time: 4.33)
   (a) Take 1 - (6.55)
   (b) Instrumental Take 2 - (4.42)
   (c) Take 3 - (4.34)
1109. Moon Is Up (Time: 3.42)
   (a) Instrumental Take 1 - (5.03)
   (b) Take 2 - (4.18)
1110. The Worst (Time: 2.24)
   (a) Take 1 - (3.08)
   (b) Take 2 - (2.26)
   (c) Take 3 - (2.27)
1114. Mean Disposition (Time: 4.07)
   (a) Instrumental Take 1 - (4.13)
   (b) Take 2 - (3.14)

1116. You Got Me Rocking (Time: 3.35)
  (a) Take 1 - (10.58)
  (b) Take 2 - (4.11)
  (c) Take 3 - (4.13)
  (d) Short Extract - (1.13)
  (e) Take 4 - (4.05)
1122. The Storm (Time: 2.49)
  (a) Take 1 - (9.56)
  (b) Take 2 - (3.19)
  (c) Take 3 - (3.17)
1124. New Faces (Time: 2.52)
  (a) Take 1 - (2.54)
  (b) Take 2 - (2.47)
1126. Sparks Will Fly (Time: 3.16)
  (a) Take 1 - (3.20)
  (b) Take 2 - Studio Extract - (14.33)
  (c) Take 3 - (3.16)
  (d) Take 4 - (3.19)
  (e) Take 5 - (3.15)
  (f) Radio Clean Version - (3.15)
1129. Out Of Tears (Time: 5.27)
  (a) Take 1 - (4.23)
  (b) Take 2 - (5.29)
  (c) Take 3 - (5.24)
1131. Jump On Top Of Me (Time: 4.24)
  (a) Instrumental Take 1 - (5.03)
1132. I'm Gonna Drive (Time: 3.42)
  (a) Instrumental Take - (5.27)
1133. Baby Break It Down (Time: 4.09)
  (a) KR Vocal Take 1 - (6.02)
  (b) Instrumental Take 2 - (5.56)
  (c) Take 3 - (4.11)
  (d) Longer Take - (5.59)
1134. Brand New Car (Time: 4.15)
  (a) Take 1 - (5.29)
  (b) Take 2 - (5.05)
  (c) Take 3 - (5.04)
1135. Sweethearts Together (Time: 4.45)
  (a) Take 1 - (3.39)
  (b) Take 2 - (5.58)
  (c) Take 3 - (5.56)
  (d) Take 4 - (5.48)
  (e) Take 5 - (5.56)
  (f) Take 6 - (5.51)
1138. I Go Wild (Time: 4.23)
  (a) Take 1 - (5.33)
  (b) Take 2 - (4.40)

1994

15 January - April 1994 Don Was' Studio and A&M Studios, Los Angeles, USA.
771. So Young (1994 Version) (Time: 3.25)
  (a) Original Take - (2.57)
772. So Young (Piano Version) (Time: 2.55)
1091. Love Is Strong (Bob Clearmountain Remix) (Time: 3.49)
1092. Love Is Strong (Teddy Riley Radio Remix) (Time: 4.08)
1093. Love Is Strong (Teddy Riley Extended Remix) (Time: 5.04)
1094. Love Is Strong (Teddy Riley Extended Rock Remix) (Time: 4.48)
1095. Love Is Strong (Teddy Riley Dub Remix) (Time: 4.07)
1096. Love Is Strong (Teddy Riley Instrumental) (Time: 4.46)
1097. Love Is Strong (Joe The Butcher Club Mix) (Time: 5.25)
1117. You Got Me Rocking (Perfecto Mix) (Time: 5.04)
  (a) Pefecto Mix Edit Version - (3.49)
1118. You Got Me Rocking (Sexy Disco Dub Mix) (Time: 6.18)
1119. You Got Me Rocking (Trance Mix) (Time: 5.00)
1127. Out Of Tears (Don Was Edit) (Time: 4.22)
1128. Out Of Tears (Bob Clearmountain Remix Edit) (Time: 4.21)
1136. I Go Wild (Scott Litt Remix) (Time: 4.39)
1137. I Go Wild (Luis Resto Straight Vocal Mix) (Time: 5.40)

1995

3 - 4 March 1995 Toshiba-EMI Studios, Tokyo, Japan.
1187. Parachute Woman *
1188. No Expectations (Time: 5.01) *
1189. Let It Bleed (Time: 1.05) *
1190. Beast Of Burden (Time: 3.30) *
1191. Memory Motel (Time: 6.21) *
1192. The Worst *
1193. Love In Vain (Time: 5.31)
1194. Slipping Away (Time: 4.55)
1195. Honest I Do (Time: 3.57)
1196. The Spider And The Fly (Time: 3.28)
1197. Wild Horses (Time: 5.09)
  (a) Edited Promo Version - (4.07)
1198. Let's Spend The Night Together (Time: 3.20) *
1119. The Last Time *
1200. Angie *
1201. Make No Mistake *
1202. Heartbeat *
1203. Little Baby (Time: 4.00)
1204. I'm Left, You're Right, She's Gone *

25-26 July 1995 Estudios Valentim De Carvalho, Lisbon, Portugal.
1254. Not Fade Away (Time: 3.06)
1255. I'm Free (Time: 3.12)
1256. Sweet Virginia (Time: 4.15)

1997

13 March - April 1997 Ocean Way Recording Studios, Hollywood, Cherokee Recording Studios, Los Angeles, California, USA.
1257. Paying The Cost To Be The Boss (Time: 3.34)

13 March - July 1997 Ocean Way Recording Studios, Hollywood, California, USA.
1103. Baby, You're Too Much II (Time: 5.24) *
1258. Precious Lips *
1249. Might As Well Get Juiced (Time: 5.23)
  (a) Keith's Revenge Remix (Bootleg) - (10.50)
  (b) Cult-Club Mix *(Bootleg)* - (7.21)
1260. Low Down (Time: 4.25)
  (a) 12 Inch Edit *(Bootleg)* - (6.21)
  (b) Master Mix *(Bootleg)* - (6.04)
1261. Anybody Seen My Baby? (Time: 4.31)
  (a) Call Out Hook (Chorus) Version - (0.09)
  (b) Armand's Tuned Club Cut - (9.32)
  (c) Armand's House Special - (13.37)
1262. Anybody Seen My Baby? (Armand's Rolling Steelo Mix) (Time: 10.30)
1263. Anybody Seen My Baby? (Soul Solution Remix Edit) (Time: 4.20)
1264. Anybody Seen My Baby? (Soul Solution Vocal Dub) (Time: 3.44)
1265. Anybody Seen My Baby? (Soul Solution Remix) (Time: 9.31)
1266. Anybody Seen My Baby? (Bonus Roll Mix) (Time: 6.04)
1267. Anybody Seen My Baby? (LP/Single Edit) (Time: 4.07)
1268. Anybody Seen My Baby? (Don Was Radio Remix) (Time: 3.45)
1269. Anybody Seen My Baby? (No Biz Edit) (Time: 4.03)
1270. Anybody Seen My Baby? (Phil Jones Remix) (Time: 4.30)
1271. Anybody Seen My Baby? (Casanova New Vocal Remix) (Time: 6.33)
1272. Flip The Switch (Time: 3.27)
  (a) Clean Version - (3.28)
  (b) Call Out Hook No. 1 - (0.13)
  (c) Call Out Hook No. 2 - (0.14)
  (d) Hyper Mix (Bootleg) - (5.59)
1273. Always Suffering (Time: 4.43)
  (a) Sentimental Remix *(Bootleg)* - (9.22)
1274. Thief In The Night (Time: 5.15)

1275. Saint Of Me (Time: 5.14)
  (a) Alternate Mix *(Bootleg)* - (5.13)
  (b) Detroit Floor RMX *(Bootleg)* - (12.42)
  (c) Call Out Hook - (0.12)
  (d) Radio Edit - (4.11)
1276. Saint Of Me (Todd Terry Extended Mix) (Time: 6.03)
1277. Saint Of Me (Todd Terry Fade) (Time: 3.32)
1278. Saint Of Me (Todd Terry Tee's Freeze Dub) (Time: 7.43)
1279. Saint Of Me (Todd Terry Dub No. 2) (Time: 7.40)
1280. Saint Of Me (Deep Dish Club Mix Part One) (Time: 7.35)
1281. Saint Of Me (Deep Dish Rolling Dub) (Time: 7.12)
1282. Saint Of Me (Deep Dish Grunge Garage Dub) (Time: 7.25)
1283. Saint Of Me (Deep Dish Grunge Garage Remix Edit) (Time: 3.22)
1284. Saint Of Me (Deep Dish Grunge Garage Remix) (Time: 14.08)
1285. You Don't Have To Mean It (Time: 3.44)
1286. Already Over Me (Time: 5.24)
  (a) Ambient Mix *(Bootleg)* - (9.04)
  (b) Ambient Remix *(Bootleg)* - (9.13)
1287. Too Tight (Time: 3.37)
1288. Gunface (Time: 5.02)
  (a) Dodge City Mix *(Bootleg)* - (6.17)
1289. Anyway You Look At It (Time: 4.20)
1290. Out Of Control (In Hand With Fluke) (Time: 8.28)
1291. Out Of Control (In Hand With Fluke - Radio Edit) (Time: 4.32)
1292. Out Of Control (In Hand With Fluke Instrumental) (Time: 5.55)
1293. Out Of Control (Saber Master With Fade) (Time: 4.42)
  (a) Danny Saber's Demo - (5.39)
  (b) Bi-Polar Horns Of Control - (5.09)
  (c) Bi-Polar Fat Controller Mix (Percussive Version) - (5.24)
  (d) S.D.S. Mix - (4.23)
  (e) S.D.S. Mix (No Samples) - (4.22)
  (f) S.D.S. Dub Mix - (4.51)
  (g) Fluke Vocal 12-Inch - (6.36)
  (h) Fluke Instrumental - (5.36)
  (i) Fluke Vocal 12-Inch #2 - (6.51)
  (j) Fluke Vocal 7-Inch #2 - (4.10)
1294. Out Of Control (Saber Final Mix) (Time: 5.45)
1295. Out Of Control (Bi-Polar At The Controls) (Time: 5.12)
1296. Out Of Control (Bi-Polar's Outer Version) (Time: 5.09)
1297. Out Of Control (Bi-Polar's Fat Controller Mix) (Time: 5.24)
1298. Out Of Control (Time: 4.43)
  (a) Papa Was A Rolling Stone Mix *(Bootleg)* - (10.21)
  (b) Reggae Version *(Bootleg)* - (5.09)
  (c) Album Radio Edit - (4.00)
  (d) Call Out Hook - (0.18)
  (e) Old School Mix *(Bootleg)* - (8.58)
1299. Young Love *
1300. How Can I Stop (Time: 6.54)

2002

May - June 2002 Encore Studios, Burbank, California, USA.
729. Miss You (Dr Dre Remix 2002) (Time: 3.42)

13 May - 8 June 2002 Studio Guillaume Tell, Paris, France; Mix This! Studios, Los Angeles, USA.
1343. Losing My Touch (Time: 5.06)
1344. Keys To Your Love (Time: 4.12)
1345. Stealing My Heart (Time: 3.42)
1346. Don't Stop (Time: 3.58)
  (a) Single Edit Version - (3.32)
  (b) Call Out Hook Version - (0.13)
1347. Don't Stop (New Rock Mix) (Time: 4.01)
1348. Extreme Western Grip (Time: 3.05)
1349. Well Well (Time: 3.01)
1350. Hurricane (Time: 1.25)

2003

April - July 2003 The Hit Factory, New York, Hovercraft Studios, Mixstar Studios, Virginia, USA.
403. Sympathy For The Devil (Neptunes Remix) (Time: 5.55)
404. Sympathy For The Devil (Neptunes Radio Remix) (Time: 4.16)

April - July 2003 HMS House, Brighton, England.
405. Sympathy For The Devil (Fatboy Slim Remix) (Time: 8.25)
406. Sympathy For The Devil (Fatboy Slim Radio Remix) (Time: 4.06)

April - July 2003 Magic Shop, New York, Flava Lab, London, England.
407. Sympathy For The Devil (Full Phatt Remix) (Time: 5.26)
408. Sympathy For The Devil (Full Phatt Radio Remix) (Time: 3.42)

2004-2005

June, November - December 2004, January, March - April; June 2005 La Fourchette Home Studio, Fourchette, Tours, France & St. Vincent's Home Studio, West Indies; Ocean Way Studio & Henson Studios, Hollywood, California, USA.
1423. Rain Fall Down (Time: 4.53)
1424. Rain Fall Down (Radio re-edit) (Time: 4.02)
1425. Rain Fall Down (will.i.am Remix) (Time: 4.05)
1426. Rain Fall Down (will.i.am instrumental) (Time: 4.05)
1427. Rain Fall Down (Ashley Beedle's 'Heavy Disco' Vocal re-edit) (Time: 6.13)
1428. Rain Fall Down (Ashley Beedle's 'Heavy Disco' Dub re-edit) (Time: 6.07)
1429. Rain Fall Down (Ashley Beedle's 'Heavy Disco' Radio re-edit) (Time: 4.06)
1430. Let Me Down Slow (Time: 4.16)
  (a) Alternative Mix 1 - (4.17)
  (b) Alternative Mix 2 - (4.16)
  (c) Alternative Mix 3 - (4.17)
1431. Streets Of Love (Time: 5.10)
  (a) Alternative Mix 1 - (5.10)
  (b) Alternative Mix 2 - (5.09)
  (c) Radio Edit Version - (4.04)
1432. It Won't Take Long (Time: 3.54)
  (a) Alternative Mix 1 - (4.12)
  (b) Alternative Mix 2 - (4.12)
1433. Back Of My Hand (Time: 3.32)
1434. She Saw Me Coming (Time: 3.12)
  (a) Alternative Mix - (3.22)
1435. Dangerous Beauty (Time: 3.48)
  (a) Alternative Mix 1 - (4.14)
  (b) Alternative Mix 2 - (4.15)
1436. Don't Wanna Go Home (Time: 3.34)
  (a) Alternative Mix 1 - (4.33)
  (b) Alternative Mix 2 - (4.32)
  (c) Alternative Mix 3 - (4.33)
1437. Oh No, Not You Again (Time: 3.46)
  (a) Clean Mix Version - (3.49)
  (b) Alternative Mix Cut - (3.48)
1438. This Place Is Empty (Time: 3.16)
1439. Under The Radar (Time: 4.36)
  (a) Alternative Take - (5.09)
1440. Driving Too Fast (Time: 3.56)
  (a) Alternative Take - (4.29)
1441. Biggest Mistake (Time: 4.06)
  (a) Alternative Take - (4.53)
  (b) Edited Single Version - (3.33)
  (c) Instrumental Single Version - (4.09)
1442. Laugh, I Nearly Died (Time: 4.54)
1443. Infamy (Time: 3.48)
1444. Look What The Cat Dragged In (Time: 3.57)
1445. Sweet Neocon (Time: 4.33)
1446. Rough Justice (Time: 3.13)

2005

9 May 2005 S.I.R. Studios, New York, USA.
1447. Brown Sugar (Time: 3.46) *
1448. Oh No, Not You Again (Time: 3.51) *

2006

6-8 July 2006 Discotheque Alcatraz, Milan, Italy.
1495. I Can't Be Satisfied (Time: 3.32)

11 September 2006 Palmdale Studios, California, USA.
1497. Only Found Out Yesterday (Time: 1.57)

2006 Various Studios.
265. I'm Free (Hot Chip Remix) (Time: 3.03)
266. I'm Free (Moby Remix) (Time: 3.43)
267. I'm Free (The Postal Service Remix) (Time: 2.27)
268. I'm Free (DJ Shadow Remix) (Time: 4.11)

2006 Norman Cook Studio, Hove, Brighton, England.
269. I'm Free (Fatboy Slim Remix) (Time: 3.58)

2007

2007 Soulwax Studios, Ghent, Belgium.
411. You Can't Always Get What You Want (Soulwax Full Length Remix) (Time: 6.07)
   (a) Soulwax Remix Radio Edit Version - (3.58)

2008-2009

2008 - 2009 Abdala Studios, Havana, Cuba.
165. Under The Boardwalk (Rhythms Del Mundo Remix) (Time: 2.44)

\

2009

September - November; December 2009 One East Studio, New York, Henson Studios, Village Recording; Mix This!, Los Angeles, USA.
432. So Divine (Aladdin Story) (Time: 4.32)
438. Loving Cup - Alternate Take (Time: 5.26)
496. Good Time Women (Time: 3.21)
497. Dancing In The Light (Time: 4.22)
504. All Down The Line (Electric) (Time: 4.09)
543. Soul Survivor - Alternate Take (Time: 3.59)
548. Following The River (Time: 4.51)
   (a) Promo Edit Version - (4.01)

367. Title 5 (Time: 1.47)
528. I'm Not Signifying (Time: 3.56)
529. Pass The Wine (Sophia Loren) (Time: 4.54)
546. Plundered My Soul (Time: 3.58)
547. Plundered My Soul (Radio Mix) (Time: 3.56)

2010

1-5 February; February; 21 October; November 2010 Helicon Mountain Studio, Blackheath, London; Chapel Studios, London; One East Studios, New York, USA; La Fourchette Home Studio, Fourchette, Tours, France.
1546. Watching The River Flow (Time: 5.09)

2011

August - September 2011 La Fourchette Home Studio, Fourchette, Tours, France, Electric Lady, New York, Berkeley St., Mix This!, Los Angeles, USA.
713. I Love You Too Much (Time: 3.10)
735. Claudine (Time: 3.42)
737. Don't Be A Stranger (Time: 4.06)
740. Keep Up Blues (Time: 4.20)
741. Do You Think I Really Care? (Time: 4.22)
748. Petrol Blues (Time: 1.35)
758. No Spare Parts (Time: 4.30)
759. When You're Gone (Time: 3.51)
773. So Young (2011 Version) (Time: 3.18)
774. You Win Again (Time: 3.00)
805. Tallahassee Lassie (Time: 2.37)
842. We Had It All (Time: 2.54)

LIVE TRACKS IN DATE ORDER INDEX

All officially released live and significant live tracks are listed. (Available as a file on stonessessions.com)
* indicates the track has not been released officially.

1964

8 February - 7 March 1964 - UK Tour - Unknown venue, BBC Radio, London, England.
83. Roll Over Beethoven (2.17) *
84. Beautiful Delilah (2.14) *

19 March 1964 - Camden Theatre, London, England.
91. Route 66 (2.45) *
92. Cops And Robbers (3.55) *
93. You Better Move On (3.01) *
94. Mona (2.51) *

10 April 1964 - Playhouse Theatre, London, England.
95. Not Fade Away (2.04) *
96. High Heeled Sneakers (1.39) *
97. Little By Little (2.30) *
98. I Just Want To Make Love To You (2.16) *
99. I'm Moving On (2.08) *

26 April 1964 - NME Poll Winners Concert, Empire Pool Wembley, London, England.
109. Not Fade Away (2.01) *
110. I Just Want To Make Love To You (2.19) *
111. I'm Alright (2.07) *

27 April 1964 - The Royal Albert Hall, London, England.
112. Not Fade Away *
113. High Heeled Sneakers *
114. I'm Alright *

28-29 October 1964 - Santa Monica Civic Auditorium, California, USA.
181. Around And Around (2.17)
182. Off The Hook (2.31)
183. Time Is On My Side (2.34)
184. It's All Over Now (3.08)
185. I'm Alright (3.02)

29 October 1964 - Santa Monica Civic Auditorium, California, USA.
186. Get Together (2.07)

1965

5-16 March 1965 - IBC Mobile Unit, London Edmonton Regal, Liverpool Empire, Manchester Palace, England.
207. Everybody Needs Somebody To Love (0.33)
208. Pain In My Heart (2.03)
209. Route 66 (2.36)
210. I'm Moving On (2.12)
211. Time Is On My Side (2.48)
212. I'm Alright (2.22)
    (a) Re-Recorded Vocal Version (2.26)

11 April 1965 - Empire Pool Wembley, London, England.
217. Everybody Needs Somebody To Love (0.23) *
218. Pain In My Heart (1.58) *
219. Around And Around (2.20) *
220. The Last Time (3.04) *
221. Everybody Needs Somebody To Love (2.55) *

17-18 April 1965 - Olympia Theatre, Paris, France.
222. Hey Crawdaddy (5.52) *

1966

28 July 1966 - Honolulu Stadium, Honolulu, Hawaii.
303. Mother's Little Helper (2.32) *
1 October 1966 - City Hall, Newcastle, England.
323. Under My Thumb (2.53)
324. Get Off My Cloud (2.54)
325. The Last Time (3.07)
326. 19th Nervous Breakdown (3.30)

7 October 1966 - Colston Hall, Bristol, England.
328. Under My Thumb (3.08)
329. Lady Jane (3.08)
330. Not Fade Away (2.03)
331. Have You Seen Your Mother, Baby, Standing In The Shadow? (2.19)
332. (I Can't Get No) Satisfaction (3.04)

1968

12 May 1968 - NME Poll Winners Concert, Empire Pool, Wembley, England.
389. Jumpin' Jack Flash *
390. (I Can't Get No) Satisfaction *

1969

5 July 1969 - Hyde Park, London, England.
444. I'm Yours And I'm Hers (3.17)
444. Jumping Jack Flash (3.19)
446. Mercy Mercy (2.55)
447. Down Home Girl (4.51) *
448. Stray Cat Blues (3.36)
449. No Expectations (3.19)
450. I'm Free (2.49)
451. Give Me A Drink (5.07) *
452. Love In Vain (4.33)
453. (I Can't Get No) Satisfaction (6.20)
454. Honky Tonk Women (3.10)
455. Midnight Rambler (4.29)
456. Street Fighting Man (3.34)
457. Sympathy For The Devil (10.18)

26 November 1969 - Baltimore Civic Centre, Madison, USA.
462. Stray Cat Blues (3.40)
463. Love In Vain (4.56)

27 November 1969 - Madison Square Garden, New York, USA.
464. Jumpin' Jack Flash (4.02)
465. Prodigal Son (2.38)
466. Under My Thumb (3.38)
467. I'm Free (2.47)
468. Honky Tonk Women (3.34)

28 November 1969 (Show One) - Madison Square Garden, New York, USA.
469. Jumpin' Jack Flash (3.17)
470. Carol (3.46)
471. Sympathy For The Devil (6.51)
472. Little Queenie (4.33)
473. (I Can't Get No) Satisfaction (5.38)
474. Street Fighting Man (4.03)

28 November 1969 (Show Two) - Madison Square Garden, New York, USA.
475. Carol (3.29)
476. Prodigal Son (4.04)
477. You Gotta Move (2.18)
478. Midnight Rambler (9.04)
479. Live With Me (3.02)

480. Honky Tonk Women (3.02)
481. Street Fighting Man (3.41)

6 December 1969 - Altamont Speedway, Livermore, California, USA.
485. The Sun Is Shining (3.44) *
486. Sympathy For The Devil (6.02)
487. Under My Thumb (3.31)
488. Gimme Shelter (2.03)

1970
7 October 1970 - Grugahalle, Essen, Germany.
507. Roll Over Beethoven (2.12) *

1971
13 March 1971 - RS Mobile, Leeds University, Leeds, England.
518. Let It Rock (2.47)

26 March 1971 - Marquee Club, London, England.
519. Live With Me (3.50) *
520. Dead Flowers (3.58) *
521. I Got The Blues (3.39) *
522. Let It Rock (2.25) *
523. Midnight Rambler (9.20) *
524. (I Can't Get No) Satisfaction (4.45) *
525. Bitch (4.05) *
526. Brown Sugar (4.16) *

1972
24 June 1972 - Tarrant County Convention Centre, Fort Worth, Texas, USA. (Show One).
562. Gimme Shelter (4.49)
563. Dead Flowers (4.09)
564. Sweet Black Angel (3.18) *
565. Happy (3.07)
566. Sweet Virginia (4.30)

24 June 1972 - Tarrant County Convention Centre, Fort Worth, Texas, USA. (Show Two).
567. Bitch (4.44)
568. Don't Lie To Me (2.38) *
569. Rip This Joint (2.23)

25 June 1972 - Hofheinz Pavilion, Houston, Texas, USA. (Show One).
570. Tumbling Dice (5.16)
571. Love In Vain (6.35)
572. You Can't Always Get What You Want (7.22)
573. Bye Bye Johnny (3.24)
574. Jumping Jack Flash (3.39)

25 June 1972 - Hofheinz Pavilion, Houston, Texas, USA. (Show Two).
575. Brown Sugar (4.23)
576. All Down The Line (5.23)
577. Midnight Rambler (12.42)
578. Street Fighting Man (7.10)

21 July 1972 - Spectrum Sports Arena, Philadelphia, USA.
579. Uptight / (I Can't Get No) Satisfaction (5.32) *

25 July 1972 - Madison Square Garden, New York, USA.
580. Brown Sugar (1.48)
581. Street Fighting Man (1.44)

1973
18 January 1973 - LA Forum, Inglewood, California, USA.
605. It's All Over Now (4.52) *

17 October 1973 (Show One) - RSM, National Forest Arena, Brussels, Belgium.
607. Brown Sugar (3.56)
608. Midnight Rambler (12.53)
609. Street Fighting Man (3.27)

17 October 1973 (Show Two) - RSM, National Forest Arena, Brussels, Belgium.
610. Gimme Shelter (5.33)
611. Happy (3.14)
612. Tumbling Dice (5.04)
613. Star Star (4.16)
614. Dancing With Mr. D (4.37)
615. Doo Doo Doo Doo (Heartbreaker) (5.03)
616. Angie (5.15)
617. You Can't Always Get What You Want (11.00)
618. Honky Tonk Women (3.11)
619. All Down The Line (4.20)
620. Rip This Joint (2.25)
621. Jumpin' Jack Flash (3.27)

1975
6 June 1975 - Arrowhead Stadium, Kansas City, USA.
661. Sure The One You Need (4.48) *

17 June 1975 - Maple Leaf Gardens, Toronto, Ontario, Canada.
662. Fingerprint File (5.17)
663. It's Only Rock 'N' Roll (4.26)

9 July 1975 - LA Forum, Inglewood, California, USA.
665. Sympathy For The Devil (7.57)

13 July 1975 - LA Forum, Inglewood, California, USA.
666. Honky Tonk Women (5.29)
667. All Down The Line (4.05)
668. If You Can't Rock Me (3.24)
669. Get Off My Cloud (4.02)
670. Star Star (4.45)
671. Gimme Shelter (6.12)
672. Ain't Too Proud To Beg (4.24)
673. You Gotta Move (4.32)
674. You Can't Always Get What You Want (15.23)
675. Happy (2.45)
676. Tumbling Dice (5.23)
677. It's Only Rock 'N' Roll (6.04)
678. Doo Doo Doo Doo (Heartbreaker) (4.22)
679. Fingerprint File (8.43)
680. Angie (5.18)
681. Wild Horses (7.25)
682. That's Life (3.17)
683. Outa-Space (4.04)
684. Brown Sugar (4.15)
686. Midnight Rambler (15.15)
686. Rip This Joint (2.06)
687. Street Fighting Man (4.05)
688. Jumping Jack Flash (6.57)
689. Sympathy For The Devil (10.21)

1976
27 May 1976 - Earl's Court, London, England.
690. If You Can't Rock Me (1.27)
691. Get Off My Cloud (3.34)

5 June 1976 - Aux Abattoirs, Paris, France.
692. Honky Tonk Women (3.20)
693. You Gotta Move (4.19)
694. Happy (2.54)

6 June 1976 - Aux Abattoirs, Paris, France.
695. Hot Stuff (4.36)
696. Star Star (4.10)
697. Brown Sugar (3.11)
698. Jumpin' Jack Flash (3.57)

7 June 1976 - Aux Abattoirs, Paris, France.
699. You Can't Always Get What You Want (7.44)
700. Tumbling Dice (3.59)
701. Nothing From Nothing (2.50) *

21 August 1976 - Knebworth, England.
702. Wild Horses (5.56)

1977
4/5 March 1977 - El Mocambo, Toronto, Canada.
703. Around And Around (4.07)
704. Little Red Rooster (4.39)
705. Mannish Boy (6.29)
706. Crackin' Up (5.40)

1978
14 June 1978 - Capitol Theatre, Passaic, New Jersey, USA.
778. Sweet Little Sixteen (2.58) *

28 June 1978 - Mid-South Coliseum, Memphis, Tennessee, USA.
779. Hound Dog (2.00) *

6 July 1978 - Masonic Hall, Detroit, Michigan, USA.
780. When The Whip Comes Down (4.25)

18 July 1978 - Will Rogers Memorial Center, Fort Worth, Texas, USA.
781. Let It Rock (2.12)
782. All Down The Line (3.56)
783. Honky Tonk Women (3.38)
784. Star Star (3.47)
785. When The Whip Comes Down (5.13)
786. Beast Of Burden (6.28)
787. Miss You (8.35)
788. Just My Imagination (Running Away With Me) (6.40)
789. Shattered (4.44)
790. Respectable (3.23)
791. Far Away Eyes (5.51)
792. Love In Vain (4.53)
793. Tumbling Dice (4.38)
794. Happy (3.12)
795. Sweet Little Sixteen (3.11)
796. Brown Sugar (3.14)
797. Jumpin' Jack Flash (6.14)

1979
22 April 1979 - Oshawa Civic Auditorium, Toronto, Canada.
837. Before They Make Me Run (3.10) *
838. Prodigal Son (3.06) *

1981
25 September 1981 - JFK Stadium, Philadelphia, USA.
853. Tops (3.58) *

26 September 1981 - JFK Stadium, Philadelphia, USA.
854. Down The Road Apiece (2.11) *
855. Mona (4.01) *

5 November 1981 - Brendan Byrne Arena, The Meadowlands, New Jersey, USA.
856. Under My Thumb (4.18)

5-6 November 1981 - Brendan Byrne Arena, The Meadowlands, New Jersey, USA.
857. Going To A Go-Go (3.23)
858. You Can't Always Get What You Want (5.57)
859. Little T&A (2.13)
860. Tumbling Dice (2.27)
861. She's So Cold (3.20)
862. All Down The Line (3.03)
863. Hang Fire (2.07)
864. Miss You (4.04)

865. Let It Bleed (2.57)
866. Start Me Up (2.34)
867. Brown Sugar (2.09)
868. (I Can't Get No) Satisfaction (3.05)

25 November 1981 - Rosemont Horizon, Chicago, Illinois, USA.
869. Beast Of Burden (4.38)
870. Start Me Up (4.21)

8 December 1981 - Capital Center, Largo, Washington, USA.
871. Let Me Go (3.32)

9 December 1981 - Capital Center, Largo, Washington. USA.
872. Twenty Flight Rock (1.51)
873. Going To A Go-Go (3.23)

13 December 1981 - Sun Devil Stadium, Tempe, Arizona, USA.
874. Under My Thumb (3.45)
875. Let's Spend The Night Together (2.59)
876. Shattered (3.31)
877. Neighbours (3.03)
878. Black Limousine (3.10)
879. Just My Imagination (Running Away With Me) (5.45)
880. Twenty Flight Rock (1.41)
881. Let Me Go (2.47)
882. Time Is On My Side (3.26)
883. Beast Of Burden (4.38)
884. Waiting On A Friend (2.56)
885. Honky Tonk Women (3.24)
886. Jumping Jack Flash (3.43)
887. (I Can't Get No) Satisfaction (4.24)

18 December 1981 - Hampton Roads Coliseum, Hampton, Virginia, USA.
888. Under My Thumb (5.04)
889. When The Whip Comes Down (5.06)
890. Let's Spend The Night Together (4.32)
    (a) Edited Version - (3.50)
891. Shattered (4.50)
    (a) Edited Version - (4.10)
892. Neighbours (4.23)
893. Black Limousine (3.28)
894. Just My Imagination (Running Away With Me) (9.46)
895. Twenty Flight Rock (1.47)
896. Going To A Go-Go (4.03)
897. Let Me Go (5.25)
898. Time Is On My Side (4.13)
    (a) Edited Version - (3.38)
899. Beast Of Burden (7.24)
900. Waiting On A Friend (5.55)
901. Let It Bleed (6.58)
902. You Can't Always Get What You Want (9.35)
903. Little T&A (3.58)
904. Tumbling Dice (4.48)
905. She's So Cold (4.25)
906. Hang Fire (2.40)
907. Miss You (7.46)
908. Honky Tonk Women (3.42)
909. Brown Sugar (3.39)
910. Start Me Up (5.06)
911. Jumpin' Jack Flash (8.43)
912. (I Can't Get No) Satisfaction (7.28)

19 December 1981 - Hampton Roads Coliseum, Hampton, Virginia, USA.
913. Just My Imagination (Running Away With Me) (5.23)

1982
25 June 1982 - Wembley Stadium, London, England.
914. Chantilly Lace (4.17) *

1989

25 November 1989 - The Gator Bowl, Jacksonville, Florida, USA.
1019. Rock And A Hard Place (4.52)
1020. You Can't Always Get What You Want (7.26)
1021. Miss You (5.55)

26 November 1989 - Death Valley Stadium, Clemson, South Carolina, USA.
1022. Start Me Up (3.54)
1023. (I Can't Get No) Satisfaction (6.09)
1024. Play With Fire (3.46)
1025. Can't Be Seen (4.17)
1026. Gimme Shelter (4.54**)**

19 December 1989 - Atlantic City Convention Center, Atlantic City, New Jersey, USA.
1027. Bitch (3.41) *
1028. Sad Sad Sad (3.33)
1029. Undercover Of The Night (3.54)
1030. Terrifying (5.20) *
1031. Salt Of The Earth (5.05) *
1032. Mixed Emotions (5.32) *
1033. Honky Tonk Women (5.14) *
1034. Midnight Rambler (10.46) *
1035. Little Red Rooster (5.15)
1036. Boogie Chillen' (5.32)
1037. Happy (4.37) *
1038. It's Only Rock 'N' Roll (4.48) *

1990

26 February 1990 - Korakuen Dome, Tokyo, Japan.
1039. Sympathy For The Devil (5.35)
　　　(a) Un-Edited Version - (7.58)

27 February 1990 - Korakuen Dome, Tokyo, Japan.
1040. Ruby Tuesday (3.33)
1041. Jumping Jack Flash (5.00)
1042. Harlem Shuffle (4.05)

14 June 1990 - Olympic Stadium, Barcelona, Spain.
1043. Paint It Black (4.02)
1044. 2000 Light Years From Home (3.27)

6 July 1990 - Wembley Stadium, London, England.
1045. Factory Girl (2.47)
1046. I Just Want To Make Love To You (4.07)

28 July 1990 - Stadio Delle Alpi, Turin, Italy.
1047. Sad Sad Sad (3.21)
1048. Rock And A Hard Place (4.57)
1049. Honky Tonk Women (5.02)
1050. Paint It Black (4.18)
1051. 2000 Light Years From Home (5.41)
1052. Brown Sugar (4.45)

14 August 1990 - Weisensee, Berlin, Germany.
1053. Happy (4.20)
1054. It's Only Rock 'N' Roll (5.00)

24 August 1990 - Wembley Stadium, London, England.
1055. Start Me Up (4.03)
1056. Tumbling Dice (4.22)
1057. Sympathy For The Devil (6.38)
1058. (I Can't Get No) Satisfaction (8.32)

25 August 1990 - Wembley Stadium, London, England.
1059. Ruby Tuesday (3.46)
1060. You Can't Always Get What You Want (7.18)
1061. Street Fighting Man (6.05)
1062. Brown Sugar (4.45)

1994

19 July 1994 RPM Club, Toronto, Canada.
1141. Can't Get Next To You (Time: 5.45)

14 August 1994 - Giants Stadium, The Meadowlands, New Jersey, USA.
1142. Not Fade Away (2.39)
1143. Tumbling Dice (4.02)
1144. You Got Me Rocking (3.45)
1145. Shattered (4.08)
1146. Rocks Off (5.05)
1147. Sparks Will Fly (4.29)
1148. (I Can't Get No) Satisfaction (5.28)
1149. Out Of Tears (5.33)
1150. Miss You (6.40)
1151. Honky Tonk Women (4.48)
1152. The Worst (2.49)
1153. Monkey Man (4.25)
1154. Start Me Up (4.02)
1155. It's Only Rock 'N' Roll (4.49)
1156. Street Fighting Man (5.13)
1157. Brown Sugar (5.47)
1158. Jumping Jack Flash (5.49)

25 November 1994 - Joe Robbie Stadium, Miami, Florida, USA.
1159. Not Fade Away (2.54)
1160. Tumbling Dice (4.01)
1161. You Got Me Rocking (3.15)
1162. Rocks Off (5.02) *
1163. Sparks Will Fly (4.19) *
1164. Live With Me (4.31) *
1165. (I Can't Get No) Satisfaction (5.28)
1166. Beast Of Burden (5.48) *
1167. Angie (3.30)
1168. Dead Flowers (4.23) *
1169. Sweet Virginia (4.34)
1170. Doo Doo Doo Doo (Heartbreaker) (3.57) *
1171. It's All Over Now (3.32)
1172. Stop Breaking Down (4.20)
1173. Who Do You Love (3.59)
1174. I Go Wild (6.30)
1175. Miss You (9.27)
1176. Honky Tonk Women (4.13)
1177. Before They Make Me Run (4.12) *
1178. The Worst (2.35)
1179. Sympathy For The Devil (5.57)
1180. Monkey Man (4.22) *
1181. Street Fighting Man (5.12) *
1182. Start Me Up (3.56)
1183. It's Only Rock 'N' Roll (4.57)
1184. Brown Sugar (5.40)
1185. Jumpin' Jack Flash (5.35)

1995

25 February 1995 - Ellis Park, Johannesburg, South Africa.
1186. Out Of Tears (5.23) *

6 March 1995 - Tokyo Dome, Tokyo, Japan.
1205. Angie (3.52)

12 March 1995 - Tokyo Dome, Tokyo, Japan.
1206. Not Fade Away (2.50)
1207. Tumbling Dice (4.03)
1208. You Got Me Rocking (3.23)
1209. Live With Me (3.52)
1210. Rocks Off (4.44)
1211. Sparks Will Fly (3.58)
1212. (I Can't Get No) Satisfaction (5.50)
1213. Angie (3.35)

1214. **Sweet Virginia** (4.22)
1215. **Rock And A Hard Place** (4.46)
1216. **Love Is Strong** (5.02)
1217. **I Go Wild** (5.59)
1218. **Miss You** (9.37)
1219. **Honky Tonk Women** (4.24)
1220. **Before They Make Me Run** (3.36)
1221. **Slipping Away** (5.05)
1222. **Sympathy For The Devil** (5.53)
1223. **Monkey Man** (4.04)
1224. **Street Fighting Man** (5.41)
1225. **Start Me Up** (4.03)
1226. **It's Only Rock 'N' Roll** (4.50)
1227. **Brown Sugar** (6.10)
1228. **Jumpin' Jack Flash** (6.02)

26 May 1995 - The Paradiso, Amsterdam, Netherlands.
1229. **Gimme Shelter** (6.53)
1230. **Street Fighting Man** (3.40)

27 May 1995 - The Paradiso, Amsterdam, Netherlands.
1231. **It's All Over Now** (3.34)
1232. **Dead Flowers** (4.11) *
1233. **Still A Fool** (5.37) *
1234. **Down In The Bottom** (5.08) *
1235. **Shine A Light** (4.56) *
1236. **Jump On Top Of Me** (4.15) *
1237. **Can't Get Next To You** (5.22) *
1238. **All Down The Line** (4.22)

3 June 1995 - Olympic Stadium, Stockholm, Sweden.
1239. **Not Fade Away** (2.58) *
1240. **You Got Me Rocking** (3.13) *
1241. **I Go Wild** (5.51) *

3 July 1995 - Olympia Theatre, Paris, France.
1242. **Tumbling Dice** (4.08)
1243. **Let It Bleed** (4.15)
1244. **Angie** (3.28)
1245. **Shine A Light** (4.38)

19 July 1995 - Brixton Academy, Brixton, London, England.
1246. **Live With Me** (3.52)
1247. **Black Limousine** (3.30)
1248. **Dead Flowers** (4.13)
1249. **Sweet Virginia** (4.05) *
1250. **Far Away Eyes** (4.43) *
1251. **Like A Rolling Stone** (5.38)
      (a) Edited Single Version - (4.20)
1252. **Connection** (3.48) *
1253. **Rip This Joint** (2.32) *

1997
18 September 1997 - The Double Door Club, Chicago, USA.
1301. **Shame, Shame, Shame** (3.59) *

25 October 1997 - Capitol Theatre, Port Chester, New York, USA.
1302. **Gimme Shelter** (6.22)
      (a) Edited Promo Version - (4.16)

12 December 1997 - TWA Dome, St Louis, USA.
1303. **(I Can't Get No) Satisfaction** (5.09)
1304. **Let's Spend The Night Together** (4.26)
1305. **Flip The Switch** (4.09)
1306. **Gimme Shelter** (6.34)
1307. **Wild Horses** (5.59)
1308. **Anybody Seen My Baby?** (4.47) *
1309. **Saint Of Me** (5.20)
1310. **Corrina** (4.17)

1311. **Out Of Control** (8.01)
1312. **Waiting On A Friend** (5.02)
1313. **Miss You** (9.15)
1314. **All About You** (4.45) *
1315. **Wanna Hold You** (4.51)
1316. **It's Only Rock 'N' Roll** (4.46)
1317. **The Last Time** (4.47)
1318. **Like A Rolling Stone** (5.26)
1319. **Sympathy For The Devil** (8.00)
1320. **Tumbling Dice** (5.31)
1321. **Honky Tonk Women** (5.02)
1322. **Start Me Up** (4.37)
1323. **Jumping Jack Flash** (7.02)
1324. **You Can't Always Get What You Want** (5.37)
1325. **Brown Sugar** (6.23)

1998
16 January 1998 - Madison Square Garden, New York, USA.
1326. **Out Of Control (Don Was Live Remix)** (6.54)

4 April 1998 - River Plate, Buenos Aires, Argentina.
1327. **Saint Of Me** (5.25)
1328. **Out Of Control** (7.59)

11 April 1998 - Praca da Apoteose, Rio De Janeiro, Brazil.
1329. **Like A Rolling Stone** (6.22) *
1330. **Little Queenie** (4.27) *

13 June 1998 - Zeppelinfield, Nuremburg, Germany.
1331. **Thief In The Night** (5.37)

1 July 1998 - Arena, Amsterdam, Netherlands.
1332. **I Just Want To Make Love To You** (5.19)
1333. **Flip The Switch** (4.12)
1334. **Live With Me** (3.54)

5 July 1998 - Arena, Amsterdam, Netherlands.
1335. **Memory Motel** (6.05)
      (a) Remix Edit Version - (4.45)
      (b) Call Out Hook - (0.15)
1336. **Respectable** (3.35)

6 July 1998 - Arena, Amsterdam, Netherlands.
1337. **You Got Me Rocking** (3.25)
1338. **Sister Morphine** (6.16)

1999
11 February 1999 - The Arrowhead Pond, Anaheim, California.
1339. **Midnight Rambler** (10.02) *

8 June 1999 - Shepherds Bush Empire, London, England.
1340. **Melody** (5.06) *
1341. **Brand New Car** (4.30)
1342. **Moon Is Up** (4.58) *

2002
16 August 2002 - Palais Royale, Toronto, Canada.
1351. **I Can't Turn You Loose** (4.49) *

3 September 2002 - Fleet Center, Boston, Massachusetts, USA.
1352. **Can't You Hear Me Knocking** (8.48) *

4 November 2002 - Wiltern Theatre, Los Angeles, USA.
1353. **Beast Of Burden** (5.19)
1354. **Everybody Needs Somebody To Love** (6.34)
1355. **You Don't Have To Mean It** (4.34)
1356. **Rock Me Baby** (3.50)
1357. **Can't You Hear Me Knocking** (10.02)
1358. **Bitch** (4.00)

2003

18 January 2003 - Madison Square Garden, New York, USA.
1359. **Street Fighting Man** (4.20)
1360. **Start Me Up** (4.02)
1361. **If You Can't Rock Me** (4.06)
1362. **Don't Stop** (4.58)
1363. **Monkey Man** (4.04)
1364. **Angie** (3.29)
1365. **Let It Bleed** (4.59)
1366. **Midnight Rambler** (12.25)
1367. **Thru And Thru** (7.12)
1368. **Happy** (3.37)
1369. **Gimme Shelter** (6.50)
1370. **You Got Me Rocking** (3.56)
1371. **Can't You Hear Me Knocking** (11.19)
1372. **Honky Tonk Women** (3.24)
1373. **(I Can't Get No) Satisfaction** (7.33)
1374. **It's Only Rock 'N' Roll** (4.54)
1375. **When The Whip Comes Down** (4.28)
1376. **Brown Sugar** (3.50)
1377. **Sympathy For The Devil** (6.15) *
1378. **Jumpin' Jack Flash** (5.55)

8 June 2003 - Circus Krone, Munich, Germany.
1379. **I Can't Turn You Loose** (7.13)

20 June 2003 - Festwiese, Leipzig, Germany.
1380. **Rock Me Baby** (7.02)

11 July 2003 - Olympia Theatre, Paris, France.
1381. **Start Me Up** (4.34)
1382. **Live With Me** (4.41)
1383. **Neighbours** (3.40)
        (a) Non-Edited Version - (4.05)
1384. **Hand Of Fate** (4.32)
1385. **No Expectations** (4.50)
1386. **Worried About You** (6.00)
1387. **Doo Doo Doo Doo (Heartbreaker)** (4.07)
1388. **Stray Cat Blues** (5.06)
1389. **Dance (Pt. 1)** (6.13)
1390. **Everybody Needs Somebody To Love** (5.48)
1391. **That's How Strong My Love Is** (5.09)
1392. **Going To A Go-Go** (7.49)
1393. **The Nearness Of You** (4.34)
1394. **Before They Make Me Run** (4.00)
1395. **Love Train** (6.03)
1396. **Respectable** (3.03)
1397. **Honky Tonk Women** (4.22)
1398. **Brown Sugar** (6.30)
1399. **Jumpin' Jack Flash** (7.07)

30 July 2003 - Downsview Park, Toronto, Canada.
1400. **Start Me Up** (5.19)
1401. **Ruby Tuesday** (3.19)
1402. **Miss You** (6.22)
1403. **Rock Me Baby** (6.49)
1404. **(I Can't Get No) Satisfaction** (9.09)
1405. **Jumpin' Jack Flash** (6.27)

24 August 2003 - Twickenham Stadium, London, England.
1406. **Brown Sugar** (4.08)
1407. **You Got Me Rocking** (4.10)
1408. **Rocks Off** (3.41)
1409. **Wild Horses** (5.04)
1410. **You Can't Always Get What You Want** (6.45)
1411. **Paint It Black** (4.44)
1412. **Tumbling Dice** (5.38)
1413. **Slipping Away** (5.54)

1414. **Sympathy For The Devil** (9.54)
1415. **Star Star** (4.08)
1416. **I Just Want To Make Love To You** (4.52)
1417. **Street Fighting Man** (3.43)
1418. **Gimme Shelter** (9.00)
1419. **Honky Tonk Women** (4.38)
1420. **(I Can't Get No) Satisfaction** (8.14)
1421. **Jumpin' Jack Flash** (7.39)

20 September 2003 - Twickenham Stadium, London, England.
1422. **Salt Of The Earth** (4.51) *

2005

10 May 2005 - Julliard School Of Music, New York, USA.
1449. **Start Me Up** (4.47) *
1450. **Oh No, Not You Again** (4.25) *
1451. **Brown Sugar** (5.32) *

10 August 2005 - Phoenix Concert Theatre, Toronto, Canada.
1452. **Back Of My Hand** (4.13)
1453. **Get Up, Stand Up** (5.53)
1454. **Mr. Pitiful** (3.18)

21 August 2005 - Fenway Park, Boston, Massachusetts, USA.
1455. **Shattered** (4.44) *
1456. **Back Of My Hand** (5.18) *

28 September 2005 - PNC Park, Pittsburgh, Pennsylvania, USA.
1457. **Wild Horses** (4.47)

2006

5 February 2006 - Ford Field, Detroit, Michigan, USA.
1458. **Start Me Up** (3.44)
1459. **Rough Justice** (2.49)
1460. **(I Can't Get No) Satisfaction** (5.25)

18 February 2006 - Copacabana Beach, Rio De Janeiro, Brazil.
1461. **Jumpin' Jack Flash** (3.53)
1462. **It's Only Rock 'N' Roll** (4.32)
1463. **You Got Me Rocking** (3.17)
1464. **Tumbling Dice** (4.19) *
1465. **Oh No, Not You Again** (4.01) *
1466. **Wild Horses** (5.24)
1467. **Rain Fall Down** (5.45)
1468. **Midnight Rambler** (11.53)
1469. **Night Time Is The Right Time** (8.38)
1470. **This Place Is Empty** (3.34) *
1471. **Happy** (3.36)
1472. **Miss You** (5.38)
1473. **Rough Justice** (3.18)
1474. **Get Off My Cloud** (3.17)
1475. **Honky Tonk Women** (4.11)
1476. **Sympathy For The Devil** (7.51) *
1477. **Start Me Up** (3.59)
1478. **Brown Sugar** (6.37)
1479. **You Can't Always Get What You Want** (7.10)
1480. **(I Can't Get No) Satisfaction** (8.18)

21 February 2006 - River Plate Stadium, Buenos Aires, Argentina.
1481. **Worried About You** (6.20)
1482. **Happy** (4.05)
1483. **Miss You** (6.49)
1484. **Paint It Black** (4.26)
1485. **(I Can't Get No) Satisfaction** (8.25)

2 April 2006 - Saitama Super Arena, Saitama, Japan.
1486. **Let's Spend The Night Together** (4.02)
1487. **Rain Fall Down** (5.45)
1488. **Rough Justice** (3.25)

8 April 2006 - The Grand Stage, Shanghai, China.
1489. Bitch (4.38)
1490. Wild Horses (5.16)
1491. Midnight Rambler (7.43)
1492. Gimme Shelter (6.18)
1493. This Place Is Empty (3.23)
1494. It's Only Rock 'N' Roll (4.32)

11 July 2006 - Stadio Giuseppe Meazza, San Siro, Milan, Italy.
1496. Con Le Mie Lacrime (3.38) *

17 October 2006 - Qwest Field, Seattle, Washington, USA.
1498. Let It Bleed (5.11)

22 October 2006 - Zilker Park, Austin, Texas, USA.
1499. You Got Me Rocking (3.35)
1500. Let's Spend The Night Together (4.22)
1501. She's So Cold (4.39)
1502. Oh No, Not You Again (4.00)
1503. Sway (3.45)
1504. Bob Wills Is Still King (3.34)
1505. Streets Of Love (5.25)
1506. Ain't Too Proud To Beg (5.06)
1507. Bitch (3.03)
1508. Tumbling Dice (7.55)
1509. Learning The Game (3.15)
1510. Little T&A (3.47)
1511. Under My Thumb (5.18)
1512. Get Off My Cloud (3.10)
1513. Honky Tonk Women (4.07)
1514. Sympathy For The Devil (7.36)
1515. Jumpin' Jack Flash (4.11)
1516. (I Can't Get No) Satisfaction (6.10)
1517. Brown Sugar (6.11)

29 October 2006 - Beacon Theatre, New York, USA.
1518. I'm Free (3.30)
1519. Undercover Of The Night (4.24)
1520. Shine A Light (4.05)
1521. Little T&A (4.09)
1522. Paint It Black (4.28)

1 November 2006 - Beacon Theatre, New York, USA.
1523. Jumpin' Jack Flash (4.22)
1524. Shattered (4.06)
1525. She Was Hot (4.44)
1526. All Down The Line (4.35)
1527. Loving Cup (4.02)
1528. As Tears Go By (3.31)
1529. Some Girls (4.19)
1530. Just My Imagination (Running Away With Me) (6.39)
1531. Far Away Eyes (4.37)
1532. Champagne & Reefer (5.58)
1533. Tumbling Dice (4.24)
1534. You Got The Silver (3.21)
1535. Connection (3.30)
1536. Sympathy For The Devil (5.56)
1537. Live With Me (3.54)
1538. Start Me Up (4.05)
1539. Brown Sugar (5.25)
1540. (I Can't Get No) Satisfaction (5.37)

25 November 2006 - BC Place Arena, Vancouver, British Columbia, Canada.
1541. Shine A Light (4.22)

2007
10 June 2007 - Isle Of Wight Festival, Isle Of Wight, England.
1542. Start Me Up (3.49) *
1543. Ain't Too Proud To Beg (4.01) *

26 August 2007 - O2 Arena, London, England.
1544. She Was Hot (4.51) *
1545. I'll Go Crazy (3.20) *

ALPHA TRACKS **INDEX**

(Available as a file on stonessessions.com)
Also known as names are placed in normal typeset.

(I Can't Get No) Satisfaction (3.53) — 232, 233, 244, 248, 251, 257, 286, 332, 390, 453, 473, 524, 868, 887, 912, 1023, 1058, 1148, 1165, 1212, 1303, 1373, 1404, 1420, 1460, 1480, 1485, 1516, 1540
   (a) Instrumental - (3.44)

(Walkin' Thru The) Sleepy City (2.52) — 61
100 Years Ago (3.59) — 596
   (a) Take 1 - (4.07)
1-2-3-4 — 724
19th Nervous Breakdown (3.57) — 277, 278, 326
   (a) Take 1 - (4.03)
2000 Light Years From Home (4.45) — 350, 1044, 1051
   (a) Early Take - (2.05)
   (b) Many Alternative Cuts - (30.32)
   (c) Single Version - (3.27)
   (d) Edited Version - (2.51)
2000 Man (3.07) — 365
   (a) Takes 1 - 15 - (38.53)
2120 South Michigan Avenue (2.38) — 131, 178, 226
   (a) Extended Version - (3.39)
32-20 Blues (1.41) — 559
365 Rolling Stones (One For Each Day Of The Year) (2.01) — 70
5 Part Jam (3.33)
   (a) Many Takes - (25.51) — 364
9/11 Hurricane — 1350
A Different Kind (6.01) — 722
A Mess With Fire — 201
Acid In The Grass — 351
Act Together (4.48) — 637
After Five — 355
After Hours (5.04) — 756
After Muddy & Charlie — 587
Aftermath — 78, 350
Again And Again And Again — 822
Ain't Gonna Lie — 528
Ain't No Use In Crying — 849
Ain't That Lovin' You Baby (1.54) — 175
Ain't Too Proud To Beg (3.31) — 623, 672, 1506, 1543
   (a) Alternative Mix - (3.51)
   (b) Edited Single Version - (2.48)
Aladdin Stomp — 432
Aladdin Story — 432
All About You (4.18) — 832, 1314
All Down The Line (3.50) — 534, 576, 619, 667, 782, 862, 1238, 1526
   (a) Take 1 - (3.53)
   (b) Instrumental Take 1 - (4.01)
   (c) Take 2 - (3.47)
All Down The Line (Acoustic) (4.22) — 442
All Down The Line (Electric) (4.09) — 504
All Mixed Up (6.36) — 921
   (a) Instrumental Take - (2.38)
All Part Of The Act — 308
All Sold Out (2.18) — 308
   (a) Take 1 - (2.48)
All The Way Down (3.14) — 922
   (a) Early Take - (3.43)
All Together — 360, 361
Almost Hear You Sigh (4.37) — 1004
   (a) Take 1 - (5.22)
   (b) Take 2 - (4.52)
   (c) Remix Version - (4.06)
Already Over Me (5.24) — 1286

   (a) Ambient Mix *(Bootleg)* - (9.04)
   (b) Ambient Remix *(Bootleg)* - (9.13)
Alright Charlie (4.09) — 1081
   (a) Take 1 - (5.04)
   (b) Take 2 - (3.09)
Alteration Boogie (4.45) — 1070
Always Suffering (4.43) — 1273
   (a) Sentimental Remix *(Bootleg)* - (9.22)
And I Know — 713
And I Was A Country Boy — 430
And The Rolling Stones Met Phil And Gene — 77
Andrew's Blues (3.03) — 77
Angeline — 760
Angie (4.33) — 595, 616, 680, 1167, 1200, 1205, 1213, 1244, 1364
Another CR (9.46) — 1115
   (a) No Strings Alternative Take - (4.27)
Anybody Seen My Baby? (4.31) — 1261, 1308
   (a) Call Out Hook (Chorus) Version - (0.09)
   (b) Armand's Tuned Club Cut - (9.32)
   (c) Armand's House Special - (13.37)
Anybody Seen My Baby? (Armand's Rolling Steelo Mix) (10.30) — 1262
Anybody Seen My Baby? (Bonus Roll Mix) (6.04) — 1266
Anybody Seen My Baby? (Casanova New Vocal Remix) (6.33) — 1271
Anybody Seen My Baby? (Don Was Radio Remix) (3.45) — 1268
Anybody Seen My Baby? (LP/Single Edit) (4.07) — 1267
Anybody Seen My Baby? (No Biz Edit) (4.03) — 1269
Anybody Seen My Baby? (Phil Jones Remix) (4.30) — 1270
Anybody Seen My Baby? (Soul Solution Remix Edit) (4.20) — 1263
Anybody Seen My Baby? (Soul Solution Remix) (9.31) — 1265
Anybody Seen My Baby? (Soul Solution Vocal Dub) (3.44) — 1264
Anything For You (8.14) — 1089
   (a) Take 1 - (5.49)
Anyway You Look At It (4.20) — 1289
Apartment No. 9 (3.44) — 708
Armpit Blues (2.39) — 755
Around And Around (3.04) — 133, 157, 174, 179, 181, 219, 703
Around And Around (Little Boy Blue & The Blue Boys) (1.21) — 1
As Now — 492
As Tears Go By — 87, 275, 287, 300, 1496, 1528
As Time Goes By (2.13) — 87
Baby Break It Down (4.09) — 1133
   (a) KR Vocal Take 1 - (6.02)
   (b) Instrumental Take 2 - (5.56)
   (c) Take 3 - (4.11)
   (d) Longer Take - (5.59)
Baby, What's Wrong? (3.24) — 19
Baby, You're Too Much I (5.13) — 958
   (a) Early Take - (1.39)
Baby, You're Too Much II (5.24) — 1103

Back In The USA (2.05) — 804
Back Of My Hand (3.32) — 1433, 1452, 1456
Back On The Streets Again (5.21) — 962
Back Street Girl (3.28) — 313
Back To The Country — 648
Back To Zero (4.00) — 986
  (a) Early Take - (4.17)
Bathroom — 359
Beast Of Burden (4.25) — 723, 786, 813, 869, 883, 899,
  (a) Take 1 - (5.34) — 1166, 1190, 1353
  (b) Take 2 - (4.05)
  (c) 8 Track Version - (5.20)
  (d) Instrumental Dub Cut - (5.49)
  (e) Single Edit Version - (3.20)
Beautiful Delilah (2.14) — 84, 103
Beautiful Delilah (Little Boy Blue
& The Blue Boys) (2.58) — 3
  (a) Alternative Take - (2.18)
Bedroom Blues — 549
Before They Make Me Run (3.25) — 714, 837, 1177, 1220, 1394
  (a) Take 1 - (4.40)
  (b) Take 2 - (4.51)
Before They Make Me Run
(Bob Clearmountain Remix) (3.14) — 715
Bent Green Needles — 510
Between A Rock (And A Hard Place) — 1003
Biggest Mistake (4.06) — 1441
  (a) Alternative Take - (4.53)
  (b) Edited Single Version - (3.33)
  (c) Instrumental Single Version - (4.09)
Bill's Tune — 351
Biscuit Blues — 769
Bitch (3.37) — 509, 525, 567, 1027, 1358,
  (a) Take 1 - (3.39) — 1489, 1507
  (b) Take 2 - (2.24)
  (c) Single Version - (3.42)
Black And Blue Jam — 649
Black Angel — 510
Black Limousine (3.33) — 627, 878, 893, 1247
  (a) Take 1 - (4.13)
  (b) Take 2 - (3.26)
  (c) Take 3 - (4.06)
  (d) Edit Take 3 - (3.39)
Black Pussy — 483
Blinded By Love (4.36) — 1014
  (a) Take 1 - (5.20)
  (b) Take 2 - (5.07)
Blinded By Rainbows (4.33) — 1108
  (a) Take 1 - (6.55)
  (b) Instrumental Take 2 - (4.42)
  (c) Take 3 - (4.34)
Blood Red Wine (5.20) — 398
Blow Me Mama — 358
Blue Turns To Grey (2.29) — 150, 260
Blues 1 — 349
Blues Jam (3.05) — 826
  (a) Alternative Take - (1.40)
Blues No. 3 (3.02) — 371
  (a) Multiple Alternative Takes - (19.21)
Blues With A Feeling (3.12) — 800
Bluesberry Jam (3.09) — 556
Bob Wills Is Still King (3.34) — 1504
Boogie Chillen' (5.32) — 1036
Brand New Car (4.15) — 1134, 1341
  (a) Take 1 - (5.29)
  (b) Take 2 - (5.05)
  (c) Take 3 - (5.04)
Break Away (4.30) — 830
Break The Spell (3.07) — 1013

  (a) Take 1 - (3.36)
  (b) Take 2 - (3.50)
Breakin' (2.55) — 978
  (a) MJ Take
Brian's Blues — 124
Bright Lights, Big City (2.25) — 20
Bright Lights, Big City (Little Boy
Blue & The Blue Boys) — 12
Broken Head Blues (2.12) — 627, 769, 770
Broken Hearts For Me And You — 954
Broken Toe (1.55) — 750
Broken Wrist — 750
Brown Leaves (1.50) — 594, 745
Brown Sugar (3.49) — 483, 517, 526, 575, 580,
  (a) Muscle Shoals Take 1 - (3.43) — 607, 684, 697, 796, 867,
  (b) Muscle Shoals Take 2 - (3.49) — 909, 1052, 1062, 1157,
  (c) Multiple Cut Segments — 1184, 1227, 1325, 1376,
  (d) Olympic Take 3 — 1398, 1406, 1447, 1451,
  (Hot Rocks Version) - (3.48) — 1478, 1517, 1539
  (e) Olympic Take 4 - (3.52)
  (f) Olympic Alternate Mix - (3.54)
Bulldog (3.50) — 835, 836
Bump And Ride (5.48) — 1104
Bye Bye Johnny (2.12) — 30, 74, 573
Cable From My Baby — 640
Call Girl Blues — 1013
Can I Get A Witness (2.58) — 80
Can You Hear The Music? (5.32) — 593
Candlewick Bedspread — 500
Can't Be Seen (4.10) — 1012, 1025
  (a) Take 1 - (5.14)
  (b) Take 2 - (5.25)
Can't Believe It — 306
Can't Find Love — 916
Can't Get Next To You (5.45) — 1141, 1237
Can't You Hear Me Knocking (7.15) — 495, 1352, 1357, 1371
Carnival — 664
Carnival To Rio (1.43) — 664
Carol (2.35) — 59, 105, 139, 155, 470, 475
Casino Boogie (3.34) — 545
Cellophane Trousers (2.26) — 648
Cellophane Y-Fronts — 648
Chain Reaction Groove — 830
Chainsaw Rocker — 924
Champagne & Reefer (5.58) — 1532
Chantilly Lace (4.17) — 914
Charlie Is My Darling (3.16) — 258
Cherry Oh Baby (3.57) — 642
  (a) Take 1 - (4.32)
  (b) Take 2 - (3.38)
  (c) 8 Track Version - (3.00)
Child Of The Moon (3.12) — 375
  (a) Early Cuts - (9.57)
  (b) Acoustic Cut - (4.16)
  (c) Alt Mix - (3.11)
  (d) No Lead Vocals - (3.11)
Child Of The Moon (rmk) — 375
Christine — 918
Christmas Issue — 940
Citadel (2.50) — 355
  (a) Alternative Instrumental Takes - (25.21)
Claudine (3.42) — 735
  (a) Take 1 - (3.31)
  (b) Acoustic Take 1 - (3.33)
  (c) Acoustic Take 2 - (7.33)
Close Together — 15
Cocksucker Blues (3.28) — 499, 777
  (a) Electric Take - (5.05)
Come And Dance With Me — 89

Come On (1.50) — 25, 34
Come On Sugar (5.31) — 651
  (a) Take 1 - (6.19)
Coming Down Again (5.55) — 582
Complicated (3.16) — 317
  (a) Instrumental - (3.25)
Con Le Mie Lacrime (2.44) — 300, 1496
  (a) No Harpsichord - (2.59)
Con Le Mie Lagrime Cosi — 300
Confessin' The Blues (3.00) — 120, 132, 154, 415
Congratulations (2.29) — 116
Connection (2.10) — 318, 344, 1252, 1535
Continental Drift (5.15) — 1018
  (a) Instrumental Take 1 - (6.21)
  (b) Take 2 - (6.22)
Cook Cook Blues (4.11) — 929
Cookin' Up (4.01) — 924
  (a) Early Take - (5.57)
Cool, Calm And Collected (4.19) — 314
Cops And Robbers (3.55) — 92
Corrina (4.17) — 1310
Cosmic Christmas (0.40) — 376
Country Honk (3.07) — 436
  (a) Early Take - (3.04)
Covered In Bruises — 724
Crackin' Up (2.14) — 160, 706
Craw-Dad — 222
Crazy Arms (1.30) — 932
Crazy Mama (4.34) — 652
  (a) Early Take 1 - (4.04)
  (b) Edited Version - (4.06)
Criss Cross (4.18) — 598
  (a) Take 1 - No Sax - (4.30)
  (b) Take 2 - (4.20)
  (c) Take 3 - (4.46)
Criss-Cross Man — 598
Crushed Pearl (3.17) — 959
Cry To Me (3.10) — 237, 253, 272
Cut Your Throat (5.59) — 975
Da Doo Ron Ron (2.21) — 163
Daddy You're A Fool To Cry — 641
Dance (4.23) — 841, 1389
  (a) Take 1 - (6.54)
  (b) Take 2 - (7.40)
  (c) Take 3 - (8.04)
Dance (Instrumental) (4.37) — 839
Dance Little Sister (4.11) — 634
  (a) Take 1 - (5.07)
Dance Mr. K — 935
Dancing Girls (2.52) — 594, 745
  (a) Alternative Take - (4.08)
Dancing In The Light (4.22) — 497
  (a) Take 1 - (2.44)
Dancing With Mr. D (4.53) — 585, 614
  (a) Take 1 - (5.01)
Dandelion (3.33) — 337, 338
Dangerous Beauty (3.48) — 1435
  (a) Alternative Mix 1 - (4.14)
  (b) Alternative Mix 2 - (4.15)
Dead Flowers (4.05) — 489, 520, 563, 1168, 1232, 1248
Dear Doctor (3.22) — 392
  (a) Take 1 - (3.28)
  (b) Take 2 - (3.24)
Deep Love (4.11) — 985
Delta Slide (2.50) — 558
Did Everybody Pay Their Dues? — 380
Diddley Daddy (2.38) — 16
Dirty Work (3.53) — 980
  (a) Early Take - (4.19)

Disco Musik (5.55) — 761
Disposition Boogie (1.32) — 1069
Do You Get Enough? — 737
Do You Think I Really Care? (4.22) — 741
  (a) Take 1 - (6.09)
  (b) Edited Take 1 - (3.02)
  (c) Edited Take 1 - (4.26)
Dog Shit — 920
Doncha Bother Me (2.41) — 279
Don't Be A Stranger (4.06) — 737
  (a) Take 1 - (5.20)
  (b) Take 2 - (4.18)
Don't Be Cruel (4.49) — 956
Don't Get Mad (0.58) — 973
Don't Know How To Stop — 1346
Don't Know Why I Love You — 443
Don't Lie To Me (1.43) — 71, 115, 568
Don't Stop (3.58) — 1346, 1362
  (a) Single Edit Version - (3.32)
  (b) Call Out Hook Version - (0.13)
Don't Stop (New Rock Mix) (4.01) — 1347
Don't Wanna Go Home (3.34) — 1436
  (a) Alternative Mix 1 - (4.33)
  (b) Alternative Mix 2 - (4.32)
  (c) Alternative Mix 3 - (4.33)
Don't Want No Woman (Little Boy Blue & The Blue Boys) (2.30) — 8
Don't Ya Follow Me — 279
Don't You Lie To Me — 115
Doo Doo Doo Doo (Heartbreaker) (3.27) — 599, 615, 678, 1170, 1387
Down Home Girl (4.08) — 187, 447
Down In The Bottom (2.46) — 117, 136, 1234
Down In The Hole (3.57) — 845
  (a) Early Take - (3.56)
Down The Road Apiece (2.05) — 121, 137, 203, 243, 854
Down The Road Apiece (Little Boy Blue & The Blue Boys) (2.12) — 7
Downtown Lucy — 427
Downtown Suzie (3.53) — 427
  (a) Take 1 - (3.45)
Dream Pipe — 370
Drift Away (4.10) — 624
  (a) Alternative Take - (3.52)
Driving Too Fast (3.56) — 1440
  (a) Alternative Take - (4.29)
Dust My Pyramids — 172
Each And Everyday Of The Year (2.49) — 62
Eliza Upchink — 934
Emotional Rescue (5.39) — 843
  (a) Short Promo Version - (4.18)
  (b) Forty Licks Edit Version - (3.42)
  (c) Alternative Take - (6.58)
Empty Heart (2.38) — 130
English Rose (1.27) — 645
English Summer — 335
Everlasting Is My Love (5.00) — 731
  (a) Acoustic Take 1 - (3.54)
  (b) Take 2 - (4.14)
Everybody Needs Somebody To Love (5.00) — 188, 204, 207, 213, 217, 221, 225, 1354, 1390
  (a) Short Version - (2.57)
Everyone Wants To Be My Friend — 629
Everything Is Turning To Gold (4.06)
  (a) Take 1 - (9.51)
  (b) Extended Take 2 - (4.28) — 711
Exile Instrumental (7.12) — 535
Exile On Main Street Blues (6.21) — 551
  (a) Original Cut - (1.37)
Extreme Western Grip (3.05) — 1348

Factory Girl (2.09)   396, 1045
Fairground   337, 338
Family (4.06)   395
    (a) Acoustic Take - (4.13)
    (b) Take 1 - (4.01)
Fancy Man Blues   1017
Fancyman Blues (5.12)   1017
    (a) Take 1 - (5.48)
    (b) Take 2 - (6.46)
Fanny Mae (2.11)   254
Far Away Eyes (4.23)   720, 791, 1250, 1531
    (a) Take 1 - (5.17)
    (b) Edited Version - (3.43)
Fast Talking Slow Walking (6.34)   536
Fat Old Man   136
Feel No Pain No More   737
Feel On Baby (5.07)   947
Feel On Baby (Instrumental Dub)   948
Feel On Baby (Instrumental Mix) (6.31)   948
Fight (3.10)   969
    (a) Take 1 - (3.59)
    (b) Instrumental Take 2 - (3.03)
    (c) Take 3 - (4.57)
Fiji Gin (4.01)   742
    (a) Alternative Take - (3.26)
Fiji Jim   742
Fingerprint File (6.33)   626, 662, 679
    (a) Original Speed Version - (7.05)
First Thing   586
Flight 505 (3.27)   297
Flip The Switch (3.27)   1272, 1305, 1333
    (a) Clean Version - (3.28)
    (b) Call Out Hook No. 1 - (0.13)
    (c) Call Out Hook No. 2 - (0.14)
    (d) Hyper Mix (Bootleg) - (5.59)
Flowers   352
Flowers In Your Barnet   352
Flowers In Your Hair   352, 362
Fly High As A Kite   370
Fly My Kite   370
Follow You (1.30)   753
Following The River (4.51)   548
    (a) Promo Edit Version - (4.01)
Fool To Cry (5.05)   641
    (a) Take 1 - (6.04)
    (b) Take 2 - (5.43)
    (c) Edited Version - (4.06)
For Your Precious Love (6.39)   1009
    (a) Take 1 - (6.21)
Fortune Teller (2.18)   27, 333
    (a) Alternative Take - (2.06)
Four And In   588
Fragile   531
Freeway Jam (0.54)   644
Fuckin' Andrew   77
Gangster's Moll (2.20)   844
Get A Line On You   431, 506
Get Back To The One You Love   195
Get It Made   1123
Get Off My Cloud (2.56)   259, 274, 324, 669, 691, 1474, 1512
Get Together (2.07)   186
Get Up, Stand Up (5.53)   1453
Get Your Hands Off (3.41)   1071
    (a) Take 1 - (6.38)
Get Yourself Together (3.10)   306
Gimme Shelter (3.51)   428, 459, 488, 562, 610, 671, 1026, 1229, 1302, 1306, 1369, 1418, 1492

Gimmie Shelter (4.30)   428
    (a) Early Take - (4.22)
    (b) KR Vocal - (4.31)
Girl With The Faraway Eyes   720
Girl, You're Too Rude   966
Give Me A Drink (6.39)   437, 451, 527
Give Me A Hamburger To Go (3.25)   394
Give Me A Little Drink   438
Give Me Some Shelter   428
Give Me Your Hand (0.06)   49
Give Us A Break   590
Giving It Up (5.32)   1010
Glimmer Twins Boogie (1.36)   1073
Go Home Girl (2.26)   39
Go On To School (Little Boy Blue
& The Blue Boys) (2.02)   5
God Bless You   360, 361
Godzi   146
Goin' Home (11.14)   280
Going To A Go-Go (3.23)   857, 873, 896, 1392
Gold Painted Fingernails (5.00)   373
    (a) Multiple Various Takes - (31.56)
Gold Painted Nails   373
Golden Caddy (1.58)   749
    (a) Take 1 - (3.18)
    (b) Take 2 - (6.15)
    (c) Take 3 - (8.56)
Golden Mile   749
Gomper (5.08)   362
    (a) Cut 1 - (8.50)
    (b) Cut 2 - (8.56)
    (c) Many Alternative Cuts - (6.49)
Good Time Women (3.21)   496, 538
    (a) Cut 1 - (3.17)
Good Times (1.59)   236
Good Times, Bad Times (2.30)   85
Goodbye Girl (2.14)   195
Goodbye To Love (2.29)   1075
Got No Oil To Change   758
Got No Spare Parts   758
Gotta Get Away (2.07)   262
Grown Up Wrong (1.59)   169
Guess I Should Know (4.06)   827
Guitar Lesson (4.06)   822
Guitar Wonderful   734
Gunface (5.02)   1288
    (a) Dodge City Mix (Bootleg) - (6.17)
Had It With You (3.20)   963, 964
    (a) Early Take - (2.55)
Hand Of Fate (4.27)   657, 1384
    (a) Take 1 - (4.43)
    (b) Take 2 - (3.46)
Hang Fire (2.20)   739, 863, 906
    (a) Take 1 - Lazy Bitch - (6.22)
    (b) Take 2 - Lazy Bitch - (6.06)
    (c) Take 1 - (2.28)
    (d) Take 2 - (2.26)
Hang On To Me Tonight   993
Hang On Tonight   993
Happy (3.05)   541, 565, 611, 675, 694, 794, 1037, 1053, 1368, 1471, 1482
Harlem Shuffle (3.26)   983, 1042
    (a) Take 1 - (4.09)
    (b) Take 2 - (3.45)
    (c) Take 3 - (5.35)
Harlem Shuffle (London Mix) (6.19)   981
Harlem Shuffle (NY Mix) (6.36)   982
    (a) NY Mix Edit Version - (5.49)
Have Mercy   197

**Have You Seen Your Mother, Baby,
Standing In The Shadow?** (2.36)   319, 322, 327, 331
   (a) Take 1 - (2.29)
   (b) No Lead Vocal - (2.33)
   (c) Stereo Version - (2.36)
He Loves You So (5.54)   1078
Hear It (3.04)   162
Heart Of Stone (3.48)   161, 190
   (a) 161 - Alternative Mix - (4.11)
   (a) 190 - Stereo Version - (2.59)
Heartbeat   942, 1202
Hearts For Sale (4.41)   1006
   (a) Take 1 - (4.30)
   (b) Take 2 - (4.35)
Heat Wave (5.00)   643
Heaven (4.22)   850
   (a) Take 1 - (5.17)
   (b) Take 2 - (5.24)
Hellhound On My Trail (1.15)   994
Hey Crawdaddy (5.52)   222
Hey Mama   501
Hey Negrita (4.59)   660
   (a) Take 1 - (5.30)
   (b) Edited Take 1 - (4.38)
Hide Your Love (4.12)   597
   (a) Take 1 - (4.12)
Hideaway   933
High And Dry (3.08)   296
High Heeled Sneakers (1.39)   96, 104, 113, 134
High Temperature (5.23)   965
Highway Child (5.02)   386
Highwire (4.45)   1063
   (a) Edited Single Version - (3.41)
Hillside Blues   458
Hip Shake   511
Hitch Hike (2.26)   191, 246
Hold Back (3.53)   991
Hold On I'm Coming (4.08)   378
Hold On To Your Hat (3.32)   1007
   (a) Take 1 - (4.10)
   (b) Take 2 - (4.07)
Hold On To Yourself   1007
Hold On You   1112
Holetown Prison   1090
Honest I Do (2.12)   64, 1195
Honest Man (4.28)   1120
   (a) Take 1 - (4.23)
Honey What's Wrong?   19
Honky Tonk Women (3.01)   434, 454, 461, 468, 480, 618,
   (a) Early Take 1 - (3.06)   666, 692, 783, 885, 908, 1033,
   (b) Take 2 - (2.52)   1049, 1151, 1176, 1219, 1321,
   (c) Single Version - (3.02)   1372, 1397, 1419, 1475, 1513
Hot Stuff (5.21)   658, 695
   (a) Take 1 - (4.52)
   (b) Special Edited Single Version - (3.30)
Hound Dog (2.00)   779
How Can I Stop (6.54)   1300
Hurricane (1.25)   1350
**I Ain't Got You (Little Boy Blue
& The Blue Boys)** (2.00)   9
I Ain't Lying   528
I Ain't Signifying   528
I Ain't Superstitious (4.21)   807
I Am Waiting (3.11)   298
I Can See It   306
I Can't Be Satisfied (3.26)   125, 159, 1495
I Can't Help It   713
I Can't Turn You Loose (4.49)   1351, 1379
I Don't Care (3.02)   550

I Don't Know The Reason Why (11.29)   458
   (a) Cut 1 - (5.57)
I Don't Know Why (3.02)   443
I Go Wild (4.23)   1138, 1174, 1217, 1241
   (a) Take 1 - (5.33)
   (b) Take 2 - (4.40)
**I Go Wild (Luis Resto Straight
Vocal Mix)** (5.40)   1137
I Go Wild (Scott Litt Remix) (4.39)   1136
I Got A Hold On You (4.37)   1112
I Got A Letter (4.26)   638
   (a) Instrumental Take - (4.23)
I Got The Blues (3.54)   494, 521
I Just Can't Be Seen   1012
I Just Want To Make Love To You (2.19)   63, 98, 102, 110, 123, 1046,
       1332, 1416
I Just Want To See His Face (2.53)   539
I Know (I'm Alright)   212
I Love Ladies (4.31)   653
I Love You Too Much (3.10)   713
   (a) Take 1 - (4.22)
   (b) Take 2 - (2.32)
   (c) Instrumental Take 3 - (3.24)
   (d) Take 4 - (4.08)
   (e) Instrumental Take 5 - (3.25)
I Miss You   730
I Need You (3.43)   738
   (a) Edited Cut - (2.41)
I Need You Baby   94
I Only Found Out Yesterday   1497
I Think I'm Going Mad (4.12)   817
   (a) No Sax - (6.49)
   (b) Alternative Take - (5.47)
   (c) Alternative KR Vocal - (14.57)
I Wanna Be Loved   18
I Wanna Be Your Man (1.43)   37, 75
I Wanna Fight   969
I Wanna Hold You   915
I Want All The People To Know   365
I Want Nobody Else   960
I Want To Be Loved (1.53)   18, 26
I Want You To Know (0.11)   50
I Was Just A Country Boy   430
I'd Much Rather Be With The Boys (2.12)   202
Identification   938
If (Moon Is Up)   1109
If I Don't Have You (3.14)   960
   (a) Take 1 - (2.41)
   (b) Take 2 - (4.23)
   (c) Take 3 - (7.07)
   (d) Take 4 - (7.23)
If I Was A Dancer (Dance Part Two) (5.50)   840
If Not For You   799
If You Can't Rock Me (3.47)   625, 668, 690, 1361
   (a) Alternative Mix - (3.49)
If You Let Me (3.18)   339
If You Need Me (2.05)   129, 153, 158, 173, 206
If You Need Someone   439
**If You Really Want To Be
My Friend** (6.16)   629
I'll Coming Home   377
I'll Feel A Whole Lot Better   306
I'll Go Crazy (3.20)   1545
I'll Hold Your Hand   49
I'll Let You Know (6.55)   806
I'm A Country Boy (4.30)   430
I'm A Hog For You Baby   24
I'm A King Bee (2.37)   65
I'm A Love You   176

I'm Alright (2.07) — 111, 114, 185, 212, 215
I'm Fallin' (6.35) — 1083
I'm Free (2.24) — 264, 450, 467, 1255, 1518
I'm Free (DJ Shadow Remix) (4.11) — 268
I'm Free (Fatboy Slim Remix) (3.58) — 269
I'm Free (Hot Chip Remix) (3.03) — 265
I'm Free (Moby Remix) (3.43) — 266
I'm Free (The Postal Service Remix) (2.27) — 267
I'm Going Down (2.52) — 440
  (a) Take 1 - (3.04)
I'm Gonna Drive (3.42) — 1132
  (a) Instrumental Take - (5.27)
I'm Just A Funny Guy — 167
I'm Left, You're Right, She's Gone — 1204
I'm Left, You're Right, She's Gone
(Little Boy Blue & The Blue Boys) (2.31) — 6
I'm Moving On — 23, 99, 210
I'm Not Signifying (3.56) — 528
  (a) Early Take - (3.39)
  (b) Take 2 (Piano) - (3.46)
I'm Relying On You (0.24) — 167
I'm Talkin' About You — 33, 40
I'm Yours And I'm Hers (3.17) — 444
I'm Yours, She's Mine — 444
In Another Land (3.15) — 351
  (a) Takes 1-19 - (8.34)
  (b) Alternative Takes 1-14 - (12.54)
In Your Hand — 926
Indian Girl (4.23) — 846
  (a) Long Take - (6.05)
Infamy (3.48) — 1443
Intermezzo — 258
Invitation (15.52) — 984
It Must Be Hell (5.04) — 930
  (a) Early Take - (5.45)
It Should Be You (1.45) — 53
It Won't Be Long (2.38) — 762
  (a) Take 1 - (2.33)
It Won't Take Long (3.54) — 1432
  (a) Alternative Mix 1 - (4.12)
  (b) Alternative Mix 2 - (4.12)
It's A Lie (4.36) — 751
It's All Over Now (3.28) — 127, 152, 184, 346, 605, 1171, 1231
  (a) USA Edit Version - (2.48)
It's All Right Babe — 22
It's All Wrong (3.37) — 757
It's Alright (4.00) — 1107
It's Cold Down There (3.37) — 816
  (a) Alternative Cut - (1.36)
It's Funny (4.36) — 1088
  (a) Early Take 1 - (2.38)
  (b) Take 2 - (6.24)
It's Not Easy (2.56) — 291
It's Only Rock 'N' Roll
(But I Like It) (5.07) — 628, 636, 663, 677, 1038, 1054,
  (a) Edited Version 1 - (4.46) — 1155, 1183, 1226, 1316, 1374,
  (b) Edited Version 2 - (4.01) — 1462, 1494
I've Been Lonely Too Long — 238
I've Been Loving You Too Long (2.57) — 238, 334
I've Gotta Get Away — 262
Ivy League (3.13) — 1076
Jah Is Not Dead (10.47) — 825
Jah Is Wonderful — 734
Jah Wonderful — 734
Jam One (4.05) — 372
  (a) More Alternative Takes - (6.20)
Jamaica — 591
Jigsaw Puzzle (6.06) — 384
  (a) Take 1 - (6.07)

  (b) Many Alternative Cuts - (53.35)
Jimmy Reed Blues Jam (6.50) — 808
Jiving Sister Fanny (3.25) — 441
  (a) Take 1 - (3.24)
Johnny B. Goode (Little Boy Blue
& The Blue Boys) (2.24) — 10
John's Jam (3.34) — 552
Jump On Top Of Me (4.24) — 1131, 1236
  (a) Instrumental Take 1 - (5.03)
Jumpin' Jack Flash (3.41) — 383, 389, 393, 418, 445, 464,
  (a) Early Guitar Riff - (2.17) — 469, 574, 621, 688, 698, 797,
  (b) Take 1 - (3.25) — 886, 911, 1041, 1158, 1185,
  (c) No Lead Vocals - (3.52) — 1323, 1378, 1399, 1405, 1228,
  (d) USA Single Edit Version - (2.42) — 1421, 1461, 1515, 1523
  (e) Promotional Film - (3.58)
Jungle Disease (3.56) — 557
Just My Imagination (Running Away
With Me) (4.38)
  (a) Alternative Take - (6.46) — 732, 788, 879, 894, 913, 1530
Just Wanna — 539
Keep Up Blues (4.20) — 740
  (a) 'Some People Tell Me' Take - (4.54)
Keith's Blues (3.33) — 1082
Key To The Highway (3.25) — 194, 561
Keys To Your Love (4.12) — 1344
Knee Trembler (5.35) — 811
Knock Your Teeth Out — 970
La Bamba (Little Boy Blue
& The Blue Boys) (0.18) — 4
Labour Swing — 633
Lady (1.32) — 400
Lady Fair — 352
Lady Jane (3.08) — 290, 321, 329
Laugh, I Nearly Died (4.54) — 1442
Lazy Bitch — 739
Learning The Game (3.15) — 1509
Leather Jacket (3.31) — 503
Leave Me Alone (1.57) — 46
Let It Bleed (5.27) — 439, 865, 901, 1189, 1243,
— 1365, 1498
Let It Loose (5.18) — 549
  (a) Instrumental Take - (5.57)
Let It Rock (2.47) — 518, 522, 781
Let Me Down Slow (4.16) — 1430
  (a) Alternative Mix 1 - (4.17)
  (b) Alternative Mix 2 - (4.16)
  (c) Alternative Mix 3 - (4.17)
Let Me Go (3.51) — 848, 871, 881, 897
  (a) Without Sax - (3.52)
Let Some Fucker Do The Dirty Work — 980
Let's Do It Right — 651
Let's Go Steady — 824
Let's Go Steady Again (2.51) — 824
Let's Spend Some Time Together (3.03) — 343
Let's Spend The Night Together (3.39) — 341, 343, 347, 875, 890, 1198,
  (a) No Lead Vocal - (3.56) — 1304, 1486, 1500
  (b) Instrumental - (3.46)
  (c) Single Version - (3.26)
  (d) Stereo Version - (3.37)
Let's Talk It Over — 115
Lies (3.11) — 712
  (a) Take 1 - (3.50)
  (b) Take 2 - (4.13)
Light Up (4.44) — 764
Like A Rolling Stone (5.38) — 1251, 1318, 1329
Linda Lu (4.34) — 833
Lisle Street Lucie — 427
Little Baby (4.00) — 1203
Little By Little (2.41) — 79, 97

Little Queenie (4.33)	472, 1330	Mean Woman Blues	528
Little Queenie (Little Boy Blue		**Mellobar**	943
& The Blue Boys) (4.32)	2	**Melody** (5.49)	654, 1340
(a) Alternative Take - (4.11)		**Memo From Turner** (4.03)	409, 412
Little Red Rooster (3.06)	166, 193, 199, 224, 227, 240,	(a) Organ Cut - (3.54)	
	704, 1035	**Memory Motel** (7.09)	659, 1191, 1335
Little T & A (3.23)	835, 836, 859, 903, 1510, 1521	(a) Instrumental - (4.14)	
(a) Take 1 - (3.41)		**Memphis Tennessee** (2.20)	35, 147
(b) Take 2 - (4.13)		**Mercy Mercy** (2.44)	197, 228, 245, 249, 446
Live With Me (3.33)	435, 479, 519, 1164, 1209, 1246,	**Mexican Divorce** (3.31)	954
	1334, 1382, 1537	**Miami**	592
Living In The Heart Of Love (2.37)	632	**Middle Of The Sea** (3.42)	1130
London Jam	400	**Midnight Rambler** (6.52)	424, 455, 478, 523, 577, 608,
Lonely At The Top (4.40)	821		685, 1034, 1339, 1366, 1468, 1491
Lonesome Schoolboy	499, 777	**Might As Well Get Juiced** (5.23)	1259
Long Long While (3.01)	294	(a) Keith's Revenge Remix *(Bootleg)* - (10.50)	
Look On Yonder Wall	416	(b) Cult-Club Mix *(Bootleg)* - (7.21)	
Look Out Baby (10.23)	1085	**Miss Amanda Jones** (2.48)	312
Look What The Cat Dragged In (3.57)	1444	**Miss You** (4.49)	730, 787, 864, 907, 1021, 1150,
Look What You've Done	90, 138	(a) Take 1 - (11.40)	1175, 1218, 1313, 1402, 1472, 1483
Looking For Trouble (3.03)	927	(b) 8 Track Version - (5.43)	
Looking Tired (2.15)	270	(c) Video Version - (3.55)	
Loose Woman	350	**Miss You (12 Inch Version)** (8.26)	727
Los Trios Guitaros (3.22)	718	(a) Remix Edit Version - (7.33)	
Losing My Touch (5.06)	1343	Miss You (Dance Version)	727
Love In Vain (4.19)	426, 452, 460, 463, 571, 792, 1193	**Miss You (Dr Dre Remix 2002)** (3.42)	729
(a) Promo Only		**Miss You (Edit)** (3.34)	728
Love Is Strong (3.50)	1098, 1216	**Misty Roads** (4.28)	743
(a) Take 1 - (5.47)		**Mixed Emotions** (4.38)	997, 1032
(b) Take 2 - (5.41)		(a) Take 1 - (6.44)	
(c) Take 3 - (5.42)		(b) Take 2 - (6.36)	
Love Is Strong		(c) Edited Single Version - (4.00)	
(Bob Clearmountain Remix) (3.49)	1091	(d) New Mix Version - (4.37)	
Love Is Strong		**Mixed Emotions**	
(Joe The Butcher Club Mix) (5.25)	1097	**(Chris Kimsey's Twelve-Inch)** (6.13)	996
Love Is Strong		**Mona** (2.11)	58, 72, 94, 106, 156, 177, 855
(Teddy Riley Dub Remix) (4.07)	1095	**Money** (2.34)	31, 32
Love Is Strong		**Monkey Man** (4.11)	433, 1153, 1180, 1223, 1363
(Teddy Riley Extended Remix) (5.04)	1093	**Monsoon Ragoon** (4.36)	1113
Love Is Strong		**Moon Is Up** (3.42)	1109, 1342
(Teddy Riley Extended Rock Remix) (4.48)	1094	(a) Instrumental Take 1 - (5.03)	
Love Is Strong		(b) Take 2 - (4.18)	
(Teddy Riley Instrumental) (4.46)	1096	**Moonlight Mile** (5.56)	493
Love Is Strong		**Mother's Little Helper** (2.45)	278, 303
(Teddy Riley Radio Remix) (4.08)	1092	**Mr Spector And**	
Love Train (6.03)	1395	**Mr Pitney Came Too** (2.47)	78
Love You Too Much	713	**Mr. Pitiful** (3.18)	1454
Lovely Lady	653	**Muck Spreading Dub** (3.23)	733
Loving Cup	437, 451, 527, 553, 1527	**Munich Hilton** (10.35)	710, 852
Loving Cup - Alternate Take (5.26)	438	(a) Take 1 - (6.57)	
Loving You Is Sweeter Than Ever (6.20)	987	(b) Take 2 - (5.41)	
Low Down (4.25)		(c) Take 3 Vocals - (7.39)	
(a) 12 Inch Edit *(Bootleg)* - (6.21)		(d) Take 4 - (5.29)	
(b) Master Mix *(Bootleg)* - (6.04)	1260	**Munich Reggae** (5.29)	655
Lucky In Love	737	(a) Edited Cut - (2.02)	
Luxury (5.01)	631	**My Baby Left Me** (3.20)	967
(a) Edited Original Release - (4.31)		**My First Plea** (4.14)	801
Majesties Honky Tonk (2.28)	363	(a) Take 1 - (4.50)	
(a) Various Takes - (20.41)		(b) Take 2 - (5.16)	
Make It Now (4.29)	1084	(c) Take 3 - (3.50)	
(a) Take 1 - (9.15)		**My Girl** (2.39)	239
(b) Take 2 - (7.35)		**My Home Is A Prison** (2.43)	377
Make No Mistake	1201	**My Love Is My Love** (9.20)	1072
Man Eating Woman (3.45)	647	**My Obsession** (3.18)	307
Manhole Cover	354	(a) Instrumental - (4.08)	
Mannish Boy (6.29)	705	**My Only Girl** (2.01)	44, 45
Mean Disposition (4.07)	1114	**Nanker Phelge**	722
(a) Instrumental Take 1 - (4.13)		**Natural Magic** (1.39)	387
(b) Take 2 - (3.14)		**Neighbours** (3.33)	851, 877, 892, 1383

(a) Alternative Take - (3.26)
Never Let Her Go (4.51)   765
Never Make Me Cry (4.01)   763
Never Make You Cry   763
Never Stop (4.27)   656
Never Too Into (5.04)   823
New Faces (2.52)   1124
    (a) Take 1 - (2.54)
    (b) Take 2 - (2.47)
Night Time Is The Right Time (8.38)   1469
No Expectations (3.56)   381, 420, 449, 1188, 1385
    (a) Alternative Take - (4.20)
No One Knows (0.09)   88
No Spare Parts (4.30)   758
    (a) Take 1 - (5.01)
    (b) Take 2 - (6.06)
No Use In Crying (3.25)   849
    (a) Take 1 - (3.35)
    (b) Take 2 - (4.28)
    (c) Take 3 - (4.26)
    (d) Take 4 - (4.28)
Not Fade Away (1.49)   60, 95, 100, 108, 109, 112, 122,
    (a) Take 1 - (1.49)   141, 330, 1142, 1159, 1206,
    1239, 1254
Not The Way To Go (9.39)   766
    (a) Alternative Take - (7.10)
Nothing From Nothing (2.50)   701
Now I've Got A Witness
(Like Uncle Phil and Uncle Gene) (2.32)   81
Off The Hook (2.34)   144, 182, 198
Oh I Do Like To See
Me On The B-Side (2.24)   69
Oh No, Not You Again (3.46)   1437, 1448, 1450, 1465, 1502
    (a) Clean Mix Version - (3.49)
    (b) Alternative Mix Cut - (3.48)
Oh, Baby (We Got A Good
Thing Going) (2.09)   192, 250, 255
On Our Knees   768
On With The Show (3.39)   374
    (a) 10 Various Takes - (25.21)
On Your Way To School   5
Once You Start   725
One Hit (To The Body) (4.44)   952
    (a) Early Take - (7.51)
    (b) Instrumental Take - (4.59)
    (c) Take 3 - (4.57)
    (d) Take 4 - (4.41)
    (e) Take 5 - (4.44)
    (f) Edit 12 Inch Single - (4.12)
One Hit (To The Body)
(London Mix) (7.00)   951
One More From Your Body   952
One More Try (1.58)   235
One Night (2.50)   803
Only Found Out Yesterday (1.57)   1497
Out Of Control (4.43)   1298, 1311, 1328
    (a) Papa Was A Rolling Stone Mix
    (Bootleg) - (10.21)
    (b) Reggae Version *(Bootleg)* - (5.09)
    (c) Album Radio Edit - (4.00)
    (d) Call Out Hook - (0.18)
    (e) Old School Mix *(Bootleg)* - (8.58)
Out Of Control
(Bi-Polar At The Controls) (5.12)   1295
Out Of Control
(Bi-Polar's Fat Controller Mix) (5.24)   1297
Out Of Control
(Bi-Polar's Outer Version) (5.09)   1296
Out Of Control

(Don Was Live Remix) (6.54)   1326
Out Of Control (In Hand
With Fluke - Radio Edit) (4.32)   1291
Out Of Control (In Hand
With Fluke Instrumental) (5.55)   1292
Out Of Control (In Hand
With Fluke) (8.28)   1290
Out Of Control (Saber Final Mix) (5.45)   1294
Out Of Control
(Saber Master With Fade) (4.42)   1293
    (a) Danny Saber's Demo - (5.39)
    (b) Bi-Polar Horns Of Control - (5.09)
    (c) Bi-Polar Fat Controller Mix
    (Percussive Version) - (5.24)
    (d) S.D.S. Mix - (4.23)
    (e) S.D.S. Mix (No Samples) - (4.22)
    (f) S.D.S. Dub Mix - (4.51)
    (g) Fluke Vocal 12-Inch - (6.36)
    (h) Fluke Instrumental - (5.36)
    (i) Fluke Vocal 12-Inch #2 - (6.51)
    (j) Fluke Vocal 7-Inch #2 - (4.10)
Out Of Tears (5.27)   1129, 1149, 1186
    (a) Take 1 - (4.23)
    (b) Take 2 - (5.29)
    (c) Take 3 - (5.24)
Out Of Tears
(Bob Clearmountain Remix Edit) (4.21)   1128
Out Of Tears (Don Was Edit) (4.22)   1127
Out Of Time (5.37)   289, 301
    (a) Edited Version - (3.42)
    (b) No Lead Vocals - (4.58)
Outa-Space (4.04)   683
Over You   86
Pain In My Heart (2.05)   189, 208, 214, 218
Paint It Black   293
Paint It, Black (3.20)   293, 302, 320, 1043, 1050,
    (a) Instrumental - (2.22)   1411, 1484, 1522
    (b) Album Version - (3.45)
    (c) Stereo Version - (3.24)
    (d) Alternative Take - (2.22)
Panama Powder Room   304
Parachute Woman (2.20)   385, 419, 1187
    (a) Take 1 - (2.15)
Pass The Wine (Sophia Loren) (4.54)   529
Pay Your Dues (3.05)   380
Paying The Cost To Be The Boss (3.34)   1257
Petrol   748
Petrol Blues (1.35)   748
    (a) Alternative Take - (3.41)
Petrol Gang   748
Piano Instrumental (4.37)   747
Pieces   352
Pink Pick   939
Play With Fire (2.15)   201, 242, 1024
Please Go Home (3.18)   311
    (a) Instrumental - (3.20)
Plundered My Soul (3.58)   546
Plundered My Soul (Radio Mix) (3.56)   547
Poison Ivy (2.36)   28, 41
Positano Grande   433
Possesses Me (7.37)   1111
Potted Shrimps (4.12)   513
Precious Lips   1258
Precious Love   1009
Pretty Beat Up (4.05)   920
    (a) XXX Take
    (b) Instrumental Take 1 - (6.08)
    (c) Instrumental Take 2 - (4.28)
Pretty Thing   21

Primo Grande	380
Prodigal Son (2.52)	393, 465, 476, 838
Pullover	936
Putty (In Your Hands)	961
Rain Fall Down (4.53)	1423, 1467, 1487
Rain Fall Down (Ashley Beedle's	
'Heavy Disco' Dub re-edit) (6.07)	1428
Rain Fall Down (Ashley Beedle's	
'Heavy Disco' Radio re-edit) (4.06)	1429
Rain Fall Down (Ashley Beedle's	
'Heavy Disco' Vocal re-edit) (6.13)	1427
Rain Fall Down (Radio re-edit) (4.02)	1424
Rain Fall Down	
(will.i.am instrumental) (4.05)	1426
Rain Fall Down	
(will.i.am Remix) (4.05)	1425
Randy Whore (7.57)	1068
(a) Take 1 - (3.58)	
Ready Yourself (3.37)	1011
Red House	508
Redeyes	759
Reelin' And A Rockin' (3.32)	128
Reelin' And A Rockin'	
(Little Boy Blue & The Blue Boys)	11
Remember These Days (4.16)	752
Respectable (3.07)	719, 790, 814, 1336, 1396
(a) Take 1 - (3.52)	
(b) Take 2 - (3.57)	
Rice Krispies Jingle	82
Ride On Baby (2.53)	283
Rip This Joint (2.22)	540, 569, 620, 686, 1253
(a) Instrumental Version - (2.32)	
Road Runner (3.02)	17
Rock And A Hard Place (5.25)	1003, 1019, 1048, 1215
(a) Early Take 1 - (5.49)	
(b) Take 2 - (5.52)	
(c) Edited Single Version - (4.10)	
Rock And A Hard Place	
(Bonus Beats Mix) (4.08)	999
Rock And A Hard Place	
(Dance Mix) (6.54)	998
Rock And A Hard Place	
(Michael Brauer Mix) (7.05)	1002
Rock And A Hard Place	
(Oh-Oh Hard Dub Mix) (6.54)	1000
Rock And A Hard Place	
(Rock Mix Edit) (5.39)	1001
Rock It	490
Rock Me Baby (0.41)	379, 1356, 1380, 1403
Rocks Off (4.33)	544, 1146, 1162, 1210, 1408
(a) Instrumental Mix - (4.33)	
Roll Over Beethoven (2.17)	36, 83, 507
Ronnie's Idea	920
Rotten Roll	714
Rough Justice (3.13)	1446, 1459, 1473, 1488
Route 66	57, 91, 107, 119, 209, 414
Ruby Tuesday (3.11)	340, 342, 345, 1040, 1059, 1401
(a) Take 1 - (3.25)	
(b) Alt Mix - (3.17)	
Sad Day (3.02)	285
Sad Ol' Day	285
Sad Sad Sad (3.35)	1005, 1028, 1047
(a) Take 1 - (3.58)	
(b) Take 2 - (3.53)	
Sad Song	550
Saint Of Me (5.14)	1275, 1309, 1327
(a) Alternate Mix (Bootleg) - (5.13)	
(b) Detroit Floor RMX (Bootleg) - (12.42)	
(c) Call Out Hook - (0.12)	

(d) Radio Edit - (4.11)	
Saint Of Me	
(Deep Dish Club Mix Part One) (7.35)	1280
Saint Of Me	
(Deep Dish Grunge Garage Dub) (7.25)	1282
Saint Of Me (Deep Dish Grunge	
Garage Remix Edit) (3.22)	1283
Saint Of Me (Deep Dish Grunge	
Garage Remix Parts 1 & 2)	1284
Saint Of Me (Deep Dish Grunge	
Garage Remix) (14.08)	1284
Saint Of Me (Deep Dish Rolling	
Dub) (7.12)	1281
Saint Of Me	
(Todd Terry Dub No. 2) (7.40)	1279
Saint Of Me	
(Todd Terry Extended Mix) (6.03)	1276
Saint Of Me (Todd Terry Fade) (3.32)	1277
Saint Of Me	
(Todd Terry Tee's Freeze Dub) (7.43)	1278
Salt Of The Earth (4.47)	388, 423, 1031, 1422
(a) Take 1 - (4.48)	
Samba (3.42)	1121
Sands Of Time	820
Satanic Organ Jam (1.44)	368
Save Me	598
Schoolboy's Blues	499, 777
See I Love You	498
Send It To Me (3.43)	847
(a) Long Take - (6.15)	
Sending Out An Invitation	984
Separately (4.18)	532
Serious Love (1.38)	809
Sex Drive (5.07)	1066
Sexdrive (Club Version) (6.18)	1065
(a) Edited Club Version - (4.33)	
Sexdrive (Dirty Hands Mix) (4.27)	1064
Sexy Night	653
Shake Your Hips (2.59)	511, 554
(a) Alternative Take - (4.11)	
Shame, Shame, Shame (3.02)	646, 746, 1301
Shang A Doo Lang (0.10)	43
Shattered (3.46)	721, 789, 815, 876, 891,
(a) Take 1 - (3.46)	1145, 1455, 1524
(b) Take 2 - (3.01)	
(c) Short Version - (2.43)	
Shaved Stone	713
She Comes In Colours	352
She Left Me	824
She Never Listens To Me (7.34)	968
She Said Yeah (1.35)	261, 273, 276
She Saw Me Coming (3.12)	1434
(a) Alternative Mix - (3.22)	
She Smiled Sweetly (2.45)	309, 348
She Was Hot (4.42)	923, 1525, 1544
(a) Early Take - (6.44)	
(b) Long Take - (9.27)	
(c) Single Promo Version - (3.59)	
(d) Video Version - (4.58)	
Sheep Dip Blues (0.37)	754
She's A Rainbow (4.35)	352
(a) Promo Only Version - (2.51)	
(b) Cut 1 - (4.10)	
(c) Takes 1 - 7 - (12.15)	
She's Doing Her Thing	357
She's So Cold (4.13)	831, 861, 905, 1501
(a) Alternative Take - (6.51)	
(b) Cleaned Up Version - (4.06)	
She's So Cold (God Damn Version)	831

Shine A Light (4.17)   431, 506, 1235, 1245, 1520, 1541
Short And Curlies (2.43)   603
Shot My Baby   377
Show Me A Woman   937
Silver Blanket   388
Silver Coated Rails (3.18)   716
Silver Train (4.26)   515
    (a) Early Take 1 - (3.36)
    (b) Take 2 - (4.36)
Sing Me Back Home (4.17)   707
Sing This All Together (3.46)   360
**Sing This All Together
(See What Happens)** (7.52)   361
    (a) Un-edited Cut - (14.54)
Sister Morphine (5.34)   397, 1338
    (a) Marianne Faithfull Version - (5.29)
    (b) Early Take - (5.35)
Sittin' On A Fence (3.02)   284
Slave (4.59)   649
    (a) Take 1 - (9.43)
    (b) Take 2 - (8.20)
    (c) Take 3 - (11.13)
    (d) Extended Version - (6.32)
Sleep Tonight (5.14)   992
    (a) Early Take - (6.50)
Slide On (5.49)   919
    (a) Short Take - (4.15)
Slipping Away (4.29)   1008, 1194, 1221, 1413
    (a) Early Take 1 - (5.25)
    (b) Take 2 - (5.38)
Slips Away (16.01)   1074
Slow Down And Stop (3.02)   622
So Divine (Aladdin Story) (4.32)   432
So Much In Love (0.11)   48
So Young (1994 Version) (3.25)   771
    (a) Original Take - (2.57)
So Young (2011 Version) (3.18)   773
So Young (Piano Version) (2.55)   772
Some Girls (4.36)   726, 1529
    (a) Take 1 - (5.12)
    (b) Take 2 - (6.29)
Some More Girls   726
Some Of Us Are On Our Knees (5.38)   977
Some People Tell Me   740
**Some Things Just Stick
In Your Mind** (2.27)   148
Something Good   639
**Something Happened To Me
Yesterday** (4.55)   315
**Sometimes Happy,
Sometimes Blue** (2.05)   337, 338
Sometimes I Wonder Why   650
Song For Andrew   77
Soon Forgotten   14
Sophia Loren   529
Soul Blues (3.53)   369
    (a) Take 1 - (1.46)
    (b) Take 2 - (2.05)
Soul Survivor (3.49)   542
    (a) Early Take - (4.02)
Soul Survivor - Alternate Take (3.59)   543
Sparks Will Fly (3.16)   1126, 1147, 1163, 1211
    (a) Take 1 - (3.20)
    (b) Take 2 - Studio Extract - (14.33)
    (c) Take 3 - (3.16)
    (d) Take 4 - (3.19)
    (e) Take 5 - (3.15)
    (f) Radio Clean Version - (3.15)
Speed Of Light   1018

Star Star (4.25)   600, 613, 670, 696, 784, 1415
    (a) Censored Version - (4.25)
Starfucker   600
Start It Up   736
Start Me Up (3.33)   656, 736, 866, 870, 910, 1022,
    (a) Alternative Take - (3.44)   1055, 1154, 1182, 1225, 1322,
    1360, 1381, 1400, 1449, 1458,
    1477, 1538, 1542
Stay Where You Are (1.43)   767
Stealing My Heart (3.42)   1345
Steel Wheels   1003, 1019
Step On It   979
Stewed And Keefed (4.12)   124
Stiff   941
Still A Fool (6.43)   399, 1233
    (a) Extended Slow - (9.48)
Still In Love (5.22)   819
    (a) Early Take 1 - (1.45)
    (b) Take 2 - (7.29)
    (c) Take 3 - (5.38)
Stoned (2.09)   38
Stones   38
Stop Breaking Down (4.34)   502, 1172
Stop That (5.40)   926
Stray Cat Blues (4.37)   382, 448, 462, 1388
    (a) Take 1 - (4.17)
Street Fighting Man (3.16)   391, 456, 474, 481, 578, 581,
    (a) USA Single Version - (3.10)   609, 687, 1061, 1156, 1181,
    1224, 1230, 1359, 1417
Streets Of Love (5.10)   1431, 1505
    (a) Alternative Mix 1 - (5.10)
    (b) Alternative Mix 2 - (5.09)
    (c) Radio Edit Version - (4.04)
Strictly Memphis (3.41)   979
    (a) Take 1 - (3.22)
    (b) Take 2 - (8.15)
Stuck In The Cold   831
Stuck Out All Alone   394
Stupid Girl (2.56)   292
Suck On The Jugular (4.28)   1090
    (a) Take 1 - (5.47)
    (b) Take 2 - (5.50)
Summer Romance (3.16)   744, 812
    (a) Take 1 - (4.42)
    (b) Take 2 - (5.37)
    (c) Take 3 - (5.11)
    (d) Take 4 - (5.32)
Summertime Blues (1.49)   776
Sunshine Glance   767
Sure I Do   47
Sure The One You Need (4.48)   661
Surprise Me   374
Surprise, Surprise (2.31)   171
Susie Q (1.48)   170
Sway (3.52)   516, 1503
    (a) Single Version - (3.33)
Sweet Black Angel (2.58)   510, 564
    (a) Instrumental Cut - (3.00)
Sweet Home Chicago (4.49)   818
Sweet Little Sixteen (2.58)   778, 795
Sweet Neocon (4.33)   1445
Sweet Virginia (4.26)   505, 566, 1169, 1214, 1249, 1256
    (a) Take 1 - (4.23)
    (b) Alternative Mix - (4.32)
Sweethearts Together (4.45)   1135
    (a) Take 1 - (3.39)
    (b) Take 2 - (5.58)
    (c) Take 3 - (5.56)
    (d) Take 4 - (5.48)

(e) Take 5 - (5.56)
(f) Take 6 - (5.51)
Sympathy For The Devil (6.18)   401, 402, 413, 422, 457, 471,
(a) Take 1 - (6.23)   486, 665, 689, 1039, 1057,
(b) Edited Cut - (5.57)   1179, 1222, 1319, 1377, 1414,
   1476, 1514, 1536

Sympathy For The Devil
(Fatboy Slim Radio Remix) (4.06)   406
Sympathy For The Devil
(Fatboy Slim Remix) (8.25)   405
Sympathy For The Devil
(Full Phatt Radio Remix) (3.42)   408
Sympathy For The Devil
(Full Phatt Remix) (5.26)   407
Sympathy For The Devil
(Neptunes Radio Remix) (4.16)   404
Sympathy For The Devil
(Neptunes Remix) (5.55)   403
Take It Or Leave It (2.47)   281
Take Me Down Slowly   1430
Talkin' About You   40
Talkin' 'Bout You (2.32)   263
Tall & Slender Blondes   716
Tallahassee Lassie (2.37)   805
(a) Original Cut - (2.37)
Tease Me (4.21)   1125
Tell Me (You're Coming Back) (3.49)   68, 140
(a) Long Cut - (4.05)
Tell Me (You're Coming Back)
(Early Version) (2.47)   54
(a) Alternative Take - (3.02)
Tell Me Baby (1.57)   135
Tell Me Baby, How Many Times?   135
Telstar II   353
Terrifying (4.53)   1016, 1030
(a) Take 1 - (5.09)
(b) Take 2 - (5.40)
(c) Seven-Inch Re-Mix Edit - (4.10)
Terrifying (Twelve Inch Re-mix) (6.56)   1015
That Girl Belongs To Yesterday   44, 45
That's How Strong My Love Is (2.25)   231, 247, 256, 1391
That's Life (3.17)   682
That's No Way To Get Along   393
The Devil Is My Name   401, 402
The Harder They Come (3.47)   810
(a) Alternative Take - (3.39)
The Japanese Thing   493
The Jimmy Miller Show   429
The Ladies The Lillies And The Lake   362
The Lantern (4.23)   370
(a) Many Alternative Takes - (26.45)
The Last Time (3.42)   200, 205, 216, 220, 223, 241,
   325, 1199, 1317

The Nearness Of You (4.34)   1393
The Right To Think   798
The Rocky Road To Dublin (5.03)   1139
(a) Edited Version - (4.17)
The Singer Not The Song (2.23)   271
The Spider And The Fly (3.39)   234, 252, 1196
The Storm (2.49)   1122
(a) Take 1 - (9.56)
(b) Take 2 - (3.19)
(c) Take 3 - (3.17)
The Sun Is Shining (3.44)   485
The Train Song   832
The Under Assistant West Coast
Promotion Man (3.07)   230
(a) Long Version - (3.20)
The Vulture   386

The Way She Held Me Tight   743
The Worst (2.24)   1110, 1152, 1178, 1192
(a) Take 1 - (3.08)
(b) Take 2 - (2.26)
(c) Take 3 - (2.27)
There Are But Five
Rolling Stones (2.23)   56
These Arms Of Mine   953
Thief In The Night (5.15)   1274, 1331
Think (3.09)   282
Think I'm Going Mad   817
Thinking About You   722
Thirty Nine And Holding (6.26)   955
This Place Is Empty (3.16)   1438, 1470, 1493
Through The Lonely Nights (4.13)   601
Thru And Thru (6.15)   1067, 1367
(a) Early Take 1 - (4.45)
(b) Early Take 2 - (3.11)
(c) Take 3 - (11.49)
(d) Take 4 - (4.11)
(e) Take 5 - (8.32)
(f) Take 6 - (8.26)
(g) Take 7 - (8.23)
Tie You Up (The Pain Of Love) (4.16)   925
(a) Early Take - (10.48)
Till The Next Goodbye (4.36)   635
(a) Alternative Mix - (4.40)
Time Is On My Side (2.56)   126, 142, 180, 183, 211, 882, 898
Time To Go   711
Time Waits For No One (6.38)   630
(a) Edited Version - (4.25)
Title 12   350
Title 15 (4.05)   366
(a) Take 1 - (4.08)
Title 5   383
Title 5 (1.47)   367
Title 8   340
To Know Him Is To Love Him (3.09)   55
Toffee Apple   350
Toilet   359
Too Much Blood (6.25)   946
(a) Early Take - (6.26)
(b) Extract Take - (2.51)
Too Much Blood (Dance Version) (12.33)   945
Too Much Blood (Dub Version) (8.00)   944
Too Rude (3.13)   966
(a) Take 1 - (3.34)
(b) Take 2 - (10.21)
Too Tight (3.37)   1287
Too Tough (3.51)   928
(a) Early Take - (5.24)
Tops (3.48)   602, 853
(a) Instrumental - (4.41)
Torn And Frayed (4.18)   533
Track With No Name   1100
Tram Song   832
Travellin' Man (5.58)   512
Travelling Tiger   491
Treat Me Like A Fool (6.40)   971
(a) Take 1 - (5.06)
(b) Take 2 - (3.10)
(c) Take 3 - (1.52)
Trident Jam (3.43)   514
Tried To Talk Her Into It (3.19)   931
Trouble In Mind (3.43)   336
Trouble Man (4.00)   1140
(a) Take 1 - (4.43)
Truckdriver Blues   720
Try A Little Harder (2.19)   151

Try Me (2.25)   229

Tumbling Dice (3.47)   496, 538, 555, 570, 612, 676, 700, 793, 860, 904, 1056, 1143, 1160, 1207, 1242, 1320, 1412, 1464, 1508, 1533

Turd On The Run (2.38)   537

Twenty Flight Rock (1.51)   872, 880, 895

Two Trains Running   399, 1233

Under My Thumb (3.41)   295, 323, 328, 466, 487, 856, 874, 888, 1511

Under The Boardwalk (2.46)   164

Under The Boardwalk (Rhythms Del Mundo Remix) (2.44)   165

Under The Radar (4.36)   1439
    (a) Alternative Take - (5.09)

Undercover Of The Night (4.33)   950, 1029, 1519
    (a) Single Edit Version - (4.13)
    (b) Take 1 - (4.26)
    (c) Take 2 - (3.54)
    (d) Take 3 - (4.48)
    (e) Take 4 - (4.53)
    (f) Promo Single Version - (4.02)

Undercover Of The Night (Dub Version) (6.21)   949

Undercover Of The Night (Extended Cheeky Version)   949

Undercover Of The Night (Special Dance Remix)   949

Untitled Instrumental   514

Untitled Jam   514

Untitled Slide Doodles   381

Up Against The Wall (6.24)   768

Uptight / (I Can't Get No) Satisfaction (5.32)   579

Vagina   649

Ventilator Blues (3.24)   530

Voodoo Brew - Untitled #1 (6.19)   1099

Voodoo Brew - Untitled #2 (3.51)   1100
    (a) Take 1 - (5.57)

Voodoo Brew - Untitled #3 (5.47)   1101

Voodoo Brew - Untitled #4 (3.50)   1102

Voodoo Brew - Untitled #5   1103

Voodoo Residue - Untitled #1 (6.57)   1086

Voodoo Residue - Untitled #2 (1.51)   1087

Waiting For A Friend   604

Waiting On A Friend (4.34)   604, 884, 900, 1312
    (a) Early Take 1 - (3.20)
    (b) Take 2 - No Sax - (4.19)
    (c) Take 3 - Sax - (3.34)
    (d) Edited Version - (3.35)

Waiting On My Friend   604

Wake Up In The Morning (0.27)   82

Walkin' Blues   417

Walking The Dog (3.11)   67, 73, 101

Wanna Hold You (3.52)   915, 1315
    (a) Take 1 - (6.28)
    (b) Take 2 - (3.22)
    (c) Take 3 - (6.57)
    (d) Edited Version - (3.15)

Watching The River Flow (5.09)   1546

Waving Hair   168

We Don't Wanna Go Home   1436

We Got To Get Our Shit Together   637

We Had It All (2.54)   842
    (a) Take 1 - (2.55)
    (b) Take 2 - (2.55)

We Love You (4.21)   356
    (a) Instrumental Alternative Take - (3.02)
    (b) Instrumental Takes - (9.52)

We Love You, Goodbye   356

We Were Falling In Love (1.20)   168

We Wish You A Cosmic Joke   376

Wee Baby Blues   5

Well Well (3.01)   1349

We're Wastin' Time (2.44)   149
    (a) Take 1 - (2.53)

What A Shame (2.59)   196

What Am I Gonna Do With Your Love? (5.29)   957
    (a) Early Take - (14.38)

What Am I Living For? (9.35)   799

What Are You Gonna Do With My Love?   957

What Are You Gonna Tell Your Boyfriend? (5.13)   972

What Gives You The Right (5.03)   798
    (a) Alternative Take - (5.23)

What To Do (2.32)   299

What You're Gonna Do With Your Boyfriend   972

What's The Matter? (4.44)   834

When A Boy Meets A Girl   51

When A Girl Loves A Boy (0.21)   51

When The Whip Comes Down (4.20)   717, 780, 785, 889, 1375
    (a) Take 1 - (9.56)
    (b) Extended Take 2 - (6.19)
    (c) Edited Extended Take 1 - (7.22)

When You Got A Good Friend (2.37)   560

When You're Gone (3.51)
    (a) Alternative Take - (3.58)   759

Where The Boys All Go   775

Where The Boys Go (3.29)
    (a) Early Take 1 - (5.15)
    (b) Take 2 - (3.48)
    (c) Take 3 - (3.52)
    (d) Intro Segment - (0.35)   775

Who Am I? (3.49)   498

Who Do You Love (3.59)   1173

Who's Been Sleeping Here? (3.57)   316

Who's Driving My Plane?   305

Who's Driving Your Plane? (3.13)   305

Who's Shagging Who? (2.04)   974

Why You Runnin'? (4.54)   1079

Wild Horses (5.42)   484, 681, 702, 1197, 1307, 1409, 1457, 1466, 1490
    (a) Pedal Steel - Pete Kleinow - (5.22)
    (b) Short Promo Version - (3.26)
    (c) Alternative Take - (5.45)
    (d) Billy Preston (Organ) Take - (5.43)

Will You Be My Lover Tonight?   42

Wind Call   606

Windmill (3.26)   606

Winning Ugly (4.33)   990
    (a) Early Take - (4.55)

Winning Ugly (London Mix) (7.55)   989

Winning Ugly (NY Mix) (7.03)   988

Winsome   966

Winter (5.30)   584
    (a) Take 1 - (5.25)

Wish I'd Never Met You (4.42)   995

Worried About You (5.16)   650, 1386, 1481
    (a) Take 1 - (7.42)
    (b) Edited Take 1 - (3.14)
    (c) Long Take 2 - (7.21)

Worried Life Blues (2.15)   709

XXX   920

Yellow Cab   741

Yellow Jacket (2.05)   1077

Yesterday's Papers (2.05)   310
    (a) Take 1 - (2.06)
    (b) Take 2 - (2.12)

(c) Extended Backing Track - (3.08)
Yonders Wall   416
You Better Move On (2.40)   29, 76, 93
You Can Make It If You Try (2.03)   66, 118
**You Can't Always Get
What You Want** (7.28)   410, 421, 572, 617, 674, 699,
  (a) Single Edit Version - (4.52)   858, 902, 1020, 1060, 1324,
                                                   1410, 1479

**You Can't Always Get What You Want
(Soulwax Full Length Remix)** (6.07)   411
  (a) Soulwax Remix Radio
  Edit Version - (3.58)
You Can't Catch Me (3.30)   145
You Can't Cut The Mustard (3.26)
  (a) Early Take - (2.55)   963
**You Can't Judge A Book
By The Cover** (0.36)   13
You Don't Have To Go (2.16)   770
You Don't Have To Mean It (3.44)   1285, 1355
You Don't Tell Me   984
You Got Away With Murder (4.42)   1080
You Got It (2.56)   976
You Got It Made (5.01)   1123
  (a) Take 1 - (4.27)
  (b) Take 2 & Conversation - (17.16)
You Got Me Rocking (3.35)   1116, 1144, 1161, 1208, 1240,
  (a) Take 1 - (10.58)   1337, 1370, 1407, 1463, 1499
  (b) Take 2 - (4.11)
  (c) Take 3 - (4.13)
  (d) Short Extract - (1.13)
  (e) Take 4 - (4.05)

**You Got Me Rocking
(Perfecto Mix)** (5.04)   1117
  (a) Pefecto Mix Edit Version - (3.49)
**You Got Me Rocking
(Sexy Disco Dub Mix)** (6.18)   1118
**You Got Me Rocking
(Trance Mix)** (5.00)   1119
You Got Some Silver Now   425
You Got The Silver (2.50)   425, 1534
  (a) MJ Vocal - (2.51)
You Gotta Move (2.18)   477
  (a) Take 1 - (2.35)   482, 673, 693
You Keep It Cool   917
You Left Me   828
You Must Be The One (0.16)   52
You Should Have Seen Her Ass (4.20)   583
You Win Again (3.00)   774
  (a) Alternative Take - (3.20)
Young Love   1299
**Your Angel Steps Out
Of Heaven** (3.05)   802
Your Love   957
You're Coming Back To Me   54, 68
You're So Beautiful   829
You're Too Much   958
You've Just Made My Day (0.38)   143
Zabadoo   589
Zip Mouth Angel (3.33)   1105
Zulu (4.37)   1106
  (a) Take 1 - (4.11)

Interviews and Information Provision

- Cheltenham & Gloucester Library October 2001
- Ronald Elliott (Editor Ready Steady Go! Magazine 1964) January 2002
- Gene Pitney (Stones musician 1964) February 2002 interview
- Jim Sullivan (Stones musician 1964) March 2002 interview
- Phil Lawton (BBC Archives) March 2002 interview
- Nikki Sudden (Musician and Stones historian) February 2004
- Mutual research with Stones author Sean Egan November 2004
- Bernard Fowler (Rolling Stones 1989 – date) June 2008 interview
- John Pasche (designer of Stones tongue 1970) November 2010, August 2011 correspondence
- Marc Roberty (author of Clapton sessions) November 2010 correspondence
- Ann Waters (Ben Waters' manager) April 2011 correspondence
- Ed Cherney (Stones engineer 1995 – date) May 2011 interview
- Ian McLagan (Rolling Stones 1978 – 1981) August 2011 interview
- Ben Waters (Stones musician 2010) September 2011 interview
- Gary Galbraith (Stones historian) November 2011 information
- Chris Kimsey (Stones producer/engineer 1969 – 1995) October, November 2011 interviews and on-going help
- Kristi Kimsey (Stones session singer 1979) November 2011 conversation
- Barry Sage (Stones engineer 1977, 1978, 1980) November 2011 interview and on-going help
- Susan McLean (Stones backing singer 1980) November 2011 conversation
- Jennifer Ruffy (Stones backing singer 1980) November 2011 conversation
- Adrienne Posta-Davis (Singer and band acquaintance 1964) November 2011 interview
- Rod Thear (Stones engineer 1974 and 1983) January 2012 interview
- Keith Grant (Olympic's Studio Manager 1958 – 1987) January 2012 interview
- Vicki Wickham (Producer, Ready Steady Go! 1963 – 1966) February 2012 correspondence
- Jane Rose (Rolling Stones' Executive Associate) February 2012 conversation
- Graham Wiltshire (Stones photographer) March, May 2012
- Dr Andrew Demery (Stones ABKCO SACD Sony expert) on-going research and advice
- Stephen Carter (Stones historian) on-going research and advice

Magazines and Books

Guitar World, Ice Magazine, Loaded, Melody Maker, Mojo, Musician, New Musical Express, Q, Record Collector, Rolling Stone, Sounds, Uncut, Vox.

Felix Aeppli: *The Rolling Stones 1962-1995 The Ultimate Guide,* Record Information Services, 1996.
Mandy Aftel: *Death Of A Rolling Stone,* Sidgwick & Jackson Ltd, 1982.
John Aldridge: *Satisfaction, The Story Of Mick Jagger,* Proteus Books, 1984.
Keith Altham: *No More Mr Nice Guy,* Blake Publishing Ltd, 1999
Steve Appleford: *The Rolling Stones It's Only Rock 'N' Roll,* Carlton Books Ltd, 1997.
Freddy Bannister: *There Must Be A Better Way,* Bath Books, 2003
Victor Bockris: *Keith Richards The Unauthorised Biography,* Omnibus Press, 2002.
Jean Michel Boris, Jean-Francois Brieu, Eric Didi: *Olympia Bruno Coquatrix,* Les Editions Hors Collection, 2003.
Stanley Booth: *The True Adventures Of The Rolling Stones,* Sphere Books Ltd, 1986.
Howard Brown: *The Rolling Stones Complete,* E.M.I. Publishing Ltd, 1981.
Phill Brown: *Are We Still Rolling?,* Tape Op Books, 2010.
Roy Carr: *The Rolling Stones, An Illustrated Record,* New English Library Ltd, 1976.
Barbara Charone: *Keith Richards Illustrated,* Futura Publications, 1979.
Nick Cowan: *Fifty Teabags And A Bottle Of Rum,* Quartet Books Ltd, 2008.
Sam Cutler: *You Can't Always Get What You Want,* ECW Press, 2010.

David Dalton: *The Rolling Stones, The First Twenty Years,* Alfred A. Knopf, Inc, 1981.

David Dalton and Mick Farren: *In Their Own Words, The Rolling Stones,* Omnibus Press, 1985.

Julian Dawson: *And On Piano... Nicky Hopkins,* Desert Hearts, 2011.

Sean Egan: *Let It Bleed, Vinyl Frontier,* Unanimous Ltd, 2005.

Murray Engleheart with Arnaud Durieux: *AC/DC Maximum Rock & Roll,* Harper Collins Publishers, 2006.

Marianne Faithfull with David Dalton: *Faithfull,* Penguin Books, 1995.

David Fricke and Robert Sandall: *Rolling Stones Images Of The World Tour 1989-1990,* Boxtree Ltd, 1990.

Bill German: *Beggars Banquet Newsletters.*

Bill German: *Under Their Thumb,* Aurum Press Ltd., 2009.

Bill German: *My Life Inside Rock And Out,* Da Capo Press, 2004

Robert Greenfield: *A Journey Through America With The Rolling Stones,* Helter Skelter Publishing, 1997.

Robert Greenfield: *A Season In Hell With The Rolling Stones,* Da Capo Press, 2005.

Geoffrey Giuliano, Chris Eborn: *Not Fade Away The Rolling Stones Collection,* Paper Tiger – Dragon's World Ltd, 1995.

Geoffrey Giuliano: *Paint It Black,* Virgin Publishing Ltd, 1994.

Jerry Hall with Jonathan Phang: *My Life In Pictures,* Quadrille Publishing Ltd, 2010.

James Hector: *The Complete Guide To The Music Of The Rolling Stones,* Omnibus Press, 1995.

Dieter Hoffmann: *Das Rolling Stones Schwarzbuck,* New Media Verlag GmbH, 1987.

A E Hotchner: *Blown Away,* Simon & Schuster, 1990.

Laura Jackson: *Heart Of Stone,* Blake Publishing Ltd, 1998.

Bill Janowitz: *Exile On Main St,* Continuum International Publishing Group, 2005.

James Karnbach and Carol Bernson: *The Complete Recording Guide To The Rolling Stones,* Aurum Press Ltd, 1997.

Bobby Keys with Bill Ditenhafer: *Every Night's A Saturday Night,* Counterpoint, 2012.

Nick Kent: *The Dark Stuff,* Faber & Faber, 1999.

Nick Kent: *Apathy For The Devil,* Faber & Faber Ltd, 2010.

Al Kooper: *Backstage Passes & Backstabbing Bastards,* Backbeat Books, 2008.

Dora Lowenstein with Philip Dodd: *A Life On The Road,* Virgin, 1998.

Dora Lowenstein with Philip Dodd: *According To The Rolling Stones,* Weidenfeld & Nicholson, 2003.

Ian 'Mac' McLagan: *All The Rage,* Sidgwick & Jackson, 1998.

Miles: *Mick Jagger, In His Own Words,* Omnibus Press, 1982.

Philip Norman: *The Stones,* Elm Tree Books, 1984.

Kris Needs: *Needs Must,* Virgin Books, 1999.

Kris Needs: *Keith Richards Before They Make Me Run,* Plexus Publishing Ltd, 2004.

Andrew Loog Oldham: *Stoned,* Secker & Warburg, 2000.

Andrew Loog Oldham: *2Stoned,* Secker & Warburg, 2002.

Mark Paytress: *Off The Record,* Omnibus Press, 2003.

John Perry: *Classic Rock Albums Exile On Main St.,* Schirmer Books, 1999.

James Phelge: *Phelge's Stones,* Buncha Asshole Books, 1998.

Terry Rawlings: *Who Killed Christopher Robin?,* Boxtree Ltd, 1994.

Terry Rawlings & Keith Badman: *Good Times Bad Times The Definitive Diary Of The Rolling Stones 1960-1969,* Complete Music Publications Ltd, 1997.

Terry Rawlings: *Rock On Wood The Origin Of A Rock & Roll Face Ronnie Wood,* Boxtree, 1999.

Keith Richards: *Life,* Orion Publishing Group Ltd, 2010.

Graham Ride: *Foundation Stone,* Broad Brush Publishing Ltd, 2001.

Ethan Russell: *Let It Bleed,* Springboard Press, 2009.

Tony Sanchez: *Up And Down With The Rolling Stones,* Blake Paperbacks, 1991.

Christopher Sandford: *Mick Jagger Primitive Cool,* Victor Gollancz, 1993.

Anthony Scaduto: *Mick Jagger,* W H Allen & Co. Ltd, 1974.

UFO Music Books Ltd 1995: *Rolling Stones Stripped A Trip Through The Voodoo Lounge Tour 1994-95.*

Sue Weiner and Lisa Howard: *The Rolling Stones, A – Z,* Omnibus Press, 1984.

Simon Wells: *Butterfly On A Wheel, The Great Rolling Stones Drug Busts,* Omnibus Press, 2011.
Anna Wohlin: *The Murder Of Brian Jones,* Blake Publishing Ltd, 2000.
Ronnie Wood: *Ronnie,* Macmillan, 2007.
Bill Wyman: *Stone Alone,* Viking, 1990.
Bill Wyman: *Bill Wyman's Blues Odyssey A Journey To Music's Heart & Soul,* Dorling Kindersley Ltd, 2001.
Bill Wyman with Richard Havers: *Bill Wyman's Blues Odyssey,* Dorling Kindersley Ltd, 2001.
Bill Wyman with Richard Havers: *Rolling With The Stones,* Dorling Kindersley Ltd, 2002.

Web Sources

http://aeppli.ch/tug.htm - The great Felix Rolling Stones database
www.allmusic.com - Artist Information
www.billboard.com - USA Chart Information
www.chartstats.com - UK Chart Information
http://dbboots.com/index.php - Stones Bootleg Database
www.eil.com - Rare record information
www.iorr.org - Stones News & Message Board
www.jasobrecht.com - Music Archive
http://krlabeat.sakionline.net - Los Angeles Music Newspaper
http://lukpac.org/stereostones/stones-cd-faq.txt - ABKCO Data Analysis
www.nzentgraf.de - The great Nico's site of Rolling Stones Works
www.theofficialcharts.com - UK Official Chart Company
www.recordproduction.com - Recording information
www.rocksbackpages.com - Music Journalism Archive
www.rockscenester.com - Music Scene Magazine Archives
www.rocksoff.org - Stones Message Board and Information
www.rollingstones.com - The official site
www.rollingstonesnet.com – Chris M's great Stones Information
www.setlist.fm - Setlist Information
http://shidoobeewithstonesdoug.yuku.com/ - Stones Message Board
www.soundonsound.com - Recording Technology Magazine
www.stevehoffman.tv - Music Forum
www.stonesarchive.com - Official Archive Site
www.stonessessions.com - Martin Elliott's website
www.timeisonourside.com - Stones Database & Articles
www.under-cover.net - Stones Mailing List
www.vinylnet.co.uk - Record Company Releases

Also available from Cherry Red Books:

Nina Antonia: *Johnny Thunders - In Cold Blood*
Andy Blade: *The Secret Life Of A Teenage Punk Rocker: The Andy Blade Chronicles*
Craig Brackenbridge: *Hells Bent On Rockin': A History Of Psychobilly*
Jake Brown: *Tom Waits: In The Studio*
Steve Bruce: *Best Seat In The House – A Cock Sparrer Story*
David Burke: *Heart Of Darkness – Bruce Springsteen's 'Nebraska'*
David Cartwright: *Bittersweet: The Clifford T Ward Story*
Jeremy Collingwood: *Kiss Me Neck – A Lee 'Scratch' Perry Discography*
Campbell Devine: *All The Young Dudes: Mott The Hoople & Ian Hunter*
Malcolm Dome / Jerry Ewing: *Celebration Day – A Led Zeppelin Encyclopedia*
Sean Egan: *Our Music Is Red - With Purple Flashes: The Story Of The Creation*
Sean Egan: *The Doc's Devils: Manchester United 1972-77*
Ian Glasper: *The Day The Country Died: A History Of Anarcho Punk 1980 To 1984*
Ian Glasper: *Burning Britain - A History Of UK Punk 1980 To 1984*
Ian Glasper: *Trapped In A Scene - UK Hardcore 1985-89*
Ian Glasper: *Armed With Anger – How UK Punk Survived the Nineties*
Stefan Grenados: *Those Were The Days - The Beatles' Apple Organization*
Phil Harding: *PWL: From The Factory Floor*
Colin Harper / Trevor Hodgett: *Irish Folk, Trad And Blues: A Secret History*
Dave Henderson: *A Plugged In State Of Mind: The History of Electronic Music*
Nick Hodges / Ian Priston: *Embryo - A Pink Floyd Chronology 1966-1971*
Jim Bob: *Goodnight Jim Bob - On The Road With Carter USM*
Barry Lazell: *Indie Hits 1980 – 1989*
Mark Manning (aka Zodiac Mindwarp): *Fucked By Rock (Revised and Expanded)*
Mick Mercer: *Music To Die For - International Guide To Goth, Goth Metal, Horror Punk, Psychobilly Etc*
Alex Ogg: *Independence Days - The Story Of UK Independent Record Labels*
Alex Ogg: *No More Heroes: A Complete History Of UK Punk 1976 To 1980*
David Parker: *Random Precision - Recording The Music Of Syd Barrett 1965-1974*
Mark Powell: *Prophets and Sages: The 101 Greatest Progressive Rock Albums*
Terry Rawlings / Keith Badman: *Good Times Bad Times - The Rolling Stones 1960-69*
Terry Rawlings / Keith Badman: *Quite Naturally - The Small Faces*
John Repsch: *The Legendary Joe Meek - The Telstar Man*
John Robb: *Death To Trad Rock – The Post-Punk fanzine scene 1982-87*
Garry Sharpe-Young: *Rockdetector: A To Zs of '80s Rock / Death Metal / Doom, Gothic & Stoner Metal and Power Metal*
Garry Sharpe-Young: *Rockdetector: Black Sabbath - Never Say Die*
Garry Sharpe-Young: *Rockdetector: Ozzy Osbourne*
Mick Stevenson: *The Motorhead Collector's Guide*
Dave Thompson: *Truth... Rod Stewart, Ron Wood And The Jeff Beck Group*
Dave Thompson: *Number One Songs In Heaven - The Sparks Story*
Dave Thompson: *Block Buster! – The True Story of The Sweet*
Dave Thompson: *Children of the Revolution: The Glam Rock Story 1970-75*
Paul Williams: *You're Wondering Now - The Specials from Conception to Reunion*
Alan Wilson: *Deathrow: The Chronicles Of Psychobilly*
Terry Wilson: *Tamla Motown - The Stories Behind The Singles*

Please visit www.cherryredbooks.co.uk for further info and mail order

We're always interested to hear from readers, authors and fans - for contact, submissions, mail order and further information, please email books@cherryred.co.uk

www.cherryredbooks.co.uk

Please check out our extensive range of CD reissues,
from Prog Rock to Hip hop, at

www.cherryred.co.uk